UNIVERSITY CASEBOOK SERIES®

ACCOUNTING FOR LAWYERS

CONCISE FIFTH EDITION

MATTHEW J. BARRETT
Professor of Law
Notre Dame Law School

DAVID R. HERWITZ
Professor Emeritus
Harvard Law School

FOUNDATION
PRESS

University Casebook Series is a trademark registered in the U.S. Patent and Trademark Office.

© 1978, 1980, 1997, 2001, 2006 FOUNDATION PRESS
© 2016 LEG, Inc. d/b/a West Academic
    444 Cedar Street, Suite 700
    St. Paul, MN 55101
    1-877-888-1330

Printed in the United States of America

ISBN: 978-1-59941-672-4

*To Kate, Kevin, Wilson, Luke, and Maggie;
my mother; and David*

*In memory of my father and
Rev. Theodore M. Hesburgh, C.S.C.*

*

PREFACE TO THE CONCISE FIFTH EDITION

Is there any such thing as "accounting for lawyers?" No matter how you answer that question, these materials attempt to highlight the importance of issues involving accounting to the practice of law.

In 2013, three professors at Harvard Law School ("HLS") surveyed 124 practicing attorneys at the eleven law firms that have hired the largest number of HLS graduates in recent years. When asked to rate the usefulness of seven business-methods classes currently offered at HLS, the practicing lawyers gave the highest overall score to "Accounting and Financial Reporting." When asked to select the three most important business-methods courses, "Accounting and Financial Reporting" again ranked first among both *corporate or transactional lawyers and litigators. See* John Coates et al., *What Courses Should Law Students Take? Harvard's Largest Employers Weigh In* (Feb. 17, 2004), http://papers.ssrn.com/sol3/papers.cfm?abstract_id=2397317. Especially after the financial frauds involving Enron Corp. ("Enron"), WorldCom, Inc. ("WorldCom"), and numerous other companies in the late 1990s and early 2000s, clients increasingly expect lawyers to have developed at least some working knowledge of accounting. *See, e.g.*, Lawrence A. Cunningham, *Sharing Accounting's Burden: Business Lawyers in Enron's Dark Shadows*, 57 BUS. LAW. 1421 (2002) (asserting that every competent business lawyer should understand basic accounting principles, arguably as a matter of professional responsibility). Accordingly, law students who acquire this knowledge enhance their attractiveness to potential employers and clients. This text seeks to facilitate that process.

Accounting issues can arise in the practice of law in many different ways. Accounting has long been called "the language of business." In addition, accounting has been described as "the language of corporate governance." Joel Seligman, *Accounting and the New Corporate Law*, 50 WASH. & LEE L. REV. 943, 945 (1993). Virtually every lawyer represents businesses, their owners, or clients with adverse legal interests, such as creditors and customers. Could you effectively practice law in China if you did not speak, or at least understand, Chinese? Moreover, accounting issues also arise regularly in the representation of not-for-profit enterprises, including governmental bodies, and even in private individual matters, such as local rent control. Almost all lawyers, therefore, will encounter financial statements at some time in their professional careers or personal lives. At one time or another, every lawyer will draft, negotiate, or sign an agreement or other legal document containing accounting terminology or concepts. Perhaps most importantly, however, potential discovery issues related to contingencies and audit inquiry letters affect every lawyer or law firm that represents businesses or legal interests adverse to those businesses. Finally, all competent lawyers should recognize certain "red flags" that suggest that their client or another party has committed financial fraud. Businesses often misstate their inventories or other assets, record revenues before they are earned, allocate expenses to the wrong accounting period, or fail to record or disclose liabilities.

Accounting issues constantly arise in different practice areas. Litigators encounter accounting issues when calculating damages in contract and tort cases, throughout securities fraud cases, and in discovery. Transactional lawyers frequently draft and negotiate contracts and other legal documents involving accounting terminology. Securities lawyers frequently advise clients about the disclosure requirements under the federal securities laws. Environmental lawyers face significant cost allocation issues and often need to disclose environmental loss contingencies. Tax lawyers, in particular, must understand the time value of money, and they depend upon accounting concepts to determine taxable income. Labor lawyers often draft, negotiate, or litigate profit-sharing agreements, while intellectual property lawyers do the same with licensing agreements. Domestic relations law frequently requires lawyers to interpret financial statements in property settlement, alimony, or child support matters. Trust, estate, and probate lawyers often encounter fiduciary accounting, which must distinguish between income and principal. Regulatory lawyers, whether representing clients in the health care, insurance, or public utility industries, use accounting to resolve reimbursement issues, to establish reserves, and petition for rate approvals. "White collar" crime, especially financial fraud, has become increasingly important to criminal lawyers.

These materials strive to make accounting as teachable as possible to law students, recognizing that many law students approach the subject with considerable trepidation and have not previously studied accounting. This edition treats its audience as the law student with no accounting background. In that regard, this edition continues to omit lengthy excerpts from official accounting publications. I hope that this book will instill confidence in its readers so that they can begin to master the principles of accounting and develop command of the basic tools that lawyers need so that they can "care about accounting, as lawyers." Bernhard Grossfeld, *Comparative Corporate Governance: Generally Accepted Accounting Principles v. International Accounting Standards*, 28 N.C. J. INT'L L. & COM. REG. 847, 877 (2003).

To accomplish this objective, I continue to develop the materials around explanatory text designed to lead the students through the subject's technical aspects. Each chapter begins with a section that explains the topic's importance to lawyers. Wherever possible, I have attempted to lay out the bookkeeping alternatives, illustrating the various entries in some detail, in the hope that students can direct their efforts more to analyzing the various alternatives' comparative merits and less to the accounting mechanics. To serve as vehicles for such analysis, I have again included alternative problems in each section, and both the materials and the problems seek to highlight the lawyer's role in dealing with accounting issues.

Before beginning the second edition, I wrote to our colleagues across the country who had taught an Accounting for Lawyers course and asked them for their response to the question: What are the top ten things that *every* lawyer should know about accounting? Grateful for the many insights that our colleagues shared and as an overview to this fifth edition, I offer my own updated list of critical accounting concepts for lawyers, arranged in the general order that these topics appear in the chapters that follow:

1. Together with the accompanying notes, the balance sheet, the income statement, the statement of changes in owners' equity, and the statement of cash flows constitute a complete set of financial statements. Accountants use these four different financial statements and the accompanying notes to describe an enterprise's financial condition and the results of its operations. The balance sheet presents an enterprise's financial assets and liabilities, and owners' equity, at a particular moment in time, and it reflects the fundamental accounting equation:

$$\text{Assets} - \text{Liabilities} = \text{Owners' Equity}$$

The income statement shows the extent to which the enterprise's operations and other changes in assets and liabilities from peripheral activities affected the amount of owners' equity, or net assets, over a period of time. The statement of owners' equity more fully reconciles the income statement with the net changes in owners' equity during the period by describing investments by, and distributions to, owners. In addition, most enterprises currently use the statement of owners' equity to report comprehensive income, an amount that summarizes all increases and decreases in net assets during a period, except those changes resulting from investments by, and distributions to, owners. Finally, the statement of cash flows explains the change in the enterprise's cash and cash equivalents during the particular period.

2. Financial statements currently use a "mixed-attribute model," which increasingly requires enterprises to report certain financial assets and liabilities at fair value. Until recently, financial accounting primarily used historical costs, rather than current values, to record financial transactions. Financial statements, therefore, have historically presented, at best, a retrospective picture of an enterprise's financial condition and the results of its operations. Increasingly, financial accounting requires enterprises to use fair value or current market value, rather than historical cost, to report certain financial assets and liabilities in an effort to provide more contemporary or prospective information. At the same time, however, financial statements do not reflect many important "assets" and "liabilities." For example, the value of an outstanding management team, good morale among the enterprise's employees, and loyal and satisfied customers do not appear on the financial statements; nor do the financial statements list weak management, labor problems, unsatisfied customers, or a poor reputation in the community as "liabilities."

3. Poor accounting can violate the law. An enterprise's financial statements represent the "ends" in a process that accountants refer to as "double-entry bookkeeping." As the "means" in this bookkeeping process, business enterprises use journals, ledgers, accounts, debits, credits, trial balances, and worksheets to prepare financial statements. As a result of the Foreign Corrupt Practices Act of 1977 and related amendments, even domestic businesses that keep poor accounting records may violate the federal securities laws.

4. When reading financial statements, pay careful attention to the accompanying notes and, if applicable, Management's Discussion and Analysis, usually called simply "MD&A." Accounting is an art, rather than a science. Accountants, like lawyers, constantly exercise judgment. Even though we often hear accountants referred to as "bean counters," accounting often involves estimates and does not always provide precise rules. Generally accepted accounting principles typically provide alternative choices or may not address a particular situation because business transactions evolve more rapidly than accounting principles. Like lawyers, accountants must examine and interpret statutes, regulations, administrative cases, and official pronouncements of accounting bodies for answers to accounting and auditing questions. Lawyers should know where and how to find and apply this body of authorities. As a general rule, an enterprise's management selects the accounting principles that the enterprise will use from among the acceptable alternatives. The notes to the financial statements address and explain these choices and judgments. MD&A gives readers an opportunity to view the business "through the eyes of management" and may provide forward-looking information about the business and significant trends, commitments, or uncertainties.

5. Generally accepted accounting principles can, and often do, change or evolve. Lawyers should specifically consider this possibility when drafting contracts and legal documents involving accounting terminology. In particular, lawyers in the new millennium should pay attention to the emergence of international accounting principles and their use and acceptance in the United States.

6. An audit does not guarantee the accuracy of financial statements. Even an unqualified audit report provides only "reasonable assurance" that the financial statements fairly present, in all material respects, the enterprise's financial condition, results of operations and cash flows. In addition to auditing financial statements, accountants also often render review and compilation services. Reviews offer only limited assurance, and compilations provide no assurance that the financial statements provide fair representations.

7. A dollar today is worth more than a dollar tomorrow. Remember the time value of money.

8. Different sets of accounting rules can apply for different purposes. An enterprise may use one set of rules for preparing financial statements for creditors and investors, another set for reporting to a regulatory agency, and still others for tax purposes. Different rules or accounting measurements may also apply for specific contracts or for trust accounting, or to determine the legality of distributions to owners, such as a dividend to corporate shareholders. As a result, enterprises may keep different sets of accounting records to maintain information necessary for the various sets of rules or accounting measurements that may apply to the enterprise.

9. Be aware of the legal issues involving contingent liabilities. Be careful when responding to an auditor's requests for information about pending or threatened litigation, claims, or assessments. You probably waive the attorney-client privilege as to any information that you provide to the auditor. Although numerous states have enacted an accountant-client privilege, no such privilege exists under federal law or under the common law. Wherever possible, seek information about a litigation opponent's reserve for a contingent liability during discovery, by examining the opponent's financial statements and public filings, books and records, and tax returns, or by requesting such information from your opponent's auditor.

10. Various lawful and unlawful motivations can influence the discretionary, and often difficult, cost allocation issues that underlie financial statements. Small businesses and their owners generally prefer accounting principles that reduce income in order to reduce income taxes. In contrast, a publicly traded enterprise may select accounting treatments that increase earnings so that management can report higher earnings to investors. All businesses incur costs that they must classify as either assets or expenses. Enterprises expect assets such as inventories, long-lived assets, and intangibles, which appear on the balance sheet, to produce future revenues or other benefits. Expenses like selling commissions, repairs, depreciation, depletion, and amortization, in contrast, offset current revenues on the income statement. Many smaller businesses use the "cash method" of accounting for tax purposes, which requires the taxpayer to report income when actually or constructively received and allows the taxpayer to deduct expenses when actually paid. The cash method, however, does not match expenses with the revenues that they produce. Financial accounting requires the "accrual method," under which a business recognizes revenue when it has completed, or has at least substantially completed, the earnings process and matches the expenses necessary to generate those revenues.

During the nine years that have elapsed since the publication of our concise fourth edition, lawyers have watched as the stock option scandals developed, the collapse in various subprime lending markets in the United States developed into a global financial crisis, and the Securities and Exchange Commission ("SEC") announced a proposed "roadmap" for adopting International Financial Reporting Standards ("IFRS") as issued by the International Accounting Standards Board ("IASB"). Although the SEC later issued a statement in support of global accounting standards, the Commission failed to meet the timetable established in the roadmap and the agency's ultimate decision regarding IFRS remains pending. Collectively, the credit crisis, the Bernard Madoff scandal, the Dodd-Frank Wall Street Reform and Consumer Protection Act of 2010, and the Jumpstart Our Business Startups Act have demanded the SEC's time and attention. Although far less publicized in the popular press, the Financial Accounting Standards Board ("FASB") completed a multi-year project to develop a single authoritative source of generally accepted accounting principles for nongovernmental entities in the United States. Effective for financial statements for interim and annual periods ending after September 15, 2009, the FASB Accounting Standards Codification (the "Codification") assembles all authoritative guidance in one place and affects the way enterprises reference accounting policies in their financial statements and related notes.

In late 2001, the country watched as corporate and accounting fraud led to the sudden collapse of Enron, then the nation's fifth largest company in terms of revenue. Even if you know very little about the Enron scandal, the corporation's collapse painfully illustrates the importance of financial accounting to *all lawyers and law students*. While accounting rules have become increasingly complex, and few law students or lawyers receive formal training in accounting, lawyers can, and should, watch financial statements and related disclosures for "red flags." Accordingly, I continue to include in this preface the following listing of my top ten accounting lessons for lawyers from the Enron scandal:

1. Where's the beef?

A complete set of financial statements includes an income statement, a balance sheet, a statement of cash flows, a statement of changes in owners' equity, and the accompanying notes. The Enron crisis accelerated when the company's 2001 third quarter earnings press release on October 16, 2001, provided only an income statement, and not a balance sheet, statement of cash flows, or statement of changes in shareholders' equity. (Remarkably, Enron failed to provide the other financial statements in its earnings releases beginning in 1996.) In response to questions from analysts, Enron's management later disclosed that Enron recorded a $1.2 billion reduction in shareholders' equity. Because the income statement does not reflect this item, without a balance sheet or statement of changes in shareholders' equity, investors could not see a complete and accurate picture of Enron's financial condition and operating results. In addition, the cash flow statement, possibly the lawyer's best friend in such situations, also would have alerted a careful reader to problems, including the business's declining profitability. As Enron's collapse demonstrates, a missing financial statement may indicate that the enterprise seeks to hide disappointing results. Enron's eventual issuance of its missing balance sheet, and the large write-down of shareholders' equity in that financial statement, triggered a loss of investor confidence, which caused Enron's share price to fall, accelerated debt repayment obligations, and ultimately led to Enron's bankruptcy. The Enron scandal illustrates that *each* financial statement offers important information necessary to maintain investor and creditor confidence. A lawyer should ask probing questions any time an enterprise does not provide a complete set of financial statements, plus accompanying notes.

2. Old dogs, new tricks.

Generally accepted accounting principles (GAAP) often offer choices in financial accounting treatments. Although the "consistency principle" generally requires enterprises to use the same accounting principles to treat the same transactions similarly from year-to-year, this consistency requirement does not apply to new business activities. The business community refers to the "rules" governing the compilation of accounting data into financial statements and the accompanying notes as "GAAP." GAAP, however, typically allows choices among permissible alternatives and almost always requires estimates and assumptions that affect the amounts shown in the financial statements, including the reported amounts of assets, liabilities, revenues and expenses. Especially in today's world, business transactions and practices evolve more rapidly than rule-makers can promulgate accounting rules. For several reasons, therefore, GAAP does not provide a set of black-and-white rules that produce a single "bottom-line" number that a lawyer can use natural law to verify. Commonly referred to as "earnings management," corporate managers can often use GAAP's flexibility to show operating results in line with projections and expectations. Especially when an enterprise's business changes (witness Enron's evolution from a regional natural gas company to a global energy and commodities trader), lawyers should pay particular attention to the accounting principles an enterprise uses to account for transactions arising from the new business activities.

3. Looks aren't everything.

Pro forma reporting can distort an enterprise's financial appearance. In its 2001 third quarter earnings release, Enron reported "recurring" net income of $393 million. Such "pro forma" reporting, which provides numbers "as if" certain (often undescribed) assumptions apply, does not follow GAAP. Even a simple analysis of the earnings release reveals that Enron actually suffered a $618 million *net loss* under GAAP. By labeling $1.01 billion as "one-time" or "non-recurring" charges, mostly related to investment and asset write-downs and restructuring charges, the company turned its $618 million net loss, purportedly using GAAP, into $393 million in net income. Such write-downs and charges, however, would seem to represent normal business expenses and losses.

In an effort to focus investors on results from "normal" business operations, an enterprise may, knowingly or innocently, mislead investors. Initially, pro forma reporting can hide troubling financial results. For instance, in its 2000 fourth quarter earnings release, Enron boasted a 25 percent increase in earnings per share ("EPS") for the full year 2000 over 1999 and a 32 percent increase in earnings per share for the 2000 fourth quarter over the 1999 fourth quarter. Buried in the last section of its earnings release, however, the company told a very different story. Enron disclosed that EPS for 2000, including non-recurring charges, increased only from $1.10 per share in 1999 to $1.12 per share in 2000. These amounts translated to an increase of only 1.8 percent, compared to the 25 percent increase Enron reported at the beginning of its earnings release. Next, Enron disclosed that 2000 fourth quarter EPS, after non-recurring charges, totaled $0.05, a *decrease* of 83.8 percent from the 1999 fourth quarter, in contrast to the 32 percent increase it reported at the beginning of the release. Interestingly, earlier in the quarter, Enron predicted that it would post fourth quarter EPS of $0.35. Excluding what it called non-recurring items allowed Enron to exceed those expectations. If Enron had included the non-recurring items, its results would have fallen below that prediction.

Second, an enterprise can use pro forma reporting to manage earnings. Earnings management typically tries to increase net income (or reduce the size of a loss), relative to what the business would otherwise report under GAAP. Enterprises, however, sometimes exclude non-recurring gains in an effort to report lower net income, which translates to smaller profit-sharing payments to employees (or reduced income tax obligations). Lawyers drafting agreements that rely on earnings to set prices or trigger payments, for example, should distinguish pro forma earnings from net income calculated in compliance with GAAP. Without distinguishing between the two benchmarks, parties to such an agreement can manipulate earnings by labeling some items as one-time or non-recurring.

4. Sometimes, looks <u>are</u> everything.

Auditor independence matters—both in appearance and in fact. During the late 1990s, the largest public accounting firms increasingly provided non-audit services, such as consulting, internal audits, and tax advising, often for the very enterprises they audited. During 2000, Enron paid $52 million to Arthur Andersen—$25 million for auditing services, and an additional $27 million for non-auditing services—and ranked as Andersen's second largest client. In addition, an internal Andersen memo regarding the retention of Enron as an audit client refers to $100 million a year in potential revenues from Enron.

Unlike lawyers who must zealously represent their clients, auditors' real responsibilities flow to the investing public, not the enterprise that hires them. By evaluating an enterprise's financial statements and expressing an opinion as to whether those statements fairly present, in all material respects, the enterprise's financial position and operating results, an auditor seeks to help maintain investor and creditor confidence. To satisfy generally accepted auditing standards, an auditor must remain independent from any enterprises it audits—both in fact and in appearance. When non-audit fees comprise a substantial piece of an auditor's income from the audit client, those fees might tempt an auditor to overlook an enterprise's "aggressive" accounting simply to retain the client's non-audit business. At a minimum, substantial fees paid to auditors for non-audit related services call the appearance of independence into question. Even if the auditor continues, in fact, to exercise objective judgment, such relationships impair the appearance of independence. As the recent malaise that has afflicted the stock markets in the United States ably demonstrates, even the *perception* of a lack of independence can shake investor confidence in the quality of financial statements. Because investors view a lack of independence, whether in appearance or in fact, with a critical eye, lawyers should encourage clients to preserve independence, both in fact and in appearance. Lawyers should also carefully scrutinize financial statements, disclosures, and transactions that involve an auditor who may have compromised independence, whether in fact or in appearance.

5. With friends like these, ...

Related-party transactions, especially those involving a special purpose entity ("SPE"), can distort an enterprise's apparent financial condition and operating results. Although related-party transactions may increase efficiency in transacting business, they may also allow an enterprise to manipulate its earnings by the way the enterprise sets prices or allocates expenses. Similarly, an enterprise may use SPEs for legitimate purposes, such as to limit exposure to risk in certain investments, including credit card receivables or residential mortgages. An enterprise, the "sponsor," generally forms an SPE to transfer risks from such investments to outside investors.

Enron's transactions with its SPEs, including the so-called Chewco and LJM partnerships, highlight the dangers that can arise from related-party transactions. As a small, but relatively simple example, Enron sold an interest in a Polish company to LJM2 for $30 million on December 21, 1999. While Enron intended to sell the interest to an unrelated party, the company could not find a buyer before the end of the year. The sale allowed Enron to record a gain of $16 million on a transaction that Enron could not close with a third party. Remarkably, Enron later bought back LJM2's interest for $31.9 million after it failed to find an outside buyer. Another deal allowed Enron to *report* a $111 million gain on the transfer of an agreement with Blockbuster Video to deliver movies on demand, even after Enron realized that no real profits would ever flow from the underlying agreement.

The related-party transactions with SPEs, often occurring at the end of a fiscal period, allowed Enron to manipulate its reported earnings, to close deals at desired amounts quickly, to hide debt, and to conceal poorly performing assets. Such transactions, which frequently closed at the end of a quarter or year, allowed Enron to meet its earnings expectations and to sustain its stock price. In fact, Enron sometimes even backdated such transactions to the previous period, in an effort to "manufacture" income for that period. Because Enron entered into those transactions with "friendly" related parties, the company could quickly and easily negotiate terms that allowed its earnings to appear on target. In addition, Enron used its earliest SPEs to obtain financing, without showing the related liability on its balance sheet. Finally, Enron used SPEs to move poorly performing assets off of its balance sheet. By transferring such assets to SPEs, Enron could hide later declines in the value of those assets.

GAAP requires an enterprise to disclose information about material related-party transactions in the notes to the financial statements. In particular, an enterprise must disclose: the nature of any relationships involved; a description of the transactions for each period for which the financial statements present an income statement, including any information necessary to understand the transactions' effects on the financial statements; the dollar amounts of the transactions and the effects of any changes in the method used to establish terms when compared to those followed in the preceding period; and amounts due from or to related parties on each balance sheet date and the related terms governing those amounts. The disclosures should not imply that the transactions contained terms equivalent to those that would have prevailed in an arm's-length transaction unless management can substantiate that claim. Enron did disclose various related-party transactions in the notes to its financial statements, but not in any detail.

Lawyers who assist in related-party transactions should carefully examine the transactions and their client's securities disclosures in an effort to assure that those disclosures accurately describe the transactions' true nature and effects on the financial statements. Likewise, lawyers negotiating other transactions or pursuing other claims, especially when future or past earnings determine legal rights and obligations, should keep in mind that an enterprise can use related-party transactions to manipulate earnings.

6. Details, details, details.

Corporations should develop and adhere to internal controls (both administrative and accounting). Administrative controls generally refer to an enterprise's plan of organization, procedures, and records that lead up to management's approval of transactions. Accounting controls, by comparison, describe the plans, procedures, and records that an enterprise uses to safeguard assets and produce reliable financial information. Enron's administrative controls included policies designed to minimize conflicts of interest and to ensure that transactions fairly benefitted the company. Not only did recent events prove Enron's administrative controls inadequate, but those events also showed that Enron failed to follow the controls that it had put in place. For example, when Enron's board approved a policy that allowed the company to enter into transactions with certain entities owned by Enron officers, the implementing procedures explicitly required management to use a "Deal Approval Sheet." By requiring certain disclosures and the approval of Enron's chief executive officer, the Deal Approval Sheets sought to ensure that the contractual provisions in such transactions would closely resemble the terms that would have materialized in an arms'-length transaction. In fact, the chief executive officer's signature does not appear on the sheets for several specific transactions. Moreover, the current absence of sheets for other transactions suggests that Enron did not complete any such document in those transactions. As another example, Andrew Fastow, Enron's former chief financial officer and, for a time, the general partner of the several partnerships that entered into transactions with Enron, reportedly earned more than $30 million from his investments in those enterprises. Even though the board seemed to recognize the conflict of interest inherent in such related-party transactions, the board failed to require that Mr. Fastow report his profits from the partnerships to the company. Such disclosures almost certainly would have alerted the board to the possibility that the underlying transactions unfairly benefitted the related parties, to the detriment of Enron and its shareholders. Other items in this list document that Enron failed to implement adequate accounting controls.

Although top management bears the initial responsibility to develop, implement, and, when necessary, revise adequate internal controls, overall oversight falls to the board of directors, who often rely on lawyers for advice. Internal controls work effectively only when those who bear responsibility for developing, implementing, and overseeing those controls stress the need to adhere to all policies and procedures and lead by adhering to those rules themselves. In recent years, the SEC has brought administrative actions and imposed so-called "tone-at-the-top liability" under the Foreign Corrupt Practices Act, which applies to all SEC registrants, including enterprises that engage only in domestic operations. Strong internal controls enhance the likelihood that the enterprise will engage in sound, beneficial transactions and reduce the chances that an enterprise will incur the enormous losses that can result from internal control failures.

7. If it walks like a duck, ...

In recognizing revenue (and accounting generally), substance prevails over form. Under GAAP, an enterprise cannot recognize revenue until the business has substantially completed performance in a bona fide exchange transaction. If a transaction does not unconditionally transfer the risks that typically accompany a "sale," the enterprise may not recognize revenue.

Enron's announcement regarding a $544 million after-tax charge to earnings in October 2001 revealed a serious flaw in its prior financial statements: Enron had improperly recognized revenue from transactions with its SPEs. In short, Enron recorded revenue after transferring certain assets to those SPEs, even though credit guarantees, promises to protect the purchasers from any loss from decline in value, or buyback agreements caused the company to retain the risks of ownership even after the transfers. As a result, Enron had not truly "earned" the revenue it reported.

Enron's "sham" transactions resemble schemes that ultimately led to the demise of Drexel Burnham and the imprisonment of Michael Milken, that appeared so frequently during the savings and loan crisis, and that accompany most financial accounting frauds today. Milken ultimately pled guilty to charges involving "parking," whereby Drexel Burnham purchased securities from third parties with the understanding that the investment banking firm would quickly resell the securities back to the third parties at a fixed price. Similarly, the Federal Home Loan Bank Board (FHLBB) took control of Lincoln Savings & Loan Association in 1989 after discovering, among other things, that Lincoln or its affiliates had recognized income on sales of real estate even though the funds for the down payments had emanated from Lincoln itself. In substance, Lincoln or its affiliates had retained the risks of ownership and could not recognize revenue from the sales.

The issue of substance over form applies not only to managers and accountants, but to attorneys as well. The litigation that follows financial frauds can impose enormous financial costs. In addition, a lawyer who fails to investigate, or perhaps spot, a "red flag," such as a side agreement or guarantee, can face staggering personal liability for malpractice. Whether drafting, negotiating, or interpreting contractual provisions that refer to "net income" or "earnings," performing "due diligence" to determine whether a particular transaction will further a client's best interests, or rendering a "true sale" opinion regarding whether a transferor that retains some involvement with the transferred asset (or the transferee) has surrendered economic control over the asset to justify treating the transaction as a sale for financial accounting purposes, substance over form requires an attorney to look beyond the form of a transaction and to try to identify any arrangements that may affect the transaction's economic realities. In particular, understanding the motivations for a transaction offers an important clue to the transaction's substance. Enron often transferred assets to SPEs to hide losses or to remove liabilities from its balance sheet. Although most clients or adversaries will not expressly state such desires, such effects should also alert attorneys to issues of substance over form.

8. Promises, promises.

Any time an enterprise guarantees the indebtedness of another in material amounts, the enterprise must disclose the nature and amount of the guarantees in the notes to the financial statements. When Enron's SPEs sought credit, the lenders often required that Enron guarantee the debt. On several occasions, Enron guaranteed amounts that various SPEs borrowed by promising to pay cash or to issue additional common shares to repay the debt, if the market price of Enron's common shares dropped under a set amount or if Enron's bond rating fell below investment grade. While the notes to Enron's financial statements disclosed guarantees of the indebtedness of others, Enron did not mention that its potential liability on those guarantees, which shared common debt repayment triggers, totaled $4 billion. When material, GAAP specifically requires an enterprise to disclose the nature and amount of guarantees of the indebtedness of others. Again, inadequate disclosure can subject enterprises to liability and lawyers to malpractice claims.

9. If it sounds too good to be true, ...

An enterprise cannot recognize income from issuing its own shares and generally should not record a net increase in shareholders' equity when it issues stock in exchange for a note receivable. At the risk of oversimplifying, Enron used related-party SPEs to hedge, or to protect itself from declines in the market value of, certain investments that Enron used current market prices to value on its books. In these arrangements, Enron transferred its own stock to an SPE in exchange for a note or cash. In addition, Enron guaranteed, directly or indirectly, the SPE's value. The SPEs in turn hedged the underlying investments, using the transferred Enron stock as the principal source of payment for the hedges. The value of the underlying investments decreased, but the hedges allowed Enron to recognize a corresponding increase, resulting in a wash. The SPEs, however, could reimburse Enron for any decline in value of the investments only as long as the market price of Enron's common shares remained stable or increased. When the value of Enron's common shares fell, Enron had to issue additional shares pursuant to its agreements with the SPEs and the related guarantees. These additional shares reduced Enron's stock value, which triggered additional guarantees. In the interim, Enron recognized about $500 million in revenues from the hedges, which had really arisen from the issuance of the company's own shares. GAAP, however, does not allow an enterprise to record gains from the increase in the value of its capital stock on its income statement.

As previously mentioned in the first item, Enron announced on October 16, 2001, that it had recorded a $1.2 billion reduction in shareholders' equity, arising, in large part, from an accounting error. When Enron issued its common shares to several SPEs in exchange for notes receivable, Enron recorded the notes receivable as assets, thereby overstating shareholders' equity by $1 billion. Although GAAP usually allows an enterprise to record notes receivable as assets, a different rule applies when an enterprise issues stock in exchange for the notes. GAAP states that an enterprise should treat any notes received in payment for the enterprise's stock as an offset to shareholders' equity. Only when the obligor pays the note can the enterprise record an increase in shareholders' equity for the amount actually paid.

Many credit agreements allow the lender to accelerate the repayment of the debt if the borrower's debt-to-shareholders' equity ratio exceeds a certain level or if the borrower fails to maintain a certain credit rating. Although Enron's $1.2 billion reduction in shareholders' equity did not itself trigger any debt repayment obligations, investment ratings companies immediately placed Enron on review for downgrade. Soon after, the ratings companies downgraded Enron's credit rating to below investment grade. Because provisions in many of Enron's credit agreements required the company to maintain an investment grade credit rating, the downgrades triggered debt repayment obligations, which accelerated Enron's bankruptcy.

10. When the going gets tough, ...

Lawyers' duties to their clients include an obligation to object when a client proposes or uses questionable accounting policies or practices. In Judge Stanley Sporkin's well-publicized opinion in the *Lincoln Savings and Loan* case in 1990, Judge Sporkin asked where the lawyers were when Lincoln consummated various improper transactions, wondering why they did not attempt to prevent those transactions or disassociate themselves from them. About a decade later, the legal profession heard similar questions directed to Enron's lawyers. While Enron's lawyers, both in-house and outside counsel, did question some practices, Enron officers and employees often either ignored the lawyers' advice, or changed the transactions just enough to get around the lawyers' particular concerns. In some cases, Enron's lawyers apparently helped to complete the very transactions they questioned.

The attorney-client privilege prevents lawyers from disclosing client confidences. That privilege, however, does not prevent lawyers from discussing concerns with their clients, attempting to persuade their clients to choose another course of action, going up the "corporate ladder," or even withdrawing from representing their clients if a client declines to follow the lawyer's advice. When Enron's lawyers questioned Enron's practices, they voiced their concerns to Enron's in-house lawyers and its management, but not to the board of directors or the audit committee. Blind deference to accountants and auditors seems unwise and dangerous. We'll never know, but without hearing the concerns of Enron's lawyers, the board of directors or the audit committee arguably could not see an objective picture of those transactions and Enron's financial accounting practices.

Standing up takes courage. The scandals at Enron, WorldCom, and other companies led to numerous reforms in the Sarbanes-Oxley Act of 2002 and taught more lawyers to watch for accounting "red flags" and to respond courageously when they see them. Although lawyers played leading roles in the stock options scandals of the mid-2000s, the profession fared much better during the 2008 credit crisis and its continuing aftermath.

With those highlights, which I hope you will reread periodically during your study of these materials, we can overview what follows. As in previous versions, this edition starts with an Introduction to Bookkeeping, Accrual Accounting, and Financial Statements, which has proved successful in introducing students to the mechanics of the accounting process. Lawyers typically must work backwards through the bookkeeping process to obtain accounting-related information relevant to various legal issues, transactions, or disputes. It remains my belief that lawyers cannot work effectively from the financial statements to the accounting records unless they understand the accounting process from the beginning. Chapter II deals with the development of accounting principles and auditing standards. Chapter III offers a set of materials on the time value of money. This edition illustrates various calculations using Microsoft Excel. Chapter IV introduces financial statement analysis and financial ratios. Chapter V focuses on legal issues involving shareholders' equity and the balance sheet. Chapter VI covers revenue recognition and issues involving the income statement. Chapter VII proceeds to discuss contingencies, a very important topic for lawyers. Chapter VIII deals with inventories and cost allocation issues. Chapter IX continues that theme in the context of long-lived assets and intangibles.

In addition to the book's dedication, I want to recognize David R. Herwitz, who first identified the need for a concise edition, and who, in addition to serving for fifty years as author or co-author of materials designed to teach the language of business to law students, developed the concise edition. During his legendary career, he taught Accounting for Lawyers to about 14,000 law students, primarily at Harvard Law School. I also want to thank him for his countless contributions to the field and his many kindnesses to me since I joined him on this text's second edition. I remain deeply grateful for the wonderful opportunity to collaborate with him on these materials, and I have thoroughly enjoyed the friendship we have shared for almost twenty years. I continue to wish him the very best as he enjoys his emeritus status and devotes more time to his family, especially his grandchildren.

As to this concise fifth edition, I gratefully acknowledge valuable assistance from Susan Good and Dan Manier; countless hours and unending patience from Sharon Loftus in preparing the manuscript; and outstanding editing, indexing, and proofreading assistance from Rachel Lynn, Notre Dame Law School Class of 2016.

I also appreciate the graciousness of two companies: Ben & Jerry's Homemade Holdings, Inc. for permission to reprint cartoons that appeared in the 1992 annual report of Ben & Jerry's Homemade, Inc.; and Starbucks Corporation for permission to reprint its annual report for the fiscal year ended September 30, 2012, its Form 10-K and earnings release for the same period, and the proxy statement for its 2013 annual meeting. © 2012 Starbucks Coffee Company. All rights reserved. Used with permission. I am especially grateful to Myron E. Ullman, III, whose kind and invaluable intervention enabled me to continue to provide the Starbucks materials in this edition for your convenience.

Portions of the *FASB Accounting Standards Codification*®, copyrighted by the Financial Accounting Foundation, 401 Merritt 7, PO Box 5116, Norwalk, CT 06856-5116, are reprinted with permission.

This book's roots date back to Professor Robert Amory, Jr.'s pioneering first casebook on accounting for law students in 1948. Five years later, Professor Covington Hardee joined Professor Amory on a second edition. In 1959, Professor Donald T. Trautman joined my co-author emeritus for an earlier third edition. These materials continue to benefit from my predecessors' contributions, helpful suggestions and valuable help from numerous colleagues, fellow teachers, and research assistants listed in the unabridged fifth edition, and the comments and questions of numerous students over the years. I also want to highlight the contributions of Delona Wilkin on the manuscripts for previous concise editions and proof-reading, editing, indexing, and general polishing efforts of Christopher Lee Wilson, Harvard Law School Class of 2006, and Melissa Anderson, Harvard Law School Class of 2009.

A note on form: I have edited most cases and other selections to delete irrelevant material, citations in the text and footnotes. Spaced asterisks indicate deletions in the text. I again have omitted citations in the text and footnotes without indication. Where footnotes appear in the edited version, I have retained the number in the original material.

Before I move on, one final comment: I want these materials to be as accurate, current, and helpful as possible, and I plan to continue our recent practice of updating them annually. Apart from isolated "subsequent events," this text uses December 31, 2013 as the cut-off date for developments. If you find any errors or omissions, I hope that you will call them to my attention so that I can incorporate any corrections into future supplements and editions. I also welcome any other comments or suggestions that you might be willing to share. You can reach me via e-mail at Barrett.1@nd.edu, by calling me at (574) 631-8121, or sending me a fax to (574) 631-8078.

Matthew J. Barrett

SUMMARY OF CONTENTS

*

TABLE OF CONTENTS

TABLE OF ACRONYMS

AAER	SEC Accounting and Auditing Enforcement Release
ABA	American Bar Association
AcSEC	AICPA Accounting Standards Executive Committee
AICPA	American Institute of Certified Public Accountants
AMEX	American Stock Exchange
APB	AICPA Accounting Principles Board
ARB	Accounting Research Bulletin
ARC	Accounting Regulatory Committee of the European Union
ARO	Asset retirement obligation
AS	PCAOB Auditing Standard
ASAF	IASB Accounting Standards Advisory Forum
ASB	AICPA Auditing Standards Board
ASC	FASB Accounting Standards Codification
ASD	AICPA Auditing Standards Division
ASR	Accounting Series Release
ASU	FASB Accounting Standards Update
AU	Codification of Statements on Auditing Standards
AudSEC	AICPA Auditing Standards Executive Committee
CAP	AICPA Committee on Accounting Procedure
CAQ	AICPA Center for Audit Quality
CAT	AICPA Committee on Accounting Terminology
CEO	Chief executive officer
CFO	Chief financial officer
CFRP	SEC Codification of Financial Reporting Policies
CON	FASB Concepts Statement
CorpFin	SEC Division of Corporation Finance
COSO	Committee of Sponsoring Organizations of the Treadway Commission
DPA	Deferred prosecution agreement
EBITDA	Earnings Before Interest, Taxes, Depreciation, and Amortization
EBIT	Earnings Before Interest and Taxes
EC	European Commission
EDGAR	SEC Electronic Data Gathering, Analysis, and Retrieval System
EFRAG	European Financial Reporting Advisory Group
EGC	Emerging growth company
EITF	Emerging Issues Task Force
EPS	Earnings per share
EU	European Union
FAF	Financial Accounting Foundation

FAS	FASB Statement of Financial Accounting Standards
FASAC	Financial Accounting Standards Advisory Council
FASB	Financial Accounting Standards Board
FCAG	Financial Crisis Advisory Group of the FASB and IASB
FEI	Financial Executives International
FIFO	First-in, first-out inventory method
FIN	FASB Interpretation
FinRec	AICPA Financial Reporting Executive Committee
FRC	SEC Codification of Financial Reporting Policies
FRR	SEC Financial Reporting Release
FSP	FASB Staff Position
FTB	FASB Technical Bulletin
GAAP	Generally accepted accounting principles
GAAS	Generally accepted auditing standards
GAO	United States Government Accountability Office
GASB	Government Accounting Standards Board
IAASB	International Auditing and Assurance Standards Board
IAPS	International Auditing Practice Statements
IAS	International Accounting Standard
IASB	International Accounting Standards Board
IASC	International Accounting Standards Committee
ICFR	Internal control over financial reporting
IDEA	Interactive Data Electronic Applications
IFAC	International Federation of Accountants
IFRIC	International Financial Reporting Interpretations Committee
IFRS	IASB International Financial Reporting Standard
IFRSAC	IFRS Advisory Council
IFRSF	IFRS Foundation
IFRSIC	IFRS Interpretations Committee
IOSCO	International Organization of Securities Commissions
IPO	Initial public offering
IPR&D	In-process research and development
IRS	Internal Revenue Service
ISA	International Standards on Auditing
ISB	Independence Standard Board
ITAC	FASB Investors Technical Advisory Committee
Libor	London inter-bank offered rate
LIFO	Last-in, first-out inventory method
MD&A	Management's Discussion and Analysis
MoU	Memorandum of Understanding between the IASB and FASB
MDPs	Multidisciplinary practices
NASBA	National Association of State Boards of Accountancy
NASD	National Association of Securities Dealers
Nasdaq	The Nasdaq Stock Market, Inc.
NIRI	National Investor Relations Institute
NPA	Non-prosecution agreement
NYSE	New York Stock Exchange
OTTI	"Other than temporary" impairment
PCAOB	Public Company Accounting Oversight Board

PCC	FAF Private Company Council
QSPE	Qualified special purpose entity
RAP	Regulatory accounting practices
S-K	Regulation S-K
S-X	Regulation S-X
S&P	Standard & Poors
SAB	SEC Staff Accounting Bulletin
SAC	IASB Standards Advisory Council
SAP	Statement of Auditing Procedure
SAS	Statement of Auditing Standards
SBAC	FASB Small Business Advisory Committee
SEC	United States Securities and Exchange Commission
SFAC	Statement of Financial Accounting Concepts
SFAS	Statement of Financial Accounting Standards
SIC	IASB Standards Interpretation Committee
SLB	SEC Staff Legal Bulletin
SMEs	Small- and medium-sized entities
SOP	AICPA Statement of Position
SOx	Sarbanes-Oxley Act of 2002
SQCS	AICPA Statement on Quality Control Standards
SPE	Special purpose entity
TB	FASB Technical Bulletin
TPA	AICPA Technical Practice Aid
UAC	FASB User Advisory Council
VIE	Variable interest entity
XBRL	eXtensible Business Reporting Language

*

TABLE OF OFFICIAL ACCOUNTING AND AUDITING PROMULGATIONS

References are to Pages.

*

TABLE OF FEDERAL STATUTES AND REGULATIONS

References are to Pages.

*

TABLE OF CASES

Principal cases are in bold type. Non-principal cases are in roman type. References are to Pages.

*

UNIVERSITY CASEBOOK SERIES®

ACCOUNTING FOR LAWYERS

CONCISE FIFTH EDITION

CHAPTER I

INTRODUCTION TO FINANCIAL STATEMENTS, BOOKKEEPING, AND ACCRUAL ACCOUNTING

A. IMPORTANCE TO LAWYERS

Accounting is often called "the language of business." Even if a lawyer does not represent businesses or their owners, almost every lawyer will represent clients with legal interests adverse to businesses or their owners. Lawyers, therefore, must understand certain fundamental concepts about accounting.

Resolving accounting problems that lawyers encounter ordinarily demands much the same kind of analysis and judgment necessary to solve other legal problems. A lawyer must unscramble other people's troubles or, even better, help avoid trouble before it develops. Before a lawyer can accept an assignment where accounting issues are involved, however, the lawyer faces a special difficulty. Accountants, and more generally people in business and finance, have their own way of expressing the data with which they are concerned. At first, it may seem akin to an unfamiliar language. But the basic principles on which this language is built are simple enough. This chapter is designed to show you that if you—rather than, as historians tell us, thirteenth century merchants in Venice, then the world's commercial center—had set out to devise a process for recording financial data, which a Renaissance monk named Luca Pacioli first described in 1494, you might well have reached the same system.

You should not assume, however, that every aspect of the current system was inevitable. Certainly the application of the system in particular situations is open to doubt and to analysis, and in later chapters of this book, which deal with the function of accounting statements in business life, we will occasionally question the appropriateness of the "language" as applied in particular contexts.

Before discussing specific accounting issues, we must first understand the system for reporting and recording financial information. Accountants use four different financial statements—the *balance sheet*, the *income statement*, the *statement of changes in owner's equity*, and the *statement of cash flows*—to describe an enterprise's financial condition and the results of its operations. We will see that both the names and the formats that accountants may use to refer to and to present the information in these financial statements may vary, but that they or their equivalents provide the same basic information.

1

Each financial statement serves a slightly different purpose. The balance sheet presents an enterprise's financial assets and liabilities–what the enterprise owns and owes–and residual equity, at a particular moment in time. Traditionally, assets typically appeared on the balance sheet at their historical cost, but an ongoing conversion to a so-called mixed attribute system now requires enterprises to report some assets and liabilities at their fair value. The income statement shows the extent to which the enterprise's operations have caused changes in the amount of residual equity over a period of time. The statement of changes in owner's equity reconciles the change in the equity section between balance sheet dates. Finally, the statement of cash flows explains the change in the enterprise's cash during the particular period. We will discuss each financial statement in this chapter.

As discussed in the preface, the Enron scandal teaches that *each* financial statement offers critical information about an enterprise's financial health and the importance of a complete set of financial statements. In fact, an incomplete set of financial statements may prevent a reader from seeing the entire picture. Adopting the custom of many other companies, Enron stopped providing a balance sheet in the press releases announcing its quarterly results in 1996. That practice became significant when Enron reported its 2001 third quarter earnings in October 2001. In response to questions from analysts, Enron's management later disclosed that the company recorded a $1.2 billion reduction in shareholders' equity during that third quarter. Because the income statement does not reflect this item, without a balance sheet or statement of changes in shareholders' equity, investors could not see a complete and accurate picture of Enron's financial condition and operating results. Enron's eventual issuance of its missing balance sheet, and the large write-down of shareholders' equity in the balance sheet, triggered a loss of investor confidence, which caused Enron's share price to fall, accelerated debt repayment obligations, and ultimately led to Enron's bankruptcy, at the time the largest in history in the United States.

Perhaps, even more significantly, the cash flow statement, possibly the lawyer's best friend in such situations, would have alerted a careful reader to the serious problems at Enron, including the business's declining profitability. As early as 1999, Enron's cash flows from operations dropped when compared to the previous year, even though net income for 1999 had increased. During the first six months of 2001, which reflects the period immediately before Enron's collapse, Enron reported negative cash flows from operations exceeding $1.3 billion.

When Pacioli developed his bookkeeping system, most business ventures did not last very long. Today, businesses usually continue indefinitely or, in other words, lack a determinate period of existence. For management purposes, most businesses prepare periodic financial statements. *Accrual accounting* seeks to allocate revenues and expenses to accounting periods regardless of when the cash expenditures or receipts occur or when the obligations to pay or the rights to receive cash arise.

The financial statements ultimately represent the "ends" in a process that accountants refer to as *double-entry bookkeeping*. As the "means" in the process, business enterprises use journals, ledgers, accounts, debits, credits, trial balances, and worksheets. These accounting records underlie the financial statements.

This chapter will also describe, and give you an opportunity to practice by doing, the bookkeeping process, which begins when a bookkeeper or accountant prepares a journal entry to record a transaction or event. Next, the bookkeeper or accountant posts the amounts from the journal entry to the applicable accounts in the ledger. At the end of the accounting period, the bookkeeper or accountant determines the balances in the accounts, adjusts those balances as necessary, and often uses a worksheet to help prepare financial statements.

Lawyers, in contrast, typically must work backwards through the bookkeeping process to obtain accounting-related information relevant to various legal issues, transactions, or disputes. Starting with the financial statements, a lawyer can often look at an underlying worksheet to determine where amounts in the financial statements came from in the ledger. Drilling down deeper and working in the opposite direction as the bookkeeper or accountant, the lawyer can follow the bookkeeping trail, first from the ledger to the journal entry, and then to any invoices, records or files that document the relevant transaction or event. If a lawyer does not understand the bookkeeping process, the lawyer risks missing the opportunity to gather or obtain extremely valuable information.

To begin our study of bookkeeping and accrual accounting, we should understand the first important financial statement, the balance sheet.

B.   THE BALANCE SHEET

The object of bookkeeping is to make it as easy as possible for anyone who understands the language to get a clear and accurate summary of how well a business is doing. As one way of determining how well a business is doing, we can compare what the business owns with what it owes. The difference between what a business owns—its *assets*—and what it owes—its *liabilities*—represents its *net worth*, which accountants sometimes refer to as *equity*. As the first basic financial statement that we will study, the balance sheet shows a business's assets, liabilities, and equity at a particular moment in time.

The following cartoons, which originally appeared in the 1992 annual report of Ben & Jerry's Homemade, Inc., and which we reprint with permission, very simply explain the balance sheet and its components, namely assets, liabilities, and equity. After that introduction, we can then proceed to discuss those components in more detail, beginning with assets.

FRAN SMILED

AAH, SMART DECISIONS ABOUT BEN & JERRY'S FINANCES - A REALLY IMPORTANT PART OF BEING SOCIALLY RESPONSIBLE - IMPORTANT FOR OUR EMPLOYEES AND OUR STOCKHOLDERS AND OUR STOCKHOLDERS TO REMEMBER, WE WOULDN'T BE AROUND TO BE SOCIALLY RESPONSIBLE IF WE DIDN'T MANAGE OUR MONEY RESPONSIBLY

YOU GET A LETTER FROM A FRIEND AT THE END OF THE YEAR...

LET'S TAKE A LOOK AT THE BALANCE SHEET & THE STATEMENT OF INCOME. THERE ARE OTHER FINANCIAL STATEMENTS, BUT WE'LL JUST TAKE THOSE TWO FOR NOW.

THE PICTURE ON THE LEFT WE'LL CALL THE BALANCE SHEET. IT'S A SNAPSHOT OF WHAT WE HAVE AT ONE MOMENT. THIS IS A PICTURE OF YOUR FRIENDS. YOU CAN SEE THEY HAVE A DOG, A BIKE FOR THEIR DAUGHTER, A NEW CAR, &... OH YES, A PAYMENT BOOK, PLUS A BUNCH OF OTHER STUFF. SO IN ACCOUNTING LANGUAGE, THIS IS A PICTURE OF THEIR ASSETS & LIABILITIES (AS IN... THEY'RE LIABLE TO COME GET OUR CAR IF WE DON'T MAKE THE NEXT PAYMENT).

THE LETTER ON THE RIGHT IS FROM YOUR FRIENDS IN THE PICTURE. OH JEEZ, IT'S ONE OF THOSE REALLY BORING HOLIDAY LETTERS. IN BUSINESS LANGUAGE, THIS WOULD BE LIKE THE STATEMENT OF INCOME. IT'S A DESCRIPTION OF ALL THE THINGS THAT THEY HAVE DONE IN THE PAST YEAR, LIKE WHAT THEY EARNED, & WHAT THEY BOUGHT & SOLD FOR HOW MUCH. (OR IF YOUR FRIENDS ARE A LITTLE LESS CRASS, WHAT THE KIDS DID IN SCHOOL & WHERE THEY ALL WENT ON VACATION).

NOW IMAGINE THAT YOUR FRIENDS CLOSED THE LETTER BY SAYING, "WE TOOK WHAT WE HAD LEFT AT THE END OF THE YEAR, & BOUGHT THE SAILBOAT YOU CAN SEE IN THE ENCLOSED PICTURE." THAT'S HOW THE STATEMENT OF INCOME CONNECTS TO THE BALANCE SHEET. EVERY YEAR, THE NET INCOME (THE END OF THE LETTER) GETS ADDED TO THE RETAINED EARNINGS (OVER IN THE CORNER OF THE PICTURE). IT'S NOT QUITE THAT SIMPLE IN A COMPANY), BUT IT'S THE SAME IDEA.

ASSETS ~ THINGS THE COMPANY OWNS.

~ CASH

~ ACCOUNTS RECEIVABLE : MONEY OWED TO THE COMPANY

~ INVENTORY : MANUFACTURED PRODUCTS WAITING TO BE SOLD, ALSO INGREDIENTS, PACKAGING & SUPPLIES

~ PROPERTY, PLANT & EQUIPMENT : BUILDINGS, MACHINERY, TRUCKS ETC. DEPRECIATION IS THE PART OF THE VALUE OF THESE ASSETS THAT HAS BEEN USED UP, BASED ON HOW LONG IT IS EXPECTED TO LAST.

~ PREPAID EXPENSES, DEFERRED INCOME TAXES, OTHER ASSETS : THESE ARE MISCELLANEOUS OTHER PURCHASED ASSETS THE COMPANY HAS THAT HAVE VALUE.

LIABILITIES ~ WHAT THE COMPANY OWES.

~ CURRENT LIABILITIES ~ BILLS, PAYROLL DUE, TAXES & OTHER OBLIGATIONS THAT HAVE TO BE PAID WITHIN A YEAR.

~ LONG TERM DEBT & OBLIGATIONS UNDER CAPITAL LEASES ~ LOANS OR AGREEMENTS TO PAY FOR USE OF EQUIPMENT A YEAR OR MORE FROM NOW.

~ OTHER LIABILITIES ~ MISCELLANEOUS OTHER FINANCIAL COMMITMENTS.

STOCKHOLDERS' EQUITY : THIS IS CALLED THE "BOOK VALUE" OF THE OWNERS' STAKE IN THE COMPANY. IT INCLUDES PROCEEDS THE COMPANY RECEIVED FROM THE INITIAL AND SUBSEQUENT SALES OF STOCK TO THE PUBLIC, PLUS ACCUMULATED PROFITS, CALLED RETAINED EARNINGS.

THIS BOOK VALUE IS NOT THE SAME AS THE VALUE OF STOCK ON THE PUBLIC STOCK MARKET WHICH IS CALLED THE "MARKET VALUE". THE STOCK MARKET DETERMINES IN ITS OWN WAYS WHETHER THE COMPANY IS WORTH MORE THAN THE BOOK VALUE OF WHAT IT OWNS MINUS WHAT IT OWES. FOR EXAMPLE, A COMPANY'S STOCK PRICE CHANGES REGULARLY WITHOUT REGARD TO THE VALUE OF THE ASSETS & LIABILITIES IT USES TO RUN ITS BUSINESS.

1. ASSETS

Suppose we want a financial picture of E. Tutt, who recently graduated from law school and has opened a law office. Certainly one important facet is how much she owns. Because we really are concerned with her business and not her personal affairs, we forget her car, her clothes, and other personal property, and we look to see what she has in her office:

(a) Office furniture

(b) Office equipment

(c) Stationery and supplies

(d) Library

(e) Cash in the bank

A layperson would understand all of these to be what the accountant calls them: assets.

Accountants view *assets* as future economic benefits that a particular accounting entity, whether a natural person, business enterprise, or charitable organization, owns or controls as a result of a past transaction or event. Accountants classify economic resources as assets when the entity satisfies three requirements pertaining to the resource. First, the entity must control the resource. Second, the entity must reasonably expect the resource to provide a future benefit. Third, the entity must have obtained the resource in a transaction so that the entity can measure the resource.

Several examples can illustrate these requirements. Would E. Tutt's friendly personality qualify as an asset that she can list on her balance sheet? No. Although Tutt can control her personality and a friendly personality should help a lawyer, she did not acquire her personality in a transaction. If Tutt purchases a computer for her office, paying $2,000 in cash, and expects the computer to last two years, can she show the computer as an asset on her balance sheet? Yes. Tutt controls the computer, which should provide at least two years of service to her law practice, and she acquired the computer in a transaction. If Tutt spends $300 to send her secretary to a training session on using software for the computer, can she treat the training cost as an asset? No. Unless Tutt and her secretary have signed an employment contract, as an at-will employee, the secretary could choose to quit her job at any time, taking along the training. Although Tutt expects to receive future benefits from the training and a transaction has occurred, Tutt does not have control over her secretary.

Before we can show an asset on a balance sheet, we need some measure for the resource. In other words, we need to assign some dollar amount to the asset. Because the price at which property was bought is ordinarily much easier to ascertain and less subjective than the current fair market value of the property, accountants generally record assets at *historical cost*. We should always remember that the balance sheet usually does not show assets at their fair market value.

We should also remember that the balance sheet shows only assets that satisfy the three requirements described above. The balance sheet does not reflect many important things that we might consider as valuable to a business. For example, the value that an outstanding management team brings to a business, good morale among the enterprise's employees, or loyal and satisfied customers, do not appear as assets on the balance sheet.

For these reasons, the balance sheet, like the other financial statements we will discuss, typically provides limited, if any, contemporary or prospective information.

2.   SOURCES

If E. Tutt bought all her property out of her own funds and has not yet earned anything, we could simply add up the assets to find out how E. Tutt stands in her business. But if she has borrowed money from a bank to buy some of her assets or, perhaps more likely, has bought some on credit, E. Tutt's personal "stake" in the business would not be as large as if she had bought everything from her own funds. To give a true picture of her financial position, we would want to know where the money came from to buy the assets. Suppose we find that she acquired the assets as follows:

(a) Office furniture: bought on credit from Frank Co. for $400;

(b) Office equipment: bought on credit from Elmer Co. for $300;

(c) Stationery and supplies: bought from Stanley for $100 on a promissory note;

(d) Library: purchased for $200 cash, out of E. Tutt's original "stake" of $1,000; and

(e) $800 cash: balance of Tutt's original "stake" remaining.

We could then list, in parallel columns, the assets and their sources:

	Assets		**Sources**	
(a)	Office furniture	$ 400	Frank Co.	$ 400 (a)
(b)	Office equipment	300	Elmer Co.	300 (b)
(c)	Stationery and supplies	100	Stanley	100 (c)
(d)	Library	200		
(e)	Cash (balance remaining)	800	E. Tutt	1,000 (d,e)
	Total	$1,800	Total	$1,800

This parallel listing of assets and their sources is what accountants usually call a *balance sheet*. As other examples, you can find the balance sheets of Starbucks Corporation ("Starbucks") on both September 30, 2012, and October 2, 2011, in Appendix A on page 747, *infra*. Appendix A contains the Form 10-K that Starbucks filed with the Securities and Exchange Commission

("SEC") for the company's fiscal year ended September 30, 2012, to illustrate the financial statements, accompanying notes, and related reports and disclosures for a publicly-traded corporation. Starbucks' consolidated financial statements and the related notes appear on pages 54 to 88 of the Form 10-K at pages 750 to 784, *infra*. At different times, this text will also refer to the financial reports of Amazon.com, Inc. ("Amazon"), Google Inc. ("Google"), and United Parcel Service, Inc. ("UPS"), which you can easily access via the Investor Relations sections of those companies' websites, to illustrate various financial accounting principles and related concepts, including the balance sheet.

Other enterprises may label their listing of assets and sources as a *statement of financial position* or a *statement of financial condition*. As preliminary matters about this first financial statement, whatever the name, we should note two things. First, the totals of the two columns must always be equal. For this reason, we will refer to this financial statement as the balance sheet. Second, no matter how complicated a business or how long its history, the balance sheet shows, at one particular point in time, what assets the business owns and where the money came from to acquire those assets. Because the balance sheet reflects one instant in time, we can compare the balance sheet to a snapshot.

To give a somewhat clearer picture of how well off E. Tutt herself is, we can separate the sources of assets into two groups: "outside" sources—money that the business owes to creditors; and "inside" sources—amounts that Tutt herself has invested in the business. We now turn our discussion to those "outside" sources.

a. LIABILITIES

The "outside" sources would also be understood by a layperson to be what the accountant calls them: liabilities. Accountants characterize duties or responsibilities to provide economic benefits to some other accounting entity in the future as *liabilities*. Liabilities arise from borrowings of cash, purchases of assets on credit, breaches of contracts or commissions of torts, receipts of services, or passage of time. Accountants treat duties or responsibilities as liabilities when the underlying debt or obligation possesses three characteristics. First, the debt or obligation must involve a present duty or responsibility. Second, the duty or responsibility must obligate the entity to provide a future benefit. Finally, the debt or obligation must have arisen from a transaction or event that has already occurred so the entity can reasonably measure the obligation.

Again, several hypotheticals can illustrate these characteristics. If E. Tutt accepts delivery of the computer on August 1 and agrees to pay for it in full on October 1, has she incurred a liability? Yes. A transaction that has already occurred has legally bound Tutt to pay $2,000 to the seller. If Tutt orders law books worth $200, but the seller has not yet delivered the books, has she incurred a liability? No. When delivery takes place, Tutt will owe the $200, but until that time Tutt has not incurred a liability. The transaction does not become complete until the delivery takes place; only then must Tutt pay for the supplies or return them. If Tutt accepts a $300 retainer from one of her clients to prepare and file articles of incorporation in advance of rendering legal services, has she incurred a liability? Yes. Tutt has an obligation to deliver legal services worth $300 to the client. If she cannot provide the services, she must refund the client's payment. She has incurred a legal obligation and a transaction has already occurred.

Just as the balance sheet does not show "positives" that do not satisfy the accounting requirements for assets, the balance sheet also may not list "negatives" that could adversely affect the business. For example, poor management, labor problems, unsatisfied customers, or a poor reputation in the community would not appear as liabilities on a balance sheet. By ignoring these factors, which obviously present difficult measurement issues, the balance sheet can convey a false impression about a business's financial condition.

Unless the business has given a creditor a security interest in a particular asset, or a law grants such an interest, liabilities attach to the business's assets generally, rather than to the specific assets that the creditor may have helped the business acquire. If the business does not pay its debts, creditors may force the business to liquidate. In that event, creditor rights laws require the entity to satisfy its liabilities before paying any "inside" claims to its owner.

b.   EQUITY

Because creditors' claims enjoy priority in liquidation over "inside" claims, any liabilities reduce E. Tutt's personal stake or equity in the business. Accountants refer to *equity* as the arithmetical amount that remains after a particular accounting entity subtracts its liabilities from its assets. In other words, if the entity sold its assets, and satisfied its liabilities, for the amounts shown on the balance sheet, we call the remainder equity because the owners could claim that residual amount.

Equity increases when the owners invest assets into the business. The equity in E. Tutt's law practice increased when she contributed $1,000 to the business. Equity decreases when the owners withdraw assets from the business.

Depending on the accounting entity involved, accountants assign different names to the residual ownership interest. Owners can use sole proprietorships, partnerships, corporations, or hybrid organizations such as limited partnerships, limited liability partnerships, and limited liability companies, to conduct business. We will now consider the residual ownership claims in these different forms of business organization.

As the name suggests, only one person owns a *sole proprietorship*. The owner usually also manages and operates the business. Many small service-type businesses, including E. Tutt's law office, operate as sole proprietorships. Sole proprietorships generally offer simplicity as an advantage. Anyone can start a sole proprietorship, and the owner can keep any profits. The owner, however, must bear any losses and remains personally liable for any debts the business incurs. Although the law does not recognize any distinction between the business and the owner, we recognize the business as a separate accounting entity. Accountants refer to the residual ownership interest in a sole proprietorship as *proprietorship*.

A *partnership* arises when two or more persons engage in business for profit as co-owners. If E. Tutt and her law school classmate, Jennifer King, decide to practice law together, they could form a partnership, which they might call "King Tutt." In many ways, a partnership resembles a sole proprietorship except that the business involves more than one owner. Again, partnerships generally offer simplicity, but the partners frequently sign partnership agreements which set forth various terms regarding the partnership, such as each partner's initial investment, responsibilities and duties, profit and loss sharing ratio, and vote in management and the procedures for ending the partnership. As a huge disadvantage, each partner incurs unlimited personal liability for the partnership's debts. Despite this unlimited personal liability, accountants recognize partnerships as separate accounting entities to segregate partnership affairs from the partners' personal activities. Accountants refer to the residual ownership interest in partnership as *partners' equity*. With multiple owners, however, partnerships keep separate equity accounts for each partner.

One or more persons owning a business could also form a *corporation* by complying with certain statutory requirements. Laws in every state treat corporations as legal entities separate from their owners. Corporate laws divide the residual ownership interest in a corporation into *shares*. Generally, each share entitles the owner to: (1) participate in corporate governance by voting on certain matters, such as the election of directors who manage the corporation's business and affairs; (2) share proportionally in any earnings, in the form of dividends, which the directors may declare and the corporation may distribute to shareholders; and (3) share proportionally in residual corporate assets upon liquidation.

The owners of the shares, usually referred to as *shareholders*, enjoy limited liability. The corporation's creditors cannot hold the shareholders personally liable for the corporation's debts. Shareholders can transfer their shares to other investors without dissolving the corporation. On the downside, federal income tax law treats corporations as separate taxpaying entities. This treatment creates double taxation because corporations must pay taxes on their income, and shareholders generally must pay taxes on any amounts that the corporation distributes as dividends.

Accountants refer to the ownership interest in a corporation as *shareholders' equity*. For practical reasons related to the free transferability of shares and the possibility that thousands, or even millions, of shareholders could own a stake in a corporation, corporations do not maintain separate equity accounts for each shareholder.

All states permit business owners to form hybrid entities such as *limited partnerships, limited liability companies,* or *limited liability partnerships.* These hybrid entities possess both partnership and corporate characteristics. The hybrid entities all follow partnership accounting.

Two or more persons can form a limited partnership in any state by complying with the applicable statutory requirements. A limited partnership requires one or more general partners and one or more limited partners. As a general rule, general partners manage the partnership's business while limited partners provide additional capital. Although the limited partners enjoy limited liability, the general partners remain personally liable for the limited partnership's debts. As with partnerships, accountants refer to the residual ownership interest in the limited partnership as partners' equity. Limited partnerships keep separate equity accounts for each partner, whether general or limited.

By following state law requirements, one or more owners can form a limited liability company ("LLC") as a separate legal entity in every state. The LLC's owners, usually referred to as *members,* enjoy limited liability. Accordingly, an LLC's creditors cannot hold the members personally liable for the LLC's debts. LLCs offer significant flexibility because the members can structure their *operating agreement* in almost any way they want. LLCs have become very popular because they can avoid the double tax problem. Accountants refer to the residual ownership interest in an LLC as *members' equity.* Because LLCs possess some partnership characteristics, LLCs keep separate equity accounts for each member.

All states now permit two or more owners to organize a limited liability partnership ("LLP") or to convert an existing partnership to an LLP. Depending on the statute, partners in an LLP enjoy limited liability from either certain tort-type liabilities or from all liabilities. LLPs, therefore, offer partners either partial or full shields against the LLP's obligations. As with any other partnership, accountants refer to the residual ownership interest in an LLP as partners' equity. Similarly, LLPs keep separate equity accounts for each partner.

We will discuss, in more detail, the different accounting treatments that accountants use to account for partners' equity and shareholders' equity later in the chapter.

3.   THE FUNDAMENTAL ACCOUNTING EQUATION

No matter what organizational form the owners choose, we can express the relationship between equity, assets and liabilities in the following mathematical equation:

$$\text{Equity} = \text{Assets} - \text{Liabilities}$$

Under this equation, E. Tutt's equity, which we might also call her *net worth,* equals the difference between the law practice's assets and liabilities.

Accountants, however, rearrange the equation in two steps. First, they reverse the equation's two sides so that the equation reads:

$$\text{Assets} - \text{Liabilities} = \text{Equity}$$

Second, they add Liabilities to both sides of the equation to produce the restated equation:

$$\text{Assets} = \text{Liabilities} + \text{Equity}$$

Accountants refer to this restatement as the *fundamental accounting equation* because the equation serves as the underlying basis for the balance sheet. In fact, the fundamental accounting equation sustains the bookkeeping process and the accrual accounting system.

We might rearrange E. Tutt's assets, listing them in the order in which they are likely to be used up. We might also separate the source of the assets between liabilities and equity. The result would be a simple balance sheet that might look like this:

E. Tutt, Esquire
Balance Sheet, After transaction (e)

Assets			**Liabilities & Proprietorship**		
			Liabilities:		
(e)	Cash	$ 800	Accounts Payable:		
(c)	Supplies	100	Frank Co.	$ 400	(a)
			Elmer Co.	300	(b)
			Note Payable:		
(b)	Equipment	300	Stanley	100	(c)
(a)	Furniture	400	Total Liabilities	$800	
(d)	Library	200	Proprietorship	1,000	(d, e)
	Total	$1,800	Total	$1,800	

Note that no change has been made except a change in presentation of the list of assets and sources which appears on page 9, *supra*. The essential meaning remains the same.

Having discussed each component in the balance sheet and the fundamental accounting equation, we should remember four very important points about the balance sheet. First, total assets must equal the sum of liabilities and equity. Second, the balance sheet speaks at, or as of, one particular instant in time. Third, the balance sheet shows only assets and liabilities that meet certain accounting requirements. The balance sheet, therefore, may not reflect many important things that we might consider as valuable or detrimental to the business. Fourth, the balance sheet generally records assets at historical cost. Because financial accounting requires that an economic resource must probably provide a future benefit before an enterprise can treat the resource as an asset, the balance sheet does offer some prospective information. Similarly, financial accounting recognizes a liability only when an enterprise probably must provide a future benefit to another individual or organization.

4. THE CLASSIFIED BALANCE SHEET

Thus far, we have purposely kept the discussion about the balance sheet simple. The balance sheet becomes more useful to managers, creditors, owners, and potential investors, however, when the entity classifies assets and liabilities into various categories.

Accountants generally classify assets into four types: *current assets, long-term investments, fixed assets*, and *intangible assets*. They generally treat cash and other assets that the particular accounting entity would normally expect to convert into cash or use within one year as *current assets*. Current assets could include: *marketable securities*, such as stocks and bonds, which the entity holds as short-term investments; *notes receivable*, amounts due to the entity under promissory notes; *accounts receivable*, uncollected amounts owed to the entity for goods or services sold on credit; *inventories*, or goods held for sale or resale; and *prepaid expenses*, such as insurance premiums paid in advance for insurance coverage during the next year. In contrast, accountants generally classify resources that an accounting entity would not normally expect to convert into cash or use within one year as *long-term investments*. Long-term investments include stocks and bonds that the entity intends to hold; notes receivable or accounts receivable that the entity cannot collect for more than a year; and prepaid expenses, such as insurance premiums paid in advance for insurance coverage more than one year into the future. *Fixed assets* include tangible resources such as land, buildings, plant and equipment, machinery, or furniture and fixtures that the entity acquired for extended use in the business. *Intangible assets* lack physical substance and include patents, copyrights, and trademarks acquired for extended use in the business.

Accountants usually show assets on the balance sheet in the order listed in the previous paragraph. Typically, a balance sheet lists current assets first and according to declining *liquidity*. Liquidity refers to the relative ease and time necessary to convert an asset into cash. Within current assets, the balance sheet starts with cash and proceeds to marketable securities, notes receivable, accounts receivable, inventory, and prepaid expenses in that order. Long-term investments typically follow current assets. The balance sheet then proceeds to list fixed assets, usually according to permanence, and finishes with intangible assets.

Turning to liabilities, accountants also divide these duties or obligations into two types: current and long-term. They generally classify liabilities that will require payment in one year or less as *current liabilities*. Current liabilities include: money borrowed under promissory notes due within one year, usually called *notes payable*; amounts owed for purchases on credit, or *accounts payable*; money owed for services already performed, usually referred to as *accrued liabilities or wages*; those portions of long-term debt that the business must repay within one year; taxes payable; and *unearned revenues*, amounts that the entity will have to refund if it does not perform the required services.

In contrast to current liabilities, accountants generally consider obligations, or parts of obligations, which would normally not require payment for more than one year as *long-term liabilities*. Long-term liabilities typically include notes payable that do not require repayment for more than one year; *bonds payable*, which usually represent borrowings from numerous investors through the financial markets, rather than a loan from one creditor which gives rise to a note payable; lease and mortgage obligations due in more than one year; and obligations under employee pension plans.

Because liabilities enjoy priority in liquidation over ownership claims, the balance sheet lists liabilities above equity. Again, accountants usually show liabilities on the balance sheet in the order listed in the previous two paragraphs. Current liabilities come first, usually starting with notes payable and, then, accounts payable. Balance sheets frequently list other current liabilities in descending order of magnitude. Long-term liabilities follow, with any *secured claims*, or liabilities for which the borrower has pledged one or more assets as collateral, usually listed first. Last, the balance sheet shows equity.

We might rearrange E. Tutt's balance sheet according to these conventions. We might also show the assets above the liabilities and equity. The result would be a somewhat more refined balance sheet that might look like this:

E. Tutt, Esquire
Balance Sheet, After transaction (e)

Assets

	Current Assets:		
(e)	Cash		$ 800
(c)	Supplies		100
	Total Current Assets		$ 900
	Fixed Assets:		
(b)	Equipment		$ 300
(a)	Furniture		400
(d)	Library		200
	Total Fixed Assets		$ 900
	Total Assets		$1,800

Liabilities & Proprietorship

	Liabilities		
	Current Liabilities:		
(c)	Note Payable: Stanley		$ 100
	Accounts Payable:		
(a)	Frank Co.	$400	
(b)	Elmer Co.	300	700
	Total Liabilities		$ 800
(d, e)	Proprietorship		1,000
	Total Liabilities and Proprietorship		$1,800

Accountants refer to such a balance sheet as a *classified balance sheet* in *report form*. Again, note that no change has been made except a change in presentation. The essential meaning again remains the same. But because clear disclosure is one of the accountant's main concerns, matters of presentation are important. The classified balance sheet helps the user to determine whether the accounting entity owns enough current assets to pay liabilities as they come due. The classified balance sheet also shows the relative claims between short-term and long-term creditors.

C.   DOUBLE-ENTRY BOOKKEEPING

As Tutt engages in practice, many events will occur to affect her financial position, and the balance sheet figures will change. If, for example, in transaction (f), she pays off the note to Stanley, her cash would decrease by $100, so that the cash balance remaining would be $700, and the liability to Stanley of $100 would disappear. If, in transaction (g), Tutt paid Elmer Co. $200 of the amount owed for equipment, cash would be further decreased, to $500, and the liability of $300 to Elmer Co. would be decreased to $100. After these two transactions, Tutt's balance sheet, shown in *simple form* where the assets appear on the left side, while the liabilities and equity share the right side, would read as follows:

E. Tutt, Esquire
Balance Sheet, After transaction (g)

	Assets		**Liabilities & Proprietorship**		
			Liabilities:		
(e,f,g)	Cash	$ 500	Accounts Payable:		
(c)	Supplies	100	Frank Co.	$ 400	(a)
(b)	Equipment	300	Elmer Co.	100	(b,g)
(a)	Furniture	400	Total Liabilities	$ 500	
(d)	Library	200	Proprietorship	1,000	(d, e)
	Total	$1,500	Total	$1,500	

Note that each of these two transactions affected two items on the balance sheet and did so in equal amounts. This is not a coincidence; the fact is that every transaction has two separate aspects of equal importance. If, (h), Tutt bought more books for $100 in cash, it would tell only half the story to record just the decrease in cash of $100; her "holdings" of books—represented by the asset, *Library*—have increased by $100. If, (i), Tutt took a chair costing $50 from her office for use thereafter at home, reducing *Furniture* by $50 would not tell the whole story because her stake in the enterprise, *Proprietorship*, has also been reduced by $50.

Tutt's balance sheet, again in simple form, after these two transactions:

E. Tutt, Esquire
Balance Sheet, After transaction (i)

	Assets			Liabilities & Proprietorship		
				Liabilities:		
(e,f,g,h)	Cash	$ 400		Accounts Payable:		
(c)	Supplies	100		Frank Co.	$ 400	(a)
(b)	Equipment	300		Elmer Co.	100	(b,g)
(a,i)	Furniture	350		Total Liabilities	$ 500	
(d,h)	Library	300		Proprietorship	950	(d,e,i)
	Total	$1,450		Total	$1,450	

You will note that recognition of the two aspects of each transaction, which are always equal in amount, may change the totals of the balance sheet columns but does not upset their equality. That should not be surprising; we have already seen that the two columns of the balance sheet mirror the two sides of the fundamental accounting equation. The balance sheet reflects the assets and their sources at any given time, and the inherent equality of the fundamental accounting equation cannot be affected by changes in the mix of assets and their sources. To illustrate, an increase in an asset may come about in one of two ways: either another asset has been exchanged for it, or an additional source of funds has been supplied to acquire it (as, for example, if Tutt bought an asset on credit from a new supplier). On the balance sheet, the increase in the asset column would either be offset by a decrease in the asset column or be balanced by an increase in the sources column. Likewise, a decrease in an asset may come about in one of two ways. If assets have been exchanged, we have the transaction already discussed, but stated in reverse order—the decrease in assets will be accompanied by an increase in assets reflecting the acquisition of the new asset. The other possibility is a decrease in the sources column, reflecting use of an asset to pay off a claim, such as the use of cash to discharge the note payable to Stanley. Finally, there can be an exchange of sources, which would be reflected by equal increases and decreases in the sources column, as, for example, if Tutt should give a note to a creditor to whom she owed money on open account.

To simplify the number of possible combinations involved, we might first set out all the possibilities:

One Effect of Transaction	Accompanying Effect
(1) Increase in Asset	(a) Increase in Source
	(b) Decrease in Asset
(2) Decrease in Asset	(a) Decrease in Source
	(b) Increase in Asset
(3) Increase in Source	(a) Increase in Asset
	(b) Decrease in Source
(4) Decrease in Source	(a) Increase in Source
	(b) Decrease in Asset

Obviously, a number of these possibilities simply restate others, but in reverse order: e.g., (1)(a) and (3)(a). Indeed, the four types of balance sheet effects involved could be grouped as follows:

Increase in Asset	Increase in Source
Decrease in Source	Decrease in Asset

because all transactions are some combination of an item on one side of this table with one of the two items on the other side of the table.

The balance sheet itself is simply the summary to date of all the individual transactions, and the inherent equality of its columns is confirmed by the fact that each individual transaction has two equal effects on the balance sheet.

A single transaction can have more than two effects. If, in transaction (j), Tutt bought another piece of office equipment from Elmer Co. for $100, paying $50 down, *Equipment* would increase $100, *Cash* would decrease $50, and *Accounts Payable: Elmer Co.* would increase $50. This transaction shows that sometimes two combinations may be involved at the same time; the transaction here involves an increase in an asset balanced half by a decrease in an asset and half by an increase in a source.

Tutt's balance sheet, in simple form, after the above transaction becomes:

E. Tutt, Esquire
Balance Sheet, After transaction (j)

	Assets		Liabilities & Proprietorship		
			Liabilities:		
(e,f,g,h,j)	Cash	$ 350	Accounts Payable:		
(c)	Supplies	100	Frank Co.	$ 400	(a)
(b,j)	Equipment	400	Elmer Co.	150	(b,g)
(a,i)	Furniture	350	Total Liabilities	$ 550	
(d,h)	Library	300	Proprietorship	950	(d,e,i)
	Total	$1,500	Total	$1,500	

Even with these few transactions, the balance sheet has been changed several times. While we could rewrite the balance sheet every time something happens, it is more efficient for a business to keep a separate record of the ups and downs of each item on the balance sheet, so that the business can determine at any time the net effect on that item of all transactions since the bookkeeper drew up the last balance sheet. Look at cash. Tutt's first balance sheet, shown earlier, showed a cash balance of $800. The bookkeeper would take a separate card, or page in a book, entitle it *Cash*, and enter the $800 from the balance sheet as the opening balance. Since we ultimately want the net result of all the ups and downs in cash, it would be convenient to divide the page into two columns, one for recording the increases in cash, the other for reflecting the decreases; and it would be sensible to use the same column for increases as the one that has the opening balance. This record is called the Cash *account*. Here, transactions (e), (f), (g), (h) and (j) would each produce an *entry* in the Cash account. When the time for drawing up a new balance sheet arrived, it would be simple to add the total of the increases in cash to the opening balance and subtract the total of the decreases to find the balance in the cash account. The process is about the same as entering the balance forward, deposits, and withdrawals in the stubs of a checkbook. The Cash account for Tutt, beginning at the date of the balance sheet on page 14, *supra*, would look like this:

Order in which entries were made

		Cash		
		(+)	(−)	
(e)	Opening balance (from last balance sheet)	(e) $800		
(f)	To pay off Stanley		$100	(f)
(g)	To pay off Elmer Co.		200	(g)
(h)	To purchase books		100	(h)
(j)	To purchase equipment		50	(j)
	Current balance	$350		

Because this record is shaped like a "T," it is often called a *T-account*. The total of the plus column of the T-account, showing the opening cash balance plus any increases, less the total of the minus column, showing decreases, gives the current balance of $350, which would appear on the new balance sheet.

The T-accounts for the other assets, with the opening balance in each case coming from the previous balance sheet, would be as follows:

		Furniture		
		(+)	(−)	
(a)	Opening balance	(a) $400		
(i)	On removal of chair from business		$50	(i)
	Current balance	$350		

		Equipment		
		(+)	(−)	
(b)	Opening balance	(b) $300		
(j)	On new purchase from Elmer Co.	(j) 100		
	Current balance	$400		

		Supplies		
		(+)	(−)	
(c)	Opening balance	(c) $100		
	Current balance	$100		

(No further entries, as nothing has happened to affect the Supplies account)

Library

	(+)		(−)
(d) Opening balance	(d)	$200	
(h) On purchase of new books	(h)	100	
Current balance		$300	

In the T-accounts for assets, it is customary to enter the opening balance in the left-hand column. This corresponds to the fact that assets are recorded on the left-hand side of the balance sheet. As noted, the increases are entered in the same column as the opening balance, just as bank deposits are added to the previous balance in a checkbook.

T-accounts similar to those illustrated for the asset accounts are also set up for the liability and the proprietorship accounts. By a convention to be analyzed in the next paragraph, the opening balance in these accounts (which, as with assets, comes from the previous balance sheet) is entered on the right-hand side of the T-account. To keep this important switch in mind, remember that these accounts are the ones on the right-hand side of the balance sheet. As with assets, increases in these accounts are entered on the same side as the opening balance; but for these accounts that means the right-hand side, with decreases on the left. Tutt's liability and proprietorship T-accounts are as follows:

Accounts Payable:
Frank Co.

	(−)		(+)	
(a) Opening balance			$400	(a)
Current balance			$400	

Accounts Payable:
Elmer Co.

	(−)		(+)	
(b) Opening balance			$300	(b)
(g) To show partial payment of the account	(g)	$200		
(j) On new purchase of equipment			50	(j)
Current balance			$150	

Note Payable: Stanley

	(−)		(+)	
(c) Opening balance			$100	(c)
(f) To show payment of note	(f)	$100		
Current balance			$0	

		Proprietorship			
		(−)		(+)	
(d,e)	Opening balance			$1000	(d,e)
(i)	On removal of chair from business	(i)	$50		
	Current balance			$950	

At first, this switch of the plus and minus columns may seem clumsy. But it has one very practical advantage that makes the bookkeeper's job easier: it results in having every transaction, no matter what accounts are affected, give rise to equal left-hand and right-hand entries in the T-accounts. To see that this is so, you should first recognize that a transaction affecting accounts on only one side of the balance sheet must produce an equal increase and decrease, and never two increases alone, or two decreases alone. Therefore, if a transaction affects only one side of the balance sheet, such as assets only or sources only, one entry will be a left-hand entry and the other a right-hand entry. In these cases there is no necessity for any convention calling for a switch between asset accounts and source accounts as to the side of the T-account on which an increase or decrease is entered.

It is when a transaction affects both sides of the balance sheet that the advantage of this convention appears. Remember that a transaction affecting accounts on both sides produces either an equal increase on both sides or an equal decrease on both sides, but never an increase on one and a decrease on the other. Whether the change on both sides of the balance sheet is an increase or a decrease, by virtue of this convention the change on one side will be a left-hand entry and the change on the other a right-hand entry. For example, an increase in assets is a left-hand entry, whereas the corresponding equal increase in liabilities or proprietorship is a right-hand entry. Again, a decrease in the assets column will be a right-hand entry, and the corresponding decrease in liabilities and proprietorship will be a left-hand entry. The table given earlier, then, actually constitutes a summary of the possible combinations of left-hand and right-hand entries:

Left-hand entries	**Right-hand entries**
Increase in Asset	Increase in Source
Decrease in Source	Decrease in Asset

This convention as to the side of the T-accounts on which increases and decreases are entered, operating in conjunction with the fact that every transaction has two equal aspects which must be recorded, forms the basis of the system that accountants call double-entry bookkeeping.

At this time, we should mention that some small businesses use *single-entry bookkeeping*. A checkbook register illustrates a single-entry bookkeeping system. If Tutt opened a checking account for her law office and deposited all cash receipts in the account and wrote checks for all cash payments, her checkbook register would tell us the balance in her checking account, where she collected cash and where she spent cash. In that example, the register would show a $350 balance in the checking account and that Tutt deposited $1,000 in the account to start the business. The register would also provide information about five cash expenditures: (1) the purchase of the library for $200, (2) the $100 payment to Stanley for stationery and supplies, (3) the $200 partial payment to Elmer Co. for office equipment that Tutt purchased on credit, (4) another $100 to purchase books for the library, and (5) the $50 down payment to Elmer Co. for another piece of office equipment. The checkbook register, however, does not tell us what other assets the business owns or what business obligations Tutt owes. For example, the checkbook register does not tell us: (1) that Tutt also owns office furniture that she bought on credit from Frank Co., (2) whether Tutt still owns the library books, (3) whether the business has used the stationary and supplies, (4) whether E. Tutt still owns the office equipment she purchased from Elmer Co., or (5) whether the business owes any other creditors. In this last regard, the checkbook register does not tell us that Tutt owes Frank Co. $400 for the office furniture that she bought on credit. Finally, the checkbook register does not reveal that Tutt took a chair that cost $50 from her office for use at home. Double-entry bookkeeping permits more comprehensive financial reports.

To see how double-entry bookkeeping is used, take another look at the transactions already considered. When Tutt paid off Stanley's note, there was a decrease in a liability, *Note Payable: Stanley*, a left-hand entry, and a decrease in an asset, *Cash*, a right-hand entry. And when Tutt bought more office equipment from Elmer Co. for $100, paying $50 down, the left-hand entry showed a $100 increase in an asset, *Equipment*; the right-hand entries included: (1) a $50 decrease in an asset, *Cash*, and (2) a $50 increase in a liability, *Accounts Payable: Elmer Co.* The left-hand and right-hand entries for each transaction are equal, no matter how many accounts are affected.

The terms "left-hand entry" and "right-hand entry" are cumbersome. Bookkeepers instead use shorthand terms. Left-hand entries are *debits* and right-hand entries are *credits*. When Tutt buys more books, the bookkeeper speaks of a *debit* to *Library*, or *debiting Library*, and a *credit* to *Cash*, or *crediting Cash*. Both debits and credits convey only positive numbers; rather than record a debit for a negative number, a bookkeeper would use a credit for that same amount, and vice versa. Whatever meaning debit and credit express in other contexts, here debit and credit, which accountants often abbreviate "Dr." and "Cr." respectively, mean nothing more than left-hand and right-hand entries in the T-accounts. We could restate the T-accounts that appear on pages 20 to 22, *supra*, as follows:

		Cash			
		Dr.		Cr.	
(e)	Opening balance (from last balance sheet)	(e)	$800		
(f)	To pay off Stanley			$100	(f)
(g)	To pay off Elmer Co.			200	(g)
(h)	To purchase books			100	(h)
(j)	To purchase equipment			50	(j)
	Current balance		$350		

Furniture

		Dr.	Cr.	
(a)	Opening balance	(a) $400		
(i)	On removal of chair from business		$50	(i)
	Current balance	$350		

Equipment

		Dr.	Cr.	
(b)	Opening balance	(b) $300		
(j)	On new purchase from Elmer Co.	(j) 100		
	Current balance	$400		

Supplies

		Dr.	Cr.	
(c)	Opening balance	(c) $100		
	Current balance	$100		

Library

		Dr.	Cr.	
(d)	Opening balance	(d) $200		
(h)	On purchase of new books	(h) 100		
	Current balance	$300		

Accounts Payable: Frank Co.

		Dr.	Cr.	
(a)	Opening balance		$400	(a)
	Current balance		$400	

Accounts Payable: Elmer Co.

		Dr.	Cr.	
(b)	Opening balance		$300	(b)
(g)	To show partial payment of the account	(g) $200		
(j)	On new purchase of equipment		$50	(j)
	Current balance		$150	

Note Payable: Stanley

		Dr.	Cr.	
(c)	Opening balance		$100	(c)
(f)	To show payment of note	(f) $100		
	Current balance		$0	

	Proprietorship		
	Dr.		Cr.
(d,e) Opening balance			$1000 (d,e)
(i) On removal of chair from business	(i)	$50	
Current balance			$950

For convenience, the bookkeeper first records transactions chronologically in a separate book, usually referred to as the *journal*. For each transaction, the journal shows the debit and credit effects on specific accounts. Businesses may use various kinds of journals, but every business will use a *general journal*. A business may also create a journal to record transactions in various functions, such as a sales journal, a purchases journal, a cash receipts journal, or a cash disbursements journal. Today, many businesses use computers to keep their journals, but the fundamental concepts remain the same.

The general journal usually contains five columns for the date, the accounts involved and any explanation of the transaction, a cross-reference for the account number to which the bookkeeper transferred the amount in the journal entry, and separate columns for debits and credits. The general journal for a business typically looks something like this:

General Journal

Date	Account	Ref.	Debit	Credit

For each transaction, the bookkeeper first enters the date. Then, the bookkeeper writes the account to be debited as a result of the transaction and the amount of the debit. Next on the following line, but indented, is written the account to be credited and the amount. Indentation separates the credits from the debits. These items are often followed by a brief description of the transaction that makes it possible to check later to see whether the transaction was recorded properly. Representative *journal entries*, in simplified form with the letter of each transaction rather than the date and without the reference column or the linear grids, for some of Tutt's transactions would be:

(f)	Note Payable: Stanley	$100	
	Cash		$100
	(To record payment of the note to Stanley)		
(h)	Library	100	
	Cash		100
	(To record the purchase of additional books)		

(j) Equipment	100	
Cash		50
Accounts Payable: Elmer Co.		50

(To record purchase of additional business
equipment from Elmer Co.)

These entries are then recorded in the appropriate accounts, a process known as *posting* from the journal to the *ledger*. Accountants refer to the ledger as the collection of all the accounts that a business maintains. The ledger, therefore, stores in one place all the information about changes in specific account balances. Again, businesses often keep various kinds of ledgers, but every business will use a *general ledger*. The general ledger contains all the asset, liability, and equity accounts for the business. A business may also keep *sub-ledgers* when it needs to keep very detailed records. For example, an accounting entity may use an accounts receivable sub-ledger to record the individual amounts that each customer owes to the business. The accounts receivable account in the general ledger would keep track of the total amount owed to the firm by all its customers. The sum of the subsidiary accounts in the sub-ledger must equal the balance in the accounts receivable account in the general ledger.

For each ledger, businesses often use a looseleaf binder or card file with each account kept on a separate sheet or card. Businesses usually number each account for identification purposes and usually place the accounts in the general ledger in balance sheet order, starting with assets. Liabilities and equity accounts usually follow. As with journals, many businesses today use computerized ledgers, but the underlying concepts still remain the same.

Most business have developed a *chart of accounts* that lists each account and the corresponding account number that identifies the account's location in the ledger. To understand a business's accounting records, you should start with the chart of accounts. For example, E. Tutt's chart of accounts might list the following accounts and account numbers:

E. Tutt, Esquire
Chart of Accounts

Number	Account
	Assets
1	Cash
5	Accounts Receivable
9	Supplies
11	Equipment
13	Furniture
15	Library
	Liabilities
21	Notes Payable
23	Accounts Payable

<u>Owner's Equity</u>

31   Proprietorship
99   Profit and Loss

<u>Revenues</u>

51   Professional Income
55   Miscellaneous Income

<u>Expenses</u>

71   Rent Expense
75   Secretary Expense
79   Telephone Expense
83   Miscellaneous Expense

We will discuss revenues, expenses, and profit and loss in the next section. For now, you should notice, however, that the account numbering system in the chart of accounts contains gaps to permit the bookkeeper to insert new accounts as needed.

To summarize the bookkeeping process, the bookkeeper first periodically records transactions in the journal. Next, the bookkeeper posts the information in the journal to the ledger by periodically transferring the information in the journal to accounts in the ledger. If the bookkeeper wants to prepare a balance sheet at any point in time, the bookkeeper determines the balance in each account by netting one side against the other and uses the balances in the asset, liability and equity accounts to prepare the balance sheet.

From this summary, you can already imagine that bookkeeping involves a tedious process. As previously mentioned, computers have become so important in bookkeeping and accounting that all large businesses and many, if not most, smaller businesses use computerized bookkeeping or accounting systems. Computerized systems can save enormous amounts of time because software can automatically record each journal entry in the ledger, concurrently compute the new balance in the account, and simultaneously prepare updated financial statements if desired. Beneath the computer software, however, lies the double-entry bookkeeping system.

PROBLEMS

You have now read about the basic foundations of bookkeeping. What is called for at this point is some practice in applying these techniques yourself.

Problem 1.1A. Immediately following is the balance sheet for E. Tutt on January 1 of her second year of practice, followed by a list of some of Tutt's transactions during the month of January, on the dates indicated.

(1) Set up T-accounts for each of the items on the balance sheet on one sheet of paper, with the opening balance on the appropriate side. Then on a separate piece of paper write the journal entry for each of the transactions listed, and then post them to the appropriate T-accounts, adding new T-accounts as necessary.

(2) Unless your professor directs otherwise, prepare a simple balance sheet for E. Tutt as of January 12.

E. Tutt, Esquire
Balance sheet, January 1 of Second Year

Assets		Liabilities & Proprietorship	
		Liabilities:	
Cash	$ 450	Accounts Payable:	
Supplies	50	Brown	$ 200
Equipment	420	Frank Co.	250
Furniture	550	Total Liabilities	$ 450
Library	630	Proprietorship	1,650
Total	$2,100	Total	$2,100

Transactions in January:

Jan. 1 Bought a new chair for the office for $75 cash.

4 Paid Brown $100 on account.

6 Purchased a new office machine from Jones Co. for $220 on credit.

7 Purchased a new copy of the Ames Code Annotated from the East Publishing Co. for $120, paying $60 down, with the other $60 due in February.

9 Received a birthday gift from her parents of $300 cash to help her stay in business—she deposited the money in her business bank account.

11 Paid Frank Co. the $250 she owed it.

12 Gave some law books she no longer needed, which cost her $100, to her law school's library.

Problem 1.1B. Immediately following is the balance sheet for Geoffrey P. Forgione's Diner on June 30, followed by a list of some of transactions during the month of July, on the dates indicated.

(1) Set up T-accounts for each of the items on the balance sheet on one sheet of paper, with the opening balance on the appropriate side. Then on a separate piece of paper write the journal entry for each of the transactions listed, and then post them to the appropriate T-accounts, adding new T-accounts as necessary.

(2) Unless your professor directs otherwise, prepare a simple balance sheet for Geoffrey P. Forgione's Diner as of July 31.

Geoffrey P. Forgione's Diner
Balance Sheet, June 30

Assets		Liabilities & Proprietorship	
		Liabilities:	
Cash	$ 4,000	Accounts Payable:	
Inventory	2,200	Thomas M. Henry Co.	$ 4,200
Equipment	12,000	Proprietorship	14,000
Total	$18,200	Total	$18,200

Transactions in July:

July   2 Geoff invested an additional $1,500 in the business.

         5 Geoff used $300 worth of inventory at cost for a personal party for which he paid $300 cash to the business.

         8 The business acquired additional inventory from Thomas M. Henry Co. on credit for $1,200.

      13 Using funds in his business bank account, Geoff purchased a new fax machine for the diner for $600 cash.

      17 Geoff withdrew $1,000 from the business for his personal use.

      20 Thomas M. Henry Co. accepted a promissory note for the total balance due to the company.

Problem 1.1C. Immediately following is the balance sheet for Kathleen M. Brannock, Wedding Planner on June 30, followed by a list of some of transactions during the month of July, on the dates indicated.

(1) Set up T-accounts for each of the items on the balance sheet on one sheet of paper, with the opening balance on the appropriate side. Then on a separate piece of paper write the journal entry for each of the transactions listed, and then post them to the appropriate T-accounts, adding new T-accounts as necessary.

(2) Unless your professor directs otherwise, prepare a simple balance sheet for Kathleen M. Brannock, Wedding Planner, as of July 31.

Kathleen M. Brannock, Wedding Planner
Balance Sheet, June 30

Assets		Liabilities & Proprietorship	
Cash	$ 7,000	Liabilities:	
Inventory	5,200	Accounts Payable:	
Equipment	19,000	Justice	$ 5,200
Total	$31,200	Proprietorship	26,000
		Total	$31,200

Transactions in July:

July   5   Kathy acquired additional inventory from Terry Pendleton on credit in the amount of $1,200.

8   Kathy sold equipment to print invitations that had cost the proprietorship $5,500 to Ron Gant for that same amount.

13   She withdrew $1,000 from the business for her personal use.

17   Kathy used proprietorship funds to purchase for the business a new computer and color printer for $3,500 in cash.

20   Justice demanded payment on the total balance due to him during a telephone call. Kathy promised payment to him by the end of the month.

29   Kathy withdrew $6,500 from the proprietorship for personal use.

D.   THE INCOME STATEMENT

We have already seen how the balance sheet gives a reader one way to determine how well a business is doing by comparing what the business owns with what it owes. The balance sheet shows the present status of the assets and their sources resulting from all transactions since the business was formed. It is drawn up at regular intervals which will vary with the needs of the business. The balance sheet, however, cannot tell a reader very much about the business's ability to earn a profit.

As another, and probably more important way, to assess how a business is doing, we could also compare the amounts which the business's activities generate—its *revenues*—with the costs incurred to produce those revenues—its *expenses*. The *income statement*, the second basic financial statement, shows the extent to which business activities have caused an accounting entity's equity, or net worth, to increase or decrease over some period of time. Before we discuss the income statement any further, you might want to read the following cartoons that originally appeared in the 1992 annual report of Ben & Jerry's Homemade, Inc. and that we reprint with permission. Again, these cartoons very simply explain the income statement.

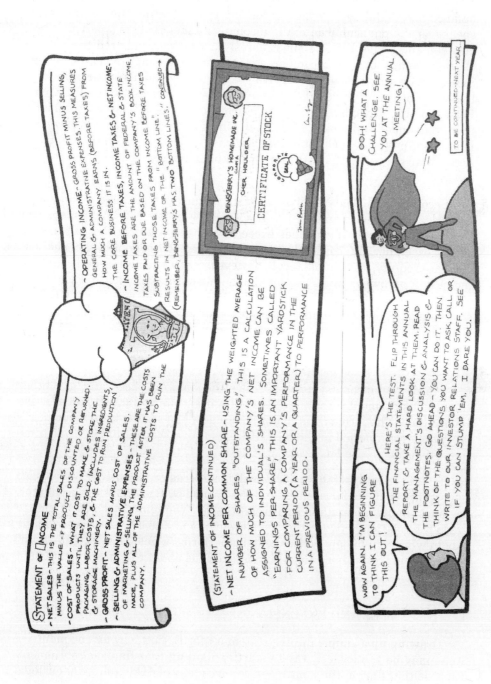

As preliminary matters, we should note three things about the income statement, which businesses sometimes call the *statement of earnings* or the *statement of operations*. First, the fundamental distinction between the balance sheet and the income statement is that, while the balance sheet speaks as of a particular date, the income statement covers a period of time between successive balance sheet dates. Just as we compared the balance sheet to a snapshot, we can compare the income statement to a motion picture. Income statements usually cover one year, either a calendar year or another twelve-month or fifty-two or fifty-three week period referred to as a *fiscal year*. For example, Appendix A contains Starbucks' financial statements for the fiscal year ended September 30, 2012. Business owners or managers, however, may also prepare such statements on a monthly or quarterly basis. Accountants usually refer to these monthly or quarterly statements as *interim reports*.

Second, the income statement only shows the extent to which a business's activities have caused an increase or a decrease in equity, or net worth, over some period of time. If revenues exceed expenses, the resulting net income increases equity. In contrast, if expenses exceed revenues, the net loss decreases equity. You should recall, however, that a business's equity can also increase if an owner invests assets in the business or decrease if an owner withdraws assets from the business. Recall that equity increased when E. Tutt contributed $1,000 as her original stake in her law office and decreased when she removed a chair from her office to use at home. The income statement, therefore, only gives a summary of earnings or losses between balance sheet dates.

Third, the income statement, like the balance sheet and the other financial statements that we will discuss, offers limited prospective information. The income statement shows only the results from a business's operations for a period in the past. Past results, however, may provide some indications about the business's prospects.

In later chapters of this book we will have occasion to consider the relative importance of the balance sheet and the income statement. For this chapter, we must simply understand their relationship. You may need a little time to grasp the relation between the two statements and to get accustomed to the way in which double-entry bookkeeping performs a neat "bridging function" between them. But there is nothing mysterious about the income statement as such.

1.   REVENUES AND EXPENSES

Drawing up a simple income statement for E. Tutt, say for the month of June, may be the easiest way to start explaining that financial statement. Suppose that during the month she receives fees of $600 and $400 for legal services.

(1)	Professional Income	$600
(2)	Professional Income	400

Accountants define *revenues* as increases in assets, decreases in liabilities, or both, resulting from delivering goods, rendering services, or engaging in ongoing major or central operations. In this example, E. Tutt produces $1,000 in revenues during June from her principal business activity, namely performing legal services. In contrast, accountants classify increases in assets or decreases in liabilities from peripheral or incidental transactions not involving investments by owners as *gains*. Because both revenues and gains increase assets or decrease liabilities, we can describe these transactions as increases in owner's equity. For these reasons, accountants occasionally describe revenues and gains as "positives." After all, revenues and gains increase equity and increase assets or decrease liabilities—consequences that a business views as favorable.

To find E. Tutt's net income, we must subtract her expenses for the month from the month's revenues. Accountants define *expenses* as decreases in assets, increases in liabilities, or both, resulting from using goods or services to produce revenue. In contrast, accountants classify decreases in assets or increases in liabilities from peripheral or incidental transactions which do not involve distributions to owners as *losses*. Once again, because both expenses and losses decrease assets or increase liabilities, these transactions decrease owner's equity. Accountants may say that expenses and losses produce a "negative" effect on a business; expenses and losses decrease equity and decrease assets or increase liabilities, all unfavorable consequences.

Suppose that E. Tutt's operating expenses were as follows:

(3)	Rent	$200
(4)	Secretary	230
(5)	Telephone	15
(6)	Heat & Light	5
(7)	Miscellaneous	5

In addition, further suppose that Tutt suffered a loss during the month when a thief broke into her office and stole $20 cash. This loss is treated as any other expense:

(8)	Theft Loss	$20

There is no particular form required for an income statement, so long as it is a clear and fair statement of the information. An acceptable one might look like this:

E. Tutt, Esquire
Income Statement
For the Month of June

(1 & 2)	Professional Income		$1,000
	Less: Expenses		
(3)	Rent	$200	
(4)	Secretary	230	
(5)	Telephone	15	
(6)	Heat & Light	5	
(7)	Miscellaneous	5	
(8)	Theft Loss	20	
	Total Expenses		$ 475
	Net Income		$ 525

To see how the income statement fits into the balance sheet we might ask where Tutt's net income shows up on her balance sheet. In lay terms, Tutt's net income is an increase in her stake in the business, which we have been calling Proprietorship. Hence, if no other change in her stake occurs, the balance sheet figure for Proprietorship on June 30 should be $525 larger than on June 1.

How does this work out in the accounts? Upon receipt of the $600 fee for legal work completed in June, Tutt will debit *Cash*, since cash has increased by $600:

Cash	$600
?	$600

Because the corresponding entry must be a credit of $600, the alternatives are a decrease in assets, an increase in liabilities, or an increase in proprietorship (or some combination thereof). But no asset has decreased, nor has any liability increased. Therefore, the credit must be an increase in proprietorship of $600.

This result makes sense. The assets of Tutt's law practice have increased, and because she is the residual owner of this enterprise, the increase redounds to her benefit; in other words, her stake in the enterprise has gone up. But common sense tells us that Tutt's "stake" has not been augmented by a full $600. Light, heat, rent, supplies, secretarial services and miscellaneous items have all gone to produce this $600 fee (and while the theft loss of $20 has not actually helped to produce any fees, it too is a cost of doing business). These items, then, should appear as decreases in proprietorship; in the same way that income increases the stake of the proprietor, expenses decrease her stake. For example, when rent is paid, the entry could be:

Proprietorship	$200
Cash	$200

If all revenues and expenses were entered in the Proprietorship account, the account would reflect the net increase or decrease in proprietorship for the period. The T-accounts for Cash and Proprietorship for Tutt would be:

	Cash		
(Bal.)	$350	$200	(3)
(1)	600	230	(4)
(2)	400	15	(5)
		5	(6)
		5	(7)
		20	(8)
(Bal.)	$875		

	Proprietorship		
(3)	$200	$950	(Bal.)
(4)	230	600	(1)
(5)	15	400	(2)
(6)	5		
(7)	5		
(8)	20		
		$1,475	(Bal.)

Just as it is inconvenient to draw up a new balance sheet every time something happens, so it would be inconvenient, and indeed uninformative, to enter all the many operating items directly in Proprietorship. Instead, the Proprietorship account is broken up into separate T-accounts. The left-hand side of the Proprietorship account, the side on which decreases in proprietorship are recorded, is subdivided into separate T-accounts, called *expense accounts*, such as Rent Expense or Utility Expense, or sometimes *loss accounts*, such as Theft Loss, and the decreases in proprietorship other than withdrawals by Tutt are entered in those accounts rather than directly in the Proprietorship account. Similarly, the right-hand side of the Proprietorship account, on which increases are recorded, is subdivided into separate T-accounts called *income accounts*, such as Professional Income or Dividend Income, or sometimes *gain accounts*, such as Gain on Sale of Equipment, and increases other than capital investments by owners are recorded in those accounts. The relationship between the expense and income T-accounts and the Proprietorship T-account might be symbolized in the following manner:

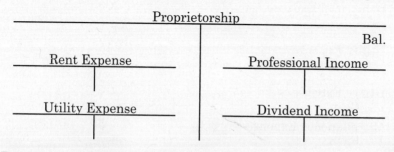

Because an expense constitutes a decrease in proprietorship, which is a debit entry, an expense is of course reflected by a debit or left-hand entry in the appropriate expense T-account. Indeed, because the expense T-accounts are subdivisions of just the left-hand side of the Proprietorship account, you may wonder why the expense accounts themselves have two sides. The answer is simply a practical one: sometimes a portion of an expense previously paid is refunded, perhaps as a rebate, or because it was inadvertently overpaid, and it seems more sensible to record this as a reduction in the expense, by a right-hand entry in the expense T-account, than as an increase in proprietorship, either by a credit directly to that account or to some income account. Again, recall that double-entry bookkeeping does not use negative numbers, only debits and credits. As we shall see shortly, right-hand entries in expense T-accounts also facilitate the mechanics of double-entry bookkeeping.

In the same vein, since income constitutes an increase in proprietorship, which is a credit, an income item is reflected by a credit or right-hand entry in the appropriate income T-account; and the presence of a left-hand side in the income T-accounts is simply to make it convenient to reflect any refund of an income item, such as a return by E. Tutt of an overpayment of a fee, as a reduction in the income by a debit to the income T-account (while also facilitating double-entry bookkeeping).

The number of different expense and income T-accounts set up depends upon the extent to which we want to identify separately in the books the various items of income and expense. For example, Tutt may want to show rent and secretarial expense as separate items, because they are individually important, but may be satisfied to lump together telephone, heat and light in a single Utility Expense account.

Tutt's journal entries for the income and expense transactions during the month would be as follows:

(1)	Cash	$600	
	Professional Income		$600
(2)	Cash	400	
	Professional Income		400
(3)	Rent Expense	200	
	Cash		200
(4)	Secretarial Expense	230	
	Cash		230
(5)	Utility Expense	15	
	Cash		15
(6)	Utility Expense	5	
	Cash		5
(7)	Miscellaneous Expense	5	
	Cash		5
(8)	Theft Loss	20	
	Cash		20

As these entries show, cash received for professional income has as its corresponding right-hand entry a credit to Professional Income, which is in effect an increase in proprietorship. When cash is paid out for expenses for the period, there are corresponding left-hand entries in the various expense accounts that are in effect decreases in proprietorship. When these entries have been posted to the T-accounts, the T-accounts would appear as follows:

Cash		Proprietorship	
Bal.$ 350	$200 (3)		$950 Bal.
(1) 600	230 (4)	[Expense Items]	[Income Item]
(2) 400	15 (5)		
	5 (6)		
	5 (7)		
	20 (8)	Rent Expense	Professional Income
Bal. $875		(3) $200	$600 (1)
			400 (2)
		Bal. $200	$1,000 Bal.

Rent Expense

(3) $200	
Bal. $200	

Secretarial Expense

(4) $230	
Bal. $230	

Utilities Expense

(5) $15	
(6) 5	
Bal. $20	

Miscellaneous Expense

(7) $ 5	
Bal. $ 5	

Theft Loss

(8) $20	
Bal. $20	

2.   THE CLOSING PROCESS

Income and expense accounts differ from other accounts in one important respect: as subsidiary accounts of proprietorship, they never appear on the balance sheet. Instead, after the accounts have performed their function of collecting in one place all items of the same kind of income or expense for the period, the net balances in these accounts are brought together in a single account. The net figure in that account, net income or loss, shows the effect of the operations of the period on proprietorship. In other words, whereas at the beginning of the period we broke the Proprietorship account down into several subaccounts for income and expense items, at the end of the period we bring these subaccounts back together, and the net figure is the increase or decrease in proprietorship due to operations.

Of course, the income and expense accounts could be brought back together in the Proprietorship account itself, by simply debiting the Proprietorship account with the various expense items, and crediting the Proprietorship account with the income items. That is ordinarily not done, however, since it is desirable to isolate in a single special account all the items relating to operations for the particular period. If the income and expense items were brought back together in the Proprietorship account, that isolation would not be achieved, since the Proprietorship account also reflects other transactions having nothing to do with the operations of the business—for example, a withdrawal from the business during the period, such as Tutt's removal of the chair from the office. A separate account is needed to show just the results of operations; that account called *Profit and Loss*, serves as the consolidating account for all the income and expense items. Accordingly, the income and expense items are transferred, or, in accounting jargon, *closed* to the Profit and Loss account.

The bookkeeper uses journal entries to transfer the balances in these individual accounts to the Profit and Loss account. Since the separate income and expense accounts are to disappear, the bookkeeper makes an entry in each of these accounts equal to and on the opposite side from the net balance found in the account. This entry, by making the two sides of the account equal, closes the account, and the bookkeeper draws a double line across the bottom of the account to show that it is closed. The corresponding opposite-hand entry is then made to the Profit and Loss account, thus putting the balance in each account on the same side of the Profit and Loss account as it was in the account from which it came, i. e., expenses on the left-hand side, income on the right. The bookkeeper would record Tutt's *closing entries* as follows:

(a)	Professional Income	$1,000	
	Profit and Loss		$1,000
(b)	Profit and Loss	200	
	Rent Expense		200
(c)	Profit and Loss	230	
	Secretarial Expense		230
(d)	Profit and Loss	20	
	Utility Expense		20
(e)	Profit and Loss	5	
	Miscellaneous Expense		5
(f)	Profit and Loss	20	
	Theft Loss		20

The T-accounts would become:

Cash	
Bal.$ 350	$200 (3)
(1) 600	230 (4)
(2) 400	15 (5)
	5 (6)
	5 (7)
	20 (8)
Bal. $875	

Proprietorship	
	$950 Bal.

[Expense Items]   [Income Item]

Rent Expense	
(3) $200	
Bal. $200	$200 (b)

Professional Income	
	$600 (1)
	400 (2)
(a) $1,000	$1,000 Bal.

Secretarial Expense	
(4) $230	
Bal. $230	$230 (c)

Utilities Expense	
(5) $15	
(6) 5	
Bal. $20	$20 (d)

Miscellaneous Expense	
(7) $ 5	
Bal. $ 5	$5 (e)

Theft Loss	
(8) $20	
Bal. $20	$20 (f)

Profit and Loss	
(b) $200	$1,000 (a)
(c) 230	
(d) 20	
(e) 5	
(f) 20	
	$525 Bal.

What has been achieved? Compare the Profit and Loss account with the income statement which we made up on page 34, *supra*, at the beginning of this section. They are of course essentially the same, for the income statement is nothing more than a somewhat more detailed presentation of the Profit and Loss account. The creation of separate income and expense accounts in effect sets up slots for recording the transactions as they occur; it permits the immediate classification of the various categories of income and expense and provides a single place for the orderly accumulation and preservation of all items of the same category. The utility of a separate Profit and Loss account, reflecting solely the operations of the business, will become increasingly apparent.

The final step is to close the Profit and Loss account into the Proprietorship account: because at present the net figure in the Profit and Loss account is a credit of $525, we need a debit to Profit and Loss of $525 to close the account, and a credit to Proprietorship in the same amount:

(g) Profit and Loss $525
        Proprietorship $525

Nothing more is happening, of course, than to transfer the credit of $525 to the Proprietorship account, where it would have been in the first place if we had not created the separate income and expense accounts. The T-accounts then appear as follows:

Cash	
Bal. $875	

Proprietorship		
	$ 950	Bal.
	525	(g)
	$1,475	Bal.

Profit and Loss			
(b)	$200	$1,000	(a)
(c)	230		
(d)	20		
(e)	5		
(f)	20		
(g)	$525	$ 525	Bal.

The circle is now complete; the resulting balances of $875 in the Cash account and $1,475 in the Proprietorship account are exactly the same as we saw earlier in this section, before we went through the bookkeeping processes for expense and income items. If no change in other assets or liabilities has occurred, so that the balances in those accounts remain as they were on page 19, *supra*, the ending balance sheet, in simple form, would be:

E. Tutt, Esquire
Balance Sheet, End of June

Assets		**Liabilities & Proprietorship**	
		Liabilities:	
Cash	$875	Accounts Payable:	
Supplies	100	Frank Co.	$400
Equipment	400	Elmer Co.	150
Furniture	350	Total Liabilities	$550
Library	300	Proprietorship	1,475
Total	$2,025	Total	$2,025

To summarize our discussion of the bookkeeping process in the context of both the balance sheet and the income statement, the bookkeeper first records transactions in the journal. Second, the bookkeeper posts the information in the journal to the ledger. At the end of an accounting period, the bookkeeper closes the books by transferring the balances in the revenue, gain, expense and loss accounts to owner's equity.

During the *closing process*, the bookkeeper first determines the balance in each account by netting one side against the other. Next, the bookkeeper prepares closing journal entries which transfer the balances in the revenue and expense accounts to the clearinghouse Profit and Loss account and posts those entries to the ledger. Then, the bookkeeper prepares a final closing entry which transfers the balance in the Profit and Loss account to the Proprietorship account and posts this entry to the ledger.

As the final step in the bookkeeping process, the bookkeeper prepares financial statements.

PROBLEMS

You have now read about the basic principles underlying the balance sheet and the income statement. At this point, we should practice the techniques we have read about.

Problem 1.2A. As a continuation of Problem 1.1A, below are the rest of E. Tutt's transactions for the month of January in her second year. Prepare the journal entries for these transactions, and post them to the appropriate T-accounts, setting up any additional T-accounts that may be needed (including, of course, the necessary expense and income accounts). Then close the expense and income accounts to the Profit and Loss account, and close the Profit and Loss account to the Proprietorship account. Prepare an income statement for the month of January and a simple balance sheet as of the end of January, using the forms set out after the list of transactions.

Additional Transactions in January:

Jan.   13   Gave Smith some legal advice and received $150.

15   Got a reminder from her landlord that she had not paid the rent of $150 for her office for January, and sent a check immediately.

16   Paid her secretary a salary of $200 for the first half of January.

20   Received $375 for her work during January on Bolton's Estate.

23   Paid an electrician $20 to repair a lighting fixture.

25   Purchased some supplies for $75 cash from Stanley Co.

27   Did some work for Sam's Book Store, and in exchange received a new East's Digest which sells for $220.

29   Prepared a deed for Ingersoll and received a fee of $250.

30   Paid her secretary $200 for the second half of January.

31   Went to Telephone Co. and paid her bill of $50 for the month of January.

E. Tutt, Esquire
Income Statement
For the Month of January

Professional Income		$_____
Less: Expenses		
Secretary	$_____	
Rent	_____	
Telephone	_____	
Miscellaneous	_____	
Total Expenses		$_____
Net Income		$_____

E. Tutt, Esquire
Balance Sheet, January 31

Assets		Liabilities & Proprietorship	
		Liabilities:	
Cash	$ _____	Accounts Payable:	
Supplies	_____	Brown	$ _____
Equipment	_____	Jones Co.	_____
Furniture	_____	East Publishing	_____
Library	_____	Total Liabilities	$ _____
		Proprietorship	_____
Total	$ _____	Total	$ _____

Problem 1.2B. The balance sheet on December 31 of James Stief, Attorney at Law, appears below.

James Stief, Attorney at Law
Balance Sheet, December 31

Assets		Liabilities & Proprietorship	
		Liabilities (all current):	
Cash	$ 4,000	Accounts Payable:	
Office Equipment	3,500	Jackson	$ 1,400
Library	3,000	Proprietorship	9,100
Total	$10,500	Total	$10,500

During January, Stief's office engaged in the transactions listed below. Prepare journal entries for those transactions and post them to the appropriate T-accounts, setting up any additional T-accounts that may be needed (including, of course, the necessary expense and income accounts). Then close the expense and income accounts to the Profit and Loss account, and close the Profit and Loss account to the Proprietorship account. Unless your professor directs otherwise, prepare an income statement for the month of January and a classified balance sheet as of the end of January, using the forms set out after the list of transactions.

Transactions in January:

Jan. 1 Paid $500 on his account due to Jackson.

  4 Rendered legal services to Lee and received payment in the amount of $700.

  5 His secretary, Lulu, purchased for cash $85 worth of office supplies that she used before the end of the month.

  8 Received payment in the amount of $1,500 for legal services rendered to Jones.

  11 Purchased a set of state reporters from West Group for $1,200 on account.

  15 Paid $1,100 rent for the month to the landlord of the office building.

  20 Received and paid a bill of $75 for printing services.

  31 Paid Lulu $500 as her monthly salary.

James Stief, Attorney at Law
Income Statement
For the Month of January

Professional Income		$_____
Less: Expenses		
Rent	$_____	
Secretary	_____	
Office Supplies	_____	
Printing	_____	
Total Expenses		$_____
Net Income		$_____

James Stief, Attorney at Law
Balance Sheet, January 31

Assets		Liabilities & Proprietorship	
Current Assets:		Liabilities (all current):	
Cash	$_____	Accounts Payable:	
Fixed Assets:		Jackson	$_____
Office Equipment	_____	West Group	_____
Library	_____	Total Liabilities	$_____
Total Fixed Assets	$_____	Proprietorship	_____
Total Assets	$_____	Total	$_____

Problem 1.2C. The balance sheet of Donna Preston, Attorney at Law, as of December 31 appears below:

Donna Preston, Attorney at Law
Balance Sheet, December 31

Assets			Liabilities & Proprietorship	
			Liabilities (all current):	
Cash		$ 5,000	Notes Payable	$ 1,400
Office Equipment		4,000	Accounts Payable:	
Library		2,500	Acme Equipment	1,600
	Total	$11,500	Total Liabilities	$ 3,000
			Proprietorship	8,500
			Total	$11,500

During January, Preston's office engaged in the transactions listed below. Prepare journal entries for those transactions and post them to the appropriate T-accounts, setting up any additional T-accounts that may be needed (including, of course, the necessary expense and income accounts). Then close the expense and income accounts to the Profit and Loss account, and close the Profit and Loss account to the Proprietorship account. Unless your professor directs otherwise, prepare an income statement for the month of January and a classified balance sheet as of the end of January, using the forms set out after the list of transactions.

Transactions in January:

Jan. 2 Rendered legal services to Lee and received payment in the amount of $1,700.

4 Paid $600 on her note payable.

5 Purchased a new copy machine from Office Devices Co. for $2,700 on account.

11 Minnie, the secretary, purchased for cash $50 of supplies for the office that she used before the end of the month.

15 Minnie paid $200 for monthly parking in the lot adjacent to the office. This fee covered all of the firm's employees and clients during the month.

20 Paid a bill for court reporter's fees in the amount of $250 from Depositions Unlimited, Inc. for services rendered during the week.

25 Paid $500 on the note payable.

31 Minnie paid $1,000 rent to the landlord for office space for January.

Donna Preston, Attorney at Law
Income Statement
For the Month of January

Professional Income		$_____
Less: Expenses		
Rent	$_____	
Court Reporting Services	_____	
Parking	_____	
Supplies	_____	
Total Expenses		$_____
Net Income		$_____

Donna Preston, Attorney at Law
Balance Sheet, January 31

Assets		**Liabilities & Proprietorship**	
Current Assets:		Liabilities (all current):	
Cash	$_____	Note Payable	$_____
Fixed Assets:		Accounts Payable:	
Office Equipment	_____	Acme Equipment	_____
Library	_____	Office Devices Co.	_____
Total Fixed Assets	$_____	Total Liabilities	$_____
Total Assets	$_____	Proprietorship	_____
		Total	$_____

3.   THE TRIAL BALANCE AND SIX-COLUMN WORKSHEET

To assist in the closing process, many bookkeepers will also prepare either a *trial balance* or a *worksheet*. Lawyers and law students can benefit from understanding both of these bookkeeping tools. The trial balance presents another application of the fundamental accounting equation while the worksheet further illustrates the relationship between the income statement and the balance sheet.

You will recall that to begin the closing process, the bookkeeper determines the balance in each account by netting one side against the other. Before proceeding any further, many bookkeepers will then prepare a *trial balance*. The trial balance lists all accounts and their temporary balances. As the final step in completing the trial balance, the bookkeeper totals the debits and credits.

Using the T-accounts above and the balances in the other accounts from the balance sheet on page 19, *supra*, because no change in those accounts has occurred, we could prepare a trial balance for E. Tutt as follows:

E. Tutt, Esquire
Trial Balance, After transaction (8) on page 36, *supra*

Account	Debit	Credit
Cash	$ 875	
Supplies	100	
Equipment	400	
Furniture	350	
Library	300	
Accounts Payable: Frank Co		$ 400
Accounts Payable: Elmer Co.		150
Proprietorship		950
Professional Income		1,000
Rent Expense	200	
Secretary Expense	230	
Utility Expense	20	
Miscellaneous Expense	5	
Theft Expense	20	
Totals	$2,500	$2,500

If the debits do not equal the credits, the bookkeeper has made an error. Under the fundamental accounting equation and double-entry bookkeeping, debits must always equal credits. In this way, the trial balance provides a minimal check on the process of recording and posting daily transactions. Preparing a trial balance will detect any addition or subtraction errors that the bookkeeper may have made, any incomplete journal entries or postings to the ledger, and any transposition errors in posting amounts to the ledger by rearranging the order of the digits in a number, such as recording the number "180" as "810." The trial balance, however, only detects errors that result in unequal debits and credits. The trial balance will not detect incorrect, but equal amounts, which the bookkeeper may have recorded in the journal entries, entries to the wrong accounts, or omitted or duplicate transactions. For example, a bookkeeper might record a $10 million sale on credit for only $1 million, a potentially disastrous error that a trial balance would not catch.

After determining that the debits equal the credits in the trial balance, many bookkeepers will use a *worksheet* to aid in the closing process and the preparation of financial statements. The worksheet allows the bookkeeper to separate the revenue, gain, expense and loss accounts in the trial balance which flow into the income statement and the asset, liability, and equity accounts which will appear on the balance sheet. The worksheet also helps the bookkeeper prepare the closing entries which we have already discussed.

Without going into elaborate detail, a common type of worksheet contains six columns of figures, preceded by a list of all the accounts in the ledger, plus a caption for net income or net loss. The first and second columns display the debit and credit balances, respectively, from the trial balance. The third and fourth columns show the debit and credit balances, respectively, for the revenue, gain, expense and loss accounts that will appear on the income statement while the fifth and sixth columns, respectively, compile the debit and credit balances for the asset, liability and equity accounts that will appear on the balance sheet. Consequently, a six-column worksheet would look something like this:

E. Tutt, Esquire
Six-Column Worksheet, After transaction (8)

Account	Trial Balance Debit	Trial Balance Credit	Income Statement Debit	Income Statement Credit	Balance Sheet Debit	Balance Sheet Credit
Cash	$ 875				$ 875	
Supplies	100				100	
Equipment	400				400	
Furniture	350				350	
Library	300				300	
Accounts Payable: Frank Co.		$ 400				$ 400
Accounts Payable: Elmer Co.		150				150
Proprietorship		950				950
Professional Income		1,000		$1,000		
Rent Expense	200		$ 200			
Secretary Expense	230		230			
Utility Expense	20		20			
Miscellaneous Expense	5		5			
Theft Expense	20		20			
Subtotals	$2,500	$2,500	$ 475	$1,000	$2,025	$1,500
Net Income			525			525
Totals			$1,000	$1,000	$2,025	$2,025

The debit entry for net income balances the income statement columns and the credit entry balances the balance sheet columns. The credit in the balance sheet column also indicates the increase in equity from net income. Consequently, the worksheet powerfully illustrates the interrelationship between the income statement and the balance sheet. Once again, we see how the income statement shows the change in equity from net income or loss resulting from operations during an accounting period.

If the total debits for the income statement exceed the total credits for the income statement, the business has suffered a net loss for the period. In that event, the bookkeeper inserts the words "Net loss" in the account column. Again, the credit entry balances the income statement columns while the debit entry balances the balance sheet columns. The debit in the balance sheet column also indicates the decrease in equity from the net loss. Just as accountants use a credit rather than a negative debit entry to record a decrease in an asset account, please note that the six-column worksheet always uses a positive number to balance the amounts in the columns for the income statement and balance sheet.

PROBLEMS

You have now read about the basic techniques underlying the trial balance and the six column worksheet. At this point, we should practice what we have learned.

Problem 1.3A. Based on the following trial balance for Chamberlain's Romance Bookstore, construct a six-column worksheet and prepare August financial statements (balance sheet and income statement only). Ignore depreciation and any other accruals or deferrals.

Chamberlain's Romance Bookstore
Trial Balance, August 31

Account	Debit	Credit
Accounts Payable		$ 3,500
Accounts Receivable	$ 1,500	
Advertising Expense	2,800	
Book Binding Expense	1,300	
Cash	8,700	
Equipment	8,000	
Notes Payable		2,400
Proprietorship		13,700
Rent Expense	5,000	
Revenue		16,000
Salary Expense	6,000	
Supplies Expense	1,500	
Traveling Expense	800	
Totals	$35,600	$35,600

Problem 1.3B. Based on the following trial balance for Dave Dutile, Attorney at Law, construct a six-column worksheet and prepare July financial statements (classified balance sheet and income statement only). Unless your professor directs otherwise, assume that Dutile reasonably expects to collect all receivables within one year and must pay the accounts and notes payable within ninety days. Ignore depreciation and any other accruals or deferrals.

Dave Dutile, Attorney at Law
Trial Balance, July 31

Account	Debit	Credit
Accounts Receivable	$ 9,800	
Accounts Payable		$ 3,300
Cash	5,700	
Notes Payable		10,000
Office Equipment	8,100	
Proprietorship		10,800
Rent Expense	800	
Revenue		2,200
Salary Expense	1,600	
Supplies Expense	100	
Telephone Expense	200	
Totals	$26,300	$26,300

Problem 1.3C. Based on the following trial balance for Glen's Ice Cream Shop, construct a six-column worksheet and prepare June financial statements (classified balance sheet and income statement only). Unless your professor directs otherwise, assume that the business reasonably expects to consume the office supplies and to collect all accounts receivable, but not the notes receivable, within one year and must pay the accounts and notes payable

within ninety days. Ignore depreciation, income taxes and any other accruals or deferrals.

Glen's Ice Cream Shop
Trial Balance, June 30

Account	Debit	Credit
Accounts Receivable	$ 3,600	
Accounts Payable		$ 3,500
Cash	13,000	
Food Expense	4,000	
Notes Payable		6,500
Notes Receivable	4,100	
Office Equipment	5,000	
Office Supplies	1,500	
Proprietorship		18,200
Rent Expense	7,500	
Revenue		14,000
Salary Expense	2,300	
Supplies Expense	1,200	
Totals	$42,200	$42,200

E.   THE STATEMENT OF CHANGES IN OWNER'S EQUITY

We have now studied both the balance sheet and the income statement. We have seen how the income statement serves as a "bridge" between two balance sheets. The income statement, however, only shows the extent to which a business's activities have caused an increase or a decrease in equity over some period of time. During that same period of time, equity also could have increased if an owner invested assets in the business, or it could have decreased if an owner withdrew assets from the business. The *statement of changes in owner's equity* fully reconciles the changes in net worth between balance sheet dates.

To distinguish between the changes in equity that arise from operations and those from investments and withdrawals by owners, accounting entities often maintain different accounts for *capital, drawings*, and *retained earnings*. Accountants use capital accounts to record an owner's investment in the business. Investments obviously increase equity and capital. An owner also may withdraw cash or some other asset for use outside the business. To illustrate, E. Tutt removed a chair from her law office for personal use. Such withdrawals decrease equity and could directly decrease capital. Accountants, however, normally prefer to use a separate account, referred to as Drawings, to track an owner's total withdrawals for an accounting period. For a corporation, accountants usually net any withdrawals, which we usually refer to as *distributions* or *dividends*, against the corporation's cumulative net income or loss in an account called Retained Earnings. We will examine the accounting treatment for the equity section in the three basic business forms, the sole proprietorship, the partnership, and the corporation.

1. THE SOLE PROPRIETORSHIP

In a sole proprietorship, accountants might describe the account to record capital as either Proprietorship or Capital. When E. Tutt invested $1,000 in her legal practice, the bookkeeper could have recorded the following entry in the general journal:

(d) Cash $1,000
        Proprietorship $1,000
    (To record original investment in business)

Similarly, when E. Tutt removed the chair from her law office, the bookkeeper could have used the following journal entry for the transaction:

(i) Drawings $50
        Furniture $50
    (To record withdrawal of chair for personal use)

At the end of the accounting period, the bookkeeper would close the Drawings account to the Proprietorship account as follows:

    Proprietorship $50
        Drawings $50
    (To close drawings)

To reconcile the equity amounts that appear in the balance sheets on pages 14 and 40, *supra*, we could prepare the following financial statement:

E. Tutt, Esquire
Statement of Changes in Owner's Equity
For the Month of June

Proprietorship, beginning of period	$1,000
Net income	525
Subtotal	$1,525
Less: Drawings	50
Proprietorship, end of period	$1,475

The statement of changes in owner's equity, therefore, reconciles the amount of the residual ownership interest from the beginning to the end of an accounting period. In other words, the statement summarizes the various changes that have occurred in equity since the last balance sheet. Either net income or additional investments can increase equity, while a net loss or withdrawals decrease equity. Depending on the accounting entity involved, the statement of changes in owner's equity can assume different forms. We will turn next to the statement in a partnership context.

2. THE PARTNERSHIP

You may recall that accountants assign different names to the residual ownership interest depending on the accounting entity involved. In a partnership, accountants call that remainder *partners' equity*. With multiple owners, however, partnerships maintain separate equity accounts for each partner. Therefore, the King Tutt partnership would keep separate equity accounts for both E. Tutt and Jennifer King. The partnership might call their capital accounts *Partner's Equity, E. Tutt* and *Partner's Equity, J. King*, respectively. Similarly, the partnership might also call their drawings accounts *Drawings, E. Tutt* and *Drawings, J. King*.

Assume that E. Tutt and Jennifer King each invested $1,000 to start King Tutt on September 1. We could record their contributions as follows in the general journal:

Cash	$2,000	
Partner's Equity, E. Tutt		$1,000
Partner's Equity, J. King		$1,000
(To record original investment in partnership)		

If during September, the partnership collected $2,000 for professional services and incurred $800 in expenses, the partnership would show $1,200 net income. Further assume that each partner withdrew $400 for living expenses during the month. When the partners withdrew $400 for living expenses, we could record the following journal entry:

Drawings, E. Tutt	$400	
Drawings, J. King	400	
Cash		$800
(To record draws)		

At the end of the accounting period, we could close the Drawings accounts to the Partner's Equity accounts as follows:

Partner's Equity, E. Tutt	$400	
Partner's Equity, J. King	400	
Drawings, E. Tutt		$400
Drawings, J. King		400
(To close the drawings accounts)		

Because the partnership earned $1,200 in net income, the Profit and Loss account would contain a $1,200 credit balance after transferring the balances in the revenue and expense accounts. To close the Profit and Loss account, we could make the following entry to divide the net income for the month equally between E. Tutt and Jennifer King:

Profit and Loss	$1,200	
Partner's Equity, E. Tutt		$600
Partner's Equity, J. King		600

To reconcile the changes in partners' equity during September, we could prepare the following financial statement:

King Tutt
Statement of Changes in Partners' Equity
For the Month of September

	Tutt	King	Total
Partners' Equity, September 1	$–0–	$–0–	$–0–
Original investment	1,000	1,000	2,000
Net income	600	600	1,200
Subtotals	$1,600	$1,600	$3,200
Less: Drawings	400	400	800
Partners' Equity, September 30	$1,200	$1,200	$2,400

If the partnership included more than two partners, the bookkeeper could add a column for each partner. At some point, however, a partnership may move to a summary approach to the statement as follows:

King Tutt
Statement of Changes in Partners' Equity
For the Month of September

Partners' Equity, September 1	$–0–
Original investment	2,000
Net income	1,200
Subtotal	$3,200
Less: Drawings	800
Partners' Equity, September 30	$2,400

3. THE CORPORATION

Rather than operate her legal practice as a sole proprietorship, E. Tutt could have formed a corporation to practice law. In fact, all fifty states allow lawyers to practice law as a professional corporation. If Tutt had so incorporated, she would have contributed her $1,000 initial investment to the corporation in exchange for shares in the corporation. Those shares represent the residual ownership interest in the corporation. One, several, or many investors can own shares in a corporation. Because, as a general rule, *shareholders*, sometimes referred to as *stockholders* or *shareowners*, can transfer their shares at any time, and the fact that thousands, or even millions, of shareholders could own shares at any time, corporations do not create separate equity accounts for each shareholder.

To incorporate a business, one or more individuals, often a lawyer or paralegal, must file *articles of incorporation*, which the specific language in some corporate statutes refers to as a *certificate of incorporation*, with the appropriate state official, such as the secretary of state. Lawyers frequently refer to either the articles or certificate of incorporation as the *corporate charter*. Among other things, the corporate charter must set forth the number of *authorized shares*, or the maximum number of shares that the corporation can lawfully issue.

Lawyers also need to understand both what the terms *issued shares*, *outstanding shares*, and *treasury shares* mean and how those descriptors differ from each other and from authorized shares. As we will soon see, financial statements, statutes, and legal agreements often use these words. For example, you will find references to authorized, issued, and outstanding shares on Starbucks' balance sheets, which appear in Appendix A on page 1215, *infra*.

The term *issued shares* refers to the number of shares that a corporation has sold or otherwise put into the hands of shareholders. As we will discuss in more detail in Chapter V on pages 329 to 332, *infra*, corporations increasingly repurchase shares from their shareholders. In that event, financial statements often refer to the repurchased shares as *treasury shares*, especially in those states that continue to follow the legal capital system that we will soon describe. Similarly, the term *outstanding shares* refers to those shares that shareholders continue to own. If a corporation that previously issued 500 shares subsequently repurchased twenty shares, then 480 shares would remain outstanding. We could also use the phrase *authorized and issued, but no longer outstanding* to describe the twenty treasury shares. In essence, the corporation can reissue those twenty shares.

Stated another way, the number of outstanding shares equals the number of issued shares minus any treasury shares that the corporation has repurchased. We could use the following equation to express that relationship:

Outstanding shares = Issued shares – Treasury shares

Given that equation, if the financial statements provide only two of the three numbers, we can calculate the third. Accordingly,

Issued shares = Outstanding shares + Treasury shares

and

Treasury shares = Issued shares – Outstanding shares

A corporation can also issue more than one class or type of shares, with one class representing the basic residual ownership rights while the corporate charter will give preference to each additional class in one way or another. For example, a corporation may issue a class of *preferred shares*, which offer special rights or privileges to the preferred shareholders. To illustrate, the articles of incorporation may give preferred shareholders the right to receive a fixed amount of dividends before the corporation can distribute any amount to the common shareholders. Preferred shares typically also entitle shareholders to receive a fixed amount of money upon liquidation from the residual assets before the corporation may distribute any amount to the common shareholders. In exchange for these privileges, preferred shareholders almost always sacrifice rights that common shareholders enjoy. For example, articles of incorporation usually provide that preferred shareholders cannot vote to elect directors, who manage the corporation's business and affairs, except in very limited circumstances, such as when the corporation has not paid dividends to preferred shareholders for some specified period of time.

Furthermore, preferred shareholders usually forego the right to share in the corporation's profits beyond the stated preference.

Corporate laws do not grant a shareholder, unlike a partner, any claim to any specified amount of the corporation's assets, whether at liquidation or otherwise. Corporate laws merely give each shareholder the right to share proportionately with all other holders of the same class, after the corporation has satisfied all prior interests. As a result, accountants typically divide shareholders' equity into three components: *capital stock, additional paid-in capital,* and *retained earnings.* These three categories of accounts track changes in the two primary sources from which a corporation derives its equity: (1) amounts that shareholders invest in the corporation, commonly referred to as *contributed capital;* and (2) *earned capital* or profits that the corporation reinvests in the business. The single *Retained Earnings account* tracks all undistributed profits that remain invested in the corporation. When a corporation has suffered losses which exceed any undistributed profits, this account may appear on financial statements as "Accumulated Deficit." Accounting for the corporation's total contributed capital, in contrast, typically requires at least two separate accounts: a capital stock account and the *Additional Paid–In Capital account.*

a.   CONTRIBUTED CAPITAL

To best understand why accountants subdivide contributed capital into two separate accounts, we must briefly introduce the so-called *legal capital system,* which we will discuss at greater length in Chapter V on pages 329 to 331, *infra,* and, especially, the concept of *legal capital,* or *stated capital.* In addition to specifying the number of authorized shares that the corporation can lawfully issue, a corporate charter historically also stated the total amount of capital that the shareholders would originally invest in the enterprise. Charters often described this total capital as being divided into a specified number of shares. For example, the articles of incorporation of Tutt, Inc. might provide that "the capital of this corporation shall be $1,000 divided into 100 shares." Each share bore the figure designating the fractional portion of the total capital that the share represented, here $10. Eventually, lawyers referred to this figure as the share's *par value.* It is unfortunate that this term included the word "value" because, except perhaps at the very outset, the figure bears no necessary relationship to the share's actual worth.

In modern corporate practice, the term *par value* refers to the nominal amount, if any, assigned to each share in a corporation's charter. For example, the certificate of incorporation may describe a corporation's shares as "$1 par value." Again, this figure bears no necessary relation to the share's fair market value. Under the legal capital system and the corporate laws still followed in about one-fifth of the states, including Delaware, which boasts that "[m]ore than 50% of all publicly-traded companies in the United States including 64% of the Fortune 500 have chosen Delaware as their legal home," the cumulative par value of all issued shares constitutes the corporation's *legal capital* or *stated capital.* As we shall discuss shortly and explain more fully in Chapter V on pages 329 to 331, *infra,* that amount creates important legal consequences. In those jurisdictions that still use the legal capital system, a corporation's *stated capital* equals the product of the total number of its issued shares times the shares' par value. If a corporation issues 1,000 shares of $100 par value stock, the corporation's stated capital equals $100,000.

Over the years, corporate statutes have required corporations to identify their legal capital for two major reasons. First, the concept of stated capital helped to assure equality and fairness among shareholders in a new corporation. By providing a stated par value on each stock certificate, the corporation assured investors that all shareholders purchased their shares for equivalent amounts. For this premise to hold true, of course, corporate statutes dictated that corporations could not give favorable treatment to a shareholder by allowing the shareholder to purchase a share for less than its par value. With the benefit of this statutory provision, an investor purchasing newly issued $100 par value stock from a corporation would know that the other shareholders also paid at least $100 per share for their shares.

Second, the concept of legal capital purportedly protected corporate creditors. As we will see in Chapter V on pages 331 to 339, *infra*, corporate statutes placed restrictions on a company's ability to distribute its legal or stated capital to its stockholders. Traditional corporate statutes under the legal capital system sought to provide a "cushion" for corporate creditors. By placing limits on a corporation's ability to distribute to shareholders amounts representing the stated capital that the shareholders contributed to the company, those statutes sought to assure the corporation's creditors that the shareholders would permanently dedicate the stated capital to the enterprise's activities and obligations, subject to operating losses, of course.

Not surprisingly, however, the ingenuity of lawyers soon rendered the legal capital system illusory. Today, in states such as Delaware that still use the legal capital system, we typically see corporations issue stock with very low par values, such as $1, $.01, or even $.001, thereby minimizing the portion of contributed capital that the corporation may not distribute to the shareholders. For example, Google's Fourth Amended and Restated Certificate of Incorporation, which you can access at http://investor.google.com/corporate/certificate-of-incorporation.html, assigns a $0.001 par value to all Google shares.

As a practical matter, even in states still following the legal capital system, corporations usually do not issue shares for consideration equal to their par value. Although these corporate statutes do not impose any requirements as to what amount a corporation should fix as the par value, the statutes require that the company not issue shares for *less than* par value. Because a corporation cannot always accurately determine beforehand the exact price that investors might pay for a share of its newly issued stock, companies using par value shares often set the figure at a low amount, thereby ensuring that the corporation will not experience any difficulty in selling a share for an amount *at least equal to* its par value. When a corporation issues shares for an amount that exceeds par value under the legal capital system, the corporation does not classify the excess as legal capital or stated capital, but instead refers to the excess as *capital surplus*. If a corporation issues 1,000 shares of $1 par value stock for $20 per share, $1,000 (1,000 shares times $1 par value per share) would represent stated capital. The legal capital system treats the remaining $19,000 (1,000 shares times the difference between (i) the $20 per share selling price and (ii) the $1 par value per share) as capital surplus. Together, then, legal capital and capital surplus represent the total capital that the shareholders contribute to a corporation. As we will see in Chapter V on page 331, *infra*, however, and depending upon the corporate statute, the restriction precluding a corporation from distributing to shareholders amounts that represent the stated capital that the original shareholders contributed to the company may not apply to capital surplus.

In addition, most corporate statutes following the legal capital system, including the Delaware General Corporation Law, permit corporations to issue shares that do not bear any specified par value. *See, e.g.*, DEL. CODE ANN. tit. 8, §§ 151(a), 153(b) (West, West through ch. 362 of 2014 Legis. Sess.). Lawyers refer to such shares as *no-par* shares. Obviously, the use of no-par shares avoids the legal restriction against issuing shares for consideration less than par value, and, as will be noted shortly, reduces concerns about distributions from stated capital to shareholders. A corporation can issue no-par shares for such consideration as the company's board of directors may determine. When a corporation issues no-par shares, its board of directors generally has discretion in allocating the price that shareholders pay for the shares between stated capital and capital surplus. Thus, those involved with corporate practice soon recognized stated capital as a wholly arbitrary number, unrelated in any way to any economic facts that are relevant to the company.

If a corporation issues more than one class of stock, the legal capital system requires the company to maintain a separate legal capital or stated capital account for each class. For example, a corporation that has issued both common shares and preferred shares will maintain two separate capital stock accounts, each recording the stated capital associated with a particular class. Accounting for contributed capital mirrors this legal capital system, although the legal and accounting terminology differ.

When the articles of incorporation authorize a corporation to issue more than one class of shares, accountants typically divide the capital stock component into *Common Stock* and *Preferred Stock accounts*. The Common Stock account will show an amount equal to the product of the total number of issued common shares times the par value per common share. Similarly, the Preferred Stock account will contain an amount equal to the product of the total number of issued preferred shares times the par value per preferred share, which usually differs from the par value per common share. If the articles of incorporation only authorize one class of shares, the corporation would use a Common Stock account as the only capital stock account.

(1) Shares with Par Value

When a corporation issues shares at par value, the company debits the appropriate asset account, whether cash, property, or other consideration, and credits a capital stock account for the par value amount. To illustrate, if Tutt, Inc. issues 100 shares, $10 par value, to E. Tutt for $1,000, the corporation's bookkeeper would record the following journal entry:

Cash	$1,000	
Common Stock, $10 par value		$1,000
(To record the issuance of 100 shares to E. Tutt)		

If instead, Tutt, Inc. issues five shares of $100 par value preferred stock to Tutt for $500 and fifty shares of $10 par value common stock to her for another $500, the bookkeeper would make the following entry:

Cash	$1,000	
Preferred Stock, $100 par value		$500
Common Stock, $10 par value		500
(To record the issuance of five preferred shares and fifty common shares to E. Tutt)		

In the common case, when a corporation issues shares for more than their stated par value under the legal capital system, the company treats the excess as capital surplus. For accounting purposes, the corporation records this excess as *additional paid-in capital* or *capital contributed in excess of par*. Because the legal capital system does not require a corporation to isolate any capital surplus derived from issuing different classes of shares, a corporation usually maintains only one additional paid-in capital account. Combined then, the accounts for capital stock, namely the Common Stock and Preferred Stock accounts, and the Additional Paid–In Capital account, represent the corporation's total contributed capital.

Thus, if Tutt, Inc. had issued all 100 shares of $1 par stock that the articles of incorporation authorize to E. Tutt for $1,000, the bookkeeper would have recorded the following entry:

Cash	$1,000	
Common Stock, $1 par value		$100
Additional Paid-In Capital		900

We should note that a corporate balance sheet or accompanying notes typically disclose important information about the company's capital structure. The shareholders' equity section, often alternatively captioned either as *shareowners' equity* or *stockholders' equity*, commonly shows the par value for each share or states that the shares are no-par. In addition, the shareholders' equity section or accompanying notes indicate the number of shares that the corporate charter authorizes the company to issue, the number of shares that the corporation has issued, and the number of shares that remain outstanding.

We can use Google to illustrate a more complicated presentation of shareholders' equity arising from a complex corporate charter. In June 2012, the company filed its Fourth Amended and Restated Certificate of Incorporation with the Secretary of State of the State of Delaware. You may recall that you can access the document at http://investor.google.com/ corporate/certificate-of-incorporation.html. Article IV authorizes Google to issue Preferred Stock, Class A Common Stock, Class B Common Stock, and Class C Capital Stock and assigns a $0.001 par value to each and every share.

Although Google had not issued any outstanding preferred shares as of December 31, 2013, the company's certificate of incorporation authorizes 100 million preferred shares. Subject to any limitations prescribed by law, the certificate of incorporation gives the board of directors the authority to issue shares of Preferred Stock in series, to establish from time to time the number of shares in each series, and to fix the preferences and rights of the preferred shares in each series.

Google can issue up to twelve billion shares of common stock, including nine billion shares of Class A Common Stock and three billion shares of Class B Common Stock. The holders of the Class A and Class B common shares enjoy identical rights, except as to voting. The Class B common shares enjoy *super-voting power*. The company's certificate of incorporation grants the holders of the outstanding Class A common shares one vote per share. By comparison, the holders of outstanding Class B common shares can cast ten votes per share. As of March 17, 2014, Larry Page, Sergey Brin, and Eric E. Schmidt, Google's founders and executive chairman, beneficially owned almost ninety-two percent of the company's outstanding Class B shares, which translated to more than sixty-one percent of the combined voting power of all outstanding common shares. The holders of Class B shares can convert their shares into Class A shares at any time. In addition, the Class B shares automatically convert to Class A shares upon sale or transfer.

Finally, Google can issue three billion shares of Class C Capital Stock. The Class C shares enjoy no voting rights, except as applicable law requires. Apart from the differences in voting rights and unless otherwise provided in the certificate of incorporation, the Class C shares rank equally, share ratably, enjoy the same rights and privileges, and mirror in all other respects the Class A and Class B shares. In April 2014, Google distributed shares of the Class C capital stock to the holders of Class A and Class B shares on a share-for-share basis.

Google's balance sheet as of December 31, 2013, which appears on page 48 of the Form 10-K for the year then ended ("Google's 2013 Form 10-K") that Google filed with the Securities and Exchange Commission ("SEC") on February 12, 2014, describes this more complicated capital structure. You can access the Form 10-K via a link on Google's website at http://investor.google. com/earnings.html, which collects pages containing various documents related to the company's quarterly and annual earnings. Alternatively, from Google's home page at www.google.com, select the "About" link at the bottom. Under the "Investor Relations" heading on the "About" page, click on the "financial information" link. From the "2013 Quarterly Earnings" page, click on the link for "Annual Report on Form 10-K." As a third approach, you could use the

SEC's Electronic Data Gathering and Retrieval ("EDGAR") database to obtain the Form 10-K via www.sec.gov. From the SEC's homepage, click on the "Search EDGAR for Company Filings" box. After entering your search information by typing "Google Inc." in the box for "Company name" and selecting the "Starts with" and "Excludes [ownership forms]" circles, click on the "Find Companies" rectangle. Scroll down the search results until you find the Form 10-K filed on February 12, 2014, and select that document.

In addition to Google's December 31, 2013 balance sheet, the text in Note 12 on page 76 of the company's Form 10-K for the year ended December 31, 2013, provides additional information about Google's shareholders' equity. From those portions of Google's 2013 Form 10-K, we can determine that as of December 31, 2013, the company's Amended and Restated Certificate of Incorporation authorized 100 million preferred shares, nine billion Class A common shares, three billion Class B common shares, and three billion Class C capital shares, and assigned a $0.001 par value to all 15.1 billion authorized shares. Over the years, Google had issued at least 279,325,564 shares of Class A common stock and approximately 62,531,000 shares of Class B common stock. On December 31, 2013, 279,325,564 Class A common shares and 56,506,728 Class B common shares remained outstanding.

(2) No–Par Shares

For no-par shares, absent some special action by the board of directors, the legal capital system treats the entire amount of consideration that the shareholder pays for the shares as legal capital or stated capital. Most statutes in this system, however, permit the board of directors to treat some of the total amount that the corporation receives for shares without par value as capital surplus. In most states that follow the legal capital system, only the amount allocated to stated capital constitutes legal capital which the corporation cannot distribute to the shareholders. Lawyers sometimes refer to the amount per share that the board of directors has allocated to stated capital with respect to no-par shares as *stated value*, a misnomer that, like par value, does not necessarily bear any relation to the shares' actual value.

From an accounting standpoint, if the board of directors does not elect to treat some of the consideration that the corporation receives for no-par shares as capital surplus, the company debits the appropriate asset account and credits the full consideration to stated capital. If instead, the board decides that less than all of the consideration received for no-par shares should constitute legal capital, the company again debits the appropriate asset account, but credits that smaller figure to stated capital, with the excess credited to capital surplus. In either case, the so-called stated value per share equals the quotient of stated capital divided by the number of no-par shares.

In summary, accountants and lawyers divide contributed capital into two categories, but they assign different names to these categories. Accountants use a capital stock account, typically either a Common Stock account or a Preferred Stock account, to portray the amount that represents the product of the number of issued shares times the par value or stated value per share.

Lawyers call this same product legal capital or stated capital. Accountants refer to any excess of the amount that a shareholder pays for shares and those shares' collective par or stated value as additional paid-in capital. Lawyers describe this excess as capital surplus.

b. EARNED CAPITAL

As already mentioned, reinvested earnings provide the second source from which a corporation derives its equity. A corporation can either use earnings to pay dividends to, or repurchase shares from, shareholders or retain those earnings in the business. Accountants use the Retained Earnings account to track the undistributed earnings, less any cumulative losses, that remain invested in the enterprise. The legal capital system usually refers to any such positive figure as *earned surplus*.

To this point, we have seen that accountants generally divide shareholders' equity into three components: capital stock accounts—either common stock or preferred stock; additional paid-in capital; and retained earnings. By comparison, the legal capital system refers to these categories as stated capital, capital surplus, and earned surplus, respectively. The following chart compares the various titles that accountants and the legal capital system assign to the different components of shareholders' equity:

SHAREHOLDERS' EQUITY CATEGORIES	
ACCOUNTING NOMENCLATURE	LEGAL TERMINOLOGY
Capital Stock: Common Stock or Preferred Stock	Stated Capital or Legal Capital
Additional Paid-in Capital	Capital Surplus
Retained Earnings	Earned Surplus

To reconcile the equity amounts from the balance sheets that appear on pages 14 and 40, *supra*, we could prepare the following financial statement:

E. Tutt, Esquire
Statement of Changes in Shareholder's Equity
For the Month of June

Shareholder's Equity, beginning of period	$1,000
Net Income	525
Subtotal	$ 1525
Less: Dividends	50
Shareholder's Equity, end of period	$1,475

Some corporations call this financial statement the *statement of shareholders' equity*, the *statement of stockholders' equity*, or the *statement of changes in stockholders' equity*. As you can see in Appendix A on page 749, *infra*,

Starbucks labels its reconciliation the Statement of Equity. In any event, we again see how the statement of changes in owner's equity reconciles the amount of the residual ownership interest from the beginning to the end of an accounting period. In this example, however, the only changes involved retained earnings. For that reason, some corporations call the reconciliation the *statement of retained earnings*. Still other corporations combine the income statement and the statement of retained earnings into a *combined statement of income and retained earnings*. Finally, some corporations disclose the changes shown in these various statements in the notes to the financial statements.

PROBLEMS

Problem 1.4A. You can obtain information about Amazon's capital structure as of December 31, 2012, from the company's Form 10-K for the year ended on that date. You can access the Form 10-K, which Amazon incorporates into its 2012 Annual Report, via http://phx.corporate-ir.net/phoenix.zhtml?c =97664&p=irol-reportsAnnual. Alternatively, from Amazon's home page at www.amazon.com, select the "Investor Relations" link at the very bottom of the page. Under the heading "Financial Documents," select "Annual Reports and Proxies" to access the company's 2012 Annual Report. Describe as fully as possible the different classes of shares in Amazon's capital structure as of December 31, 2012. For each class or type of shares: (1) state the par or stated value, if any; (2) describe any dividend or liquidation preferences or other features; and (3) list the number of (a) authorized, (b) issued, (c) outstanding, and (d) treasury shares. Explain exactly where you found any relevant information.

Problem 1.4B. Using the materials in Appendix A on pages 691-805, *infra*, describe as fully as possible the different classes of shares in Starbucks' capital structure as of September 30, 2012. For each class or type of shares: (1) state the par or stated value, if any; (2) describe any dividend or liquidation preferences or other features; and (3) list the number of (a) authorized, (b) issued, (c) outstanding, and (d) treasury shares. Explain exactly where you found any relevant information.

Problem 1.4C. You can obtain information about UPS's capital structure as of December 31, 2012, from the company's Form 10-K for the fiscal year ended on that date. You can access the Form 10-K, which UPS incorporates into its 2012 Annual Report, via the company's Investor Relations website at http://www.investors.ups.com/phoenix.zhtml?c=62900&p=irol-reportsannual. Alternatively, from UPS's home page at www.ups.com., select the "Investors" link near the bottom of the page. Under the heading "Financials," select "Annual Report" to access the company's 2012 Annual Report. Describe as fully as possible the different classes of shares in UPS's capital structure as of December 31, 2012. For each class or type of shares: (1) state the par or stated value, if any; (2) describe any dividend or liquidation preferences or other features; and (3) list the number of (a) authorized, (b) issued, (c) outstanding, and (d) treasury shares. Explain exactly where you found any relevant information.

F. ACCRUAL ACCOUNTING

Thus far, we have been studying bookkeeping, or the technique for recording a business's transactions. In addition to recording transactions, *accrual accounting*, or *accounting* for short, seeks to allocate revenues and expenses to accounting periods, regardless of when the cash receipts or expenditures actually occur. From an accounting standpoint, earning revenue does not require a cash receipt. Similarly, an expense may not require a cash expenditure in the accounting period in which the business incurred the expense. Under accrual accounting, an accounting entity recognizes revenues when earned and expenses when incurred, without regard to the actual cash receipts or payments.

We can illustrate these points by returning to our example involving E. Tutt. You will recall that during the month of June, Tutt received $1,000 in fees for legal services that she performed during the month. What if Tutt had sent a $300 bill to a client on June 29 for services she had performed earlier in the month, but the client did not pay the bill until July 3? Under the *cash method*, an accounting entity recognizes revenues when the enterprise actually receives cash or payment for goods or services. If Tutt used the cash method, she would not recognize the $300 revenue until the client paid the bill in July, even though she actually performed the services in June. In contrast, under the accrual method, an accounting entity recognizes revenues when the business delivers the goods or performs the services. If Tutt had adopted the accrual method, she would have included the $300 in June's revenues because she performed the services during the month.

These same distinctions apply to expenses. An accrual method business records expenses when it actually incurs them. Under the cash method, the business would not record the expenses until it paid them. To illustrate, assume that Tutt hired a company supplying janitorial services to clean her office for $50 per month starting June 1. The company performed the requested services during June, but did not bill Tutt until July 1. Tutt paid the bill promptly on July 5. When should she record the expense? If Tutt uses the cash method, she would not record the expense until July, when she paid the bill. Under the accrual method, however, Tutt would have recorded a $50 janitorial expense in June because the company performed the requested services during June, which means that Tutt incurred those expenses during the month.

In both examples, the underlying event preceded payment. Sometimes, however, cash precedes the underlying event. For example, Tutt could collect a retainer, or legal fee prepayment, from a client in July for services that she would not perform until August. Under the cash method, Tutt would include the retainer in July's revenue, even though she has not earned anything yet. The accrual method would require her to wait until she performed the services to recognize the income. Similarly, during July, Tutt might prepay a registration fee for a seminar that she planned to attend in September. If she used the cash method, she would record the prepayment as an expense in July. Under the accrual method, Tutt would treat the prepayment as an asset until she attended the seminar in September, at which point she would eliminate the asset and record an expense.

Accrual accounting seeks to recognize revenues when earned, and to match expenses with the revenues that they produce. Accrual accounting includes the processes of deferral and accrual, which we will discuss in detail shortly. Very briefly, *deferral* refers to the process whereby the accountant delays an event involving cash or cash's worth in the current period until a subsequent accounting period or periods. In deferral, the accountant "pushes" a past payment into the future. In our example, at the end of July, the accountant would defer the retainer and the seminar prepayment until August and September, respectively. By comparison, *accrual* refers to the process whereby an accountant records a revenue or expense in the current accounting period even though no payment occurred during the current period. In accrual, the accountant "pulls" the future payment into the current period. In our example, during June, the accountant would accrue the income from the billed, yet unpaid, legal services and the expense from the janitorial services.

In summary, accrual accounting refers to those rules and principles that accountants use to classify and measure "real world" economic events in numbers to fit into the bookkeeping process. Before we begin our detailed study of accrual accounting, as an additional application of bookkeeping, we should understand the basic assumptions, principles, and constraints or modifying conventions underlying the process.

1.   INTRODUCTION

Many accounting practices make sense only if you understand the assumptions, principles, and constraints or modifying conventions underlying accrual accounting. As we discuss and attempt to resolve various accounting issues, we should ask whether the general assumptions still apply in the specific circumstances and whether the basic principles and constraints or modifying conventions suggest a particular accounting treatment.

a.   ASSUMPTIONS

Several basic assumptions underlie accrual accounting. These suppositions include the economic entity assumption, the monetary unit assumption, the periodicity assumption, and the going concern assumption. Thus far, we have only implicitly considered these suppositions. We will now explicitly consider each assumption and its implications.

(1) Economic Entity Assumption

Accountants presuppose that they can separate the activities of a business from those of its owners and any other business. Under this assumption, accountants identify economic activity with a particular accounting entity even though the law may not recognize the accounting entity as a distinct legal entity. Recall that we kept separate accounting records for E. Tutt's legal practice even though the law holds a sole proprietor personally liable for a business's obligations. In addition, the accounting records for the law office did not include E. Tutt's personal expenses even though E. Tutt undoubtedly had to eat and pay various housing, transportation, and clothing expenses.

(2) Monetary Unit Assumption

Accountants recognize that money serves as the common denominator that enables businesses to conduct economic activity. In the United States, the applicable monetary unit, the dollar, theoretically provides an appropriate basis for accounting measure and analysis. This assumption implies that the monetary unit best communicates economic information regarding exchanges of goods and services, as well as changes in owners' equity, and assists in rational, economic decision-making.

As a practical matter, accountants use the monetary unit because that measure offers a simple, universally available, and easy-to-understand standard. This selection assumes that the unit of measure—again, the dollar in the United States—remains reasonably stable. As a result, accountants add 1960 dollars to 2010 dollars without any adjustment for inflation. Accountants, therefore, assume that we can ignore the difference in purchasing power between 1960 dollars and 2010 dollars. In a period of inflation with continuous and significant rises in prices, users of financial statements should question this assumption. In the inflationary period of the 1970s and early 1980s, accountants required and provided additional information to reflect the effect of inflation on financial statements. With inflation in relative control thus far in the new millennium, accountants usually do not provide that supplemental information.

(3) Periodicity Assumption

As we have already suggested, an accountant could most accurately measure an enterprise's financial results by waiting until the enterprise's liquidation. The accountant could then determine the enterprise's net profit by calculating the difference between what the owners contributed to the business and what they received at liquidation. Management, investors, lenders, and governments cannot wait indefinitely to assess an enterprise's financial performance. Consequently, periodic evaluation of an enterprise's operations becomes important.

The periodicity assumption presupposes that an accountant can divide an accounting entity's economic activities into artificial time periods. In dividing continuous operations into separate time periods, accountants must determine the relevance of each business transaction or event to distinct accounting periods. The shorter the time period, the more difficult it becomes to determine what belongs in the period.

(4) Going Concern or Continuity Assumption

Under the going concern or continuity assumption, accountants presume that the accounting entity will continue normal operations into the foreseeable future. Accountants use this continuity assumption because experience indicates that modern business enterprises will carry on indefinitely, or at least until they can fulfill their contractual commitments and plans. The going concern assumption creates several implications. First, the assumption lends credibility to the historical cost principle. If accountants adopted a liquidation approach to valuing assets, the balance sheet would show assets at net realizable value rather than at historical cost. Second, without a continuity assumption, classifying assets and liabilities as either current or non-current loses its significance.

The going concern assumption does not apply where liquidation, whether or not in connection with bankruptcy, appears imminent. If an accountant doubts a business's ability to continue as a going concern, she will want to provide different information to the users of the financial statements. In particular, the accounting entity should show assets at net realizable value, which means expected selling price less estimated selling costs, rather than use figures based upon historical costs.

b.   BASIC PRINCIPLES

Given the fundamental assumptions underlying accounting, accountants follow certain basic principles and rules in recording transactions. We have already met some of these principles. The basic principles include the historical cost principle, the objectivity or verifiability principle, the revenue recognition principle, the matching principle, the consistency principle, the full disclosure principle, and an emerging fair value or relevance principle. We will discuss various exceptions to these principles in subsequent chapters.

(1) Historical Cost Principle

As we have already seen, accountants initially record assets at original or historical cost. Thereafter, accountants have historically continued to use a figure based on historical cost because that measure offers a definite and determinable standard. Once established, historical cost remains fixed as long as the accounting entity owns the asset. At the same time, however, historical cost usually does not provide the most relevant or helpful information for decision-making purposes because the measure will only coincidentally reflect an asset's fair market value. Users of financial statements increasingly want contemporary or prospective information. Opponents have also criticized the historical cost principle on the grounds that during inflationary periods, original cost soon becomes out of date.

As an alternative to historical cost, accountants could use current fair value. Using that measure, however, would offer less precision and require more estimates. With this background, we will soon discuss the currrent movement toward a "mixed-attribute" system that combines historical cost reporting with a fair value model.

(2) Objectivity or Verifiability Principle

As an ideal, accountants prefer a system that will reach essentially similar measures and conclusions if two or more qualified persons examine the same data. The objectivity principle seeks to attain that goal and provides additional support for the historical cost principle. If we asked two accountants to record the transaction in which E. Tutt purchased her office equipment from Elmer Co., they would record the office equipment at $300. If we asked the accountants to determine the equipment's fair market value, they would probably give us two different answers. Under the verifiability principle, which most accountants consider as a corollary to the objectivity principle, accountants prefer accounting treatments that available and reliable evidence can support. To further illustrate, financial accounting generally uses historical cost because the two accountants in our previous example could verify that E. Tutt paid $300 by examining the invoice from the transaction.

We should not overstate this objectivity principle. As we will see in this section on accrual accounting, financial accounting requires estimates. Consequently, financial statements do not present completely objective information. Nevertheless, as long as others can corroborate supporting data and methodology, accountants consider an estimate to be objective and verifiable.

(3) Revenue Recognition Principle

Apart from income tax considerations, most businesses would prefer to recognize income as soon as possible and to defer expenses as long as possible. Under the revenue recognition principle, however, accountants usually recognize revenue only when: (1) an exchange transaction has occurred; and (2) the accounting entity has completed, or virtually completed, the earnings process. We will discuss this principle and its exceptions at length in Chapter VI on pages 359 to 465, *infra*.

(4) Matching Principle

At periodic intervals, accountants compute the results of operations, seeking as much accuracy as possible. The matching principle dictates that an accounting entity offset expenses against the resulting revenues in the same accounting period wherever feasible. If the revenue recognition principle precludes an entity from recognizing certain revenue, the income statement should not subtract the expenses necessary to produce that revenue. On the other hand, the income statement should show those expenses that the accounting entity incurred to generate reported income for an accounting period, even though no cash outflow has occurred for those expenses.

(5) Consistency Principle

Under the consistency principle, accounting entities must give economic events the same accounting treatment from accounting period to period. If readers can compare financial statements with similar reports for prior periods, accounting statements and records become much more useful. The consistency principle restricts an accounting entity from changing an accounting method between accounting periods to those situations in which accountants would consider the newly adopted principle as preferable to the old method. If an accounting entity does change an accounting principle, the entity must disclose the change's nature and effect, as well as the justification, for the accounting period in which the entity adopts the change. We should not, however, overstate the consistency principle. Because accounting practices vary from business to business, comparisons between the financial statements of different businesses can prove quite difficult.

(6) Full Disclosure Principle

This basic accounting principle generally requires an accounting entity to report in financial statements any fact important enough to influence an informed reader's judgment. Because enterprises can often choose from alternative accounting treatments, unless explicitly informed a reader might assume that the organization had followed an entirely different accounting practice. Common methods for satisfying this disclosure requirement include presenting an account as a line item in the financial statements, adding an accompanying parenthetical disclosure, and including an explanatory footnote. For this reason, remember to read the footnotes! At the same time, accountants recognize that financial statements must reasonably condense and summarize the details of the enterprise's operations and financial position to convey meaningful information to a user of financial statements. Too much detail and information can overwhelm and confuse a reader.

(7) An Emerging Fair Value or Relevance Principle

Because financial statements based solely on historical costs typically do not provide the most relevant or helpful information for decision-making purposes, financial accounting increasingly requires enterprises to use fair value or market value, rather than historical cost, to report certain assets and liabilities. As a result, current financial accounting technically uses a so-called "mixed-attribute" system that combines historical cost-reporting with a fair value model. Professor Stanley Siegel has highlighted this development and predicted that the "accounting principles of the twenty-first century may bear little resemblance to their forbears." In addition to replacing the historical cost principle, the movement to fair value calls into question the objectivity, revenue recognition, consistency, and full disclosure principles. Stanley Siegel, *The Coming Revolution in Accounting: The Emergence of Fair Value as the Fundamental Principle of GAAP*, 42 WAYNE L. REV. 1839, 1841, 1847–49, 1859 (1996).

In 1999, the leading body of accounting rulemakers began what seems like an inevitable move toward accounting standards that will eventually compel enterprises to use fair value to report most, if not all, financial assets and liabilities. As we will read later in this text, more and more accounting standards, both domestically and internationally, require that enterprises report certain assets and liabilities at fair value. To date, however, the rulemakers have not resolved all the conceptual and practical issues related to determining the fair values of financial assets and liabilities. Accordingly, they have not decided when, if ever, the basic financial statements should report such fair values. As possible alternatives, the rulemakers have observed that they could require enhanced disclosures about fair values or a separate set of financial statements based upon fair value. Because market prices do not exist for many financial assets, enterprises would need to develop valuation models to determine fair value. Such valuation models would inherently depend upon subjective assumptions. In 2006, the standard setters issued a final pronouncement on fair value measurements that codified and simplified the guidance that previously existed for developing fair value measurements, improved their consistency and comparability, and enhanced disclosures about those measurements.

The new rules on fair value measurements took effect at about the same time that the credit crisis began. In response to criticisms that fair value accounting exacerbated the ongoing financial crisis by requiring enterprises to write-down assets in inactive markets, the standard setters have repeatedly announced significant clarifications, improvements, and technical corrections. The rules, which Chapter VI describes in more detail on pages 409 to 415, *infra*, establish a uniform methodology for obtaining the fair value measurements that other standards require; offer guidance on calculating fair value for assets in an illiquid market and on determining whether an asset has suffered an other-than-temporary impairment in value; and require additional disclosures. Although controversial, the new rules do not obligate enterprises to measure any additional items at fair value. Not surprisingly, banks and other financial institutions have repeatedly asked the rulemakers to suspend fair value accounting and have consistently objected to any rule that requires enterprises to use fair value accounting.

In response to certain developments in international accounting principles, rules promulgated in 2007 allow an irrevocable, one-time election to use fair value to measure and report certain financial assets and financial liabilities on a contract-by-contract basis, with any changes in fair value recognized in earnings as those changes occur. We will describe those rules in more detail in Chapter VI on pages 434 and 436, *infra*.

c. CONSTRAINTS OR MODIFYING CONVENTIONS

Accountants realize that they cannot regard the basic accounting principles as infallible rules. Not only do exceptions apply to almost every basic accounting principle, but certain practical considerations, which we will refer to as *constraints or modifying conventions*, often help to shape accounting practices. Such constraints or modifying conventions, which include cost-benefit, materiality, conservatism, and industry practices, also merit our attention.

(1) Cost-Benefit

Accounting's rulemakers realize that the costs of gathering and providing information can exceed its usefulness. For example, although investors may want information about an enterprise's expected exposure to litigation, the plaintiffs in such litigation might use any disclosures to the enterprise's detriment in the underlying litigation. In other circumstances the costs to gather information may outweigh any reasonably expected benefits. Accordingly, accounting standard setters attempt to consider all such costs when they weigh new accounting rules and disclosures. Unless the expected benefits of a proposed standard exceed the estimated costs, both admittedly difficult, if not impossible, to quantify, the rulemakers should not promulgate the standard.

(2) Materiality

As another constraint, accounting's practical side also recognizes that precise attention to theory can impose unreasonable costs and burdens. At times, the added complication and cost involved in complying with an accounting requirement do not justify the insignificant benefit that any user of the financial statements would likely derive. When other, more important items dwarf a small and unimportant amount, the concept of materiality permits the accountant to disregard otherwise applicable accounting principles and rules.

Materiality includes quantitative as well as qualitative components, and hence involves questions of both relative size and importance. Quantitatively, materiality depends not only on an item's size, but also on the business's size. To illustrate, an accountant would consider $20,000 in missing inventory to be material for a small business showing $100,000 in annual sales, while that amount in missing inventory would not qualify as material for Starbucks Corporation. From a qualitative standpoint, materiality can vary with an item's nature. For example, an accountant might consider any illegal payment, even a very small payment, as material for certain businesses.

(3) Conservatism

Accountants frequently refer to conservatism as a modifying convention. Over the years, accountants have tried to avoid overly optimistic financial statements by anticipating and recording possible losses, while at the same time refusing to recognize potential income. In a nutshell, the convention pushes accountants toward the pessimistic side, to offset the natural optimism, if not exuberance, of business owners or managers in reporting the results of their operations. Accountants have summed up this convention's theme in the adage, "Recognize all losses, anticipate no gains." To avoid later unpleasant surprises, accountants should undertake an effort to reflect all losses or expenses as soon as they appear likely, while delaying the recognition of income or gain until it is virtually assured.

When various measurements exist and none qualifies as the best alternative, conservatism counsels the accountant to choose the approach least likely to overstate assets and income or to understate liabilities and expenses. As a result, this modifying convention can lead to an accounting entity understating its income, assets, and equity and overstating its expenses and liabilities. Although conservatism still enjoys considerable influence, accountants increasingly recognize that undue pessimism in reporting financial results can cause almost as many undesirable consequences as over-optimism. For example, unduly discouraging financial statements could lead an investor to sell an investment for a lower price. As a result, we should remember that application of this convention, as with any other accounting doctrine, requires the exercise of sound judgment. The convention only applies when uncertainty or doubt exists.

(4) Industry Practices

As a final modifying convention, peculiarities in some industries and businesses allow departure from basic accounting principles. For example, while accounting entities generally use historical cost to value their inventories, businesses engaged in the meat-packing industry sometimes carry inventories at sales price less distribution cost because a meat-packer cannot allocate the cost of an animal to the ribs, chucks, and shoulders with any ease or precision.

Having discussed the assumptions, principles, and constraints or modifying conventions underlying accrual accounting, we can now turn to discuss the process itself in some detail. The process involves both accrual and deferral. We begin our detailed discussion with deferral.

PROBLEMS

Problem 1.5A. In 1960, Bellia Company purchased land costing $10,000. For real estate tax purposes, the county assessor has valued the land at $75,000 for tax year 201X. A local real estate agent has suggested to the company's president that the land is worth at least $100,000. Based on increases in the consumer price index, which reveals that $1 in 1960 bought six times as much as $1 in 201X, one could say that the original cost of the land in 201X dollars is $60,000.

(1) At what amount should the land appear on the company's books and in its 201X financial statements?

(2) Which financial accounting assumptions, basic principles or constraints or modifying conventions require your result? Explain briefly.

Problem 1.5B. The Beck Corporation has a policy of recording all purchases of supplies as expenses at the time of purchase, even though the company might not use the supplies during that accounting period. The value of unused

Modifying
conversion
cost v. ben
materiality
cost benefit
F.   ACCRUAL ACCOUNTING   **71**

supplies represents a large portion of the firm's assets and varies greatly from period to period. What financial accounting assumptions or basic principles, if any, does this accounting treatment violate? Explain briefly.

Problem 1.5C. Sunburst Partners lists office stationery purchased two years ago on its balance sheet at its $1,260 cost, although no one else would buy all this stationery for more than $25 as scrap paper. What financial accounting assumptions, basic principles, or constraints or modifying conventions dictate this treatment? Explain briefly.

2.   DEFERRAL OF EXPENSES AND INCOME

As briefly mentioned already, deferral refers to the process whereby an accountant delays a payment in the current period until a subsequent accounting period or periods. Accountants defer both prepaid expenses and unearned revenues. In the first instance, the accountant delays treating a cash expenditure as an expense until some subsequent accounting period when the business will enjoy the benefit of the expenditure. Similarly, she delays recognizing a cash receipt as income when the business will not earn the income until a subsequent period.

a.   EXPENSES

As a practical matter, the fact that assets and expenses are each increased by a debit and decreased by a credit is not coincidental. There is a significant relationship between assets and expenses. In fact, dishonest corporate executives have used this relationship to perpetrate financial frauds. At WorldCom, senior financial officers improperly treated about $11 billion in operating expenses as assets, which tremendously overstated the company's income and led, in 2002, to the then-largest bankruptcy filing in U.S. history.

(1) In General

To illustrate the relationship between assets and expenses, suppose that when Tutt first hangs out her shingle, she pays $60,000 to purchase a small building to use as her office. She would debit the asset Building for $60,000, and would credit the Cash account in the same amount, and no income or expense account would be affected. If she pays a week's rent for an office instead, a debit to the Rent Expense account would be appropriate. But what if she pays advance rent for six months? Ten years? Ninety-nine years? Clearly, at some point it no longer can be said that Tutt is "out" or "poorer" by the amount of the advance payment, or that her stake in the enterprise has been reduced in that amount. Rather, she has exchanged cash for an asset, just as she did when she purchased a building; here, the asset would be the right to occupy the office for the period covered by the payment.

Actually, any expense paid in advance creates an asset, although that asset may be short-lived; even the advance payment of rent for a week gives rise to an asset—the right to occupy for one week. By the end of the week, however, the asset has been used up, and the payment has become an expense. By the same token, almost all assets are simply prepaid expenses, since ultimately they will be used up and will disappear. For the key to deciding how much of an advance payment is an expense and how much is an asset, remember that the income and expense accounts collect the items affecting the enterprise's equity *in a particular period*. The amount of an advance payment that is used up during the period is an expense for that period; any portion of the payment not used up in the current period is something the business still owns, and hence is an asset as of the end of the period. Thus, if Tutt pays $60,000 advance rent for ten years, at the end of the first year $6,000 is an expense, and $54,000 remains as an asset. If, as we have been assuming, Tutt prepares statements each month, then for the first month $500 (1/120 times $60,000) is an expense, and the remaining $59,500 is an asset at the end of the first month.

If, for simplicity, we assume that the useful life of a building can be estimated with precision, and we ignore scrap or other salvage value at the end of the useful life, the purchase of a building with a useful life of, say, ten years for $60,000 may be thought of in exactly the same way as an advance rent for ten years. Like the advance rent, the cost of the building will be completely used up at the end of the tenth year; that cost, therefore, should be apportioned among the periods in which the building helps to produce income under the matching principle.

To see how the bookkeeper uses entries to handle prepaid expenses, suppose that on January 1 of her first year Tutt pays $15,000 for rent for three years in advance. At the end of the first year, no matter how the entries are made during the year, she should end up with an expense of $5,000 and an asset of $10,000. Because at first blush a payment for rent seems like an expense, Tutt's bookkeeper might make this entry on January 1:

Rent Expense	$15,000	
Cash		$15,000

Assuming, for the moment, that we are only concerned with Tutt's annual statements, the various income and expense accounts will be closed into the Profit and Loss account at the end of the year. But only $5,000 of the $15,000 now in the Rent Expense account "belongs" to the first year; thus if the whole $15,000 is closed to the Profit and Loss account, rent expense for that year will be overstated, and net income will be understated. At the same time, Tutt's balance sheet for December 31 will not include all of her assets because the asset representing the right to occupy the premises for two more years will be missing. What is needed, then, is a reduction of the expense to the amount actually used up and the creation of an asset to show what Tutt actually still owns. To show the existence of the asset, that is, the right to occupy, a debit of $10,000 should be made to an asset account, such as Deferred Rent Cost. To decrease the expense from $15,000 to $5,000, a credit to the Rent Expense account of $10,000 is needed. A single entry would accomplish both objectives. Such an entry could appear as follows:

| Deferred Rent Cost (asset) | $10,000 | |
| Rent Expense | | $10,000 |

The term deferral describes this process of reducing an expense to the amount actually used up during the accounting period while creating an asset to show something the business still owns at the end of the period. The word appropriately connotes the fact that part of the expenditure is held back from the current period because it has not yet been used. Accordingly, the asset created is often called a *deferred cost* or, perhaps, a *deferred expense*—here, the asset might also be called *Deferred Rent Expense*. An accounting purist would hesitate to use the word "Expense" in a balance sheet account, preferring to limit the use of the word to income statement accounts, but not everyone in the real world agrees.

Accountants commonly refer to such an asset as a *prepaid expense*, in this case, *Prepaid Rent*, or *Prepaid Rent Cost*, which, of course, connotes the fact that a future expense has been paid in advance. The fact that a single entry, often referred to as an *adjusting entry*, accomplishes both the reduction in the expense and the creation of the asset in the proper amount is another example of the neat "bridging function" that double-entry bookkeeping performs between the balance sheet and the income statement.

Look now at the case in which, at the beginning of her first year, Tutt purchases a building with a useful life of ten years, to use as her office. This is clearly a purchase of an asset, and the entry would be:

| Building | $60,000 | |
| Cash | | $60,000 |

Unless some entry is made at the end of the first year, however, the balance sheet drawn up then will show the asset Building at $60,000. That would be an overstatement of Tutt's assets, because the building would have a remaining useful life of only nine years. In addition, Tutt's net income for the first year would be overstated, since there would be no deduction for the expense of using the building, although one-tenth of the total life of the building has been used up during the year. What is called for, then, is the creation of an expense of $6,000, which we could call *Building Expense*, and a reduction of the asset Building to $54,000. Again, a single entry would do the job:

| Building Expense | $6,000 | |
| Building | | $6,000 |

As we will see on pages 75 to 76, *infra*, the accountant would not normally call the expense Building Expense nor credit the Building account. In any event, the adjusting entry properly puts an expense of $6,000 into the current year and reduces the asset figure to $54,000 to show what is really left for future years.

It might be noted, incidentally, that the advance payment for rent could have been handled in exactly the same way, rather than as we did it above.

Upon payment of the $15,000 on January 1 of the first year, the entire payment could have been recorded as a Deferred Rent asset:

Deferred Rent	$15,000	
Cash		$15,000

In that event, on December 31 an adjusting entry creating an expense of $5,000 and decreasing the asset by the same amount would have been necessary to show that one-third of the asset had been used up:

Rent Expense	$5,000	
Deferred Rent		$5,000

The product of these two entries is exactly the same as the one we obtained by first recording the entire advance payment as an expense and then deferring the portion not used up during the period.

As a third alternative, upon payment of the $15,000 on January 1 of the first year, the bookkeeper could have simply reflected the obvious split between rent expense for the first year and deferred rent as follows:

Rent Expense	$5,000	
Deferred Rent	10,000	
Cash		$15,000

The one entry produces exactly the same effect as the earlier illustrations where we: (1) first recorded the entire advance payment as an expense and then deferred the portion not used up during the period; or (2) first recorded the entire advance payment as an asset and then decreased the asset by the amount of the asset that had been used up. With the single entry, the bookkeeper would not need to record an adjusting entry at the end of the first year. In the two subsequent years, as in the earlier illustrations, however, the bookkeeper would need to make an adjusting entry to create an expense of $5,000 and decrease the asset by the same amount to show that the business had used up one-third of the asset in each of those years.

Whichever of these methods the bookkeeper uses depends entirely upon whether she initially records an expenditure as an asset, an expense, or a combination; the end result is the same. Therefore, if you find it easier, handle any advance payment that may not be used up in the current period just as you would an obvious asset like a building—that is, first record the payment as an asset, and then at the end of the period reduce the asset and create an expense to the extent that the asset was used up during the period. In practice, however, the initial entry for an expenditure often depends upon whether it looks more like an expense or an asset in the lay sense; hence, a payment of rent to a landlord will normally be debited to an expense account initially, even though it may cover far more than the current period. That is because the bookkeeper's functions are fairly mechanical and do not include, except in obvious cases, deciding how much of a particular expenditure the business will use up during the current period. That often difficult question, which will receive considerable attention in later chapters of this book, is then resolved by the accountant who supervises the closing of the books at the end of the period and makes whatever adjusting entries are necessary.

(2) Depreciation Accounting

We have already seen that a close relationship exists between deferred expenses and fixed assets, such as buildings, which may benefit several, or even many, accounting periods. For example, suppose E. Tutt purchases computer equipment for her law office for $2,000. Because this expenditure will benefit the business in future months and years, Tutt must not treat the entire amount as an expense in the month she buys the computer equipment. Rather, most of the expenditure reflects a future benefit or unexpired cost, which she should record as an asset. Computer equipment, however, like most tangible fixed assets other than land, will not last forever. Ultimately, Tutt will retire the computer equipment. At some point, the computer will physically wear out or become inefficient to operate. Alternatively, technological changes may cause Tutt to replace the machine. In any event, the $2,000 that she spent to acquire the computer equipment, less any *salvage value* that Tutt will receive in exchange for the equipment when she decides to retire it, constitutes an expense of producing revenues during the time she uses the computer equipment, a period accountants usually refer to as the computer's useful life. If we assume that Tutt will sell the computer for $200 in three years, she should allocate $1,800, the difference between the $2,000 cost and the $200 salvage value, to expense in some reasonable and systematic manner during the computer's useful life. Accountants refer to this allocation process as *depreciation* for fixed assets and as *amortization* for intangible assets. We should note that the term depreciation in this context does not refer to any diminution in the asset's value. Although almost all equipment declines in value as time passes, depreciation does not attempt to measure that decrease.

Assuming Tutt decides to use the straight-line method to allocate the $1,800 equally among the three years that she plans to use the computer equipment in her law office, she should treat $600 per year, or $50 per month, as depreciation expense for the computer equipment. We could express this computation as the following formula:

$$\text{Monthly Depreciation Expense} = \frac{(\text{Cost} - \text{Salvage Value})}{\text{Useful life in months}}$$

At the end of the first month, therefore, Tutt might record the following entry:

Depreciation Expense	$50	
Computer Equipment		$50

If Tutt bought the computer in the middle of the month, she might only treat $25, or one-half the normal monthly amount, as depreciation expense.

Using a general term like *Depreciation Expense* enables Tutt to lump together, under one heading, all of the expenses of using up fixed assets during an accounting period. Although Tutt does not own many fixed assets, a large company might own thousands or even millions of individual fixed assets.

As another practical matter, an accountant would normally not credit the Computer Equipment account. Instead, he would credit a separate *contra-asset* account called *Accumulated Depreciation*, which would appear as an offset to, or reduction from, the Computer Equipment account on the balance sheet. As the name suggests, a contra-asset account records reductions in a particular asset account separately from the relevant asset account. Basically, the Accumulated Depreciation account at any time simply represents the cumulative amount of the fixed asset's cost that the accounting entity has charged to expense. Accountants use this account so that they can preserve the fixed asset's original cost in the accounting records and show that amount on the balance sheet. Hence, we could restate the previous journal entry as:

Depreciation Expense	$50	
Accumulated Depreciation: Computer		
Equipment		$50

At the end of the first month, the computer equipment would appear as a fixed asset on Tutt's balance sheet, perhaps as follows:

Fixed Assets:	
Computer Equipment	$2,000
Less: Accumulated Depreciation	50
Net Computer Equipment	$1,950

Accountants often refer to the net amount–original cost less accumulated depreciation–as the asset's *book value*. The book value, therefore, represents the amount of the original cost remaining to be allocated to future periods, plus any estimated salvage value. If Tutt purchases additional equipment for her office, such as a copy machine or a fax machine, her bookkeeper will likely lump together all such office equipment so that only a single figure showing the total cost of all office equipment would appear on Tutt's balance sheet together with an offsetting figure for the total accumulated depreciation on that equipment.

b. REVENUES

A relation similar to that between expenses and assets exists between income items and liabilities, both of which are decreased by a debit and increased by a credit. Consider the bookkeeping for Ohner, the lessor of the building in which E. Tutt rents office space for three years by paying $15,000 in advance. When Ohner receives the $15,000, he might make the following entry in his books:

Cash	$15,000	
Rent Income		$15,000

Without some further entry, this $15,000 item will be closed into the Profit and Loss account along with the other income and expense items at the end of the year. We should remember, however, that the income accounts, like the expense accounts, are supposed to collect items affecting proprietorship *in the current period*. The entire $15,000 of rent income does not belong to the first year; $10,000 of that amount was received for the second and third years. Thus, if the whole $15,000 is closed to the Profit and Loss account for the first year, rent income for that year will be overstated, which will result in an overstatement of net income for the year. And net income for each of the next two years would be understated, because there would be no rent income for those years, although there would still be such expenses as insurance, janitor service, property taxes, and the like.

At the same time, there would be an item missing from Ohner's balance sheet for the end of the first year. If for some reason Ohner defaulted in his agreement to furnish Tutt with office space for the next two years, presumably Ohner would at least be required to refund to Tutt the $10,000 paid for those two years. To put it another way, as of the end of the first year, Ohner has an obligation to provide office space to Tutt for the next two years, and the most convenient measure of this obligation is the $10,000 Tutt paid for those two years. This obligation should appear on Ohner's balance sheet as a liability at the end of the first year.

What is needed, then, is a reduction of rent income to the amount actually applicable to the current period, here $5,000, and the creation of a liability in the amount of $10,000 to show Ohner's future obligation. To reduce rent income to $5,000, a debit of $10,000 should be made to that account. To create the liability account, which is typically called *Unearned Rent*, or perhaps, *Deferred Income*, or even, *Deferred Rent Income*, because it results from deferring income from the current period, a credit of $10,000 should be made to that account. Again, a purist would not use the word "Income" in a balance sheet account, but you may encounter such account titles in your practices. We might prepare a journal entry as follows:

Rent Income	$10,000	
Unearned Rent		$10,000

Once again a single adjusting entry has accomplished both objectives—and we see here another example of the bridging function of double-entry bookkeeping.

Just as it is permissible to record an advance payment which may not be used up during the current period initially as an asset rather than as an expense, so an advance receipt can properly be recorded first by a credit to the appropriate liability account rather than as income. Such an entry for Ohner would be:

Cash	$15,000	
Unearned Rent		$15,000

In that event, at the close of the period it would be necessary to make an adjusting entry crediting the Rent Income account in the amount of $5,000 and decreasing the liability by the same amount. Again, a single entry will do the job:

Unearned Rent	$5,000	
Rent Income		$5,000

This entry properly puts income of $5,000 into the current year, and reduces the liability to $10,000 to show a more meaningful measure of Ohner's obligation for future years. The result of these two entries is exactly the same as the one we obtained by first recording the entire advance receipt as income and then deferring the amount not applicable to the current period.

As a third alternative, the bookkeeper for Ohner could have split the $15,000 advance payment between rent income and unearned rent as follows:

Cash	$15,000	
Rental Income		$5,000
Unearned Rent		10,000

Again, the one entry produces exactly the same effect as the earlier illustrations where we: (1) first recorded the entire advance payment as income and then deferred the portion not earned during the period or (2) first recorded the entire advance payment as a liability and then decreased the liability by the amount earned during the period. With the single entry, the Ohner's bookkeeper would not need an adjusting entry at the end of the first year. In the two subsequent years, as in the earlier illustration, however, the bookkeeper would need to make an adjusting entry to create income of $5,000 and decrease the liability by the same amount to show that Ohner had earned one-third of the total $15,000 in each of those years.

Determination of the period or periods in which to reflect, or as the accountants say, *recognize*, the income represented by a payment received in advance is not always as easy as in the foregoing illustration. Actually, the advance rent example, in which the total income involved is allocated pro rata among the periods affected, is somewhat atypical; in many situations, all of the income from a single transaction is recognized in just one period, and not allocated among several periods. That treatment flows from the general rule governing revenue recognition which has been mentioned before and will be developed in more detail later in Chapter VI on pages 359 to 465, *infra*. Under that rule, accountants recognize income only in the period in which it is earned. Based in part on conservatism, accountants do not consider any of the income from a particular transaction earned until the recipient has "substantially performed" everything required under the contract. As you might expect, some close questions arise as to what constitutes "substantial performance" or a single transaction, whether in the practice of law, the sale of goods, or whatever the activity. We will also examine these issues in Chapter VI, specifically on pages 440 to 465, *infra*.

Returning to our example involving Ohner's receipt of an advance payment of rent for three years, it might seem that Ohner would not have completed his agreed-upon performance until the end of the third year, and therefore would not have earned any of the income involved in the transaction until that time. However, transactions in which the performance by the recipient of income consists primarily of permitting another to enjoy the use of property or money for a period of time, as in the case of rent or interest, are usually treated differently from the standard types of business activity like the practice of law or the sale of goods. These transactions involving leasing property or lending money at interest, which produce income by virtue of the passage of time, are viewed as though they consist of a series of separable agreements covering the consecutive accounting periods over which the entire transaction runs, and the income proportionate to the passage of time during each accounting period is regarded as having been earned in that period. Hence, one-third of the income from Ohner's advance receipt of three years' rent would be treated as earned at the end of the first of the three years. Similarly, for anyone interested in monthly periods, one-twelfth of the one-third earned in the first year would be regarded as earned during each of the twelve months of that first year. Accountants find some justification for this difference in treatment in the fact that even under the most conservative view of things the lender of money or the lessor of property will almost invariably perform their agreement in full.

3.   Accrual of Expense and Income

Thus far we have been considering the proper treatment of expense and income items when cash has been paid or received. We have seen that cash payments or receipts do not necessarily determine the amount of expense or income for the current period. As a matter of fact, the time when cash changes hands in a business transaction is often governed by factors which have little to do with the question of when the expense or income represented by the cash should be reflected. That holds true whether the cash moves beforehand, as in the deferral cases we have been considering, or moves afterward, as in accrual. The absence of cash payment or receipt does not negate current expense or income.

a. IN GENERAL

Accrual refers to the process whereby an accountant records an expense or revenue during the current accounting period even though no payment occurred during the current period. In accrual, the accountant "pulls" the future event involving cash or cash's worth into the current period. In our original example, you will recall that the accountant would accrue in June both: (1) the expense from the janitorial services, even though no cash changed hands during the month, and (2) the income from the billed, yet unpaid, legal services.

(1) Expenses

Let us look in more detail at a situation where no cash has moved. Suppose Tutt signed a three-year lease of office space calling for rent of $5,000 per year, payable at the end of each year. Obviously, if Tutt paid the $5,000 due for rent at the end of the first year, an entry debiting Rent Expense in the amount of $5,000 and crediting Cash in the same amount would be routine. But suppose instead that due to inadvertence, or otherwise, Tutt failed to pay the rent due at the end of the first year. If the movement of cash were controlling, then there would not be any entry reflecting rent expense during the first year; hence, when Tutt closes her books at the end of that first year, net income for the year would be overstated because there would be no deduction for the expense of using the office during the year. Moreover, when Tutt pays the $5,000 for the first year's rent shortly into the second year, presumably it would be debited to the current Rent Expense account at that time; but if Tutt also pays the rent for the second year by the end of that year, as she is supposed to, that too would be charged to current rent expense, with the result that the income statement for the second year would be burdened with $10,000 of rent expense, and net income for the year would be seriously understated.

What is needed, then, is the creation of an expense in the first year in the amount properly allocable to that year. That is, the first year should bear its fair share of the total cost of utilizing office space, even though none of that cost was actually paid during the first year. A bookkeeping entry can be used to accomplish this purpose. The debit part is simple enough, for that is dictated by the judgment that rent expense in the amount of $5,000 belongs in the current (first) year. There is only one way to reflect an expense in a particular year, and that is to debit the appropriate expense account in that year, so that it will be closed to the Profit and Loss account at the end of the year and netted with all of the other expense and income items for the period.

| Rent Expense | $5,000 | |
| ? | | $5,000 |

As to the credit, of course if cash had been paid that would be easy. But since Tutt has not paid, as she was supposed to, is it not clear that she owes the $5,000 at the close of the year, just as clearly as if she had bought more office equipment for $5,000 on account? The credit, therefore, should be to a liability account to reflect her obligation to pay. This process of pulling an expense into the current period even though it has not yet been paid, while creating a liability account reflecting the obligation to pay, constitutes accrual. Taken together with deferral, accrual makes it possible to free the reporting of expense items from the movement of cash. When cash has moved in an amount greater than the expense that belongs in the current period, deferral makes it possible to charge only the proper amount to expense for the current period. When an expense belongs in the current period even though the cash has not moved as yet, accrual makes it possible to reflect the expense in the current period.

Incidentally, with regard to the name given the liability account which is created when an expense is accrued, it would probably not be called an Account Payable, because that term is usually reserved for credit purchases of goods and supplies; moreover, it is often helpful to identify other liabilities as to their source. Hence, the liability would more likely be called *Accrued*

Rent Payable, which serves as a reminder that the liability results from the accrual of an expense into the current period. Other common terms for such a liability include *Expense Payable* or *Accrued Expense Payable*, or in this example *Rent Expense Payable*, *Accrued Rent Expense Payable*, *Rent Payable* or *Accrued Rent Payable*. These terms connote that the liability arises from an accrual. So the entry here might be:

Rent Expense	$5,000	
Accrued Rent Payable		$5,000

This entry puts $5,000 of rent expense into the current year, and creates a liability account to show that Tutt owes this amount for rent at the end of the first year.

Now suppose that Tutt's lease of office space for three years had not called for payments at the end of either of the first two years, but instead provided that the total of $15,000 should all be paid at the end of the third year. Once again, unless some entry is made when Tutt closes her books at the end of the first year, net income for the first year will be overstated since there will be no deduction for the expense of using an office during the year. Moreover, presumably the entire $15,000 payment in the third year would have to be treated as an expense of that year, with the result that net income for the third year would be greatly understated. Here, too, we need to accrue in the first year the amount of rent expense properly applicable to that year, even though no amount has been paid during that year. Because one-third of the total rent of $15,000 is properly applicable to the first year, an entry exactly the same as before is called for, with a debit of $5,000 to Rent Expense, and a credit of $5,000 to Accrued Rent Payable or Rent Payable.

To be sure, because Tutt has agreed to pay only at the end of the third year, strictly speaking, she is under no legal obligation to pay anything at the end of the first year. Nevertheless, in an accounting sense, Tutt does owe $5,000 at the end of the first year, since she must pay it ultimately, and, what is more significant, $5,000 of the total commitment has been used up in the current period. Hence, it is entirely appropriate to credit either Accrued Rent Payable, Rent Payable, Accrued Rent Expense Payable, Rent Expense Payable, Accrued Rent Expense or some similarly titled liability account. Tutt, however, may want to segregate liabilities of this sort, which do not have to be paid for quite some time, from current liabilities which she must pay within one year on the balance sheet. The important point is that an expense which belongs in the period may be accrued, that is, reflected in a current expense account, even though it not only has not been paid but there is not yet even a current obligation to pay it.

Notice that in this case when the rent expense is accrued for the first year, the Accrued Rent Payable, Rent Payable, Accrued Rent Expense Payable, Rent Expense Payable, Accrued Rent Expense or similar liability account reflects only an amount equal to the expense related to that year, not the entire rent obligation for the three-year period. That is because the very purpose of an accrual is to reflect an expense currently, with the creation of the liability being simply a corollary, to provide a companion credit to go along with the debit to an expense account, and obviously that credit must be in the same amount as the debit. Indeed, unlike the case of an advance payment, when of course some entry must be made to reflect the reduction in cash even though not all of the payment is chargeable to current expense, which is where deferral comes in, in the case of an expected future payment, usually no entry at all need be made in the current period unless, and then only to the extent that, a charge to current expense is called for. So if Tutt signed a three-year lease for office space during the year before the beginning of the lease, no entry at all relating to the lease commitment would be called for in that year. If material, however, it would be desirable to disclose the existence of the lease commitment scheduled to start the following year in the financial statements for the current year. In fact, an accounting entity must disclose the future minimum rental payments required under leases as of the latest balance sheet date presented for each of the five succeeding years. As we shall see, the use of footnotes or other adjuncts to the financial statements may provide suitable mechanisms for such disclosure.

When the rent for the three years is ultimately paid, the debit will be to Accrued Rent Payable, Rent Payable, Accrued Rent Expense Payable, Rent Expense Payable, Accrued Rent Expense or the similar liability account, just as any debtor who pays money owed on open account debits the account payable:

Accrued Rent Payable	$15,000	
Cash		$15,000

The important fact is that no account on the income statement is affected by the actual payment, which is as it should be since the expense has already been reflected at an earlier time.

At this point, we should also observe that there may be some occasions when the full amount of the obligation should be recorded on the balance sheet, rather than only disclosed, say, in a footnote, even though some, or even all, of the obligation is not yet properly chargeable to current expense. This situation can arise when some, or even all, of the benefit remains to be enjoyed in future periods. These occasions might include scenarios where an obligation to make future payments is relatively very large or the obligation is all currently due as a matter of contract. In those events, the entire amount of the obligation would have to be credited to the liability account, which might then need a different name. As to the accompanying debit in such a case, the only sensible one, except for any amount charged to current expense, would be a debit to a prepaid or deferred asset account. Recording the liability functions as a kind of substitute for the payment of cash which is the usual basis for creating a deferred asset.

(2) Revenues

Similar accrual techniques are available where income should be recognized in a period prior to the receipt of cash. Look at the bookkeeping for Ohner when he leases an office to Tutt for three years, for a total rent of

$15,000. Ohner's recognition of income from this transaction should not depend upon when he receives the cash; the amount of income reflected in the first year, or any subsequent year for that matter, should be the same, whether Ohner (1) received cash during the year or (2) was entitled to receive cash but Tutt inadvertently failed to pay, or (3) was not entitled to receive any cash until the end of the three years. As to the amount of income to be reflected in the first year, recall that under the rules for recognizing income noted earlier, the income represented by rent and interest is regarded as earned uniformly with the passage of time. Accordingly, at the end of the first year Ohner has earned $5,000 of the rent, and therefore he should recognize $5,000 in current income, even though no cash has been received, or is even due as yet.

Once a judgment has been made that $5,000 of rent income belongs in the first year, it follows that a credit in that amount must be made to the Rent Income account for that year. As with the counterpart reflection of an expense, the only way that any income item can ever be put into a particular year is to credit a current income account during that year. This is another example of accrual; the rent income is accrued, i. e., pulled into the current period, although the cash has not yet been received. As to the accompanying debit, which would of course have been to cash if the $5,000 had been received, a receivable should be created, to reflect the fact that although the cash has not been received Ohner has a right to receive it in the future. This receivable might be called *Accrued Rent Receivable* or *Rent Receivable*, or perhaps even *Accrued Rent Income Receivable*, *Accrued Rent Income*, or *Rent Income Receivable*, terms which connote the fact that the receivable reflects the right to receive an amount which has been recognized as income prior to the receipt of cash. So the entry might be:

Accrued Rent Receivable	$5,000	
Rent Income		$5,000

Notice that if the lease provided that none of the rent was due until the end of the third year, then technically Ohner would not have any legal right to $5,000 at the end of the first year. Nevertheless, in the same sense that Tutt owed $5,000 at the end of the first year even though she was not obligated to pay anything until the end of the third year, so Ohner would have a right to $5,000 at the end of the first year since he is entitled to receive it ultimately, and it has been earned during the first year. Therefore, it is entirely appropriate to debit an account like Accrued Rent Receivable, Rent Receivable, Accrued Rent Income Receivable, Accrued Rent Income, or Rent Income Receivable. On a balance sheet, Ohner may again want to segregate long-term receivables like this, on which the cash will not be received for more than one year, from receivables which qualify as current assets because they will be converted into cash within one year. Note that, paralleling the accrual of expenses, the primary purpose of accrual of income is to reflect an item in current income even though cash has not yet been received, and the creation of a receivable account is merely an adjunct needed to show that there is a right to receive the cash in the future. Hence, as with the counterpart payables discussed earlier, these receivables will normally show only that portion of a future receipt which has been earned, rather than the full amount of the expected future payment.

When Ohner ultimately receives the money for the entire three-year period, the credit will be to the Accrued Rent Receivable or a similar account, just as a creditor who receives money owed to him on open account credits the account receivable:

Cash	$15,000	
Accrued Rent Receivable		$15,000

The important fact is that no account on the income statement is affected by the actual receipt, which is as it should be since the income has already been recognized.

As we noted in connection with advance receipts, transactions involving the rental of property, as here, or lending money at interest, are atypical so far as recognition of income is concerned, because in such cases the income is viewed as earned by the passage of time. For standard types of income-producing activity, like the practice of law or the sale of goods, the general rule applies, to the effect that all of the income from a transaction is to be recognized in the period in which substantial completion occurs. Sometimes, recognition of income from performance of services is delayed until a bill has been sent, to avoid the need for estimation, and perhaps also provide greater assurance that performance has indeed been completed. The important point is that it does not matter whether the cash has been received as yet, so long as the income has been earned. Accrual provides the mechanism for recognizing the income in the period in which it is earned, even though no cash has been received.

Notice that, unlike the case of an advance receipt where some entry must be made to reflect the receipt of cash even though the related income has not been earned in the current period, in the case of an expected future receipt no entry is called for in the current period if the income has not yet been earned. An entry will be made only in the period when the income is finally earned, unless, of course, the cash moves sooner, in which event the case becomes simply one of an advance receipt.

One special aspect of the treatment of an expected receipt deserves brief mention here. It arises because accounting, mirroring business in this regard, still attributes considerable importance to the ultimate receipt of cash, even though it does not make such receipt a pre-condition for the recognition of income. Obviously, however, no question about the ultimate receipt of cash can arise in cases involving advance receipts, because the cash has already been received. In the case of an expected future receipt, if there is substantial doubt as to the ultimate collectibility of cash, because of the insolvency of the debtor or otherwise, no income is recognized from the transaction even though it has been earned in the current period. It should be emphasized that this qualification applies only when there is some special reason for concern about collectibility, not just the general risk of non-payment that is inherent in any business done on credit. For the latter, other tools exist, which will be introduced when this subject is discussed in more detail in Chapter VI on pages 458 to 465, *infra*.

PROBLEMS

The following problems present situations involving both deferrals and accruals. Drawing a time line of the underlying economic events and cash transactions and dividing the time line into the relevant accounting periods often helps when analyzing situations where cash moves in an accounting period before or after from the underlying economic event.

Problem 1.6A. Andrew Company borrowed $50,000 from Bradford, Inc. at twelve percent annual interest on January 1. Twelve percent annual interest on a $50,000 loan translates to $6,000 in interest per year, or $500 in interest each month. The promissory note requires Andrew Company to pay the $500 monthly interest on, or before, the last day of each month. Andrew Company made three interest payments, $600 on January 15, $250 on February 20, and $350 on March 10.

(1) Prepare appropriate journal entries for Andrew Company for the months of January, February and March, assuming each month is a separate accounting period.

(2) Prepare appropriate journal entries for Bradford, Inc. for the months of January, February and March, assuming each month is a separate accounting period.

Problem 1.6B. Jones Company leased a machine from Smith, Inc. on January 1. Under the terms of the lease, Jones Company agreed to pay $250 rent per month, due on the first day of each month. Jones Company made two rental payments, one of $300 on January 1 and the other of $350 on February 14.

(1) Prepare appropriate journal entries for Jones Company for the months of January, February, and March, assuming each month is a separate accounting period.

(2) Prepare appropriate journal entries for Smith, Inc. for the months of January, February, and March, assuming each month is a separate accounting period.

Problem 1.6C. Dallas Inc. borrowed $30,000 from Crayne Corporation at eight percent annual interest on January 1. Eight percent annual interest on a $30,000 loan translates to $2,400 in interest per year, or $200 in interest each month. The promissory note requires Dallas Inc. to pay the $200 monthly interest on, or before, the last day of each month. Dallas Inc. made three interest payments, $100 on January 15, $250 on February 25, and $150 on March 5.

(1) Prepare appropriate journal entries for Dallas Inc. for the months of January, February and March, assuming each month is a separate accounting period.

(2) Prepare the appropriate journal entries for Crayne Corporation for the months of January, February and March, assuming each month is a separate accounting period.

b. INCOME TAX ACCOUNTING

Income taxes present a special application of accrual accounting for corporations that do not file a subchapter S election under the Internal Revenue Code. Such an election treats income as taxable to the corporation's shareholders rather than to the corporation. Sole proprietorships, partnerships and most subchapter S corporations do not pay federal income taxes. Instead, the owners must report their allocable share of the business's income on their federal income tax returns and pay taxes on that income. As separate legal and taxable entities, corporations generally must file federal income tax returns, compute taxable income according to the Internal Revenue Code and related Treasury Regulations, and pay taxes on their taxable income. State and local laws may also require corporations and other businesses to pay income taxes. In most cases, a business will not pay all of its income taxes attributable to income from a particular accounting period during that period. As a result, corporations, in particular, frequently must accrue income tax expense during the closing process.

If we assume that Tutt, Inc. earned $525 in taxable income during the month and that the corporation will pay taxes at a forty percent total rate for all federal, state and local income taxes, the corporation will owe $210 in income taxes on the month's income. To properly match expenses against revenues, Tutt, Inc. should accrue $210 as income tax expense for the month as an adjusting journal entry. To reflect this income tax expense, at the end of the month, the bookkeeper could record the following entry:

Income Tax Expense	$210	
Accrued Income Taxes Payable		$210

Accountants usually show *Income Tax Expense* as a separate caption on the income statement immediately above net income. Accordingly, assuming the facts from the income statement on page 34, *supra*, we could restate this portion of Tutt, Inc.'s income statement for the month of June as follows:

Operating Income Before Income Taxes	$ 525
Income Taxes	210
Net Income	$ 315

On the company's balance sheet, Accrued Income Taxes Payable would normally appear as a current liability because an income tax obligation will usually require a cash payment within one year.

4. PRACTICE PROBLEM

The following problem is designed to afford some additional practice in bookkeeping. Set out after the list of transactions are the appropriate journal entries, with explanatory comments, the completed T-accounts, and the final balance sheet and income statement. However, you would do best to work out the problem on your own, before looking at the recommended solution and the comments.

Assume that E. Tutt's balance sheet on June 30 was as follows:

E. Tutt, Esquire
Balance Sheet, June 30

Assets		Liabilities & Proprietorship	
Cash	$1,150	Liabilities:	
Accounts Receivable:		Accounts Payable:	
Southacre Corp.	300	Robertson Law	
Georgina Hats, Inc.	100	Book Co.	$ 40
Jack Self Clothes	125		
Office Equipment	575		
Library	650	Proprietorship	2,860
Total	$2,900	Total	$2,900

Although you should ignore depreciation, the following transactions occurred during the month of July:

July 1 Purchased a piece of land for a contemplated new office building for $1,800. She paid $600 down, and gave a one-year 5% note for the balance, interest payable at maturity.

2 Paid $75 cash to landlord for rent for July.

3 Paid $100 cash to Douds for painting interior of office.

5 Bought adding machine for $200 from P.M. Ryan on account.

9 Received $150 cash for legal services rendered on July 7 and 8 to Jones.

11 Mailed bill for $225 to Potter for legal services rendered in July.

13 Paid Ryan $100 cash on account.

15 Received check from Southacre Corp. for $200 on account.

16 Paid temporary secretarial replacement $180 cash for salary for first three weeks in July.

18 Jack Self settled account with $25 cash and a suit of clothes for Ms. Tutt.

20 Paid Robertson Law Book Company $40 cash.

21   Uncle Zeke Tutt's executor delivered law books worth $100 which had been bequeathed to E. Tutt.

25   Paid $15 filing fee to Clerk of County for client Coogan in Coogan v. Sargeant. The engagement letter requires Coogan to reimburse Tutt for any fees advanced.

26   Tutt carelessly dropped a cigarette, starting a fire that destroyed books costing $120, for which she had no insurance.

28   Received $200 advance retainer from Annan.

29   Received telephone bill of $25 for July.

30   Probate court allowed $1,000 fee for services to executor of Estate of Smith.

31   Paid temporary secretary $180 salary for last week in July and first two weeks in August.

RECOMMENDED SOLUTION

July
1   Land $1,800
    Cash $600
    Note Payable   1,200

Comment: This entry records Tutt's purchase of land, partly for cash, and partly on credit by giving a note. The Note Payable account is basically the same kind of account as an Account Payable, except that the term "Note Payable" or, in the case of bonds, "Bonds Payable" is used when a written instrument is given. A separate account is particularly desirable when the written instruments are negotiable. Notice that nothing is done at this time to record the obligation for interest, since no interest is yet due, but an adjusting entry for interest will be necessary at the end of the month.

2   Rent Expense $75
    Cash $75

Comment: Tutt debits Rent Expense because she wants a separate record of her rent payments. If she had no interest in identification of rent payments, the debit might be simply to Miscellaneous Expense. Because this payment is all for July, it is all an expense for July, and no asset will appear on the balance sheet on July 31.

3   Miscellaneous Expense $100
    Cash $100

Comment: Tutt might have used a separate account for Maintenance Expense, in which case the debit would have been to that account. Note also that there is a deferral problem: Because the paint job will doubtless have utility beyond the month of July, should all this expense be considered a cost of doing business in the month of July? Factors affecting the accounting judgment of whether some of the $100 should be allocated to later periods will be considered in Chapter IX on pages 630 to 634, *infra*; here, for simplicity, Tutt treats this item as an expense of the current period.

| 5 | Office Equipment | $200 | |
| | Accounts Payable: P.M. Ryan | | $200 |

Comment: If Tutt distinguished among the various kinds of office equipment that she owned, such as computers, copiers, and printers, the debit would then be to the appropriate one of these accounts, which would be in effect subaccounts of Office Equipment. Note that, in fact, Tutt has moved in the opposite direction, and now includes both Furniture and Equipment in the Office Equipment account.

| 9 | Cash | $150 | |
| | Professional Income | | $150 |

Comment: Because Tutt has performed all the services called for by the agreement, the income arising from this receipt has been earned and is therefore income for the current period.

| 11 | Accounts Receivable: Potter | $225 | |
| | Professional Income | | $225 |

Comment: Although no cash has yet been received, Tutt has earned the income in July. Therefore, unless Potter is insolvent or for some other reason collection is not reasonably assured, the income should be recognized in the current period. The debit might just as appropriately be to Fees Receivable: Potter; there is no uniform practice where income from personal services is involved.

If Tutt had not yet sent a bill, she might postpone the recognition of this income; the recognition of income from services is often postponed until the sending of a bill, even though the services have been completed and collection of the income is reasonably assured, because of uncertainty as to the amount to be charged.

| 13 | Accounts Payable: P.M. Ryan | $100 | |
| | Cash | | $100 |

Comment: This is exactly like payment of the amount due Elmer Co., described earlier in this chapter on pages 17 to 26, *supra*; note that the transaction affects both sides of the balance sheet, resulting in a decrease on both sides of $100.

| 15 | Cash | $200 | |
| | Accounts Receivable: Southacre Corp. | | $200 |

Comment: Note that the income account is not affected. An entry like that of July 11 had already been made in a prior period, and Tutt is now simply converting into cash the asset she then recorded.

| 16 | Secretarial Expense | $180 | |
| | Cash | | $180 |

Comment: Because this payment will be completely used up in July, it is recorded immediately as an expense for the current period, and no deferral problem will arise.

18	Cash	$25	
	Proprietorship	100	
	Accounts Receivable: Jack Self Clothes		$125

Comment: The troublesome element, the debit of $100 to Proprietorship, is exactly the same in theory as the entry upon Tutt's removal of a chair from the office for use at home.

| 20 | Accounts Payable: Robertson Law Book Co. | $40 | |
| | Cash | | $40 |

Comment: This is exactly like payment of the amount due Ryan on July 13. Once again, the transaction affects both sides of the balance sheet, resulting in a decrease on both sides of $40.

| 21 | Library | $100 | |
| | Proprietorship | | $100 |

Comment: Here, in effect, Tutt has contributed $100 more assets to the business, and there is an increase in Proprietorship.

| 25 | Accounts Receivable: Coogan | $15 | |
| | Cash | | $15 |

Comment: The $15 is chargeable to Coogan and is not an expense of Tutt's.

| 26 | Fire Loss | $120 | |
| | Library | | $120 |

Comment: Tutt lost one of her assets other than cash. Nevertheless, this loss, like the theft loss described earlier in the text, is one of the costs of doing business, and is therefore treated like an expense. Fire Loss may be regarded as simply shorthand for Fire Loss Expense. The credit to Library reduces that account by the amount of the books lost.

| 28 | Cash | $200 | |
| | Client Advances | | $200 |

Comment: Because Tutt has not yet performed the services for which this fee was received, the income arising from this advance receipt has not been earned. The income, therefore, should not be recognized in the current period, and the credit is to Client Advances, or Deferred Income. If, by the end of the current period, Tutt were to complete performance of all the services called for by the agreement, the income would be recognized currently, by a debit to Client Advances and a credit to Professional Income; because she did not,

Client Advances will appear as a liability account on the balance sheet at the end of July.

| 29 | Telephone Expense | $25 | |
| | Accrued Telephone Costs Payable | | $25 |

Comment: This is an example of accrual of expense. Because this expense is clearly applicable to the current period, it should be reflected in this period. Even if no bill had been received, Tutt would still reflect this expense in the current period. Recognition of an expense applicable to the current period is usually not postponed until the receipt of a bill, even though there is uncertainty as to the amount of the charge; instead, a reasonable estimate of the charge is made. This differs somewhat from the treatment often adopted in connection with accrual of income. See the Comment to the entry on July 11.

| 30 | Accounts Receivable: Estate of Smith | $1,000 | |
| | Professional Income | | $1,000 |

Comment: The accrual problem here is exactly like that in the transaction of July 11.

| 31 | Prepaid Salary | $180 | |
| | Cash | | $180 |

Comment: Here, the payment will not be completely used up by the end of the period. If, as here, Tutt initially records the payment as an asset, she must make an adjusting entry at the end of the period, to create an expense and to reduce the asset in the amount used up during the period. The adjusting entry:

| (a) | Salary Expense | $60 | |
| | Prepaid Salary | | $60 |

Alternatively, it would be equally proper to record the payment as an expense, first. In that event, the initial entry would be:

| 31 | Salary Expense | $180 | |
| | Cash | | $180 |

Upon closing her books at the end of the period, Tutt's adjusting entry would defer the amount not used up during the period as follows:

| (a) | Prepaid Salary | $120 | |
| | Salary Expense | | $120 |

As a final alternative, Tutt could split the original entry between expense and unexpired asset. The split entry eliminates the need for an adjusting entry at the end of July.

31	Salary Expense	$60	
	Prepaid Salary	120	
	Cash		$180

As the net effect of each alternative, Tutt treats $60 as salary expense for July and defers $120 to August. In each alternative, Tutt will also have to make an adjusting entry in August to record the salary expense for that month.

One other adjusting entry is necessary:

(b)   Interest Expense $5
           Accrued Interest Payable $5

Comment: Recall that no entry reflecting interest expense was made at the time of the borrowing transaction on July 1, because the note had then just been given. The interest that Tutt will ultimately have to pay, however, should not all be treated as an expense in the month when she makes the payment. This is just like the situation in the text above, in which we saw that Tutt should not charge the entire payment for rent for three years to the third year simply because it was all paid during that year. Instead, Tutt should attribute a *pro rata* share of the total interest expense to each month during the time that she has the use of the money, just as she charged a *pro rata* share of the rent expense to each of the years in which she had the use of the office premises. Because the interest charge per year is five percent of $1,200, or $60, one-twelfth of $60, or $5, should be treated as an expense in each month. Hence, Tutt should debit an expense account, here Interest Expense, to reflect this expense in the current period; the credit is to a liability account, here Accrued Interest Payable, to reflect the eventual liability for this current expense. Tutt will make similar entries during the next eleven months. When Tutt ultimately pays the interest at maturity, she will record the following entry:

Accrued Interest Payable $60
    Cash $60

Please note that the need to repay the note's principal amount in one year does not give rise to an expense in the current month or in any future accounting period. Keep in mind that the payment of a liability for the recorded amount, like the collection of a receivable in full, does not affect owner's equity. As a result, no entry is called for to reflect the fact that the due date of the principal amount of the note is one month closer. Just as the borrowing of the funds did not affect Tutt's income statement, neither will the repayment. Therefore, no further entry need be made in connection with the ultimate liability to pay the principal until the note is actually discharged, at which time the entry will be simply:

Note Payable $1,200
    Cash $1,200

The T-accounts that follow reflect the journal entries we have been discussing:

Cash

Bal.	$1,150	$600	7-1
7-9	150	75	7-2
7-15	200	100	7-3
7-18	25	100	7-13
7-28	200	180	7-16
		40	7-20
		15	7-25
		180	7-31
Bal.	$435		

Accounts Receivable: Coogan

7-25	$15		
Bal.	$15		

Accounts Receivable: Estate of Smith

7-30	$1,000		
Bal.	$1,000		

Accounts Receivable: Georgina Hats, Inc.

Bal.	$100		
Bal.	$100		

Accounts Receivable: Jack Self Clothes

Bal.	$125	$125	7-18
Bal.	–0–		

Accounts Receivable: Potter

7-11	$225		
Bal.	$225		

Accounts Receivable: Southacre Corp.

Bal.	$300	$200	7-15
Bal.	$100		

Prepaid Salary

7-31	$180	$60	(a)
Bal.	$120		

Land

7-1	$1,800		
Bal.	$1,800		

Office Equipment

Bal.	$575		
7-5	200		
Bal.	$775		

Library

Bal.	$650	$120	7-26
7-21	100		
Bal.	$630		

Note Payable

		$1,200	7-1
		$1,200	Bal.

Accounts Payable: Robertson Law Book Co.

7-20	$40	$40	Bal.
Bal.	–0–		

Accounts Payable: P.M. Ryan

7-13	$100	$200	7-5
		$100	Bal.

Accrued Telephone Costs Payable

		$25	7-29
		$25	Bal.

Accrued Interest Payable

		$5	(b)
		$5	Bal.

Client Advances

		$200	7-28
		$200	Bal.

Proprietorship

7-18	$100	$2,860	Bal.
		100	7-21
		$2,860	Bal.
		810	(j)
		$3,670	Bal.

Professional Income

		$150	7-9
		$225	7-11
		$1,000	7-30
(i)	$1,375	$1,375	Bal.

Interest Expense

(b)	$5		
Bal.	$5	$5	(h)

Miscellaneous Expense			
7-3	$100		
Bal.	$100	$100	(d)

Fire Loss			
7-26	$120		
Bal.	$120	$120	(g)

Rent Expense			
7-2	$75		
Bal.	$75	$75	(c)

Secretarial Expense			
7-16	$180		
(a)	60		
Bal.	$240	$240	(e)

Profit and Loss			
(c)	$75	$1,375	(i)
(d)	100		
(e)	240		
(f)	25		
(g)	120		
(h)	5		
(j)	$810	$810	Bal.

Telephone Expense			
7-29	$25		
Bal.	$25	$25	(f)

Using the T-accounts, we can prepare the following income statement for the month of July and balance sheet as of July 31:

E. Tutt, Esquire
Income Statement
For the Month of July

Professional Income		$1,375
Expenses:		
Rent	$ 75	
Secretarial	240	
Telephone	25	
Miscellaneous	100	
Fire Loss	120	
Interest	5	565
Net Income		$ 810

E. Tutt, Esquire
Balance Sheet, July 31

Assets

Cash		$ 435
Accounts Receivable:		
Estate of Smith	$1,000	
Potter	225	
Southacre Corp.	100	
Georgina Hats, Inc.	100	
Coogan	15	1,440
Prepaid Salary		120
Land		1,800
Office Equipment		775
Library		630
Total Assets		$5,200

Liabilities & Proprietorship

Liabilities:		
Note Payable		$1,200
Accounts Payable: P.M. Ryan		100
Accrued Costs Payable		30
Client Advances		200
Total Liabilities		$1,530
Proprietorship		3,670
Total Liabilities and Proprietorship		$5,200

PROBLEMS

Problem 1.7A. Below is the balance sheet for E. Tutt on March 1, followed by Tutt's transactions during March. Prepare the journal entries and post them to the appropriate T-accounts; then make up the income statement for the month of March and the balance sheet as of March 31. Ignore depreciation and income taxes. Blank forms for these financial statements are set out after the list of transactions.

E. Tutt, Esquire
Balance Sheet, March 1

Assets		Liabilities & Proprietorship	
Cash	$ 345	Liabilities:	
Accounts Receivable:		Accounts Payable:	
Estate of Smith	500	Jones Co.	$ 220
Potter Corp.	225	Stanley	100
Supplies	110	Accrued Telephone	
Prepaid Salary	200	Costs Payable	40
Office Furniture &		Client Advances	300
Equipment	1,250	Total Liabilities	$ 660
Library	870	Proprietorship	2,840
Total	$3,500	Total	$3,500

Transactions in March:

March 1 Purchased a three-section Super Fireproof Safe for $480 from Jarald Co. on credit.

2 Paid the landlord $150 rent for her office for March.

5 Paid $120 for a one-year liability insurance policy ordered the week before and running through next February 28.

7 Paid $60 for a one-year subscription to the local weekly legal journal, to start on April 1.

9 Purchased a $100 treatise on bankruptcy from East Publishing Company on credit.

11 Received $350 from Homer Co. for legal advice given during the week.

13 A new client, Fashion Corp., sent her $250 as a retainer for an argument on a motion scheduled for April 10.

14 Completed the work for which Anderson paid her $300 in advance last month.

15 Borrowed $480 from First State Bank on a one-year note, with interest at ten percent, payable at maturity, and immediately paid her debt to Jarald Co.

16 Paid $50 to Manpower, Inc. for temporary typing assistance last week.

17 Received bill from landlord for additional rent of $15 due for March under the fuel-adjustment clause in her lease.

20 Sent $40 to the telephone company to pay her outstanding bill.

21 Gave tax advice to Olson and received $200 for it.

22 Prepared and filed incorporation papers for Nelson, Inc. and sent a bill for $250.

24 Received $300 of the $500 due from Estate of Smith.

26 Rented a section of her new safe to Bilder, a lawyer in the adjacent office, for ninety days, at a rental of $90 payable at the end of the term.

30 Paid her secretary $100 of the $200 owed for the second half of March.

31 Checked with telephone company and learned that her bill for March would be $45.

E. Tutt, Esquire
Income Statement
For the Month of March

Professional Income	$_____	
Rent Income	_____	$_____
Less Expenses:		
Rent	$_____	
Insurance	_____	
Secretarial	_____	
Telephone	_____	
Interest	_____	$_____
Net Income		$_____

E. Tutt, Esquire
Balance Sheet, March 31

<u>Assets</u>		<u>Liabilities & Proprietorship</u>	
		Liabilities:	
Cash	$_____	Note Payable	$_____
Accounts Receivable	_____	Accounts Payable	_____
Accrued Rent		Accrued Costs	
Receivable	_____	Payable	_____
Supplies	_____	Client Advances	_____
Prepaid Costs	_____	Total	$_____
Office Furniture &			
Equipment	_____		
Library	_____	Proprietorship	_____
Total	$_____	Total	$_____

Problem 1.7B. Tomlin Realty Company began business on January 1 and engaged in the transactions listed below during its first month.

(1) Unless your professor directs otherwise, prepare journal entries, including any adjusting entries, post them to T-accounts, complete the closing process, and prepare an income statement for January and a classified balance sheet as of January 31. Ignore income taxes and depreciation on all assets except for the building. The company uses straight-line depreciation for the building.

Jan.   1   Issued all 1,000 authorized shares of $1 par value common stock as follows:

200 shares to Michael Smith for $20,000.

300 shares to Gregory Myers for marketable securities worth $30,000.

500 shares to Steven Braggs for land worth $50,000.

1 Purchased land and building from William Marzano for $25,000, $5,000 down and the balance pursuant to a 9% simple interest per annum note secured by a mortgage. Interest on the unpaid balance of the note is payable annually on December 31. The note is due in ten annual installments of $2,000 each at the end of each calendar year, plus accrued interest. The land is valued at $5,000. The useful life of the building is 25 years and estimated salvage value is $5,000.

7 Purchased for $365 in cash a one-year liability insurance policy, effective through next January 6, for the building.

12 Mrs. Hayes, a sales agent, sold a parcel of real estate for a client and the company received a $6,000 commission, half of which it paid to Mrs. Hayes.

15 Paid Angie Roberts, a secretary, $500 salary for the first half of January.

17 Made a down payment of $250 for office equipment costing $750 which was ordered but not received.

19 Received a $1,000 dividend check on the marketable securities.

21 Mailed a check for $120 to South Bend News, Inc. for a six month subscription beginning February 1 to Realty News.

22 Sold marketable securities which were worth $10,000 at the time of their transfer to the company on January 1 for $10,500.

29 Paid Angie Roberts, the secretary, $300 of the $500 the company owed her as salary for the second half of January.

31 The previously ordered office equipment arrived.

31 Received a telephone bill for January for $30.

(2) Use the same facts as above, but assume that the corporation pays income taxes at a forty percent (40%) rate.

Problem 1.7C. Nemo Hand, a great grandchild of a prominent high-court judge, decided to pursue the field of optometry after receiving an F in his first-year torts class.

(1) Unless your professor directs otherwise, prepare journal entries, including any adjusting entries, post them to T-accounts, complete the closing process, and prepare an income statement for June and a classified balance sheet as of June 30 from the following information for Hand Optometry, Inc. Treat the costs of any glasses sold to customers as an expense captioned "Cost of Glasses Sold." Ignore depreciation on all assets except for the building. The company uses straight-line depreciation for the building.

June 1 Issued 500 of the 1000 authorized shares of $5.00 par value common stock as follows:

  (1) 150 shares to Benjamin Cardizi for $3,000
  (2) 250 shares to Brian White for marketable securities worth $5,000
  (3) 100 shares to Sandy Connors for farmland worth $2,000

1 Paid $730 for a one-year professional liability insurance policy effective through next May 31.

2 Purchased eyeglasses and contact lenses for inventory on account from Rice Optometry for $3,150.

4 Paid an assistant named Charlie his $300 salary for the first two weeks of June in advance because Charlie was strapped for cash.

7 Made a down payment of $500 to Tidmarsh Supply for optometry equipment costing $1,500, which was ordered but not received.

9 Received a $100 dividend check on the marketable securities.

12 Received a check for $450 from a customer, $250 of which was for optometry services rendered and the remainder was for a pair of glasses which Nemo purchased from Rice Optometry on June 2 for $100.

16 Purchased land and a building adjacent to the farmland for $31,000, $1,000 down and the balance pursuant to a 10% simple interest per annum note secured by a mortgage. Interest on the unpaid balance of the note is payable annually on December 31. The note is due in five annual installments of $6,000 each at the end of this year and each of the next four calendar years, plus accrued interest. The land is valued at $3,000. The useful life of the building is thirty years and its estimated salvage value is $10,000.

19 Sold the following investments in marketable securities:

  (1) Received $2,200 for marketable securities worth $2,000 at the time of their transfer to the company on June 1.

  (2) Received $2,250 for other marketable securities. Nemo expected this investment to decline drastically in value in the near future. These securities were worth $2,500 when transferred to the company on June 1.

22 Mailed a check for $360 to the Journal of Optometry for a one-year subscription beginning on August 1.

25 Tidmarsh Supply received the equipment that was ordered on June 7.

28 Received a telephone bill for June for $40.

29 Paid Charlie's $300 salary for the last two weeks of June.

30 Sent bills totaling $2,250 to various insurance companies for services provided during the month. These bills reflected optometric services of $1,400 and $850 for glasses and contact lenses which Nemo purchased from Rice Optometry on June 2 for $450.

(2) Use the same facts as above, but assume that the corporation pays income taxes at a forty percent (40%) rate.

G. ACCOUNTING FOR MERCHANDISE INVENTORY

Many businesses earn profits from the sale of goods rather than, like Tutt, from providing services. In such a business, inventory, or goods held for sale or resale in the ordinary course of business, comprises one of the business's basic assets. Inventory differs from the assets which Tutt owns because the goods in inventory are constantly turning over; sales take goods out of inventory, and purchases are made to replace them. As we will see in Chapter VIII on pages 593 to 597, *infra*, for an enterprise engaged in manufacturing, the process is a bit more complex: the manufactured, or, as they are often termed, "completed," goods are sold and replaced by purchases of raw materials which will be turned into completed goods through the manufacturing operations. This section is designed to introduce you to the special techniques used to deal with the problems that this constant turnover creates.

To take a simple example, suppose Marty Jones operates a retail store which sells inexpensive shoes. Further suppose that during the month of January he sells 1,000 pairs of shoes for $10 per pair. To calculate his net income, Jones must include in his expenses not only the ones that Tutt had, such as rent, utilities, and salaries, but also the cost of the shoes sold. In bookkeeping language, the business sold shoes for $10,000 from which Jones must deduct the cost of the goods sold, as well as his other operating expenses, to determine his net income. If the shoes cost Jones $7 per pair, and his other operating expenses for the month came to $1,000, his net income would be $2,000. A simplified version of his income statement might look something like this:

Jones Shoes
Income Statement
For the Month of January

Sales	$10,000
Cost of Goods Sold	7,000
Gross Profit	$ 3,000
Operating Expenses	1,000
Net Income	$ 2,000

The chief differences between this statement and Tutt's are: the different name given to the income account; the introduction of the Cost of Goods Sold account; and the new caption "Gross Profit." We will discuss these differences in sequence.

1.   SALES

Sales, or Sales Revenues, are simply another type of income (i. e., increase in proprietorship resulting from operations), and the Sales account reflects the total amount of sales completed during the period. Invariably, however, some customers will bring back goods for various reasons. Customers may return damaged, defective, unwanted or unneeded goods for credit or a cash refund. Accountants call these transactions *sales returns*. Sometimes, the customer may decide to keep the goods if the seller grants an allowance or deduction from the selling price. Accountants refer to these transactions as *sales allowances*, but usually combine sales returns and sales allowances into a single account, *Sales Returns and Allowances*. We can describe this account as a contra-revenue account to the Sales account. The Sales Returns and Allowances account normally contains a debit balance. Accountants use this contra-revenue account, rather than debiting the Sales account directly, to separately identify and disclose sales returns and allowances in both the accounts and in the income statement. Debiting the Sales account directly would hide the comparative size of the returns and allowances relative to sales. Large returns or allowances suggest inferior goods, sloppy sales techniques, or poor handling, shipping or delivery practices. Lawyers might want information about sales returns and allowances in product liability litigation or cases alleging fraudulent revenue recognition. The caption *Net Sales* simply shows the numerical difference between the Sales and Sales Returns and Allowances accounts.

To illustrate, suppose that Jones actually sold 1,020 pairs of shoes during January, but that customers returned twenty pairs for refunds and Jones restored those shoes to inventory. In bookkeeping language, Jones sold shoes for $10,200, from which he must subtract $200 in sales returns, leaving him with $10,000 in net sales. We could restate his income statement as follows:

Jones Shoes
Income Statement
For the Month of January

Sales	$10,200
Less: Sales Returns and Allowances	200
Net Sales	$10,000
Cost of Goods Sold	7,000
Gross Profit	$ 3,000
Operating Expenses	1,000
Net Income	$ 2,000

From net sales, he must deduct the cost of the goods sold, as well as his other operating expenses, to determine his net income.

2.   COST OF GOODS SOLD

There are various ways to determine the figure for the cost of goods sold during an accounting period. For example, Jones might keep a record of the cost of each pair of shoes as they are purchased for resale and then sold. Accountants usually refer to such a system as a *perpetual inventory system* because the accounting records continuously show the quantity and cost of the goods which the business holds as inventory at any time. As the business sells goods, the bookkeeper transfers their cost from the Inventory account to the Cost of Goods Sold account. At the end of the period, the balance in the Cost of Goods Sold account would give Jones the cost of all the shoes sold during the period. Ordinarily, however, it might be difficult, and it would certainly be time-consuming, to identify the cost of each pair of shoes.

As an alternative, Jones could merely keep a record of the cost of the shoes on hand at the beginning of the period and the cost of the shoes acquired during the period. Then at the end of the period Jones can *take inventory*, that is, count up the number of shoes he has left and determine their total cost. By subtracting the cost of what he has left from the sum of what he had at the beginning of the period and what he acquired during the period, he can compute the cost of what he sold. Accountants call this system the *periodic inventory method* because the accounting entity determines inventory only at the end of an accounting period.

Suppose, for example, that Jones had an inventory at the beginning of January of 300 pairs of shoes which cost $7 per pair, and that during the month he purchased another 1,200 pairs of shoes at $7 per pair. Because Jones sold 1,020 pairs of shoes during January, but customers returned 20 pairs which Jones placed back in inventory, upon taking inventory at the end of the month, he would find 500 pairs of shoes which cost a total of $3,500. The difference between that figure and the sum of what Jones had on hand and what he acquired, $10,500, gives the cost of goods sold figure of $7,000 which we had previously assumed.

A somewhat more detailed version of his income statement might then look like this:

Jones Shoes
Income Statement
For the Month of January

Net Sales		$10,000
Cost of Goods Sold:		
Beginning Inventory	$ 2,100	
Purchases	8,400	
Goods Available for Sale	$10,500	
Less: Closing Inventory	3,500	7,000
Gross Profit		$3,000
Operating Expenses		1,000
Net Income		$2,000

At this point, we can explain *gross profit* and its presentation on the income statement.

3.   GROSS PROFIT AND THE MULTI-STEP INCOME STATEMENT

The "Gross Profit" caption in the income statement reflects the difference between net sales and the cost of goods sold. Accountants call an income statement which lists gross profit as an intermediate figure in computing net income or loss as a *multi-step* income statement. The income statement for Jones Shoe shows two steps: (1) the statement calculates gross profit by subtracting the cost of goods sold from net sales and (2) the statement computes net income by deducting operating expenses from gross profit. Although gross profit does not measure the business's overall profitability, users of financial statements often pay particular attention to that figure, which frequently serves as a better guide to market conditions and the efficiency of the selling operations than net income.

A multi-step income statement may also provide additional information by separating the business's operating activities and non-operating activities and presenting more detailed information about revenues and expenses. You will recall that businesses derive revenues and incur expenses from normal operating activities while gains and losses flow from peripheral or incidental transactions. The non-operating section for Jones Shoe might show interest income, rental income from subleasing part of the store, gain from the sale of office equipment, interest expense, fire damage, and loss from the sale of office equipment.

If we assume that Jones has incorporated the business and that the corporation pays income taxes at a forty percent tax rate, a multi-step income statement for Jones Shoe Co. might look something like:

Jones Shoe Co.
Income Statement
For the Month of January

Sales		$10,200
Less: Sales Returns and Allowances		200
Net Sales		$10,000
Cost of Goods Sold:		
Beginning Inventory	$ 2,100	
Purchases	8,400	
Goods Available for Sale	$10,500	
Less: Closing Inventory	3,500	7,000
Gross Profit		$ 3,000
Operating Expenses		
Rent Expense	$ 600	
Selling Commission Expense	250	
Utility Expense	100	950
Operating Income		$ 2,050
Non–Operating Items		
Rental Income	$ 50	
Interest Expense	(100)	(50)
Earnings Before Income Taxes		$ 2,000
Income Taxes		800
Net Income		$ 1,200

You will note that the multi-step income statement shows non-operating items immediately after the company's operating income and nets the non-operating items. In this case, the company subtracted the non-operating items from operating income to determine earnings before income taxes.

For comparison purposes, we should also mention that some companies use a so-called *single-step* income statement. The single-step income statement classifies all items into two categories: (1) revenues, which includes both operating revenues and gains, and (2) expenses, which includes cost of goods sold, operating expenses and losses. To determine net income or loss, the single-step income statement subtracts total expenses from total revenues. The following illustrates a single-step income statement for Jones Shoe Co.:

Jones Shoe Co.
Income Statement
For the Month of January

Revenue		
Net Sales		$10,000
Rental Income		50
Total Revenues		$10,050
Expenses		
Cost of Goods Sold	$7,000	
Operating Expenses	950	
Income Taxes	800	
Interest Expense	100	
Total Expenses		8,850
Net Income		$ 1,200

Even though Starbucks' statements of earnings, which appear on page 50 of the company's Form 10-K for the year ended September 30, 2012, and in Appendix A on page 746, *infra*, do not contain a line for gross profit, we might describe the presentation as a hybrid income statement because the company shows subtotals for operating income and earnings before income taxes.

4.   PERIODIC INVENTORY SYSTEM

Let us now see how the bookkeeper uses T-accounts and entries to make these computations under the periodic inventory system. On his balance sheet at the beginning of the period, Jones has an asset, Inventory, in the amount of $2,100. This account, which was derived by taking inventory at the close of the period just ended, becomes beginning inventory for the new period. During the period, Jones opens a T-account called *Purchases* to which the amount of purchases made during the period is debited; the corresponding credit is to Cash or an account payable, depending upon whether the purchase is made for cash or on credit. Actually, the purchases during the period could as well be debited directly to the Inventory T-account, thus eliminating the need for opening a new Purchases T-account; but in practice a separate account for purchases is commonly used.

If Jones returns any purchases or a seller grants any allowance for defective or damaged goods, the bookkeeper would credit an account called *Purchase Returns and Allowances*. Again, we can describe this account as a contra account to Purchases. The Purchase Returns and Allowances account normally contains a credit balance. Similar to Sales Returns and Allowances, accountants use this contra account, rather than crediting the Purchases account directly, to identify and disclose purchase returns and allowances in the accounts and in the income statement. Crediting the Purchases account directly would hide the comparative size of the returns and allowances relative to purchases. Large returns or allowances suggest sloppy purchasing procedures or unreliable suppliers. If shown on the income statement, the caption *Net Purchases* simply shows the difference between the Purchases and Purchases Returns and Allowances accounts.

Thus, if Jones purchased the entire $8,400 worth of goods acquired in January in a single cash transaction, the entry would be:

(a) Purchases $8,400
      Cash $8,400

Whether or not Jones purchased all the goods at the same time, or purchased them all for cash, the T-account for Purchases would show a total debit of $8,400 at the end of the month of January.

At the end of the period the bookkeeper sets up a new T-account called *Cost of Goods Sold*. As we have already seen, Cost of Goods Sold is an expense and therefore this account should be increased by a debit and decreased by a credit. The bookkeeper then closes [Beginning] Inventory, Purchases, and Purchase Returns and Allowances to the Cost of Goods Sold account in much the same way that expense and income accounts are closed to the Profit and Loss account. Because Jones did not return any purchases, the entries would consist of debits to the Cost of Goods Sold account, and credits to the [Beginning] Inventory and Purchases accounts respectively to close them out:

(b) Cost of Goods Sold $2,100
      Inventory $2,100

(c) Cost of Goods Sold   8,400
      Purchases   8,400

If the Purchase Returns and Allowances account contained a credit balance, the bookkeeper would have closed that account by debiting Purchase Returns and Allowances and crediting the Cost of Goods Sold account.

The bookkeeper then learns from the person who took inventory at the end of the month how much inventory remains unsold—here $3,500. This information has two aspects of equal significance to the bookkeeper. It tells the bookkeeper that there remains at the end of the period an asset of $3,500 of closing inventory which should appear on the balance sheet at the end of the period. It also tells the bookkeeper that the cost of goods sold is $3,500 less than would be indicated simply by adding together the beginning inventory and the purchases. The bookkeeper can reflect both these facts by a single journal entry:

(d) Inventory $3,500
      Cost of Goods Sold $3,500

The amount debited to the Inventory account is balanced by a credit to the Cost of Goods Sold account. The Cost of Goods Sold account performs the subtraction of what Jones has left from the sum of what he had at the beginning of the period plus what he bought during the period; the net debit in the Cost of Goods Sold account is the cost of what was sold during the period.

A little thought will show that this entry debiting the amount of the goods still on hand at the close of the period to Closing Inventory, and crediting the same figure to the Cost of Goods Sold account, is just another example of deferral. The sum of what Jones originally had on hand and what he bought during the period constitutes an overstatement of the expense applicable to the current period; the cost of merchandise remaining at the end of the period should not be included as an expense of the current period, but rather should be deferred to later periods. Thus *Closing Inventory* is just another, but more descriptive, name for *Deferred Cost of Goods Sold Expense*. The closing inventory will appear as an asset, usually called simply Inventory, on the balance sheet at the end of the period, like any other deferred item. The Inventory account on the balance sheet will then become [Beginning] Inventory for the new period, and the cycle will start all over again.

It is not necessary to use separate T-accounts for beginning inventory and closing inventory. Instead, the bookkeeper usually uses a single T-account called simply Inventory. At the close of each period, this account is temporarily closed out with a credit in the amount of the beginning inventory and an equal debit to the Cost of Goods Sold account. The bookkeeper then reopens the Inventory account with a debit in the amount of the closing inventory.

Once the net figure in the Cost of Goods Sold account is arrived at, here $7,000, that cost, like any other expense, is closed to Profit and Loss:

(e) Profit and Loss	$7,000	
Cost of Goods Sold		$7,000

Here is a summary of the journal entries described above, along with the related T-accounts.

(a) Purchases	$8,400	
Cash		$8,400
(b) Cost of Goods Sold	2,100	
Inventory		2,100
(c) Cost of Goods Sold	8,400	
Purchases		8,400
(d) Inventory	3,500	
Cost of Goods Sold		3,500
(e) Profit and Loss	7,000	
Cost of Goods Sold		7,000

Inventory				Cost of Goods Sold			
Bal.	$2,100	$2,100	(b)	(b)	$2,100	$3,500	(d)
(d)	$3,500			(c)	8,400		
Purchases				Bal.	$7,000	$7,000	(e)
(a)	$8,400	$8,400	(c)				

The Profit and Loss account would then look like this (after Cost of Goods Sold, together with Sales Income of $10,000 and other expenses of $1,000 have been closed to it):

Profit and Loss			
(e)	$7,000	$10,000	
	1,000		
		$2,000	Bal.

and this balance of $2,000 would be closed to Proprietorship.

The foregoing illustrates the mechanics of handling inventory under what is known as the periodic inventory system. This system relies upon a physical count of closing inventory at the end of a period to determine the amount of inventory sold during the period. As you might expect, some difficult problems can arise in particular situations, such as determining the cost of the closing inventory when the price has been fluctuating during the period. It is not necessary to do more than allude to such problems here; however, they are considered in detail in Chapter VIII on pages 599 to 623, *infra*.

5. SUMMARY OF THE BOOKKEEPING AND ACCRUAL ACCOUNTING PROCESS

At this point, we should summarize our entire discussion of the bookkeeping and accrual accounting process in outline form and provide a format for a classified balance sheet and multi-step income statement:

A. Prepare original journal entries
B. Post journal entries to accounts in the ledger after entering beginning balances from previous balance sheet, if applicable
C. If applicable, complete periodic inventory accounting to determine Cost of Goods Sold
   1. Transfer beginning balance in Inventory account to Cost of Goods Sold
   2. Transfer balances in Purchases and Purchase Returns and Allowances accounts to Cost of Goods Sold
   3. Record ending inventory and reduce Cost of Goods Sold
      a. Physically count inventory at end of period
      b. Calculate cost of ending inventory

D. Prepare necessary adjusting entries after reviewing the beginning balance sheet and current period transactions:
1. Record depreciation
2. Defer any other paid but unused expenses
3. Defer received but unearned revenues
4. Accrue incurred but unrecorded expenses
5. Accrue earned but unrecorded revenues
6. Accrue income taxes

E. Post entries related to periodic inventory accounting and adjusting entries to the ledger

F. Close revenue and expense accounts
1. Determine the account balances
2. Prepare trial balance
3. Prepare worksheet
4. Make closing journal entries
   a. Transfer debit balances to Profit and Loss account
   b. Transfer credit balances to Profit and Loss account
   c. Transfer balance in Profit and Loss account to Owner's Equity
5. Post closing journal entries to the ledger

G. Preparing the financial statements
1. Balance Sheet
   Assets
      Current Assets
         Cash
         Marketable Securities
         Notes Receivable
         Accounts Receivable
         Inventory
         Prepaid Costs
            Total Current Assets
      Long–Term Investments
      Fixed Assets
         Land
         Buildings
            Less: Accumulated Depreciation
         Equipment
            Less: Accumulated Depreciation
            Total Fixed Assets
      Intangible Assets
            Total Assets
    Liabilities and Owners' Equity
      Liabilities
         Current Liabilities
            Notes Payable
            Accounts Payable
            Accrued Liabilities
            Taxes Payable
            Unearned Items
               Total Current Liabilities
         Other Liabilities
             Total Liabilities

Owners' Equity
Proprietorship
Partners' Equity
Partners' Capital
Drawings
Shareholders' Equity
Capital Stock
Preferred Stock
Common Stock
Additional Paid–In Capital
Retained Earnings
Total Owners' Equity
Total Liabilities and Owners' Equity
2.   Income Statement
Sales
Less: Sales Returns and Allowances
Net Sales
Cost of Goods Sold
Beginning Inventory
Purchases
Less: Purchase Returns and Allowances
Net Purchases
Cost of Goods Available for Sale
Less: Ending Inventory
Cost of Goods Sold
Gross Profit
Operating Expenses
Operating Income
Non–Operating Items (interest and non-recurring items)
Earnings Before Income Taxes
Income Taxes
Net Income

PROBLEMS AND QUESTIONS

The following problems and questions are designed to provide some experience in handling the mechanics of accounting for inventory, as well as some additional practice in bookkeeping generally.

Problem 1.8A.

(1) The Nifty-Novelty Company was organized as a partnership on February 1, to operate a wholesale knick-knack business at rented premises formerly occupied by Samuel Nifty. The following transactions during February are to be recorded on the firm's books. Using the periodic inventory method, make the appropriate journal entries and post them to the T-accounts. Draw up a simplified income statement for the month and a balance sheet as of February 28. Ignore depreciation and taxes.

Feb.   1   Samuel Nifty contributed store fixtures valued at $10,000; Hiram Novelty contributed merchandise valued at $2,000 and $8,000 in cash.

1   Paid February rent for store of $200.

2   Paid painter $72 for lettering on store front which will not have to be redone for a year.

3   Purchased costume jewelry on account from Acme, Inc., for $1,000.

4   Purchased counter and trays for displaying merchandise from Blake & Co. for $1,500 on account.

6   Sold merchandise for $550 cash.

8   Received $400 from Ritter for goods to be delivered in March.

9   Sold party decorations and favors to Lincoln Hotel on account for $310.

11   Paid February wages of $260 to salesperson.

12   Paid $500 on account to Acme, Inc.

15   Sold merchandise for $2,150 cash.

17   Purchased merchandise from Klips Corp. giving note for $1,300 due in six months.

20   A display tray which cost $19 was accidentally destroyed.

22   Received $100 on account from Lincoln Hotel.

24   Paid Blake & Co. $1,000 on account.

26   Sold merchandise for $700 cash.

28   Determined that telephone bill for February will amount to $20.

28   Distributed $100 to each of the partners.

Assume further that:

(i)   Rent of $105 will be due Smith Corp. on April 30 for storage space leased to Nifty-Novelty on Feb. 1 for 3 months.

(ii)   A physical inventory on February 28 discloses $1,700 worth of merchandise on hand.

Nifty-Novelty Company
Income Statement
For the Month of February

Sales		$_____
Cost of Goods Sold		
Beginning Inventory	$_____	
Purchases	_____	
Goods Available for Sale	$_____	
Less: Closing Inventory	_____	$_____
Gross Profit		$_____
Less: Expenses		_____
Net Income		$_____

Nifty-Novelty Company
Balance Sheet, February 28

<u>Assets</u>		<u>Liabilities & Partners' Equity</u>	
		Liabilities:	
Cash	$_____	Note Payable	$_____
Accounts Receivable	_____	Accounts Payable	_____
Inventory	_____	Accrued Costs Payable	_____
Prepaid Costs	_____	Customer Deposits	_____
Store Fixtures	_____	Total Liabilities	$_____
Total	$_____	Partners' Equity	$_____
		Total Liabilities & Equity	$_____

(2) Suppose the Nifty-Novelty bookkeeper was not aware of the lease of storage space from Smith Corp. referred to in (i) above, and made no entry reflecting this transaction. What would the effect of this omission be on Nifty-Novelty's financial statements?

(3) Could any of the transactions listed on the previous page, *supra*, have been overlooked by the bookkeeper, and hence not recorded, without changing either the balance sheet totals or the net income figure?

Problem 1.8B

(1) The balance sheet of Camera Sales Co. as of March 31, Year 1 is presented below:

Camera Sales Co.
Balance Sheet, March 31, Year 1

Assets

Current Assets:

Cash	$14,800
Accounts Receivable	2,700
Inventories (21 cameras)	2,100
Prepaid Insurance (representing the unused cost of a one-year policy purchased on January 1, Year 1 at a cost of $300)	225
Total Current Assets	$19,825

Fixed Assets:

Land		$10,000
Buildings	$40,000	
Less: Accumulated Depreciation	11,700	
Net Buildings		28,300
Furniture and Fixtures	$ 3,600	
Less: Accumulated Depreciation	480	
Net Furniture and Fixtures		3,120
Total Fixed Assets		$41,420
Total Assets		$61,245

Liabilities and Stockholders' Equity

Liabilities:

Current Liabilities:

Accounts Payable	$ 7,900
Accrued Interest Payable	225
Total Current Liabilities	$ 8,125

Long–Term Liabilities:

Note Payable, due December 31, Year 5, bearing nine percent interest payable annually on December 31 of each year	$10,000
Total Liabilities	$18,125

Shareholders' Equity:

Common Stock (1,000 shares, $10 par value, authorized, issued and outstanding)	$10,000
Retained Earnings	33,120
Total Shareholders' Equity	$43,120
	$61,245

Total Liabilities and Shareholders' Equity

Unless your professor directs otherwise, prepare journal entries for the following transactions which occurred during April, prepare any necessary adjusting entries, post to T-accounts, construct a six-column worksheet, prepare and post closing entries and prepare April financial statements (multi-step income statement and classified balance sheet only). Assume that Camera Sales Co. pays income taxes at a flat rate of thirty percent (30%) of net income and uses the periodic inventory method and separate accounts for sales returns and allowances and purchase returns and allowances. The building has an estimated useful life of thirty years and a salvage value of $4,000. The furniture and fixtures have an estimated useful life of ten years and no salvage value.

Apr.   1   Purchased ten cameras for $100 each on account from Kojak, Inc.

2   Returned one camera to Kojak, Inc. for credit because of a slight defect.

4   Sold eight cameras in various cash sales totaling $1,325.

6   Sold three cameras to *The Observer* for $675. *The Observer* paid $75 down and issued a promissory note, due in three months, for the $600 balance with interest at the rate of ten percent per annum.

9   Sold fourteen cameras for $2,300, $1,700 on account and $600 cash.

11   Sold camera to Thelma Bird for $175 on account.

14   Thelma Bird returned the camera she purchased for credit on her account.

15   Paid salaries of $500 for the first half of the month.

18   Purchased fifteen cameras on account at $100 each from Nikon Inc.

21   Gave George Land, the President, a $600 advance for May salary.

23   Paid $100 in back wages, which had been accidentally overlooked, after a former employee who had been fired in January complained.

25   Paid $24 for April telephone bill.

27   Accepts a $100 down payment from a customer to order a camera costing $200, which the company will sell to the customer for $500.

30   Physical inventory reveals seventeen cameras in inventory. All cameras were purchased for $100 each. Bookkeeper decides not to pay $500 in salaries for the second half of the month until May.

(2) Suppose the bookkeeper for Camera Sales Co. was not aware of prepaid insurance described in the balance sheet as of March 31, and made no entry during April regarding this insurance. What would the effect of this omission be on the company's financial statements?

(3) Could any of the transactions listed above have been overlooked by the bookkeeper, and hence not recorded, without changing the figures on the balance sheet, the balance sheet totals, or net income?

Problem 1.8C

(1) The balance sheet of the Tortious Toys Company, as of March 31, Year 1 is presented below:

Tortious Toys Company
Balance Sheet, March 31, Year 1

Assets

Current Assets:

Cash		$12,000
Accounts Receivable		4,500
Inventory		8,500
Prepaid Insurance (representing the unused cost of a one-year policy purchased on January 1, Year 1 at a cost of $1,500)		1,125
Total Current Assets		$26,125

Fixed Assets:

Land		$ 8,000
Buildings	$50,000	
Less: Accumulated Depreciation	6,375	
Net Buildings		43,625
Furniture and Fixtures	$12,000	
Less: Accumulated Depreciation	5,100	
Net Furniture and Fixtures		6,900
Total Fixed Assets		$58,525
Total Assets		$84,650

Liabilities & Shareholders' Equity

Liabilities:

Current Liabilities:

Accounts Payable	$14,750
Accrued Interest Payable	450
Wages Payable	1,100
Total Current Liabilities	$16,300

Long–Term Liabilities:

Note Payable (due December 31, Year 3, bearing nine percent interest payable annually on December 31 of each year)	$20,000
Total Liabilities	$36,300

Shareholders' Equity:

Common Stock (5,000 shares authorized, $5 par value; 3,000 shares issued and outstanding)	$15,000
Retained Earnings	33,350
Total Shareholders' Equity	$48,350
Total Liabilities and Shareholders' Equity	$84,650

Unless your professor directs otherwise, prepare journal entries for the following April transactions, prepare any necessary adjusting entries, post to T-accounts, construct a six-column worksheet, prepare and post closing entries, and prepare the April financial statements (income statement and classified balance sheet only). Assume that Tortious Toys Co. pays income taxes at a flat rate of thirty percent (30%) of net income and uses the periodic inventory method and separate accounts for sales returns and allowances and purchase returns and allowances. The building has an estimated useful life of thirty years and a salvage value of $5,000. The furniture and fixtures have an estimated useful life of ten years and no estimated salvage value.

Apr. 1 Sold five "Inspector Troy's Obtain–O–Confession" kits to Toys–R–Us for $1,700 total. Toys–R–Us paid $500 down and issued a promissory note, due in six months, for the balance with interest at the rate of ten percent (10%) per annum. The company had purchased the kits for a total of $500 last month.

4 Purchased twenty "Easy Bake Ovens" for $15 each on account from the manufacturer.

6 Sold three "My First Shuttle Ride" kits to a German retailer and four "Debbie's Doggie Dentist" kits to a French outlet store for cash totaling $6,000. The company had purchased the shuttle kits two months ago for $750 each. The dentist kits cost the company $500 each last year.

9 After reading a news release mentioning that the popular "Easy Bake Ovens" were being recalled due to burn-related injuries, the company's attorney determined that two of the ovens were poorly manufactured and unacceptable even for Tortious Toys. The company returned the two ovens to the manufacturer for credit to account due to the obvious defects.

11 Paid $1,100 to the store employees for wages for the last two weeks of March after they threatened to turn over confidential files to the "60 Minutes" crew that stopped by earlier in the day. The amount paid represented the entire wages payable liability on the March 31, Year 1 balance sheet.

14 Sold six of the ever-popular "My First Sternos" to Gloria Vanderpohl on account for $150. Each sterno cost $10 when purchased in February.

15 Paid salaries for the month of April totaling $1,075.

16 Mrs. Vanderpohl returned all six of the "My First Sternos" which she purchased two days earlier for credit to her account.

18 Gave Ted Tungstra, a manager, a $500 advance on his May salary.

21 Sold five "Little Bubble Boy Suits" to Bud's Discount Sales for $365 in cash and twenty "Johnny Switchblade Adventure Punk Dolls." The dolls are worth $240 in total. The company purchased the five suits for a total of $200 last year.

23 Purchased thirty boxes of date-expired "Silly Putty" for $30 on account.

24 Paid $50 for the April telephone bill.

25 Paid $150 to Jack & Jill Magazine for advertisements which will appear in the issues published in May and June.

27   Accepted a $500 down payment from a valued customer to order two "My First Shuttle Ride Kits" which will cost the company $600 each and which the company will sell to the customer for $900 each.

30   Physical inventory revealed that the closing inventory balance was $3,750.

(2) Suppose the bookkeeper for Tortious Toys was not aware of note payable described in the balance sheet as of March 31, and made no entry during April to reflect the interest on the note. What would the effect of this omission be on the company's financial statements?

(3) Could any of the transactions listed above or on the previous page have been overlooked by the bookkeeper, and hence not recorded, without changing the figures on the balance sheet, the balance sheet totals, or net income?

H.   THE STATEMENT OF CASH FLOWS

Under accrual accounting, as we have seen, the movement of cash does not control the determination of expenses and income for an accounting period. A business's *cash flow*, which refers to the movement of cash into and out of the enterprise, however, often determines the business's financial success. To remain in business, an enterprise must either own or have access to the cash needed to meet recurring expenses, such as payroll and rent, to pay its accounts payable to suppliers, and to pay its outstanding debt obligations as they come due. In addition, any distributions which the enterprise returns to its owners normally come from cash. Accordingly, judging a business's future prospects calls for some consideration, and comparison, of the business's cash-generating potential and cash needs, over both the short and long terms.

Obviously, an enterprise's revenues from operations provide its primary source of cash, while its expenses serve as the principal cash drain. Estimated future earnings, therefore, provide some indication as to expected cash resources. But operations afford only a starting point, because transactions not reflected in the income statement, such as borrowing money, paying cash dividends, or purchasing long-lived assets, including buildings, machinery, and equipment, may significantly increase or decrease a business's cash. We must also keep in mind, as a corollary of accrual accounting, that some expenses will not require any current or future cash outflow. For example, the periodic charge off, or amortization, of a deferred expense asset, like E. Tutt's deferred insurance expense, illustrates this common occurrence. As a practical matter, depreciation on tangible fixed assets purchased for cash epitomizes those situations in which the actual cash expenditure occurred in an earlier accounting period. The enterprise acquired and paid for the asset in an earlier accounting period, but did not expense the cost at that time. As the enterprise allocates the unexpired cost to subsequent accounting periods, the business records a depreciation expense, but does not make any additional cash payments. The only cash outlay occurred when the enterprise purchased the asset. In contrast to situations where the cash expenditure precedes expense recognition on the income statement, income recognition under the accrual method normally reflects an expected cash receipt. In this situation, however, a substantial time lag can separate the income recognition and the actual cash receipt. This delay can significantly affect an enterprise's overall financial picture.

By comparing an enterprise's current balance sheet with a previous balance sheet, a reader can glean some useful information relating to cash flow. For example, the relative amounts of cash and accounts receivable, and the change in those figures from the prior year, may indicate significant trends. A number of important transactions, however, such as borrowing, issuing new stock, or buying capital assets, greatly affect cash but do not appear in the income statement for the period and emerge on the balance sheet at the end of the period only as accomplished facts. While a reader may surmise what happened by comparing the current balance sheet with the prior balance sheet, users of financial statements often want more explanatory information.

In any event, prudent investors and creditors want a statement of cash flows, which details the effect on cash of an enterprise's regular operations during the fiscal period and those other types of significant transactions. Unlike the balance sheet, which we described as a snapshot, but like the income statement, we can compare the statement of cash flows to a motion picture. Common cash inflows include sales for cash; collection of accounts receivable; short and long-term borrowings; sale of property, plant, and equipment; and issuance of stock for cash. Common cash outflows include current operating costs; acquisition of property, plant, equipment, and other long-term assets; repayment of short and long-term debt; and distributions to owners. As enterprises increasingly rely on debt to finance activities such as expanded operations, buy-outs and mergers, attorneys as well as accountants, financial analysts, creditors, investors and others must increase their awareness of the mechanics and usefulness of the statement of cash flows. Both the Enron and Tyco scandals show that lawyers should understand not only the statement of cash flows, but also the ways that enterprises can manipulate that financial statement.

The W.T. Grant Company illustrates the importance of the statement of cash flows to both investors and creditors. In 1975, the W.T. Grant Company, then the nation's largest retailer, filed for protection under the federal bankruptcy laws because the company did not have enough cash to pay its debts. For almost ten years before the company filed for bankruptcy, its income statement reported steady profits, but its operations produced a cash deficit, which required W.T. Grant to borrow huge sums of money to continue the business. If investors and creditors had benefitted from access to a statement of cash flows, they would have noticed that the company's operations did not generate any positive cash flow and that the company borrowed cash year after year to compensate for the deficits. *See* James A. Largay, III & Clyde P. Stickney, *Cash Flows, Ratio Analysis and the W.T. Grant Company Bankruptcy*, FIN. ANALYSTS J., July–Aug. 1980, at 51, 51–54.

1.   HISTORY

Accountants have prepared statements that explain flows of cash and other financial resources for many years. The names of these statements have included *Statement of Sources and Uses of Funds, Funds Statement, Statement of Changes in Financial Position*, and most recently, *Statement of Cash Flows*. In fact, the statement of cash flows replaced the statement of changes in financial position for financial statements for fiscal years ending after July 15, 1988. Several problems inherent in the previous cash flow reporting practice caused the change to the statement of cash flows. These problems included the ambiguity of terms, such as "funds," lack of comparability among statements resulting from different definitions, different formats and the reporting of net changes in amounts of assets and liabilities rather than gross inflows and outflows of cash.

We should note that statutes, regulations, and legal documents may use outdated terminology. More than twenty-five years after the adoption of the current accounting standards, thirty-four states and the District of Columbia continue to use "statement of changes in financial position" instead of "statement of cash flows" in their state codes or administrative regulations.

Today, the statement of cash flows complements the other major financial statements. The statement of cash flows reports the changes in cash and cash equivalents during an accounting period and, most importantly, *explains* those changes. Whereas the balance sheet summarizes an enterprise's assets, liabilities and owner's equity at a specific point in time and the income statement summarizes the enterprise's performance on an accrual basis, the statement of cash flows allows its reader to assess an enterprise's cash transactions.

2.   THE PURPOSE OF THE STATEMENT OF CASH FLOWS

According to accounting pronouncements, the statement of cash flows should provide relevant information about an enterprise's cash receipts and payments during an accounting period. The information provided in a statement of cash flows, if used with related disclosures and information in the other financial statements, should help investors, creditors and other users of financial statements to:

(a) assess the enterprise's ability to generate positive future net cash flows;

(b) assess the enterprise's ability to meet its obligations, its ability to pay dividends, and its needs for external financing;

(c) assess the reasons for differences between net income and associated cash receipts and payments; and

(d) assess the effects on an enterprise's financial position of both its cash and noncash investing and financing transactions during the period.

To achieve this purpose, the statement of cash flows should report the cash effects during a period of an enterprise's operations, investments in capital assets, and financing transactions. As an example, Starbucks includes its statements of cash flows on page 52 of its Form 10-K for the fiscal year ended September 30, 2012, which appears in Appendix A at page 748, *infra*.

3.   CASH AND CASH EQUIVALENTS

The statement of cash flows explains the change during the period in *cash and cash equivalents*. To establish consistency in financial reporting, companies must report the changes in "cash and cash equivalents" rather than in the ambiguous term "funds." Cash includes not only currency, but bank accounts that the enterprise can access "on demand." The applicable accounting pronouncement defines cash equivalents as "short-term, highly liquid investments." To satisfy this definition, cash equivalents must meet two requirements:

1.   An enterprise must be able to convert the equivalents to cash readily, and

2.   These equivalents' original maturity dates must not exceed three months, so that changes in interest rates do not threaten to affect adversely their value.

Examples of cash equivalents include United States Treasury bills, certificates of deposit, commercial paper and money market funds. The original maturity date means the maturity date when an enterprise acquires the investment. For example, a five-year U.S. Treasury note purchased three months from maturity qualifies as a cash-equivalent because the note will mature in three months. A five-year U.S. Treasury note purchased two years before its maturity date does not become a cash equivalent three months before its maturity because the note's maturity exceeded three months on the acquisition date. According to accounting standards, an enterprise must combine cash and cash equivalents on the balance sheet and on the statement of cash flows. These same standards require an enterprise to include its definition of cash equivalents in a related disclosure to its statement of cash flows. As an example, Starbucks includes its definition of cash and cash equivalents on page 54 of its 2012 Form 10-K, which appears in Appendix A on page 750, *infra*.

The credit crisis uncovered certain ambiguities in the requirements necessary to qualify as a "cash equivalent" for financial accounting purposes. After the relevant accounting rule's promulgation, new financial instruments, such as auction-rate securities and variable-rate demand notes, which typically offered higher returns than short-term commercial paper and Treasury securities, became very popular. Although these securities sometimes carried maturities up to thirty years, they also contained features, such as provisions allowing the holder to sell the securities back to the issuer every ninety days, designed to qualify as "highly liquid." As a result, numerous enterprises treated these securities as cash equivalents for financial accounting purposes. As the credit crisis worsened, some issuers defaulted and most securities in the $330 billion market suddenly became illiquid.

4.   CLASSIFICATION OF THE STATEMENT OF CASH FLOWS

An enterprise must classify its statement of cash flows into three separate categories: operating, investing, and financing activities. These three categories represent an enterprise's three major functions and help the readers of the statement of cash flows recognize important relationships between the three activities. Each activity can produce a cash inflow or outflow to the enterprise. Once again, note Starbucks' statements of cash flows on page 52 of its 2012 Form 10-K in Appendix A at page 748, *infra*. Along with separating these three sections, the statement of cash flows must reconcile the total change in cash and cash equivalents for the period with the beginning and ending balances which appear on the current and prior balance sheets.

The **operating activities** of an enterprise involve acquiring and selling the enterprise's products and services. For example, Starbucks' operating section would mainly report cash disbursements and receipts from roasting coffee beans; selling them, handcrafted coffee, tea, and other beverages, and fresh food items; and licensing its trademarks. For a service organization, such as a law firm, this section may include inflows from legal fees collected and outflows for associate and secretarial salaries, rents, and utilities. Cash inflows from operating activities include interest and dividends from loans to and ownership investments in other enterprises, while cash outflows from operating activities include cash interest payments to lenders and other creditors, but not dividends to shareholders. The operating category also serves as a "catch all" for any cash flows from transactions which do not qualify as investing or financing activities.

The **investing activities** of an enterprise include acquiring and disposing of long-term investments and long-lived assets. Manufacturing enterprises typically spend the largest amount of cash on long-lived assets, such as property, plant, and equipment, which accountants sometimes refer to as *capital expenditures*. The investing section also shows cash expenditures to acquire other companies through mergers or stock acquisitions. During its fiscal year ended September 30, 2012, for example, Starbucks spent more than $856 million on additional property, plant, and equipment and more than $1.7 billion to purchase investments, not counting business acquisitions. Note that investing activities do not refer to all investments in the usual sense of the word. The term, for example, does not apply to the purchase or sale of U.S. Treasury bills that qualify as cash equivalents. The term also does not apply to interest and dividends from those long-term investments.

The **financing activities** of an enterprise include the obtaining of resources from owners and providing them with a return on, and a return of, their investment. Financing activities also include the issuance and retirement of short and long-term debt from creditors. Cash outflows from financing activities include cash dividends or other distributions to owners. During Starbucks' 2012 fiscal year, for example, the company raised almost $237 million by issuing common stock, but spent more than $549 million to repurchase common shares, paid $513 million in dividends, and repaid almost $31 million in short-term debt.

5. THE OPERATING SECTION

An enterprise may use the direct or indirect method to report its cash flows from operations. The direct method requires an enterprise to report major classes of cash receipts and cash payments which relate to the enterprise's operations. Enterprises that use the direct method must report, at a minimum, the following seven classes of cash transactions, if they exist:

1. Cash collected from customers, including lessees and licensees

2. Interest and dividends received

3. Other operating cash receipts

4. Cash paid to employees and other suppliers of goods or services, including suppliers of insurance and advertising

5. Interest paid

6. Income taxes paid

7. Other operating cash payments

Although the authoritative accounting pronouncement expresses a preference for the direct method, only a very small percentage of large, publicly-traded companies actually use that method. Illustration 1–1 illustrates the direct method.

Illustration 1–1: Direct Method of Reporting Cash Flows from Operating Activities

Widgets, Inc. Statement of Cash Flows For the Year Ended December 31, 201X	
Cash Flows From Operating Activities:	
Cash receipts from:	
Customers	$1,150,000
Interest	15,000
Other Receipts	100,000
Total Cash Receipts	$1,265,000

Cash Payments for:	
Inventory	$(650,000)
Salaries and Wages	(140,000)
Utilities	(40,000)
Interest	(55,000)
Income Taxes	(90,000)
Total Cash Payments	$(975,000)
Net Cash Provided from Operating Activities	$ 290,000

Under the indirect method of presenting net cash flows from operations, an enterprise must reconcile net income, determined pursuant to accrual accounting, to net cash from operations. This reconciliation involves adjusting net income to remove the effect of any current recognition of income or expense attributable to a past deferral of operating cash receipts or payments and all accruals in the current period of future operating cash receipts and payments. The reconciliation also eliminates any recognized gains or losses from the sale of long-term investments and property, plant, and equipment because the full amount of the proceeds from such sales will appear as inflows from investing activities. These adjustments require an enterprise to add back (1) depreciation, amortization and other non-cash expenses, (2) so-called "sources" of cash from decreasing accounts receivable, inventories, or prepaid expenses, and from increasing payables, and (3) losses from the sale of long-term investments and property, which reduced net income. The enterprise must also subtract so-called "uses" of cash to increase accounts receivable, inventories or prepaid expenses, or to reduce payables, as well as any gains from the sale of long-term investments and property, which increased net income. Because the indirect method starts with net income, any inaccuracies in the income statement directly affect the statement of cash flows. Starbucks' statements of cash flows in its 2012 Form 10-K, which you can find on page 748 in Appendix A, use the indirect method of reporting cash flows from operations.

Starbucks' consolidated statement of cash flows for the year ended October 2, 2011, illustrates the adjustment necessary under the indirect method of determining cash flows from operating activities when a business sells a long-term investment or property, plant, and equipment. That statement of cash flows subtracts $30.2 million from net earnings for "[g]ain on sale of properties" in deriving net cash provided from operating activities for the year ended October 2, 2011. In addition, that statement shows $117.4 million as "[c]ash proceeds from sale of property, plant, and equipment" in the cash flows from investing activities for that same year. Putting the pieces together, the property, plant, and equipment that Starbucks sold had a book value of $87.2 million. Because Starbucks actually sold the property, plant, and equipment for $117.4 million cash (which produced the $30.2 million gain), $117.4 million must appear as a cash inflow from investing activities for the year ended October 2, 2011. Because the resulting $30.2 million gain already appears in "[n]et earnings" for fiscal 2011, Starbucks had to subtract that amount in determining the net cash flow from operating activities for the year or the statement of cash flows would double-count the cash inflow from that gain, appearing both in the operating section and in the investing section. In addition, the statement would not reconcile to the ending amount of cash and cash equivalents. Finally, please observe that the $30.2 million gain did not arise from an operating activity, but rather from the sale of property, plant, and equipment. In fact, text in Note 7: Supplemental Balance Sheet Information on the bottom of page 71 of Starbucks' 2012 Form 10-K confirms this analysis. Note 7 states in pertinent part that: "On August 8, 2011, we completed the sale of two office buildings for gross consideration of $125 million. As a result of this sale, we recognized a $30.2 million gain within operating income on the consolidated statements of earnings in fiscal 2011." We can further infer that Starbucks incurred $7.6 million in real estate commissions, closing costs, or other expenses in connection with the sale of the buildings, which reduced the net cash received from the sale to $117.4 million.

Regardless of whether an enterprise uses the direct or indirect method for reporting cash flows from operations, a user of financial statements should note several important disclosures. First, accounting standards require an enterprise that uses the direct method of reporting net cash flows from operations to include an indirect operating section in its financial statements. On the other hand, because the indirect method does not disclose certain details involving operating receipts and disbursements, an enterprise that chooses the indirect method must also disclose the amounts of interest and income taxes paid during the period, either on the face of the statement of cash flows or in the notes to the financial statements. The indirect operating section must also report separately the changes in inventory, receivables and payables. You can find all of these disclosures on Starbucks' consolidated statements of cash flows, which appear on page 52 of the company's 2012 Form 10-K in Appendix A at page 748, *infra*.

Until the Enron fraud came to light, many readers of financial statements erroneously assumed that dishonest corporate executives could not manipulate the statement of cash flows, especially cash flows from operating activities. Because the indirect method starts with net income, however, any inaccuracies in the income statement directly affect cash flows from operating activities. In addition, numerous public companies that provided vendor financing to customers, either directly or indirectly through subsidiaries, incorrectly reported increases in receivables from customers as investing outflows rather than as cash outflows from operating activities, which overstated consolidated operating cash flows. Michael Rapoport, *GE Cuts Past Operating Cash Flows*, WALL ST. J., Mar. 7, 2005, at C3; Jonathan Weil, *'Cash Flow Never Lies'—Or Does It?*, WALL ST. J., Apr. 16, 2004, at C3.

The scandals at Enron and Tyco International Ltd. ("Tyco") further illustrate devious techniques that so-called "financial engineers" can use to manufacture fictitious operating cash flows. In a series of complex transactions, usually referred to simply as "prepays," Enron treated more than $6 billion in advances that it obtained from J.P. Morgan Chase & Co. and Citigroup, Inc. as cash from operating activities rather than as cash from financing activities. In the so-called "Mahonia transactions," Mahonia Ltd. functioned as a front for J.P. Morgan Chase. Enron entered into contracts that purported to sell various commodities to Mahonia, which obtained the necessary funds to pay for the commodities from the bank. At the same time, the bank sold the identical commodities back to Enron on credit. The net effect left Enron as the seller and purchaser of the same amounts of a commodity, at the same price on the same day. Enron received billions in cash from the transactions and treated those receipts as operating cash flows. Later, Enron paid back those sums, plus interest. Nevertheless, Enron treated the transactions as sales that generated operating cash flows, rather than as loans that gave rise to financing cash flows. Citicorp engaged in similar transactions with Enron, using Delta Energy Corporation as its front. In 2003, the leading body of accounting rulemakers in the United States issued a new pronouncement that clarifies that when such "prepays" contain a borrowing element, the borrower must report all cash inflows and outflows from the transaction as financing activities.

Tyco relied upon a different technique to boost its cash flows from operations. Rather than treat as operating cash outflows about $830 million that Tyco spent in 2001 to buy about 800,000 individual customer contracts for its security-alarm business from a network of independent dealers, Tyco treated these amounts as investing outflows. Since Tyco treated every penny of the monthly fees that those individual customers paid as operating cash flows, this technique both increased operating cash inflows and reduced operating outflows. In early 2003, however, Tyco announced its plans to change the accounting treatment for the amounts to acquire customer accounts. Mark Maremont & William M. Bulkeley, *Tyco Cuts Outlook, Fires Executive*, WALL ST. J., Mar. 13, 2003, at A5; Mark Maremont, *How Is Tyco Accounting for Its Cash Flow?*, WALL ST. J., Mar. 5, 2002, at C1.

Users of financial statements, including lawyers, should keep in mind that legitimate, but unsustainable, strategies for boosting operating cash flows for a particular accounting period involve selling receivables for quick cash or slowing down payments for goods and services purchased on credit. Michael Rapoport, *Quick Cash via Receivables Deals Can Leave a Blurry Fiscal Picture*, WALL ST. J., June 16, 2006, at C3.

6.   NONCASH INVESTING AND FINANCING ACTIVITIES

Occasionally, an enterprise will engage in an activity that does not involve a cash transfer and which, therefore, does not fall into any of the three prescribed sections. For example, an enterprise may exchange stock for the assets of another company. Although this exchange involves both an investing and financing activity, accounting standards do not require the enterprise to report the transaction on the statement of cash flows because cash did not change hands. Because of the possible significance of these types of events to readers of the financial statements, accounting standards require any enterprise which engages in a material noncash activity to disclose the transaction in the footnotes to the financial statements. Other examples of noncash activities include converting debt to equity, acquiring assets by assuming related liabilities, entering into a lease to obtain a capital asset, exchanging noncash assets for other noncash assets, and converting preferred stock to common stock.

7.   DISCLOSURES

An attorney should know that accounting standards require certain disclosures and reporting techniques by an enterprise preparing a statement of cash flows. First, an enterprise should disclose its policy for determining which items it treats as cash equivalents; remember the Starbucks illustration. If an enterprise changes that policy, a change in accounting principle has occurred and the enterprise must restate any financial statements for earlier years which the financial statements present for comparative purposes. Second, as we have already mentioned, a business choosing to report its net cash flow from operations under the direct method must also disclose in footnotes to its financial statements its net cash flows from operations using the indirect method. When an enterprise reports its net cash flow from operations under the indirect method, the enterprise must disclose the amounts of interest and income taxes paid during the period on its statement of cash flows or in the notes to the financial statements. The indirect section of an enterprise's statement of cash flows must also separately report changes in inventory, receivables and payables. Third, the notes to the financial statements must disclose any material noncash investing or financing activities. Finally, accounting standards forbid the reporting of the cash flow per share ratio in an enterprise's financial statements.

PROBLEMS

Problem 1.9A. Explaining where you found the relevant information, answer the following questions about Amazon's cash flows for the year ended December 31, 2012:

(1) How does the company define the term "cash and cash equivalents"?

(2) Did the company's cash and cash equivalents increase or decrease during the year? By what amount?

(3) Does the company use the direct or indirect method to calculate operating cash flows? Explain briefly.

(4) What was the company's net cash used in, or provided by:
   (a) Operating activities?
   (b) Investing activities?
   (c) Financing activities?

(5) What amount, if any, did the company pay for:
   (a) Interest?
   (b) Income taxes?

(6) How does the amount that the company paid for interest during the year compare with the amount that the company treated as interest expense for the year? Describe what amount, if any, the company treated as interest expense for the year.

(7) How does the amount that the company paid for income taxes during the year compare with the amount that the company treated as income tax expense for the year? Describe what amount, if any, the company treated as income tax expense for the year.

(8) How did operating activities affect the following operating assets and liabilities:
   (a) Inventories?
   (b) Receivables?
   (c) Payables?

(9) Did the company report any material noncash investing or financing activities? Explain briefly.

Problem 1.9B. Explaining where you found the relevant information, answer the following questions about Google's cash flows for the year ended December 31, 2012:

(1) How does the company define the term "cash and cash equivalents"?

(2) Did the company's cash and cash equivalents increase or decrease during the year? By what amount?

(3) Does the company use the direct or indirect method to calculate operating cash flows? Explain briefly.

(4) What was the company's net cash used in, or provided by:
   (a) Operating activities?
   (b) Investing activities?
   (c) Financing activities?

(5) What amount, if any, did the company pay for:
   (a) Interest?
   (b) Taxes?

(6) How does the amount that the company paid for interest during the year compare with the amount that the company treated as interest expense for the year? Describe what amount, if any, the company treated as interest expense for the year.

(7) How does the amount that the company paid for income taxes during the year compare with the amount that the company treated as income tax expense for the year? Describe what amount, if any, the company treated as income tax expense for the year.

(8) How did operating activities affect the following operating assets and liabilities:
- (a) Inventories?
- (b) Receivables?
- (c) Payables?

(9) Did the company report any material noncash investing or financing activities? Explain briefly.

Problem 1.9C. Explaining where you found the relevant information, answer the following questions about UPS's cash flows for the year ended December 31, 2012:

(1) How does the company define the term "cash and cash equivalents"?

(2) Did the company's cash and cash equivalents increase or decrease during the year? By what amount?

(3) Does the company use the direct or indirect method to calculate operating cash flows? Explain briefly.

(4) What was the company's net cash used in, or provided by:
- (a) Operating activities?
- (b) Investing activities?
- (c) Financing activities?

(5) What amount, if any, did the company pay for:
- (a) Interest?
- (b) Income taxes?

(6) How does the amount that the company paid for interest during the year compare with the amount that the company treated as interest expense for the year? Describe what amount, if any, the company treated as interest expense for the year.

(7) How does the amount that the company paid for income taxes during the year compare with the amount that the company treated as income tax expense for the year? Describe what amount, if any, the company treated as income tax expense for the year.

(8) How did operating activities affect the following operating assets and liabilities:
- (a) Inventories?
- (b) Receivables?
- (c) Payables?

(9) Did the company report any material noncash investing or financing activities? Explain briefly.

I.   Consolidated Financial Statements

A corporation that carries on two or more businesses may own them directly or may use a wholly- or substantially-owned subsidiary or other legal entity, such as partnership, limited liability company or trust, to hold one or more indirectly. Although corporate law treats a corporation and its subsidiaries and affiliated organizations (collectively, "its investees") as separate legal entities, accountants aggregate financial data for a parent company and its investees as if the parent and the investees constitute a single economic or accounting entity because such treatment provides more meaningful information to users of financial statements. To take the simplest example, it should not make any difference in the overall evaluation of an enterprise whether the firm owns all of its businesses directly or indirectly through a wholly-owned subsidiary. Similarly, as long as the parent enjoys as much control over a substantially-owned investee as over directly-owned assets, the same conclusion should apply even if the parent does not completely own the investee.

Accountants refer to the process of combining the accounts of two or more affiliated enterprises to present a unified, composite picture of the overall enterprise as *consolidating*. Today, companies must consolidate all majority-owned investees, whether foreign or domestic, unless control does not rest with the majority owner. Circumstances in which a parent may not control an investee include bankruptcy, legal reorganization, foreign exchange restrictions, or other governmentally imposed limitations or uncertainties so severe that they cast significant doubt on the parent's ability to control the investee.

An accountant, however, cannot simply add the assets of the affiliated enterprises together because the parent's assets will include any investment in an affiliate, which reflects the affiliate's residual ownership interest, or, in other words, the affiliate's assets less liabilities. Similarly, an entity cannot report earnings by entering into revenue-producing transactions with itself. Therefore, in the consolidating process the accountant or bookkeeper eliminates reciprocal accounts, which track the dealings between the parent and the affiliate, and combines only nonreciprocal accounts.

The Enron scandal caused the subject of consolidating controlled entities to explode in importance. Enron demonstrated that an enterprise could use contractual agreements, the entity's organizational instruments, or other governing documents to obtain or retain control or significant influence over an entity without holding a majority voting interest. In its "financial engineering," Enron designed a number of so-called "special purpose entities" ("SPEs"), which appeared independent, but which Enron or its officers controlled in fact. Enron used these SPEs to generate manipulated profits, to conceal poorly performing assets, and to hide large amounts of debt. Following Enron's collapse, accounting standard-setters in the United States issued rules that adopted a new model for consolidation, in addition to the so-called "voting interest model." For fiscal years that began on or before November 15, 2009, a quantitative "risk and rewards model" applied. Under that model, the primary beneficiary of a "variable interest entity" ("VIE"), a term that includes not only entities that the business community referred to as SPEs, but also other entities, was required to consolidate the VIE when the beneficiary received a majority of the VIE's expected residual returns, absorbed a majority of the entity's expected losses, or both. Starting with fiscal years beginning after November 15, 2009, a primarily qualitative approach now applies to identifying a controlling financial interest in a VIE. The new rules require ongoing assessments as to whether an entity falls within the definition of VIE and whether a particular interest makes the holder the VIE's primary beneficiary. This newest approach focuses on which enterprise holds the power to direct a VIE's activities that most significantly effect the entity's economic performance and (1) the obligation to absorb the entity's losses or (2) the right to receive benefits from the entity. We will pursue this important topic in more detail in Chapter VI on pages 431 to 434, *infra*. For now, we need only an introduction to the process of consolidation. Please keep in mind, however, that this consolidation process applies to situations where an enterprise either owns a controlling voting interest or holds a controlling economic interest in another entity.

To illustrate the consolidation process, assume that X Corp. plans to purchase all of Y Corp.'s stock. Before the purchase, simplified balance sheets for X and Y show the following:

X Corp.
Balance Sheet, Before Transaction

Assets		Liabilities & Equity	
Cash	$300,000	Liabilities	$250,000
Plant	400,000	Common Stock	300,000
	$700,000	Retained Earnings	150,000
			$700,000

Y Corp.
Balance Sheet, Before Transaction

Assets		Liabilities & Equity	
Cash	$ 50,000		
Plant	150,000	Common Stock	$200,000
	$200,000		$200,000

If X purchases all of Y's stock for $200,000 in cash, X's balance sheet might then be:

X Corp.
Balance Sheet, After Transaction

Assets		Liabilities & Equity	
Cash	$100,000	Liabilities	$250,000
Investment	200,000	Common Stock	300,000
Plant	400,000	Retained Earnings	150,000
	$700,000		$700,000

Because each share of capital stock in a corporation is a proportionate interest in the equity of the corporation and consequently an indirect interest in its net assets, X's purchase of all of Y's stock amounts to an indirect purchase of Y's net assets. If X and Y engage in related operations, we might want to show, both to the outside world and to X's stockholders, the enterprise's composite picture. Because X's investment indirectly represents Y's assets, we can achieve this composite or *consolidated* picture by substituting Y's assets for the asset *Investment* which appears on X's balance sheet. X's balance sheet would then appear as follows:

X Corp. and Subsidiary
Consolidated Balance Sheet, After Transaction

Assets		Liabilities & Equity	
Cash	$100,000	Liabilities	$250,000
Cash (Y)	50,000	Common Stock	300,000
Plant (Y)	150,000	Retained Earnings	150,000
Plant	400,000		$700,000
	$700,000		

and, after combining similar items:

X Corp. and Subsidiary
Consolidated Balance Sheet, After Transaction

Assets		Liabilities & Equity	
Cash	$150,000	Liabilities	$250,000
Plant	550,000	Common Stock	300,000
	$700,000	Retained Earnings	150,000
			$700,000

This last statement presents the consolidated balance sheet for X and its affiliated subsidiary, Y. Although X and Y must maintain their separate legal entities for most legal purposes, as a practical matter X could dissolve Y at any time and bring all the assets together under one corporate roof. Even without dissolution or merger, consolidating the corporations' accounts may provide a more meaningful picture—both to outsiders interested in the enterprise as a whole and to X's stockholders—about the assets that X actually controls.

We assumed, for the sake of simplicity, that Y did not owe any liabilities. Unless "intra-family" obligations between X and Y exist, the consolidation process remains about the same if Y had owed amounts to creditors. Assume that Y's balance sheet at the time of acquisition reflected the following financial position:

Y Corp.
Balance Sheet, Before Transaction

Assets		Liabilities & Equity	
Cash	$150,000	Liabilities	$100,000
Plant	150,000	Common Stock	200,000
	$300,000		$300,000

You will note that Y's net assets remain the same as before. Other things being equal, the purchase price might stay the same. To consolidate the accounts of the two corporations, we replace the asset Investment on X's balance sheet with the actual assets and liabilities which that investment represents. This presentation provides the most meaningful picture of what the composite enterprise owns and owes as a whole. The consolidated balance sheet would appear as follows:

X Corp. and Subsidiary
Consolidated Balance Sheet, After Transaction

Assets		Liabilities & Equity	
Cash	$250,000	Liabilities	$350,000
Plant	550,000	Common Stock	300,000
	$800,000	Retained Earnings	150,000
			$800,000

"Intra-family" obligations between X and Y do not belong in the composite picture. An accountant would eliminate any liabilities between X and Y in the consolidation process by canceling the receivable in one corporation's accounts against the payable on the other corporation's books.

The same consolidation procedure applies when the acquired corporation's balance sheet shows retained earnings on the acquisition date. Suppose that Y's balance sheet appeared as follows:

Y Corp.
Balance Sheet, Before Transaction

Assets		Liabilities & Equity	
Cash	$ 50,000	Common Stock	$100,000
Plant	150,000	Retained Earnings	100,000
	$200,000		$200,000

Here again X's purchase of Y's stock amounts to an indirect acquisition of Y's net assets. The source of the subsidiary's net assets, whether capital stock, additional paid-in capital, or retained earnings does not matter. Because the net assets remain the same as before, the purchase price for the investment might still stay the same. To accomplish the consolidation, we again replace the asset Investment on X's balance sheet with the actual assets and liabilities which that investment represents. The consolidated balance sheet would then appear as follows:

X Corp. and Subsidiary
Consolidated Balance Sheet, After Transaction

Assets		Liabilities & Equity	
Cash	$150,000	Liabilities	$250,000
Plant	550,000	Common Stock	300,000
	$700,000	Retained Earnings	150,000
			$700,000

Note that the consolidated retained earnings do not include the retained earnings which appeared on Y's balance sheet at the acquisition date. In a cash purchase, X in effect buys Y's net assets. Consequently, whether those residual assets arise from capital stock, additional paid-in capital or retained earnings does not matter. Any shareholders' equity which Y accumulated prior to X's acquisition does not belong in the composite picture when X acquires the net assets for cash.

To summarize, when preparing a consolidated balance sheet the accountant or bookkeeper eliminates the parent's investment in the subsidiary, substituting instead the subsidiary's assets and liabilities, while eliminating the subsidiary's equity accounts. In addition, the consolidation process eliminates any intercompany transactions, such as intercompany loans or intercompany sales, to avoid duplication and premature revenue recognition. Finally, the consolidation process reclassifies any transaction arising from the sale of inventory in which one member of the consolidated group recorded an operating cash inflow from financing that another member of the group recorded as an investing cash outflow. Just as the elimination avoids duplication and premature revenue recognition, the reclassification prevents the enterprise from recognizing operating cash inflow from the sale of any inventory until a member of the consolidated group actually receives cash from the customer.

The first note to an enterprise's financial statements typically summarizes the significant accounting policies used. Under the heading "Principles of Consolidation" in "Note 1: Summary of Significant Accounting Policies" on page 54 of Starbucks' Form 10-K for the fiscal year ended September 30, 2012, which appears on page 750, *infra*, Starbucks explains that its consolidated financial statements include its wholly owned subsidiaries and any investees that the company controls. Starbucks also states that the consolidated financial statements have eliminated any intercompany transactions and balances.

Thus far, we have considered only very simple consolidations. When X acquires Y's stock by issuing its own shares rather than paying cash, the accounting becomes more complex. Additionally, in the real world, unlike our simplistic examples, the price that the acquiring corporation pays would ordinarily differ from the book value of the acquired corporation's net assets, which again requires complicated adjustments that we will ignore. Finally, as described above, the accounting rules do not limit consolidated financial statements to wholly-owned subsidiaries.

As long as the parent holds majority ownership in a subsidiary or economically controls an investee, consolidated financial statements typically present more meaningful information than separate company statements. In such cases, an account called *noncontrolling interests*, now shown within the equity section, reflects the carrying amount of the shares or ownership interests that the parent enterprise or other affiliates do not own. In Starbucks' financial statements for its fiscal year ending September 30, 2012, for example, Starbucks reported $5.5 million and $2.4 million as "[n]oncontrolling interests" within equity on the company's consolidated balance sheets as of September 30, 2012, and October 2, 2011, respectively. See page 747, *infra*. Previously, most enterprises called this account *minority interests* and typically, but not always, listed the account as a long-term liability. The account balance reflected the net book value of, or other amount necessary to purchase, the ownership interests, usually shares, that the parent and other affiliates did not own. Because these minority interests did not represent present obligations of the parent to pay cash or to distribute other assets to minority owners, other enterprises sometimes reported these amounts in the "mezzanine," or in a section between liabilities and equity on the balance sheet. For example, note 11 to Starbucks' financial statements for the fiscal year ended October 2, 2005, showed that Starbucks included $11,153,000 as "[m]inority interest liabilities" in the $193,565,000 in "[o]ther long-term liabilities" that the company listed on its consolidated balance sheet as of that date. Starbucks Corp., Annual Report (Form 10-K), at 63 (Dec. 16, 2005).

In an effort to improve comparability and converge accounting principles applying to consolidated financial statements globally, accounting standard setters in the United States decided to use the term "noncontrolling interests" rather than the previous "minority interests." These standard setters also decided that an enterprise should treat a noncontrolling interest in a subsidiary or investee as an ownership interest in the consolidated entity that would appear as equity in the consolidated financial statements, albeit separate from the parent's equity. Previous practice in the United States, which had typically classified minority interests as liabilities or reported such amounts in the "mezzanine" section between liabilities and equity on the balance sheet.

The SEC requires enterprises subject to its jurisdiction to list their significant subsidiaries, the subsidiaries' state or other jurisdiction of incorporation or organization, and the names under which such subsidiaries do business in the annual reports that such registrants file with the Commission. *See* 17 C.F.R. § 229.601(b) (21)(2014). In Exhibit 21 to Starbucks' Form 10-K for the fiscal year ended September 30, 2012, the company lists eighty-nine domestic and foreign corporations, limited liability companies, limited partnerships, and other entities as significant subsidiaries, including Starbucks Coffee International, Inc., a Washington corporation; Starbucks CPG International G.K., a Japanese corporation; Olympic Casualty Insurance

Company, a Vermont corporation; and Starbucks Capital Asset Leasing Company, LLC, a Delaware limited liability company. Once again, you can obtain a copy of the exhibits to Starbucks' Form 10-K filed on November 16, 2012, via the SEC's EDGAR database at www.sec.gov or the Investor Relations section of the company's website.

We should also briefly mention two other presentation formats before finishing this chapter. *Consolidating financial statements* present not only consolidated financial statements, but also the financial statements of the consolidated group's individual components in different columns plus a separate column for any eliminations. A consolidating balance sheet for X and Y might appear, therefore, as follows:

X Corp. and Subsidiary
Consolidating Balance Sheet

	X Corp.	Y Corp.	Eliminations	Consolidated
Assets				
Cash	$100,000	$ 50,000	–0–	$150,000
Investment	200,000	–0–	($200,000)	–0–
Plant	400,000	150,000	–0–	550,000
Totals	$700,000	$200,000	($200,000)	$700,000
Liabilities & Equity				
Liabilities	$250,000	–0–	–0–	$250,000
Common Stock	300,000	$200,000	($200,000)	300,000
Retained Earnings	150,000	–0–	–0–	150,000
Totals	$700,000	$200,000	($200,000)	$700,000

Similar to consolidating statements, *combined financial statements* aggregate the accounts of commonly-controlled companies that do not share a corporate parent. For example, an individual Zoe Zendejas may own both X Corp. and Y Corp. In this situation, accountants and business people sometimes refer to X Corp. and Y Corp. as *brother-sister* corporations. *Combining financial statements* present not only combined statements but also the separate financial statements for each member of the combined group plus a separate column for any eliminations. A combining balance sheet for X and Y might appear as follows:

X Corp. and Y Corp.
Combined Balance Sheet

	X Corp.	Y Corp.	Eliminations	Combined
Assets				
Cash	$100,000	$ 50,000	–0–	$150,000
Investment	50,000	–0–	($50,000)	–0–
Plant	400,000	150,000	–0–	550,000
Totals	$550,000	$200,000	($50,000)	$700,000
Liabilities & Equity				
Liabilities	$150,000	–0–	–0–	$150,000
Common Stock	300,000	$200,000	($50,000)	450,000
Retained Earnings	100,000	–0–	–0–	100,000
Totals	$550,000	$200,000	($50,000)	$700,000

An important caution for both litigators and transactional lawyers: an attorney representing a client in a matter adverse to one of the eighty-nine domestic and foreign corporations, limited liability companies, limited partnerships, or other entities listed as significant subsidiaries in Exhibit 21 to Starbucks' 2012 Form 10-K cannot simply rely on Starbucks' consolidated financial statements when providing legal advice to the client. As a practical matter, few knowledgeable lawyers want to bring a contingent fee case against an insolvent parent, subsidiary, or affiliate, or to advise an hourly-rate client to sue such an adversary without carefully evaluating the likely recovery if the client prevails in the litigation. Absent a guarantee from a financially capable third party, few clients seek to enter into a transaction with a struggling enterprise.

Neither consolidated nor combined financial statements allow a reader to evaluate the separate financial condition, liquidity, or operating results of the parent enterprise or any individual subsidiary or affiliate. Only the financial statements for the particular entity provide that information. As a result, lawyers often need to secure consolidating financial statements, combining financial statements, the worksheets used to prepare consolidated or combined financial statements, or the separate financial statements for the parent itself, a specific subsidiary, or a particular affiliate to obtain information about that enterprise's financial condition, liquidity, or operating results. When reading consolidated and combined financial statements, lawyers need to remember that the "accounting entity" includes more than one legal entity and to keep that distinction between the separate legal entities and the aggregated accounting entity in mind during any representation.

PROBLEMS

Problem 1.10A. What principles of consolidation did Amazon use to prepare its financial statements for the year ended December 31, 2012? Explain briefly how and where you found your answer.

Problem 1.10B. What principles of consolidation did Google use to prepare its financial statements for the year ended December 31, 2012? Explain briefly how and where you found your answer.

Problem 1.10C. What principles of consolidation did UPS use to prepare its financial statements for the year ended December 31, 2012? Explain briefly how and where you found your answer.

Problem 1.11A. Did Amazon report any noncontrolling interest in its financial statements for the year ended December 31, 2012. Explain briefly how and where you found your answer.

Problem 1.11B. Did Google report any noncontrolling interest in its financial statements for the year ended December 31, 2012. Explain briefly how and where you found your answer.

Problem 1.11C. Did UPS report any noncontrolling interest in its financial statements for the year ended December 31, 2012. Explain briefly how and where you found your answer.

Problem 1.12A. How many significant subsidiaries did Amazon list in its Form 10-K for the year ended December 31, 2012? Name up to ten, providing as much variety in locations of organization and forms of organization as possible. Explain briefly how and where you found your answer.

Problem 1.12B. How many significant subsidiaries did Google list in its Form 10-K for the year ended December 31, 2012? Name up to ten, providing as much variety in locations of organization and forms of organization as possible. Explain briefly how and where you found your answer.

Problem 1.12C. How many significant subsidiaries did UPS list in its Form 10-K for the year ended December 31, 2012? Name up to ten, providing as much variety in locations of organization and forms of organization as possible. Explain briefly how and where you found your answer.

J.   ILLUSTRATIVE FINANCIAL STATEMENTS

Although the consolidated financial statements of Starbucks, Amazon, Google, and UPS, which this text uses to illustrate various financial accounting principles and concepts, contain numerous complexities not present in E. Tutt's financial statements, the same principles that we have discussed in this chapter determined the preparation and presentation of those consolidated statements. The most important difference lies in the numerous difficult judgment questions, many of which this text will discuss in later chapters, that Starbucks, Amazon, Google, and UPS had to resolve when preparing their financial statements.

*

CHAPTER II

THE DEVELOPMENT OF ACCOUNTING PRINCIPLES AND AUDITING STANDARDS

A.   IMPORTANCE TO LAWYERS

After completing Chapter I, you may think that financial accounting produces precise answers in all circumstances. This chapter and later chapters will attempt to dispel that myth. In particular, this chapter will address accounting principles and auditing standards.

As a starting point, lawyers must understand the difference between accounting principles and auditing standards because they give rise to very different legal issues. Although we often hear accountants referred to as "bean counters," the term mischaracterizes the profession. The "rules" governing the compilation of accounting data into financial statements in the United States and the form and content of those statements, rules which the business community refers to as *generally accepted accounting principles* domestically or U.S. generally accepted accounting principles internationally and often abbreviates as *GAAP* or *U.S. GAAP*, often offer choices among permissible alternatives. In addition, GAAP frequently does not provide specific rules for treating various transactions. But perhaps most significantly for our purposes, lawyers need to keep in mind that the vast majority of businesses in the United States need not follow any particular rules in preparing financial statements. Unless an enterprise's owners, a lending agreement or other contract, or some legal requirement call for audited financial statements, the enterprise's management need not follow GAAP or any other set of rules in preparing the financial statements.

Enterprises frequently supply financial statements to owners, creditors, potential investors and lenders, and governmental bodies. These users often want assurances that the financial statements contain reliable representations about the enterprise's financial health because management can face temptations to fudge the numbers to keep their jobs, to qualify for bonuses, to satisfy contractual requirements, and for various other reasons. As a result, a certified public accountant or a public accounting firm, retained as an independent third party, serves as an auditor to examine the financial statements that management has presented. In an audit, the auditor seeks to gather evidence about the various representations that management asserts in the financial statements about the enterprise's assets and liabilities at a specific date and transactions during a particular accounting period. Ultimately, an auditor wants to express an opinion as to whether the financial statements fairly present the enterprise's financial condition, results of operations, and cash flows in accordance with generally accepted accounting principles. During the audit, the auditor must act in certain ways and perform certain procedures, which accountants refer to collectively as *auditing standards*, before expressing an opinion on the financial statements.

The economic downturns that followed the internet bubble in the late 1990s; the financial scandals involving Enron, WorldCom, Tyco, and numerous other public companies in the early 2000s; and the 2008 credit crisis illustrate the importance of investor confidence to our economic system. Investor confidence in turn depends upon management's integrity, good accounting systems and processes, effective oversight, independent assurance, and strong regulation.

In the Sarbanes-Oxley Act of 2002 ("Sarbanes-Oxley" or "SOx"), Pub. L. No. 107-204, § 108, 116 Stat. 745, 768, Congress gave the Securities and Exchange Commission ("SEC" or the "Commission") the legal authority to recognize accounting principles established by a private standard setting body as "generally accepted" for purposes of the federal securities laws. Pursuant to that authority, the SEC has designated the Financial Accounting Standards Board ("FASB"), the private sector's official standards-setter in the United States. In 2009, FASB adopted the FASB Accounting Standards Codification™ (the "Codification" or "ASC"), which now compiles all authoritative accounting principles in the United States in a single location.

Subject to certain limitations described below involving the auditor and any audit committee, an enterprise's management selects the accounting principles that the enterprise will use. If the enterprise needs audited financial statements—typically because the enterprise's owners, a lending agreement or other contract arrangement, or a law, such as the federal securities laws, require—management can choose from among the alternatives that FASB considers acceptable. Thus, management plays the leading role in selecting accounting principles. Once again, however, lawyers should keep in mind that most enterprises, at least in terms of sheer number, as opposed to size, need not follow GAAP.

To protect a client's interests, a competent lawyer must understand not only GAAP, but also GAAP's shortcomings. The footnotes to the financial statements address and explain the choices and judgments that management has made. As a result, lawyers and all users of financial statements should pay close attention to the footnotes. In addition, and as described more fully in Chapter IV at pages 318 to 319, *infra*, the SEC has urged public companies to describe their critical accounting policies.

Sarbanes-Oxley substantially enhanced the role of the audit committees of companies listed on national securities exchanges, such as the New York Stock Exchange ("NYSE") or the NASDAQ Stock Market ("NASDAQ"). Publicly traded companies have historically used committees, or subsets, of the board of directors to oversee various aspects of the enterprise's activities.

The audit committee oversees the accounting, financial reporting and disclosure processes, and the audits of the enterprise's financial statements. In listed companies, SOx now effectively requires an audit committee, composed only of directors independent from management, to hire, to set compensation for, and to fire the auditor.

To maintain investor confidence in the capital markets in the United States, the federal securities laws require so-called "public companies" to follow certain sound accounting and financial reporting practices. These enterprises have issued securities, such as stocks and bonds, that the public can buy and sell on the national stock exchanges or an over-the-counter market. In fact, notwithstanding the tight employment market for new lawyers generally, more and more attorneys work in compliance, both for law firms and as in-house counsel, trying to ensure that their clients design and follow internal procedures that satisfy these legal requirements.

First, under the Foreign Corrupt Practices Act of 1977 and its amendments, which apply to all issuers, even those that do not engage in any operations outside the United States, such enterprises must (a) keep books and records that accurately reflect the enterprise's transactions and (b) establish and maintain adequate internal accounting controls. Internal accounting controls refer to those systems, procedures, and policies that an enterprise implements to provide reasonable assurances that the enterprise's representatives appropriately execute transactions according to management's authorization, then records them, and safeguards assets. As a result, poor bookkeeping, lousy record keeping, or inadequate internal accounting controls can violate the federal securities laws.

Second, Sarbanes-Oxley imposes certification requirements and contains provisions designed to strengthen the internal control over financial reporting at public companies. Pursuant to the directive in SOx to implement the certification requirements, the SEC adopted rules that, among other items, require registrants to disclose the conclusions of the chief executive officer ("CEO") and chief officer financial officer ("CFO") about the effectiveness of the issuer's disclosure controls as of the end of each reporting period. Such controls encompass the policies and procedures designed to ensure that the enterprise records, processes, summarizes and reports within the time periods specified in the SEC's rules and forms any information that the issuer must disclose in the reports that it files or submits under the periodic reporting requirements in the federal securities laws.

SOx also requires an issuer's management to assess the enterprise's internal control over financial reporting annually and to include a report on internal control over financial reporting in the enterprise's annual report. Internal control over financial reporting refers to the process designed by, or under the supervision of, the CEO and CFO and that the company's board of directors implements to provide reasonable assurance regarding the reliability of financial reporting and the preparation of financial statements for external purposes in accordance with GAAP. In addition, the largest public companies must include a separate report from their auditor that expresses an opinion as to whether the company maintained effective internal control over financial reporting.

To prevent or timely detect unauthorized transactions, misappropriation of corporate assets, or fraudulent financial reporting, many enterprises have established hotlines to encourage employees, customers, or others to report suspicious transactions or suspected fraud, often anonymously. Various laws, including SOx and the Dodd-Frank Wall Street Reform and Consumer Protection Act ("Dodd-Frank"), Pub. L. No. 111-203, 124 Stat. 1376 (2010), provide incentives and protections to so-called "whistleblowers," who report fraudulent or otherwise illegal activities. Dodd-Frank, for example, now requires the SEC to pay eligible whistleblowers between ten and thirty percent of any recovery exceeding $1 million, which translates to at least a $100,000 minimum reward if the SEC or another government or self-regulatory agency brings a successful enforcement action and collects more than $1 million.

Lawyers must understand the difference between the role of an auditor and the role of a lawyer. Independence serves as the cornerstone of the auditing profession. In some circumstances, the federal securities laws or auditing standards may require an auditor to inform others, including perhaps the SEC, about illegal acts that may affect an enterprise's financial statements. By comparison, a lawyer generally must remain loyal to a client and represent the client zealously. As described more fully in Chapter VI on pages 399 and 401, *infra*, and pursuant to a direction in Sarbanes-Oxley, new SEC regulations may require a lawyer for a public company to report any illegal acts to the company's chief legal officer and, potentially, to the board of directors.

In Sarbanes-Oxley, Congress overhauled the regulation of auditing of public companies, turning complete control over to a new Public Company Accounting Oversight Board ("PCAOB"), subject to the SEC's watchful eye. As an initial matter, Congress gave the PCAOB the power to establish or adopt auditing standards, including rules governing quality control and independence, for audits of public companies. Previously, the American Institute of Certified Public Accountants ("AICPA") and particularly its Auditing Standards Board ("ASB"), together with custom and practice, had determined *generally accepted auditing standards* ("GAAS") in the United States. Almost immediately, the PCAOB adopted the ASB's existing standards. After that, the PCAOB began adopting its own standards, and the ASB joined an international effort to clarify and harmonize auditing standards, which led to new AICPA standards. Today, the PCAOB standards apply to audits of public companies, while the AICPA's clarified standards specify GAAS for other non-governmental audits. Although usually similar, the different auditing standards sometimes contain important differences, which the text tries to highlight.

In an effort to "further the public interest in the preparation of informative, accurate and independent reports" for investors in public companies, SOx requires all accounting firms that audit public companies to register with the PCAOB, and the Board to inspect those firms regularly. Indeed, if an accounting firm regularly audits more than 100 public companies annually, the PCAOB must conduct an annual inspection. When the PCAOB finds deficiencies, the Board can discipline both the auditing firm and individual auditors, subject to SEC oversight.

Sarbanes-Oxley also directed some important changes in previous auditing practices beyond the requirement that only the audit committees of public companies can hire, fire, and compensate the independent auditor. To address potential impairment of auditor independence resulting from the auditor having lucrative consulting arrangements with auditing clients, which often generated much larger fees than the auditing, SOx prohibits auditors of public companies from providing certain consulting services to audit clients and requires the audit committee to preapprove any permissible non-audit services.

Lawyers should understand the important role that *internal control* plays in both accounting and the law. As an important step in every audit, the auditor must assess an enterprise's internal controls. Before Sarbanes-Oxley, if the enterprise had designed and implemented strong internal control, the auditor could generally rely on the accounting records and could reduce the necessary testing otherwise applied to the data that the accounting system had produced. While auditors for private enterprises can still use internal control testing for this purpose, the federal securities laws now also generally require public companies with a market capitalization of at least $75 million to include an audit report from its independent auditor as to the effectiveness of the company's internal control over financial reporting. As a result, such public companies now undergo a so-called integrated audit in the sense that the same auditor performs examinations of the company's financial statements and internal control over financial reporting at the same time and usually executes the procedures supporting the opinion on the financial statements concurrently with the procedures that involve testing the related control over financial reporting. As in audits before SOx, this control testing usually influences the extent, nature, and timing of the substantive testing related to the financial statements.

If the examination of an enterprise's accounting records satisfies the auditor that the financial statements fairly present the enterprise's financial position, operating results and cash flows in conformity with generally accepted accounting principles, then the auditor will issue an unqualified or "clean" opinion. Similarly, if the examination allows the auditor to obtain reasonable assurance that the enterprise's has maintained effective internal control over financial reporting, the auditor will issue an unqualified opinion. Lawyers should understand that an auditor does not guarantee the accuracy of financial statements or the effectiveness of the enterprise's internal control over financial reporting. Even unqualified opinions provide only "reasonable assurance" that the financial statements fairly present, in all material respects, the enterprise's financial condition, results of operations, and cash flows in conformity with generally accepted accounting principles or effective internal control over financial reporting.

The reach of Sarbanes-Oxley extends well beyond accounting principles, audit committees, certification requirements, internal controls, and auditing standards. Returning to the certification requirement, as to any financial report filed with the SEC, each public company's CEO and CFO must certify that, based on such officer's knowledge, the financial statements and other financial information included in the report fairly present in all material respects the company's financial condition and results of operations. This certification very much parallels an auditor's unqualified opinion, but with one very important exception: the required corroboration does not contain any reference to generally accepted accounting principles, which could qualify the executives' certification. In other words, conformity with GAAP may not satisfy the obligation to provide full and fair disclosure under the federal securities laws. Especially in our post-Enron world, important questions arise when "fairly present" and literal compliance with generally accepted accounting principles do not coincide.

Lawyers should also recognize that many businesses do not need audited financial statements. Nevertheless, these businesses may engage an outside accountant to perform a *review* or a *compilation*. Reviews offer only limited assurance that the financial statements fairly present the enterprise's financial position, operating results and cash flows in conformity with generally accepted accounting principles. Compilations merely report data which management has supplied, with no independent testing or review, so they offer no assurance that the financial statements provide fair representations.

Like lawyers, accountants must examine and interpret various authorities—statutes, regulations, administrative rulings and releases, and official pronouncements of accounting bodies—for answers to accounting and auditing questions. Lawyers should know where and how to find and apply these authorities.

The typical lawsuit involving a failed enterprise's financial statements illustrates the difference between accounting principles and auditing standards. A plaintiff, perhaps either a shareholder who invested in the business or a creditor who lent money to the enterprise based on its financial statements, seeks to recover from the enterprise or its management because the financial statements that management prepared failed to portray properly the enterprise's financial condition and operating results. To collect damages from the independent auditor, the plaintiff must prove that the auditors should have detected and called attention to the deficiencies in the financial statements.

In summary, the enterprise's management and accounting staff prepare financial statements, while an independent auditor examines those statements. Whether assisting management in preparing financial statements or auditing those statements, accountants, like lawyers, must exercise judgment. As a result, lawyers should always consider accounting as an art, rather than a science.

B.   THE NEED FOR ACCOUNTING PRINCIPLES AND AUDITING STANDARDS

Take a look at the following data relating to a hypothetical corporation that J. Evans and C. Lewis formed in 2010 to manufacture and sell souvenir plastic cups for the 2012 Olympic Games in London, England. At the conclusion of the games, Evans and Lewis decided to liquidate the business rather than to design a similar product for the 2016 Olympics in Rio de Janeiro, Brazil. The following summary tabulates the corporation's receipts and expenditures from organization to liquidation:

Receipts		Expenditures		
Original investment	$ 100,000	Organization expenses	$	10,000
		Office rent		60,000
Borrowings	200,000	Purchase of computer		
		equipment		25,000
Payments from		Raw materials		200,000
customers	750,000	Freight charges		10,000
		Salaries and wages		250,000
Damages collected		Utility charges		15,000
on trademark		Insurance premiums		30,000
infringement	50,000	Miscellaneous expenses		25,000
		Interest paid		20,000
Interest received on		Income taxes		100,000
bank deposits	15,000	Dividends		100,000
		Repayment of loans		200,000
Proceeds of sale of		Amount left for		
computer equipment	5,000	shareholders upon		
		liquidation		75,000
Total	$1,120,000	Total		$1,120,000

Because the corporation has ceased operations, sold its assets and paid its liabilities, we can easily determine how well the enterprise performed during its existence and how much the owners received on their investment. If accounting involved only the orderly collection of data and this simple arithmetic exercise, no one would consider accounting as a profession or devote much time to learning about it. Usually, however, bookkeepers and accountants prepare financial statements for an on-going enterprise—indeed, very few people care about the financial statements for a business winding up its affairs. The various parties concerned with an on-going enterprise's welfare and prospects, particularly existing and prospective investors and creditors, need a picture of the business's financial position and results of operations on an interim basis, typically, at least annually. Because enterprises do not just stop to facilitate preparing periodic financial statements, measurement problems abound, and accountants must exercise their professional judgment. Thus, at the end of any period, whether it be a year, a quarter or a month, a business is likely to be in various stages of many different transactions, and the matter of how to reflect, or "account for," these partially completed transactions in the most meaningful fashion poses a host of difficult questions.

Obviously, businesses need ground rules and guidelines for presenting various types of financial data in the financial statements. Some rules are virtually self-evident: for example, businesses should treat similar transactions similarly, so that users of financial statements can compare the financial statements with those for different enterprises and from successive periods for the same business. But with regard to the question on the merits as to what presentation most meaningfully shows any particular type of transaction or item, reasonable minds can disagree. For example, some accountants believe that enterprises should treat costs to develop new products as assets that benefit future accounting periods, while others maintain that businesses should classify these outlays as expenses because the expenditures provide only speculative benefits outside the current accounting period. If accountants recognize two or more acceptable modes, how should an enterprise choose between them? Ground rules and conventions covering these kinds of matters constitute accounting principles, and one may properly ask where these principles come from.

Before pursuing that topic, however, we must consider the question of who bears the ultimate responsibility for a company's financial statements, and what role the accounting profession plays in that process. Historically, the business community has always assumed that management supplies the representations in the financial statements. After all, the managers of the company are intimately acquainted with its affairs, and they are well-positioned to prepare the financial statements. One of the important functions of the financial statements, however, is to report on how the managers have employed the resources entrusted to them, and how successful they have been—their "stewardship," as it is often termed. But of course the managers are not the most objective reporters of their own performance; accordingly, from the beginning the owners of an enterprise who did not manage it often engaged independent accountants to review the records of the managers and verify the financial statements prepared by these "stewards." As the ownership of business enterprises passed into the hands of disparate groups of public investors, it became all the more important to have independent accountants "audit" the managers' reports, to confirm that they were not manipulated to give an unduly rosy hue to the picture, or, even worse, to conceal improprieties.

Hence, the practice developed of having an independent public accountant—the auditor—report on, or in other words, express an opinion as to, whether management's financial statements were consistent with fact and presented in accordance with accounting principles which are generally accepted as sound and appropriate in the circumstances. Notice the two-fold responsibility involved in the auditing process: (1) some check on the underlying facts represented in the financial statements (e.g., physically observing that the company actually has the inventory it shows, and confirming that the company owes no more than the liabilities indicated); and (2) a review of the principles applied in portraying the information (e.g., whether a particular expenditure should be recorded as an expense of the current year). If the auditor finds that the financial statements suffer from a deficiency in any material respect, the auditor will not give an unqualified report, but instead will qualify the opinion or perhaps even give an adverse opinion, depending upon the particular circumstances. After Sarbanes-Oxley, however, the financial statements that a public company files with the SEC must reflect all material adjustments that the auditor identified, so the agency no longer accepts financial statements accompanied by a qualified or adverse opinion.

From management's point of view, any response other than an unqualified opinion constitutes a most unwelcome development, even for a private enterprise. Either an accounting disagreement with the auditor for a public company or a qualified opinion issued to a private enterprise can lower an enterprise's credit rating, discourage potential investors and creditors, attract scrutiny from governmental regulators, generally harm the enterprise's reputation in the business community, and potentially breach covenants in loan agreements and other contracts. Such consequences almost always lead to a lower valuation for the enterprise's securities. Because managers often invest in the enterprises that they manage, management's own stake in the enterprise, along with the desire to retain the support of the enterprise's shareholders, provide powerful incentives to obtain an unqualified opinion. For an illustration of an unqualified opinion, see page 89 of Starbucks' Form 10-K for the fiscal year ended September 30, 2012 in Appendix A at page 785, *infra*.

To instill greater public confidence in the role of the certified public accountants that serve as independent auditors, the various states developed standards of education and experience as minimum qualifications for accountants authorized to perform this function. For example, most states require that a certified public accountant earn an undergraduate degree in accounting, satisfy an experience requirement, and pass a uniform, multi-part exam that the AICPA administers in all fifty states. We can compare the AICPA to the American Bar Association ("ABA") in the sense that both organizations represent national, voluntary membership, trade associations. In general, both the ABA and the AICPA enjoy limited authoritative, but no regulatory, power. Similar to the ABA's role in accrediting law schools whose graduates qualify to take the bar exam in numerous states, the AICPA administers this uniform exam.

The financial scandals involving Enron, WorldCom Inc. ("WorldCom"), Tyco, and other companies during the early 2000s battered investor confidence. The resulting "Enronitis," a crisis in confidence in which investors questioned the integrity of financial corporate statements, erased literally trillions of dollars in value from the stock markets in the United States and around the world. Then SEC Commissioner Paul Atkins estimated that accounting failures had caused the loss of $5 trillion in market value and cost the average U.S. household nearly $60,000. After Enron's collapse, many public companies, including General Electric Co., then the company with the largest market value in the world, and computer giant International Business Machines Corp., voluntarily began providing more detailed financial information and disclosures about their operations. When those efforts appeared inadequate to restore investor confidence and news about the scandal at WorldCom broke, Congress responded by enacting Sarbanes-Oxley, which seeks "[t]o protect investors by improving the accuracy and reliability of corporate disclosures made pursuant to the securities laws, and for other purposes." Accordingly, this complex legislation, which we will discuss at great length, strives to strengthen both the corporate governance of public enterprises and the process of auditing their financial statements. This landmark legislation, however, reached well beyond audit committees and auditors, imposing a number of obligations on the top executives of public companies. By dealing extensively with various aspects of corporate governance that affect financial reporting and disclosure, SOx also required changes by other participants in the financial reporting process by public companies, namely regulators and oversight bodies, accounting and auditing standard setters, gatekeepers, including lawyers, and analysts. Many of the reforms in Sarbanes-Oxley have influenced the best practices among private enterprises and not-for-profit organizations as well.

Investor confidence suffered again during and following the 2008 financial crisis. Auditors in particular attracted criticism that they failed to identify problems at financial institutions and investment banking firms in the years leading up to the financial crisis and issued unqualified opinions just months before numerous companies failed or almost collapsed. Although less focused on financial accounting and auditing, Dodd-Frank nevertheless brought important reforms affecting the financial reporting process. Our financial system depends upon accurate information. Setting aside fraud and potential criminal sanctions, erroneous data also leads to poor allocations of resources that can destroy jobs, cause investment losses, damage reputations, and often lead to lawsuits and insurance claims.

C.   GENERALLY ACCEPTED ACCOUNTING PRINCIPLES

Accountants define "accounting principles" as those guidelines, rules or procedures which enterprises use to prepare financial statements. Accordingly, the term "generally accepted accounting principles" refers to those practices which enjoy substantial support at a particular time. GAAP reflects a consensus of what the accounting profession and financial community consider good accounting practices. Even though GAAP provides rules for many situations, plenty of flexibility remains. Often, these rules offer acceptable alternatives. At other times, the rules do not address a particular situation at all, largely because business transactions evolve more rapidly than accounting principles. For example, *derivatives*, or financial contracts that base their value on some underlying asset, such as bonds or foreign currency, emerged in the 1980s. Accounting for transactions involving derivatives did not fit neatly into existing accounting principles, with the result that financial statements did not contain adequate disclosures about the financial risks underlying derivatives.

Management selects the accounting principles that an enterprise uses to prepare financial statements from the acceptable alternatives. The independent auditor then examines the financial statements seeking reasonable assurance that they fairly present the enterprise's financial condition, results of operation and cash flows in accordance with GAAP.

Today, the auditor of a public company must disclose any concerns about the company's accounting principles, even though they may comply with GAAP, to the audit committee. If the auditor believes that management has selected an accounting principle which does not conform with GAAP, the auditor can qualify an opinion, significantly increasing an enterprise's costs to raise capital.

Despite the consistent use of the word "principles" to describe the current accounting regime reflected in GAAP, standard setters in the United States have relied historically upon rather specific rules to establish and define the governing standards. Although the specific, detailed provisions that result from this approach can give helpful guidance, that very detail can allow enterprises to structure transactions to circumvent a rule's intent. In contrast, other countries and, as we shall see, the body that establishes international accounting standards have adopted an approach that articulates broad principles and policies, and relies more on professional judgment to determine how an enterprise should present any particular transaction. Commentators generally refer to the latter approach as "principles-based," describing the U.S. system as "rules-based." In the aftermath of Enron's financial engineering, Sarbanes-Oxley directed the SEC to conduct a study to determine whether the financial reporting system in the United States should switch to a principles-based standard-setting process and to submit a report to Congress within one year.

In 2003, the SEC's staff issued the mandated report, which concluded that "objectives-oriented" standard setting offered the best approach to establishing accounting standards. The report observed that imperfections arise when standard setters use either a rules-based or principles-only basis to establish accounting principles. The SEC staff warned that exceptions, bright-line tests, and internal inconsistencies can cause financial reporting under a rules-based system to degenerate into "an act of compliance rather than an act of communication." At the other extreme, principles alone typically offer insufficient guidance to financial statement preparers and auditors. The significant judgment necessary to apply the broad standards to specific transactions and events can reduce comparability among enterprises and give rise to litigation with both regulators and private plaintiffs.

The SEC's staff described an optimal standard as a concise statement of substantive accounting principle, derived from a coherent conceptual framework of financial reporting. The statement should include the accounting objective, provide sufficient detail and structure so that users can apply the standard on a consistent basis, and avoid exceptions and percentage tests that might allow financial engineers to achieve technical compliance, while evading the standard's intent. The report opined that neither generally accepted accounting principles in the United States nor international accounting standards, as then comprised, implemented "objectives-oriented" standards. The report noted, however, that standard setters in the United States had already begun the shift to objectives-oriented standard setting. OFFICE OF THE CHIEF ACCOUNTANT & OFFICE OF ECON. ANALYSIS, U.S. SEC. & EXCH. COMM'N, STUDY PURSUANT TO SECTION 108(d) OF THE SARBANES-OXLEY ACT OF 2002 ON

THE ADOPTION BY THE UNITED STATES REPORTING SYSTEM OF A PRINCIPLES-BASED ACCOUNTING SYSTEM (July 25, 2003), *available at* http://www.sec.gov/news/studies/principlesbasedstand.htm.

1. THE ESTABLISHMENT OF ACCOUNTING PRINCIPLES

As to public companies, Congress long ago gave the SEC the authority under the federal securities laws to establish accounting principles for enterprises which fall within its jurisdiction. In exercising this authority, the SEC historically deferred to the private sector to establish accounting principles, but occasionally exercises its power to prescribe accounting methods. Sarbanes-Oxley explicitly gave the SEC discretion to recognize a separate board in the private sector as the institution designated to establish accounting principles for federal securities law purposes. As Congress contemplated, the SEC has designated the Financial Accounting Standards Board ("FASB") for that role, but the requirement that FASB report to the SEC annually indicates that the latter retains ultimate authority over accounting principles for public companies. In addition, listing standards at stock exchanges increasingly influence corporate governance at public companies and could shape accounting principles and disclosure policies in the future. Because most businesses do not fall within the SEC's jurisdiction, but may nevertheless need to provide audited financial statements to investors, banks, or other lenders, we first review the development of accounting principles in the private sector, which historically is where the process began, but where leadership has shifted from the accounting professor to the private sector more broadly.

a. THE PRIVATE SECTOR

The private accounting profession's first formal efforts to develop accounting principles occurred in 1939, when the AICPA created two committees, the Committee on Accounting Procedure ("CAP") and the Committee on Accounting Terminology ("CAT"). The Institute asked CAP to determine the proper accounting approach or approaches in particular areas of concern. At the same time, the Institute invited CAT to submit recommendations regarding the definition of certain accounting terms and their subsequent use in financial statements. The two committees published their views in the form of Accounting Research Bulletins ("ARBs") which the Institute widely circulated. At that time, however, these pronouncements did not bind the profession, much less anyone else. Each ARB bore the concluding comment that "the authority of the bulletins rests upon the general acceptability of opinions so reached." While promulgations from subsequent principle-setting groups have modified most of these early statements, some remain incorporated in U.S. GAAP today.

Although the ARBs represented a useful start, they did not carry great weight in the profession. Because no significant amount of research supported the ARBs, they simply represented a consensus of committee members and reflected the members' experiences and viewpoints. As a result, the ARBs frequently approved alternative practices or otherwise equivocated and often reflected the compromises on conclusions and wording necessary to obtain the required two-thirds vote of the committee members.

In an effort to give more effective leadership in the determination of accounting principles, the AICPA established the Accounting Principles Board ("APB") in 1959. The APB's membership included AICPA members, mostly in public practice, with representatives from each of the largest accounting firms, at that time the "Big Eight," a number of smaller firms and academia. Because a greatly expanded research capacity supported the APB, the Board considered and reached some conclusions on basic concepts and accounting principles. The Board also tried to resolve the more important problem areas involving accounting practices and financial reporting in an attempt "to narrow the areas of difference and inconsistency in practice" in as expeditious a manner as practicable. By the time the AICPA dissolved the APB in 1973, the Board had issued thirty-one "Opinions" and four "Statements," which defined and narrowed the acceptable perimeters of accounting methodology. In these materials, we will sometimes refer to APB Opinions as "APB Opinion No. —."

Despite the added research dimension, the APB suffered from some of the same deficiencies which marked its predecessor. The compromises needed to secure the required two-thirds vote of the members often led to results that failed to satisfy anyone and sometimes produced long delays in reaching any conclusion. A continuing disquiet about whether the practicing members could sufficiently divorce themselves from their major clients' desires on various issues also plagued the APB.

In an effort to improve the process, in 1971 the AICPA appointed a Committee on the Establishment of Accounting Principles. Pursuant to that committee's recommendations, the accounting profession created the Financial Accounting Standards Board in 1972 as a new body to replace the APB as the organization responsible for determining and promulgating accounting principles.

FASB differs structurally from the CAP and the APB in one major respect: FASB exists independently from the AICPA. Except on technical, standard-setting matters, an independent charitable corporation, the Financial Accounting Foundation ("FAF"), oversees FASB. FAF's trustees select FASB's seven full-time members to serve staggered terms, which usually last five years. In the trustees' judgment, FASB's members shall possess "knowledge of and experience in investing, accounting, finance, business, accounting education and research and a concern for the investor and the public interest in matters of investing, financial accounting and reporting." To assure independence, FASB's members must terminate all other employment ties in exchange for a generous salary, which amounted to more than $820,000 for the chairman and $646,000 for the other board members in 2012.

The FAF's trustees also appoint, from the sponsoring organizations' various constituencies, approximately thirty members of the Financial

Accounting Standards Advisory Council ("FASAC"). FASAC functions as an advisory body to FASB. In this capacity, FASAC meets quarterly to evaluate and discuss FASB's preliminary positions on pending projects and to counsel FASB about priorities for pending and proposed projects. Following the accounting scandals in the late 1990s, FASB established the now defunct User Advisory Council ("UAC") in 2002 to increase participation by securities analysts and other users of financial statements, such as mutual funds, commercial banks, other institutional investors, and rating agencies, in the accounting standard-setting process. Today, the Investor Advisory Committee facilitates user participation. In 2012, the FAF established the Private Company Council ("PCC") to improve the process that sets accounting standards that potentially apply to the nation's 28 million private firms. For years, private companies have complained that GAAP imposes overly burdensome accounting rules and disclosure requirements.

Although FAF and FASB historically relied upon contributions and sales of publications to fund their operations, SOx section 109 included a mechanism that requires issuers to pay annual support fees to fund FASB's operations and now that the SEC has designated FASB as the private standard-setting body that may establish " 'generally accepted' accounting principles" for federal securities law purposes.

FASB operates under two basic premises in establishing financial accounting standards. First, the Board attempts to respond to the needs and viewpoints of the entire economic community, not just the public accounting profession. Second, FASB strives to operate in full public view through a "due process" system that gives interested persons ample opportunity to share their views. This due process, however, can significantly enlarge the time necessary to issue pronouncements. For example, after twelve years FASB and IASB completed a joint project on revenue recognition in 2014.

Under FASB's due process procedures, the Board works from a public agenda which its constituencies help to establish, employs a technical staff to research and analyze various issues and solutions, issues detailed discussion memoranda which attempt to focus issues under the Board's consideration, publishes exposure drafts of contemplated pronouncements, conducts public hearings, and promulgates accounting standards only after a majority of the seven FASB members approve the pronouncement. FASB's due process procedures enable financial statement preparers, auditors, financial statement users, government officials, academics and members of the general public to participate in establishing accounting principles.

Over the years, FASB has adopted a "problem-approach" towards setting accounting standards. Areas and issues where disparities already exist in accounting treatments usually comprise the Board's agenda. FASB has only rarely acted before a controversy or dispute arises. In 1984, FASB created the Emerging Issues Task Force ("EITF") to promulgate timely guidance within existing GAAP to reduce diversity in practice arising from narrow issues. Today, EITF seeks to assist FASB in improving financial reporting by timely identifying, discussing, and resolving financial accounting issues. The task force's members include technical experts from the four largest public accounting firms, Deloitte & Touche LLP, Ernst & Young LLP, KPMG LLP, and PricewaterhouseCoopers LLP (collectively, the "Big Four" or "Final Four"); representatives from other public accounting firms; individuals that the Financial Executives Institute, the Institute of Management Accountants and the Business Roundtable nominate to represent enterprises that prepare financial statements; two investors or other users of financial statements; and FASB's Technical Director, who serves as chair. In addition, the SEC's Chief Accountant or Deputy Chief Accountant regularly attends meetings as an observer with the right to speak during the task force's deliberations, which try to reach a consensus. A designate from IASB and the chairman of the AICPA's FinRec, the Institute's senior technical committee on financial accounting and reporting matters, enjoy similar privileges. FASB members also attend meetings and participate in the discussion.

If EITF can reach a consensus, which the rules treat as occurring when no more than three of the task force's voting members present at the meeting object to a proposed position on the issue, FASB exposes the consensus for public comment. After considering the public comments, FASB can ratify the consensus position, which leads to an ASU that incorporates the consensus into the FASB ASC. EITF's failure to reach a consensus on an issue, or negative feedback on an consensus for exposure, may suggest that FASB should add the issue to its agenda. Although FASB members do not vote at Task Force meetings, a majority of FASB must approve all consensus positions.

In 1973, the AICPA adopted Rule 203 in its Code of Professional Conduct. Rule 203 provides that, subject to a rare exception, an independent auditor cannot issue an unqualified opinion if the financial statements contain any material departure from an accounting principle promulgated by the body that the AICPA Council, the Institute's governing body, designated to establish such principles—for our purposes, currently FASB and, at least until May 2016, the International Accounting Standards Board ("IASB"). Auditors have almost never asserted the exception, which applies only if unusual circumstances would otherwise cause misleading financial statements.

Although the AICPA can admonish or expel a member for violating the Code of Professional Conduct, the Institute cannot bar a person from practicing accounting because only state accountancy boards can grant or revoke an accountant's license to practice. Nevertheless, potential liability for misrepresentation, fraud, or other legally recognizable claims deters an auditor from issuing an unqualified opinion if the financial statements contain a material departure from GAAP.

In 2009, FASB adopted the FASB Accounting Standards Codification™ (the "Codification" or "ASC"). For financial statements issued for interim and annual periods ending after September 15, 2009, the Codification supersedes all nongrandfathered, non-SEC accounting and reporting standards for nongovernmental entities. Just as the United States Code organizes federal legislation, the Codification assembles and distills thousands of pages in promulgations from FASB, the AICPA, and the SEC. Consequently, the

Codification marks a major milestone in the development of accounting principles in the United States.

Recall that even though the SEC has designated FASB as the standard setter, public companies must still follow SEC disclosure requirements. For this reason, the Codification also includes separate sections containing guidance from the SEC related to issues within the basic financial statements. These SEC materials carry the designation "S" before the applicable section number, so that users can distinguish between the SEC requirements and other authoritative GAAP. To date, the SEC has yet to ratify these materials. The Codification does not replace or affect how the SEC or the SEC staff issues or updates SEC content. Please also keep in mind that the SEC staff content does not constitute Commission approved rules or interpretations. Nevertheless, the Codification has simplified accounting research, improved the accessibility and usability of the entire body of literature relevant to each topic, and provided real-time updates as the FASB releases new standards. Moving forward, the Codification seems likely to assist FASB and other standard setters in the efforts to converge accounting standards worldwide.

When changing the content in the Codification, FASB now issues a transient document, called an Accounting Standards Update ("ASU"), regardless of which standard setter issued the original guidance on the particular topic. In addition, the Board issues ASUs both for amendments to the SEC content in the Codification and for editorial changes. Because the SEC and its staff plan to continue to use existing SEC procedures to communicate new or revised SEC content, however, users should expect delays between SEC changes and corresponding updates to the Codification. In all situations, FASB updates the Codification concurrently with an ASU's release, presents current and transitional text together to allow access to all relevant content in the same location, and identifies any new guidance as "Pending Text" until the passage of time means that the prior guidance no longer applies.

Each ASU summarizes the key conclusions of the project that led to the update, details the specific amendments to the Codification, and explains the basis for the Board's decisions. The Board will not amend ASUs; it will only amend the FASB Codification. Although each ASU updates the Codification, the FASB does not consider these updates authoritative in their own right. Nevertheless, the Board numbers these updates sequentially by year, such as 2014-01.

Even before the financial crisis, FASB spent a steadily increasing portion of its time on international accounting issues and convergence projects with the IASB in an effort to achieve a single set of high quality, global accounting standards. Dating at least back to a joint meeting with IASB during 2002 in Norwalk, Connecticut, which gave rise to the so-called "Norwalk Agreement," FASB has acknowledged its commitment to, and worked toward, the goal of developing a common set of high-quality, global accounting standards, which led to converged standards in areas including business combinations and revenue recognition. To date, however, the boards have been unable to find a converged approach to their ongoing joint projects on financial instruments, leases, and insurance.

b.   THE SECURITIES AND EXCHANGE COMMISSION

The enactment of the Securities Act of 1933 (the "1933 Act") and the Securities Exchange Act of 1934 (the "1934 Act") tremendously boosted the significance of accounting within the business community. Congress enacted those laws in response to the 1929 stock market crash and sought to ensure that the investing public could rely on financial statements, particularly those of companies whose stocks were traded in the nation's securities markets. The 1934 Act created the SEC and gave the Commission the responsibility to oversee the reporting requirements for companies subject to its jurisdiction.

The federal securities laws generally require any *issuer*, another name for a business desiring to offer securities to the public, to file a registration statement, including the firm's most recent financial statements, with the SEC. If the SEC finds a registration statement deficient or misleading after notice and hearing, the agency can issue a "stop order" that halts the sale of any securities under the registration statement. In addition, periodic reporting requirements apply to *registrants*. Registrants include most of the country's largest corporations, specifically those companies whose shares are listed on a national securities exchange, such as NYSE or NASDAQ. Following the Jumpstart Our Business Startups Act of 2012 (the "JOBS Act"), the term "registrant" now includes only those entities with (1) total assets exceeding $10 million on the last day of their fiscal years *and* (2) a class of equity securities, other than an exempted security, owned by at least either (a) 2,000 persons or (b) 500 persons who do not qualify as "accredited investors" as the SEC defines. For banks and bank holding companies, only the 2,000 person threshold applies. In addition, the legislation excludes from the shareholder threshold calculations any person who received the securities pursuant to an employee compensation plan in a transaction exempt from the registration requirements under the federal securities laws. Although the provisions apply immediately, the SEC must adopt conforming rules and safe harbor provisions. (Prior to the JOBS Act, the federal securities laws required a company that owned more than $10 million in assets on the last day of its fiscal year and had a class of nonexempted securities held of record by 500 or more persons to register the class of securities and to satisfy periodic reporting requirements.) The JOBS Act also allows banks and bank holding companies to deregister more easily, permitting them to do so if the number of holders of all classes of securities drops below 1,200, compared to the previous 300-shareholder threshold, which continues to apply to all other registrants. Deregistration avoids the costs of filing quarterly and annual financial reports, which can reach $200,000 a year.

Different requirements apply to registrants depending upon whether the SEC's rules classify the enterprise as a non-accelerated filer, accelerated filer, large accelerated filer, or smaller reporting company. *Non-accelerated filer* serves as the default category. A registrant becomes an *accelerated filer* when it (1) has been subject to the SEC's periodic reporting requirements for at least twelve months and has filed one annual report and (2) reaches a "public float" that equals or exceeds $75 million. "Public float" means the worldwide market value of outstanding voting and non-voting common equity that non-affiliates own. Only the largest reporting companies, those accelerated filers with a public float of at least $700 million, including Starbucks, become *large accelerated filers*. The checked box towards the bottom of the cover page of Starbucks' Form 10-K for the fiscal year ended September 20, 2012, which appears in Appendix A on page 695, *infra*, indicates that Starbucks filed that annual report as a large accelerated filer.

A registrant generally can qualify as a *smaller reporting company*, once known as a "small business issuer," which allows the enterprise to take advantage of scaled disclosure requirements that reflect the characteristics and needs of smaller companies and their investors, if it (1) has a common equity public float that does not equal or exceed $75 million or (2) cannot calculate its public float and has annual revenue that does not equal or exceed $50 million. The SEC's rules, however, preclude certain enterprises, such as majority-owned subsidiaries of an ineligible parent, investment companies, including business development companies, and asset-based issuers, from qualifying as smaller reporting companies.

The JOBS Act created a new designation, *emerging growth company* ("EGC"), which applies to certain enterprises with less than $1 billion in total annual gross revenues during their most recently completed fiscal year and that did not sell equity securities publicly on or before December 8, 2011. The legislation offers these companies certain accommodations relating to their initial public offerings ("IPOs") of equity securities and subsequent reporting obligations. Once within the category, an enterprise remains an EGC until the earliest of: (1) the last day of its fiscal year during which it had total annual gross revenues of at least $1 billion; (2) the last day of its fiscal year following the fifth anniversary of the date of its IPO; (3) the date of which it has, during the previous three-year period, issued more than $1 billion in nonconvertible debt; or (4) the date it becomes a large accelerated filer.

Non-accelerated filers, including smaller reporting companies, must submit a quarterly report, known as Form 10-Q and often referred to simply as a "10-Q," within forty-five days after the end of a fiscal quarter. These registrants must also file an annual report on Form 10-K, usually called simply a "10-K," within ninety days after the end of a fiscal year. Shorter deadlines apply to both accelerated filers and large accelerated filers. Accelerated filers must submit their quarterly reports within forty days and their annual reports within seventy-five days after the end of the relevant fiscal period. Large accelerated filers have only sixty days after the end of their fiscal years to file their annual reports.

We can summarize the current filing deadlines as follows:

Type of filer	Form 10-K annual reports	Form 10-Q quarterly reports
Large accelerated filer	60 days	40 days
Accelerated filer	75 days	40 days
Non-accelerated filer and smaller reporting company	90 days	45 days

In 2008, the SEC adopted a new system of disclosure rules for smaller companies filing periodic reports. Those rules, which served as a forerunner to various provisions for emerging growth companies in the JOBS Act, contain scaled requirements to reflect the characteristics and needs of smaller companies and their investors. Unless further loosened in the JOBS Act, the scaled requirements apply to "smaller reporting companies," which generally and primarily means "non-accelerated filers."

In addition to the quarterly and annual filings, registrants must file a current report, denominated a Form 8-K, to report certain significant events, such as earnings releases or similar announcements, generally within four business days following the event.

Under the federal securities statutes, the SEC can prescribe accounting rules for those financial statements that enterprises must include in their public filings with the Commission, and perhaps as to all financial statements for those businesses. More specifically, SOx section 108 allows the SEC to recognize as "generally accepted" for purposes of the federal securities laws any accounting principles established by a private standard setting body that meets certain criteria. In 2003, the SEC determined that FASB, and its parent organization, the FAF, satisfied those criteria and recognized FASB's financial accounting and reporting standards as generally accepted for purposes of the federal securities law. The SEC's statement of policy stated that the agency would continue to monitor FASB's procedures, qualifications, capabilities, activities, and results. Commission Statement of Policy Reaffirming the Status of FASB as a Designated Private-Sector Standard Setter, Financial Reporting Release No. 70, 68 Fed. Reg. 23,333-01 (May 1, 2003).

In the most recent illustration of the SEC's ability to set accounting standards for public companies, in 2005 the agency overruled FASB and allowed public companies an additional six months to comply with then-new Board rule that still requires corporations to treat the fair value of stock options as an expense. The SEC's action came after FASB had already granted one six-month extension, but had rejected the SEC's request for an additional six-month delay.

The federal securities laws also give the SEC the authority to approve listing standards at the national securities exchanges, meaning the rules and criteria that publicly traded enterprises must observe or jeopardize losing their listing on the exchange. SOx section 301 directed the SEC to prescribe rules that prohibit the national securities exchanges and national securities associations, including NYSE and NASDAQ, from listing any issuer that does not satisfy certain standards relating to its audit committee, a subset of its board of directors that must oversee both the accounting and financial reporting processes and the audits of an issuer's financial statements. The listing standards require listed companies to give their audit committees direct responsibility to hire, compensate, oversee, and fire the independent auditor. In addition, Dodd-Frank section 954 requires the SEC to issue rules directing the national securities exchanges to bar from listing any issuer that does not develop, disclose, and implement a so-called "clawback" policy. Such a policy would require any current or former executive officer who received incentive-based compensation, such as a bonus on stock options, based on erroneous financial information required under any federal securities law in the three-year period before an accounting restatement, to repay the excess over what the issuer would have paid under the restatement. By mid-2014, the SEC had neither issued, nor proposed, the implementing regulations, and Dodd-Frank does not impose any deadline for any action on the agency. Subject to SEC oversight, the various national stock exchanges could potentially use these listing standards to require certain accounting principles, to impose various disclosure policies, or to observe certain corporate governance standards.

By regulation, the SEC imposes numerous reporting and disclosure requirements on registrants. Regulation S–X contains lengthy and detailed requirements prescribing the specific items which registrants must disclose or address in financial statements that they file with the Commission. Regulation S–K provides standard instructions for filing forms under the 1933 Act and the 1934 Act, including directions related to certain financial information that those forms require. In addition, over the years the SEC has issued many types of administrative releases relating to accounting topics, including particularly Accounting Series Releases ("ASRs"), which expressed the opinions of the Commission and its Chief Accountant, who probably qualifies as the most influential accountant in the world, regarding various accounting and financial reporting issues. By 1982, when the SEC promulgated the Codification of Financial Reporting Policies (the "CFRP") to consolidate the accounting positions in the ASRs, the agency had issued more than 300 ASRs. The SEC also announced that it would issue Financial Reporting Releases ("FRRs") to update the CFRP, mostly to provide guidance in areas the private sector had failed to address. As of December 31, 2013, the SEC had issued eighty-three FRRs, but none since 2010.

Since 1975, the SEC has also published informal guidance concerning accounting matters. As one of twenty-two offices in the SEC, the Office of the Chief Accountant helps to develop, subject to Commission approval, policy and rules on accounting and auditing issues relating to the federal securities laws. Responsibility for recommending administrative proceedings relating to such matters and for assisting in such proceedings also rests with the Office of the Chief Accountant, which the Chief Accountant oversees. The Division of Corporation Finance ("CorpFin"), probably the most influential of the SEC's five divisions on accounting issues, strives to ensure that the financial information which registrants present to the public complies with the SEC's rules and regulations. In particular, CorpFin reviews the reports that public companies file with the Commission. The staff of CorpFin also posts and periodically updates several other sources of information about the statutes, rules and regulations that the Division administers, some of which involve accounting issues. To access this guidance, first select the "Divisions" dropdown at the top of the SEC's home page, http://www.sec.gov, and then select the "Corporation Finance" link.

In 1975, the SEC announced a series of Staff Accounting Bulletins ("SABs") to present interpretations and practices that the Chief Accountant and CorpFin follow in reviewing financial statements and administering the disclosure requirements in the federal securities laws. Though SABs do not carry the SEC's official approval, they often provide useful guidance. Today, the SEC incorporates all subsequently issued SABs into the Codification of Staff Accounting Bulletins by adding questions and staff interpretations under topic headings.

The SEC also exerts significant influence over the financial statements which registrants do not file with the Commission, notably the annual report which corporations customarily send to shareholders. Under federal securities laws, certain rules apply to registrants that solicit proxies. In particular, registrants that solicit proxies in connection with an annual meeting at which the shareholders will elect directors must send, either previously or concurrently, an annual report that meets detailed requirements. These proxy rules also require registrants to send substantially equivalent information to security holders even if the registrant does not solicit proxies.

Immediately after the original revelations in 2002 that WorldCom had engaged in a staggering $3.8 billion fraud, an amount which the company subsequently pegged at $11 billion, the SEC issued an order requiring the senior officers of more than 900 of the nation's largest public companies to file sworn statements regarding the accuracy of their company's financial statements. Congress codified similar duties in Sarbanes-Oxley. SOx section 302 directed the SEC to issue rules that require a registrant's chief executive and financial officers to certify in each quarterly and annual report filed with the SEC that, among other things, based on such officer's knowledge the report does not contain any material misrepresentations or omissions and financial statements and other financial information included in the report fairly present in all material respects the entity's financial condition and results of operations. SOx section 906 also added a provision containing a separate certification requirement that creates new criminal penalties for a knowing or willful false certification. The SEC quickly adopted rules to implement these provisions. For Starbucks' Form 10-K for the year ended September 30, 2012, you can find certifications, dated November 16, 2012, by Howard Schultz, chairman, president and chief executive officer, and Troy Alstead, chief financial officer and chief administrative officer, respectively, as Exhibits 31.1, 31.2, and 32. These exhibits appear in Appendix A on pages 803-05, *infra*.

Sarbanes-Oxley also directed the SEC to review the periodic disclosures and financial statements of all public companies at least once every three years. In recent years, the SEC has conducted about 5,000 reviews each year on the approximately 9,000 companies that currently report to the SEC. In 2005, the SEC began posting staff comment letters and responses related to disclosure filings made after August 1, 2004 on the agency's website in the EDGAR database.

The SEC's Division of Enforcement also influences the application of accounting standards. The agency's enforcement staff conducts investigations into possible violations of the federal securities laws, including accounting fraud, and prosecutes the Commission's administrative proceedings as well as the agency's civil suits in the federal courts. We will read about both administrative proceedings and civil suits in later chapters. When the SEC announced the CFRP and the FRRs, the Commission also published the first in a series of Accounting and Auditing Enforcement Releases ("AAERs") which address administrative or enforcement matters only. As of December 31, 2013, the SEC had published more than 3,500 AAERs, including ninety during 2013, down significantly from a record 240 in 2002.

Although the SEC has long called for the development of global accounting standards, the Commission seems unlikely to require domestic companies to use international financial reporting standards ("IFRS") any time soon. Under the Administrative Procedure Act, the SEC must give formal notice and allow a period for public comment before adopting international accounting principles. In 2007, the SEC issued final rules that allow foreign private issuers to use IFRS to prepare the financial statements required under the federal securities laws without any reconciliation to U.S. GAAP. In 2008, the SEC published a proposed "roadmap" for public companies to transition to IFRS for public filings. The credit crisis, the Madoff scandal, the Congressional mandates in Dodd-Frank and the JOBS Act, however, have diverted the SEC's focus away from global accounting principles, especially when combined, first with an inadequate budget, and then sequestration.

c. CONGRESS

Congress created the federal securities laws and the SEC. Because Congress has granted the SEC the power to designate a private standard setter to establish accounting principles recognized as "generally accepted" for purposes of the federal securities law and to prescribe accounting principles, Congress also retains, at least implicitly, the right to legislate on accounting principles and standards that implicate interstate commerce or the federal securities exchanges. Even though Congress has only rarely, if ever, mandated any specific accounting treatment, Congress has used its legislative power to influence the SEC, FASB, AICPA, and the financial community.

Since the publication of the concise fourth edition, Congress twice turned its attention to the controversy surrounding the role of fair value accounting in the credit crisis. In the so-called "bailout bill," the Emergency Economic Stabilization Act of 2008, Congress specifically authorized the SEC "to suspend, by rule, regulation, or order," FASB's controversial promulgation on fair value accounting "for any issuer . . . or with respect to any class or category of transaction" if necessary or appropriate in the public interest and consistent with the protection of investors. The legislation also directed the SEC, in consultation with Board of Governors of the Federal Reserve System and the Secretary of the Treasury, to study mark-to-market accounting standards applicable to financial institutions and to submit a report to Congress within ninety days. At a minimum, the study needed to consider the effects of the accounting standards on a financial institution's balance sheet; the impacts of such accounting on bank failures in 2008; the impact of such standards on the quality of financial information available to investors; the process that FASB used to develop accounting standards; the advisability and feasibility of modifications to such standards; and alternative accounting standards.

During a Congressional hearing in 2009, bipartisan pressure from members of the House Financial Services Subcommittee on Capital Markets, Insurance, and Government Sponsored Entities essentially forced FASB to issue additional guidance on inactive markets and impairments on an accelerated basis during the following month to avoid Congressional intervention. The events caused some observers to question FASB's continued independence and credibility. *The Wall Street Journal* published a front-page article reporting that a group of thirty-one financial firms and trade groups marshalled a multimillion-dollar lobbying campaign, formed the "Fair Value Coalition" to change the accounting rules, and then directed $286,000 in campaign contributions to thirty-three legislators on the House Financial Services Committee. *See* Susan Pulliam & Tom McGinty, *Congress Helped Banks Defang Key Rule*, WALL ST. J., June 3, 2009, at A1. These developments again raised important questions about the extent to which Congress should participate in the establishment of specific accounting rules.

Likely as no surprise, Dodd-Frank contained provisions on accounting and auditing issues. Among other reforms, the legislation established the Financial Stability Oversight Council and empowered it to review and, as appropriate, submit comments to the SEC and any standard-setting body with respect to an existing or proposed accounting principle, standard, or procedure. Earlier in the legislative process, the House Financial Services Committee approved an amendment containing that provision rather than alternative language which would have allowed future systemic risk regulators to override FASB rules.

The most recent Congressional reach into accounting rules occurred in the JOBS Act, which restricts FASB's ability to set effective dates for new accounting standards. When promulgating new accounting standards in recent years, FASB has often established different effective dates for public and non-public enterprises in an effort to give the latter additional time to transition to the new standard. Pursuant to the JOBS Act, an EGC can now elect not to comply with new or revised financial accounting standards that apply to public companies until the standards become mandatory for private companies.

d. INTERNATIONAL ACCOUNTING STANDARDS

In today's global economy, investors, businesses and their lawyers need to understand local financial accounting and reporting practices. Different taxation systems, economic conditions, political processes and cultural traditions contribute to a diversity in accounting practices between nations in matters such as inventory valuation, depreciation, consolidations, and disclosure requirements. To illustrate, as we saw in Chapter I, the accounting standards in the United States generally follow the historical cost principle to value assets. In many foreign countries, particularly nations experiencing high inflationary rates, businesses use current values to record their assets. As another example, German and Japanese businesses have traditionally turned to banks rather than the equity markets for financing. Accordingly, the needs of creditors, rather than investors, have disproportionately influenced the financial reporting in those countries, at least relative to the United States and the United Kingdom, where the accounting profession largely developed the financial reporting systems. By comparison, tax reporting and creditor concerns influenced the laws that established very different accounting systems in various European countries and Japan.

The international business community desires globally accepted accounting practices to facilitate the flow of capital between markets. Multinational enterprises around the world, especially in Germany, Switzerland and other European countries, increasingly seek to raise capital across borders and to list their securities on more than one stock market. At the same time, the New York Stock Exchange and exchanges in Canada, Europe, London and Japan have been pressing for international accounting rules.

Serious efforts to harmonize accounting standards world-wide got started in 1973, when an agreement among professional accountancy bodies from Australia, Canada, France, Germany, Japan, Mexico, the Netherlands, the United Kingdom and Ireland, and the United States established the International Accounting Standards Committee ("IASC"). By 1983 IASC's members included every professional accountancy body that belonged to the International Federation of Accountants ("IFAC"). Between 1973 and 1987 the IASC's board issued some twenty-six accounting standards, but most of them were relatively loose; permitting optional treatment, and so they were adopted mainly in developing countries which had no accounting standards of their own. Ironically, the IASC standards were largely ignored by the founder countries, virtually all of which by then had developed their own programs for issuing accounting standards, which they viewed as superior to those of the IASC. In 1988, however, the IASC, with strong support from the International Organization of Securities Commissions ("IOSCO"), embarked on a program of reviewing its earlier standards to eliminate most of the optional treatments, and to enhance the required disclosures plus specify in greater detail how each standard was to be interpreted. In 1995, the IASC and IOSCO agreed to develop and endorse international accounting standards so that businesses could raise capital across borders.

By 1999, the IASC had reviewed most of its earlier standards, and even issued some new ones in particularly troublesome areas. IOSCO endorsed IASC's standards in 2000, although IOSCO did permit each country's securities regulators to impose additional requirements, such as additional disclosure, more specific interpretations of the standards, and reconciliation of IASC-based financial statements with the country's own GAAP.

Meanwhile, the SEC was pressing the IASC to restructure itself into a more independent body, along the lines of the FASB, to earn legitimacy in the eyes of the world's capital markets. Until this point, critics often referred to the core standards as "IASC Lite" or "FASB Lite." In 2000, IASC's members, the professional accountancy bodies in more than 100 countries, adopted a new constitution that restructured IASC into an independent foundation that paralleled the FAF on an international level. Following additional constitutional amendments, governance of the IFRS Foundation ("IFRSF"), which until 2010 was known as the International Accounting Standards Committee Foundation ("IASCF"), rests with two main bodies, the Trustees and the Monitoring Board. In addition to continuing the standard-setting responsibilities of IASB, which was previously known as IASC, the 2000 constitution also created both the IFRS Interpretations Committee ("IFRSIC") and the IFRS Advisory Council ("IFRSAC"), which until 2010, were known as the International Financial Reporting Interpretation Committee ("IFRIC") and the Standards Advisory Council ("IASB-SAC").

In 2002, the European Union ("EU") approved a regulation requiring all listed companies in the EU, currently about 8,000 in all, to comply with IFRS in preparing consolidated financial statements for each fiscal year beginning in or after 2005. By 2008, more than 100 countries required or permitted IFRS, or a variant thereof. Since 2007, Brazil, Canada, India, Japan, Korea, Mexico, and Russia all adopted similar requirements or announced plans to adopt or converge with IFRS.

In 2009, amid calls to enhance the foundation's governance because IASB lacked any link to an elected body or a body linked to national authorities responsible for overseeing compliance with IFRS, the Trustees completed the first phase of their periodic review of the organization's structure and amended the constitution to create a Monitoring Board over the Trustees to enhance the foundation's public accountability. This change created formal interaction between national authorities responsible for establishing or recognizing accounting standards for listed companies and the IFRSF. The Monitoring Board includes leaders from the Emerging Markets and Technical Committees of IOSCO, the European Commission ("EC"), the Japan Financial Services Agency, and the SEC. In addition, the Basel Committee on Banking Supervision sits as a formal observer at Monitoring Board meetings. The Monitoring Board meets with the Trustees at least once a year, or more often if necessary, and approves the appointment or reappointment of Trustees, who serve staggered, three-year terms, appoint the members of IASB, raise the more than $25 million needed each year to fund the organization's operations, and exercise general oversight over the foundation's operations. After the 2010 constitutional amendments, three-fourths of the Trustees can waive IASB's normal due process requirements.

The 2009 amendments to the IFRSF's constitution expanded IASB from fourteen to sixteen members. Guidelines ensure a broad international basis for membership. IASB holds sole responsibility for setting accounting standards. In an effort to balance perspectives and experience, the constitution directs the Trustees to select Board members so that as a group the Board provides an appropriate mix of individuals with recent and practical experience as auditors, preparers, users, and academics. The constitution, however, designates professional competence and practical experience as the main qualifications for membership on the Board.

In an effort to secure a more streamlined and effective dialogue between the IASB and the accounting standard setters around the world, the IFRSF established the Accounting Standards Advisory Forum ("ASAF") in 2013 to provide technical advice and feedback to the IASB and to support the IFRSF in achieving its objectives. The forum, which the IASB chairs, brings together geographically balanced representatives from twelve national accounting standard setters and regional bodies that share an interest in financial reporting. After a nomination process, in 2013 the Trustees announced the forum's initial members, which include the FASB. The Trustees have agreed to review the ASAF and its membership after two years.

Two changes in accounting standard-setting across the globe precipitated the ASAF's creation. First, the number of countries adopting IFRS has grown significantly, which as a practical matter precluded the IASB from entering into MoUs with each national or regional standard setter that had adopted or might adopt IFRS. Second, different areas around the world have established regional accounting standard-setting organizations to discuss matters related to IFRS and financial reporting. In an effort to respond to these developments, the ASAF essentially replaces multiple bilateral MoUs, that the IASB signed with the national standard setters in Brazil, China, Japan, and the United States, with a single 2013 agreement between IFRSF and the ASAF members.

For each project, the IASB must publish an exposure draft for public comment and consider any comments before issuing a final International Financial Reporting Standard (also "IFRS"). If the Board includes fewer than sixteen members, nine of the them must approve the publication of an exposure draft or a final IFRS. When the Board contains sixteen members, ten must approve such an action.

The IFRSF's constitution empowers the IFRSIC, again previously known as IFRIC, a fourteen-member panel whose members serve three-year terms, to meet when required to decide "contentious" accounting issues arising in the application of IFRS. In essence, IFRSIC performs the same function for IASB as the Emerging Issues Task Force does for FASB, that is, interpret IFRS, publish draft interpretations for public comment, consider timely comments before finalizing interpretations, and obtain IASB approval for final interpretations. If no more than four members of the panel vote against an interpretation, IFRSIC will ask the IASB to issue an interpretation. Again, depending upon the Board's size, either nine or ten members must approve the publication of a final interpretation. A former, but then-SEC Chief Accountant referred to IFRSIC as "NIFRIC," for "No IFRIC" because the panel typically refuses to accept an issue for interpretation. According to SEC staff research, IFRSIC and the now defunct IFRIC accepted only 27 of the 233 issues that came before them between 2002 and early 2012. Of the remaining 206 requests for guidance, the panels rejected seventy outright, another eighty-three with guidance, and fifty-three with referral to IASB. *See* Steve Burkholder, *SEC Chief Accountant Targets How Interpretations of IFRS, GAAP Are Done*, 44 Sec. Reg. & L. Rep. (BNA) 952 (May 7, 2012).

IFRSAC is comprised of thirty or more individuals with renewable, three-year terms, having diverse geographic and functional backgrounds and an interest in international financial reporting. These individuals assist the Board on agenda decisions and priorities for the Board's work, inform the Board of their views on major rulemaking projects, and otherwise advise the Trustees and Board, especially on any proposed changes to the constitution. The 2009 constitutional amendments sought to engage the investor community by changing the advisory council's structure, so that members would serve primarily as representatives of organizations.

IASB has obtained a competitive advantage as to accounting standards for SMEs. In 2009, IASB issued the much anticipated IFRS for SMEs. Described as "a self-contained standard of fewer than 230 pages," the rules seem likely to appeal to more than ninety-five percent of all enterprises globally that publish general purpose financial statements for external users, but need not comply with public filing or accountability requirements. By 2013, more than eighty countries worldwide had adopted the standards. Departing from its usual practice, IASB immediately upon issuance posted the accompanying basis for conclusions, illustrative examples, and a disclosure checklist on its website, where registered users can access the materials, free of charge. In 2008, the AICPA Council designated the IASB as "the body which is authorized to establish professional standards with respect to international financial accounting and reporting principles under Rule 202 (Compliance With Standards) and Rule 203 (Accounting Principles) of the AICPA Code of Professional Conduct." As a result, private companies can potentially use IFRS, including IFRS for SMEs, and obtain audited financial statements in the United States.

Until the global credit crisis, virtually every signal indicated that the IFRS would soon become the applicable accounting principles for securities law filings in the United States. In 2005, the EU internal market commissioner and the SEC chairman reached an agreement to mutually recognize each others' accounting standards before 2009. In 2007, the SEC issued final rules that allow foreign private issuers to use IFRS to prepare financial statements for submission to the agency without any reconciliation to U.S. GAAP. The rules, which became effective in early 2008, removed a barrier that discouraged some foreign private issuers from accessing the U.S. capital markets.

After the SEC announced its proposed roadmap for public companies to transition to IFRS for securities filings, *supra* at page 160, the financial crisis battered large companies and threatened even entire economies. Ironically, while the global credit crisis has highlighted the need for international accounting standards, the downturn also slowed the momentum for the SEC to mandate IFRS for public companies and weakened IASB's future as the international standard setter.

Unlike FASB, which enjoys financial independence via the annual support fees that SOx section 109 requires public companies to pay to the Board, IASB still relies on contributions, subscriptions to electronic databases, and sales of publications to fund its operations. In addition, IASB's responses during the credit crisis generated enormous political controversy in the EU and beyond. First, in 2008, pressure from the EC persuaded IASB to suspend its normal due process procedures and to change its rules governing financial instruments to allow banks to reclassify certain assets, thereby avoiding losses. The EC had threatened to legislate a carve-out from the relevant standard. Then, after IASB declined to amend IFRS to incorporate what the FASB had published on accounting for other-than-temporary impairments and fair value measurement in inactive markets in 2009, the EC threatened to create its own accounting rules and to revoke the 2002 directive that mandated that public companies in the EU use IFRS. Current EU rules allow the EC to decide, standard by standard, whether to accept or reject new guidance. In fact, the EU enjoys a carve-out from the current international accounting standards on the recognition and measurement of financial instruments. Equally important, IASB has yet to obtain stable funding, its reliance on funding from the largest accounting firms continues to raise concerns about its independence, and its net assets as of December 31, 2013 stood at slightly more than fifty percent of its annual operating expenses.

In addition to independence, both financially and politically, one other significant hurdle for a single set of global accounting principles lies in the realm of enforcement of the applicable standards. On that score the U.S. has historically been well ahead of other countries, due to the strong role of the SEC with its broad administrative and regulatory powers. The U.K. and its close cousins in Canada and Australia have been moving in that direction, with the development of either public or private sector institutions which provide some oversight of company compliance with accounting standards. In the EU, the EC saw that the need for stronger regulation of financial reporting was likely to be met most effectively within the framework of securities regulation. The result was the promulgation in 2002 of a proposed Statement of Principles of Enforcement of Accounting Standards in Europe by a committee of European securities regulators, which was designed to assist member states in the development of their securities law regulation, including the effort to achieve conformity with accounting standards.

In late 2010, IASB and FASB prioritized their joint work on financial instruments, revenue recognition, and leases. Accordingly, the Boards each decided to defer deliberations on several independent standard-setting projects and agreed to modify their work plan to defer substantive deliberations on four joint projects until after June 30, 2011. At their joint meeting in early spring 2011, the Boards extended the timetable for the three priority convergence projects on financial instruments, revenue recognition, and leases "beyond June 2011 to permit further work and consultation with stakeholders." By mid-2014 the Boards had reached converged standards for revenue recognition, but had failed to reach any framework for convergence on the impairment phase of the financial instruments project and had not completed the project on leases.

With more than 120 countries permitting or requiring IFRS, much of the world, especially many multinational companies based outside the United States, has already adopted IFRS, subject to the caveat that some countries have approved local variations or special applications. By 2010, more than 200 of the 500 largest companies in the world used IFRS for financial reporting. More than 500 foreign private issuers, including forty percent of banks, representing market capitalizations in the trillions of dollars, file financial statements using IFRS with the SEC without reconciliation to U.S. GAAP.

In the aftermath of the credit crisis and in the midst of rulemaking to implement Dodd-Frank and the JOBS Act, the SEC ultimately must decide whether to allow domestic companies to use IFRS for purposes of the federal securities laws, especially given the need to train preparers, auditors, investors, analysts, regulators, tax authorities, educators, and eventually even lawyers. In its 2008 proposed roadmap, the SEC estimated that a transition to IFRS would cost the average public company about 0.125 percent of revenues. Former SEC chairman Mary Schapiro shared reports placing the cost for a single company to move from U.S. GAAP to IFRS in a range from $300,000 to $20 million. Numerous commentators have suggested that the SEC should instead allow the FASB to continue its efforts to converge accounting standards as completely as possible before adopting IFRS. As discussed on page 166, *supra*, the European Union's threats to adopt its own accounting rules in response to the credit crisis raised doubts about IASB's future, let alone its financial and political independence. Observers worldwide have also voiced concerns as to whether moving to IFRS offers the best path for establishing a single set of high-quality accounting principles. Within the United States, opponents have asked whether regulators should allow an international body to create accounting standards for U.S. companies and who can enforce international standards globally. Finally, some opponents have objected to any system that would allow domestic registrants to adopt IFRS because such a framework would create diversity, rather than uniformity, in accounting principles in this country and not improve financial reporting for investors in the United States.

While the IASB seems willing to continue to work with national and regional standards setters, including FASB, to converge global accounting standards, the "most preferred nation status" that the United States has enjoyed during the convergence process seems unlikely to survive. The IASB chair has repeatedly called for a clear signal from the SEC that it wants to incorporate IFRS into the financial reporting system that public companies in the United States use in their securities filings; warned that without public support from the SEC, international concern about the SEC's inaction could turn into international skepticism; and indicated that future standard-setting will become more multilateral, involving rulemakers from other countries and regions. *See* Steve Burkholder, *'Tangible Sign' of U.S. Commitment to IFRS Essential, Says IASB Chief*, 44 Sec. Reg. & L. Rep. (BNA) 2266 (Dec. 10, 2012).

Although the eventual emergence of a single set of high-quality, global accounting standards eventually seems inevitable, the exact timing and identity of those standards remain very uncertain. As the movement toward harmonization continued, leaders in the accounting community in the United States speculated about FASB's decline or even demise. If not internationally, FASB appears likely to continue to set accounting standards domestically. At some point, a two-tier reporting system in the United States remains a definite possibility. Under such a scenario, domestic companies could continue to apply U.S. GAAP, while multinational firms listed on certain exchanges or specialized markets within an exchange would use international accounting standards. Critics, however, complain that such a scenario would create an unlevel playing field in accounting. *See generally* James D. Cox, *Regulatory Duopoly in U.S. Securities Markets*, 99 COLUM. L. REV. 1200, 1202, 1214 n.35 (1999) (concluding that the SEC should continue to promote convergence between international and domestic standards and describing the biggest political issue as whether to limit international standards to foreign issuers or to permit domestic firms to use international standards to satisfy SEC reporting requirements).

2. HOW DO ACCOUNTING PRINCIPLES BECOME "GENERALLY ACCEPTED?"

You will recall that accounting principles refer to the rules, procedures and conventions that enterprises use to maintain accounting records and to prepare financial statements. The phrase "generally accepted accounting principles" refers to those conventions, rules and procedures which define accepted accounting practice at a particular time. Experience, reason, custom, usage and practical necessity develop these principles. As a result, GAAP evolves and changes. Furthermore, to say that an accounting method conforms with GAAP does not always imply precision. GAAP often leaves considerable leeway and may not provide definite rules for treating various transactions. In addition, various federal and state laws may also require an enterprise to file financial reports with regulatory agencies which require accounting treatments differing from GAAP. In *Shalala v. Guernsey Memorial Hospital*, 514 U.S. 87 (1995), the Supreme Court held that neither the Medicare statute nor the implementing regulations require the Secretary of Health and Human Services to adhere to GAAP in reimbursement determinations for Medicare providers. In that case, Justice Kennedy's majority opinion states:

> Financial accounting is not a science. It addresses many questions as to which the answers are uncertain, and is a "process [that] involves continuous judgments and estimates." * * *

GAAP is not the lucid or encyclopedic set of pre-existing rules that the dissent might perceive it to be. Far from a single-source accounting rulebook, GAAP "encompasses the conventions, rules, and procedures that define accepted accounting practice at a particular point in time." GAAP changes and, even at any one point, is often indeterminate.

514 U.S. at 101 (citations omitted). In 2009 and more than a decade after Justice Kennedy wrote that dicta, the Financial Accounting Standards Board released the FASB Accounting Standards Codification™ (the "Codification," "FASB ASC," or simply "ASC"), culminating a landmark project that compiled all authoritative accounting principles in the United States in a single location. We turn now to the Codification.

a. THE FASB ACCOUNTING STANDARDS CODIFICATION

Before FASB completed the Codification, no one source fully supplied or detailed generally accepted accounting principles in the United States. In fact, twenty different sources and more than 2,000 promulgations set forth GAAP in a hierarchy that listed four collections of sources for accounting principles and another grouping for accounting literature. Now superseded SFAS No. 162, *The Hierarchy of Generally Accepted Accounting Principles,* ranked the four collections levels (a) through (d), with level (a) designating the highest level of authority. The grouping for accounting literature fell below level (d). The previous grouping for so-called "accounting literature," sometimes referred to as "level (e)," has become non-authoritative. In essence, the Codification flattened the previous GAAP hierarchy from five levels to two camps—authoritative and non-authoritative, and the Codification contains the authoritative materials. Although the FASB did not expect the Codification to change existing GAAP in any material way, the Codification now sets forth official GAAP.

To appreciate the Codification's significance more fully, keep in mind that accounting principles sometimes offer alternative treatments and typically require judgment in their application. As a result, management occasionally must determine whether a particular rule, procedure or treatment enjoys general acceptability. In addition, auditing standards require an auditor to opine in the audit report whether the financial statements fairly present the enterprise's financial position, results of operations, and cash flows in conformity with GAAP. Accordingly, an important interrelationship exists between accounting principles and auditing standards. To help management select an appropriate accounting principle or application and to assist the auditor in evaluating whether the financial statements conform to GAAP, the Codification now establishes the rules used to prepare financial statements presented in conformity with U.S. GAAP, apart from any guidance from the SEC.

Keep in mind that the Codification really only binds enterprises that need audited financial statements prepared pursuant to U.S. GAAP. Most of the estimated 28 million private corporations and other small businesses in the

United States do not need audited financial statements for their owners or lenders; those businesses need not, and typically do not, observe GAAP. Press Release, Fin. Acct. Found., The American Institute of Certified Public Accountants and the Financial Accounting Foundation Form "Blue-Ribbon Panel" to Address Standards for Private Companies (Dec. 17, 2009), http://www.fasb.org/cs/ContentServer?c=FASBContent_C&pagename=FAS B%2FFASBContent_C%2FNewsPage&cid=1176156582312.

Finally, recall that SEC registrants need to follow Regulations S-K and S-X, the CFRP, and other SEC rules and releases. Smaller reporting companies can benefit from scaled disclosure under Regulation S-K. Regardless of size, registrants that do not follow Staff Accounting Bulletins ("SABs") and other promulgations from the SEC's Office of the Chief Accountant and CorpFin can expect challenges from the SEC staff. Such guidance continues to announce practices that the SEC staff will follow in administering the disclosure and periodic reporting requirements in the federal securities laws.

Because the AICPA Council designated IASB as the body to establish international financial reporting standards for both private and public entities pursuant to the Institute's Rule 203, publicly traded, domestic enterprises not within the SEC's jurisdiction can use either the Codification or IFRS to obtain audited financial statements. Absent a contractual requirement to the contrary, private enterprises that need audited financial statements can choose between GAAP, IFRS, and IASB's new 230-page IFRS for small- and medium-sized enterprises ("SMEs"). With acquiescence from the owners and any lender that may require audited financial statements, these closely held firms now can also adopt the AICPA's FRF for SMEs or another comprehensive basis of accounting, such as the cash method or income tax basis accounting, all of which avoid GAAP's complexity. As a practical matter, many small businesses and sole proprietors use software like QuickBooks. Because the program "can be modified to meet the needs of every business," users can establish their own accounting principles. The following chart summarizes the accounting principles that domestic enterprises in the United States, ranging from large, publicly traded corporations to small proprietorships, can use after the JOBS Act:

Publicly traded enterprises			Closely held firms	
SEC registrants		Not traded on a national securities exchange <u>and</u> either: (i) less than $10 million in assets or (ii) no class of equity securities owned by at least (a) 2,000 persons or (b) 500 persons who do not qualify as "accredited investors"	Owners or lenders require audited financial statements	Audited financial statements not required
Non-accelerated filers, accelerated filers, and large accelerated filers	Smaller reporting companies			
Codification, subject to: •Regulations S–K and S–X •SEC's rules and releases and SABs	Codification, subject to: •Scaled disclosure under Regulation S–K •SEC's rules and releases and SABs	Codification or IFRS	Codification, IFRS, IFRS for SMEs, or with owner or lender permission, FRF for SMEs or other comprehensive basis of accounting	Codification, IFRS, IFRS for SMEs, FRF for SMEs, and any other comprehensive basis of accounting all optional

As you might imagine, situations will exist where the Codification does not provide any direct guidance about accounting for a particular event or transaction. For example, the business community, particularly the finance industry, constantly develops new business transactions. When no prior accounting precedent exists, the Codification encourages management in the first instance, and then any auditor, to look to the transaction's substance, to consult the accounting literature, and to select an accounting treatment that appears appropriate.

b. BEFORE THE CODIFICATION

Although the Codification superseded all previous level (a) through level (d) standards for fiscal periods ending after September 15, 2009, accounting issues may arise in legal disputes involving fiscal periods ending on or before that date. At least for the immediate future, and especially in litigation, lawyers must pay attention to the Codification's effective date and should understand the GAAP hierarchy that previously applied. You may need to identify and evaluate the various sources of generally accepted accounting principles before the Codification's "effective date." For a comprehensive discussion of the various authorities and their level within the previous GAAP hierarchy, see DAVID R. HERWITZ & MATTHEW J. BARRETT, MATERIALS ON ACCOUNTING FOR LAWYERS 182-87(4th ed. 2006 & Supp. 2013).

c. REGULATORY ACCOUNTING PRACTICES

Over the years, various federal and state governmental bodies and agencies that regulate certain industries, such as banks, thrifts, credit unions, utilities and insurance companies, have issued their own accounting rules and requirements for businesses subject to their jurisdiction. Although the governmental organizations usually based these regulatory accounting practices ("RAP") on GAAP, RAP often modified or supplemented GAAP. As a result, differences between GAAP and RAP often required businesses in regulated industries to prepare separate financial statements, and in some instances to keep separate sets of accounting records, for financial accounting and regulatory purposes. In *Shalala v. Guernsey Memorial Hospital, supra,* the Supreme Court's opinion explicitly recognized that GAAP's underlying goal to inform investors does not always advance regulatory objectives. 514 U.S. at 100-01. In the midst of the economic downturn and the debate about the role that fair value accounting played in the global credit crisis, for example, international bank regulators and accounting standard setters alike correctly recognized that regulatory capital need not depend upon financial reporting under GAAP, which ultimately strives to provide useful information to investors and creditors. Indeed, the primary goals of banking regulators, namely safety and soundness, may dictate different approaches and rules than the transparency that financial reporting standards seek. Until all regulatory bodies adopt GAAP, RAP will continue to impose potentially different standards on various regulated enterprises. When handling matters involving any of these regulated industries, lawyers should keep in mind the specialized, non-GAAP rules and requirements that may apply.

3. WHO SELECTS AMONG GENERALLY ACCEPTED ACCOUNTING PRINCIPLES?

Given the various accounting estimates and permissible choices in accounting methods, one academic calculated that a typical business enterprise could select from more than a million possible bottom lines. Moreover, the fact that the Codification does not, and indeed could not, address every conceivable situation leaves additional choices. Consequently, the question becomes: Who selects among the permissible alternatives?

We have already read the answer: Accounting practice has long placed the responsibility for an enterprise's financial statements on management. As a result, management chooses, in the first instance, the accounting principles from among the acceptable alternatives or selects an accounting treatment when the Codification does not address a particular transaction or event. If an independent auditor examines the financial statements, the auditor can often influence, at least to some extent, the accounting principles that management selects. If an auditor believes that the accounting principles that management has chosen do not fairly present the enterprise's financial condition, operating results, or cash flows, the auditor can threaten to issue a qualified opinion. As mentioned earlier in the chapter, Sarbanes-Oxley now prohibits a public company from filing financial statements subject to a qualified opinion with the SEC. Even for a private enterprise, a qualified opinion can significantly and negatively affect the enterprise's financial status and ability to generate capital.

Until Sarbanes-Oxley, management usually selected, either directly or indirectly, the independent auditor. Even today, many closely held firms continue to follow that practice. Subject to oversight from a corporation's audit committee, which we will discuss shortly, management at private companies can conceivably exercise pressure on the auditor to approve, or at least to acquiesce in, questionable accounting treatments by threatening to terminate the auditor's engagement, a practice often referred to as "opinion shopping." At public companies, the SEC largely curtailed this pressure by adopting rules that require full disclosure of the circumstances any time a registrant changes auditors, plus a letter to the SEC from the former auditor either concurring or disagreeing with the registrant's statements. As no surprise, the financial community views changes in auditors after an accounting disagreement with considerable suspicion.

Sarbanes-Oxley effectively requires the audit committees of listed companies to hire, to set compensation for, and to decide when and if to replace the auditor. In particular, SOx section 301 directed the SEC to prescribe rules that, among other things, prohibit the national securities exchanges and national securities associations from listing any issuer that does not satisfy certain standards relating to audit committees. Since 2004, the new listing standards require those public companies that list their shares on national securities exchanges and associations, including NYSE and NASDAQ, to comply with certain standards. Perhaps most importantly, a listed company's audit committee must hold the direct responsibility to hire, compensate, oversee, and fire the independent auditor, and the auditor must report directly to the audit committee. In addition, only independent directors can serve on the audit committee. To qualify as independent, a board member generally cannot: (a) accept directly or indirectly any consulting, advisory, or other compensatory fee, other than director's fees, from the listed company or its subsidiaries, or (b) qualify as an affiliate of the listed company or any subsidiary. Pursuant to these listing standards, each audit committee member of a listed company also must qualify as "financially literate," or obtain that literacy qualification within a reasonable period after appointment to the audit committee. In addition, at least one audit committee member must have "accounting or related financial management expertise."

SOx section 407 directed the SEC to adopt rules that require public companies to disclose whether at least one "financial expert" serves on the company's audit committee and, if not, why not. In addition, that provision authorizes the SEC to define the term "financial expert." Ultimately, the SEC decided to create the more distinct label "audit committee financial expert" because that descriptor better conveys that the designated person should possess experience specifically applicable to the duties of an audit committee member. The term "audit committee financial expert" means a person with the following attributes: (i) an understanding of financial statements and GAAP; (ii) an ability to assess GAAP's application regarding accounting for estimates, accruals, and reserves; (iii) experience preparing, auditing, analyzing or evaluating financial statements that contain a breadth and complexity reasonably similar to the issuer's financial statements, or experience actively supervising one or more persons engaged in such activities; (iv) an understanding of internal controls and procedures for financial reporting; and (v) an understanding of audit committee functions. Although the NYSE's rules deem any director who satisfies the SEC's "audit committee financial expert" definition as also satisfying the NYSE's "accounting or related financial management expertise" requirement, a director who qualifies under the NYSE's rules may not necessarily satisfy the SEC's standards.

PROBLEMS

Problem 2.1A. Suppose that the Nifty-Novelty "management" in Problem 1.10A on pages 110 to 112, *supra*, had decided not to defer the sales income involved in the transaction of February 8, on the ground that "these things even up over time." As the outside auditor, how would you respond?

Problem 2.1B. Suppose that the Camera Sales "management" in Problem 1.10B on pages 112 to 114, *supra*, had decided not to accrue the salaries for the second half of the month on the ground that "these things even up over time." As the outside auditor, how would you respond?

Problem 2.1C. Suppose that the Tortious Toys "management" in Problem 1.10C on pages 114 to 117, *supra*, had decided not to defer the potential income involved in the transaction of April 27, on the ground that "these things even up over time." As the outside auditor, how would you respond?

D. AUDITS AND GENERALLY ACCEPTED AUDITING STANDARDS

Recall that an audit involves a process whereby an independent accountant examines an enterprise's accounting books and records, transactions, and other related information to consider whether the enterprise's financial statements contain any material misstatements. Ultimately, the auditor seeks to express an opinion as to whether the financial statements fairly present, in all material respects, the enterprise's financial position, results of operations, and cash flows in conformity with GAAP. In addition to auditing financial statements, auditors often also assess the effectiveness of the enterprise's internal control over financial reporting for external purposes. In that regard, a public company's management must design and implement procedures intended to provide reasonable assurance regarding the reliability of the enterprise's financial reporting in accordance with GAAP. In both ways, auditors serve to enhance the reliability and credibility of financial statements for the investing public and other interested users.

As another preliminary point, we should mention an important factor that motivates the demand for audit services. In any agency relationship, a person, usually referred to as the principal, authorizes another person, the agent, to act on the former's behalf and subject to the principal's control. In a corporation, the shareholders, through the board of directors, in effect function as principals that hire the corporation's management as agents to operate the business.

The interests of the principal and the agent can, and often do, diverge. For example, an enterprise's management may want to keep their jobs, even though their continued employment may not further the principals' best interests. Indeed, in some situations the shareholders would likely replace management if the shareholders knew all relevant information about the existing management's past efforts and results. As we saw earlier, however, the ultimate responsibility for an enterprise's financial statements rests with management, which either prepares the financial statements or oversees their preparation.

In most situations, an absent principal does not enjoy the agent's access to information. As a result, the absent principal encounters *information risk*–or more simply, the chance that the agent has not shared all details relevant to the relationship, leading principals to want an independent monitor's services to reduce information risk. Similar incentives encourage agents, in this case management, to accept such monitoring arrangements. If monitoring reduces information risk to the principal, the corresponding cost of capital drops for the agent because the lower risk means that the principal will accept a lower return. For this reason, the demand for auditing services would exist, and does exist, even absent the regulatory requirement that publicly traded enterprises file audited financial statements with the SEC.

As an additional, but related, explanation for audits, the various users of financial statements, including owners, creditors, potential investors and lenders, and regulatory bodies, want assurances that the financial statements accurately portray the enterprise's financial condition and operating results. In an audit, therefore, the auditor seeks to verify the underlying transactions and events reported in the financial statements and to test the application of GAAP to those facts. For this reason, the Supreme Court has described auditors as "public watchdogs." *United States v. Arthur Young & Co.*, 465 U.S. 805, 818 (1984).

During an audit, the auditor must follow certain standards and perform certain procedures, which accountants refer to collectively as "auditing standards." After Sarbanes-Oxley and Dodd-Frank, the PCAOB, subject to SEC approval, can establish the auditing and related standards that registered public accounting firms must use in audits for issuers and broker-dealers subject to the SEC's jurisdiction. Setting aside broker-dealers, please keep in mind that the PCAOB's rules apply only to accounting firms that audit issuers. For audits involving nonissuers, the accounting profession, through the AICPA and ASB, still establishes generally accepted auditing standards in the United States. Although usually not significant, differences exist between the PCAOB and ASB standards. Following closely behind global accounting principles, international auditing standards seem likely to continue to grow in importance in the years ahead. To date, neither the PCAOB nor ASB has adopted international auditing standards.

1. INDEPENDENCE AND THE AUDIT PROCESS

By requiring that a report from an independent auditor accompany the financial statements that registrants file with the SEC, the Commission has endorsed the accounting profession's role as the auditor of management's financial statements. As a prerequisite to a successful audit, an auditor needs independence from management so that the auditor can hold the public's trust and approach the audit with the necessary professional skepticism. If the auditing firm, or a member of the firm, owns a direct, or material indirect, financial interest in the audit client, its parent entity, or any subsidiaries or other affiliates, or holds a close connection with the client as a director, officer, or employee, the auditing firm lacks independence.

a. INDEPENDENCE

To understand why independence serves as the cornerstone for the auditing profession, we must recognize the distinct role that auditors play and appreciate the difference between the responsibilities of an auditor and an attorney. In *United States v. Arthur Young & Co.*, 465 U.S. 805 (1984), the Supreme Court contrasted these roles and responsibilities before holding that an auditor must disclose audit workpapers in response to a subpoena from the Internal Revenue Service. As we already know, attorneys serve as confidential advisors and advocates for clients. The lawyer's duty of loyalty requires a lawyer to present the client's case in the most favorable possible light. By comparison, the Supreme Court described an auditor as "a disinterested analyst charged with public obligations." The Supreme Court wrote:

> By certifying the public reports that collectively depict a corporation's financial status, the independent auditor assumes a public responsibility transcending any employment relationship with the client. The independent public accountant performing this special function owes ultimate allegiance to the corporation's creditors and stockholders, as well as to the investing public. This "public watchdog" function demands that the accountant maintain total independence from the client at all times and requires complete fidelity to the public trust.

465 U.S. at 817-18.

To maintain the public's confidence, an auditor must remain independent. To do so, and thereby to avoid violating professional standards and SEC rules, auditors must not only comply with the strict financial interest limitations already noted, but must also maintain not only an independent mental attitude in all matters related to the assignment, but also the appearance of independence. To qualify as independent in appearance, an auditor must avoid any circumstance that a reasonable person might consider likely to influence independence adversely. For example, the general public would likely question an auditor's independence if the auditor's spouse worked for the client even though the auditor exercised intellectual honesty during the audit. Other examples illustrating compromised independence include owning stock in a client, simultaneously representing the client as an attorney, participating in an audit after accepting an employment offer from the client, and accepting business or personal loans from a client.

Recall the temptation and the threats to independence that lucrative consulting contracts caused in the years leading up to Sarbanes-Oxley. After the accounting profession, with the SEC's support, had tried to strengthen independence standards, Congress codified those initiatives and created the Public Company Accounting Oversight Board ("PCAOB"), whose responsibilities to oversee firms that audit public companies include establishing rules regarding independence.

In an effort to reduce conflicts of interest, Sarbanes-Oxley flatly prohibits auditors from providing certain types of non-audit services to audit clients. The legislative history states that three basic principles informed the list of prohibited activities that Congress established for registered public accounting firms to qualify as independent: an auditing firm (1) should not audit its own work; (2) should not function as part of client management or as a client employee; and (3) should not act as an advocate for the audit client. The "prohibited activities" for auditors include bookkeeping or other services related to the audit client's accounting records or financial statements; financial information systems design and implementation; appraisal or valuation services, fairness opinions, or contribution-in-kind reports; actuarial services; internal audit outsourcing; management functions; human resources; broker-dealer, investment adviser or investment banking services; legal services; expert services unrelated to the audit; and, subject to the SEC's approval, any other service that the PCAOB decides to prohibit via regulation. An auditor may perform services not included on the prohibited list, such as tax services, for an audit client only if the client's audit committee approves those services in advance.

During the hearings that ultimately led to Sarbanes-Oxley, Congress considered a total ban that would have prevented auditing firms from providing any non-audit services, including so-called "tax services," to publicly traded audit clients. Tax services can range from tax compliance work, such as preparing tax returns, to sophisticated tax minimization strategies, or "tax shelters," that aggressively seek to use quirks in the Internal Revenue Code to avoid taxes. Ultimately, Congress decided against an absolute ban on non-audit services and to omit tax services from the list of prohibited services. Subsequently, the release that announced the SEC's final rules on auditor independence specifically reiterated the agency's "long-standing position that an accounting firm can provide tax services to its audit clients without impairing the firm's independence." Strengthening the Commission's Requirements Regarding Auditor Independence, 68 Fed. Reg. 6006, 6017

(Feb. 5, 2003). Various commentators, however, have continued to argue that various conflicts of interest arise anytime an auditor offers significant tax advice to an audit client or promotes a tax shelter to anyone. *See, e.g.*, Bernard Wolfman, *SEC Let Investors Down*, 98 TAX NOTES 1019 (2003) (opining that the SEC "has left the investing public in the lurch" and urging the SEC and Congress to prohibit auditors for public companies from promoting tax shelters or providing tax planning and consulting services); Matthew J. Barrett, *"Tax Services" as a Trojan Horse in the Auditor Independence Provisions of Sarbanes-Oxley*, 2004 MICH. ST. L. REV. 463 (further arguing that auditors for public companies should also not provide tax compliance services to audit clients or their executives). While management can no longer hire or fire the auditor, under the guise of increasing auditor independence, management can use "enhanced independence" to support a recommendation to the audit committee to hire another firm to provide tax services, other permissible non-audit services, or future audit services. Thus, if the auditor does not approve, or at least acquiesce in, certain accounting treatments or disclosures that management prefers, the auditor conceivably jeopardizes potentially significant future professional fees.

In 2006 the SEC approved new PCAOB ethics and independence rules concerning tax services. These rules prohibit auditors from providing non-audit services to audit clients related to (1) confidential transactions, as defined under Treasury regulations, (2) aggressive tax position transactions, described as significantly motivated by tax avoidance, unless the applicable tax laws more likely than not allow the proposed tax treatment, and (3) any tax service to any person who fills a financial reporting oversight role at an audit client, or to an immediate family member of such a person. *See* Pub. Co. Accounting Oversight Bd. R. 3522-23, *available via* http://pcaobus.org/rules/pcaobrules/pages/section_3.aspx; *see also* Order Approving Proposed Ethics and Independence Rules Concerning Independence, Tax Services, and Contingent Fees, 71 Fed. Reg. 23,971, 23,971–72 (April 25, 2006).

b. THE AUDIT PROCESS

Financial statements represent assertions that fall into five broad categories: (1) that reported assets and liabilities exist and that recorded transactions occurred during the particular accounting period; (2) that the financial statements present all transactions and accounts; (3) that the listed assets represent the enterprise's rights and the reported liabilities show the business's obligations; (4) that the financial statements record the enterprise's assets, liabilities, revenues and expenses at appropriate amounts; and (5) that the enterprise has properly classified, described, and disclosed the financial statements' components. *See* 1 AM. INST. OF CERTIFIED PUB. ACCOUNTANTS, AICPA PROFESSIONAL STANDARDS AU-C ¶ 315.A114 (Jan. 2014), *available at* http://www.aicpa.org/Research/Standards/AuditAttest/Downloadable Documents/AU-C-00315.pdf; *see also* AM. INST. OF CERTIFIED PUB. ACCOUNTANTS, PCAOB STANDARDS AND RELATED RULES (AS OF JANUARY 2014)

AS § 15.11, *available at* http://pcaobus.org/Standards/Auditing/Pages/Auditing _Standard_15.aspx. An audit gathers evidence about these five assertions.

At one time in history, auditors reviewed each transaction during the period which the financial statements covered to ensure that the enterprise properly recorded each transaction. As commerce developed, however, the number of transactions grew and became too numerous to review individually. Today, auditors often relied on the enterprise's internal controls over its accounting processes, plus sampling techniques to test selected transactions, to obtain reasonable assurance that the financial statements do not contain any material misstatement. "Internal control" refers to those systems, procedures, and policies that an enterprise uses to ensure that an appropriate individual authorizes all transactions and that the enterprise properly executes and records those transactions.

As the number of transactions actually reviewed decreases, an auditor's professional judgment becomes exceedingly important. In seeking the reasonable assurance that the financial statements do not contain any material misstatements or omissions, auditors strive to design an effective and efficient audit that holds *audit risk* below a reasonable level. Audit risk refers to the possibility that an auditor will unknowingly fail to detect materially misleading financial statements.

Because GAAS does not define "reasonable assurance," the standard depends on the facts and circumstances underlying a particular audit engagement. Although the same auditor may examine a business's financial statements every year, each audit probably will vary in scope and detail. Accepted auditing practices require the auditor to assemble sufficient evidence to form an opinion regarding whether the financial statements fairly present the client's financial condition and operating results. An auditor, however, may encounter various problems during the audit. For example, the client's management or employees may not follow internal control procedures. Clients may blunder certain transactions or omit certain liabilities. When testing sample transactions, observed deviations may indicate larger, more significant problems. Auditors rely on their experience and professional judgment to decide whether such deficiencies likely indicate a material error in the financial statements. Until the auditor issues the audit report, the auditor must constantly exercise professional judgment and, if necessary, modify the audit strategy to attain the requisite reasonable assurance.

A standard audit includes three phases: planning the audit, implementing the audit program, and reporting the results. We will discuss these phases in order.

(1) Planning the Audit and Assessing Internal Control

To plan an audit properly, the auditor must gather information about the client and assess the enterprise's internal control before developing an audit program. After accepting an audit engagement, the independent auditor will investigate the client's business and accounting policies. In this process, the auditor will gather information about conditions in the industry, the business's products or services, sales trends, major customers, production and marketing techniques, characteristics of management, personnel, budgeting and accounting systems, affiliations with outside influences, such as foreign governments or political groups, and similar matters. In particular, the auditor will review prior years' audit results.

During this phase, the auditor will also obtain and document an understanding of the client's accounting system. Generally accepted auditing standards require the auditor to assess the enterprise's *internal control*, which, as noted above, means those systems, procedures, and policies that an enterprise uses to help assure that the organization properly authorizes, executes, and records transactions. The mechanisms for internal control include both administrative controls, which comprise an enterprise's plan of organization, procedures, and records that lead up to management's authorization of transactions, and accounting controls that describe the plans, procedures, and records that the enterprise uses to safeguard assets and produce reliable financial records.

An enterprise's internal controls should segregate the responsibilities for authorizing and recording transactions and safeguarding assets between different individuals to detect errors and prevent fraud, thereby insuring greater accuracy and reliability in the accounting records and financial statements. Illustrative internal controls include cash registers that display prices and totals to customers and allow management to total all transactions during a shift to discourage clerks from "pocketing" sales revenues; consecutive numbers on checks, purchase orders, and invoices to allow better accountability; rules that require certain employees, especially in banks and other financial institutions, to take continuous, two-week vacations each year to reduce the chance that those employees can hide any irregularities; arrangements that require at least two authorized individuals to sign any check exceeding a certain amount; the division of accounting functions so that different individuals write checks and reconcile bank statements against the cash account; and the separation of purchasing, receiving, and accounting functions so that the same individual does not order, accept, and pay for goods.

As a practical matter, auditors rely extensively on client internal controls because an audit cannot test every transaction. Accordingly, the auditor performs compliance tests to determine whether the internal controls function properly. The auditor may also examine sample transactions or records to ascertain how accurately the client's financial and accounting systems document transactions. In a process that accountants refer to as *vouching*, an auditor selects a transaction recorded in the business's books to determine whether underlying data supports the recorded entry. Alternatively, an auditor may use a process known as *tracing*, which involves following a particular item of data through the accounting and bookkeeping process to determine whether the business has properly recorded and accounted for the data. Based upon this evaluation, the auditor decides whether to rely on some or all of the internal control systems to reduce the need to test actual transactions and account balances. To the extent that the business does not regularly observe the internal controls or those controls do not adequately prevent errors or frauds, however, the auditor must design auditing procedures that gather additional audit evidence to permit the auditor to render an opinion regarding the financial statements.

a) INTERNAL CONTROL UNDER THE FOREIGN CORRUPT PRACTICES ACT

In the mid-1970s, the Watergate scandal that forced President Richard Nixon's resignation also led to the prosecution of executives who had used corporate slush funds to make illegal political contributions to candidates for public office in the United States, including President Nixon. Investigations into how the companies had recorded the payments ultimately caused more than 400 U.S. companies to admit questionable payments exceeding $300 million to foreign governmental officials and politicians. Fearing that the United States could not enforce any law that banned bribes outside the country, officials at the SEC lobbied for a new law that would penalize companies for failing to keep accurate books and records or to maintain strong internal accounting controls. For enterprises subject to Congress's power to regulate interstate commerce, namely companies traded on the national securities exchanges and other registrants, poor record-keeping or inadequate internal accounting controls can violate the Foreign Corrupt Practices Act of 1977 (the 1977 FCPA") and the Foreign Corrupt Practices Act Amendments of 1988 (the "1988 Amendments") (collectively, the "FCPA"). Notwithstanding their titles, these statutory provisions apply to all SEC registrants, *including enterprises that do not engage in any operations outside the United States.*

The 1977 FCPA contained two parts: antibribery provisions and accounting requirements. Presumably, Congress enacted the accounting rules to improve corporate accountability on the theory that any failure in record-keeping or internal controls threatened the disclosure requirements under the federal securities laws. In any event, the legislation imposes two distinct accounting requirements on all SEC registrants, including those that engage only in domestic operations, which create federally mandated, minimum record-keeping and internal controls standards for all registrants.

First, the record-keeping obligations require all registrants to "make and keep books, records, and accounts, which, in reasonable detail, accurately and fairly reflect the transactions and dispositions of the assets of the issuer." Under this provision, the SEC promulgated two rules, the first prohibiting any person from falsifying any book, record or account that the statute requires, and the second forbidding any officer or director from, directly or indirectly, making a materially false or misleading statement or failing to state a material fact to an accountant in connection with any audit or other required filing.

Second, to establish adequate internal accounting controls all registrants must "devise and maintain a system of internal accounting controls sufficient to provide reasonable assurances" that the enterprise: (1) executes transactions in accordance with management's authorization, (2) records transactions in such a way as to permit the enterprise to prepare financial statements in conformity with GAAP and to maintain accountability for assets; (3) permits access to assets only in accordance with management's authorization; and (4) compares recorded assets against actual assets at reasonable intervals and takes appropriate action regarding any differences. These four clauses came directly from an authoritative auditing promulgation offering guidance to auditors to helo them evaluate internal control during an audit. The FCPA provisions, on the other hand, impose a statutory obligation on registrants and, hence their managements, to comply with the requirements. In 2013, for example, the SEC imposed a $200 million civil penalty against JPMorgan Chase & Company for violating the books and records and internal controls provisions as part of a broader $920 million agreement that resolved claims brought by regulators in the United States and the United Kingdom in response to the infamous "London whale" transactions that led to more than $6 billion in trading losses at the global banking and financial services firm. *See In re* JPMorgan Chase & Co., Accounting and Auditing Enforcement Release No. 3490 (Sept. 19, 2013), http://www.sec.gov/litigation/admin/2013/34-70458.pdf.

Congress amended the 1977 FCPA in 1988 to provide that the "reasonable detail" and "reasonable assurances" with which registrants must keep "books, records, and accounts" and maintain the requisite internal controls, respectively, mean "such level of detail and degree of assurance as would satisfy prudent officials in the conduct of their own affairs." The 1988 Amendments also limit criminal liability to knowing violations. In an administrative bulletin, the SEC staff has reminded registrants that immaterial, but intentional, misstatements can indeed violate the FCPA record-keeping and internal controls requirements.

In 1998, a private sector group issued a report that highlighting recent regulatory and legal developments that increasingly compel businesses to focus on internal fraud detection. As basic principles in the "battle against fraud and other illegal activity," the report identified setting the tone at the top through example and communication to create a clear policy against improper conduct, explicitly focusing on fraud risk, and developing an effective communication process between directors, officers, senior managers, and employees.

Although a company's top management bears the initial responsibility to develop and implement adequate internal controls, and, when necessary, revise them, overall oversight falls to the board of directors, who often rely on lawyers for advice. Internal controls work effectively only when those who bear responsibility for developing, implementing, and overseeing those controls stress the need to adhere to all policies and procedures and set a good example themselves. Strong internal controls enhance the likelihood that the enterprise will engage in sound, beneficial transactions and reduce the chances that an enterprise will incur the enormous losses that can result from internal control failures. In the early 2000s, the scandals at Enron, WorldCom, Tyco, and numerous other companies all involved internal control failures.

At least two major internal control failures occurred at Enron. First, when Enron's board of directors approved a policy that allowed the company to enter into transactions with certain entities owned by Enron officers, the implementing procedures explicitly required management to use a "Deal Approval Sheet." By requiring certain disclosures and the approval of Enron's chief executive officer, the Deal Approval Sheets sought to ensure that the contractual provisions in such transactions would closely resemble the terms that would have materialized in an arms'-length transaction. In fact, the chief executive officer's signature did not appear on the sheets for several specific transactions, and no sheet existed for other transactions. Second, when Andrew Fastow, Enron's former chief financial officer, reportedly earned more than $30 million from partnerships that entered into transactions with Enron, the board failed to require that he report those profits from the partnerships to the company. Such disclosures almost certainly would have alerted the board to the possibility that the underlying transactions unfairly benefitted Fastow, to the detriment of Enron and its shareholders.

b) Sarbanes-Oxley and Internal Controls

Congress reacted to the revelations about lax internal controls at Enron and other large companies by requiring in SOx section 404 that the SEC create and enforce regulations intended to foster a more stringent internal control environment in public companies. That provision also directed the SEC to adopt rules requiring public companies to include in each annual filing a report from management on the company's internal control over financial reporting. The required report must (1) state management's responsibility for establishing and maintaining an adequate internal control structure and procedures for financial reporting and (2) contain an assessment, as of the end of the company's most recent fiscal year, of the effectiveness of the company's internal controls and procedures. In addition, the registered public accounting firm that audits the company must also opine on the internal controls over financial reporting.

When implementing these provisions, the SEC defined "internal control over financial reporting" as the procedures that a company's principal executive and financial officers design, or supervise such design, and that the company's board of directors implements to provide reasonable assurance regarding the reliability of the company's financial reporting and the preparation of financial statements for external purposes in accordance with GAAP. These controls include procedures designed to ensure that a company maintains records that reasonably reflect the company's transactions and dispositions of assets to enable the company to prepare financial statements in accordance with GAAP. Further, the internals controls should aim to provide reasonable assurances that management or the board of directors appropriately authorized all transactions and that the unauthorized acquisition, use, or disposition of the company's assets would not occur without detection. You can find management's report on Starbucks' internal control over financial reporting in Item 9A, Controls and Procedures, on page 90 of the company's 2012 Form 10-K, which appears in Appendix A on page 786, *infra*.

The registered public accounting firm auditing the company's financial statements must also express an opinion on the effectiveness of the company's internal controls over financial reporting. This requirement has significantly increased audit costs for public companies and exposes auditors to heightened legal liability because they formerly tested internal controls before the end of each reporting period, but now they must opinion on the controls' quality as of the last date of the reporting period. Thus, auditors cannot claim that errors in their reports result from management making changes to internal controls after an interim review. As discussed in more detail on page 187, *infra*, Deloitte's audit report on the effectiveness of Starbucks' internal controls over financial reporting appears on page 91 of the company's 2012 Form 10-K and on page 787 in Appendix A, *infra*.

Collectively, the new internal control requirements seemingly occasioned more criticism and complaints from companies and their auditors than all the other provisions in SOx, combined. The objections centered on the very large increase in the cost of both internal accounting and outside auditing fees, plus the considerable drain on senior management's time and energy. On six separate occasions, the last in 2009, the SEC postponed the compliance date to meet the auditor attestation requirement for non-accelerated filers (recall generally those public companies with a market capitalization under $75 million, an amount which exceeds the market capitalization for the vast majority of public companies). Then, Dodd-Frank section 989G finally exempted those non-accelerated filers from the requirement. With that Congressional directive, the SEC quickly amended its rules to remove the requirement that non-accelerated filers include an attestation report on internal control over financial reporting from the filer's registered public accounting firm.

Dodd-Frank also mandated that the SEC study how the agency could reduce compliance burdens associated with section 404(b) for companies with market capitalizations between $75 million and $250 million and whether a reduction in those burdens, or a complete exemption for issuers in that range, would encourage companies to list their initial public offerings on United States exchanges. In 2011, the SEC staff completed the study and recommended against any exemption for such companies, which have comprised only about ten percent of issuers over the last five years. The study further concluded that, by itself, an exemption for issuers that would expect a public float in the $75-$250 million range after going public would not encourage companies to list their initial public offerings in the United States.

More recently, the JOBS Act completely exempts any EGC from the need to obtain an audit report on the enterprise's internal control over financial reporting or any attestations as to internal control reports.Please note that the separate exemptions in the JOBS Act and in Dodd-Frank apply *only* to the auditor attestation requirement. For fiscal years ending after December 15, 2007, *all* registrants must evaluate their internal control over financial reporting, disclose that management performed such evaluation, and state management's conclusions about the controls' effectiveness.

c) Whistleblower Incentives and Protections

Public companies must design and implement internal controls to prevent or detect unauthorized transactions or misappropriation of corporate assets. For years, many enterprises established hotlines or other mechanisms to encourage employees, customers, or others to report suspicious transactions. Various other laws, including the False Claims Act, seek to provide incentives to individuals who report fraudulent or otherwise illegal activities. In an effort to encourage whistleblowers, Dodd-Frank section 922 requires the SEC to pay between ten and thirty percent of any recovery exceeding $1 million, which translates to a $100,000 minimum reward if the SEC can collect any amount more than $1 million, to those persons who voluntarily provide "original information" to the Commission regarding a securities law violation that leads the SEC or other government or self-regulatory agency to bring a successful enforcement action. The new provision, however, generally denies awards to certain individuals, notably auditors; officials and employees at regulatory, self-regulatory and law enforcement organizations; and any whistleblower who fails to submit information to the SEC in such form as the Commission, by rule, may require. In 2011, the SEC issued final rules to implement the new provision. The final rules do not require whistleblowers to report violations internally, but do provide incentives to use internal compliance and reporting systems when appropriate. One incentive gives whistleblowers 120 days from the date they internally report alleged misconduct to contact the SEC and have the information provided qualify as "original information."

To protect whistleblowers, Sarbanes-Oxley section 806 prohibits an employer from discharging, demoting, suspending, threatening, harassing, or in any other manner discriminating against, a whistleblower in the terms and conditions of employment because of any lawful act that the whistleblower did, including, among other things, providing information to the SEC. The provision also created a civil action to redress a violation. *See* 18 U.S.C. § 1514A (2012). Dodd-Frank section 922(c)(2) further mandated that no "agreement, policy form, or condition of employment" could waive any such right or remedy. *See* 18 U.S.C. § 1514(e) (2012). The whistleblower protections apply to individuals who report accounting-related violations of the federal securities laws to the SEC, including accounting fraud, false or misleading disclosures in public filings, and violations of the FCPA books, records, and internal controls provisions. In addition, the Office of the Whistleblower has warned against using confidentiality, severance, or other agreements to discourage employees or other individuals from reporting perceived wrongdoing.

(2) Implementing the Audit Program

After gathering information about the client and assessing the internal control, the auditor develops a plan, which accountants refer to as the *audit program*, that sets forth the detailed procedures that the auditor will perform to test transactions and account balances to in an effort to reach that reasonable assurance that the financial statements present fairly, in all material respects, the business's financial condition and operating results.

Based on the information that the auditor has gathered about the client and the internal control, the auditor makes a preliminary materiality judgment and risk assessment which determine the nature, timing, and extent of the procedures which the auditor will perform during the engagement. Most large auditing firms use a standard audit program that they tailor to each engagement according to the reliability of the internal control and the specific audit risks that the client presents.

Professional standards require an auditor to obtain sufficient competent evidence, either through inspection, observation, inquiries, or confirmations to reach an opinion about the financial statements. In a typical audit, the auditor verifies that tangible assets exist, observes business activities, confirms account balances, checks mathematical computations, and seeks representations from management and outside counsel. The audit procedures may include substantive testing where the auditor uses statistical sampling to test the financial records. For example, in auditing the accounts receivable ledger, which contains information about all customers that owe money to the client, an auditor might select customers on a random basis to confirm their outstanding balances.

The auditor documents the various procedures and findings in audit *working papers*, which lawyers may hear referred to as "workpapers." In any legal dispute involving a failed audit or other accounting issue, a lawyer will want to examine the working papers. Those documents contain the schedules, memoranda and analyses that the auditor prepared while carrying out the various audit procedures and tests, the corresponding results and information obtained, and the pertinent conclusions reached regarding significant matters.

During an audit, the auditor constantly examines the findings to determine whether they provide a "reasonable basis" to enable the auditor to express an opinion on the financial statements. If the findings have not reached that level, the auditor must conduct additional tests or procedures. For example, suppose that the auditor selects twenty random customers to confirm their outstanding balances and six customers affirmatively disagree with the balances which appear in the client's accounting records. In those circumstances, the auditor must exercise "professional skepticism" and expand the test sample or seek alternative procedures to gain assurance that the accounting system properly recorded the accounts receivable.

(3) Reporting the Audit Results

As the most important step in the audit process, the auditor prepares an audit report which represents the audit's end product. If the examination allows the auditor to reach reasonable assurance that the financial statements fairly present the enterprise's financial position, operating results and cash flows in conformity with GAAP, the auditor will issue an unqualified or "clean" opinion. Limitations in the auditor's examination, deficiencies in the client's financial statements, or other unusual conditions, however, may prevent the auditor from rendering the standard report. In those circumstances, the auditor must carefully modify the audit report to highlight those problems or conditions for the users of the financial statements. The SEC, however, will not accept audited financial statements accompanied by anything other than an unqualified opinion.

a) STANDARD REPORT

The auditor's standard report identifies the financial statements audited in an opening or introductory paragraph, describes the nature of an audit in a scope paragraph, and expresses the auditor's opinion in a separate opinion paragraph. Generally, the financial statements present the enterprise's financial condition and operating results on a comparative basis, showing the numbers from both the present and one or more previous years. The audit report from Starbucks' Form 10-K for the fiscal year ended September 30, 2012, which you can also find in Appendix A on page 785, *infra*, illustrates an audit report issued in accordance with PCAOB standards.

Notice that the introductory paragraph highlights the fact that the responsibility for the financial statements rests with the enterprise's management. In contrast, the auditor must express an opinion on the financial statements based on the audit. The second paragraph describes the scope of the audit, including the need to conduct the examination in accordance with GAAS and what that entails, and states whether the auditor believes that the audit provides a reasonable basis for an opinion.

As the most important paragraph in the audit report, the opinion paragraph states the auditor's opinion as to whether the financial statements present fairly, in all material respects, the enterprise's financial position as of the balance sheet date, plus the results of its operations and its cash flows for the period then ended, in conformity with generally accepted accounting principles. If the auditor can attain reasonable assurance that the financial statements satisfy this standard, the auditor will render the standard unqualified opinion.

You should also note that Deloitte & Touche's audit report contains a final paragraph that cross-references a separate audit report on the effectiveness of the audit client's internal control over financial reporting. As described above, SOx section 404 added an important new element to the auditor's reporting function for accelerated filers. If a registered public accounting firm issues separate audit reports on a public company's financial statements and on the company's internal control over financial reporting, the audit report on the financial statements must contain a paragraph cross-referencing the audit report on the effectiveness of the company's internal control over financial reporting.

The auditor's standard report expressing an unqualified opinion on the effectiveness of a company's internal control over financial reporting also contains the following discrete and essential paragraphs: an opening or introductory paragraph, a scope paragraph, a definition paragraph, an inherent limitations paragraph, an opinion paragraph, and a paragraph that references the audit report on the company's financial statements. The report on page 91 of Starbucks' Form 10-K for the fiscal year ended September 30,

2012, which you can find in Appendix A on page 787, *infra*, illustrates these different paragraphs.

b) OTHER REPORTS

Instead of the standard unqualified opinion, an auditor may render one of four other reports:

(i) Explanatory Language Added to an Unqualified Opinion

Certain circumstances, while not affecting the auditor's unqualified opinion on the financial statements, may require the auditor to add explanatory language to the audit report. These situations include when: (1) the auditor uses another auditor's work, (2) a change in accounting principles or in the method of their application has materially affected the comparability of financial statements between accounting periods, or (3) the financial statements must depart from a promulgated accounting principle to avoid a misleading presentation.

(ii) Qualified Opinion

In a qualified opinion, the auditor states that, *except for* the effects of the matter to which the qualification relates, the financial statements present fairly, in all material respects, the enterprise's financial picture. An auditor may issue a qualified opinion if: (1) inadequate accounting records prevent the auditor from performing a full audit, (2) the auditor could not observe the counting of physical inventories at year-end, or (3) a departure from GAAP, including when the financial statements fail to disclose information that GAAP requires, materially affects the financial statements. A qualified opinion will always contain the words "except for" or "with the exception of."

(iii) Adverse Opinion

An adverse opinion states that the financial statements do not present fairly the financial position, results of operations, or cash flows of the entity in conformity with generally accepted accounting principles. When an enterprise departs from GAAP, the auditor may issue either an adverse opinion or a qualified opinion, depending upon materiality of the departure. The SEC does not accept adverse opinions from registrants because the registrant can correct the reporting that gave rise to the adverse opinion. Because adverse opinions virtually destroy an enterprise's ability to raise capital or borrow money, as a practical matter, the client will do almost anything to prevent the auditor from issuing an adverse opinion. Nevertheless, auditors sometimes need to issue adverse opinions as in the following example where the enterprise did not consolidate a subsidiary:

As described in Note X, the Company has not consolidated the financial statements of subsidiary XYZ Company that it acquired during 20X1 because it has not yet been able to ascertain the fair values of certain of the subsidiary's material assets and liabilities at the acquisition date. This investment is therefore accounted for on a cost basis by the Company. Under accounting principles generally accepted in the United States of America, the subsidiary should have been consolidated because it is controlled by the Company. Had XYZ Company been consolidated, many elements in the accompanying consolidated financial statements would have been materially affected. The effects on the consolidated financial statements of the failure to consolidate have not been determined.

Adverse Opinion

In our opinion, because of the significance of the matter discussed in the Basis for Adverse Opinion paragraph, the consolidated financial statements referred to above do not present fairly the financial position of ABC Company and its subsidiaries as of December 31, 20X1, or the results of their operations or their cash flows for the year then ended in accordance with accounting principles generally accepted in the United States of America.

* * *

1 Am. Inst. of Certified Pub. Accountants, AICPA Professional Standards AU-C ¶ 705.A32, illus. 3 (Jan. 2014); *available at* http://www.aicpa.org/Research/Standards/AuditAttest/Downloadable Documents/AU-C-00705.pdf.

(iv) Disclaimer of Opinion

A disclaimer of opinion states that the auditor does not express an opinion on the financial statements. An auditor, for example, must disclaim an opinion when the auditing firm has not performed an examination sufficient in scope to enable the auditor to form an opinion on the financial statements. The following excerpt illustrates a disclaimer of opinion when the auditor could not obtain audit evidence about the enterprise's inventories and accounts receivable:

We were not engaged as auditors of the Company until after December 31, 20X1, and, therefore, did not observe the counting of physical inventories at the beginning or end of the year. We were unable to satisfy ourselves by other auditing procedures concerning the inventory held at December 31, 20X1, which is stated in the balance sheet at $XXX. In addition, the introduction of a new computerized accounts receivable system in September 20X1 resulted in numerous misstatements in accounts receivable. As of the date of our audit report, management was still in the process of rectifying the system deficiencies and correcting the misstatements. We were unable to confirm or verify by alternative means accounts receivable included in the balance sheet at a total amount of $XXX at December 31, 20X1. As a result of these matters, we were unable to determine whether any adjustments might have been found necessary in respect of recorded or unrecorded inventories and accounts receivable, and the elements making up the statements of income, changes in stockholders' equity, and cash flows.

Disclaimer of Opinion

Because of the significance of the matters described in the Basis for Disclaimer of Opinion paragraph, we have not been able to obtain sufficient appropriate audit evidence to provide a basis for an audit opinion. Accordingly, we do not express an opinion on these financial statements.

1 AM. INST. OF CERTIFIED PUB. ACCOUNTANTS, AICPA PROFESSIONAL STANDARDS AU-C ¶ 708.A32, illus. 6 (Jan. 2014), *available at* http://www.aicpa.org/Research/Standards/AuditAttest/DownloadableDocuments/AU-C-00705.pdf.

PROBLEMS

Problem 2.2A. If a creditor asked you to audit the financial statements of Nifty-Novelty as of the close of February from the problem on pages 110 to 112, *supra*, what steps would you take? What questions would you ask and to whom would you address them?

Problem 2.2B. If a shareholder asked you to audit the financial statements of Camera Sales Co. as of the close of April from the problem on pages 112 to 114, *supra*, what steps would you take? What questions would you ask and to whom would you address them?

Problem 2.2C. If a potential creditor asked you to audit the financial statements of the Tortious Toys Company as of the close of April from the problem on pages 114 to 117, *supra*, what steps would you take? What questions would you ask and to whom would you address them?

2. THE ESTABLISHMENT OF GENERALLY ACCEPTED AUDITING STANDARDS

Modern audit procedures trace their development to a famous scandal and failed audit involving McKesson & Robbins Incorporated, a company whose shares were traded on the New York Stock Exchange. Price, Waterhouse & Co. audited the financial statements for McKesson & Robbins and its subsidiaries for the year ended December 31, 1937. The consolidated financial statements reported total assets exceeding $87 million. This total, however, contained approximately $19 million in fictitious assets, including about $10 million in feigned inventories and approximately $9 million in fabricated receivables. For 1937, fictitious sales amounted to more than $18 million on which the consolidated income statement reported fictitious gross profit exceeding $1.8 million.

To accomplish this fraud, Philip M. Musica, a previously convicted swindler who served as the corporation's president under the alias Frank Donald Coster, and his three brothers devised a clever scheme. McKesson & Robbins pretended to purchase merchandise from fictitious vendors that supposedly retained the goods for shipment directly to the corporation's customers. The perpetrators also prepared invoices to document fabricated sales to customers. Musica caused McKesson & Robbins to issue checks to the fictitious vendors, intercepted and cashed the checks, and used the proceeds for partial payments to the corporation on the fabricated sales to customers. Musica and his assistants, however, pocketed about $2.8 million in the scheme. Because the auditors did not observe the inventories or confirm the receivables, the audit did not detect the fraud.

The SEC held administrative hearings to review this failed audit and issued ASR No. 19, which concluded that:

> auditing procedures relating to the inspection of inventories and confirmation of receivables, which, prior to our hearings, had been considered optional steps, should . . . be accepted as normal auditing procedures in connection with the presentation of comprehensive and dependable financial statements to investors.

Accounting Series Release No. 19, 11 Fed. Reg. 10,918 (Dec. 5, 1940), *reprinted in* [1937–1982 Transfer Binder] Fed. Sec. L. Rep. (CCH) ¶ 72,020.

In response to the McKesson-Robbins fraud, the AICPA established the Committee on Auditing Procedures (the "Committee") to develop a set of auditing standards. Like ARBs, however, SAPs did not bind the profession. Nevertheless, the SEC refrained from establishing separate auditing procedures and decided to let the accounting profession develop auditing standards, thereby following the same path which the Commission had adopted regarding accounting principles. Compared to matters involving accounting principles, however, until Sarbanes-Oxley, the SEC consistently exhibited even greater deference to the accounting profession regarding auditing standards, largely because the profession willingly addressed issues that the SEC deemed significant. While the accounting profession had turned the responsibility to develop and promulgate GAAP over to FASB, until Sarbanes-Oxley the AICPA largely retained the corresponding duty to establish auditing standards through the Auditing Standards Board ("ASB"), which set the rules that the AICPA's professional standards required members to follow in all audits. Following the high profile financial frauds in the late 1990s and early 2000s that raised questions about the audit process because auditors failed to detect seriously misstated financial statements at numerous public companies, most notably Enron and WorldCom, Sarbanes-Oxley created the PCAOB. Subject to SEC approval, the legislation gives the PCAOB the authority to establish the auditing and related standards that registered public accounting firms need to use to prepare and issue audit reports for public companies subject to the SEC's jurisdiction. As we will soon discuss in more detail, SOx also required firms that audit public companies to register with the PCAOB and allowed the PCAOB to inspect those firms and to bring disciplinary actions against individual auditors and firms that audited public companies.

Please again remember that PCAOB's rules apply only to accounting firms that audit issuers. Consequently, the accounting profession, through the AICPA and its ASB, still establishes "generally accepted auditing standards in the United States," or "GAAS in the United States" or "U.S. GAAS," for audits involving all other nonissuers. In 2008, the ASB Chairman estimated that the body's standards applied to hundreds of thousands of businesses and almost 90,000 government entities.

Historically, the emergence of auditing standards follows closely behind the development of accounting principles. As today's global economy focuses increased attention on international accounting principles in the United States and throughout the world, we can expect international auditing standards to develop and grow in significance. Just as the financial crisis has spread globally, the accounting scandals and audit failures at Dutch grocer Ahold NV, Italian dairy and multinational food company Parmalat SpA, and Japanese camera and medical equipment company Olympus Corp. document that accounting fraud crosses international boundaries.

After Sarbanes-Oxley, separate standards apply to audits involving (1) issuers and (2) so-called nonissuers. We proceed now to discuss the creation of auditing standards in the United States.

a. ISSUERS

Simply stated, Sarbanes-Oxley ended accountant self-regulation and standard setting concerning audits of issuers. The term "issuer" generally means any registrant subject to the periodic reporting requirements and any person or entity who has filed, but not withdrawn, a registration statement that has not yet become effective. Subject to the SEC's oversight, SOx section 101 established the PCAOB, a private-sector, non-profit corporation, to oversee auditors that issue audit reports to issuers and, among other responsibilities, to establish or adopt auditing, quality control, ethics, independence, and other standards for such audits to protect investors and further the public's interest in fair, informative, and independent audit reports. As a result, both the SEC and the PCAOB establish auditing standards for audits of public companies. In addition, Congress certainly retains the power to intervene in, or at least to influence, auditing standards and did so in the recent JOBS Act. Although Sarbanes-Oxley eliminated the AICPA's ability to establish auditing standards for audits involving issuers, the accounting profession, typically through public comment and the AICPA, still enjoys considerable influence in the establishment and revision of those standards.

(1) THE SECURITIES AND EXCHANGE COMMISSION

The Private Securities Litigation Reform Act of 1995 specifically requires any audit that the securities laws mandate to include, among other things, procedures designed to provide reasonable assurance that the audit will detect any illegal acts that would directly and materially affect the determination of financial statement amounts. In addition, the legislation specifically gives the SEC authority to modify or supplement certain generally accepted auditing standards in at least three areas—illegal acts, related party transactions, and the registrant's ability to continue as a going concern. A financial reporting release issued in response to that legislation expressed the SEC's desire to alert auditors and issuers to the possibility that, in certain circumstances, the Commission might mandate additional audit procedures, beyond those that GAAS required.

After Sarbanes-Oxley, the SEC enjoys the power to approve any rules that the PCAOB may adopt and the PCAOB's budget. For example, the PCAOB's first auditing standard requires auditors' reports on financial statements for public companies to state that the auditor performed the audit in accordance with the Board's standards rather than the previously required reference to generally accepted auditing standards. By January 1, 2014, the SEC had approved seventeen PCAOB auditing standards.

As another way to influence auditing standards, the SEC can impose disciplinary sanctions on accountants and other professionals, including lawyers. Rule 102(e) of the Commission's Rules of Practice allows the SEC to prohibit an accountant from practicing before the Commission for a variety of reasons, including lack of the requisite qualifications, character, or integrity; engaging in violations of the securities laws; or engaging in unethical or improper conduct. Even though Sarbanes-Oxley established the PCAOB in part to discipline auditors of public companies, the Board cannot exercise any unrestrained authority over discipline because the SEC retains authority to modify any sanction that the PCAOB imposes.

The SEC has also recently begun enforcement efforts against foreign accounting firms that audit foreign-based companies whose securities trade on U.S. stock exchanges. To date, those enforcement efforts have focused on auditors of registrants involved in *reverse mergers*, which occur when a private company, typically based in a foreign country, acquires a shell public company, enabling the private company to go public without the securities filings and due diligence that typically accompany a public offering. Since 2007, more than 600 companies have used this "backdoor" technique, including more than 150 based in China. Dating back to 2011, dozens of Chinese companies have either acknowledged accounting problems or watched accounting questions cause either the SEC or U.S. exchanges to halt trading in their shares. As no surprise, regulatory scrutiny has turned to these firms' auditors, which often include fewer than five partners and ten professional staff members and which have frequently resigned their engagements.

(2) PUBLIC COMPANY ACCOUNTING OVERSIGHT BOARD

As one of the most important reforms in Sarbanes-Oxley, section 101 established the PCAOB as a five-member body to register, regulate, and inspect public accounting firms that audit publicly traded companies; to establish or adopt auditing, quality control, ethics, independence, and other standards for such audits, subject to SEC approval; and to conduct investigations and disciplinary proceedings when appropriate to enforce compliance with the law and professional standards.

While the PCAOB continues to develop its own auditing standards, the Board has adopted those standards that the accounting profession, through the AICPA and the organization's ASB, had promulgated as of April 16, 2003 as "Interim Professional Auditing Standards." The PCAOB took this action to assure continuity and certainty in the standards that govern audits of public companies. In its first auditing standard, Auditing Standard No. 1 ("AS 1"), however, the PCAOB required that auditors change the reference in audit reports to state explicitly that the audit complied with the PCAOB's auditing standards. Through June 2014, the PCAOB had issued seventeen auditing standards.

Under SOx section 104(a), the PCAOB must conduct a continuing program of inspections to assess each registered public accounting firm's compliance with SOx, SEC and PCAOB rules, and professional standards. SOx requires the PCAOB to inspect firms auditing 100 or more public companies every year, which translates to annual inspections in 2014 for the "Big Four," plus BDO USA, Crowe Horwath, Grant Thornton, MaloneBailey, and McGladrey. In contrast, the PCAOB must inspect those firms with less than 100 public companies as audit clients at least every three years. When circumstances warrant, the Board can order a special inspection.

The Board's inspections include an intensive review of audit engagements and financial statements and have focused on audit firm culture, the free flow of information between predecessor and successor auditors, the detection of fraud, inadequate documentation, and risk assessment. Various recent PCAOB reports contain troubling data about audit deficiencies. Perhaps most troubling, the Board found deficiencies in thirty-nine percent of the Big Four audits inspected during 2013, compared to thirty-seven percent in 2012. The PCAOB has also found record numbers of deficiencies in audits of internal control over financial reporting during recent annual inspections of the eight largest domestic registered firms. Although a third report shows a decrease in significant audit performance deficiencies identified among smaller firms inspected at least once every three years, the results leave much room for improvement. The report states inspections identified significant deficiencies at 44 percent of the audit firms inspected from 2007 to 2010, compared to 61 percent during the 2004 through 2006 period. Inspectors found at least one significant deficiency in 28 percent of the individual audits reviewed during 2007-2010, an improvement relative to the 36 percent in the 2004-2006 period.

Today, SOx section 101 gives the PCAOB the authority to discipline both public accounting firms and associated persons that audit public companies.

The PCAOB can suspend or bar both public accounting firms and associated persons from auditing public companies, impose civil penalties, censure, require additional professional education or training, or impose other sanctions any time any auditor does not observe GAAP or other professional standards. *See* 15 U.S.C. § 7211 (2012). As a result, at least as to auditors of public companies, SOx ended accountant self-regulation.

Audit deficiencies can lead to sanctions against accounting firms and individual auditors, but rarely involve the Big Four and their professionals. In 2007, however, the PCAOB applied its first disciplinary actions against a Big Four accounting firm, assessing a one million dollar fine on Deloitte & Touche ("Deloitte") and barring a former Deloitte audit partner from association with a registered public accounting firm for at least two years. More recently, the PCAOB announced a settled disciplinary order censuring Ernst & Young LLP and imposing a $2 million civil penalty, which matches the Board's largest fine to date, to resolve charges arising from three audits involving Medicis Pharmaceutical Corporation and an internal review consultation after one of the audits. In addition, four current or former partners also agreed to sanctions, ranging from a two-year ban from associating with a PCAOB-registered accounting firm and a $50,000 penalty to a censure. Most significantly, the PCAOB imposed discipline against the partners involved in the audits, rather than only against the firm.

Overseeing an international auditing profession may rank as the most critical challenge facing the PCAOB. SOx section 106 requires foreign audit firms that prepare audit reports for companies whose securities are publicly traded in the United States to register with the PCAOB. The Board continues to work with the European Commission in an effort to reach agreement on audit regulations that likely will result in the joint supervision of the accounting profession. This provision originally engendered strong opposition from the European Union, but the recent accounting scandals and corresponding audit failures at Dutch grocer Ahold NV and Italian dairy and multinational food company Parmalat SpA have seemingly changed attitudes on both sides of the Atlantic Ocean.

Inspecting auditing firms outside the United States has presented an enormous challenge to the PCAOB. As of September 2014, over 900 non-U.S. audit firms from more than eighty-five countries had registered with the PCAOB. At least fifteen nations, including several EU countries, and until very recently, China, have refused to cooperate with PCAOB inspectors. (The Chinese refusal also affected registered auditors in Hong Kong to the extent that they audited clients that operated in China.) In addition, foreign auditors that have not registered with the PCAOB often render assistance, sometimes substantial, to the registered auditors for public companies, who rely on that audit work. In either event, no one should assume that the PCAOB has reviewed the quality control practices or audit procedures at these foreign auditing firms. As of December 31, 2013, the PCAOB had conducted inspections in forty-three foreign jurisdictions, but was prevented from inspecting the U.S.-related audit work and practices in three of those jurisdictions—Greece, Ireland, and Hong Kong. As of that date, the PCAOB had not conducted inspections in twelve jurisdictions, including Austria, Belgium, China, and Italy. Dating back to 2010, the PCAOB has published and regularly updated lists containing those foreign companies whose securities trade in U.S. markets and that have filed financial statements with the SEC, but for which asserted non-U.S. legal obstacles prevent the Board from inspecting the companies' PCAOB-registered auditors. Once again, no one should assume that the PCAOB has reviewed the quality control practices or audit procedures at these auditing firms.

When reading financial statements from a foreign-based, public company, lawyers should ask the following questions:

(1) How long has the company been publicly traded in the United States?
(2) Is the company current in its periodic filings with the SEC?
(3) How long has the company published audited financial statements?
(4) Has the PCAOB inspected the auditor?
(5) Has the PCAOB inspected any other auditing firms that the auditor may have relied on during the audit?
(6) Do the company's management and directors bring significant public company experience to their current positions?

See Nicolas Morgan & Patrick Hunnius, *Regulators Ramp Up China Reverse Merger Scrutiny*, 9 Corp. Accountability Rep. (BNA) 1168 (Sept. 30, 2011).

(3) CONGRESS

As with generally accepted accounting principles, Congress retains, again at least implicitly, the ability to legislate, or at a minimum influence, auditing standards for public companies. In the JOBS Act, Congress exercised its power and prospectively excused EGCs from complying with any new PCAOB rules requiring either mandatory audit firm rotation or an auditor discussion and analysis to supplement the auditor's report. In addition, unless "after considering the protection of investors and whether the action will promote efficiency, competition, and capital formation," the SEC determines that any new rule that the PCAOB adopts qualifies as "necessary or appropriate in the public interest," that rule will not apply to any audit involving an EGC.

b. NONISSUERS

As previously mentioned, after the McKesson-Robbins scandal the AICPA created the Committee on Auditing Procedures and later renamed the group first the Auditing Standards Executive Committee ("AudSEC") and most recently the Auditing Standards Board ("ASB"). Those bodies have issued many authoritative standards, called Statements on Auditing Standards ("SASs"). Rule 202 of the AICPA's Code of Professional Conduct requires members to adhere to auditing standards promulgated by bodies that the AICPA Council has designated to establish such standards. The Council has designated the ASB to establish auditing standards. With the 2011 issuance of SAS No. 122, *Statements on Auditing Standards: Clarification and Recodification*, the ASB completed a "clarity" project that recodified its auditing standards. During the process, the ASB brought the AICPA standards for audits involving nonpublic companies closer toward convergence with the standards from the International Auditing and Assurance Standards Board ("IAASB"). The clarified AICPA standards apply to audits of financial statements for periods ending on or after December 15, 2012. As of June 1, 2014, the ASB and its predecessor, AudSEC, had published 128 Statements on Auditing Standards ("SASs"). The SASs interpret GAAS for nonissuers.

The AICPA's bylaws empower the joint trial board to admonish, suspend, or expel a member from the Institute for violating the Code of Professional Conduct. In addition, most state CPA societies use the same trial board. In an effort to enforce professional standards uniformly, the trial board hears and adjudicates charges alleging that a member has violated the Code of Professional Conduct or a state society's rules or bylaws after the Institute's Professional Ethics Division has completed an investigation. Although the trial board cannot impose fines or bar a person from practicing accounting, its decisions affect both AICPA and state society memberships. In addition, disciplinary action typically damages the accountant's professional reputation and can also cause the appropriate state accountancy board to revoke the accountant's license.

c.   INTERNATIONAL AUDITING STANDARDS

Even if some organization or group promulgates a core set of international accounting principles that gain worldwide acceptance, those principles will not achieve their purpose unless adequate auditing and enforcement ensure application of the principles. The International Federation of Accountants ("IFAC"), a group of 157 national professional accountancy bodies, including the AICPA, from 123 countries and jurisdictions, represents 2.5 million accountants worldwide. Pursuant to IFAC's mission to protect the public interest by encouraging high quality practices by the world's accountants, the organization formed the IAASB, previously known as the International Auditing Practices Committee ("IAPC"). IAASB develops and promulgates standards and statements on auditing and related services. Among other pronouncements, IAASB issues International Standards on Auditing ("ISAs") and International Auditing Practice Statements ("IAPSs") and seeks to promote their voluntary acceptance. ISAs describe basic principles and essential procedures and offer guidance through explanatory and other material. In contrast, IAPSs provide practical assistance to auditors in implementing ISAs or promoting good practice. IAPSs enjoy less authority than ISAs. In 2009, IAASB completed its so-called "clarity project," during which reviewed and revised all thirty-six of its auditing standards in an effort to advance convergence.

At this point, neither ISAs nor IAPSs establish standards which auditors in the United States must follow under either the PCAOB's rules or the AICPA's Code of Professional Conduct. Before an ISA or related IAPS will apply to audits in the United States, either the PCAOB or the ASB must specifically adopt the ISA. So far, the PCAOB has yet to take an official position on international auditing standards. While the PCAOB has shown support for global auditing standards, opponents have voiced concerns that convergence to international auditing standards could harm investors in the United States, noting that Congress established the PCAOB as independent from the auditing profession and that the auditing profession funds and controls both the IAASB and ASB.

3. COMPONENTS

The audit process incorporates both accepted auditing standards and recognized auditing procedures. Auditing standards differ from auditing procedures in that the former broadly addresses an audit's objectives and seeks to ensure a certain performance level, while the latter refers to the specific acts that an audit entails.

a. AUDITING STANDARDS

Auditing standards involve not only the auditor's professional qualities but also the judgment that the auditor exercises in the audit and the audit report. The AICPA's membership has adopted ten basic statements which the profession refers to as "generally accepted auditing standards." Collectively, these ten basic statements, plus the SASs that build upon them by providing additional specificity, comprise GAAS, which Rule 202 of the AICPA Code of Professional Conduct requires members to follow.

The ten basic statements fall into three groups: (1) general standards, (2) standards of fieldwork, and (3) standards of reporting.

The accounting profession recognizes three general standards for audits and auditors. An auditor must, first, possess adequate technical training and proficiency before undertaking an audit to ensure that qualified persons perform the examination; second, maintain an independent mental attitude in all matters relating to the assignment; and third, exercise due professional care while performing the examination and preparing the audit report.

Three separate tenets comprise the standards of field work. An auditor must: (1) adequately plan the work and properly supervise any assistants; (2) properly study and evaluate the existing internal controls to assess the extent to which the auditor can either rely on those controls or must perform additional tests and procedures; and (3) appropriately obtain sufficient competent evidence, whether through inspection, observation, inquiries, or confirmation, to afford a reasonable basis for an opinion regarding the financial statements under examination.

As perhaps the most important step in the audit process, the auditing profession recognizes four basic standards for reporting. First, the audit report generally must express an opinion as to whether the financial statements comply with generally accepted accounting principles. Second, the report must identify any inconsistency in the application of those principles between the current period and the preceding period. Third, the profession regards informative disclosure in the financial statements as reasonably adequate unless the audit report specifically states otherwise. Finally, the report shall either express an opinion regarding the financial statements, taken as a whole, or explain why the auditor must disclaim an opinion. In either event, the report should describe the auditor's examination, if any, and the degree of responsibility that the auditor assumes.

b. AUDITING PROCEDURES

Audit procedures refer to the various acts that an auditor performs during an audit. These acts include tests that the auditor makes to obtain comfort that the financial statements fairly present the enterprise's financial condition and results. Common audit procedures include reconciling the cash amounts reflected in the business's ledger with the balances reflected in statements from the financial institution, observing physical inventories, price testing inventories, confirming assets and liabilities, transactional testing involving expenses, purchases, sales, and payroll, performing cut-off tests between accounting periods, reading minutes of shareholder and director meetings, and obtaining representation letters from management and attorneys. The SASs specifically require very few audit procedures in interpreting the ten basic standards and do not establish specific requirements to guide auditors' decisions, such as establishing minimums for determining sample size, rules for selecting sample items for testing, or evaluating results. Although more bright line requirements might help address difficult audit situations, such rules might not keep pace with today's rapidly changing business environment.

4. WHO SELECTS THE AUDITING PROCEDURES?

In definite contrast to accounting principles, the client's management does not choose the auditing procedures that the auditor will perform. Although the financial statements remain management's responsibility, the auditor assumes full responsibility for the audit and the audit opinion. As a result, the auditor selects the auditing procedures that the auditor will use to reach an opinion about whether the financial statements present fairly, in all material respects, the financial condition, results of operations, and cash flows. In selecting auditing procedures and performing the audit, the auditor must act within the confines of GAAS.

5.   THE EXPECTATION GAP

Differing perceptions exist between the assurance auditors provide and that which investors and other users of financial statements expect. A study in the early 1990s revealed that almost half of the investors surveyed believed that audited financial statements provide absolute assurance against errors or unintentional misstatements. In that same survey, more than seventy percent expressed a belief that audited financial statements provide absolute assurance against fraud or intentional misstatements. As we have seen, however, an audit provides only reasonable assurance against material misstatements, whether intentional or unintentional, in the financial statements. Moreover, experience shows that frauds, especially forgery and collusion, can more easily avoid detection even in a properly planned and executed audit than unintentional errors. The survey indicates, however, that investors set a higher standard for auditors to uncover fraud than to discover errors and that expectations exceed the assurance actually provided. The accounting profession has labeled these misconceptions as the "expectation gap."

In reality, an audit does not guarantee that error or fraud has not affected the financial statements. Similarly, an audit does not offer any assurance about the safety of an investment in the enterprise. At the same time, however, GAAS requires the auditor to assess the risk that error or fraud may cause the financial statements to contain a material misstatement, and the auditor must design an audit to provide reasonable assurance that the audit will detect material errors and misstatements and then must properly perform and evaluate audit procedures to attain the required assurance.

We must keep in mind, however, that the legal standard for materiality may differ from the auditing standard. The Codification states that enterprises need not apply its provisions to immaterial items, but does not define either material or immaterial. *See* FASB ASC ¶ 105-10-05-6. Historically, auditors generally treated any amount that did not exceed five percent of income before taxes as immaterial. Conversely, auditors usually considered any item that exceeded ten percent of income before taxes as material. Both the courts and the SEC, however, have rejected these mathematical standards, preferring a facts and circumstances analysis. Under the federal securities laws, the Supreme Court has concluded that an omitted fact qualifies as material if a substantial likelihood exists that a reasonable investor would have considered the omitted fact important because disclosure would have significantly altered the "total mix" of available information. *Basic Inc. v. Levinson*, 485 U.S. 224, 231–32 (1988); *TSC Indus., Inc. v. Northway*, 426 U.S. 438, 449 (1976); *see also* 17 C.F.R. §§ 230.405, 240.12b-2 (2014) ("The term 'material,' when used to qualify a requirement for the furnishing of information as to any subject, limits the information required to those matters to which there is a substantial likelihood that a reasonable investor would attach importance in determining whether to purchase [or sell] the securit[ies] registered.").

One example from the late 1990s may illustrate how a quantitatively immaterial item might nevertheless qualify as material. A 1998 *Wall Street Journal* article described BankAmerica Corp.'s failure to disclose information about its $372 million write-down of a loan to D.E. Shaw & Co., a New York investment firm. Even though bank officials knew about possible losses on the loan as early as August, the bank did not disclose the extent of the losses before shareholders voted in late September to approve a $43 billion merger with NationsBank, which created the nation's second-largest bank. The article quotes the merged bank's chief financial officer as saying that " [$372 million is] a big number but it's not material to a company' that is as big as Bank America." When the merged bank announced the write-down in mid-October, the stock price dropped eleven percent in a single day. Plaintiffs quickly filed multiple class action securities fraud actions related to the merger against new BankAmerica and other defendants.

In Staff Accounting Bulletin No. 99, the SEC's staff explicitly rejected the automatic classification of financial statement misstatements or omissions that fall under a five percent threshold as immaterial. The staff emphasized that registrants and their auditors must consider qualitative factors in materiality determinations. For example, a quantitatively small misstatement or omission could nevertheless qualify as material when it:

- arises from an item capable of precise measurement;

- masks a change in earnings or other trends;

- hides a failure to meet analysts' consensus expectations for the enterprise;

- changes a loss into income or vice versa;

- concerns a segment or other portion of the registrant's business that has been identified as playing a significant role in the registrant's operations or profitability;

- determines the registrant's compliance with regulatory requirements;

- affects the registrant's compliance with loan covenants or other contractual requirements;

- increases management's compensation—for example, by satisfying requirement for the award of bonuses or other forms of incentive compensation; or

- involves concealment of an unlawful transaction.

In assessing multiple misstatements, the bulletin reminds registrants and auditors that they must consider all misstatements or omissions both separately and in the aggregate to determine whether, in relation to the individual line item amounts, subtotals or totals in the financial statements, the misstatements or omissions materially misstate the financial statements taken as a whole. Finally, the SAB reminds registrants that immaterial, but intentional misstatements can violate the federal securities laws, particularly the FCPA record-keeping and internal controls requirements. Materiality, Staff Accounting Bulletin No. 99, 64 Fed. Reg. 45,150 (Aug. 19, 1999), *available at* http://www.sec.gov/interps/account/sab99.htm.

Following SAB No. 99, the agency became aware of diversity in how enterprises determined the materiality of financial statement errors that span multiple periods. The SEC staff indicated that many registrants did not consider the effect of prior year errors on current year financial statements, potentially resulting in material misstatements as the errors accumulate. Accordingly, Staff Accounting Bulletin No. 108 seeks to improve financial reporting practices in that regard. SAB No. 108 directs registrants to consider prior year misstatements when examining misstatements in the current year.

The staff explained that enterprises have largely applied two methods in practice to accumulate and quantify misstatements: the "rollover" and "iron curtain" approaches, both of which contain shortcomings. The "rollover" approach focuses on the materiality of such errors in terms of the current income statement, potentially allowing the accumulation of errors on the balance sheet. By comparison, the "iron curtain" approach analyzes the materiality of the errors accumulated on the current balance sheet, but may produce errors in the income statement.

In SAB No. 108, the SEC staff advises against exclusive reliance on either the "rollover" or "iron curtain" approach. Instead, registrants should quantify errors under both approaches and adjust the financial statements when either approach indicates a material misstatement, "considering all relevant quantitative and qualitative factors." The staff indicated that registrants need not restate prior period financial statements when applying the guidance; instead, registrants may post a cumulative effect adjustment to the opening balance of retained earnings and disclose the nature and amount of the individual errors included in the adjustment. Considering the Effects of Prior Year Misstatements when Quantifying Misstatements in Current Year Financial Statements, Staff Accounting Bulletin No. 108, 71 Fed. Reg. 54,580 (Sept. 18, 2006), *available at* http://www.sec.gov/interps/account/sab108.pdf.

In 2010 and 2011, the FASB and the ASB, respectively, while trying to converge GAAP and GAAS with IFRS and international auditing standards, have adopted changes, without explanation, which seemingly lower the definition of materiality for financial accounting and auditing purposes from a "would influence" to a "could influence" standard. In between those actions, the SEC approved the PCAOB's new Auditing Standard No. 11, *Consideration of Materiality in Planning and Performing an Audit*, which describes thresholds auditors should apply to evaluate materiality during an audit of an SEC registrant. The PCAOB explicitly relied on *TSC Industries, Inc. v. Northway, Inc.*, cited on page 200, *supra*, which applied a "would influence" test. Thus, the guidance from the FASB and ASB has seemingly created inconsistent definitions of materiality in the United States. *See* Samuel P. Gunther, *What is Materiality? SEC & PCAOB v. FASB & ASB*, 10 Corp. Accountability Rep. (BNA) 496 (May 18, 2012).

a. "PRESENT FAIRLY"

As indicated in the introductory sections A and B to this chapter, the ultimate goal of the independent outside auditor in examining the financial statements proposed by the management is to express an opinion as to whether those statements "present fairly" the enterprise's financial condition, operating results, and cash flows "in accordance with generally accepted accounting principles." This language, which has traditionally been used by auditors in their report accompanying the financial statements when they are distributed to the shareholders and the financial markets at large, poses a dilemma: what should an auditor do if despite scrupulous application of GAAP the resulting statements do not fairly present the financial picture, whether because of a misleading representation in some respect, or a failure to disclose some relevant information, or whatever. To put it another way, the traditional language raises the question of whether compliance with GAAP may be presumed in and of itself to satisfy the "present fairly" test. Over the years, the accounting profession has at least leaned toward the position that an auditor's responsibilities end with making sure that the financial statements comply with GAAP. In the profession's mind, the application of GAAP conveys a "fair" presentation.

Investors and other users, however, have believed, and continue to believe, that accountants accept an additional burden of ensuring that the financial statements present the underlying transactions in a reasonable and fair manner. That view got a significant boost from the very influential decision in *United States v. Simon*, 425 F.2d 796 (2d Cir. 1969). In that case, Roth, the president of Continental, caused the company to lend substantial sums to an affiliated entity, which Roth also controlled. Roth in turn borrowed the money from the affiliate to use for his personal purposes. Roth's financial picture had deteriorated, leaving him in no position to repay the affiliate, and the collateral he put up, consisting mostly of stock and securities of Continental, was worth substantially less than the amount of the loan, so the loan receivable from the affiliate on Continental's books was of doubtful collectibility. For failing to insist upon fuller disclosure of these facts, the three accountants from the large firm auditing Continental were charged under various federal statutes with conspiracy to commit fraud. At the jury trial, eight outstanding accounting experts testified that GAAP did not require disclosure of either the make-up of the collateral or the fact of Roth's borrowings from the affiliate. The trial judge refused to give the defendants' requested instruction that the defendants could be found guilty only if according to GAAP the financial statements did not constitute a fair presentation. Instead, the judge instructed the jury that the critical test was whether the financial statements fairly presented Continental's financial position, and if not, whether the defendants had acted in good faith, as to which compliance with GAAP would be "evidence which may be very persuasive but not necessarily conclusive." The conviction of the defendants was upheld on appeal, in a much cited opinion by Judge Friendly, holding that if literal compliance with GAAP produces a materially misleading impression, the auditors with knowledge could be held criminally liable for their unqualified acceptance.

It should be noted that the Simon case could be construed narrowly, and limited to the special fact that the auditors were aware that the president was running the business for his own benefit rather than in the best interests of the shareholders. As the following excerpt indicates, Judge Friendly's opinion certainly stressed this point:

> We join defendants' counsel in assuming that the mere fact that a company has made advances to an affiliate does not ordinarily impose a duty on an accountant to investigate what the affiliate has done with them or even to disclose that the affiliate has made a loan to a common officer if this has come to his attention. But it simply cannot be true that an accountant is under no duty to disclose what he knows

when he has reason to believe that, to a material extent, a corporation is being operated not to carry out its business in the interest of all the stockholders but for the private benefit of its president . . . . Generally accepted accounting principles instruct an accountant what to do in the usual case where he has no reason to doubt that the affairs of the corporation are being honestly conducted. Once he has reason to believe that this basic assumption is false, an entirely different situation confronts him. Then . . . he must "extend his procedures to determine whether or not such suspicions are justified." If . . . he finds his suspicions to be confirmed, full disclosure must be the rule, unless he has made sure the wrong has been righted and procedures to avoid a repetition have been established.

425 F.2d at 806–07.

Later cases have followed the *Simon* approach, at least for the purpose of imposing civil rather than criminal liability upon accountants. In *Herzfeld v. Laventhol, Kreckstein, Horwath & Horwath*, 378 F. Supp. 112 (S.D.N.Y. 1974), *rev'd in part on other grounds*, 340 F.2d 27 (2d. Cir. 1976), the District Court put it this way:

The policy underlying the securities laws of providing investors with all the facts needed to make intelligent investment decisions can only be accomplished if financial statements *fully and fairly portray* the actual financial condition of the company. In those cases where application of generally accepted accounting principles fulfills the duty of full and fair disclosure, the accountant need go no further. But if application of accounting principles alone will not adequately inform investors, accountants, as well as insiders, must take pains to lay bare all the facts needed by investors to interpret the financial statements accurately.

378 F. Supp. at 121–22.

Of course these decisions rest upon construction of federal securities laws, such as SEC Rule 10b-5, and do not necessarily fix the test for the responsibility of auditors pursuant to generally accepted auditing standards. But the liability of auditors, criminal or civil, is just as painful on either basis, and that probably represents the ultimate influence on auditor conduct. Nevertheless, the profession continued to display considerable ambivalence about the scope of the auditor's duty. For example, SAS No. 69, *The Meaning of Present Fairly in Conformity with Generally Accepted Accounting Principles in the Independent Auditor's Report*, while broadening the responsibility of the auditor somewhat beyond mere literal compliance with GAAP, still stopped short of adopting the standard enunciated in Simon. The PCAOB's auditing standards require an auditor to assess whether:

(1) the accounting principles that management has selected and applied enjoy general acceptance;

(2) the accounting principles are appropriate in the circumstances;

(3) the financial statements, including the related notes, provide information about those matters that may affect their use, understanding and interpretation;

(4) the financial statements classify and summarize the information that they present in a reasonable manner that neither provides too much detail nor too few specifics; and

(5) the financial statements reflect the underlying transactions and events in a manner that presents the financial position, results of operations, and cash flows stated within a range of acceptable limits that the enterprise can reasonably and practicably attain.

AM. INST. OF CERTIFIED PUB. ACCOUNTANTS, PCAOB STANDARDS AND RELATED RULES (AS OF JANUARY 2014) AU ¶ 411.04, *available at* http://pcaobus.org/Standards/Auditing/Pages/AU411.aspx.

In any event, the issue of fair presentation versus GAAP appears back on center stage by virtue of the two Sarbanes-Oxley provisions requiring certification of financial statements by the top corporate executives. While there are some differences between sections 302 and 906, such as criminal liability rather than civil, or the breadth of the information covered, the two provisions are identical in casting the obligation in terms of certifying that the information involved "fairly present[s] in all material respects the financial condition and results of operations of the issuer," with no qualifying reference to generally accepted accounting principles. In the light of the long history of the traditional language of the auditor's report, it is hard to believe that this failure to refer to GAAP was inadvertent, and, not surprisingly, the SEC expressly takes that view in its release adopting the implementing rules that SOx section 302 required. In that release, the SEC put it this way (after adding "cash flows" to the financial information specifically required by section 302 to be certified as "fairly presented"):

The certification statement regarding fair presentation of financial statements and other financial information is not limited to a representation that the financial statements and other financial information have been presented in accordance with "generally accepted accounting principles" and is not otherwise limited by reference to generally accepted accounting principles. We believe that Congress intended this statement to provide assurance that the financial information disclosed in a report, viewed in its entirety, meets a standard of overall material accuracy and completeness that is broader than financial reporting requirements under generally accepted accounting principles. In our view, a "fair presentation" of an issuer's financial condition, results of operations and cash flows encompasses the selection of appropriate accounting policies, disclosure of financial information that is informative and reasonably reflects the underlying transactions and events and the inclusion of any additional disclosure necessary to provide investors with a materially accurate and completer picture of an issuer's financial condition, results of operations and cash flows."

Certification of Disclosure in Companies' Quarterly and Annual Reports, 67 Fed. Reg. 57,276, 57,279 n.56 (Sept. 9, 2002).

While this Release relates only to the required certification by corporate officers, its message is likely to be extended to auditors' duties: there is little reason to impose a heavier burden on the corporate officers with respect to fair presentation than on the outside auditor, as long as the auditor knows or has reason to know the facts. As indicated in the discussion of international accounting standards at pages 162 to 168, *supra*, proponents of converging U.S. and international accounting standards would welcome such an extension.

b. THE AUDITOR'S RESPONSIBILITY TO DETECT AND REPORT ERRORS, FRAUD, AND ILLEGAL ACTS

An audit does not attempt to detect all errors that the financial statements may contain or all frauds or illegal acts which may underlie the financial statements. Errors can include unintentional misstatements or omissions, either in actual amounts or in disclosures which appear in the financial statements. In contrast, recall that accountants have historically used the term "irregularities" to refer to intentional misstatements or omissions, which lawyers would probably better understand as fraud or theft. Illegal acts refer to acts or omissions by the enterprise's management or employees related to the enterprise's activities that violate laws or governmental regulations.

Once again, an unqualified opinion only provides reasonable assurance against material misstatements in the financial statements. While designing the audit strategy, the auditor must assess the risk that errors, fraud or illegal acts may cause the financial statements to contain material misstatement. In addition, the auditor must plan and perform appropriate procedures to enable the audit to attain the required assurance.

Because of the characteristics of certain frauds and illegal acts, particularly those involving forgery and collusion, a properly designed and executed audit may not detect a material irregularity. For example, GAAS does not require an auditor to authenticate documents. Additionally, audit procedures that effectively detect unintentional misstatements may not uncover collusion between the client's employees and third parties or among management and employees.

In the recent past, public perceptions and court decisions, especially *United States v. Simon*, have caused the accounting profession to reassess the role which auditors play in society and the public opinion about the level of assurance that an audit should provide. To close the expectation gap, the accounting profession could either educate the public or increase the level of assurance to meet expectations. Over the years, the profession has chosen to do both. In 1988, the ASB changed the language in the standard audit opinion in an attempt to provide better information about what an unqualified opinion means and issued two SASs on the auditor's responsibility to detect errors, fraud and illegal acts. SAS No. 53, which the ASB later revised on multiple occasions, required an auditor to exercise (a) due care in planning, performing, and evaluating the results of audit procedures, and (b) increased sensitivity about the possibility that material fraud exists in every audit. THE AUDITOR'S RESPONSIBILITY TO DETECT AND REPORT ERRORS AND IRREGULARITIES, Statement on Auditing Standards No. 53 (Am. Inst. of Certified Pub. Accountants 1988). Similarly, SAS No. 54 originally prescribed the consideration that an auditor should give to the possibility that a client's illegal acts or omissions may materially affect the financial statements and provides guidance when the auditor detects a possible illegal act. ILLEGAL ACTS BY CLIENTS, Statement on Auditing Standards No. 54 (Am. Inst. of Certified Pub. Accountants 1988).

When those efforts did not produce the anticipated results, the AICPA supported the Private Securities Litigation Reform Act of 1995 which, as discussed on page 193, *supra*, requires any audit that the securities laws mandate to include, among other things, procedures designed to provide reasonable assurance that the audit will detect any illegal acts that would directly and materially effect the determination of financial statement amounts. In addition, the legislation continues to require auditors to take certain actions if they uncover an illegal act or suspect that such an act may have occurred. If an illegal act has likely occurred, unless it qualifies as "clearly inconsequential" the auditor must assure that the audit committee or the entire board of directors obtains adequate information about the illegal act as soon as practicable. If the registrant does not notify the SEC within one business day, the auditor must do so. *See* Pub. L. No. 104-67, § 301(a), 109 Stat. 737, 762–64 (adding Section 10A(b) to the 1934 Act, codified at 15 U.S.C. § 78j-1 (2012)); *see also* 17 C.F.R. § 240.10A-1 (2014).

In 1997, the ASB issued SAS No. 82, Consideration of Fraud in a Financial Statement Audit, which toughened auditing standards and required auditors to assess specifically and document the risk that fraud may cause material misstatements in every audit. In this context, fraud includes both intentional misrepresentations in financial statements, sometimes referred to as "cooking the books," and misappropriation or theft of assets. SAS No. 82 expanded an auditor's responsibilities to plan and perform an audit to require that the auditor obtain reasonable assurance that neither error nor fraud had caused material misstatements in the financial statements. The pronouncement described various frauds and accompanying characteristics, identified factors that an auditor should consider in assessing the risk that fraud had caused material misstatements in the financial statements, and provided guidance about how the auditor should respond to the assessment's results. In addition, the standard suggested how an auditor should evaluate test results as they relate to the possibility that fraud may cause material misstatements, required the auditor to document the risk assessment and response, and finally reaffirmed the requirement that the auditor inform management, the audit committee and perhaps government regulators about any material fraud that an audit detected. CONSIDERATION OF FRAUD IN A FINANCIAL STATEMENT AUDIT, Statement on Auditing Standards No. 82 (Am. Inst. of Certified Pub. Accountants 1997).

Later, SAS No. 99, *Consideration of Fraud in a Financial Statement Audit*, superseded SAS No. 82. CONSIDERATION OF FRAUD IN A FINANCIAL STATEMENT AUDIT, Statement on Auditing Standards No. 99 (Am. Inst. of Certified Pub. Accountants 2002). In addition to previous expectations, SAS No. 99 required an auditor to extend the exercise of professional skepticism to the possibility that fraud may cause a material misstatement. In particular, auditors must evaluate specific fraud risks and document the plan and procedures used to evaluate those risks. *Id.*

Until SAS No. 128, *Using the Work of Internal Auditors*, becomes effective for audits ending on or after December 31, 2014, SAS No. 122, *Consideration of Fraud in a Financial Statement Audit*, sets forth the auditor's responsibilities relating to fraud in an audit of financial statements. Even after SAS No. 128, a lawyer should remember that audits provide only reasonable assurance, not absolute assurance, that fraud has not caused a material misstatement in the financial statements. As a result, even an audit conducted according to GAAS may not detect a material misstatement. *See* 1 AM. INST. OF CERTIFIED PUB. ACCOUNTANTS, AICPA PROFESSIONAL STANDARDS AU-C § 240, ¶ 610.A49 (Mar. 2014); *available at* http://www.acipa.org/ Research/Standards/AuditAttest/DownloadableDocuments/AU-C-00240.pdf (for audits for periods ending on or after December 15, 2012, but before December 15, 2014).

E. ALTERNATIVES TO AUDITS

Privately owned enterprises do not need to file audited financial statements with the SEC. Unless a loan agreement or some other contract requires audited financial statements, these enterprises often prefer to avoid the costs that accompany an audit. Nevertheless, these same firms may want accountants to help prepare their financial statements. As a result, at least two other types of reports may accompany unaudited financial statements. In a *review*, the independent accountant performs certain analytical and other procedures to reach a reasonable basis for expressing limited assurance that the financial statements do not require any material modification to comply with GAAP. The independent accountant will compare financial data to corresponding data for prior periods to ascertain whether or not the data appears reasonable, while also discussing the enterprise's operations with management to determine whether any changes in the business or operating procedures might explain variations in the financial data or suggest that the financial data from a previous period should change. SEC rules require an independent public accountant to review a registrant's interim financial statements before the registrant files its quarterly report with the Commission on Form 10-Q. In a *compilation*, the independent accountant does not express any assurance or opinion on the accompanying financial statements. Instead, the accountant simply prepares financial statements based upon information that management has supplied. The standards for performing reviews are much less demanding than the GAAS that applies to audits and the standards for compilations are even lower. Nevertheless, the same accounting principles apply: the review and compilation standards both state that the Codification also applies to those engagements.

F.   ACCOUNTANTS' LEGAL LIABILITY

Arthur Andersen's quick and stunning demise illustrates the staggering consequences that can flow from an auditor's malpractice. The audit failure at Enron destroyed the auditor's reputation, left thousands looking for new jobs, and spawned lawsuits seeking more than $25 billion from the firm for Enron's investors and former employees. In addition to a $500,000 fine and probation for five years, the conviction barred Andersen from auditing public companies. Although the Supreme Court later reversed Andersen's conviction for obstructing justice on the ground that the trial court's instructions failed to convey properly the requisite consciousness of wrongdoing, the decision came too late to save the firm. Arthur Andersen LLP v. United States, 544 U.S. 696 (2005). In 2005, KPMG accepted a deferred prosecution agreement, admitted criminal wrongdoing, and agreed to pay $456 million in an effort to avoid an indictment arising from the firm's sale of tax shelters.

Although Andersen's demise ranks as the most serious consequence ever visited upon an accounting firm for improper conduct, accountants have long faced serious penalties and liabilities for failure to perform properly. Back in 1990, Laventhal & Horwath, at the time the seventh largest accounting firm, went out of business after declaring bankruptcy in the face of liability claims. Between 1991 and 1995, Ernst & Young agreed to a $400 million settlement with federal banking regulators to settle various cases arising from failed audits involving financial institutions; Deloitte & Touche paid $312 million to settle federal regulators' claims involving flawed audits of several banks and savings and loan associations; and KPMG Peat Marwick agreed to pay $186.5 million to settle claims that the Federal Deposit Insurance Corp., the Resolution Trust Corp., and the Office of Thrift Supervision brought against the firm.

This sad parade continued into the 21st century as audit failures related to the corporate scandals in the early 2000s left each of the Big Four facing potentially enormous legal liability. A 2006 study estimated that the total costs of judgments, settlements, legal fees, and related expenses that the U.S. audit practices of the Big Four firms incurred had risen to 14.2 percent of revenue in 2004, up from 7.7% in 1999. David Reilly, *Booming Audit Firms Seek Shield From Suits*, WALL ST. J., Nov. 1, 2006, at C1. As an example, Deloitte reportedly paid about $250 million during 2005 to settle litigation related to the collapse of Fortress Re, once the largest aviation reinsurer in the world. Interestingly, Deloitte never received more than $100,000 in any year from that engagement. Mark Maremont & Miho Inada, *Deloitte Pays Insurers More Than $200 Million*, WALL ST. J., Jan. 6, 2006, at C3. In 2007, PricewaterhouseCoopers paid $225 million, the firm's largest settlement to date, to resolve malpractice claims arising from audits at Tyco International Ltd. The following year, the firm agreed to pay $97.5 million to settle a securities-fraud class action arising from the audits of American International

Group Inc. The settlement reportedly ranked as one of the ten highest amounts that an accounting firm had agreed to pay to resolve a securities-fraud class action. In 2009, Ernst & Young agreed to the seemingly eighth highest amount, $109 million, to settle a similar suit arising from the financial fraud at HealthSouth Corp.

In 2007, before the economy collapsed, a Florida jury found BDO Seidman, LLP ("BDO"), a second-tier accounting firm, grossly negligent in failing to detect a loan-fraud scheme during its audit of E.S. Bankest, LLC, a Miami-based financial services company. The jury awarded a staggering $521 million, including $351 million in punitive damages. A Florida appellate court reversed the award in 2010 and remanded the case to the trial court for a new trial. In 2011, BDO agreed to confidential settlements with the plaintiffs. Nevertheless, the case illustrates how a single jury verdict can potentially destroy a large auditing firm. *See* Sophia Pearson, *BDO USA Settles Bankest Suit With Former Client Banco Espirito Santo*, BLOOMBERG (May 5, 2011), http://www.bloomberg.com/news/print/2011-05-05/bdo-usa-settles-bankest-suit-with-former-client-banco-espirito-santo.html; Drew Douglas, *Florida Appeals Court Reverses, Remands $521 Million Verdict Against BDO Seidman*, 42 Sec. Reg & Law. Rep. (BNA) 1268 (June 28, 2010). In another case, the United States District Court for the Southern District of New York denied the motions for summary judgment that the international firm Deloitte Touche Tohmatsu and its U.S. affiliate, Deloitte & Touche LLP, filed to dismiss claims seeking to hold the firms liable for alleged fraud at an Italian affiliate, Deloitte & Touche, S.p.A, during audits of Parmalat S.p.A., and related companies. *In re* Parmalat Sec. Litig., 594 F. Supp. 2d 444, *reconsideration denied*, 598 F. Supp. 2d 537, *motion for order certifying interlocutory appeal denied*, 599 F. Supp. 2d 535 (S.D.N.Y. 2009). Because both the Big Four and the second-tier accounting firms market themselves as worldwide, seamless organizations, the decision marks an important development. For the first time, an influential court recognized that plaintiffs can potentially hold a global accounting firm and its U.S. affiliate responsible for an audit failure at a foreign affiliate. *See* Steven Marcy, *Parmalat Ruling Will Cause Audit Firms to Rethink Liability Threat, Lawyers Say*, 41 Sec. Reg. & L. Rep. (BNA) 381 (Mar. 2, 2009).

In the mid-2000s, accountants began inserting clauses in engagement letters that require arbitration, mediation, or alternative dispute resolution; bar punitive damages in any dispute; and obligate the client to indemnify the accountant for any losses arising from the client's misrepresentations, willful misconduct or fraudulent behavior. So far, those clauses appear to have significantly reduced the publicly reported amounts of recent settlements because each of the Big Four issued unqualified audit opinions just months before various financial institutions failed during the credit crisis. Deloitte audited Bear Stearns and Washington Mutual; Ernst & Young inspected Lehman Brothers; KPMG examined Countrywide, Fannie Mae, and New Century Financial Corp.; and PricewaterhouseCoopers tested AIG and Freddie Mac. In 2010, the New York attorney general's office filed a civil fraud lawsuit against Ernst & Young, alleging that the auditor collected $125 million in fees in the seven years before Lehman Brothers collapsed and watched while the investment bank misstated its financial statements. KPMG agreed in 2010 to pay $24 million to settle a federal securities class action arising from its Countrywide audits. During 2012, the U.S. District Court for the Southern District of New York approved a class action settlement in which Deloitte agreed to pay $19.9 million to certain Bear Stearns shareholders. In 2013, KPMG reportedly agreed to pay $76.5 million to settle a class action lawsuit arising from its audits of Fannie Mae, while Ernst & Young reached a $99 million settlement to resolve class-action allegations arising from its Lehman audits.

The SEC has imposed seemingly ever-growing fines against audit firms. In 2005 Deloitte agreed to pay a $25 million civil penalty to the SEC and another $25 million into a fund to compensate victims of the financial fraud at Adelphia Communications Corp. Even though Deloitte had identified Adelphia as one of its highest risk clients, the accounting firm allegedly failed to implement audit procedures designed to detect illegal acts. To date, the amount stands as the largest fine that the SEC has ever imposed on an auditing firm, surpassing the previous-record $22.475 million collected from KPMG after inadequate audits at Xerox Corp. *See* Siobhan Hughes, *Deloitte Auditors Are Charged by SEC in Adelphia Case*, WALL ST. J., Oct. 1, 2005. Kara Scannell, *KPMG Apologizes for Tax Shelters*, WALL ST. J., June 17, 2005, at A3. The Xerox case also involved the largest civil penalties, $150,000, that the SEC has ever imposed against individual auditors. *See* David Reilly, *SEC Obtains Record Penalties From KPMG Auditors of Xerox*, WALL ST. J., Feb. 23, 2006, at C3.

In 2004, the SEC suspended Ernst & Young from accepting any new public audit clients for six months because of violating the SEC's auditor independence rules. The SEC found that while auditing PeopleSoft, Inc., E&Y had significant business relationships with the client, including partnership arrangements and licensing agreements intended to boost E&Y's consulting revenues. The State of California Board of Accountancy (CBA) served a reminder of the ever-present but rarely exercised power of state regulators under their licensing authority, pressing the same charges against E&Y under state law. E&Y agreed to a settlement with CBA calling for a three-year probation for the firm; payment for an independent consultant to conduct an investigation to determine whether the firm has taken steps reasonably calculated to remedy the violations; reimbursement of up to $100,000 for CBA's expenses incurred pursuing E&Y; and contribution of the funds needed for CBA to host a continuing education program of no less than eight hours, which all the firm's personnel licensed in California must attend. Tom Gilroy, *E&Y Accepts Probation, Fine To Settle Calif. Independence Charges*, 36 Sec. Reg. & L. Rep. (BNA) 1804 (Oct. 4, 2004).

In the typical suit involving a failed audit against an auditor, a creditor or shareholder alleges that management did not prepare the financial statements in conformity with GAAP. To collect damages from the independent auditor, the plaintiff, however, must also prove that auditor should have detected and called attention to the failure to comply with GAAP. Accountants' potential liability extends to their review and compilation engagements, as well as to their tax, consulting and litigation services.

NOTES

1. Due to the complexity of the materials involving accountants' legal liability, our coverage is limited and should not be considered comprehensive. Nevertheless, accountants can face two major types of liabilities—common law liability and statutory liability. Accountant's liability usually results in monetary damages. Both private parties, such as creditors or shareholders, or administrative agencies, like the SEC, can bring lawsuits seeking damages. Intentional misconduct, however, can also result in criminal sanctions. In addition, state licensing authorities and the SEC can revoke an accountant's license to practice.

We can divide common law liability into two categories, contract and tort. In appropriate circumstances, liability can flow to both clients and third parties. As superbly summarized in *Bily v. Arthur Young & Co.*, 834 P.2d 745 (Cal. 1992), courts have recognized three separate tort causes of action against auditors—negligence, negligent misrepresentation, and intentional conduct or fraud. Under a negligence theory, courts have applied at least three different standards: (1) requiring something akin to privity of relationship for recovery, (2) allowing recovery to third parties whose reliance on the audit report was "foreseeable" and (3) limiting liability to third parties that the audit intended to benefit. Only two states, Pennsylvania and Virginia, currently require privity. Landell v. Lybrand, 107 A. 783 (Pa. 1919); Ward v. Ernst & Young, 435 S.E.2d 628 (Va. 1993). Three states have adopted the requirement of foreseeability. First Cmty. Bank & Trust v. Kelley, Hardesty, Smith and Co., Inc., 663 N.E.2d 218 (Ind. Ct. App. 1996); Touche Ross & Co. v. Commercial Union Ins. Co., 514 So.2d 315 (Miss. 1987); Citizens State Bank v. Timm, Schmidt & Co., S.C., 335 N.W.2d 361 (Wis. 1983).

At least thirty states have now adopted Restatement 552 as the basis for negligent misrepresentation claims against accountants. *See, e.g.*, Coleman v. PricewaterhouseCoopers LLC, 2005 WL 1952844 (Del. Super. Ct. 2005); First Florida Bank, N.A. v. Max Mitchell & Co., 558 So. 2d 9 (Fla. 1990); McCamish, Martin, Brown & Loeffler v. F.E. Appling Interests, 991 S.W.2d 787 (Tex. 1999). In one way or another, twelve states and the District of Columbia require the auditor to know about the third party's existence, including five states that require conduct linking the auditor to the third party. See e.g., ARK. CODE ANN. § 16-114-302 (West 2010); Credit Alliance Corp. v. Arthur Andersen & Co., 483 N.E.2d 110 (N.Y. 1985). The law remains unclear in four states--Nevada, Ohio, South Dakota, and Vermont. *See generally* Leon P. Gold & Richard L. Spinogatti, *The Liability of Accountants to Non-Clients for Professional Malpractice*, 5501-1st Tax & Accounting Portfolio (BNA) VI.B. (accessed via Bloomberg Law); Joyce Holley & Dannye Holley, *Auditor Common Law Liability in the State Courts: A Recent (1980-94) Outcome Restatement and Perspectives of the Accounting and Legal Professions*, 6 U. MIAMI BUS. L.J. 1 (1997) (analyzing almost fifty cases since 1980 and identifying unanswered questions concerning auditor common law liability);

see also Walpert, Smullian & Blumenthal, P.A. v. Katz, 361 Md. 645, 762 A.2d 582 (2000) (a case that lists and updates those jurisdictions that had adopted each standard).

Several cases have recognized comparative fault defenses in actions for negligent misrepresentations. *See, e.g.*, ESCA Corp. v. KPMG Peat Marwick, 939 P.2d 1228 (Wash. Ct. App. 1997), *aff'd,* 959 P.2d 651 (Wash. 1998) (based on state comparative negligence statute); Standard Chartered PLC v. Price Waterhouse, 945 P.2d 317 (Ariz. 1997) (as corrected on denial of reconsideration) (based on both constitutional and statutory provisions).

Statutory liability can flow from professional malpractice statutes, civil RICO, the federal securities laws and the blue sky laws. *See generally* George Spellmire, Wayne Baliga, & Debra Winiarski, Accountants' Legal Liability: Prevention and Defense (1993); *see also* Lewis D. Lowenfels & Alan R. Bromberg, *Liabilities of Lawyers and Accountants Under Rule 10b-5*, 53 Bus. Law. 1157 (1994) (analyzing decisions involving accountants after *Central Bank v. First Interstate Bank*, 511 U.S. 164 (1994), abolished aiding and abetting liability in certain private securities fraud actions); Barry S. Augenbraun, *Liability of Accountants Under The Federal Securities Laws*, CPA J., Dec. 1994, at 34–35, 56–57. More recently, the Private Securities Litigation Reform Act of 1995 replaced joint and several liability with proportionate liability for accountants and other persons that unknowingly violate the federal securities laws. Pub. L. No. 104-67, § 201, 109 Stat. 737, 758-59 (codified at 15 U.S.C. § 78u-4(f) (2012)).

In 2008, the Supreme Court of the United States narrowed statutory liability under the federal securities laws by rejecting so-called "scheme liability." The Court refused to allow a private action by investors against a third-party that did not violate the antifraud provisions in the federal securities laws but that may have aided or abetted another entity's fraudulent scheme. Stoneridge Inv. Partners, LLC v. Scientific-Atlanta, Inc., 128 S. Ct. 761 (2008). Accounting and law firms closely followed the case, fearing the Court could expand their liability for their clients' frauds. In *Stoneridge*, investors sued Charter Communications, Inc. ("Charter") for fraudulent securities violations, along with Scientific-Atlanta, Inc. and Motorola, Inc. ("respondents"), who supplied set-top cable boxes to Charter. Charter had devised a fraudulent revenue recognition scheme to increase reported revenue and operating cash flow. In the 5-3 decision, the Court upheld an earlier precedent that investors cannot pursue a private right of action against third-party aiders and abettors. *Id.* at 767-69 (citing Cent. Bank of Denver v. First Interstate Bank of Denver, 511 U.S. 164, 191 (1994)). Because the respondents did not commit a primary violation of the securities law, the investors could not maintain their claims against the respondents. *Id.* at 774. The Court, however, noted that secondary actors remain subject to criminal penalties, civil enforcement actions by the SEC, and state securities laws. *Id.* at 773-74.

Dodd-Frank now allows the SEC to recover monetary damages in civil enforcement actions from any person, including an auditor or an attorney, who "knowingly or recklessly" aids or abets a violation of specified federal securities laws, including the 1933 Act and the 1934 Act. *See* 15 U.S.C. §§ 78j, 78t, 80b-9 (2012). In addition, Dodd Frank section 929Z directed the Comptroller General to study whether Congress should create a private cause of action for aiding and abetting securities violations and to submit a report to Congress within one year. 124 Stat. at 1871. In 2011, the GAO issued the report, which set forth arguments for and against private actions, but did not include any recommendation. U.S. Gov. Accountability Office, Securities Fraud Liability of Secondary Actors, No. 11-664 (July 21, 2011), *available at* http://www.gao.gov/new.items/d11664.pdf.

As an example of state legislation affecting accountants' legal liability, Texas enacted a statute which limits the legal liability of accountants involved in issuing securities of small businesses to no more than three times their fees, provided that the accountant did not engage in intentional wrongdoing. *See* 1997 Tex. Gen. Laws ch. 638, § 1 (codified at Tex. Rev. Civ. Stat. Ann. art. 581-33, subsec. N (West, Westlaw through end of 2013 Third Called Session of the 83rd Legislature)). Other states have enacted privity statutes that raise often insurmountable obstacles to a third party's ability to maintain a professional liability action against an accountant. *See, e.g.*, H. Keith Morrison & Robert W. George, *Arkansas's Privity Requirement for Attorney and Accountant Liability*, 51 ARK. L. REV. 697, 705–11 (1998) (also discussing privity statutes in Illinois, Kansas, Utah and Michigan).

2. The subject of accountants' legal liability raises several important policy questions. Do accountants profit from the value which anticipated third party reliance on audit opinions produces, yet to escape liability when negligence causes injury to relying third parties? Does the threat of liability reinforce the accountant's independence from the client, preventing loyalty to the client from affecting, either consciously or unconsciously, the auditor's professional judgment? Does potential liability against accountants prevent harm by deterring negligent conduct? Do cases involving accountants' legal liability present an inherently legislative problem?

3. Upon the dissolution of an enterprise due to management fraud, the auditing firm often finds itself as the only solvent entity for the shareholders to seek restitution. Aggressive auditing firms, however, have begun seeking damages from the corporate officials. Several cases have recognized that an auditor may recover substantial damages from corporate officials in shareholder litigation, even damages the auditor itself paid to settle shareholder claims. But more significantly, the mere existence of auditor claims can preclude corporate officials from settling a lawsuit against them, because the corporate officials, even after consummation of the settlement, may still be vulnerable to litigation from the outside auditor. By bringing such claims, the auditor can virtually preclude any settlement, no matter how much money corporate officials are willing to pay. Michael R. Young, *The Liability of Corporate Officials to Their Outside Auditor for Financial Statement Fraud*, 64 FORDHAM L. REV. 2155 (1996).

*

CHAPTER III

THE TIME VALUE OF MONEY

A. IMPORTANCE TO LAWYERS

Any lawyer who has ever filled out a time sheet knows that "time is money." Although almost every lawyer has heard about billable hours, lawyers should also understand the time value of money, which provides an alternative application for the saying that "time is money." As a fundamental principle, lawyers must always remember that "A dollar today is worth more than a dollar tomorrow." This chapter will discuss various situations in which the time value of money can affect the practice of law.

We can compare borrowing money to renting a car, in the sense that the borrower usually agrees to pay "rent" for the use of either asset. With money, we describe this rent as *interest*. For the borrower, the time value of money refers to the interest expense of borrowing money over a period of time. For the lender, the time value of money refers to the interest earned from lending or investing money.

Issues involving the time value of money arise in both litigation and transactional work. The lawyer who understands the time value of money has learned a useful tool for settling cases, resolving bargaining disputes, advising clients on money-related issues, and financial planning. For instance, suppose you represent a plaintiff who has been offered $5 million, after any applicable legal fees, to settle a case. Your client must decide whether to accept the settlement or to go to trial where the client ultimately expects to recover $6 million, again after legal fees, in three years. If the relevant interest rate is six percent per year, compounded annually, and in the absence of tax and other considerations, should your client accept the settlement offer? Would your recommendation change if the relevant interest rate was seven percent per year, again compounded annually?

The time value of money can also affect defendants. The lawyer representing a defendant against a plaintiff seeking future lost profits should ask the court to reduce any such award to present value. After all, a dollar in the future is not worth as much as a dollar today. Remarkably, however, lawyers, and therefore judges and juries, sometimes do not consider this issue. If the defendant does not raise the issue at trial, an appellate court may refuse to reduce an undiscounted award.

Creative lawyering, and specifically an appreciation of the time value of money, reportedly allowed Exxon Corporation in 1991 to agree to pay $1 billion in civil damages and criminal fines, then "by far the largest single amount ever paid as a result of environmental violations" to settle all federal and state civil claims and criminal charges arising from the 1989 Exxon Valdez oil spill. By stretching the payments out over ten years, the present value of the settlement, even before the savings from tax deductions, did not come close to $1 billion. Similarly, in 1981 the Los Angeles Lakers signed Earvin "Magic" Johnson to a twenty-five year contract, starting in 1984, at $1 million per year, for a total of $25 million, the longest and richest contract in professional sports history when signed. The arrangement allowed Johnson to brag that he had signed the largest contract in professional sports history, while the Lakers committed to payments with a present value much less than $25 million.

Lawyers encounter time value of money concepts in various contexts. When drafting and negotiating legal agreements, for instance, lawyers must recognize the difference between simple interest and compound interest. Lawyers often need to help clients select either an expected rate of return by which an investment will grow over time or an appropriate discount rate to allow the client to compare a future amount to a current sum. Both situations usually require the lawyer to understand the factors that influence interest rates, to reference various market rates, and to exercise professional judgment.

A lawyer specializing in wills and trusts, for example, will use time value of money concepts to estimate the value of estates, to set up charitable remainder trusts, and to advise beneficiaries in selecting payment options under life insurance policies. Tax lawyers use time value of money concepts to defer income and accelerate deductions. In *Atlantic Mutual Insurance Co. v. Commissioner*, 523 U.S. 382 (1998), an insurance tax case, for example, the Supreme Court observed that the relevant Internal Revenue Code provisions enabled the insurer to claim "a current deduction for future loss payments without adjusting for the 'time value of money'—the fact that ' "[a] dollar today is worth more than a dollar tomorrow. " ' " *Id.* at 384 (quoting the second edition).

We often see applications of time value of money concepts in life. Almost all law students borrow money to attend law school. Any borrower should understand the payments necessary to repay a particular loan, whether the underlying transaction involves educational expenses, a car, a home, an investment, or personal expenses on a credit card. Corporations and state lotteries frequently spread payments on large prizes and contests over multiple years. To illustrate, the 2013 winner of America's Got Talent will receive $25,000 a year for forty years, the recipient of the $1 million grand prize in McDonald's 2013 Monopoly game will collect $50,000 a year for twenty years without interest, and the holder of the winning ticket in the May 18, 2013 Powerball lottery had to decide whether to claim the record $590.5 million jackpot over twenty-nine years or to elect an immediate $377 million payout.

Not surprisingly, lawyers also use time value of money concepts for financial planning. Whether planning for their own retirements, saving for college educations for their children or grandchildren, or advising clients about these same matters, every lawyer should understand the power of compound interest. The brilliant Albert Einstein, *Time*'s "Person Of The [20th] Century," reportedly described compound interest at different times as "the greatest invention in human history," "the most powerful force in the universe," and "the eighth wonder of the world."

This chapter will acquaint you with the basics of time value of money analysis. Throughout this chapter, notice how smaller amounts—whether single sums or streams of equal, periodic payments called annuities—grow to larger amounts in the future. Accountants use the term *annuity* to refer to a sequence of periodic and equal amounts. For example, an individual can buy an annuity from an insurance company. Such a contract requires the issuer to remit specified amounts regularly for a certain period of time, usually for the duration of the life of an individual, and perhaps the life of the individual's spouse or another beneficiary. Promises to repay a loan in equal, regular installments, whether monthly, quarterly, or annually, also give rise to annuities. Please keep in mind that all annuities involve a payer and a recipient.

As the following diagram illustrates, we use the term *compounding* to describe the accretive process by which smaller amounts, again whether a lump sum or annuity payments, grow to larger amounts in the future.

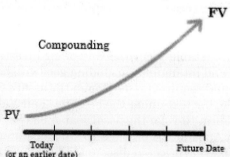

Because a dollar tomorrow is worth less than a dollar today, lawyers also often must determine what unknown amount today, or *present value*, will grow to a certain amount at some point in the future when invested at a given interest rate. Therefore, a process known as *discounting* allows a lawyer to compute the present value of a future amount, again whether a single sum or a stream of future payments.

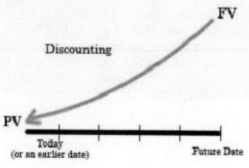

We learned at an early age that tiny acorns grow into huge oak trees and oak trees come from acorns. Indeed, while working on this chapter, this text's principal author opened a fortune cookie with the message: "Little acorns lead to mighty oaks." In this chapter, we will see how compound interest allows smaller amounts to grow into much larger future values. We will also learn how discounting allows us to determine where a larger future value came from.

By chapter's end, you will be able to analyze and resolve problems involving the time value of money, by both compounding given amounts to future values and discounting future sums to present values. Given the accessibility and widespread availability of Microsoft Excel, this chapter will illustrate various calculations using the 2010 version of that software for Windows after first describing the analysis underlying the computations. The 2013 version of Excel and Excel for Mac 2011 share similar organizations and use identical formulas as the version used in this chapter.

As we proceed through this chapter, please keep in mind that the Codification often requires, or allows, an enterprise to use time value of money concepts, especially discounted future cash flows, to determine amounts appearing in the financial statements or in the notes to the financial statements. As described in Chapter VI on pages 404 to 405, *infra*, the Codification sometimes requires enterprise to discount anticipated future receipts to present value in recognizing revenue. As also discussed in Chapter VI on pages 413 and 413, *infra*, and in Chapter IX on pages 664, 666, and 667, *infra*, the Codification often allows enterprises to use discounted cash flows to determine whether marketable securities and other investments; property, plant and equipment; and intangibles, including goodwill, have suffered any impairment, which would require a reduction in the asset's carrying value to fair value. For example, the text under the heading "Fair Value" in Note 1 on page 55 of Starbucks' Form 10-K for the fiscal year ended September 30, 2012, which can be found in Appendix A on page 751, *infra*, states that Starbucks used available quoted market prices or discounted cash flows to determine fair values for certain investments. Other enterprises use time value of money concepts to value stock options and to determine the fair value of certain liabilities, including estimated pension liabilities and lease obligations.

B. INTEREST

As previously mentioned, interest represents a charge for the use of money. Borrowers agree to pay interest when they believe that the benefit they receive from spending the money outweighs the interest they must pay to borrow the money. Lenders and investors lend money when they believe that the interest income they will earn in the future outweighs the opportunity cost of spending today.

1. FACTORS DETERMINING INTEREST RATES

Numerous and complex factors affect interest rates. Financial analysts often divide a stated interest rate into various components that can help to explain the different factors which can influence the market rate. These components include a pure rate of interest, the inflation premium, the maturity premium, the default premium, and the illiquidity premium.

Economists often describe the *pure rate of interest* as the rate which lenders would charge and borrowers would agree to pay if the risks which we will discuss shortly did not exist. Financial analysts generally believe that this pure rate of interest falls between two and three percent per year. Until the Federal Reserve held interest rates artificially low in an effort to stimulate the economy after the 2008 credit crisis, the interest rate on short-term U.S. Treasury obligations in periods of stable prices best approximated the risk-free rate. Interest rates, however, usually exceed this pure rate of interest because various premiums compensate lenders for the different risks that they assume by lending money.

Inflation risk refers to the general loss in purchasing power that rising prices cause. Accordingly, interest rates tend to rise when inflation increases and drop when the price level declines. The *inflation premium* compensates the lender for the increase in prices that the lender expects over the loan's term. Next, the *maturity premium* offsets the risks associated with committing funds for longer periods. Various general market, business and economic risks underlie the maturity premium. Historically, long-term interest rates have exceeded short-term interest rates for investments presenting similar risks. The maturity premium helps explain this difference. The difference in interest rates between long-term U.S. Treasury bonds and short-term U.S. Treasury obligations illustrates maturity premium.

The *default premium* reflects the risk that the borrower will default on the loan and that the lender will lose the loan principal and any accrued interest. In August 2011, the ratings firm Standard & Poor's downgraded long-term United States government obligations below the triple-A rating they had held for about seventy years. Even after the historic, and still controversial, downgrade, the rates for U.S. Treasury obligations seemingly do not include a default premium. The differences in interest rates between bonds with similar maturities in different risk categories, such as low-risk U.S. Treasury bonds and higher-risk corporate bonds, document a default premium. The following diagram illustrates the relationship between the pure rate of interest and the inflation, maturity and default premiums in explaining the typical differences in interest rates among short-term Treasury bills, longer-term Treasury bonds, and higher-risk corporate bonds with the same maturity as the Treasury bonds:

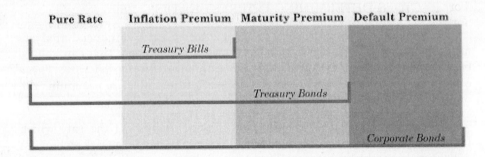

Please also note that the default premium varies depending upon the borrower's credit worthiness. Below investment grade bonds, often referred to as *junk bonds*, carry a higher default premium than high grade corporate bonds.

Finally, the *illiquidity premium* compensates a lender for lack of marketability and the resulting price concession that the lender may have to grant if unexpected circumstances force the lender to sell the debt instrument before maturity, particularly if the lender needs to raise cash quickly. The spread between interest rates on nonpublicly traded bonds and highly marketable bonds with similar maturities, credit ratings, and other characteristics exhibits an illiquidity premium. Likewise, the following diagram shows the relationship between the pure rate of interest and the inflation, default, and illiquidity premiums to explain the typical differences in interest rates among Treasury bills, marketable corporate obligations, and non-marketable certificates of deposit with the same maturity dates.

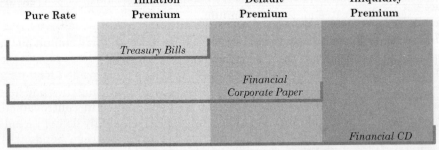

In today's global economy, large commercial lenders, including financial institutions, less frequently rely on their *prime rate*, or the interest rate that they charge their best and most creditworthy borrowers. Historically, such lenders would charge higher interest rates, such as prime plus something, on loans that carried higher risk. Beginning in the late 1980s, Libor, the London interbank offered rate, which the British Bankers' Association ("BBA") has called the " 'world's most important number,' " has often served as a benchmark to fix the cost of borrowing for hundreds of trillions of dollars in mortgages, corporate debt, and financial contracts worldwide. Using information that sixteen large, mostly European, international banks submit, the trade association calculated average interest rates at which banks borrowed dollars and other currencies from each other on an unsecured basis for periods ranging from one month to one year. As the credit crisis in the United States both deepened and widened, critics complained that the use of Libor rendered global markets especially susceptible to financial troubles in Europe. In 2008, *The Wall Street Journal* further raised questions about Libor's use, as well as its accuracy, by publishing a front-page story detailing an analysis that suggested that several participating banks had understated their borrowing rates in an effort to mask their own financial difficulties. Such understatements would have translated to an estimated $45 billion reduction in interest payments by borrowers during the first four months in 2008 alone. Early in 2012, *The Wall Street Journal* reported that at least one bank told regulators that various traders successfully manipulated the yen Libor as recently as June 2010. By mid-2012, regulators in the United States and European Union had fined global banks more than$6 billion and those banks had admitted that their traders and executives had tried to manipulate Libor and the Euro interbank offered rate, or Euribor, another key interest rate. Prosecutors have filed criminal charges against more than a dozen individuals who allegedly orchestrated the schemes, and a growing number of bank and brokerage employees remain under investigation. The banks also find themselves defending various civil suits, including antitrust and RICO claims seeking treble damages, from various plaintiffs alleging massive damages from manipulations involving Libor, Euribor, and other rates, including the Tokyo interbank offered rate, or Tibor. Legal analysts predict Libor litigation could last for ten years or more and estimate that the ultimate cost to the banks at between $7.8 billion and $176 billion.

Lawyers should, but often do not, consider the various components and different factors that may determine market interest rates in contractual negotiations and litigation. Contracts and pleadings frequently use risk-free or statutory interest rates that bear no resemblance to market rates. *See, e.g.*, Medcom Holding Co. v. Baxter Travenol Labs., Inc., 200 F.3d 518, 520 (7th Cir. 2000) (concluding that the district court should have awarded prejudgment interest at a market rate rather than the statutory rate of five percent simple interest).

2.   COMPUTATIONS

We generally state interest as a rate over a specified period of time, such as four percent per annum. To compute the actual dollar amount of interest, we start with the basic equation:

Interest = Principal x Rate x Time

where *Interest* represents the dollar amount of interest; *Principal*, the amount of money that the debtor borrows; *Rate*, the stated cost of borrowing one dollar per unit of time; and *Time*, the number of units of time that the principal remains unpaid.

We normally count one year as one unit of time because people usually express the interest rate as an annual rate. You should note, however, that when someone expresses the rate in something other than an annual rate or the time in something other than years, we can still use this equation as long as we adjust the formula for the proper units of time. For example, if someone charges interest at one percent per month, we would use months as the unit of time.

When the loan period extends over several units of time, the borrower and lender decide whether the borrower will pay *simple* interest or *compound* interest. With simple interest, the borrower pays interest on the original principal amount only, regardless of any interest that has accrued in the past. Under compound interest, the borrower pays interest on the unpaid interest of past periods, as well as on the original principal amount.

Example 1: *Simple Interest Calculation*

Susan borrows $10,000 from Larry, who charges simple interest at a rate of four percent per year. At the end of the first year, Susan owes Larry $400 interest, calculated as follows:

$$\begin{aligned} \text{Interest} &= \text{Principal x Rate x Time} \\ &= \$10,000 \text{ x } .04/\text{year x 1 year} \\ &= \$400 \end{aligned}$$

Now suppose that the $10,000 loan remains outstanding for another year. Under simple interest, we calculate the second year's interest based upon the original principal amount only. The $400 first year's interest does not affect the interest calculation in the second year. For the second year, therefore, Larry earns another $400 interest. Thus, at the end of the second year Susan owes Larry a total of $10,800, representing $10,000 original principal plus $800 simple interest at $400 per year.

Example 2: *Compound Interest Calculation*

Assume Carla deposits $10,000 in a bank account that pays interest at a rate of four percent per year, compounded annually. At the end of the first year, the bank owes Carla $400 interest, calculated as above.

Now suppose that Carla keeps the original $10,000 plus the $400 interest in the bank account for another year. The bank adds, or compounds, the $400 first year's interest to the $10,000 original principal amount before calculating the interest for the second year. In the second year, Carla earns $416 interest, calculated as follows:

$$\begin{aligned} \text{Interest} &= \text{Principal x Rate x Time} \\ &= \$10,400 \text{ x } .04/\text{year x 1 year} \\ &= \$416 \end{aligned}$$

Thus, at the end of the second year the bank owes Carla a total of $10,816, which represents $10,000 original principal plus interest at $400 for year one, which we added to unpaid principal to compute interest for year two, and $416 for year two. Because of compounding, Carla earned $16 more interest than she would have earned under simple interest.

Example 3: *Another Compound Interest Calculation*

Same facts as **Example 2**, except that Carla deposits $100,000 instead of $10,000. At the end of the first year, the bank owes Carla $4,000 interest, and in the second year, Carla earns $4,160 interest. Thus, at the end of the second year, the bank owes Carla a total of $108,160.

Comparing the amount the bank owes Carla at the end of year two with the original principal in **Examples 2** and **3**, the ratio remains constant at 1.08160. In other words, $10,816 bears the same relationship to $10,000 as $108,160 does to $100,000. This relationship exists because the Rate and the Time remained constant, and only the Principal changed. We can use this ratio as a shortcut for making similar calculations involving the same Rate and Time.

Examine Table I in Appendix B on page 827, *infra*, which lists Rates across the top and Periods down the left side. Find the column with four percent at the top and the row for two periods. They intersect at 1.08160, the same number as the ratio that we calculated above. Someone has similarly precalculated the other numbers in the body of the table for different Rates and Times, each ratio representing the shortcut for a specific combination of Rate and Time.

As we will describe in more detail, Appendix B contains a total of four tables, each table embodying a shortcut for four different types of time value of money calculations. Tables I and II compute future values for a dollar or the future value of a series of equal amounts at the end of each period by compounding interest. In comparison, Tables III and IV discount the value of an amount at some time in the future or discount a stream of equal payments at the end of a given number of periods in the future to determine the present value of that sum or stream of payments.

Please note that the tables in Appendix B only contain amounts for particular interest rates expressed in whole numbers, such as one percent, two percent, three percent, et cetera and certain periods. In the real world, arrangements between debtors and creditors and other payors and payees often involve interest rates expressed in decimals or fractions of a percent, such as 3.4% or five and one-eighth percent, or whole interest rates not included on the tables in Appendix B, such as eleven percent and eighteen percent. In addition, an arrangement might contemplate more than 100 periods, such as a ten-year loan that requires monthly payments, which translates to 120 periods. In such common situations, a scientific calculator, numerous websites, or various software can readily perform such compounding and discounting. Throughout the remainder of this chapter, we will often illustrate various calculations using Microsoft Excel.

With that background, we will now examine the concepts of both future value and present value, beginning with future value.

C.   FUTURE VALUE

We can describe *future value* as the sum to which an amount or a series of periodic and equal amounts will grow at the end of a certain amount of time, invested at a particular compound interest rate. Future value, therefore, can apply either to one amount or a series of equal amounts. In this section, we will discuss two different future value calculations: the first for single amounts and the second for annuities. We begin with the future value of a single amount.

1.   SINGLE AMOUNTS

Examples 2 and 3 both involve the concept of *future value*. We can define *future value* as the amount to which a current Principal *p* will grow at the end of *n* periods of Time, invested at *i* compound interest Rate. Accountants sometimes refer to future value as the *future amount of $1* or the *amount of a given sum*. Table I lists the amounts to which one dollar invested will grow at the end of various periods of time, at various compound interest rates. Using the table, we can easily compute the future value of a current principal amount if we know the interest rate and the length of time over which the amount will remain invested. Let's continue with another simple example:

Example 4: *Future Value—Simple Illustration*

Maria contributes $10,000 to an investment account which earns four percent, compounded annually. How much money will the account contain at the end of ten years? $14,802.40. Using Table I, we find the future value factor for ten periods at four percent compound interest. The column for four percent interest and the row for ten periods intersect at 1.48024, which means that one dollar will grow to approximately $1.48 at the end of ten years at four percent compound interest per year. We multiply Maria's original investment of $10,000 times the 1.48024 future value factor to arrive at a $14,802.40 future value. Now let's try a more complicated calculation:

Example 5: *Future Amount—More Complicated Illustration*

In 1901, the monetary reward to Nobel Prize winners was $40,000. By 2013, the prize, actually awarded in Swedish kronor, had grown to approximately $1.2 million. If a 1901 Nobel Prize winner invested the proceeds from the award at five percent interest, compounded annually, would the 1901 winner have more or less than $1,200,000 in 2013?

If the 1901 prize winner had invested the proceeds at five percent interest, compounded annually, by 2013 the proceeds would have grown to over $9 million. To answer the question, we must calculate the future value of $40,000 after 112 years at five percent, compound interest. Although Table I shows the amounts to which one dollar invested will grow at the end of various periods of time, at five percent compound interest, the Table does not list a factor for 112 periods. Nevertheless, we can use Table I to answer the question if we make an intermediate calculation.

First, using Table I, we find the factor for 100 periods and five percent compound interest, or 131.5013. Table I tells us that one dollar would have grown to about $131.50 if invested at five percent compound interest for 100 years. Using this factor, we can compute that $40,000 would have grown to $5,260,052, or $40,000 times 131.5013, at the end of 100 years. Next, we use Table I to find the factor for twelve periods and five percent interest, or 1.79586. During the last twelve years, $5,260,052 would have grown to $9,446,317, which equals $5,260,052 times 1.79586. To summarize:

Year	Factor	Amount
1901		$40,000
2001	131.5013	5,260,052
2013	1.79586	9,446,317

Rather than use Table I, which requires us to perform an intermediate calculation, we could use Microsoft Excel to calculate the future amount as follows. First, after starting Excel, click the Formulas tab at the top of the screen. Next, click on the Financial box on the ribbon that appears under the Formulas tab. Then, from the drop down menu, select the FV [Future Value] function, which enables the user to compute the future value of a current lump sum invested at a constant interest rate. The following window will appear:

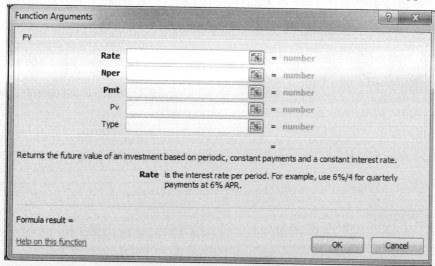

In the **Rate** box, enter the applicable interest rate per period, either "5%" or ".05" for this example because the facts specify five percent interest, compounded annually. In the **Nper** box, enter "112" for the number of periods for the investment because the interest would compound 112 times between 1901 and 2013. Because this example involves only one single amount, the $40,000 the Nobel laureate won in 1901, we leave the **Pmt** and the **Type** boxes blank. (As we will see shortly during our discussion about annuities, these boxes potentially apply to streams of equal, periodic payments.) Finally, enter "-40000" in the **Pv** box, the amount our Nobel Prize winner invested in 1901. We enter a negative number because that sum represents an outlay to our Nobel laureate. Please note that Excel does not use dollar signs or commas, so you will get an error message if you enter "$" or a "40,000" in the **Pv** box. The correctly filled-in window will appear as follows:

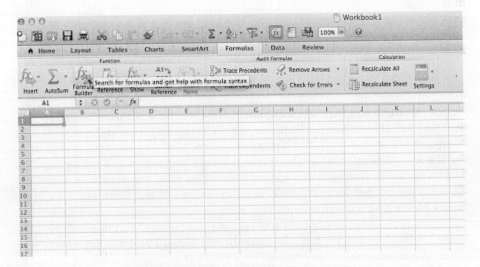

We could express this Excel argument, which computes the future value of $40,000 in 112 years at five percent interest, compounded annually, as "=FV(0.05,112,,-40000)." As the graphic above indicates, Excel calculates the future value of that single sum at almost $9,446,295. The twenty-two dollar difference between the amount calculated in Excel and the $9,446,317 figure we computed using Table I arises from rounding imperfections that occurred when we computed the future value in 100 years and then used that figure to compute the future value in an additional twelve years.

If you use Excel 2011 for Mac, first click the Formulas tab just above the Functions ribbon at the top of the screen as shown in the following picture:

Then, click the Formula Builder button, which is located in the Functions ribbon. Next, insert FV in the search bar which should produce the following:

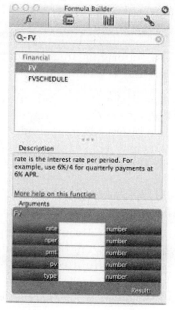

After you select FV, complete the arguments as in Excel for Windows. Future illustrations will show only Excel for Windows.

a. CONSEQUENCE OF MORE FREQUENT COMPOUNDING

You will recall from **Example 4**, that $10,000 will grow to $14,802.40 after ten years at four percent interest, compounded annually. But what if the investment will compound interest semiannually? To calculate future value when the lending agreement requires compounding more than once a year, we must first adjust for the length of the compounding period, as in the following examples.

Example 6: *Future Value—Interest Compounded Semiannually*

Sheila contributes $10,000 to an investment account earning four percent interest, compounded *semi-annually*. How much will Sheila have at the end of ten years? $14,859.50. Because the investment accrues interest twice a year, in ten years the account will have earned interest twenty different times. Every six months, Sheila will earn two percent interest, or one-half the four percent annual rate. Using Table I, we find a future value factor of 1.48595 for $1 invested for twenty periods of time at two percent compound interest. Multiplying the $10,000 original investment times the 1.48595 future value factor yields a $14,859.50 future value.

Example 7: *Future Value—Interest Compounded Quarterly*

Quincy deposits $10,000 into an account earning four percent interest, compounded *quarterly*. How much will the account contain at the end of ten years? $14,888.60. Because the investment compounds interest four times a year, over ten years the account will receive interest forty different times. Every three months, Quincy will earn one percent interest or one-fourth the four percent annual rate. Using Table I, we find a future value factor of 1.48886 for $1 invested for forty periods of time at one percent compound interest. Multiplying the $10,000 original investment times the 1.48886 future value factor yields a future value of $14,888.60.

At this point, we can also discern a general rule to determine the future value factor from Table I when the contract requires interest compounding more than once a year. When interest is compounded c times a year, multiply the number of years the principal will be invested times c, divide the annual interest rate by c, then use the future value factor located at this adjusted Time and Rate.

Example 8: *Future Value—Interest Compounded Daily using Excel*

David contributes $10,000 to an account earning four percent interest, compounded *daily*. To what amount will the account grow in ten years? We cannot use Table I to determine this future amount because Table I does not provide amounts for any interest rate less than one percent, and four percent annual interest, compounded daily, would translate to an interest rate of .0001095% a day, assuming 365 days in a year. Again, Microsoft Excel provides an easy alternative for determining this future amount. In Excel, open the FV function under the Financial box. For an annual rate that is compounded more than once a year, we divide the annual rate by the number of compounding periods. Thus, we enter "4%/365" in the **Rate** box to represent four percent interest compounded daily, assuming 365 days in a year. For semiannual or quarterly compounding, we would divide by two or four, respectively. In the **Nper** box, we multiply the number of compounding periods in each year by the number of years. Thus, for the future value of an amount after ten years, compounded daily, we enter "10*365" in the **Nper** box. Because we are dealing with a single outlay, we again leave the **Pmt** and **Type** boxes blank. In the **Pv** box, we input "-10000" because David has invested $10,000. The completed function argument will appear as follows:

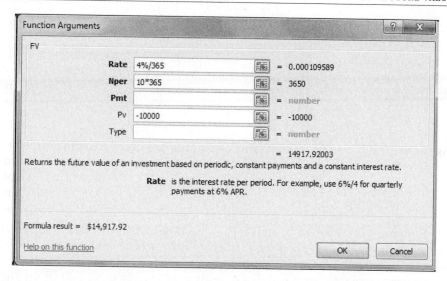

We could express this Excel argument, which calculates the future value of $10,000 in ten years at four percent annual interest, compounded daily, as "=FV(0.04/365,3650,,-10000)," which translates to $14,917.92 in ten years.

From **Examples 4, 6, 7, and 8**, we can see that, assuming the same stated interest rate, in these illustrations four percent annual interest, lenders and investors prefer more frequent compounding because the compounding produces a higher effective interest rate. In contrast, at any particular interest rate, borrowers prefer simple interest or compound interest with less frequent compounding. The investors in **Examples 4, 6, 7, and 8** all invested in accounts which earned interest at a four percent stated rate. At the end of ten years, however, David has earned more interest on the same investment than either Maria, Sheila, or Quincy. Similarly, the borrowers in **Examples 4, 6, 7, and 8** all agreed to pay four percent interest. Maria's borrower paid less interest for the ten year period than both Sheila's and Quincy's borrowers, and those borrowers paid less interest than David's borrower.

b.   RULE OF 72s: DOUBLING AN INVESTMENT

Dividing 72 by the interest rate gives us the approximate number of years in which an investment will double at compound interest. For example, an investment earning six percent interest, compounded annually, will double in approximately twelve years. To illustrate, Table I shows the future value factor for six percent and twelve periods as 2.01220. Thus, the Rule of 72s enables us to estimate quickly how soon an investment will double.

To illustrate, we can use the Rule of 72s to estimate how much money a twenty-five year old person needs to retire as a millionaire at age sixty-five, assuming a nine percent return, compounded annually. At a nine percent compounded annual return, an investment will double every eight years. Even if the twenty-five year old never saves another penny, we can work backwards as follows:

Age	Amount
65	$1,000,000
57	500,000
49	250,000
41	125,000
33	62,500
25	31,250

As the table illustrates, relative small amounts can grow to significant sums over time.

2.   ANNUITIES

Suppose that instead of making a one-time deposit to her IRA, Erica decided to invest $5,000 every year. In an *annuity*, the investor makes a series of equal payments at regular time intervals, such as depositing an amount from every paycheck into a savings account or investing $5,000 in an IRA every year. In an *ordinary annuity*, which accountants sometimes refer to as an *annuity in arrears*, the investor starts making payments at the end, rather than at the beginning, of the first period. In contrast, under an *annuity due*, which accountants might call an *annuity in advance*, the investor makes payments at the beginning of each period. We can calculate the future value of both ordinary annuities and annuities due using the same principles to determine the future value for a single amount.

a.   ORDINARY ANNUITY

With an *ordinary annuity*, or *annuity in arrears*, the first payment occurs at the end of the first period. The future value of an ordinary annuity represents the sum accumulated at the time of the last payment. To illustrate, suppose that Dianne contributes $1,000 at the end of each year for four years to an annuity paying five percent compound interest. How much will Dianne have at the end of four years? By examining the timing of the payments, we can use Table I to compute the future value of this annuity.

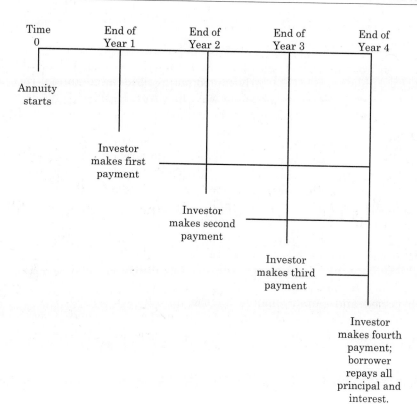

We notice that the first payment at the end of year one will compound three times before the end of year four; the second payment will compound twice; the third payment will compound once; and the fourth payment does not earn any interest, because we are determining the value as of the date of the fourth and last payment. Summarizing the future value factors from Table I for five percent interest for these periods, we get:

First payment (three periods)	1.15763
Second payment (two periods)	1.10250
Third payment (one period)	1.05000
Fourth payment (no interest)	1.00000
Total	4.31013

If Dianne contributed $1 at the end of each year, she would have $4.31 at the end of four years. But Dianne invested $1,000 each year. Multiplying Dianne's $1,000 annuity payment times this sum of future value factors, we see that Dianne will have $4,310.13 at the end of four years.

Alternatively, we could use Table II in Appendix B on page 828, *infra*, to determine the future amount of this annuity. Table II uses the future value factors from Table I for single amounts to calculate the future value factors for an ordinary annuity. Assuming the same facts as above, we find a future value factor at Table II of 4.31013 for an annuity of $1 for four payments at five percent compound interest. Multiplying the $1,000 annuity payment times the

4.31013 future value factor yields a $4,310.13 future value, the same amount that we calculated earlier, but with much less effort.

When working with Tables I and II, recall that we can adjust Table I to reflect semiannual and quarterly compounding of a stated annual rate. We cannot adjust Table II in the same way, however, because Table II would require an additional payment at the end of each semiannual or quarterly period.

We could also use Microsoft Excel to determine the future amount of this annuity. Using the FV function located within the Financial box on the ribbon that appears under the Formula tab, we insert "5%" into the **Rate** box because the annuity pays Dianne five percent interest annually. Next, we would enter "4" in the **Nper** box because the annuity lasts four years. Finally, we input "-1000" in the **Pmt** box to represent the $1,000 payment or investment that Dianne will make each period, in this case at the end of each year. When calculating the future value of an ordinary annuity, whether in Excel or by using Table II, please recall that the each payment must remain the same each period and cannot change for the annuity's duration. Because this example involves a stream of payments occurring at the end of each period and not a single payment, we leave both the **Pv** and **Type** boxes blank. We leave the **Type** box blank or enter a "0" in that field because the payments in an ordinary annuity occur at the end of each period. Inputting those figures into Excel results in the following function argument:

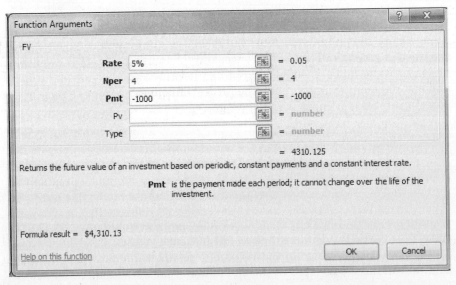

We can express this Excel argument, which calculates the future value of a four-year, $1,000 ordinary annuity at five percent interest, simply as "=FV(0.05,4,-1000)." The argument yields a $4,310.13 future value, the exact same amount that we calculated earlier using Table II.

Example 9: *Future Value of an Ordinary Annuity*

Paul's parents plan to invest $2,000 at the end of each year for the next fifteen years in his college fund. Assuming that the fund will earn six percent compound interest, how much will Paul have in fifteen years? $46,551.94. Using Table II, we find a future value factor of 23.27597 for an annuity of $1 for fifteen payments at six percent compound interest. Multiplying the $2,000 annuity payment times the 23.27597 future value factor yields a future value of $46,551.94.

But what if Paul's parents decide to invest $2,000 at the beginning of each year to fund his college education? How much will the college fund contain at the end of fifteen years? We turn now to the future amount of an annuity due.

b. ANNUITY DUE

Recall that with an *annuity due*, unlike an ordinary annuity, the investor makes payments at the beginning of the each period. The future value of an annuity due represents the sum accumulated one period *after* the last payment. Thus, each payment compounds for one more period than the payment would under an ordinary annuity. To illustrate, let us recalculate Dianne's $1,000 annuity, previously described as an ordinary annuity, as an annuity due instead. By examining the timing of the payments, we can use Table I to compute the future value of her annuity due.

The first payment at the beginning of year one will compound four times by the end of year four; the second payment will compound three times; the third payment will compound twice; and the fourth payment will compound once, because we determine the future value of an annuity due one period after the last payment. Summarizing the future value factors from Table I for five percent for these periods, we get:

First payment (four periods)	1.21550
Second payment (three periods)	1.15763
Third payment (two periods)	1.10250
Fourth payment (one period)	<u>1.05000</u>
Total	4.52563

Multiplying Dianne's $1,000 annuity payment times this sum of future value factors, we see that Dianne will have $4,525.63 at the end of four years.

You will not find this total of future value factors in Table II because Table II lists future value factors for ordinary annuities, not annuities due. We can, however, use the FV function in Microsoft Excel to calculate the future value of an annuity due. In the **Rate** box, we enter "5%" for the annuity's annual interest rate. We insert "4" in the **Nper** box for the number of payments that Dianne will make. We again input "-1000" in the **Pmt** box as the annual annuity payment and leave the **Pv** box blank. As you may have noticed, to this point the function argument for an annuity due mirrors the function argument we used for an ordinary annuity. The only difference between the function arguments for an annuity due and an ordinary annuity is the logical function entered into the **Type** box. When calculating an annuity due, we enter "1" into the **Type** box to represent that each payment occurs at the beginning of the period. Recall that whenever we leave the **Type** box blank or enter "0" into that box, Excel will calculate the future value based on payments occurring at the end of each period. The completed Excel function argument for Dianne's annuity due, which we can express as "=FV(0.05,4,-1000,,1)," appears as follows:

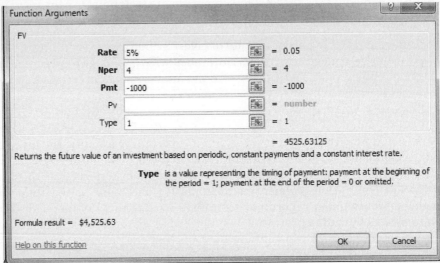

Thus, Excel computes a $4,525.63 future value, the same amount we calculated early, but with much less effort.

D.   PRESENT VALUE

Future value analysis tells us how much a given amount or annuity, invested at compound interest, will grow to at some time in the future. Conversely, present value analysis tells us how much a given future sum or stream of future payments, discounted at a specified interest rate, is worth today. In this section, we will discuss present values in two different contexts: the first for single amounts and the second for annuities. We again start with the present value of a single amount.

1.   SINGLE AMOUNTS

We can define *present value* as the amount that will grow to a larger sum at the end of n periods of time in the future, at r compound interest rate. Accountants sometimes refer to this present value amount as the *present value of $1* or the *present value of a single sum*. Just as someone precalculated Table I for future value computations, we can also use a precalculated table for present value calculations. In fact, Table III in Appendix B on page 829, *infra*, lists the amount that will grow to one dollar at the end of n periods of time in the future, at r compound interest rate. In other words, Table III shows the present value of one dollar at the end of n periods, *discounted* at r compound interest. We say discounted because we start with a larger known amount in the future and determine the lower present value. Several examples can illustrate the concept.

Example 10: *Present Value—Simple Illustration*

Amy promised to give Thomas, her twelve year old brother, $10,000 on his twenty-second birthday. What is the present value, discounted at eight percent interest annually, of this promise? Using Table III, we find a present value factor of .46319 at ten periods and eight percent interest. Multiplying the $10,000 promised payment times the .46319 present value factor yields a $4,631.90 present value.

We have determined that the promise to pay $10,000 in ten years, discounted at eight percent interest each year, is worth $4,631.90 today. Using Table I, we can verify our calculation. We first find 2.15892 as the future value factor for ten periods at eight percent compound interest on Table I. That factor means that one dollar will grow to approximately $2.16 at the end of ten years at eight percent compounded annually. We then multiply the $4,631.90 we determined above times the 2.15892 future value factor to arrive at a $9,999.90 future value, which we can round to $10,000 to eliminate some slight imprecision in the tables.

Just as we observed for future values, Microsoft Excel can be used to compute quickly the present value of a known amount in the future. Under the Formulas tab in Excel, select the Financial drop box. Then, click on the PV [Present Value] function, which enables the user to determine how much a given amount in the future is worth now. Next, enter "8%" or ".08" in the **Rate** box for the annual interest rate. In the **Nper** box, insert "10" for the total number of periods necessary to discount the known future amount to present value. Because this example involves only a single future outlay, we will leave the **Pmt** and **Type** boxes blank. (As we will see once again during our discussion about annuities, these boxes potentially apply when we want to determine the present value of a stream of equal, periodic amounts involving at least one future transfer.) Finally, enter "-10000" into the **Fv** box, which represents the $10,000 Amy has promised to pay in ten years. (Again, please note that Excel does not use dollar signs or commas, so you will get an error message if you enter a "$" or "40,000" in the **Fv** box.) The correctly filled-in window appears as follows:

We could express this Excel argument, which computes the present value of $10,000 in ten years, discounted at eight percent interest, compounded annually, as "=PV(0.08,10,,-10000)." Excel calculates the present value of that single sum as $4,631.93. Again, the three cent difference between the amount calculated in Excel versus the $4,631.90 answer we found using Table III arises from rounding.

Having verified our present value calculation, we can see what happens when we compound interest more frequently than annually. Recall the general rule that we derived in the future value context: when the scenario requires compounding interest c times a year, we multiply the number of years times c, divide the annual interest rate by c, then use the future value factor located at this adjusted Time and Rate. We apply the same rule in present value calculations.

Example 11: *Present Value—Interest Compounded Semiannually*

Same facts as **Example 10**, except assume that we will compound interest semiannually. Because this scenario requires us to compound interest twice a year, in ten years, we must compound interest twenty times. Every six months, we will compound interest at four percent or one half the eight percent annual rate. Using Table III, we look at twenty periods and four percent interest and find a .45639 present value factor. Multiplying the $10,000 promised payment times the .45639 present value factor yields a $4,563.90 present value.

Notice that the more frequently we compound interest, the lower the present value drops, because more frequent compounding produces a higher effective rate of interest. Recall **Examples 4, 6, 7, and 8**. A higher effective rate of interest means that we can invest less now, which means a lower present value, to arrive at a given sum in the future.

Example 12: *Present Value—Interest Compounded Daily using Excel*

Same facts as **Example 10**, except that we will compound interest daily. As noted when we calculated future values, the tables in Appendix B only provide factors for computing up to one hundred periods. Using Excel, however, we can easily and quickly compound interest for any number of periods. For daily compounding, we divide the stated annual interest rate by 365 and multiply the number of years by 365, assuming 365 days in a year. Thus, enter "8%/365" or ".08/365" in the **Rate** box to represent the daily interest rate that corresponds to eight percent annual interest. In the **Nper** box, type "10*365" to represent the total number of periods. Because we are dealing with a single outlay and not daily payments, we leave the **Pmt** and **Type** boxes blank. In the **Fv** box, we input "-10000" because Amy has promised to pay her brother $10,000 in ten years. The completed function argument appears as follows:

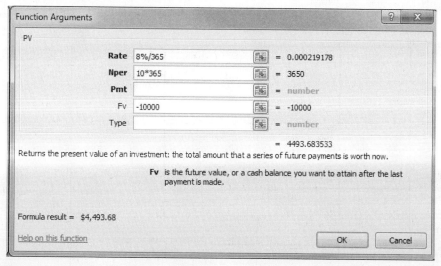

We could express this Excel argument, which computes the present value of $10,000 in ten years, discounted at eight percent annual interest, compounded daily, as "=PV(0.08/365,10*365,,-10000)," and which produces a $4,493.68 present value. Again, please note that daily compounding results in a present value $138.25 less than the $4,631.93 amount we calculated with annual compounding in Excel. The more frequent compounding produces a higher effective discount rate, which in turn means that a lower present value will produce a given sum in the future.

2.   ANNUITIES

Suppose that instead of promising to make a one-time payment, someone promises to make a *series* of equal payments, such as agreeing to pay regular amounts on a loan. In an annuity, this person promises to make these payments at regular intervals of time. The present value of an annuity represents the present value of this series of payments discounted at compound interest. You can also think of this present value as the lump-sum that someone must invest now, at compound interest, to permit a series of equal withdrawals at regular intervals, and end up with nothing after the final withdrawal. In either event, we can calculate the present value of an annuity using the principles developed above.

a. ORDINARY ANNUITY

Recall that in an ordinary annuity or an annuity in arrears, the first periodic payment or investment occurs at the end of the first period. If we turn the transaction around, we could say that the first withdrawal also occurs at the end of that first period. For example, suppose that Steve enters a four-year lease on his apartment, promising to pay $1,000 at the end of each year. Steve can earn eight percent on his investments. How much would Steve have to invest now to meet his rental obligations? By examining the timing of the withdrawals, we can use Table III to compute the present value of this annuity.

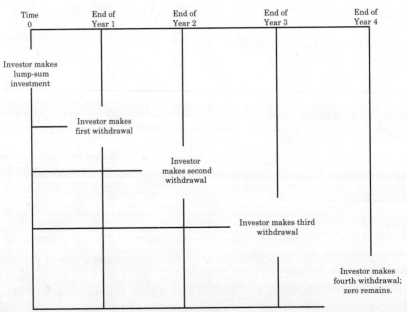

We notice that we will discount the first withdrawal at the end of year one once to the beginning of year one. Similarly, we will discount the second withdrawal twice; the third withdrawal three times; and the fourth withdrawal four times. Summarizing the present value factors from Table III for eight percent interest for these periods, we get:

First withdrawal (one period)	.92593
Second withdrawal (two periods)	.85734
Third withdrawal (three periods)	.79383
Fourth withdrawal (four periods)	.73503
Total	3.31213

Multiplying Steve's $1,000 rental payment times this sum of present value factors, we see that Steve must invest $3,312.13 at eight percent interest today to have enough money to withdraw $1,000 at the end of each of the next four years.

Alternatively, we could use Table IV in Appendix B on page 830, *infra*, to determine the present value of this annuity. Table IV uses the future value factors from Table III for one-time payments to calculate the present value factors for an ordinary annuity. Assuming the same facts as above, we find a present value factor at Table IV of 3.31213 for an annuity of $1 for four payments at eight percent compound interest. Multiplying the $1,000 annuity payment times the 3.31213 present value factor yields a $3,312.13 present value.

We can verify these calculations as follows: In the first year, the $3,312.13 initial deposit earns eight percent interest or $264.97, bringing the account balance to $3,577.10. After subtracting the first $1,000 withdrawal at the end of the first year, $2,577.10 remains available to earn interest during the second year. During the second year, that remaining balance earns $206.17 interest, which increases the balance to $2,783.27. The second withdrawal reduces the balance to $1,783.27. In the third year, the $1,783.27 earns $142.66 interest, raising the balance to $1,925.93. After subtracting the third withdrawal, $925.93 remains in the account to earn interest during the fourth year. In the final year, $74.07 interest on the previous balance increases the balance to $1,000, which the fourth withdrawal entirely consumes. Summarizing these calculations, we could develop the following chart:

Description	Interest	Principal	Balance
Initial Deposit			$3,312.13
Interest During Year 1	$264.97		3,577.10
First Withdrawal		$1,000.00	2,577.10
Interest During Year 2	206.17		2,783.27
Second Withdrawal		1,000.00	1,783.27
Interest During Year 3	142.66		1,925.93
Third Withdrawal		1,000.00	925.93
Interest During Year 4	74.07		1,000.00
Fourth Withdrawal		1,000.00	–0–

Recall that we could adjust Table I, but not Table II, to reflect semiannual and quarterly compounding of a stated annual rate. Similarly, we cannot adjust Table IV because the table would require an additional payment or withdrawal at the end of each semiannual or quarterly period.

We can also use the PV function in Microsoft Excel to calculate the present value of an ordinary annuity. Here, we enter "8%" or ".08" into the **Rate** box for the annual eight percent interest that Steve could earn on his investments and "4" into the **Nper** box for the four annual lease payments set forth in the example. Since the example involves an annuity rather than a single outlay, we put "-1000," the amount of each lease payment, in the **Pmt** box. Accordingly, we leave the the **Fv** box blank. Because each lease payment occurs at the end of the year, we can also leave the **Type** box blank. Alternatively, because the example involves an ordinary annuity, we could enter "0" into the **Type** box. The completed Excel argument appears as follows:

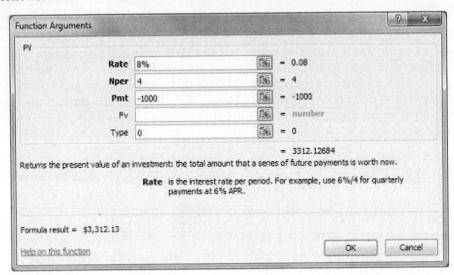

We can express this Excel argument, which calculates the present value of a four-year $1,000 ordinary annuity, discounted at eight percent annual interest, either as "=PV(0.08,4,-1000)" or "=PV(0.08,4,-1000,,0)." Both arguments yield a $3,312.13 present value, the exact amount we calculated earlier using Table IV.

b. ANNUITY DUE

Recall that the first period payment or investment in an annuity due or an annuity in advance occurs at the beginning, rather than at the end, of the first period. We can also use the PV function in Microsoft Excel to calculate the present value of an annuity due. To determine the present value of Steve's lease as an annuity due, we again enter "8%" or ".08" in the **Rate** box because he could earn eight percent annually on his investments; "4" in the **Nper** box; and "-1000" in the **Pmt** box. Because the example involves an annuity, rather than a single future payment, we again leave the **Fv** box blank. Finally, we must input "1" into the **Type** box because this example involves an annuity due, as Steve will make the lease payments at the beginning of each period. Note that this "1" in the **Type** box is the only difference between the function arguments for an annuity due and an ordinary annuity. Recall that for an ordinary annuity, we can leave the **Type** box blank or can enter "0" in that field to indicate that the payments occur at the end of each period. The completed Excel function appears as follows:

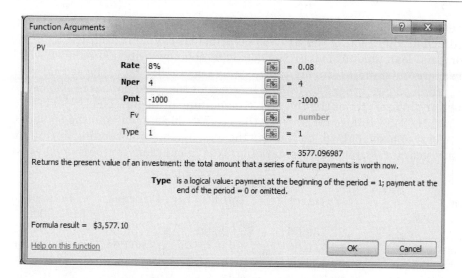

We can express this Excel argument, which calculates the present value of a four-year $1,000 annuity due, discounted at eight percent annual interest, as "=PV(0.08,4,-1000,,1)," which computes to $3,577.10.

c.   CALCULATING THE AMOUNT OF THE ANNUITY PAYMENT

So far, we have determined the present value of an annuity, given the amount of the annuity payment. Because the present value of an annuity equals the annuity payment times the factor from Table IV, we can also solve for the amount of an annuity payment, given the present value of the annuity.

To illustrate, assume that Brianna borrows $100,000 for five years at six percent interest. The lender requires repayment of the loan through equal, annual payments at the end of each of the next five years. The lender will credit each payment to accrued interest first, and then to principal. What annual payment will the lender require Brianna to make?

We know that the present value of the annuity is $100,000, because the lender is giving Brianna $100,000 cash today. We can find a 4.21236 present value factor in Table IV for an ordinary annuity of $1 for five payments at six percent compound interest. Because the present value of an annuity equals the annuity payment times the factor from Table IV, we get:

$$\$100,000 = \text{Annuity Payment} \times 4.21236$$

Solving this equation, we see that the annuity payment equals $23,739.66. Therefore, Brianna must pay the lender $23,739.66 at the end of each year for five years to repay her $100,000 loan.

Let us examine how much of each $23,739.66 payment the lender credits to interest and principal. For the first year, the interest equals the six percent interest rate times the $100,000 original principal amount outstanding during the year, or $6,000. Of the $23,739.66 that Brianna pays at the end of the first year, the lender credits $6,000 to interest and the remaining $17,739.66 to principal. Subtracting the $17,739.66 principal payment from the $100,000 original loan amount leaves $82,260.34 as the new principal balance which remains outstanding during the second year. At the end of the second year, Brianna pays another $23,739.66. Interest for that year equals $4,935.62, six percent interest times the $82,260.34 remaining principal. The lender credits the $18,804.04 difference between the $23,739.66 payment and the $4,935.62 interest to principal, which reduces the loan balance outstanding during the third year to $63,456.30. Summarizing these calculations for the five years, we get:

Year	Payment	Interest	Principal	Balance
0				$100,000.00
1	$23,739.66	$6,000.00	$17,739.66	82,260.34
2	23,739.66	4,935.62	18,804.04	63,456.30
3	23,739.66	3,807.38	19,932.28	43,524.02
4	23,739.66	2,611.44	21,128.22	22,395.80
5	23,739.66	1,343.75	22,395.91	(.11)

Rounding creates the eleven cent overpayment, which we will ignore as insignificant.

Microsoft Excel also calculates payment amounts easily. After clicking on the Formulas tab at the top of the screen in Excel, select the Financial box on the ribbon that appears under the Formulas tab. From the drop down menu, next choose the PMT [Payment] function, which calculates the payment for a loan based on equal payments and a fixed interest rate. We then enter the annual interest rate, either "6%" or ".06," in the **Rate** box and "5" in the **Nper** box for the number of years. For the **Pv** box, we enter "-100000" because the bank loaned Brianna $100,000, which also represents the present value of the series of future payments that Brianna must make to repay the loan. We leave the **Fv** and **Type** boxes blank because Brianna wants to repay the entire loan, leaving no balance after the last payment, and each loan payments is payable at the end of each year. The completed Excel function appears as follows:

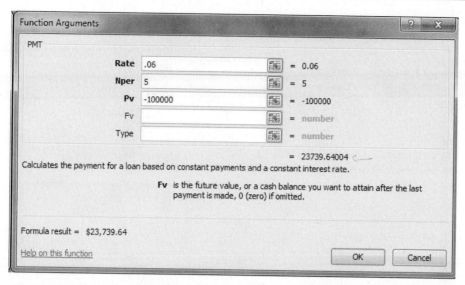

We can express this Excel argument, which calculates the payment amount necessary at the end of each year to repay a five-year, $100,000 loan at six percent interest, compounded annually, as "=PMT(0.06,5,-100000)." Thus, Brianna will need to make annual payments of $23,739.64 at the end of each year to repay the $100,000 loan in five years.

We can also use Microsoft Excel to calculate the amount of the periodic payment for an annuity due. After selecting the PMT function from the drop down menu under the Financial box under the Formulas tab, we again enter the annual interest rate in the **Rate** box, here either "6%" or ".06"; "5" in the **Nper** box for the number of years; and "-100000" in the **Pv** box because the bank loaned Brianna $100,000. This amount also represents the present value of the series of future payments that Brianna must make to repay the loan. We again leave the **Fv** box blank because Brianna wants to repay the entire loan, leaving no balance after the last payment. In this example, we must enter a "1" in the **Type** box because Brianna wants to make each payment at the beginning of each year. The completed Excel function appears as follows:

We can express this Excel argument, which calculates the five annual payments necessary to repay a $100,000 loan at five percent interest, with the first payment due immediately, as "=PMT(0.06,5,-100000,,1)." Thus, Brianna will need to make five annual payments of $10,998.80, beginning immediately, to repay the $50,000 loan.

Microsoft Excel enables users to compute payment amounts easily even when a loan involves an interest rate that is not a whole number, when the loan requires compounding more frequently than annually, and when the number of payments does not appear in the tables in Appendix B. For example, assume that Alex borrows $200,000 from a bank on October 1, 201X, to finance the purchase of a home. Alex agrees to pay five and a half percent interest per annum, compounded monthly, for thirty years. What monthly payment will the bank require Alex to make starting November 1, 201X, or at the end of the first monthly period, to repay the loan in thirty years?

Once again, select the PMT function from the Financial drop down box under the Formulas tab in Excel. In the **Rate** box, enter the annual interest rate, five and a half percent, divided by the number of compounding periods per year, here twelve for monthly compounding, which means either "5.5%/12" or ".055/12" in the present example. In the **Nper** box, enter "30*12," or "360," for the number of years in the loan, thirty, times the number of compounding periods per year, twelve. In the **Pv** box, enter "-200000" because the bank loaned Alex $200,000, which also represents the present value of the series of future payments that Alex must make to repay the loan. Because Alex wants to repay the entire loan, leaving no balance after the last payment, and with loan payments due at the end of each monthly period, leave the **Fv** and **Type** boxes blank. The completed Excel function argument appears as follows:

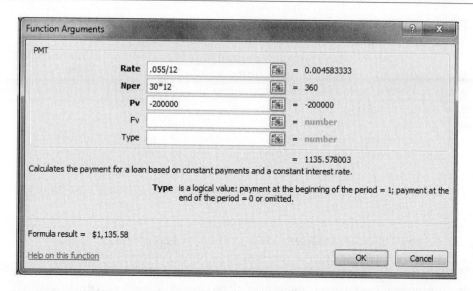

We can express this Excel argument, which calculates the monthly payment amount necessary to repay a thirty year, $200,000 loan at 5.5 percent annual interest, compounded monthly, as "=PMT(0.055/12,30*12,-200000)." Thus, Alex will need to make monthly payments of $1,135.58 to pay off the $200,000 mortgage in thirty years.

E. PERPETUAL ANNUITIES

All the annuities we have examined so far, whether in the future value or present value context, have been of limited duration. Unlike the previous annuities, with a perpetual annuity the investor intends the annuity to continue forever. For an annuity to continue forever, the investor may withdraw only the interest earned; the investor cannot withdraw any of the original principal.

To illustrate, assume that Ann, who plans to retire soon, wants to make sure she will have $60,000 per year in annual income. Assuming a five percent interest rate, how much money must Ann have in her retirement fund to guarantee $60,000 in annual income? This time, we can easily compute an answer. To determine what principal amount at five percent interest will produce $60,000 annual income, simply solve for X in the following equation, where X represents the principal amount:

$$.05X = \$60,000$$

$$X = \frac{\$60,000}{.05}$$

$$X = \$1,200,000$$

Ann, therefore, must invest $1,200,000 at five percent interest to guarantee $60,000 in annual income.

F. COMPREHENSIVE ILLUSTRATIONS

Thus far, we have examined perpetual annuities and four different types of compound interest calculations: future value of an amount, future value of a series of equal amounts, present value of an amount, and present value of a series of equal amounts. In all our previous examples, we have used one and only one of these computations. In the real world, however, we may have to apply more than one of these computations to solve a particular problem. Two common examples include evaluating payment options and valuing bonds.

1. CHOOSING AMONG A PRESENT AMOUNT, A FUTURE SUM, AND AN ANNUITY

Assume that under the terms of a settlement agreement, plaintiff has the option of receiving either: (1) an immediate cash payment of $200,000, (2) a deferred payment of $400,000 payable in ten years, or (3) a five-year annuity, beginning one year after the plaintiff signs the settlement agreement, which will pay $50,000 annually. Ignoring tax considerations and assuming a relevant interest rate of seven percent, compounded annually, which settlement option should plaintiff accept?

Before comparing these offers, we must find a common denominator to evaluate each offer, so that we are comparing "apples to apples." The $200,000 payment would give plaintiff cash immediately. The $400,000 payment would require plaintiff to wait ten years before collecting any cash. The annuity will pay $50,000 at the end of each of the next five years. In most situations, present value offers the easiest and simplest point to compare options.

Recall that we already know that Option 1 offers a $200,000 present value. Using Table III, we can calculate the present value of Option 2. Table III lists .50835 as the present value of $1 for ten years at seven percent, compound interest. Multiplying the $400,000 proposed payment times the .50835 present value factor yields a $203,340 present value for Option 2. Alternatively, the Excel argument "=PV(0.07,10,,-400000)" calculates a more precise $203,339.72 present value for Option 2. We can compute the present value of Option 3 using Table IV. In that table, we find 4.10020 as the factor for five periods and seven percent compound interest. Multiplying the $50,000 annual payments times the 4.10020 present value factor yields a $205,010 present value for Option 3. Likewise, the Excel argument "=PV(0.07,5,-50000)" yields a $205,009.87 present value for Option 3.

Because Option 3 has the highest present value, we should advise the plaintiff to select that option. Under Option 3, plaintiff will receive five $50,000 payments, totaling $250,000. Assume that our engagement letter entitles us to a one-fifth contingent fee. Does the plaintiff owe us $50,000 immediately upon accepting Option 3 and signing the settlement agreement? Common sense suggests that if we want to collect our fee immediately, we can charge only one-fifth of the present value of all the future payments or approximately $41,000. As a practical matter, absent an explicit agreement to the contrary, a court may permit a client to pay legal fees attributable to an annuity as the client collects each payment.

2. CALCULATING THE MARKET VALUE OF BONDS

Bonds generally give the owner two separate rights: (1) the right to periodic interest payments and (2) the right to the repayment of principal at the bond's maturity. The periodic interest payments give rise to an annuity while the principal represents a single amount. To determine a bond's market value, we must determine the present value of the interest payments and the principal.

Assume that Starbucks Corporation uses bonds to borrow money at ten percent interest per year, payable semiannually. Further assume that after Starbucks issues the bonds, interest rates increase to twelve percent annual interest, compounded semiannually. If the bonds will mature in exactly three years, how much would a reasonable investor pay for such a bond with a $10,000 principal amount?

This bond gives its owner two separate rights: (1) the right to the six semiannual interest payments of $500, or one half of the ten percent annual rate times $10,000; and (2) the right to repayment of the $10,000 bond principal at maturity, or in this case after three years. The value of the bond, therefore, equals the sum of the present values of these two rights discounted at the market interest rate of twelve percent annual interest, compounded semiannually.

By contract, the bond's terms set $500 as the amount of the semiannual interest payments. As a result, the amount of the annuity does not change as the market interest rate fluctuates. The present values of the rights to those semiannual interest payments and the principal amount, however, do vary as the market interest rate changes. Consequently, we discount the semiannual interest payments and the principal amount at the market rate.

Using Table IV, we find a 4.91732 present value factor for an annuity of $1 for six payments at six percent compound interest which represents one half of the twelve percent annual market rate. Multiplying the $500 semiannual interest payment times the 4.91732 present value factor yields a $2,458.66 present value for the interest payments. Likewise, the Excel argument "=PV(0.12/2,3*2,-500)" calculates the same $2,458.66 present value for the interest payments. Next, we turn to the present value of the $10,000 principal which the borrower will repay in three years. Because the semiannual compounding requires us to discount interest twice a year for three years, we must discount the principal amount to present value over six periods. Every six months, we will discount the principal at six percent or one half the twelve percent annual rate. Using Table III, we look at six periods and six percent interest and find a .70496 present value factor. Multiplying the $10,000 principal amount times the .70496 present value factor yields a $7,049.60 present value. Alternatively, the Excel argument

"=PV(0.06,3*2,,-10000)" calculates a $7,049.61 for the $10,000 principal at maturity in three years. Therefore, the bond should trade for $9,508.26, the sum of the $2,458.66 present value of the semiannual interest payments and the $7,049.60 present value of the principal, or a penny more using Excel.

Now assume the same facts as above, except that, after Starbucks issues the bonds, the market interest rate on comparable bonds falls to eight percent annual interest, compounded semiannually. Still assuming that the bond will mature in exactly three years, how much would a reasonable investor pay for this $10,000 bond?

Again, we must determine present values for both (1) the right to the six semiannual interest payments which the bond's terms still fix at $500 each and (2) the right to repayment of the $10,000 bond principal at maturity in three years. Using Table IV, we find a 5.24214 present value factor for an annuity of $1 for six payments at four percent compound interest which represents one half of the eight percent annual market rate. Multiplying the $500 semiannual interest payment times the 5.24214 present value factor yields a $2,621.07 present value. Likewise, the Excel argument "=PV(0.08/2,3*2,-500)" calculates the same $2,621.07 present value for the interest payments.

As to the present value of the repayment of the $10,000 bond principal in three years, the semiannual compounding again requires us to discount interest twice a year, or six times. Every six months, we will discount the principal at four percent or one half the eight percent annual rate. Using Table III, we look at six periods and four percent interest and find a .79031 present value factor. Multiplying the $10,000 principal amount times the .79031 present value factor yields a $7,903.10 present value. Alternatively, the Excel argument "=PV(0.08/2,3*2,,-10000)" calculates a $7,903.15 present value for the $10,000 principal at maturity in three years, an additional five cents than the amount calculated using Table III. Therefore, the bond should trade for $10,524.17 using Appendix B, the sum of the $2,621.07 present value of the semiannual interest payments and the $7,903.10 present value of the principal, or a nickel more using Excel.

As we have just seen, the value of bonds varies inversely with the current market interest rate. When the market interest rate rises, the value of bonds decreases. When the market interest rate falls, the value of bonds increases.

G. CAUTIONS ABOUT TIME VALUE ANALYSIS

To become acquainted with basic time value analysis, we have used nothing more than a simple calculator and the Tables in the back of this book. As we have seen, business calculators and electronic spreadsheets can quickly perform more complex time value of money computations. Excel has demonstrated that if a lender charges interest at a rate other than a whole percentage point, interest compounds frequently, or the loan term extends over many periods, then Excel, another electronic spreadsheet, or a business calculator can easily perform these more challenging computations.

In time value analysis, notwithstanding mathematical precision, an invalid underlying assumption can yield extremely inaccurate and unreliable results. For example, although we can calculate the future value of an investment at 800 percent per year for the next 40 years, only a complete fool would assume that any investment could perform that well. Similarly, time value analysis assumes that we can reinvest the earnings of an investment at the same interest rate, period after period, when in fact, interest rates fluctuate all the time.

Moreover, time value analysis ignores taxes and other considerations, such as terminal illnesses. For instance, suppose that a plaintiff, under the terms of a settlement offer, can select either an immediate cash payment of $1,000,000 or twenty annual, but nonassignable, payments of $200,000 each, beginning one year after the plaintiff signs the settlement agreement. If the plaintiff suffers from a terminal illness, the plaintiff might select the immediate payment, even if the twenty annual payments would normally offer a greater present value. We could also explain this decision on the grounds that the illness has caused the plaintiff to use a very high discount rate which exceeds the market rate.

In conclusion, time value analysis provides one factor for lawyers and their clients to consider when making decisions. Remember to consider these other factors, and the limitations of time value analysis, before you base a decision solely on time value analysis.

PROBLEMS

Problem 3.1A. Red, White, and Blue, believing themselves to be astute investors, each deposited $5,000 in different banks on January 1, 2000. Red deposited his $5,000 in an account that paid six percent simple interest per year; White deposited his $5,000 in an account that paid six percent annual interest, compounded annually; and Blue deposited his $5,000 in an account that paid six percent interest per year, compounded semiannually. How much would each person have had in his savings account on January 1, 2013? Explain briefly.

Problem 3.1B. In 1803, the United States purchased the Louisiana Territory from France for $15 million.

(1) If France had invested the $15 million in a savings account on November 1, 1803 at three percent simple interest per year, how much would France have had in the account on November 1, 2013? Explain briefly.

(2) If France had invested the $15 million in a savings account on November 1, 1803 at three percent annual interest, compounded semiannually, how much would France have had in the savings account on November 1, 2013? Explain briefly.

Problem 3.1C. In 1626, Native Americans sold Manhattan Island for $24. If the Native Americans had invested the $24 in a savings account on October 1, 1626, at three percent annual interest, compounded quarterly, how much would they have had in the account on October 1, 2013? Explain briefly.

Problem 3.2A. Molly's grandparents plan to give her $3,000 each year for her college fund.

(1) If they give her $3,000 at the end of each year for the next eighteen years, how much will she have at the end of eighteen years, assuming that she is able to earn five percent interest per year, compounded annually? Explain briefly.

(2) If her grandparents had given her the $3,000 each year at the beginning of the year (i.e., January 1), how much would she have at the end of the eighteenth year, again assuming that she is able to earn five percent annual interest, compounded annually? Explain briefly.

Problem 3.2B. Martha's employment contract requires her employer, D Corp., to deposit $4,000 per year into the company's pension plan on Martha's behalf.

(1) If, at the end of each year, D Corp. deposits $4,000 for the next twelve years, how much will Martha have at the end of the twelfth year, assuming that D Corp. is able to earn six percent interest per year, compounded annually? Explain briefly.

(2) If D Corp. deposits $4,000 each year at the beginning of the year, how much will Martha have at the end of the twelfth year, again assuming that D Corp. is able to earn six percent interest per year, compounded annually? Explain briefly.

Problem 3.2C. Mary Ann's parents will celebrate their 50th anniversary in seven years, and she would like to start saving money now so that she can surprise them with a marvelous gift on their anniversary.

(1) If Mary Ann can save $100 at the end of each month for the next seven years, how much will she have at the end of the seventh year, assuming that she is able to earn two percent interest per year, compounded monthly? Explain briefly.

(2) If Mary Ann deposits $100 at the beginning of each month, how much will she have at the end of the seventh year, again assuming that she is able to earn two percent interest per year, compounded monthly? Explain briefly.

Problem 3.3A. Under the terms of a settlement agreement, Defendant promised to pay Plaintiff $180,000 fifteen years from now. If Defendant can earn five percent per year on his investments, compounded annually, what is the present value of his promise? Explain briefly.

Problem 3.3B. A prestigious law school has just accepted Mark's application, and his parents are so proud that they promise to give him $20,000 upon his graduation in three years.

(1) If his parents can earn seven percent per year on their investments, compounded annually, what is the present value of their promise? Explain briefly.

(2) What is the present value of their promise if the interest compounds semiannually? Explain briefly.

Problem 3.3C. Thomas bequeaths $300,000 in trust to pay the income at the end of each year to Ellen for life, remainder to Maria. The trust can earn 7.5% interest per year, compounded quarterly. Ellen has a life expectancy of 18 years.

(1) What is the present value of Maria's remainder interest? Explain briefly.

(2) What is the present value of Ellen's income interest? Explain briefly.

Problem 3.4A. In 2012, the dog trick act "Olate Dogs" and trainers Richard and Nicholas Olate earned $1 million for winning the seventh season of *America's Got Talent*. The prize remains payable $40,000 a year for twenty-five years, with the first payment occurring immediately after the season finale. If the applicable interest rate was four percent, compounded annually, what was the present value of the prize to Olate Dogs in 2012? Explain briefly.

Problem 3.4B. Noelle won $20,000,000 in the state lottery, payable $1,000,000 a year for twenty years. The applicable interest rate is three percent per year, compounded annually.

(1) If the lottery payments are payable at the end of each year, what is the present value of all the lottery payments? Explain briefly.

(2) What is the present value if the lottery payments are payable at the beginning of each year? Explain briefly.

Problem 3.4C. Under the terms of a settlement agreement, Defendant must pay Plaintiff ten annual installments of $100,000 each. The applicable interest rate is 3.85% per year, compounded annually. Assume that the Internal Revenue Service will allow the Defendant to claim a one-time deduction in the current year for the present value of the payments.

(1) If the payments are payable at the end of each year, what is the amount of Defendant's deduction? Explain briefly.

(2) What is the amount of Defendant's deduction if the payments are payable at the beginning of each year? Explain briefly.

Problem 3.5A. Melanie owes the bank $25,000 from the purchase of her new sports car. The debt bears interest of eight percent per year, payable annually. Melanie wants to pay the debt and interest in four annual installments beginning in one year. What equal annual installments will pay the debt and interest? Explain briefly.

Problem 3.5B. Sarah, a first year law student, plans to finance her law school education by borrowing $150,000 from her parents. Her parents have agreed not to charge her any interest on the loans until she graduates. The loans require her to pay three percent interest, compounded annually, starting on the date of her graduation. She has agreed to repay the loans in ten, equal annual installments, with payments due on the first ten anniversaries of her graduation. What annual payment will enable Sarah to repay the loans and any accrued interest over ten years? Explain briefly.

Problem 3.5C. Jose purchases a new home by borrowing $240,000 from his local bank. Under the terms of the mortgage, the bank charges Jose 5.125 percent annual interest, compounded monthly, and requires him to make equal payments at the end of each month for thirty years. How much will Jose owe the bank monthly? Explain briefly.

Problem 3.6A. Disturbed about the lack of financial aid that his alma mater provides to its students, I. M. Generous decides to set up an endowment fund to provide a $50,000 annual scholarship for a needy student. Assuming a eight percent annual interest rate, how much must Generous donate to his alma mater to fund the endowment permanently? Explain briefly.

Problem 3.6B. Planning to retire soon, Patricia wants to set up a retirement fund that will provide $80,000 in annual income. Assuming a six percent annual interest rate, how much must Patricia have in her retirement fund to guarantee $80,000 in annual income forever? Explain briefly.

Problem 3.6C. John wants to save enough to ensure himself the equivalent of $100,000 in current income each year during his retirement. In addition, he wants $150,000 available on the date of his retirement so that he can travel widely and leave immediately once he retires. Given his fiscal conservatism, he wants to assume that he will live forever. He also expects four percent inflation each year. If John expects to earn eight percent on his retirement savings, how much will he need when he retires?

Problem 3.7A. Blue Chip, Inc. patented a microchip that revolutionized the computer industry. This chip allows all computers and computer software to communicate with each other without converting the software or changing the computer language. Blue Chip has received offers from several major computer and computer software companies to purchase the patent. Maxihard offered $200,000,000, payable in ten years. MBI proposed paying $20,000,000 each year over the next 10 years, payable at the beginning of each year. Orange offered $100,000,000 immediately, and a $100,000,000 bond with stated interest of four percent annual interest, payable at the end of each year, with the principal due in ten years. The company's president has asked you to determine the highest offer assuming an eight percent interest rate, compounded annually. What advice would you give Blue Chip? Explain briefly.

Problem 3.7B. Your best friend is the proud parent of a new baby girl. Your friend's parents want to pay for their granddaughter's freshman year of college. Your friend estimates that one year of college will cost $50,000 at a public university in eighteen years.

(1) If your friend's parents can earn an after-tax rate of return of five percent per year, compounded annually, how much should they set aside today to pay for their granddaughter's freshman year? Explain briefly.

(2) If they want instead to make equal, annual payments at the end of each of the next five years, how much should they set aside each year? Explain briefly.

Problem 3.7C. You are trying to decide whether to purchase or lease your next car. The dealer is willing to sell you a new Saturn for $18,000. At the end of six years, you estimate that the fair market value of the Saturn will be $6,000. The dealer is also willing to lease the car to you for seventy-two monthly payments of $219 beginning in one month, plus a $3,600 "rental reduction" or non-refundable down payment at the time you accept delivery. Assume that the applicable interest rate is 5.9 percent per year, compounded monthly. Applying present value principles, which option would you choose? Explain briefly.

Problem 3.8A. List as many different accounting issues or topics as possible in which Amazon used time value of money concepts to determine amounts included on its financial statements for the year ending December 31, 2012. Explain briefly where you found this information.

Problem 3.8B. List as many different accounting issues or topics as possible in which Google used time value of money concepts to determine amounts included on its financial statements for the year ending December 31, 2012. Explain briefly where you found this information.

Problem 3.8C. List as many different accounting issues or topics as possible in which UPS used time value of money concepts to determine amounts included on its financial statements for the year ending December 31, 2012. Explain briefly where you found this information.

*

CHAPTER IV

INTRODUCTION TO FINANCIAL STATEMENT ANALYSIS AND FINANCIAL RATIOS

A. IMPORTANCE TO LAWYERS

In the first chapter, we discussed the four basic financial statements: the balance sheet, the income statement, the statement of owners' equity, and the statement of cash flows. A lawyer must understand the form and content of these financial statements to be able to interpret and analyze them. In this chapter, we will examine how lawyers can use the basic financial statements and related information to counsel clients. As one lesson from Enron's collapse, attorneys should remember that a missing financial statement may indicate a desire to hide disappointing results, or perhaps the business lacks sufficiently complete or reliable books and records. As a starting point, therefore, a lawyer should ask probing questions any time an enterprise does not provide a complete set of financial statements, plus accompanying notes.

The notes to the financial statements explain the accounting policies that the enterprise has adopted and contain additional disclosures about important matters affecting the financial statements and the business. As a result, any knowledgeable user of financial statements will carefully read the notes, which the legal community may refer to as *footnotes*. As we discussed in Chapter II, generally accepted accounting principles often provide alternatives, and the accounting principles chosen and their application to particular situations can greatly influence the amounts reported in the financial statements. The notes sometimes explain why management chose a particular accounting principle from among the acceptable alternatives. A reader should consider whether the policies that management has used fit the industry and whether a change in accounting policies has affected the enterprise's financial position, especially for comparative purposes. In short, the notes help a reader to assess how the applicable accounting principles and policies affected the numbers in the financial statements.

The notes also provide additional detail about items and amounts which appear in summary form in the financial statements. We will discuss many of these additional disclosure requirements in later chapters. In particular, businesses use the notes to divulge information about acquisitions, debt and borrowing arrangements, operating lease commitments, pension and retirement benefits, and financial information relating to different business segments. The notes also commonly disclose information about commitments and contingencies. The term *commitments* generally refers to quantifiable transactions that management has affirmatively entered into on the enterprise's behalf, such as capital expenditures to expand operating facilities. In contrast, *contingencies* reflect more uncertain future events, such as litigation and guarantees, whose ultimate consequences, if they do occur, will adversely affect the company.

The experienced user will also request and read financial statements for more than one accounting period. In academic terms, the financial statements and the accompanying notes represent the business's report card and cumulative grade point average. Just as a seasoned job interviewer usually prefers to evaluate grades from more than one academic term, a knowledgeable reader of financial statements favors financial statements covering more than one accounting period. As we will discuss in more detail later, a thoughtful reader will want to review a series of financial statements to assess the business's general direction. Financial statements for a single accounting period do not reveal whether the business's operating results and financial position are improving, holding steady or declining.

Finally, an experienced reader of financial statements will look for the reports, if any, from the independent accountant or auditor. If no such report exists, the reader must view the statements with considerable skepticism. If the financial statements do include a report from an independent accountant, the report will indicate whether the engagement involved an audit, review, compilation, or some other agreed-upon procedures. As we saw in Chapter II, an experienced reader prefers an unqualified audit opinion, even though such an opinion does not guarantee the financial statement's accuracy. In addition, lawyer reading a public company's financial statements will look for the auditor's report on internal control over financial reporting. As we discussed in Chapter II, nonaccelerated filers and emerging growth companies need not obtain such a report from their auditors. In any event, a reader should watch for any "material weaknesses" in internal control over financial reporting that either management or the independent auditor have identified and carefully consider such weaknesses.

A lawyer who can read and understand these documents has developed a valuable tool for understanding business transactions, appreciating investment and credit decisions, and advising clients. The required section called Management's Discussion & Analysis ("MD&A") in various filings that public companies must submit to the SEC also often provides additional valuable information to knowledgeable readers. MD&As explain and analyze the company's financial condition, operating results, and liquidity. This discussion gives the reader the opportunity to see the company through the "eyes of management." The SEC has urged public companies to use this venue to disclose important information about trends affecting the business and critical accounting policies.

B.   ANNUAL REPORTS

As previously mentioned, most businesses, including all publicly-traded corporations, present their financial statements in an annual report. The astute reader of an annual report understands the purpose behind each section. But before discussing those sections, we must understand why businesses prepare annual reports.

State corporate laws require corporations to hold annual meetings to elect directors and to conduct other business. Especially in publicly-traded corporations, shareholders live throughout the country, and increasingly around the world. For various reasons, shareholders often cannot, and usually do not, attend such meetings. Corporate laws, however, require a *quorum* before the corporation can validly conduct any business. A quorum means that the holders of a certain number of shares, most often a majority, must attend a shareholders' meeting, either in person or by *proxy*. Unless shareholders that do not attend a meeting appoint proxies, or agents, to represent them at the meeting, the quorum requirement may prevent the shareholders as a group from electing directors or transacting any other business. For that reason, a corporation's management usually solicits proxies before each shareholders' meeting.

Pursuant to the regulation of proxy solicitation under federal securities law, enterprises that have issued securities traded on a national securities exchange, or have $10 million or more in assets *and* a class of non-exempt equity securities owned by at least either 2,000 persons or 500 persons who do not qualify as accredited investors, must send, either before or concurrently with the solicitation, an annual report that meets detailed requirements. Special rules, however, permit small business issuers to send only specified financial statements. The proxy rules also require registrants to provide substantially equivalent information to security holders even if the registrant does not solicit proxies.

An annual report summarizes an enterprise's financial and operational activities for the most recent calendar or other fiscal year. SEC regulations require registrants to include the following in their annual reports: (1) audited financial statements for the most recent year, plus several immediately preceding years for comparative purposes; (2) quarterly financial data; (3) a historical summary of selected financial data for the most recent five years or the registrant's entire life, if less than five years; (4) a description of the business; (5) business segment information, if applicable; (6) information about executive officers and directors; (7) historical data about the market prices of the business's equity securities during the past two years and dividends on those securities during that period; (8) perhaps most importantly, management's discussion and analysis of the enterprise's financial condition and the results of its operations; and (9) management's report on internal control over financial reporting and, if applicable, the related report from the independent auditor as to whether the enterprise maintained effective control over financial reporting.

Research shows that most investors, on average, spend only a few minutes glancing at an annual report. As a result, registrants have used various gimmicks, including coupons for free or discounted merchandise, supermodels, and scented annual reports, to try to impress readers. Registrants typically highlight positive information in such attention-getting sections while placing negative information in technical sections that intimidate the common reader. As attorneys, we must expend the extra time and energy to read carefully the technical sections and analyze an annual report. By doing so, we can glean important information that may affect our client's business interests or investments.

In addition to supplying the financial statements, notes, and report of independent auditor discussed in the previous section, registrants usually disseminate the other required information in the following standardized sections:

Business Profile: This section describes the enterprise's business. As an example, please see page 2 of Starbucks Corporation's Form 10-K for the fiscal year ended September 30, 2012, which appears in Appendix A on page 698, *infra*. The business profile often contains the names of the directors, officers or senior executives. You can find the names of Starbucks' board of directors and senior officers in Appendix A on page 798, *infra*.

The business profile frequently contains the business's *mission statement*—a broad statement about the enterprise's purpose and future goals. The mission statement should give the reader some sense about the business's values and direction. For example, a computer software company may stress innovation in its mission statement; as a result, the reader should expect that the business will incur substantial costs to research and develop new software. Overly-broad mission statements obviously do not help in this regard, but may indicate that management has not developed a focused strategy for the business.

Financial Highlights: The contents of this section will vary among registrants, but generally contain quantitative information on sales or revenues, income or loss per ownership unit, balance sheet items, financial ratios, and other information. Supporting graphs often accompany this quantitative data. We can find Starbucks' financial highlights from its fiscal 2012 annual report in Appendix A on page 692, *infra*. We should keep in mind that management carefully selects the information presented in this section, usually with an eye to portraying the enterprise's financial condition and results as favorably as possible. As we will discuss in considerable detail later in this chapter, a reader should keep in mind that nonrecurring or unusual items, rather than normal operations, may have caused significant fluctuations between periods. Only carefully examining the financial statements and the relevant footnotes may reveal such nonrecurring or unusual items.

Letter to the Owners: For the annual report, the enterprise's highest ranking executive, typically the chairperson of the board of directors or the president, usually writes the *letter to shareholders*. We should read this letter with considerable skepticism because this part of the annual report functions as another public-relations piece. Experienced readers and financial analysts watch for euphemisms, such as the word "challenging," to describe bad situations or to predict tough financial times. The "Dear Shareholders" letter from Starbucks' fiscal 2012 annual report appears in Appendix A on pages 693 and 694, *infra*.

Operational Overview: This section summarizes the enterprise's normal business functions. For large, multi-segmented enterprises, such as General Electric Co. or Procter & Gamble, this part of the annual report describes each business segment's products, markets and key financial data. Consequently, experienced readers often find this section helpful in analyzing the financial statements.

Historical Summary of Financial Data: As mentioned earlier, the proxy rules require registrants to present five years of income statements, balance sheets and other data. Financial analysts describe this section as the business's "medical record" because the summary compares the business's financial vital signs over the years given. You can find this selected financial data on page 22 of Starbucks' 2012 Form 10-K in Appendix A on page 718, *infra*.

Management's Discussion and Analysis: This extremely important section should contain (1) management's "crystal ball" expectations or predictions regarding prospective results of operations, capital resources, and liquidity, and (2) pursuant to pressure from the SEC after the financial frauds in the early 2000s, identification of critical accounting policies, including those assumptions, estimates, and other judgments or uncertainties that affect the application of the chosen accounting policies to the financial statements. We will discuss this section in greater detail later in the chapter, but in the meantime, remember that the independent accountants do not audit the information contained in this section. You can find Starbucks' MD&A for the fiscal year ended September 30, 2012 in Appendix A on pages 721 to 745, *infra*.

Report on Internal Control over Financial Reporting: Please recall that SOx section 404(a) requires registrants to file a report from management on the effectiveness of internal control over financial reporting as of the end of the fiscal year and to describe any changes to such controls during the period. The report of Starbucks' management on internal control over financial reporting appears in Appendix A on page 786, *infra*. Excepting emerging growth companies, most "accelerated filers," again which generally means the largest and most established public companies, must also provide an attestation report from the independent auditor on the effectiveness of the company's internal control over financial reporting. The report from Deloitte & Touche LLP, Starbuck's independent auditor, appears in Appendix A on page 787, *infra*.

C. ANALYTICAL TECHNIQUES

Financial statements seek to provide useful information to help existing and potential investors, creditors, and other users reach rational investment, credit, and similar decisions. Normally, these decision-makers try to predict an enterprise's financial future on the basis of the enterprise's experience to date. This process requires the user to analyze the financial data available, and a number of analytical techniques and ratios have proved quite helpful. Of course, much depends upon the decision-maker's objective. A potential buyer of common stock focus on different aspects of the financial data than those facets that will gain the attention of a banker considering a short-term loan. The holder of a twenty-year bond will contemplate yet a third set of concerns. But these decision-makers will consider some common themes, and, as to many of these, ratios derived from data collected on the financial statements can provide relevant and helpful information. In this chapter, we will look at some of these procedures and ratios, not to try to qualify as financial analysts, but to develop an understanding of the basic tools and techniques that accountants and analysts use to interpret financial statements.

The most common procedures that accountants and financial analysts use to evaluate an enterprise's financial statements include trend analysis, common-sized analysis and financial ratios. All these methods permit an analyst to look beyond the financial statements themselves to assess whether changing general economic or industry conditions, such as fluctuating interest rates, inflation, or vacillating consumer confidence, will affect the enterprise.

1. TREND ANALYSIS

Trend analysis involves comparing financial statements for an enterprise over several periods. This comparison allows the reader to determine where the enterprise generated and spent its resources over a longer period of time. By analyzing an enterprise over a series of reporting periods, a reader may notice various patterns or trends, such as increasing sales or decreasing accounts payable.

2. COMMON-SIZED ANALYSIS

Common-sized analysis, which accountants and financial analysts also refer to as *vertical analysis*, consists of reducing a financial statement, such as the income statement or the statement of cash flows, to a series of percentages of a given base amount, such as net sales or total cash flow for the period. On pages 27 to 29 of Starbucks' Form 10-K for the fiscal year ended September 30, 2012, which you can find in Appendix A on pages 723 to 725, *infra*, three different tables set forth the percentages of the various line items in the consolidated statements of earnings to the company's total net revenues. A reader of financial statements can take these percentages and compare them either to prior years for the same enterprise or to the current percentages for comparable businesses. As another example, an investor may want to compare the percentage that an enterprise's cash flow from operations currently bears to its total cash flows from all sources with the counterpart percentages in previous accounting periods.

3.   FINANCIAL RATIOS

Creditors and investors frequently rely on ratios to assess the financial health of an enterprise. In general, financial ratios basically fall into four groupings. These categories include *liquidity ratios, leverage or coverage ratios, profitability ratios*, and *activity ratios*. Liquidity and leverage ratios provide information on an enterprise's ability to cover its anticipated operating expenses, such as payroll, to meet its debt obligations in the short and long run, and to distribute profits to owners. Coverage ratios measure the relative claims that creditors and owners hold on the business's assets. Profitability ratios assess how effectively the business operates. Activity ratios provide information about how effectively a business uses its assets.

Lawyers will often use financial ratios in contracts and loan agreements and to evaluate business transactions. Whether representing the borrower or the lender, lawyers should understand how to apply financial ratios and negotiate loan covenants to their client's advantage. To illustrate, most loan agreements give the lender the right to demand immediate repayment in full if the borrower defaults. Loan agreements frequently define "default" as including the borrower's failure to maintain certain financial ratios. If such a default gives a lender the right to demand immediate repayment, accounting rules require the business to treat the entire loan balance as a current liability. Reclassifying long-term debt as a current liability could cause similar defaults under other lending arrangements.

Lawyers representing borrowers can avoid such defaults by carefully drafting and negotiating realistic covenants or by obtaining a waiver prior to any anticipated defaults. If a lender agrees to waive a default for at least one year from a balance sheet date, the accounting rules will not require the borrower to treat the liability as a current liability, which gives the borrower the opportunity to improve its financial condition.

Because alternative definitions potentially apply to certain ratios, an attorney should insist that contracts or loan documents explicitly define any ratios. An attorney should also consult the client's accountant about these ratios, their definitions, and their applications to the client's situation. Moreover, the understanding necessary for competent representation does not disappear if litigation arises and the lawyer's role changes from advisor to advocate.

Some of these financial ratios, like some analytical techniques more generally, utilize the figures on the balance sheet, some look to the income statement, and others incorporate cash flow data. We now take a closer look at each of these financial statements in turn, together with their related analytical tools and ratios.

D. THE BALANCE SHEET

By focusing on the recognition of assets and liabilities, the balance sheet supplies useful information to investors, creditors and others in reaching investment, credit and similar decisions.

1. CHANGES IN OWNERS' EQUITY

To understand the role of the balance sheet in stating a business's financial position, we should reexamine the relationship between the balance sheet and the income statement. Consider, for example, what happens in the balance sheet accounts during the period which the income statement covers. In general, a business earns net income by obtaining cash or other assets in excess of the amount of the assets expended or liabilities incurred. Thus, E. Tutt generated net income because the amount of cash and accounts receivable that she obtained from professional fees during the period exceeded the total of the cash expended and the liabilities incurred for expenses during the same period. Similarly, Marty Jones realized net income by obtaining a total of cash and receivables during the period which exceeded the cost of the shoes which he sold plus the expenses which he paid or became obligated to pay. Notice that whenever a business earns a profit its net assets, or assets less liabilities, will increase; conversely, a decline in net assets will accompany a loss for the period. After all, net income affects owners' equity, because net assets always equal owners' equity. But remember, transactions with owners, such as capital contributions from the owners, and distributions to them, neither of which indicate how the enterprise has performed, also affect owners' equity. To illustrate, look at E. Tutt's balance sheets for June 30 and July 31 in the problem that begins at page 87, *supra*. Net assets totaled $2,860 on June 30 and $3,670 on July 31. Ignoring the offsetting $100 contribution to and withdrawal from the proprietorship during the period, which exactly offset each other, the increase in net assets during July of $810 exactly equaled the net income for that period.

Every once in a while, we may encounter situations in a legal setting in which someone uses the change in net assets between successive balance sheet dates to determine net income or loss for the intervening period. As an example, the Internal Revenue Service ("IRS") has long recognized that taxable income, including unreported income, causes an increase in net assets. For many years, the IRS has used the *net worth method* to prove that taxpayers failed to report income when their net assets increased by more than their reported taxable income, and they could not explain the difference. Notably, the net worth method helped send the famous gangster Al Capone to jail in the early 1930s for tax evasion. For the years 1922, 1923, 1924 and 1925, Capone filed delinquent tax returns reporting $20,000 income for each of three years and $15,000 income for one year. During a period including those same years, Capone deposited sums totaling $1,851,840.08 in various banks under fictitious names. The Seventh Circuit affirmed the convictions. Capone v. United States, 51 F.2d 609 (7th Cir. 1931).

Whenever we use the balance sheet to measure an enterprise's financial performance by computing the change in net assets between successive balance sheet dates, we must ask whether we should revalue the assets. Recall that in Chapter I, we decided to record E. Tutt's assets at cost, rather than current market value, on the ground that accountants can easily and objectively ascertain cost while reasonable minds can disagree about current fair market value. Especially before the advent of accrual accounting, some accountants and financial analysts urged that the balance sheet should show the current market value of the assets on the balance sheet, because the balance sheet would thereby present a more meaningful picture of the enterprise's current condition and worth. Even if the balance sheet did not actually list those current market values, the business could disclose that information in the notes to the financial statements. In either event, a financial analyst could take account of any increase or decrease in the value of those assets when computing the change in net assets between particular balance sheet dates. Obviously, periodic revaluation of assets could significantly impact the picture of the enterprise's business fortunes that the financial statements portray.

Look at E. Tutt's balance sheet for July 31, on page 95, *supra*. Suppose that on July 31, E. Tutt finds that her office equipment, recorded at $775, has appreciated in value to $1,000, presumably because of an increase in the price of such equipment in the second-hand market. If despite GAAP's disapproval she records the asset at that figure, her net assets, and the amount in the Proprietorship account, on July 31 would increase to $3,895. Ignoring the contribution to, and withdrawal from, the enterprise during July of $100 each, which offset one another, comparing that amount to the amount of net assets, or Proprietorship, of $2,860 on June 30 would indicate that the enterprise had gained $1,035 since June 30, rather than the $810 shown on the income statement. We will consider in Chapter V whether one of these figures presents a more meaningful picture than the other; for the moment we need understand only how we derived each number.

During the late 1990s FASB adopted accounting rules that recognize that the change in net assets between successive balance sheets can effectively measure an enterprise's financial performance. FASB ASC Topic 220, *Comprehensive Income*, which codified SFAS No. 130, requires enterprises to report the net changes in their equity from all transactions other than with owners during a period in the financial statements and to display this so-called "comprehensive income" and its components with the same prominence as other financial statements. The Codification describes "comprehensive income" as the change in an enterprise's net assets, or owners' equity, during a period from transactions and other events and circumstances from nonowner sources. The term, therefore, includes all increases and decreases in net assets during the period except those changes resulting from investments by and distributions to owners. We will discuss comprehensive income in more detail later in this chapter on pages 291 to 294, *infra*, and in Chapter VI on pages 422 to 424, *infra*, as an exception to the exchange transaction requirement.

Despite the emphasis on the income statement with its indication of enterprise earning power and on the statement of cash flows, which gives some intimation of the enterprise's capacity to generate cash in the future, see pages 117 to 126, *supra,* the business community has certainly not yet sent the balance sheet to the financial junk heap. Indeed, the data on the balance sheet still provides a basis for making some relevant judgments about an enterprise's financial performance.

2.   ANALYTICAL TERMS AND RATIOS

In addition to showing changes in owners' equity over time, the data on the balance sheet continues to offer a basis for making some relevant judgments about an enterprise's financial condition. We now turn to some of the terms and ratios which accountants and business analysts use to interpret and evaluate the figures that appear on the balance sheet.

Consider the following balance sheet for a small corporation:

X Corp.
Balance Sheet, December 31

Assets		Liabilities & Shareholders' Equity	
Cash	$ 2,000	Accounts Payable	$10,000
Accounts Receivable	3,000	Bonds Payable	5,000
Inventory	16,000		$15,000
Plant	19,000	Shareholders' Equity	25,000
	$40,000		$40,000

Is this corporation in good financial shape? Because the corporation failed to subdivide the $25,000 in shareholders' equity into contributed capital and retained earnings components, we cannot tell whether the company has produced earnings, either recently or at some time in the past. But did you also notice that X Corp. may well have some trouble meeting its accounts payable in the near future? In fact, unless X raises cash through some other means, such as borrowing or issuing more stock, X cannot pay off its accounts payable until the company has sold the inventory and collected payment. This kind of information particularly interests short-term creditors, and would also benefit long-term creditors and stockholders. Indeed, because of the importance of such timing considerations, as we previously discussed in Chapter I, accountants usually arrange both assets and liabilities on the balance sheet in the order of their currentness, with the most current items at the top. Most modern balance sheets go further and expressly classify their assets and liabilities as between current and noncurrent, including fixed or long-term, as the consolidated balance sheets for Starbucks in Appendix A on page 747, *infra,* illustrate. Remember that current assets usually include cash, cash equivalents, and any other assets which the business expects to convert into cash within a year, which normally means accounts receivable, inventory, probably any marketable securities, and possibly short-term prepaid expenses, even though, strictly speaking, the business will not convert the prepaids into cash. Current liabilities would encompass those obligations that the business expects to pay within one year, which would typically include accounts payable, accrued expenses payable, plus any portion of a long-term indebtedness coming due within one year. Assuming that X does not have to repay any portion of the bonds payable within a year, an accountant might recast X Corp.'s balance sheet in classified form as follows:

X Corp.
Classified Balance Sheet, December 31

Assets		Liabilities & Shareholders' Equity	
Current Assets		Liabilities	
Cash	$ 2,000	Current	
Accounts Receivable	3,000	Accounts Payable	$10,000
Inventory	16,000	Bonds payable	5,000
Total	$21,000	Total Liabilities	$15,000
Plant	19,000	Shareholders' Equity	25,000
	$40,000		$40,000

a. WORKING CAPITAL

Because of the importance attached to both current assets and current liabilities, accountants and financial analysts pay special attention to the excess of current assets over current liabilities, usually referred to as *working capital*. Subject to the caveat " too much of a good thing can be bad for you," the more working capital, the better. A simple net figure for working capital, however, does not tell the entire story. For example, if one company has $25,000,000 in current assets and $20,000,000 in current liabilities, and another has $10,000,000 in current assets and $5,000,000 in current liabilities, both have working capital of $5,000,000 but their financial conditions differ quite significantly. A ratio would provide more instructive information. As we will shortly see, accountants and financial analysts have developed a ratio, the *current ratio*, which compares current liabilities to current assets.

If an enterprise's current liabilities exceed its current assets, the firm shows a negative working capital. Although some businesses, such as fast-food restaurants, can survive with a negative working capital because they sell their inventory before they have to pay for it, more current liabilities than current assets usually spells trouble for most businesses.

b. FINANCIAL RATIOS

Accountants and financial analysts frequently use liquidity ratios and leverage ratios to analyze a balance sheet.

(1) Liquidity Ratios

You will recall that liquidity ratios help an accountant or financial analyst to evaluate a business's ability to pay its short-term obligations. The most commonly-used liquidity ratios include the current ratio and the acid test.

The *current ratio* compares the amount of current assets to current liabilities. Returning to our previous example about the two companies each having $5,000,000 in working capital, the difference between them becomes immediately apparent. The first company's ratio of current assets to current liabilities is 1.25 ($25,000,000/$20,000,000), while the second company's is 2.0 ($10,000,000/$5,000,000). Accountants and financial analysts commonly use the current ratio to evaluate the financial condition of a business, especially its ability to pay its debts as come due.

Financial professionals often say that a current ratio less than 1.0 suggests a problem, while a current ratio exceeding 2.0 generally indicates satisfactory liquidity, a test which X Corp. meets. We, however, must qualify these generalizations according to the type of industry (recall our fast-food restaurant example), seasonal business factors, and similar considerations. As an example, banks usually need greater liquidity than manufacturers.

We must also keep in mind that accountants and financial analysts primarily use any ratio in comparative terms. In other words, accountants and financial analysts compare a ratio as of one date or for a particular period with the same business's ratio for an earlier date or period, or with the ratio of some other enterprise, or at least with some standard. Although creditors and investors generally prefer a higher current ratio, an abnormally high current ratio can also evidence a problem. If a business keeps too many of its resources in liquid assets, the business may not be replacing long-lived assets or making other investments necessary for long-term success or know what to do with its cash or other liquid assets.

Because a good deal of time may elapse before a business can convert inventory into cash, and short-term creditors want some assurance that the business will repay its debts if calamity suddenly strikes, short-term creditors often look to a related ratio, the *acid test* or *quick ratio*. This ratio compares so-called *quick assets* to current liabilities. You should note, however, that the definition of "quick assets" can vary. Most lenders and analysts include only cash, cash equivalents, other highly-liquid assets, such as marketable securities held as short-term investments, and accounts receivable in the numerator. Notice, therefore, that this ratio typically ignores inventories and prepaid expenses. Some analysts, however, simply subtract inventories and prepaid expenses from current assets, which might keep an income tax refund receivable in the numerator. Still other analysts subtract only inventories from current assets.

However labeled or defined, accountants and financial analysts usually consider a ratio approximating 1.0 as satisfactory. You should observe that X Corp., with an acid test of .50 [($2,000 cash + $3,000 accounts receivable)/$10,000 current liabilities], does not come close to meeting this test, which somewhat confirms the concern expressed earlier about its liquidity. Even though X Corp.'s ratio falls below 1.0, the company will survive as long as the business can convert inventory into cash before the company's debts mature. The acid test comes close to applying a worst-case analysis because the ratio implicitly assumes that the business could not sell any more inventory. At the same time, even a quick ratio greater than 2.0 does not mean that an enterprise has the financial ability to pay its bills in a timely manner. Imagine a company that owes $50,000 in thirty days, but owns only a nonmarketable note receivable not due for nine months.

(2) Leverage Ratios

As you might expect, accountants and financial analysts do not confine their analysis to current assets and liabilities. These analysts also use leverage ratios, such as debt to equity and debt to total assets, to assess the business's overall ability to pay its debts. For example, both investors and lenders usually consider the composition of a company's long-term financing, particularly the long-term debt, both in absolute and relative amounts.

Debt financing represents both a special opportunity and a significant risk. The opportunity lies in the fact that if the company can borrow at, say, seven percent interest, and earn a return of, say, ten percent on the borrowed funds by utilizing them in the business, the excess of three percent benefits the shareholders. Under these circumstances, the more debt the company issues, the greater the return to the shareholders. The financial community often refers to this phenomenon as *leverage*: the greater the proportion of debt, the more highly leveraged the company. But the more debt the company incurs, the greater its risk. After all, the company normally must pay interest in any event, even if the company earns less than the interest rate on the borrowed funds, or perhaps does not earn anything at all. In addition, the debtor company must repay the borrowed funds on the agreed date or face the prospect of bankruptcy.

Financial analysts most commonly use the ratio of debt to total owners' equity, which they usually call the *debt to equity ratio* or the *debt-equity ratio*, to measure the relative amount of debt in a business's financial structure. Again, the definition of "debt" can vary under this ratio. Many lenders and analysts will compare total liabilities to total equity. Under this definition, those analysts would compute a .60 debt to equity ratio by comparing $15,000 in total liabilities to $25,000 in shareholder's equity. Other lenders and analysts will compare only long-term debt to total equity, usually including the current portion of long-term debt in the debt factor. Under both those applications, X Corp.'s balance sheet reveals a .20 debt to equity ratio from comparing the $5,000 bonds payable to the $25,000 shareholder's equity. In any event, the relationship of the amount of an enterprise's debt, however defined, to the amount of equity provides lenders with some indication about the likelihood that the business will repay a loan, in that the amount of equity serves as a safety net for the creditors in case of financial difficulty, because creditors come ahead of stockholders in any liquidation. Hence, the more highly leveraged a company, the greater the risk that the company will not repay creditors if it encounters hard times. As with any financial ratio, judgment as to how much leverage may be desirable depends upon the type of business and other circumstances. For example, financial analysts might consider a debt-equity ratio of 1.5 as quite high for a typical industrial concern, but relatively normal for many public utilities.

Among the biggest casualties in the credit crisis, the inability to repay short-term obligations led to the demise of Bear Stearns Companies and Lehman Brothers Holdings Inc., both highly leveraged investment bank. In its final report, the Financial Crisis Inquiry Commission observed that at the end of 2007, Bear Stearns' $11.8 billion in equity supported $383.6 billion in liabilities, which translates to a debt to equity ratio of more than 32 to 1. In addition, the investment bank was borrowing as much as $70 billion each day in the overnight market. The Commission compared the situation to "a small business with $50,000 in equity borrowing $1.6 million, with $296,750 of that due each and every day." Fannie Mae and Freddie Mac, two government-sponsored enterprises, carried even more leverage. At the end of 2007, the loans that these two firms either owned or guaranteed produced a combined leverage ratio of 75 to 1.

Alternatively, some accountants and financial analysts use the *debt to total assets ratio* to compare the business debt to the sum of the debt and equity. Once again, the definition of "debt" can vary, ranging from an all-inclusive total liabilities to long-term debt exclusive of its current portion. Under the all-inclusive meaning, we would compute a .375 debt to total asset ratio by comparing $15,000 in total liabilities to $40,000 in total assets; the more narrow definitions produce a .125 debt to total asset ratio by dividing the $5,000 bonds payable by the $40,000 total assets.

c. NET BOOK VALUE

Accountants, in particular, frequently use one other term, *net book value* when discussing the balance sheet. One of the cartoons from Ben & Jerry's Homemade, Inc.'s 1992 annual report, which appears as the last cartoon on page 7, *supra*, refers to the term as *book value*. In any event, the term refers to the difference between an enterprise's assets and its liabilities as reflected in the business's accounting records, usually expressed as an amount per outstanding common share or other ownership interest.

If we assume that X Corp. has 100 common shares outstanding, we can readily calculate X Corp.'s net book value as $250 per share ($25,000 shareholders' equity divided by 100 outstanding shares). To determine the net book value per common share in a corporation that has also issued preferred stock, the accountant or financial analyst will subtract the preferred stock's liquidation preference to determine the net book value attributable to the common shares. By dividing that amount by the number of common shares outstanding, the accountant or financial analyst can calculate the net book value.

d. CAUTIONS AND APPLICATION

As the credit crisis illustrated, we should always remember that the balance sheet does not pretend to report the assets or liabilities at fair market value. As a result, the balance sheet figures do not necessarily tell the whole story: the amount that the assets would bring upon liquidation may fall significantly below the figures at which they appear in a business's accounting records. Accordingly, absent unusual circumstances a business's net book value does not reflect what a buyer might pay for the business.

We should also keep in mind that the amounts of working capital or net book value and the various ratios that the accountant or financial analyst may compute are only as good as the balance sheet from which they are derived. If, for example, a balance sheet overstates inventory, the balance sheet will also overstate owners' equity unless the erroneous balance sheet also overstates a liability or understates another asset. Thus, the accountant, analyst or lawyer using the balance sheet will compute greater working capital, a higher current ratio, a lower debt to equity ratio, and larger net book value than without the overstatement.

Notwithstanding these cautions, lawyers and their clients frequently use financial ratios derived from the balance sheet, often in lending and other legal agreements. Table 4–1 computes the terms and ratios discussed in this section from the numbers contained in Starbucks' consolidated balance sheet as of September 30, 2012 on page 51 of the company's 2012 Form 10-K, which appears in Appendix A on page 747, *infra*.

Table 4–1—Balance Sheet Terms and Ratios (millions omitted)

Term or Ratio	Formula	Starbucks for 2012	Ratio
Liquidity			
1. Working Capital	Current Assets — Current Liabilities	$1,989.8 a	N/A
2. Current Ratio	$\dfrac{\text{Current Assets}}{\text{Current Liabilities}}$	$\dfrac{\$4,199.6}{\$2,209.8}$	1.90
3. Acid Test	$\dfrac{\text{Cash and Cash Equivalents + Short-Term Investments + Accounts Receivables}}{\text{Current Liabilities}}$	$\dfrac{\$2,522.9\ b}{\$2,209.8}$	1.14
Leverage			
4. Debt to Equity	$\dfrac{\text{Total Liabilities}}{\text{Total Equity}}$	$\dfrac{\$3,104.7}{\$5,114.5}$	.607
5. Debt to Total Assets	$\dfrac{\text{Total Liabilities}}{\text{Total Assets}}$	$\dfrac{\$3,104.7}{\$8,219.2}$	.378
6. Net Book Value	$\dfrac{\text{Net Book Value Attributable to Common Shares}}{\text{Common Shares Outstanding}}$	$\dfrac{\$5,109.0\ c}{749.3\ \text{shares}}$	$6.82 per share

a. $4,199.6 (Total current assets) − $2,209.8 (Total current liabilities)

b. $1,188.6 (Cash and cash equivalents) + $848.4 (Short-term investments) + $485.9 (Accounts receivable, net)

c. $5,109.0 (Total shareholders' equity) − $0 (no outstanding preferred stock)

At the conclusion of the fiscal year ended October 2, 2011, we could compute the same ratios for Starbucks as follows (millions omitted):

Term or Ratio	Formula	Starbucks for 2011	Ratio
Liquidity			
1. Working Capital	Current Assets — Current Liabilities	$1,719.1 a	N/A
2. Current Ratio	$\dfrac{\text{Current Assets}}{\text{Current Liabilities}}$	$\dfrac{\$3,794.9}{\$2,075.8}$	1.83
3. Acid Test	$\dfrac{\text{Cash (and Equivalents)} + \text{Short-Term Investments} + \text{Receivables}}{\text{Current Liabilities}}$	$\dfrac{\$2,437.2 \text{ b}}{\$2,075.8}$	1.17
Leverage			
4. Debt to Equity	$\dfrac{\text{Total Liabilities}}{\text{Total Owners' Equity}}$	$\dfrac{\$2,973.1}{\$4,387.3}$	.678
5. Debt to Total Assets	$\dfrac{\text{Total Liabilities}}{\text{Total Assets}}$	$\dfrac{\$2,973.1}{\$7,360.4}$	.404
6. Net Book Value	$\dfrac{\text{Net Book Value Attributable to Common Shares}}{\text{Common Shares Outstanding}}$	$\dfrac{\$4,384.9 \text{ c}}{744.8 \text{ shares}}$	$5.89 per share

a. $3,794.9 (Total current assets) − $2,075.8 (Total current liabilities)

b. $1,148.1 (Cash and cash equivalents) + $902.6 (Short-term investments) + $386.5 (Accounts receivable, net)

c. $4,384.9 (Total shareholders' equity) − $0 (no outstanding preferred stock)

Between the ends of fiscal 2011 and fiscal 2012, Starbucks' liquidity improved. During the 2012 fiscal year, Starbucks added more than $270 million in working capital, as that liquidity measure increased from more than $1.7 billion to almost $2 billion. The current ratio rose from 1.83 to 1.90. The acid test, however, decreased from 1.17 to 1.14.

During fiscal 2012, Starbucks' leverage declined slightly. The debt-to-equity ratio dropped from 0.678 on October 2, 2011 to 0.607 on September 30, 2012. Similarly, the debt to total assets ratio dropped from 0.404 to 0.378 during fiscal 2012. Successful operations allowed the company's net book value to grow by almost sixteen percent, jumping from $5.89 per common share on October 2, 2011 to $6.82 per share on September 30, 2012.

Although usually not a task for lawyers, we could access Starbucks' liquidity and leverage further by comparing the ratios computed above to industry norms for a particular period.

PROBLEMS

Problem 4.1A. Using the consolidated balance sheets and any necessary miscellaneous information for Amazon.com for the years ended December 31, 2012 and December 31, 2011:

(1) Compute the financial terms and ratios listed in Table 4–1 for 2012 and 2011.

(2) Do you see any trends compared to 2011 worth noting?

Problem 4.1B. Using the consolidated balance sheets and any necessary miscellaneous information for Google for the years ended December 31, 2012 and December 31, 2011:

(1) Compute the financial terms and ratios listed in Table 4–1 for 2012 and 2011.

(2) Do you see any trends compared to 2011 worth noting?

Problem 4.1C. Using the consolidated balance sheets and any necessary miscellaneous information for UPS for the years ended December 31, 2012 and December 31, 2011:

(1) Compute the financial terms and ratios listed in Table 4–1 for 2012 and 2011.

(2) Do you see any trends compared to 2011 worth noting?

E.   THE MEASUREMENT OF INCOME

As we saw in Chapter I, transactions that do not involve operations can increase or decrease shareholders' equity. For example, when E. Tutt took home a chair from her law office, the net assets of her sole proprietorship decreased even though the transaction did not relate to her professional activities. By comparison, when Tutt contributed law books to her law office, her business activities did not cause the resulting increase in net assets. Thus, comparing successive balance sheets does not necessarily measure an enterprise's performance during a particular period. Instead, measuring the enterprise's profitability, which considers only transactions and events related to the enterprise's operations that caused owners' equity to increase or decrease, can also assess how the enterprise performed between balance sheet dates. Long ago, creditors, investors, and analysts realized that an enterprise's past profitability can often help them predict whether the business will likely generate profits in the future. Finally, ratios derived from various performance measures often provide useful information.

1. RESULTS OF OPERATIONS

Publicly traded companies must follow GAAP when preparing the financial statements, including the income statement, that they must include in various SEC filings, such as 10-Ks and 10-Qs. Starting during the dot-com bubble in the late 1990s, companies increasingly have been using alternative presentations, including unaudited pro forma metrics to gauge their operating results. These "as if" numbers, now more commonly referred to simply as "non-GAAP," such as pro forma income, recurring earnings, core earnings, earnings before interest and taxes ("EBIT"), and earnings before interest, taxes, depreciation, and amortization ("EBITDA"), often allowed enterprises to present a more favorable picture than GAAP and, in some instances, to distort their financial performance. In addition, the Codification now requires enterprises to report all nonowner changes in equity in either a single continuous statement of comprehensive income or in two separate, but consecutive statements, the first calculating net income or loss and the second presenting total comprehensive income or loss. We will take a look at these two alternatives to the "net income" reported on the income statement shortly.

a. THE INCOME STATEMENT

Before looking at the various measures that the financial community uses to gauge an enterprise's profitability, however, we should first observe that unsophisticated readers of financial statements frequently concentrate unduly on net income on the income statement, the so-called "bottom line." The financial press often publicizes that figure, or the related *earnings per share* that we will discuss shortly, while ignoring the presence of unusual or nonrecurring items or other considerations, such as taxes and the interest on any debt that the enterprise may have incurred.

GAAP attempts to resolve various questions that arise when enterprises present their operating results via an income statement. One recurring difficulty stems from the fact that the income statement reports the operating results for a particular *period*. To take a simple illustration, how should an enterprise's financial statements reflect a recovery in an antitrust suit for lost profits from prior years? Obviously, the enterprise cannot recall the income statements for those prior years and amend them. On the other hand, including a material recovery in income for the current period might give the false impression that the enterprise is operating more profitably than actually is the case.

As an alternative, an enterprise could perhaps include the recovery in current income under a separate caption, such as "Income Unrelated to Current Operations," or "Extraordinary Item," which would appear on the income statement after a figure for "Net Income from Current Operations." The latter figure would then provide a picture about current operations, which excludes the special item. Because the income statement would still reflect the special item in the final "Net Income" figure for the period, however, this approach would not entirely resolve the problem, especially from the viewpoint of average, financially unsophisticated investors. These investors, who constitute an important group of financial statement users, frequently concentrate unduly upon the final "Net Income" figure, particularly because, as noted above, the financial press often publicizes that figure, or the closely related earnings per share, without discussing the presence of special items.

If the enterprise had recorded these "lost profits" in the earlier years in which they really had "belonged," they would have increased the respective net income figures for those prior years, and those profits would now appear in retained earnings. Unlike the income statements for prior years, an enterprise can effectively amend the retained earnings figure during the current period, simply by recording an entry directly to that account. Thus, the enterprise might credit, or debit, a special item directly to Retained Earnings, so that the amount would neither affect, nor appear in, the income statement for the current year. Accountants use the term "prior period adjustment" to refer to this process that by-passes the income statement, connoting the fact that such a direct entry to Retained Earnings in effect adjusts the results from a prior period, because an item that the enterprise realized currently really "belongs" in a prior period.

This approach, however, also presents difficulties. For one thing, how would an enterprise decide whether a particular item qualified as "special" enough to omit entirely from the income statement, and hence from the determination of net income? After all, the desire to impress creditors and owners could tempt management to err on the side of regarding losses as special, and therefore excludable, while viewing most gains as ordinary and therefore includable. Such a situation would not make the income statement more meaningful. In addition, each individual income statement becomes a part of a series of consecutive income statements. Collectively, the series may reveal significant trends from which users of financial statements can more readily assess the enterprise's future prospects. Ideally, any series of consecutive income statements should portray as complete a picture as possible of the business's fortunes over the total period that the series covers. By-passing the income statement, however, excludes such items from the entire series of income statements, which could cloud the picture that the series presents. An individual reader might prefer that the enterprise include every item of gain or loss in the income statement for some year, with an appropriate caption if the item does not theoretically belong in that year. In that situation, the individual reader can assess the significance of particular special items.

As distinguished from clearly operational items that "belong" to some prior period, transactions that do not directly relate to operations pose a related problem. For example, suppose an enterprise sells a manufacturing plant. Should the enterprise include the gain or loss from this relatively unusual transaction in the income statement for the current period? In this event, if any income statement should report the transaction, it should appear on the income statement for the current period. Once again, however, a risk exists that including such an item in the income statement could lead those unsophisticated investors who rely too heavily on the single "net income" figure to conclude that the enterprise's operations had been considerably more, or less, successful this year than the results from ordinary, recurring operations would otherwise suggest. On the other hand, by-passing the income statement in favor of a direct credit, or debit, to Retained Earnings would exclude this very significant item from the series of income statements. Especially if the enterprise sells manufacturing plants from time to time, this exclusion would impair the validity of the data on those income statements.

The conflict between these two objectives—making each individual income statement as meaningful a picture as possible of the enterprise's operations for that period, and having any series of income statements represent a virtually complete portrayal of the enterprise's fortunes for the time-span that the series covers—creates considerable difficulty. For many years, the accounting profession regarded the question of which way to treat any particular unusual item as mainly a judgment call, which enterprises could resolve as they saw fit. Predictably, such flexibility caused considerable trouble, both in comparing an enterprise's current performance with its earlier years, and in making current comparisons with other businesses that may have treated similar items differently.

To address these problems, FASB and its predecessors issued several pronouncements to guide enterprises in reporting and classifying certain special, unusual or nonrecurring items in the financial statements. Today, via the Codification, GAAP strives to provide the relevant information in the most meaningful format to enable a reader of the income statement to determine an enterprise's true "operational" results and to assess the extent to which such historical performance suggests future earnings. The relevant standards pertain to unusual or nonrecurring events or transactions, changes in accounting principles and estimates, prior period adjustments, discontinued operations, and extraordinary items. We will discuss each of these topics in turn.

(1) *Unusual* or *Nonrecurring Operating Items*

Anyone interested in using a measure of profitability to try to predict how a business will perform in the future must however pay particular attention to unusual or nonrecurring items that affect profitability in one period, but which will most likely not affect the business's performance in subsequent periods. Enterprises can present these items: (1) as a separate line on the income statement; (2) in a parenthetical on the income statement itself, or (3) in an explanatory note to the financial statements. As discussed in more detail below, public companies must identify any unusual or infrequent events or transactions or any significant economic changes that materially affected the amount of reported income from continuing operations, and, in each case, review the extent to which that item affected reported income in the MD&A section of various securities filings. The sophisticated reader watches carefully for such information and disclosures.

To illustrate, the face of the consolidated statements of earnings on page 50 of Starbucks' Form 10-K for the fiscal year ended September 30, 2012, which appears in Appendix A on page 746, *infra*, identifies two such items.

First, Starbucks reports $53.0 million in restructuring charges for the fiscal year ended October 3, 2010, but no amounts for the fiscal years ended October 2, 2011 and September 30, 2012, respectively. Second, Starbucks shows $30.2 million in gain on sale of properties during the fiscal year ended October 2, 2011, but no amounts for the fiscal years ended October 3, 2010 or September 30, 2012. In addition, under the heading "Fiscal Year End" in Note 1 on page 54 of the 2012 Form 10-K, which appears in Appendix A on page 750, *infra*, Starbucks discloses that fiscal year 2010 included fifty-three weeks, while fiscal years 2012 and 2011 contained the normal fifty-two weeks. The last sentence under the heading "Goodwill" in that same note on page 57 of the 2012 Form 10-K and page 753, *infra*, in Appendix A, states that Starbucks recorded $1.6 million in charges related to goodwill impairment during fiscal 2010, but no amounts during fiscal 2011 or 2012. Two pages later, under the heading "Stored Value Cards," again in Note 1, Starbucks discloses that a court ruling enabled the company to recognize an undisclosed amount of additional income associated with unredeemed gift cards during fiscal 2012. In the first paragraph on page 29 of the 2012 Form 10-K, which appears in Appendix A on page 725, *infra*, the MD&A quantifies this amount as "approximately $29 million." Finally, that same paragraph also discloses that Starbucks recognized "approximately $55 million" in fiscal 2011 by acquiring the remaining interest in the company's previous joint venture operations in Switzerland and Austria.

Attorneys and other users of financial statements must exercise caution because enterprises may broadly construe the terms "unusual" or "nonrecurring" to include particular items when in fact they can expect such items, or similar circumstances, to occur again in the future. For example, Motorola Inc. reported at least one "special" item, albeit not the same item, in fourteen consecutive earnings reports. Representatives from the company assert that failure to highlight such items, which include restructuring expenses and write-offs for bad investments and obsolete inventory, would hinder a user from reliably predicting future operating results. If a company reports such items periodically, even if not every quarter, do those items qualify as "special," or do they merely reflect a normal cost of doing business? Jesse Drucker, *Motorola's Profit: 'Special' Again?*, Wall St. J., Oct. 15, 2002, at C1.

We should keep in mind that financial statements become more useful if readers can compare them with similar reports for previous periods. As a result, knowledgeable users of financial statements typically want information about any unusual or infrequent items that materially affect the financial statements in a particular accounting period. Such information enables readers to decide whether to factor in, or to ignore, the effects of the item, especially relative to future periods. For this reason, the Codification requires an enterprise to report a material event or transaction that qualifies as either unusual in nature or infrequent in occurrence, but not both, as a separate item in computing income or loss from continuing operations. Such an item must appear at its gross amount, without adjusting for any income tax effect. In addition, the enterprise should disclose the nature and any financial effect of each such event or transaction, either on the income statement itself or in the notes to the financial statements. FASB ASC ¶¶ 225-20-45-16, 225-20-50-3 (codifying REPORTING THE RESULTS OF OPERATIONS—REPORTING THE EFFECTS OF DISPOSAL OF A SEGMENT OF A BUSINESS, AND EXTRAORDINARY, UNUSUAL AND INFREQUENTLY OCCURRING EVENTS AND TRANSACTIONS, Accounting Principles Board Opinion No. 30, ¶ 26 (Am. Inst. of Certified Pub. Accountants 1973)).

As we will see later in this chapter, the federal securities laws often require public companies to disclose information about material unusual or nonrecurring items in the MD&A section of certain securities filings. In addition, an enterprise's management may want to highlight the effect of a particular event, transaction, or other circumstance even if it does not materially affect the financial statements by itself. In that circumstance, management can report the item: (1) as a separate line on the income statement; (2) in a parenthetical on the income statement; or (3) in an explanatory note to the financial statements. Knowledgeable readers watch carefully for such disclosures in all four locations.

(2) Accounting Changes

As we saw in Chapter II on page 168, *supra*, GAAP does not always establish a rigid rule as to how to report every type of transaction. More specifically, GAAP often allows alternative accounting methods or calls for management to exercise judgment in determining the most appropriate accounting for particular transactions or events. In addition, GAAP constantly changes and evolves.

This flexibility, however, does not mean that an enterprise can shift from one accounting approach to another on management's whim, even if GAAP treats both methods as equally acceptable. Switching methods seriously interferes with the reader's ability to compare an enterprise's current financial statements to those from previous accounting periods. Just as the manner in which an enterprise reports a particular transaction or event can significantly affect the current period's financial statements, changing approaches in different accounting period can seriously distort the trends revealed in a series of income statements, which reduces their usefulness.

Accordingly, GAAP imposes significant limitations on an enterprise's ability to change its accounting. For this purpose, the term "accounting change" connotes a change in (1) an accounting principle, (2) an accounting estimate, or (3) the reporting entity. The term "accounting change," however, explicitly does not include the correction of an error made in previously issued financial statements. With respect to a change in the reporting entity, as a practical matter GAAP treats such changes in much the same way as a change in an accounting principle. Consequently, the text that follows discusses only changes in an accounting principle or an accounting estimate.

a) CHANGES IN AN ACCOUNTING PRINCIPLE

A change in an accounting principle occurs whenever an enterprise adopts a principle that differs from the one that the enterprise previously used for financial reporting purposes. In this regard, the term *accounting principle* includes not only accounting principles and practices, but the methods that an enterprise uses to apply them. As we will see in Chapter VIII on page 626 and 626, *infra*, a change in an accounting principle would include a switch from last-in, first-out ("LIFO") to first-in, first-out ("FIFO") when accounting for inventories. In contrast, adopting a new principle to handle events that have occurred for the first time or that previously qualified as immaterial does not constitute a changes in accounting principle.

Because the consistency principle requires an enterprise generally to give the same accounting treatment to similar transactions and events in different accounting periods, under GAAP an enterprise can only change an accounting principle if the new principle qualifies as "preferable." Unfortunately, GAAP does not define that term. As a practical matter, GAAP may *require* an enterprise to adopt a change in accounting principle when a revision to the Codification (1) creates a new accounting principle, (2) interprets an existing principle, (3) expresses a preference for a particular principle, or (4) rejects a specific principle. In that event, the Codification treats the revision as "sufficient support" for the change. If the Codification does not require the change, the enterprise bears the burden to justify the switch. In any event, Accounting Standards Updates that revise the Codification typically include specific transition provisions, which enterprises must follow.

FASB ASC Topic 250, *Accounting Changes and Error Corrections*, which codified identically named SFAS No. 154, allows an enterprise to apply any voluntary changes in accounting principles retroactively. New pronouncements typically include specific transition provisions, which enterprises must follow. SFAS No. 154 altered the rules in the United States for recording and reporting accounting changes to converge U.S. GAAP with international accounting standards. Unless an enterprise cannot reasonably determine the period-specific effects, ASC Topic 250 requires an enterprise to revise past earnings to show the effect of the change in each period presented and, if necessary, (1) reflect the cumulative effect of the change to the new accounting principle on all periods prior to those presented in the appropriate asset or liability accounts as of the beginning of the first accounting period presented to reflect the change's cumulative effect on periods prior to those presented, and (2) record any necessary corresponding adjustment directly to either the beginning balance in the Retained Earnings account or other appropriate components of equity. In addition, the enterprise must disclose: (1) the change and the reason for it, explaining why the newly adopted principle qualifies as preferable; (2) the change's effect on income from continuing operations, net income, any other affected line item on the financial statements, and any affected per-share amounts for the current period and any prior period restrospectively adjusted; and (3) any cumulative effect of the change on retained earnings or other components of equity as of the beginning of the earliest period presented. FASB ASC Topic 250, *Accounting Changes and Error Corrections* (a codification of ACCOUNTING CHANGES AND ERROR CORRECTIONS, Statement of Fin. Accounting Standards No. 154 (Fin. Accounting Standards Bd. 2005)).

As mentioned in the discussion on audit reports on page 188, *supra*, a change in accounting principle has generally required the auditor to add explanatory language to an unqualified opinion, even though the new method qualifies as "preferable." If the new method does not qualify as "preferable" and causes a material effect on the financial statements, the auditor must issue either a qualified or adverse opinion. Financial statement users should view enterprises that change accounting principles without sufficient support very skeptically.

b) *Changes in Accounting Estimates*

In connection with preparing financial statements, management must estimate various items, such as useful life, salvage value, and warranty expenses, that affect the recorded amounts for various assets, liabilities, revenues, and expenses. Naturally, the actual results may differ from those estimates. When the estimate involved future projections, as for example estimating the useful life of an asset for depreciation or amortization purposes, after a few years an enterprise's experience may indicated that the asset's originally estimated useful life no longer accurately predicts how long the asset will continue to provide benefits. By definition, estimates can, and often do, change when new events occur, or as management acquires more experience and information. For this reason, ASC Topic 250 codifies the rules originally set forth in APB Opinion No. 20, *Accounting Changes,* and limits the accounting for changes in estimates to (a) the period of change, if the change affects that period only, or (b) the period of change and future periods, if the change affects both. In accounting for a change in estimate, an enterprise should not restate amounts reported in financial statements for prior periods or report pro forma amounts for those periods. An enterprise, however, should disclose the effect on income from continuing operations, net income, and any related per-share amounts for the current period if the change in estimate affects future periods, such as a change in estimated useful lives. As we will suggest in Chapter VI on page 380, *infra*, enterprises engaging in so-called "earnings management" commonly revise accounting estimates. As a result, readers of financial statements should watch the notes to the financial statements for disclosures about any changes in, or revisions to, accounting estimates.

(3) *Prior Period Adjustments*

Over the years, generally accepted accounting principles have significantly narrowed the items that enterprises may treat as prior period adjustments. Today, the Codification limits prior period adjustments to corrections of errors in previously issued financial statements and requires an enterprise to restate the prior period financial statements. Errors in financial statements can arise from mathematical mistakes, misapplying accounting principles, overlooking or misusing facts that existed at the time the enterprise prepared the statements, or changing from an accounting principle that the business community does not generally accept to one that it does. In these limited circumstances, the enterprise: (1) debits or credits the appropriate asset or liability accounts as of the beginning of the first accounting period presented to reflect the cumulative effect of the error on periods prior to those presented; (2) records any necessary corresponding adjustment directly to either the beginning balance in the Retained Earnings account or any other appropriate component of equity; and (3) adjusts the financial statements for each individual prior period presented to reflect correction of the error's effects in that period. Such treatment does not affect the income statement in the current accounting period.

To illustrate the correction of an error, assume that in 20X3 an enterprise discovers that it improperly recognized $100,000 of revenue in a transaction on open account in 20X2 that included a right of return, which prevented the enterprise from completing the earnings process. If the only related expenses include $60,000 in cost of goods sold and $15,000 in sales commissions that the enterprise prepaid, the enterprise must restate the financial statements for 20X2 to eliminate the $25,000 profit. The enterprise might make the following "adjusting" entry for 20X2:

Inventory	$60,000	
Prepaid Sales Commissions	15,000	
Retained Earnings	25,000	
Accounts Receivable		$100,000

Observe that the enterprise must correct the entire $25,000 error upon discovery. The enterprise cannot amortize the error over some period of time. *See, e.g., In re* Boston Company, Inc., Accounting and Auditing Enforcement Release No. 439, [1991–1995 Transfer Binder] Fed. Sec. L. Rep. (CCH) ¶ 73,898 (Feb. 4, 1993) (amortizing the correction of various accounting errors over time, rather than recognizing the entire amount upon discovery, violated GAAP).

Assuming that the enterprise uses the periodic inventory method, when the right of return expires in 20X3, the enterprise would record the transaction as follows:

Accounts Receivable	$100,000	
Sales Commissions Expense	15,000	
Sales		$100,000
Prepaid Sales Commissions		15,000

In setting up the ending inventory, the enterprise would automatically include the cost of the items in the cost of goods sold for the period under the periodic inventory system.

In an effort to converge accounting standards worldwide, FASB added some new disclosure requirements when an enterprise restates its financial statements to correct an error. As a result, an enterprise that restates must disclose: (1) the nature of the error; (2) the correction's effect on each financial statement line item and any per-share amounts affected for each prior period presented; and (3) the change's cumulative effect on retained earnings or other appropriate component of equity as of the beginning of the earliest period presented. FASB ASC ¶¶ 250-10-45-23, 250-10-50-7 (codifying Accounting Changes and Error Corrections, Statement of Fin. Accounting Standards No. 154, ¶¶ 25, 26 (Fin. Accounting Standards Bd. 2005)).

Apart from the limited circumstance related to error corrections, enterprises must include all other items of profit or loss in the income statement. While this treatment may not best match expenses and losses against revenues, the approach ensures that all of these items will flow through the income statement. By separately identifying material items related to previous years, either on the income statement or in the notes to the financial statements, an enterprise can enable investors to interpret more intelligently the enterprise's operating results. FASB ASC ¶ 250-10-45-22 (codifying Prior Period Adjustments, Statement of Fin. Accounting Standards No. 16, ¶ 11 (Fin. Accounting Standards Bd. 1977), *as amended by* Accounting for Income Taxes, Statement of Fin. Accounting Standards No. 109, ¶ 288(n) (Fin. Accounting Standards Bd. 1992)).

(4) Discontinued Operations

Discontinued operations refers to a distinct component of an entity that an enterprise has sold or otherwise transferred, eliminated, abandoned, or designated for sale. A component comprises operations and cash flows that the enterprise can distinguish, both operationally and for financial reporting purposes, from its other operations. A segment, reporting unit, subsidiary, consolidated joint venture, division, department, or asset group can qualify as a component.

An enterprise must separately report the results of any discontinued operations, net of any related income tax expense or benefit, on the income statement, as well as in the operating section of the statement of cash flows, if (1) the disposition or sale has eliminated, or will eliminate, the component's operations and cash flows from the entity's ongoing operations, and (2) the enterprise will not have any significant continuing involvement in the component's operations. For example, assume that an entity owns and operates retail stores that selling household goods, each of which qualifies as a component because the entity can clearly distinguish the operations and cash flows for each store. Even though each store qualifies as a component, a decision to close two stores to open a new superstore in the same region, which would continue to sell the household goods previously sold in the retail stores as well as other related products, would not meet the requirements for reporting the closed stores' results in discontinued operations. Such a consolidation would not eliminate either the retail operations in the region or the related cash flows from the sale of household goods.

The separate listing for discontinued operations, which appears just before any extraordinary items on the income statement and in the sections for operating, investing and financial activities on the statement of cash flows, enables the reader to assess the results of continuing operations in the current period and to compare those results to prior periods on a consistent basis. As a practical matter, discontinued operations, if material, require an enterprise to reclassify amounts previously included in income from continuing operations and cash flows from the various activities in financial statements for prior years to the separate listing for discontinued operations in those same years for the purpose of presenting comparative financial statements. Although the enterprise's net income or loss and overall cash flows for each year remain unchanged, the shift from continuing operations to discontinued operations can affect contract drafting and interpretation.

This separate category for discontinued operations on the income statement will also contain any loss (or gain for a subsequent increase in value) that the enterprise must recognize pursuant to the rules for the impairment or disposal of long-lived assets, which we will discuss later in Chapter IX, less any applicable income taxes or plus any related tax benefit. If the enterprise expects a loss from a proposed sale, then pursuant to the doctrine of conservatism the enterprise must immediately include the estimated loss on the income statement under the heading for discontinued operations. By comparison, an enterprise cannot recognize future operating losses from these discontinued operations until they occur. If the enterprise expects a net gain on the sale, both the revenue recognition principle and conservatism require the enterprise to wait until it recognizes the income, which ordinarily occurs at the actual disposal. *See* FASB ASC ¶¶ 205-20-45-1 to -5 (codifying ACCOUNTING FOR THE IMPAIRMENT OR DISPOSAL OF LONG-LIVED ASSETS, Statement of Fin. Accounting Standards No. 144, ¶¶ 41–44 (Fin. Accounting Standards Bd. 2001)).

(5) Extraordinary Items

GAAP defines *extraordinary items* as gains and losses from events or transactions, other than the sale, abandonment, or other disposal of a business segment, that qualify as both *unusual in nature* **and** *infrequent in occurrence*. To qualify as "unusual in nature," an event or transaction must possess a high degree of abnormality and either not relate to, or only incidentally relate to, the enterprise's ordinary activities. To satisfy the "infrequent in occurrence" requirement, the enterprise must not reasonably expect the underlying event or transaction to recur in the foreseeable future. FASB ASC ¶¶ 225-20-45-2 to -7, 225-20-55-1 to -2 (codifying REPORTING THE RESULTS OF OPERATIONS—REPORTING THE EFFECTS OF DISPOSAL OF A SEGMENT OF A BUSINESS, AND EXTRAORDINARY, UNUSUAL AND INFREQUENTLY OCCURRING EVENTS AND TRANSACTIONS, Accounting Principles Board Opinion No. 30, ¶¶ 20–23 (Am. Inst. of Certified Pub. Accountants 1973)).

In determining whether an item qualifies as either unusual or infrequent, an enterprise must consider the business's operating environment, which includes industry characteristics, geographical location, and governmental regulations. As a result, an event or transaction may qualify as unusual or infrequent for one enterprise but not another, given differences in their respective operating environments. For example, if a hail storm destroys a large portion of a tobacco grower's crops, the enterprise can treat the loss as an extraordinary item if severe damage from hail storms occurs only rarely in the locality. In contrast, because severe frosts typically occur every three or four years in Florida, frost damage to a citrus grower's crops in Florida would not qualify. After Mount St. Helens erupted in 1980, Weyerhauser Co. treated a $36 million loss arising from destroyed timber, inventory, and buildings as extraordinary on its financial statements because no eruption had occurred at the volcano in 130 years. Diya Gullapalli, *For Annual-Report Purposes, Hurricane Katrina Is 'Ordinary,'* WALL ST. J., Sept. 2, 2005, at C3. Events and transactions that do not qualify as extraordinary items because they recur frequently in normal business activities include write-offs of receivables, losses attributable to labor strikes, and "[o]ther gains and losses from sale or abandonment of property, plant, or equipment used in the business." FASB ASC ¶ 225-20-45-4 (codifying REPORTING THE RESULTS OF OPERATIONS—REPORTING THE EFFECTS OF DISPOSAL OF A SEGMENT OF A BUSINESS, AND EXTRAORDINARY, UNUSUAL AND INFREQUENTLY OCCURRING EVENTS AND TRANSACTIONS, Accounting Principles Board Opinion No. 30, ¶ 23 (Am. Inst. of Certified Pub. Accountants 1973)).

After the terrorist attacks on September 11, 2001, the Emerging Issues Task Force ultimately reached a consensus that enterprises could not treat losses or costs resulting from the attacks as extraordinary items under GAAP. In reaching this conclusion, some Task Force members believed that although the terrorist attacks qualified as "unusual in nature" for many businesses, those events did not satisfy the "infrequent in occurrence" requirement. Those members reasoned that terrorist attacks had occurred in the United States in the past and that enterprises could reasonably expect such attacks to recur in the United States in the foreseeable future. Although other members felt that the sheer magnitude of the attacks might allow certain losses and costs arising from the events to qualify as extraordinary items, in the end the Task Force decided against such treatment. Given an already weakening economy, the members agreed that no one line on a financial statement could possibly isolate the extensive and pervasive losses directly attributable to the attacks from those arising from the general economic slowdown. The Task Force, however, did conclude that enterprises should, at a minimum, disclose the nature and amounts of any losses or contingencies resulting from the terrorist attacks and any related insurance recoveries in the notes to the financial statements. ACCOUNTING FOR THE IMPACT OF THE TERRORIST ATTACKS OF SEPTEMBER 11, 2001, Emerging Issues Task Force Issue No. 01-10 (Fin. Accounting Standards Bd. 2001).

More recently, and in response to a question during the aftermath of Hurricane Katrina in 2005, a spokesman for the FASB issued a statement that concluded that losses from the storm and subsequent flooding and evacuation did not qualify as extraordinary because " 'every year many businesses across the country are affected by [hurricanes and other natural disasters] and thus they do not represent an unusual and infrequent occurrence to businesses or to insurers.' " Diya Gullapalli, *For Annual-Report Purposes, Hurricane Katrina Is 'Ordinary,'* WALL ST. J., Sept. 2, 2005, at C3.

At least for the present, extraordinary items, assuming they qualify as material, appear in a separate section on the income statement, immediately after discontinued operations and following the caption "Income before extraordinary items." The Codification requires an enterprise to show these extraordinary items net of any taxes, whether incurred upon a gain or saved upon a loss. As part of a simplification initiative, however, FASB has proposed to eliminate the concept of extraordinary items. Even though events and conditions rarely qualify for treatment as extraordinary items under GAAP, preparers, auditors, and regulators often need to devote time and expend resources to decide whether the circumstances satisfy the two requirements. In mid-2014, FASB proposed an accounting standards update designed to reduce the income statement's complexity and cost while at least maintaining the usefulness of the information provided in financial statements. *See* Income Statement–Extraordinary and Unusual Items (Subtopic 225-20): Simplifying Income Statement Presentation by Eliminating the Concept of Extraordinary Items, Proposed Accounting Standards Update (Fin. Accounting Standards Bd. July 15, 2014), *available via* http://www.fasb. org/jsp/FASB/Page/SectionPage&cid=1175805074609. The comment period closed on September 30, 2014. Interested readers can access updates on the project via http://www.fasb.org/jsp/FASB/Page/TechnicalAgendaPage&cid=1175805470156#tab_1175805471978.

Again, please keep in mind that even if FASB eliminates the concept of extraordinary items, or an event or transaction does not qualify as both "unusual" and "infrequent in occurrence," (1) an enterprise can nevertheless highlight the event, transaction, or other circumstance (a) as a separate line on the income statement, (b) in a parenthetical on the income statement itself, or (c) in an explanatory note to the financial statements and (2) the federal securities laws may require a public company to disclose information about a material unusual or nonrecurring item in MD&A.

PROBLEMS

Problem 4.2A. Do any unusual or nonrecurring items appear in the consolidated statements of operations for Amazon.com for the years ended December 31, 2012, 2011, or 2010, respectively? Describe briefly any such items, and explain where you found this information.

Problem 4.2B. Do any unusual or nonrecurring items appear in the consolidated statements of income for Google for the years ended December 31, 2012, 2011, or 2010, respectively? Describe briefly any such items, and explain where you found this information.

Problem 4.2C. Do any unusual or nonrecurring items appear in the statements of consolidated income for UPS for the years ended December 31, 2012, 2011, or 2010, respectively? Describe briefly any such items, and explain where you found this information.

b. PRO FORMA METRICS

As indicated above, the financial community historically referred to financial measures that do not conform to GAAP as "pro forma" numbers, or simply "pro formas." Enterprises now more commonly describe such figures as "non-GAAP." When computing net income, GAAP—with its fairly conservative approach to measuring an enterprise's performance—requires a firm to include all expenses incurred during the reporting period and prohibits recognizing income that the firm merely expects will materialize in the future. In contrast, pro forma metrics typically exclude some expenses related to an enterprise's normal operations, while sometimes including projected benefits that the firm will not realize until later.

Enterprises originally used pro formas to adjust GAAP financials to exclude the effects of major, nonrecurring events or to show what an enterprise's financial statements would look like if a proposed merger or other acquisition occurred. These metrics gained popularity during the internet stock surge in the 1990s, eventually becoming common in all industries because the approach allowed enterprises to present more positive earnings reports by minimizing large asset write-downs and other expenses that dragged down net income under GAAP. By the early 2000s, public companies repeatedly emphasized such non-GAAP metrics as "pro forma income," "recurring earnings," "core earnings," EBIT, EBITDA, and the like. Today, public companies more commonly use terms like "non-GAAP operating income," "non-GAAP net income," and "non-GAAP free cash flow" to describe such metrics. For example, the second page of Starbucks' 2012 Annual Report, which appears in Appendix A on page 692, *infra*, contains bar graphs comparing GAAP and Non-GAAP amounts for Operating Income, Operating Margin, and Earnings per Diluted Share for fiscal years 2008-2011. Such numbers can allow enterprises to present a more optimistic picture of their financial results, highlight favorable financial data, and dismiss, or even ignore, less-flattering GAAP reporting measures.

For example, assume that a newspaper publishing company generated $1 million from its business operations in 20X4 before a $15 million settlement following a jury verdict for libel arising from an article that the company published. Under GAAP, the company would report a $14 million net loss. If the company hired "Legally Blonde" business law expert Elle Woods to advise the company, she might recommend that the company prepare pro forma statements that ignore the "totally heinous" jury verdict and related settlement and report $1 million as income before special items. Given the potential to mislead investors, some financial experts, including a former SEC chief accountant, routinely criticize such gauges of performance, referring to some pro forma metrics as "EBS," or "everything but the bad stuff."

While no specific definition of the term "pro forma" exists, an attorney should understand that these non-GAAP numbers essentially allow businesses to establish their own accounting standards and rules for financial reporting, sometimes even presenting results "as if" certain events or transactions did not occur, or assuming that certain other things will happen exactly as planned. As a result, attorneys evaluating financial statements must distinguish between GAAP reporting measures and pro forma metrics.

(1) Advantages

The good news: pro forma metrics can indeed serve legitimate purposes. Knowledgeable investors and analysts can find pro formas helpful in measuring an enterprise's current profitability and trying to predict its future operating results. Even the SEC has recognized that "[p]ublic companies may quite appropriately wish to focus investors' attention on critical components of quarterly or annual financial results in order to provide a meaningful comparison to results for the same period of prior years or to emphasize the results of core operations." Cautionary Advice Regarding Use of "Pro Forma" Financial Information in Earnings Releases, Financial Reporting Release No. 59, 66 Fed. Reg. 63,731, 63,732 (Dec. 10, 2001). In addition, pro forma metrics such as EBITDA can produce more useful comparisons between enterprises that (1) finance their operations largely with borrowed funds, on which the businesses must pay interest, and those firms that rely more on equity capital that owners contribute and, which therefore, incur less interest expense, and (2) pay income taxes and partnerships, limited liability companies, and S corporations that generally do not; instead, the owners must report their share of the enterprise's profit or loss on their separate income tax return.

Standard & Poors ("S&P"), an independent provider of investment data used in analyzing and valuing companies, employs a pro forma metric called "core earnings" to measure operating income. S&P introduced a new definition of core earnings in mid-2002 to enhance consistency in financial reports on different companies and to provide greater transparency in the computations and adjustments underlying the measure. S&P's core earnings metric focuses on earnings after taxes generated from an enterprise's principal business activities and entails making adjustments to net income calculated in conformity with GAAP. In particular, S&P ignores certain items, such as gains from pensions and charges for goodwill impairment or litigation settlements, which GAAP requires enterprises to take into account when they calculate their net income. Before the new rules on stock options took effect, S&P included the value of employee stock options, which then-GAAP did not require an enterprise to treat as an expense, in computing net income. Unlike most pro forma numbers, which enterprises develop using their own criteria, S&P has used these guidelines consistently in arriving at core earnings. Whatever the measure, however, all users of financial statements, including lawyers, need to understand how any pro forma figure differs from its counterpart GAAP reporting number.

(2) The Pitfalls

To start, a specific enterprise's pro formas may lack comparability to that company's prior period numbers or the results of competitors. More generally, pro forma metrics can mislead investors and other users of financial information if they obscure GAAP results or distort an enterprise's financial appearance. For example, Enron obscured poor GAAP results by focusing investor attention on dubious pro forma metrics. In its 2000 fourth-quarter earnings release, Enron boasted a twenty-five percent increase in earnings per share ("EPS") for the full year 2000 when compared to 1999, and a thirty-two percent increase in EPS for the 2000 fourth quarter over the same period in 1999. Buried in the last section of its earnings release, however, the company revealed a very different story. Enron disclosed that EPS for 2000, including nonrecurring charges, increased only from $1.10 per share in 1999 to $1.12 per share in 2000. These amounts translated to a 1.8 percent increase, in stark contrast to the twenty-five percent increase that Enron touted at the beginning of its earnings release. Similarly, in 2001 Enron used a pro forma metric called "recurring net income" to announce a $393 million profit in its earnings release for the third quarter of 2001, just weeks before the company filed for bankruptcy protection. Later in that release, Enron reported that it actually sustained a $618 million net loss for that period under GAAP. Enron turned its GAAP loss into a pro forma profit by labeling $1.01 billion in charges as "one-time" or "nonrecurring" and excluding those charges from "recurring net income." Those charges, which included restructuring charges and investment and other asset write-downs, however, arose from the company's normal business activities. Enron's pro forma metrics seem calculated to mislead the public.

The chances that a pro forma metric will convey a distorted picture increases when the reporting enterprise does not disclose where the underlying numbers come from or does not reconcile the metric to a comparable GAAP measure. In addition, pro formas should allow for comparison to previous results for the same business and current results for competitors.

(3) Regulation G

In the aftermath of the corporate scandals during the late 1990s and early 2000s, SOx section 401(b) directed the SEC to issue regulations to protect investors from false or misleading pro forma information. In response to that mandate, the SEC issued Regulation G, which now applies whenever a public company discloses material information that includes a pro forma metric. Conditions for Use of Non-GAAP Financial Measures, Financial Reporting Release No. 65, 68 Fed. Reg. 4820 (Jan. 30, 2003) (codified at 17 C.F.R. 244.100–.102 (2014)). Regulation G contains two important components: (1) a general prohibition against materially false or misleading pro forma metrics; and (2) a specific requirement to reconcile any pro forma metric reported with the most closely comparable GAAP reporting measure. In addition, the accompanying release explicitly endorsed the Earnings Press Release Guidelines that the Financial Executives International ("FEI") and the National Investor Relations Institute ("NIRI") have jointly promulgated.

Consistent with the FEI/NIRI guidelines, Regulation G prohibits public companies from giving non-GAAP financial metrics greater prominence than comparable GAAP reporting measures in their earnings releases. In essence, pro forma metrics may not supplant GAAP numbers, they may clarify current period results and future prospects. In addition, the new rules bar public companies from using "titles or descriptions of non-GAAP financial measures that are the same as, or confusingly similar to, titles or descriptions used for

GAAP financial measures." Neither the final regulations nor the answers to frequently asked questions about Regulation G that the staff in the Division of Corporation Finance has posted on the SEC's web site, however, provide any examples of "confusingly similar" terms. Given their resemblance to "income from continuing operations," "income before extraordinary items," and "net income," public companies should keep in mind that labels such as "net income from operations," "earnings before marketing expenses," "earnings before special items," or "recurring net income" may invite SEC scrutiny. To help users of financial information better understand the nature and relevance of any pro forma metrics reported, the SEC now requires explanations and reconciliations of pro forma metrics to GAAP reporting measures, specifically in tabular format, in any release that uses pro forma metrics. This rule seeks to ensure that public companies provide users of financial statements information detailing where the pro forma metrics come from and why management believes them useful, so that users can better determine how much weight to give to the pro forma metrics presented.

Regulation G also expressly prohibits the use of non-GAAP measures to smooth earnings and bans companies from designating items as "special," "nonrecurring," or "unusual" in certain public filings, specifically 10-Ks and 10-Qs, if similar items have occurred in the previous two years or if the enterprise expects such events or transactions to occur again within two years. Public companies, however, may still use such designations to define pro forma metrics in earnings or other releases, and post that information on the corporate website, as long as the enterprise explains where the pro forma metric comes from and includes the necessary reconciliation to GAAP. As a result, a two-tiered reporting system has developed, where enterprises use press releases and the corporate website to disseminate information about such items, but then omit such information from SEC annual or quarterly reports. To illustrate, Starbucks' Earnings Release for Fourth Quarter and Fiscal 2012, dated November 1, 2012 , which appears in Appendix A on pages 807 to 824, *infra*, contains various non-GAAP numbers and disclosures. Page 18 reconciles "Non-GAAP operating margin" to "Operating margin, as reported (GAAP)" and "Non-GAAP Diluted EPS" to "Diluted EPS, as reported (GAAP)." In addition, recall that the second page of Starbucks' 2012 Annual Report, which also appears in Appendix A on page 692, *infra*, contains bar graphs comparing GAAP and non-GAAP amounts for Operating Income, Operating Margin, and Earnings per Diluted Share for fiscal years 2008-2011, but interestingly does not provide any non-GAAP figures for fiscal 2012. Notably, none of these metrics appear in Starbucks' Form 10-K for the year ended September 30, 2012. More troublesome from a Regulation G standpoint, the Annual Report relies on asterisks for the reconciliation between the non-GAAP and GAAP numbers, rather than use a tabular format, and does not offer any explanation as to why management considers the non-GAAP metrics useful.

In 2010, the Division of Corporation Finance updated its Compliance and Disclosure Interpretations on non-GAAP measures and opined that the prohibition against designations as "non-recurring, infrequent or unusual" arises from the description and not from the item's nature. The staff continued: "The fact that a registrant cannot describe a charge or gain as nonrecurring, infrequent or unusual, however, does not mean that the registrant cannot adjust for that charge or gain. Registrants can make adjustments they believe are appropriate, subject to Regulation G and [Regulation S-K]." Staff of the Sec. & Exch. Comm'n, Non-GAAP Financial Measures, Q. 102.03 (Jan. 15, 2010), *available at* http://www.sec.gov/divisions/corpfin/guidance/nongaapinterp.htm. In essence, such disclosures cannot mislead, must provide a reconciliation to the most directly comparable GAAP number, and should explain why the presentation provides information useful to investors.

FASB ASC Topic 718, Compensation–Stock Compensation, which codified SFAS No. 123(R), Share-Based Payment, now requires public companies to treat the fair value of any share-based payments, more commonly referred to as "stock options," determined on the grant date, as an expense that reduces net income. Until 2006, corporations did not need to treat stock options as an expense as long as they supplied additional disclosures that showed the effects of stock-based compensation on net income and earnings per share if the company had used the fair value method for the various periods in the notes to the financial statements. In response to the rules codified in ASC Topic 718, numerous corporations, including Google, now distribute pro forma numbers that, often exclude from expenses, among other items, the value of stock options when calculating non-GAAP operating income and non-GAAP net income.

Both Regulation S-X and FASB ASC Topic 805, *Business Combinations*, require a public entity to disclose certain pro forma information to show what the entity's financial statements would look like if a business combination had occurred at the beginning of the first annual accounting period presented in the financial statements. *See* FASB ASC ¶ 805-10-50-2(h). After a recent update to the Codification, entities must now describe the nature and amount of any material, nonrecurring pro forma adjustments directly attributable to a business combination. *Id.* at -2(h)(4). Because the Codification requires such data and disclosures, any resulting pro forma numbers technically do not qualify as "non-GAAP." As a consequence, Regulation G contains an important exception for such disclosures. Any such disclosures, however, remain subject to SEC regulations regarding mergers and business combinations that predate SOx.

(4) Practical Tips for Lawyers

Knowing the difference between GAAP and non-GAAP reporting measures allows lawyers to represent and advise clients more effectively and to reach more informed investment decisions. Although Regulation G applies only to public companies, the administrative rule also offers important insights and suggests best practices to lawyers working on legal matters involving private firms. Any user or reader of non-GAAP metrics, including a lawyer, would do well to follow the SEC's advice and to keep the following questions in mind when analyzing non-GAAP numbers:

What is the company assuming? "Pro forma" financial results can be misleading, particularly if they change a loss to a profit or hide a significant fact. For example, they may assume that a proposed transaction that benefits the company has actually occurred. Or they may fail to account for costs or charges. Be sure to look behind the numbers, and find out what assumptions the numbers are based on.

What is the company not saying? Be particularly wary when you see "pro forma" financial results that only address one component of a company's financial results—for example, [EBITDA]. These kinds of statements can be misleading unless the company clearly describes what transactions are omitted and how the numbers might compare to other periods.

How do the "pro forma" results compare with GAAP-based financials? Because "pro forma" information comes from selective editing of financial information compiled in accordance with GAAP, "pro forma" financial results can raise a serious risk of misleading investors—even if they do not change a loss to a profit. Look for a clear, comprehensible explanation of how "pro forma" results differ from financial statements prepared under GAAP rules, and make sure you understand any differences before investing on the basis of "pro forma" results.

Are you reading "pro forma" results or a summary of GAAP-based financials? Remember that there is a big difference between "pro forma" financial information and a summary of a financial statement that has been prepared in accordance with GAAP. When financial statements have been prepared in compliance with regular accounting rules, a summary of that information can be quite useful, giving you the overall picture of a company's financial position without the mass of details contained in the full financial statements. It is always best, however, to compare any summary financial presentation you read with the full GAAP-based financial statements.

Staff of the Securities & Exchange Commission, "Pro Forma" Financial Information: Tips for investors (Dec. 4, 2001).

In addition, lawyers should remember that understanding financial statements puts an attorney at a great advantage in a number of legal arenas. At a minimum, therefore, lawyers should also remember to:

(1) Read earnings releases, public announcements, and annual reports in their entirety and with healthy skepticism. Decide for yourself whether any pro forma metrics accurately portray the enterprise's financial health and performance. Remember that Enron tried to hide a $1 billion loss by labeling it as "non-recurring" and excluding it from pro forma metrics.

(2) Assess the quality of earnings. Gains from one-time events, such as litigation recoveries and sales of major assets, usually do not reliably predict future earnings performance. In its 10-Q for the second quarter in 2001, Enron gushed: "Profits from North American power marketing operations, which

increased significantly, included the sale of three peaking power plants." Which earnings are likely to recur?

(3) Watch out for "everything but bad stuff" reporting. Has the enterprise reported similar expenses and charges in the past? Are the events or economic circumstances underlying these items likely to recur in the future?

PROBLEMS

Problem 4.3A. Before the adoption of Regulation G, Amazon.com's Form 10-K for the fiscal year ended December 31, 1999 contained the following section entitled "Pro Forma Information:"

Pro forma information regarding our results, which excludes amortization of goodwill and other intangibles, stock-based compensation, equity in losses of equity-method investees and merger, acquisition and investment-related costs, is as follows:

	Year ended December 31, 1999
	(in thousands, except per share amount)
Pro forma loss from operations	$(352,371)
Pro forma net loss	$(389,815)
Pro forma basic and diluted loss per share	$ (1.19)
Shares used in computation of pro forma basic and diluted loss per share	326,753

Using the methodology described above to derive pro forma loss from operations, our US books business was profitable in the fourth quarter of 1999 and we expect this business to be profitable in 2000. The pro forma results are presented for informational purposes only and are not prepared in accordance with generally accepted accounting principles.

Amazon.com, Inc., Annual Report (Form 10-K), at 28 (Mar. 30, 2000). For the year, Amazon.com reported a $605,755,000 loss from operations, which included $30,618,000 in stock-based compensation, $214,694,000 in amortization of goodwill and other intangibles, and $8,072,000 in merger, acquisition and investment-related costs. Amazon.com also reported a $719,968,000 net loss, which included $76,769,000 in losses from equity-method investees. *Id.* at 34. Assume that you serve as assistant general counsel for Amazon.com shortly after the SEC adopts Regulation G. Your boss, the general counsel, has asked you to review the company's pro forma information and the related discussion to assess the company's compliance with the new regulation. Your boss wants to know whether the disclosures in that Form 10-K would comply with Regulation G. If not, the boss wants to know what changes you would recommend to the pro forma information and disclosures.

Problem 4.3B. What non-GAAP numbers, if any, did Google include in its 2012 fourth quarter earnings release, which you can access at http://investor.google.com/earnings/2012/Q4_google_earnings.html? Can you find any of those numbers in Google's Form 10-K for the year ended December 31, 2012?

Problem 4.3C. Your law firm serves as outside counsel to Keough-Hall Health Corp. ("Keough"), a health care provider listed on the NYSE. Keough's audit committee has asked your firm to review a proposed earnings release announcing the company's results for the quarter ended March 31, 20X1, when Keough posted a $55 million net loss, which included $245 million for various write-offs and restructuring charges. The first paragraph of Keough's proposed release declares, "net income from operations was $190 million, or $.40 per share." The draft release, however, does not mention the net loss until the final sentence of the tenth paragraph. From your previous work for Keough, you know that the company has used the term "net income from operations" for years. What advice would you give to the audit committee?

c. COMPREHENSIVE INCOME

As mentioned on page 263, *supra*, FASB ASC Topic 220, *Comprehensive Income*, which codified SFAS No. 130, *Reporting Comprehensive Income,* now generally requires enterprises to report an all-inclusive "comprehensive income" for an accounting period in a full set of financial statements and as prominently as the other financial statements. Section 220-10-20 defines "comprehensive income" as "the change in equity (net assets) of a business entity during a period from transactions and other events and circumstances from nonowner sources." The term comprehensive income encompasses "all changes in equity during a period except those resulting from investments by owners and distributions to owners." FASB ASC § 220-10-20.

FASB ASC Topic 220 divides comprehensive income into *net income* and *other comprehensive income*. "Net income" includes the revenues, expenses, gains, and losses that give rise to income from continuing operations, discontinued operations, and extraordinary items. "Other comprehensive income" includes certain gains and losses that the Codification requires an enterprise to include in comprehensive income, but exclude from net income for an accounting period. The Codification later reclassifies these gains and losses out of accumulated other comprehensive income and into net income.

At the risk of oversimplifying, "net income" measures current operating performance, while "other comprehensive income" seeks to capture changes in items longer-term in nature. For example, and as discussed in more detail in Chapter VI on pages 416 to 426, *infra*, the rules for reporting certain investments in debt and equity securities require enterprises to include changes in the fair values of those investments in a separate component of the equity section of the balance sheet in such a way that bypasses net income but gives rise to other comprehensive income. This treatment prevents fluctuations in fair value from unnecessarily increasing volatility in net income, while informing the reader about the gain or loss that the enterprise would recognize if it sold the investments at fair value. To avoid double counting in comprehensive income realized gains or losses recognized in net income during an accounting period after an enterprise had previously included unrealized gains or losses related to that investment in other comprehensive income in an earlier accounting period, the enterprise must reverse the net unrealized gain or loss previously recorded when reporting the realized gain or loss. The Codification refers to such adjustments for items that an enterprise has previously included in other comprehensive income as "reclassification adjustments." FASB ASC ¶ 220-10-20.

Similar rules apply to other items, which remain beyond the scope of these materials. These items include various translation adjustments arising from converting a foreign entity's financial statements from foreign currency to U.S. dollars, changes in the fair value of certain derivatives that qualify as hedges, and certain gains or losses and prior service costs or credits associated with pension or other postretirement benefits that the accounting rules do not require an enterprise to recognize immediately in the cost of providing pension or other postretirement benefits to employees. See FASB ASC ¶ 220-10-45-10A. Please observe that Note 11 to the financial statements in Starbucks' 2012 Annual Report, which you can find in Appendix A on pages 771 and 772, *infra*, shows a $10.5 million gain from a reclassification adjustment for net losses realized in net income for cash flow hedges, net of tax, during the fiscal year ending September 30, 2012. Because Starbucks earlier included unrealized losses in other comprehensive income, the reclassification adjustment appears as a gain.

Because the effects of these items bypass the income statement, the Codification requires enterprises to report and present such items of other comprehensive income and the all-inclusive "total comprehensive income" somewhere in the basic financial statements. Notably, under IFRS, enterprises report fewer items in *other comprehensive income*, presumably to avoid these often arbitrary distinctions.

The Codification does not require firms to use the term "comprehensive income" or any specific format, but does mandate that an enterprise display an amount representing total nonowner changes in equity for the period with the same prominence as other financial statements. If an enterprise does not have any items of "other comprehensive income" during any accounting period presented, the enterprise need not report comprehensive income. FASB ASC ¶¶ 220-10-15-3, 220-10-45-4 to -8.

Most corporations originally reported the necessary amounts in the statement of changes in stockholders' equity. AM. INST. OF CERTIFIED PUB. ACCOUNTANTS, ACCOUNTING TRENDS & TECHNIQUES 446 (66th ed. 2012). Note that the consolidated statements of equity on page 53 of Starbucks' 2012 Form 10-K, which you can find in Appendix A on page 749, *infra*, use the third alternative, combined with additional disclosures in note 11 on pages 75 and

76 of the Form 10-K or pages 771 and 772 in Appendix A, *infra.* For the fiscal years ended October 3, 2010, October 2, 2011, and September 30, 2012, Starbucks reported total comprehensive income, excluding noncontrolling interest, of $937.4 million, $1,234.8 million, and $1,360.2 million, respectively. For the fiscal year ended September 30, 2012, Starbucks reported ($23.6) million in other comprehensive income (loss), which included a $26.4 million net unrealized holding loss and a $2.8 million translation gain, both net of tax. As of September 30, 2012, Starbucks' consolidated balance sheet and statement of equity reported $22.7 million in accumulated other comprehensive income. Note 11 states that the cumulative amount, net of $6.6 million of tax, includes (in millions):

Net unrealized gains (losses) on available-for-sale securities	$ (0.1)
Net unrealized gains (losses) on hedging instruments	(72.1)
Translation adjustment	94.9
Accumulated other comprehensive income	$22.7

For public entities beginning for fiscal years starting after December 15, 2011, and for interim periods within those years, the amendments in Accounting Standards Update No. 2011-05, *Comprehensive Income (Topic 220), Presentation of Comprehensive Income*, eliminate the option to present comprehensive income as part of the statement of shareholders' equity. As a result, enterprises now need to present retrospectively all nonowner changes in owners' equity either in a single continuous statement of comprehensive income or in two separate, but consecutive, statements. In the two-statement approach, an enterprise would first present net income and its components in the statement of net income. Then, a statement of other comprehensive income would show three things: the components of other comprehensive income, total other comprehensive income, and total comprehensive income.

Keep in mind that the certain gains and losses that the Codification requires enterprises to report in other comprehensive income eventually affect net income in at least one future accounting period. As a result, at some point enterprises must reclassify those gains and losses out of accumulated other comprehensive income and into net income. The recent amendments in Accounting Standards Update No. 2013-02, *Comprehensive Income (Topic 220), Reporting of Amounts Reclassified Out of Accumulated Other Comprehensive Income*, require enterprises to disclose the effect on any specific line items on the income statement caused when the enterprise reclassifies any significant amount out of accumulated other comprehensive income and entirely into net income in the same reporting period. (In some situations, the enterprise might transfer a portion of the amount to a balance sheet account, such as inventory or another account for deferred costs that benefit a subsequent accounting period, rather than directly to income or expense.) This disclosure can appear either on the face of the income statement or in the notes to the financial statements as long as all of the required information appears in one place. The new rules generally apply to reporting periods beginning after December 31, 2012, but do not apply to private companies until reporting periods beginning after December 31, 2013. By comparison, IFRS does not require enterprises to reclassify all amounts of accumulated other comprehensive income to net income. When necessary, however, IFRS requires enterprises to present reclassifications by component of other comprehensive income, again either in the notes to the financial statements or on the face of the income statement, the statement of comprehensive income, or the combined statement of income and comprehensive income.

PROBLEMS

Problem 4.4A. Explaining where you found the relevant information, answer the following questions about Amazon.com, Inc.'s comprehensive income for the year ended December 31, 2012:

(1) What was the company's comprehensive income (loss) for the year?

(2) What was the company's other comprehensive income (loss) for the year? What items did Amazon.com include in this amount?

(3) Did the company record any reclassification adjustments during the year? If so, what was the nature and net amount of any reclassifications?

(4) What was the company's accumulated other comprehensive income (loss) on December 31, 2012?

Problem 4.4B. Explaining where you found the relevant information, answer the following questions about Google's comprehensive income for the year ended December 31, 2012:

(1) What was the company's comprehensive income (loss) for the year?

(2) What was the company's other comprehensive income (loss) for the year? What items did Google include in this amount?

(3) Did the company record any reclassification adjustments during the year? If so, what was the nature and net amount of any reclassifications?

(4) What was the company's accumulated other comprehensive income (loss) on December 31, 2012?

Problem 4.4C. Explaining where you found the relevant information, answer the following questions about UPS's comprehensive income for the year ended December 31, 2012:

(1) What was the company's comprehensive income (loss) for the year?

(2) What was the company's other comprehensive income (loss) for the year? What items did UPS include in this amount?

(3) Did the company record any reclassification adjustments during the year? If so, what was the nature and net amount of any reclassifications?

(4) What was the company's accumulated other comprehensive income (loss) on December 31, 2012?

2.   RATIO ANALYSIS

When studying the income statement, knowledgeable users frequently analyze the financial statement by converting each line to a percentage of sales. In fact, the annual report or the financial statements commonly include a breakdown showing net income, as well as the major expense categories for the period, as a percentage of net sales. As an example, again please refer to the charts on pages 27 to 30 of Starbucks' Form 10-K for the fiscal year ended September 30, 2012, which appear in Appendix A on pages 723 to 726, *infra*, and express various line items from the income statements as a percentage of total net revenues. An experienced analyst can compare those percentages to the corresponding figures either from Starbucks in previous years or from competitors for the current year.

Accountants and financial analysts have also developed a number of financial ratios based upon net income or other numbers appearing in the income statement. Once again, however, keep in mind that these financial ratios are only as good as the financial statements from which they are derived. An erroneous income statement or balance sheet can produce misleading financial ratios. That caution aside, the ratios that use numbers from the income statement fall into three categories: coverage, profitability and activity.

a.   COVERAGE RATIOS

Coverage ratios measure the extent to which income, usually determined before interest and taxes, covers certain payments related to an enterprise's long-term debt. The most commonly-used coverage ratios include times interest earned and debt coverage. Similarly, the dividend coverage ratio measures the extent to which net income, this time after interest and taxes, covers regular dividend payments.

(1) Times Interest Earned

Creditors, especially bondholders, often focus on the ratio of earnings to interest charges. This ratio provides some indication about how much the enterprise's earnings can decline without endangering the interest payments. For this purpose, financial analysts usually recompute the earnings figure by adding back to net income both the interest charges and income taxes, which come after interest. Financial analysts usually refer to this ratio as *times interest earned* or *interest coverage*. If a company has net income before taxes of $500,000 and interest charges of $250,000, it would cover its interest 3.0 times [($500,000 income before taxes plus $250,000 interest)/$250,000 interest].

(2) Debt Coverage

Some analysts also use a *debt coverage ratio* which determines how many times a business can cover both interest and any debt, including the current portion of long-term debt, that the enterprise must repay in the next twelve months. If the company in our previous example must also repay $250,000 principal, as the current portion of its long-term debt, in addition to paying the $250,000 interest charges, the debt coverage ratio would drop to 1.5 times [($500,000 income before taxes plus $250,000 interest)/($250,000 interest plus $250,000 principal)]. If the debt coverage ratio does not equal or exceed 1.0, the enterprise's operating income before interest and taxes will not cover the firm's debt service. As a result, the enterprise would need to draw upon cash reserves, borrow, or sell additional shares to pay the loan. In fact, lenders prefer debt coverage ratios greater than 1.0, typically at least 1.2 or greater.

(3) Dividend Coverage, Dividend-Payout, and Dividend Yield

Investors, particularly preferred shareholders, may focus on the ratio of net income, this time computed after interest charges and taxes, to regular dividends. This ratio provides some indication about how much the enterprise's net income can decline without jeopardizing the regular dividend payments. Financial analysts usually refer to this ratio as *dividend coverage*. If a company has net income of $200,000 and 10,000 outstanding preferred shares offering a $4 dividend preference annually, the company can cover the preferred dividend preference 5.0 times [$200,000 net income/(10,000 preferred shares times $4 preference per share)].

The dividend-payout ratio shows the percentage of a company's net income that the firm paid out in dividends. In 2012, companies in the S&P 500 index paid out just thirty-six percent of their net income in dividends, significantly below a more than fifty percent historical payout since 1925. As the dividend payout ratio approaches 100 percent, the company must maintain earnings each year, or face the likely need to reduce the dividend. Any payout above about two-thirds of earnings usually raises questions about sustainability.

The dividend yield equals a company's per share dividend payout over the last twelve months divided by the share's market price, such as the closing price on a certain date or the average between the high and low price on that same date or over a specified period, perhaps the same twelve months used in the numerator. Keep in mind that a higher dividend yield does not always signal a better investment; the paying company may have neglected reinvestment in its business.

b. PROFITABILITY RATIOS

Recall that profitability ratios assess how effectively a business operates. These profitability ratios include earnings per share, the price-earnings ratio, return on sales, gross profit percentage, operating profit margin, and the returns on assets and equity. Consider the following income statement for X Corp., which has issued 100 common shares, all of which remained outstanding during the entire year.

X Corp.
Income Statement
For the Year Ended December 31

Net Sales		$100,000
Cost of Goods Sold:		
Opening Inventory	$14,000	
Purchases	72,000	
Goods Available for Sale	$86,000	
Less: Closing Inventory	16,000	70,000
Gross Profit		$ 30,000
Operating Expenses		20,000
Income Before Taxes		$ 10,000
Income Taxes		4,000
Net Income		$ 6,000

(1) Earnings Per Share

When analyzing a corporation's income statement, lawyers will perhaps most frequently encounter the term *earnings per share*, sometimes abbreviated *EPS*, which usually refers to the net income attributable to the company's common shares. To compute the net income attributable to the common shares, the accountant or financial analyst subtracts any preferred stock dividends from the company's net income and then divides the remaining amount by the weighted average of common shares outstanding during the period. Because X Corp. has not issued any preferred shares and 100 common shares remained outstanding during the entire year ended December 31, we can compute $60 ($6,000 net income/100 weighted average common shares outstanding) as the earnings per share for that year.

The business community uses this ratio as an important yardstick, perhaps the most important one, for comparing an enterprise's performance in the current accounting period to that in a prior period. Although accounting standards generally require enterprises to show information regarding earnings per share or net loss per share on the face of the income statement, GAAP exempts nonpublic enterprises from this requirement. These rules state that enterprises should also show per share amounts for income from continuing operations. Finally, the rules encourage businesses to explain the numbers used in the earnings per share calculation in the notes to the financial statements.

When evaluating a corporation's earnings per share, lawyers should consider adding another step to their analysis by going beyond the standard per-share amounts reported to the nearest penny on the face of the income statement and computing the amount to the tenth of a cent. An academic study at Stanford University, which examined almost 500,000 quarterly earnings reports for more than 20,000 companies from 1980 to 2006, found that when earnings per share figures were calculated down to a tenth of a cent, the number "4" appeared less frequently in the tenths place than any other digit and only 8.5 percent of the time. The numbers "2" and "3" also appeared less frequently than expected. This effect, which the authors dubbed "quadrophobia," suggests that companies nudge earnings up until at least a "5" appears in the tenths place, which then lets them round earnings per share up to the next highest cent. Such a practice can enable the company to meet analyst and investor expectations. Investors often aggressively purchase shares in companies that beat earnings estimates, even by a penny, and dump shares of companies that fall short. During the trial of former Enron executives Jeffrey Skilling and Kenneth Lay, the company's head of investor-relations testified that Skilling managed Enron's earnings per share to meet or exceed Wall Street expectations in an effort to avoid a significant drop in Enron's stock price and that Lay at least acquiesced in the practice. *See* Scott Thurm, *For Some Firms, a Case of 'Quadrophobia,'* WALL ST. J., Feb. 13, 2010, at B1; Gary McWilliams & Kara Scannell, *Profit Tweaking May Lose Favor After Enron Trial*, WALL ST. J., Feb. 16, 2006, at C1.

In a collaborative effort with what was then known as the International Accounting Standards Committee, in 1997 the FASB issued SFAS No. 128, *Earnings per Share*, now codified in the identically named FASB ASC Topic 260, to simplify the standards for computing earnings per share and to conform the applicable rules more closely to international accounting standards. ASC Topic 260 requires enterprises with publicly held common stock, or with outstanding contractual obligations that could allow holders to obtain common stock either during, or after the end of, the reporting period, to report figures for *basic earnings per share* and, if applicable, *diluted earnings per share*. The new terms "basic earnings per share" and "diluted earnings per share" replace the previously used labels "primary earnings per share" and "fully diluted earnings per share," respectively. Under the Codification, *basic earnings per share* describes the amount of earnings for the period available to each share of common stock outstanding during the period, computes as illustrated above by dividing income available to common shareholders by the weighted average of common shares outstanding during the period. The Codification defines *diluted earnings per share* as the amount of earnings for the period available to each share of common stock, taking into account not only the shares in fact outstanding during the period, but also all shares that would have been outstanding if the enterprise had issued common shares for all *dilutive potential common shares* outstanding during the period. Dilutive potential common shares, such as options, warrants and convertible securities, give the holder the right to acquire common shares either during, or after the end of, the reporting period; the resulting increase in the number of shares would normally reduce the earnings per share, often considerably, even after taking into account any potential increase in earnings resulting from the exercise of the rights, such as the reduction in interest expense when a holder converted bonds into stock. Computing diluted earnings per share can present quite a challenge, so we will not discuss the actual mechanics here.

As a result of these rules, enterprises with simple capital structures, meaning those with only common shares outstanding, must report basic per-share amounts for income from continuing operations and for net income on the face of the income statement. All other enterprises must present both basic and diluted per share amounts for income from continuing operations and for net income with equal prominence on the face of the income statement. The rules also encourage businesses to explain the numbers used in the earnings per share calculations in the notes to the financial statements. Note that the consolidated statements of earnings that appear on page 50 of Starbucks' Form 10-K for the fiscal year ended September 30, 2012, reprinted in Appendix A on page 746, *infra,* show net income per common share–both basic and diluted–and the weighted average number of common shares outstanding for the three fiscal years reported. In addition, the portion of Note 1 captioned "Earnings Per Share" on page 61 of the 2012 Form 10-K, which appears in Appendix A on page 757, *infra,* further explains the computations. Enterprises that report a discontinued operation or an extraordinary item can present basic and diluted per share amounts for those line items either on the face of the income statement or in the notes to the financial statements. In addition to applying to companies with publicly held common stock or complex capital structures, these rules pertain to any enterprise that chooses to present earnings per share in the financial statements and that seeks to comply with GAAP. FASB ASC ¶¶ 260-10-15-2 to -3, 260-10-45-2 to -3, -5 (codifying EARNINGS PER SHARE, Statement of Fin. Accounting Standards No. 128, ¶¶ 6, 36, 37 (Fin. Accounting Standards Bd. 1997)).

(2) Price-Earnings Ratio

Once an analyst has found or determined earnings per share, the analyst will usually compute the *price-earnings ratio.* This ratio, which the business community often refers to simply as the *P/E* or the *P/E ratio*, compares the market price of the common shares to the earnings per share. Although the price-earnings ratio does not apply to privately-held corporations, whose shares are not publicly traded, we can illustrate the computation using X Corp. as an example. Suppose its common shares were trading at $300 per share. Using the $60 earnings per share figure which we previously computed for X Corp., we can calculate an 5.0 P/E ratio ($300 per share market price/$60 earnings per share). As with the other ratios discussed in this chapter, the investor, creditor or other user must compare the P/E ratio against industry and market standards to interpret the number.

(3) Return on Sales or Net Profit Margin

Another common profitability ratio, the ratio of net income to sales for an accounting period, usually stated in percentage terms, provides some index to the enterprise's efficiency. This ratio, which financial analysts typically refer to as either *return on sales* or *net profit margin*, shows the percentage of each dollar in sales that becomes net income. For the year ended December 31, X Corp.'s income statement shows a 6.0 percent return on sales ($6,000 net income/$100,000 sales). The higher the return on sales, the more profitably, and presumably the more efficiently, the business sells goods or provides services.

(4) Gross Profit Percentage

Closely related to the return on sales, the *gross profit percentage* reflects the business's profitability from selling its products, ignoring operating expenses, such as general, selling and administrative expenses. You will recall from Chapter I that gross profit represents the difference between sales and cost of goods sold. This ratio compares the gross profit to sales, again commonly expressed in percentage terms. Using the income statement, we can compute a 30.0 percent gross profit percentage ($30,000 gross profit/$100,000 sales) for X Corp. for the year ended December 31. A higher gross profit percentage usually suggests that the business's products enjoy some advantage over the competition, whether technological, legal, or marketing.

(5) Operating Profit Margin

The *operating profit margin* measures income from operations, typically before income taxes, interest, and other nonoperating items, relative to operating revenue. To determine income from operations, an enterprise subtracts both cost of goods sold and operating expenses, such as general, selling and administrative expenses, from sales. In our example involving X Corp., subtracting the $20,000 in operating expenses from the $30,000 in gross profit leaves $10,000 in operating income. If we divide the $10,000 in operating income by the $100,000 in net sales, we get a 10.0 percent operating profit margin for the year ended December 31.

(6) Return on Assets

The return on assets ratio measures a business's profitability relative to its total assets, usually expressed in terms of average assets, however defined. Most simply, analysts define "average assets" as the average of beginning and ending assets for the period. If X Corp.'s average assets for the year equaled the $40,000 December 31 amount shown on page 264, *supra*, the return on assets would 15.0 percent ($6,000 net income/$40,000 average assets). The higher the return on assets, the better job management is doing utilizing its resources in the business.

(7) Return on Equity

Another net income test in common use is the ratio of net income to owners' equity, representing the amounts that owners have invested in the business, whether directly as a capital contribution or indirectly by leaving accumulated earnings in the business. This ratio, which the business community sometimes refers to as *return on equity* or *ROE*, gives a measure of how successfully the management is utilizing the owners' capital. If we subtract X Corp.'s $6,000 net income from its $25,000 total shareholders' equity on December 31 set forth on page 264, *supra*, we can assume that shareholders' equity at the beginning of the year equaled $19,000. As a result, we will use $22,000 [($19,000 beginning equity + $25,000 ending equity)/2] as average equity. Thus, we can compute a 27.3 percent ROE for the year ended December 31 ($6,000 net income/$22,000 average equity). Because analysts cannot compute a P/E ratio for privately held businesses, they often use return on equity to measure these businesses' profitability.

(8) Earnings Before Interest, Taxes, Depreciation and Amortization

In the late 1990s, a non-GAAP measure known as *EBITDA*, or earnings before interest, taxes, depreciation and amortization, became important both as a measure of operating results and as the numerator in coverage ratios. Because depreciation and amortization do not involve the current expenditure of cash, readers of financial statements have used this measure to compare the enterprise's current operating results to a prior period or to its competitors' numbers or to quantify the extent to which an enterprise's "adjusted" income, before interest and taxes, can service the enterprise's debt obligations.

Using amounts shown on the consolidated statements of earnings found on page 50 of Starbucks' 2012 Form 10-K, and in Appendix A on page 746, *infra*, we could compute the company's EBITDA (in millions) for the fiscal years ending September 30, 2012 and October 2, 2011, respectively, as follows:

	2012	2011
Net earnings attributable to Starbucks	$1,383.8	$1,245.7
Interest expense	32.7	33.3
Income taxes	674.4	563.1
Depreciation and amortization expenses	550.3	523.3
EBITDA	$2,641.2	$2,365.4

As a practical matter, however, many enterprises do not list exact amounts for interest, depreciation, or amortization expense on their financial statements. A lawyer can often find figures or proxies for these items in the notes to the financial statements or in the operating section of the statement of cash flows. For example, the Note 10 to the Starbucks financial statements used in the fourth edition of this text listed the company's interest expense as $1.3 million and $0.4 million for fiscal 2005 and 2004, respectively, even though no explicit amounts appeared on the consolidated statements of earnings. *See* DAVID R. HERWITZ & MATTHEW J. BARRETT, MATERIALS ON ACCOUNTING FOR LAWYERS 1008, 1030 (unabr. 4th ed. 2006). In addition, a lawyer representing Starbucks could likely get the company's exact interest expense for any particular period from the company. In the absence of an exact amount for interest expense, another lawyer could use: (a) an amount shown for "Interest expense" in the notes to the financial statements; (b) the amount of cash shown as paid as interest during the period from the supplemental information on the face of the company's consolidated statement of cash flows, or (c) some other estimate for interest expense. Given the various possibilities, any legal agreement using EBITDA should define exactly how the parties will compute the figure.

c.   ACTIVITY RATIOS

We should also mention three activity ratios which compare amounts from the balance sheet and the income statement and measure how effectively the business utilizes its resources. In many loan transactions, often referred to as *asset-based lending*, the borrower pledges accounts receivables or inventory to secure the loan. Lenders in such transactions frequently focus on an activity ratio, such as receivables or inventory turnover, in making credit decisions.

(1) Receivables Turnover

The ratio of credit sales to average accounts receivable, however defined, for a period provides some measure of the liquidity of the accounts receivable. Thus if X Corp.'s credit sales for the year amounted to $30,000 and its average accounts receivable during the year equaled the $3,000 balance on December 31, we can compute a 10.0 *receivables turnover* ratio. In other words, the accounts receivable turn over 10 times a year. In effect, this means that, on average, the company collected its accounts receivable in 36.5 days or one-tenth of a year.

Along these same lines, analysts frequently compare the terms for payment which businesses in the industry typically offer to customers against a particular enterprise's days of receivables outstanding to evaluate the enterprise's efficiency in collecting receivables. As an example, if the industry generally gives customers thirty days to pay their bills, but receivables turnover indicates that on average a business collects its receivables every fifty days, those facts may suggest inefficiencies in the enterprise's collection process and could even indicate a problem with the receivables' collectibility. In addition, analysts often compare the payment terms which a business extends to its customers against the terms that vendors offer to the business. A business can face liquidity difficulties if suppliers require the business to satisfy its accounts payable over a shorter period than the business can collect accounts receivables from customers.

(2) Inventory Turnover

Financial analysts commonly perform similar analysis regarding the relationship between the cost of goods sold for the year and the average inventory figure during the year, which they often compute by simply averaging the opening and closing inventories. Because X's average inventory amounted to $15,000 [($14,000 opening inventory plus $16,000 closing inventory)/2], a financial analyst might say that the *inventory turnover* ratio equaled 4.67 times ($70,000 cost of goods sold/$15,000 average inventory). Thus, the inventory turnover ratio measures how often a business sells and replaces inventory during a fiscal period. Grocery stores and fast-food restaurants operate in industries with high inventory turnover ratios. By dividing the number of inventory turns into the number of days in the fiscal period, we can also determine how may days it takes a business to turnover its inventory. This means that, on average, X completely sells and replaces its inventory about every 78.2 days. A low inventory turnover suggests that the business may have overinvested in inventory, may own obsolete or slow moving goods, or suffer from a poor sales force.

(3) Asset Turnover

Finally, the ratio of sales to average assets for the period, which analysts usually call the *asset turnover*, indicates how many dollars of sales the business generates for each dollar of assets that the business owns. Thus if X Corp.'s average assets for the year equaled the $40,000 December 31 amount, the financial statements reveal a 2.5 asset turnover ($100,000 sales/$40,000 average total assets). In effect, this means that, on average, each dollar in assets produced $2.50 in sales.

Table 4–2 computes the income statement ratios discussed in this section from the numbers contained in Starbucks' consolidated balance sheets as of September 30, 2012 and October 2, 2011, respectively, and consolidated statement of earnings for the fiscal years ending on those dates, which appear in Appendix A on pages 747 and 746, *infra*.

Table 4–2—Income Statement Ratios (millions omitted)			
Term or Ratio	Formula	Starbucks for 2012	Ratio
Coverage			
1. Times Interest Earned	$\dfrac{\text{Net Income Before Interest and Taxes}}{\text{Interest Expense}}$	$2,090.9 a $32.7	63.9 times
2. Debt Coverage	$\dfrac{\text{Net Income Before Interest and Taxes}}{\text{Interest Expense + Current Portion of Long-Term Debt}}$	$2,090.9 a $34.4 b	60.8 times
3a. Dividend Coverage	$\dfrac{\text{Net Income}}{\text{Preferred Stock Dividend Preferences}}$	Not meaningful c	
3b. Dividend Payout	$\dfrac{\text{Dividends Paid}}{\text{Net Income Attributable to Company}}$	$513.0 d $1,383.8	37.1%
3c. Dividend Yield	$\dfrac{\text{Dividends Paid Per Share}}{\text{Average Market Price}}$	$0.68 e $48.56 f	1.4%
Profitability			
4. Basic Earnings Per Share	$\dfrac{\text{Net Income Attributable to Common Shares}}{\text{Weighted Average Common Shares Outstanding}}$	$1,383.8 g 754.4 shares	$1.8343 per share
5. Price-Earnings Ratio	$\dfrac{\text{Market Price}}{\text{Basic Earnings Per Share}}$	$48.66 h $1.83	26.6 times
6. Return on Sales	$\dfrac{\text{Net Income}}{\text{Net Revenue}}$	$1,383.8 i $13,299.5	10.4%

7. Gross Profit Percentage [company-owned stores only]	$\dfrac{\text{Gross Profit}}{\text{Net Revenues}}$	$\dfrac{\$4,721.2\ j}{\$10,534.5\ k}$	44.8%
8. Operating Profit Margin	$\dfrac{\text{Operating Income}}{\text{Net Revenues}}$	$\dfrac{\$1,997.4}{\$13,299.5}$	15.0%
9. Return on Assets	$\dfrac{\text{Net Income}}{\text{Average Total Assets}}$	$\dfrac{\$1,383.8\ i}{\$7,789.8\ l}$	17.8%
10. Return on Equity	$\dfrac{\text{Net Income}}{\text{Average Shareholders' Equity}}$	$\dfrac{\$1,383.8\ i}{\$4,746.95\ m}$	29.2%
11. EBITDA	Earnings Before Interest, Taxes, Depreciation and Amortization (see page 301, *supra*)	$2,641.2	N/A

Activity

12. Receivables Turnover	$\dfrac{\text{Credit Sales}}{\text{Average Accounts Receivable}}$	$\dfrac{\$2,765.0\ n}{\$436.2\ o}$	6.3 times
13. Inventory Turnover	$\dfrac{\text{Cost of Goods Sold}}{\text{Average Inventory}}$	$\dfrac{\$5,813.3\ p}{\$1,103.65\ q}$	5.3 times
14. Asset Turnover	$\dfrac{\text{Net Revenues}}{\text{Average Total Assets}}$	$\dfrac{\$13,299.5}{\$7,789.8\ l}$	1.7 times

a. $1,383.8 (Net earnings attributable to Starbucks) + $32.7 (Interest expense) + $674.4 (Income taxes)

b. Debt obligations, including principal maturities and scheduled interest payments, on long-term debt due in less than one year (from page 43 of the 2012 Form 10-K)

c. Starbucks has not issued any preferred shares, so the company did not pay any preferred stock dividends.

d. From the financing section in the consolidated statements of cash flows

e. Note 11 ($0.17 per share paid on December 2, 2011, February 24, 2012, May 25, 2012, and August 24, 2012)

f. ($62.00 high price during fiscal 2012 + $35.12 low price during same period)/2

g. ($1,383.8 (Net earnings attributable to Starbucks) – $0 (no preferred stock preferences)

h. ($54.28 high price during fiscal 2012 fourth quarter + $43.04 low price during same period)/2

i. Net earnings attributable to Starbucks

j. $10,534.5 (Net revenues from company-operated stores) – $5,813.3 (Cost of sales including occupancy costs)

k. Net revenues from company-operated stores

l. [$8,219.2 (Total assets on September 30, 2012) + $7,360.4 (Total assets on October 2, 2011)]/2

m. [$5,109.0 (Shareholders' equity on September 30, 2012) + $4,384.9 (Shareholders' equity on October 2, 2011)]/2

n. $1,210.3 (Net revenues from licensed stores) + $1,554.7 (Net revenues from CPG, foodservice and other)

o. [$485.9 (Accounts receivable, net on September 30, 2012) + $386.5 (Accounts receivable, net on October 2, 2011)]/2

p. Cost of sales including occupancy costs

q. [$1,241.5 (Inventories on September 30, 2012) + $965.8 (Inventories on October 2, 2011)]/2

If we obtain a copy of Starbucks' Form 10-K for the fiscal year ended October 2, 2011, we would see that page 36 lists $34.4 million as debt obligations, including principal maturities and scheduled interest payments, on long-term debt due in less than one year. The consolidated balance sheets on page 44 list the following assets as of October 3, 2010:

Item	Amount (in millions)
Accounts receivable, net	$302.7
Inventories	543.3

Note 11 on page 64 discloses that Starbucks paid a $0.13 dividend on December 3, 2010. For Starbucks' fiscal year ended October 2, 2011, we could use those figures to compute the same income statement ratios as follows (millions omitted):

Term or Ratio	Formula	Starbucks for 2011	Ratio
Coverage			
1. Times Interest Earned	$\dfrac{\text{Net Income Before Interest and Taxes}}{\text{Interest Expense}}$	$\dfrac{\$1,842.1 \text{ a}}{\$33.3}$	55.3 times
2. Debt Coverage	$\dfrac{\text{Net Income Before Interest and Taxes}}{\text{Interest Expense + Current Portion of Long-Term Debt}}$	$\dfrac{\$1,842.1 \text{ a}}{\$34.4 \text{ b}}$	53.5 times
3a. Dividend Coverage	$\dfrac{\text{Net Income}}{\text{Preferred Stock Dividend Preferences}}$	Not meaningful c	
3b. Dividend Payout	$\dfrac{\text{Dividends Paid}}{\text{Net Income Attributable to Company}}$	$\dfrac{\$389.5 \text{ d}}{\$1,245.7}$	31.3%
3c. Dividend Yield	$\dfrac{\text{Dividends Paid Per Share}}{\text{Average Market Price}}$	$\dfrac{\$0.52 \text{ e}}{\$33.685 \text{ f}}$	1.5%
Profitability			
4. Basic Earnings Per Share	$\dfrac{\text{Net Income Attributable to Common Shares}}{\text{Weighted Average Common Shares Outstanding}}$	$\dfrac{\$1,245.7 \text{ g}}{748.3 \text{ shares}}$	$1.6647 per share
5. Price-Earnings Ratio	$\dfrac{\text{Market Price}}{\text{Basic Earnings Per Share}}$	$\dfrac{\$37.86 \text{ h}}{\$1.66}$	22.8 times
6. Return on Sales	$\dfrac{\text{Net Income}}{\text{Net Revenue}}$	$\dfrac{\$1,245.7 \text{ i}}{\$11,700.4}$	10.6%
7. Gross Profit Percentage [company-owned stores only]	$\dfrac{\text{Gross Profit}}{\text{Net Revenues}}$	$\dfrac{\$4,683.1 \text{ j}}{\$9,632.4 \text{ k}}$	48.6%
8. Operating Profit Margin	$\dfrac{\text{Operating Income}}{\text{Net Revenues}}$	$\dfrac{\$1,728.5}{\$11,700.4}$	14.8%
9. Return on Assets	$\dfrac{\text{Net Income}}{\text{Average Total Assets}}$	$\dfrac{\$1,245.7 \text{ i}}{\$6,873.15 \text{ l}}$	18.1%

10. Return on Equity	$\dfrac{\text{Net Income}}{\text{Average Shareholders' Equity}}$	$\dfrac{\$1,245.7}{\$4,029.8 \text{ m}}$	30.9%
11. EBITDA	Earnings Before Interest, Taxes, Depreciation and Amortization (see page 301, *supra*)	$2,365.2	N/A

Activity

12. Receivables Turnover	$\dfrac{\text{Credit Sales}}{\text{Average Accounts Receivable}}$	$\dfrac{\$2,068.0 \text{ n}}{\$344.6 \text{ o}}$	6.0 times
13. Inventory Turnover	$\dfrac{\text{Cost of Goods Sold}}{\text{Average Inventory}}$	$\dfrac{\$4,915.5 \text{ p}}{\$754.55 \text{ q}}$	6.5 times
14. Asset Turnover	$\dfrac{\text{Net Revenues}}{\text{Average Total Assets}}$	$\dfrac{\$11,700.4}{\$6,873.15 \text{ l}}$	1.7 times

a. $1,245.7 (Net earnings attributable to Starbucks) + $33.3 (Interest expense) + $563.1 (Income taxes)

b. Debt obligations, including principal maturities and scheduled interest payments, on long-term debt due in less than one year (from page 36 of the 2011 Form 10-K)

c. Starbucks has not issued any preferred shares, so the company did not pay any preferred stock dividends.

d. From the financing section in the consolidated statements of cash flows

e. Note 11 to the 2012 and 2011 Form 10-Ks ($0.13 per share paid on December 3, 2010, February 25, 2011, May 27, 2011, and August 26, 2011)

f. ($42.00 high price during fiscal 2011 + $25.37 low price during same period)/2

g. $1,245.7 (Net earnings attributable to Starbucks) – $0 (no preferred stock preferences)

h. ($42.00 high price during fiscal 2011 fourth quarter + $33.72 low price during same period)/2

i. Net earnings attributable to Starbucks

j. $9,632.4 (Net revenues from company-operated stores) – $4,915.5 (Cost of sales including occupancy costs)

k. Net revenues from company-operated stores

l. [$7,360.4 (Total assets on October 2, 2011) + $6,385.9 (Total assets on October 3, 2010)]/2

m. [$4,384.9 (Shareholders' equity on October 2, 2011) + 3,674.7 (Shareholders' equity on October 3, 2010)]/2

n. $1,007.5 (Net revenues from licensed stores) + $1,060.5 (Net revenues from CPG, foodservice and other)

o. [$386.5 (Accounts receivable, net on October 2, 2011) + $302.7 (Accounts receivable, net on October 3, 2010)]/2

p. Cost of sales including occupancy costs

q. [$965.8 (Inventories on October 2, 2011) + $543.3 (Inventories on October 3, 2010)]/2

During the fiscal year ended September 30, 2012, Starbucks' times interest earned and debt coverage ratios improved, but not meaningfully. Even based upon fiscal 2011 figures, Starbucks could still cover its combined interest and principal payments more than fifty times.

Starbucks enjoyed increased profitability during fiscal 2012, and at least two of the company's profitability ratios improved. Basic earnings per share rose from $1.66 per share in fiscal 2011 to $1.83 per share in fiscal 2012. While the company's price-to-earnings ratio rose from 22.8 to 26.6, Starbucks and its investors may not view the increase as a positive development. The operating profit margin also improved during fiscal 2012, increasing from 14.8% to 15.0%. All the other profitability ratios slipped during fiscal 2012. The gross profit percentage fell from 48.6% to 44.8%, return on sales declined slightly from 10.6% to 10.4%, return on assets decreased from 18.1% to 17.8%, and return on equity dropped from 30.9% to 29.2%.

During fiscal 2012, receivables turnover rose from 6.0 times to 6.3 times, meaning that Starbucks collected its receivables more efficiently when compared to fiscal 2011. Asset turnover held steady at 1.7 times. Inventory turnover decreased from 6.6 times to 5.3 times.

Again, we could compare the ratios compute above to industry norms to assess more fully Starbucks' profitability and efficiency, but clients rarely expect lawyers to perform such analysis.

PROBLEMS

Problem 4.5A. Using the consolidated statements of operations and miscellaneous information for Amazon.com for the years ended December 31, 2012 and December 31, 2011, and the consolidated balance sheets as of those dates:

(1) Compute the financial ratios listed in Table 4–2 for 2012 and 2011.

(2) Do you see any trends compared to 2011 worth noting?

Problem 4.5B. Using the consolidated statements of income and miscellaneous information for Google for the years ended December 31, 2012 and December 31, 2011, and the consolidated balance sheets as of those dates:

(1) Compute the financial ratios listed in Table 4–2 for 2012 and 2011.

(2) Do you see any trends compared to 2011 worth noting?

Problem 4.5C. Using the statements of consolidated income and miscellaneous information for UPS for the years ended December 31, 2012 and December 31, 2011, and the consolidated balance sheets as of those dates:

(1) Compute the financial ratios listed in Table 4–2 for 2012 and 2011.

(2) Do you see any trends compared to 2011 worth noting?

F.   The Statement of Cash Flows

As one of the basic financial statements, a statement of cash flows can provide important insights into a business. Through careful scrutiny of this statement, a reader can assess how well an enterprise manages its cash. In addition to using common-sized and trend analysis and computing various financial ratios based on cash flow information, readers can use three other important analytical techniques regarding the statement of cash flows: *examining the patterns among the cash flow from operating, investing and financing activities; calculating free cash flow; comparing cash flows from operations to net income;* and *preparing monthly cash flow statements.* We begin by describing these analytical techniques unique to the statement of cash flows before discussing those financial ratios derived from the cash flows statement.

1. PATTERNS

Because the statement of cash flows includes three separate sections, eight possible patterns of cash flows from the various sections exist. Chart 4–1 displays these possibilities.

Chart 4–1. Cash Flow Patterns								
Pattern	1.	2.	3.	4.	5.	6.	7.	8.
1. Operating Cash Flows	+	+	+	+	–	–	–	–
2. Investing Cash Flows	+	–	+	–	+	–	+	–
3. Financing Cash Flows	+	–	–	+	+	+	–	–

The first four patterns contain situations where an enterprise generated positive net cash flows from its operations, which usually denote a healthy enterprise that can use this cash to expand operations, satisfy long-term obligations, or provide a return on investment to its owners. In fact, if the enterprise is not investing in new equipment, a reader must wonder when the existing equipment will simply wear out or become obsolete.

The second four patterns describe situations in which the enterprise generated negative net cash flow from operations, which indicates that the enterprise's cash inflows from operations do not cover operating expenses. At some point, these cash flow deficits from operations will force the venture to sell assets, borrow from creditors, or raise additional funds from the owners to continue its operations. If this pattern continues over an extended period, the business will almost assuredly go bankrupt, like the W.T. Grant Company, as described on page 118, *supra.*

In pattern one, the enterprise generated cash from all three activities. In other words, the business generated a positive cash flow from operations, sold off capital assets, and raised additional capital. Although very unusual, such an enterprise obviously wants to increase its cash on hand. An enterprise usually uses positive cash from operations to expand by buying capital assets, to satisfy creditors by paying off debt, or to distribute profits to its owners.

Pattern two, arguably the pattern that all enterprises hope to fall under, shows that the business generated cash flow from internal operations and used the cash for investing activities, such as the purchase of property, plant, or equipment, and also spent the cash on its financing activities, like paying its debts or distributing earnings to owners. Mature businesses usually fall into this scenario. For example, Starbucks fell into this pattern during its fiscal 2010, 2011, and 2012.

In pattern three, the enterprise generated positive cash flow from operations and investing activities, most likely from selling capital assets. The business used this cash for financing activities, such as paying its creditors, investors, or both. This pattern may suggest that the enterprise has decided to downsize or restructure by selling assets to repay its debt or to buy out owners. The cash from operations did not cover the financing needs, so the sale of long-term assets raised additional cash to cover the difference.

Pattern four, typical of a growing business, demonstrates an enterprise that generated cash from operating and financing activities to buy long-term assets, which may include investments in non-operating assets, like securities.

In pattern five, the enterprise generated a negative cash flow from its operations. To cover this deficit and stay in business, the enterprise generated a positive cash flow from its investing activities, such as selling capital assets, and its financing activities, like seeking additional investments from owners or taking loans. An enterprise may endure this situation temporarily in hopes of a turnaround, but eventually the venture will face bankruptcy, as occurred with the W.T. Grant Company.

In pattern six, the enterprise generated cash from its financing activities by raising capital from creditors, owners or both to cover its operating cash flow deficit and provide resources to purchase additional capital assets. Young, fast-growing businesses typically fall into this category. The negative cash flow from operations may have resulted from large increases in inventory to prepare for expanded operations and sales. Investors may invest cash in such ventures, anticipating a return in the future. An enterprise may also fall under this pattern while expecting increased future sales.

In pattern seven, the enterprise probably sold off capital assets to support its operations and to pay creditors, to distribute cash to investors, or both. An enterprise in the process of liquidation or downsizing would fall under this pattern.

Finally, in pattern eight, an extremely unusual situation, the enterprise generated a negative cash flow in all of its activities. An enterprise could only survive these unusual circumstances until any cash originally on hand runs out.

When an unusual pattern, such as patterns one, three, five, seven, or eight, appears, an attorney should try to understand why the enterprise finds itself in that category. In such situations, the attorney should also consider the relative size of the cash inflows and outflows.

2. FREE CASH FLOW AND CASH FLOW FROM OPERATIONS COMPARED TO NET INCOME

Just as EBITDA has been used increasingly to measure and evaluate operating results, *free cash flow*, typically defined as cash flow from operating activities minus (1) capital expenditures for property, plant and equipment, (2) amounts spent to acquire businesses, net of any cash acquired, (3) investments in affiliated businesses, and (4) dividend payments, has become more important regarding cash flows. Once again, potential proceeds from the sale of property, plant and equipment, amounts from the sale of businesses, distributions from affiliated businesses illustrate the need to define this term precisely in any legal agreement. We can use Starbucks' Form 10-K for the fiscal year ended September 30, 2012 to calculate the company's free cash flow (in millions) for the fiscal years ending September 30, 2012 and October 2, 2011, respectively, as follows:

	2012	2011
Net cash provided by operating activities	$1,750.3	$1,612.4
Additions to property, plant and equipment	(856.2)	(531.9)
Acquisitions, net of cash acquired	(129.1)	(55.8)
Cash dividends paid	(513.0)	(389.5)
Free cash flow (in thousands)	$252.0	$635.2

As we can see, Starbucks' free cash flow dropped significantly during fiscal 2012.

While analyzing the patterns between the various activities, financial analysts also compare the cash flow from operations with net income. Four possible combinations exist as shown in Chart 4–2.

Chart 4–2. Cash Flow from Operations Compared to Net Income:				
Pattern	1.	2.	3.	4.
Cash Flows from Operating Activities	+	+	−	−
Net Income	+	−	+	−

Net cash flow from operations generally correlates to net income, but significant differences between the two may exist. We have already noted that a gain or loss upon the sale of a capital assets for cash will appear in net income but not in cash flow from operations. For another example, a capital intensive business, such as steel manufacturing with large depreciation expenses, may operate at a slight profit or even show a loss, but nevertheless generate significant cash flows from its operations. This normal situation should not alarm a reader of the enterprise's financial statements. On the other hand, non-normal situations, such as a net loss coupled with negative cash flows from operations for several periods, will occasionally arise, and the reader should scrutinize them carefully.

The difference between net income and operating cash flows results most commonly arises from timing differences. Recognition of revenue and expense under accrual accounting may or may not involve an inflow or outflow of cash. For example, as noted earlier, depreciation expense will affect net income, but not the cash flow from operations. Conversely, an item may affect cash in the period, but not net income, such as a prepayment of rent.

Predictable patterns do not exist. The user of the financial statements must investigate all the timing differences to see if they explain any disparity that may exist between net income and operating cash flow.

3.   MONTHLY CASH FLOW STATEMENTS

To supplement annual statements of cash flows, management typically uses budgeted monthly, and sometimes weekly or daily, cash flow statements to determine the amount of cash surplus or deficit that an enterprise will generate over a short period of time. Through the use of a budgeted monthly cash flow statement, management can readily determine if an enterprise will have excess cash or a cash shortfall in the near future. Armed with this knowledge, management may decide to make accelerated payments on its outstanding debt with any excess cash or to obtain short-term financing to cover any cash shortfalls.

4.   RATIO ANALYSIS

Historically, readers of financial statements usually limited their use of ratios to balance sheet and income statement amounts. The increased attention to cash flows in the business community, however, has led to greater interest in however, creditors and investors must increasingly rely on ratios based on cash flow information. For example, a study from the 1990s documents the importance of cash flow information in the loan assessment process. When ranking fifty-nine different ratios in order of importance to the processing of a loan, cash flow to current maturities of long term debt ranked third behind the debt to equity ratio and the current ratio. In addition, the cash flow to total debt ratio ranked ninth. The study also concluded that over sixty percent of all loan agreements included clauses involving the cash flow to current maturities of long term debt ratio. As the importance of the statement of cash flows increases, attorneys can expect to see and use these ratios much more frequently. Cash flow ratios typically fall into three categories: liquidity and coverage; profitability; and quality of income.

a.   LIQUIDITY AND COVERAGE

You will recall that liquidity and coverage ratios help assess an enterprise's ability to meet its debt obligations in the short and long run, pay dividends, and to cover anticipated operating expenses, such as payroll. Cash flow ratios in these categories typically provide information on the business's ability to meet its scheduled cash payments. Table 4–3 lists some of these ratios.

Most of the names for the liquidity and coverage formulas in Table 4–3 explain what information the ratios will provide to users. *Cash interest coverage* assesses whether an enterprise generates enough cash from operations to pay its interest payments. *Debt service coverage*, like cash interest coverage, relates to the ability of an enterprise to meet and retire its debt obligations, which include interest and principal payments. *Cash dividend coverage* demonstrates the business's ability to pay dividends with cash generated from operations after payment of taxes and interest. Finally, *cash flow from operations to capital expenditures ratio* informs the user about an enterprise's ability to purchase its current capital assets with cash flows from operations.

b. PROFITABILITY

As we have already seen, profitability ratios convey information about the ability of an enterprise to provide its investors with a return on their investment. Although many profitability cash flow ratios exist, Table 4–3 shows two important ratios. *Cash return on investment* provides information on the cash-generating ability of an enterprise's assets. *Cash flow per common share*, perhaps the most important ratio for closely-held companies, including private equity firms, furnishes the analyst with information about how much cash the enterprise generated for every share of common stock outstanding. This ratio almost mirrors earnings per share, a profitability ratio based on accrual accounting, so accounting pronouncements forbid its disclosure in the financial statements to avoid confusion. Because these cash return ratios contain no provision for the replacement of assets or existing contractual commitments, the cash returns will usually exceed their counterparts based on net income, especially for industrial enterprises.

c. QUALITY OF INCOME

Finally, cash flow ratios can fall into a new category called *quality of income*, or the ability of an enterprise to actually generate cash from the amount it reports as income from operations. These ratios allow the reader to assess how readily the enterprise converts net income to cash. For example, under accrual accounting, an enterprise may "book" revenues as an account receivable before the business actually receives cash from sales. The venture may also record expenses as accrued liabilities before it actually spends cash by paying the bill. An enterprise that takes a long time to receive cash from its sales and promptly pays its expenses would generate a low *cash quality of income ratio* because the net income significantly exceeds cash flow from operations. Although more difficult to calculate because of potentially unavailable information, *cash quality of income before interest, taxes, depreciation, and amortization*, more accurately reflects the effect of accrual accounting on net income as mentioned above. By removing the effects of interest, taxes, depreciation, and amortization on net income, this later ratio further highlights the timing differences arising from accrual accounting.

Enterprises obviously prefer positive cash flows from operations. In any event, a larger, positive difference between the numerator and the denominator in either ratio indicates a better cash quality of income. With regard to these quality of income ratios, however, please keep in mind that a negative number in either the numerator or the denominator signals danger. Although two negative numbers produce a positive ratio, please do not let such a situation mislead you!

Table 4–3 computes the cash flow ratios described in this section for Starbucks for the fiscal year ended September 30, 2012, using information obtained primarily from the consolidated statement of cash flows end on that date, which appears on page 52 of the company's Form 10-K for that fiscal year and in Appendix A on page 748, *infra*.

Table 4–3—Cash Flow Ratios (millions omitted)

Term or Ratio	Formula	Starbucks for 2012	Ratio
Liquidity and Coverage			
1. Cash Interest Coverage	$\dfrac{\text{CFFO}^a \text{ before Interest \& Taxes}}{\text{Interest Payments}}$	$2,201.6 b $34.4 c	64.0 times
2. Debt Service Coverage	$\dfrac{\text{CFFO before Interest \& Taxes}}{\text{Interest and Principal Payments}}$	$2,201.6 b $65.2 d	33.8 times
3. Cash Dividend Coverage	$\dfrac{\text{CFFO}}{\text{Total Cash Dividends}}$	$1,750.3 $513.0 e	3.4 times
4. Cash Flows from Operations to Capital Expenditures	$\dfrac{\text{CFFO – Total Dividends Paid}}{\text{Cash Paid to Acquire Property, Plant and Equipment}}$	$1,237.3 f $856.2 g	1.4 times
Profitability			
5. Cash Return on Investment	$\dfrac{\text{CFFO before Interest \& Taxes}}{\text{Average Total Assets}}$	$2,201.6 b $7,789.8 h	28.3%
6. Cash Flow per Common Share	$\dfrac{\text{CFFO – Preferred Stock Dividend Preferences}}{\text{Weighted Average Common Shares Outstanding}}$	$1,750.3 i 754.4 shares j	$2.32 per share
Quality of Income			
7. Cash Quality of Income	$\dfrac{\text{CFFO}}{\text{Net Income}}$	$1,750.3 $1,383.8 k	1.26
8. Cash Quality of Income before Interest, Taxes, Depreciation, and Amortization	$\dfrac{\text{CFFO before Interest and Taxes}}{\text{Net Income before Interest, Taxes, Depreciation, and Amortization}}$	$2,201.6 b $2,641.2 l	0.83

a. CFFO means Cash Flows from Operating Activities

b. $1,750.3 (Net cash provided by operating activities) + $34.4 (Interest, net of capitalized interest, paid during year) + $416.9 (Income taxes paid during year)

c. Interest, net of capitalized interest, paid during year

d. $34.4 (Interest, net of capitalized interest, paid during year) + $30.8 (Payments on short-term borrowings)

e. Cash dividends paid during year

f. $1,750.3 (CFFO) - $513.0 (Cash dividends paid)

g. Additions to property, plant and equipment

h. [$8,219.2 (Total assets on September 30, 2012) + $7,360.4 (Total assets on October 2, 2011)]/2

i. $1,750.3 (Net cash provided by operating activities) – $0 (no preferred stock preferences)

j. Weighted average number of common shares (basic) from income statement

k. Net earnings attributable to Starbucks from consolidated statement of earnings

l. $1,383.8 (Net earnings attributable to Starbucks) + $674.4 (Income taxes from consolidated statements of earnings) + $32.7 (Interest expense from consolidated statements of earnings) + $550.3 (Depreciation and amortization expenses from consolidated statements of earnings)

For the fiscal year ended October 2, 2011, we could compute the same ratios for Starbucks as follows (millions omitted):

Term or Ratio	Formula	Starbucks for 2011	Ratio
Liquidity and Coverage			
1. Cash Interest Coverage	$\dfrac{\text{CFFO}^a \text{ before Interest \& Taxes}}{\text{Interest Payments}}$	$1,996.9 b $34.4 c	58.0 times
2. Debt Service Coverage	$\dfrac{\text{CFFO before Interest \& Taxes}}{\text{Interest and Principal Payments}}$	$1,996.9 b $34.4 d	58.0 times
3. Cash Dividend Coverage	$\dfrac{\text{CFFO}}{\text{Total Cash Dividends}}$	$1,612.4 $389.5 e	4.1 times
4. Cash Flows from Operations to Capital Expenditures	$\dfrac{\text{CFFO – Total Dividends Paid}}{\text{Cash Paid to Acquire Property, Plant and Equipment}}$	$1,222.9 f $531.9 g	2.3 times
Profitability			
5. Cash Return on Investment	$\dfrac{\text{CFFO before Interest \& Taxes}}{\text{Average Total Assets}}$	$1,996.9 b $6,873.15 h	29.1%
6. Cash Flow per Common Share	$\dfrac{\text{CFFO – Preferred Stock Dividend Preferences}}{\text{Weighted Average Common Shares Outstanding}}$	$1,612.4 i 748.3 shares j	$2.15 per share
Quality of Income			
7. Cash Quality of Income	$\dfrac{\text{CFFO}}{\text{Net Income}}$	$1,612.4 $1,245.7 k	1.29
8. Cash Quality of Income before Interest, Taxes, Depreciation, and Amortization	$\dfrac{\text{CFFO before Interest and Taxes}}{\text{Net Income before Interest, Taxes, Depreciation, and Amortization}}$	$1,996.9 b $2,365.4 l	0.84

a. CFFO means Cash Flows from Operating Activities

b. $1,612.4 (Net cash provided by operating activities) + $34.4 (Interest, net of capitalized interest, paid during year) + $350.1 (Income taxes paid during year)

c. Interest, net of capitalized interest, paid during year

d. $34.4 (Interest, net of capitalized interest, paid during year) + $0 (Principal payments on debt)

e. Cash dividends paid during year

f. $1,612.4 (CFFO) - $389.5 (Cash dividends paid)

g. Additions to property, plant and equipment

h. [$7,360.4 (Total assets on October 2, 2011) + $6,385.9 (Total assets on October 3, 2010)]/2

i. $1,612.4 (Net cash provided by operating activities) – $0 (no preferred stock preferences)

j. Weighted average number of common shares (basic) from income statement

k. Net earnings attributable to Starbucks from consolidated statement of earnings

l. $1,245.7 (Net earnings attributable to Starbucks) + $563.1 (Income taxes from consolidated statements of earnings) + $33.3 (Interest expense from consolidated statements of earnings) + $523.3 (Depreciation and amortization expenses from consolidated statements of earnings)

For the fiscal year ended September 30, 2012, Starbucks' cash interest coverage ratio increased, but not meaningfully. Even at the end of fiscal 2011, Starbucks could still cover its interest payments more than fifty-eight times. The debt service coverage dropped from this same number to almost thirty-four times, which still reflects excellent debt service coverage. Between fiscal 2011 and fiscal 2012, the company's cash dividend coverage ratio declined from 4.1 times to 3.4 times. More troubling, the ratio comparing cash flows from operations to capital expenditures fell from 2.3 times in fiscal 2011 to 1.4 times in fiscal 2012, in part because Starbucks paid more than an additional $300 million to acquire property, plant and equipment as cash outlays rose from $531.9 million in fiscal 2011 to $856.2 million in fiscal 2012.

Starbucks' profitability also declined during fiscal 2012. The cash return on investment dropped from 29.1 percent in fiscal 2011 to 28.3 percent in fiscal 2012. Although no industry figures exist in the public domain, even the 28.3 percent seems quite impressive, considering that the company's cash flow per common share increased from $2.15 per share in fiscal 2011 to $2.32 per share in fiscal 2012, an almost eight percent increase.

Starbucks' quality of income dropped according to both measures during fiscal 2012. The cash quality of income ratio declined from 1.29 in fiscal 2011 to 1.26 in fiscal 2012. Similarly, the cash quality of income before interest, taxes, and depreciation inched down from 0.84 in fiscal 2011 to 0.83 in fiscal 2012. While Starbucks' cash quality of income ratio exceeded 1.0 during both fiscal years, the cash quality of income before interest, taxes, and depreciation did not exceed 1.0 in either year.

Of course, financial analysts find many other ratios useful in evaluating financial statements. For our purposes, it is enough to get some sense of what such ratios might involve and to pay attention to the potential implications of financial analysis. Soon, we will turn our primary attention to the accounting processes which underlie the figures recorded on the financial statements.

PROBLEMS

Problem 4.6A. Using the consolidated statement of cash flows and miscellaneous information for Amazon.com for the years ended December 31, 2012 and December 31, 2011, the consolidated balance sheets as of those dates, and the consolidated statements of operations for the years ended on those dates:

(1) Compute the financial ratios listed in Table 4–3 for 2012 and 2011.

(2) Do you see any trends compared to 2011 worth noting?

Problem 4.6B. Using the consolidated statement of cash flows and miscellaneous information for Google for the years ended December 31, 2012 and December 31, 2011, the consolidated balance sheets as of those dates, and the consolidated statements of income for the years ended on those dates:

(1) Compute the financial ratios listed in Table 4–3 for 2012 and 2011.

(2) Do you see any trends compared to 2011 worth noting?

Problem 4.6C. Using the statements of consolidated cash flows and miscellaneous information for UPS for the years ended December 31, 2012 and December 31, 2011, the consolidated balance sheets as of those dates, and the statements of consolidated income for the years ended on those dates:

(1) Compute the financial ratios listed in Table 4–3 for 2012 and 2011.

(2) Do you see any trends compared to 2011 worth noting?

G. MANAGEMENT'S DISCUSSION AND ANALYSIS

As one of the essential parts of an annual report which we discussed earlier in the chapter, the federal proxy rules applicable to publicly-held companies direct a registrant to discuss and analyze the enterprise's financial condition and results of operations. This requirement, as well as other rules that compel a registrant to file periodic reports with the SEC, help furnish information about the enterprise to the investing public. For these and other purposes, the SEC has adopted Regulation S–K to provide standard instructions for registrants filing forms under the federal securities laws.

Item 303 of Regulation S–K requires registrants to discuss their financial condition, including liquidity and capital resources, changes in financial condition and operating results, and other information necessary to understand the financial statements, in both the annual report sent to shareholders and the periodic reports filed with the SEC. The financial community refers to these requirements as *Management's Discussion and Analysis*, sometimes abbreviated to *MD&A*. Recognizing that the traditional dry recitation of numbers and the accompanying often boilerplate notes to financial statements rarely allowed an investor "to judge the *quality of earnings* and the likelihood that past performance is indicative of future performance" the MD&A rules seek to offer the reader both historical and prospective analysis of the financial statements, with an emphasis on the future of the business. Fundamentally, the MD&A section strives to give investors an opportunity to view the business "through the eyes of management." Management's Discussion and Analysis of Financial Condition and Results of Operations; Certain Investment Company Disclosures, Financial Reporting Release No. 36, 54 Fed. Reg. 22,427, 22,428 (May 24, 1989) (emphasis added).

1. THE PURPOSE OF REQUIRED DISCLOSURE IN MD&A

After reviewing the MD&A filings of more than 200 registrants in 1988, the SEC found that nearly all of the MD&A sections did not comply with the regulations. Consequently, the SEC published the following release to clarify its position on required MD&A disclosures. The following excerpts represent the SEC's best statement of the goals and purposes of MD&A.

Financial Reporting Release No. 36

Securities and Exchange Commission, 1989.
54 Fed. Reg. 22,427, 22,428–29, 22,436.

III. Evaluation of Disclosure—Interpretive Guidance

A. Introduction

The MD&A requirements are intended to provide, in one section of a filing, material historical and prospective textual disclosure enabling investors and other users to assess the financial condition and results of operations of the registrant, with particular emphasis on the registrant's prospects for the future. * * *

The Commission has long recognized the need for a narrative explanation of the financial statements, because a numerical presentation and brief accompanying footnotes alone may be insufficient for an investor to judge the quality of earnings and the likelihood that past performance is indicative of future performance. MD&A is intended to give the investor an opportunity to look at the company through the eyes of management by providing both a short and long-term analysis of the business of the company. * * *

* * *

B. Prospective Information

Several specific provisions in Item 303 require disclosure of forward-looking information. MD&A requires discussions of "known trends or any known demands, commitments, events or uncertainties that will result in or that are reasonably likely to result in the registrants' liquidity increasing or decreasing in any material way." * * * Disclosure of known trends or uncertainties that the registrant reasonably expects will have a material impact on net sales, revenues, or income from continuing operations is also required. Finally, the Instructions to Item 303 state that MD&A "shall focus specifically on material events and uncertainties known to management that would cause reported financial information not to be necessarily indicative of future operating results or future financial condition."

* * * [T]he distinction between prospective information that is required to be discussed and voluntary forward-looking disclosure is an area requiring additional attention. * * *

* * * The distinction between the two rests with the nature of the prediction required. Required disclosure is based on *currently known trends, events, and uncertainties that are reasonably expected to have material effects,* such as: A reduction in the registrant's product prices; erosion in the registrant's market share; changes in insurance coverage; or the likely non-renewal of a material contract. In contrast, optional forward-looking disclosure involves *anticipating a future trend or event or anticipating a less predictable impact of a known event, trend or uncertainty.*

* * *

IV. Conclusion

In preparing MD&A disclosure, registrants should be guided by the general purpose of the MD&A requirements: to give investors an opportunity to look at the registrant through the eyes of management by providing a historical and prospective analysis of the registrant's financial condition and results of operations, with particular emphasis on the registrant's prospects for the future. The MD&A requirements are intentionally flexible and general. Because no two registrants are identical, good MD&A disclosure for one registrant is not necessarily good MD&A disclosure for another. The same is true for MD&A disclosure of the same registrant in different years. * * *

NOTES

1. The SEC has promulgated rules that establish a safe harbor for disclosure of "forward-looking information." 17 C.F.R. §§ 230.175(c), 240.3b–6 (2014). The rules define "forward-looking information" to include statements regarding "future economic performance contained in" MD&A. In FRR No. 36, the SEC observed that these safe harbors apply to both required statements concerning the future effect of known trends, demands, commitments, events or uncertainties and optional forward-looking statements.

2. In the Private Securities Litigation Reform Act of 1995, Congress added safe harbor provisions for forward-looking statements to both the Securities Act of 1933 and the Securities Exchange Act of 1934. Both safe harbors specifically apply to qualifying statements in MD&A unless the plaintiff can prove that the person making or the executive officer approving the statement had "actual knowledge * * * that the statement was false or misleading."

3. Shortly after Enron filed its bankruptcy petition in December 2001, the SEC issued a statement that encouraged public companies to explain in plain English in their MD&A their "critical accounting policies;" the assumptions, estimates, and other judgments or uncertainties affecting the application of those policies; and the likelihood that the company would report different amounts under different conditions or using different objectives. Cautionary Advice Regarding Disclosure About Critical Accounting Policies, Financial Reporting Release No. 60, 66 Fed. Reg. 65,013 (Dec. 17, 2001).

Less than six months later, the SEC issued proposed rules that would require issuers and registrants to include a separately captioned section regarding the application of critical accounting policies in the MD&A section of various securities filings. The rules would require disclosures about both the critical accounting estimates used to apply the company's accounting policies and the initial adoption of certain accounting policies. Disclosure in Management's Discussion and Analysis about the Application of Critical Accounting Policies, 67 Fed. Reg. 35,620 (proposed May 20, 2002). Although the SEC never adopted the proposed rules, the SEC did announce additional interpretive guidance regarding MD&A. The guidance came in a release that sought to elicit more meaningful disclosure about, among other things, critical accounting estimates. Commission Guidance Regarding Management's Discussion and Analysis of Financial Condition and Results of Operations, Financial Reporting Release No. 72, 68 Fed. Reg. 75,056 (Dec. 29, 2003).

4. Of particular relevance to MD&A, SOx section 401(a) directed the SEC to issue final rules to require each annual and quarterly report that registrants file with the Commission to disclose "all material off-balance sheet transactions, arrangements, obligations (including contingent obligations), and other relationships of the issuer with unconsolidated entities or other persons, that may have a material current or future effect on financial condition, changes in financial condition, results of operations, liquidity, capital expenditures, capital resources, or significant components of revenues or expenses." Pursuant to that charge, the SEC issued final regulations in early 2003 that require registrants to explain their off-balance sheet arrangements in a separately captioned subsection of the MD&A portion of various disclosure documents. The rules also require a registrant other than a small business issuer to disclose in tabular format somewhere in the MD&A section the amounts of payments due under certain known contractual obligations, as of the latest fiscal year-end balance sheet date. Disclosure in Management's Discussion and Analysis About Off-Balance Sheet Arrangements and Aggregate Contractual Obligations, 68 Fed. Reg. 5982 (Feb. 5, 2003), *available at* http://www.sec.gov/rules/final/33-8182.htm.

5. The MD&A in Starbucks' Form 10-K for the fiscal year ended September 30, 2012 appears on pages 25 to 49 of that document, which you can find in Appendix A on pages 721 to 745, *infra.* The overview appears on page 25 to 27. The sections addressing results of operations; financial condition, liquidity and capital resources; contractual obligations; off-balance sheet arrangements; and critical accounting policies begin on pages 27, 41, 43, 44, and 46, respectively.

We highlight several items in Starbucks' MD&A for fiscal 2012. The company's consolidated net revenues increased fourteen percent during fiscal 2012 compared to fiscal 2011. Comparable store sales at company-operated establishments increased seven percent during fiscal 2012. A six percent growth in the number of customer transactions and a one percent increase in the average value per transaction explained the rise in comparable store sales. Starbucks expected "mid single-digit increased comparable store sales" during fiscal 2013. Starbucks Corp., Annual Report (Form 10-K) 25-26 (Nov. 16, 2012).

Increased sales and the absence of charges in fiscal 2012 related to the closing of Seattle's Best Coffee stores in Border's bookstores during fiscal 2011 more than offset higher commodity costs in fiscal 2012 and gains from the sale of real estate and a fair market value adjustment arising from the acquisition of the Starbucks' joint venture in Switzerland and Austria in the fiscal 2011 to boost the company's operating profit margin from 14.8 percent in fiscal 2011 to 15.0 percent in fiscal 2012. *Id.* at 25. In fiscal 2013, Starbucks expected "robust consolidated operating margin and EPS improvement compared to fiscal 2012." *Id.* at 26.

With regard to financial condition, liquidity and capital resources, Starbucks's foreign subsidiaries held approximately $703 million of the consolidated group's $1,188.6 million in cash and cash equivalents on September 30, 2012. If Starbucks needed to repatriate any of those foreign funds to the United States, the company would owe additional income taxes in the United States. For fiscal 2013, Starbucks expected to spend approximately $1.2 billion for capital expenditures to remodel and refurbish existing company-owned stores, to upgrade equipment in those stores, to enhance systems and technology in the stores and in the support infrastructure, to open new company-operated stores, and to add manufacturing capacity. The company believed that future cash flows from operations and existing cash and short-term investments would fund such capital expenditures and distributions to shareholders for the foreseeable future. To provide additional liquidity, in 2013, Starbucks entered into an arrangement with various banks that enabled the company to borrow up to $500 million, and perhaps an additional $500 million, on an unsecured basis. This credit facility also backed a commercial paper program that allowed Starbucks to issue unsecured commercial paper with maturities that could not exceed 397 days from the date of issue. As of September 30, 2012, only $18 million in letters of credit remained outstanding under the credit facility. *Id.* at 41-42.

Starbucks' management listed the company's policies on asset impairment, goodwill impairment, self insurance reserves, income taxes, and litigation accruals as the company's most critical accounting policies. *Id.* at 46-49. Finally, the MD&A cross-referenced the first note to the consolidated financial statements for a detailed description about the expected immaterial effects from various new accounting pronouncements on the company's financial statements. *Id.* at 49.

Although not included in the MD&A, by 2014 Starbucks expected to operate or license 20,000 stores on six continents. In addition, Starbucks planned to open 3,000 new stores over the next five years in the Americas region alone, which included the United States, Canada, and Latin America. Starbucks Corp., Fiscal 2012 Annual Report 2 (2012). As of September 30, 2012, the company reported 18,066 stores globally. This number included 11,128 stores in the United States (6,866 company-operated establishments and 4,262 licensed locations) and 6,938 international locations (2,539 company-operated establishments and 4,399 licensed locations). During fiscal 2012, Starbucks opened 398 net stores, up from 141 net openings in fiscal 2011. The bankruptcy of Borders Bookstores caused 475 licensed Seattle's Best Coffee locations to close during fiscal 2011. Starbucks Corp., Annual Report

(Form 10-K) 3-4, 6 (Nov. 16, 2012). (At one point, Starbucks' long-term plans called for 20,000 retail locations in the United States, plus at least an additional 20,000 stores worldwide. Starbucks Corp., Annual Report (Form 10-K) 21 (Dec. 16, 2005).)

2.   COMPLIANCE WITH GAAP ALONE DOES NOT SATISFY MD&A REQUIREMENTS

In the 1990s, the MD&A section became a focal point for the SEC's enforcement activities. Linda Quinn, former director of the SEC's Division of Corporation Finance, described MD&A as one of the "linchpin[s] of the disclosure system." She also emphasized that the SEC intended to continue to "press heavily" for companies to disclose information not reflected in their historic financial statements that would likely affect their future. In 1992, the SEC announced the settlement of its first enforcement action against a registrant for alleged shortcomings in its MD&A, although its financial statements complied with GAAP. *See In re* Caterpillar Inc., Accounting and Auditing Enforcement Release No. 363, [1991–1995 Transfer Binder] Fed. Sec. L. Rep. (CCH) ¶ 73,830 (Mar. 31, 1992), 1992 WL 71907 (S.E.C.). Caterpillar's wholly owned Brazilian subsidiary, Caterpillar Brasil, S.A. ("CBSA"), enjoyed an unusually good year in 1989, accounting for some twenty-three percent of Caterpillar's net profits, though CSBA's revenues represented only five percent of the consolidated revenues. Nonoperating items, many of which arose from the hyper-inflation in Brazil and the related currency exchange rate, explained Caterpillar's success. As GAAP permitted, Caterpillar presented CBSA's financial results on a consolidated basis with the remainder of Caterpillar's operations, which essentially hid the impact of CBSA's contributions to Caterpillar's overall results. Early in 1990, political and economic developments in Brazil sent strong signals that not only was CBSA unlikely to repeat its exceptional 1989 performance, but that the subsidiary was likely to suffer a loss, which would produce an material adverse effect on Caterpillar's bottom line in 1990.

The SEC pointed out that Item 303(a) of Regulation S-K required Caterpillar to describe "any unusual or infrequent events or transactions . . . that materially affected the amount of reported income" and to discuss "any known trends or uncertainties that . . . the registrant reasonably expects will have a material favorable or unfavorable impact on net sales or revenues or income . . . ." Hence, Caterpillar should have described CBSA's impact on the consolidated operating results and disclosed the known uncertainty as to CBSA's ability to repeat its 1989 performance in Caterpillar's MD&A.

The SEC has continued to bring enforcement actions against registrants for inadequate disclosures about their financial statements even though those statements complied with GAAP. These actions document the SEC's positions that (a) the disclosures must occur in the MD&A section, rather than in press releases, (b) MD&A must discuss material unusual or nonrecurring items and their effect on the "quality of [both current and expected future] earnings;"

and (c) MD&A must discuss "known trends" or practices likely to affect future financial statements in a material way.

In another case involving a registrant that did not violate GAAP, Sony Corporation ("Sony") settled administrative charges arising from the company's failure to disclose losses in its Sony Pictures Entertainment Inc. subsidiary ("SP") in the MD&A sections of its annual reports for the fiscal year ended March 31, 1994. This inadequate disclosure occurred during the several months before Sony wrote down about $2.7 billion in goodwill related to SP's acquisition. Despite the expressed preference of its outside auditors and own financial officers, Sony did not report the results of SP as a separate industry segment. Instead, the company reported the combined results of SP and Sony's profitable music business as a single "entertainment" segment. This treatment obscured the approximately $967 million in net losses that SP had incurred after the acquisition and before the close of the fiscal year ended March 31, 1994, which the SEC described as a "known trend." In addition, Sony's filings failed to disclose that the company had been considering for more than a year the possible need to write down a substantial part of the goodwill attributable to SP for more than a year. As part of the settlement, Sony agreed among other things to engage an independent auditor to examine its MD&A presentation for the fiscal year ending March 31, 1999. In March 1998, the AICPA had issued standards setting forth the procedures that an auditor should undertake when examining a registrant's MD&A in such an engagement. *In re* Sony Corp., Accounting and Auditing Enforcement Release No. 1061, [1995-1998 Transfer Binder] Fed. Sec. L. Rep. (CCH) ¶ 74,574 (Aug. 5, 1998), 1998 WL 439898 (S.E.C.).

In 2005, the SEC brought and settled cease-and-desist proceedings against The Coca-Cola Company ("Coca-Cola") on the grounds that the company failed to disclose certain end-of-quarter sales practices used to meet earnings expectations and that would likely affect the company's future operating results. Through a process known as "gallon pushing," or more generically as "channel stuffing," between 1997 and 1999 Coca-Cola offered Japanese bottlers favorable credit terms to induce them to purchase beverage concentrate that they otherwise would not have purchased until a later fiscal period. Without admitting or denying the SEC's findings, Coca-Cola consented to an administrative order finding that the company had violated antifraud and periodic reporting requirements in the federal securities laws. The company also voluntarily implemented measures to strengthen its internal disclosure review process. *In re* Coca-Cola Co., Accounting and Auditing Enforcement Release No. 2232, 7 Fed. Sec. L. Rep. (CCH) ¶ 75,894 (Apr. 18, 2005), http://www.sec.gov/litigation/admin/33- 8569.pdf.

More recently, in 2007 Tenet Healthcare Corporation ("Tenet") agreed to pay a $10 million civil penalty to settle SEC charges that, among other things, the company's MD&As misled the investing public. In particular, Tenet failed to disclose that the company had exploited a loophole in the Medicare reimbursement system related to so-called "outlier payments," designed to compensate hospitals for caring for extraordinarily sick Medicare patients. This unsustainable strategy allowed Tenet to report strong growth in revenues and earnings from 1999 to 2002. Once Tenet admitted that it could not sustain this strategy, its shares lost more than $11 billion in market value. SEC v. Tenet Healthcare Corp., Accounting and Auditing Enforcement Release No. 2591 (Apr. 2, 2007), http://www.sec.gov/litigation/litreleases/2007/lr20067.htm. In addition, a federal district court enjoined Tenet's former chief compliance officer, executive vice president, and general counsel from violating various federal securities laws and ordered her to pay one dollar in disgorgement and a $120,000 civil penalty for either knowingly or recklessly failing to grasp Tenet's unsustainable strategy to inflate its Medicare revenues and failing to disclose that unsustainable strategy. The SEC also issued an administrative order suspending her from appearing or practicing before the agency as an attorney. *See In re* Sulzbach, Accounting and Auditing Enforcement Release No. 3000 (June 25, 2009), http://www.sec.gov/litigation/admin/2009/34-60170.pdf.

Although the SEC has pursued only a limited number of these disclosure cases, these administrative proceedings document the importance that the SEC places on MD&A and highlight the types of prospective information that a reader can expect to find in MD&A in the future.

3. Enforcement Issues Arising From Liquidity Problems

The SEC has brought other enforcement actions involving failures to disclose known liquidity problems. In one such proceeding against America West Airlines Inc., the SEC criticized the airline for failing to disclose in the MD&A section serious financial difficulties that made continuing operations unlikely:

> Specifically, America West's MD&A disclosure in its Report on Form 10–K for the year ended December 31, 1990, failed to discuss fully uncertainties related to its ability to meet its financial covenants. Instead, the MD&A discussion stated the following:

> > At December 31, 1990, the Company was not in compliance with certain of the covenants. Waivers were secured for such violations and during the first quarter of 1991, amended covenants were established. The Company anticipates to be in compliance with such amended covenants . . . .

> Such disclosure did not adequately address the known uncertainties relating to America West's liquidity position at that time. The Company had failed to comply with the leverage covenant provision in November 1990. Subsequently, management faced uncertainties about the Company's ability to comply with its covenants. These uncertainties are illustrated by management's request to the Board in January 1991 for authority to amend the Company's financial covenants as needed to avoid violating such covenants. In fact, on January 31, 1991, two days after management received authority from the Board to amend its financial covenants on an ongoing basis, the Company did fail to comply with its January $100 million cash covenant provision. Furthermore, the

Company's failure to comply with its covenant provisions in November and January gave rise to events of default. Consequently, in both instances the lenders had the option of rendering the debt immediately due and payable.

Furthermore, the MD&A disclosure failed to discuss as required the known material uncertainties relating to the Company's ability to obtain the financing necessary to remedy its liquidity problems. Indeed, rather than addressing America West's liquidity position directly, the MD&A disclosure stated the following about the Company's efforts to obtain financing:

> In spite of the net loss incurred in 1990 and the anticipated net loss for the first quarter of 1991, the Company believes that its present capital commitments can be met as they become due with existing capital resources, its ability to obtain additional financing and its anticipation of improved operating results beyond the first quarter 1991.

While the MD&A did state that the Company's ability to meet its capital commitments was, in part, dependent upon its ability to obtain additional financing, it did not disclose that the Company was primarily dependent on external financing to remedy its liquidity problems. Further, the MD&A did not discuss as required the known uncertainties related to its ability to obtain such financing.

In re America West Airlines, Inc., Accounting and Auditing Enforcement Release No. 562, [1991–1995 Transfer Binder] Fed. Sec. L. Rep. (CCH) ¶ 74,022 (May 12, 1994). Management's failure to discuss these known liquidity problems in the MD&A section prevented investors from seeing the company "through the eyes of management."

More recently, the SEC brought separate public administrative proceedings against Terex Corporation ("Terex"), its former chairman, and others for inadequately disclosing an accounting adjustment and its effect on the current liabilities of Terex and Fruehauf Trailer Corp. ("Fruehauf"). The accounting adjustment caused Fruehauf to fail to meet specified financial ratios in long-term loans totaling $82.7 million from various financial institutions and to violate certain loan covenants, which gave the lenders the right to accelerate the loans. In such circumstances, FASB ASC Topic 470, *Liabilities*, which codified SFAS No. 78, *Classification of Obligations that are Callable by the Creditor*, requires that the borrower reclassify the underlying long-term obligation as a current liability. Because Fruehauf continued to classify the $82.7 million as long-term liabilities, both Fruehauf and its ultimate parent, Terex, understated their current liabilities. *In re* Terex Corp., Accounting and Auditing Enforcement Release No. 1126, [1999–2001 Transfer Binder] Fed. Sec. L. Rep. (CCH) ¶ 74,633 (Apr. 20, 1999), 1999 WL 228426 (S.E.C.).

Even before the credit crisis, which has only highlighted the importance of discussions about liquidity in MD&A, SEC officials publicly stated that

MD&A disclosure failures remained a top enforcement priority. In 2009, a jury returned a verdict in the SEC's favor on civil charges the agency filed against Kmart's former CEO for material misrepresentations and omissions about the company's liquidity in the MD&A section of Kmart's Form 10-Q for the third quarter and nine months ended October 31, 2001. Kmart filed for bankruptcy in early 2002. The SEC's complaint alleged the company's former CEO and former CFO failed to disclose the reasons for a massive inventory overbuy in the summer of 2001 and the impact it had on the company's liquidity. The former CFO agreed to settle shortly before trial. In 2010, the district court entered an amended final judgment that ordered the former CEO to pay $5.5 million, including $3 million in disgorgement and a $2.5 million civil penalty. SEC v. Conaway, Litigation Release No. 21,745 (Nov. 17, 2010), http://www.sec.gov/litigation/litreleases/2010/lr21745.htm; *see also* Michael Bologna, *Firms Getting Disclosure Message, But MD&A Still Enforcement Priority*, 38 Sec. Reg. & L. Rep. (BNA) 867 (May 15, 2006).

In 2010, the SEC provided additional guidance on the disclosures related to liquidity and capital resources in MD&A. The SEC observed that liquidity constraints caused numerous failures in the recent financial crisis. The SEC also identified certain additional known trends and uncertainties that materially affect liquidity and that may require disclosure, including difficulties accessing debt markets, reliance on commercial paper or other short-term financing arrangements, and maturity mismatches between borrowing sources and the assets that those sources fund. In addition, the SEC suggested that if borrowings during a reporting period differ materially from the period-end amounts reported in the financial statements, an enterprise should disclose information about variations during the period so that investors can better understand the enterprise's liquidity. Commission Guidance on Presentation of Liquidity and Capital Resources Disclosures in Management's Discussion and Analysis, Financial Reporting Release No. 83, 75 Fed. Reg. 59,894 (Sept. 28, 2010), *available at* http://www.sec.gov/rules/interp/2010/33-9144fr.pdf. The release offers the insight that liquidity analysis should focus on a period in time rather than a point in time and highlights issues that all lawyers, including those working on matters involving private companies, should keep in mind when evaluating an enterprise's liquidity and leverage.

PROBLEMS

Problem 4.7. Locate Starbucks' MD&As for the most recent fiscal periods. You can obtain this information from EDGAR at http://www.sec.gov or via the "Investor Relations" link under "the Company" heading on Starbucks' home page at http://www.starbucks.com. You can find Starbucks' MD&A for the fiscal year ended September 30, 2012 in Appendix A on pages 721 to 745, *infra*. In addition to the discussion on those pages, do you find anything in the 2013 or more recent MD&As that conveys Starbucks' prospects for the future? Explain briefly.

Problem 4.8A. Locate Amazon.com's MD&As for the year ended December 31, 2012 and for the most recent fiscal period. You can obtain this information from EDGAR at http://www.sec.gov or via the "About Amazon.com" link at the bottom of the company's home page at www.amazon.com. Do you find anything in the 2013 or more recent MD&As that forecasts Amazon.com's prospects for the future? Explain briefly.

Problem 4.8B. Locate Google's MD&As for the year ended December 31, 2012 and for the most recent fiscal period. You can obtain this information from EDGAR at http://www.sec.gov or via Google's home page at www.google.com (select the "About Google" link; under the "Our Company" section, select the "Investor Relations" link). Do you find anything in the 2013 or more recent MD&As that forecasts Google's prospects for the future? Explain briefly.

Problem 4.8C. Locate UPS's MD&As for the year ended December 31, 2012 and for the most recent fiscal period. You can obtain this information from EDGAR at http://www.sec.gov or via the company's Investor Relations website at http://www.shareholder.com/ups/ (under the heading "Investor Kit," select "SEC Filings"). Do you find anything in the 2012 or more recent MD&As that forecasts UPS's prospects for the future? Explain briefly.

H.   THE FUTURE OF FINANCIAL AND NON-FINANCIAL REPORTING

Investment analysts and other users of financial statements often criticize the current financial accounting model, which generally uses historical cost to present quantitative information and ignores many intangibles that have dramatically influenced the "new economy." As mentioned in Chapter I on pages 67 to 68, *supra*, FASB has already begun to take steps toward a fair value-based system, which could eventually require enterprises to report all financial assets and liabilities at fair value.

More fundamentally, critics of the current model increasingly have called upon enterprises to reveal indicators that management tracks on a regular basis to assess the business's performance. For example, an enterprise might disclose key trends in operating or performance data; management's analysis of changes in such data; forward-looking information about such things as opportunities, risks and management's plans; or information about order backlogs, market share, new products, revenue per transaction, revenue per employee, customer acquisition costs, customer satisfaction, costs per unit, and intangible assets, especially those intangibles not currently included in financial statements. Ultimately, securities regulators or accounting rule-makers may develop a framework regarding the types of supplemental and non-financial information that enterprises should provide to investors. In the meantime, however, leadership in this area will likely come from individual companies and industries that provide voluntary disclosures. Public companies increasingly disclose such information in MD&A. *See generally* Richard I. Miller & Michael R. Young, *Financial Reporting and Risk Management in the 21st Century*, 65 FORDHAM L. REV. 1987 (1997) (discussing (1) the potential liability arising from improvements in financial reporting systems, which would presumably move away from objectively verifiable data and towards more subjective information, thereby increasing the opportunity for second-guessing and hence the enterprise's exposure to litigation, and (2) how individuals and organizations responsible for structuring financial reporting relationships can manage that liability both to facilitate honest financial reporting and to give financial reporting systems the flexibility to evolve).

Without setting a deadline, SOx section 409 directed the SEC to move towards "real-time" disclosure. That section authorized the Commission to issue any rules requiring rapid and current disclosures regarding material changes in financial condition or operations deemed "necessary or useful for the protection of investors and in the public interest." Sarbanes-Oxley Act of 2002, Pub. L. No. 107-204, § 409, 116 Stat. 745, 791.

In 2009, and after a successful voluntary program that allowed public companies to file financial reports using eXtensible Business Reporting Language ("XBRL"), a computer language that makes financial data interactive, the SEC issued a final rule that obligates public companies to provide their financial statements to the agency and on their corporate websites in interactive data format using XBRL. By October 31, 2014, the grace and amnesty periods that the SEC had announced for any tagging mistakes during the first twenty-four months that the XBRL requirements applied to a particular company had expired. When preparers accurately "tag" various kinds of information, users can retrieve and efficiently analyze data found in financial reports. Using XBRL, for example, could enable users to compare financial results under U.S. GAAP and IFRSs.

The SEC believes that XBRL will make financial data more useful to investors because the technology allows them to download the information from the financial statements directly into spreadsheets, analyze it using commercial off-the-shelf software, and use the information within investment models in other software formats. Critics have complained that the actual benefits have not exceeded the costs necessary to tag the data in the financial statements and related notes. In early 2013, a Columbia Business School study reported responses showing that less than ten percent of investors and analysts surveyed actually used XBRL-tagged data.

In addition to formalizing arrangements to modernize the online EDGAR filing database to accommodate the XBRL format, the SEC announced plans in 2008 to replace the EDGAR system with the Interactive Data Electronic Application ("IDEA") system. The SEC expected that IDEA would facilitate the use and analysis of information submitted to the agency in interactive data format and allow quick comparisons of different companies or various fiscal periods, but the financial crisis, other priorities, and budget cuts have postponed, if not cancelled, the project. The financial crisis and other priorities have postponed, if not cancelled, the project.

In 2010, FASB and FAF, its parent organization, assumed ongoing development and maintenance responsibilities for the [U.S.] GAAP Financial Reporting Taxonomy ("UGT"), a task that contemplates a new UGT each year. In June 2014, the SEC approved the 2014 U.S. GAAP Financial Reporting

Taxonomy, which organizes and standardizes thousands of elements that public companies can use to identify and tag pieces of data in their financial reports. The number of elements changes each year as new versions adopt tags that users suggest, add tags to reflect new rules in the Codification, and ongoing reviews remove elements redundant or no longer necessary under current GAAP. The SEC's website maintains only the current-year taxonomy and the immediately prior version so the agency's staff strongly encourages public companies to use the most recently approved UGT to access all the up-to-date tags relating to new accounting standards and other improvements.

On the international front, in March 2014 the IASCF released *IFRS Taxonomy 2014*, which translates both IFRS and IFRS for SMEs into XBRL. The 2014 taxonomy also contains XBRL tags for all IFRS disclosure requirements.

*

CHAPTER V

LEGAL ISSUES INVOLVING SHAREHOLDERS' EQUITY AND THE BALANCE SHEET

A. IMPORTANCE TO LAWYERS

As explained more fully in Chapter I, shareholders own the residual claim to a corporation's assets, which is usually called shareholders' equity. This residual claim appears on a corporation's balance sheet as the difference between the company's assets and liabilities, both traditionally recorded at historical cost, but increasingly reported at fair value. Shareholders' equity increases when the enterprise succeeds, and shrinks, or may disappear entirely, when the business struggles.

In our initial discussion of the corporate balance sheet, we saw that accountants generally divide shareholders' equity into three components: capital stock accounts—either common stock or preferred stock, additional paid-in capital and retained earnings. In contrast, the legal capital system, which traditionally attracted more attention from lawyers, refers to these categories as stated capital, capital surplus and earned surplus, respectively. We can compare the various titles which accountants and the legal capital system assign to the different components of shareholders' equity as follows:

SHAREHOLDERS' EQUITY CATEGORIES	
ACCOUNTING NOMENCLATURE	LEGAL TERMINOLOGY
Capital Stock: Common Stock or Preferred Stock	Stated Capital or Legal Capital
Additional Paid-in Capital	Capital Surplus
Retained Earnings	Earned Surplus

The legal capital system affects lawyers because the underlying corporate statutes: (1) require corporations to issue shares for consideration that equals or exceeds the shares' par value and (2) restrict a company's ability to distribute assets to shareholders, using a test based upon legal or stated capital. The second restriction seeks to protect creditors, plus those shareholders entitled to dividend and liquidation preferences, and even the residual shareholders, by prohibiting distributions to shareholders that would reduce a corporation's net assets to an amount less than the legal capital safety margin. An unlawful transaction may give rise to claims against the corporation, its directors, and the shareholder recipients. Because corporations can take lawful measures to circumvent the protections that the legal capital system purportedly offered, most modern corporate statutes, including the 1984 Model Business Corporation Act ("MBCA")--as revised, now entirely or substantially adopted in thirty states, have eliminated the concepts of stated capital and par value. Instead, these statutes base their limitations on distributions to shareholders on the corporation's solvency. Despite major shortcomings, the legal capital system continues to survive in eight states, including commercially important jurisdictions like Delaware, New York, and Texas. Until the legal capital system becomes a historical footnote, corporate lawyers, bankruptcy specialists and attorneys representing creditors holding claims against insolvent corporations should understand the important ramifications that the system presents, especially when corporations distribute assets to shareholders.

In all states, whatever the test for assessing whether a corporation can lawfully declare and pay a dividend or repurchase shares, lawyers should remember that important accounting issues can underlie these determinations and that different sets of accounting rules can apply for distinct purposes. In this chapter, we will see that a corporation may use one set of rules for preparing financial statements, another set for determining if the corporation can lawfully distribute assets to shareholders, and yet another when deciding whether the corporation remains in compliance with a covenant in a loan agreement or other contract. Similarly, lawyers should also recognize that regulators may apply completely different rules when assessing whether the decision of a financial institution's board of directors to declare a dividend leaves the regulated institution in an unsafe and unsound condition to transact business.

B.   DISTRIBUTIONS AND LEGAL RESTRICTIONS

Savvy creditors and their lawyers long ago recognized that the legal capital system did not effectively safeguard creditors' rights. Rather than rely on the easily avoidable statutory restrictions, sophisticated lenders enjoying sufficient bargaining power began using contractual provisions, often referred to as *restrictive covenants*, to protect their interests. The previous chapter mentioned how some legal agreements contain provisions requiring a party to conform to a certain financial ratio. These restrictive covenants also often prohibit or limit distributions that the legal capital system would not prevent. Like the dividend statutes, these covenants often present accounting issues, and once again GAAP may not control. Because lawyers frequently draft and negotiate, and occasionally even litigate, these covenants, attorneys must understand how accounting concepts and terminology can affect such agreements.

1. STATUTORY RESTRICTIONS

Statutory restrictions on distributions flow from two sources: corporate law and creditors' rights statutes. The corporate laws in eight states, including Delaware, continue to follow the legal capital system and to use the traditional par value rules, limiting distributions to *surplus* under various definitions. Recall that the legal capital system traditionally divides surplus into two components: capital surplus and earned surplus. These surplus tests basically limit the assets a corporation can distribute to shareholders to the amount by which total shareholders' equity exceeds stated capital. Sometimes, however, these surplus statutes only allow distributions from capital surplus under specified circumstances, such as with disclosure to shareholders.

Another statutory formulation, which amounts to the same thing, prohibits distributions to shareholders if the payment will impair stated capital. This approach, too, forbids distributions that leave the amount of a corporation's net assets less than its stated capital. In other words, a corporation can declare and pay a dividend or redeem shares only in an amount no greater than the corporation's surplus, which illustrates stated capital's role as a "cushion" for the benefit of the corporation's creditors (and shareholders with a liquidation preference).

To illustrate how such surplus statutes operate, suppose that the balance sheet for Maledon, Inc. reflects the following:

Assets		Liabilities & Shareholders' Equity	
Cash	$13,000	Liabilities	
Equipment	2,000	Current Liabilities	$ 2,000
Other Assets	4,000	Long-Term Debt	5,000
Total Assets	$19,000	Total Liabilities	$ 7,000
		Shareholders' Equity:	
		Stated Capital (2,000 shares, $2 par)	4,000
		Capital Surplus	5,000
		Earned Surplus	3,000
		Total Equity	$12,000
		Total Liabilities & Equity	$19,000

You will recall that on a real balance sheet, accountants would use the titles "Common stock," "Additional paid-in capital" and "Retained earnings" in place of stated capital, capital surplus and earned surplus, respectively. Unless Maledon's articles of incorporation provide otherwise, the company can lawfully declare a dividend which does not exceed $8,000. As a practical matter, however, paying a $8,000 dividend would reduce Maledon's cash to $5,000, which would mean that the corporation could not then immediately repay both its current liabilities and long-term debt.

Most modern corporate statutes apply one or more *insolvency* tests to determine whether a corporation can lawfully distribute assets to shareholders, and whether or not some other test, such as one based upon stated capital, also applies. These economic tests forbid distributions unless: (1) the corporation can continue to pay its obligations as they come due (the equity insolvency test); (2) the corporation's assets after the distribution exceed its liabilities plus any liquidation preferences belonging to preferred shares; or, most commonly (3) the corporation can satisfy both previous requirements. Similarly, creditors' rights statutes, namely state fraudulent transfer statutes and the federal Bankruptcy Code, may protect creditors from distributions that leave a corporation with: (1) more liabilities than assets, (2) not enough liquid resources to pay bills as they come due, or (3) an unreasonably small amount of capital for continuing operations.

The equity insolvency test prohibits any distribution that would leave the corporation unable "to pay its debts as they become due in the usual course of business." Usually, if a corporation is carrying on its operations in normal fashion, that fact itself probably indicates that no issue arises under this requirement. Alternatively, if an auditor has examined the financial statements and has not expressed any qualification in the auditor's report about the corporation's ability to continue as a going concern, the absence of any subsequent adverse events would normally satisfy the standard. If a corporation has encountered liquidity or operational difficulties, the directors may want "to consider a cash flow analysis, based on a business forecast and budget, covering a sufficient period of time to permit a conclusion that known obligations of the corporation can reasonably be expected to be satisfied over the period of time that they will mature." 1 MODEL BUS. CORP. ACT ANN. § 6.40 cmt. 2 (4th ed. 2008).

As to the balance sheet test, notice that a corporation can reduce its assets down to its liabilities, which eliminates the "cushion" for creditors that stated capital once sought to provide. These statutes, however, often provide that if the corporation has outstanding any shares with a liquidation preference, then the assets remaining after a distribution must at least equal the sum of the liabilities plus the total liquidation preference, which coincidentally preserves some cushion for the creditors.

2. RELATIONSHIP OF GAAP TO STATUTORY RESTRICTIONS

Whenever a dividend statute uses the balance sheet to judge an enterprise's financial position, a question arises as to whether the user may or should revalue the assets. Under corporate statutes that prohibit distributions "which impair capital" or allow them only "out of surplus," tests that call for a balance sheet computation, should a lawyer measure the assets at current value, or at the balance sheet figure based on historical cost, often referred to as the "book value" in determining the amount by which net assets exceed stated capital?

Up until now, we have ignored the interpretive questions of what the dividend statutes mean when they use accounting terms such as "assets" and "liabilities." Thus, in our earlier examples concerning Maledon, Inc., we simply accepted the amounts listed on the balance sheet for the company's assets and liabilities in applying the dividend statute. If the company prepared its balance sheet according to GAAP, these amounts generally reflect historical cost. Can the company write up its assets to reflect their current fair values? Dividend statutes often fail to address this question, leaving the issue for the courts to resolve, usually as a matter of statutory interpretation, perhaps as informed by various policy considerations. To illustrate, look again at the balance sheet of Maledon, Inc., on page 331, *supra*. Suppose that the value of Maledon's equipment has appreciated to, say, $5,000. If we construe the dividend statute consistent with GAAP, the accounting bar against recognizing unrealized appreciation would apply, and Maledon could not take the unrealized appreciation into account for dividend purposes either, which would limit any dividend to $8,000. In determining the amount available for distribution, could a lawyer legitimately advise Maledon's board of directors to increase its surplus by $3,000 to $11,000 by writing-up its equipment account, solely for dividend purposes, from its $2,000 book value to $5,000 to reflect the equipment's fair market value? The following case addresses that question.

Randall v. Bailey

Supreme Court of New York, Trial Term, New York County, 1940.
23 N.Y.S.2d 173, aff'd 288 N.Y. 280, 43 N.E.2d 43 (1942).

■ WALTER, JUSTICE.

A Lender of Bush Terminal Company, appointed in a proceeding under Section 77B of the Bankruptcy Act, 11 U.S.C.A. § 207, here sues former directors of that company to recover on its behalf the amount of dividends declared and paid between November 22, 1928, and May 2, 1932, aggregating $3,639,058.06. At the times of the declarations and payments, the company's books concededly showed a surplus which ranged from not less than $4,378,554.83 on December 31, 1927, down to not less than $2,199,486.77 on April 30, 1932. The plaintiff claims, however, that in fact there was no surplus, that the capital was actually impaired to an amount greater than the amount of the dividends, and that the directors consequently are personally liable to the corporation for the amount thereof under Section 58 of the Stock Corporation Law. Defendants claim that there was no impairment of capital and that the surplus was actually greater than the amount which plaintiff concedes as the amount shown by the books.

The claims of the plaintiff, although branching out to a multitude of items, are basically reducible to [two]:

1. It was improper to "write-up" the land values above cost and thereby take unrealized appreciation into account.

2. It was improper not to "write-down" to actual value the cost of investments in and advances to subsidiaries and thereby fail to take unrealized depreciation into account.

* * *

I next turn to the subject of unrealized appreciation and depreciation.

Until 1915 the company's land was carried upon its books at cost. In 1915 the land was written up to 80% of the amount at which it was then assessed for taxation, and in 1918 it was written up to the exact amount at which it was then so assessed. Those two writeups totalled $7,211,791.72, and the result was that during the period here in question the land was carried on the books at $8,737,949.02, whereas its actual cost was $1,526,157.30. Plaintiff claims that the entire $7,211,791.72 should be eliminated because it represents merely unrealized appreciation, and dividends cannot be declared or paid on the basis of mere unrealized appreciation in fixed assets irrespective of how sound the estimate thereof may be. That obviously and concededly is another way of saying that for dividend purposes fixed assets must be computed at cost, not value, and plaintiff here plants himself upon that position, even to the point of contending that evidence of value is immaterial and not admissible. If that contention be sound, the company indisputably had a deficit at all the times here involved in an amount exceeding the dividends here in question. The importance of the question so presented, both to this case and to corporations and corporate directors in general, is thus apparent, and it is, I think, surprising that upon a question so important to and so often occurring in the realm of business there is, not only no decision which can be said to be directly in point, but, also, no discussion in text-book or law magazine which does much more than pose the question without answering it. * * *

It is to be emphasized at the outset that the question is not one of sound economics, or of what is sound business judgment or financial policy or of proper accounting practice, or even what the law ought to be. My views of the business acumen or financial sagacity of these directors, as well as my views as to what the legislature ought to permit or prohibit, are entirely immaterial. The question I have to decide is whether or not an existing statute has been violated. The problem is one of statutory construction.

The words of the statute, as it existed during the period here involved, are: "No stock corporation shall declare or pay any dividend which shall impair its capital or capital stock, nor while its capital or capital stock is impaired * * *."

* * *

In summary, I think that it cannot be said that there is a single case in this State which actually decides that unrealized appreciation cannot be taken into consideration, or, stated in different words, that cost and not value must be used in determining whether or not there exists a surplus out of which dividends can be paid. I think, further, that such a holding would run directly counter to the meaning of the terms capital and capital stock as fixed by decisions of the Court of Appeals construing the earlier statutes, and that such construction of those terms must be deemed to have been adopted by the legislature in enacting the statute here involved. I thus obviously cannot follow decisions to the contrary in other States or any contrary views of economists or accountants. If the policy of the law be bad it is for the legislature to change it.

* * * I am of the opinion that the same reasons which show that unrealized appreciation must be considered are equally cogent in showing that unrealized depreciation likewise must be considered. In other words, the test being whether or not the value of the assets exceeds the debts and the liability to stockholders, all assets must be taken at their actual value.

I see no cause for alarm over the fact that this view requires directors to make a determination of the value of the assets at each dividend declaration. On the contrary, I think that is exactly what the law always has contemplated that directors should do. That does not mean that the books themselves necessarily must be altered by write-ups or write-downs at each dividend period, or that formal appraisals must be obtained from professional appraisers or even made by the directors themselves. That is obviously impossible in the case of corporations of any considerable size. But it is not impossible nor unfeasible for directors to consider whether the cost of assets continues over a long period of years to reflect their fair value, and the law does require that directors should really direct in the very important matter of really determining at each dividend declaration whether or not the value of the assets is such as to justify a dividend, rather than do what one director here testified that he did, viz. "accept the company's figures." The directors are the ones who should determine the figures by carefully considering values, and it was for the very purpose of compelling them to perform that duty that the statute imposes upon them a personal responsibility for declaring and paying dividends when the value of the assets is not sufficient to justify them. What directors must do is to exercise an informed judgment of their own, and the amount of information which they should obtain, and the sources from which they should obtain it, will of course depend upon the circumstances of each particular case. * * *

   * * *

Defendants' motions for judgment at the close of the whole case are granted * * *.

NOTES

1. Other courts have shared the judicial attitude expressed in *Randall v. Bailey*. For example, in *British Printing & Communication Corp. v. Harcourt Brace Jovanovich, Inc.*, 664 F. Supp. 1519 (S.D.N.Y. 1987), the court approvingly cited *Randall v. Bailey* and held that, under New York law, a corporation may measure its assets at their fair market value rather than their accounting book value for purposes of determining the amount available for distribution to shareholders. *Id.* at 1531–32. More recently, the Supreme Court of Delaware expressly adhered to principles that allow a corporation to revalue assets and liabilities for purposes of determining whether the corporation can lawfully redeem shares. Klang v. Smith's Food & Drug Ctrs., Inc., 702 A.2d 150, 154 (Del. 1997). In the unanimous opinion, Chief Justice Veasey wrote: "Balance sheets are not, however, conclusive indicators of surplus or a lack thereof." *Id.* at 152.

2. Most established corporations' balance sheets show surpluses which enable the corporation to pay its regular dividends. In the 1980s, however, corporations began paying large extraordinary dividends as a defense to unwelcomed takeover attempts, so the question of whether corporations could pay dividends from unrealized appreciation became very important in that context. More recently, corporations have proposed large stock redemptions, sometimes in response to takeover efforts, which has raised similar questions in those contexts.

3. Suppose that in the example involving Maledon, Inc. on page 331, *supra*, the equipment had decreased in value to $500. Would the company's board of directors need to take that into account in determining the amount available for distribution? If so, would the directors need to reduce earned surplus or capital surplus? Would the corresponding reduction matter?

4. In *Resolution Trust Corp. v. Fleischer*, 826 F. Supp. 1273 (D. Kan. 1993), a case involving the legality of dividends that a savings and loan association had paid, the governing statute prohibited dividends "except from the earnings and undivided profits," with a further condition that the company meet "the net worth requirement" for federal insurance of accounts, plus a provision imposing liability of the directors for "an impairment of capital." The plaintiff government agency contended that because the association's net worth determined on a fair market value basis was negative, the court should hold the directors liable for declaring unlawful dividends. The court, however, held that the statutory provisions did not require a fair market value determination. After noting the absence of any express statutory requirement to use fair market value, the court said:

> The court finds that indeed such an interpretation would create severe practical problems for the industry. Every time an institution desired to pay dividends, it would be required, in effect, to conduct a liquidation analysis of its assets. Such an analysis would conceivably require separate appraisals of all the properties owned by an institution. Such appraisals can be highly subjective, with the fair market value of specified property often resting in the eyes of the appraiser. * * *
>
> * * * The Kansas statutes are phrased in accounting terms such as "earnings" and "undivided profits." This court finds it much more likely that the legislature intended net earnings and capital of an institution to be evaluated according to the institution's ability to pay as a going concern, not based on a fair market liquidation analysis. The court therefore finds that Kansas law does not require that an institution's capital, net worth and earnings be determined on a fair market value basis.

Id. at 1281. Was the court correct that adopting the fair market value interpretation would require a "liquidation analysis" of the corporation's assets?

As the principal case and related notes illustrate, the applicable statutes often fail to provide any insight as to how a company should compute its assets and liabilities. In the following report, a task force of the Corporate Law and Accounting Committee of the Section of Corporation, Banking and Business Law, American Bar Association, now the Association's Section of Business Law, concluded that GAAP offered the most practical answer to the question as to which accounting principles directors and courts should apply in assessing issues which arise under dividend statutes.

Current Issues on the Legality of Dividends from a Law and Accounting Perspective: A Task Force Report[*]

39 Bus. Law. 289, 292–94 (1983).

GAAP AS A LEGAL STANDARD

Under the statutes, the accounting principles to be applied in determining net assets and liabilities are generally unspecified. What, then, are the accounting principles to be applied under these statutes prescribing a financial statement test? GAAP is by far the most practical standard for the courts.

First, with the exception of some closely regulated industries, GAAP accounting is required by the Securities and Exchange Commission for publicly held companies and is effectively required by the American Institute of Certified Public Accountants (AICPA) for both public and private companies. These requirements have resulted in a single set of accounting principles for most publicly traded and larger private companies. Thus lenders, trade creditors, and, especially important for our purposes, equity investors receive GAAP statements for such companies.

Second, the objectives of the financial accounting standards for general purpose external financial reporting, as set forth in the FASB's summary of its Statement of Financial Accounting Concepts No. 1, include:

§ 1210.34: Financial reporting should provide information that is useful to present and potential investors and creditors and other users in making rational investment, credit, and similar decisions. The information should be comprehensible to those who have a reasonable understanding of business and economic activities and are willing to study the information with reasonable diligence.

§ 1210.37: Financial reporting should provide information to help present and potential investors and creditors and other users in assessing the amounts, timing, and uncertainty of prospective cash receipts from dividends or interest and the proceeds from the sale, redemption, or maturity of securities or loans. Since investors' and creditors' cash flows are related to enterprise cash flows, financial reporting should provide information to help investors, creditors, and others assess the amounts, timing, and uncertainty of prospective net cash inflows to the related enterprise.

§ 1210.40: Financial reporting should provide information about the economic resources of an enterprise, the claims to those resources (obligations of the enterprise to transfer resources to other entities and owners' equity) and the effects of transactions, events, and circumstances that change resources and claims to those resources.

These objectives have not been and may never be fully achieved, but they demonstrate that GAAP financial statements are designed, in part, to show the ability of a corporation that is a going concern to pay cash dividends. Such objectives are consistent in a realistic way with the purposes of the dividend statutes: the protection of creditors, shareholders, and the relationships among the shareholders. For a going concern, a basic assumption of GAAP, these objectives come far closer to carrying out these protective functions than the fair valuation standard of the Bankruptcy Law, the fair salable value standard of the Uniform Fraudulent Conveyance Act, * * * or the continuing process of valuation and revaluation such as that contemplated by *Randall v. Bailey*. For a going concern considering the declaration of dividends, it seems inappropriate to require a valuation of assets on the basis of theoretical current realization when such assets are not going to be the subject of current realization. * * *

Third, the courts are quite unequipped to choose among and revise accounting principles. It is not a question of accepting, rejecting, or revising a particular item: instead an interrelated set of principles that focus on agreed objectives must be devised. Beneath the concepts of assets, liabilities, net income, and surplus is a complex network of definitions, assumptions, and judgments which are often individually, and always collectively, complex.

Fourth, some jurisdictions implicitly recognize GAAP as the standard for accounting determinations through statutes permitting directors to rely on financial statements prepared by public accountants. Several states expressly permit the use of generally accepted accounting principles. * * *

NOTES

1. Contrary to the opinions expressed in the preceding article, the MBCA does not mandate that corporations use GAAP in valuing assets and liabilities for purposes of determining the amount available for distribution. The MBCA provides that the board of directors may base its determination "either on financial statements prepared on the basis of accounting practices and principles that are reasonable in the circumstances *or on a fair valuation or other method that is reasonable in the circumstances*." 1 MODEL BUS. CORP. ACT ANN. § 6.40(d) (4th ed. 2008) (emphasis added). As the official commentary to MBCA § 6.40 articulates, "the revised Model Act contemplates that generally accepted accounting principles are always 'reasonable in the circumstances' * * *." 1 MODEL BUS. CORP. ACT ANN. § 6.40 cmt. 4(A) (4th ed. 2008). Departure from GAAP, therefore, depends on the "reasonableness of the circumstances."

2. Until 2012, California's corporate law generally required the board of directors to use GAAP in determining the company's assets, liabilities, and retained earnings when evaluating a distribution's lawfulness. Unless expressly specified elsewhere, the applicable provision still states that all references to financial statements and accounting items "mean those financial statements or comparable statements or items prepared or determined in conformity with generally accepted accounting principles then applicable." CAL. CORP. CODE § 114 (West, West through ch. 185 of 2014 Legis. Sess.). Thus, the previous California statute prohibited, in determining the amount of a corporation's assets or retained earnings for distribution purposes, the inclusion of any appreciation in value not yet realized. Current California law follows the approach in the MBCA that allows a board to use a fair valuation or any other reasonable method under the circumstances to determine a proposed distribution's lawfulness. *See* CAL. CORP. CODE § 500(c) (West, West through ch. 185 of 2014 Legis. Sess.).

3.   CONTRACTUAL RESTRICTIONS

The corporate statutes require, either implicitly or explicitly, that any distribution not violate the corporation's articles of incorporation. We can easily characterize such a prerequisite to a distribution as a contractual restriction because the articles of incorporation serve as a contract between the shareholders and the corporation. Indeed, every once in a while, a corporation's articles will contain a clause regarding distributions. These provisions can specifically prohibit, or require, distributions in certain situations. In one recent case, the Ninth Circuit cited the unabridged version of this text's fourth edition on several occasions in an opinion that interpreted a corporation's articles of organization. Affirming the district court's decision granting summary judgment for a preferred shareholder, the appellate court concluded that because the corporation's net worth exceeded $5 million, determined in accordance with GAAP and as shown on the relevant balance sheet, the articles required the corporation to redeem certain preferred shares. Bolt v. Merrimack Pharm., Inc., 503 F.3d 913, 915–17 (9th Cir. 2007).

Given the weaknesses in the statutory restrictions limiting distributions, however, sophisticated creditors enjoying superior bargaining power more commonly require borrowers to agree to various contractual limitations or prohibitions as a condition to any loan. These restrictive covenants frequently limit distributions to owners, require the borrower to maintain certain financial ratios, prohibit the debtor from incurring any additional indebtedness, and compel the borrower to pay withholding and sales taxes. In 2005, for example, Cablevision Systems Corp. cancelled plans to pay a special $3 billion dividend after the company discovered that it had technically violated a provision in a bank loan. Sara Silver, *Cablevision Calls Off Special Dividend*, WALL ST. J., Dec. 20, 2005, at A3. Absent the lender's approval, such restrictive covenants may also prohibit or limit pledges of assets, purchases, capital expenditures or leases exceeding a certain amount, sales or issuance of capital stock, mergers, consolidations or sales of assets, salaries paid to officers and directors, or management changes. Large borrowers, however, often refuse to accept such covenants, which lenders increasingly demand.

As an example of these restrictive covenants, see Note 9 to Starbucks' consolidated financial statements for the fiscal year ended September 30, 2012, which begins on page 73 of the company's 2012 Form 10-K and appears in Appendix A on page 769, *infra*. Note 9 discloses that the company's $500 million unsecured credit facility with various banks requires the company to maintain compliance with certain covenants, including a minimum fixed charge coverage ratio.

Covenants restricting distributions to shareholders typically limit such distributions to an amount derived from three components:

(1) all or part of the borrower's accumulated net earnings from the *peg date*, which is nothing more than a fixed date, often the beginning of the fiscal year in which the borrower issues the debt, to the end of some period preceding a distribution's declaration or payment,

(2) the proceeds from the sale of stock after the peg date, and

(3) the *dip*, a specified amount of existing retained earnings.

AM. BAR FOUND., COMMENTARIES ON INDENTURES 410–11 (1971). *Alleco, Inc. v. IBJ Schroder Bank & Trust Co.*, 745 F. Supp. 1467 (D. Minn. 1989), involved a covenant that illustrates these components and an additional allowance. The covenant provided in pertinent part:

Restrictions on Dividends and Redemption of Capital Stock. No dividend whatever shall be declared or paid nor shall any distribution be made on any capital stock of the Company (except in shares of capital stock of the Company), nor shall any shares of capital stock of the Company be acquired or redeemed by the Company or any Subsidiary, unless after giving effect to such dividend, distribution, acquisition or redemption, the aggregate payments for all such purposes subsequent to June 30, 1985 would not exceed the sum of (A) 50% of the Net Income of the Company (determined on a cumulative basis) for the period commencing July 1, 1985 and ending on the last day of the immediately preceding calendar month (or in the event that such Net Income (determined on a cumulative basis) is a negative amount, 100% of such Net Income); (B) the aggregate of the net proceeds received by the Company from the sale for cash or other property (including issuance in any merger, consolidation or similar transaction) of shares of its capital stock subsequent to September 1, 1985; (C) the aggregate of the net proceeds received by the Company from the issuance of the Debentures or the issuance of sale of any other debt obligation of the Company, which Debentures or debt obligation shall have been converted into shares of Common Stock of the Company after September 1, 1985; and (D) $12,000,000.00.

Id. at 1474 n.5. The covenant, therefore, designated June 30, 1985 as the peg date, allowed the borrower to distribute fifty percent of cumulative net income after the peg date, permitted the issuer to distribute the proceeds from the sale of stock or the issuance of any debt instrument converted into common shares after September 1, 1985, and set a $12 million dip.

The *Alleco* case also demonstrates that litigation occasionally arises regarding the interpretation of these restrictive covenants. In that case, a dispute arose regarding, among other things, whether a tender offer and merger violated the covenant. In the accompanying loan transaction, Alleco issued $105 million in *debentures*, another name for an unsecured long-term debt security, and signed an *indenture* or agreement which granted IBJ Schroder Bank & Trust Co., as the successor to the original indenture trustee, certain rights and powers to exercise for the benefit of the debenture holders or lenders. The district court held that the transactions violated the indenture and that Alleco's failure to honor the covenant constituted an event of default which permitted Schroder properly to give written notice of default and to declare the principal and accrued interest immediately due and payable.

In fact, loan agreements typically treat the borrower's failure to comply with the restrictive covenants as a "default," which may give the lender the right to demand immediate repayment or require the borrower to cure the default before a grace period expires. In connection with the scandals involving backdated stock options in the mid-2000s, numerous companies delayed filing financial statements with the SEC until they could complete internal investigations. In response, bondholders declared technical defaults and either demanded immediate repayment or charged additional fees, sometimes in the millions of dollars, to extend the default deadlines. In 2006, for example, Mercury Interactive Corp., one of the first companies implicated in the stock options scandals, agreed to pay $7.1 million to creditors and granted an option, which could have potentially cost the company an additional $40.2 million, to redeem certain notes at a premium to avoid default on certain bonds. Peter Lattman & Karen Richardson, *Hedge Funds Play Hardball With Firms Filing Late Financials*, WALL ST. J., Aug. 29, 2006, at A1 (also describing other examples involving companies that missed SEC deadlines after accounting woes).

Before the credit crisis began in 2007 and then again after 2012, the financial markets witnessed a steady erosion of covenants in debt agreements. *The Wall Street Journal* has reported that in the late 1990s, the traditional secured loan contained between three and six so-called "maintenance tests," which required the borrower to meet certain performance targets. By 2006, however, the safest secured loans typically contained fewer than three covenants. At least in partial response to the trend toward so-called "covenant-lite" loan agreements, the credit crisis, and concerns about voluntary issuer actions that erode bondholder value, such as debt-financed distributions, more than fifty large lenders banded together to form the Credit Roundtable. In 2007 that organization issued a white paper setting forth certain model covenants that the group would like borrowers to include in bond indentures.

Credit Roundtable, Improving Covenant Protections in the Investment Grade Bond Market (Dec. 17, 2007), http://www.creditroundtable.org/Article.aspx? EID=40037; *see also* Cynthia Koons, *Risky Business: Growth of 'Covenant-Lite' Debt*, WALL ST. J., June 18, 2007, at C2.

As the credit crisis deepened, lenders toughened loan terms, including restrictive covenants that would force borrowers to maintain cash flows or EBITDA to fund scheduled interest and principal payments, to limit overall debt amounts or ratios, or to cap distributions. When the Federal Reserve continued to keep interest rates at historically low levels, lenders sought higher-yielding investments, easier lending terms returned, and debt agreements increasingly omitted meaningful covenants designed to protect lenders in exchange for higher interest rates. Reacting to these developments in 2013, the Office of the Comptroller of the Currency, the Federal Deposit Corporation, and the Board of Governors of the Federal Reserve jointly issued final guidance regarding leveraged lending to all supervised financial institutions, along with their subsidiaries and affiliates. In issuing the guidance, the regulatory agencies cited industry practices that raised safety and soundness concerns, including inadequate maintenance covenants and borrower reporting requirements in leveraged debt agreements. When discussing the minimum regulatory expectations for underwriting standards, the final guidance explicitly identifies credit agreement covenant protections, including debt to cash flow and interest coverage; reporting requirements; and compliance monitoring. The expectations explicitly state that a debt to EBITDA ratio that exceeds 6.0 "raises concerns for most industries." The guidelines at least discourage, if not completely deter, supervised financial institutions from originating covenant-lite loans. Interagency Guidance on Leveraged Lending, 78 Fed. Reg. 17,766, 17,773 (Mar. 22, 2013), *available at* http://www.gpo.gov/fdsys/pkg/FR-2013-03-22/pdf/2013-06567.pdf.

The number of covenant-lite loans, presumably from non-supervised lenders, jumped significantly in 2013, however, and became even more prevalent during the first five months of 2014, growing to 53.8 percent of the J.P. Morgan Leveraged Loan Index in mid-2014. *See* Katy Burne, *More Loans Come With Few Strings Attached*, WALL ST. J., June 13, 2014, at C1.

As the preface observes, accounting has been accurately described as the "language of corporate governance." Law students and lawyers should keep in mind that, whether for better or for worse, restrictive covenants can allow "lender activism" in corporate governance.

PROBLEMS

Problem 5.1A. In 20X1, Noelle Ries incorporated Ries, Inc. (the "Company"). The Company issued its 100 authorized shares, $100 par value common stock, to her in exchange for $15,000. About the same time, the Company borrowed $55,000, payable on demand, from Melanie Rubocki. The Company immediately used the loan proceeds to purchase land which cost $30,000. Although the Company has not repaid any principal on the loan, the corporation has not incurred any other indebtedness. At the end of 20X3, the

Company's only assets include the land, a bank account containing $25,000 and a $5,000 account receivable from a customer.

During 20X1, the Company lost $4,000. The Company earned a $2,000 profit in 20X2. In 20X3, an uninsured tort claim against the Company caused an $8,000 loss for the year.

(1) Assuming no contractual limitations on distributions and based on the Company's financial position at the end of 20X3, can the Company declare and pay a $2,000 dividend in early 20X4 under:

(a) a surplus test?

(b) a retained earnings statute?

(c) an equity insolvency test?

(d) the MBCA's balance sheet test?

Explain your answers briefly.

(2) How, if at all, would your answers to the questions in part (1) change if the land has appreciated in value to $50,000?

Problem 5.1B. X Corp. had the following balance sheet on January 1:

X Corp.
Balance Sheet, January 1

Assets		Liabilities & Shareholders' Equity	
Cash	$ 11,000	Shareholders' Equity	
Plant	90,000	Stated Capital	$100,000
		Earned Surplus	1,000
Total	$101,000	Total	$101,000

On February 1, X borrowed $5,000, giving a note due three years later, with interest at twelve percent per year. X Corp. agreed to pay the $600 annual interest in two installments each year, $300 on April 30 and $300 on October 31. Assume for simplicity that X Corp. did not earn any income or incur any other expenses during the calendar year. How large a dividend could X Corp. properly pay at the close of the calendar year, under a statute which permits dividends only "out of net assets in excess of capital"?

Problem 5.1C. Your law firm has represented The Cougar Company ("Cougar") for many years. The senior partner at your law firm describes the following facts:

Cougar, which is incorporated in Pacioli, the fictional fifty-first state, has paid dividends on its common stock every year for the past twenty-five years. For the fiscal year beginning December 1, 20X1, Cougar had stated capital of $1,000,000, capital surplus of $200,000, and an earned surplus of $500,000. As a result of the recession, fiscal year 20X2 was a bad year for the company and the income statement for the fiscal year ended November 30, 20X2 showed a net loss of $600,000. Given the slow economic recovery, Cougar expects to lose $150,000 from operations during fiscal year ending November 30, 20X3. As a result of borrowings, the Company nevertheless had $150,000 cash on deposit in various local banks on October 1, 20X3.

The Board of Directors would like to declare the regular cash dividend of $100,000 at the board meeting scheduled for October 31, 20X3. The dividend would be payable on January 1, 20X4. The senior partner, however, is not certain that such a dividend would be legal.

The senior partner also tells you that Cougar owns an investment in LMN Corporation ("LMN"). In 1975, Cougar purchased 1,000 shares of LMN for $50,000. As a result of stock splits and dividends, Cougar currently owns 10,000 shares which are trading at a market price of $25 per share. The Board of Directors, however, does not want to sell any of the LMN shares because the Board believes that the shares are an excellent investment. Cougar also owns a fully depreciated factory. Cougar has accepted an offer to sell the factory for $150,000 cash. The closing on that contract, however, will not take place until February 1, 20X4.

Finally, the senior partner mentions that Cougar owns some property in California. Cougar paid $500,000 for the property in 20X0. The recession has been particularly severe in California and an appraiser recently valued the property at $250,000. The Board of Directors does not want to sell the property because the Board reasonably believes that the decline in value is only temporary. The senior partner states that you can assume that all other assets are worth what the company paid for them.

Section 100 of the Pacioli Corporations Code governs distributions and provides: "The board of directors of a corporation may declare and the corporation may pay dividends on its outstanding shares in cash provided that no dividend shall be declared or paid if such dividend shall render its net assets less than its stated capital." There are no other applicable statutory provisions in Pacioli and no cases have interpreted the provisions of Section 100.

The senior partner wants to determine whether the proposed dividend would be legal under Pacioli law. The senior partner also wants to know whether the Board of Directors should consider any other legal restrictions.

Problem 5.2A. As of December 31, 2012, does Amazon.com's 2012 Form 10-K disclose any restrictive covenants that limit the company's ability to pay dividends or redeem shares? If so, describe any restrictions. Explain how you determined your answer.

Problem 5.2B. As of December 31, 2012, does Google's 2012 Form 10-K disclose any restrictive covenants that limit the company's ability to pay dividends or redeem shares? If so, describe any restrictions. Explain how you determined your answer.

Problem 5.2C. As of December 31, 2012, does UPS's 2012 Form 10-K disclose any restrictive covenants that limit the company's ability to pay dividends or redeem shares? If so, describe any restrictions. Explain how you determined your answer.

C. Drafting & Negotiating Agreements & Other Legal Documents Containing Accounting Terminology and Concepts

At one time or another in virtually every lawyer's career, a lawyer will draft or negotiate an agreement or legal document containing accounting terminology or concepts. The following excerpts, adapted from written materials prepared for a seminar that the Practising Law Institute sponsored, offer some very practical suggestions for those situations.

Terry Lloyd, *Financial Language in Legal Documents**
adapted and revised from Accounting for Lawyers 1994 at 361–409.

From time to time almost every attorney is called on to draft an agreement containing some accounting concepts or principles. Such agreements might include a shareholders' agreement with a buy/sell provision based on a corporation's net worth, an "earn out" clause in a sale, or a supply contract with a termination provision triggered by one party becoming insolvent. Even litigators are occasionally required to draft settlement documents with accounting or financial provisions. * * * The following principles may save you and your clients that trouble and expense.

General Principles of Drafting

All too often, the drafting process consists of going to the files, locating a similar agreement or agreements, and modifying those documents to the terms of the new transaction. Just as frequently, attorneys simply state that all accounting issues are to be governed by "generally accepted accounting principles" (GAAP) under the (mistaken) assumption that GAAP is useful for all purposes and unchanging. Although these approaches are better than simply stating that "all computations shall be made in accordance with good accounting standards," they are not likely to achieve the best results for your client. Set forth below is a list of principles of legal drafting that should be considered in drafting any agreement involving accounting or financial issues. The first five of these principles apply generally to all legal documents; the remaining five apply only to those with accounting concepts.

1. *Completely Mutual Terms are Not Necessarily Even—or Best for Your Client.*

Attorneys often make the mistake of thinking that if all the covenants in an agreement are parallel, (i.e. the terms apply equally to both parties), the document is fairly drawn. This fallacy was memorably put to rest by the

---

French social commentator, who observed that the law in its majestic equality prohibits the rich as well as the poor from sleeping under the bridges of Paris. Before you accept a purely parallel contract, ask yourself whether you are representing the "rich" party or the "poor" party and whether some of those mutual clauses impose greater restrictions on (or fewer benefits for) your client. * * *

2. When Relying On Past Agreements, Be Careful Which Document You Choose.

* * *[The fallacy of relying] heavily on what some attorneys used to call the "form file[" is that] you may be using a document drawn for the benefit of your opposition [perhaps because your firm represented the other side of the transaction in the earlier matter]. * * *

3. Long Forms are Not Necessarily Superior.

* * * As a practical matter, if your client controls a situation (such as a majority partner in a joint venture) the less said the better, as your client is likely to be more constrained by a longer agreement. Control typically includes the ability to pick accounting methods, which is discussed in more detail below, under Rule Six. On the other hand, if your client is not in control of the situation, the more matters reduced to writing, the more likely he is better protected. There is one exception to this general rule and that pertains to agreements in which there is a large disparity in bargaining power. In such cases the courts often resolve ambiguities in favor of the party that did not prepare the agreement.

4. Make Sure the Mechanics Work.

* * * The agreement, especially calculations, must be reviewed carefully both before and after modification for use by your client. * * * When calculations are called for, have someone (such as the client's accountant, see below) actually do the calculation for amounts likely to occur under various scenarios such as high/low interest rates or high/low earnings amounts. Software programmers call this test by various names, including "idiot proofing," since only idiots (or unexpected circumstances) can find the real flaws in a program or calculation.

5. Clear the Documents with Your Client's Accountants.

* * * While there is no shame in not knowing GAAP, it really is fairly easy to have someone who does understand the implications look at the calculations. * * *

6. If your Client is in Control, Use a Bottom Line Concept; If the Opposing Party is in Control, Use a Top Line Concept.

The prior discussion of Rule Three, suggested that if your client is in control of a situation, usually the less said in an agreement, the better. The corollary to that rule is that when your client isn't in control, base calculations on items not subject to judgment or manipulation by either party. In the course of preparing financial statements, numerous accounting judgments and estimates are made, such as the useful lives of depreciable assets, the collectibility of receivables, the obsolescence of inventory, and the recognition of liabilities. Alone, or in combination, such estimates can have a profound effect on the bottom lines (net income and equity) of the resulting financial statements. On the other hand, "creative accounting" is less likely to have a significant effect on the "top lines" (revenues and cash) of those same statements. For this reason, if the accounting judgments are to be made by your client, you will want to use a bottom line concept, since she will enjoy the ability to shape the outcome by appropriate selection of accounting methods and estimates. On the other hand, if the opposing party is in charge of the accounting, you will want to key the agreement to the top lines, which are less susceptible to manipulation through creative accounting.

* * *

7. *The Longer the Term of the Agreement, the Less Important the Control of Accounting.*

Control over accounting can be a powerful tool if manipulated to a specific end. However, if the agreement provides for payments or computations over many years, the method of accounting, *if consistently applied,* should not greatly vary the overall results, unless the accounting is dishonest, in which case the problem is not in the selection of the appropriate accounting methods, but the application and verification of those methods. If control of accounting is in the hands of the other party, you might wish to minimize that advantage by utilizing a long measuring period. You should also consider using some variation of cash flow, which is much less susceptible to manipulation. * * *

* * *

8. *Use Proper Accounting Terminology.*

Nothing marks an amateur faster than a failure to use proper terminology. Even today some agreements still refer to "good accounting practices." (The form file lives!) This expression has no meaning in the accountant's world and the lawyer who uses it is likely to get "pot luck" if its meaning is ever adjudicated—especially by a jury. The guiding principles for the preparation of most financial statements are "generally accepted accounting principles" (or "GAAP").

The accounting profession performs three types of services concerning historical financial statements and uses three words very carefully when describing them: an "audit," or an examination in accordance with generally accepted auditing standards, the highest level of an outside accountant's work; a "review" of financial statements, which requires the accountant to perform significantly less pervasive checks and analytical procedures than those performed in an audit; and a "compilation" in which the accountant merely prepares financial statements from the books and records of the company but makes no effort to verify the accuracy or completeness of those records.

* * *

A phone call to a qualified accountant will help you in drafting or testing the language. Such consultations are usually brief and often handled over the phone for little or no cost. Using your client's accountant is often most valuable since he or she knows more about the company, the industry and may have worked on similar agreements in the past.

9. GAAP May Not be Best for Your Client.

Generally accepted accounting principles are filled with assumptions, estimates and practices that may not necessarily reflect the true circumstances and economic health of an entity. GAAP accounting is, admittedly, a conservative discipline and leans heavily toward *understating* assets and profits when judgment is required. The underlying theory here is that management, who is responsible for accounting and the financial statements, tends to overstate assets and earnings, so GAAP and the auditors should be inclined in the other direction. * * *

Existing accounting principles also use *historical* costs (the purchase prices of the assets), rather than the current or fair values of the assets. Some observers call these "hysterical costs," since the numbers presented on the financial statements may bear little relationship to true economic values of the assets. This is increasingly true in an age of intellectual property and other intangible assets. * * *

* * * In too many cases, reality (true economic value) and GAAP simply do not agree.

* * * In simple terms, GAAP is probably a good place to begin the calculations, but not a place to end.

10. GAAP is Not a Static Set of Principles.

* * * Reliance on an old form of agreement could have disastrous consequences if you are dealing in an area in which there has been a major change in GAAP.

More importantly, if the agreement you are preparing is to be in effect for an extended period, you must also take into consideration *which* GAAP you are adopting, that which is in effect now or that which will be in effect when the required computations are to be made. It is also possible to utilize the latter formula with a built-in time delay to allow the parties to adjust for any GAAP changes or to utilize new GAAP methods but at the same time adjust the numerical bases on which financial computations are to be made as if the new principles were in effect at the time the agreement was executed. Remember also that GAAP allows for elections and changes of methods. Most parties are well served by including language stating that methods and elections will be consistent throughout the agreement's period. Often lenders like some certainty in their agreements and loan covenants (such as how loan-to-value ratios are calculated), but enjoy the fact that GAAP tends to become more restrictive over time in its treatment of income and assets. This is a case where more or less specificity on accounting practices and the definitions of some calculations may help your client.

* * *

Agreements Employing Balance Sheet Items

The operative provisions of many agreements are keyed to financial balance sheet items, such as amount and quality of accounts receivable. * * * Balance sheet concepts are commonly employed in legal agreements in the following types of provisions:

- The termination provision of commercial agreements, where either party is given the right to terminate in the event the other party becomes "insolvent."

- The pricing provision of acquisition agreements, where the purchase price is based on the book value, net income, net worth or total assets of the acquired entity.

- Negative covenants in loan agreements, where the borrower is required to maintain a specified minimum working capital, current ratio, tangible assets or net worth; and

- The funding limit provision in a loan or commercial financing or factoring agreement, where the amount of available credit is limited by the reported (book) value of the borrower's inventory, machinery and equipment and/or accounts receivable.

These four types of provisions share in common the fact that one or more of their operative clauses is based on a line item in a company's balance sheet. When the determination of each line item involves complex accounting principles and estimates, an understanding of those principles and judgments is important in drafting documents that help your client.

* * * [I]f a loan agreement contains a covenant requiring the borrower to maintain a current ratio (the borrower's current assets divided by its current liabilities) of at least 2 to 1, the borrower might be placed in default under that covenant in the final year of the loan because, under GAAP, the outstanding balance of the loan would become a current liability in the final year of the loan, since any amount due in less than one year is considered "current" by accounting standards. * * *

* * *

Finally, it's important to understand the effect on accounting data that may result from the exercise of accounting estimates. One observer has called GAAP a six-lane highway. For example, management is given wide latitude in determining the useful lives of its assets. If management concludes that a class of assets should be expensed over three instead of ten years, that decision will have a profound effect on both the balance sheet and income statement. * * *

Basic Considerations

An attorney drafting an agreement utilizing accounting concepts should first be aware of which financial values are relevant to the measurements called for in the agreement. For example, he should help the client decide whether or not a given payment or condition of default or termination should be based on the subject enterprise's total assets, specific assets, current assets, working capital or net worth (among other measures). In making this determination, the attorney should consult with the client about her ability (or the other party to the agreement) to manipulate the chosen accounting measurement through the selection of accounting methods and estimates, based on surrounding circumstances, such as material transactions with related parties.

* * *

Specific Accounting Concerns

As noted above, it may be appropriate to provide that certain financial determinations are to be made on a basis other than GAAP, such as the cash method or modified GAAP. * * * [For example, in] drafting contracts involving balance sheet concepts, consider whether or not it is to your client's advantage to utilize a "hard" or "realizable" asset concept. If you are drafting the default provisions in a loan agreement on behalf of the lender, you should be concerned with whether or not the borrower will have sufficient assets to repay the loan at the time a default occurs. Accordingly, you should provide maximum assurance that sufficient assets of the borrower will always exceed a specified level. * * * [I]t would be of little comfort to your client if an unrealized intangible asset such as "goodwill" represents the borrower's entire net worth.

* * *

Similarly, it is often advisable to specify the treatment of certain balance sheet accounts to suit your client's needs. For example, * * * [l]enders commonly place a cap on the amount they will loan on the basis of the borrower's receivables. [When representing a lender,] you should draft a provision specifying that, for the purposes of computing the borrower's eligible receivables, only receivables not older than a specified period (commonly 90 days, sometimes 60 days) should be counted.

* * *

Dealing With Changing Accounting Principles

* * * The changing nature of generally accepted accounting principles poses significant problems to the attorney drafting an agreement. She should try to anticipate their likely impact in devising contractual payment provisions. The drafting attorney essentially has five choices in dealing with this problem:

1.   She may ignore generally accepted accounting principles and specify with particularity the manner in which a given account or transaction is to be treated;

2.   She may invoke such generally accepted accounting principles as are in effect at the time the agreement is executed;

3.   She may invoke generally accepted accounting principles as may be in effect from time to time;

4.   She may invoke generally accepted accounting principles as they may be changed from time to time, but provide that no change shall be taken into effect for a period sufficiently long to enable the parties to renegotiate in the event that the change has a material effect on the agreement; and

5 .   She may specify that certain proposed changes in generally accepted accounting principles, if adopted by a standard setting authority, will (or will not) be given effect for the purposes of the agreement.

While these alternatives may not be wholly satisfactory, they at least offer an alternative to having one's contract being rewritten by an authoritative accounting body with little or no concern for the interests of the parties.

* * *

Individual Balances

When including *cash* in the overall asset base, be aware that all cash is not "free" or available for unrestricted use. Some restrictions include collateralized balances, security deposits made by others, escrow amounts and compensating balances. There may be maturity restrictions on some amounts.

* * * There is a particular problem when receivables are for services provided. Unlike goods, services (like legal advice) cannot be repossessed and liquidated. * * * Are longer than normal or stated credit terms interest bearing? What other leverage does the service provider have to force (if necessary) payment of the receivable?

* * *

Intangibles must be evaluated individually. In liquidation, goodwill counts for nothing and, conversely, some companies may have explicit goodwill with no asset on the books to reflect this competitive advantage. * * *

Unearned or prepaid items (such as retainers or subscriptions paid to a publisher) are booked as liabilities since the recipient has an obligation to provide goods or services in the future. Hopefully, the cost of providing that good or service is less than the amount paid, so prepaids really have an equity portion in them. GAAP requires the full amount to be carried as a liability until it is earned. * * *

* * *

NOTES

1. Lawyers, especially those representing borrowers, should not underestimate the possibility that changing accounting principles can drastically impact restrictive covenants and other legal documents. In 1990, the FASB issued Statement of Financial Accounting Standards No. 106, entitled "Employers' Accounting for Postretirement Benefits Other Than Pensions," and now codified in FASB ASC Subtopic 715-60, *Compensation—Retirement Benefits—Defined Benefit Plans—Other Postretirement.* Before the pronouncement, many employers used a "pay-as-you-go" basis, or the cash method, to account for the costs incurred to provide postretirement health care benefits. The pronouncement, however, required employers to accrue the expected costs necessary to provide those benefits during the years that the employee renders the services required to earn the benefits. In addition, the new rule required companies to establish a reserve for previously earned benefits. *The Wall Street Journal* reported that the new rules would reduce profits, and therefore equity, by as much as $1 trillion starting in 1993, "a record for any accounting rule." Lee Berton & Robert J. Brennan, *New Medical-Benefits Accounting Rule Seen Wounding Profits, Hurting Shares,* WALL ST. J., Apr. 22, 1992, at C1.

Imagine a restrictive covenant based on financial results under an accounting system that suddenly converts to new rules. On January 1, 2005, many lawyers representing public companies in the European Union faced that exact scenario, when an EU regulation took effect that required all listed companies to use IFRS to prepare consolidated financial statements for fiscal years beginning on or after January 1, 2005. As a result, lawyers in the United States often need to consider IFRS in transactions with EU companies and their subsidiaries.

As discussed earlier on pages 165 to 168, *supra,* although the momentum to incorporate IFRS into the financial reporting system in the United States has slowed to a crawl, FASB and IASB nevertheless have continued to work on various projects intended to converge accounting principles worldwide, most recently completing a joint project on revenue recognition, as described in the next chapter. In addition, the likelihood remains that the industrialized world will eventually embrace some system of global accounting standards. This likelihood deserves serious consideration, especially when drafting or negotiating agreements involving enterprises interested in cross-border securities listings.

Given the drastic effects that changes in accounting principles can cause in restrictive covenants and other legal documents, lawyers in the United States should try to stay abreast of the agenda at the FASB, especially as to any further movement toward IFRS, and perhaps the IASB. Interested readers can monitor developments at the FASB via the Project Roster & Status webpage at http://www.fasb.org/jsp/FASB/Page/SectionPage&cid= 1218220137074.

2. Given that GAAP often sanctions alternate treatments for the same transaction or event and accounting standards cannot begin to address every conceivable situation, knowledgeable lawyers have long advised borrowers or sellers to avoid provisions in covenants that represent or warrant the financial statements as "true, correct, and complete" or as "full and accurate presentations" of the enterprise's financial picture. Now that SOx requires the chief executive officer and chief financial officer of each public company to certify quarterly and annually that to their knowledge the financial statements fairly present in all material respects the financial condition, operating results, and cash flows, without any limitation to GAAP, counsel for lenders and buyers increasingly ask for warranties and representations containing similar language from public companies. In view of the different burdens of proof for criminal convictions under the federal securities and for civil judgments in contract or misrepresentation cases, borrowers and sellers remain well advised to refuse.

3. Some covenants require borrowers to supply lenders or indenture trustees with financial statements and related information within a certain period, typically fifteen days, after filing periodic reports with the SEC. Disagreements have arisen in at least two different circumstances.

First, does the failure to submit timely filings to the SEC breach the loan agreement? Trial courts have reached opposite conclusions on this question. *Compare* Bank of N.Y. v. BearingPoint, Inc., No. 600169/06, 824 N.Y.S.2d 752 (unpublished table decision), 2006 WL 2670143 (N.Y. Sup. Ct. Sept. 18, 2006), *appeal withdrawn*, No. M-6818X, 2007 N.Y. App. Div. LEXIS 524 (N.Y. App. Div. Jan. 16, 2007) (granting the indenture bank trustee's motion for summary judgment, holding the agreement "unambiguously obligates BearingPoint to make the required SEC filings," finding the company liable for breach of contract, and ruling that trial would determine the amount of damages arising from the breach), *with* Cyberonics, Inc. v. Wells Fargo Bank, N.A., No. H-07-121, 2007 WL 1729977 (S.D. Tex. June 13, 2007) (granting borrower Cyberonics' motion for summary judgment because the indenture agreement only required delivery of copies of documents that the borrower had actually filed with the SEC and setting a timetable for Cyberonics to file an affidavit in support of its request for attorneys' fees and for the bank to respond to that affidavit). To date, the federal appellate courts have uniformly affirmed decisions granting summary judgment in such lawsuits. *See, e.g.,* Affiliated Computer Servs., Inc. v. Wilmington Trust Co., 565 F.3d 924 (5th Cir. 2009) (affirming district court order granting summary judgment for borrower because neither the indenture nor the Trust Indenture Act required the borrower to file timely reports with the SEC).

In *Cyberonics*, the district court observed that if "the parties desired to impose a filing obligation rather than a delivery obligation, they could have easily done so." Cyberonics, Inc. v. Wells Fargo Bank, N.A., No. H-07-121, 2007 WL 1729977, at *4 (S.D. Tex. June 13, 2007). Prudent lawyers for lenders and indenture trustees will follow that advice. Interestingly, BearingPoint ultimately reached an agreement with its bondholders that waived the requirement that the company file reports with the SEC, but increased the interest rate on the obligations "by an amount ranging from 0.1 to 0.85 percentage points." *BearingPoint Reaches Deal With Bondholders,* Wash.

POST, Nov. 4, 2006, at D01. Thanks in part to the stock option scandals in the mid-2000s and during an eighteen-month period in 2006 and 2007, missed deadlines for filing periodic reports forced at least twenty-five companies to redeem bonds on an accelerated basis or to pay multimillion dollar fees for waivers. Peter Lattman & Karen Richardson, *Hedge Funds Play Hardball With Firms Filing Late Financials*, WALL ST. J., Aug. 29, 2006, at A1.

Second, what happens if the SEC's filing requirements no longer apply because the borrower has deregistered with the agency? In its recent white paper on improving covenant protections, the Credit Roundtable observed that "[o]n more than a few occasions in recent years, issuers of investment grade bonds have withdrawn from the periodic reporting requirements" in the federal securities laws. Credit Roundtable, Improving Covenant Protections in the Investment Grade Bond Market 6 (Dec. 17, 2007), http://www.creditroundtable.org/Article.aspx?EID=40037. In an effort to ensure that bondholders can obtain reasonable access to financial information about an issuer for as long as its bonds remain outstanding, the Roundtable has proposed a model covenant. *Id.* at 6, 21-23 (rider 4).

4. The Codification changes the way knowledgeable lawyers reference accounting principles and promulgations in legal documents. References to now superseded accounting pronouncements indicate that person who prepared the document qualifies as either careless or "accounting-challenged."

PROBLEM

Problem 5.3. Assume that in mid-20X1 the Mooney Company (the "Company") would like to borrow $2,000,000 at eight percent interest from the First National Bank ("Lender") to build a new manufacturing facility. The proposed loan requires the Company's largest shareholder ("Individual Guarantor") to guarantee the loan, which the Company will repay over fifteen years. If the Company breaches the loan agreement and the breach continues for more than thirty days, the loan agreement treats the breach as a default, which requires immediate repayment. The Company, which the guarantor aspires to "take public" as soon as reasonably possible, has reported $(55,000), $60,000 and $210,000 in net income (loss) during the last three years and has shown $150,000 and $1,050,000 in shareholders' equity at the end of the last two years. For the last two years, the balance sheets list $255,000 and $1,375,000 in total current assets and $195,000 and $700,000 in total current liabilities, respectively. Your client has sent you a loan agreement (the "Loan Agreement") that contains the following provisions for your review and comments:

I. AFFIRMATIVE COVENANTS

Until payment in full of all sums due under this Loan Agreement and unless the prior written consent of the Lender is otherwise obtained, the Company will:

A. *Financial Statements*. Deliver to the Lender: (a) within thirty (30) days after the end of each fiscal month, an unaudited balance sheet as of the end of such month, and a statement of income through the end of such month; (b) within one hundred twenty (120) days after the end of each fiscal year, a balance sheet as of the end of such fiscal year and a statement of income and retained earnings and a statement of changes in financial position through the end of fiscal year, all audited by independent certified public accountants satisfactory to the Lender; and (c) within one hundred twenty (120) days after the end of each calendar year, a personal financial statement of Individual Guarantor for such year in form and substance satisfactory to the Lender. Miller, Zimmerman & Associates are acceptable independent certified accountants for the purpose hereof; provided that the Lender reserves the right in the future to require a different independent certified public accountant. Each set of financial statements delivered under (b) above shall be accompanied by a no-default certificate executed by the independent certified public accountant preparing such financial statements.

B. *Net Working Capital.* Maintain at all times net working capital of at least $100,000 through December 31, 20X2, $150,000 through December 31, 20X3, $200,000 through December 31, 20X4, $250,000 through December 31, 20X5, $300,000 through December 31, 20X6, and $350,000 thereafter, all computed in accordance with good accounting practices.

C. *Current Ratio.* Maintain at all times a ratio of current assets to current liabilities of at least 1.15 to 1 computed in accordance with good accounting practices.

D. *Other.* Maintain net worth of not less than $750,000.

E. *Taxes.* Promptly pay and discharge all of its taxes, assessments and other governmental charges prior to the date on which penalties are attached thereto, establish adequate reserves for the payment of taxes and assessments and make all required withholding and other tax deposits; provided, however, that nothing herein contained shall be interpreted to require the payment of any tax, assessment or charge so long as its validity is being contested in good faith and by appropriate proceedings diligently conducted.

F. *Insurance.* (a) Keep all its property so insurable insured at all times with responsible insurance carriers against fire, theft and other risks in coverage, form and amount satisfactory to the Lender; (b) keep adequately insured at all times in reasonable amounts with responsible insurance carriers against liability on account of damage to persons or property, against business interruption, products liability and under all applicable workers' compensation laws; (c) promptly deliver to the Lender certificates of insurance or any of those insurance policies required to be carried by the Company pursuant hereto, with appropriate endorsements designating the Lender as a named insured or loss payee as requested by the Lender; (d) cause each such insurance policy to contain a notice of cancellation provision satisfactory to the Lender.

II. *NEGATIVE COVENANTS*

So long as any portion of the indebtedness evidenced by the Loan Agreement remains outstanding and without the written consent of the Lender, the Company will not:

A. *Borrowed Money.* Create, incur, assume or suffer to exist any liability for borrowed money except (i) the Loan, (ii) money borrowed from the Lender, and (iii) the liabilities set forth on Schedule A annexed hereto.

B. *Encumbrances.* Create, incur, assume or suffer to exist any mortgage, lien, security interest, pledge or other encumbrance on any of its property or assets, whether now owned or hereafter owned or acquired, except in favor of (i) the Lender and (ii) liens related to this transaction.

C. *Guaranties.* Become a guarantor, surety or otherwise liable for the debts or other obligations of any other person, firm or corporation, whether by agreement to purchase the indebtedness of any other person, firm or corporation, or agreement for the furnishing of funds to any other person, firm or corporation through the purchase of goods, supplies or services (or by way of stock purchase, capital contribution, advance or loan) for the purpose of paying or discharging the indebtedness of any other person, firm or corporation, or otherwise, except as an endorser of instruments for the payment of money deposited to its bank account for collection in the ordinary course of business and as related to this transaction.

D. *Sale of Assets.* Convey, sell, transfer, lease, or sell and lease back all or any substantial portion of its property, assets or business to any other person, firm or corporation, except in the ordinary course of business.

E. *Dividends.* Pay or declare any dividends on capital stock; provided, however, that Company may declare such dividends after June 30, 20X2, as long as the dividends paid in any fiscal year do not exceed 50% of after-tax profits for such fiscal year (after deducting for all debt service requirements for such fiscal year).

F. *Capital Stock.* Purchase, redeem or retire any of its capital stock or issue any additional capital stock.

G. *Leases.* Enter, as lessee, or assume or suffer to exist any leases or rental agreements of real or personal property other than leases requiring payments of less than $18,000 per year in the aggregate.

H. *Merger.* Merge or consolidate with or into any other firm or corporation, or enter into any joint venture or partnership with any other person, firm or corporation.

I. *Investments and Loans.* Make or suffer to exist any investments in, or loans or advances to, any other person, firm or corporation, including, without limitation, loans or advances to its shareholders, directors, officers or employees, except (i) investments in the form of obligations of the United States of America or any agency thereof, (ii) deposits for purchases in the ordinary course of business, and (iii) loans or advances up to an aggregate amount of $3,000 to any officer or employee of the Company.

J. *Capital Expenditures*. Make or incur any capital expenditures in any fiscal year of the Company in excess of $100,000.

III. *SPECIAL COVENANT*

Until payment in full of all the sums due under this Loan Agreement, or as otherwise indicated below, the Individual Guarantor will pledge to the Lender 210,000 shares of the Company's common stock (the "Shares") owned by him subject to the following:

A. The Lender will release to the Individual Guarantor on June 30, 20X3, upon written request from the Individual Guarantor, 105,000 Shares, provided that the Company has a net worth in excess of $1,000,000 and a net after-tax profit plus depreciation exceeding 120% of all debt service requirements as determined by either

(i) certified financial statements of the most recent fiscal year-end of the Company and statements covering the period from the last fiscal year-end audit to a date within sixty (60) days prior to the date of the request; or

(ii) if the request is made subsequent to June 30, 20X3, certified interim review statements for a period not less than six (6) months after the most recent fiscal year-end and statements covering the period from the certified review statement to a date within sixty (60) days prior to the date of the request.

B. The Lender further agrees to release 35,000 Shares annually, or such lesser number as may be held by the Lender, on each June 30 after the date of the original request on the same basis each year as set forth above.

QUESTIONS:

A. If you represent the Company, what advice would you give your client regarding the accounting terminology and concepts used in the Loan Agreement? Would you give your client any other advice?

B. If you represent the Lender, what advice would you give your client regarding the accounting terminology and concepts used in the Loan Agreement? Would you give your client any other advice?

C. If you represent the Individual Guarantor, what advice would you give your client regarding the accounting terminology and concepts used in the Loan Agreement? Would your give your client any other advice?

*

CHAPTER VI

REVENUE RECOGNITION AND ISSUES INVOLVING THE INCOME STATEMENT

A.   IMPORTANCE TO LAWYERS

Beginning in the 1930s, both existing and potential creditors and investors typically turned to the income statement to try to predict an enterprise's potential. After all, any financial returns–whether from interest, dividends, or appreciation in an investment's value–will usually flow from the business's earnings. As mentioned in Chapter I, most businesses prefer to recognize revenue as soon as possible and to defer expenses for as long as possible for financial accounting purposes. Under the Codification, and based on the revenue recognition principle and conservatism, however, a business cannot recognize revenue until the enterprise has substantially completed performance in a bona fide exchange transaction. These *exchange transaction* and *substantial completion* requirements force businesses, and their accountants and lawyers, to focus on substance rather than form in analyzing various problems involving revenue recognition.

Businesses normally can recognize revenue when they exchange goods or services for cash or current claims to future cash and deliver the goods or substantially perform the services that entitle the enterprise to the promised consideration. In certain situations, however, a transaction may not unconditionally transfer the risks that typically accompany a "sale." Sometimes, the circumstances suggest that the consideration received lacks a readily ascertainable value in money or money's worth. In other instances, the vendor has not delivered the goods or performed important obligations under the contract. A seller may even offer the purchaser the right to return the item purchased with no obligation. In all these examples, the circumstances preclude revenue recognition.

Against this background, the matching principle seeks to offset expenses against related revenues wherever possible in determining an enterprise's net income. In other words, accrual accounting strives to match interrelated items of expense and income to the appropriate accounting period. For example, if Marty Jones sells shoes which cost $10,000 for $15,000, treating the $10,000 cost of goods sold as an expense in a different accounting period than that in which the sales occurred would grossly distort Jones' operating results. If an enterprise recognizes income related to a prospective expense in the current accounting period, then the enterprise should accrue the related expense, even if the enterprise must estimate the expense (as accurately as possible), to achieve the desired matching. In contrast, if an expenditure relates to revenues that an enterprise cannot currently recognize or that will benefit a future accounting period generally, then the expenditure represents an asset, perhaps more accurately an unexpired cost, which the enterprise should not charge against income in the current period.

This chapter, therefore, also addresses the use of some deferral and accrual techniques to achieve the most informative periodic reflection of expense and income. Although these materials generally deal with income and expense items separately, we should keep in mind that as a practical matter the problems of choosing the appropriate period for reflecting items of income and expense often arise together rather than as separate questions. After all, business operations usually involve a continuous series of transactions in which the enterprise incurs expenses to produce income. We consider the limitations on revenue recognition first, however, because those more stringent requirements sometimes control the ultimate decision. Every once in a while, an enterprise must defer expenses because they directly relate to revenues which the enterprise cannot recognize until a subsequent accounting period.

In addition to revenue recognition and matching, several other accounting principles influence the income statement. As a practical matter, conservatism affects both revenue recognition and matching. To provide meaningful financial data, a business must also consistently apply the same accounting treatment from period to period and properly disclose the methods used to recognize revenues and record costs in the financial statements. Accordingly, our discussion focuses on five central themes: revenue recognition, conservatism, matching, consistency and disclosure.

Throughout this chapter, we will discuss various situations in which revenue recognition and other issues involving the income statement, such as allocating and matching costs, affect the practice of law. Lawyers should understand the rules governing revenue recognition and the income statement to provide sound legal advice, both prospectively and retrospectively. Increasingly, all lawyers, whether litigators or those in transactional practice and whether representing publicly traded or privately owned enterprises, risk legal liability arising from malpractice if they do not recognize and respond to "red flags" signaling potentially fraudulent revenue recognition issues. An enterprise or its owners or managers, for example, can defraud investors by prematurely recognizing revenues, or by deferring expenses that the business should match against current revenues. Alternatively, the enterprise can shortchange employees entitled to profit-sharing payments by accelerating expenses or deferring revenues.

As a starting point, corporate lawyers, who often serve as critical "gatekeepers" under the federal securities laws, must understand revenue recognition methods to prevent, identify, and remedy financial frauds. As another example, lawyers often perform *due diligence* to determine whether a prospective transaction will further their client's best interests. During this process, the attorney investigates an underlying business in an effort to obtain a deeper understanding about the business's future prospects. Historically, approximately half of the attorney malpractice cases involving due diligence arise from an accounting failure. Among those cases, about forty percent contain issues involving revenue recognition. In such cases, the courts typically look for "red flags" indicating improper or fraudulent revenue recognition. An attorney who fails to spot and investigate such "red flags" can face personal liability for professional malpractice. Rochelle D. Jackson, *Due Diligence[:] Careful Use of the Process Helps to Minimize Liability Exposure*, CORP. COUNS. WEEKLY (BNA), May 10, 2004, at 4. Finally, lawyers often draft, negotiate or interpret contractual provisions that refer to "net income" in employment, collective bargaining, partnership, buy-sell and other agreements. Lawyers must grasp the concepts of revenue recognition to provide legal services competently for such prospective business transactions.

Beginning in the late 1990s, numerous financial frauds involving improper revenue recognition sent shockwaves throughout the financial markets. Enron's sudden collapse in 2001 distinctly marked an escalating accounting crisis in corporate America. In addition to the highly publicized frauds at WorldCom and Tyco, other accounting scandals occurred at well-known companies, including AOL Time Warner, Citigroup, Coca-Cola Co., Freddie Mac, IBM, KMart, Lucent Technologies, Merck, Qwest, and Xerox. In a 2003 study that the Sarbanes-Oxley Act of 2002 required, the SEC discovered that over half of the actions brought for financial reporting violations during the five-year period ended July 30, 2002 involved improper revenue recognition. SEC. & EXCH. COMM'N, REPORT PURSUANT TO SECTION 704 OF THE SARBANES-OXLEY ACT OF 2002 (Jan. 24, 2003), *available at* http://www.sec.gov/news/studies/sox704report.pdf.

Schemes to recognize revenue improperly take many deceptive forms, including fictitious sales, "sham" transactions, related party arrangements, prematurely recognized revenue, and nonmonetary sales agreements engineered solely to create the false appearance of revenues. Although revenues generally represent the largest item on the income statement, until recently multiple commentators have observed that the smallest number of accounting rules governs the largest income statement item.

In May 2014, FASB and IASB issued new and converged accounting rules on revenue recognition for contracts with customers, completing a joint project that began in 2002 to simplify the rules on revenue recognition; to increase comparability across companies, industries and capital markets; and to improve disclosures. Previously, different industries applied various methods and standards for recognizing revenue, a situation that arose from disjointed and sometimes inconsistent accounting principles. FASB's new rules, announced in Accounting Standards Update No. 2014-09, become effective for public companies for fiscal years beginning after December 15, 2016, including interim periods within those years. For non-public companies, the new rules become effective for fiscal years beginning after December 15, 2017, and for interim reports beginning after December 15, 2018. Enterprises can choose between the full retrospective method and the simplified transition method. Under the full retrospective method, an enterprise would apply the new rules to each prior accounting period presented. This alternative will require adopting public companies using the calendar year to report figures under the new rules for 2015, 2016, and 2017 when the enterprises release their financial statements for 2017 in early 2018. As a result, these public companies want the capability to apply the new rules beginning January 1, 2015. Under the simplified transition method, a public company using the calendar year would recognize the cumulative effect of the new rules in retained earnings as of January 1, 2017, the date of initial application. *See* Revenue from Contracts with Customers (Topic 606), Accounting Standards Update No. 2014-09 (Fin. Accounting Standards Bd. 2014), *available via* http://www.fasb.org/cs/ContentServer?c=Document_C&page name=FASB%2FDocument_C%2FDocumentPage&cid=1176164076069.

When effective, the new rules supersede most of the guidance in FASB ASC Topic 605, *Revenue Recognition*. ASU 2014-09 added Topic 606, *Revenue from Contracts with Customers*, as well as Subtopic 340-40, *Other Assets and Deferred Costs—Contracts with Customers,* to the Codification. The new guidance seeks to implement the core principle that "an entity should recognize revenue to depict the transfer of promised goods or services to customers in an amount that reflects the consideration to which the entity expects to be entitled in exchange for those goods or services." To apply that principle, an enterprise would: (i) identify the contract with the customer; (ii) designate the separate performance obligations in the contract; (iii) determine the transaction price; (iv) allocate the transaction price to any separate performance obligations; and (v) recognize revenue when the enterprise satisfies a performance obligation. *See* Revenue from Contracts with Customers (Topic 606), Accounting Standards Update No. 2014-09 (Fin. Accounting Standards Bd. 2014), *available via* http://www.fasb.org/cs/Content Server?c=Document_C&pagename=FASB%2FDocument_C%2FDocument Page&cid=1176164076069. The Boards believe that the new rules will make the area more uniform, and easier for financial statement users to compare statements not just across industries, but on an international scale. In addition, new disclosure requirements aim to provide more useful information to financial statement users.

As mentioned earlier, almost all financial frauds involve income measurement issues, either premature revenue recognition or improper expense deferral. For example, Enron fraudulently recognized revenue from a now infamous "Nigerian barge" agreement with Merrill Lynch. As a result, the energy trader recorded $12 million in profit even though the firm promised to repurchase the barges and, therefore, retained the risk of loss. *See, e.g., Judge Refuses Defendants' Bid To Have Trials Held Separately*, Wall St. J., Apr. 26, 2004, at C5. WorldCom improperly treated about $11 billion in current operating expenses as assets.

Because investigators often find the "fingerprints" and failings of lawyers behind various financial frauds, lawyers can no longer avoid responsibility for such accounting shenanigans by blaming unscrupulous executives and rogue auditors. In response to the accounting scandals, Congress enacted SOx section 307 that directed the SEC to establish rules requiring lawyers who practice before the SEC to report evidence of financial frauds that may violate the securities laws or breach fiduciary duties to the appropriate corporate officer or body, including the audit committee or board of directors.

After disturbing increases in the number of public companies restating prior financial statements beginning in the late 1990s and peaking in 2006, a study that the Center for Audit Quality commissioned using data for the years 2003-2012 from Audit Analytics shows that restatements declined rapidly until 2009 and then remained essentially flat through 2012. In 2006, SEC registrants filed 1,784 restatements. The number of restatements fell to 1,268 in 2007 and then to 929 in 2008, before bottoming at 711 in 2009. Restatements rose to 817 in 2010, declined slightly to 810 in 2011, and then dropped to 738 in 2012.

Beginning in late 2004, the SEC has required public companies to file Form 8-K to disclose certain restatements. Item 4.02, Non-Reliance on Previously Issued Financial Statements or a Related Audit Report, requires a registrant to file a current report within four business days when either the registrant or the independent auditor concludes that the investing public should no longer rely on the financial statements. The financial community often refers to such disclosures as "4.02" or "Big R" restatements. Since 2010, the percentage of restatements filed *without an Item 4.02*, so-called "revision" or "small r" restatements, has continued to grow. In 2012, registrants treated a record sixty-five percent of all restatements as revisions, up from thirty-nine percent in 2005, the first year that SEC rules required public companies to file Item 4.02 notices.

Over the years, lawyers have occasionally felt the consequences from the SEC's efforts to remedy widespread problems in revenue recognition and financial accounting reporting. The SEC can censure or bar attorneys from practicing before the agency for negligence or intentional conduct, unethical behavior, or improper activities, such as obstructing an investigation. The stock option backdating scandals that began drawing attention in 2006, and ultimately involved more than 180 companies, cost lawyers their positions as general counsel at Apple Inc., Comverse Technology Inc., Juniper Networks Inc., McAfee Inc., Mercury Interactive, LLC, Monster Worldwide Inc, and UnitedHealth Group. Inc. *See Thomsen Cites Attorneys' Roles in Backdating, Offering Frauds, Insider Suits*, 6 Corp. Accountability Rep. (BNA) 457 (May 2, 2008); Marc B. Dorfman, *Top 10 Securities and Exchange Commission Enforcement Developments of 2005*, 38 Sec. Reg. & L. Rep. (BNA) 385 (Mar. 6, 2006) (ranking the volume and variety of SEC enforcement proceedings against lawyers as "the Number One SEC enforcement development of 2005").

Since the publication of the fourth edition, involvement in financial frauds has continued to cost various lawyers their jobs, their ability to practice law, their professional reputations, and, in some cases, their freedom. Recent examples include the following:

- David Lubben, the former general counsel at United Health during its stock option scandal, agreed to a final judgment that ordered him to pay more than $1.4 million in disgorgement, $350,000 in prejudgment interest, and a $575,000 civil penalty. Lubben also consented to an antifraud injunction, a five-year bar from serving as an officer or director for a public company, and a three-year suspension from appearing or practicing as an attorney before the SEC. *In re* Lubben, Accounting and Auditing Enforcement Release No. 2939 (Feb. 19, 2009), http://www.sec.gov/litigation/admin/2009/34-59423.pdf; SEC v. UnitedHealth Grp. Inc., Litigation Release No. 20,836 (Dec. 22, 2008), http://www.sec.gov/litigation/litreleases/2008/lr20836.htm.

- Jordan H. Mintz, a former Enron vice president and general counsel of Enron's Global Finance Group, and Rex R. Rogers, a former Enron vice president and associate general counsel, who served as Enron's top securities lawyer, consented to judgments that ordered them each to pay one dollar in disgorgement and $25,000 in civil penalties and suspended them from appearing or practicing before the SEC as an attorney for two years. The charges arose from the lawyers' participation in a fraudulent transaction involving a Brazilian power plant intended to inflate Enron's earnings. *In re* Mintz, Accounting and Auditing Enforcement Release No. 2926 (Jan. 26, 2009), http://sec.gov/litigation/admin/2009/34-59296.pdf; *In re* Rogers, Accounting and Auditing Enforcement Release No. 2927 (Jan. 26, 2009), http://sec.gov/litigation/admin/2009/34-59297.pdf.

- Christi R. Sulzbach, formerly the chief compliance officer, executive vice president and general counsel at Tenet Healthcare Corporation, received an administrative order suspending her from appearing or practicing before the Commission as an attorney. Previously, a federal district court ordered Sulzbach to pay one dollar in disgorgement and a $120,000 civil penalty for intentionally or recklessly failing to know about Tenet's unsustainable strategy to inflate its Medicare revenues and failing to disclose that unsustainable strategy. *In re* Sulzbach, Accounting and Auditing Enforcement Release No. 3000 (June 25, 2009).

When an attorney actively participates in a financial fraud, the Justice Department has also brought criminal charges. In late 2012, a federal jury in New York again convicted Joseph P. Collins, a former partner at Mayer Brown LLP, on conspiracy, securities fraud, wire fraud, and false statement charges. Although Collins remains free on bail pending appeal, the court in 2013 sentenced him to one year and one day in prison and two years of supervised release. For years, Collins served as the primary outside counsel for Refco Inc., a commodity broker that collapsed in 2005, and its predecessor, Refco Group Ltd. The convictions arose from his participation in a scheme that failed to disclose hundreds of millions of dollars in related party transactions and that ultimately led to Refco's bankruptcy. Earlier in 2012, the Second Circuit vacated Collins' 2009 conviction based on a faulty jury instruction and remanded the case for a new trial. After the first conviction, the SEC issued an administrative order suspending Collins from appearing or practicing before the agency as an attorney. Later, the district court entered a settled final judgment on related civil charges that enjoins Collins from violating antifraud provisions in the federal securities laws. In 2010, the Second Circuit affirmed the dismissal of a class action federal securities lawsuit that Refco investors brought against Collins and Mayer Brown. As set forth more fully on page 213, *supra*, Dodd-Frank now allows the SEC to recover money damages in civil enforcement actions from any person, including a lawyer, who knowingly or recklessly aids or abets a violation of specified federal securities laws. *See* SEC v. Collins, Accounting and Auditing Enforcement Release No. 3145 (June 14, 2010), http://www.sec.gov/litigation/litreleases/2010/lr221555.htm; *see also Attorney Collins Convicted on Charges Stemming From Role in Refco Collapse*, 44 Sec. Reg. & L. Rep. (BNA) 2205 (Dec. 3, 2012).

Several state courts have brought disciplinary actions against lawyers involved in financial frauds. For example, the Appellate Division, Second Department, of the New York Supreme Court disbarred Steven Woghin, the former general counsel of Computer Associates, a company that used so-called "thirty-five day months" to recognize revenue prematurely and to meet revenue and earnings expectations. In 2004, Woghin pled guilty to conspiracy to commit federal securities fraud and obstruction of justice, admitting that he not only supervised attorneys who routinely backdated agreements or reported them as having been signed within the earlier quarter, but also that he personally participated in such activities and sought to conceal such practices from the authorities. *In re* Woghin, 880 N.Y.S.2d 74 (N.Y. App. Div. 2009). Previously, Woghin agreed to a suspension from appearing or practicing before the SEC as an attorney. *In re* Woghin, Accounting and Auditing Enforcement Release No. 2133 (Nov. 10, 2004), *available at* http://www.sec.gov/litigation/admin/34-50653.htm. In 2007, the Supreme Court of Oregon ordered a 120-day suspension from the practice of law for an in-house lawyer who violated a disciplinary rule prohibiting dishonesty, fraud, deceit, and misrepresentation. The lawyer signed a management representation letter to his company's independent auditor when he knew that the letter contained false statements. Based on the letter, the auditor allowed the company to recognize a $4.1 million sale even though the purported purchaser never entered into a fixed contract. *In re* Fitzhenry, 162 P.3d 260 (Or. 2007); *see also In re* FLIR Systems, Inc., Accounting and Enforcement Release No. 1637, [2001-2003 Transfer Binder] Fed. Sec. L. Rep. (CCH) ¶ 75,152 (Sept. 30, 2002), *available at* http://www.sec.gov/litigation/admin/33-8135.htm; *In re* Fitzhenry, Accounting and Enforcement Release No. 1670, [2001-2003 Transfer Binder] Fed. Sec. L. Rep. (CCH) ¶ 75,185 (Nov. 21, 2002), *available at* http://www.sec.gov/litigation/admin/34-46870.htm (barring the accused from practice before the SEC for five years).

The litigation that follows from financial frauds can impose catastrophic costs. Not surprisingly, several companies have paid enormous financial damages after financial scandals. In 2007, Tyco International Ltd. agreed to pay a record approximately $3 billion to resolve a class action arising from the financial fraud at that company. *See Tyco Shareholder Suit Ends in Record $3 Billion Settlement*, 5 Corp. Accountability Rep. (BNA) 508 (May 18, 2007).

That amount surpassed the at least $2.83 billion that Cendant Corp. agreed to pay to settle the class action lawsuit that arose from accounting irregularities within the company's consolidated group, which previously stood as the largest settlement by a corporate defendant in the history of class action securities fraud litigation. *See Cendant Corp. Agrees to Record Payment To Settle Class Financial Fraud Allegations*, 31 Sec. Reg. & L. Rep. (BNA) 1618 (Dec. 13, 1999). In 2006, Nortel Networks Corp. agreed to a settlement worth about $2.4 billion to resolve two class actions arising from the company's accounting scandal. The company agreed to pay $575 million in cash and to issue more than 625 million additional shares to end the litigation. Mark Heinzl, *Nortel Networks to Pay $2.4 Billion to Settle Suits*, WALL ST. J., Feb. 9, 2006, at B5.

The SEC and other governmental regulators may also impose monetary penalties in response to financial frauds. Notably, for WorldCom's multi-billion dollar fraudulent inflation of income, in 2003 the SEC imposed a $2.25 billion fine, $1.5 billion suspended, against the company, the largest civil money penalty ever imposed against a corporation not a broker-dealer. *See, e.g., U.S. Court Approves Record Settlement To Resolve SEC Case Against WorldCom*, CORP. L. DAILY (BNA), July 8, 2003. In 2006, and as described in more detail on pages 378 to 379, *infra*, insurance giant AIG agreed to pay more than $1.6 billion to resolve SEC, New York state, and Justice Department charges arising from its accounting fraud and other misconduct.

Companies also can incur significant legal costs for accounting investigations and often bankruptcies resulting from financial frauds. *The Wall Street Journal* reported that Enron's bankruptcy has generated a record-breaking and "eye-popping" almost $1 billion in fees to lawyers, financial advisors, and turnaround experts. Some observers have estimated that in slightly more than one year Qwest spent as much as $75 million in legal fees for outside attorneys alone during an accounting investigation and continued to spend about $7 million per month, the equivalent of approximately 100 lawyers billing $350 per hour for 50 hours per week. Dennis K. Berman, *Qwest Is Spending Top Dollar to Defend Accounting Practices*, WALL ST. J., Mar. 10, 2003, at C1. In addition to the "out-of-pocket" costs, these frauds prevent company management from devoting attention to other business matters.

Finally, financial frauds have demonstrated that such scandals can severely damage a company's reputation, inflicting a cost extremely detrimental to the "bottom line," yet less capable of financial measurement. Significantly, corporate reputations fell to depressing lows in the days after the accounting scandals. *See, e.g.,* Ronald Alsop, *Reputations of Big Companies Tumble in Consumer Survey; 'Money Can Rob the Goodness,'* WALL ST. J., Feb. 19, 2004, at B1 (discussing the continued decline in corporate reputations). As expected, following their financial scandals, Enron, Global Crossing, and WorldCom ranked among the "bottom 10 losers." *Id.* These damaged reputations can affect consumer decisions and ultimately result in lost customers. A study examining all 585 companies that the SEC brought enforcement actions against from 1978 to 2002 for financial misrepresentation found that the largest financial losses from the misconduct arose from damaged reputations rather than penalties paid to regulators. For each dollar that a company misleadingly inflated its market value, on average the company lost that dollar, plus an additional $3.08, when the misbehavior came to light. Moreover, the study estimated the reputational damage amounted to more than 7.5 times any penalties that the legal and regulatory system imposed. Steve Burkholder, *Money Loss from Cooking the Books Stems from Hurt Reputation, Study Says*, 4 Corp. Accountability Rep. (BNA) 1160 (Nov. 17, 2006). An even more recent study found that the companies that the SEC cited for fraud in accounting and auditing enforcement releases ("AAERs") between 2000 and 2007 show higher incidences of significant drops in stock prices, investor lawsuits, and bankruptcy. *Deloitte Group Finds Companies Take Major Hits for Fraud Involvement*, Sec. L. Daily (BNA), Dec. 17, 2008. Rebuilding a damaged corporate reputation and regaining the public's trust can take years.

Continuing a theme from Chapter V, we will again see that an enterprise may use GAAP for preparing financial statements for creditors and investors, another set of rules for tax purposes and still another for reporting to a regulatory agency. Different standards may also apply for specific contracts. For this reason, an enterprise may keep different sets of accounting records to maintain information necessary for the various sets of rules that may apply to the enterprise. We will also see, however, that separate sets of financial records can indicate financial fraud.

B.   ESSENTIAL REQUIREMENTS FOR REVENUE RECOGNITION

According to the Codification, an enterprise can recognize revenue only when (1) realized or realizable, a threshold that generally requires a bona fide exchange transaction with an outsider; and (2) earned, a standard that seeks to ensure that the enterprise has substantially accomplished the earnings process. *See* FASB ASC ¶ 605-10-25-1 (a codification of RECOGNITION AND MEASUREMENT IN FINANCIAL STATEMENTS OF BUSINESS ENTERPRISES, Statement of Fin. Accounting Concepts No. 5, § 83 (Fin. Accounting Standards Bd. 1984). Not every case or administrative authority, however, identifies two prerequisites for revenue recognition in just this way. For example, the SEC staff lists *four* conditions that an enterprise must meet before recognizing revenue. In Staff Accounting Bulletin No. 101, *Revenue Recognition in Financial Statements*, the SEC's staff attempted to put together, in a single document, all the authoritative literature found in various standards on revenue recognition. In addition, the staff expressed its belief that enterprises can recognize revenue only upon satisfying the following four conditions: (1) the evidence must persuasively demonstrate that an arrangement exists; (2) the enterprise must have delivered the product or performed the services; (3) the arrangement must contain a fixed or determinable sales price; and (4) the circumstances must reasonably assure collectibility. Revenue Recognition in Financial Statements, Staff Accounting Bulletin No. 101, 64 Fed. Reg. 68,936 (Dec. 9, 1999), *available at* http://www.sec.gov/interps/

account/sab101.htm. Subsequently, the SEC staff revised this interpretative guidance to rescind material that private sector developments in U.S. GAAP had addressed and to incorporate portions of the frequently asked questions and answers document. Staff Accounting Bulletin No. 104, 68 Fed. Reg. 74,436 (Dec. 23, 2003), *available at* http://www.sec.gov/interps/account/sab104rev.pdf.

Given the different approaches, this chapter will organize our discussion about revenue recognition around the two most commonly identified requirements: a bona fide exchange transaction and substantial completion. Please note, however, that even the distinctions between these two requirements can blur. Regardless of how we present these requirements, lawyers should keep in mind that significant incentives can motivate individuals and businesses to report good operating results, which they can do by overstating revenues for the accounting period. For publicly-traded enterprises, the financial markets' tendency to focus on the most recent, quarterly results can encourage managers to inflate or smooth earnings in an attempt to produce or maintain a higher market price for the business's securities, often so that the executives can profit from stock options. A higher market price may also enable an enterprise to use overvalued ownership interests as "currency" in corporate acquisitions. Management's desire to obtain a loan or more credit can also provide motivation for prematurely recognizing revenue and overstating accounts receivable. A desire to postpone addressing financial difficulties or to avoid violating a restrictive covenant can also explain financial frauds for both publicly-traded and closely-held businesses. In either context, managers, accountants and other employees may feel that their job or compensation depends upon results. Some individuals commit financial frauds to qualify for larger bonuses or promotions. These same motivations also explain actions which some owners or managers in closely-held businesses take to *understate* earnings to reduce income taxes. Understated earnings may also enable companies to grant stock options to executives at lower prices and to minimize payments to employees under profit-sharing plans and labor agreements or to owners under buy-sell agreements or share repurchases.

Lawyers should learn to recognize ways that unscrupulous individuals have perpetrated financial frauds involving revenue recognition. Fraudulent practices have included creating fictitious transactions; backdating transactions, or turning back computer clocks, to record revenue in an earlier period; prematurely shipping goods or sending items not ordered; shipping goods to a warehouse; selling goods to customers that lack the financial ability to pay; and recording "sales" when the transaction remains subject to contingencies. Side letters may attempt to hide various contingencies that can arise from return or cancellation privileges, sales subject to resale, which the business community often refers to as *consignments*, or the vendor's agreement to provide future services. Walter Schuetze, formerly chief accountant at the SEC's Division of Enforcement, repeatedly stated that "premature revenue recognition remains 'the recipe of choice for cooking a company's books.' " Phyllis Diamond, *Accounting Fraud Is Top Priority, Enforcement Officials Tell CPAs*, 30 Sec. Reg. & L. Rep. (BNA) 1757 (Dec. 11, 1998).

Warning signs indicating ideal conditions for accounting fraud include unrealistic financial goals and revenue targets; large transactions at the end of an accounting period; transactions involving related parties; unusual or complex transactions; auditor changes; stray invoices or monthly statements; and high employee turnover, especially unexplained resignations, in the accounting or finance departments. An important report concluded that the so-called *tone at the top*, the atmosphere that top management establishes and the related corporate environment or culture, serves as the most important deterrent to fraudulent financial reporting. A lax tone will more likely give rise to fraudulent financial reporting. National Commission on Fraudulent Financial Reporting, Report of the National Commission on Fraudulent Financial Reporting 32 (1987).

Financial frauds often require cooperation from lower-level employees or customers to deceive auditors. In *In re* Kurzweil Applied Intelligence, Inc., Accounting and Auditing Enforcement Release No. 689, [1995–1998 Transfer Binder] Fed. Sec. L. Rep. (CCH) ¶ 74,204 (S.E.C. July 25, 1995), sales representatives forged signatures on sales quotes and altered documents. Employees in the accounting department destroyed records relating to the fraudulent sales, helped to hide inventory, and created fictitious accounts receivable collection sheets. The perpetrators in *Kurzweil* also enlisted customers to sign false audit confirmations and to misrepresent the status of negotiations which the company had fraudulently recorded as sales. The participants in the scheme gave a warehouse a false list to use in completing another audit confirmation. Finally, following instructions from one of the executives, a sales person obtained an audit confirmation from a customer, signed the customer's name and used the customer's telefacsimile cover sheet to transmit the confirmation directly to the auditors.

In response to the frequent involvement by lower-level employees and third parties in financial frauds, SOx section 303 directed the SEC to establish rules to prohibit any officer or director of an issuer, or any other person acting under the direction of an officer or director, from taking any action to fraudulently influence, coerce, manipulate, or mislead the issuer's independent auditor for the purpose of rendering a financial statement materially misleading. In 2003, the SEC promulgated final rules to implement that provision. See 17 C.F.R. § 240.13b2-2(b) (2014); *see also* Improper Influence on Conduct of Audits, Financial Reporting Release No. 71, 68 Fed. Reg. 31,820 (May 28, 2003). In the release adopting the final rules, the SEC emphasized that the statute only requires "fraudulent" action with regard to conduct to "influence" the auditor. 68 Fed. Reg. at 31,823. At least with respect to the verbs "coerce, manipulate, or mislead," the SEC's final rules prohibit such conduct that a person "knew or should have known" could result in rendering the financial statements materially misleading. By seemingly adopting a negligence standard, the SEC arguably ignored the provision in SOx section 303 that prohibits conduct "for the purpose of rendering such financial statements materially misleading." Although the SEC admits that the language "knew or should have known" historically reflected a negligence standard, the SEC maintained that SOx's objective to restore investor confidence justifies the Commission's interpretation. *Id.* at 31,826-27. In addition, the SEC stressed that persons "under the direction" of an officer or director encompasses a broader category than supervision or control and could include third parties such as outside lawyers, customers, or vendors. Notably, the SEC specifically described "inaccurate or misleading legal analysis" as conduct that could violate Rule 13b2-2(b). *Id.* at 31,821-23. Although the new rule extends to a broad category of actors, only the SEC can enforce the provision in a civil proceeding. In essence, the new rules supplement regulations issued under the Foreign Corrupt Practices Act that prohibit, among other things, falsifying books and accounting records, providing false or misleading statements, or omitting to state any material fact to an accountant in connection with an audit.

NOTES

1. Lawyers should recognize that the criminal penalties arising from the financial frauds in the late 1990s and early 2000s reflect the government's desire to "reward" persons who cooperate with investigators and to punish severely defendants who do not. After jury convictions arising from the corporate scandals in the early 2000s, judges have imposed the following prison sentences on prominent corporate executives:

- Bernard Ebbers, former WorldCom CEO (twenty-five years)
- Dennis Kozlowski, former Tyco CEO (up to twenty-five years)
- Mark Swartz, former Tyco CFO (up to twenty-five years)
- Walter A. Forbes, former Cendant Corp. chairman (twelve years and seven months)
- Sanjay Kumar, former Computer Associates International CEO (twelve years).

In 2013, the U.S. District Court for the South District of Texas resentenced former Enron CEO Jeffrey Skilling to fourteen years in prison after the Fifth Circuit vacated his original sentence of more than twenty-four years in a case that reached the Supreme Court.

Improper revenue recognition can also lead to criminal penalties against the enterprise involved. Sarbanes-Oxley added several new federal white-collar crimes and significantly increased the maximum potential criminal fines and imprisonment for other offenses. As a notable example, SOx section 1106 enhanced the maximum potential criminal penalties for persons who violate the Securities Exchange Act of 1934 from a $1,000,000 fine and ten years imprisonment to $5,000,000 and twenty years imprisonment, as well as increasing the maximum fine for corporations from $2,500,000 to $25,000,000. Moreover, SOx sections 805, 905, and 1104 directed the U.S. Sentencing Commission to review and amend the federal sentencing guidelines to increase the criminal penalties for certain white-collar crimes. Accordingly, in 2003 the U.S. Sentencing Commission issued "emergency amendments" that established the sentence guidelines for SOx's newly created white-collar crimes and significantly enhanced the federal prison term for financial frauds that: (1) adversely affect more than 250 victims; (2) substantially jeopardize the solvency or financial security of 100 or more victims, an organization employing 1,000 or more employees, or a publicly traded company; (3) involve an officer or director; or (4) cause losses exceeding $200 million and $400 million, respectively. Sentencing Guidelines for United States Courts, 68 Fed. Reg. 2615, 2617 (Jan. 17, 2003). Later in 2003, the Sentencing Commission voted unanimously to make these amendments permanent. Sentencing Guidelines for United States Courts, 68 Fed. Reg. 26,960, 26,963 (May 16, 2003).

Additionally, lawyers should know that the SEC may impose a broad array of civil sanctions for financial frauds. As mentioned in the chapter overview, the SEC can impose monetary fines for misconduct. Recall the $2.25 billion fine, $1.5 billion suspended, that the SEC imposed against WorldCom in 2003, the largest civil money penalty ever imposed against a non broker-dealer, and the more than $1.6 billion that the SEC, New York authorities, and the Justice Department collected from AIG in 2006. Moreover, SOx sections 305 and 1105 authorized the SEC for the first time to bar, either temporarily or permanently, "unfit" officers and directors from serving in such capacity for any public company. 15 U.S.C. §§ 77h-1(f), 77t(e), 78u(d)(2), 78u-3(f) (2012). Finally, pursuant to SOx section 304, the SEC regularly seeks to disgorge any benefits that officers and directors received from their fraudulent conduct. As only one illustration, for fraudulently inflating revenues by approximately $3 billion, in 2003 the SEC fined two former Xerox officers $1 million each, the largest fines ever imposed against individuals for financial fraud, barred four officers from serving as officer or directors for any public company, and ordered six former senior executives to pay almost $20 million in disgorgement and prejudgment interest. SEC v. Allaire, Accounting and Auditing Enforcement Release No. 1796, 7 Fed. Sec. L. Rep. (CCH) ¶ 75,456 (June 5, 2003). More recently, Richard M. Scrushy, the former chairman and CEO of HealthSouth Corporation, consented to a final judgment that, among other things, ordered him to pay $77.5 million in disgorgement, subject to an offset for any amounts paid in certain other lawsuits. SEC v. Scrushy, Accounting and Auditing Enforcement Release No. 2599 (Apr. 23, 2007), http://www.sec.gov/litigation/litreleases/2007/lr20084.htm. In 2005, a federal jury acquitted Scrushy on thirty-six criminal fraud charges after he became the first CEO indicted under SOx. The final judgment in the SEC action, which also permanently bars Scrushy from serving as an officer or director of a public company, further imposed $3.5 million in civil penalties, illustrating some important differences between civil and criminal liability. Earlier, the Alabama Supreme Court affirmed a partial summary judgment ordering Scrushy to repay almost $48 million, including more than $46 million in bonuses he received from HealthSouth and prejudgment interest. Scrushy v. Tucker, 955 So. 2d 988 (Ala. 2006). Multiplying Scrushy's financial woes exponentially, in early 2011, the Supreme Court of Alabama affirmed a $2.88 billion judgment against him in a shareholders' derivative action for HealthSouth, reportedly the largest judgment against a single executive. *See* Scrushy v. Tucker, 70 So. 3d 289 (Ala. 2011); *see also* Valerie Bauerlein & Mike Esterl, *Judge Orders Scrushy to Pay $2.88 Billion in Civil Suit*, Wall St. J., June 19, 2009, at B1.

2. In late 2007, the SEC announced a record $468 million settlement in an enforcement action in a stock options backdating case against Dr. William W. McGuire, the former CEO and chairman of UnitedHealth Grp. Inc. The SEC's release described the settlement as "the first with an individual under the 'clawback' provision (Section 304) of the Sarbanes-Oxley Act to deprive corporate executives of their stock sale profits and bonuses earned while their companies were misleading investors." McGuire agreed to "reimburse UnitedHealth for all incentive- and equity-based compensation he received from 2003 through 2006, totaling approximately $448 million in cash bonuses, profits from the exercise and sale of UnitedHealth stock, and unexercised UnitedHealth options." He also agreed to disgorge other ill-gotten gains, plus prejudgment interest, and to pay a $7 million civil penalty. In addition, the order bars McGuire from serving as an officer or director of a public company for ten years. SEC v. McGuire, Accounting and Auditing Enforcement Release No. 2754 (Dec. 6, 2007), http://www.sec.gov/litigation/litreleases/2007/lr20387.

SOx section 304, which requires a CEO or CFO to return incentive-based or equity-based compensation to an issuer when an accounting restatement occurs "as a result of misconduct," suffers from important limitations. First, the provision applies only to CEOs and CFOs. Second, the disgorgement only applies to compensation received during the twelve-month period following the misstated financials. Third, section 304 requires an accounting restatement. At least one federal district court has held that the SEC cannot invoke the statute without the actual filing of a restatement, potentially after the SEC compels or orders the company to restate its financial statements. SEC v. Shanahan, 624 F. Supp. 2d 1072, 1078 (E.D. Mo. 2008). Fourth, to date the federal courts have rejected the argument that the provision creates a private right of action to address violations. In a case of first impression in the federal appellate courts, the Ninth Circuit agreed with dicta in an earlier Third Circuit decision and the decisions of at least eight different district courts and held that no private remedy exists under section 304. *See In re* Digimarc Corp. Deriv. Litig., 549 F.3d 1223, 1230-33 (9th Cir. 2008); *see also* Pirelli Armstrong Tire Corp. Retiree Med. Benefits Trust *ex rel.* Fed. Nat. Mortg. Ass'n v. Raines, 534 F.3d 779, 793 (3rd Cir. 2008).

The statute also does not clearly set forth what misconduct can trigger a so-called "clawback." Does misconduct encompass negligence? Must the CEO or CFO engage in wrongdoing? In 2009, the SEC brought the first action under section 304 that sought only reimbursement and that did not allege that the defendant engaged in fraudulent conduct. The SEC filed suit to recover more than $4 million in bonuses and profits from the stock sales that the former CEO of CSK Auto Corporation received while the company was committing accounting fraud. *See* SEC v. Jenkins, Accounting and Auditing Enforcement Release No. 3025 (July 23, 2009), http://www.sec.gov/litigation/litreleases/2009/lr21149a.htm. In 2010, the United States District Court for the District of Arizona denied the former CEO's motion to dismiss. The court held that SOx did not require personal misconduct to trigger a reimbursement obligation. SEC v. Jenkins, 718 F. Supp. 2d 1070 (D. Ariz. 2010). In 2011, the SEC announced that, subject to court approval, the former CEO had agreed to settle the case by reimbursing the company $2.8 million in bonuses and stock profits. The SEC has also brought other no-fault actions against the CEOs at Diebold Inc. and Beazer Homes USA Inc., which settled upon filing. *See, e.g.,* SEC v. McCarthy, Accounting and Auditing Enforcement Release No. 3250 (Mar. 4, 2011), *available at* http://www.sec.gov/litigation/litreleases/ 2011/lr21873.htm (CEO agreed to reimburse Beazer for a $5.7 million incentive bonus, 40,103 restricted stock units, $772,000 in stock sale profits, and 78,763 restricted shares awarded in, or for, fiscal 2006). When approving the settlement with the Beazer CEO, the United States District Court for the Northern District of Georgia ordered the CEO not to seek any indemnification for the payments under the settlement. *See Settlement Between SEC, Beazer CEO in Clawback Case Wins Court Approval,* 9 Corp. Accountability Rep. (BNA) 371 (Apr. 1, 2011). After these developments, any accounting restatement now creates worries for any CEO or CFO who received incentive-based or equity-based compensation during the twelve-month period that begins when the issuer issued or filed the misstated financial document. *See* Yin Wilczek, *CSK's Jenkins, SEC Reach Tentative Accord to Settle Agency's No-Fault Clawback Action,* 9 Corp. Accountability Rep. (BNA) 370 (Apr. 1, 2011); Tina Chi, *SEC's Latest Use of SOX 'Clawback' Statute Seen Shifting Calculus About Restatements,* 7 Corp. Accountability Rep. (BNA) 1050 (Aug. 28, 2009).

Recognizing the limitations in SOx section 304, various institutional investors encouraged public companies to adopt broader "clawback" or executive compensation recoupment policies than section 304 authorized and to disclose such policies. In particular, these investors wanted, first, policies that apply to all senior executives, for longer periods of time, and in situations beyond misconduct and, then, actual enforcement of the policies. Increasingly, such corporate policies also apply to excessive risk-taking or detrimental conduct, which can include failing to "blow the whistle" when someone else violates a corporate policy. *See* Tina Chi, *Companies Assessing Risk Should Review Pay Programs, Implement Clawback Policies,* 8 Corp. Accountability Rep. (BNA) 162 (Feb. 19, 2010); *see also* Robin Sidel, *Wall Street Toughens Its Rules on Clawbacks,* WALL ST. J., Jan. 27, 2010, at C1. According to the executive compensation research firm Equilar Inc., by the end of 2008 almost seventy-two percent of *Fortune 100* companies had adopted clawback policies that allow those firms to recoup executive compensation following a financial restatement or misconduct. *See* Mary Hughes, *Firm Clawback Polices Go Beyond SOX to Recoup Ill-Gained Profits, Study Finds,* 7 Corp. Accountability Rep. (BNA) 1364 (Nov. 20, 2009).

Dodd-Frank section 954 requires the SEC to issue rules directing the national securities exchanges to bar from listing any issuer that does not develop, disclose, and implement a clawback policy. Such policies must apply to any current or former executive officer who received incentive-based compensation, including stock options, based on erroneous financial information required under any federal securities law in the three-year period before an accounting restatement. These policies must also require the executive to repay the excess over what the issuer would have paid under the restatement. *See* 15 U.S.C. § 78j-4 (2012). As a practical matter, this provision's implementation can only apply after: (1) the SEC proposes and issues implementing regulations; (2) the securities exchanges draft listing standards that comply with the final regulations; (3) the SEC approves the listing standards; and (4) listed companies adopt policies that satisfy the listing standards. In the meantime, all public companies—and most private firms—should consider adopting new, or modifying existing, clawback policies. *See* Pierre Greene, *Experts Advise Compensation Committees to Prepare for SEC Clawback Requirements*, 9 Corp. Accountability Rep. (BNA) 891 (July 29, 2011) (containing examples offering sample language).

Although the SEC has not yet issued final regulations pursuant to Dodd-Frank section 954, and the provision does not impose any deadline for any action on the agency, companies continue to adopt, expand, and enforce clawback policies. According to the executive compensation firm Equilar Inc., the number of *Fortune 100* companies disclosing clawback policies increased from less than twenty percent in 2009 to more than eighty-five percent in 2012. *See* Mary Hughes, *Clawbacks Gain Favor, Raise Issues In Absence of Guidance, Speakers Say*, 11 Corp. Accountability Rep. (BNA) 685 (June 28, 2013). In response to trading scandals at their banks, UBS AG and J. P. Morgan Chase & Co. clawed back compensation. UBS cancelled half of the share-based bonuses awarded to investment bankers whose bonuses exceeded $2 million, or two million Swiss francs, in 2011. In response to the "London Whale" fiasco in 2012, J.P. Morgan Chase reportedly seized about two years of total annual compensation from three London-based traders responsible for the blunder by voiding restricted stock and stock option grants. In addition, Credit Suisse Group AG, Goldman Sachs Group Inc., and Morgan Stanley have reportedly used clawbacks in the past. *See* Dan Fitzpatrick, *J.P. Morgan: 'Whale' Clawbacks About Two Years of Compensation*, WALL ST. J., July 13, 2012, http://wsj.com/article/SB1000142405270230374070457752473099 4899406.html; Suzanne Kapner & Aaron Lucchetti, *Pay Clawbacks Raise Knotty Issues*, WALL ST. J., May 17, 2012, at C1; Deborah Ball, *A First for UBS: Bonus Clawbacks*, WALL ST. J., Feb. 9, 2012, at C3; Richard Hill, *Dimon Tells Senators Loss Was Part of Hedging Strategy, to Expect Clawbacks*, 44 Sec. Reg. & L. Rep. (BNA) 1191 (June 18, 2012).

Lawyers designing clawback policies, which have become "best practices" should consider the following questions when implementing or designing a clawback policy:

- Who does the clawback policy cover? Should the policy cover current and former upper management, current and former officers, or any current or former employee?
- What will trigger a clawback? Does a clawback require a restatement, any misconduct, or personal responsibility for a defined event?
- What compensation does the clawback cover? Bonuses, stock options, performance-based awards? State wage laws may not allow an employer to clawback any previously earned compensation, including certain bonuses.
- Who will administer the policy?

- How much discretion, if any, should the policy give to the administrator?
- Can the administrator exercise "self help" and hold-back other compensation that the individual has earned?

3. In one all too common way that enterprises improperly recognize revenue, known as "channel stuffing," a business uses bargaining power or financial incentives, such as cash payments, price discounts, reimbursements or other arrangements, to persuade customers to order and to keep—and not return—more goods than currently needed so that the business can record additional revenue in the current period and thereby reach a desired level of net income. "Channel stuffing" more fundamentally involves disclosure issues because an enterprise's sales practices in the current period adversely affect the likely prospects for sales in future accounting periods by forcing sales into the current accounting period. One dramatic example involved Bristol-Myers Squibb Co., one of the world's major drug companies. Bristol-Myers indulged in a practice of paying incentives to its wholesalers to buy extra products, and in effect stockpile the inventory, so that the drug company could show higher current income. This practice inflated revenue from 1999 to 2001 by $2.5 billion, and earnings by $900 million. In 2005, the company reached a settlement to end the Justice Department's criminal investigation by agreeing to pay $300 million to a shareholders' restitution fund. When added to $150 million that the company had previously paid to settle the SEC's civil charges, then the second-largest ever SEC settlement payment involving accounting fraud, and $339 million to settle a class-action suit over the matter, this improper revenue recognition cost Bristol-Myers almost $800 million. At the same time, federal prosecutors indicted two former company executives. The company avoided indictment by agreeing to a deferred prosecution arrangement, under which the company will escape a criminal charge if it complies with all the terms and conditions of the agreement, which included appointment of an independent party to monitor the company's activities. More than a year later, Bristol-Myers terminated both its chief executive and general counsel after the federal monitor recommended their dismissal. After the agreed two-year oversight period ended, the U.S. Attorney in New Jersey dismissed the criminal charges.

4. Some new wrinkles in overstating earnings have received special attention, particularly in connection with retail enterprises. In the food industry, suppliers and retailers often agree that a volume discount will reduce the stated price for goods if the retailer's purchases exceed a specified level for the year. Similarly, a corporate retailer that advertises a supplier's products often qualifies for an allowance from the stated price for some portion of those advertising costs, a so-called "promotional allowance." But these arrangements have often tempted retailers to take larger discounts or allowances than allowed under the agreement, perhaps in the hope that the supplier will not want to challenge a valued customer. More to the immediate point, retailers have sometimes baldly claimed grossly inflated discounts or allowances, in an effort to show a higher net income. A $800 million financial fraud involving U.S. Foodservice, Inc. ("USF"), a subsidiary of the major Dutch food conglomerate Royal Ahold N.V., illustrates this illicit practice. Four executives at USF, in an attempt to reach certain earnings targets that would entitle them to virtually double their salaries, grossly inflated the amount of USF's promotional allowances, and then not only supplied that false information to the company's outside auditors, but also persuaded employees at several of its major suppliers to provide false confirmations regarding the overstated promotional allowances. Federal regulators brought criminal as well as civil charges against those now-former executives, which eventually led to four guilty pleas. In addition, more than a dozen employees or agents of USF suppliers who signed those false confirmations in an effort to retain a profitable business relationship pleaded guilty to criminal charges. In 2006, federal prosecutors in New York reached a non-prosecution agreement with the company, shortly after a federal district court approved a $1.1 billion settlement in a class action arising from the scheme.

Similar improprieties have turned up in the financial statements of several large department store companies. In that industry, department stores historically have expected clothing manufacturers and other merchandise suppliers to share in their sales risk by refunding part of the price that the retailers paid for items that did not sell well at full price, such that the retailer needed to mark those items down. In addition, retailers typically discount the price owed to vendors to take account of defects in the goods received, errors in the mix of products shipped, or shortfalls in the number actually received. Here too, the retailers generally enjoy the upper-hand, except when the vendor has a particularly high-powered name or brand. Retailers have sometimes seemingly taken advantage of the situation by claiming larger mark-down allowances than had been agreed to, and in some cases even misstating the amount of markdowns, defective goods, or number of items received. Obviously, the desire, particularly among publicly-traded retailers, to shore up net income for financial accounting purposes provides the impetus for such conduct, but once again, booking an unjustified allowance or discount results in a false financial statement. This issue hit the financial headlines in 2005 when a giant Japanese apparel manufacturer sued Saks Fifth Avenue ("Saks"), one of the best-known retailers in the country, for taking substantial, but unjustified, deductions and credits. Saks subsequently admitted that it "overcollected" money from its suppliers; fired three executives, including its general counsel, who were involved in the practice; and announced that it would repay vendors about $48 million in improper markdown allowances and interest. In 2007, Saks's parent corporation settled civil charges that it violated financial reporting, books-and-records, and internal control provisions under the federal securities laws. SEC v. Saks Inc., Accounting and Auditing Enforcement Release No. 2674 (Sept. 5, 2007), http://www.sec.gov/litigation/litreleases/2007/lr20266.htm.

Ironically, the practices by retailers, at least the deductions for markdowns, actually may have started as a result of sales practices by vendors that pressured retailers to order more goods than they really needed or wanted, in a forerunner of channel stuffing described above. In response, retailers would agree to place the larger order as long as the vendor would guarantee that if the retailer could not sell some of the goods at full price, the vendor would refund enough to protect the retailer's profit margin. That practice eventually led to a more general expectation that vendors should share the burden of retail markdowns, which retailers have now carried to these illegitimate extremes.

5. Regulators investigating possible financial statement abuses have focused on insurance companies, after learning that buyers had used certain novel insurance products to manage, or smooth, their earnings. The spotlight has shone especially brightly on American International Group Inc. ("AIG"), perhaps the largest insurance company in the world, and once a favorite of Wall Street because of its history of continuous, steady earnings growth over many years. In addition, the company's apparent ability to keep the ratio of its underwriting losses (payments on insurance claims) to its premium revenues at the lowest levels in the industry impressed investors. While we could accurately describe the financial accounting rules for the insurance business as especially complex, particularly with respect to reinsurance transactions, some of the efforts to manage earnings were fairly straightforward. The most controversial scenario involved so-called "finite insurance," developed in the 1980s and designed to limit an insurance company's maximum risk if a covered loss did occur, while also providing both an accounting and a tax advantage for the insured. In its simplest form, finite insurance consists of a multi-year contract calling for total premiums almost equaling the amount of the potential losses being covered, but with the further proviso that at the end of the contract the insurance company would refund most of the total amount of premiums paid in excess of any reimbursed losses. Thus, such policies limited the insurance company's risk to the difference between the maximum of losses that the policy covered and the total premiums paid by the insured. Buyers, on the other hand, could avoid paying significantly more in premiums than their actual loss experience, as often happened to insureds with favorable loss experiences. Of course, self-insurance could provide these same advantages, but at a cost of much greater earnings volatility, which investors have frowned upon. In other words, with finite insurance the buyer could provide for its losses over a period of years in a stable, budgeted manner, while also securing an annual deduction for tax purposes.

When an insurance company assumes little, if any, risk, however, the question arises as to whether the arrangement really constitutes insurance, or whether the parties should instead treat the agreement as akin to loan from the customer to the insurance company, which the latter will repay, except to the extent of losses incurred. In 1992, after intense debate, the FASB ruled that to qualify for being treated as insurance for accounting purposes the arrangement had to include a "reasonable possibility" that the insurer might "realize a significant loss." While the FASB never formally defined these terms, industry practices developed an informal guideline of at least a ten percent chance of a ten percent loss. Because management determined the chance and possible amount of loss, the informal guideline offered ample opportunity to stretch to find compliance.

So-called "income smoothing," or "earnings management," seeks to reduce variability in net income over accounting periods by shifting revenues or expenses from good quarters or years to bad reporting periods. Depending upon its desires, management shifts future income or deductions to the present or vice versa. The technique results in financial statements that reflect economic results not as they are, but rather as management wants them to look. Finite insurance became a particularly tempting vehicle for abuse because it could help to hide losses and thereby avoid full disclosure in financial statements. In one notable case involving AIG, another company, Brightpoint, Inc., had suffered a $29 million trading loss. Brightpoint's management wanted to avoid disclosing the full amount because the company had earlier indicated that the loss would fall between $13 million and $18 million. Brightpoint arranged to purchase a policy from AIG under which in exchange for $15 million in future premiums Brightpoint immediately received $11.9 million in "insurance" proceeds, which the company set off against its trading loss and hence avoided showing the full amount of the loss. Because AIG never incurred any risk of loss, however, the arrangement did not qualify as an insurance transaction, so no basis existed for such a set-off. In 2007, a federal jury found the Brightpoint official who helped to devise and execute the scheme civilly liable for aiding and abetting the fraud. The Second Circuit affirmed the ruling in 2009. Both AIG and Brightpoint had previously settled SEC charges arising from the transaction, with AIG paying a $10 million civil penalty. SEC v. Brightpoint, Inc., Accounting and Auditing Enforcement Release No. 2632 (July 9, 2007), http://www.sec.gov/litigation/litreleases/2007/lr20185.htm.

Although not involving AIG, one other relatively recent case illustrates the abuse of a purported reinsurance transaction, only this time to defer earnings from a good quarter to an accounting period in the future, creating a so-called "cookie jar" reserve that management could save for a "rainy day" to boost earnings at some point in the future. In this case, the "round-trip" transaction enabled RenaissanceRe Holdings Ltd. ("RenRe") to "bank" excess revenue from a good year for a future accounting period. To accomplish this desired result, RenRe used two seemingly unrelated contracts with another reinsurance company. In the first contract, RenRe purported to assign $50 million in receivables to the other company for $30 million, which resulted in a $20 million net transfer to the other company. The second contract, disguised as a reinsurance contract even though the arrangement did not transfer any risk, allowed the other company to refund the $20 million, plus investment income earned on that amount in the interim, less transactional fees and costs, to RenRe. Among other things, RenRe agreed to pay a $15 million civil penalty and to retain an independent consultant to resolve securities fraud charges. SEC v. RenaissanceRe Holdings Ltd., Accounting and Auditing Enforcement Release No. 2550 (Feb. 6, 2007), http://www.sec.gov/litigation/litreleases/2007/lr19989.htm.

The AIG transaction that has received by far the most attention (and criticism) arose at a time when investors were expressing some concern that AIG's loss reserves, the amount that AIG estimated as necessary to pay for losses that its policyholders had incurred, might not in fact prove sufficient to cover the total of those losses. As an obvious cure for this problem, AIG could have charged additional expense against income to increase the reserve, but the insurer did not want to incur the resulting reduction in net income. Instead, AIG entered into a putative reinsurance deal—an arrangement in which an insurance company itself in effect buys insurance from another company to obtain protection against the possibility of incurring a particularly large loss claim on an existing policy—with an insurance company called General Reinsurance Corp. ("General Re"), a subsidiary of Berkshire Hathaway Inc., the company run by fabled investor Warren Buffet, which only added to the media attention this transaction ultimately received. In exchange for a $5 million fee, General Re purportedly helped AIG boost its loss reserves by $500 million. In two transactions, AIG received $500 million in premiums in exchange for providing reinsurance to General Re for $500 million of possible losses on which General Re had issued insurance policies. Although AIG did not undertake any risk in the transactions, AIG treated the $500 million received from General Re as income from reinsurance premiums. When coupled with a $500 million charge against income for additional potential losses, AIG raised its loss reserve by that amount while its net income remained the same as it would have been without these transactions. General Re treated the transactions not as the purchase of reinsurance, but rather as loans, which AIG would repay, presumably with interest for the use of the money, or some other compensation to General Re for entering into the deal. By mid-2005, the new top management at AIG acknowledged that the company had improperly accounted for these transactions, along with a number of others. AIG restated its financial statements through 2004 to correct these accounting improprieties, which reduced the company's shareholders' equity by several billion dollars, or about three percent. After two former senior General Re executives pled guilty to criminal conspiracy to commit fraud in 2005, a federal grand jury indicted three other former senior General Re executives, including an assistant general counsel, and one former senior executive of AIG for their alleged involvement in the financial fraud at AIG. Shortly thereafter in 2006, AIG agreed, without admitting or denying wrongdoing, to pay more than $1.6 billion to resolve SEC, New York state, and Justice Department charges arising from the accounting fraud and other alleged misconduct. In 2011, the Second Circuit vacated the convictions of four former General Re executives and one AIG executive on conspiracy, securities fraud, and other charges arising from their alleged roles in the scheme, but remanded their cases for another trial. In 2009, former AIG CEO Maurice "Hank" Greenberg, without admitting or denying wrongdoing, agreed to settle SEC charges that alleged his involvement in material misstatements that enabled AIG to create the false impression that the company consistently met or exceeded key earnings and growth targets. In so doing, Greenberg consented to a judgment directing him to pay $7.5 million in disgorgement and a $7.5 million penalty. In 2010, General Re agreed to pay about $92 million and to implement certain corporate-governance changes to enter into a nonprosecution agreement with the federal government. *See* SEC v. Greenberg, Accounting and Auditing Enforcement Release No. 3032 (Aug. 6, 2009), http://www.sec.gov/litigation/litreleases/2009/lr21170.htm; SEC v. Ferguson, Accounting and Auditing Enforcement Release No. 2369 (Feb. 2, 2006), http://www.sec.gov/litigation/litreleases/lr19552.htm.

Over the years, questionable management conduct with regard to financial statements has consistently occurred. This conduct, which may not constitute fraud, has not advanced the goal that financial statements should present as much meaningful and objective information as possible. Because stock markets have historically given higher price-earnings ratios to companies that have shown an ability to report steady, predictable earnings growth, many business executives have far too willingly accommodated investors' desires for such growth, and unabashedly see nothing wrong with the practice. In this regard, the financial community often refers to managerial actions that increase or decrease a business's current reported earnings without producing any real increase or decrease in the unit's long-term economic profitability as *earnings management* or *income smoothing*. As mentioned earlier, the latter term refers to efforts to keep the business growing at a steady rate. When business executives manage or smooth earnings, whether by a change in accounting method or estimate, or by an operating decision like offering customers special discounts at year-end to accelerate sales, the financial statements do not accurately reflect the enterprise's economic strength. In those circumstances, such executives violate the trust that users place in financial statements and may cause users to reach decisions different from those that they might have made if they had enjoyed access to all relevant information. Understood in this context, earnings management and income smoothing raise important issues involving business and legal ethics.

The following speech by then SEC Chairman Arthur Levitt identifies certain problem areas in financial accounting and reporting. Although Sarbanes-Oxley and related reforms have addressed these problems in public companies, the opportunity for abuse persists in closely-held businesses.

"The 'Numbers Game,'" remarks by Arthur Levitt

Chairman, Securities and Exchange Commission
NYU Center for Law and Business, September 28, 1998.
(available at <http://www.sec.gov/news/speech/speecharchive/1998/spch220.txt>).

* * *

I'd like to talk to you about [a] widespread, but too little-challenged custom: earnings management. This process has evolved over the years into what can best be characterized as a game among market participants. A game that, if not addressed soon, will have adverse consequences for America's financial reporting system. A game that runs counter to the very principles behind our market's strength and success.

Increasingly, I have become concerned that the motivation to meet Wall Street earnings expectations may be overriding common sense business practices. Too many corporate managers, auditors, and analysts are participants in a game of nods and winks. In the zeal to satisfy consensus earnings estimates and project a smooth earnings path, wishful thinking may be winning the day over faithful representation.

As a result, I fear that we are witnessing an erosion in the quality of earnings, and therefore, the quality of financial reporting. Managing may be giving way to manipulation; integrity may be losing out to illusion.

Many in corporate America are just as frustrated and concerned about this trend as we, at the SEC, are. They know how difficult it is to hold the line on good practices when their competitors operate in the gray area between legitimacy and outright fraud.

A gray area where the accounting is being perverted; where managers are cutting corners; and, where earnings reports reflect the desires of management rather than the underlying financial performance of the company.

[I] want to talk about why integrity in financial reporting is under stress and explore five of the more common accounting gimmicks we've been seeing. Finally, I will outline a framework for a financial community response to this situation.

This necessary response involves improving both our accounting and disclosure rules, as well as the oversight and function of outside auditors and board audit committees. I am also calling upon a broad spectrum of capital market participants, from corporate management to Wall Street analysts to investors, to stand together and re-energize the touchstone of our financial reporting system: transparency and comparability.

This is a financial community problem. It can't be solved by a government mandate: it demands a financial community response.

THE ROLE OF FINANCIAL REPORTING IN OUR ECONOMY

Today, America's capital markets are the envy of the world. Our efficiency, liquidity and resiliency stand second to none. Our position, no doubt, has benefited from the opportunity and potential of the global economy. At the same time, however, this increasing interconnectedness has made us more susceptible to economic and financial weakness half a world away.

The significance of transparent, timely and reliable financial statements and its importance to investor protection has never been more apparent. The current financial situations in Asia and Russia are stark examples of this new reality. These markets are learning a painful lesson taught many times before: investors panic as a result of unexpected or unquantifiable bad news.

If a company fails to provide meaningful disclosure to investors about where it has been, where it is and where it is going, a damaging pattern ensues. The bond between shareholders and the company is shaken; investors grow anxious; prices fluctuate for no discernible reasons; and the trust that is the bedrock of our capital markets is severely tested.

THE PRESSURE TO "MAKE YOUR NUMBERS"

While the problem of earnings management is not new, it has swelled in a market that is unforgiving of companies that miss their estimates. I recently read of one major U.S. company, that failed to meet its so-called "numbers" by one penny, and lost more than six percent of its stock value in one day.

I believe that almost everyone in the financial community shares responsibility for fostering a climate in which earnings management is on the rise and the quality of financial reporting is on the decline. Corporate management isn't operating in a vacuum. In fact, the different pressures and expectations placed by, and on, various participants in the financial community appear to be almost self-perpetuating.

This is the pattern earnings management creates: companies try to meet or beat Wall Street earnings projections in order to grow market capitalization and increase the value of stock options. Their ability to do this depends on achieving the earnings expectations of analysts. And analysts seek constant guidance from companies to frame those expectations. Auditors, who want to retain their clients, are under pressure not to stand in the way.

ACCOUNTING HOCUS-POCUS

Our accounting principles weren't meant to be a straitjacket. Accountants are wise enough to know they cannot anticipate every business structure, or every new and innovative transaction, so they develop principles that allow for flexibility to adapt to changing circumstances. That's why the highest standards of objectivity, integrity and judgment can't be the exception. They must be the rule.

Flexibility in accounting allows it to keep pace with business innovations. Abuses such as earnings management occur when people exploit this pliancy. Trickery is employed to obscure actual financial volatility. This, in turn, masks the true consequences of management's decisions. These practices aren't limited to smaller companies struggling to gain investor interest. It's also happening in companies whose products we know and admire.

So what are these illusions? Five of the more popular ones I want to discuss today are "big bath" restructuring charges, creative acquisition accounting, "cookie jar reserves," "immaterial" misapplications of accounting principles, and the premature recognition of revenue.

"Big Bath" Charges

Let me first deal with "Big Bath" restructuring charges.

Companies remain competitive by regularly assessing the efficiency and profitability of their operations. Problems arise, however, when we see large charges associated with companies restructuring. These charges help companies "clean up" their balance sheet--giving them a so-called "big bath."

Why are companies tempted to overstate these charges? When earnings take a major hit, the theory goes, Wall Street will look beyond a one-time loss and focus only on future earnings.

And if these charges are conservatively estimated with a little extra cushioning, that so-called conservative estimate is miraculously reborn as income when estimates change or future earnings fall short.

When a company decides to restructure, management and employees, investors and creditors, customers and suppliers all want to understand the expected effects. We need, of course, to ensure that financial reporting provides this information. But this should not lead to flushing all the associated costs--and maybe a little extra--through the financial statements.

Creative Acquisition Accounting

Let me turn now to the second gimmick.

In recent years, whole industries have been remade through consolidations, acquisitions and spin-offs. Some acquirers, particularly those using stock as an acquisition currency, have used this environment as an opportunity to engage in another form of "creative" accounting. I call it "merger magic."

* * *

So what do [these acquirers] do? They classify an ever-growing portion of the acquisition price as "in-process" Research and Development, so--you guessed it--the amount can be written off in a "one-time" charge--removing any future earnings drag. Equally troubling is the creation of large liabilities for future operating expenses to protect future earnings--all under the mask of an acquisition.

Miscellaneous "Cookie Jar Reserves"

A third illusion played by some companies is using unrealistic assumptions to estimate liabilities for such items as sales returns, loan losses or warranty costs. In doing so, they stash accruals in cookie jars during the good times and reach into them when needed in the bad times.

I'm reminded of one U.S. company who took a large one-time loss to earnings to reimburse franchisees for equipment. That equipment, however, which included literally the kitchen sink, had yet to be bought. And, at the same time, they announced that future earnings would grow an impressive 15 percent per year.

"Materiality"

Let me turn now to the fourth gimmick--the abuse of materiality--a word that captures the attention of both attorneys and accountants. Materiality is another way we build flexibility into financial reporting. Using the logic of diminishing returns, some items may be so insignificant that they are not worth measuring and reporting with exact precision.

But some companies misuse the concept of materiality. They intentionally record errors within a defined percentage ceiling. They then try to excuse that fib by arguing that the effect on the bottom line is too small to matter. If that's the case, why do they work so hard to create these errors? Maybe because the effect can matter, especially if it picks up that last penny of the consensus estimate. When either management or the outside auditors are questioned about these clear violations of GAAP, they answer sheepishly[,] "It doesn't matter. It's immaterial."

In markets where missing an earnings projection by a penny can result in a loss of millions of dollars in market capitalization, I have a hard time accepting that some of these so-called non-events simply don't matter.

Revenue Recognition

Lastly, companies try to boost earnings by manipulating the recognition of revenue. Think about a bottle of fine wine. You wouldn't pop the cork on that bottle before it was ready. But some companies are doing this with their revenue--recognizing it before a sale is complete, before the product is delivered to a customer, or at a time when the customer still has options to terminate, void or delay the sale.

ACTION PLAN

Since U.S. capital market supremacy is based on the reliability and transparency of financial statements, this is a financial community problem that calls for timely financial community action.

Therefore, I am calling for immediate and coordinated action: technical rule changes by the regulators and standard setters to improve the transparency of financial statements; enhanced oversight of the financial reporting process by those entrusted as the shareholders' guardians; and nothing less than a fundamental cultural change on the part of corporate management as well as the whole financial community.

This action plan represents a cooperative public-private sector effort. It is essential that we work together to assure credibility and transparency. * * *

          * * *

And, finally, qualified, committed, independent and tough-minded audit committees represent the most reliable guardians of the public interest. Sadly, stories abound of audit committees whose members lack expertise in the basic principles of financial reporting as well as the mandate to ask probing questions. In fact, I've heard of one audit committee that convenes only twice a year before the regular board meeting for 15 minutes and whose duties are limited to a perfunctory presentation.

Compare that situation with the audit committee which meets twelve times a year before each board meeting; where every member has a financial background; where there are no personal ties to the chairman or the company; where they have their own advisers; where they ask tough questions of management and outside auditors; and where, ultimately, the investor interest is being served.

The SEC stands ready to take appropriate action if that interest is not protected. But, a private sector response that empowers audit committees and obviates the need for public sector dictates seems the wisest choice. * * *

* * *

Need for a Cultural Change

Finally, I'm challenging corporate management and Wall Street to re-examine our current environment. I believe we need to embrace nothing less than a cultural change. For corporate managers, remember, the integrity of the numbers in the financial reporting system is directly related to the long-term interests of a corporation. While the temptations are great, and the pressures strong, illusions in numbers are only that--ephemeral, and ultimately self-destructive.

To Wall Street, I say, look beyond the latest quarter. Punish those who rely on deception, rather than the practice of openness and transparency.

CONCLUSION

Some may conclude that this debate is nothing more than an argument over numbers and legalistic terms. I couldn't disagree more.

* * *

Our mandate and our obligations are clear. We must rededicate ourselves to a fundamental principle: markets exist through the grace of investors.

Today, American markets enjoy the confidence of the world. How many half-truths, and how much accounting sleight-of-hand, will it take to tarnish that faith?

As a former businessman, I experienced all kinds of markets, dealt with a variety of trends, fads, fears, and irrational exuberances. I learned that some habits die hard. But, more than anything else, I learned that progress doesn't happen overnight and it's not sustained through short cuts or obfuscation. It's induced, rather, by asking hard questions and accepting difficult answers.

For the sake of our markets; for the sake of a globalized economy which depends so much on the reliability of America's financial system; for the sake of investors; and for the sake of a larger commitment not only to each other, but to ourselves, I ask that we join together to reinforce the values that have guided our capital markets to unparalleled supremacy. Together, through vigilance and trust, I know, we can succeed.

NOTES

1. Chapter IX discusses "big bath" charges and creative acquisition accounting. See pages 629 and 678 to 687, *infra*. We will further consider "cookie jar reserves" and revenue recognition in this chapter. Chapter II previously mentioned the "abuse of materiality." See pages 200 to 202, *supra*.

2. Accountants sometimes classify actions to manage earnings into two types: those which involve changing accounting methods and those which involve operating decisions. Adjusting the reserve, or the amount the enterprise has accrued as an expense to satisfy a contingency, illustrates a change in accounting method. In contrast, offering special terms to customers at year-end in an attempt to accelerate sales which would normally not occur until the next accounting period into the current accounting period exemplifies an operating decision.

3. You may recall from the discussion in Chapter II on page 172, *supra*, that given the various permissible choices in alternative accounting treatments, some companies could select from more than a million possible bottom lines. If no true "bottom line" exists, do earnings management and income smoothing simply reflect efforts by businesses "'to put their best foot forward?'"

4. Even before Sarbanes-Oxley, the SEC brought well-publicized enforcement actions against at least three registrants and their high-ranking officers for managing earnings.

About three months before then-Chairman Levitt's speech, the SEC instituted public administrative proceedings against Venator Group, Inc., the company formerly known as Woolworth Corporation ("Woolworth"), and four former senior officers in response to a scheme to manage Woolworth's reported earnings. In the cease-and-desist proceeding against Woolworth, which the company settled by agreeing to cease and desist from future financial reporting violations without admitting or denying the Commission's allegations, the SEC found that the former officers at Woolworth and two of its major subsidiaries, Kinney Shoe Corporation ("Kinney") and Woolworth Canada Inc. ("Canada"), engaged in a scheme to manage the company's reported earnings by inflating profits by understating cost of sales and improperly deferring certain operating expenses that the subsidiaries incurred in the first two quarters of the company's 1993 fiscal year. This fraudulent conduct enabled Woolworth to report a profit for each of the first two quarters of fiscal 1993, even though the company actually lost money during those quarters. The former officers then adjusted results in the third and fourth quarters, so that the company could report accurate results by year-end, when the outside auditor examined the company's financial statements. *In re* Venator Group, Inc., Accounting and Auditing Enforcement Release No. 1049, [1995-1998 Transfer Binder] Fed. Sec. L. Rep. (CCH) ¶ 74,564 (June 29, 1998).

Less than three months after then-Chairman Levitt's speech, the SEC announced a civil action against W.R. Grace & Co. ("Grace") and public administrative and cease-and-desist proceedings against seven former executives, including the company's former president and chief financial officer, for financial fraud involving earnings manipulation. The complaint in the civil action alleges that Grace, through its subsidiary National Medical Care, Inc., falsely reported operating results between 1991 and 1995 by deferring income to smooth earnings. Rather than report the income, the Company allegedly established reserves that did not conform with GAAP and then used those reserves to manipulate quarterly and annual earnings. The SEC's complaint further alleges that when Grace reversed the excess reserves during the 1995 fourth quarter, the company improperly netted the excess reserves with other amounts and "misleadingly described the reversal as a 'change in accounting estimate.'" SEC v. W.R. Grace & Co., Accounting and Auditing Enforcement Release No. 1091, [1995–1998 Transfer Binder] Fed. Sec. L. Rep. (CCH) ¶ 74,599F (Dec. 22, 1998); In re Bolduc, Accounting and Auditing Enforcement Release No. 1090, [1995–1998 Transfer Binder] Fed. Sec. L. Rep. (CCH) ¶ 74,599E (Dec. 22, 1998). In 1999, Grace consented to a cease-and-desist order and agreed to set aside $1 million to establish a fund, and then to use that fund within one year, to develop at least one program to further awareness and education relating to financial statements and generally accepted accounting principles. In re W.R. Grace & Co., Accounting and Auditing Enforcement Release No. 1140, [1999–2001 Transfer Binder] Fed. Sec. L. Rep. (CCH) ¶ 74,647 (June 30, 1999).

In addition to the finite insurance and purported reinsurance schemes described earlier on pages 377 to 379, supra, the SEC has continued to bring enforcement actions against companies that improperly manage or "smooth" earnings, whether via "cookie jar" reserves or so-called "top-side adjustments." With "top-side adjustments" or "top-side journal entries," senior executives, such as the CFO, or upper-level accountants use special (and sometimes manual) entries at the end of a fiscal period to change the books, avoiding the normal accounting process, usually to attain or avoid significantly exceeding a financial target. See, e.g., SEC v. Dell Inc. Accounting and Auditing Enforcement Release No. 3156 (July 22, 2010), http://www.sec.gov/litigation/litreleases/2010/lr21599.htm (announcing that the company agreed to pay a $100 million penalty to resolve various securities disclosure and accounting fraud charges, including that the company's most senior former accounting personnel engaged in improper accounting by maintaining and using "cookie jar" reserves to hide shortfalls in operating results during fiscal years from 2002 to 2005); SEC v. Gen. Elec. Co., Accounting and Auditing Enforcement Release No. 3029 (Aug. 4, 2009), http://www.sec.gov/litigation/litreleases/2009/lr21166.htm (announcing a $50 million penalty to settle civil charges that the company used improper accounting methods to increase its reported earnings or revenues and avoid reporting negative financial results on four separate occasions in 2002 and 2003).

In the credit crisis, senior executives sometimes failed to recognize expenses and create reserves or understated expenses and established inadequate reserves for impaired assets or known liabilities arising from credit or investment losses. See, e.g., SEC v. Strauss, Accounting and Auditing Enforcement Release No. 2967 (Apr. 28, 2009), http://www.sec.gov/litigation/litreleases/2009/lr21014.htm (senior executive at American Home Mortgage Investment Corp. agreed to permanent injunction, approximately $2.2 million in disgorgement and rejudgment interest, and a $250,000 penalty for allegedly under stating loan loss reserves).

5. In the years immediately after then-Chairman Levitt's speech, the SEC staff published staff accounting bulletins on materiality, restructuring charges, and revenue recognition. Materiality, Staff Accounting Bulletin No. 99, 64 Fed. Reg. 45,150 (Aug. 19, 1999), *available at* http://www.sec.gov/interps/account/sab99.htm; Restructuring and Impairment Charges, Staff Accounting Bulletin No. 100, 64 Fed. Reg. 67,154 (Dec. 1, 1999), *available at* http://www.sec.gov/interps/account/sab100.htm; Revenue Recognition in Financial Statements, Staff Accounting Bulletin No. 101, 64 Fed. Reg. 68,936 (Dec. 9, 1999), *available at* http://www.sec.gov/interps/account/sab101.htm; *see also* Staff Accounting Bulletin No. 104, 68 Fed. Reg. 74,436 (Dec. 23, 2003), *available at* http://www.sec.gov/interps/account/sab104rev.pdf.

1. A BONA FIDE EXCHANGE TRANSACTION

As the name implies, an *exchange transaction* for revenue recognition purposes occurs when two or more individuals or enterprises exchange products, services, or other assets for cash, claims to cash or other consideration. As a fundamental component, a transfer of risk must occur to qualify a transaction as an "exchange" for revenue recognition purposes. The amount of cash or the cash equivalent in value that the purchaser pays or promises to pay provides objective evidence about the amount of revenue that the seller should recognize. In those situations where the consideration received lacks value in money or money's worth, conservatism indicates that an exchange transaction has not really occurred. As a result, both the objectivity principle and the conservatism convention support the exchange transaction requirement.

A recent and important exception to the exchange transaction requirement arises from "fair value accounting." With a new accounting standard establishing a unified approach to measuring fair values and a second standard granting enterprises the option to record more assets and liabilities at fair value, businesses will increasingly report unrealized holding gains and losses in the income statement without a corresponding exchange transaction. While fair value accounting involves a potential sacrifice of reliability for relevance and has generated significant controversy during the global credit crisis, both the FASB and the IASB remain committed to developing rules that will require enterprises to report additional assets and liabilities at fair value.

a. THE NATURE OF THE EXCHANGE TRANSACTION

Financial statement users do not view all exchange transactions equally. Just as a professor's letter of recommendation probably assesses your skills more objectively than a letter from your grandmother, exchange transactions between unrelated parties determine revenue more objectively than sales between related parties. Therefore, financial statement users prefer to use exchange transactions between unrelated parties to measure current revenue and to predict future revenue. Accountants and lawyers commonly call exchange transactions between unrelated parties *arms-length* transactions. To understand the concept of an arms-length transaction, consider a prom chaperone's perspective on dancing couples. Just as the chaperone probably suspects that couples who dance at less than "arms-length" are more likely to behave improperly, financial statement users suspect that enterprises who transact business with related parties are more likely to engage in financial shenanigans.

(1) In General

Accountants normally require exchange transactions before allowing a business to recognize revenue. Another simple analogy may help illustrate why GAAP requires an exchange transaction before recognizing revenue. Imagine that you compile a brilliant law school survival guide. Because the survival guide leads to excellent grades, you want to "share" your masterpiece with your classmates. Although generous by nature, you need cash more than gratitude and decide to sell the survival guides for ten dollars each rather than give them away. Reasoning that at least 4,800 law students nationwide seek excellent grades each year, you recognize $4,000 [(4,800 guides times $10 per guide) divided by 12 months] in revenue for the first month, say January, and head to the bank to finance the Porsche that you have dreamed about since your sixteenth birthday. Impressed with your loan application, the loan officer commends you on selling 400 survival guides during your first month in business. You clear your throat and say, "Well, I haven't exactly sold any survival guides yet." As the loan officer shreds your loan application, she explains that the bank cannot afford to share in your optimism. Until law students actually buy the survival guide, which would give rise to an exchange transaction, the loan officer cannot verify that you can sell 400 survival guides each month at ten dollars each. According to the objectivity principle and conservatism, you can only recognize revenue as you sell each survival guide.

a) MARKET TRANSACTION

We could describe an exchange transaction as an "external" event which involves mutual transfers of value between two or more persons or enterprises. Therefore, transferring materials between the purchasing division and the manufacturing division of a single enterprise does not qualify as an exchange transaction. For this same reason, the SEC instituted cease-and-desist proceedings against a registrant which recognized revenue when the company shipped equipment to its field representatives. Under the circumstances, GAAP would not recognize an exchange until the company shipped the equipment to a customer, rather than to a field representative. The registrant consented to a finding that it violated the federal securities laws. *In re* Advanced Medical Products, Inc., Accounting and Auditing Enforcement Release No. 812, [1995–1998 Transfer Binder] Fed. Sec. L. Rep. (CCH) ¶ 74,327 (Sept. 5, 1996).

As mentioned earlier, financial statement users prefer that these external transactions occur at arms-length. But where can an enterprise find another firm willing to transact business? The "market." The market represents the group of enterprises that want to purchase particular services, goods, or other assets. The amount of cash or cash equivalent in value that this group pays represents the market value for the underlying services, goods, or other assets. Until an enterprise actually sells goods held for resale in a market transaction, accountants cannot verify the goods' market value and, therefore, cannot determine the amount that the enterprise should recognize as revenue. "Solid" exchange transactions help to minimize the risk that an enterprise will recognize income prematurely or otherwise overstate revenue.

b) SHAMS

Although some transactions facially appear to qualify as market transactions, a closer examination into the underlying circumstances may reveal that the exchange lacks economic substance or that the parties have not transferred the risks that usually accompany ownership. In other words, while "form" satisfies the exchange transaction requirement, the "substance" or economic realities do not.

As one type of "sham" transaction, so-called "round-trips" involve two or more parties exchanging the same amount of consideration, usually money, in transactions lacking economic substance. Enterprises use these "round-trip" transactions, which typically do not affect net income, to inflate revenue or transaction volumes. In such transactions, the entity records both the revenue and the equivalent expense upfront, resulting in no effect on net income. During the Internet bubble, when the markets typically valued enterprises based upon their revenues or revenue growth, rather than on net income, nascent "dot-com" companies found this manipulative accounting practice particularly attractive. During the boom, devising "round-trip" schemes would increase revenues for both parties involved, a seemingly "win-win" situation.

Perhaps the most publicized cases of "round-tripping" during the Internet boom occurred at America Online, Inc. ("AOL"). Investors and analysts closely followed AOL's advertising revenue as a key measure of the company's success. Between mid-2000 and 2002, as sales of online advertising declined, AOL used fraudulent "round-trip" arrangements to bolster online advertising revenue. AOL, in essence, funded its own revenue by giving customers the money to pay for advertising they would not otherwise have purchased from AOL. While AOL attempted to portray the "round-trip" schemes as separate, legitimate transactions, the purported "purchasers" of the advertising often had little or no control over the advertising received. Time Warner, Inc., the parent of AOL, eventually paid $300 million to settle SEC charges and $2.65 billion to settle a shareholder class action suit related to the sham revenue scheme and other fraudulent practices. SEC v. Time Warner Inc., Accounting and Auditing Enforcement Release No. 2216, [2003-2006 Transfer Binder] Fed. Sec. L. Rep. (CCH) ¶ 75,878 (Mar. 21, 2005), *available at* http://www.sec.gov/litigation/litreleases/lr19147.htm; *In re* AOL TimeWarner, Inc., No. MDL 1500, 02 Civ. 5575(SWK), 2006 WL 903236 (S.D.N.Y. Apr. 6,

2006). The SEC now estimates that AOL overstated revenue by more than $1 billion and has continued to bring new enforcement actions stemming from the schemes.

By comparison, an enforcement action that the SEC brought against Motorola, Inc. illustrates another situation where a registrant at least allowed, and perhaps actively enabled, Adelphia Communications Corp. ("Adelphia") to use "round trips" to increase its profits and operating cash flows artificially. For facilitating Adelphia's false and misleading financial statements, Motorola agreed to pay a $25 million in disgorgement and prejudgment interest. *In re* Motorola, Inc., Accounting and Auditing Enforcement Release No. 2607 (May 8, 2007), http://www.sec.gov/litigation/admin/2007/34-55725.pdf. In the transactions at issue, Adelphia paid Motorola for retroactive "price increases" on set-top cable boxes, but only after Motorola agreed to pay the same amount back to Adelphia for "marketing support." The transactions lacked economic substance because Motorola had already sold the set-top boxes to Adelphia, and the latter did not undertake any actual marketing pursuant to the agreement. Adelphia improperly accounted for the transactions in two ways. First, Adelphia recorded the "marketing support" payments as an offset to decrease other marketing expenses. Second, Adelphia treated the "price increases" on the set-top boxes as a capital expenditure, depreciable over time, rather than treating the costs as an immediate expense, which overstated net income and operating cash flow. To illustrate the financial accounting consequences, suppose that Adelphia and Motorola consummate the agreement at the start of the year. Adelphia pays $1,000,000 in cash to Motorola for "price increases" on cable boxes, and Motorola then pays Adelphia $1,000,000 for "marketing support." Adelphia improperly records the $1 million cable-box payment as an asset and applies company accounting policy to depreciate the expenditure over five years, the estimated useful life of the cable boxes. During the first year, Adelphia will record a $200,000 depreciation expense, but will decrease total marketing expenditures by $1,000,000, thereby fraudulently increasing net income by $800,000. This treatment would also overstate operating cash flow by $1,000,000 because Adelphia could add back the $200,000 in depreciation to $800,000 in additional net income when computing operating cash flows. The SEC enforcement actions against Motorola illustrates the need for public companies to maintain appropriate policies and internal controls, to train personnel adequately, and to foster a culture that will not allow participation in financial frauds either within the corporation itself or that third parties might commit. This responsibility falls upon top management and the board of directors, both of whom often rely on lawyers for assistance.

As in other contexts, especially tax, appearances may belie a transaction's true substance. Parties can often structure a transaction to appear as a bona fide exchange with an outsider, when in fact the parties have not transferred the risks that usually accompany ownership. In *In re* Reliance Group Holdings, Inc., Accounting and Auditing Enforcement Release No. 529, [1991–1995 Transfer Binder] Fed. Sec. L. Rep. (CCH) ¶ 73,989 (Feb. 17, 1994), a major insurance company, Reliance, owned some appreciated debt securities on which the company wanted to recognize gain to avoid reporting an overall loss for the current quarter. At the same time, however, the officer in charge of fixed income securities did not want to give up the company's investment in these bonds. Accordingly, the officer worked out a deal with a salesman at Reliance's regular brokerage firm under which the broker-dealer would purchase the bonds, and then thirty-one days later, would sell them back to Reliance, in effect, but not in form, for the same price. The broker-dealer would receive a specified fee for this service. The SEC condemned Reliance's gain on the transaction, stating that to recognize revenue, an exchange transaction must take place that transfers the risks and rewards of ownership, and that never happened in that situation.

The following case further illustrates circumstances where economic substance prevents an enterprise from recognizing income even though the transaction's form resembles a "sale."

Lincoln Savings & Loan Association v. Wall

United States District Court, District of Columbia, 1990.
743 F. Supp. 901

■ SPORKIN, DISTRICT JUDGE.

In this consolidated action, plaintiffs American Continental Corporation and Lincoln Savings and Loan Association seek to regain operational control of Lincoln Savings and Loan Association. Plaintiff American Continental Corporation ("ACC") is an Ohio corporation with its principal place of business in Phoenix, Arizona. Plaintiff Lincoln Savings and Loan Association ("Lincoln") is a California corporation chartered as a savings and loan institution by the State of California Department of Savings and Loans. Lincoln is a wholly owned subsidiary of ACC. The deposits in Lincoln were insured by the Federal Savings and Loan Insurance Corporation ("FSLIC"). Defendant Office of Thrift Supervision is the successor agency of the Federal Home Loan Bank Board ("FHLBB" or "Bank Board"). On April 14, 1989, the Bank Board pursuant to its statutory authority appointed a conservator to take over the management of Lincoln.

* * *

I. BACKGROUND

* * *

Plaintiffs here contend that they at all times managed and operated Lincoln on a sound financial basis. Plaintiffs allege that defendant was not justified in seeking and obtaining their removal from control of Lincoln which was effectuated by the Bank Board's appointment of a conservator * * * for Lincoln. Plaintiffs claim that the Bank Board's actions were arbitrary and capricious and that these actions were so ill founded that they precipitated Lincoln's severe financial crisis.

* * * It is defendant's contention that plaintiffs engaged in numerous unsafe and unsound banking practices and that as a result of these and other improper practices there had been a substantial dissipation of the thrift's assets. The Bank Board asserts that it was these practices that led to Lincoln's downfall.

In the post-deprivation hearing conducted before this Court, the Board justified its actions by introducing proof on a number of specific transactions which it claims fully sustain its position. Plaintiffs have countered by alleging that the transactions enumerated were perfectly proper and have introduced expert testimony to demonstrate the accounting treatment afforded these transactions fully conformed with all the professional norms that existed at the time the transactions were effected. Plaintiffs also introduced evidence from their independent auditors which plaintiffs claim fully support the accounting treatment taken.

* * *

III. DISCUSSION

* * *

Before examining the specific transactions that were the subject of the evidentiary hearing, some background discussion is necessary. It is quite clear that the thrift industry has had a number of problems over the past two decades. In the 1970s, the limits that were placed on both the borrowing and investing activities of thrifts drove a number of savings and loan associations into financial difficulty. First, because of limits on the amount of interest thrifts could pay to investors, savings and loans became noncompetitive with other financial institutions. This resulted in Congress' removing the interest rate ceiling that limited the rate that thrifts could pay to the savings public. Later when Congress learned that the thrifts continued to face severe financial problems, it enacted certain deregulatory measures to provide additional investment opportunities for thrifts, aside from the traditional one of financing the purchase of single family homes. With the number of thrifts facing financial difficulties, Congress believed that it could stave off bailing out the thrift industry of its financial problems by deregulating it and thereby inducing investors to pour private funds into sick thrifts. Congress chose this tack to avoid having to bail out the industry with taxpayers' money. * * * As will later be seen by what happened with Lincoln, the privatization gambit failed miserably and today * * * the magnitude of the S & L debacle is probably 5 to 10 [times what it would have been]. * * *

Charles Keating, Jr., ("Keating"), the chairman and chief executive officer of ACC, was one of those entrepreneurs who was willing to enter the S & L industry once Congress lessened the regulatory restrictions. [In 1976, he acquired] American Continental Corporation ("ACC"). Keating moved the company to Phoenix, Arizona and continued to focus its operations on single-family home construction and development. When Keating first took over the company, it was in a loss posture. Over the years, Keating was able to turn it around to where it was moderately successful. In the late 1970s and early 1980s, ACC became very active in building large single-family housing developments in Phoenix and Denver. In addition to the actual construction of homes, ACC started a mortgage company in 1978 to assist home buyers with financing. Building on this experience, in 1981, ACC created a system for packaging and selling groups of single family home mortgages—the investment instrument became known as mortgaged backed securities.

With the passage of the Depository Institutions Deregulation Act of 1980 and the Garn-St. Germaine Depository Institutions Act of 1982, Keating decided to look for a savings and loan association to add to his real estate empire. After analyzing various thrifts that were for sale, Keating decided to see if Lincoln Savings & Loan could be acquired. Keating was attracted to Lincoln for three primary reasons 1) he was impressed with its fine reputation in the industry; 2) the controlling block of Lincoln's stock was owned by one family; and 3) Lincoln was a California chartered savings and loan. According to Keating's testimony, this accumulation of stock in the hands of one family would make Lincoln easier to acquire if the family was interested in selling. The fact that Lincoln had a California State Charter attracted Keating because the California legislature had embarked on a course aimed at deregulating the state's thrift industry in 1982 with the passage of the Nolan Act. By removing restrictions that had previously been in place, the Nolan Act further broadened the field of direct investments that California savings and loans would be permitted to make.

Although Lincoln had not been formally offered for sale, it had been losing money and the principal owners agreed to entertain an offer from ACC. After a short negotiating period, ACC agreed to acquire Lincoln for $51 million, which represented a premium of some $17 million over the institution[']s net worth of $34 million. ACC closed the Lincoln acquisition on February 24, 1984. The financing was provided through the issuance and sale in December of 1983 of approximately $55 million in exchangeable preferred stock. This preferred stock issue was underwritten by Drexel, Burnham, Lambert, which had previously underwritten for ACC a high yield debt offering of $125 million in August of 1983.

At the time Lincoln was acquired, it was conducting a traditional savings and loan business. It was largely in the business of lending money to purchasers of single family dwelling units in Southern California. While its business was conservative, it was not thriving financially. At the time of the acquisition, Lincoln had assets of approximately $1 billion and a net worth of $34 million. When ACC took over, it was required to and did obtain approval of both the California and Federal thrift regulators. In the change of control application that ACC filed with the federal regulators prior to its acquisition of Lincoln, it stated that "While it is anticipated that the current officers of the Holding Company and the Institution [Lincoln] will remain upon consummation of the proposed transaction, the Applicant [ACC] intends to augment this management team." ACC also reaffirmed its commitment to maintain Lincoln's current level of community lending * * *.

These commitments, however, were short lived. Once ACC was given approval, it deviated from its original plan. Contrary to ACC's representations to the federal regulators that it would retain existing management, the former management team was soon replaced by ACC officials. Although virtually all of Lincoln's pre-acquisition activities had been conducted in the Los Angeles and surrounding areas, after its sale a good portion of Lincoln's business was transferred to Phoenix, Arizona, ACC's home base. Indeed, by 1986, most of Lincoln's operations were conducted out of a newly-constructed Phoenix office, which was located next to ACC corporate offices in downtown Phoenix.

* * * While ACC employed many lawyers, accountants, and other professionals to watch over and handle Lincoln's investments, an inordinate amount of business was originated by Keating himself. This was so even though Keating held no official position with Lincoln. Numerous multi-million dollar deals were negotiated by Keating personally with ACC's staff of professionals left to work out the precise details.

* * *

The Bank Board's case is fairly straightforward. It asserts that Lincoln engaged in a number of imprudent transactions in order to improperly upstream monies to ACC, its parent, which was experiencing financial difficulties.

* * *

B.   The Wescon Transaction

One of Lincoln's direct investments involved the development of 20,000 acres of land outside Phoenix known as the Estrella Project. The most remote part of the project, the southern half, consists of some 8500 acres and is referred to as Hidden Valley.

The evidence shows that on March 31, 1987, a Lincoln subsidiary sold 1000 acres of raw land in Hidden Valley to a company called West Continental Mortgage and Investment Corporation (Wescon). The terms of the sale involved a cash down payment of $3.5 million, along with a non-recourse note for the balance of $10.5 million for a total sales price of $14 million.

Since Lincoln's pro rata cost of the property sold was only $3 million, it was able to book a gain of $11 million along with $250,000 in accrued interest.
* * *

Wescon never made a payment against the balance on the outstanding note. Wescon was a company of little means. It had a net worth of only $31,000, and it really had no intention of developing the property. Fernando Acosta, the President of Wescon, was quite blunt in his testimony at the hearing. He stated that his company was acting only as a "straw" for Mr. Garcia, the head of E.C. Garcia & Company. Indeed, when Wescon was being pressed to fulfill its obligations under the transaction, Acosta went to Garcia who agreed to assume Wescon's obligation under the agreement but, like Wescon, made no payments to Lincoln.

It is clear, and this Court finds, that the sole reason for the Wescon transaction was to enable the ACC complex to record an $11 million profit * * *. ACC justifies its action by stating that certain arcane accounting provisions allowed it to book the $11 million profit. Indeed a great deal of testimony at the trial was devoted to the propriety of the accounting treatment of this and a number of Lincoln's other profit-recording transactions. If ACC, its accountants and experts are correct, that $11 million can be booked as profit from this transaction * * *, then the system of accounting that exists in the United States is in a sorry state. Here we have a sham transaction from the start with the identity of the real party in interest being shielded from those who must exercise appropriate oversight of the transaction. Because of the use of a straw buyer the accounting audit trail does not disclose all the salient points associated with the transaction. According to the appraisal obtained by Lincoln, the appraised value of the property was only $9 million, or some $5 million under the designated sales price. The purported buyer was woefully underfinanced and on the basis of its financial statements unable to repay its loan or even service the debt. Since under the terms of the transaction the seller had no recourse against the buyer for the unpaid balance of the debt and since the pay downs on the debt were to be made on a deferred basis, it is clear the seller was not looking for the debt to be repaid in any realistic time frame.

Of particular importance as to this aspect of the transaction was the fact that the actual 25% down payment ($3.5 million) emanated from a loan E.C. Garcia made to Wescon. This meant that Wescon had not invested a single dollar of its own money in the transaction. Moreover, when the entire series of transactions between the Garcia and ACC complex of companies is reviewed, it emerges that in fact the money for the down payment actually emanated from Lincoln itself. The Garcia stable of companies was a heavy borrower from Lincoln. Indeed, at about the time of the Wescon transaction approximately $30 million in loans were being finalized between the Garcia companies and Lincoln. It is also clear from the record that E.C. Garcia was really not interested in buying the Hidden Valley parcel, but was doing so because he did not want to jeopardize a loan of over $20 million he was in the process of obtaining from Lincoln that was going to be used in a transaction that was extremely important to Garcia. It is more than a coincidence that this $20-million loan from Lincoln to Garcia closed on the same day as the $14.5 million sale of the property to Wescon was concluded.

A review of the Wescon transaction demonstrates the booking of an $11 million profit by Lincoln * * *, even though when reviewed in the light most favorable to plaintiffs, Lincoln only received cash of $3.5 million. [In addition,] Lincoln itself was the indirect source of the $3.5 million Wescon down payment.

* * * The Court was quite surprised by [ACC's accounting] experts' rationalization which supported plaintiffs' position as to the appropriate accounting for this transaction. To be generous to the position expounded by plaintiffs' experts, the Court will attribute the position they took to the abstract application of accounting principles.

What it is hoped the accounting profession will learn from this case is that an accountant must not blindly apply accounting conventions without reviewing the transaction to determine whether it makes any economic sense and without first finding that the transaction is realistic and has economic substance that would justify the booking of the transaction that occurred. [Accountants must be particularly skeptical where a transaction has little or no economic substance. This is so despite the fact that the transaction might technically meet GAAP standards.] Moreover, they should be particularly skeptical of any transaction where the audit trail is woefully lacking and the audited entity has failed to comply with the record keeping requirements established by a federal regulatory body. * * *

* * *

IV.   CONCLUSIONS OF LAW

Based upon the above findings, it is this Court's conclusions of law that the Bank Board acted appropriately in all respects in it * * * placing Lincoln in conservatorship * * *. * * * None of the Bank Board's material findings were arbitrary or capricious and accordingly the Court will enter judgment in favor of the Bank Board and dismiss plaintiffs' action in its entirety. Based upon the facts found by this Court, to return Lincoln to ACC, a defunct entity, would be the height of irresponsibility.

* * *

NOTES

1. Near the end of the decision in the principal case, the following passage attracted considerable public attention and created an uproar in both the legal and accounting professions:

> There are other unanswered questions presented by this case. Keating testified that he was so bent on doing the "right thing" that he surrounded himself with literally scores of accountants and lawyers to make sure all the transactions were legal. The questions that must be asked are:

> Where were these professionals, a number of whom are now asserting their rights under the Fifth Amendment, when these clearly improper transactions were being consummated?

> Why didn't any of them speak up or disassociate themselves from the transactions?

> Where also were the outside accountants and attorneys when these transactions were effectuated?

> What is difficult to understand is that with all the professional talent involved (both accounting and legal), why at least one professional would not have blown the whistle to stop the overreaching that took place in this case.

While we in this nation have been trying to place blame for the savings and loan crisis on the various governmental participants in the crisis and on the government's fostering of deregulation within the thrift industry, this Court believes far too little scrutiny has been focused on the private sector. * * *

743 F. Supp. at 919–20. Was Judge Sporkin unfairly criticizing members of the legal profession that owed a duty of loyalty to their client?

2. At least two prominent law firms agreed to multimillion dollar settlements to resolve malpractice claims arising from their representation of Lincoln Savings & Loan Association, the nation's most famous failed thrift. In 1992, Kaye, Scholer, Fierman, Hays & Handler, a New York law firm, agreed to pay $41 million after federal regulators sought $275 million because the firm allegedly concealed damaging information about Lincoln. In a separate action, Jones, Day, Reavis & Pogue, a Cleveland-based firm, agreed to a $24 million settlement.

3. We pose the same general question that Judge Sporkin rhetorically asked in the *Lincoln Savings and Loan* case: where were all the lawyers and why did they not speak up or blow the whistle to prevent or remedy the financial frauds. While the lawyers played diverse roles with varying degrees of involvement, investigators have found lawyers behind many corporate scandals. As an overview, we might divide lawyers' involvement into four broad categories.

First, some lawyers simply failed to recognize "red flags," even when whistle-blowers called the circumstances to their attention. For example, notwithstanding prior concerns about Enron's financial accounting and securities law disclosures, Vinson & Elkins LLP, Enron's principal outside law firm, concluded, after conducting only a limited inquiry, that Enron's former vice president Sherron Smith Watkin's infamous memo warning of an "accounting scandal" neither raised serious alarms nor warranted a deeper investigation of financial fraud. *Limited Partners: Lawyers for Enron Faulted Its Deals, Didn't Force Issue*, WALL ST. J., May 22, 2002, at A1; *see also* Dennis K. Berman, *Global Crossing Board Report Rebukes Ex-Outside Counsel*, WALL ST. J., Mar. 11, 2003, at B9 (criticizing Simpson Thacher & Bartlet, Global Crossing's former outside law firm, for inadequately investigating a former employee's letter that questioned the company's multibillion dollar "capacity swaps" used to inflate revenues).

Second, while some lawyers recognized the "red flags," they failed to express their concerns to the appropriate corporate officers or directors. Although Vinson & Elkins sometimes objected to Enron's dealings that posed conflict-of-interest concerns or disregarded Enron's best interests, once lawyers from Enron's legal department and Andrew Fastow, Enron's chief financial officer, ignored the concerns or slightly modified the transaction to sidestep the particular concern, the law firm failed to inform Enron's general counsel or board of directors because the law firm concluded it had no basis for such "extraordinary action." See *Limited Partners: Lawyers for Enron Faulted Its Deals, Didn't Force Issue*, WALL ST. J., May 22, 2002, at A1.

Third, some lawyers passively facilitated, whether negligently or ignorantly, the corrupt executives with their fraudulent accounting schemes. *See, e.g.*, WILLIAM C. POWERS, JR. ET AL., REPORT OF INVESTIGATION BY THE SPECIAL INVESTIGATIVE COMMITTEE OF THE BOARD OF DIRECTORS OF ENRON CORP. 10 (2002), *available at* http://news.findlaw.com/hdocs/docs/enron/ sicreport/sicreport020102.pdf (finding that Vinson & Elkins provided advice and drafted documents, including "true sales" opinion letters, involving many of the transactions with the special purpose entities ("SPEs")—which Enron created either to keep debt off its books or to transfer the risks related to the ownership of certain assets to outside investors—and assisted with Enron's disclosures of related-party transactions, but concluding that the law firm failed to provide "objective and critical professional advice").

Finally, some lawyers knowingly and actively participated in various fraudulent accounting schemes. Juries have already convicted Franklin C. Brown, Rite-Aid Corp.'s former general counsel, and Jamie Olis, a lawyer and former Dynegy vice president for their roles in financial frauds at those companies. Brown participated in schemes that included improperly reporting certain expenses, prematurely reporting vendor rebates, and retroactively increasing the useful life of some assets, in an effort to inflate the company's net income by $1.6 billion, and then obstructing the federal investigation by attempting to conceal the fraud. Olis spearheaded Dynegy's efforts to disguise a $300 million loan as cash flow from operations and to boost net income by $79 million. *See, e.g.*, SEC v. Bergonzi, Accounting and Auditing Enforcement Release No. 1581, [2001–2003 Transfer Binder] Fed. Sec. L. Rep. (CCH) ¶ 75,096 (June 21, 2002) (detailing the charges against Brown); SEC v. Foster, Accounting and Auditing Enforcement Release No. 1800, 7 Fed. Sec. L. Rep. (CCH) ¶ 75,460 (June 12, 2003) (setting forth the charges against Olis).

In response to lawyers' involvement in the corporate scandals during the late 1990s and early 2000s, Congress enacted SOx section 307, which directed the SEC to issue rules establishing "minimum standards of professional conduct for attorneys appearing and practicing before the Commission in any way in the representation of issuers" that require "an attorney to report evidence of a material violation of securities law or breach of fiduciary duty or similar violation" up-the-ladder to the chief legal counsel or chief executive officer and, if those officers do not "appropriately respond" then to report the evidence to the audit committee, another committee composed solely of independent directors, or the board of directors. 15 U.S.C. § 7245 (2012). In early 2003, the SEC timely issued final rules, implementing SOx section 307. *See* 17 C.F.R. Part 205 (2014); *see also* Implementation of Standards of Professional Conduct for Attorneys, 68 Fed. Reg. 6296 (Feb. 6, 2003).

As an initial matter, the SEC's final rules emphasize that an attorney represents the issuer as an entity rather than the officers or other individuals with whom the attorney may interact with during the representation. 17 C.F.R. § 205.3(a) (2014). In addition, the final rules broadly define "appearing and practicing" before the SEC to *include* any attorney, whether in-house or outside counsel: (1) transacting any business with the SEC; (2) representing an issuer in any SEC administrative proceedings or investigation; (3)

providing advice regarding securities laws or rules with respect to any document that the attorney has notice will be filed with the SEC; or (4) advising an issuer whether the securities laws require it to file information with the SEC. The rules, however, explicitly *exclude* any attorney not providing services within the context of an attorney-client relationship and certain foreign attorneys. 17 C.F.R. § 205.2(b) (2014).

The SEC's final rules specify that the obligation to report up to the issuer's chief legal officer, chief executive officer, or both triggers when, under an objective standard of reasonableness, an attorney becomes aware of credible evidence of a material violation. 17 C.F.R. § 205.3(b)(1) (2014). In addition, the final rule provides that attorney's obligation to report up to the issuer's audit committee or the board of directors, as discussed above, automatically triggers unless the reporting attorney reasonably believes that the chief legal officer or the chief executive officer provided an "appropriate response." 17 C.F.R. § 205.3(b)(3) (2014). Alternatively, the SEC's final rules provide that an issuer may establish a qualified legal compliance committee or designate another existing committee to serve in that capacity in which case after an attorney informs the committee of the evidence of a material violation any further obligations by the reporting attorney cease. 17 C.F.R. § 205.3(c) (2014).

The SEC's proposed rules contained "noisy withdrawal" provisions that under certain circumstances would have permitted or required attorneys to notify the Commission when they withdraw from representing an issuer and would have allowed attorneys to report evidence of material violations of the federal securities laws to the Commission. *See* Implementation of Standards of Professional Conduct for Attorneys, 67 Fed. Reg. 71,670, 71,705–06 (proposed Dec. 2, 2002). After numerous commentators expressed concerns involving the attorney-client privilege, the SEC extended the comment period and proposed a narrower alternative. *See* Implementation of Standards of Professional Conduct for Attorneys, 68 Fed. Reg. 6324 (proposed Feb. 6, 2003). Upon receiving a written withdrawal notice from an attorney, the SEC's alternative proposal would give an issuer two business days to notify the SEC. If the issuer does not so notify the SEC, the proposed rules would *permit*, but not require, an attorney to notify the SEC. *Id*. at 6328. More than a decade later, those proposed rules remain pending.

Following these developments, the American Bar Association ("ABA") amended its Model Rules of Professional Conduct, rules which have no legal effect unless adopted by the appropriate state authority, to address the SEC's rules on professional conduct. One amendment, directed to lawyers representing organizations, parallels the SEC's obligation to report up-the-ladder and, if the reporting lawyer fails to receive an appropriate response, *permits* the lawyer to reveal information relating to the representation only to the extent the lawyer reasonably believes necessary to prevent substantial injury to the organization. MODEL RULES OF PROF'L CONDUCT R. 1.13(b), (c) (2014); *see also* Judith Burns, *Attorneys Face a Paradox in the SEC Conduct Rules*, WALL ST. J., Aug. 19, 2003, at C1. Another amendment applies more generally to all lawyers and *permits*, but does not require, lawyers to disclose client information when the client is using or has used the lawyer's services to commit a crime or fraud reasonably certain to result in substantial injury to another's financial interests or property. MODEL RULES OF PROF'L CONDUCT R. 1.6(b)(2) (2014). Lawyers should keep in mind that to the extent state laws conflict with the SEC's rules, the latter will likely prevail under the Supremacy Clause.

(2) Special Circumstances

In two other situations, nonmonetary transactions and related party transactions, special rules apply to deals that would otherwise satisfy the exchange transaction requirement. An enterprise cannot recognize revenue in a nonmonetary transaction if major uncertainties exist about the fair market value of the assets transferred and received in exchange. In related party transactions, GAAP requires additional disclosures.

a) NONMONETARY EXCHANGES

In most exchange transactions, a business provides or transfers services, goods or other assets for cash or claims to cash, such as notes receivable or accounts receivable. The monetary amount of the cash or claim to cash usually provides an objective basis for measuring revenue or the gain or loss from the exchange. Some transactions, however, involve only nonmonetary assets, such as inventories, investments or long-lived assets.

Via FASB ASC Topic 845, *Nonmonetary Transactions*, which codified APB Opinion No. 29, *Accounting for Nonmonetary Transactions*, as amended by SFAS No. 153, *Exchanges of Nonmonetary Assets* in an effort to conform U.S. GAAP to IFRSs, the Codification generally uses the fair values of the assets or services involved to account for nonmonetary exchanges. As a basic principle, a business should recognize a gain or loss on any such exchange. Thus, the fair value of any assets relinquished becomes the cost of any nonmonetary assets acquired, and the enterprise should recognize gain or loss on the exchange. An enterprise should use the fair value of any assets acquired to measure the cost if the enterprise can more clearly determine that amount relative to the fair value of the asset surrendered. ASC Topic 845, however, directs an enterprise to use the recorded amount, after reduction for any indicated impairment, when: (1) the enterprise cannot determine fair value of either the received or relinquished assets within reasonable limits; (2) the transaction qualifies as an exchange to facilitate a sale to a customer other than the parties to the exchange; or (3) the transaction lacks commercial substance. In those circumstances, the enterprise should not recognize a gain or loss on the transaction. Topic 845 further provides that an enterprise should regard fair value as "not determinable within reasonable limits" if major uncertainties exist about a business's ability to realize value from an asset obtained in a nonmonetary exchange. The Codification also requires that enterprises disclose the basis for accounting for nonmonetary transactions and the gains and losses recognized on such transactions in the financial statements. FASB ASC ¶¶ 845-10-05-2 to -3, 845-10-30-1 to -3, -8, 845-10-50-1 (codifications of ACCOUNTING FOR NONMONETARY TRANSACTIONS, Accounting Principles Board Opinion No. 29, ¶¶ 1, 18, 20, 26, 28 (Am. Inst. of Certified

Pub. Accountants 1973), as amended by EXCHANGES OF NONMONETARY ASSETS, Statement of Fin. Accounting Standards No. 153 ¶ 2 (Fin. Accounting Standards Bd. 2004)).

If the circumstances do not reasonably assure that an enterprise will collect the sales price reflected in a receivable, and the enterprise also cannot reasonably estimate the degree of collectibility, FASB ASC Topic 310, *Receivables*, which codifies certain rules set forth in APB Opinion No. 10, permits the business to use either the installment method or the cost recovery method to account for the transaction. Such circumstances would include sales to financially troubled purchasers, as well as transactions requiring little or no down payments and periodic payments over an extended period. FASB ASC ¶ 310-10-35-11 (a codification of OMNIBUS OPINION—1966, Accounting Principles Board Opinion No. 10, ¶ 12 n.8 (Am. Inst. of Certified Pub. Accountants 1966)).

We can use the Wescon transaction in the *Lincoln Savings & Loan Association* case to illustrate the installment and cost recovery methods. You will recall that a Lincoln subsidiary sold 1000 acres in Hidden Valley, which cost $3 million, for a total of $14 million, a $3.5 million down payment plus a $10.5 million non-recourse note. For purposes of this illustration, suppose that Wescon did not indirectly obtain the $3.5 million down payment from Lincoln.

(i) Installment Method

The installment method requires the vendor to allocate all cash received from the buyer between cost recovery and profit. Because Lincoln sold the property for $14 million and the land cost $3 million, Lincoln would allocate 3/14ths, or approximately .214286, of each payment to cost recovery and 11/14ths, or about .785714, to profit.

Lincoln could record the following journal entry to record the sale:

Cash	$3,500,000	
Note Receivable	10,500,000	
Land		$3,000,000
Deferred Profit on Sale		11,000,000

The installment method would treat $2.75 million, or 11/14ths of the $3.5 million collected, as profit. Accordingly, Lincoln could also make another entry to record the profit as follows:

Deferred Profit on Sale	$2,750,000	
Profit from Sale of Land under Installment Method		$2,750,000

Suppose that Wescon paid an additional $1 million on the note before defaulting. In that event, Lincoln would first record the $1 million payment as follows:

Cash	$1,000,000	
Notes Receivable		$1,000,000

In addition, Lincoln would recognize 11/14ths of the $1 million as profit and could record the following entry:

Deferred Profit on Sale	$785,714	
Profit from Sale of Land		
under Installment Method		$785,714

(ii) Cost Recovery Method

Under the cost recovery method, an enterprise recognizes equal and offsetting amounts of revenue and expense as the business collects payments on the receivable until the enterprise has recovered all costs. As a result, the cost recovery method postpones any profit recognition until that time and any subsequent collections generate additional profits.

Under the cost recovery method, Lincoln could use the same original journal entry to record the sale as follows:

Cash	$3,500,000	
Note Receivable	10,500,000	
Land		$3,000,000
Deferred Profit on Sale		11,000,000

Because the $3.5 million down payment exceeds the $3 million cost of the land, Lincoln can recognize $500,000 in profit and could record the following journal entry:

Deferred Profit on Sale	$500,000	
Profit on Land Sale under		
Cost Recovery Method		$500,000

Assuming again that Wescon paid an additional $1 million on the note before defaulting, Lincoln would first record the $1 million payment as follows:

Cash	$1,000,000	
Notes Receivable		$1,000,000

In addition, Lincoln would recognize the entire $1 million as profit because Lincoln had already recovered the $3 million cost of the land. As a result, Lincoln could also record the following entry:

Deferred Profit on Sale	$1,000,000	
Profit on Land Sale under		
Cost Recovery Method		$1,000,000

(iii) Illustration of the Effects of the Accrual, Installment, and Cost Recovery Methods

If the facts had supported full income recognition under the accrual method, Lincoln would have recognized $11 million in gain at the time of sale. Lincoln could have used the following journal entry to record the sale:

Cash	$3,500,000	
Note Receivable	10,500,000	
Land		$3,000,000
Gain on Sale of Land		11,000,000

When Wescon paid $1 million on the note, Lincoln would record the payment as follows:

Cash	$1,000,000	
Notes Receivable		$1,000,000

Because Lincoln had already recognized $11 million in gain under the accrual method, Lincoln would not recognize any additional income as it collects payments on the note.

To recap, the different accounting methods produce different gains at different times. Assuming that Lincoln ultimately collects all amounts due under the note, it will recognize $11 million in income from the transaction. The timing of that income, however, varies under the different accounting methods. The following chart summarizes the timing differences in this relatively simple example:

Time	Accrual Method	Installment Method	Cost Recovery Method
Sale	$11,000,000	$-0-	$-0-
Down Payment	-0-	2,750,000	500,000
First Installment	-0-	785,714	1,000,000
Later Installments	-0-	7,464,286	9,500,000
Total	$11,000,000	$11,000,000	$11,000,000

The chart demonstrates that the selection of a method for recognizing revenue can significantly affect the financial statements.

NOTE

When a transaction involves a promissory note or other obligation, another important issue arises as to whether the face amount of a note or other obligation provides reliable evidence for properly recording an exchange transaction. A promissory note exchanged for services, goods or other property represents two separate elements even though the note may not refer to these components: (1) the principal amount which equals the bargained price for the services, goods or other property that the supplier and the purchaser established and (2) interest to compensate the supplier during the promissory note's life for the use of the funds that the supplier would have received in a cash transaction at the time of the exchange. If the note does not provide interest or uses an interest rate which differs from the market rate, the note's face amount does not reasonably represent the present value of the consideration given or received in the exchange. Unless the supplier and purchaser both record the note at its present value, the parties will misstate the sales price and profit to the seller, the buyer's purchase price, and interest income and interest expense in subsequent accounting periods.

You may recall from Chapter III on the time value of money and the example involving the Nobel Prize on pages 224 to 226, *supra*, that $40,000 invested in 1901 at five percent interest, compounded annually, would have grown to $9,446,317 by 2013 after 112 years. Assume that a car dealer sells a sports car in exchange for the buyer's promissory note for $9.44 million, payment due in exactly 112 years. Can the dealer recognize $9.44 million in sales revenue? Of course not. If we assume that five percent interest, compounded annually, represents the market rate, the car dealer can record no more than $40,000 in sales revenue. The remaining $9,400,000 represents unearned interest. Accountants call the $9,400,000 difference between the promissory note's $9.44 million face amount and the note's present value *discount,* which the seller will *amortize* and recognize as interest income over the note's life. At the time of the sale, the car dealer might record the following journal entry:

Note Receivable	$9,440,000	
Sales		$40,000
Discount on Note Receivable		9,400,000

The Discount on Note Receivable serves as a contra asset account which the seller would report on the balance sheet as a direct deduction from the note's face amount. The note's description on the balance sheet or in the notes to the financial statements should mention the effective interest rate. As a result, the promissory note might appear as a non-current asset on the car dealer's balance sheet as follows:

Note Receivable ($9,440,000 face amount, noninterest bearing, due in 112 years (less unamortized discount of $9,400,000, based on five percent per annum imputed interest, compounded annually))	$40,000

Each year, the car dealer would recognize five percent of the "real" amount of the note or, in other words, the face amount discounted at the imputed interest rate to reflect present value, as interest income and reduce the unamortized discount by that amount. In the first year after the sale, the dealer would have earned $2,000 in interest income, representing the $40,000 discounted amount of the note times five percent interest. For that first year, the dealer might record the following journal entry:

Discount on Note Receivable	$2,000	
Interest Income		$2,000

The entry would reduce the unamortized discount to $9,398,000, so that the promissory note might again appear as a non-current asset on the car dealer's balance sheet as:

Note Receivable ($9,440,000 face amount,
noninterest bearing, due in 112 years (less
unamortized discount of $9,398,000, based on
five percent per annum imputed interest,
compound annually)) $42,000

In the second and following years, the car dealer would continue to recognize five percent of the note's discounted amount as interest income until the car dealer had recognized the entire $9,400,000 as interest income. For the second year, the dealer would recognize $2,100 as interest income ($42,000 discounted amount times five percent interest). *See* FASB ASC Subtopic 835-30, *Interest—Imputation of Interest* (a codification of INTEREST ON RECEIVABLES AND PAYABLES, Accounting Principles Board Opinion No. 21 (Am. Inst. of Certified Pub. Accountants 1971)).

b) *RELATED PARTY TRANSACTIONS*

The Enron scandal and the more recent and sudden 2005 collapse of Refco Inc., one of the world's largest commodities brokerages, remind us that related-party transactions can distort an enterprise's apparent financial condition and operating results. Although related-party transactions may increase efficiency in transacting business, they may also allow an enterprise to manipulate its earnings by the way the enterprise sets prices or allocates expenses. Enron's transactions with the so-called Chewco and LJM partnerships, highlight the dangers that can arise from related-party transactions. As a small, but relatively simple example, Enron sold an interest in a Polish company to LJM2 for $30 million on December 21, 1999. While Enron intended to sell the interest to an unrelated party, the company could not find a buyer before the end of the year. The sale allowed Enron to record a gain of $16 million on a transaction that Enron could not close with a third party. Remarkably, Enron later bought back LJM2's interest for $31.9 million after the partnership failed to find an outside buyer. Often occurring at the end of a fiscal period, the related party transactions allowed Enron to manipulate its reported earnings, to close deals at desired amounts quickly, to hide debt, and to conceal poorly performing assets. Until uncovered, these transactions allowed Enron to meet its earnings expectations and to sustain its stock price.

If an enterprise transacts business with a related party, the enterprise can manipulate revenue by selling to the related party at higher or lower prices, especially if no cash changes hands in the transaction. To illustrate, imagine that the following events develop in the law school survival guide example. During February, law students purchase 200 survival guides at five dollars each. After you agree to share Porsche-privileges, your younger sister promises to pay $3,000 for 200 survival guides. With a new loan application in hand, you triumphantly return to the bank. The loan officer again commends you on selling 400 survival guides at what appears to be ten dollars each. You mention how fortunate you are that your younger sister appreciates both great literature and fast cars. You watch in dismay as the loan officer again shreds your loan application. The loan officer explains that your younger sister's fifteen dollar purchase price, or the $3,000 total consideration divided by 200 survival guides, represents the value of Porsche-privileges rather than the survival guide's value. The loan officer further explains that, unless you grant Porsche-privileges to future purchasers, the 200 survival guides your younger sister purchased do not forecast future demand. In contrast, the 200 survival guides your classmates purchased at five dollars each reflect the survival guide's true market value and future demand. As we can see, loan officers and investors who know the nature of an enterprise's exchange transactions can better assess current revenue and predict future demand.

Slightly more than two months after a $583 million initial public offering in 2005, Refco Inc. ("Refco") filed for bankruptcy protection. Its collapse began when the company disclosed a series of transactions used to conceal bad debts. Beginning in 1999, Refco's former CEO Philip R. Bennett allegedly devised a scheme that allowed the company to hide as much as $720 million in bad debts from customers. When customers suffered trading losses and could not repay the funds that Refco had advanced to them, Bennett reportedly had a company he controlled, conveniently named Refco Group Holdings Inc. ("RGHI"), assume the bad debts so that Refco would not have to write off the loans and reduce its net income. The amounts due from RGHI, however, were related party transactions on Refco's books. Shortly before the end of Refco's fiscal years, an Austrian bank, Bawag P.S.K., which once owned a part of Refco, extended short-term loans to RGHI to enable it to "pay off" at least part of its debt to Refco. A deposit from Refco to an account at Bawag secured, at least in part, RGHI's debt to Bawag. Early in Refco's new fiscal years, the companies would reverse the transactions so that Bennett's RGHI owed the sums to Refco. To settle civil charges and to avoid criminal prosecution, Bawag agreed to pay at least $675 million, including $337.5 million that the company forfeited to the United States for distribution to victims of the Refco fraud. *See Austria's BAWAG to Pay $675M to Avoid U.S. Prosecution, Settle Claims*, 38 Sec. Reg. & L. Rep. (BNA) 1006 (June 12, 2006); Paul Davies, *Former CEO Bennett Is Indicted in Refco Collapse*, Wall St. J., Nov. 11, 2005, at C3.

Businesses do not account for related party transactions differently than for unrelated party transactions. If related party transactions, other than compensation arrangements, expense allowances, and other similar items in the ordinary course of business, qualify as material, however, GAAP requires that enterprises disclose the following information in their financial statements:

(1) The nature of any relationships involved;

(2) A description of the transactions for each period for which the financial statements present an income statement, including any information necessary to understand the transactions' effects on the financial statements;

(3) The dollar amounts of the transactions and the effects of any change in the method used to establish terms when compared to those followed in the preceding period; and

(4) Amounts due from or to related parties on each balance sheet date and the related terms governing those amounts.

FASB ASC Topic 850, *Related Party Disclosures* (a codification of RELATED PARTY DISCLOSURES, Statement of Fin. Accounting Standards No. 57 (Fin. Accounting Standards Bd. 1982)). Entities that belong to a group that files a consolidated tax return shall disclose additional information concerning tax-related balances due to or from affiliates on each balance sheet date. FASB ASC ¶ 740-10-50-17 (a codification of ACCOUNTING FOR INCOME TAXES, Statement of Fin. Accounting Standards No. 109, ¶¶ 49, 288s (Fin. Accounting Standards Bd. 1992).

Significant related party relationships or transactions can conceivably preclude an auditor from issuing an unqualified opinion because an underlying relationship or transaction can prevent the financial statements from "fairly present[ing]" the enterprise's financial condition, operating results and cash flows. Generally accepted auditing standards require an auditor to identify related party relationships and transactions and to obtain and evaluate competent evidence regarding the purpose, nature, extent of any relationship or transaction and their effect on the financial statements. Before issuing an unqualified opinion, the auditor must conclude that the financial statements adequately disclose any related party transaction or relationship. In particular, any disclosure should not imply that the enterprise consummated a transaction on terms equivalent to those that would have prevailed in an arms-length transaction unless management can substantiate the representation. If management cannot substantiate any such representation which appears in the financial statements, then the auditor should express either a qualified or adverse opinion, depending on materiality. OMNIBUS STATEMENT ON AUDITING STANDARDS—1983, Statement on Auditing Standards No. 45 (Am. Inst. of Certified Pub. Accountants 1983), *reprinted at* 1 AM. INST. OF CERTIFIED PUB. ACCOUNTANTS, PROFESSIONAL STANDARDS AU § 334 (Dec. 1997).

b.   EXCEPTIONS TO THE EXCHANGE TRANSACTION REQUIREMENT

In the first survival guide example, the loan officer explained that the bank could not afford to share in your "optimism." In other words, the bank needed actual exchange transactions or sales to demonstrate that you could generate cash to repay your loan. As mentioned in Chapter I, accountants often use conservatism to avoid overly optimistic financial statements. Under conservatism, GAAP accrues all losses and expenses as soon as they appear likely but generally waits to recognize revenues and gains until the underlying events appear certain. Banks and other users of financial statements, however, cannot afford undue "pessimism." No one benefits when a bank denies a loan to a borrower who needlessly understates income, assets or equity.

Realizing that financial statement users need "realism," GAAP authorizes several exceptions to the exchange transaction requirement for revenue recognition. First, in an effort to provide more relevant information, the FASB has begun to implement a movement to fair value accounting. Under a fair value system, enterprises measure certain assets and liabilities at fair value, or current value, rather than at historical cost as GAAP has traditionally required. At each financial statement date, enterprises report changes in fair value in earnings even though no exchange of these assets and liabilities has occurred. To assist the transition to such a system, in 2006 the Board released a new standard establishing a unified approach to measuring fair value. As explained on pages 416 through 426, *infra*, GAAP already required most enterprises to use fair value accounting to report investments in certain debt and marketable equity securities. In limited circumstances, an enterprise must include unrealized holding gains and losses on the income statement without an exchange transaction. More commonly, an enterprise's net unrealized holding gain and loss appeared in "other comprehensive income" when computing "comprehensive income." Another provision in the Codification, however, grants entities an option to record more assets and liabilities at fair value and expands the unrealized holding gains and losses that enterprises can report on the income statement without an exchange transaction. Second, if changing circumstances impair an asset's value, conservatism requires the enterprise to recognize an immediate loss for any non-temporary decline in value. Both the fair value rules and the requirement to recognize a loss when an asset has suffered an other-than-temporary impairment ("OTTI") attracted considerable attention and generated significant controversy during the credit crisis. Finally, the accounting profession has used current fair market values on personal financial statements for many years.

(1) Fair Value Accounting

Both the FASB and the IASB continue to work to develop a comprehensive scheme for incorporating fair value measurements into financial reporting. This new approach stands in contrast with the historical-cost principle and exchange transaction requirement for revenue recognition. Financial statement users can benefit from fair value reporting, which provides more timely and relevant asset and liability valuation data. As the credit crisis powerfully illustrates, however, fair value reporting also increases volatility in reported earnings and amounts shown on the balance sheet. Reporting at fair value also comes at the cost of reliability and comparability if companies use different sources and methods for measuring the current values of assets and liabilities. To address these concerns, the FASB issued SFAS No. 157, *Fair Value Measurements*. Those rules, now codified in FASB ASC Topic 820, *Fair Value Measurements and Disclosures*, and as amended by ASU No. 2011-04, *Fair Value Measurement (Topic 820): Amendments to Achieve Common Fair Value Measurement and Disclosure Requirements in U.S. GAAP and*

IFRSs, define fair value, establish a unified framework for measuring fair value, and expand disclosures about fair value measurements.

FASB ASC Topic 820 defines "fair value" as the "exit price," meaning "the price at which an orderly transaction to sell the asset or to transfer the liability would take place between market participants at the measurement date under current market conditions." The standard establishes a three-tier "hierarchy" for inputs used to determine fair value. First, a quoted price in an active market typically provides the most reliable evidence of fair value. Hence, only "quoted prices (unadjusted) in active markets for identical assets or liabilities that the reporting entity can access at the measurement date" qualify as "Level 1 inputs," which explains the expression "mark-to-market," which the Codification now refers to as "subsequently measure at fair value." Next, the hierarchy recognizes other directly or indirectly observable inputs as "Level 2 inputs." These second-tier inputs include quoted market prices for similar assets or liabilities in active markets; quoted prices for identical or comparable assets in inactive markets; interest rates and yield curves observable at commonly quoted intervals; and other market-corroborated inputs. By comparison, FASB ASC Topic 820 defines "Level 3 inputs" as "unobservable inputs for the asset or liability," including the reporting entity's own analysis of the underlying data that market participants would factor into the pricing of the asset or liability. As a result, most commentators refer to those valuations based on Level 2 or Level 3 inputs as "mark-to-model," although some individuals refer to valuations based on Level 2 inputs as "mark-to-comparables." To enhance transparency, the disclosure rules in FASB ASC section 820-10-50 now require enterprises to describe their valuation processes used to reach measurements categorized within Level 3, including, for example, some explanation as to how the enterprise decides its valuation policies and procedures and analyzes changes in fair value measurements from period to period, and to set forth any corresponding effect on earnings.

As originally issued, SFAS No. 157, again now codified in ASC Topic 820, required companies using the calendar year for financial accounting purposes to adopt the new rules no later than the first quarter in 2008. Subsequently, FASB approved a one-year partial deferral for fair value measures of non-financial assets and non-financial liabilities, noting challenges arising in implementation. Non-financial assets include goodwill and other intangible assets, while contingencies and asset retirement obligations exemplify non-financial liabilities. FASB ASC ¶¶ 820-10-65-1, 820-10-15-1A, 820-10-50-8A, 820-10-55-23A to -23B (codifications of EFFECTIVE DATE OF FASB STATEMENT NO. 157, FASB Staff Position No. FAS 157-2 (Fin. Accounting Standards Bd. 2008).

Critics feared that granting leeway to managers in measuring the fair values of assets without readily-available market prices potentially invited manipulation and fraud similar to Enron's deceitful accounting practices. At Enron, managers used favorable internal valuation models and data to overvalue energy contracts and artificially boost earnings. Given the use of management's analysis in Level 3 valuations, some commentators have continued to refer to fair value accounting as "mark-to-management," or more skeptically, "mark-to-myth." In promulgating the rules on fair value measurements, however, FASB concluded the expanded disclosure requirements provide financial statement users with better information on the inputs that management used to measure fair value. The board emphasized that a single definition and framework for measuring fair value also enhanced consistency and comparability.

The debate over the merits of fair value accounting and the fair value option intensified as the subprime mortgage crisis spread to other credit markets. Investment banks, which adopted the fair value measurement rules early, struggled to value their holdings as markets for securities and derivatives connected to American subprime mortgages crashed. Commentators feared that businesses would turn to outdated or inaccurate Level 3 inputs for fair value estimates. In 2007, the SEC warned public companies that the agency would carefully scrutinize Level 3 valuations and disclosures. The agency subsequently launched several investigations into valuations and the timeliness of disclosures of subprime risks.

As the crisis continued and deepened, Wall Street's largest investment banks took multi-billion dollar write-downs on subprime-related instruments. Critics of fair value accounting blamed the new standards for exacerbating the credit crunch. As banks wrote down investments, regulatory capital requirements limited the banks' ability to lend money. Some investors and executives faulted fair value accounting for exaggerating losses, thereby causing market downturns. A "domino effect" resulted, they argued, with market downturns triggering further writedowns. Many executives felt forced to recognize current losses on holdings they did not intend to sell in the near-term. Analysts acknowledged that fair value accounting increased volatility and reduced comparability from quarter to quarter. David Reilly, *Wave of Write-Offs Rattles Market*, Wall St. J., Mar. 1, 2008, at A1. At the core, however, no one trusted the financial statements and the numbers that enterprises used for fair values. The market capitalizations at many banks fell below their tangible book values.

Nevertheless, most investors and leaders in the accounting community have continued to defend fair value accounting as part of the solution to the credit crisis, not part of the problem. In their view, misguided lending decisions and the creation of complex instruments based on subprime loans caused the crisis, not accounting rules. Even under the historical-cost system, GAAP required enterprises to write bad loans down to fair value, the amount expected to be recovered in the future. These supporters also observe that international regulators increasingly demand fair value information to reduce the uncertainty in valuations. Proponents emphasize that fair values provide more relevant and helpful information for investment decision-making. Numerous commentators have observed that when management enjoys the latitude to "mark" assets and liabilities, most surprises have been—and will likely continue to be—on the downside. One analyst noted that Lehman Brothers Holding Inc.'s insolvency approximated $150 billion, while Enron's liabilities did not exceed its assets by any more than $70 billion. Advocates of fair value accounting also point to the savings-and-loans crisis of the 1980s, which resulted partly from banks carrying loans at historical cost when the loans had sharply declined in value.

Recall that the definition of fair value explicitly requires "an orderly transaction." In contrast to a forced transaction, such as a distressed sale or rushed liquidation, an orderly transaction "assumes exposure to the market for a period prior to the measurement date to allow for marketing activities that are usual and customary for transactions involving such assets." As the financial crisis expanded, numerous banks and other financial institutions contended that regulators or rulemakers should repeal, or at least suspend, fair value accounting because the crisis had frozen many markets.

Under intense political pressure to dump or suspend "mark-to-market" accounting as then set forth in SFAS No. 157 during the 2008 financial crisis, especially as applied to banks and other financial institutions, FASB provided additional guidance on issues related to fair value accounting and disclosures on multiple occasions. The guidance included pronouncements on inactive markets, distressed transactions, and, as described in the discussion on losses on page 437, *infra*, other-than-temporary impairments.

Culminating a "fast-track" project, FASB issued guidance on determining the fair value of a financial asset in an inactive market. The guidance followed a short comment period that lasted less than a week. Using an example that sought to illustrate key considerations in determining the fair value of a financial asset in an inactive market, the guidance, now codified in FASB ASC Subtopic 820-10, *Fair Value Measurements and Disclosures*, *Overall*, recognized that when a market becomes inactive such that the enterprise must apply significant adjustments using unobservable inputs to previously used observable inputs, the resulting and appropriate valuation would fall within the Level 3 category. In addition, the Board approved the use of a discounted, present value technique, as long as it incorporated the expectations of market participants. Among other factors indicating an inactive market, the guidance identified a significant widening in the spread between bid and ask prices, a decrease in volumes, stale prices, and prices that vary substantially either over time or among market makers. FASB ASC ¶¶ 820-10-35-15A, -55A, -55B, 820-10-65-2 (codifications of Determining the Fair Value of a Financial Asset When the Market for That Asset Is Not Active, FASB Staff Position No. FAS 157-3 (Fin. Accounting Standards Bd. 2008)).

During a Congressional hearing in early 2009, both Democratic and Republican members of the House Financial Services Subcommittee on Capital Markets, Insurance, and Government Sponsored Entities essentially gave FASB Chairman Robert Herz an ultimatum to issue additional guidance within the month or Congress would suspend fair value accounting. Within days, FASB again expedited its process and soon issued three staff positions within a month, two involving fair value accounting and disclosures and the third related to accounting for impaired securities, such as mortgage-backed securities. The pronouncements provided guidelines for making fair value measurements more consistent with the principles now codified in FASB Topic

820, *Fair Value Measurements and Disclosures*, sought more consistency in financial reporting by increasing the frequency of fair value disclosures, and included guidance to improve clarity and consistency in recording and presenting impairment losses on securities.

With regard to fair value accounting, the first staff position addressed how to determine fair values when no active market exists or where the relevant price inputs represent distressed sales. In short, the new rules, now codified in sections 820-10-35 and 820-10-50 of the Codification, sought to dispel the notion that the measurement rules imposed a "last price" model. In essence, the guidance affirms the need for management to use judgment when evaluating whether a market has become inactive and tries to both expand and guide that judgment. In addition, the new rules required an enterprise to disclose changes in valuation techniques and related inputs for fair value measurements in both interim and annual periods. FASB ASC §§ 820-10-35, -50 (codifications of Determining Fair Value When the Volume and Level of Activity for the Asset or Liability Have Significantly Decreased and Identifying Transactions That Are Not Orderly, FASB Staff Position No. FAS 157-4 (Fin. Accounting Standards Bd. 2009)).

FASB ASC section 820-10-35 states that fair value measurements seek to reflect how much the enterprise would sell the asset for in an orderly transaction—as opposed to a distressed or forced transaction—at the date of the financial statements under current market conditions. The Codification proceeds to list numerous factors that enterprises should evaluate to ascertain whether a formerly active market has become inactive. If the market has become inactive, an enterprise must next evaluate whether any observed prices or broker quotes obtained represent distressed transactions. The circumstances that may indicate disorderly transactions include inadequate exposure to the market before the measurement date to allow usual and customary marketing activities, marketing to only a single market participant, a need to sell to meet regulatory or legal requirements, or a transaction price that falls outside other recent prices for the same or similar asset or liability. In inactive or disorderly markets, the Codification proceeds to recognize that management could use a discounted cash flow model to estimate fair value, as long as fair value measurement includes "a risk premium reflecting the amount market participants would demand because of the risk (uncertainty) in the cash flows [in an orderly transaction at the measurement date under current market conditions]." FASB ASC ¶¶ 820-10-35-36, -48, -51A to -53, 820-10-50-2, -5 (codifications of FSP No. FAS 157-4).

The second staff position on fair value, now codified in FASB ASC section 825-10-50, addressed disclosures regarding any financial instruments that an enterprise does not report on the balance sheet at fair value. The previous rules only required enterprises to disclose fair values once a year. The new rules require such disclosures on a quarterly basis. As a result, commercial banks must now disclose information about the fair value of their loans outstanding each quarter. FASB ASC ¶ 825-10-50-10 (a codification of Interim Disclosures About Fair Values of Fin. Instruments, FASB Staff Position No. FAS 107-1 & APB 28-1 (Fin. Accounting Standards Bd. 2009)).

Seeking to reduce ambiguity and to improve consistency in applying the rules for measuring liabilities at fair value, FASB issued ASU No. 2009-05, *Measuring Liabilities at Fair Value*, to amend FASB ASC Subtopic 820-10, *Fair Value Measurements and Disclosures—Overall*. The amendments to the Codification clarify that when an enterprise cannot obtain a quoted price in an active market for the identical liability, the enterprise should, as usual, look to the views of marketplace participants and use one or more acceptable valuation techniques. Suitable means for measuring liabilities include techniques that use a quoted price for the identical liability when traded as an asset or quoted prices for similar liabilities or similar liabilities when traded as assets. In addition, other techniques consistent with the principles set forth in FASB ASC Topic 820, *Fair Value Measurements and Disclosures*, qualify. For example, both an income approach or a market approach would satisfy those principles. Under an income approach, an enterprise would use a present value technique to calculate the liability's fair value, while a market approach would try to determine the amount that the enterprise would pay to transfer the liability or would receive to enter into the identical liability.

In response to continued calls from investors for additional information regarding fair value measurements, early in 2010 the FASB issued ASU 2010-6, *Improving Disclosures About Fair Value Measurements*. The amendments, again to Subtopic 820-10, sought to increase transparency in financial reporting by mandating additional information and clarifying existing disclosures. The rules require enterprises to make new disclosures about significant transfers in and out of Level 1 and Level 2 categories and activity in Level 3 fair value measurements. In the reconciliation for changes in amounts for Level 3, an enterprise should present information about purchases, sales, issuances, and settlements on a gross basis. The amendments clarify the level of disaggregation required and address disclosures about inputs and valuation techniques. An enterprise should provide disclosures about fair value measurements for each class of assets and liabilities. A class refers to a subset of assets or liabilities within a line item on the balance sheet. For fair value measurements that fall within Level 2 or Level 3, an enterprise should describe the inputs and techniques used to determine both recurring or nonrecurring measurements.

In 2011, FASB and IASB completed a joint project to develop common requirements for measuring fair value and for disclosing information about fair value measurements. The converged standards give fair value the same meaning in U.S. GAAP and IFRS and, except for minor differences in wording and style, impose the same fair value measurement and disclosure requirements. While the amendments do not require additional fair value measurements, the guidance changed the wording used to describe numerous rules in FASB ASC Topic 820, *Fair Value Measurements,* and clarified that an enterprise should disclose quantitative information about the unobservable inputs used in a fair value measurement categorized as Level 3 within the fair value hierarchy in an effort to improve comparability. In addition, the new rules require additional disclosures about fair value measurements. For fair value measurements categorized within Level 3, the enterprise must disclose the valuation processes used and the fair value measurement's sensitivity to changes in unobservable inputs and any interrelationships between those inputs. Finally, the amendments, and a related clarification, exempt nonpublic enterprises from certain disclosure requirements. For example, nonpublic enterprises need not disclose transfers between Level 1 and Level 2, explain the reasons for such transfers, provide a narrative description as to how changes in unobservable inputs affect Level 3 measurements, or show the hierarchy levels for items disclosed, but not measured at fair value for the balance sheet. *See* Fair Value Measurements (Topic 820): Amendments to Achieve Common Fair Value Measurement and Disclosure Requirements in U.S. GAAP and IFRSs, Accounting Standards Update No. 2011-04 (Fin. Accounting Standards Bd.); Financial Instruments (Topic 825): Clarifying the Scope and Applicability of a Particular Disclosure to Nonpublic Entities, Accounting Standards Update No. 2013-03 (Fin. Accounting Standards Bd.) (exempting nonpublic companies from the need to provide hierarchy levels for fair value amounts disclosed, but not included on the balance sheet).

When reading financial statements containing "fair value" amounts and disclosures, law students and lawyers should pay special attention to the percentage of assets and liabilities shown in Level 3 and disclosures about those assets and liabilities. In particular, readers should keep in mind the following questions:

- How have the percentages of assets and liabilities shown in Level 3 changed from period to period?
- How has the amount of unrealized gains and losses in Level 3 assets changed?
- Does the firm explain fully the methods used to value Level 3 assets and liabilities?
- Has the firm changed its valuation methods? If so, how do any changes affect reported results?

For public companies, readers should also study the portions of MD&A addressing fair value measurements and disclosures.

Dating back to 2005, the FASB and the IASB have been working together to try to improve and simplify the financial accounting for financial instruments, such as investments, derivatives, loans, and long-term receivables. The financial crisis that exploded in 2008 spurred increased attention to credit impairment and loan losses. As a long-term goal, both Boards aspire to require enterprises to measure all financial instruments at fair value, with realized and unrealized gains and losses reported in earnings in the period in which they occur. Banks and other financial institutions have resisted the ultimate objective. This wide-ranging project sought, but seems unlikely, to converge international accounting standards for financial instruments, to provide greater transparency, and to reduce complexity.

a) INVESTMENTS IN SECURITIES

Businesses often invest in debt or equity securities that governmental entities or other enterprises issue. Debt securities include U.S. Treasury obligations, government bonds, municipal securities, corporate bonds and debentures, commercial paper and other instruments representing a right to receive payment from a borrower. In contrast, common and preferred shares and options to acquire or sell those investments represent equity securities.

For our purposes, we can divide these investments in debt or equity securities into two categories: passive and active. In a passive investment, the investing enterprise does not and cannot exert any significant influence over the investee. When an enterprise owns less than twenty percent of an investee's voting stock, GAAP generally treats the investment as passive. Conversely, accountants presumptively classify situations in which the investing enterprise owns twenty percent or more of the investee's voting stock as an active investment.

Under financial accounting, five different "methods" can apply to an enterprise's investment in debt or equity securities. Depending on the underlying circumstances, enterprises will use either "fair value," "cost" or "amortized cost" to report passive investments on their balance sheets. Where applicable, changes in "fair value" can affect either "net income" or "other comprehensive income," which collectively determine "comprehensive income." For active investments by comparison, GAAP requires enterprises either to use the "equity method" or to prepare consolidated financial statements.

Before we describe these methods and discuss when each applies in greater detail, we want to set forth some basic rules as an overview for the materials that follow. As an important exception to the historical cost principle, FASB ASC Topic 320, *Investments—Debt and Equity Securities*, which codified SFAS No. 115, generally requires enterprises to use "fair value," rather than historical cost, to account for "passive investments" that have readily determinable fair values. As a result, most passive investments will appear on an enterprise's balance sheet at "fair value," and the enterprise must include the net unrealized holding gains and losses as "other comprehensive income" in computing "comprehensive income."

Three exceptions exist to these general rules regarding passive investments. First, the "cost method" applies to passive investments in equity securities that do not have readily determinable market values. Second, the "amortized cost" method applies to "held-to-maturity debt securities." Third, enterprises must report unrealized holding gains and losses from "trading securities" directly on the income statement. As a practical matter, however, very few firms hold "trading securities."

(i) Passive Investments

The accounting treatment for passive investments depends upon a multi-pronged analysis:

> (1) Does the underlying investment fall into a debt or equity classification?

> (2) If the investment qualifies as an equity security, does it have a readily determinable market value?

For equity securities without readily determinable market values, enterprises must use the *cost method* to account for such investments. Under the cost method, an enterprise records an investment at historical cost and treats any dividends that the investee distributes from net accumulated earnings after the acquisition date as income. The enterprise treats any dividends which exceed net accumulated earnings subsequent to the acquisition date as a return of investment that reduces the cost of the investment on the enterprise's books.

Because dividends serve as the event for recognizing income from an investment accounted for under the cost method, the enterprise's financial statements may not reflect substantial changes in the investee's affairs. The dividends that the investing enterprise includes in income during an accounting period may not relate to the investee's earnings, or losses, for that period. To illustrate, an investee may pay no dividends for several accounting periods and then pay dividends substantially in excess of earnings in that particular period. As a result, the cost method prevents the investing enterprise from adequately reflecting the earnings related to investments in common stock either cumulatively or in the appropriate periods.

GAAP modifies the cost method if the investee incurs a series of operating losses or other factors indicate that the investment has suffered a decrease in value which does not qualify as a mere temporary condition. In that event, the *lower of cost or market method* requires the enterprise to recognize a loss. Conservatism, and for that matter realism, dictates this result even though no exchange transaction has occurred. FASB ASC Subtopics 323-10 (equity method), 325-20 (cost method) (codifications of The Equity Method of Accounting for Investments in Common Stock, Accounting Principles Board Opinion No. 18, ¶ ¶ 5–7 (Am. Inst. of Certified Pub. Accountants 1971)).

For marketable equity securities and all debt securities which qualify as so-called passive investments, however, an enterprise must classify the investment into one of three categories at acquisition: (1) held-to-maturity securities, (2) trading securities, or (3) available-for-sale securities. *See* FASB ASC Topic 320, *Investments—Debt and Equity Securities* (a codification of Accounting for Certain Investments in Debt and Equity Securities, Statement of Fin. Accounting Standards No. 115 (Fin. Accounting Standards Bd. 1993)). As we will see below, the accounting treatment for each category differs. Enterprises must report trading securities and available-for-sale securities at fair value. This treatment represents a significant departure from the historical cost principle. In addition, enterprises will report the related unrealized gains and losses on either the income statement or in the owners' equity section of the balance sheet.

(a) Held-to-Maturity Debt Securities

Accountants define held-to-maturity securities as debt securities that the enterprise has the positive intent and ability to hold until maturity, that is, the date when the borrower must repay any unpaid principal and accrued interest. Until one year before maturity, an enterprise normally lists held-to-maturity securities as noncurrent assets on a classified balance sheet. Because equity securities do not mature, this category applies only to debt securities. Certain changes in circumstances can cause an enterprise to alter its intent to hold a particular security to maturity without affecting its intent to hold other debt securities to maturity in the future. By comparison, if an enterprise anticipates selling a debt security in response to fluctuations in market interest rates, needs for liquidity, or changes in alternative investment opportunities or yields or funding sources and terms, the enterprise may not classify a debt security as held-to-maturity.

Enterprises report held-to-maturity securities at *amortized cost*. Before explaining amortized cost, however, we should review some concepts from Chapter III. You may recall from the examples on pages 247 to 248, *supra*, that the market value of bonds moves in the opposite direction as interest rates. If interest rates increase so that the current market interest rate for similar investments exceeds a bond's stated interest rate, the bond's market value will decrease. In that regard, remember that as interest rates increased from ten percent to twelve percent, both compounded semiannually, the market value of a $10,000 face amount bond fell to $9,508.26. The difference between the $10,000 face amount and the $9,508.26 market value represents *market discount*. When the market interest rate rises above the stated interest rate, a reasonable investor will only purchase the bond at a discount from the bond's face amount. In contrast, if interest rates drop, the bond's value will increase. When interest rates fell from ten percent to eight percent, both compounded semiannually, the market value of a $10,000 face amount bond, paying ten percent annual interest semiannually, rose to $10,524.17. In that situation, the bond will trade at a premium because a reasonable investor will be willing to pay more than the $10,000 face amount to obtain the right to a higher-than-market interest rate and a reasonable owner would only sell if a potential buyer offered such a premium. The difference between the $10,524.17 market value and the face amount represents *market premium*. If the interest rate stated in a debt security and the market rate for similar investments differ, the security will trade at either a discount or a premium. The purchaser will amortize any discount or premium to interest income over the debt security's remaining term to maturity. As a general rule, GAAP requires the purchaser to use the effective interest method for this purpose, unless another method will not produce materially different results. Amortized cost, therefore, reflects the original cost to acquire a debt security, adjusted to reflect the amortization of any discount or premium.

To illustrate amortized cost, assume that ABC Corporation ("ABC") purchases a $10,000 face amount bond bearing ten percent annual interest, payable semiannually, exactly three years before maturity and when the market interest rate stands at twelve percent interest, again compounded semiannually. From our previous discussion, assume that ABC pays $9,508.26 for the bond. At the time of the purchase, ABC might record the following journal entry:

| Investments in Bonds | $9,508.26 | |
| Cash | | $9,508.26 |

Every six months until maturity, ABC would recognize six percent of the bond's cost, adjusted for any earlier amortization of the market discount, as interest income. At the end of the first six months, the borrower would pay $500 interest on the bond ($10,000 face amount times the five percent interest for that six month period provided in the contract). Under the effective interest method, therefore, ABC would have earned $570.50 in interest income ($9,508.26 purchase price times six percent market interest rate). For that first interest payment, ABC might record the following journal entry:

Cash	$500.00	
Investments in Bonds	70.50	
Interest Income		$570.50

The entry would increase the bond's amortized cost or carrying value to $9,578.76 ($9,508.26 plus $70.50 amortized discount).

In the second six-month period and following periods, ABC would continue to recognize six percent of the bond's amortized cost amount as interest income for the next period. For the second six-month period, ABC would recognize $574.73 as interest income ($9,578.76 amortized cost times six percent interest). For that second interest payment, ABC might record the following journal entry:

Cash	$500.00	
Investments in Bonds	74.73	
Interest Income		$574.73

The entry would increase the amortized cost or carrying value of the bonds to $9,653.49 ($9,578.76 plus $74.73 amortized discount). *See* FASB ASC Subtopic 835-30, *Interest—Imputation of Interest* (a codification of INTEREST ON RECEIVABLES AND PAYABLES, Accounting Principles Board Opinion No. 21 (Am. Inst. of Certified Pub. Accountants 1971)).

The following table summarizes the amortization of the market discount during the three years or six semiannual periods until maturity:

Period	Interest Income	Cash Received	Amortization of Discount	Amortized Cost
0				$9,508.26
1	$570.50	$500.00	$70.50	9,578.76
2	574.73	500.00	74.73	9,653.49
3	579.21	500.00	79.21	9,732.70
4	583.96	500.00	83.96	9,816.66
5	589.00	500.00	89.00	9,905.66
6	594.34	500.00	94.34	10,000.00

Similarly, we can illustrate the amortization of market premium by assuming that DEF Company ("DEF") purchases a $10,000 face amount bond bearing ten percent annual interest, payable semiannually, exactly three years before maturity and when the market interest rate stands at eight percent interest, again compounded semiannually. From our previous example, assume that DEF pays $10,524.17 for the bond. Every six months until maturity, DEF would recognize four percent of the bond's carrying amount as interest income. At the end of the first six months, the borrower would pay $500 interest on the bond ($10,000 face amount times the five percent contract interest rate for that six month period). Under the effective interest method, DEF would have only earned $420.97 in interest income ($10,524.17 purchase price times four percent market interest rate for this semiannual period). Accordingly, DEF might record the following journal entry for that first interest payment:

Cash	$500.00	
Interest Income		$420.97
Investments in Bonds		79.03

The entry would treat $79.03 as a return of the original investment and reduce the amortized cost or carrying value of the bonds to $10,445.14 ($10,524.17 minus $79.03 amortized premium).

In the second six-month period and following periods, DEF would continue to recognize four percent of the bond's amortized cost amount as interest income for the next period. For the second six-month period, DEF would recognize $417.81 as interest income ($10,445.14 amortized cost times four percent interest). For that second interest payment, DEF might record the following journal entry:

Cash	$500.00	
Interest Income		$417.81
Investments in Bonds		82.19

The entry would decrease the amortized cost or carrying value of the bonds to $10,362.95 ($10,445.14 minus $82.19 amortized premium).

The following table summarizes the amortization of the market premium during the three years or six semiannual periods until maturity:

Period	Interest Income	Cash Received	Amortization of Premium	Amortized Cost
0				$10,524.17
1	$420.97	$500.00	$79.03	10,445.14
2	417.81	500.00	82.19	10,362.95
3	414.52	500.00	85.48	10,277.47
4	411.10	500.00	88.90	10,188.57
5	407.54	500.00	92.46	10,096.11
6	403.84	500.00	96.16	9,999.95

Rounding creates the five cent difference between the bond's amortized cost at the end of the sixth semiannual period and the bond's face amount, which we can ignore as insignificant.

(b) Trading Securities

If a business purchases and holds either debt or marketable equity securities principally intending to sell them in the near term, accountants treat the securities as trading securities. In other words, an enterprise intends to hold trading securities only for a short period of time. Trading typically involves frequent buying and selling, intending to generate profits on short-term differences in price.

Businesses report trading securities at fair value and include the related unrealized holding gains and losses in income. If an enterprise presents a classified balance sheet, trading securities will appear as current assets. To illustrate, assume that a brokerage firm that uses the calendar year for financial accounting purposes and prepares quarterly financial statements, including a classified balance sheet, purchases 10,000 common shares of Starbucks Corporation for $37.50 per share on September 20, 201X, because the trading department thinks the company can derive a quick profit from a short-term price swing. Further assume that Starbuck's common shares increase in value to $39.50 per share on September 30, 201X. On the company's balance sheet for September 30, 201X, the company will report the 10,000 shares at $39.50 per share for a $395,000 total as a current asset. In addition, the income statement will reflect $20,000 in income from the unrealized holding gain on the 10,000 shares. In contrast, if the market price declines to $35 per share on September 30, 201X, the company will show $350,000 as an investment in current assets on the balance sheet and the income statement will show a $25,000 unrealized loss on the 10,000 shares.

(c) Available-for-Sale Securities

Accountants treat all remaining debt and marketable equity securities as available-for-sale securities. Enterprises record this catch-all category at fair value, but include the related unrealized holding gains and losses as a net amount in a separate component of the equity section of the balance sheet until realized, rather than in income. Depending upon whether an enterprise intends to sell an available-for-sale security within a certain period, normally one year, the enterprise will treat available-for sale securities as either current or noncurrent assets. You may recall from Chapter I on page 15, *supra*, that an enterprise normally lists investments that the enterprise plans to sell within one year as current assets on a classified balance sheet.

Building upon the above example involving the 10,000 common shares of Starbucks, assume instead that the company plans to hold those shares indefinitely because the board of directors believes that Starbucks offers an excellent investment opportunity. If Starbucks common shares again increase in value to $39.50 per share on September 30, 201X, the company's balance sheet for that date will again show the 10,000 shares at $39.50 per share for a $395,000 total. The income statement, however, will not reflect a $20,000 unrealized gain. Instead, the $20,000 will appear as a separate item in shareholders' equity on the balance sheet. If the market price declines to $35 per share on September 30, 201X, and the company believes that the drop reflects only a temporary decline, the company will show $350,000 as an investment on the balance sheet and shareholders' equity will now reflect a $25,000 unrealized loss as a separate item in shareholders' equity.

As discussed earlier in Chapter IV, *supra* at 291 to 294, FASB ASC Topic 220, *Comprehensive Income*, which codified SFAS No. 130, *Reporting Comprehensive Income*, requires enterprises to report an amount for "comprehensive income" in the financial statements. To illustrate the concept of comprehensive income further, assume that, as its only investment, Vogt Corporation ("Vogt"), a calender year corporation, purchases 10,000 shares of Keller, Inc. ("Keller"), a publicly traded corporation with total market value exceeding $1 billion, on March 1, 20X1 for $100,000 (i.e., $10 per share). Further assume that by the end of 20X1, the market value of each share of Keller stock has increased to $13 per share. At the end of 20X2, the market price equals $18 per share. On February 1, 20X3, Vogt sells its Keller shares for $17 per share. How much income and comprehensive income does Vogt recognize from these events?

At the time of the original investment, Vogt would make the following journal entry:

Investments (debit)	$100,000	
Cash (credit)		$100,000

As available-for-sale securities, the Keller shares will appear on Vogt's balance sheet at the end of 20X1 and 20X2 at their fair values of $130,000 and $180,000, respectively. The increase in value would appear in a separate section of shareholders' equity. At the end of 20X1, Vogt would make the following journal entry to reflect the increase in fair value:

Investments (debit)	$30,000	
Unrealized Gain on Marketable Equity		
Securities (credit) (an equity account)		$30,000

After the $30,000 debit to the Investments account, that account would show a $130,000 debit balance. In addition to appearing in the equity section of the balance sheet, the $30,000 unrealized gain would appear in both "other comprehensive income" and comprehensive income. Although Vogt would not recognize any net income from the increase in fair value (because no exchange transaction has occurred), the company's financial statements would show $30,000 in "other comprehensive income" and comprehensive income of $30,000 ($-0- net income plus $30,000 in "other comprehensive income").

At the end of 20X2, Vogt would make the following journal entry to reflect the increase in the fair value of the Keller shares to $180,000 during the year:

Investments (debit)	$50,000	
Unrealized Gain on Marketable Equity		
Securities (credit) (an equity account)		$50,000

After the $50,000 debit to the Investments account, that account would show a $180,000 debit balance. After the $50,000 credit, $80,000 would appear as unrealized gain in the equity section of the balance sheet. In addition, the $50,000 increase in the unrealized gain during 20X2 would appear in both "other comprehensive income" and comprehensive income. Although Vogt would not recognize any net income from the increase in fair value (again because no exchange transaction has occurred), the company's financial statements would show $50,000 in "other comprehensive income" and comprehensive income of $50,000 ($-0- net income plus $50,000 in "other comprehensive income").

When Vogt sells the Keller shares on February 1, 20X3, Vogt would record the following journal entry:

Cash (debit)	$170,000	
Unrealized Gain on Marketable Equity		
Securities (debt)	80,000	
Investments (credit)		$180,000
Gain on Sale of Investments (credit)		70,000

Because Vogt has sold its only investment, which appeared at $180,000 in the Investment account after the $80,000 increases in value during 20X1 and 20X2, Vogt can no longer show the unrealized gain as a separate item in shareholder's equity and must reverse the $80,000 that previously appeared as unrealized gain. Although Vogt can recognize $70,000 in gain, representing the difference between the $170,000 sales proceeds and the $100,000 original investment, the company must also report an $80,000 loss as a *reclassification adjustment* in "other comprehensive income." ASC Topic 220 refers to such adjustments for items that an enterprise has previously included in "other comprehensive income" as "reclassification adjustments." FASB ASC ¶ 220-10-45-15 (a codification of REPORTING COMPREHENSIVE INCOME, Statement of Fin. Accounting Standards No. 130 ¶ 18 (Fin. Accounting Standards Bd. 1997)). Although not related to available-for-sale securities, please observe that Note 11 to the financial statements in Starbucks' 2012 Annual Report, which you can find in Appendix A on page 772, *infra*, shows a $10.5 million gain from a reclassification adjustment for net losses realized in net income for cash flow hedges, net of tax, during the fiscal year ending September 30, 2012. Because Starbucks recognized losses in net income, the reclassification adjustment appears as a gain.

Combining Vogt's $70,000 in net income from the sale of investments and the $80,000 loss arising from the reclassification adjustment, the company would report a net $10,000 loss in comprehensive income for 20X3. We could summarize the effects on comprehensive income as follows:

	Net Income	Other Comprehensive Income	Comprehensive Income
20X1	$-0-	$30,000	$30,000
20X2	$-0-	$50,000	$50,000
20X3	$70,000	($80,000)	($10,000)
Totals	$70,000	$ –0–	$70,000

Note that all $70,000 in gain appears in net income during 20X3, while that same collective amount appears in comprehensive income over the same period as $30,000 income in 20X1, $50,000 income in 20X2, and net $10,000 loss—$70,000 realized gain minus the $80,000 reclassification adjustment—in 20X3. The requirement to report comprehensive income precludes an enterprise from recognizing all the income related to the increase in the value of an investment in the year of sale. Under the previous accounting rules, enterprises could decide when to recognize gains from investments. In that regard, please recall the *In re Reliance Group Holdings* administrative proceedings briefly discussed on page 391, *supra*.

Finally, ASC Topic 220 also requires an enterprise to transfer "other comprehensive income" for each accounting period to an equity account such as *accumulated other comprehensive income* and to display that account separate from retained earnings and additional paid-in capital on the balance sheet. Such account shows cumulative other comprehensive income for the period and previous periods. FASB ASC ¶ 220-10-45-14 (a codification of REPORTING COMPREHENSIVE INCOME, Statement of Fin. Accounting Standards No. ¶ 26 (Fin. Accounting Standards Bd. 1997)). Accordingly, Starbucks' consolidated balance sheets and consolidated statements of shareholders' equity in Appendix A on pages 747 and 749, *infra*, respectively, both show accumulated other comprehensive income of $22.7 million and $46.3 million on September 30, 2012 and October 2, 2011, respectively.

(d) Comparison of the Accounting Treatments for the Different Categories of Debt and Marketable Equity Securities Held as Passive Investments

The following chart summarizes the different categories of debt and marketable equity securities and their accounting treatments:

FINANCIAL STATEMENT EFFECTS OF DIFFERENT CLASSIFICATIONS FOR CERTAIN DEBT AND MARKETABLE EQUITY SECURITIES

Classification of Investment	Type of Security	Balance Sheet Valuation of the Investment	Other Balance Sheet and Income Statement Effects
Held-to-Maturity	Debt	Amortized Cost	None
Trading Securities	Debt or Equity	Fair Value	Unrealized Holding Gains and Losses Included in Income Statement
Available-for-Sale	Debt or Equity	Fair Value	Unrealized Holding Gains and Losses Reported Net in Equity Section

An investing enterprise includes dividend and interest income, including any amortization of market discount or premium existing at acquisition, from all three categories of passive investments on the income statement. The income statement also reports any realized gains or losses from held-to-maturity or available-for-sale securities. For individual securities which an enterprise has classified as either held-to-maturity or available-for-sale, the enterprise must determine whether any security has suffered an "other than temporary" decline in fair value below amortized cost or carrying value. If such a decline has occurred, the enterprise must write down the security to fair value and treat the write down as a realized loss. The fair value becomes the new amortized cost for held-to-maturity securities and the enterprise may not use any subsequent recoveries to change the new amortized cost. For available-for-sale securities, the enterprise must include any subsequent increases and temporary decreases in other comprehensive income pursuant to the usual rules for available-for-sale securities.

An investing enterprise must treat any transfers between categories as a recognition event at fair value according to the previously described rules. Thus, if an enterprise transfers a debt security from the held-to-maturity category to the available-for-sale category, the enterprise must recognize the unrealized holding gain or loss on the transfer date in other comprehensive income. Conversely, if an enterprise transfers a debt security from available-for-sale into the held-to-maturity category, the enterprise must continue to report the unrealized holding gain or loss on the transfer date in a separate component of shareholders' equity, such as accumulated other comprehensive income, but must amortize that amount over the security's life to maturity similar to the amortization of any market discount or premium. Given the definitions for held-to-maturity and trading securities, transfers from held-to-maturity and into or from trading securities should only rarely occur. But, if an enterprise transfers a debt security from held-to-maturity to the trading category, the enterprise must immediately recognize the unrealized holding gain or loss in income. FASB ASC ¶¶ 320-10-35-4, -10 to -

12, -18 to -34, 320-10-45-9 (codifications of ACCOUNTING FOR CERTAIN INVESTMENTS IN DEBT AND EQUITY SECURITIES, Statement of Fin. Accounting Standards No. 115, ¶ ¶ 14–16 (Fin. Accounting Standards Bd. 1993)).

(ii) Active Investments

When an enterprise owns, directly or indirectly, at least twenty percent of an investee's voting stock, GAAP presumes that the enterprise can exercise significant influence over the investee and generally treats such investments as "active" investments. If an enterprise owns more than fifty percent of the voting shares, the enterprise generally must prepare consolidated financial statements. When an enterprise owns at least twenty percent, but not more than fifty percent, GAAP generally requires the enterprise to use the equity method to account for the investment. An enterprise that prepares consolidated financial statements recognizes gains or losses attributable to a subsidiary's operations even though the enterprise has not sold its investment in the subsidiary. Similarly, the equity method of accounting for investments in other enterprises adopts a nearly identical approach.

(a) Consolidated Financial Statements

You may recall that pages 129 to 135, *supra*, in Chapter I introduced consolidated financial statements. At that time, we saw that such statements combine financial data for a parent company and its majority-owned subsidiaries as if the parent and any subsidiaries represent a single accounting entity. GAAP requires an enterprise's financial statements to consolidate all majority-owned subsidiaries unless the enterprise does not hold actual control or holds only temporary control. For example, contract, court order or other circumstances may deprive a majority shareholder of actual control. In addition, bankruptcy or legal reorganization may give the majority shareholder only temporary control. FASB ASC ¶¶ 810-10-15-8, -10 (codifications of CONSOLIDATION OF ALL MAJORITY–OWNED SUBSIDIARIES, Statement of Fin. Accounting Standards No. 94, ¶ ¶ 10, 13 (Fin. Accounting Standards Bd. 1987)).

In Chapter I, we focused solely on how accountants aggregate nonreciprocal assets and liabilities. In this chapter, we consider how the parent company should reflect a subsidiary's earnings subsequent to its acquisition in the consolidated accounts. Because the make-up of the subsidiary's balance sheet does not affect the process, for the sake of simplicity consider the following balance sheets for X and Y:

X Corp.
Balance Sheet, Immediately After Acquisition

Assets		Liabilities & Equity	
Cash	$100,000	Liabilities	$250,000
Investment	200,000	Common Stock	300,000
Plant	400,000	Retained Earnings	150,000
	$700,000		$700,000

Y Corp.
Balance Sheet, Immediately After Acquisition

Assets		Liabilities & Equity	
Cash	$ 50,000	Common Stock	$200,000
Plant	150,000		$200,000
	$200,000		

Suppose that during the first year after the acquisition, Y earned $50,000 while X remained completely inactive. Y's balance sheet might then look like this:

Y Corp.
Balance Sheet, One Year After Acquisition

Assets		Liabilities & Equity	
Cash	$100,000	Common Stock	$200,000
Plant	150,000	Retained Earnings	50,000
	$250,000		$250,000

X's balance sheet would have remained:

X Corp.
Balance Sheet, One Year After Acquisition

Assets		Liabilities & Equity	
Cash	$100,000	Liabilities	$250,000
Investment	200,000	Common Stock	300,000
Plant	400,000	Retained Earnings	150,000
	$700,000		$700,000

Since Y's net assets now exceed X's cost of the investment in Y, the consolidation technique of replacing the asset Investment on X's balance sheet with Y's net assets appears to make the columns of the consolidated balance sheet unequal:

X Corp.
Consolidated Balance Sheet, One Year After Acquisition

Assets		Liabilities & Equity	
Cash	$200,000	Liabilities	$250,000
		Common Stock	300,000
Plant	550,000	Retained Earnings	150,000
	$750,000		$700,000

Why does the balance sheet not balance? To balance, we must increase the consolidated retained earnings in an amount equal to the $50,000 increase in the subsidiary's retained earnings after acquisition. After all, we can attribute this increase to the consolidated enterprise. The increase, therefore, properly belongs in the consolidated retained earnings. The consolidated balance sheet should appear as follows:

X Corp.
Consolidated Balance Sheet, One Year After Acquisition

Assets		Liabilities & Equity	
Cash	$200,000	Liabilities	$250,000
		Common Stock	300,000
Plant	550,000	Retained Earnings	200,000
	$750,000		$750,000

Notice that if Y subsequently paid a dividend to X, the payment would not affect the consolidated balance sheet. The increase in X's net assets and retained earnings arising from the dividend would offset the corresponding decrease in Y's net assets and retained earnings.

Once again, the foregoing consolidation technique applies whenever a parent corporation owns at least a majority voting interest in a subsidiary, unless the parent does not hold actual control or maintains only temporary control. If the parent corporation owns less than complete control, you may recall from Chapter I on page 134, *supra*, that *noncontrolling interests* represent the ownership stake that does not belong to the parent or another subsidiary. In that circumstance, the parent must deduct the minority interest's share of the subsidiary's net income for a particular accounting period in determining consolidated net income. In calculating consolidated net income, the parent corporation must also remove the effects of any intercompany transactions. For example, if the parent sold goods to the subsidiary or vice versa, the consolidated financial statements must eliminate those transactions so that the consolidated income statement will only reflect sales to enterprises outside the consolidated group.

(b) Equity Method

Suppose, however, that X only owns fifty percent of Y's outstanding voting shares and, therefore, does not hold a controlling financial interest in Y. You will recall that under the cost method, X would simply treat the investment in Y as an asset on X's balance sheet. Under this approach, X's books would reflect Y's subsequent earnings only when and to the extent that Y actually paid dividends to X, at which time X would include the dividend in its income and ultimately in its retained earnings. An intermediate position, which accountants refer to as the *equity method* and which resembles a "quasi-consolidation," exists between the cost method and full consolidation.

Under the equity method, an enterprise initially records an investment in an investee's stock at cost, and adjusts the investment's carrying amount to recognize the investing enterprise's share of the investee's earnings or losses after the acquisition date. The investing enterprise includes this pro rata share in net income. This process, however, requires adjustments similar to those which an enterprise would make in preparing consolidated statements, such as eliminating intercompany gains and losses. As a result, the enterprise recognizes its share of the investee's earnings or losses in the periods for which the investee reports them on its financial statements. Under the cost method, in contrast, the investing enterprise only reports income in the period in which the investee declares a dividend.

The investing enterprise also adjusts the investment in the investee to reflect its share of changes in the investee's capital. For example, any dividends that the investee pays reduce the investment's carrying amount. Once again, a series of operating losses or other factors may indicate that the investment has suffered a non-temporary decline in value. The investing enterprise must recognize this decline even though the decrease exceeds the loss that the enterprise would otherwise recognize under the equity method. Operating losses or a decline in an investment's market price below the carrying amount, however, does not necessarily indicate a non-temporary loss in value. The investing enterprise's management must evaluate all factors.

The Codification requires an enterprise to use the equity method to account for investments in common stock if an investment in voting stock enables the investing enterprise to exercise significant influence over the investee's operating or financial decisions. FASB ASC Topic 323, *Investments—Equity Method and Joint Ventures*, which codified APB No. 18, *The Equity Method of Accounting for Investments in Common Stock*, presumes that an investment of twenty percent or more of an investee's voting stock carries the ability to exercise significant influence, while an investment of less than twenty percent does not. In the appropriate circumstances, however, an investing enterprise can rebut those presumptions. Representation on the board of directors, participation in policy making processes, material intercompany transactions, interchange of managerial personnel or technological dependency can all indicate an ability to exercise significant influence.

Under the equity method, X's balance sheet would show merely its investment in Y, rather than Y's net assets which would appear in consolidated financial statements. X's financial statements, however, will reflect Y's subsequent earnings or losses whether or not Y declares any dividends, just as would occur under consolidation.

To illustrate, assume again that Y had earned $50,000 during the first year after X acquired fifty percent of its voting stock for $200,000, while X was completely inactive. Y's balance sheet at the end of that year looked like this:

Y Corp.
Balance Sheet, One Year After Acquisition

Assets		Liabilities & Equity	
Cash	$100,000	Common Stock	$200,000
Plant	150,000	Retained Earnings	50,000
	$250,000		$250,000

Because a fifty percent ownership interest does not qualify for consolidation, under the cost method X would have to wait for Y to declare a dividend before reflecting any of Y's post-acquisition earnings on X's financial statements. Until then, X's balance sheet would remain the same as it appeared immediately after X purchased Y's stock:

X Corp.
Balance Sheet, One Year After Acquisition

Assets		Liabilities & Equity	
Cash	$100,000	Liabilities	$250,000
Investment	200,000	Common Stock	300,000
Plant	400,000	Retained Earnings	150,000
	$700,000		$700,000

Under the equity method, in contrast, X would write up the investment in Y to reflect its share in Y's earnings subsequent to acquisition. An increase in X's retained earnings would balance the increase in the investment account. As a result, X's balance sheet would appear as follows:

X Corp.
Balance Sheet, One Year After Acquisition

Assets		Liabilities & Equity	
Cash	$100,000	Liabilities	$250,000
Investment	225,000	Common Stock	300,000
Plant	400,000	Retained Earnings	175,000
	$725,000		$725,000

Notice that the equity method produces a balance sheet which resembles the consolidated balance sheet with two important exceptions. First, because X only acquired fifty percent of Y's voting stock, X can only write up its investment in Y to reflect one-half of Y's earnings. Second, X does not substitute Y's net assets for the asset "Investment" on X's balance sheet. To summarize, enterprises use the equity method to account for significant, but unconsolidated, stock investments, connoting the fact that an enterprise writes up the investment on the books to conform with the increases in the investee's equity arising from its earnings.

(c) Consolidation of Variable Interest Entities

In response to the Enron scandal, GAAP now requires enterprises to consolidate certain entities known as variable interest entities ("VIEs"), a term which encompasses the special purpose entities ("SPEs") at root in Enron's "financial engineering." These new rules apply even if the enterprise does not own a majority of the voting shares. Recall from our discussion on pages 426 to 428, *supra*, that an enterprise must generally consolidate an entity if it owns a controlling financial interest, usually defined as a majority voting interest in the entity. Enron, however, illustrated that an enterprise may retain effective control or significant influence over an entity through arrangements other than voting stock, including contractual agreements, the entity's organizational documents, and other governing documents. Significantly, Enron designed its SPEs to avoid including the assets and debt on its consolidated balance sheet as the consolidation method would generally dictate. In addition, Enron created some SPEs to inflate revenues by recognizing sales on transactions with the SPEs, a treatment that both the consolidation and equity methods would otherwise disallow. Accordingly, Enron either evaded or disregarded fragmented and incomplete accounting literature for consolidating SPEs as well as the SEC's general rule that required an independent investor with ownership of at least three percent of the SPE's assets and control over the SPE for an enterprise to avoid consolidation. *See* FASB ASC ¶¶ 958-810-25-8 to -10 (codifications of IMPACT OF NONSUBSTANTIVE LESSORS, RESIDUAL VALUE, GUARANTEES, AND OTHER PROVISIONS IN LEASING TRANSACTIONS, Emerging Issues Task Force Issue No. 90-15 (Fin. Accounting Standards Bd. 1990)); *see also* William W. Bratton, *Enron and the Dark Side of Shareholder Value*, 76 TUL. L. REV. 1275 (2002) (discussing in greater detail how Enron abused its extraordinarily complex web of SPEs to avoid consolidating the entities under previous accounting rules).

Notably, while accountants and lawyers alike have integrated the term SPE into their common business vernacular, even has FASB recognized that no clear or generally accepted definition exists. *See, e.g.*, CONSOLIDATION OF VARIABLE INTEREST ENTITIES (AN INTERPRETATION OF ARB NO. 51), FASB Interpretation No. 46 (rev. 2003), ¶ E1 (Fin. Accounting Standards Bd. 2003). As a general starting point, a report on Enron's collapse defines an SPE as "an entity created for a limited purpose, with a limited life and limited activities, and designed to benefit a single company." WILLIAM C. POWERS, JR. ET AL., REPORT OF INVESTIGATION BY THE SPECIAL INVESTIGATIVE COMMITTEE OF THE BOARD OF DIRECTORS OF ENRON CORP. app. A, at 95 (2002), *available at* http://news.findlaw.com/hdocs/docs/enron/sicreport/sicreport020102.pdf. Although SPEs may take any legal form, including a corporation, partnership, or trust, the organizational documents or contractual arrangements often limit or predetermine activities and powers.

Both law students and lawyers may find this general description unhelpful, but enterprises use these SPEs for legitimate financing, investing, or leasing functions to increase efficiency in transacting business and to limit exposure to risk. For example, enterprises often legitimately use SPEs for securitization, the process by which a business assembles a pool of financial assets, such as mortgage loan or credit card receivables, and transfers them to an SPE, potentially recognizing the transfer as a sale. While enterprises primarily benefit from securitization by isolating the risk to the financial assets within the pool, which often allows a higher credit rating and more favorable financing terms, benefits generally flow to consumers as well. *See, e.g.*, Christine Richard, *Investors Come to the Defense of Securitization, Special Purpose Entities Tainted by Enron's Fall,* WALL ST. J., Mar. 19, 2002, at C15 (noting that securitization contributed to the increased availability of credit cards to Americans).

Because commercial lawyers often draft the organizational documents for SPEs and assist with subsequent transactions, lawyers should generally understand the form, purpose, and the accounting treatment of VIEs, including legitimate SPEs. Estimates indicated that trillions of dollars of assets resided in such off-balance sheet entities and the new accounting rule governing VIEs could add as much as $379 billion of assets and $377 billion of liabilities to the balance sheets of companies in the Standard & Poor's 500-stock index. Cassell Bryan-Low, *Accounting Board Clarifies Rule*, WALL ST. J., Nov. 3, 2003, at A11.

Although SPEs can serve legitimate business purposes, after Enron popularized SPEs under such infamous names as Braveheart, Chewco, and JEDI, many lawyers and law students nonetheless associate SPEs with complex transactions designed to distort an enterprise's financial condition and operating results. Enron-era SPEs often existed as highly leveraged, shell entities that enterprises exploited to inflate revenues and to move liabilities and poorly performing assets off the balance sheet. For example, Enron conducted a joint venture investment partnership known as JEDI that involved debt totaling $1.6 billion by 1999. John R. Emshwiller, *Enron Transaction Raises New Questions*, WALL ST. J., Nov. 5, 2001, at A3. As mentioned in the preface and earlier in this chapter, Enron recorded a $16 million gain by selling an interest in a Polish company to an SPE known as LJM2 for $30 million after failing to find an unrelated buyer, and, remarkably, later bought the interest back from LJM2 for $31.9 million. In another deal with the SPE code-named Braveheart, Enron reported a $111 million gain by transferring an agreement with Blockbuster Video for movies on demand after Enron determined that it would never realize any real profits from the agreement.

In response to the gaps in the prior consolidation rules exposed by the Enron scandal, in 2003 FASB adopted, and then quickly revised, rules determining when enterprises should consolidate certain entities. *See*

Consolidation of Variable Interest Entities (An Interpretation of ARB No. 51), FASB Interpretation No. 46 (rev. 2003) (Fin. Accounting Standards Bd.) ("FIN 46(R)"), now codified at FASB ASC Topic 810, *Consolidation*. FASB essentially adopted a substance over form approach by focusing on the enterprise's actual "variable interests" in the entity, which include contractual, ownership, or other pecuniary interests. FASB ASC § 810-10-20 (a codification of Consolidation of Variable Interest Entities (An Interpretation of ARB No. 51), FASB Interpretation No. 46 (rev. 2003) ¶ 2(c) (Fin. Accounting Standards Bd.)). As mentioned earlier, accountants and lawyers both commonly referred to VIEs simply as SPEs, but FIN 46(R) substituted, and now FASB ASC Topic 810 uses, the former term to emphasize that the guidelines apply to a broader spectrum of entities. Very simply stated, ASC Topic 810 specifies two general inquiries to determine whether an investing enterprise must consolidate an entity that may otherwise escape consolidation under the voting stock analysis.

First, FASB ASC Topic 810 broadly treats any entity, including SPEs, that meet *any of the following conditions* as a VIE and, therefore, subject to consolidation:

(1) The entity's total equity investment at risk does not permit the entity to finance its activities without additional financial support.

(2) The equity investors as a group *lack* any one of the following characteristics of a controlling financial interest:

(a) the ability through voting rights to make decisions about an entity's activities; or

(b) the obligation to absorb the entity's expected loss; or

(c) the right to receive the entity's expected returns.

(3) Some equity investors have voting rights disproportionate to their obligation to absorb the entity's expected losses, their right to receive the entity's expected returns, or both, and substantially all of the entity's activities either involve or are conducted on behalf of the equity investor that has disproportionately few voting rights.

Second, the Codification generally considers an investing enterprise the primary beneficiary of a VIE, and, therefore, the enterprise must consolidate the VIE, if the investor or related parties own interests in the VIE that will absorb a majority of the VIE's expected losses, receive a majority of the VIE's expected returns, or both.

In response to the substantial losses that banks, investors, and other financial institutions incurred during the credit crisis from off-balance-sheet affiliates, particularly in the subprime residential mortgage industry, FASB completed two projects in 2009. In addition to the project described above to revise SFAS No. 140, now codified in FASB ASC Topic 860, *Transfers and Servicing*, FASB completed a project to amend the consolidation rules in ASC Topic 810. Until ASU No. 2009-17 amended the Codification, SFAS No. 167,

Amendments to FASB Interpretation No. 46(R), contained the amendments. The new rules eliminate the exception that allowed QSPEs to avoid consolidation; replace the quantitative-based "risk and rewards model" discussed in Chapter I on page 129, *supra*, for determining which enterprise, if any, must consolidate a variable interest entity ("VIE") with a qualitative test; and require additional disclosures about an enterprise's involvement in VIEs. FASB believes these changes will improve transparency by providing more relevant and timely information about an enterprise's involvement with other controlled entities that may contain significant risk.

Transactional lawyers in particular should understand that the new criteria in FASB ASC Topic 810 now requires enterprises to consolidate entities that previously qualified for off-balance sheet treatment as QSPEs. The new rules may also require an enterprise to consolidate previously unconsolidated VIEs. In lieu of the "risks and rewards model," Topic 810 now contains a primarily qualitative approach for identifying which enterprise holds the power to direct a VIE's activities that most significantly affect the entity's economic performance and (1) the obligation to absorb the entity's losses or (2) the right to receive benefits from the entity. In addition, enterprises holding interests in VIEs must periodically assess whether the enterprise has become the VIE's primary beneficiary, such as to require consolidation. Finally, the new rules require additional disclosures about an enterprise's involvement in VIEs, whether as a primary beneficiary or otherwise, which will enhance the information provided to users of financial statements. *See* FASB ASC ¶¶ 810-10-25-37 to-38G, 810-10-35-4, 810-10-50 (a codification of SFAS No. 167).

b) FAIR VALUE OPTION FOR OTHER ASSETS AND LIABILITIES

FASB ASC Topic 825, *Financial Instruments*, which codified SFAS No. 159, *The Fair Value Option for Financial Assets and Financial Liabilities*, grants enterprises the option to expand fair value reporting beyond investments in securities. The rules permit the reporting of many financial assets and financial liabilities at fair value with unrealized gains and losses included in income, an exception to the exchange transaction principle. Simply stated, financial assets involve contractual rights to receive cash; financial liabilities involve contractual obligations to pay cash. FASB ASC § 825-10-20 (a codification of SFAS No. 159, ¶ 6). For instance, financial assets include accounts receivable, but not fixed assets like buildings; financial liabilities include bonds payable, but not loss contingencies for pending or threatened litigation. Companies choosing the fair value option: (1) may apply the option selectively, instrument by instrument; (2) cannot revoke the option once elected; and (3) must apply the option to whole instruments, not parts of instruments. FASB ASC ¶ 825-10-25-2 (a codification of SFAS No. 159, ¶ 5). The FASB viewed these rules as the culmination of the first phase of a comprehensive fair value project. Subsequently, the Board abandoned the second phase of the project which originally planned to consider expansion of the fair value option to non-financial assets and liabilities. Fin. Accounting Standards Bd., Project Updates, Fair Value Option (Oct. 22, 2007).

Recall from Chapter III, pages 247 to 248, *supra*, that the value of bonds and other debt obligations moves inversely to changes in the interest rate. As interest rates drop, the value of bonds increases, and vice versa. Numerous financial institutions, especially banks, have elected to value their own debt at fair value. This election requires them to include any changes in the value of their own debt in net income. During the credit crisis, as the value of banks' debt fell, they recorded the decline as income, which they typically used to offset partially their loan losses and other operating expenses. The justification under the accounting rules: the lower market prices made it cheaper for the banks to repurchase their own debt. Then, as the economy stabilized and the value of their debt recovered, the banks recognized losses from the increase in value. When concerns rose about Bank of America's solvency during the 2011 third quarter, the value of the bank's debt fell by $6.2 billion, which enabled the bank to recognize that amount as income. When the value of that debt recovered in the 2012 first quarter, Bank of America recognized a $4.8 billion charge against earnings, labeled "debit value adjustment," or "DVA." Ironically, improving perceptions about an enterprise's creditworthiness hurt its earnings, while growing concerns about a debtor's ability to repay debt help the borrower's earnings. Complicating matters further, individual financial institutions and other enterprises typically use various terms to describe the gains and losses arising from these changes in value, and the banks disclose them in different ways. In 2014, the IASB revised IFRS 9, *Financial Instruments*, effective for annual periods beginning on or after January 1, 2018, to remove DVA gains and losses from net income, shifting them into other comprehensive income. As part of its financial instruments project on classification and measurement, FASB has tentatively decided to adopt a similar rule. *See* Michael Rapoport, *Banks Outside U.S. Get New Rules on Accounting for Bad Loans*, WALL St. J., July 25, 2014, at C3; Michael Rapoport, *Odd Debt Rule to Lose Bite*, Oct. 1, 2012, WALL St. J., at C1; David Reilly, *Wall Street Reaps Profit Volatility It Sowed*, WALL St. J., Oct. 31, 2011, at C12; Paul Vigna, *What Are These Banks Really Worth Anyway?*, WSJ.com, Apr. 19, 2012, http://blogs.wsj.com/marketbeat/2012/04/19/what-are-these-banks-really-worth-anyway/.

Controversy and lengthy debate has accompanied the movement toward fair value accounting. Two members of the FASB dissented from the "fair value option" rules, explaining that selective, instrument-by-instrument fair value reporting increases complexity, distorts evaluation of entities' economic exposures, and reduces the relevance of earnings. The dissenters favored a comprehensive fair value requirement instead of a fragmented, optional approach. Other critics decried the new standard for arbitrarily allowing managers to select the financial assets and liabilities measured at fair value, providing an opportunity for earnings management. The FASB, in defense, emphasized that the standard requires extensive disclosures on management's selection of the fair value option. The board highlighted that the fair value option reduces volatility in earnings that can result from the mismatch in reporting some assets and liabilities at historical cost and other related assets and liabilities at fair value. The new standard also achieves further convergence with International Accounting Standards, which already provided a fair value option for financial instruments.

(2) Losses

As mentioned in Chapter I and repeated earlier in this chapter, conservatism generally requires an enterprise to recognize expenses and losses immediately. As we have already seen in this chapter and will see again in later chapters, this general rule regarding losses applies to investments, accounts receivable, inventory and long-lived assets. In the previous section, we mentioned that GAAP requires an enterprise to treat any "other than temporary" decline in an investment's value as a loss.

As early as 1985, the SEC's staff expressed its belief that the phrase "other than temporary" does not mean permanent. Accounting for Noncurrent Marketable Equity Securities, Staff Accounting Bulletin No. 59 (Sept. 5, 1985), *reprinted in* 7 Fed. Sec. L. Rep. (CCH) ¶ ¶ 75,522, 75,721 at Topic 5–M (May 28, 2003). Today, FASB ASC Topic 320, *Investments—Debt and Equity Securities*, which codified FSP FAS 115-1 & 124-1, *The Meaning of Other-Than-Temporary Impairment and Its Application to Certain Investments*, addresses the steps that an enterprise must follow to determine whether circumstances have impaired an investment, whether the impairment qualifies as temporary, and the how to measure any other-than-temporary impairment loss. The Codification concludes that an investment becomes impaired when its fair value falls below its cost. In determining whether an investment has experienced a non-temporary decline, the enterprise must consider various factors originally set forth in SAB No. 59 and other pronouncements, including the length of time and the extent to which fair value has remained less than cost, the enterprise's intent and ability to hold the investment for such time as to allow for any anticipated recovery in fair value, and the investee's financial condition and near-term prospects. If an investment has suffered a non-temporary decline, the enterprise must write down the investment to its fair value and may not recognize any partial recoveries subsequent to that date through the income statement. In other words, the investment's then-fair value becomes its new cost basis from which the enterprise determines any future other-than-temporary impairments. In addition, the enterprise must sell the investment to recognize income from any subsequent increase in value after the write-down. FASB ASC ¶ ¶ 320-10-35-17 to -34 (codifications of FSP FAS 115-1 & FAS 124-1).

In 2008 the SEC's Office of the Chief Accountant and the FASB's staff jointly issued a press release regarding various issues involving fair value measurements and the credit crisis. Relevant to this discussion, the statement acknowledged that existing GAAP did not provide safe harbors or bright-line rules for exercising judgments about other-than-temporary impairments. The release reiterated, however, that generally speaking, "the greater the decline in value, the greater the period of time until anticipated recovery, and the longer the period of time that a decline has existed," the greater the evidence necessary to conclude that the decline remains temporary. SEC Office of the

Chief Accountant & FASB Staff, Clarifications on Fair Value Accounting (Sept. 30, 2009), http://www.sec.gov/news/press/2008/2008-234.htm.

Early in 2009 and on an expedited basis, FASB issued a staff position retaining the other-than-temporary assessment guidance and required disclosures now found in FASB ASC Subtopic 325-40, *Investments—Other, Beneficial Interests in Securitized Financial Assets*, which codified FSP EITF 99-20-1, *Amendments to the Impairment Guidance of EITF Issue No. 99-20*. In an other-than-temporary impairment analysis, an enterprise seeks to determine whether it will probably realize some portion of the unrealized loss on an impaired security. Such a loss realization could occur because either the enterprise will not collect all of the contractual or estimated cash flows, considering both the timing and amount, or the enterprise lacks the intent and ability to hold the security until its value recovers. The Codification cautions that an enterprise cannot automatically conclude that a security has not suffered an other-than-temporary impairment simply because the enterprise has received all of the scheduled payments to date. At the same time, the guidance observes that not every decline in fair value represents an other-than-temporary impairment. Although other-than-temporary assessments require analysis and judgment, the longer or more severe the decline in fair value, the more persuasive the evidence that management needs to overcome the premise that the enterprise will not collect all of the contractual or estimated cash flows. When FASB issued the staff position during the credit crisis, two board members dissented on the grounds that financial accounting standards should serve the needs of investors and the investor community did not request and did not support the guidance, especially on an expedited basis with limited due process. FASB ASC ¶¶ 325-40-35-3, -4, -10A, -10B (codifications to FSP EITF 99-20-1).

More recently, in 2009, FASB released guidance now contained in FASB ASC Topics 320, *Investments—Debt and Equity Securities*, and 325-40, *Investments—Other—Beneficial Interests in Securitized Financial Assets*, which codified FSP FAS 115-2 & 124-2, *Recognition and Presentation of Other-Than-Temporary Impairments*, that enables enterprises to avoid taking impairment charges against current earnings on certain investments in debt securities. The new rules, however, bring more consistency to the recognition of impairments and provide more information to investors about the credit risk and illiquidity components of impaired debt securities that the enterprise does not expect to sell until their maturity. Notably, the guidance could change when and where an enterprise records a write-down for held-to-maturity and available-for-sale debt securities. Under previous rules, an enterprise need not reduce net income for a temporary impairment as long as the enterprise could and planned to hold the security until its fair value recovered. Under the new rules, an enterprise need not record an impairment charge as long as the enterprise does not intend to sell the security and evidence indicates on a "more likely than not" basis that regulatory requirements, legal obligations, or other circumstances will not compel the enterprise to sell the security before recovering its remaining basis. Next, the guidance changed the presentation of an impairment charge, splitting it into two components. First, the amount of the impairment related to credit losses will appear on the income statement and will reduce net income. Second, enterprises will show the amount of the impairment related to other factors, such as illiquidity, in other comprehensive income in the equity section of the balance sheet. An enterprise, however, must present the total other-than-temporary impairment on the income statement, with an offset for the portion recognized in other comprehensive income. Last, the guidance now requires interim disclosures about impairments for both debt and equity, including the aging of securities with unrealized losses. Previously, enterprises only provided such disclosures annually. *See* FASB ASC §§ 320-10-35, 320-10-65-1, 325-40-35 (codifications of FSP FAS 115-2 & FAS 124-2).

In the materials that follow, we will discuss the requirements for recognizing losses, even absent an exchange transaction, in a variety of different contexts. Later in this chapter, for example, we consider the problem of uncollectible accounts. In Chapters VII, VIII, and IX, we will consider losses on contingencies, inventories, and long-lived assets, respectively.

(3) Personal Financial Statements

One other commonly encountered situation deviates from the historical cost principle and the exchange transaction requirement. Banks and other lenders frequently rely on personal financial statements for making credit decisions about individuals, often focusing on an individual's assets and liabilities. Similarly, attorneys consider current values in estate, gift and income tax planning for clients. Elected public officials and candidates for public offices often disclose personal financial information. In all these situations, current values, even if estimated, usually provide more relevant information than historical costs.

FASB ASC Topic 274, *Personal Financial Statements*, which codifies Statement of Position 82–1, *Accounting and Financial Reporting for Personal Financial Statements*, sets forth the accounting standards for personal financial statements. The Codification states that personal financial statements should present all assets and liabilities at their estimated current values or amounts. In addition, a personal balance sheet should treat any estimated income taxes on the differences between the assets' current values and costs as a liability in determining net worth.

PROBLEMS

Problem 6.1A. Explaining where you found the relevant information, answer the following questions about the financial statements and related notes included in Amazon's Form 10-K for the year ended December 31, 2012:

(1) For what amount and percentage of Amazon's cash equivalents and marketable securities did the company use significant unobservable inputs to determine amounts reported on its December 31, 2012 balance sheet?

(2) How, if at all, did those figures change from the amounts reported as of December 31, 2011?

(3) How, if at all, did the amount of any unrealized gains or losses related to such investments change during 2012?

(4) Did Amazon change its fair valuation methods during 2012? If so, how did any changes affect reported results?

(5) Did Amazon recognize any impairment losses on marketable securities during 2012?

(6) What was the fair value of Amazon's long-term debt, including any current portion, as of December 31, 2012?

Problem 6.1B. Explaining where you found the relevant information, answer the following questions about the financial statements and related notes included in Google's Form 10-K for the year ended December 31, 2012:

(1) For what amount and percentage of Google's cash equivalents and marketable securities did the company use significant unobservable inputs to determine amounts reported on its December 31, 2012 balance sheet?

(2) How, if at all, did those figures change from the amounts reported as of December 31, 2011?

(3) How, if at all, did the amount of any unrealized gains or losses related to such investments change during 2012?

(4) Did Google change its fair valuation methods during 2012? If so, how did any changes affect reported results?

(5) Did Google recognize any impairment losses on marketable securities during 2012?

(6) What was the fair value of Google's unsecured senior notes, including any current portion, as of December 31, 2012?

Problem 6.1C. Explaining where you found the relevant information, answer the following questions about the financial statements and related notes included in UPS's Form 10-K for the year ended December 31, 2012:

(1) For what amount and percentage of UPS's non-pension or postretirement marketable securities and investments did UPS use significant unobservable inputs to determine numbers reported on its December 31, 2012 balance sheet?

(2) How, if at all, did those figures change from the amounts reported as of December 31, 2011?

(3) How, if at all, did the amount of any unrealized gains or losses related to such investments change during 2012?

(4) Did UPS change its fair valuation methods during 2012? If so, how did any changes affect reported results?

(5) Did UPS recognize any impairment losses on marketable securities during 2012?

(6) What was the fair value of UPS's long-term debt, including any current portion, as of December 31, 2012?

2. EARNINGS PROCESS SUBSTANTIALLY COMPLETE

In addition to satisfying the bona fide exchange transaction requirement, an enterprise must substantially complete the earnings process before recognizing revenue. To satisfy this substantial completion requirement, especially under the requirements in SAB No. 101, as revised in SAB No. 104 and as described on page 368, *supra*, an enterprise must normally deliver the underlying goods or render the contemplated services. Delivery itself, however, does not automatically satisfy the substantial completion requirement. Various arrangements may give the customer the right to return or to refuse to pay for the delivered item. "Side letters" may contain material contingencies which the seller must resolve before the agreement would become final. Some agreements condition "sales" to distributors upon the distributor's ability to resell the product. In such conditional transactions, which the business community sometimes refers to as *consignments*, GAAP normally prohibits revenue recognition because the seller has not substantially completed the earnings process. We proceed now to consider the different rules affecting substantial completion.

a.   GENERAL RULES

The Codification prevents an enterprise from recognizing revenue until earned, which usually requires the enterprise to deliver goods or render services. *See* FASB ASC ¶ 605-10-25-1 (referencing RECOGNITION AND MEASUREMENT IN FINANCIAL STATEMENTS OF BUSINESS ENTERPRISES, Statement of Fin. Accounting Concepts No. 5 ¶ 83(b) (Fin. Accounting Standards Bd. 1984). To illustrate the substantial completion requirement, imagine that your seven-foot, 290 pound brother pays you five dollars to wash his car. Although the down payment resembles an exchange transaction, logic, fear, and your accountant tell you that you can not recognize five dollars as revenue until you actually wash the car. We proceed now to consider the different rules affecting substantial completion.

(1) Delivery, Passage of Title, or Performance

When a customer orders goods from a manufacturer, with or without a down payment, the manufacturer cannot recognize revenue at that time. At a minimum, the manufacturer must wait until completing the manufacturing process because production represents the principal requirement that the manufacturer must perform under the contract. In most cases, full performance for a public company after SAB No. 101 requires the seller to deliver the goods, either to the buyer or to a carrier, destined for the buyer. Some sales contracts will require other necessary steps as well, such as labeling the goods, installing the products at the buyer's premises, or the like. Keep in mind, however, that substantial performance justifies revenue recognition. The seller need not complete every element of performance. As a result, the question often becomes: "At what point does the seller achieve substantial performance?" The answer often requires professional judgment. Although accountants typically view the passage of title to the goods from the seller to the buyer as a sensible demarcation, lawyers cannot always agree when that has occurred. As a general rule, any reasonable cut-off point, *consistently applied* and adequately *disclosed*, should qualify. If an enterprise must still complete some steps, presumably insubstantial, the enterprise should accrue the estimated costs to perform at the same time, so that the income statement will match the entire expense of performance against the revenue from the transaction.

The following case illustrates these issues in a tax setting.

Pacific Grape Products Co. v. Commissioner

United States Court of Appeals, Ninth Circuit, 1955.
219 F.2d 862.

■ Pope, Circuit Judge.

Petitioner is a canner of fruit and fruit products. It regularly billed its customers for all goods ordered by them, but not yet shipped and remaining in petitioner's warehouse, on December 31 in each year. It accrued upon its books the income from the sales of such unshipped goods in the taxable years ending on the days of such billing. On the same date it also credited to the accounts of brokers the brokerage due on account of sales of such unshipped goods, and accrued the cost of such unshipped goods including therein the anticipated cost of labeling, packaging and preparing the same for shipment. For many years the petitioner reported its income accordingly. (It filed its returns on the calendar year, accrual basis.)

The Commissioner, in determining deficiencies for the years 1940 to 1944, held petitioner's method of accounting did not clearly reflect its income and made adjustments by excluding from the computation of income for the years 1939, 1940 and 1941, the sales prices of unshipped goods billed on December 31 of those years, and included such amounts in the computations of income for the years 1940, 1941 and 1942 respectively. He likewise transferred to these later years the brokerage fees and the estimated costs mentioned which related to these goods. The result was a deficiency in income tax for the years 1940 and 1943, and in excess profits tax for the years 1940, 1941, 1942 and 1944, and in declared value excess profits tax for the year 1944. The determinations mentioned were upheld by the Tax Court on petition for redetermination.

Since its organization in 1926 petitioner has operated its cannery at Modesto, California. Its product was limited to fruit and fruit products. Its canning season in each year extends from about July 1st to November 1st.

During such season it enters into numerous contracts for the sale of its current pack. * * *

The contracts described the quantity, price, grade, size of cans, and variety of fruit or fruit products to be sold. Some provided for labels bearing petitioner's name; others provided for the use of labels bearing the buyer's trade name, in which case the labels were furnished by the buyer to whom an allowance was made for the labels. A large portion of the goods covered by the contracts are shipped during the calendar year in which the fruits are packed. On occasion some buyers request petitioner to withhold shipment of all or part of their contract amounts until the following year and petitioner normally complies with such request. In that connection the contract form used provides: "Goods to be shipped in seller's discretion as soon as practicable after packing. * * * If seller shall elect to withhold shipment at buyer's request, then the goods unshipped shall be billed and paid for on the following dates respectively hereinafter specified. * * * Fruits, Fruit Products or Sundry Vegetables, December 31." Accordingly goods remaining unshipped on December 31 of each year were billed by the petitioner to their respective buyers on that date.

On December 31 of each year the petitioner always has on hand a sufficient quantity of goods of every variety, grade and size of can to fill all contracts. * * * The fruits of different varieties, grades and sizes of cans were separately arranged in separate stacks with no commingling of variety, grade or size in any one stack. It was stipulated in the Tax Court that all of the canned fruits and fruit products here involved were fungible goods within the meaning of the Uniform Sales Act * * *. The evidence showed that in accruing and entering upon its books in these years the expense of brokerage fees, petitioner calculated the amount of such fees in accordance with the customary trade practice of the California canning industry. That practice was to accrue the expenses of such fees as of the dates the unshipped goods were billed. With respect to the expenses of shipment of the goods, that is, the cost of labeling, packing and freight, it accrued and entered upon its books as an item of deduction the anticipated cost of these items. What the cost would be was known from the petitioner's past experience with such expenditures.

The Tax Court, six judges dissenting, upheld the Commissioner's determination that the method employed by the petitioner of computing accrued income from its sales did not clearly reflect its income. The court based its conclusion entirely upon its determination that title to the goods in question did not pass to the buyers on the billing dates. * * *

* * * In this we think that the Tax Court was in error.

* * *

It is true that the goods here had to be labeled, packed and shipped at a subsequent date. Such a circumstance is a matter to be taken into consideration in ascertaining the intention of the parties as to when the property in the goods is to pass under Rule 2 of the California Civil Code, § 1739, § 19 of the Uniform Sales Act. But that circumstance is not controlling, for all of the rules specified in that section are subject to the initial qualification of the section,—"unless a different intention appears", etc. Not only is the different intention indicated by the proof of the custom here referred to, but the language of the contract provides that the goods unshipped shall be billed and paid for on December 31. While there is no evidence to show that the buyers actually paid for those goods on December 31 (the implication is quite otherwise), yet the contract clearly specifies that payment was due on that date, which would further confirm an understanding that title had then passed.

Since title had thus passed to the buyers, it is plain that petitioner's method of accounting and accruing in such years its gross income from sales of such merchandise clearly reflected its income. Consistently, and to make reflection of income complete, it properly accrued its shipping expenses relating to this merchandise as part of its cost of goods sold in the respective years billed. The record shows that the items making up these expenses were either precisely known or determinable with extreme accuracy. Labels and cases for packing were on hand. The expenses of labor in labeling and casing were determinable on the basis of petitioner's past experience. Freight costs were available from published rate schedules. * * *

We think also that petitioner correctly treated the brokerage fees relating to the goods billed on the December 31 dates as deductible expenses in those years. The Tax Court disapproved this procedure on the ground that it thought there was a failure to introduce evidence of the contracts with the brokers to show that there was any fixed liability for the brokerage fees prior to the payment of the purchase price for the goods. The evidence, however, showed that the brokers doing business with the industry contracted in accordance with the established trade practice of considering that title to the unshipped goods passed on the billing dates, and that the brokerage fees accrued to the broker on those dates. In our view the finding that there was want of proof on this point is clearly erroneous.

* * *

Finally, we are of the view that the petitioner's method of accounting clearly and accurately reflected its income wholly apart from the question whether title to the goods did or did not pass to the buyers on the dates of billing. Upon this aspect we are agreed with what the six dissenting judges said in this case.[10]

---

[10]"Opper, J. dissenting: The practice of disapproving consistent accounting systems of long standing seems to me to be exceeding all reasonable bounds. Methods of keeping records do not spring in glittering perfection from some unchangeable natural law but are devised to aid business men in maintaining sometimes intricate accounts. If reasonably adapted to that use they should not be condemned for some abstruse legal reason, but only when they fail to reflect income. There is no persuasive indication that such a condition exists here. On the contrary, a whole industry apparently has adopted the method used by petitioner."

"It will not do to say that respondent should not have disturbed petitioner's accounting method, but that since he has done so, we are powerless to do other-

Not only do we have here a system of accounting which for years has been adopted and carried into effect by substantially all members of a large industry, but the system is one which appeals to us as so much in line with plain common sense that we are at a loss to understand what could have prompted the Commissioner to disapprove it. Contrary to his suggestion that petitioner's method did not reflect its true income it seems to us that the alterations demanded by the Commissioner would wholly distort that income. It is reasonable that both the taxpayer and the Government should be able accurately to ascertain the income accruing to the taxpayer on account of each annual pack. The Commissioner would break up the petitioner's product for the year 1940 and throw the receipts from the portion shipped before December 31 into gross income for that year and the receipts from the unshipped portion into the following year. If in a succeeding year there arose a market shortage which led to a demand which brought about almost complete shipment of the pack before December 31, the Commissioner's accounts for that succeeding year would cover one nearly complete pack and portions of the income and deductions relating to the preceding pack. We see no reason for any such requirement on the part of the Commissioner.

The judgment of the Tax Court is reversed and the cause is remanded with directions to modify the judgment in accordance with this opinion.

NOTES

1. Today, Treasury Regulations allow an accrual-method taxpayer engaged in manufacturing to account for sales when the taxpayer ships or delivers the product, when the customer accepts delivery, or when title to the goods passes to the customer—whether or not the taxpayer bills the customer, depending on the method that the taxpayer regularly uses for financial accounting purposes. Treas. Reg. § 1.446-1(c)(1)(ii)(C) (as amended in 2011).

2. The substantial completion requirement finds support in the *matching principle* which Chapter I introduced on page 66, *supra,* and which we will discuss in more detail shortly. When an enterprise recognizes revenue under the substantial completion rule, the enterprise will have rendered most, if not all, of the required performance. By waiting until substantial completion, the enterprise will have already incurred most related costs, thus removing any doubt about whether performance will occur and eliminating the need to estimate most expenses.

3. As previously mentioned, when the seller delivers goods to a buyer the revenue recognition principle generally treats the goods as sold because the seller has substantially completed its obligations. When some relatively minor uncertainty remains, such as a warranty obligation, the seller could

wise. As long as we continue to approve the imposition of theoretical criteria in so purely practical a field, respondent will go on attempting to seize on such recurring fortuitous occasions to increase the revenue, even though he may actually accomplish the opposite. I think it evident that petitioner's generally recognized accounting system did not distort its income and that it should be permitted to continue to use it. * * *"

theoretically delay at least a portion of the revenue until the warranty period expires. In the real world, however, most enterprises estimate the likely costs to honor the warranties for the goods sold and accrue those estimated expenses at the time of the sale to achieve the desired matching.

4. In Note 1: Summary of Significant Accounting Policies under the headings "Revenue Recognition," "Company-operated Stores Revenues," "Licensed Stores Revenues," "[Consumer Product Group], Foodservice and Other Revenues," and "Stored Value Cards" on pages 58 and 59 of Starbucks' Form 10-K for the fiscal year ended September 30, 2012, which appears in Appendix A on pages 754 and 755, *infra*, the company discloses various accounting policies related to revenue recognition. Under those policies, Starbucks recognizes revenue from company-operated retail stores when customers tender payment at the point of sale, net of sales, use or other transaction taxes that the company collects from customers and remits to taxing authorities. For product sales to customers other than through company-operated retail stores, and subject to contrary contract terms, Starbucks generally recognizes revenue, including shipping charges billed to customers, upon shipment to customers. The company treats cash payments received in advance of product or service delivery as deferred revenue. The company recognizes revenue from Starbucks cards and other stored value cards upon redemption or when the company deems the likelihood of redemption, based upon historical experience, remote. *Id.*

(2) Right of Return and Buy-Back Arrangements

Even if a seller has delivered goods, however, the underlying contract may give the buyer the right to return the goods and recover the purchase price or negate any obligation to pay for the goods. As we saw earlier in *Lincoln Savings & Loan Association v. Wall*, at pages 392 to 397, *supra*, substance over form represents an important principle in financial accounting. If an enterprise sells a product in one accounting period, but the buyer can return the item in the next period, has the enterprise really "sold" the product? Although in form the seller has transferred legal title, the transaction's economic substance suggests that the seller has retained the risks of ownership, which would preclude revenue recognition.

FASB ASC Subtopic 605-15, *Revenue Recognition—Products*, which codified SFAS No. 48, *Revenue Recognition When Right of Return Exists*, sets forth the accounting and reporting standards for sales in which either the contract or existing practice gives the buyer the right to return the product. Under the Codification, a seller can recognize revenue immediately only if the surrounding circumstances satisfy the following six conditions:

(1) The underlying agreement substantially fixes or determines the price to the buyer on date of the sale;

(2) The buyer has paid the seller, or the underlying agreement obligates the buyer to pay the seller whether or not the buyer resells the product;

(3) The product's theft, physical destruction or damage will not change the buyer's obligation to the seller;

(4) The buyer acquiring the product for resale has economic substance apart from any resources that the seller has provided;

(5) The underlying agreement does not impose significant obligations on the seller for future performance to directly bring about the product's resale; *and*

(6) The seller can reasonably estimate future returns.

If a sales transaction satisfies all six requirements, ASC Subtopic 605-15 specifies that the seller report the sales revenues and cost of sales in the income statement and reduce those amounts to reflect estimated returns.

In many cases, an exchange transaction satisfies the first five requirements and revenue recognition hinges on whether the seller can reasonably estimate future returns. That determination, in turn, depends on many factors and circumstances which vary from case to case. Subtopic 605-15, however, provides that the following factors may impair the seller's ability to establish a reasonable estimate:

(a) The product's susceptibility to significant external factors, such as technological obsolescence or changes in demand;

(b) A relatively long return period;

(c) Insufficient or no historical experience with similar sales or similar products;

(d) Changing circumstances, such as modifications in the seller's marketing policies or relationships with customers, which preclude the enterprise from applying historical experience; or

(e) Inadequate volume of relatively homogeneous transactions.

If the seller cannot reasonably estimate returns or satisfy one of the other five requirements necessary for revenue recognition at the time of sale, the enterprise should recognize sales revenue and cost of sales when either: (1) the return privilege has substantially expired or (2) the underlying circumstances subsequently satisfy the six conditions, whichever occurs first.

(3) Nonmonetary Transactions

In addition to the limitations on recognizing sales when a right of return exists, an enterprise should not recognize revenue in certain nonmonetary exchanges if the transaction does not have commercial substance. FASB ASC Topic 845, *Nonmonetary Transactions*, which codified APB Opinion No. 29, as amended by SFAS No. 153, identifies two types of transactions which fall under this rule: (1) an exchange of property held for sale in the ordinary course of business for a product or property that the enterprise will promptly sell in the same line of business to a customer other than another party to the exchange, and (2) an exchange that will not result in significant changes in the risk, timing or amount of future cash flows of the reporting enterprise. Transactions in this second category would include so-called tax shelters that do not serve a legitimate business purpose other than tax avoidance. In either situation to which nonrecognition applies, the enterprise should account for the asset that the enterprise acquired in the exchange at the recorded amount for the nonmonetary asset relinquished. FASB ASC ¶¶ 845-10-30-3 to -4 (codifications of Accounting for Nonmonetary Transactions, Accounting Principles Board Opinion No. 29 ¶ 20–21 (Am. Inst. of Certified Pub. Accountants 1973), as amended by Exchanges of Nonmonetary Assets, Statement of Fin. Accounting Standards No. 153 ¶ 2 (Fin. Accounting Standards Bd. 2004)).

In a barter transaction, a type of nonmonetary exchange, two or more enterprises exchange goods or services, but not money. ASC Topic 845 generally requires enterprises to account for barter transactions based on the fair value of the assets or services exchanged. In addition, FASB ASC Subtopic 605-20, *Revenue Recognition—Services*, which codified EITF Issue No. 99-17, *Accounting for Advertising Barter Transactions*, specifically addresses the proper accounting for advertising barter transactions involving check swaps. Under Subtopic 605-20, enterprises can recognize revenue and expense from an advertising barter transaction only if they can determine the fair value of the advertising surrendered based on their own historical practice. FASB ASC ¶¶ 605-20-25-14 to -18 (a codification of EITF Issue No. 99-17, ¶ 4). Check swaps do not evidence the fair value of the transaction. Where an enterprise cannot determine the fair value of the advertising surrendered, the enterprise records the barter transaction based on the carrying amount of the advertising surrendered, likely zero. The enterprise, however, should still disclose the volume and type of the advertising surrendered and received. FASB ASC ¶¶ 605-20-25-14 to -18, 605-20-50-1 (codifications of EITF Issue No. 99-17, ¶¶ 4, 80).

(4) Software Revenue Recognition

As the computer software industry has grown in importance in this country, the accounting profession has recognized the need for specific revenue recognition rules for software transactions. These transactions can range from agreements that provide a license for a single software product to arrangements that require the supplying enterprise not only to deliver software or a software system, but also to expend significant efforts to produce, modify or customize the software. FASB ASC Subtopic 985-605, *Software—Revenue Recognition*, which codified Statement of Position 97-2, *Software Revenue Recognition*, and other promulgations, sets forth the applicable revenue recognition rules.

Although the following discussion does not attempt to describe the Codification's rules in any detail, several general statements can convey the rules' importance. If a software transaction does not require significant production, modification or customization services, the vendor should recognize revenue when the transaction meets the following four criteria: (1)

persuasive evidence of the arrangement, such as a signed contract, purchase order or on-line authorization, exists; (2) delivery has occurred; (3) the arrangement fixes the vendor's fee or allows its determination; *and* (4) collectibility appears probable. By comparison, when a transaction requires the supplying enterprise to perform significant production, modification or customization activities, the vendor must follow the rules for long-term contracts, discussed on pages 455 to 457, *infra*. Those rules either limit the enterprise's ability to recognize revenue to an amount that represents the actual percentage of estimated work that the enterprise actually performed during the period or force the vendor to wait until substantially completing the required services before recognizing any revenue.

Early in the technology revolution, software enterprises enjoyed the leeway to record revenue upon delivery of the first part of the software package. Several pronouncements, now codified at FASB ASC Subtopic 985-605, *Software—Revenue Recognition*, then required vendors required vendors to defer revenue on software contracts if the vendor had not yet provided all promised services or software components, which delay the recording of revenues for months, or even years. *See, e.g.*, Software Revenue Recognition, Statement of Position 97-2 (Am. Inst. of Certified Pub. Accountants 1997)); Deferral of the Effective Date of a Provision of SOP 97-2, "Software Revenue Recognition," Statement of Position 98-4 (Am. Inst. of Certified Pub. Accountants 1998); Modification of SOP 97-2, Software Revenue Recognition, With Respect to Certain Transactions, Statement of Position 98-9 (Am. Inst. of Certified Pub. Accountants 1998).

In 2009, the FASB concurrently issued two new rules on related revenue recognition issues that have changed how technology, biotech, medical device, auto, and appliance companies account for sales of products that bundle software, hardware, and services. Previous rules usually required companies to defer the majority of the revenues from such sales, gradually recognizing those revenues over time, rather than immediately upon sale. The new rules allow enterprises to recognize revenue sooner.

ASU 2009-13, *Multiple-Deliverable Revenue Arrangements*, amended FASB ASC Topic 605, *Revenue Recognition*, to enable vendors to account for products or services, referred to as "deliverables," separately rather than as a combined unit. Under previous rules, an enterprise could recognize revenue from such arrangements only if the vendor could show vendor-specific objective evidence or third-party evidence as to any undelivered elements' selling price. Under the so-called residual method, the vendor could allocate the residual amount in the arrangement to the delivered element. As a result, the residual method allocated any discount in selling prices from the combined transaction entirely to the delivered elements. The new rules eliminate the residual method. By comparison, the relative selling price method allocates any discount in the arrangement proportionately to each deliverable, which enables enterprises to recognize all the expected revenue from the completed parts of the transaction.

The guidance also removes the previous rules that required management to obtain vendor-specific objective evidence or third-party evidence of fair value for each deliverable in an arrangement with multiple elements or the enterprise could not immediately recognize revenue from that deliverable. Now, when an enterprise cannot obtain such evidence, management nevertheless can estimate the proportion of the selling price attributable to each deliverable. The revised rules, however, require additional disclosures about how a vender allocates revenue to deliverables, the significant judgments involved and any changes to those judgments in allocating revenue, and how those judgments affect when the enterprise reports revenue and its amount.

ASU 2009-14, *Certain Revenue Arrangements That Include Software Elements*, changes FASB ASC Topic 985, *Software*, and addresses concerns that constituents had expressed about the accounting for transactions that contained tangible products and software. Investors and vendors had argued that the previous rules forced them to delay recognizing revenue for certain products, such as Apple Inc.'s iPhone, that bundled tangible products and software. Previously, Apple recognized iPhone revenue over a two-year period, the time it expected the customer to use the device. The new rules remove tangible products from the scope of the software revenue recognition guidance. *See* Michael Rapoport, *FASB, as Expected, Approves Accounting Change That Benefits Tech Companies*, WALL ST. J., Sept. 24, 2009, at C6.

(5) Revenue Recognition and the Internet

As the Internet and e-commerce exploded during the late 1990s, interesting and important accounting questions emerged. With the business community and financial markets often using multiples of revenues to value Internet firms, the determination of revenues becomes crucial. The following six situations illustrate the revenue recognition issues that have arisen:

Situation One. A purchaser buys an item from an Internet auction company's customer for $1,000. Under the customer's agreement with the Internet auction company, the customer must remit ten percent of the sales price to the Internet firm.

Situation Two. An Internet auction company distributes goods for a wholesale supplier. The company incurs no obligation to pay the supplier until the purchaser actually pays for the goods. The Internet auction company sells goods for $1,000. When the purchaser remits the $1,000, the company electronically transfers $800 to the supplier's bank account.

Situation Three. An Internet service provider ("ISP") offers a $400 rebate to purchasers of personal computers who contract for three years of Internet service at $25 per month.

Situation Four. A purchaser buys an item from an Internet company for $25, plus $3 shipping and handling, uses a $15 coupon, and remits $13.

Situation Five. An Internet company offers "free" overnight shipping. A customer buys an item for $25. The company pays $10 to ship the item overnight.

Situation Six. Two Internet companies enter into a barter agreement in which they agree to "purchase" advertising space on each other's Internet site. The agreement sets the value of the advertising on each site at $100,000. One company charges other customers $90,000 for similar advertising services. The other company plans to unveil its Internet site within sixty days and has never sold advertising space to anyone else.

How should these Internet companies account for each of these transactions? How much should they report as revenues? What amounts, if any, should they record as cost of goods sold or marketing expenses? *See* Staff Accounting Bulletin No. 104, 68 Fed. Reg. 74,436 (Dec. 23, 2003), *available at* http://www.sec.gov/interps/account/sab104rev.pdf; FASB ASC ¶¶ 605-20-25-14 to -18, 605-20-50-1 (codifications of ACCOUNTING FOR ADVERTISING BARTER TRANSACTIONS, Emerging Issues Task Force Issue No. 99-17 (Fin. Accounting Standards Bd. 2000)); FASB ASC ¶¶ 605-45-45-1 to -18, 605-45-50-1 (codifications of REPORTING REVENUE GROSS AS A PRINCIPAL VERSUS NET AS AN AGENT, Emerging Issues Task Force Issue No. 99-19 (Fin. Accounting Standards Bd. 2000)); FASB ASC ¶¶ 605-45-45-19 to -21, 605-45-50-2 (codifications of ACCOUNTING FOR SHIPPING AND HANDLING REVENUES AND COSTS, Emerging Issues Task Force Issue No. 00-10 (Fin. Accounting Standards Bd. 2000); FASB ASC Subtopic 605-50, *Revenue Recognition—Customer Payments and Incentives* (a codification of ACCOUNTING FOR COUPONS, REBATES, AND DISCOUNTS, Emerging Issues Task Force Issue No. 00-14 (Fin. Accounting Standards Bd. 2000)) (concluding enterprises should report certain shipping and handling fees billed to customers as revenues at their gross amounts).

b.   EXCEPTIONS TO THE SUBSTANTIAL COMPLETION REQUIREMENT

Notwithstanding the general rules that an enterprise must have substantially completed the earnings process before recognizing revenues, several important exceptions exist. These exceptions apply to situations in which the earnings occur over time.

(1) Accounting for Rent, Interest, and Certain Services

As the first exception to the substantial completion requirement, if an enterprise grants rights to use an asset or agrees to render certain services continuously over time, the enterprise may recognize the related revenues, such as interest, rent or periodic service charges, as time passes. For example, a business renting property or equipment for an annual lease payment or providing security services for an annual fee need not wait until the full year has ended to record any revenue. Instead, the business should accrue revenue as time elapses or it provides the contemplated services. Similarly, a lender that extends a five-year loan normally should not wait until the borrower repays the loan to recognize any interest income.

With regard to interest income, three different methods—the straight-line method, the effective interest method and the Rule of 78s—exist to allocate interest to the different accounting periods during which a loan remains outstanding. To illustrate these different methods, let us return to an example which we discussed in Chapter III. In that example, which appears on pages 241 to 243, *supra*, we determined that if Brianna borrows $100,000 at ten percent interest, compounded annually, she must pay the lender $26,379.73 at the end of each of the next five years to repay the loan. Because Brianna must make five $26,379.73 payments to repay the loan, she will pay the lender $131,898.65 ($26,379.73 times five payments) over the loan's life. Subtracting the $100,000 principal amount, Brianna will pay $31,898.65 in interest over that period. How should the lender allocate that amount between the different accounting periods involved?

a) STRAIGHT-LINE METHOD

The lender would treat $6,379.73 of each $26,379.73 payment as interest income under the straight-line method for allocating interest between different accounting periods. The remaining $20,000 of each payment would reduce the unpaid principal balance as follows:

Year	Payment	Interest	Principal	Balance
0				$100,000.00
1	$26,379.73	$6,379.73	$20,000.00	80,000.00
2	26,379.73	6,379.73	20,000.00	60,000.00
3	26,379.73	6,379.73	20,000.00	40,000.00
4	26,379.73	6,379.73	20,000.00	20,000.00
5	26,379.73	6,379.73	20,000.00	-0-

The straight-line method offers simplicity, but does not accurately match interest income to the various accounting periods. In this regard, you should note that the $100,000 outstanding loan balance during the first year generates $6,379.73 in interest income, which translates to a 6.38 percent interest rate ($6,379.73 interest divided by $100,000 principal balance). Conversely, the $20,000 outstanding loan balance in the fifth year generates the same $6,379.73 in interest income, a 31.9 percent interest rate ($6,379.73 interest divided by $20,000 principal balance). Although the $6,379.73 interest income remains the same in each year, the effective interest rate varies from year to year.

b) EFFECTIVE INTEREST METHOD

Under the effective interest method, the lender recognizes a constant rate of interest on the outstanding loan balance from period to period. We used the effective interest method in Chapter III. Because the lender agreed to loan money to Brianna at ten percent annual interest, the effective interest method treats ten percent of the outstanding loan balance as interest income for each period. In the first year, therefore, interest income equals the ten percent interest rate times the $100,000 original principal amount outstanding during the year, or $10,000. Of the $26,379.73 that Brianna pays at the end of the first year, the lender treats $10,000 as interest income and the remaining $16,379.73 reduces principal. Subtracting the $16,379.73 principal payment from the $100,000 original loan amount leaves $83,620.27 as the unpaid principal balance which remains outstanding during the second year. At the end of the second year, Brianna pays another $26,379.73. Interest income for the second year equals $8,362.03, ten percent interest times the $83,620.27 remaining principal. The lender treats the $18,017.70 difference between the $26,379.73 payment and the $8,362.03 interest as principal, which reduces the loan balance outstanding during the third year to $65,602.57. Summarizing these calculations for the five years, we get:

Year	Payment	Interest	Principal	Balance
0				$100,000.00
1	$26,379.73	$10,000.00	$16,379.73	83,620.27
2	26,379.73	8,362.03	18,017.70	65,602.57
3	26,379.73	6,560.26	19,819.47	45,783.10
4	26,379.73	4,578.31	21,801.42	23,981.68
5	26,379.73	2,398.17	23,981.56	.12

As in Chapter III, we will again ignore the twelve cent balance that remains at the end of year five as an insignificant rounding difference. Although the lender records a different amount as interest income for each year, the interest income always equals ten percent of the outstanding principal balance. As we have already suggested on pages 405 and 406, *supra*, FASB ASC Subtopic 835-30, *Interest—Imputation of Interest*, which codified Accounting Principles Board Opinion No. 21, *Interest on Receivables and Payables*, encourages, and may even require, enterprises to use the effective interest method to recognize interest income.

c) RULE OF 78S

Although less commonly used and illegal in numerous states, consumer loans often use the Rule of 78s to allocate payments between interest and principal. Lenders prefer this approach because the Rule of 78s allows them to allocate a greater portion of early payments to interest than under either the effective interest or straight-line methods. If a loan remains outstanding for its entire term, the Rule of 78s will not affect the interest that the lender recognizes as income or that the borrower pays. If the borrower repays the loan early, however, the Rule of 78s may cause the borrower to pay substantially more interest than under the other methods. For this reason, laws in numerous states prohibit lenders from using the Rule of 78s under various circumstances. In any event, because the Rule of 78s treats a greater percentage of early payments as interest, rather than as reductions in principal, borrowers should avoid loan agreements that adopt the Rule of 78s for computing interest wherever possible.

To illustrate the Rule of 78s, assume that on January 1, Ellen borrows $10,000 from a bank for one year at twelve percent annual interest. For the one year loan, Ellen agrees to pay $1,200 interest, plus the $10,000 principal, or $11,200 on the following January 1. Under the Rule of 78s, each month's share of $1,200 total interest represents a fraction which contains the number of remaining months in the loan as the numerator and the sum of the numbers from one to the number of months in the loan as the denominator. For a one year loan, the denominator would, therefore, equal seventy-eight (1 + 2 + 3 + 4 + 5 + 6 + 7 + 8 + 9 + 10 + 11 + 12 = 78). To quickly compute the sum of the numbers from one to the number of accounting periods in the loan for the denominator, we can use the following formula:

$$\text{Denominator} = \frac{n(n+1)}{2}$$
$$= \frac{12(12+1)}{2}$$
$$= 78$$

In January, the loan has twelve remaining periods. Interest for January equals the fraction 12/78ths times the $1,200 total interest for the loan or $184.62. If Ellen wants to repay the loan in full, she must pay $10,184.62 to discharge her obligations under the loan at the end of January. Similarly, the interest attributable to February equals the fraction 11/78ths times the $1,200 total interest or $169.23 because eleven months remain in the loan's term. At the end of February, Ellen must pay $10,353.85 to completely satisfy the loan. You will note that although only two months have elapsed in the loan, the $353.85 represents almost thirty percent of the interest for the entire year. Under the Rule of 78s, the lender would allocate interest on the loan for the entire year as follows:

Month	Numerator	Interest Calculation	Interest	Loan Balance
				$10,000.00
January	12	12/78 x $1,200	$184.62	10,184.62
February	11	11/78 x $1,200	169.23	10,353.85
March	10	10/78 x $1,200	153.85	10,507.70
April	9	9/78 x $1,200	138.46	10,646.16
May	8	8/78 x $1,200	123.08	10,769.24
June	7	7/78 x $1,200	107.69	10,876.93
July	6	6/78 x $1,200	92.31	10,969.24
August	5	5/78 x $1,200	76.92	11,046.16
September	4	4/78 x $1,200	61.54	11,107.70
October	3	3/78 x $1,200	46.15	11,153.85
November	2	2/78 x $1,200	30.77	11,184.62
December	1	1/78 x $1,200	15.38	11,200.00
Totals	78		$1,200.00	

Like the effective interest method, the Rule of 78s allocates a decreasing amount of each payment to interest. Unlike the effective interest method, however, those decreasing amounts do not bear any relationship to the outstanding loan balance, which actually increased in this example at the same time that interest was decreasing.

Although the Rule of 78s derives its name from the number of months in a year (in other words, the sum of the numbers from 1 to 12 equals 78), we can apply the Rule of 78s to a loan of any length of time. Returning to our earlier example involving the $100,000 loan to Brianna, recall that she must make five $26,379.73 payments, which include $31,898.65 in total interest, to repay the loan. If we treat each year as a separate accounting period, we could use the previously given formula to determine the denominator in the fractions which will allocate interest to the different years involved as follows:

$$\text{Denominator} = \frac{n(n + 1)}{2}$$
$$= \frac{5(5 + 1)}{2}$$
$$= 15$$

In the first year, the loan has five remaining periods. Interest for that year, therefore, equals the fraction 5/15ths times the $31,898.65 total interest on the loan or $10,632.88. If Brianna wants to repay the entire loan at the end of the first year, she must therefore pay $110,632.88, or the $100,000 original principal amount plus the $10,632.88 interest for the first year. Assuming Brianna remits the $26,379.73 first installment payment, the principal balance would drop to $84,253.15 at the end of that first year. Similarly, the interest attributable to the second year equals the fraction 4/15ths times the $31,898.65 total interest or $8,506.31 because four years remain in the loan's term. At the end of second year, Ellen must pay $92,759.47, which represents the $84,253.16 previous principal balance plus $8,506.31 interest for the second year, to completely satisfy her obligation under the loan. Under the Rule of 78s, the lender would allocate interest income on the loan for the five years as follows:

Year	Payment	Interest Computation	Interest	Principal	Balance
0					$100,000.00
1	$26,379.73	5/15 x $31,898.65	$10,632.88	$15,746.85	84,253.15
2	26,379.73	4/15 x $31,898.65	8,506.31	17,873.42	66,379.73
3	26,379.73	3/15 x $31,898.65	6,379.73	20,000.00	46,379.73
4	26,379.73	2/15 x $31,898.65	4,253.15	22,126.58	24,253.15
5	26,379.73	1/15 x $31,898.65	2,126.58	24,253.15	-0-

Once again note that the Rule of 78s attributes exactly one-third of the interest for the five-year loan term to the first year.

d) COMPARISON OF THE THREE METHODS FOR ALLOCATING INTEREST TO DIFFERENT ACCOUNTING PERIODS

The following chart summarizes the alternatives for allocating the $31,898.65 interest income among the different years under the straight-line and effective interest methods and the Rule of 78s:

Year	Straight-Line Method	Effective Interest Method	Rule of 78s
1	$6,379.73	$10,000.00	$10,632.88
2	6,379.73	8,362.03	8,506.31
3	6,379.73	6,560.26	6,379.73
4	6,379.73	4,578.31	4,253.15
5	6,379.73	2,398.17	2,126.58
Totals	$31,898.65	$31,898.77	$31,898.65

Ignoring the twelve cent additional interest under the effective interest method attributable to rounding, the chart demonstrates that the selection of a method for recognizing interest income can significantly affect an enterprise's financial statements. Once again, GAAP arguably requires an enterprise to use the effective interest method to recognize interest income, but does permit other methods as long as the results do not significantly differ from the effective interest method.

(2) Long-Term Contracts

GAAP recognizes the percentage-of-completion method as a second exception to the substantial completion requirement. Under the percentage-of-completion method, an enterprise can recognize a portion of the estimated profit on a long-term contract spanning several accounting periods even though the enterprise has not substantially completed the project. In contrast, the completed-contract method requires full completion, or at least substantial completion, before an enterprise may treat revenue as earned.

Under the completed-contract method, an enterprise does not recognize revenue and gross profit from a contract until the enterprise has substantially completed the contract. In the meantime, the enterprise defers all construction costs in an asset account, usually referred to as *Construction in Process*, and records payments and any amounts due, but not collected, on the contract in *Billings on Construction in Process*. If the costs incurred exceed the billings, which equal payments and receivables, the enterprise reports the excess as a current asset on the balance sheet. In contrast, if billings exceed costs, the excess appears as a current liability. In the year in which the enterprise substantially completes the contract, it would report all revenues and all expenses attributable to the contract on the income statement for that year.

Under the percentage-of-completion method, on the other hand, the recognition of revenue does not depend upon the contract's substantial completion. Instead, an enterprise recognizes estimated revenues based on the progress that it made on the contract during the accounting period. For each period, the income statement shows the actual expenses incurred on the contract during the period and an amount of estimated revenue which bears the same ratio to the total expected revenue as the costs incurred during the period bear to the total estimated costs to perform the contract, subject to any adjustments to reflect changes in estimated costs.

To illustrate, assume that in the first year of a $1 million contract an enterprise incurs $200,000 in expenses. Further assume that the enterprise expects to spend another $600,000 performing the contract. Because the enterprise has incurred $200,000 of the total $800,000 expected costs on the contract, the enterprise would recognize $50,000 in gross profit, or twenty-five percent of the $200,000 expected gross profit ($1 million contract price less $800,000 estimated costs), in the first year under the percentage-of-completion method. Although the actual bookkeeping mechanics get very complex quite quickly, the enterprise would debit an asset account for $50,000 to offset the $50,000 credit balance that arises from recognizing the gross profit. In all other respects, the balance sheet treatment mirrors the presentation for the completed-contract method. The income statement under the percentage-of-completion method, however, would show $50,000 gross profit, the difference between the $250,000 in revenue and the $200,000 in costs actually incurred during the year. *See* DONALD E. KIESO ET AL., INTERMEDIATE ACCOUNTING 909-13 (11th ed. 2005).

If an enterprise expects to incur a loss on a contract under either method, conservatism technically requires the enterprise to recognize the loss immediately. If a close relationship exists, however, between profitable and unprofitable contracts and those contracts constitute parts of the same project, an enterprise may treat the group as a unit when determining whether to recognize a loss immediately.

FASB ASC Subtopic 605-35, *Revenue Recognition—Construction-Type and Production-Type Contracts*, which also codified Statement of Position 81–1, states that the percentage-of-completion and completed-contract methods do not offer "acceptable alternatives for the same circumstances." The Codification requires an enterprise to use the percentage-of-completion method when the enterprise can reasonably and reliably estimate progress towards completion, contract revenues and total costs and the following three conditions exist: (1) the contract clearly specifies the enforceable rights involving the underlying goods or services, the applicable consideration and the settlement terms; (2) the seller expects the buyer to satisfy all obligations under the contract; and (3) the seller expects to perform any contractual obligations. Because ASC Subtopic 605-35 describes the ability to produce reasonably dependable estimates as an essential element of the contracting business, the Codification presumes that enterprises that produce and deliver goods or services on a continuing basis and for which such contractual arrangements represents a significant part of their operations can reach such estimates. If an enterprise's estimates cannot satisfy the reasonable dependability standard or the other conditions for the percentage-of-completion method, then the enterprise must use the completed-contract method. *See* FASB ASC ¶¶ 605-35-25-1 to -2, -56 to -57, -94, 605-35-50-1 (codifications of ACCOUNTING FOR PERFORMANCE OF CONSTRUCTION–TYPE AND CERTAIN PRODUCTION–TYPE CONTRACTS, Statement of Position 81–1, ¶¶ 21, 23, 32 (Am. Inst. of Certified Pub. Accountants 1981)).

Enterprises sometimes also adopt the *program method*. Under the program method, an enterprise first estimates both (1) aggregate total revenues from the product or service under both existing and anticipated future contracts and (2) aggregate total costs to produce those revenues. Then the enterprise matches the average cost per unit, based on aggregate total costs in the "program," against current contract revenues. Through this process, the enterprise averages the net profit from both current and *anticipated* future contracts, even though no exchange transaction exists for the future contracts.

To illustrate, assume that a defense contractor builds a prototype aircraft which costs $100 million to develop, design and build which the contractor sells to the government for $80 million with the expectation that the government will order at least five more aircraft at that same price, but which will only cost another $40 million each to produce. Aggregate total revenues equal $480 million (six aircraft at $80 million each). Aggregate total costs equal $300 million ($100 for the first unit and $40 million each for the next five units), or a $50 million average cost per unit. Under the program method, the contractor matches the $50 million average cost per unit against the $80 million contract price and reports a $30 million gross profit on the sale of the prototype. In contrast, if the contractor had matched the $100 million in costs necessary to develop, design and build the prototype against the $80 million contract price, the contractor would have recognized a $20 million loss.

As a result, the program method generates a higher profit, or smaller loss, for the current contract than if the enterprise accounted for the contract separately. If the anticipated future contracts do not materialize, the enterprise must then recognize larger losses, or smaller profits, in subsequent years. *See, e.g.,* Polin v. Conductron Corp., 552 F.2d 797 (8th Cir. 1977) (affirming the district court's conclusion that defendant did not commit securities fraud because the proxy statement and annual report warned that recovery of various costs related to aircraft simulators would depend upon future contracts). Given the potential to mislead investors, however, the SEC requires additional disclosures about long-term contract and program activities. "Notice of Adoption of Amendments to Regulation S–X to Provide for Improved Disclosures Related to Defense and Other Long–Term Contract Activities," Accounting Series Release No. 164, 39 Fed. Reg. 43,621 (S.E.C. 1974), codified in the Codification of Financial Reporting Policies, § 206, *reprinted in* 7 Fed. Sec. L. Rep. (CCH) ¶ 73,007 (May 18, 1988).

PROBLEMS

Problem 6.2A. Explaining where you found the relevant information, answer the following questions about Amazon's revenue recognition and reporting policies?

(1) When does Amazon recognize revenue?

(2) Where does Amazon report shipping revenue? How much did such revenue total in the year ended December 31, 2012?

(3) Where does Amazon report outbound shipping costs? How much did the company incur for such costs in the year ended December 31, 2012?

Problem 6.2B. Explaining where you found the relevant information, when does Google recognize revenue?

Problem 6.2C. Explaining where you found the relevant information, when does UPS recognize revenue?

Problem 6.3. Your law firm represents Data Control Inc. ("DCI"), a company with a fiscal year ending August 31 that manufactures and sells computer tape and tape cartridges. DCI is considering an initial public offering and has retained your firm to prepare the registration statement necessary for the public offering. During your preparation of the registration statement, you learn that during the last week of August 201X, John Ward, the company's chief financial officer, convinced Fred Engel, who currently owns sixty-percent of DCI's outstanding shares, to accept a $100,000 shipment of computer cartridges to enable DCI to meet sales projections for the fiscal year ending August 31, 201X. Engel also owns and operates Engel Enterprises, a sole proprietorship which sells computer cartridges. Engel agreed to accept the shipment on credit with the understanding that he would have no obligation to pay for the shipment unless he could resell the cartridges and that he could return the shipment at any time within ninety days for full credit. On October 30, 201X, Engel resold the last portion of the shipment to an unrelated third party. Can DCI recognize revenue on the transaction during its fiscal year ending August 31, 201X, if it complies with the related party disclosure requirements in Statement of Financial Accounting Standards No. 57? If so, what information must DCI disclose to satisfy GAAP? If not, explain briefly.

Problem 6.4. Crimson Company began operations on January 1, 201X. On December 31, 201X, Crimson Company owned the following investments in the following publicly traded marketable securities:

	Cost	Fair Value
Best Company Bonds	$20,000	$17,000
Domers Ltd. Common Stock	100,000	82,000
Falcon, Inc. Common Stock	35,000	49,000

Best Company Bonds are classified as a held-to-maturity security. Domers Ltd. common stock is a trading security. Falcon, Inc. common stock is an available-for-sale security. Crimson Company reasonably determines that the changes in fair value are temporary in nature.

(a) How much income or loss, if any, should Crimson Company report to reflect the changes in value of the investments? Explain briefly.

(b) Would your answer differ if the changes are "other than temporary?" If so, how would your answer differ? In any event, explain briefly.

3. CUSTOMER DEPOSITS AND PREPAYMENTS

Sometimes, an enterprise collects cash in advance for services that the enterprise will perform or provide in the future. Under the accrual method, the enterprise cannot recognize income before rendering the required services. You may recall from Chapter I, page 62, *supra*, that under accrual accounting E. Tutt could not include the retainer that she collected from a client in July for services that she would not perform until August in July's revenue because she had not yet earned anything. The following case further illustrates income deferral and also explains how and why financial accounting rules can differ from tax rules.

Boise Cascade Corp. v. United States

United States Court of Claims, 1976.
530 F.2d 1367, *cert. denied*, 429 U.S. 867 (1976).

■ Per Curiam:

These are consolidated cases, in which plaintiffs seek the recovery of nearly $2,400,000 in income taxes plus interest thereon, paid for the years 1955 through 1961. They now come before the court on exceptions by the parties to the recommended decision filed by Trial Judge Lloyd Fletcher, on September 20, 1974, * * * having been submitted to the court on the briefs and oral argument of counsel. He held for the plaintiffs on all the significant issues. After briefing and oral argument, the court agrees with the trial judge in part, and disagrees in part.

* * *

We agree substantially with the portions of the recommended opinion that hold the Commissioner of Internal Revenue to have abused his discretion under IRC § 446(b), in determining that Ebasco's method of accounting failed to reflect income clearly for Federal Income Tax purposes and in requiring a change in such method as set forth below. The portions of the said trial judge's opinion that deal with this subject are set forth below and are adopted as our opinion with some modifications made by the court.

* * *

Trial Judge Fletcher's opinion, as modified by the court, follows:

The plaintiffs are Boise Cascade Corporation and several of its subsidiary companies. The original petition was filed by Ebasco Industries Inc. and its subsidiary companies which [later] merged with Boise Cascade * * *. Ebasco Industries was engaged in holding various investments [including] ownership interests in various operating subsidiaries which were (and continue to be) engaged primarily in rendering engineering, construction, architectural, and consulting services. * * *

The plaintiffs' annual shareholder reports included a certification by independent accountants that the financial statements were prepared in conformity with generally accepted accounting principles applied on a basis consistent with that of the preceding year.

In its business, Ebasco Services enters into contracts to perform engineering and similar services. Under the various terms of these contracts, Ebasco is entitled to bill fixed sums either in monthly, quarterly, or other periodic installments, plus such additional amounts as may be provided for in a particular contract. Depending on the terms of the different contracts, payments may in some cases be due prior to the annual period in which such services are to be performed, and in some cases subsequent thereto.

For a number of years prior to 1959 and continuing to the time of trial, Ebasco included in its income for both book and tax purposes amounts attributable to services which it performed during the taxable year, a procedure accepted by the Internal Revenue Service on prior audits. Ebasco determined the amounts so earned by dividing the estimated number of service hours or days required to complete the particular contract into the contract price. The resulting quotient represents an hourly or daily rate which is then multiplied by the number of hours or days actually worked on the contract during the taxable year. As the contract is performed, the rate is adjusted to reflect revised estimates of the work required to complete the contract.

Where Ebasco billed for services prior to the tax year in which they were performed, it credited such amounts to a balance sheet account called "Unearned Income[."] Where the services were performed in a subsequent period, the "Unearned Income" account was debited, and such amounts were included in an income account called "Service Revenues." The amount recorded in the latter account was included in income for both book and tax purposes. In determining the amount which was to be included in the "Unearned Income" account, the costs of obtaining the [contract, which included the cost of preparing bids, proposals, and estimates, advertising, selling and other expenses,] were not taken into account; and, with the exception of prepaid insurance and similar items, all such amounts were expensed in the tax year during which they were incurred. The amounts in the "Unearned Income" account were treated as liabilities and were excluded from gross income for each tax year consistently in Ebasco's books, records, and shareholder reports, as well as in its tax returns. All of the amounts included in the account during one tax year were earned through the performance of services during the following year and were included in income for such following tax year. When the amounts credited to the "Unearned Income" account were collected, Ebasco had an unrestricted right to the use of such funds.

During the three tax years in issue, an average of over 94 percent of the amounts included in the "Unearned Income" account was received by Ebasco under contracts which obligated it to perform engineering services in connection with the design and construction of electric generating plants. These contracts either required that services be performed by a specified date or required that Ebasco should perform those services "with all reasonable dispatch and diligence," as "expeditiously as possible," or some comparable requirement. The small remaining amounts in the account were received either under contracts which required Ebasco to perform specific services in connection with a specific project of a client, or required Ebasco to provide consultation and advice on an annual basis for an annual fee.

In addition to its "Unearned" account, Ebasco maintained an "Unbilled Charges" account computed in the same manner as the "Unearned Income" account. The balance in such account represented amounts earned through the rendering of services, or on partially completed contracts, or earned prior to contracting under all of which payment was not then due by the terms of a contract or was not billable and due prior to execution of a future contract. Stated another way, the amounts included in this account were those which Ebasco was not entitled to bill or receive until a year subsequent to the year in which the services were actually rendered. Such amounts were recorded in "Service Revenues" and included in income for tax as well as book purposes in the taxable year in which the services were rendered. Likewise, the costs attributable to the rendering of services which produced the year-end balance in the "Unbilled Charges" account were deducted from gross income in the year such services were rendered. In 1959, 1960, and 1961 there were approximately $405,000, ($56,000), and $179,000 of such net amounts, respectively, carried in the "Unbilled Charges" account.

Plaintiffs' consolidated income tax returns for 1959 through 1961 were audited by the Government, and the amounts in the "Unearned Income" account were included in taxable income for Federal tax purposes. These adjustments were made pursuant to section 446(b) of the 1954 Code under which the Commissioner determined that plaintiffs' deferral method of accounting did not clearly reflect income. During the same examination for the same tax years, no adjustments were made to the "Unbilled Charges" or the "Service Revenues" accounts.

At trial Ebasco presented expert testimony related solely to the accounting practices described above. The sole witness was a qualified certified public accountant and a partner in a major accounting firm. Based on his broad experience with comparable service companies and his personal familiarity with the accounting practices of Ebasco, he expressed his expert opinion with respect to the accounts in issue and the changes made by the Commissioner.

He testified that the method of accounting used by Ebasco which employs both an "Unearned Income" account and an "Unbilled Charges" account and is based on [recognizing] amounts as income at the time the related services are performed is in accordance with * * * generally accepted accounting principles and clearly reflects Ebasco's income. He indicated that this method properly matched revenues with costs of producing such revenues and is particularly appropriate in this case because almost all of Ebasco's income is derived from the performance of services by its own personnel. He further testified that this method of accounting was widely used by companies engaged in rendering engineering and similar services, and that such method clearly reflected the income of Ebasco.

With respect to costs incurred in obtaining contracts, such as bid preparation, overhead, advertising, and other selling expenses, the witness considered them to be properly deducted in the year incurred as continuing costs of doing and developing business. [The witness distinguished such costs from commissions which in some instances may properly be amortized where they relate directly to the contract involved and thus reduce the amount realizable under such contract.] He explained that these costs should not properly be amortizable over the life of any particular contract since they were costs connected with new business development and were unrelated to performance of the contract.

The accounting method proposed by the Commissioner requires Ebasco to accrue as income the amounts included in the "Unearned Income" account and also requires the accrual, consistent with plaintiffs' accounting method, of amounts in the "Unbilled Charges" account. In the opinion of plaintiffs' expert, this method of accounting was not in accordance with generally accepted accounting principles and did not clearly reflect Ebasco's income. To him, the Commissioner's method was erroneous in that it required the inclusion in income of amounts billed but not yet earned on contracts in one accounting period without at the same time acknowledging the obligations and costs to be incurred by Ebasco in the future performance of such contractual commitments. He termed such method as "hybrid" in that while it recognized the accrual method with respect to unbilled charges which were earned but not yet billable, it had the effect of imposing a cash basis method as to the billed but unearned charges in the "Unearned Income" account.

Finally, the witness testified that if Ebasco were to use a method of accounting under which amounts in the "Unearned Income" account would be accrued as income and amounts in the "Unbilled Charges" account would *not* be accrued as income, such method would more clearly reflect the income of Ebasco than the method of accounting proposed by the Commissioner. He stated that, while such method was not technically in accordance with generally accepted accounting principles, it was a more logical and consistent approach to use in determining the income of Ebasco than the Commissioner's method.

* * *

These issues present but another facet in the continuing controversy over the proper timing for Federal income tax purposes of various income and expense items incurred by an accrual basis taxpayer. Based on expert accounting testimony presented by Ebasco at trial, it can hardly be disputed that Ebasco's system for deferral of unearned income is in full accord with generally accepted accounting principles as that phrase is used in financial or commercial accounting. But such a showing alone is not determinative for income tax purposes. The taxpayer must also show that its method clearly reflects income for the purposes of the Internal Revenue Code. Thus, while generally accepted methods of accounting are of probative value and are treated with respect by Treas. Reg. § 1.446–1(a)(2), they are not necessarily synonymous with the proper tax accounting to be afforded an accrual item in a given situation.

This variance is especially noticeable in cases where the taxpayer's accounting method results in the deferment of income. The taxpayer in such a situation is generally relying on well-known accounting principles which essentially focus on a conservative matching of income and expenses to the end that an item of income will be related to its correlative expenditure. Tax accounting, on the other hand, starts from the premise of a need for certainty in the collection of revenues and focuses on the concept of ability to pay. Thus, under this theory, where an item of income has been received even though as yet unearned, it should be subject to taxation because the taxpayer has in hand (or otherwise available) the funds necessary to pay the tax due.

[The Court then reviewed three important Supreme Court decisions.]

It seems clear to me that, despite defendant's vigorous contention to the contrary, this trilogy of Supreme Court decisions cannot be said to have established an unvarying rule of law that, absent a specific statutory exception, a taxpayer may never defer recognition of income received or accrued under a contract for the performance of future services, no matter whether such deferral clearly reflects income.

Defendant persuasively argues, however, that its interpretation of the cases is justified by the Court's additional ground for decision in [two of the cases, in which] the Court's majority and minority opinions gave close consideration to the legislative history of sections 452 and 462 of the 1954 Code. These sections contained the first explicit legislative sanctions of deferral of income (§ 452) and deduction of future estimated expenses (§ 462). In the next year, however, both sections were retroactively repealed. To the majority in [one of the cases], this repealer action constituted "clearly a mandate from the Congress that petitioner's system was not acceptable for tax purposes." The dissent, of course, viewed the legislative history in different perspective.

To me, the dilemma and its likely solution, have been gracefully and accurately stated by the able and comprehensive opinion of the Fifth Circuit Court of Appeals in *Mooney Aircraft, Inc. v. United States*, 420 F.2d 400, 408–409 (5th Cir., 1969) where the court observed:

> This alternative ground, based on legislative intent, would seem to dispose of the entire question: *all* deferrals and accruals are bad unless specifically authorized by Congress. But the Court was careful to discuss the legislative history as dictum and restricted its holding to a finding that the Commissioner did not abuse his discretion in rejecting the *AAA*'s accounting system. It specifically refrained from overruling *Beacon* [*Beacon Publishing Co. v. Commissioner of Internal Revenue*, 218 F.2d 697 (10th Cir. 1955) (deferral of prepaid subscriptions)] and *Schuessler* [*Schuessler v. Commissioner of Internal Revenue*, 230 F.2d 722 (5th Cir. 1956) (accrual of expenses of 5–year service period)], distinguishing them on the ground that future performance was certain. * * *

The *Mooney Aircraft* approach was foreshadowed by the Seventh Circuit's decision in *Artnell Company v. Commissioner of Internal Revenue*, 400 F.2d 981 (7th Cir., 1968). There, Chicago White Sox, Inc. had received and accrued in a deferred unearned income account amounts attributable to advance ticket sales and revenues for other services related to baseball games to be played thereafter during the 1962 season. Prior to such performance, however, Artnell acquired Chicago White Sox, Inc., liquidated it, and continued operation of the team. In the final short-year return filed as transferee by Artnell in behalf of White Sox, Inc., Artnell excluded the deferred unearned income previously received by White Sox. The Commissioner required such amounts to be accrued as income to White Sox on receipt, and the Tax Court sustained him. In reversing and remanding, the Seventh Circuit analyzed the Supreme Court's trilogy, *supra*, and said at 400 F.2d 984–985:

* * *

It is our best judgment that, although the policy of deferring, where possible, to congressional procedures in the tax field will cause the Supreme Court to accord the widest possible latitude to the commissioner's discretion, there must be situations where the deferral technique will so clearly reflect income that the Court will find an abuse of discretion if the commissioner rejects it.

Prior to 1955 the commissioner permitted accrual basis publishers to defer unearned income from magazine subscriptions if they had consistently done so in the past. He refused to allow others to adopt the method. In 1955 his refusal was held, by the tenth circuit, in *Beacon*, to be an abuse of discretion. In *Automobile Club of Michigan*, the Supreme Court distinguished Beacon, on its facts, because "performance of the subscription, in most instances, was, in part, necessarily deferred until the publication dates after the tax year." The Court, however, expressed no opinion upon the correctness of *Beacon*. In 1958, Congress dealt specifically with the [*Beacon* problem]. It is at least arguable that the deferral as income of prepaid admissions to events which will take place on a fixed schedule in a different taxable year is so similar to deferral of prepaid subscriptions that it would be an abuse of discretion to reject similar accounting treatment.

* * *

Judicial reaction to *Artnell* has been mixed.

* * * Defendant's reaction, of course, is simply that "*Artnell* was wrongly decided."

Out of this mélange, one must choose a path. To use one of Justice Holmes' favorite expressions, I "can't help" but conclude that what Ebasco is pleased to call its "balanced and symmetrical" method of accounting does in fact clearly reflect its income. It achieves the desideratum of accurately matching costs and revenues by reason of the fact that the costs of earning such revenues are incurred at the time the services are performed. *See, Mooney Aircraft*, *supra*, 420 F.2d at 403. Entirely unlike the factual situations before the Supreme Court in the automobile club and dance studio cases, Ebasco's contractual obligations were fixed and definite. In no sense was Ebasco's performance of services dependent solely upon the demand or request of its clientele.

Based upon the foregoing considerations, it is necessary to conclude that Ebasco's method of accounting under which income is accrued as the related services are performed clearly reflects its income, and, accordingly, the Commissioner is not authorized by § 446(b) to impose another method of accounting. That this is true becomes particularly obvious when it is realized that the accounting method imposed upon Ebasco by the Commissioner is a classic example of a hybrid system combining elements of the accrual system with a cash system, a mixture generally viewed with disfavor. Thus, where Ebasco's billing precedes the rendition of its contracted-for services, the Commissioner proposes to tax as income amounts billed even though such amounts have not then been earned by performance. On the other hand, where the performance of services precedes billing, the Commissioner would tax amounts as income at the time the services are rendered even though, under such contracts, Ebasco has no present right to bill, or receive payment of such amounts. The inconsistency within the Commissioner's method is strident.

His method would appear to the ordinary mind to distort income instead of clearly reflecting it. Judging both by what he has rejected and what he would impose he has abused his discretion within the meaning of the authority cited, *Mooney Aircraft* and *Artnell*. Ebasco has demonstrated not only that its method of accounting is in accordance with generally accepted accounting principles but, in addition, clearly reflects its income, treating these issues to be discrete, as we must. Therefore, the amounts accrued in Ebasco's "Unearned Income" account are not taxable until the year in which Ebasco performs the services which earn that income.

* * *

NOTES

1. The principal case involved income taxes for the years 1955 through 1961. In Revenue Procedure 71–21, 1971–2 C.B. 549, the Internal Revenue Service announced an administrative decision to allow accrual method taxpayers to defer prepaid income for services as long as the taxpayer will perform the services before the end of the following taxable year. The deferral, however, applies no longer than to the end of that following year. Similarly, Treasury Regulations permit an accrual method taxpayer to elect to defer advance payments for goods and long-term contracts. Treas. Reg. § 1.451–5 (as amended in 2001). Neither authority, however, authorizes an accrual method taxpayer to defer prepaid interest or rent.

2. In the principal case, Ebasco expensed the costs for obtaining the contracts, which included the cost of preparing bids, proposals and estimates, advertising, selling and other expenses, and the Commissioner did not challenge that treatment. As we will discuss more fully in the next section, this treatment technically does not match those expenses with the revenues that they produced.

C. THE MATCHING PRINCIPLE FOR EXPENSES

As important as revenues are in financial accounting, they do not equal profits: an enterprise cannot show a profit unless its revenues exceed its expenses. *See, e.g.*, Pashman v. Chemtex, Inc., 825 F.2d 629, 631 (2d Cir. 1987) ("Perhaps the first rule of accounting is that the black ink of profit is not entered into the ledger until expenses are deducted from gross revenues."). To provide a meaningful picture about an enterprise's operations, therefore, the income statement attempts to compare revenues for an accounting period against the expenses necessary to produce those revenues.

This objective produces two consequences. First, if an enterprise reasonably expects a particular expenditure to produce revenues in a subsequent accounting period, the matching principle precludes the enterprise from treating the expenditure as an expense in the current accounting period. Instead, the enterprise should defer the expenditure to that future period. In other words, the enterprise should treat the expenditure as an asset, or, perhaps more accurately, an unexpired cost. You may recall from the practice problem in Chapter I on pages 87 to 95, *supra*, that E. Tutt paid her temporary secretary $180 in salary on July 31 for the last week in July and the first two weeks in August. Although E. Tutt could use various journal entries to reach the end result, Tutt treated $60 as salary expense for July and postponed $120 to August as deferred salary expense. Second, and conversely, the matching principle also requires an enterprise to assign any expenses, including prospective expenses, related to revenues that the enterprise recognizes during an accounting period to that period. In the practice problem referred to above, you will recall that when E. Tutt received the $25 telephone bill for July on July 25, she accrued $25 in telephone expense for the month even though she did not pay the bill at that time.

These simple examples illustrate deferral and accrual, the techniques which accountants use to match expenses and revenues. In reality, more difficult judgment questions often arise as to whether an expenditure will actually benefit a future accounting period or whether an enterprise should charge a future expected expenditure or loss against income in the current period. In resolving these questions, enterprises should consider and apply the following basic rules: (1) an enterprise should match expenditures and losses against revenues that result directly and jointly from the same transactions or events; (2) if an expenditure or loss does not directly relate to any particular revenue-producing transaction, but does generally relate to revenues earned in an accounting period, the enterprise should recognize an expense or loss for that accounting period; (3) if an expenditure does not relate to a particular transaction, but generally aids in the production of revenues in more than one accounting period, the enterprise should systematically and rationally allocate the expenditure among the different accounting periods that the enterprise expects to benefit from the expenditure; (4) if an enterprise can not relate an expenditure or loss to a particular revenue transaction or to any future accounting period, the enterprise should recognize the item in the accounting period in which the business incurred the cost or discerned the loss. *See*

Recognition and Measurement in Financial Statements of Business Enterprises, Statement of Fin. Accounting Concepts No. 5, ¶ ¶ 85–87 (Fin. Accounting Standards Bd. 1984); *see also* Elements of Financial Statements, Statement of Fin. Accounting Concepts No. 6, ¶ ¶ 144–152 (Fin. Accounting Standards Bd. 1985).

1. Deferral of Expenditures and Declines in Value

Way back in Chapter I on pages 71 to 76, *supra*, we saw that if an enterprise expects an expenditure to benefit a future accounting period, the enterprise does not treat the expenditure as an expense, but reports the item as an asset on its balance sheet. You will recall that assets represent economic resources which an enterprise acquired in a transaction, expects to provide future benefits, and controls. For most purposes we can view an asset, whether tangible or intangible, as the balance of a previous cash outlay which an enterprise has not yet allocated to current expense because whatever the enterprise acquired remains available for use or consumption in the future. To the extent that an expenditure relates to future activities or benefits subsequent accounting periods, the expenditure represents an unexpired cost which the enterprise should defer.

a. ALTERNATIVE THEORIES FOR DEFERRING EXPENSES FOR FINANCIAL ACCOUNTING PURPOSES

In deferral, the important judgment question is to what extent will an expenditure benefit a future accounting period. As general rules, an enterprise should defer expenditures based on "cause and effect" relationships and systematic and rational allocations.

(1) "Cause and Effect" Relationships

As the first theory for matching expenses and losses, accountants determine whether a "cause and effect" relationship exists between an expense or loss and the enterprise's revenues in a particular accounting period. For example, a merchandise sale involves both revenue, namely sales revenue, and an expense for cost of goods sold. Other expenses that may directly relate to a sales transaction include shipping costs to deliver the item to the customer, sales commissions, and any other variable selling expense. As a general rule, a merchandiser recognizes revenue when it delivers the underlying goods to the customer. The cost of the goods, shipping costs and selling expenses, which we can describe as the "cause," produce an "effect," namely the sales revenue. Given this "cause and effect" relationship, the enterprise treats the cost of the goods, shipping costs, sales commissions and related selling costs as expenses in the accounting period in which the business recognizes the sales revenue.

If an enterprise has not yet recognized the revenue from a particular transaction or event, it should defer any directly related expense items to achieve the necessary matching. For example, if an enterprise cannot recognize revenue from the sale of an item because a right of return exists, the enterprise should not include the item's cost in the cost of goods sold for the period. Instead, the item, plus any shipping costs, sales commissions or related selling costs, should continue to appear on the enterprise's balance sheet as an asset until the accounting period in which the business recognizes the revenue.

We have previously observed that assets and expenses both appear as debits in an enterprise's accounting records. Perpetrators of financial frauds have not overlooked this relationship. In fact, numerous financial frauds over the years have involved hiding expenses as assets, but none larger than the effort at WorldCom to treat as much as $11 billion in operating expenses as assets by pretending that those expenditures would provide some future benefit to the enterprise.

(2) Systematic and Rational Allocation

Some expenditures do not relate to any particular transaction, but generally aid in the production of revenues. For example, casualty insurance represents one of the general costs of doing business. Since an enterprise enjoys the benefit that expenditure produces, namely financial protection against loss, ratably over the policy's duration, the enterprise should allocate the policy's cost ratably among the accounting periods that the policy covers. Thus, if an enterprise purchases a three-year policy for $300 on January 1, 20X1, the enterprise should treat $100 as an expense for 20X1, while deferring $200. The $200 appears on the balance sheet as an asset, Deferred Insurance Cost or, perhaps, Prepaid Insurance, at the end of 20X1. The bookkeeper would then charge off, or in other words, *amortize*, this Deferred Insurance Cost asset to current expense ratably over the next two years. In 20X2, the enterprise would charge $100 to current expense, so that $100 would remain in the Deferred Insurance Cost account at the end of that year. The enterprise would treat the remaining $100 as current expense in 20X3. Notice that this treatment mirrors the way we handled E. Tutt's prepayment of rent for three years back in Chapter I. Similarly and as we will discuss further in Chapter IX, accountants use depreciation, depletion and amortization to allocate the costs to acquire a long-lived asset over the accounting periods expected to benefit from the asset's use.

Whenever an expense's benefit occurs as a function of time, as in the case of insurance, the basis for allocation among current period and any future periods involved appears obvious. Thus, if an enterprise purchases a two-year policy on July 1 of 20X1 for $200, the enterprise would treat $50 as expense in 20X1, $100 in 20X2, and $50 in 20X3. The amount that the enterprise has not yet charged to current expense would appear in the Deferred Insurance Cost account on the balance sheet at the end of each intervening year.

Occasionally, an expenditure may provide benefits in succeeding periods which do not correspond to the passage of time. Suppose an enterprise spends $300 on July 1 of 20X1 for a promotional campaign for one of its products. As a preliminary matter, a judgment question arises as to whether this expenditure will provide any benefit beyond the end of 20X1. If not, of course, the enterprise must treat the entire $300 as an expense in 20X1. But suppose that the enterprise concludes that the business will continue to derive benefit from the promotion through June 30, 20X2, at which time the enterprise plans to incur another promotional expenditure. The enterprise should not automatically charge half of the total expenditure to expense for each year. Instead, these facts present another judgment question, namely how much of the total benefit from the $300 expenditure does the enterprise enjoy in each of 20X1 and 20X2. If the enterprise determines, based on past experience, professional advice, or otherwise, that the business derived twice as much benefit in the first six months after the expenditure as in the next six months, then that determination would suggest that the enterprise should charge $200 to current expense in 20X1, and $100 in 20X2.

PROBLEM

Problem 6.5. Suppose that two months before the end of 20X1 Pacific Grape had contracted for four months of spot advertising on radio for $10,000 per month, designed to pave the way for a new product which the company plans to introduce to the market early in 20X2. Pacific Grape paid the entire $40,000, covering the last two months of 20X1 and the first two months of 20X2, on December 31, 20X1. How should Pacific Grape reflect this payment on its financial statements for 20X1?

b. DEFERRED LOSSES

Although GAAP generally requires enterprises to recognize losses and non-temporary declines in value immediately, certain statutory or regulatory schemes may require an enterprise to defer some portion of the loss to a later accounting period for other purposes. A Supreme Court case, *Shalala v. Guernsey Memorial Hospital*, 514 U.S. 87 (1995), illustrates a dispute regarding whether an enterprise should immediately recognize a loss or defer the loss. In that case, the hospital issued bonds in 1972 and 1982 to fund capital improvements. In 1985, the hospital refinanced the debt by issuing new bonds. Although the refinancing saved an estimated $12 million in future interest expense, the transaction resulted in a $672,581 loss for financial accounting purposes. The hospital sought Medicare reimbursement for about $314,000 of the loss, requesting full reimbursement for that amount in the year of the refinancing. After applying section 233 of the Medicare Provider Manual ("PRM"), the Secretary of Health and Human Services denied the claim, concluding that the hospital must amortize the $314,000 loss over the life of the old bonds.

The Supreme Court described the issue in the case as "whether the Medicare regulations require reimbursement according to generally accepted accounting principles (GAAP) * * *." 514 U.S. at 90. The Supreme Court held that the Medicare regulations do not mandate reimbursement according to GAAP. In discussing the differences between the objectives of financial accounting and Medicare reimbursement, the Supreme Court stated:

Although one-time recognition in the initial year might be the better approach where the question is how best to portray a loss so that investors can appreciate in full a company's financial position, see APB Opinion 26, ¶¶ 4–5, the Secretary has determined in [the Regulations] that amortization is appropriate to ensure that Medicare only reimburse its fair share. The Secretary must calculate how much of a provider's total allowable costs are attributable to Medicare services, which entails calculating what proportion of the provider's services were delivered to Medicare patients. * * * Given the undoubted fact that Medicare utilization will not be an annual constant, the Secretary must strive to assure that costs associated with patient services provided over time be spread, to avoid distortions in reimbursement. * * * Should the Secretary reimburse in one year costs in fact attributable to a span of years, the reimbursement will be determined by the provider's Medicare utilization for that one year, not for later years. This leads to distortion. If the provider's utilization rate changes or if the provider drops from the program altogether the Secretary will have reimbursed up front an amount other than that attributable to Medicare services. * * *

> * * *

Contrary to the Secretary's mandate to match reimbursement with Medicare services, which requires her to determine with some certainty just when and on whose account costs are incurred, GAAP "do[es] not necessarily parallel economic reality." R. Kay & D. Searfoss, Handbook of Accounting and Auditing, ch. 5, p. 7 (2d ed. 1989). Financial accounting is not a science. It addresses many questions as to which the answers are uncertain, and is a "process [that] involves continuous judgments and estimates." Id., at ch. 5, pp. 7–8. In guiding these judgments and estimates, "financial accounting has as its foundation the principle of conservatism, with its corollary that 'possible errors in measurement [should] be in the direction of understatement rather than overstatement of net income and net assets.'" Thor Power Tool Co. v. Commissioner, 439 U.S. 522, 542, 99 S.Ct. 773, 786, 58 L.Ed.2d 785 (1979) (citation omitted). This orientation may be consistent with the objective of informing investors, but it ill-serves the needs of Medicare reimbursement * * *.

514 U.S. at 97–101. Four Justices dissented, concluding that the Medicare regulations had incorporated GAAP as the reimbursement default rule.

For a case which rejected the use of deferred losses, see *Fidelity-Philadelphia Trust Co. v. Philadelphia Transportation Co.,* 173 A.2d 109 (Pa. 1961). That case arose in a dispute about income bonds which required Philadelphia Transportation Co. ("PTC"), the issuer, to pay a fixed three percent interest per annum and up to an additional three percent each year to the extent that the issuer's "net income" allowed. The trustee for the bondholders contested the issuer's determination that it did not earn any net income for the years 1957 and 1958, contending, among other things, that PTC had improperly deferred two losses from earlier years.

Prior to the years in question, PTC decided to retire certain tracks and convert to motor buses, a process which the company completed in 1956. Rather than charging off the track's $7,200,000 remaining book value as a loss at the end of 1956, PTC decided to amortize this amount, that is, write it off over future years, at the rate of $1,200,000 per year, on the ground that future years would benefit from savings in maintenance costs and the overall advantages from the new bus system. Affirming the lower court's holding, the Supreme Court of Pennsylvania concluded that such "benefits are at most incidental, ancillary outgrowths of the track retirement program" and that the total "retirement loss * * * was reasonably foreseeable by the end of 1956." 173 A.2d at 112.

In addition, the Pennsylvania Public Utility Commission had ruled in 1953 that certain amounts paid to pave and repave streets while installing and maintaining tracks could not be included among the assets viewed as devoted to providing utility services, usually referred to as the *rate base* and historically the starting point for determining the prices the utility could lawfully charge its customers. For accounting purposes, however, PTC had kept these paving costs on its balance sheet, to be amortized over a number of future years. As a result, PTC had charged off $450,000 against income in both 1957 and 1958. The Court concluded that when the Commission removed these costs from the rate base, the Commission's action stripped the "asset" of its only corporate benefit, and hence the company should have written off the paving costs completely by the end of 1953, so that PTC had understated its income by $450,000 in both 1957 and 1958.

PROBLEM

Problem 6.6. Niagara Power Co. is a large public utility. The public utility commission regulates the rates that the company may charge and uses a formula which lets the company charge rates based on its rate base, that is assets which the company has committed to providing public utility services. One of the company's three main plants, carried on the corporation's books (at original cost less depreciation) at $100,000,000, was located at the head of Niagara Falls. During the company's most recent fiscal year, a rock slide caused that plant to collapse into the Niagara River. The company's earned surplus at the beginning of the year was $600,000,000; gross revenues for the year amounted to $1,800,000,000, and "regular" expenses were $1,500,000,000. Should the $100,000,000 book value of the plant be charged against current income for the year? Past income? Future income?

2.   ACCRUAL OF EXPENSES AND LOSSES

If an enterprise recognizes income related to a prospective expense in the current accounting period, then the enterprise must also accrue the expense to achieve the necessary matching. In these circumstances, the enterprise debits the appropriate current expense account and credits an Expense

Payable or Accrued Expense liability account. Such an entry reflects the fact that although the business has not paid the expense yet, the enterprise faces an obligation to pay the amount in the future. Neither the fact that cash has not moved nor that an enterprise cannot determine an expense's precise amount precludes recording the expense in the current period. Even if the exact amount remains uncertain, as long as an expense belongs in the current period, the enterprise should estimate the expense as accurately as possible and accrue the estimated figure in the usual manner.

In reality, such estimation serves as the norm rather than the exception, as businesses commonly estimate unpaid expenses. Suppose the Pacific Grape company in the case at page 441, *supra*, expected that shipping costs would total $25,000 under the contracts for the goods ordered, but not yet shipped at the end of a calendar year. If Pacific Grape recognizes the income from those sales contracts in the current year, the company must also accrue and record those estimated expenses in the current year as illustrated in the following entry:

Shipping Expense	$25,000	
Shipping Expense Payable		$25,000

One significant distinction exists, however, between this Pacific Grape hypothetical and the accrual in the practice problem involving E. Tutt. In the latter case, the telephone company had already supplied the services for which E. Tutt had accrued the expense, and, by using the telephone during July, she had enjoyed the benefits from those services in the current accounting period. In addition, no uncertainty existed regarding the obligation which the Expense Payable represented. The same situation would apply to the $50 worth of janitorial services that E. Tutt would accrue to reflect services performed during June on page 62, *supra*. Under the accrual method, E. Tutt would accrue the expense so that June would bear the burden of all the janitorial services which aided the production of revenues during the month. In the Pacific Grape hypothetical, on the other hand, the shippers would not have performed any of their expected services by the end of the year in which the company recognized the revenues. As a result, Pacific Grape would not have enjoyed any of the benefit of these services as yet, and presumably Pacific Grape's actual liability to pay for the services would depend upon their actual performance.

In effect, however, an accountant could view Pacific Grape as having enjoyed the benefit from these expenses, even though the shippers had not yet performed the underlying services, because the services function as a necessary condition precedent to earning the income involved. As a corollary, an accountant might say that Pacific Grape became obligated to pay for these services, in an accounting sense even if not legally speaking, thus justifying the creation of an Expense Payable type of liability account.

Nevertheless, the fact that the business has not yet performed the services representing the expense in question does make accountants a little more reluctant to accrue the expense. Among other things, businesses usually encounter greater difficulty in estimating the cost of unperformed services rather than those that the vendor has already completed. Fortunately, the rule that a business should not recognize the income from a transaction until the enterprise has substantially completed the required performance largely avoids that problem. By hypothesis, when an accounting entity has substantially completed overall performance, not many related services can remain unperformed. As a result, the circumstances should not provide much opportunity to accrue expenses for services which the enterprise has not yet performed. In other words, delaying income recognition until the enterprise has substantially completed the work not only assures that the business will not prematurely record revenue, but also assures that the enterprise will have completed practically all services related to the income. Accordingly, any expenses which the business accrues likely relate to services already performed, which means that the corresponding liability created will represent an unconditional obligation which probably facilitates any needed estimation.

Recall, however, that since the revenue recognition rules do not require absolute completion, only substantial completion, by definition, some matters, presumably relatively unimportant, may remain unfinished, and that is when a business may need to accrue expenses for services before they have been performed. For example, assume that a manufacturer of machinery has completed the machines for a particular order and shipped them to the customer by the end of the current period, but the manufacturer has not totally completed performance because it remains responsible for installing the machines in the customer's plant. In such a case, a judgment question arises as to whether the manufacturer has completed performance to such an extent that the enterprise can recognize income on the transaction. If the enterprise can recognize the income, that normally means, as we have seen, that the enterprise will report all the income from the transaction. As a corollary, the enterprise will also accrue all related expenses, including those like the costs of installation, which have not been performed yet, to achieve a proper matching with the underlying income.

We should also briefly mention one other point about accrued expenses. Some accountants have suggested that in any case in which an enterprise must estimate the amount of an accrued expense, the enterprise should use a different name for the liability created. Such nomenclature would presumably allow a reader to separate such liabilities from others which qualify as unconditional, whether or not due yet, and certain in amount. Particularly when the vendor has not performed the services involved, an enterprise often cannot claim much confidence in the estimate. In any event, these accountants consider any estimated liability as inherently conditional. For this reason, some enterprises use the term "Estimated Liability" to describe these accrued expenses. Thus, an enterprise might call the liability created when accruing an expense for future installation of machines "Estimated Liability for Installation" rather than "Installation Costs Payable" or "Accrued Installation Costs." No uniform practice exists on this matter, however, and many enterprises lump all their accrued expense liabilities under a single heading like "Accrued Costs" or "Accrued Expenses."

Because lawyers will often encounter various terminology to describe accrued liabilities, we should also mention some history about this vocabulary. At one time, accountants used the term "Reserve," as in "Reserve for Installation Expense," to signify estimated or conditional liabilities. Because the term connotes setting something aside, presumably assets, to satisfy the underlying liability, the term can easily mislead an unsophisticated reader.

An enterprise, however, can also set aside cash or other assets and specifically earmark those assets for a particular purpose, such as discharging a debt or paying for a new plant. For example, the enterprise might establish a formal escrow arrangement or, less formally, simply open a special bank account. The term "Reserve," unfortunately, suggests that the enterprise has established some such arrangement. In fact, however, calling the liability a "Reserve" means nothing more than that the enterprise created a liability and estimated the amount in conjunction with accruing an expense.

Loose terminology has often accompanied the term "Reserve" in related contexts. Particularly in judicial opinions, you may encounter references, for example, to "deducting the reserve from income," or "reserves out of income." Presumably, this language seeks to express the fact that the enterprise created a Reserve account in conjunction with a charge against income in exactly the same amount. Such phrases, however, can confuse a reader, because we know that the term "Reserve" describes a liability which appears on the balance sheet, and liabilities, themselves, do not affect the determination of net income.

Given these concerns, Accounting Terminology Bulletin No. 1 urged that the accounting profession narrowly confine the word "Reserve" and recommended that enterprises discontinue the term's use to describe the liability accompanying an accrued expense. In fact, however, the term "Reserve" still occasionally appears in accounting and legal materials. The AICPA's 2004 survey of accounting practices followed in 600 annual reports showed that the term "Reserve" sometimes appeared in financial statements, usually to describe either deductions from assets or accruals for estimated expenses relating to property abandonments or discontinued operations, environmental costs, insurance, or litigation. *See* AM. INST. OF CERTIFIED PUB. ACCOUNTANTS, ACCOUNTING TRENDS & TECHNIQUES 307 (58th ed. 2004).

Note that we have now developed a hierarchy of credits that can accompany the recognition of an expense in the current period. An enterprise credits:

a. a Prepaid or Deferred Cost
     account. . . . . if the business has prepaid the
     expense in a prior period.

b. Cash. . . . . if the business paid the expense
     in the current period.

c. an Expense Payable (Or Accrued
     Expense) account. . . . . if the business has not yet paid
     the expense, but a fixed liability
     to pay a fixed amount of money
     exists.

d. an Estimated Liability account (or,
     sometimes, a Reserve account). if the business has not paid the
     expense, but a liability to pay an
     uncertain, but estimable,
     amount of money or to perform
     or provide services exists and
     the enterprise desires to
     segregate these kinds of
     liabilities.

Whatever the name given to the liability when an enterprise accrues an expense, when the business pays the expense the enterprise treats the payment the same as when the enterprise pays any other liability, such as an account payable. The enterprise debits the liability account to record the reduction in the liability and credits cash. As we would expect, the income statement for the subsequent accounting period in which the enterprise discharges the liability does not reflect that expense. The enterprise already recognized the expense in the earlier period.

When an enterprise could only estimate the size of the liability at the time the enterprise accrued the expense, the amount actually required to discharge the liability will rarely exactly equal the figure originally estimated and charged against income. The enterprise will reflect any difference in the income statement for the period in which the enterprise discharges the liability. So, if in the foregoing hypothetical Pacific Grape had accrued an estimated $25,000 in shipping expenses in the year of revenue recognition, with an accompanying credit to an Estimated Liability account, and in the later year of performance the shipping actually cost $28,000, Pacific Grape would record the following entry in the latter year:

Estimated Liability for Shipping	$25,000	
Shipping Expense	3,000	
Cash		$28,000

Such normal, recurring corrections simply reflect adjustments in estimated expenses which, as we will discuss further shortly, the enterprise must treat as an additional expense in the year paid. Conversely, if the actual shipping expense falls below the original estimate, the enterprise would include the difference in income, or as a reduction in related expenses, for the year paid.

a. ALTERNATIVE THEORIES FOR ACCRUING EXPENSES AND LOSSES FOR FINANCIAL ACCOUNTING PURPOSES

The previous discussion illustrates the mechanics for accruing an expense before an enterprise pays or incurs the underlying liability. The more important judgment question, however, remains as to the extent to which an enterprise should charge a future expected expenditure or loss against income in the current period. GAAP basically requires an enterprise to record an expense when the enterprise uses or consumes economic resources to deliver or produce goods, render services, or engage in other activities that constitute the enterprise's primary or central operations. In addition, an enterprise must recognize a loss when the enterprise expects previously recognized assets to provide reduced or no further benefits.

Building upon the principles that we examined to resolve deferral questions, accrual problems add two more overarching considerations to the general rules that accountants use to match expenses and revenues. First, if an expenditure or loss does not directly relate to any particular revenue-producing transaction, but does generally relate to revenues earned in the current accounting period, the enterprise should accrue an expense or loss. Second, if an enterprise can not relate an expenditure or loss to a particular revenue transaction or to any future accounting period, the enterprise should accrue the item in the accounting period in which the business incurred the cost or discerned the loss. Consequently, an enterprise should match expenditures or losses based on "cause and effect" relationships, systematic and rational allocations and lack or loss of future benefits.

(1) "Cause and Effect" Relationships

As the first theory for accruing expenses and losses, accountants determine whether a "cause and effect" relationship exists between the item and the enterprise's revenues in the current accounting period. Such a cause and effect relationship can exist in two different ways. As we saw in our earlier discussion about deferral, revenues and expenses can result directly and jointly from the same transaction or other event. For this reason, an enterprise treats the cost of the goods, shipping costs, sales commissions and related selling costs as expenses in the accounting period in which the business recognizes the sales revenue.

In addition, enterprises usually incur some costs that aid in the production of revenues, but which the business cannot directly relate to any specific revenue. For example, monthly salaries paid to business executives and sales representatives, office rent, interest paid on working capital, and electricity used to operate an office building do not directly relate to any particular revenues. Nevertheless, these expenditures represent some of the general costs of doing business. Because enterprises typically incur such costs to obtain benefits that they will exhaust in the same accounting period in which the costs are incurred, they usually recognize these costs as expenses in that same period.

(2) Systematic and Rational Allocation

As we observed in the deferral discussion, some expenditures do not relate to any particular transaction, but generally aid in the production of revenues in more than one accounting period. For example, an enterprise may enter into a multi-year lease, sign a long-term loan, or purchase a long-lived asset. An enterprise should charge the underlying costs, whenever actually paid, against the revenues for the periods in which the costs contribute generally to the enterprise's ability to produce revenues. To illustrate, assume that on January 1 of year one, an enterprise signs a three-year lease, agreeing to pay $30,000 in total rent on December 31 of year three. Because the enterprise will enjoy the benefit that the $30,000 expenditure produces ratably over the lease's duration, the enterprise should allocate the total rent ratably among the accounting periods that the lease covers. Thus, the enterprise should treat $10,000 as rent expense for year one and record an offsetting $10,000 long-term liability. Similarly, the enterprise will accrue $10,000 as rent expense for year two, increase the accrued rent liability account by $10,000, and treat the entire $20,000 as a current liability because the enterprise must pay that entire amount by December 31 of year three. Finally, the enterprise will record the remaining $10,000 in rent expense in year three when the enterprise actually pays the $30,000 rent due under the lease. Notice that this treatment mirrors the way we handled E. Tutt's three-year lease of office space on pages 79 and 82, *supra*, when the lease did not require her to pay the $15,000 rent until the end of the third year.

An expenditure may provide benefits in succeeding periods which do not correspond ratably to the passage of time. Suppose that on January 1 of year one an enterprise borrows $100,000 for three years at ten percent interest, compounded annually. If the loan does not require the borrower to pay any interest or principal until the loan matures, the borrower will owe $133,100, representing $100,000 principal and $33,100 interest, at maturity. You may recall that Table I in Appendix B tells us that one dollar will grow to $1.33100 if invested at ten percent compound interest for three years. Using that factor, we can readily see that the $100,000 original loan balance will grow to $133,100 at the end of three years.

Under the effective interest method, which we described on page 451, *supra*, however, the enterprise cannot automatically allocate one-third of the $33,100 interest to each of the loan's three years. Instead, the enterprise should treat ten percent of the $100,000 original loan balance, or $10,000, as interest expense for year one. This accrued interest increases the unpaid loan balance to $110,000. In year two, the enterprise would accrue ten percent of the $110,000 loan balance, or $11,000, as interest expense, which would bring the unpaid loan balance to $121,000. In year three, the enterprise would record $12,100, or ten percent of the $121,000 loan balance, as interest, even though the enterprise actually pays $33,100 in interest when repaying the loan.

(3) Lack or Loss of Future Benefit

Enterprises immediately recognize costs and losses that do not relate to specific or current revenues and do not provide future benefits beyond the period in which they are incurred. For example, amounts that an enterprise pays to settle litigation or to satisfy a judgment arising from matters arising in an earlier accounting period generally do not provide future benefits to the business. To the extent that the enterprise did not accrue an expense or loss in an earlier accounting period, the business immediately expenses such amounts. Similarly, enterprises immediately recognize losses when a business no longer expects a cost that the business recorded as an asset in a prior period to provide discernible future benefits. Finally, enterprises sometimes recognize costs as expenses in the period incurred because the enterprise either cannot determine the period to which the costs otherwise relate or concludes that the expense necessary to make such a determination does not justify the benefit.

PROBLEM

Problem 6.7. Assume that at the close of its fiscal year just ended the Pacific Grape Products Company had on hand $300,000 of completed canned goods inventory which had been ordered by customers but not yet labeled or shipped, the sales price of these goods was $420,000, the brokers' commissions were five percent of sales price, and the estimated cost of labeling and shipping the goods was $15,000. Assume further that if the company had treated these goods as not having been sold during the year just ended, and hence had not recognized the income and related expenses during that year, its balance sheet as of the close of that year would have appeared as follows:

Pacific Grape Products Company
Balance Sheet, End of 201X

Assets		Liabilities & Equity	
Cash	$ 90,000	Liabilities	
Accounts Receivable		Note Payable	$ 500,000
(net of $14,000		Accounts Payable	334,000
allowance for		Expenses Payable	75,000
doubtful accounts)	686,000	Estimated Liabilities	12,000
Inventory	580,000	Total Liabilities	$ 921,000
		Equity	
Fixed Assets (after		Common Stock	$1,500,000
depreciation)	1,634,000	Retained Earnings	579,000
Deferred Expenses	10,000	Total Equity	$2,079,000
Total Assets	$3,000,000	Total Liabilities & Equity	$3,000,000

How would the balance sheet look if the company treated these goods as sold during the year just ended? How would that treatment have affected the company's income statement? Which approach do you favor?

b. THE PROBLEM OF UNCOLLECTIBLE ACCOUNTS

As we saw during our discussion about revenue recognition, unless some special doubt exists about the buyer's ability to pay, a seller normally recognizes revenue from a sales transaction at the point when the seller has substantially completed the required performance. The fact that the buyer has not yet paid for the goods does not matter. If L Corp. completes a sale of goods in 20X1 to Jones Company for $1,000 on credit, L Corp. would record the following entry:

Accounts Receivable: Jones Co.	$1,000	
Sales Income		$1,000

Suppose that in 20X2 L Corp. learns that Jones Company has filed for bankruptcy and that the company's insolvency means that L Corp. will not collect any amount on the account receivable. Since that account receivable has become worthless, L Corp. should "write off" the account or eliminate the receivable from its books. To do so, L Corp. can simply credit the asset Accounts Receivable: Jones Co. As for the corresponding debit, L Corp. should theoretically reduce current revenue to reflect the fact that it inaccurately estimated sales revenue in the previous year. As a practical matter, however, most enterprises charge a current loss or expense account. But query, does reducing current revenues or charging the loss due to an uncollectible account against the year in which the account happens to become uncollectible meaningfully show current revenues or match expenses against the related income? Realistically, any losses stemming from uncollectible accounts are part of the cost of selling goods on credit, so L Corp. should offset those uncollectible amounts against the revenues from the sales which gave rise to the losses. L Corp., therefore, needs an entry each year to reflect the likely future losses resulting from credit sales made during that year. Of course, as already noted, if doubts about the buyer's solvency create a special risk that the buyer will default on the obligation to pay for the goods in a particular credit transaction, the seller should not recognize income until payment actually occurs. But, in fact, in the great majority of credit sales the seller collects the receivable in the ordinary course of business. Moreover, based on prior experience or other factors, the seller can usually reasonably predict the amount of defaults which will occur. Theoretically, each year a seller should estimate the expected uncollectible amounts on credit sales made during the year and reduce revenues by that amount. For whatever reason—perhaps historical practice, a desire to report current revenues as high as possible, or both—however, most enterprises record an expense to match such uncollectible amounts with the revenues to which they relate.

The technique for reflecting these future expected losses as an expense in the current year resembles the process for accruing any other expense before the enterprise pays the underlying amount. The seller debits a current expense account, often called "Bad Debt Expense" or perhaps "Uncollectible Accounts Expense," for the estimated amount of uncollectible credit sales during that year. Paralleling the normal practice of crediting an estimated liability account when an enterprise accrues an expense or loss prior to payment, the seller correspondingly credits an account which we can describe as an estimated liability. Two important differences, however, distinguish this account from other estimated liability accounts. First, this estimated-liability-type account does not represent a liability to pay money, or perform services, but rather represents the fact that the business will not actually collect some money which, by recording various accounts receivable, the enterprise projected it would receive in the future. Second, the account created to reflect estimated losses on credit sales usually appears on the balance sheet as an offset to accounts receivable, or, in accounting terminology, as a *contra asset* account, rather than separately as a liability, to give a more accurate picture about how much cash the enterprise actually expects to obtain from the receivables. Perhaps for these reasons, enterprises usually do not use an "Estimated Liability" caption for this account. Most enterprises commonly call the account something like "Allowance for Doubtful Accounts" or "Allowance." *See* AM. INST. OF CERTIFIED PUB. ACCOUNTANTS, ACCOUNTING TRENDS & TECHNIQUES § 2.23 (67th ed. 2013).

Historically, accountants have often referred to estimated-liability-type accounts, which an enterprise creates when accruing a conditional expense (or one requiring estimation of the amount) as a "Reserve." You should recognize that "Reserve for Bad Debts" means exactly the same thing as "Allowance for Doubtful Accounts."

An Allowance for Doubtful Accounts enables an enterprise to handle an account receivable which becomes uncollectible in a later period without affecting current income in that period. Upon determining that a particular account receivable has become either wholly or partly uncollectible, the enterprise can debit the Allowance for Doubtful Accounts to balance the credit to the account receivable which has become uncollectible. This entry does not affect the income statement, because both the account receivable and the *contra asset* Allowance for Doubtful Accounts affect only the balance sheet. This treatment differs from the normal practice regarding liability accounts only in the fact that the enterprise credits the worthless account receivable rather than cash. As a result, if L Corp. in the example above had previously created an Allowance for Doubtful Accounts, upon discovering in 20X2 that the account receivable from Jones had become totally uncollectible, S would record the following entry:

Allowance for Doubtful Accounts	$1,000	
Accounts Receivable: Jones Co.		$1,000

Occasionally, an enterprise receives some payment on an account receivable which the enterprise previously wrote off. Suppose, for example, that in 20X3 the Jones Company experienced some unexpected good fortune and paid $100 on its account with L Corp. Since the write-off of the account receivable did not affect current income, such a recovery should not affect current income either. Instead, L Corp. would view this collection as an indication that the company erroneously wrote off the entire account receivable. As a result, L Corp. would partially reverse that earlier entry and record an entry to reflect the cash receipt as follows:

Accounts Receivable: Jones Co.	$100	
Allowance for Doubtful Accounts		$100
Cash	100	
Accounts Receivable: Jones Co.		100

In practice, L Corp. might well combine the two entries into a single entry, which reaches the same end point, as follows:

Cash	$100	
Allowance for Doubtful Accounts		$100

This single entry, however, would not reflect the fact that Jones Company eventually paid a portion of its account.

Incidentally, the Allowance for Doubtful Accounts does not attempt to isolate the credit losses from different years in separate accounts. Instead, enterprises use a single continuing Allowance for Doubtful Accounts. An enterprise increases the Allowance account each year by a credit, corresponding to the debit to current expense, in the amount of the year's credit sales that the enterprise estimates will become uncollectible. As we noted, the Allowance account also increases for any credits to reflect collections on accounts receivable that the enterprise had previously written off as worthless. Conversely, the Allowance account decreases by the amount of the accounts receivable which the enterprise wrote off because the receivables actually become worthless during the year.*

---

*We should mention one mechanical bookkeeping refinement at this point. An enterprise may write off worthless accounts receivable directly against the Allowance for Doubtful Accounts, and likewise credit receipts from accounts receivable previously written off directly to that account. But bookkeepers often prefer to keep a separate account to reflect the amount of accounts receivable which have become uncollectible during the period and another separate account to show the collections on accounts receivable previously written off. Accordingly, some bookkeepers set up special temporary subaccounts for the Allowance for Doubtful Accounts, typically called "Bad Debts Charged Off" and "Bad Debts Collected," respectively, to reflect these items. In that event, when an enterprise writes off an account receivable as uncollectible, the bookkeeper debits the Bad Debts Charged Off account. At the end of the period, the bookkeeper would close that account to the left-hand side of the Allowance for Doubtful Accounts. Similarly, when an enterprise receives a payment on an account receivable previously written off as uncollectible, the bookkeeper credits the Bad Debts Collected account. At the end of the period, the bookkeeper would close the total in that account to the right-hand side of the Allowance for Doubtful Accounts. While management may use the Bad Debts Charged Off and Bad Debt Collected accounts to analyze the enterprise's overall credit picture, these subaccounts represent mechanical refinements which we can easily dispense with.

In estimating the amount to credit to the Allowance for Doubtful Accounts for an accounting period, an enterprise encounters a challenge not present when estimating the amount for an expense which the enterprise has incurred but not yet paid. As we have already discussed, the Allowance account reflects the expense of doing business on a credit basis in the respective years in which the enterprise sold items or rendered services on credit. In this respect, the Allowance for Doubtful Accounts functions much like an ordinary estimated liability account, such as estimated telephone expense payable. As with an ordinary estimated liability account, experience normally serves as the best guide for determining the proper amount. In fact, for a new enterprise, or one which has not previously extended credit to customers, information from similar enterprises can help the enterprise reach a fairly accurate estimate about the percentage of credit transactions which will result in uncollectible accounts in that industry. As a result, the enterprise might consider this figure as the *prima facie* cost of doing business on credit for the period.

But the Allowance for Doubtful Accounts performs a second important function not served by ordinary estimated liability accounts. In terms of liquidity, the accounts receivable on a balance sheet rank second only to cash, and perhaps marketable securities. As a result all kinds of investors, but particularly short-term creditors, pay particular attention to accounts receivable. Accordingly, in recording accounts receivable on the balance sheet, an enterprise must give special consideration to the amount that the enterprise actually expects to collect or, in other words, the asset's real value. If an enterprise lists the gross amount of outstanding accounts receivables without in some way indicating the likelihood that not all of those receivables will prove collectible, the enterprise will mislead both current and potential investors and creditors. For this reason, GAAP dictates that the Allowance for Doubtful Accounts appear on the balance sheet as a deduction from Accounts Receivable, rather than on the right-hand side of the balance sheet as a liability. FASB ASC ¶ 310-10-45-4 (a codification of Omnibus Opinion—1967, Accounting Principles Board Opinion No. 12, ¶ 3 (Am. Inst. of Certified Pub. Accountants 1967)).

The Allowance for Doubtful Accounts, therefore, serves a vital function in reducing the gross amount of accounts receivable to the net amount that an enterprise actually expects to collect. This important role, however, also means that an enterprise should not leave the size of the Allowance account entirely to the annual additions that the enterprise bases upon the percentage of credit sales during the period which previous experience indicates will become uncollectible. Instead, an enterprise should carefully analyze the existing accounts receivable at the end of each year to determine whether the figure in the Allowance account represents the best possible estimate of the amount of the receivables that will prove uncollectible. As a practical matter, business experience confirms that the "age" of the outstanding receivables significantly affects their collectibility. As a receivable becomes progressively overdue, the likelihood of non-payment increases dramatically. An enterprise, therefore, should pay careful attention to how old the existing accounts receivable have become. For example, an enterprise may divide receivables among such categories as, say, less than three months old, between three and six months, between six and twelve months, and more than twelve months old. An enterprise should also consider any other special circumstances that may affect particular accounts. The figure that this process produces should appear in the Allowance account at the end of the year. An enterprise should therefore record a corresponding increase or decrease in the charge to current expense, typically the Bad Debt Expense account, to set the amount in the Allowance account at the desired level.

As an example of the "miscellaneous 'cookie jar reserves'" that then-SEC Chairman Arthur Levitt described as the "third [accounting] illusion," he specifically listed "loan losses." See page 383, *supra*. These loan losses are nothing more than the "Bad Debt Expense" for the estimated uncollectible amounts in the loan portfolio of a bank or other financial institution. As one of the its financial reporting initiatives following then-Chairman Levitt's "The 'Numbers Game'" remarks, the SEC expressed concern that financial institutions have intentionally created and maintained large reserves, or allowances for loan losses, in good economic times to pad against potential losses during economic downturns. During its acquisition of Crestar Financial Corp., SunTrust Banks Inc. agreed with the SEC in 1998 to revise its reported earnings and reduce its expenses for loan losses by $100 million for the three-year period from 1994 to 1996. Seeking to avoid another savings and loan-type crisis, banking regulators have repeatedly cautioned banks to manage credit risk exposure prudently and warned that the SEC's efforts could cause banks to ignore conservatism and to cut reserves for loan losses.

The recent financial crisis has reignited the debate among investors, regulators, standard-setters, and executives about how enterprises, especially banks and other financial institutions, should calculate their reserves for loan losses—similar to the allowance for doubtful accounts at a retailer or wholesaler—and the appropriate time to increase those reserves. During the crisis, many companies, especially banks and thrifts, have suffered huge losses from bad loans. As the economic downturn began and credit quality started to deteriorate, some companies anticipated more defaults and increased their bad-loan reserves, thereby lowering reported earnings. Other companies preferred to rely on their historical experience and did not increase their reserves, which kept current profits high. *See, e.g.*, Peter Eavis, *New Threat: Loan Losses*, WALL ST. J., Apr. 22, 2008, at C3; Robin Sidel & David Reilly, *No Worries: Banks Keeping Less Money in Reserve*, WALL ST. J., Feb. 27, 2007, at C7.

PROBLEM

Problem 6.8. Suppose that it was the practice of Pacific Grape Products to charge Bad Debt Expense each month in the amount of one-quarter percent of the credit sales made during the month, with a corresponding credit to Allowance for Doubtful Accounts. On $5,000,000 of sales during the year (not including, it will be recalled, the $420,000 relating to the goods ordered but not shipped at year end), this practice produced $12,500 of Bad Debt Expense for the year. The $14,000 in the Allowance account was the product of $12,000 in the account at the beginning of the year, plus the $12,500 charged to current expense and $1,000 received during the year on accounts previously written off, less $11,500 of accounts receivable written off during the year and charged against the Allowance account.

The company follows the practice of fixing the amount in the Allowance account at year end on the basis of "aging" its account receivables. Under the company's credit terms, payment is due within thirty days, and the company's experience is that once thirty days has passed without payment the percentage of loss rises steeply, the older the accounts. This past experience indicates that the figure in the Allowance account should be at least equal to the sum of the following percentages of the respective age categories: one-quarter percent of the existing receivables less than one month old; two percent of the receivables between one and three months; seven percent of the receivables between three and six months old; twenty-five percent of those between six and twelve months old; and seventy-five of those over a year old. The following table shows the breakdown of the company's receivables among the various age categories at the end of its recent fiscal year, and the percentage of each category which should be reflected in the allowance account:

Age Category	Amount of Receivables	Percentage
Less than one month old	$440,000	¼%
One to three months	200,000	2%
Three to six months	40,000	7%
Six to twelve months	16,000	25%
Over twelve months	4,000	75%

(a) What entry should the company make at the close of the year as a result of this aging procedure?

(b) Would your answer change if the issue arose in the context of applying an employee bonus provision based upon "annual net profits from operations?"

(c) If the board of directors asked whether the company could lawfully declare a dividend under a statute which provides that a corporation may "declare and pay dividends upon the shares of its capital stock out of its surplus," would your answer change?

(d) If the company recognizes in the year just ended the sale of those goods ordered but not shipped at year end, how, if at all, would that treatment affect the Allowance account?

c. MATCHING EXPENSES FOR INCOME TAX PURPOSES

As we saw earlier in the *Boise Cascade* case, *supra* at pages 459 to 465, different objectives underlie financial accounting and federal income tax reporting. In *United States v. Hughes Properties, Inc.*, 476 U.S. 593, 603, the Supreme Court observed that financial accounting strives "to provide useful and pertinent information to management, shareholders, and creditors," while federal income tax accounting seeks "to protect the public fisc." While prudent businesses often accrue reasonably foreseeable expenses, section 461(h) of the

Internal Revenue Code requires a taxpayer to satisfy both an "all events" test and an "economic performance" requirement to claim a deduction for an accrued expense. *See* 26 U.S.C. § 461(h) (2012). As a result, not all financial accounting accruals give rise to immediate tax deductions. A taxpayer meets the all events test if all events have occurred that determine the fact of liability and the taxpayer can ascertain the liability's amount with reasonable accuracy. A taxpayer cannot deduct contingent or contested expenses. The related Treasury Regulations provide, subject to various exceptions, that economic performance occurs when the taxpayer pays the person to which the liability is owed. Treas. Reg. § 1.461–4(g)(1) (as amended in 1999). Time value of money concepts explain and support the economic performance requirement. Before Congress added the economic performance requirement to the Internal Revenue Code, a taxpayer could claim a deduction for expenses that related to amounts that the taxpayer would pay in future years. The immediate deduction, however, created a windfall to the taxpayer to the extent that the deduction exceeded the future payment's present value.

3. OTHER ISSUES INVOLVING ACCRUAL OF EXPENSE AND DEFERRAL OF INCOME

The issues which we have been discussing, namely whether an enterprise should charge off an expenditure in the current period, or whether an expenditure will provide benefits beyond the end of the current period, and if so, for how long and in what amount, illustrate the kinds of judgment questions that accountants constantly face and which concern lawyers. Although an enterprise should attempt to match related revenues and expenses, very close questions can arise as to in which accounting period to do so. An enterprise probably satisfies the accounting requirements as long as it uses reasonable criteria in making these decisions, applies those criteria consistently to similar transactions and from accounting period to period, and, if material, discloses the criteria. In the common case where an expense's payment precedes receipt of the related income, however, the more stringent limitations on income recognition control the decision, and the enterprise must defer the expense until it can recognize the income. Whatever period the enterprise selects, deferral and accrual of expense or income items provide the mechanics for implementing the enterprise's decision.

We should note that businesses can conceivably accomplish matching in ways other than deferring advance receipts until the business incurs the related expenses. For example, an enterprise could instead recognize the advance receipts in current income, and then accrue the estimated amount of related future expenses into that year, thereby matching the two in the period the enterprise received the advances. But that would require a great deal of estimating with respect to the related future expenses, which would reduce the reliability of the enterprise's financial reporting. As observed earlier, accountants follow the general rule that a business should not recognize the income from a transaction until the required performance has been at least substantially completed, because by that point the business will have incurred most of the related expenses, reducing the need to estimate future expenses.

Notice that whenever the liability account which an enterprise creates to accrue an expense reflects an obligation to perform or provide services, the liability bears some resemblance to a Deferred Income account, which also reflects an obligation to perform services or deliver goods. On page 82, *supra*, we suggested that under some circumstances an enterprise should record an obligation to pay an expense in the future as a liability on the balance sheet even though the enterprise does not charge the underlying expense against current income. Take the brokers' commissions in Problem 6.7 on page 478, *supra*. If Pacific Grape treats the $300,000 in goods which customers ordered, but which the company had not shipped at the end of the year, as not sold during that year, then the principles of matching dictate that the company should not charge these commissions to expense for that year. In this circumstance, the company would normally not create an Expense Payable account, and the liability for the brokers' commissions would not appear on the balance sheet at the close of that year. Suppose, however, as suggested in the *Pacific Grape* case, pages 441 to 444, *supra*, that the brokers had earned their commissions as of the end of the year. Query whether Pacific Grape potentially misleads investors if the balance sheet does not show this liability. If Pacific Grape records the liability, the company must make a corresponding debit, and, as the discussion on page 82, *supra*, suggests, creating a deferred cost asset would appear to offer the only acceptable alternative, even though cash has not moved.

Similar issues may arise regarding decisions to reflect receivables prior to recognizing the related income. For example, take the $420,000 which the customers had contracted to pay Pacific Grape for the goods which they had ordered, but that the company had not shipped at year end. Although traditional accounting would seem to suggest that Pacific Grape should not record the right to receive this amount until the company recognizes the income from the transaction, notice how Ebasco, in the *Boise Cascade* case, accounted for amounts billed for services not yet performed, as described in the last full paragraph on page 460, *supra*.

PROBLEMS

Problem 6.9. How, if at all, would your answer to Problem 6.5 change if Pacific Grape did not pay the $40,000 on December 31, 20X1, even though that amount became payable on that date. How should Pacific Grape reflect the spot advertising on its financial statements for 20X1?

Problem 6.10A. Assume that early in its most recent calendar year Ebasco (E) learned that a large utility, P Corp., might be interested in obtaining engineering and consulting services in connection with construction of a new generating plant. One of E's three sales representatives, who work full-time soliciting this kind of business for E, on a straight salary of $60,000 per year each, without commissions, spent all of his time for four months trying to land a contract with P. In addition, since P was considering a number of unusual features for its new plant, E retained a well-known scientist to work with its regular staff during the spring on the preparation of a proposal to P Corp., for which the scientist was paid $39,000. In July E got the contract, which called for specified engineering and other consulting services over the following fifteen to eighteen months in connection with building the new plant. Under the contract, E was to receive a total of $500,000, payable at the rate of $100,000 every three months, starting on September 15, regardless of when E's services were actually performed. Due to delays in P's construction schedule, E had in fact performed no services for P by the close of the calendar year.

(1) How should these facts be reflected in E's financial statements for the year?

(2) Suppose instead that by the end of the first year E had incurred costs of $45,000 in performing under the contract with P, having originally estimated that the total cost of its performance under the contract would amount to $300,000. How should E reflect the transaction in its financial statements for that year (a) assuming, as before, that P has paid $100,000 of the total contract price by the end of the year, or (b) assuming instead that P has not made any payment by the end of the year because the contract did not require any payment until E finished the job?

Problem 6.10B. X Corp. sells and services computers, mostly to individuals for personal use. As a feature of its general sales policy, X provides to each buyer a right to have the computer thoroughly checked and serviced on one occasion during the calendar year following the purchase. X adds $60 to the computer's selling price to cover this feature, because its experience has confirmed that the average cost of fulfilling this commitment to check and service has averaged about $50 per computer. For the year of sale, how should X account for the $60 cash received and the prospective $50 cost to be incurred in the following year?

Problem 6.10C. Suppose that in 20X1 the O'Hara Company entered into a contract calling for the manufacture and delivery of goods in 20X2 for $1,000,000. The company estimated that it would cost $612,000 to perform the contract. What entries would the company make at the close of 20X1 if it wanted to reflect the profit on this contract in 20X1? Would that be proper? What if the issue was how large a dividend O'Hara Company could pay?

Problem 6.11. Culinary Corporation (CC) is a large, publicly-owned corporation operating a chain of rapid service restaurants under the name "Chicken Counter" throughout the country. CC keeps its books of account on a fiscal year basis, and its most recent fiscal year just ended last month. After considerable growth earlier, a few years ago CC's net income leveled out at around $3,000,000, on sales revenues of approximately $50,000,000. In an effort to expand its operations, CC's management decided to embark on a franchising program, under which local entrepreneurs would be awarded a permanent franchise to operate a restaurant under the name and distinctive style of "Chicken Counter." The cost of a franchise was set at $50,000, payable $10,000 down and $10,000 per year for each of the next four years; in case of default in such payments, CC reserved the right to cancel the franchise and treat payments made to date as liquidated damages. In addition, the franchisee is required to pay CC annual royalties in the amount of 2% of the franchisee's sales. The franchise agreements also required that the enterprise be operated in strict accordance with CC's rules and regulations, and many of the items sold in the restaurant were expected to be purchased from CC.

The new franchise program was formally adopted by CC's board of directors about eighteen months ago, with sales of the franchises to start a couple of months later. Management believed that for the foreseeable future the optimum number of franchises which CC could properly service and supervise would be about 120, and they planned to award about forty new franchises a year until that number was reached. It was expected that the cost of getting forty franchises started, consisting of such things as site selection, start-up advertising and promotion, and pre-operation training of franchise personnel, would amount to approximately $720,000.

The new franchise program got off to a slow start in the first year (20X1), and no franchises had been sold by the beginning of CC's most recent fiscal year (20X2). While there was no dearth of applicants for franchises, it proved to be more difficult than expected to screen the applicants and decide which ones should receive franchises. In fact, CC's initial lack of standardized procedures for selecting applicants had led to substantial controversy with some of the applicants, who claimed that they had been promised franchises by certain of CC's representatives. Several lawsuits had been commenced or threatened by the end of 20X1, with damages sought in amounts ranging from $30,000 to $70,000 per claim. In the opinion of CC's counsel, ten of the disappointed applicants had strong claims for breach of contract against CC, for amounts ranging from $20,000 to $30,000 each; CC's financial statements for that fiscal year contained a footnote making general reference to the company's possible liability on this account. However, by the beginning of 20X2 CC had substantially improved its procedures for dealing with applicants for franchises, and no additional claims of this sort were expected.

Early last year, CC's management decided that a substantial promotional campaign should be undertaken to publicize the new franchise program. After consulting with its long-time advertising firm about the most effective promotion program for the sale of franchises, CC adopted a plan under which $800,000 was expended last year (20X2) in promoting the sale of franchises, and another $400,000 is to be spent during the current year (20X3); no further franchise advertising is expected to be needed next year (20X4) to sell the last 40 franchises.

As the sale of new franchises began to pick up momentum during 20X2, CC's management decided that it would be advisable not to incur the risk of unfavorable publicity that might result from trial of the claims of the disappointed applicants for franchises. Accordingly, CC instructed its counsel to settle all of these claims on as favorable terms as possible, which counsel succeeded in doing well before the end 20X2, at a total cost of $240,000. By the close of 20X2, CC had sold its first forty franchises for $2,000,000, of which it had received down payments totaling $400,000.

CC's management is aware that franchise companies have been the subject of special attention in the stock market, with a good deal of concern expressed about not only the picture of current operations for such companies but also their long-term growth rate. Accordingly, management wants to be very careful about how the facts relating to the franchise program are reflected in the company's financial statements for 20X2, which are already in the process of preparation. CC's management had consulted the senior partner in your office, who in turn has asked for your views on the matter, particularly with regard to whether income should be recognized on the sale of the forty franchises, and, if so, in what manner.

D. Drafting and Negotiating Agreements and Other Legal Documents Containing Terminology Implicating the Income Statement

At the end of Chapter V on pages 345 to 351, *supra*, we reviewed in some detail accounting terminology and concepts involving the balance sheet and their appearance in agreements and legal documents. Attorneys also frequently draft and negotiate agreements and documents that implicate the income statement, such as an employment agreement or a labor contract with a bonus provision based upon the business's net income. The following excerpts, again adapted from written materials distributed at a seminar that the Practising Law Institute sponsored, offer some very practical suggestions focus on terminology and concepts underlying the income statement.

Terry Lloyd, *Financial Language in Legal Documents**
adapted and revised from Accounting for Lawyers 1994 at 261, 276–77, 283, 290–322 (1994).

Specific Accounting Concerns

* * *

Although reliance on GAAP has advantages, in some cases it may be appropriate to disregard or modify GAAP and use a different basis of accounting. GAAP is based on accrual accounting, [which] is believed to more accurately portray the financial status and results of operations of an economic enterprise–and is less susceptible to distortion. There are, nevertheless, circumstances in which it may be more appropriate to use cash basis accounting[–for example,] in connection with the sale of a professional practice, which typically operates on a cash basis accounting system.

The notion that GAAP "is what it is" is wrong and should not be used as an excuse for not making the effort to draft accounting provisions which more appropriately reflect the intentions of the parties.

Agreements Employing Revenue and Earnings Concepts

Many agreements use an enterprise's revenues or earnings as the basis of determining the amount of a payment or payments to be received by one or more of the parties. Attorneys drafting such agreements should be aware of the various possible accounting choices so that their clients will not be deprived of their rightfully anticipated compensation. Revenue or earnings formulas are typically found in the following types of agreements:

- acquisition agreements where the purchase price is based in whole or in part on the future earnings of the acquired business (an "earn out");

- employment or consulting agreements providing for the payment of a bonus based on the revenues or earnings of the employing enterprise;

- license, royalty and franchise agreements where the compensation paid to the licensor or franchisor is based on the revenues or earnings of the licensee or franchisee;

- partnership or joint venture agreements providing for distributions to partners to be based on the earnings of the partnership or venture during each accounting period;

- preferred stock provisions which provide for the payment of dividends out of the earnings (as defined) of the corporation; and

- pension or other employment termination benefits based on the earnings of the sponsor.

Primary Considerations

Perhaps the first question faced in drafting a revenue or earnings formula is to determine which of these measurements is more appropriate. A revenue basis is generally best suited in situations where the party to be compensated makes a direct or indirect contribution to the enterprise's revenues but has little or no control over the enterprise's overall operations. For this reason, sales and marketing personnel as well as independent contractors and trademark and patent licensors are typically compensated on the basis of the other party's revenues (top line), as opposed to its earnings (bottom line) which can be manipulated. Franchise agreements also tend to look to revenues for calculating the fee paid to the franchisor, especially where the franchisor's business format has a proven track record (like McDonald's). However, where the business format is relatively untried, the net results of the franchisee's operations are likely to be as much a reflection of the franchisor's operating formula as the franchisee's managerial skills. In such circumstances, the franchisor should not be entitled to any compensation unless the franchisee is generating a profit.

A second primary consideration is to determine the nature of the revenues or earnings to be used as the basis for determining the compensation to be paid. For example, will the determining revenues or earnings be those of a single company or those of the consolidated group; will the earnings be before or after income taxes; will they be computed on a cash basis or on an accrual basis; and will they include or exclude any unusual or nonrecurring items, gains or losses arising from discontinued operations, or extraordinary items? The answers to each of these questions will materially affect the amount of compensation payable under the formula.

* * *

Normally computations of earnings are made on an after-tax basis; however, where the subject company has a net loss carry forward or is a part of a consolidated group which includes companies generating losses, the after-tax earnings may not fairly represent the results of operations of the subject company. In such circumstances, it may be preferable to base payments on pretax earnings. Extraordinary items may similarly distort the earnings of an enterprise. Unlike the issues presented above, extraordinary revenues and expenses do not necessarily result from the subject company's operations during the measuring period. For example, a substantial portion of the subject company's assets or operations might be sold during the measuring period, the proceeds of which might reflect value generated over many prior periods. Conversely, the subject company's earnings might be reduced by reason of an uninsured casualty loss. Neither of these events may accurately reflect the value of the subject enterprise or the efforts of the formula's beneficiary during the actual measurement period. On the other hand, if extraordinary gains are excluded, the purchaser of a business could sell off parts, thereby reducing its earnings capacity and the resulting payments required to be made under the earnings formula to the seller. For these reasons, the effect of extraordinary items should be carefully considered before adopting any revenues or earnings formula.

In normal usage, "earnings" and "net income" include extraordinary items, while "operating income" does not. Under GAAP, extraordinary items are defined as "events and transactions that are distinguished by their unusual nature and the infrequency of their occurrence." This definition is quite restrictive and would exclude a number of items which a layman might view as being "extraordinary" * * *.

* * *

Specific Accounts

There is a great tendency in drafting any earnings or revenue formula to simply use the subject enterprise's revenues or earnings (as the case may be) "as determined in accordance with generally accepted accounting principles consistently applied." Doing so, however, ignores the fact that GAAP leaves to business enterprises wide latitude in selecting accounting methods as well as operational decisions that could materially affect the magnitude of their reportable earnings. For this reason, it is absolutely essential to consider the various available accounting elections and make those choices at the outset that will benefit your client. These elections need only be for the purpose of computing payments under the agreement and need not prevent the enterprise from making different choices for other purposes, such as regulatory or tax filings. * * *

* * *

Changes in Accounting Methods and Estimates. Most agreements for determining payments using earnings or income formulas require that the generally accepted accounting principles applied will be consistent with those previously applied. Although this simple restriction will eliminate many questions, it may not answer all-important accounting choices. For example, the determination of cost allocations or useful lives of assets or the percentage of allowance for bad debts are referred to in accounting language as "estimates" and are not considered generally accepted accounting principles. It takes little imagination to see that changes in "estimates" can have an equal, if not greater, impact on reportable earnings than changes in principles. As a result, the consistency clause should, at a very minimum, encompass accounting estimates. Changes in the company's operations could mandate the application of different accounting principles. For example, if the reporting company (previously only a manufacturing company) decided to open retail outlets, it might be required (or at least permitted) to calculate its finished goods inventory under a different generally accepted accounting principle. Similarly, if it changed the terms on which it sold its products (for example, by adopting a liberal return policy), it might be required under GAAP to alter the method by which it recognized its revenues.

Lastly, there is the realistic possibility that GAAP itself might change during the term of the agreement, raising the issue of whether earnings are to be computed in accordance with GAAP or on a basis consistent with past accounting practices ("old GAAP") or what the party is currently doing ("new GAAP"). This is not merely an academic consideration. The FASB is constantly rethinking previously established generally accepted accounting principles (including those established by the FASB itself) and every such change could have a serious effect on an outstanding contractual arrangement. * * *

Unfortunately, there is no simple answer to the problems posed by operational changes or changes in GAAP. Nevertheless, attorneys drafting agreements in situations where such changes may be likely should try to deal with these issues by at least setting general guidelines as to how they should be handled.

* * *

Operational Changes. One potential problem is posed by expansion of operations which are likely to generate losses during the measurement periods. For example, consider the situation of a seller of a small chain of retail stores who is to receive a portion of the purchase price based on the earnings of the chain over the next three years. Immediately following the sale, the new owner embarks on an ambitious expansion program whereby all profits (in addition to borrowed funds) are immediately poured back into new stores which operate at a loss for their first 18 months. This results in no reportable earnings—and no contingent payment to your client, the seller. In order to protect the seller under such circumstances, her attorney may wish to employ one or more of the following covenants:

- No changes in the operations of the acquired company during the payout period without the consent of the seller;

- No losses from new operations will be offset against the earnings of the operations in existence at the time of the sale; or

- For the purposes of the payout arrangement, new operations shall be deemed to have earned the same percentage of their sales as existing operations.

* * *

Repairs and Maintenance. A variation on the expanded operations gambit is for the new owner of an acquired business to embark on a campaign of extensive repairs and preventive maintenance during the measuring period, with the result that reportable "earnings" and the seller's contingent payment will be sharply reduced. To protect against this possibility, seller's counsel might seek to place a cap on repair and maintenance costs either in dollar or percentage terms. Rather than concern himself with every potential area of distortion, the lawyer drafting the agreement may avoid this detail (and potential for oversight) by dealing with an appropriate "top line" concept [as described on page 346, *supra*].

Related Party Transactions. Related party transactions come in numerous forms and always carry the potential of distorting financial results. Accordingly, where the reporting company buys or sells goods or services from or to an affiliated company or will likely do so during the measuring period, the parties must reach an understanding regarding the pricing of such goods or services to insure that earnings are not diverted to another enterprise. Similarly, where the reporting company shares resources with an affiliate, the allocation of those shared costs can have a substantial impact on reportable earnings. To guard against such pricing and allocation abuses, payee's counsel might wish to specify that the subject company will buy goods and services from affiliated companies at their cost or on a "most favored nation" basis and all cost allocations must be expressly approved by the payee.

* * *

NOTE

1. You may recall from the discussion in Chapter V that given the devastating effects that changes in accounting principles can cause in restrictive covenants and other legal documents, lawyers should try to stay abreast of the FASB's activities and agenda. With that suggestion in mind, we highlight several developments and areas to watch regarding the income statement.

(a) *Comprehensive Income.* Now that FASBASC Topic 220, *Comprehensive Income*, which codified SFAS No. 130, requires enterprises to report and display "comprehensive income" to reflect all nonowner changes in equity, will or should "comprehensive income" replace the terms "income" or "net income" in various financial contracts? Do references to "income" or "net income" in existing contracts really mean "comprehensive income" as the new "bottom line?" For example, can management include increases in unrealized holding gains on securities when computing bonuses based upon a certain percentage of "income?" Can management exclude unrealized losses on derivatives contracts that only affect "comprehensive income?"

(b) *Earnings Per Share*. How do the requirements in FASB ASC Topic 260, *Earnings Per Share*, which codified SFAS No. 128, that enterprises compute "basic earnings per share" and "diluted earnings per share" affect references to "primary earnings per share" and "fully diluted earnings per share" in previously existing contracts that do not address changes in generally accepted accounting principles? How should courts interpret contracts entered into after SFAS No. 128's effective date, but that use the old terms "primary earnings per share" or "fully diluted earnings per share?"

(c) *Stock options*. In a so-called "share-based payment" transaction, which often refers to a "stock option," an enterprise issues certain ownership interests in exchange for services. FASB ASC Topic 718, *Compensation—Stock Compensation*, which codified SFAS No. 123(R), *Share-Based Payment*, requires companies to treat the fair value of any such awards, determined on the grant date, as an expense, which would reduce net income. Enterprises must select and apply a valuation model for this purpose. FASB ASC § 718-10-30 (a codification of SFAS No. 123(R)). Even before many companies began issuing financial statements adopting the new rules, *The Wall Street Journal* published a front-page, Pulitzer prize-winning story in 2006 that exposed widespread scandals involving backdated stock options. By the end of 2013, a study by Audit Analytics found that 181 lawsuits, including civil and criminal government investigations, arising from alleged stock-option backdating had been resolved. According to the analysis, the companies involved adjusted their earnings downward by $11.1 billion. Collectively, the litigation cost companies and their executives, auditors, and advisors about $7.3 billion. Dozens of executives also lost their jobs. *See* Emily Chason, *The Big Number[: 181]*, WALL. ST. J., Nov. 26, 2013, at B5; Mark Maremont & John Hechinger, *Brocade Settles Suit for $160 Million*, WALL ST. J., June 3, 2008, at B4; Mark Maremont & Charles Forelle, *Bosses' Pay: How Stock Options Became Part of the Problem*, WALL ST. J., Dec. 27, 2006, at A1; Charles Forelle & James Bandler, *The Perfect Payday*, WALL ST. J., Mar. 18, 2006, at A1.

(d) *Uncertain tax positions*. In 2006, the FASB issued a new promulgation on uncertain income taxes that has established consistent criteria for reporting uncertain tax positions. Prior to the pronouncement, diverse accounting practices for income tax reserves provided opportunities for earnings management, and few companies disclosed details on the nature or amount of the reserves. Under the new rules, enterprises must record a liability for "unrecognized tax benefits," tax benefits claimed on tax returns which may not withstand scrutiny by taxing authorities. Most enterprises have recorded greater provisions for income tax and recognized more liabilities for income taxes than under previous practice.

FASB ASC Subtopic 740-10 (a codification of FASB Interpretation No. 48, *Accounting for Uncertainty in Income Taxes (an Interpretation of FASB Statement No. 109))* requires enterprises to examine each open tax position that constitutes a "unit of account," a judgment based on how the enterprise prepares its tax return and how the enterprise believes the taxing authority will approach the return. A two-step process then applies to analyze each uncertain tax position. The first step involves recognition: the enterprise can recognize only those tax benefits "more likely than not" sustainable, on their technical merits, upon examination. The enterprise must presume taxing authorities with full knowledge of all relevant information will examine the position. The second step focuses on measurement: the enterprise measures tax positions meeting the recognition criteria at the largest amount of benefit "more likely than not" realizable upon ultimate settlement. The enterprise makes measurements in light of the facts, circumstances, and information available at the reporting date. The rules require disclosures to provide more information for financial statement users regarding an enterprise's uncertain tax positions, including descriptions regarding any material positions for which unrecognized tax benefits will reasonably possibly and significantly increase or decrease within the next twelve months. For public entities, the disclosures include a tabular reconciliation of the total amount of unrecognized tax benefits at the beginning and end of the period. FASB ASC ¶¶ 740-10-25-6 to -7, -13, 740-10-30-7, 740-10-50-15, 740-10-50-15A (codifications of FIN 48, ¶¶ 5-8, 21, as amended by ASU 2009-06, *Implementation Guidance on Accounting for Uncertainty in Income Taxes and Disclosure Amendments for Nonpublic Entities*).

If the uncertain tax benefit fails to meet the recognition criteria, the enterprise must establish a liability for "unrecognized tax benefits," with a corresponding increase in tax expense. The liability, often referred to as a "reserve," reflects tax benefits claimed on tax returns but not allowed for financial reporting purposes. In 2007, a Credit Suisse Group study examined the financial reporting consequences at 361 large companies. The resulting research report found that those companies had recognized a combined $141 billion in tax liabilities under the new interpretation. Analysts have noted that the new approach may overstate tax liabilities and artificially increase debt ratios because the liabilities recorded will likely exceed the cash ultimately paid to taxing authorities. In addition, as facts and circumstances change, management's assessment of these estimated liabilities will likely fluctuate over time, which increases earnings volatility. *See* Jesse Drucker, *Lifting the Veil on Tax Risk*, WALL ST. J., May 25, 2007, at C1.

The FASB designed the new required disclosures to provide investors with more information about the uncertainty in income tax assets and liabilities. Tax authorities, predictably, will also read these new disclosures carefully, as discussed in Chapter VII on page 575, *infra*.

(e) *Securitizations and Consolidations.* As discussed earlier on page 433 and 434, *supra*, amendments to FASB ASC Topic 810, *Consolidation*, and Topic 860, *Transfers and Servicing*, which codified new rules in SFAS No. 166, *Accounting for Transfers of Financial Assets[–]an amendment of FASB*

Statement No. 140, and SFAS No. 167, *Amendments to FASB Interpretation No. 46(R),* have enlarged the balance sheets of the nation's banks and financial institutions by forcing QSPEs—and their hundreds of billions of dollars in underlying assets and liabilities—onto the banks' balance sheets. Discover Financial Services Inc., for example, disclosed that the rules, which FASB issued in 2009, forced the company to bring $21 billion in assets onto its books and to increase its loss reserves by $2.1 billion, which caused a $1.3 billion after-tax reduction in shareholders' equity in 2010's first quarter. J.P. Morgan Chase & Co. needed to consolidate about $145 billion in assets after the new rule. Aparajita Saha-Bubna, *Discover Financial Plans New Accounting Rule,* WSJ.com, Mar. 12, 2010; Susan Pulliam, *Banks Try to Stiff-Arm New Rule,* Wall. St. J., June 4, 2009, at C1. In addition to requiring additional regulatory capital to support the larger balance sheets, the new financial accounting requirements affected leverage and coverage ratios in loan agreements and other contracts.

Still more changes to the financial accounting standards governing consolidations appear likely. In 2011, and as part of a joint project with the IASB on consolidation policy and procedures, the FASB issued a proposed accounting standards update that would affect all companies that must evaluate whether they should consolidate another entity. When evaluating whether the Codification treats an affiliate as an VIE, and, if so whether a reporting entity should consolidate the affiliate, the reporting entity would need to consider whether the applicable decision-maker is exercising its power as a principal or an agent. *See* Consolidations (Topic 810), Principal versus Agent Analysis Accounting, Proposed Standards Update (Fin. Accounting Standards Bd. Nov. 3, 2011), *available via* http://www.fasb.org/cs/Content Server?site=FASB&c=Page&pagename=FASB%2FPage%2FSectionPage& cid=1175801893139. In addition, the proposed update would rescind an indefinite deferral for certain investment funds. This change could require financial institutions to consolidate affiliated money-funds in the $2.6 trillion money market industry, which currently qualify for "off-balance-sheet" treatment. *See* Martin Gonzalez & David Reilly, *Banks: Show Investors the Money (Funds),* Wall St. J., Mar. 26, 2012, at C10. Once again, any amendments could necessitate additional regulatory capital and might affect leverage and coverage ratios in loan agreements and other contracts. According to the FASB's Project Roster and Status listing, the board plans to issue final guidance in early 2015. Interested readers can monitor developments in the "Consolidation: Policy and Procedures" project via http://www.fasb.org/jsp/FASB/Page/SectionPage&cid=1218220137074.

(f) *Pensions.* The so-called funding gaps between the estimated liabilities and available assets in both private and public pensions grew significantly after the 2008 financial collapse, until reversing course during 2013, when rising stock markets significantly reduced those gaps, at least temporarily. According to data from J.P. Morgan Asset Management and reported in *The Wall Street Journal,* the deficit in pension plans at the companies in the Russell 3000-stock index increased from an estimated $392 billion in 2009 to $441 billion in 2012. The newspaper previously reported that from 2005 to 2009, companies in the S&P 500 with pension plans expected their pension assets to generate about $475 billion in returns, an amount that dwarfed the $239 million actually produced. *See* Gregory Zuckerman & Michael Corkery, *Pensions Make the Most of Stocks' Surge*, WALL. ST. J., Dec. 12, 2013, at C1; Vipal Monga, *Why the Corporate Pension Gap is Soaring*, WALL ST. J., Feb. 26, 2013, at B1; David Reilly, *Pension Gaps Loom Larger*, WALL ST. J., Sept. 18, 2010, at A1.

Even with rising stock markets since 2009, abnormally low interest rates have reduced the discount rates that enterprises use to determine the present value of the expected benefits owed to employees. As we recall from Chapter III on the time value of money, the lower the discount rate, the higher the pension obligations. In addition, higher regulatory costs and rising life expectancies have added to post-retirement costs and liabilities. *See* Vipal Monga, *Pension Plans Brace For a One-Two Punch*, WALL ST. J., Mar. 25, 2014, at B1.

Since the 2006 edition, several large, public companies changed their method of accounting for pension plans, switching from an approach that smoothed gains and losses arising from pension assets and liabilities over a period of years to a treatment that counts all pension gains and losses in the period incurred. For example, such an accounting change increased AT&T's pension costs for 2008 by $24.9 billion, which after taxes, turned a $12.9 billion profit for the year into a $2.6 billion loss. Although such changes increase transparency, they typically allow companies to recognize immediately any past losses that the firms were waiting to smooth into their future results. The accounting switch also forced AT&T to recognize a $10 billion reduction in operating profit during 2012 as interest rates fell. *See* Michael Rapoport, *Pendulum Swings for Retirement Charges*, WALL ST. J., Jan. 9, 2014, at B1; Michael Rapoport, *Rewriting Pension History*, WALL ST. J., Mar. 9, 2011, at C1.

After completing the first phase in a project on postretirement benefit obligations, including pensions, which required enterprises to move their pension assets and liabilities from the notes to the balance sheet, FASB started a second phase intended to reexamine how enterprises record and report expenses related to postretirement benefits. Specifically, the project sought to improve the quality of information provided to investors, creditors, employees, retirees, donors, and other users of financial statements. In an effort to leverage resources, FASB decided to start that phase separate from a parallel IASB project and to assess opportunities for convergence later. In 2009, however, FASB removed the second phase from its listing of active projects on its technical plan and began describing the project as "not active." Meanwhile, IASB promulgated a new standard effective for reporting periods beginning January 1, 2013, which prohibits enterprises from smoothing changes in their pension obligations.

Shortly after IASB promulgated its new standard, FASB announced plans to hold education sessions to consider the next steps in the second phase, which at the time appeared under the heading "FASB Research Projects" on the project roster. In January 2014, FASB voted against activating the project.

Instead, FASB decided to develop improvements to pension reporting during a comprehensive project on financial performance reporting. *See* Thomas Jaworski, *FASB Removes Projects on Income Taxes and Pensions From Agenda*, 2014 Tax Notes Today 20-8 (Jan. 30, 2014). At some point in the not too distant future, we can expect the FASB to discuss eliminating the smoothing option and how enterprises should estimate expected returns on their pension assets. Interested readers can access and monitor updates regarding this "Financial Performance Reporting (formerly Financial Statement Presentation)" research project via http://www.fasb.org/jsp/FASB/Page/TechnicalAgendaPage&cid=1175805470156.

Lawyers should keep all these recent and potential changes and issues in mind when reading financial statements and drafting and negotiating legal agreements.

PROBLEMS

Problem 6.12A. X Corp. had the following balance sheet on January 1 (in thousands):

Assets		Liabilities & Shareholders' Equity	
Cash	$ 11,000	Shareholders' Equity	
Plant	90,000	Stated Capital	$100,000
Total	$101,000	Earned Surplus	1,000
		Total	$101,000

On February 1, X borrowed $5 million, giving a note due three years later, with twelve percent annual interest; the $600,000 interest each year was to be paid in two installments, $300,000 on April 30, and $300,000 on October 31. Suppose X Corp. had $1,000,000 in income during the calendar year, and no expenses other than the interest on this note. How much should the general manager receive under an employment contract which entitles him to "ten percent of the net profits, before deduction of such salary, of each calendar year"? If you represent the general manager, what changes, if any, would you suggest to the contractual language?

Problem 6.12B. Assume that the B Bank was organized on January 1 last year with $2,000,000 of paid in capital. B immediately began to accept deposits from the public and had accumulated $3,000,000 in deposits by the end of the year. On July 1 of that year B made a loan of $500,000 to the Y Manufacturing Corporation, taking a one-year note with interest of eight percent payable at maturity (on the following June 30). On August 1, B invested $1,000,000 in six percent, twenty year, $1,000 government bonds. The annual interest of $60 per bond was payable in quarterly installments, beginning on October 31 of that year, when B collected $15,000. B also invested $2,800,000 in listed marketable securities, on which B received $250,000 in cash dividends during the year. B's total expenses for the year, including interest on its deposits, amounted to $180,000, and all but $40,000, representing accrued interest owed to depositors, was paid in cash during the year.

(1) To how much additional compensation is the president of B entitled under a contract which provides for a bonus of "ten percent of annual net profits, computed without deduction of the bonus"?

(2) If you represent the bank in negotiating an employment contract with the next bank president, what contractual language would you recommend?

Problem 6.12C. Prior to its sale to Unilever Plc, Ben & Jerry's historically set aside "five percent of pre-tax net income" for employee bonuses under the company's bonus and profit sharing plan. Before accepting the acquisition offer from Unilever Plc, the company would like to establish a written policy that describes the arrangement.

(1) If you represent the company's employees, what changes, if any, would you suggest to the language quoted above for the written policy? Explain briefly.

(2) If you represent Unilever Plc, what changes, if any, would you suggest to the language quoted above? Explain briefly.

*

CHAPTER VII

CONTINGENCIES

A. IMPORTANCE TO LAWYERS

Perhaps the most troublesome questions involving accrual arise regarding conditional expenses and losses, which may or may not ever occur and which accountants refer to as *contingencies*. Should an enterprise reflect such items in the financial statements despite their uncertainty? This question poses a real dilemma, particularly when the contingent loss or expense contributed to revenue production in the current period, because the matching principle requires an enterprise to match expenses with the revenues that they helped to produce. If the enterprise does not charge the loss or expense against income in the earlier period and the loss or expense subsequently occurs, the business will regret the failure to charge the item against income in the earlier period to which it "belonged." On the other hand, if the enterprise accrues the loss or expense and then it never actually materializes, the company will rue having accrued it in the earlier period. In most cases, the enterprise cannot tell exactly how the future will turn out. If the business decides to accrue the expense or loss in the current period, then the enterprise will debit a current expense or loss account and credit an accrued liability or, perhaps, an asset account. The business might give the liability a special name, such as "Contingent Liability," to distinguish that type of item on the balance sheet from unconditional liabilities.

Suppose that Neiers Company ("Neiers"), a corporation engaged in the shipbuilding business, usually builds and sells one cruise ship a year. Neiers warrants that each ship can maintain a certain speed for a specified number of years and agrees to refund $250,000 of the purchase price if the ship does not live up to the warranty. If Neiers must make good on such a warranty in some future period, the matching principle would treat that cost as an expense to offset against revenue in the year of sale. At the same time, Neiers may never incur this cost. A question of judgment, therefore, arises: Does the likelihood that Neiers will ultimately incur the cost justify a charge against income in the year of sale? If the circumstances require a charge, Neiers might record the following entry:

Warranty Expense	$250,000	
Contingent Liability on Warranty		$250,000

If the chances that Neiers will incur this cost do not rise to the level which justifies a charge against income, a question remains whether Neiers should reflect the contingent liability in some other way in the financial statements, perhaps simply by disclosing the contingent liability's existence in a footnote.

If Neiers does not record a charge against income in the year of sale and the company actually incurs the cost in some later year, Neiers must charge the refund against income in that later year. You may recall from Chapter IV on pages 278 and 280, *supra*, that the refund would not qualify as a prior period adjustment.

Notice the difference between a contingent liability, where uncertainty exists as to whether the enterprise will incur any expense or loss, and an unliquidated liability, where the enterprise has incurred an expense or loss attributable to the current period but uncertainty remains as to the exact amount. As we have seen, accountants usually handle the latter by trying to estimate the likely amount. Occasionally, however, management cannot ascertain the amount with any reasonable accuracy. In this situation, enterprises have hesitated to record any charge against current income, preferring instead to disclose the liability, perhaps in a footnote. Of course, uncertainty can also exist as to the amount for a contingent expenditure or loss. That uncertainty presents another reason against charging the contingent item against current income.

Sometimes a number of related contingent expenses or losses arise in the same year. Suppose, for example, that Neiers sells many ships per year, each with the same warranty described above. Although each particular warranty remains entirely contingent, assume a statistical certainty exists that Neiers will ultimately issue some refunds. In these circumstances, the previous experience of Neiers or some similar shipbuilder likely provides a fairly sound guide as to the percentage of the total potential refunds which Neiers will eventually pay. In other words, the situation becomes more like a fixed liability which remains uncertain as to amount, rather than a truly contingent liability. Therefore if, as is often the case, the enterprise can estimate the amount with reasonable accuracy, the business should record a charge against current income in the current period, with a corresponding credit to an estimated liability account.

All lawyers should recognize the various legal issues that can arise regarding contingent liabilities. As an initial matter, GAAP includes rules that require enterprises to accrue, disclose, or both accrue and disclose contingent losses and liabilities in certain circumstances. If an enterprise's financial statements do not follow these requirements, the enterprise may find itself defending a lawsuit alleging financial statement fraud or securities fraud. *See, e.g., In re* Corning, Inc. Securities Litigation, No. 92 Civ. 345 (TPG), 1997 WL 235122 (S.D.N.Y. May 7, 1997) (concluding that the consolidated and amended class action complaint sufficiently alleged that Corning's consolidated financial statements and periodic reports failed to reveal information about potential liabilities that a subsidiary, Dow Corning Corp., may have incurred in manufacturing and selling breast implants to approximately 800,000 women), a case that the district court subsequently dismissed more than seven years later on Corning's motion for summary judgment in an opinion reported at 349 F. Supp. 2d 698 (S.D.N.Y. 2004); SEC v. Trans Energy, Inc., No. 1-01-CV-02060, 2002 SEC LEXIS 465 (D.D.C. Feb. 27, 2002) (entering permanent injunction against registrant and two officers and imposing civil penalties against the officers for failing to disclose the existence of material lawsuits that resulted in more than $1 million in consent judgments against the company in its 1998 through 2000 SEC filings). In addition, issues about whether or how to disclose information about contingencies frequently perplex securities lawyers, particularly given the SEC's emphasis on the Management's Discussion and Analysis ("MD&A") requirements. For this reason, you may want to review our earlier discussion about MD&A in Chapter IV on pages 316 to 325, *supra*, at this time. The financial accounting standards under GAAP and the MD&A requirements may establish different standards. If the MD&A rules in fact impose a higher standard for disclosure, a registrant could theoretically observe the GAAP requirements but still violate the federal securities laws. In that event, a lawyer who relied on GAAP in advising a registrant about disclosure obligations for securities law purposes could end up liable for malpractice.

The Enron crisis illustrates the importance of disclosing financial guarantees in the notes to the financial statements. When various Enron affiliates—commonly referred to as SPEs, which Enron formed to keep debt off its books—sought credit, the lenders often required that Enron guarantee the debt. On several occasions, Enron guaranteed amounts that various SPEs borrowed by promising to pay cash or to issue additional common shares to repay the debt, if the market price of Enron's common shares dropped under a certain amount or if Enron's bond rating fell below investment grade. While the notes to Enron's financial statements disclosed guarantees of the indebtedness of others, Enron did not mention that its potential liability on those guarantees, which shared common debt repayment triggers, totaled $4 billion. *See* William W. Bratton, *Enron and the Dark Side of Shareholder Value*, 76 Tul. L. Rev. 1275 (2002). When material, GAAP specifically requires an enterprise to disclose the nature and amount of guarantees of the indebtedness of others. Again, inadequate disclosure can subject enterprises to liability and lawyers to malpractice claims.

Issues involving contingencies can also arise when drafting, negotiating and interpreting contracts. To repeat an earlier theme, although an enterprise almost always uses GAAP to prepare financial statements for creditors and investors, different rules may apply for specific contracts, establishing rates for public utilities, or tax purposes. *See, e.g.,* Commonwealth Transp. Commissioner v. Matyiko, 481 S.E.2d 468 (Va. 1997) (concluding that even though the corporation did not need to record a contingent liability in the financial statements, the directors could not vote to distribute all the corporation's assets to shareholders without making arrangements for the potential need to pay the liability and holding the directors personally liable when the liability materialized). In particular, transactional lawyers should always consider how to treat contingent liabilities when working on mergers and acquisitions, partnership agreements, or buy-sell agreements. With regard to tax issues, recall our discussion of the economic performance requirement in Chapter VI on page 485, *supra*.

Perhaps most importantly, however, all attorneys, whether litigators or transactional lawyers, who represent enterprises that undergo financial statement audits must respond to inquiries from independent auditors about litigation, claims and assessments involving their clients. You may recall from Chapter II on pages 178 to 179, *supra*, that financial statements present various assertions, including that reported liabilities actually exist; expenses and losses occurred during the particular accounting period; the financial statements record the enterprise's liabilities, expenses and losses at appropriate amounts; and the financial statements contain any necessary disclosures. In every audit engagement, therefore, the auditor must obtain evidence about contingent liabilities arising from litigation, claims, assessments and other uncertainties to determine whether the enterprise has properly treated those items in the financial statements. In particular, the auditor must use reasonable efforts to determine whether any material unrecorded or undisclosed liabilities exist. In addition to requesting information and representations from an enterprise's management about contingencies, the auditor must request corroborating information from the enterprise's outside counsel. To satisfy this second obligation, the auditor typically requests the client to send an audit inquiry letter directing and authorizing outside counsel to provide information about litigation, claims and assessments to the auditor. INQUIRY OF A CLIENT'S LAWYER CONCERNING LITIGATION, CLAIMS, AND ASSESSMENTS, Statement of Auditing Standards No. 12 (Am. Inst. of Certified Pub. Accountants 1976). If the enterprise's lawyers fail or refuse to reply to these inquiries, presumably under some theory of confidentiality arising from the attorney-client privilege, the auditor may qualify the audit opinion. In other circumstances, the auditor may issue an adverse opinion or disclaim an opinion. As we discussed in Chapter II on page 147, *supra*, any report other than an unqualified opinion can adversely affect the enterprise's ability to attract capital, borrow funds, or even to continue in business.

If the auditor issues an unqualified opinion with respect to financial statements which do not appropriately treat contingencies, the auditor, as well as the enterprise, can face staggering legal liability. *See, e.g.,* Endo v. Albertine, 863 F. Supp. 708 (N.D. Ill. 1994) (denying motions for summary judgment by issuer and auditor in class action presenting claims for alleged failure to disclose material facts regarding contingent tax deficiencies exceeding $100 million and environmental liabilities over $60 million). Such potential liability, plus a desire to maintain their professional reputations, motivates auditors to seek as much information about contingent liabilities as possible from an enterprise's outside counsel.

As you might surmise, lawyers must exercise great care in responding to these audit inquiry letters. A lawyer may not disclose confidential information to the auditor without the client's consent. If the client authorizes the lawyer to disclose information to the auditor, lest the auditor refuse to render an unqualified opinion, the client potentially waives the attorney-client privilege, at a minimum as to any information disclosed. Although numerous states have enacted an accountant-client privilege, the common law did not recognize such a privilege and no such privilege exists generally under federal law.

For this reason, the disclosure requirements may present discovery opportunities for litigators and pitfalls for attorneys representing businesses which need audited financial statements. Litigators should recognize the discovery possibilities of obtaining accounting information and supporting data regarding contingencies. Sophisticated litigators will carefully examine the opponent's financial statements for information about any contingency related to the dispute. In appropriate circumstances, savvy litigators will seek information about relevant contingent liabilities during discovery, by examining the opponent's books, records and tax returns or requesting such information from the opponent's auditor.

To put these issues in some perspective, assume that your law firm represents Ace Oil Corporation ("Ace"), a small publicly-traded company which distributes heating oil from four storage and distribution facilities located in Pacioli, the fictional fifty-first state. Various federal, state and local laws and regulations govern the operation of the company's facilities. You and your law firm have advised Ace that, beginning in the coming year, regulations will go into effect in stages over the next seven years that will require the company to remove, replace or modify the storage tanks and various other equipment which the company currently uses in its operations. In addition, the company faces an existing legal obligation to decontaminate the soil near its largest facility.

At your firm's suggestion, Ace hired an environmental consultant with whom you have worked in the past to evaluate the applicable technological, regulatory and legal factors involved. The consultant estimated that the total environmental expenditures over the next seven years related to the tanks and equipment will total approximately $5 million. Of that amount, about $4.75 million represents capital expenditures which the company expects to recover through operations. The existing tanks and equipment currently appear on the company's books with net book values of $500,000 and $475,000 respectively. The consultant estimates that the soil decontamination costs will exceed $1 million, an amount material to the company's operations, and could reach $3 million. The company has filed an insurance claim regarding the contaminated soil. The insurance company, which faces insolvency from similar claims, has denied coverage, however. In addition, the insurance policy contains a $500,000 deductible. *See* FASB ASC ¶¶ 410-30-55-7 to -13 (codifications of DISCLOSURE OF CERTAIN SIGNIFICANT RISKS AND UNCERTAINTIES, Statement of Position 94–6, at A–28 to A–33 (Am. Inst. of Certified Pub. Accountants 1994)). The following questionnaire from the Audit Inquiry Committee and addressed to you and a number of other lawyers at your firm arrives on your desk:

CONFIDENTIAL QUESTIONNAIRE—Please return as soon as possible

Client: Ace Oil Company

Insert "None"
where appropriate

1. Please identify any lawyer in our firm (other than those listed above) who performed services for the client since December 31, 201X. _____

2. If we have represented the client in any litigation or administrative proceeding pending or settled since December 31, 201X, please attach a description including (A) the court or agency; (B) case style and number; (C) nature of claim; and (D) amount in controversy or nature of relief sought. _____

3. Please attach a description of any of the following matters as to which we have been specifically engaged by the client to provide legal advice or representation since December 31, 201X: (A) threats of litigation; (B) assessments or threatened assessments of additional taxes; and (C) other asserted claims. _____

4. Please attach a brief description of any unasserted possible claim or assessment by or against the client, but only if (A) you have recognized it in the course of performing legal services for the client since December 31, 201X and (B) it is more likely than not that it will be asserted. _____

5. Please attach a brief description of any advice you have given the client concerning disclosure or non-disclosure either in financial statements or to the SEC of any unasserted possible claim or assessment since December 31, 201X. _____

Date: _____

_____
Responding Attorney

How should you respond? What legal consequences can result from your firm's response? Although this example involves an environmental contingency, similar issues can arise in antitrust, data security, employment discrimination, false claims, FCPA, fiduciary liability, government contract, intellectual property, privacy, product liability, real estate, securities, tax, and other legal matters.

B.   THE FINANCIAL ACCOUNTING RULES

FASB ASC Topic 450, *Contingencies*, which codified Statement of Financial Accounting Standards No. 5, *Accounting for Contingencies* ("SFAS No. 5"), which FASB issued in 1975, establishes a framework for recording and reporting contingencies for financial accounting purposes. Subject to a general, but specific, exception for immaterial items, the Codification provides as follows:

[Topic] 450 Contingencies*

[Subtopic] 10 Overall

450-10-00 Status

General Note: The Status Section identifies changes to this Subtopic resulting from Accounting Standards Updates. The Section provides references to the affected Codification content and links to the related Accounting Standards Updates. Nonsubstantive changes for items such as editorial, link and similar corrections are included separately in Maintenance Updates.

General

[No updates pertinent to this text have been made to this subtopic.]

450-10-05 Overview and Background

General Note: The Overview and Background Section provides overview and background material for the guidance contained in the Subtopic. It does not provide the historical background or due process. It may contain certain material that users generally consider useful to understand the typical situations addressed by the standards. The Section does not summarize the accounting and reporting requirements.

General

450-10-05-1 The Contingencies Topic includes the following Subtopics:

   a. Overall
   b. Loss Contingencies
   c. Gain Contingencies.

450-10-05-2 This Subtopic, in combination with Subtopics 450-20 and 450-30, provides general guidance regarding gain and loss contingencies. Other Topics

*Copyright © 2014 by the   Reprinted with permission.
Financial Accounting Foundation.

include gain or loss contingencies related to those specific Topics. Therefore, the Contingencies Topic does not include all standards related to contingencies. * * *

450-10-05-3 The Overall Subtopic establishes the scope and scope exceptions for the Contingencies Topic, provides definitions, and includes links to the standards that appear in Subtopics 450-20 and 450-30.

450-10-05-4 The Contingencies Topic establishes standards of financial accounting and reporting for loss contingencies and gain contingencies, including standards for disclosures.

450-10-05-5 Resolution of the uncertainty may confirm any of the following:

  a. The acquisition of an asset
  b. The reduction of a liability
  c. The loss or impairment of an asset
  d. The incurrence of a liability.

450-10-05-6 Not all uncertainties inherent in the accounting process give rise to **contingencies**. Estimates are required in financial statements for many ongoing and recurring activities of an entity. The mere fact that an estimate is involved does not of itself constitute the type of uncertainty referred to in the definition of a loss contingency or a gain contingency. Several examples of situations that are not contingencies are included in Section 450-10-55.

450-10-15 Scope and Scope Exceptions

General Note: The Scope and Scope Exceptions Section outlines the items (for example, the entities, transactions, instruments, or events) to which the guidance in the Subtopic does or does not apply. In some cases, the Section may contain definitional or other text to frame the scope.

General

> Overall Guidance

450-10-15-1 The Scope Section of the Overall Subtopic establishes the pervasive scope for all Subtopics of the Contingencies Topic. Unless explicitly addressed within specific Subtopics, the following scope guidance applies to all Subtopics of the Contingencies Topic.

> Entities

450-10-15-2 The guidance in the Contingencies Topic applies to all entities.

> Transactions

450-10-15-2A The guidance in the Contingencies Topic does not apply to the recognition and initial measurement of assets or liabilities arising from contingencies that are measured at fair value or assets arising from contingencies measured at an amount other than fair value on the **acquisition date** in a business combination or an **acquisition by a not-for-profit entity** * * *. Those [standards] provide the recognition and initial measurement requirements for assets and liabilities arising from contingencies measured at fair value and for assets arising from contingencies measured at an amount other than fair value as part of a business combination or an acquisition by a not-for-profit entity.

> Other Considerations

450-10-15-3 In some cases, there may be uncertainty about whether a situation is a **contingency**. Section 450-10-55 includes several situations that are not contingencies, and thus are outside the scope of the Contingencies Topic.

450-10-20 Glossary

General Note: The Master Glossary contains all terms identified as glossary terms throughout the Codification. * * * The Master Glossary may contain identical terms with different definitions, some of which may not be appropriate for a particular Subtopic. For any particular Subtopic, users should only use the glossary terms included in the particular Subtopic Glossary Section (Section 20).

* * *

Contingency

An existing condition, situation, or set of circumstances involving uncertainty as to possible gain (gain contingency) or loss (loss contingency) to an entity that will ultimately be resolved when one or more future events occur or fail to occur.

Gain Contingency

An existing condition, situation, or set of circumstances involving uncertainty as to possible gain to an entity that will ultimately be resolved when one or more future events occur or fail to occur.

* * *

Loss Contingency

An existing condition, situation, or set of circumstances involving uncertainty as to possible loss to an entity that will ultimately be resolved when one or more future events occur or fail to occur. The term loss is used for convenience to include many charges against income that are commonly referred to as expenses and others that are commonly referred to as losses.

* * *

450-10-55 Implementation Guidance and Illustrations

General Note: The Implementation Guidance and Illustrations Section contains implementation guidance and illustrations that are an integral part of the Subtopic. The implementation guidance and illustrations do not address all possible variations. Users must consider carefully the actual facts and circumstances in relation to the requirements of the Subtopic.

General

> Implementation Guidance

450-10-55-1 This Section includes several situations that do not meet the definition of a **contingency**, and thus are outside the scope of this Topic.

> > Depreciation

450-10-55-2 The fact that estimates are used to allocate the known cost of a depreciable asset over the period of use by an entity does not make depreciation a contingency; the eventual expiration of the utility of the asset is not uncertain. Thus, depreciation of assets is not a contingency, nor are such matters as recurring repairs, maintenance, and overhauls, which interrelate with depreciation. This Topic is not intended to alter present depreciation practices * * *.

> > Estimates Used in Accruals

450-10-55-3 Amounts owed for services received, such as advertising and utilities, are not contingencies even though the accrued amounts may have been estimated; there is nothing uncertain about the fact that those obligations have been incurred.

> > Changes in Tax Law

450-10-55-4 The possibility of a change in the tax law in some future year is not an uncertainty.

* * *

[Subtopic] 20 Loss Contingencies

* * *

450-20-05 Overview and Background

General

450-20-05-1 This Subtopic provides guidance for the recognition and disclosure of a **loss contingency**.

450-20-05-2 This Subtopic, in combination with Subtopics 450-10 and 450-30, provides general guidance regarding gain and loss contingencies. Other Topics include gain or loss contingencies related to those specific Topics. Therefore, the Contingencies Topic does not include all standards related to contingencies. * * *

450-20-05-3 The following are examples of loss contingencies for which links are provided in Section 450-20-60:

a. Collectibility of receivables
b. Obligations related to product warranties and product defects
c. Risk of loss from catastrophes assumed by property and casualty insurance entities including reinsurance entities
d. Guarantees of indebtedness of others
e. Obligations of commercial banks under standby letters of credit
f. Agreements to repurchase receivables (or to repurchase the related property) that have been sold.

> Dealing with Uncertainty when Accounting for Losses

450-20-05-4 Accounting standards use two primary approaches to dealing with uncertainty in loss circumstances:

a. Recognition using a probability threshold
b. Measurement using a fair value objective.

450-20-05-5 This Subtopic deals with uncertainty by requiring a probability threshold for recognition of a loss contingency and that the amount of the loss be reasonably estimable. As noted in paragraph 450-20-30-1, when both of those recognition criteria are met, and the reasonably estimable loss is a range, it requires accrual of the amount that appears to be a better estimate than any other estimate within the range, or accrual of the minimum amount in the range if no amount within the range is a better estimate than any other amount.

450-20-05-6 In contrast, fair value is not an estimate of the ultimate settlement amount or the present value of an estimate of the ultimate settlement amount. Uncertainty in the amount and timing of the future cash flows necessary to settle a liability and the likelihood of possible outcomes are incorporated into the measurement of the fair value of the liability. For example, a third party would charge a price to assume an uncertain liability even though the likelihood of a future sacrifice is less than **probable**. Similarly, when the likelihood of a future sacrifice is probable, the price a third party would charge to assume an obligation incorporates expectations about some future events that are less than probable. Recognizing the fair value of an obligation results in recognition of some obligations for which the likelihood of future settlement, although more than zero, is less than probable from a loss contingencies perspective.

450-20-05-7 Because this Subtopic deals with uncertainty differently, the recognition guidance in Section 450-20-25 is inconsistent with standards in other Topics that have an objective of measuring fair value.

>Accruals of Loss Contingencies Do Not Provide Financial Protection

450-20-05-8 Accrual of a loss related to a **contingency** does not create or set aside funds to lessen the possible financial impact of a loss. Confusion exists between accounting accruals (sometimes referred to as accounting reserves) and the reserving or setting aside of specific assets to be used for a particular purpose or contingency. Accounting accruals are simply a method of allocating costs among accounting periods and have no effect on an entity's cash flow. Those accruals in no way protect the assets available to replace or repair uninsured property that may be lost or damaged, or to satisfy claims that are not covered by insurance, or, in the case of insurance entities, to satisfy the claims of insured parties. Accrual, in and of itself, provides no financial protection that is not available in the absence of accrual.

450-20-05-9 An entity may choose to maintain or have access to sufficient liquid assets to replace or repair lost or damaged property or to pay claims in case a loss occurs. Alternatively, it may transfer the risk to others by purchasing insurance. The accounting standards set forth in this Subtopic do not affect the fundamental business economics of that decision. That is a financial decision, and if an entity's management decides to do neither, the presence or absence of an accrued credit balance on the balance sheet will have no effect on the consequences of that decision. Insurance or reinsurance reduces or eliminates risks and the inherent earnings fluctuations that accompany risks. Unlike insurance and reinsurance, the use of accounting reserves does not reduce or eliminate risk. The use of accounting reserves is not an alternative to insurance and reinsurance in protecting against risk. Earnings fluctuations are inherent in risk retention, and they are reported as they occur.

> Types of Loss Contingencies

450-20-05-10 The following are examples of loss contingencies that are discussed in this Subtopic:

    a.   Injury or damage caused by products sold
    b.   Risk of loss or damage of property by fire, explosion, or other hazards
    c.   Actual or possible claims and assessments
    d.   Threat of expropriation of assets
    e.   Pending or threatened litigation.

* * *

450-20-20 Glossary

General

* * *

Probable

The future event or events are likely to occur.

Reasonably Possible

The chance of the future event or events occurring is more than remote but less than likely.

Remote

The chance of the future event or events occurring is slight.

450-20-25 Recognition

General Note: The Recognition Section provides guidance on the required criteria, timing, and location (within the financial statements) for recording a particular item in the financial statements. Disclosure is not recognition.

General

> General Rule

450-20-25-1 When a **loss contingency** exists, the likelihood that the future event or events will confirm the loss or impairment of an asset or the incurrence of a liability can range from **probable** to **remote**. As indicated in the definition of **contingency**, the term *loss* is used for convenience to include many charges against income that are commonly referred to as expenses and others that are commonly referred to as losses. The Contingencies Topic uses the terms *probable*, **reasonably possible**, and *remote* to identify three areas within that range.

450-20-25-2 An estimated loss from a loss contingency shall be accrued by a charge to income if both of the following conditions are met:

a. Information available before the financial statements are issued or are available to be issued (as discussed in Section 855-10-25) indicates that it is probable that an asset had been impaired or a liability had been incurred at the date of the financial statements. Date of the financial statements means the end of the most recent accounting period for which financial statements are being presented. It is implicit in this condition that it must be probable that one or more future events will occur confirming the fact of the loss.

b. The amount of loss can be reasonably estimated.

The purpose of those conditions is to require accrual of losses when they are reasonably estimable and relate to the current or a prior period. Paragraphs 450-20-55-1 through 55-17 and Examples 1–2 (see paragraphs 450-20-55-18 through 55-35) illustrate the application of the conditions. As discussed in paragraph 450-20-50-5, disclosure is preferable to accrual when a reasonable estimate of loss cannot be made. Further, even losses that are reasonably estimable shall not be accrued if it is not probable that an asset has been impaired or a liability has been incurred at the date of an entity's financial statements because those losses relate to a future period rather than the current or a prior period. Attribution of a loss to events or activities of the current or prior periods is an element of asset impairment or liability incurrence.

> Assessing Probability of Incurrence of a Loss

450-20-25-3 The conditions in the preceding paragraph are not intended to be so rigid that they require virtual certainty before a loss is accrued. Instead, the condition in (a) in the preceding paragraph is intended to proscribe accrual of losses that relate to future periods.

> Assessing Whether a Loss Is Reasonably Estimable

450-20-25-4 The condition in paragraph 450-20-25-2(b) is intended to prevent accrual in the financial statements of amounts so uncertain as to impair the integrity of those statements.

450-20-25-5 That requirement shall not delay accrual of a loss until only a single amount can be reasonably estimated. To the contrary, when the condition in paragraph 450-20-25-2(a) is met and information available indicates that the estimated amount of loss is within a range of amounts, it follows that some amount of loss has occurred and can be reasonably estimated. Thus, when the condition in paragraph 450-20-25-2(a) is met with respect to a particular loss contingency and the reasonable estimate of the loss is a range, the condition in paragraph 450-20-25-2(b) is met and an amount shall be accrued for the loss.

> Events After the Date of the Financial Statements

450-20-25-6 After the date of an entity's financial statements but before those financial statements are issued or are available to be issued * * *, information may become available indicating that an asset was impaired or a liability was incurred after the date of the financial statements or that there is at least a reasonable possibility that an asset was impaired or a liability was incurred after that date. The information may relate to a loss contingency that existed at the date of the financial statements, for example, an asset that was not insured at the date of the financial statements. On the other hand, the information may relate to a loss contingency that did not exist at the date of the financial statements, for example, threat of expropriation of assets after the date of the financial statements or the filing for bankruptcy by an entity whose debt was guaranteed after the date of the financial statements. In none of the cases cited in this paragraph was an asset impaired or a liability incurred at the date of the financial statements, and the condition for accrual in paragraph 450-20-25-2(a) is, therefore, not met.

450-20-25-7 If a loss cannot be accrued in the period when it is probable that an asset had been impaired or a liability had been incurred because the amount of loss cannot be reasonably estimated, the loss shall be charged to the income of the period in which the loss can be reasonably estimated and shall not be charged retroactively to an earlier period. All estimated losses for loss contingencies shall be charged to income rather than charging some to income and others to retained earnings as prior period adjustments.

> Business Risks

450-20-25-8 General or unspecified business risks do not meet the conditions for accrual in paragraph 450-20-25-2, and no accrual for loss shall be made.

450-20-30 Initial Measurement

General

450-20-30-1 If some amount within a range of loss appears at the time to be a better estimate than any other amount within the range, that amount shall be accrued. When no amount within the range is a better estimate than any other amount, however, the minimum amount in the range shall be accrued. Even though the minimum amount in the range is not necessarily the amount of loss that will be ultimately determined, it is not likely that the ultimate loss will be less than the minimum amount. Examples 1–2 (see paragraphs 450-20-55-18 through 55-35) illustrate the application of these initial measurement standards.

450-20-50 Disclosure

General

> Accruals for Loss Contingencies

450-20-50-1 Disclosure of the nature of an accrual made pursuant to the provisions of paragraph 450-20-25-2, and in some circumstances the amount accrued, may be necessary for the financial statements not to be misleading. Terminology used shall be descriptive of the nature of the accrual, such as estimated liability or liability of an estimated amount. The term *reserve* shall not be used for an accrual made pursuant to paragraph 450-20-25-2; that term is limited to an amount of unidentified or unsegregated assets held or retained for a specific purpose. Examples 1 (see paragraph 450-20-55-18) and 2, Cases A, B, and D (see paragraphs 450-20-55-23, 450-20-55-27, and 450-20-55-32) illustrate the application of these disclosure standards.

450-20-50-2 If the criteria in paragraph 275-10-50-8 [regarding significant estimates] are met, paragraph 275-10-50-9 requires disclosure of an indication that it is at least **reasonably possible** that a change in an entity's estimate of its **probable** liability could occur in the near term. Example 3 (see paragraph 450-20-55-36) illustrates this disclosure for an entity involved in litigation.

> Unrecognized Contingencies

* * *

450-20-50-3 Disclosure of the **contingency** shall be made if there is at least a reasonable possibility that a loss or an additional loss may have been incurred and either of the following conditions exists:

   a. An accrual is not made for a **loss contingency** because any of the conditions in paragraph 450-20-25-2 are not met.
   b. An exposure to loss exists in excess of the amount accrued pursuant to the provisions of paragraph 450-20-30-1.

Examples 1–3 (see paragraphs 450-20-55-18 through 55-37) illustrate the application of these disclosure standards.

450-20-50-4 The disclosure in the preceding paragraph shall include both of the following:

   a. The nature of the contingency
   b. An estimate of the possible loss or range of loss or a statement that such an estimate cannot be made.

450-20-50-5 Disclosure is preferable to accrual when a reasonable estimate of loss cannot be made. For example, disclosure shall be made of any loss contingency that meets the condition in paragraph 450-20-25-2(a) but that is not accrued because the amount of loss cannot be reasonably estimated (the condition in paragraph 450-20-25-2[b]). Disclosure also shall be made of some loss contingencies that do not meet the condition in paragraph 450-20-25-2(a)—namely, those contingencies for which there is a reasonable possibility that a loss may have been incurred even though information may not indicate that it is probable that an asset had been impaired or a liability had been incurred at the date of the financial statements.

450-20-50-6 Disclosure is not required of a loss contingency involving an unasserted claim or assessment if there has been no manifestation by a potential claimant of an awareness of a possible claim or assessment unless both of the following conditions are met:

    a.   It is considered probable that a claim will be asserted.
    b.   There is a reasonable possibility that the outcome will be unfavorable.

450-20-50-7 Disclosure of noninsured or underinsured risks is not required by this Subtopic. However, disclosure in appropriate circumstances is not discouraged.

450-20-50-8 No disclosure about general or unspecified business risks is required by this Subtopic, however, Topic 275 requires disclosure of certain business risks.

> Losses Arising After the Date of the Financial Statements

450-20-50-9 Disclosure of a loss, or a loss contingency, arising after the date of an entity's financial statements but before those financial statements are issued, as described in paragraphs 450-20-25-6 through 25-7, may be necessary to keep the financial statements from being misleading if an accrual is not required. If disclosure is deemed necessary, the financial statements shall include both of the following:

    a.   The nature of the loss or loss contingency
    b.   An estimate of the amount or range of loss or possible loss or a statement that such an estimate cannot be made.

450-20-50-10 Occasionally, in the case of a loss arising after the date of the financial statements if the amount of asset impairment or liability incurrence can be reasonably estimated, disclosure may best be made by supplementing the historical financial statements with pro forma financial data giving effect to the loss as if it had occurred at the date of the financial statements. It may be desirable to present pro forma statements, usually a balance sheet only, in columnar form on the face of the historical financial statements.

450-20-55 Implementation Guidance and Illustrations

General

> Implementation Guidance

450-20-55-1 This Section includes implementation guidance for the application of the conditions for accrual of **loss contingencies** and for the disclosure requirements of this Subtopic. This guidance does not address all possible applications of the requirements of this Subtopic. Therefore, accrual and disclosure of loss contingencies should be based on an evaluation of the facts and circumstances in each particular situation.

> > Injury or Damage Caused by Products Sold

450-20-55-2 If it is **probable** that a claim resulting from injury or damage caused by a product defect will arise with respect to products or services that have been sold, accrual for losses may be appropriate. The condition in paragraph 450-20-25-2(a) would be met, for instance, with respect to a drug product or toys that have been sold if a health or safety hazard related to those products is discovered and as a result it is considered probable that liabilities have been incurred. The condition in paragraph 450-20-25-2(b) would be met if experience or other information enables the entity to make a reasonable estimate of the loss with respect to the drug product or the toys.

> > Risk of Loss or Damage of Property

450-20-55-3 At the date of an entity's financial statements, it may not be insured against risk of future loss or damage to its property by fire, explosion, or other hazards. Some risks, for all practical purposes, may be noninsurable, and the self-assumption of those risks is mandatory.

450-20-55-4 The absence of insurance against losses from risks of those types constitutes an existing condition involving uncertainty about the amount and timing of any losses that may occur, in which case a **loss contingency** exists. Uninsured risks may arise in a number of ways, including the following:

a. Noninsurance of certain risks
b. Co-insurance or deductible clauses in an insurance contract
c. Insurance through a subsidiary or investee to the extent not reinsured with an independent insurer. * * *

450-20-55-5 The absence of insurance does not mean that an asset has been impaired or a liability has been incurred at the date of an entity's financial statements. Fires, explosions, and other similar events that may cause loss or damage of an entity's property are random in their occurrence. With respect to events of that type, the condition in paragraph 450-20-25-2(a) is not satisfied prior to the occurrence of the event because until that time there is no diminution in the value of the property. There is no relationship of those events to the activities of the entity prior to their occurrence, and no asset is impaired prior to their occurrence. Further, unlike an insurance entity, which has a contractual obligation under policies in force to reimburse insureds for losses, an entity can have no such obligation to itself and, hence, no liability.

> > Risk of Loss from Future Events

450-20-55-6 An entity may choose not to purchase insurance against risk of loss that may result from injury to others, damage to the property of others, or interruption of its business operations. Exposure to risks of those types constitutes an existing condition involving uncertainty about the amount and timing of any losses that may occur, in which case a **contingency** exists.

450-20-55-7 Mere exposure to risks of those types, however, does not mean that an asset has been impaired or a liability has been incurred. The condition in paragraph 450-20-25-2(a) is not met with respect to loss that may result from injury to others, damage to the property of others, or business interruption that may occur after the date of an entity's financial statements. Losses of those types do not relate to the current or a prior period but rather to the future period in which they occur. Thus, for example, an entity with a fleet of vehicles should not accrue for injury to others or damage to the property of others that might be caused by those vehicles in the future even if the amount of those losses may be reasonably estimable.

450-20-55-8 On the other hand, the conditions in paragraph 450-20-25-2 would be met with respect to uninsured losses resulting from injury to others or damage to the property of others if both of the following are true:

a. The event took place prior to the date of the financial statements, even though the entity may not become aware of those matters until after that date.
b. The experience of the entity or other information enables it to make a reasonable estimate of the loss that was incurred prior to the date of its financial statements.

Injury or damage resulting from products that have been sold are discussed in paragraph 450-20-55-2.

> > Threat of Expropriation

450-20-55-9 The threat of expropriation of assets is a contingency (as defined) because of the uncertainty about its outcome and effect. The condition in paragraph 450-20-25-2(a) is met if both of the following are true:

a. Expropriation is imminent.
b. Compensation will be less than the carrying amount of the assets.

Imminence may be indicated, for example, by public or private declarations of intent by a government to expropriate assets of the entity or actual expropriation of assets of other entities. The condition in paragraph 450-20-25-2(b) requires that accrual be made only if the amount of loss can be reasonably estimated. If the conditions for accrual are not met, the disclosures described in paragraphs 450-20-50-3 through 50-8 would be made if there is at least a reasonable possibility that an asset has been impaired.

> > Litigation, Claims, and Assessments

450-20-55-10 The following factors should be considered in determining whether accrual and/or disclosure is required with respect to pending or threatened litigation and actual or possible claims and assessments:

a. The period in which the underlying cause (that is, the cause for action) of the pending or threatened litigation or of the actual or possible claim or assessment occurred
b. The degree of probability of an unfavorable outcome
c. The ability to make a reasonable estimate of the amount of loss.

Examples 1 through 2 (see paragraphs 450-20-55-18 through 55-35) illustrate the consideration of these factors in determining whether to accrue or disclose litigation.

> > > Losses Arising Before the Date of the Financial Statements

450-20-55-11 Accrual may be appropriate for litigation, claims, or assessments whose underlying cause is an event occurring on or before the date of an entity's financial statements even if the entity does not become aware of the existence or possibility of the lawsuit, claim, or assessment until after the date of the financial statements. If those financial statements have not been issued or are not yet available to be issued (as discussed in Section 855-10-25), accrual of a loss related to the litigation, claim, or assessment would be required if the probability of loss is such that the condition in paragraph 450-20-25-2(a) is met and the amount of loss can be reasonably estimated.

> > > > Assessing Probability of the Incurrence of a Loss

450-20-55-12 If the underlying cause of the litigation, claim, or assessment is an event occurring before the date of an entity's financial statements, the probability of an outcome unfavorable to the entity must be assessed to determine whether the condition in paragraph 450-20-25-2(a) is met. Among the factors that should be considered are the following:

a. The nature of the litigation, claim, or assessment
b. The progress of the case (including progress after the date of the financial statements but before those statements are issued or are available to be issued * * *)
c. The opinions or views of legal counsel and other advisers, although, the fact that legal counsel is unable to express an opinion that the outcome will be favorable to the entity should not necessarily be interpreted to mean that the condition in paragraph 450-20-25-2(a) is met

    d.   The experience of the entity in similar cases

    e.   The experience of other entities

    f.   Any decision of the entity's management as to how the entity intends to respond to the lawsuit, claim, or assessment (for example, a decision to contest the case vigorously or a decision to seek an out-of-court settlement).

450-20-55-13 The filing of a suit or formal assertion of a claim or assessment does not automatically indicate that accrual of a loss may be appropriate. The degree of probability of an unfavorable outcome must be assessed. The condition in paragraph 450-20-25-2(a) would be met if an unfavorable outcome is determined to be probable. Accrual would be inappropriate, but disclosure would be required, if an unfavorable outcome is determined to be **reasonably possible** but not probable, or if the amount of loss cannot be reasonably estimated.

450-20-55-14 With respect to unasserted claims and assessments, an entity must determine the degree of probability that a suit may be filed or a claim or assessment may be asserted and the possibility of an unfavorable outcome. If an unfavorable outcome is probable and the amount of loss can be reasonably estimated, accrual of a loss is required by paragraph 450-20-25-2. For example:

    a.   A catastrophe, accident, or other similar physical occurrence predictably engenders claims for redress, and in such circumstances their assertion may be probable.

    b.   An investigation of an entity by a governmental agency, if enforcement proceedings have been or are likely to be instituted, is often followed by private claims for redress, and the probability of their assertion and the possibility of loss should be considered in each case.

    c.   An entity may believe there is a possibility that it has infringed on another entity's patent rights, but the entity owning the patent rights has not indicated an intention to take any action and has not even indicated an awareness of the possible infringement. In that case, a judgment must first be made as to whether the assertion of a claim is probable.

450-20-55-15 If the judgment is that assertion is not probable, no accrual or disclosure would be required. On the other hand, if the judgment is that assertion is probable, then a second judgment must be made as to the degree of probability of an unfavorable outcome. The disclosures described in paragraphs 450-20-50-3 through 50-8 would be required in either of the following circumstances:

    a.   An unfavorable outcome is probable but the amount of loss cannot be reasonably estimated.

    b.   An unfavorable outcome is reasonably possible but not probable.

> > > > Assessing Whether a Loss Is Reasonably Estimable

450-20-55-16 As a condition for accrual of a loss contingency, the condition in paragraph 450-20-25-2(b) requires that the amount of loss can be reasonably estimated. In some cases, it may be determined that a loss was incurred because an unfavorable outcome of the litigation, claim, or assessment is probable (thus satisfying the condition in paragraph 450-20-25-2[a]), but the range of possible loss is wide. Examples 1 and 3 (see paragraphs 450-20-55-18 and 450-20-55-36) illustrate the application of the standards in this Subtopic when the range of possible loss is wide.

> > > Losses Arising after the Date of the Financial Statements

450-20-55-17 As a condition for accrual of a loss contingency, the condition in paragraph 450-20-25-2(a) requires that information available before the financial statements are issued or are available to be issued (as discussed in Section 855-10-25) indicate that it is probable that an asset had been impaired or a liability had been incurred at the date of the financial statements. Accordingly, accrual would clearly be inappropriate for litigation, claims, or assessments whose underlying cause is an event or condition occurring after the date of financial statements but before those financial statements are issued or are available to be issued. For example, an entity would not accrue a suit for damages alleged to have been suffered as a result of an accident that occurred after the date of the financial statements. However, disclosure may be required by paragraphs 450-20-50-9 through 50-10.

> > Net Loss on Insurance Policies

450-20-55-17A This Subtopic does not prohibit (and, in fact, requires) accrual of a net loss (that is, a loss in excess of deferred premiums) that probably will be incurred on insurance policies that are in force, provided that the loss can be reasonably estimated.

> Illustrations

> > Example 1: Litigation Open to Considerable Interpretation

450-20-55-18 An entity may be litigating a dispute with another party. In preparation for the trial, it may determine that, based on recent developments involving one aspect of the litigation, it is probable that it will have to pay $2 million to settle the litigation. Another aspect of the litigation may, however, be open to considerable interpretation, and depending on the interpretation by the court the entity may have to pay an additional $8 million over and above the $2 million.

450-20-55-19 In that case, paragraph 450-20-25-2 requires accrual of the $2 million if that is considered a reasonable estimate of the loss.

450-20-55-20 Paragraphs 450-20-50-1 through 50-2 require disclosure of the nature of the accrual, and depending on the circumstances, may require disclosure of the $2 million that was accrued.

450-20-55-21 Paragraphs 450-20-50-3 through 50-8 require disclosure of the additional exposure to loss if there is a reasonable possibility that the additional amounts will be paid.

> > Example 2: Multiple Case Litigation Example

450-20-55-22 The following Cases illustrate application of the accrual and disclosure requirements in the following stages of litigation:

  a. The trial is complete but the damages are undetermined (Case A).
  b. The trial is incomplete but an unfavorable outcome is probable (Case B).
  c. The trial is incomplete and unfavorable outcome is reasonably possible (Case C).
  d. There is a range of loss and one amount is a better estimate than any other (Case D).

> > > Case A: Trial Is Complete but Damages Are Undetermined

450-20-55-23 An entity is involved in litigation at the close of its fiscal year and information available indicates that an unfavorable outcome is probable. Subsequently, after a trial on the issues, a verdict unfavorable to the entity is handed down, but the amount of damages remains unresolved at the time the financial statements are issued or are available to be issued (as discussed in Section 855-10-25). Although the entity is unable to estimate the exact amount of loss, its reasonable estimate at the time is that the judgment will be for not less than $3 million or more than $9 million. No amount in that range appears at the time to be a better estimate than any other amount.

450-20-55-24 In this Case, paragraph 450-20-30-1 requires accrual of the $3 million (the minimum of the range) at the close of the fiscal year.

450-20-55-25 Paragraphs 450-20-50-1 through 50-2 require disclosure of the nature of the contingency and, depending on the circumstances, may require disclosure of the amount of the accrual.

450-20-55-26 Paragraphs 450-20-50-3 through 50-8 require disclosure of the exposure to an additional amount of loss of up to $6 million.

> > > Case B: Trial Is Incomplete but Unfavorable Outcome Is Probable

450-20-55-27 Assume the same facts as in Case A, except it is probable that a verdict will be unfavorable and the trial has not been completed before the financial statements are issued or are available to be issued (as discussed in Section 855-10-25). In that situation, the condition in paragraph 450-20-25-

2(a) would be met because information available to the entity indicates that an unfavorable verdict is probable. An assessment that the range of loss is between $3 million and $9 million would meet the condition in paragraph 450-20-25-2(b).

450-20-55-28 In this Case, if no single amount in that range is a better estimate than any other amount, paragraph 450-20-30-1 requires accrual of $3 million (the minimum of the range) at the close of the fiscal year.

450-20-55-29 Paragraphs 450-20-50-1 through 50-2 require disclosure of the nature of the contingency and, depending on the circumstances, may require disclosure of the amount of the accrual.

450-20-55-30 Paragraphs 450-20-50-3 through 50-8 require disclosure of the exposure to an additional amount of loss of up to $6 million.

> > > **Case C: Trial Is Incomplete and Unfavorable Outcome Is Reasonably Possible**

450-20-55-31 Assume the same facts as in Case B, except the entity had assessed the verdict differently (for example, that an unfavorable verdict was not probable but was only reasonably possible). The condition in paragraph 450-20-25-2(a) would not have been met and no amount of loss would be accrued. Paragraphs 450-20-50-3 through 50-8 require disclosure of the nature of the contingency and any amount of loss that is reasonably possible.

> > > **Case D: Range of Loss and One Amount Is a Better Estimate than Any Other**

450-20-55-32 Assume that in Case A and Case B the condition in paragraph 450-20-25-2(a) has been met and a reasonable estimate of loss is a range between $3 million and $9 million but a loss of $4 million is a better estimate than any other amount in that range.

450-20-55-33 In this Case, paragraph 450-20-30-1 requires accrual of $4 million.

450-20-55-34 Paragraphs 450-20-50-1 through 50-2 require disclosure of the nature of the contingency and, depending on the circumstances, may require disclosure of the amount of the accrual.

450-20-55-35 Paragraphs 450-20-50-3 through 50-8 require disclosure of the exposure to an additional amount of loss of up to $5 million.

> > **Example 3: Illustrative Disclosure**

450-20-55-36 Entity A is the defendant in litigation involving a major competitor claiming patent infringement (Entity B). The suit claims damages of $200 million. Discovery has been completed, and Entity A is engaged in settlement discussions with the plaintiff. Entity A has made an offer of $5 million to settle the case, which offer was rejected by the plaintiff; the plaintiff has made an offer of $35 million to settle the case, which offer was rejected by Entity A. Based on the expressed willingness of the plaintiff to settle the case along with information revealed during discovery and the likely cost and risk to both sides of litigating, Entity A believes that it is probable the case will not come to trial. Accordingly, Entity A has determined that it is probable that it has some liability. Entity A's reasonable estimate of this liability is a range between $10 million and $35 million, with no amount within that range a better estimate than any other amount; accordingly, $10 million was accrued.

450-20-55-37 Entity A provides the following disclosure in accordance with Section 450-20-50.

> On March 15, 19X1, Entity B filed a suit against the company claiming patent infringement. While the company believes it has meritorious defenses against the suit, the ultimate resolution of the matter, which is expected to occur within one year, could result in a loss of up to $25 million in excess of the amount accrued.

* * *

[Subtopic] 30 Gain Contingencies

* * *

450-30-05 Overview and Background

General

450-30-05-1 This Subtopic provides guidance for the recognition and disclosure of a **gain contingency**.

450-30-05-2 This Subtopic, in combination with Subtopics 450-10 and 450-20, provides general guidance regarding gain and **loss contingencies**. Other Topics include gain or loss contingencies related to those specific Topics. Therefore, the Contingencies Topic does not include all standards related to contingencies. * * *

450-30-15 Scope and Scope Exceptions

General

> Overall Guidance

450-30-15-1 This Subtopic follows the same Scope and Scope Exceptions as outlined in the Overall Subtopic, see Section 450-10-15.

* * *

450-30-25 Recognition

General

450-30-25-1 A contingency that might result in a gain usually should not be reflected in the financial statements because to do so might be to recognize revenue before its realization.

450-30-50 Disclosure

General

450-30-50-1 Adequate disclosure shall be made of a contingency that might result in a gain, but care shall be exercised to avoid misleading implications as to the likelihood of realization.

* * *

NOTES

1. FASB ASC Topic 450, *Contingencies*, sets forth the analytical framework for analyzing accounting issues for loss contingencies, including both pending litigation, claims, and assessments, and unasserted claims and assessments. Because the Codification allows an enterprise's management to exercise considerable discretion in determining whether the enterprise should accrue a loss contingency in its accounts or, if not, at least disclose the possibility of a loss in the notes to the financial statements, financial accounting for such items more closely resembles an art than a science.

The different, but acceptable, approaches that McDonnell Douglas Corp., which later became a subsidiary of The Boeing Co., and General Dynamics Corp. as two joint venturers (collectively, the "Team") used to account for the U.S. Navy's decision in early 1991 to terminate the A-12 aircraft contract and to demand repayment of $1.4 billion in unliquidated progress payments illustrate the underlying judgment and discretion involved. All auditors–originally Ernst & Young for McDonnell Douglas, but later Deloitte & Touche LLP for Boeing, and Arthur Andersen & Co. for General Dynamics through 2001, and then KPMG LLP–always issued unqualified opinions for the different accounting treatments under similar, if not identical, facts.

The joint venture secured the fixed price, incentive contract with the Navy for the full-scale development and initial production of a carrier-based Advanced Tactical Aircraft, known as the A-12. Under the contract, both contractors undertook full responsibility for performance and agreed to joint and several liability for potential obligations arising from termination. After the Navy terminated the contract for alleged default, the Team filed a lawsuit to contest the default termination, to assert the joint venture's rights to convert the termination to one for the convenience of the government, and to obtain payment for work done and costs incurred, but not paid. The United

States agreed to defer the collection of the $1.4 billion in progress payments pending a negotiated settlement or other resolution.

Following the termination, McDonnell Douglas' inventories included about $583 million of recorded costs on the contract. Based at least in part on an opinion from outside counsel, McDonnell Douglas believed that either the parties or the courts would convert the dispute into a termination for convenience. McDonnell Douglas further determined that its best estimate of loss was $350 million, which the company established as a loss provision against the inventory costs in 1990. *See* McDonnell Douglas Corp., Annual Report (Form 10-K) Exhibit 13, pp.15, 66-67 (Mar. 22, 1994), *available at* http://www.sec.gov/Archives/edgar/data/63917/0000063917-94-000013.txt.

In contrast, General Dynamics recorded charges totaling $724 million before tax for 1990 related to the termination of the A-12 program and earlier identified cost overruns, which the company reported in earnings from discontinued operations. In connection with that treatment, General Dynamics wrote off as uncollectible the balance in its contracts in process account and recognized estimated termination liabilities, primarily to its vendors. General Dynamics did not recognize any claim revenue from the Navy nor any obligation to return unliquidated progress payments in its financial statements. *See* Gen. Dynamics Corp., Annual Report (Form 10-K) Exhibit 13, pp.18, 22 (Mar. 29, 1994), *available at* http://www.sec.gov/Archives/edgar/data/40533/0000950133-94-000045.txt; *see also* McDonnell Douglas Corp., Annual Report (Form 10-K) Exhibit 13, pp.15, 66-67 (Mar. 22, 1994), *available at* http://www.sec.gov/Archives/edgar/data/63917/0000063917-94-000013.txt (stating that even though General Dynamics reported a $450 million pre-tax provision as a loss on the A-12 contract for the quarter ended June 30, 1990, which included reversing $24 million of earnings that General Dynamics had previously recognized on the contract, based on different cost estimates, McDonnell Douglas did not report any loss at that time; McDonnell Douglas also disclosed that for the quarter ended December 31, 1990, General Dynamics announced an additional $274 million provision on the contract).

During litigation that lasted more than twenty years, the U.S. Court of Federal Claims as the trial court, the United States Court of Appeals for the Federal Circuit, and the Supreme Court of the United States issued various rulings, some decisions favored the government and others held in Team's favor. In the third quarter of 2013, the Navy and the Team signed a written settlement agreement that provided for in-kind consideration by the contractors in exchange for the case's dismissal, contingent upon Congressional legislation to authorize the Navy to receive and retain payment in-kind for the settlement. Under the settlement agreement, General Dynamics agreed to provide a $198 million credit to the Navy toward the design, construction and delivery of portions of a ship in another defense program, while Boeing agreed to provide three EA-18G Growlers, which are carrier-based electronic warfare aircraft, at no cost to the Navy. In December 2013, President Obama signed the National Defense Authorization Act, which contained a provision authorizing the A-12 settlement. Accordingly, General Dynamics recognized a $198 million, pre-tax loss ($129 million after taxes) in discontinued operations during the fourth quarter of 2013, while Boeing recorded a $406 million pre-tax charge in 2013, which included writing off inventory related to the A-12 and the three Growlers. The parties filed a stipulation of dismissal of the A-12 litigation with prejudice with the Court of Federal Claims in early 2014, and the Court dismissed the A-12 litigation on January 23, 2014. *See* Boeing Co., Annual Report (Form 10-K) 103-104, 110 (Feb. 14,2014), *available via* http://phx.corporate-ir.net/phoenix.zhtml?c=85482 &p=irol-sec; Gen. Dynamics Corp., Annual Report (Form 10-K) 71, 93 (Feb. 7, 2014); *available via* http://investorrelations.gd.com/phoenix.zhtml?c=85778&p =irol-sec.

2. When the Codification requires accrual, U.S. GAAP may also require disclosure about the nature or identity of the particular accrual, and perhaps the specific amount accrued, to prevent the financial statements from being misleading. So, depending upon the underlying circumstances, an enterprise faced with a loss contingency may need to choose among: (a) fully accruing and specifically identifying the potential loss; (b) fully accruing but not specifically disclosing the particular potential loss; (c) accruing a part and disclosing the possibility of more; (d) merely disclosing the contingency; or (e) if the contingency qualifies as sufficiently unlikely to occur, not even disclosing it.

3. ASC paragraph 450-20-25-2, which codified paragraph 8 of SFAS No. 5, as amended by paragraph B3.a. of SFAS No. 165, *Subsequent Events* (Fin. Accounting Standards Bd. 2009), requires an enterprise to accrue an estimated loss if: (a) information available prior to the financial statements being issued or being available to be issued indicates that the enterprise probably, or at least more likely than not, incurred a liability or suffered the impairment of an asset on or before the date of the financial statements; *and* (b) the enterprise can reasonably estimate the loss. As to the first set of conditions in (a), notice that the event that gave rise to the contingency must have occurred by the last day of the period that the financial statements cover, thus ruling out, for example, a lawsuit seeking damages arising from an accident that occurred *after* the date of the financial statements. Nevertheless, ASC paragraph 450-20-50-9 might require the enterprise to *disclose* the existence of a potential loss incurred from a so-called "subsequent event" occurring after the last date of the period that the financial statements cover. Such disclosure provides a more complete picture of the enterprise's financial status. On the other hand, please keep in mind that the Codification does not require, as a condition for accrual or disclosure, that the enterprise learn about the occurrence of the underlying event and the resulting possibility of loss before the end of the period covered by the financial statements. ASC section 450-20-55-11 specifically provides that as long as the underlying event occurred before the end of the period covered by the financial statements, any information available prior to the completion of the financial statements can affect the proper accounting treatment of the loss contingency in those financial statements.

4. Turning to the requirement in ASC section 450-20-25-2 that an enterprise can only accrue an estimated loss when it is "probable" that one or more future events will confirm the fact of a loss, notice that paragraph 450-20-20 defines

the term "probable" as "likely to occur." Although the Codification provides almost no additional guidance about what the words "probable" or "likely" mean, the related explanation in section 450-20-25-3 states that the word "probable" does not infer "virtual certainty." *See* FASB ASC ¶ 450-20-25-3 (a codification of ACCOUNTING FOR CONTINGENCIES, Statement of Fin. Accounting Standards No. 5, ¶ 84 (Fin. Accounting Standards Bd. 1975)). As a result, readers can easily assign different meanings to the terms "probable" or "likely to occur." At first glance, a lawyer, especially a litigator, might interpret the terms as meaning "more likely than not" or "anything greater than fifty percent." With little explanation, however, one commentator asserts that "on average, accountants interpret 'probable' as more than 75% likely," up from "say 60 to 70 percent" in an earlier edition. GEORGE MUNDSTOCK, A FINANCE APPROACH TO ACCOUNTING FOR LAWYERS 227 n.3 (2d ed. 2006) (citing Joseph Aharony & Amihud Dota, *A Comparative Analysis of Auditor, Manager and Financial Analyst Interpretations of SFAS 5 Disclosure Guidelines*, 31 J. BUS. FIN. & ACCT. 475 (2004)); GEORGE MUNDSTOCK, A FINANCE APPROACH TO ACCOUNTING FOR LAWYERS 149 n.6 (1999). A leading accounting text sets the level even higher: "most accountants and auditors appear to use *probable* to mean 80 to 85 percent or larger." Clyde P. Stickney & Roman L. Weil, Financial Accounting[:] An Introduction to Concepts Methods and Uses 520 n.5 (8th ed. 1997) (emphasis in original).

Based on comment letters and discussions at a 2005 public roundtable on the FASB's project on uncertain income taxes, FASB concluded that constituents do not consistently apply the confidence level that the term "probable" expresses. *See* ACCOUNTING FOR UNCERTAINTY IN INCOME TAXES–AN INTERPRETATION OF FASB STATEMENT NO. 109, FASB Interpretation No. 48, ¶ B32 (Fin. Accounting Standards Bd. 2006). During that project, the FASB indicated its belief that "more likely than not" conveys a lower percentage threshold than "probable." By comparison, for purposes of IAS 37, *Provisions, Contingent Liabilities and Contingent Assets*, the IASB interprets "probable" as meaning "more likely than not." PROVISIONS, CONTINGENT LIAB. & CONTINGENT ASSETS, Int'l Accounting Standard No. 37, ¶ 23 (Int'l Accounting Standards Bd. rev. 2013), *reprinted in* INT'L ACCOUNTING STANDARDS BD., INT'L FIN. REPORTING STANDARDS (AS ISSUED AT 1 JANUARY 2014), at A1104 (2014).

At the other end of the spectrum from "probable," section 450-20-20 defines the likelihood of an unfavorable outcome as "remote" when "[t]he chance of the future event or events occurring is slight." The Codification's third category, "reasonably possible," which most commentators treat as the default category, lies between the other two likelihoods. The glossary in section 450-20-20 assigns "reasonably possible" to circumstances that are "more than remote but less than likely."

In trying to determine the likelihood of a loss stemming from a pending claim or existing litigation, an enterprise should consider factors, such as the following: (a) progress of the case – whether the claimant has filed a complaint or initiated proceedings, and if so, the current stage of the claim or litigation, such as discovery or trial; (b) opinion of legal counsel – even if counsel cannot give a favorable opinion, the potential loss may not satisfy the conditions necessary for accrual; (c) prior experience of the enterprise, or other enterprises, in similar matters; and (d) management's intended response – whether management intends to settle or defend the case.

5. As to the second condition for accrual under ASC paragraph 450-20-25-2, the ability to reasonably estimate the potential loss, in many circumstances where an enterprise has probably incurred a loss, the enterprise cannot reasonably estimate any single amount, but can only identify a wide range of possible losses. When some amount within a range seems like a better estimate than any other amount within the range, the enterprise should accrue that amount. If an enterprise cannot determine a best estimate within the range, ASC section 450-20-30-1, which codified FASB Interpretation No. 14, *Reasonable Estimation of the Amount of Loss, an interpretation of FASB Statement No. 5* (Fin. Accounting Standards Bd. 1976), specifies that the enterprise should accrue the minimum amount in the range and disclose any reasonably possible additional loss that satisfies the other requirements in the Codification.

The following chart summarizes the rules in FASB ASC Topic 450 for treating material, asserted claims that arise from underlying events that occurred before the date of the financial statements:

ACCOUNTING TREATMENT FOR ASSERTED CLAIMS			
		Ability to Reasonably Estimate the Potential Loss	
		Reasonable Estimate	No Reasonable Estimate
Likelihood of an Unfavorable Outcome	Probable	Accrue and, if necessary, disclose to avoid misleading financial statements	Disclose contingency and range of possible loss or state that no reasonable estimate possible
	Reasonably Possible	Disclose contingency and estimated amount of possible loss	Disclose contingency and range of possible loss or state that no reasonable estimate possible
	Remote	Neither accrue nor disclose, unless guarantee	Neither accrue nor disclose, unless guarantee

Once again, recall that an enterprise must also disclose information about (1) contingencies from underlying events that occurred after the date of the financial statements, but before the enterprise issued the financial statements which could have a material effect on the financials and (2) guarantees.

6. In the case of unasserted claims, a business must first assess the probability of assertion. If the enterprise concludes that the circumstances suggest that the potentially adverse party will not assert the claim, ASC Topic 450 does not require accrual or disclosure. By comparison, if assertion seems probable, the enterprise must proceed in exactly the same manner as if someone had asserted the claim. You should note that weird outcomes can result from applying the rules regarding unasserted claims. Assume that an enterprise assigns a fifty-one percent chance to the probability that the claimant will assert a $100 million claim and a fifty-one percent chance to an unfavorable outcome on the full claim. Under a broad construction of "probable," the enterprise might need to accrue, and perhaps identify, a $100 million loss even though the overall chance that the enterprise will incur the loss equals 26.01 percent (fifty-one percent times fifty-one percent).

7. ASC paragraph 450-20-25-8, which codified paragraph 14 of SFAS No. 5, prohibits enterprises from recording accruals for general or unspecified business risks. Such "general" reserves illustrate the "cookie jar reserves" that then-SEC Chairman Arthur Levitt listed as one of the five most popular accounting illusions in his famous "The 'Numbers Game'" speech. See pages 380 to 385, *supra*. In 2002, the SEC initiated cease-and-desist proceedings against Microsoft Corporation because the company maintained between about $200 million and $900 million in unsupported and undisclosed reserves, accruals, allowances, and liability accounts during its fiscal years ended June 30, 1995 through June 30, 1998, which understated the company's income for that period. Although not related to any litigation, these reserves lacked properly documented support and substantiation. Microsoft consented to a cease-and-desist order to resolve the proceedings. *In re* Microsoft Corp., Accounting and Auditing Enforcement Release No. 1563, [2001–2003 Transfer Binder] Fed. Sec. L. Rep. (CCH) ¶ 75,078 (June 3, 2002); *see also* SEC v. Bennett, Accounting and Auditing Enforcement Release No. 2281, http://www.sec.gov/litigation/litreleases/lr19310.htm (July 26, 2005) (defendant consented to injunction, $25,000 civil penalty, and officer or director bar for five years for approving the use of reserves without a specific contingency or insufficient support).

8. FASB ASC ¶ 450-20-S99-2, which codified Emerging Issues Task Force Topic No. D-77, *Accounting for Legal Costs Expected to Be Incurred in Connection with a Loss Contingency* ("EITF No. D-77), observed that enterprises typically expensed legal costs related to a loss contingency as incurred, but recognized that some companies had accrued estimated legal costs. Pursuant to FASB ASC Topic 235, *Notes to Financial Statements*, which codified APB Opinion No. 22, *Disclosure of Accounting Policies*, enterprises should disclose any material accounting policies, as well as the methods used to apply those policies, and apply those policies consistently. *See* FASB ASC ¶ 450-20-S99-2 (a codification of ACCOUNTING FOR LEGAL COSTS EXPECTED TO BE INCURRED IN CONNECTION WITH A LOSS CONTINGENCY, Emerging Issues Task Force Topic No. D-77 (Fin. Accounting Standards Bd. Jan. 23, 1997; Mar. 24-25, 1999)). Presumably pursuant to EITF No. D-77 and in response to litigation arising from the drug Vioxx, Merck & Co., Inc. ("Merck") first disclosed an accounting policy regarding "Legal Defense Costs" in the company's 2004 annual report. According to this policy, Merck accrues "[l]egal defense costs expected to be incurred in connection with a loss contingency . . . when probable and reasonably estimable." MERCK & CO., 2004 ANNUAL REPORT 40 (2005). As of December 31, 2004, the company had established a reserve of $675 million solely for its future legal defense costs related to the Vioxx litigation. Note 11 to the financial statements states: "This reserve is based on certain assumptions and is the *minimum amount* that the Company believes at this time it can reasonably estimate will be spent *over a multi-year period.*" *Id.* at 48 (emphasis added). During 2005, Merck spent $285 million in legal defense costs related to Vioxx-related litigation. In the fourth quarter, Merck recorded a $295 million charge to increase the reserve solely for its future legal defense costs related to the Vioxx litigation to $685 million on December 31, 2005. Note 11 to the financial statements continues: "This reserve is based on certain assumptions and is the *best estimate* of the amount that the Company believes, at this time, it can reasonably estimate will be spent *through 2007.*" MERCK & CO., 2005 ANNUAL REPORT 54 (2005) (emphasis added). In addition, the same note states that, as of December 31, 2005, "[t]he Company has not established any reserves for any potential liability relating to the [Vioxx litigation]." *Id.*

In November 2007, Merck settled the principal Vioxx litigation for $4.85 billion, which the company treated as an expense during the fourth quarter. Throughout that year, Merck spent $616 million on legal defense costs related to Vioxx cases and also increased the related reserve by $280 million. At year-end, Merck's total "*Vioxx* Reserve" stood at $5.372 billion, reflecting the settlement amount and $522 million in reserve for future legal defense costs. MERCK & CO., 2007 ANNUAL REPORT (Form 10-K), at 78 (Feb. 28, 2008). During 2008, Merck spent about $305 million on legal defense costs worldwide related to Vioxx litigation, recorded a $62 million charge for future legal defense costs, and paid $750 million pursuant to the settlement, which left the "Vioxx Reserve" at approximately $4.379 billion on December 31, 2008. MERCK & CO., 2008 ANNUAL REPORT (Form 10-K), at 35 (Feb. 27, 2009). In 2009, Merck paid $4.1 billion into various settlement funds, spent approximately $244 million in legal defense costs worldwide related to Vioxx litigation, and recorded a $75 million charge for future legal defense costs, which left the "Vioxx Reserve" at approximately $110 million on December 31, 2009. MERCK & CO., 2009 ANNUAL REPORT (Form 10-K), at 102 (Mar. 1, 2010). During 2010, spent approximately $140 million in legal defense costs worldwide related to Vioxx litigation, and recorded $106 million in charges for future legal defense costs, which left the "*Vioxx* Legal Defense Costs Reserve" at approximately $76 million on December 31, 2010. MERCK & CO., 2010 ANNUAL REPORT (Form 10-K), at 127-28 (Feb. 28, 2011). Merck indicated that it "will continue to monitor its legal defense costs and review the adequacy of the associated reserves and may determine to increase the *Vioxx* Legal Defense Costs Reserve at any time in the future if . . . it believes it would be appropriate to do so." *Id.* at 128. Other than a reserve established with respect to a Department of Justice investigation, Merck did not establish any reserves for any potential liability related to ongoing Vioxx product liability lawsuits or investigations because, among other reasons, the company "cannot reasonably estimate the possible loss or range of loss with respect to the *Vioxx* Lawsuits not included in the Settlement Program." *Id.*

Interestingly, the first paragraph in Note 12 to the Merck's financial statements, entitled "Contingencies and Environmental Liabilities," also provided in pertinent part:

> The Company records accruals for contingencies when it is probable that a liability has been incurred and the amount can be reasonably estimated. These accruals are adjusted periodically as assessments change or additional information becomes available. For product liability claims, a portion of the overall accrual is actuarially determined and considers such factors as past experience, number of claims reported and estimates of claims incurred but not yet reported. Individually significant contingent losses are accrued when probable and reasonably estimable. Legal defense costs expected to be incurred in connection with a loss contingency are accrued when probable and reasonably estimable.

Id. at 124.

9. The Codification also sets forth rules on accounting for and disclosing financial guarantees. FASB ASC Topic 460, *Guarantees*, provides that, at the inception of a guarantee, the guarantor must recognize a liability for the fair value of the obligation undertaken. *See* FASB ASC ¶¶ 460-10-25-3 to -4 (codifications of GUARANTOR'S ACCOUNTING AND DISCLOSURE REQUIREMENTS FOR GUARANTEES, INCLUDING INDIRECT GUARANTEES OF INDEBTEDNESS OF OTHERS: AN INTERPRETATION OF FASB STATEMENTS NO. 5, 57 AND 107 AND RESCISSION OF FASB INTERPRETATION NO. 34, FASB Interpretation No. 45 ("FIN 45"), at ¶ 9 (Fin. Accounting Standards Bd. 2002)). The rules also elaborate on the disclosures that a guarantee must provide in interim and annual financial statements about its obligations under certain guarantees. In particular, a guarantor must disclose: (1) the nature of the guarantee, including how the guarantee arose, its approximate term, and the events or circumstances that would require the guarantor to perform under the guarantee; (2) the maximum potential amount of future payments under the guarantee; (3) the carrying amount of the liability, if any, for the guarantor's obligations under the guarantee; and (4) the nature and extent of any recourse provisions or available collateral that would enable the guarantor to recover any amounts paid under the guarantee. *See* FASB ASC ¶ 460-10-50-4 (a codification of FIN 45, ¶ 13). Special rules about disclosures, however, apply to product warranties. Rather than disclose information about the maximum potential amount of future payments under the guarantee, a guarantor must disclose its accounting policy and methodology used to determine its liability for product warranties and provide a tabular reconciliation that sets forth the changes in the guarantor's product warranty liability for the reporting period. *See* FASB ASC ¶ 460-10-50-8 (a codification of FIN 45, ¶ 14).

10. FASB ASC Topic 805, *Business Combinations*, which codified SFAS No. 141(R) on that same subject, generally requires an enterprise to recognize the assets acquired and liabilities assumed in a business combination, including litigation contingencies, at their fair values on the acquisition date. *See* FASB ASC ¶ 805-20-30-1 (a codification of SFAS No. 141(R) ¶ 20). Following SFAS No. 141(R)'s issuance, preparers, auditors, and lawyers expressed concerns that the requirement to determine a legal contingency's fair value could prejudice the underlying legal dispute. Responding to those concerns, FASB announced a return to the rules in the original SFAS No. 141. Under the original, and now again applicable, rules codified in FASB ASC Subtopic 805-20, *Identifiable Assets and Liabilities, and Any Noncontrolling Interest*, an enterprise only recognizes an acquired contingency at fair value if the enterprise can determine that amount during the measurement period, which typically ends no later than one year after the transaction's closing. Otherwise, enterprises would follow the rules contained in FASB ASC Subtopic 450-20, *Loss Contingencies*, and originally set forth in SFAS No. 5 and FIN 14. As a result, unless an acquirer can resolve a legal contingency during the measurement period, the acquirer typically will not record any liability for the legal contingency as of the acquisition date. *See* FASB ASC ¶¶ 805-20-25-19 to -20B & 805-20-30-9, -23 (codifications of ACCOUNTING FOR ASSETS ACQUIRED AND LIABILITIES ASSUMED IN A BUS. COMBINATION THAT ARISE FROM CONTINGENCIES, FASB Staff Position No. FAS 141(R)-1, at ¶¶ 7-9 (Fin. Accounting Standards Bd. 2009)). Incidentally, the same rules apply when a not-for-profit acquirer obtains control of one or more nonprofit activities or businesses. *See* FASB ASC ¶ 805-20-20 (acquisition by a not-for-profit entity).

11. With respect to gain contingencies, two general principles apply. First, pursuant to the conservatism doctrine an enterprise should not record gain contingencies which the enterprise may never in fact realize. Second, an enterprise must adequately disclose gain contingencies, but should exercise care to avoid overstating the likelihood that a gain will materialize.

The following excerpts from financial statements for E.I. du Pont de Nemours and Company and JLG Industries for periods ending in December 1999 and July 1994, respectively, illustrate how enterprises have treated various contingencies:

E.I. DU PONT DE NEMOURS AND COMPANY

NOTES TO FINANCIAL STATEMENTS
(Dollars in millions, except per share)

1. Summary of Significant Accounting Policies

* * *

Environmental Liabilities and Expenditures

Accruals for environmental matters are recorded in operating expenses when it is probable that a liability has been incurred and the amount of the liability can be reasonably estimated. Accrued liabilities do not include claims against third parties and are not discounted.

Costs related to environmental remediation are charged to expense. Other environmental costs are also charged to expense unless they increase the value of the property and/or mitigate or prevent contamination from future operations, in which case they are capitalized.

* * *

26. Commitments and Contingent Liabilities

* * *

The company is subject to various lawsuits and claims with respect to such matters as product liabilities, governmental regulations and other actions arising out of the normal course of business. While the effect on future financial results is not subject to reasonable estimation because considerable uncertainty exists, in the opinion of company counsel, the ultimate liabilities resulting from such lawsuits and claims may be significant to results of operations in the period recognized but management does not anticipate they will have a material adverse effect on the consolidated financial position or liquidity of the company.

DuPont has been served with several hundred lawsuits in connection with the 1991 stop-sale and recall of Benlate® 50 DF fungicide; approximately 140 cases are pending. The majority of these lawsuits were filed by growers who allege plant damage from using Benlate® 50 DF and have been disposed of by trial, settlement or dismissal. However, certain plaintiffs who previously settled with the company have filed cases alleging fraud and other misconduct relating to the litigation and settlement of Benlate® 50 DF claims. DuPont believes that Benlate® 50 DF did not cause the damages alleged in these cases and denies the allegations of fraud and misconduct. DuPont intends to defend itself in these cases. DuPont and other major defendants have been served with lawsuits, including several class actions, which claim damages from allegedly defective plumbing systems made with polybutylene pipe and acetal fittings. In the fourth quarter of 1995, the company settled two of the class actions limiting its liability to 10 percent of the cost of repairing the allegedly defective plumbing systems up to a total company payout of $120. Other lawsuits, including the unsettled class actions, are pending in several states and Canada. The related liability for each of these matters included in the Consolidated Balance Sheet is not reduced by the amount of any expected insurance recoveries. Adverse changes in estimates for such costs could result in additional future charges.

The company is also subject to contingencies pursuant to environmental laws and regulations that in the future may require the company to take further action to correct the effects on the environment of prior disposal practices or releases of chemical or petroleum substances by the company or other parties. The company has accrued for certain environmental remediation activities consistent with the policy set forth in Note 1. At December 31, 1999, such accrual amounted to $435 and, in management's opinion, was appropriate based on existing facts and circumstances. Under adverse changes in circumstances, potential liability may exceed amounts accrued. In the event that future remediation expenditures are in excess of amounts accrued, they may be significant to results of operations in the period recognized but management does not anticipate that they will have a material adverse effect on the consolidated financial position or liquidity of the company.

The company has indirectly guaranteed various debt obligations under agreements with certain affiliated and other companies to provide specified minimum revenues from shipments or purchases of products. At December 31, 1999, these indirect guarantees totaled $19, and the company had directly guaranteed $821 of the obligations of certain affiliated companies and others. No material loss is anticipated by reason of such agreements and guarantees.

* * *

E.I. du Pont de Nemours & Co., 1999 ANNUAL REPORT 47–48, 66–67 (2000).

JLG INDUSTRIES, INC.

NOTES TO CONSOLIDATED FINANCIAL STATEMENTS

Commitments and Contingencies (In Part)

The Company is a party to personal injury and property damage litigation arising out of incidents involving the use of its products. Annually the Company sets its product liability litigation insurance program based on the Company's current and historical claims experience and the availability and cost of insurance. The combination of these annual programs constitutes the Company's aggregate product liability insurance coverage. The Company's program for fiscal year 1994 was comprised of a self-insurance retention of $5 million and catastrophic coverage of $10 million in excess of the retention.

Cumulative amounts estimated to be payable by the Company with respect to pending product liability claims for all years in which the Company is liable under its self-insurance retention have been accrued as liabilities, including $2.2 million for incidents the Company believes may result in claims. Estimates of such accrued liabilities are based on an evaluation of the merits of individual claims and historical claims experience; thus, the Company's ultimate liability may exceed or be less than the amounts accrued. Amounts accrued are paid over varying periods, which generally do not exceed 5 years. The methods of making such estimates and establishing the resulting accrued liability are reviewed continually, and any adjustments resulting therefrom are reflected in current earnings.

AM. INST. OF CERTIFIED PUB. ACCOUNTANTS, ACCOUNTING TRENDS & TECHNIQUES 80–81 (49th ed. 1995).

C.   SECURITIES DISCLOSURE ISSUES

Various legal issues involving contingencies, particularly environmental liabilities, product liability cases and tax disputes, can arise as an enterprise seeks to comply with disclosure requirements under the federal securities laws. In recent years, asbestos liabilities have also received widespread attention. In 2001, the Rand Institute conducted a study that estimated that the U.S. courts have already adjudicated $30 billion in asbestos claims. The study anticipated that the courts will need to resolve another $200 billion in pending or future claims. Steven Harras, *Asbestos Reform Summit Held on Capitol Hill; Congress, Business, Lawyers Seek Solutions*, Corp. L. Daily (BNA), Apr. 4, 2003.

Beginning in the 1970s, businesses have spent increasing amounts to comply with various federal and state environmental standards. Perhaps more significantly, however, both federal and state statutes often impose liabilities on businesses that own or operate, or once owned or operated, properties that contain environmental contamination. Due to these liabilities' sheer size, issues related to accounting for environmental cleanup liabilities have pushed to the forefront in the accounting and securities fields. Today, environmental contingencies present some of the most difficult, and important, applications of FASB ASC Topic 450, *Contingencies*, which you probably recall codified SFAS No. 5.

Businesses in the United States currently face massive liabilities for environmental clean-up costs. For example, a Congressional Budget Office study estimated that the costs to clean up only non-government sites under the Comprehensive Environmental Response, Compensation and Liability Act, as reauthorized and amended, could reach $463 billion. *AICPA Issues Proposed Guidelines for Environmental Liabilities Accounting*, 27 Sec. Reg. & L. Rep. (BNA) 1123 (July 7, 1995). In addition, businesses spend enormous amounts each year to comply with the various federal environmental laws and related regulations, and similar state legislation and administrative rules, in part because noncompliance can cause both civil and criminal penalties.

Lawyers can encounter accounting issues involving environmental contingencies in at least three different ways. First, both the SEC and the accounting profession have focused on environmental accounting and disclosure because many businesses, especially publicly-traded enterprises, did not properly accrue or disclose their environmental clean-up liabilities in their financial statements. Staff Accounting Bulletin No. 92, which follows below, signaled the Commission's commitment to improving accounting and disclosure practices in this area. Second, SEC rules require registrants to discuss their environmental obligations in Management's Discussion and Analysis. Finally, lawyers must increasingly consider environmental contingencies in responding to audit inquiry letters. Auditors have increasingly focused their attention on environmental contingencies because they fear legal liability for improperly reported or disclosed environmental liabilities.

Staff Accounting Bulletin No. 92

Securities and Exchange Commission, 1993.
58 Fed. Reg. 32,843 (June 14, 1993).

[You may recall from Chapter II on page 159, *supra*, that Staff Accounting Bulletins present interpretations and practices that the Office of the Chief Accountant and the Division of Corporation Finance follow in administering the disclosure requirements in the federal securities laws. The statements in SABs, however, do not bear the SEC's official approval. SAB No. 92 provides the following guidance regarding accounting and disclosures relating to loss contingencies:]

Facts: A registrant believes it may be obligated to pay material amounts as a result of product or environmental liability. These amounts may relate to, for example, damages attributed to the registrant's products or processes, clean-up of hazardous wastes, reclamation costs, fines, and litigation costs. The registrant may seek to recover a portion or all of these amounts by filing a claim against an insurance carrier or other third parties.

Paragraph 8 of *Statement of Financial Accounting Standards No. 5,* "Accounting for Contingencies," ("SFAS 5") [now codified in FASB ASC Topic 450, *Contingencies,*] states that an estimated loss from a loss contingency shall be accrued by a charge to income if it is probable that a liability has been incurred and the amount of the loss can be reasonably estimated. The Emerging Issues Task Force ("EITF") of the Financial Accounting Standards Board reached a consensus on EITF Issue 93–5, "Accounting for Environmental Liabilities," that an environmental liability should be evaluated independently from any potential claim for recovery. Under that consensus, any loss arising from the recognition of an environmental liability should be reduced by a potential claim for recovery only when that claim is probable of realization. The EITF also reached a consensus that discounting an environmental liability for a specific clean-up site to reflect the time value of money is appropriate only if the aggregate amount of the obligation and the amount and timing of the cash payments are fixed or reliably determinable for that site. * * *

Because uncertainty regarding the alternative methods of presenting in the balance sheets the amounts recognized as contingent liabilities and claims for recovery from third parties was not resolved by the EITF and current disclosure practices remain diverse, the staff is publishing its interpretation of the current accounting literature and disclosure requirements to serve as guidance for public companies. * * *

Question 1: Does the staff believe that it is appropriate to offset in the balance sheet a claim for recovery that is probable of realization against a probable contingent liability, that is, report the two as a single net amount on the face of the balance sheet?

Interpretive Response: Not ordinarily. The staff believes that separate presentation of the gross liability and related claim for recovery in the balance sheet most fairly presents the potential consequences of the contingent claim on the company's resources and is the preferable method of display. Recent reports of litigation over insurance policies' coverage of product and environmental liabilities and financial failures in the insurance industry indicate that there are significant uncertainties regarding both the timing and the ultimate realization of claims made to recover amounts from insurance carriers and other third parties. The risks and uncertainties associated with a registrant's contingent liability are separate and distinct from those associated with its claim for recovery from third parties.

* * *

Question 2: If a registrant is jointly and severally liable with respect to a contaminated site but there is a reasonable basis for apportionment of costs among responsible parties, must the registrant recognize a liability with respect to costs apportioned to other responsible parties?

Interpretive Response: No. However, if it is probable that other responsible parties will not fully pay costs apportioned to them, the liability that is recognized by the registrant should include the registrant's best estimate, before consideration of potential recoveries from other parties, of the additional costs that the registrant expects to pay. Discussion of uncertainties affecting the registrant's ultimate obligation may be necessary if, for example, the solvency of one or more parties is in doubt or responsibility for the site is disputed by a party. A note to the financial statements should describe any additional loss that is reasonably possible.

Question 3: Estimates and assumptions regarding the extent of environmental or product liability, methods of remedy, and amounts of related costs frequently prove to be different from the ultimate outcome. How do these uncertainties affect the recognition and measurement of the liability?

Interpretive Response: The measurement of the liability should be based on currently available facts, existing technology, and presently enacted laws and regulations, and should take into consideration the likely effects of inflation and other societal and economic factors. Notwithstanding significant uncertainties, management may not delay recognition of a contingent liability until only a single amount can be reasonably estimated. If management is able to determine that the amount of the liability is likely to fall within a range and no amount within that range can be determined to be the better estimate, the registrant should recognize the minimum amount of the range * * *. The staff believes that recognition of a loss equal to the lower limit of the range is necessary even if the upper limit of the range is uncertain.

* * * In measuring its environmental liability, a registrant should consider available evidence including the registrant's prior experience in remediation of contaminated sites, other companies' clean-up experience, and data released by the Environmental Protection Agency or other organizations. * * * While the range of costs associated with the alternatives may be broad, the minimum clean-up cost is unlikely to be zero. As additional information becomes available, changes in estimates of the liability should be reported in the period that those changes occur * * *.

* * *

Question 5: What financial statement disclosures should be furnished with respect to recorded and unrecorded product or environmental liabilities?

Interpretive Response: Paragraphs 9 and 10 of SFAS 5 [now codified in FASB ASC ¶¶ 450-20-50-1 to -6] identify disclosures regarding loss contingencies that generally are furnished in notes to financial statements. The staff believes that product and environmental liabilities typically are of such significance that detailed disclosures regarding the judgments and assumptions underlying the recognition and measurement of the liabilities are necessary to prevent the financial statements from being misleading and to inform readers fully regarding the range of reasonably possible outcomes that could have a material effect on the registrant's financial condition, results of operations, or liquidity. * * *

Registrants are cautioned that a statement that the contingency is not expected to be material does not satisfy the requirements of SFAS 5 [or ASC Topic 450] if there is at least a reasonable possibility that a loss exceeding amounts already recognized may have been incurred and the amount of that additional loss would be material to a decision to buy or sell the registrant's securities. In that case, the registrant must either (a) disclose the estimated additional loss, or range of loss, that is reasonably possible, or (b) state that such estimate cannot be made.

Question 6: What disclosures regarding loss contingencies may be necessary outside the financial statements?

Interpretive Response: Registrants should consider the requirements of Items 101 (Description of Business), 103 (Legal Proceedings), and 303 (Management's Discussion and Analysis) of Regulations S–K and S–B. * * *

* * *

NOTES

1. In 1996, the AICPA issued SOP 96-1, now codified in FASB ASC Subtopic 410-30, *Asset Retirement and Environmental Obligations—Environmental Obligations*, to provide authoritative guidance on specific accounting issues regarding the recognition, measurement, display and disclosure of such liabilities. SOP 96–1 provided that enterprises should accrue environmental remediation liabilities when the underlying facts and circumstances satisfied the criteria in SFAS No. 5, now codified in FASB ASC Topic 450, Contingencies. In addition, the statement of position contained benchmarks to help determine whether SFAS No. 5 required accrual. The document further provided that any accrual should include (1) incremental direct costs for the remediation effort and (2) an allocable portion of the compensation and benefits for those employees that the enterprise expects to devote a significant amount of time directly to the remediation effort.

2. According to FASB ASC Subtopic 410-30, *Asset Retirement and Environmental Obligations—Environmental Obligations*, which codified a conclusion originally reached in EITF Issue No. 93-5, *Accounting for Environmental Liabilities* ("EITF Issue No. 93-5"), as modified by Statement of Position 96-1, *Environmental Remediation Liabilities* ("SOP 96-1"), an enterprise should evaluate an environmental liability independently from any potential claim for recovery. The Codification provides that an enterprise can reduce the loss arising from an environmental liability only when the claim for recovery qualifies as probable of realization. On a related matter, an enterprise can discount liabilities accrued for a specific site to reflect the time value of money only if the obligation and the scheduled payments qualify as fixed or reliably determinable. As a practical matter, the best available estimates to remediate environmental liabilities generally provide only a range of possible losses. In these circumstances, therefore, the Codification prohibits discounting. In those circumstances where an enterprise can use discounting, the financial statements must disclose any underlying assumptions and any material effects that arise from the discounting.

3. You may recall from Chapter IV on page 316, *supra*, that Item 303 of Regulation S–K requires MD&A disclosure of certain forward-looking information, including any "currently known trends, events, and uncertainties" that the registrant reasonably expects will have a material impact on its liquidity, financial condition or results of operation. In Financial Reporting Release No. 36, 54 Fed. Reg. 22,427 (May 24, 1989), the SEC sets forth the following two-part test for mandatory disclosure regarding forward-looking information and gives an example involving an environmental contingency:

> Where a trend, demand, commitment, event or uncertainty is known, management must make two assessments:
>
> (1) Is the known trend, demand, commitment, event or uncertainty likely to come to fruition? If management determines that it is not reasonably likely to occur, no disclosure is required.
>
> (2) If management cannot make that determination, it must evaluate objectively the consequences of the known trend, demand, commitment, event or uncertainty, on the assumption that it will come to fruition. Disclosure is then required unless management determines that a material effect on the registrant's financial condition or results of operations is not reasonably likely to occur.
>
> * * *
>
> Application of these principles may be illustrated using a common disclosure issue which was considered in the review of a number of Project registrants: designation as a potentially responsible party ("PRP") by the Environmental Protection Agency (the "EPA") under

The Comprehensive Environmental Response, Compensation, and Liability Act of 1980 ("Superfund").

Facts: A registrant has been correctly designated a PRP by the EPA with respect to cleanup of hazardous waste at three sites. No statutory defenses are available. The registrant is in the process of preliminary investigations of the sites to determine the nature of its potential liability and the amount of remedial costs necessary to clean up the sites. Other PRPs also have been designated, but the ability to obtain contribution is unclear, as is the extent of insurance coverage, if any. Management is unable to determine that a material effect on future financial condition or results of operations is not reasonably likely to occur.

Based upon the facts of this hypothetical base, MD&A disclosure of the effects of the PRP status, quantified to the extent reasonably practicable, would be required. For MD&A purposes, aggregate potential cleanup costs must be considered in light of the joint and several liability to which a PRP is subject. Facts regarding whether insurance coverage may be contested, and whether and to what extent potential sources of contribution or indemnification constitute reliable sources of recovery may be factored into the determination of whether a material future effect is not reasonably likely to occur.

Id. at 22,430. FRR No. 36, therefore, purportedly establishes a "reasonably likely to have a material effect" standard for disclosing forward-looking information and specifically applies that standard to an environmental contingency. At least one important issue, however, seemingly remains unresolved. Does the "reasonably likely" standard differ from the "reasonably possible" likelihood which would otherwise require disclosure under ASC Topic 450?

In *Greenstone v. Cambex Corp.*, 975 F.2d 22 (1st Cir. 1992), the court of appeals explicitly recognized, but did not decide, the issue under SFAS No. 5. In that case, the First Circuit affirmed the district court's decision dismissing a securities fraud claim because the investor did not plead "with particularity" any specific factual allegations supporting the conclusion that Cambex or its officers knew that the company faced a significant possibility of loss arising from certain IBM Credit leases prior to the time that IBM Credit filed the lawsuit. In the opinion's last paragraph, then Chief Judge, now Justice, Breyer wrote:

We need not * * * decide whether the appropriate standard is knowledge (1) that an IBM Credit lawsuit was "probable" or (2) that the lawsuit (or some similar loss) was "reasonably likely[."] Whether the standard is one or the other or yet some third similar standard (such as "reasonably expects"), we should reach the same result.

975 F.2d at 28.

More recently, in 2002, the SEC indicated its view that the words "reasonably likely" express a lower disclosure threshold than "more likely than not." Commission Statement about Management's Discussion and Analysis of Financial Condition and Results of Operations, Financial Reporting Release No. 61, 67 Fed. Reg. 3746, 3748 (Jan. 25, 2002), *available at* http://www.sec.gov/rules/other/33-8056.htm. Unfortunately, the SEC did not compare "reasonably likely" and "reasonably possible." In the years ahead, we can expect lawyers and the courts to face this potentially important issue. In addition, to the extent that the "reasonably likely to have a material effect" standard in the MD&A requirements mandates disclosure in situations which would not qualify as "material" for accounting purposes, compliance with GAAP may once again not satisfy disclosure obligations under the federal securities laws. Recall our discussion about MD&A in Chapter IV, on pages 316 to 325, *supra*.

4. Late in 2008, FASB proposed to enhance the disclosure requirements for loss contingencies. FASB ultimately removed the project from its agenda in 2012, but not before critics of the proposed standards complained that the existing rules simply suffered from noncompliance. That message appears to have reached the SEC staff, who have increasingly reminded public companies about their disclosure obligations under the federal securities laws. In 2010, the Division of Corporation Finance sent letters to the chief financial officers of various public companies to remind the executives about their disclosure obligations under both FASB ASC Topic 450 and the MD&A requirements, especially given continued market concerns about potential risks and costs related to mortgage and foreclosure-related activities or exposures. *See* Staff of the Sec. & Exch. Comm'n, Sample Letter Sent to Public Companies on Accounting and Disclosure Issues Related to Potential Risks and Costs Associated with Mortgage and Foreclosure-Related Activities or Exposures (Oct. 2010), *available at* http://www.sec.gov/divisions/corpfin/guidance/cfoforeclosure1010.htm. Importantly, FASB ASC Subtopic 450-20, *Loss Contingencies*, requires an enterprise to disclose information when a reasonable possibility exists that the enterprise will incur a material loss. Such disclosures should include both information about the "nature of the contingency" and "[a]n estimate of the possible loss or range of possible loss or a statement that such an estimate cannot be made." *See* FASB ASC § 450-20-50-4.

In particular, the SEC staff has urged public companies to disclose information about the possible range of losses arising from lawsuits during the litigation so that large settlements do not surprise investors or the SEC staff. In that regard, and based upon the specific facts and circumstances disclosed, the staff focuses on whether the enterprise recognized any expense or loss in the proper period for an appropriate amount and does not hesitate to ask questions when settlements vary significantly from accruals, whether favorably or unfavorably, or when the facts and circumstances suggest that income smoothing has occurred. In addition, the staff has cautioned public companies that they must try to estimate potential losses from contingencies before declaring the effort impossible. To enable a public company to avoid announcing to an actual or potential litigation opponent how much the company either might pay to resolve the matter or expects to lose in a lawsuit, the SEC does not object to aggregating potential losses on separate situations into a single range. At least anecdotally, these efforts have produced an increase in disclosures related to possible litigation losses, especially by the largest financial institutions. *See, e.g.,* Stephen Joyce, *Largest Banks' Legal Exposure $19.2 Billion; Issues Include Mortgages, Securities, Libor,* Sec. L. Daily (Bloomberg BNA), Aug. 19, 2013 (reporting that the largest U.S. banks estimated the following amounts as their collective litigation exposure above their accrued liabilities as of June 30, 2013: $6.8 billion (JPMorgan Chase & Co.),$5 billion (Citigroup Inc.), $3.5 billion (Goldman Sachs Group Inc.), $2.8 billion (Bank of America Corp.), and $1.1 billion (Wells Fargo & Co.)).

5. After its 1994 bankruptcy, Orange County filed a lawsuit on January 12, 1995 seeking more than $2 billion from Merrill Lynch & Co., Inc. for the brokerage firm's role in the risky derivatives-based investment scheme that ultimately led to the nation's largest municipal bankruptcy. On June 2, 1998, Orange County and Merrill Lynch announced a $400 million settlement to end the lawsuit. In one of the ensuing press releases, Merrill Lynch "announced that it was fully reserved for the settlement and 'that the payment will have no financial impact on earnings reported in the 1998 second quarter or subsequent quarters.'" *Merrill Lynch to Pay $400 Million to Settle Orange County Bankruptcy Suit,* 30 Sec. Reg. & L. Rep. (BNA) 846 (June 5, 1998). A close examination of the supplemental table for "Non-Interest Expenses" in the MD&A in Merrill Lynch's Form 10-K for the fiscal year ended December 27, 1996 (filed March 21, 1997) reveals that other non-interest expenses increased from $697 million in fiscal 1995 to $859 million in fiscal 1996. At the very end of the textual discussion in that section, the following statement appears: "Other expenses rose 23% due in part to provisions related to various business activities and goodwill amortization." The same supplemental table in the MD&A in Merrill Lynch's Form 10-K for the fiscal year ended December 26, 1997 (filed March 3, 1998) also reveals that other non-interest expenses increased from $859 million in fiscal 1996 to $1,136 million in fiscal 1997. At the end of the third paragraph in textual discussion for that section, the MD&A comments: "Other expenses increased 32% from 1996 due to increases in provisions for various business activities and legal matters, and higher office and postage costs." The very last sentence in that section repeats the statement that appeared in the 1996 MD&A: "Other expenses rose 23% due in part to provisions related to various business activities and goodwill amortization." As counsel for Orange County would you find this information helpful? How might you use those disclosures to gather additional information, financial or other, that might help your client? *See* Matthew J. Barrett, *Opportunities for Obtaining and Using Litigation Reserves and Disclosures,* 63 OHIO ST. L. J. 1017 (2002) (illustrating how the disclosures in the MD&A section of various securities filings and several other sources of accounting-related information could provide, or lead to, information about litigation reserves related to the underlying litigation); Matthew J. Barrett, *New Opportunities for Obtaining and Using Litigation Reserves and Disclosures,* 64 OHIO ST. L.J. 1183 (2003) (describing how new MD&A requirements regarding certain contractual obligations and other developments could provide additional opportunities).

Press reports and securities filings repeatedly document that public companies continue to record accruals for estimated amounts that management considers necessary to resolve pending or expected litigation, especially in matters involving accounting fraud, asbestos, health-care fraud or product liability, patent infringement, and tax disputes. Pending litigation and recently settled cases offer the following examples:

• As of June 30, 2014, BP p.l.c. reported on its consolidated balance sheet almost $9 billion in accrued liabilities related to the oil spill in the Gulf of Mexico during 2010, including about $1.6 billion for future environmental costs, almost $3.9 billion to resolve litigation and claims, and $3.5 billion in estimated Clean Water Act penalties on its balance sheet. Through June 30, 2014, BP had recognized almost $43 billion in pre-tax charges related to the spill. BP recorded $40.9 billion in pre-tax charges related to the spill during 2010 and has recognized additional net charges during accounting periods from 2011 to the present. During the second quarter of 2014, BP recognized an additional $260 million before taxes in expenses from the spill. *See* Press Release, BP p.l.c., Group results Second quarter and half year results 2014, at 18, 20 (July 29, 2014), *available at* http://www.bp.com/content/dam/bp/pdf/ investors/bp_second_quarter_2014_results.pdf; *see also* Press Release, BP p.l.c., Group results First quarter 2011, at 21, 24 (Apr. 27, 2011), *available at* http://www.bp.com/liveassets/bp_internet/globalbp/STAGING/global_assets/ downloads/B/bp_first_quarter_2011_results.pdf.

• BP has not been the only company to accrue reserves for likely losses arising from the Deepwater Horizon accident. In January 2013, *The Wall Street Journal* published a story that the U.S. Department of Justice had announced that the Swiss offshore driller Transocean Ltd. had agreed to pay $1.4 billion to settle all federal civil and criminal claims relating to the incident. The article reported that Transocean had disclosed in securities filings that it had discussed a $1.5 billion settlement with the Justice Department to resolve the criminal and civil claims and had set aside a $2 billion reserve. Interestingly, the article included an observation from a former head of the Justice Department's environmental-crimes unit, who found it curious that the government had agreed to a settlement that was more favorable than what Transocean had proposed–and presumably recorded in its financial statements. The article also mentioned that Halliburton, the project's cementing contractor, had recorded a $300 million loss contingency related to civil lawsuits arising from the accident. *See* Tom Fowler, *Transocean Is Set to Pay $1.4 Billion in Gulf Spill*, WALL ST. J., Jan. 4, 2013, at A3.

• In September 2014, Halliburton announced an agreement to settle a substantial majority of the class action claims that Gulf Coast residents, businesses, and local governments asserted against the company after the incident. Subject to court approval and any appeals, the approximately $1.1 billion settlement, which included legal fees, covers claims against Halliburton that BP assigned to the settlement class in an earlier settlement and suits that the commercial fishing industry and other plaintiffs brought against Halliburton after the spill seeking punitive and other damages. Halliburton's press release announcing the settlement stated: "The company's previously accrued loss contingency provision relating to the multi-district proceedings is currently $1.3 billion." Press Release, Halliburton, Halliburton Reaches Settlement on Claims Related to Macondo (Sept. 2, 2014), http://www.halliburton.com/public/news/pubsdata/press_release/2014/corp news_090214.html; *see also* Daniel Gilbert, *Halliburton to Settle Deepwater Horizon Claims for $1.1 Billion*, WALL ST. J., Sept. 3, 2014, at B2.

• In October 2013, JPMorgan Chase & Co. ("JPM") reported a net loss of $0.4 billion for the third quarter of 2013. The third quarter results included a $9.15 billion pretax charge, or $7.2 billion after-tax, for legal expense, including reserves for litigation and regulatory proceedings. The PowerPoint slides accompanying this earnings release included a chart on the second slide that summarized firmwide litigation reserves for 2010 through third quarter of 2013 on a pretax basis in billions of dollars as follows:

Reserves for litigation – beginning balance (1/1/10)	~$3
Add: Net increase to reserves	~28
Less: Settlements and judgments	(~8)
Reserves for litigation – ending balance (9/30/13)	~$23

The reserves related to "a broad range of matters, and include a significant reserve for mortgage-related matters, including securities and repurchase litigation exposure." The slide explicitly acknowledged that "[r]eserves reflect what is probable and estimable." In addition, the slide announced an estimated $5.7 billion as the high-end range of reasonably possible losses in excess of reserves as of September 30, 2013. *See* Press Release, JPMorgan Chase & Co., JPMorgan Chase Reports Third-Quarter 2013 Net Loss of $0.4 Billion, or $(0.17) Per Share, on Revenue of $23.9 Billion (Oct. 11, 2013), http://files.shareholder.com/downloads/ONE/3470255360x0x696268/0a242e 6d-65a7-4c3c-bfef-652b4daaaf2e/3Q13_Earnings_Press_Release.pdf (footnote omitted); JPMorgan Chase & Co., Financial Results 3Q13 (Oct. 11, 2013), http://files.shareholder.com/downloads/ONE/3470255360x0x696269/53cac7f 7-de8d-4e28-aeeb-412271c2d40b/3Q13_Earnings_Presentation.pdf (footnotes omitted); *see also* David Reilly, *J.P. Morgan Lets Investors Judge*, WALL ST. J., Oct. 12, 2013, at B16.

Over the next three months, and before issuing its earnings release for the 2013 fourth quarter, JPM agreed to payments exceeding $21 billion to resolve various civil litigation and regulatory claims. The agreements included settlements totaling $5.1 billion with the Federal Housing Finance Agency ("FHFA"), Freddie Mac and Fannie Mae to resolve mortgage-backed securities litigation; a $4.5 billion agreement with twenty-one major institutional investors to resolve repurchase and servicing claims related to residential mortgage-backed securities ("RMBS") that JPM and certain subsidiaries issued between 2005 and 2008; a $13 billion settlement with the President's RMBS Working Group of the Financial Fraud Enforcement Task Force, which included a previously announced $4 billion payment to resolve FHFA's litigation claims; and almost $2.6 billion in connection with a deferred prosecution agreement with federal prosecutors to resolve charges that the bank failed to alert authorities about Bernard Madoff's Ponzi scheme. The press release announcing the agreement with the institutional investors stated: "The firm believes it is appropriately reserved for this and any remaining RMBS litigation matters." The press release publicizing the settlement with the President's Task Force stated: "JPMorgan Chase is fully reserved for this settlement." In connection with the Madoff settlements, *The Wall Street Journal* reported that JPM added $400 million to its litigation reserves and that the settlements would reduce fourth quarter earnings by $850 million. *See* Press Release, JPMorgan Chase & Co., JPMorgan Chase Reaches Settlements with The Federal Housing Finance Agency, Freddie Mac and Fannie Mae (Oct. 25, 2013), http://investor.shareholder.com/jpmorgan chase/releasedetail.cfm?ReleaseID=800566; Press Release, JPMorgan Chase & Co., JPMorgan Chase Reaches An Agreement With 21 Institutional Investors to Resolve Repurchase and Servicing Claims (Nov. 15, 2013), http://investor.shareholder.com/jpmorganchase/releasedetail.cfm?ReleaseID=807792; Press Release, JPMorgan Chase & Co., JPMorgan Chase Reaches Settlement with the President's Task Force on Residential Mortgage-Backed Securities (Nov. 19, 2013), http://investor.shareholder.com/jpmorganchase/releasedetail. cfm?ReleaseID=808446; Dan Fitzpatrick, *J.P. Morgan Settles Its Madoff Tab*, WALL ST. J., Jan. 8, 2014, at C1; Press Release, JPMorgan Chase & Co., JPMorgan Chase Reports Fourth-Quarter 2013 Net Income of $5.3 Billion, or $1.30 Per Share, on Revenue of $24.1 Billion, http://files.shareholder.com/downloads/ONE/3470255360x0x718336/c27a32b6-9827-4c51-ad6c-17c5b9fce c19/JPM_News_2014_1_14_Current.pdf.

• In July 2012, GlaxoSmithKline plc ("GSK") pled guilty to criminal charges involving illegally marketing three drugs and withholding safety data from U.S. regulators. The company agreed to pay $3 billion, an amount reached in principle in November 2011, to the federal government and various states in what the Justice Department called the largest health-care fraud settlement in U.S. history. According to the company's press release: "GSK will make payments totalling $3bn which are covered by existing provisions and will be funded through existing cash resources." The release continued: "The finalisation[sic] of the terms of the settlement mean this matter can be resolved within the existing pre-tax provision. The after tax cost will be approximately $150m lower than provided. As a result a credit will be recorded to the non-core charge for the second quarter 2012." Press Release, GlaxoSmithKline plc, GlaxoSmithKline concludes previously announced agreement in principle to resolve multiple investigations with US Government and numerous states (July 2, 2012), http://us.gsk.com/html/media-news/pressreleases/2012/2012-pressrelease-1164685.htm; *see also* Jeanne Whalen *et al.*, *Glaxo Sets Guilty Plea, $3 Billion Settlement*, WALL ST. J., July 3, 2012, at B1. As early as February 2009, GSK had reported that its profit attributable to shareholders for the 2008 fourth quarter fell to [$1.4 billion] from [$1.5 billion] during the previous year, adversely affected by a [$750 million] legal charge related to a Colorado investigation into GSK's market practices. The company's earnings release also disclosed that GSK's aggregate provision for legal and other disputes (not including tax matters) stood at [$2.7 billion] on December 31, 2008. Press Release, GlaxoSmithKline plc, GSK delivers EPS of 104.7p before major restructuring[;] Dividend increased 8% to 57p, at 16, 21 (Feb. 5, 2009), http://www.gsk.com/investors/reports/q42008/q42008.pdf; *see also* Jeanne Whalen, *Glaxo Net Falls 7.1%; Job Cuts Planned*, WALL ST. J., Feb. 6, 2009, at B5.

• In February 2007, Merck & Co., Inc. announced that it had reached an agreement to settle previously disclosed tax disputes with the IRS arising from examinations covering the period 1993-2001 at a net cash cost to Merck approximating $2.3 billion. The company's press release states: "Merck has previously reserved for these items and this settlement is not expected to have any material impact on the Company's annual earnings for 2007." Press Release, Merck & Co., Merck Settles Tax Dispute with Internal Revenue Service (Feb. 14, 2007), http://www.merck.com/newsroom/press_releases/corporate/2007_0214.html.

• In November 2006 and in connection with the closing of Google Inc.'s acquisition of YouTube, Google announced that it had placed "12.5% of the [$1.65 billion in] equity issued and issuable in the transaction . . . [in] escrow for one year to secure certain indemnification obligations." Press Release, Google Inc., Google Closes Acquisition of YouTube (Nov. 13, 2006), http://investor.google.com/releases/20061114.html. The press release at least hints that Google held back approximately $206.25 million "to cover expenses related to copyright-infringement lawsuits or content-licensing fees that YouTube already has agreed to pay, or may be forced to pay, in the future." *YouTube Deal Is Completed With Set-Aside for Suits, Fees*, WALL ST. J., Nov. 15, 2006, at B10.

• In March 2006, Research In Motion Ltd. ("RIM") agreed to pay $612.5 million to settle its highly publicized patent dispute with NTP Inc. RIM had previously accrued $450 million related to the patent infringement action and announced that the company would record a $162.5 million charge in its fiscal fourth quarter. Mark Heinzl & Amol Sharma, *RIM to Pay NTP $612.5 Million To Settle BlackBerry Patent Suit*, WALL ST. J., Mar. 4, 2006, at A1.

• Halliburton Company reached an agreement in December 2002 to pay about $4 billion in cash and stock to settle more than 300,000 asbestos claims. When Halliburton announced its results for the 2002 fourth quarter in February 2003, *The Wall Street Journal* reported that those results included only a $214 million charge for asbestos liability, suggesting that the company had previously established reserves for the uninsured balance. Indeed, Halliburton's Form 10-K for the fiscal year ended December 31, 2002 discloses that the company used a $2.2 billion estimate, the low end of an outside expert's range of liabilities, to accrue liability and defense costs for various asbestos claims during the second quarter of 2002 and, then, $3.5 billion, the upper end of that range, during that year's fourth quarter.

See also DAVID R. HERWITZ & MATTHEW J. BARRETT, 2013 SUPPLEMENT TO MATERIALS ON ACCOUNTING FOR LAWYERS 196–200 (2013) (giving other examples involving Merck & Co. Inc., J.P. Morgan Chase & Co., UBS AG, State Street Corp., Citigroup Inc., BP, and Xerox); DAVID R. HERWITZ & MATTHEW J. BARRETT, MATERIALS ON ACCOUNTING FOR LAWYERS 728–731 (unabr. 4th. ed. 2006) (giving still more examples involving AT&T Inc., Caremark Rx Inc., Citigroup Inc., JPMorgan Chase & Co., and Time Warner Inc.).

6. As discussed in the MD&A materials in Chapter IV on page 319, *supra*, SOx section 401(a) directed the SEC to issue final rules that require disclosures about all material off-balance sheet transactions and similar arrangements, obligations, and other relationships. Accordingly, in early 2003, the SEC issued final regulations that require new disclosures about off-balance sheet arrangements and aggregate contractual obligations. Even though those regulations specifically exclude "[c]ontingent liabilities arising out of litigation, arbitration or regulatory actions" from the definition of off-balance sheet arrangements, separate rules apply to contractual obligations. At a minimum, those rules would reach any obligations arising from settlement agreements that registrants reach in similar cases. Using categories including "Other Long-Term Liabilities Reflected on the Registrant's Balance Sheet under GAAP," which may well apply to any liability, including a litigation reserve, that a registrant expects to satisfy in more than one year, the final rules require certain registrants to disclose in tabular format the amounts due within specified time periods, as of the latest fiscal year-end balance sheet date. The rules apply to filings that must include financial statements for fiscal years ending on or after December 15, 2003. Disclosure in Management's Discussion and Analysis About Off-Balance Sheet Arrangements and Aggregate Contractual Obligations, 68 Fed. Reg. 5982 (Feb. 5, 2003), *available at* http://www.sec.gov/rules/final/ 33-8182.htm.

Although the proposed rules would have imposed additional disclosure requirements for contingent liabilities and commitments, the SEC decided to delete those provisions from the final regulations. The release that accompanied the final regulations, however, stated that the SEC would continue to assess the costs and benefits of an MD&A disclosure requirement for aggregate contingent liabilities and commitments during the Commission's ongoing review of MD&A.

7. In Chapter IV on pages 327 and 328, *supra*, the discussion on the future of financial and non-financial reporting describes how SEC rules now require all registrants to provide their financial statements to the agency and on their corporate websites in interactive data format using XBRL. When registrants accurately tag their financial statements and related notes, users can efficiently obtain and analyze various embedded information. Of particular interest to litigators, the following titles describe XBRL elements or tags appearing in the 2014 U.S. GAAP Financial Reporting Taxonomy that reference paragraphs in ASC Subtotpic 450-20: Accrual for Environmental Loss Contingencies; Accrual for Environmental Loss Contingencies, Period Increase (Decrease); Accrual for Environmental Loss Contingencies, Provision for New Losses; Accrued Environmental Loss Contingencies, Current; Accrued Environmental Loss Contingencies, Noncurrent; Environmental Exit Costs, Costs Accrued to Date; Environmental Exit Costs, Reasonably Possible Additional Loss [added in 2011]; Environmental Exit Costs, Reasonably Possible Additional Losses, Best Estimate; Estimated Litigation Liability;

Estimated Litigation Liability, Current; Estimated Litigation Liability, Noncurrent; Gain (Loss) Related to Litigation Settlement; Loss Contingency Accrual [all with this general title added in 2012]; Loss Contingency Accrual, Period Increase (Decrease); Loss Contingency Accrual, Provision; Loss Contingency, Accrual, Current; Loss Contingency, Accrual, Noncurrent; Loss Contingency, Estimate of Possible Loss; Loss Contingency, Loss in Period; Loss Contingency, Opinion of Counsel; Loss Contingency, Range of Possible Loss; Loss Contingency, Range of Possible Loss, Portion Not Accrued [added in 2012]; Loss on Contracts; Malpractice Loss Contingency, Accrual Not Recognized, Estimate of Possible Loss [added in 2011]; Malpractice Loss Contingency, Accrual, Discounted; Movement in Accrual for Environmental Loss Contingencies Disclosures; Product Liability Accrual, Period Expense; Product Liability Contingency, Loss Exposure Not Accrued, Best Estimate; Product Liability Contingency, Unasserted Claims; Product Warranty Accrual, Noncurrent; Schedule of Environmental Loss Contingencies by Site; Site Contingency, Unasserted Claims; and Unasserted Claim [Member] [added in 2012]. *See* ASC § 450-20-75. As software developers release functions that allow users to retrieve information corresponding to specific tags efficiently, we can imagine numerous legal applications.

8. In any legal matter involving a publicly-traded adversary, a lawyer can obtain the adversary's periodic securities filings. Within those filings, the lawyer should pay particular attention to the financial statements, the related notes, any relevant XBRL codes, and MD&A. Within MD&A, the lawyer should watch for legal matters affecting the "quality of earnings," liquidity, and the schedule of contractual obligations. The sections in the periodic filings that describe the business, detail various business risks, and discuss legal proceedings also may contain helpful information. In addition, a lawyer may obtain other detectable information about the adversary and the underlying legal matter in other regulatory filings, such as state public utility commission or insurance commission reports; corporate news releases; press reports; and even investment analysts reports.

D.   AUDIT INQUIRIES AND RELEVANT PROFESSIONAL STANDARDS

Any business requiring audited financial statements must provide information regarding legal claims against the enterprise to its auditors. An enterprise must send a letter, which accountants usually refers to as the *management letter*, to its auditor regarding asserted and unasserted claims against the business. In addition, the enterprise requests its lawyer to send a letter to the enterprise's auditor regarding asserted and usually specified unasserted legal claims against the business. Lawyers regularly receive these *audit inquiry letters* directly from clients that require audited financial statements.

While many small businesses do not require audited financial statements, many mid-sized and most larger businesses do. Remember that all publicly traded enterprises must provide audited financial statements to the Securities and Exchange Commission. In addition, many privately held companies must supply audited financial statements to lenders or to shareholders. Finally, even governmental entities, not-for-profit organizations, churches and other organizations frequently undergo audits.

In December 1975, the American Bar Association (the "ABA") issued the following Statement of Policy to set forth the legal profession's official policy on audit inquiry letters:

Statement of Policy Regarding Lawyers' Responses to Auditors' Requests for Information*

American Bar Association, 1975.
31 Bus. Law. 1709 (1976) (emphasis in original).

Preamble

The public interest in protecting the confidentiality of lawyer-client communications is fundamental. The American legal, political and economic systems depend heavily upon voluntary compliance with the law and upon ready access to a respected body of professionals able to interpret and advise on the law. The expanding complexity of our laws and governmental regulations increases the need for prompt, specific and unhampered lawyer-lawyer-client communication. The benefits of such communication and early consultation underlie the strict statutory and ethical obligations of the lawyer to preserve the confidences and secrets of the client, as well as the long-recognized testimonial privilege for lawyer-client communication.

Both the Code of Professional Responsibility and the cases applying the evidentiary privilege recognize that the privilege against disclosure can be knowingly and voluntarily waived by the client. It is equally clear that disclosure to a third party may result in loss of the "confidentiality" essential to maintain the privilege. Disclosure to a third party of the lawyer-client communication on a particular subject may also destroy the privilege as to other communications on that subject. Thus, the mere disclosure by the lawyer to the outside auditor, with due client consent, of the substance of communications between the lawyer and client may significantly impair the client's ability in other contexts to maintain the confidentiality of such communications.

Under the circumstances a policy of audit procedure which requires clients to give consent and authorize lawyers to respond to general inquiries and disclose information to auditors concerning matters which have been communicated in confidence is essentially destructive of free and open communication and early consultation between lawyer and client. The institution of such a policy would inevitably discourage management from discussing potential legal problems with counsel for fear that such discussion might become public and precipitate a loss to or possible liability of the business enterprise and its stockholders that might otherwise never materialize.

It is also recognized that our legal, political and economic systems depend to an important extent on public confidence in published financial statements. To meet this need the accounting profession must adopt and adhere to standards and procedures that will command confidence in the auditing process. It is not, however, believed necessary, or sound public policy, to intrude upon the confidentiality of the lawyer-client relationship in order to command such confidence. On the contrary, the objective of fair disclosure in financial statements is more likely to be better served by maintaining the integrity of the confidential relationship between lawyer and client, thereby strengthening corporate management's confidence in counsel and encouraging its readiness to seek advice of counsel and to act in accordance with counsel's advice.

Consistent with the foregoing public policy considerations, it is believed appropriate to distinguish between, on the one hand, litigation which is pending or which a third party has manifested to the client a present intention to commence and, on the other hand, other contingencies of a legal nature or having legal aspects. As regards the former category, unquestionably the lawyer representing the client in a litigation matter may be the best source for a description of the claim or claims asserted, the client's position (e. g. denial, contest, etc.), and the client's possible exposure in the litigation (to the extent the lawyer is in a position to do so). As to the latter category, it is submitted that, for the reasons set forth above, it is not in the public interest for the lawyer to be required to respond to general inquiries from auditors concerning possible claims.

It is recognized that the disclosure requirements for enterprises subject to the reporting requirements of the Federal securities laws are a major concern of managements and counsel, as well as auditors. It is submitted that compliance therewith is best assured when clients are afforded maximum encouragement, by protecting lawyer-client confidentiality, freely to consult counsel. Likewise, lawyers must be keenly conscious of the importance of their clients being competently advised in these matters.

Statement of Policy

NOW, THEREFORE, BE IT RESOLVED that it is desirable and in the public interest that this Association adopt the following Statement of Policy regarding the appropriate scope of the lawyer's response to the auditor's request, made by the client at the request of the auditor, for information concerning matters referred to the lawyer during the course of his representation of the client:

(1) *Client Consent to Response.* The lawyer may properly respond to the auditor's requests for information concerning loss contingencies * * * to the extent hereinafter set forth, subject to the following:

(a) Assuming that the client's initial letter requesting the lawyer to provide information to the auditor is signed by an agent of the client having apparent authority to make such a request, the lawyer may provide to the auditor information requested, without further consent, unless such information discloses a confidence or a secret or requires an evaluation of a claim.

(b) In the normal case, the initial request letter does not provide the necessary consent to the disclosure of a confidence or secret or to the evaluation of a claim since that consent may only be given after full disclosure to the client of the legal consequences of such action.

(c) Lawyers should bear in mind, in evaluating claims, that an adverse party may assert that any evaluation of potential liability is an admission.

(d) In securing the client's consent to the disclosure of confidences or secrets, or the evaluation of claims, the lawyer may wish to have a draft of his letter reviewed and approved by the client before releasing it to the auditor; in such cases, additional explanation would in all probability be necessary so that the legal consequences of the consent are fully disclosed to the client.

(2) *Limitation on Scope of Response.* It is appropriate for the lawyer to set forth in his response, by way of limitation, the scope of his engagement by the client. It is also appropriate for the lawyer to indicate the date as of which information is furnished and to disclaim any undertaking to advise the auditor of changes which may thereafter be brought to the lawyer's attention. *Unless the lawyer's response indicates otherwise, (a) it is properly limited to matters which have been given substantive attention by the lawyer in the form of legal consultation and, where appropriate, legal representation since the beginning of the period or periods being reported upon, and (b) if a law firm or a law department, the auditor may assume that the firm or department has endeavored, to the extent believed necessary by the firm or department, to determine from lawyers currently in the firm or department who have performed services for the client since the beginning of the fiscal period under audit whether such services involved substantive attention in the form of legal consultation concerning those loss contingencies referred to in Paragraph 5(a) below but, beyond that, no review has been made of any of the client's*

transactions or other matters for the purpose of identifying loss contingencies to be described in the response.

(3) *Response may be Limited to Material Items.* In response to an auditor's request for disclosure of loss contingencies of a client, it is appropriate for the lawyer's response to indicate that the response is limited to items which are considered individually or collectively material to the presentation of the client's financial statements.

(4) *Limited Responses.* Where the lawyer is limiting his response in accordance with this Statement of Policy, his response should so indicate (see Paragraph 8). If in any other respect the lawyer is not undertaking to respond to or comment on particular aspects of the inquiry when responding to the auditor, he should consider advising the auditor that his response is limited, in order to avoid any inference that the lawyer has responded to all aspects; otherwise, he may be assuming a responsibility which he does not intend.

(5) *Loss Contingencies.* When properly requested by the client, it is appropriate for the lawyer to furnish to the auditor information concerning the following matters if the lawyer has been engaged by the client to represent or advise the client professionally with respect thereto and he has devoted substantive attention to them in the form of legal representation or consultation:

(a) *overtly threatened or pending litigation*, whether or not specified by the client;

(b) *a contractually assumed obligation* which the client has specifically identified and upon which the client has specifically requested, in the inquiry letter or a supplement thereto, comment to the auditor;

(c) *an unasserted possible claim or assessment* which the client has specifically identified and upon which the client has specifically requested, in the inquiry letter or a supplement thereto, comment to the auditor.

With respect to clause (a), overtly threatened litigation means that a potential claimant has manifested to the client an awareness of and present intention to assert a possible claim or assessment unless the likelihood of litigation (or of settlement when litigation would normally be avoided) is considered remote. With respect to clause (c), where there has been no manifestation by a potential claimant of an awareness of and present intention to assert a possible claim or assessment, consistent with the considerations and concerns outlined in the Preamble and Paragraph 1 hereof, the client should request the lawyer to furnish information to the auditor only if the client has determined that it is probable that a possible claim will be asserted, that there is a reasonable possibility that the outcome (assuming such assertion) will be unfavorable, and that the resulting liability would be material to the financial condition of the client. Examples of such situations might (depending in each case upon the particular circumstances) include the following: (i) a catastrophe, accident or other similar physical occurrence in which the client's involvement is open and notorious, or (ii) an investigation by a government agency where enforcement proceedings have been instituted or where the likelihood that they will not be instituted is remote, under circumstances where assertion of one or more private claims for redress would normally be expected, or (iii) a public disclosure by the client acknowledging (and thus focusing attention upon) the existence of one or more probable claims arising out of an event or circumstance. In assessing whether or not the assertion of a possible claim is probable, it is expected that the client would normally employ, by reason of the inherentuncertainties involved and insufficiency of available data, concepts parallel to those used by the lawyer (discussed below) in assessing whether or not an unfavorable outcome is probable; thus, assertion of a possible claim would be considered probable only when the prospects of its being asserted seem reasonably certain (i.e., supported by extrinsic evidence strong enough to establish a presumption that it will happen) and the prospects of non-assertion seem slight.

It would not be appropriate, however, for the lawyer to be requested to furnish information in response to an inquiry letter or supplement thereto if it appears that (a) the client has been required to specify unasserted possible claims without regard to the standard suggested in the preceding paragraph, or (b) the client has been required to specify all or substantially all unasserted possible claims as to which legal advice may have been obtained, since, in either case, such a request would be in substance a general inquiry and would be inconsistent with the intent of this Statement of Policy.

The information that lawyers may properly give to the auditor concerning the foregoing matters would include (to the extent appropriate) an identification of the proceedings or matter, the stage of proceedings, the claim(s) asserted, and the position taken by the client.

In view of the inherent uncertainties, the lawyer should normally refrain from expressing judgments as to outcome except in those relatively few clear cases where it appears to the lawyer that an unfavorable outcome is either "probable" or "remote;" for purposes of any such judgment it is appropriate to use the following meanings:

> (i) *probable*—an unfavorable outcome for the client is probable if the prospects of the claimant not succeeding are judged to be extremely doubtful and the prospects for success by the client in its defense are judged to be slight.

> (ii) *remote*—an unfavorable outcome is remote if the prospects for the client not succeeding in its defense are judged to be extremely doubtful and the prospects of success by the claimant are judged to be slight.

If, in the opinion of the lawyer, considerations within the province of his professional judgment bear on a particular loss contingency to the degree necessary to make an informed judgment, he may in appropriate circumstances communicate to the auditor his view that an unfavorable outcome is "probable" or "remote," applying the above meanings. No inference should be drawn, from the absence of such a judgment, that the client will not prevail.

The lawyer also may be asked to estimate, in dollar terms, the potential amount of loss or range of loss in the event that an unfavorable outcome is not viewed to be "remote." In such a case, the amount or range of potential loss will normally be as inherently impossible to ascertain, with any degree of certainty, as the outcome of the litigation. Therefore, it is appropriate for the lawyer to provide an estimate of the amount or range of potential loss (if the outcome should be unfavorable) only if he believes that the probability of inaccuracy of the estimate of the amount or range of potential loss is slight.

The considerations bearing upon the difficulty in estimating loss (or range of loss) where pending litigation is concerned are obviously even more compelling in the case of unasserted possible claims. In most cases, the lawyer will not be able to provide any such estimate to the auditor.

As indicated in Paragraph 4 hereof, the auditor may assume that all loss contingencies specified by the client in the manner specified in clauses (b) and (c) above have received comment in the response, unless otherwise therein indicated. The lawyer should not be asked, nor need the lawyer undertake, to furnish information to the auditor concerning loss contingencies except as contemplated by this Paragraph 5.

(6) *Lawyer's Professional Responsibility.* Independent of the scope of his response to the auditor's request for information, the lawyer, depending upon the nature of the matters as to which he is engaged, may have as part of his professional responsibility to his client an obligation to advise the client concerning the need for or advisability of public disclosure of a wide range of events and circumstances. The lawyer has an obligation not knowingly to participate in any violation by the client of the disclosure requirements of the securities laws. The lawyer also may be required under the Code of Professional Responsibility to resign his engagement if his advice concerning disclosures is disregarded by the client. The auditor may properly assume that whenever, in the course of performing legal services for the client with respect to a matter recognized to involve an unasserted possible claim or assessment which may call for financial statement disclosure, the lawyer has formed a professional conclusion that the client must disclose or consider disclosure concerning such possible claim or assessment, the lawyer, as a matter of professional responsibility to the client, will so advise the client and will consult with the client concerning the question of such disclosure and the applicable requirements of FAS 5 [now codified in FASB ASC Topic 450, *Contingencies*].

(7) *Limitation on Use of Response. Unless otherwise stated in the lawyer's response, it shall be solely for the auditor's information in connection with his audit of the financial condition of the client and is not to be quoted in whole or in part or otherwise referred to in any financial statements of the client or related documents, nor is it to be filed with any governmental agency or other person, without the lawyer's prior written consent. Notwithstanding such limitation, the response can properly be furnished to others in compliance with court process or when necessary in order to defend the auditor against a challenge of the audit by the client or a regulatory agency, provided that the*

lawyer is given written notice of the circumstances at least twenty days before the response is so to be furnished to others, or as long in advance as possible if the situation does not permit such period of notice.

(8) *General.* This Statement of Policy, together with the accompanying Commentary (which is an integral part hereof), has been developed for the general guidance of the legal profession. In a particular case, the lawyer may elect to supplement or modify the approach hereby set forth. If desired, this Statement of Policy may be incorporated by reference in the lawyer's response * * *.

NOTES

1. The new Codification affects audit response letters because the ABA Statement of Policy and the illustrative response letters refer to SFAS No. 5, which now appears in FASB ASC Topic 450, *Contingencies*. Although the ABA Section of Business Law's Committee on Audit Responses believes that readers should construe any references to SFAS No. 5 in either the Statement of Policy or a response letter to encompass the corresponding material in the Codification, the Committee suggests that lawyers consider whether to reference FASB ASC Subtopic 450-20, *Loss Contingencies*, in their responses regarding fiscal periods ending after September 15, 2009. For example, lawyers could either: (1) add the appropriate reference to the Codification after any mention of SFAS No. 5, or (2) refer to the Codification rather than to SFAS No. 5, perhaps with an explanation that the Codification replaces prior accounting pronouncements, including SFAS No. 5, as generally accepted accounting principles for financial statements for periods ending after September 15, 2009. *See* Comm. on Audit Responses, A.B.A., *Statement of the Effect of the FASB Codification on Audit Response Letters*, 65 BUS. LAW. 491 (2010).

2. The American Bar Association's Section of Business Law has compiled, and occasionally updates, the principal official pronouncements and unofficial commentaries discussing audit inquiries and lawyers' responses. In 2013, the Audit Responses Committee, the current name for the group referenced in the previous note, published a second edition of the Auditor's Letter Handbook to update the original 1990 edition. This second edition contains an introductory update and includes the PCAOB auditing standards governing audit inquiry letters. *See* AUDIT RESPONSES COMM., A.B.A., AUDITOR'S LETTER HANDBOOK (2d ed. 2013); *see also* COMM. ON AUDIT INQUIRY RESPONSES, A.B.A., AUDITOR'S LETTER HANDBOOK (1990). In addition, *The Business Lawyer*, the Section of Business Law's quarterly publication, has periodically contained articles which discuss developments in this area. *See, e.g.,* Subcomm. on Audit Inquiry Responses, A.B.A., *Inquiry of a Client's Lawyer Concerning Litigation, Claims, and Assessments: Auditing Interpretation AU Section 337*, 45 BUS. LAW. 2245 (1990); James J. Fuld, *Lawyers' Responses to Auditors—Some Practical Aspects*, 44 BUS. LAW. 159 (1988). More recently, the Ad Hoc Committee on Audit Responses has created a listserv to discuss various issues regarding audit inquiries. The committee's first report on the listserv's activity identified two non-standard requests worth highlighting. First, any request from the auditor to confirm that no unasserted claims exist departs from the ABA Statement of Policy, which provides for comments only on unasserted claims that the client has specifically identified. Second, at least one major auditing firm requested that counsel confirm that any illegal activity that had come to counsel's attention had been reported to the audit committee and the auditors. The auditing firm acquiesced to a reply expressly refusing to respond to the request. Ad Hoc Comm. on Audit Responses, A.B.A., Report on Listserv Activity 1 (Inception to August 3, 2004) (Aug. 2004).

3. Two major problems arise in the lawyer's letters area. First, auditors and lawyers have different concerns related to the disclosure of information about legal claims. Auditors primarily want to encourage public disclosure of more information, to ensure that investors receive all potentially relevant information. Full disclosure helps to protect the auditor from liability if the client experiences future financial problems. Lawyers, on the other hand, strive to protect the attorney-client privilege. These goals conflict, because a lawyer's disclosure of information to auditors can waive the attorney-client privilege.

A second problem regarding lawyer's letters arises because attorneys and auditors may use different standards to determine the likelihood that a claim will result in a loss. The two professions define "remote" and "probable" in different terms, which may result in divergent standards for disclosure. Kenneth E. Harrison & Thomas C. Pearson, *Communications Between Auditors and Lawyers for the Identification and Evaluation of Litigation, Claims, and Assessments*, ACCT. HORIZONS, June 1989, at 76. The Codification classifies a loss as "probable" if the future events confirming the loss are "likely to occur." In contrast, the foregoing ABA Statement of Policy treats an unfavorable outcome as "probable" when "the prospects of the claimant not succeeding are judged to be extremely doubtful and the prospects for success[ful defense] are judged to be slight." Moreover, the Codification describes a loss contingency as "remote" if the chance of future events confirming the loss are "slight," while the ABA considers the possibility of an unfavorable outcome as "remote" when "the prospects of the client['s defense] not succeeding * * * are judged to be extremely doubtful and the prospects of success by the claimant are judged to be slight."

The following chart illustrates these different standards:

DIVERGENCE BETWEEN FASB AND ABA PROBABILITY REGIONS

Chances of an Unfavorable Outcome

ABA

0% remote		inferential reasonably possible		probable	100%
remote		reasonably possible		probable	

FASB

Note, *Attorney Responses To Audit Letters: The Problem of Disclosing Loss Contingencies Arising From Litigation and Unasserted Claims*, 51 N.Y.U. L. REV. 838, 877 (1976).

The standards for unasserted claims similarly diverge. An auditor must determine whether the enterprise has properly treated any unasserted claims. If the likelihood of assertion is "probable," ASC Topic 450 may require the enterprise to accrue, disclose, or both accrue and disclose the claim. Although ASC section 450-20-20, which codified the definition in paragraph 3 of SFAS No. 5, does not expressly apply to this determination, presumably the term "probable" still means "likely to occur," or at least "more likely than not" or "anything greater than fifty percent." In contrast, the ABA Statement of Policy considers an unasserted claim "probable only when the prospects of its being asserted seem reasonably certain * * * and the prospects of non-assertion seem slight."

These different definitions and standards can obviously cause problems. For example, the ABA definition of "probable" could lead lawyers to consider fewer unasserted claims than auditors, thereby revealing fewer claims. This creates difficulties for auditors in determining whether to accrue or disclose a claim. The ABA also has a narrower definition of "remote" than the FASB, so lawyers may consider fewer losses remote than auditors.

These conflicting standards can leave clients caught in the middle. Public companies generally need an unqualified opinion from their auditors for their creditors and shareholders. The client also ultimately bears responsibility for any improper disclosures. In this latter regard, the client may face lawsuits from disgruntled shareholders or the SEC if the company does not properly disclose contingencies. *See, e.g., In re* Westinghouse Securities Litigation, 90 F.3d 696 (3d Cir. 1996) (reinstating class action securities fraud claims alleging that a $975 million pre-tax accrual for loan losses did not adequately cover estimated losses).

4. In an attempt to preserve the attorney-client privilege regarding unasserted possible claims or assessments, some lawyers refuse to respond to general inquiries relating to the existence of such items in auditors' requests for information. In a 1997 interpretation, the Auditing Standards Board concluded that such refusals do not thereby limit the scope of the audit. The ASB, however, reiterated that the lawyer should confirm the assumption underlying the understanding between the legal and accounting professions that, when the circumstances require, the lawyer will advise the client concerning the client's obligation to make financial statement disclosures regarding unasserted possible claims or assessments. USE OF EXPLANATORY LANGUAGE CONCERNING UNASSERTED POSSIBLE CLAIMS OR ASSESSMENTS IN LAWYERS' RESPONSES TO AUDIT INQUIRY LETTERS, Auditing Interpretation No. 10 of Section 337 (Auditing Standards Bd. 1997), codified at 1 AM. INST. OF CERTIFIED PUB. ACCOUNTANTS, PROFESSIONAL STANDARDS AU § 9337.31–.32 (Feb. 1997).

PROBLEMS

Problem 7.1. X Corp., a closely held company that uses the calendar year for financial accounting purposes, publishes a magazine which until a few years ago was a rather placid periodical. Several years earlier, the company borrowed money from a local bank to expand its printing facilities and the loan agreement requires X Corp. to submit audited financial statements to the bank each year.

In 20X1, or about four years ago, and in an effort to boost lagging sales, X adopted a new policy of featuring more exciting, even sensational articles. On January 10, 20X2, the magazine published an alleged exposé in which the coach of a major football team was accused of fixing a game. On January 9, 20X3, the coach brought suit for libel, claiming damages of $5,000,000. X was advised by counsel that (1) there was a good chance X would be held liable, and (2) if so, the damages were most likely to run between $50,000 and $100,000, with an outside possibility that the amount would be much greater, perhaps even in seven figures. During 20X4, which ended a couple of months ago, the case was tried before a jury, which found against X and awarded general damages of $60,000 plus punitive damages of $3,000,000. The trial court reduced the total damages to $460,000. Pursuant to the advice of counsel, X appealed, primarily on the ground that it was error to award the plaintiff any punitive damages; but just last week the judgment of $460,000 was affirmed, and that amount was paid by X.

X's earnings for the past four years, without taking any account of this lawsuit, have been as follows:

20X1	20X2	20X3	20X4 (recently ended)
$375,000	$600,000	$700,000	$750,000

X's balance sheet at the close of 20X4 (recently ended) was as follows:

X Corp.
Balance Sheet, Close of 20X4

Assets		Liabilities & Equity	
Current Assets		Accounts Payable	$1,250,000
Cash	$ 800,000	Note Payable	600,000
Accounts Receivable	1,100,000	Total Liabilities	$1,850,000
Inventory	1,300,000	Shareholders' Equity	
Total	$3,200,000	Stated Capital	$4,000,000
Fixed Assets		Earned Surplus	3,150,000
Plant	5,800,000	Total	$7,150,000
Total Assets	$9,000,000	Grand Total	$9,000,000

X has faced libel suits from time to time in the past, but never one as large as this. In all of the prior actions, X either defended successfully or settled for some modest amount, the largest settlement being some $30,000 two years ago.

How, if at all, should the events relating to the coach's libel claim have been reflected in X's financial statements in each of the last four years?

Problem 7.2. Scary Air Airlines, Inc., a small publicly traded corporation that uses the calendar year for financial accounting purposes, publishes its audited annual financial statements in mid-March each year. On March 1, 20X2, a Scary Air turboprop plane crashed while flying on a sunny, warm day. The crash did not kill anyone, but all twelve passengers suffered injuries requiring medical treatment. The pilot, Sleepy Joe, escaped unharmed. A hospital near the crash site treated and released nine passengers for relatively minor injuries. The hospital admitted the other three passengers and they remained hospitalized for periods which did not exceed two weeks.

Scary Air had never had a crash until this accident, so management did not have any first hand experience at predicting potential losses. Scary Air's Chief Financial Officer ("CFO") estimated, however, based on industry experience, that if the company was liable for the accident it would likely end up paying between $20,000 and $50,000 to each of the nine passengers who were not hospitalized. The CFO also estimated that the company may have to pay between $100,000 and $250,000, but most likely about $150,000, to each of the three passengers who were hospitalized.

After the accident, the National Transportation Safety Board ("NTSB") immediately opened an investigation into the crash. In September, 20X2, Scary Air learned that several passengers, including two passengers that had been hospitalized, had been meeting with a personal injury attorney.

On January 15, 20X3, the NTSB announced its findings that pilot error caused the accident. The NTSB concluded that Sleepy Joe had fallen asleep in the cockpit. The NTSB's investigation also revealed Sleepy Joe had flown 30 hours more than the monthly maximum under the applicable safety regulations of the Federal Aviation Administration ("FAA"). After the NTSB's announcement, counsel advised management that the FAA could fine Scary Air $250,000 and suspend its license for ninety days.

Management immediately decided to offer $25,000 to the nine passengers that were not hospitalized and $100,000 to the three passengers that were hospitalized. On April 2, 20X3, shortly after Scary Air issued its financial statements for 20X2, the company agreed to pay six passengers that were not hospitalized $35,000 each and $190,000 to one of the passengers that was hospitalized in exchange for their releases of any and all claims arising from the accident. When the company refused to increase the settlement offers to the remaining five passengers, they filed suit, collectively seeking $2.5 million in compensatory damages and $5 million in punitive damages. Counsel advised management that (1) there was about a ninety percent chance that Scary Air would be held liable, and (2) if so, the damages were most likely to run between $500,000 and $1,500,000, with an outside possibility that the amount could reach $5 million. Later in 20X3, Scary Air consented to a $200,000 fine after the FAA agreed not to suspend the company's license.

Late in 20X4, which ended a couple of months ago, the company decided to accept a settlement offer from the five passengers to settle the case for a total of $2 million.

Scary Air's earnings for the past four years, without taking any account of this crash, have been as follows:

20X1	20X2	20X3	20X4 (recently ended)
$2,000,000	$1,750,000	$2,600,000	$3,250,000

How, if at all, should the events relating to the accident have been reflected in Scary Air's financial statements in each of the last four years?

Problem 7.3. Assume that you are working as a senior associate in a large law firm in Pacioli, the fictional fifty-first state. In this morning's mail, you opened a letter from Panton & Russ, CPAs, the accounting firm that audits your client Gunn Products, Inc., a publicly traded company. The standard audit inquiry letter requests your reply regarding the company's litigation, claims and assessments.

Your reply would require only a few moments except for one seemingly insignificant, but perhaps not so minor, item. You recall that about six months ago an investigator from the Federal Trade Commission visited the company's headquarters and asked some presumably routine questions about the company's pricing policies. The investigator's focus centered on several profitable products which have enjoyed no price competition for several years.

Shortly after the investigator's visit, you and the company's president talked to several employees in the marketing department. Following a long discussion, the marketing vice president admitted that she and several peers from competitors met each winter in Florida to discuss product pricing. She denied fixing prices, but admitted that the company's competitors charge the same prices for their products. You counseled her not to attend such meetings in the future and you and the president decided that the company should wait and see if the FTC takes any further action.

On several occasions after the meeting with the marketing vice president, the company's treasurer has warned you not to disclose the investigator's visit to the company's auditors. You are not certain whether the matter qualifies as a material contingency that could require disclosure in the financial statements. How should you respond to the audit inquiry letter? See Don E. Giacomino, *Resolving the "Lawyers' Letters Controversy,"* SAM Advanced Mgmt. J., Autumn 1987, at 37, 39–40.

E.   DISCOVERY ISSUES

Contingencies raise several important legal issues in a litigation context. If an enterprise accrues an expense or loss for a pending claim or assessment under FASB ASC Topic 450, *Contingencies*, again which codified SFAS No. 5, can the enterprise's opponent in litigation involving the contingency obtain information about the accrual during discovery? Would any such accrual constitute an admission against interest? Will the accrual become a de facto "floor" which the litigation opponent will refuse to drop below in any settlement negotiations?

What can an enterprise do if it wants to avoid these problems but needs audited financial statements, and the independent auditor refuses to issue an unqualified opinion unless the enterprise accrues a contingent liability? Remember that an auditor must determine whether the financial statements properly treat any material contingent liabilities. Even if the auditor decides that the Codification does not require the enterprise to accrue a contingent liability, can the litigation opponent discover underlying facts which led to, but which may not entirely support, the auditor's conclusion? Presumably, the auditor asked the enterprise's lawyer about any contingent liabilities. Can the litigation opponent discover the attorney's response to that audit inquiry? As you can imagine, disclosure to a litigation opponent could place the enterprise's lawyer in a very uncomfortable situation. Can a litigation opponent use any information produced to uncover other relevant facts or to gather insights about the enterprise's litigating strategy? Can an enterprise protect any information relating to its contingencies by invoking the attorney-client or accountant-client privileges? Does the work product doctrine exempt such information from discovery?

1.   AUDIT INQUIRY LETTERS

The Preamble to the ABA Statement of Policy emphasizes that a lawyer must consider whether a response to an audit inquiry letter will waive the attorney-client privilege. The few courts that have addressed the issue in the last forty years have split on the question of whether or not parties can discover the lawyer's response to these letters for use in litigation. In *Tronitech, Inc. v. NCR Corp.*, 108 F.R.D. 655 (S.D. Ind. 1985), an antitrust case alleging that NCR had unfairly interfered with Tronitech's business, NCR's auditor had asked NCR's counsel for a legal opinion on the lawsuit's financial implications. Tronitech sought discovery of that audit letter. After reviewing the document in camera and determining that the letter did not contain any factual references that Tronitech could discover, the court concluded that since such an opinion by an attorney as to liability or the settlement value of a case would not be admissible at trial, the letter was not legally relevant and was not within the scope of discovery. The court also determined that the work product doctrine, which we will discuss in the next section, protected the letter from discovery.

In contrast, the court in *United States v. Gulf Oil Corp.*, 760 F.2d 292 (Temp. Emerg. Ct. App. 1985), took the opposite view and required production for documents prepared for, and at the request of, a company's auditors. Although conceding that the discovery dispute did not provide an obvious answer, the court of appeals decided that documents prepared to allow the auditor to complete the audit were not "prepared in anticipation of litigation or for trial," but neither were created primarily for the business purpose of compiling appropriate financial statements. The court rejected the argument that its holding would cause lawyers to respond less candidly to auditors, writing: "there is no reason to believe that attorneys will violate their legal and ethical obligations to render candid and complete opinions."

NOTES

1. In most discovery disputes over accounting information regarding contingencies generally and audit inquiry letters in particular, the attorney-client privilege does not apply. In the first place, no confidential communication between an attorney and the client may have even occurred; any communication may not have been confidential. Second, disclosing a confidential communication to a third party, such as the client's auditor, normally waives the privilege. Remaining legal issues, however, typically involve legal relevancy, the work product doctrine, and in some states, the accountant-client privilege.

2. Rule 26(b)(1) of the Federal Rules of Civil Procedure generally allows a party to a lawsuit to discover any nonprivileged matter that is relevant to any party's claim or defense. The rule specifically provides that: "Relevant information need not be admissible at the trial if the discovery appears reasonably calculated to lead to the discovery of admissible evidence." Rule 26(b)(2)(C), however, allows a court to limit the discovery when:

> (i) the discovery sought is unreasonably cumulative or duplicative, or can be obtained from some other source that is more convenient, less burdensome, or less expensive;

> (ii) the party seeking discovery has had ample opportunity to obtain the information by discovery in the action; or

> (iii) the burden or expense of the proposed discovery outweighs its likely benefit, considering the needs of the case, the amount in controversy, the parties' resources, the importance of the issues at stake in the action, and the importance of the discovery in resolving the issues.

Fed. R. Civ. P. 26(b). Could an audit inquiry letter contain any information that could reasonably lead to the discovery of admissible evidence?

3. An attorney cannot simply avoid the issues arising from audit inquiry letters by refusing to respond, since that approach could cause a client to receive a qualified opinion from its auditors. For example, the outside counsel to Advanced Monitoring Systems, Inc. apparently refused to respond to requests for information regarding pending litigation or unasserted claims. As a result, the auditor issued a qualified opinion, as illustrated by the "except for" language in the second paragraph below, which, as discussed earlier in Chapter II of the text on pages 147 and 188, *supra*, could adversely affect the enterprise:

> We were unable to obtain a response from legal counsel representing the Company in the lawsuit described in note 8 to the consolidated financial statements regarding the current status of the

suit or other pending or threatened litigation or unasserted claims and assessments at September 30, 1993 and 1992. Therefore, we were unable to obtain sufficient competent evidential matter supporting the Company's representations regarding the contingent liability discussed in note 8 to the consolidated financial statements.

In our opinion, except for the effects of such adjustments at September 30, 1993 and 1992, if any, as might have been determined to be necessary had a response from the Company's legal counsel been obtained as discussed in the preceding paragraph, the consolidated financial statements referred to above present fairly, in all material respects, * * * in conformity with generally accepted accounting principles.

4. As discussed in Chapter VI on pages 369 and 370, *supra*, SOx section 303, directed the SEC to prescribe regulations to prohibit any officer or director of an issuer, or any other person acting under the direction of an officer or director, from taking any action to fraudulently influence, coerce, manipulate, or mislead the issuer's independent auditor for the purpose of rendering the issuer's financial statements materially misleading. The SEC's final rules seem to try to impose a negligence standard with respect to the statutory terms "coerce, manipulate, or mislead." *See* 17 C.F.R. § 240.13b2-2(b) (2014); *see also* Improper Influence on Conduct of Audits, Financial Reporting Release No. 71, 68 Fed. Reg. 31,820, 31,823, 31,826–27 (May 28, 2003), *available at* http://www.sec.gov/rules/final/34-47890.htm. Some lawyers have expressed concerns about the effects of the new rules on the accord between the ABA and the AICPA (the "Accord") that led to the ABA's Statement of Policy. These lawyers worry that if law firms become overly concerned about violating Rule 13b2-2, they may begin to disclose more information in audit responses for public companies than they have in the past. As we have already suggested and will explain in more detail shortly, disclosure to the auditor typically destroys the attorney-client privilege as to the subject matter under federal law.

2.   WORK PRODUCT PROTECTION

Rule 26(b)(3) of the Federal Rules of Civil Procedure precludes discovery of "opinion" work product reflecting the mental impressions, conclusions, opinions, and theories of attorneys. Because disclosure to a third party, such as an auditor, waives the attorney-client privilege, and multiple states and federal law generally do not recognize an accountant-client privilege, the work product doctrine typically offers the best argument against discovery.

The work product doctrine provides protection only for materials "prepared in anticipation of litigation or for trial" and does not apply to materials prepared in the ordinary course of business or otherwise for some purposes not concerned with litigation. Most federal appellate courts have adopted a "because of" test in determining whether a document was "prepared in anticipation of litigation," rejecting the previously more restrictive "primary motivating purpose test" formulated in *United States v. El Paso Co.*, 682 F.2d

530, 542 (5th Cir. 1982). Although not the first federal appellate court to apply the "because of anticipated litigation" standard, the Second Circuit's articulation in *United States v. Adlman*, 134 F.3d 1194 (2d Cir. 1998), quickly spread to First, Third, Sixth, Seventh, Eighth, Ninth, and D.C. Circuits. Under *Adlman*'s "because of" formulation, the work product doctrine protects documents that "'can fairly be said to have been prepared or obtained because of the prospect of litigation.'" *Id.* at 1202 (quoting CHARLES ALAN WRIGHT, ARTHUR R. MILLER & RICHARD L. MARCUS, 8 FEDERAL PRACTICE & PROCEDURE § 2024, at 343 (1994)). Under that standard, a document does not lose the protection under the work product doctrine merely because the document was created to assist with a business decision. In dicta, however, the *Adlman* court observed that the "because of" formulation would withhold work product protection from "documents that are prepared in the ordinary course of business or that would have been created in essentially similar form irrespective of the litigation." Even in such circumstances, however, Rule 26(b)(3) gives a trial court "the authority to protect against disclosure of the mental impressions, strategies, and analyses of the party or its representative concerning the litigation." *Id.* at 1202–03.

In *United States v. Textron Inc.*, 577 F.3d 21 (1st Cir. 2009) (en banc), *cert. denied*, 130 S. Ct. 3320 (2010), a majority of the First Circuit, sitting en banc, seemingly created and applied a "prepared *for use* in possible litigation" standard when determining whether tax accrual workpapers qualified for work product protection. The court held that the work product doctrine did not protect workpapers that Textron's attorneys had prepared from an IRS summons. Because Textron's lawyers prepared the workpapers "to support a financial statement and the independent audit of it," the 3-2 decision concluded that the lawyers did not prepare the documents for potential use in litigation if and when it might arise. In essence, the majority in *Textron* focused on the document's function rather than its subject matter or content. Whether or not the "prepared *for use* in possible litigation" standard seemingly applied by the First Circuit emerges as an alternative to both the majority "because of anticipated litigation" and the "primary motivating purpose" tests, we can expect courts to continue to struggle with discovery questions arising from so-called "dual purpose" documents. More recently, *United States v. Deloitte LLP*, 610 F.3d 129 (D.C. Cir. 2010), discussed the various tests that courts have applied in determining when a document qualifies for work product protect, refused to follow the *Textron* standard, and applied the majority "because of the prospect of litigation" test.

If materials qualify for work product protection, does sharing such materials with the company's independent auditor waive the protection? Courts have disagreed, but *Deloitte* marks the first federal appellate court to address the question. In that case, the government sought to compel Dow Chemical Co.'s independent auditor, Deloitte & Touche USA, LLP, to produce three documents related to ongoing tax litigation in another federal district court. After concluding that two of the documents qualified as work product, the *Deloitte* court held that because the auditor was not an adversary to Dow, and the AICPA's Code of Professional Conduct prohibits disclosure of confidential client information, Dow had a reasonable expectation of privacy.

If followed by other courts, the reasoning in *Deloitte* will protect the confidentiality of counsel's oral and written communications with auditors about pending or anticipated litigation.

NOTES

1. Given the importance of discovery, why have relatively few courts addressed the various issues involving the work product doctrine? The fact that parties generally cannot appeal discovery orders until the court has entered a judgment perhaps explains the paucity of appellate opinions. By that time, the litigants may have concluded that the legal issues that arose in discovery do not merit pursuing on appeal or decided to base any appeal on other issues. In *Deloitte*, the government issued the subpoena and filed the motion to compel in a different venue than the underlying tax litigation, which produced an appealable final judgment separate from the civil tax case.

Anecdotal evidence suggests that litigators rarely request accounting information related to contingencies or working papers. Some litigators may decide that the expected benefits from such accounting data does not outweigh the costs to obtain the information. Many litigators, however, do not know that this information exists or underestimate its strategic and practical value.

Before requesting any information regarding contingencies from a litigation opponent, smart litigators will consider whether the opponent can request similar information from their client. In this regard, attorneys representing individuals, especially tort plaintiffs, governmental bodies and agencies, and businesses that do not require audited financial statements generally need not worry about this downside. Discovery disputes, however, can become expensive and time-consuming.

2. Federal district courts and state courts have disagreed as to whether sharing work product with an independent auditor waives work product protection. *See, e.g.*, Merrill Lynch & Co. v. Allegheny Energy, Inc., No. 02 Civ. 7689(HB), 2004 WL 2389822 (S.D.N.Y. Oct. 26, 2004) (discussing cases that reach different results as to whether disclosure to a corporation's auditors waives work product protection before denying a request for the production of two reports produced during an internal investigation, which the company later disclosed to its auditor); Laguna Beach County Water District v. Superior Court, 22 Cal. Rptr. 3d 387 (Cal. App. 2004) (observing that federal courts have come down on both sides of the issue, but concluding that California's work product doctrine protects attorney's responses to audit inquiries); *In re* Raytheon Securities Litig., 218 F.R.D. 354 (D. Mass. 2003) (ordering in camera inspection of audit opinion letters and related affidavits to determine whether the company must disclose the information in the letters in its public financial statements and whether the auditor would likely turn those letters over to the company's adversaries, absent public disclosure under the securities laws or accounting standards). Because the work product doctrine prevents disclosure to the opposing party and counsel, transmission to third parties, including accountants, may not waive work product protection. *See, e.g., In re* Pfizer Inc. Securities Litigation, No. 90 Civ. 1260 (SS), 1993 WL 561125 (S.D.N.Y. Dec.

23, 1993) (disclosure to independent auditor did not waive work product protection, but eliminates argument that attorney-client privilege applies); *see also* Gramm v. Horsehead Industries, Inc., No. 87 CIV. 5122 (MJL), 1990 WL 142404 (S.D.N.Y. Jan. 25, 1990) (disclosure to an accounting firm which did not work on matters related to the case did not waive work product rule). Other courts have disagreed. In *In re Diasonics Securities Litigation*, No. C 91-20377 RMF (EAI), 1986 WL 53402 (N.D. Cal. June 15, 1986), plaintiffs filed a motion to compel Arthur Young & Co. to produce documents prepared by or disclosed to Diasonics' auditor so that the accounting firm could assess how pending litigation, including the underlying lawsuit, would affect Diasonics' financial condition. The court granted the motion, finding that neither the attorney-client privilege nor the work product doctrine excused production. The court found, first, that the attorney-client privilege did not apply because Arthur Young prepared or obtained the documents for accounting purposes rather than for securing legal advice. The documents also did not qualify for work product protection because they "were generated for the business purpose of creating financial statements which would satisfy the requirements of the federal securities laws and not to assist in litigation." *Id.* at *1. The court reasoned that although disclosure to someone sharing a common interest under a guarantee of confidentiality does not necessarily waive the work product protection, an independent accountant's responsibilities to creditors and the investing public transcend any such guarantee. See also Medinol, Ltd. v. Boston Scientific Corp., 214 F.R.D. 113 (S.D.N.Y. 2002) (holding that the disclosure of minutes of special litigation committee meetings to the company's independent auditor waived work product protection because the auditor's responsibilities to the investing public create an " 'adversarial tension' " between the auditor and the client, and ordering production of those minutes within twenty days).

3. FASB ASC paragraph 450-20-25-8, which codifies paragraph 14 of SFAS No. 5, provides that general or unspecified business risks do not satisfy the conditions for accrual in the Codification. Even though enterprises often try to aggregate accruals or disclosures related to separate matters into a lump sum for financial statement purposes, and the SEC staff has encouraged this approach, the Codification requires specific amounts for individual matters. At what point, do those specific amounts, and their underlying justifications, become discoverable? Even when management discusses a matter with counsel before deciding whether or not to accrue an amount or to disclose a reasonably possible loss related to the matter, some accounting record, if nothing more than a bookkeeper's memory, must support the accrual or disclosure, or the financial statements will not comply with GAAP. Can a litigation opponent depose the bookkeeper, or the chief accounting officer responsible for the financial statements, and request production of any accounting record or documentation that supports the accounting treatment? Does any journal entry or supporting documentation become an ordinary business record necessary to prepare financial statements or to comply with the federal securities laws and fall outside any protection that the attorney-client privilege and work product doctrine offer?

3.   ACCOUNTANT-CLIENT PRIVILEGE

The Supreme Court of Colorado has noted that "[a]t least thirty states have codified some form of protection for communications between an accountant and a client." Colorado State Board of Accountancy v. Zaveral Boosalis Raisch, 960 P.2d 102, 106 n.3 (Colo. 1998). Even when no statutory privilege exists, businesses have try to persuade the courts to create some barrier to prevent litigation opponents from discovering work papers and other documents that their employees or independent auditor prepared, which could reveal the enterprise's estimate of a contingent liability, data that the business used to compute the estimate, or other information which the auditor gathered to verify the appropriateness of the enterprise's treatment. Although the Internal Revenue Service Restructuring and Reform Act of 1998 created an accountant-client privilege in civil tax matters before the Internal Revenue Service or in federal courts, the legislation does not protect accountant-client communications from disclosure in other contexts and does not change the "ability of any other body, including the [SEC], to gain or compel information." H.R. Conf. Rep. No. 105-599, at 88 (1998).

In *FMC Corp. v. Liberty Mutual Assurance Co.*, 236 Ill. App. 3d 355, 603 N.E. 2d (1992), FMC sought a declaratory judgment against several insurance companies that it was entitled under certain insurance policies to defense and indemnity coverage for prospective environmental liabilities. The insurance companies sought to subpoena from FMC's long-time auditor its workpapers relating to FMC's contingent environmental liabilities. Relying upon an earlier decision of the Illinois Supreme Court that the statutory accountant's privilege did not apply to documents or information turned over to an accountant in connection with the preparation of a tax return because the client could reasonably expect they would be disclosed to third parties, the appellate court required the production of any documents that related to FMC's tax return. The court also refused to protext any other material or communications between FMC and its auditor regarding FMC's potential environmental liabilities if received from or by, or given to, third parties. The court, however, held that the accountants privilege statute protected any materials or communications between FMC and its auditor, not conveyed to or received from third parties.

On the federal side, the Supreme Court has held that no confidential accountant-client privilege existed under federal law, and no state-created privilege has been recognized in cases involving a federal claim. *See* United States v. Arthur Young & Co., 465 U.S. 805 (1984). In that case, the Internal Revenue Service sought to obtain from a taxpayer's auditor the tax accrual workpapers prepared by the auditor in analyzing and evaluating the taxpayer's reserves for contingent tax liabilities. Such workpapers sometimes contain information pertaining to the taxpayer's financial transactions, identify questionable positions taken on the tax return, and reflect the auditor's opinions regarding the validity of such positions. The District Court ordered production of the workpapers pursuant to section 7602 of the Internal Revenue Code, which authorizes the IRS to summon and "examine any books, papers, records, or other data, which may be relevant or material" to a particular tax inquiry. The Court of Appeals reversed, holding that the public interest in promoting full disclosure to auditors, and in turn enhancing the integrity of the securities markets, required protection of the work of the auditor, which called for a kind of work-product immunity docutrine for the tax accrual workpapers prepared by the auditor.

The Supreme Court reversed, finding in the Code provision no legislative intention to restrict the broad summons power of the IRS. The Court viewed the limitation imposed by the Court of Appeals as less a wrok-product immunity than a sort of testimonial accountant-client privilege, which was not recognized under federal law. But the court also rejected the analogy between work-product immunity for accountants' tax accrual workpapers and the attorney work-product immunity. The Court pointed out that, unlike the attorney, who is the client's confidential advisor and advocate, the auditor "assumes a public responsibility" and "owes ultimate allegiance to the investing public." Accordingly, in the Court's view, even if there were some risk that the absence of work-product immunity would lead some managements to consider being less forthcoming with their auditors, the auditors could not and would not accept a lack of candor and completeness and would instead respond with qualified opinions. Indeed, the Court expressed concern that work-product immunity for auditors could interfere with the appearance of independence, creating the impression that the auditor is an advocate for the client.

NOTES

1. Courts universally recognize that the person asserting a privilege bears the burden of proving the privilege's existence. *See, e.g.*, *In re* Horowitz, 482 F.2d 72, 83 (2d Cir. 1973) (attorney-client privilege). The Supreme Court has consistently directed federal courts to construe privileges narrowly in an effort to avoid suppressing probative evidence. *See, e.g.*, Univ. of Pennsylvania v. EEOC, 493 U.S. 182, 189 (1990). In applying the Illinois accountant-client privilege at issue in *FMC Corp. v. Liberty Mutual Insurance Co.*, a federal court of appeals held that the privilege did not protect documents that an accountant generated while rendering nonfinancial consulting services. Pepsico, Inc. v. Baird, Kurtz & Dobson, LLP, 305 F.3d 813 (8th Cir. 2002).

2. An accountant can generally rely upon the attorney-client privilege when an attorney employs the accountant to assist in rendering legal services. Although courts initially rejected this argument, recent cases regularly recognize the attorney-client privilege in appropriate situations. The cases, however, often draw subtle distinctions, based on who retained and paid the accountant or exactly what services the accountant performed. In addition, where the accountant uses the client's books and records to prepare a report for the lawyer, the privilege protects the report, but not the books and records. The mere delivery of pre-existing accounting records to the lawyer cannot create a privilege.

3. Assuming an accountant-client privilege does not apply, does disclosing to an accountant a communication that would otherwise qualify for the attorney-client privilege generally waive the attorney-client privilege? The attorney-client privilege does not usually apply to communications that are disclosed to others for purposes other than to enable the recipient to assist the attorney in rendering legal services. *See, e.g., In re* Horowitz, 482 F.2d 72, 81 (2d Cir. 1973) (subsequent disclosure to accountant waived the attorney-client privilege); First Fed. Sav. Bank of Hegewisch v. United States, 55 Fed. Cl. 263 (2003) (concluding that the disclosure of unredacted board minutes to an accounting firm during the performance of special accounting procedures for a law firm did not waive the attorney-client privilege, but that the disclosure of those same minutes to the accounting firm during annual audits did waive the privilege).

At least one decision, *In re Pioneer Hi-Bred Int'l, Inc.*, 238 F.3d 1370 (Fed. Cir. 2001), suggests that proxy statement disclosures waive the attorney-client privilege. In that case, Pioneer asked outside counsel to provide an opinion concerning the tax consequences of a proposed merger, which Pioneer intended to include in its proxy statement. The court held that Pioneer's reliance on and disclosure of outside counsel's opinion in its proxy statement waived the attorney-client privilege, but only with respect to the documents that formed the basis for the advice, the documents that outside counsel considered when it rendered that advice, and all reasonably contemporaneous documents that reflected discussions concerning that advice. The *Pioneer* court did not rule on the issue of work product protection, finding the record insufficient to make such a ruling. The court did, however, rule that Pioneer's disclosure of confidential information to expert witnesses waived both the attorney-client privilege and work product protection to the same extent as any other disclosure.

4. When a litigant requests the production of documents from an adversary's auditor, whether the request seeks responses to audit letters to attorneys, information about specific contingencies or reserves, or working papers generally, numerous tensions arise. First, the auditor must decide how to respond. As a practical matter, in most cases the auditor wants to keep the client happy so that the client remains a client. Because working papers usually provide the easiest roadmap to the client's business organization and financial statements, the client almost always prefers that the auditor not produce the working papers. In addition, the client normally does not want the auditor to release any responses to audit inquiry letters or information relating to specific contingencies. At the same time, the auditor must fulfill conflicting legal and professional responsibilities. These obligations require the auditor to comply with legitimate discovery requests, preserve client confidences, protect possible proprietary information about the auditor's procedures and maintain independence. In such situations, auditors often ignore the production request. At that time, the litigation opponent must decide whether to incur the costs necessary to serve and then to enforce a third party subpoena in an action usually separate from the underlying litigation.

If the litigation opponent decides to try to enforce a third party subpoena, unless and until the court allows the client to intervene the client does not become a party in that dispute and must view the proceedings as a spectator. To illustrate, if litigation opponent B tries to enforce a subpoena against accountant A to obtain documents relating to client C, legally speaking the enforcement action does not involve C. This situation also creates some practical concerns for C's counsel. Even if C intervenes in the dispute between B and A, C's counsel does not represent A. As a result, any communications between C's counsel and A or A's counsel do not qualify for the attorney-client privilege.

5. Some courts have explicitly rejected the argument that a defendant waives the right to deny liability by accruing an expense or loss on a claim. *See, e.g.*, Continental Ins. Co. v. Beecham, Inc., 836 F. Supp. 1027, 1047 n. 12 (D.N.J. 1993) (ruling that an insurer's establishment of a reserve did not constitute an admission in a policy coverage dispute). Other courts have refused to permit a party to discover information pertaining to reserves that enterprises, especially insurance companies, may have set aside to satisfy future claims. *See, e.g.*, Nat'l Union Fire Ins. Co. v. Stauffer Chemical Co., 558 A.2d 1091 (Del. Super. 1989) (denying request to produce information related to reserves on relevancy grounds because the fact that insurance company had established reserves did not necessarily mean that insurer believed applicable policies would cover hazardous waste claims). Several courts, however, have concluded that communications concerning individual case reserves qualified for work product protection, while ordering defendants to produce information regarding aggregate reserve figures. *See, e.g.*, Simon v. G.D. Searle & Co., 816 F.2d 397 (8th Cir. 1987) (ruling that risk management documents prepared by corporate officials to aggregate information from individual case reserve figures obtained from the company's legal department were not protected from discovery by the work product doctrine in product liability action against intrauterine contraceptive device manufacturer); General Electric Capital Corp. v. DirectTV, Inc., 184 F.R.D. 32 (D. Conn. 1998) (drawing a distinction between individual case reserves and aggregate figures and concluding, after in camera review, that five documents pertaining to defendants' loss reserves were both relevant and not privileged under either the work-product doctrine or the attorney-client privilege).

Dicta from at least one decision suggests that information about litigation reserves might even qualify as admissible evidence. In *In re Amino Acid Lysine Antitrust Litigation*, No. 95 C 7679, 1996 WL 197671 (N.D. Ill. Apr. 22, 1996), Senior District Judge Shadur ordered disclosure of any reserves that defendant Archer-Daniels-Midland Company had established for the underlying antitrust litigation before the court would rule that the proposed settlement in the class action fell within the range of fairness, reasonableness and adequacy. The judge wrote: "In this Court's experience in representing public companies, or in separately representing the outside directors of public companies, it has found such reserves to be a material indicium of the fair value of a liability, estimated by those who are presumably in the best position to make such an evaluation." *Id*. at *5.

What are the competing considerations in deciding whether the courts should allow litigants to use the discovery process to try to uncover litigation reserves or to point to such reserves as evidence of liability? Our adversary system's desire to give the parties the opportunity to obtain all relevant information in advance of trial, the courts' presumption against privilege, and the preference, whenever possible, to settle cases without trial all justify broad access during discovery to information about litigation reserves. In addition, to the extent that a securities filing suggests a reserve related to the specific matter, a litigant seeking discovery can portray any resulting disclosure as nothing more than a cost of taking advantage of the securities markets in the United States. At the same time, a party seeking to quash a request to obtain information about a litigation reserve during discovery should seek to portray any accruals, certainly all amounts recorded after the defendant learned the claimant had asserted the claim in any way, as "mental impressions" formed and prepared at least "in anticipation of litigation" so as to qualify for work product protection. In addition, a defendant might try to highlight the unfairness of the request by analogizing the situation to a poker game. No poker game requires only one player to show all his or her cards to another player before all bets have been placed. Finally, while allowing the discovery of information about litigation reserves might encourage some cases to settle, such a result might also encourage litigants to file actions or claims that they might not otherwise bring in an effort to determine whether an opponent has recorded a litigation reserve.

With regard to admissibility, Federal Rule of Evidence 403 provides in pertinent part: "Although relevant, evidence may be excluded if its probative value is substantially outweighed by the danger of unfair prejudice, confusion of the issues, or misleading the jury . . . ." FED. R. EVID. 403. If a litigant's accounting policies treat "probable" as anything greater than fifty percent, the danger of unfair prejudice seems to outweigh any probative value. In contrast, when a litigant's accounting policies interpret "probable" to mean at least an eighty percent chance of an unfavorable outcome, the arguments for admissibility get quite compelling. *See* Matthew J. Barrett, *Opportunities for Obtaining and Using Litigation Reserves and Disclosures*, 63 OHIO ST. L. J. 1017, 1102–06 (2002) (concluding that the Advisory Committee on the Federal Rules of Evidence should recommend that the Supreme Court adopt a new rule of evidence that would allow the discovery of information related to litigation reserves, but would bar the admission into evidence on the issues of whether the enterprise has admitted liability on a claim or the amount of liability).

6. Discovery of an enterprise's tax returns may enable a litigation opponent to uncover evidence related to contingencies. You may recall from Chapter VI on page 485, *supra*, that for tax purposes enterprises cannot deduct accrued liabilities until they satisfy the "all events test" and the economic performance requirements in section 461(h) of the Internal Revenue Code. As a result, enterprises frequently cannot deduct, for tax purposes, accrued expenses that they include in their financial statements. Subject to exceptions described below, Schedule M-1, Reconciliation of Income (Loss) per Books With Income per Return, generally requires corporations, limited liability companies, and partnerships to reconcile their taxable incomes to income for financial accounting purposes. Line 5 in Schedule M-1 on Form 1120, for example, requires corporations to itemize "[e]xpenses recorded on books this year not deducted on this return." Corporations, limited liability companies, and partnerships owning at least $10 million in assets, however, must file a more detailed Schedule M-3, Net Income (Loss) Reconciliation for Corporations With Total Assets of $10 Million or More. Lines 12, 13 and 37 in Part III, Reconciliation of Net Income (Loss) per Income Statement of Includible Corporations With Taxable Income per Return – Expense/Deduction Items, of Schedule M-3 require corporations, for example, to report on separate lines: (1) fines and penalties, (2) judgments, damages, awards, and similar costs, and (3) other expense/deduction items with differences. By carefully examining these reconciliations on either Schedule M-1 or Schedule M-3 from all tax returns after an "incident," opposing counsel may uncover an accrual not otherwise discoverable.

7. Within the discussion of critical accounting policies in Starbucks' MD&A on page 48 of the company's Form 10-K for the year ended December 31, 2012, which appears in Appendix A on page 744, *infra*, Starbucks states:

> We record reserves related to legal matters when it is probable that a loss has been incurred and the range of such loss can be reasonably estimated. Such assessments are reviewed each period and revised, based on current facts and circumstances and historical experience with similar claims, as necessary.

On page 54 of the 2012 Form 10-K, reprinted in Appendix A on page 750, *infra*, under the heading "Estimates and Assumptions" in Note 1, Starbucks cautions that the preparation of financial statements in conformity with accounting principles generally accepted in the United States requires management to make estimates and assumptions that affect the reported amounts of liabilities and expenses, including self-insurance reserves and the potential outcome of future tax consequences of events that have been recognized in the financial statements. As a result, actual results can differ from those estimates.

In Note 15 on commitments and contingencies on pages 84 and 85 of Starbucks' 2012 Form 10-K, which appears on pages 780 and 781, *infra*, Starbucks discloses an arbitration proceeding arising from the termination of a distribution agreement with Kraft Foods Global, Inc. ("Kraft"). During a hearing that commenced on July 11, 2012 and concluded on August 3, Starbucks presented evidence that Kraft materially breached the distribution agreement after earlier submitting an expert report claiming up to $62.9 million in damages from the loss of sales resulting from Kraft's failure to use commercially reasonable efforts to market Starbucks' coffee, plus attorney fees. In response, Kraft presented evidence denying any breach and sought $2.9 billion in damages for the termination, plus attorney fees. Although Starbucks offered Kraft $750 million in August 2010 to avoid litigation and to ensure a smooth transition in distribution, an amount that Kraft disclosed to the press and in federal court, Starbucks had not recorded any loss contingency for the dispute. To support this decision, Starbucks expressed its belief that an unfavorable outcome was not probable, but acknowledged that such an outcome was reasonably possible. In addition, Starbucks opined that Kraft had used faulty analysis to arrive at highly inflated damage estimates. Because Kraft immediately rejected the $750 million offer, which was based on the facts and circumstances at that time and before Starbucks had investigated Kraft's alleged breaches that would allow Starbucks to terminate the agreement without consideration, Starbucks additionally concluded that it could not reasonably estimate the possible loss. (On November 12, 2013, or more than a year after the close of Starbucks' 2012 fiscal year, the arbitrator ordered Starbucks to pay Kraft $2,227.5 million damages plus prejudgment interest and attorney fees, which Starbucks estimated at $556.6 million. Even though the arbitrator issued the order after the end of Starbucks' 2013 fiscal year, because the order came before Starbucks issued its financial statements for fiscal 2013, the company recorded a $2,784.1 million litigation charge in its fiscal 2013 operating results.) *See* Starbucks Corp., 2012 Annual Report (Form 10-K) 73 (Nov. 18, 2013).)

The last paragraph in Note 15 to the fiscal 2012 financial statements discloses that Starbucks was a party to various other legal proceedings arising in the ordinary course of business, including certain employment litigation cases that courts have certified as class actions. Finally, Note 15 states management's belief that none of these other proceedings could have a material adverse effect on the company's consolidated financial position or operating results.

Based upon these disclosures, Starbucks' opposing counsel in any such legal proceeding might focus particular attention on, and seek to discover information about, possible accruals included in the $167.7 million in "Insurance reserves" listed under "Current liabilities" on the consolidated balance sheet as of September 30, 2012 on page 51 of the 2012 Form 10-K, which appears in Appendix A on page 747, *infra*; the $329.6 million in "Other" in the detail of the $1,133.8 million in "Accrued liabilities" on page 72 of that same Form 10-K, and page 768, *infra*, in Note 7: Supplemental Balance Sheet Information; and the $22.4 million in "Other" under "Other Long-Term Liabilities" in that same Note 7. Potential discovery might include a request for a breakdown of all litigation reserves, insurance reserves, or other accrued liabilities over a certain amount, say $500,000, to determine whether Starbucks has reserved any amount to satisfy the relevant contingent liability associated with the particular matter. By obtaining such detail, a lawyer may discover information relevant to a specific matter or lawsuit and could then request additional documents related to that specific matter.

Starbucks also reports $78.4 million in "Unrecognized tax benefits" among the $345.3 million in "Other Long-Term Liabilities" detailed in Note 7. Under the heading "Uncertain Tax Positions" within Note 13 on income taxes on page 83 of the 2012 Form 10-K, which appears on page 779, *infra*, in Appendix A, Starbucks discloses $75.3 million of gross unrecognized tax benefits. This amount essentially constitutes a reserve account for potential future obligations to taxing authorities for tax positions that did not satisfy the more-likely-than-not recognition threshold, assuming that tax authorities audit all tax positions. Sophisticated taxing authorities watch for such disclosures.

Finally, the chart of deferred tax assets within Note 13 on page 82 of the 2012 Form 10-K, which appears in Appendix A on page 778, *infra*, details $15.7 million for "Other accrued liabilities" and $80.9 million for "Other" as of September 30, 2012. These sums could include anticipated tax benefits for amounts that Starbucks treated as accrued expenses for financial accounting purposes, but for which the economic performance requirement in section 461(h) of the Internal Revenue Code precluded any deduction until Starbucks pays the obligation.

8. In addition to deciding whether to track down any detectable information summarized earlier in this chapter in note 9 on page 550, *supra*, a litigator should consider trying to use discovery to obtain, whether via deposition, interrogatory, or request for the production of documents, the following potentially discoverable information: financial statements and related notes for privately-owned businesses; the opponent's accounting policies regarding contingencies, particularly how the opponent interprets "probable" and the "likely to occur" in ASC Subtopic 450-20; accounting records related to any accruals, including the chart of accounts, relevant ledgers, accounts, journals, journal entries, and any supporting documentation; tax returns and attachments, particularly Schedule M-3; the outside accountant's working papers that document various audit or review procedures, including any reconciliations, representations of management, and attorney responses to audit inquiry letters; and, if not obtained elsewhere, attorney responses to audit inquiry letters. Before initiating any discovery requests, the litigator should consider any likely defenses and responses, including relevancy, the attorney-client and accountant-client privileges, and work product protection.

9. The Codification, the federal securities laws, and the Internal Revenue Code offer litigators and general counsel several strategic opportunities to use accounting-related information and rules to their client's advantage. Below we briefly set forth some opportunities and suggestions for attorneys for plaintiffs and both general counsel and defense counsel and describe some settlement considerations for all litigators.

a. Counsel for plaintiffs. As a starting point, an attorney for a plaintiff should trying to track down and evaluate any detectable information about the defendant's treatment of underlying litigation. Counsel should assert all claims as soon as possible, so that the accounting rules for asserted claims, rather than unasserted claims, apply and then patiently wait. Attorneys for plaintiffs typically want to wait as long as possible before initiating any discovery requests for accounting-related information. Patience allows the defendant, internal accountant staff, any independent auditor, and defense counsel time to disclose any material litigation in the financial statements, to gather relevant information about the claim, to assess the likelihood of an unfavorable outcome, and to estimate any loss or damages. A premature request could alert the defendant's team that the counsel for the plaintiffs recognizes these opportunities and keep any accruals as conservative as possible. If the plaintiff prepares financial statements, counsel for the plaintiff should carefully consider the consequences of any reciprocal request from the defendant before seeking to discover accounting-related information. When appropriate, counsel for the plaintiff should argue that any information obtained is admissible at trial.

b. General counsel and defense counsel. General counsel and defense counsel must anticipate the opportunities for a potential adversary, whether in transactional negotiations or litigation, to use accounting-related information. The best litigation defenses require advance planning. Whenever possible, general counsel and defense counsel want to try to keep any accruals related to loss contingencies as low as permissible. In addition, potential defendants need to remember the prohibition against so-called "cookie jar" reserves for general or unspecified business risks set forth in ASC paragraph 450-20-25-8. No defendant wants improper financial reporting to cloud a lawsuit or to create a windfall for a plaintiff. General counsel and defense counsel want to establish and preserve any attorney-client or accountant client privileges and work product protections so that they can raise any potential defenses to discovery. If a plaintiff seeks accounting-related information in discovery, defense counsel should consider submitting a reciprocal request.

c. Settlement considerations. All lawyers should keep in mind that settlement discussions, negotiations, and agreements related to a claim that arose prior to the end of an accounting period can occur after the end of the accounting period, but before the issuance of the financial statements for that period. See ASC ¶¶ 450-20-25-2a, 450-20-55-11. After finishing an unusually good or disappointing fiscal period, and assuming no previous accrual related to the litigation, a settlement before the defendant has issued financial statements for the period could give the defendant the opportunity to resolve the litigation and to use the settlement either to downplay a "great" year into a "good" one or to convert a "bad" quarter into a so-called "big bath," but with better prospects for the future. Sophisticated plaintiffs might propose a more favorable settlement than they expected to otherwise reach, and find the defendant very willing to reach a settlement, especially when reminded to consider the financial accounting rules. Similarly, and without making any offer that could potentially necessitate an accrual, a defendant could invite the plaintiff to propose a settlement amount after the fiscal period has ended, but before the defendant issues financial statements.

Especially in litigation involving intellectual property, a settlement could include a provision whereby the defendant acquires an asset, such as the contested patent, or a future right, perhaps a license to use the patent for the next five years. Such a provision, accompanied by an arms' length allocation of the total settlement between damages and consideration for the asset or future right, could mean that even a defendant with no previous accrual related to the litigation need not immediately expense the entire announced settlement amount.

A recent settlement between Medtronic, Inc. and Edwards Lifesciences Corp. seemingly illustrates both opportunities. On May 19, 2014, or almost three weeks after Medtronic's 2014 fiscal year ended, the companies agreed to settle all pending patent litigation between them and not to sue each other for eight years. The settlement required Medtronic to make a $750 million one-time payment and to pay ongoing royalties on certain valve sales, with minimum annual payments of $40 million through April 9, 2022. Net of an undisclosed existing accrual, Medtronic recognized a $589 million expense for fiscal year 2014. The settlement nevertheless allowed Medtronic to state in its next day's earnings release: "After adjusting for this charge [and other items], fourth quarter net earnings and diluted earnings per share on a non-GAAP basis were $1.135 billion and $1.12, an increase of 1 percent and 2 percent, respectively, over the same period in the prior year." Later, the earnings release announced: "[F]iscal year 2014 non-GAAP net earnings and diluted earnings per share were $3.868 billion and $3.82, flat and an increase of 2 percent, respectively." Edwards, for its part, allocated the consideration in the settlement to the following elements (in millions):

Past damages	$ 754.3
License agreement	238.0
Covenant not to sue	77.7
Total	$1,070.0

See Edwards LifesciencesCorp., Quarterly Report (Form 10-Q) 7 (Aug. 4, 2014), *available via* http://ir.edwards.com/sec.cfm; Medtronic, Inc., Annual Report (Form 10-K) 116-117 (June 20, 2014), *available via* http://phx.corporate-ir.net/phoenix.zhtml?c=76126&p=irol-sec; Press Release, Medtronic, Inc., Medtronic Reports Fourth Quarter and Fiscal 2014 Earnings (May 20, 2014), *available via* http://newsroom.medtronic.com/phoenix. zhtml?c=251324&p=irol-news.

PROBLEMS

Problem 7.4. Do the excerpts from the financial statements on pages 534 to 536, *supra*, suggest any discovery opportunities? What additional accounting-related information, if any, might you seek to obtain in connection with any described litigation. Explain your rationale for requesting, or deciding not to request, any additional information. What arguments would you expect counsel for those companies to advance in opposing any requests for information? How would you respond? Which arguments are most likely to prevail?

Problem 7.5A. Do the financial statements of Amazon.com in its Form 10-K for the fiscal year ended December 31, 2012 suggest any discovery opportunities? Does the text in the Management's Discussion and Analysis section offer any additional insights? What additional accounting-related information, if any, might you seek to obtain in connection with any described litigation. Explain your rationale for requesting, or deciding not to request, any additional information. What arguments would you expect counsel for Amazon.com to advance in opposing any requests for information? How would you respond? Which arguments are most likely to prevail?

Problem 7.5B. Do the financial statements of Google in the Form 10-K for the fiscal year ended December 31, 2012 suggest any discovery opportunities? Does the text in the Management's Discussion and Analysis section offer any additional insights? What additional accounting-related information, if any, might you seek to obtain in connection with any described litigation. Explain your rationale for requesting, or deciding not to request, any additional information. What arguments would you expect counsel for Google to advance in opposing any requests for information? How would you respond? Which arguments are most likely to prevail?

Problem 7.5C. Do the financial statements of UPS in the Form 10-K for the fiscal year ended December 31, 2012 suggest any discovery opportunities? Does the text in the Management's Discussion and Analysis section offer any additional insights? What additional accounting-related information, if any, might you seek to obtain in connection with any described litigation. Explain your rationale for requesting, or deciding not to request, any additional information. What arguments would you expect counsel for UPS to advance in opposing any requests for information? How would you respond? Which arguments are most likely to prevail?

Problem 7.6. For several years, your law firm has represented the plaintiff Myron Ulman, an inventor, in a patent infringement case against The Russ Company ("the Company"), a company with about eighty shareholders and more than $15 million in assets. The lawsuit seeks more than $1 million in damages. Although the Company's shares are not traded on any stock exchange, the accounting firm of Barth and McKnight, CPAs, audits the Company's financial statements and has rendered unqualified opinions on the financial statements for the each of the last nine years.

One of the notes to the Company's 20X2 audited financial statements (dollars in thousands) provides in pertinent part:

Contingent Liabilities

Product Liability and Other Matters–The Company is subject to various legal actions arising out of the conduct of its business, including those related to product liability, patent infringement, and claims for damages alleging violations of federal, state or local statutes or ordinances dealing with civil rights. Total amounts included in accrued expenses related to these actions were $576 and $265 at December 31, 20X2 and 20X1, respectively. In the opinion of management of the Company, amounts accrued for awards or assessments in connection with these matters are adequate and ultimate resolution of these matters will not have a material effect on the Company's financial position, results of operations, or cash flow.

QUESTIONS:

(1) Under what circumstances can the Company accrue expenses related to the various legal actions described above?

(2) What discovery opportunities does this note suggest for your client? What additional information, if any, would you seek to obtain in connection with the litigation? Describe your methodology and explain fully your rationale for requesting any additional information.

(3) What arguments would you expect counsel for the Company to advance in opposing any requests for information? How would you respond? Which arguments are most likely to prevail?

*

CHAPTER VIII

INVENTORY

A. IMPORTANCE TO LAWYERS

Review the introductory materials on accounting for inventories in Chapter I on pages 100 to 108, *supra*. As those materials suggest, inventory accounting presents another deferral issue. Under generally accepted accounting principles, a business must allocate certain costs related to goods purchased or produced for sale in the ordinary course of business between the current period and future accounting periods. We can express this process in the form of an equation, as follows:

$$\underset{\substack{\text{Total inventory}\\\text{costs incurred}}}{1} = \underset{\substack{\text{Costs allocable}\\\text{to current period}}}{2} + \underset{\substack{\text{Costs deferred}\\\text{to later periods}}}{3}$$

The difficulty lies in the fact that items 2 and 3 represent unknown amounts. While a business could determine the costs allocable to the current period by keeping a careful record of the cost of each item sold during the period, such record keeping normally would prove too time-consuming and expensive. Instead, most businesses attempt to ascertain item 3 by "taking inventory" at the end of an accounting period.

Pricing the ending inventory serves two important functions. First, the procedure calculates the amount that the business should defer as ending inventory to match against revenues in some later period. Second, the process determines what amount of the total inventory costs for the period the business should treat as an expense of the current period to match against current revenues. In effect, we could rewrite the equation above as follows:

$$\underset{\substack{\text{Total inventory}\\\text{costs incurred}}}{1} - \underset{\substack{\text{Costs deferred}\\\text{to later period}}}{2} = \underset{\substack{\text{Costs allocable}\\\text{to current periods}}}{3}$$

In this form, the restated equation helps to explain the operation of the Cost of Goods Sold account under a periodic inventory system.

The Cost of Goods Sold account portrays the expense for goods "used up" (presumably sold) during an accounting period. To calculate this expense, a business adds together on the debit, or left hand, side of the Cost of Goods Sold account the opening inventory and the purchases for the period. Together, the beginning inventory and the purchases during the period equal the cost of goods available for sale. From the total cost of goods that the business could have sold, the business subtracts the amount of the goods still on hand at the end of the period--in other words, the closing inventory. As we suggested in

Chapter I, inventory accounting provides another example of deferral. We could just as appropriately refer to the Ending Inventory account as Cost of Unsold Goods or Deferred Cost of Unsold Goods.

With respect to the income statement, inventory accounting attempts to match the cost of goods sold during an accounting period with the corresponding revenues from those sales. Without matching revenues and corresponding costs, a business cannot accurately determine its net profit or loss for a particular accounting period. As a practical matter, the cost of goods sold often represents the largest deduction from revenues on the income statement. For example, page 28 of Starbucks' 2012 Form 10-K, which appears on page 724 in Appendix A, shows that the cost of sales including occupancy costs represented 43.7 percent of total net revenues during the fiscal year ended September 30, 2012.

We should also keep in mind that a direct relationship exists between the ending inventory and net income. Holding everything else constant, as ending inventory increases, cost of goods sold decreases, which increases net income for the current period. Conversely, the lower the ending inventory, the higher the cost of goods sold, and the lower the net income for the current period. (Notice also that errors in ending inventory will carry over to the next accounting period: if we overstate ending inventory, we will also overstate beginning inventory in the following period.) Assuming we properly determine ending inventory in that following period, we will necessarily overstate cost of goods sold in that period, which will produce lower earnings. In contrast, if we understate ending inventory in the earlier period, we will understate beginning inventory in the next accounting period, thereby understating cost of goods sold and overstating net income for the next period.

As to the balance sheet, inventories appear as a current asset. Users of financial statements particularly concerned about the business's immediate financial resources, such as short-term creditors, often pay close attention to inventories and other current assets. Under the conservatism principle, a business should not carry inventory, or any other asset, at any amount greater than the asset's current realizable value. That balance sheet objective can sometimes pull in the opposite direction from the income statement's desire to present fairly the results of operations from accounting period to accounting period. In this chapter, we shall consider how to try to resolve such conflicts in different situations.

Throughout this chapter, we will discuss various situations in which inventory accounting and reporting affect the practice of law. Lawyers should understand the importance of inventory accounting and reporting for various reasons. For example:

- Lawyers often draft, negotiate or interpret employment contracts, labor agreements, and partnership agreements which contain profit-sharing provisions. In addition, buy-sell agreements often require shareholders to sell their shares back to the corporation at a set price, based on earnings or net book value, upon certain events. An entity or its owners or managers can manipulate the entity's profit or loss to shortchange employees or minority investors by expensing costs which properly belong in inventory, thus increasing the entity's expenses and decreasing its profit and equity. Alternatively, management could overstate inventory, thus overstating the venture's profits, to qualify for a larger bonus.

• An enterprise's method of accounting for inventories may affect the taxes which the business or its owners owe. Closely-held businesses often understate closing inventory to keep taxable income, and hence income taxes, as low as possible. In contrast, publicly traded businesses may overstate inventory to show higher earnings. Improperly including various expenses in ending inventory, for example, would decrease the business's cost of goods sold and thereby increase its income. Like other financial frauds, intentionally misstating inventory can create criminal liability.

• As we saw in Chapters IV and V, loan agreements often contain clauses that require the borrower to maintain certain financial ratios. For example, a loan agreement may require the borrower to maintain a specified ratio of current assets to current liabilities. As a current asset, the amount of inventory can determine whether the borrower continues to satisfy such a covenant.

• Pursuant to the various legal limitations on distributions to shareholders which we discussed in Chapter V, a corporation's valuation of inventories can affect the amount that the entity can distribute to its owners.

• Inventory issues sometimes arise in securities fraud actions. Investors, for example, may allege that an issuer fraudulently overstated inventories, ignored losses from obsolescent goods, or failed to disclose material information related to inventories. *See, e.g.*, Newman v. Warnaco Grp., Inc., 335 F.3d 187 (2d Cir. 2003) (the defendants included the company's general counsel).

• The cost allocation issues present in accounting for inventories can also affect the computation of damages in breach of contract disputes, utility rate cases, Medicare reimbursements to hospitals and other medical care providers, payments under government contracts, and the allocation of environmental clean-up costs under federal and state environmental laws.

• Inventory accounting can impact antitrust litigation. The Robinson–Patman Act effectively outlaws quantity discounts unless differences in the cost of manufacture, sale or delivery justify such discounts. The method which a business uses to allocate costs to inventories directly impacts the cost of manufacture, sale and delivery.

• An entity's method of valuing inventory can also influence international trade disputes. Antidumping laws prohibit foreign manufacturers from selling goods in the United States at less than their full cost. The antidumping laws specify costs that companies must include in their calculation of inventory cost to ensure a fair playing field in U.S. markets.

In addition to the basic objective of matching the cost of goods which a business sold during an accounting period with the corresponding revenues from those sales, several other accounting principles influence inventory accounting. Under the conservatism principle, a business should not carry inventory at any amount greater than the asset's current realizable value. Occasionally, businesses must "write down" inventories to reflect circumstances which have impaired the realizable value.

Finally, to provide meaningful financial data, a business must consistently apply the same accounting treatment from period to period and properly disclose the methods used to determine inventories for the financial statements. Accordingly, our discussion will focus on four central themes: matching, conservatism, consistency and disclosure.

B. DETERMINING ENDING INVENTORY

As we have already seen, inventory accounting seeks to allocate certain costs between the present accounting period and future accounting periods. For more than fifty years, the guidance set forth in Chapter 4 (entitled "Inventory Pricing") of Accounting Research Bulletin No. 43, Restatement and Revision of Accounting Research Bulletins, now codified in FASB ASC Topic 330, *Inventory*, has provided the accounting standards regarding inventory pricing. *See* RESTATEMENT AND REVISION OF ACCOUNTING RESEARCH BULLETINS, Accounting Research Bulletin No. 43, Chapter 4 (Am. Inst. of Certified Pub. Accountants 1953) (codified at FASB ASC Topic 330, *Inventory*).

When a business calculates its inventory at any point in time, the business must focus on three considerations: (1) what goods and costs to include in inventory; (2) an accounting method, or flow assumption, to assign costs to those goods which remain in inventory; and (3) whether the assigned costs exceed the good's market value. Before we can grapple with the problems of valuing ending inventory, we must deal with the first consideration.

1. WHICH GOODS AND COSTS TO INCLUDE IN INVENTORY

As the first step in calculating its inventory at any point in time, a business must decide what quantity of goods and which costs to include in inventory. We can describe these two considerations as the "physical count" and "allocation" aspects of inventory accounting. We turn first to quantity issues.

a. WHICH ITEMS TO COUNT AS INVENTORY

As the initial step in the matching process, a business seeks to apportion product costs between closing inventory and goods sold during the period. You may recall that the closing inventory figure serves two important functions in the accounting process. First, closing inventory distributes inventory costs between the present accounting period and future accounting periods. The inventory costs allocated to the current period represent an expense on the income statement. Second, the inventory costs deferred to future periods appear as a current asset on the balance sheet. Both these functions emphasize the need for an accurate physical count.

To calculate the amount in inventory, a business *takes inventory* or physically counts its goods on hand. As a general rule, the quantity aspect of inventory accounting tends to focus on who holds title to the goods. Lawyers, however, should recognize that issues can arise as to what a business may or may not include in this count. For example, questions arise as to whether to include goods "belonging" to the company but in the possession of someone else, or goods in the company's possession which "belong" to someone else, in the count. As we saw during the discussion of revenue recognition, if a firm recognizes income from the "sale" of certain goods which remain in the firm's warehouse, the firm cannot count those goods in ending inventory.

Unless an enterprise increases a corresponding liability, such as accounts payable, or decreases another asset, like deposit on purchases commitment, improperly including an item in closing inventory will understate cost of goods sold, overstate earnings, and overstate owners' equity on the balance sheet. In contrast, and subject to the same caveat about corresponding liabilities or other assets, omitting an item from the final count will overstate the cost of goods sold, understate earnings, and understate inventory and owners' equity on the balance sheet.

The following excerpt from a leading accounting treatise discusses accepted inventory practice regarding which goods an enterprise should count in inventory. Although legal title generally controls for these purposes, we will see that accountants sometimes adopt certain rules of convenience.

Lee J. Seidler & D. R. Carmichael, eds.

Accountants' Handbook 18.36–18.39 (6th ed. 1981)*

SPECIAL INVENTORY ITEMS. At the end of an accounting period, questions often arise as to what constitutes proper treatment of the following items:

1. Goods in transit on the inventory date, either from vendors or to customers.

2. Goods on hand that have been segregated for certain customers, or goods on order that have been segregated by the vendor.

3. Goods on order and advances on orders.

4. Merchandise either acquired or delivered on approval or under conditional sales contracts.

5. Goods consigned to agents or acquired on consignment.

6. Pledged or hypothecated merchandise.

Whether such items should be included in, or excluded from, inventory is usually determined by applying a legal test—the **passage of title**. There are a number of limitations to the legal test as a practical solution to inventory questions, and other more practical criteria are often employed. It is important, however, for the accountant to remember that use of a criterion other than the legal test rests on the assumption that no significant information is concealed by failure to apply the legal test.

Goods in Transit. Where goods are shipped f.o.b. [free on board or, less commonly, freight on board] shipping point and are in the hands of a common carrier on the last day of the period, strict application of the legal test requires inclusion in inventory of in-transit purchases and exclusion of customer shipments. Occasionally, however, accountants object to the application of this rule to purchases on the grounds that it is impractical, preferring instead to employ the **criterion of receipt** on or before the last day of the period. Although the use of the receipt criterion, consistently applied, does not in most instances seriously distort the statement of financial position, the ease with which in-transit purchases can ordinarily be segregated by reviewing the receiving reports for the first few days of the new period leaves little support for the use of any method other than the legal criterion.
* * *

In the case of goods shipped f.o.b. destination, application of the legal test requires exclusion of in-transit purchases and inclusion of in-transit merchandise sold to customers. Common accounting procedure, however, while adhering to the legal test for purchases, employs the more practical **criterion of shipment** to exclude the merchandise shipped. Consistent application of the shipment rule causes little distortion of income and its usage eliminates the difficult task of locating merchandise en route to customers.

Segregated Goods. Where goods for filling customers' orders have been segregated by the vendor, title may pass upon segregation. If title has passed and the purchaser is aware of it, cost of the goods should be included in the purchaser's inventory and the payable recognized. Obviously, however, if the purchaser is unaware of the passage of title, such goods will be overlooked in the compilation of his inventory. The small error caused by failure to include these goods in inventory is usually considered preferable to the adoption of a procedure for surveying vendors to determine the legal status of goods on order. The effect of segregation on the passage of title is often dependent on legal technicalities difficult for even a lawyer to decide. For this reason many accountants are inclined to adopt the practice of recognizing revenue on shipment of goods, a practice resulting in the inclusion of segregated goods in the inventory of the vendor.

Purchase Orders and Advances. In general, goods on order are not included in inventory. Although the purchase contract is binding on both parties, the goods either do not exist or, if they do, title has not passed. Ordinarily, no entry should be made upon the books of the purchaser until actual delivery takes place. This, however, should not be construed as prohibiting the use of **financial statement notes** to call attention to any unusual conditions with respect to purchase commitments. The AICPA (ARB no. 43 [now codified in FASB ASC Topic 330, *Inventory*]) calls for the recognition of a loss on purchase commitments when the current "market" price of the goods falls below the contract price. * * *

Advances on purchase contracts are not inventory items. They are more in the nature of **prepayments**, being cash payments in advance for services (i.e., goods) to be received in the future. Since the advance is realized in the form of goods, not cash, it is the first step in the **working capital cycle**. It constitutes the working capital element furthest removed from the cash realization point: that is, it must pass through the successive phases of inventory and accounts receivable before disinvestment. For this reason, treatment of the item as a receivable is as poor a practice as considering it inventory. Cashin and Owens (*Auditing*) state that advances on purchase contracts and any other noninventory items not properly classifiable as raw materials and supplies, work in process, or finished goods should be segregated and appropriately shown in the financial statements. Care should be taken by vendors receiving advances to see that they are properly recorded as liabilities.

Conditional and Approval Transactions. The treatment accorded approval and other conditional sales is largely a matter of expediency. A great deal depends on the probability of the return of such goods. Legally, title to the goods is vested in the vendor until the customer accepts, makes payment, or otherwise performs on the contract in the manner specified for the passage of title. As a matter of convenience, when returns of goods sold on approval are small proportionate to total shipments, the **simplest procedure** is to consider shipment equivalent to sale. When the more conservative practice of deferring revenue recognition until receipt of the customer's approval is adopted, the cost of the goods shipped conditionally and now in the hands of customers should be displayed in the financial statement as a separate inventory element.

Where goods are sold conditionally on **installment contracts**, the cost of the goods held on such contracts, less the buyers' equity in such goods, should be carried as a special inventory account. * * *

Consignments. The title to goods shipped or received on consignment remains with the consignor while possession of such goods is transferred to the consignee who acts as the agent of the consignor. Goods on consignment should be included in the inventory of the consignor as a special type of inventory and should be excluded from the inventory of the consignee. Where arbitrary mark-ons are added to the cost of goods shipped on consignment, they must be deducted from the dollar amount of consigned goods before inclusion in the final inventory. Shipping and other appropriate charges for transfer of the goods to the consignee are legitimate additions to the cost of goods shipped on consignment and are therefore a proper portion of inventory. Care should be taken to see that shipping and other charges added to the manufacturing cost of the goods on consignment are reasonable and do not include charges for double freight, etc. The probability of eventual sales of these goods is an important consideration in assigning dollar amounts to them.

Pledged or Hypothecated Goods. When goods have been pledged or hypothecated as security on a contract, title is not transferred by the pledge or hypothecation. Such goods should be included in the inventory of the owner, with the special conditions indicated in a note to the financial statements.

NOTE ON INVENTORY FRAUD

Throughout history, unscrupulous individuals have cunningly devised schemes involving inventories either to disguise theft, enhance a business's financial position, or evade taxes. Because management and auditors can typically verify the accuracy of an inventory account by taking a physical count of the goods included in ending inventory, the perpetrators must devise elaborate schemes to evade the auditors' watchful eyes. The following examples illustrate fraudulent inventory swindles.

Hieron II, King of Syracuse, commissioned an artist to create a crown of pure gold, but upon receiving the crown, the King suspected that the artist substituted less precious metals for the gold. Archimedes, a Greek mathematician, physicist, and inventor, validated the King's suspicion by calculating the ratio of the weight of the crown to the weight of the water that the crown displaced when completely immersed. After comparing the gravity of the material in the crown with the gravity of pure gold, Archimedes concluded the crown did not contain pure gold. Physicists recognize Archimedes for this aptly named "Archimedes' Principle," while accountants view him as one of the first auditors.

We have already noted, in Chapter II, the massive inventory fraud that the management of McKesson & Robbins, Inc. ("McKesson") committed in the late 1930s, which became the driving force behind modern audit procedures requiring the verification of physical inventory. Auditors did not detect the fraud because they failed to confirm physical inventory. After regulators and the auditing profession recovered from the McKesson & Robbins scandal, the "Great Salad Oil Swindle" emerged, prompting further concern. Like Archimedes, Anthony "Tino" DeAngelis utilized the laws of physics, but in a more devious fashion. When auditors visited the site where his company, Allied Crude Vegetable Oil and Refining Corp. ("Allied"), stored oil to verify the physical inventory, they inserted dip sticks into the tanks to measure the level of oil present. Unfortunately, the auditors did not verify that the tanks contained only oil; DeAngelis had created phantom inventory records with forged warehouse receipts. In fact, only a small amount of oil floated on top of the water-filled tanks. Further, Allied reported owning more holding tanks than actually existed. During the audit, as the auditors moved from tank to tank, company employees repainted numbers on the tanks. Not only did auditors count water as oil, but they counted the same water as oil more than once!

b.   COSTS INCLUDABLE IN INVENTORY

As a preliminary matter, we should note that inventories include not only a merchandiser's goods available for resale, but also, in the case of a manufacturer, raw materials and supplies consumed directly or indirectly in the production process, plus partially completed goods, as well as finished goods awaiting sale. Inventories do not include long-lived assets, such as manufacturing plants, machinery, equipment, and office furniture, which a business enterprise does not hold for sale in the regular course of business.

Both merchandisers and manufacturers use historical cost to account for inventories, but they use slightly different rules to determine which *product costs* to include in inventory. Accountants treat all costs incurred to purchase or manufacture goods for sale as part of the cost of those goods and refer to these costs as *product costs*. Product costs, therefore, include all expenditures "directly or indirectly incurred in bringing [inventory] to its existing condition and location." FASB ASC ¶ 330-10-30-1 (a codification of RESTATEMENT AND REVISION OF ACCOUNTING RESEARCH BULLETINS, Accounting Research Bulletin No. 43, Chapter 4, Statement 3 (Am. Inst. of Certified Pub. Accountants 1953)). In contrast, accountants use the term *period costs* to refer to those costs which both merchandisers and manufacturers incur, such as administrative salaries, advertising costs, and selling expenses, that will generate revenues only in the current accounting period. The name *period costs* fits because a business expenses these costs in the accounting *period* in which they are incurred. Because periodic costs do not relate to individual inventory items, a business cannot treat such costs as part of the cost of the inventory.

The case *Berkowitz v. Baron*, 428 F. Supp. 1190 (S.D.N.Y. 1977), illustrates why the distinction between product costs and period costs matters. In that case, the plaintiffs purchased all the outstanding shares of two small manufacturers of children's clothing that had fallen on hard times. The businesses failed shortly after the acquisition, and the plaintiffs complained that the financial statements contained material misrepresentations, which the defendants had warranted as fully and fairly reflecting the companies' financial picture. In holding for the plaintiffs, the court wrote:

> The most troublesome aspect of the financial statement is the treatment accorded certain items reported therein. One such item is shipping cost and expenses totaling $145,281.76 [and which include shipping salaries, the costs of supplies and charges incurred for express and parcel post]. This sum was included as a component of manufacturing overhead. Expert testimony established that this method of presentation was not in accord with generally accepted accounting principles of the time. The appropriate procedure would

have been to treat such shipping costs as an operating expense, as was done in the 1969 financial statement, and take it as a deduction against gross profit, instead of including it in cost of goods sold, above the gross profit line.

The effect of this treatment was to cast a false picture of the companies' net income and inventory value. Because manufacturing overhead is a component of cost of goods sold, which in turn is one element of inventory value, improper incorporation of shipping costs and expenses in manufacturing overhead resulted in an overstatement of inventory computed to be approximately $44,560 by plaintiffs' expert witness. The enlarged inventory entry had a direct effect on the net loss/net income figure reported in the financial statement. Had the shipping costs and expenses been treated according to generally accepted accounting principles, the companies would have shown a net loss of approximately $24,960 (less the tax effect) for the fiscal year ending April 30, 1970, instead of a net income of $19,603, as was reported. * * *

* * *

Without going into detail, it can be seen that these charges created a financial picture for the companies that was inaccurate. The slightly inflated inventory figure gave rise to an overoptimistic estimate by plaintiffs of the revenues anticipated from liquidation of the inventory. Reporting the items above the gross profit line altered the gross profit percentage. The appearance of a small net income instead of a small net loss falsely supported the view that with good management a profit could be made.

Given these conditions, a finding that the financial statement is "materially misleading" is fully supported * * *. * * * [T]he net income/net loss and inventory value entries on a corporate financial statement are of material importance to parties interested in purchasing all of the outstanding shares of the company. This is especially true where, as here, little other information about the business is transmitted to the purchasers prior to the consummation of the sale.

NOTES

1. As a result of treating the shipping costs as manufacturing overhead, rather than operating expenses, the defendants overstated both inventory and net income. Publicly traded corporations, which must report their results of operations to the public, occasionally overstate earnings in this manner. Inflated inventories increase the apparent worth of a business and can give rise to securities fraud. Overstated inventories may also enable a business to obtain a loan or qualify for a lower interest rate than a lender would otherwise charge the business. Insurance companies may pay inflated claims for lost or destroyed inventories when insureds base claims on overstated rather than actual inventory values. *See, e.g.,* Cenco Inc. v. Seidman & Seidman, 686 F.2d

449, 451 (7th Cir. 1982). Finally, exaggerated inventories can qualify management for larger bonuses based on net income.

In contrast, federal income tax laws provide an equally strong incentive for businesses, especially those privately owned, to understate inventories, and therefore, to understate profits and their tax liabilities. *See, e.g.,* D. Loveman & Son Exp. Corp. v. Comm'r, 34 T.C. 776 (1960), *affirmed* 296 F.2d 732 (6th Cir. 1961) (holding that the taxpayer could not deduct "freight-in" as a current expense and requiring the taxpayer to treat the expenditures as part of the cost of acquiring merchandise). Another temptation to understate inventory, and hence net income, comes from profit-sharing agreements or buy-sell agreements that require the entity or its owners to pay amounts based on earnings or net book value to employees or other owners under certain circumstances. By expensing costs that properly belong in inventory, management or majority owners can increase the entity's expenses and decrease its profit and equity, thereby reducing the required payments. *See, e.g.,* Chick v. Tomlinson, *infra* at pages 623 to 626.

2. Because the financial statements that the defendants provided in the *Berkowitz* case used a different accounting treatment for the shipping costs than in the previous period, the financial statement violated the consistency requirement. See Section C, *infra*.

3. The defendant sellers "warranted that the financial statement for the year ending April 30, 1970 'fully and accurately present(s) as of its date the financial condition and assets and liabilities of the Companies and fully and accurately present(s) the results of operations of the Companies for the period indicated.'" Given that GAAP often sanctions alternative treatments for the same transaction and also cannot begin to address every conceivable situation, well-advised sellers would seemingly never agree to such a warranty. For these same reasons, counsel for sellers should similarly avoid words like "true, correct, and complete" when referring to financial statements. Whenever possible, sellers should limit any such representations and warranties to language that tracks the words used in an unqualified audit opinion. For example, the defendants might have instead warranted that "The financial statements present fairly, in all material respects, the financial position of the Companies as of April 30, 1970, and the results of their operations [and cash flows] for the year ended April 30, 1970 in conformity with generally accepted accounting principles."

(1) Merchandiser

A merchandiser's inventory usually includes goods offered for resale in the ordinary course of business. In addition to the actual price paid to acquire the goods, the merchandiser should include in inventory the costs incurred to bring the goods to the place of sale and to convert them to a salable condition. These charges include freight-in, inspection, packaging, and other costs directly related to the acquisition of the goods and their preparation for sale. A merchandiser, however, cannot include selling expenses and the cost of delivering goods to customers, sometimes referred to as "freight out," in product costs. As to shipping and handling fees billed to customers, the Codification requires that enterprises treat such fees as revenues at their gross amount, rather than as reductions in shipping expenses. FASB ASC ¶¶ 605-45-45-19 to -21, 605-45-50-2 (a codification of ACCOUNTING FOR SHIPPING AND HANDLING REVENUES AND COSTS, Emerging Issues Task Force Issue No. 00-10 (Fin. Accounting Standards Bd. 2000)). Most significantly, please keep in mind that businesses must treat selling expenses as period costs.

(2) Manufacturer

Accounting for the inventory of a manufacturing business presents some special problems because that inventory includes three separate components: raw materials, goods in process and finished goods ready for sale. In fact, product costs for a manufacturer include expenditures for raw materials, labor, and indirect expenses, such as light, heat, depreciation, insurance and property taxes, that a business incurs to manufacture a product. While the raw materials inventory creates no particular difficulty, goods in process and finished goods present special problems. Obviously, the cost of these assets at the end of an accounting period must, at a minimum, include not only the raw materials used but also the cost of the labor employed to bring the goods to their present condition. Manufacturers can often determine the costs of materials and the expense of labor directly involved in the production process, which accountants usually refer to together as *direct*, or *prime*, costs, from the manufacturing records. These records typically show the amount and kind of raw materials used and the number of hours and type of labor expended.

In addition, accountants view the normal expenses of operating the factory, frequently referred to as *factory overhead costs*, as just as much a part of production expense as the prime costs of raw material and labor. Factory overhead includes the normal expenses of operating a factory, including utilities, depreciation, insurance, and property taxes. In an effort to converge accounting standards worldwide, the Codification now clarifies that enterprises must recognize abnormal amounts of idle facility expense, excessive spoilage, double freight, or rehandling expense as period costs rather than as product costs. In addition, the rules require enterprises to allocate fixed overhead costs based on the relevant production facilities' normal capacity. FASB ASC ¶¶ 330-10-30-1 to -8 (codifying INVENTORY COSTS—AN AMENDMENT OF ARB NO. 43, CHAPTER 4, Statement of Fin. Accounting Standards No. 151 (Fin. Accounting Standards Bd. 2004)).

Even though a manufacturing business cannot readily assign the normal overhead costs to any particular goods, the manufacturer must defer the appropriate amount of overhead expense and add that amount to the goods in process and finished goods included in ending inventory. In accounting terms, no valid justification permits a manufacturer to treat those overhead costs allocable to the goods in process and finished goods on hand at the end of the period as a period expense, any more than the manufacturer can charge off the raw material, or direct labor, incorporated in that inventory. The difficulty comes in deciding what portion of the total factory overhead for the period a manufacturer should allocate to the goods in process and finished goods on hand at the end of the period. Once again, however, a manufacturer cannot treat selling expenses as product costs. Manufacturers, like merchandisers, must treat such expenses as period costs.

Accountants often describe certain factory overhead costs as *fixed*, meaning that most overhead costs do not change within a specified production range. In contrast, *variable costs*, such as raw materials and direct labor, change depending on production levels. As production levels increase or decrease, costs for raw materials and direct labor change accordingly. In addition to most overhead costs, *fixed costs* include general administrative expenses, like executive salaries, or interest on debt. Unlike factory overhead, businesses do not allocate these latter fixed costs to inventory, but treat those costs entirely as expenses of the period in which they were incurred. We should note, however, that accountants do not classify all factory overhead expenses as fixed, or entirely independent of the amount and type of goods produced. Some factory overhead costs may vary with the total, or the mix, of production. For example, if machines wear out more rapidly in one type of manufacturing process than another, the depreciation on those machines represents a variable, rather than a fixed, factory overhead item. Similarly, a business may employ a single foreman to supervise a particular manufacturing process at one level of production, but hire a second foreman if the level of production expands beyond that point. General administrative expenses may also qualify as variable expenses; a business may need to hire additional executives at higher levels of operation or incur greater interest expenses from borrowing more funds to finance the increased operations.

Cost accounting attempts to allocate overhead, or indirect, costs. Like most accounting processes, cost accounting is an art, not a science, which strives to find a reasonable and practical approach rather than a precisely accurate solution. Especially when a business produces a number of different products in various processing stages, cost accounting can become quite complicated. Even for a relatively simple, one-product business, difficult questions arise when the business seeks to allocate costs between goods in process and those which the factory completed during the period. Further complicating matters, the business sold some of the finished goods, but other finished goods still remain in ending inventory.

The following chart illustrates a sample statement of cost of goods sold for a manufacturing concern:

Statement of Cost of Goods Sold
XYZ Company, Inc.
For the Year Ended December 31, 20X5

(In thousands)

Beginning Inventory, Finished Goods			$10,000
Cost of Goods Manufactured			
Beginning Inventory, Goods in Process		$ 1,000	
Raw Materials			
Beginning Inventory, Raw Materials	$ 3,000		
Net Purchases	$19,000		
Raw Materials Available for Use	$22,000		
Less: Ending Inventory,			
Raw Materials	5,000		
Cost of Raw Materials Consumed	$17,000		
Direct Labor	30,000		
Manufacturing Overhead			
Supervisors' Salaries	$ 3,000		
Depreciation on Plant			
and Factory Equipment	2,600		
Factory Rent	1,400		
Utilities	1,200		
Indirect Labor	900		
Factory Supplies	500		
Miscellaneous Factory Expense	400	$10,000	
Total Overhead		$57,000	
Total Manufacturing Costs for Period		$58,000	
Subtotal		9,000	
Less: Ending Inventory, Goods in Process			$49,000
Cost of Goods Manufactured			$59,000
Cost of Goods Available for Sale			15,000
Less: Ending Inventory, Finished Goods			$44,000
Cost of Goods Sold			

The following case involving a manufacturer's overhead illustrates how businesses may understate inventories. Remember, understating inventories causes the business to understate income and tax liability.

Photo-Sonics, Inc. v. Commissioner

United States Court of Appeals, Ninth Circuit, 1966.
357 F.2d 656.

■ ELY, CIRCUIT JUDGE:

We face a petition for review of a Tax Court decision upholding the assessment of a deficiency in the payment of income taxes.

The controversy stems from taxpayer's method of accounting for its inventory of goods which it manufactured. Under the method, generally described as "prime costing" or "prime cost", only the cost of direct labor and materials were allocated to inventory value. No portion of factory-overhead expense, variable or fixed, was included.

The key to validity of an accounting method is, in accounting terms, a matching of costs and revenues and, in terms of the taxing statute, a clear reflection of income * * *. The Government urges that, just as labor and materials cannot be expensed in the year in which such expenses are incurred without giving due regard to whether the manufactured product remains on hand, factory-overhead expenses which constitute a portion of the cost of unsold manufactured products cannot be expensed as they are incurred but rather should be allocated to the manufactured products and deducted, as a cost of sale, when the goods are sold. It contends that proper allocation of factory-overhead expenses, both fixed and variable, to the inventory is the only manner by which the taxpayer's income for a given period may be clearly reflected.

It may be that "direct costing", the allocation to inventory of labor, materials, and variable factory overhead, is an accurate method by which to account for inventory. If consistently applied, it would not seem to be less satisfactory than the method advanced by the Government, *i.e.*, the "absorption costing" method under which labor, material, and both fixed and variable factory overhead are allocated. Both methods are accepted, although "absorption costing" seems now to be preferred by most American accountants. The Tax Court arrived at its determination "without attempting to lay down any broad principles applicable to inventories." 42 T.C. at 936. We, exercising similar restraint, are concerned with a particular accounting method only as it relates to the particular facts which are before us.

Here, the taxpayer allocated no portion of its factory-overhead expense to inventory. The regulations clearly specify that such be done. Treas. Reg. § 1.471–3(c) (1964). A method which excludes all factory-overhead costs is not an acceptable accounting practice. See American Institute of Certified Public Accountants, Accounting Research Bull. No. 43 [now codified in FASB ASC Topic 330, *Inventory*]. The significance of failure to allocate any of such costs to inventory is emphasized by looking in this case, as an example, to one of the items of unallocated factory overhead, shop and tool expense. This expense represented items purchased during the year which were either too inexpensive to depreciate or were consumed during the year. The Tax Court found that it amounted to $8,215.34 in 1958, $40,397.22 in 1959, and $103,896.18 in 1960. Thus, in an expanding business in which some of the products manufactured in one fiscal period are sold in a subsequent fiscal period, the expenses which are attributable to the cost of sales in a subsequent year are matched against the lower sales revenues of a prior year. The effect of such a practice, if allowed, would obviously permit taxpayer to report less income than the amount which was truly earned. It would not be an "accounting practice * * * clearly reflecting the income" as required by section 471.

In reviewing the proceedings below, it is seen that certain testimony of accountants produced by the taxpayer cast doubt upon the validity of taxpayer's accounting method. One such witness admitted, in the Government's cross examination, that an opinion given by a Certified Public Accountant as to the accuracy of financial statements prepared by taxpayer's method would require qualification if factory-overhead expense were material; otherwise, an examiner of the financial statement would be misled. It cannot be denied that, here, factory-overhead expense was significantly material.

We are not persuaded that the Commissioner's determination was arbitrary. It follows that the Tax Court's decision, not clearly erroneous, must be Affirmed.

(3) Other Illustrations of "Cost Accounting"

Lawyers often need to understand cost accounting issues and their relevance to the practice of law. For example, lawyers may encounter cost accounting concepts in a simple breach of contract action brought by a seller against a defaulting buyer. In calculating damages, a lawyer for the seller should recognize that each potential sale contributes to paying the seller's fixed overhead costs. Any amount of the selling price in excess of variable costs will offset the seller's fixed costs. By losing a sale, the seller loses not only the profit from that particular sale, but also that sale's contribution to the total fixed costs for the period. Failing to recognize the contribution to fixed overhead would understate the seller's damages. *See, e.g.,* Sure–Trip, Inc. v. Westinghouse Eng'g & Instrumentation Servs. Div., 47 F.3d 526 (2d Cir. 1995) (instructing that under Pennsylvania law a plaintiff can recover lost profits equal to the difference between (i) the revenue that the plaintiff would have derived under the contract and (ii) any additional or variable costs that the plaintiff would have incurred in performing the contract).

A case from the early twentieth century, *L.P. Larson, Jr., Co. v. William Wrigley, Jr., Co.*, 20 F.2d 830 (7th Cir. 1927), *rev'd in part on other grounds*, 277 U.S. 97 (1928), illustrates cost accounting concepts in an infringement action. Although Larson proved that Wrigley's "Doublemint" gum had infringed Larson's "Wintermint" gum, Larson could not calculate the lost profits attributable to the infringement and instead requested that the district court award all the net profits arising from "Doublemint" sales as damages. Both parties appealed the district court's decision awarding almost $1.4 million as net profits. Wrigley asserted that the district court should have deducted additional amounts for advertising expenses, unredeemed profit--sharing coupons, and certain other expenses from revenues in calculating the net profit figure. Larson objected to various deductions from revenues which the lower court had allowed. Obviously a lower profit on the infringing product results in smaller damages for the plaintiff and visa versa. Lawyers should recognize their ability to advocate profitability and damages through cost accounting.

Cost accounting issues also arise in environmental law and in numerous other areas of law. In *United States v. R.W. Meyer, Inc.*, 889 F.2d 1497 (6th Cir. 1987), the Environmental Protection Agency ("EPA") sought reimbursement for the costs incurred to clean up a site, as the federal statute authorized. The EPA included in its claim not only the approximately $181,000 in direct costs that the agency incurred for its personnel and on-site cleanup expenses, but almost another $53,000 in "indirect costs," which represented an allocable share of the administrative and other costs inherent in operating the environmental cleanup program. Those "overhead costs" included rent and utilities for site and non-site office space, plus payroll and benefits for program managers, clerical support, and other administrative staff. The defendant argued that the EPA could only obtain reimbursement for costs incurred in the cleanup at the defendant's site, but the district court concluded that the agency could recover all of its costs, including direct overhead. The court of appeals affirmed, saying:

> [T]he statute contemplates that those responsible for hazardous waste at each site must bear the full cost of cleanup actions and that those costs necessarily include both direct costs and a proportionate share of indirect costs attributable to each site. In essence then, the allocation of the indirect costs to specific cleanup sites effectively renders those costs direct costs attributable to a particular site. We are confident that had Meyer or the other defendants undertaken the cleanup operation by contracting with another company to perform the cleanup, the costs of that cleanup, whether characterized as costs, direct costs plus indirect costs, or otherwise, would include the type of indirect costs challenged here.

889 F.2d at 1504.

In the public utility context, rate regulation cases frequently involve cost accounting issues. To illustrate, regulators frequently approve different rates for different service classifications, such as commercial and industrial versus residential, peak versus off-peak, etc. To establish and justify different rates, regulators need to allocate costs among the different service classifications.

Cost accounting issues also arise in antitrust disputes. The Robinson–Patman Act essentially bars manufacturers from giving price discounts unless "differences in the cost of manufacture, sale or delivery" justify the discounts. Businesses may pass reductions in direct costs on to customers. A business relies on cost accounting to determine its costs to manufacture, sell and deliver goods. Improperly treating product costs as period expenses would lower the cost of manufacturing the goods, which would otherwise justify a discounted price.

PROBLEMS

Problem 8.1A. A large cotton mill company contemplated a public issue of its securities and ordered a sudden audit of its books by auditors designated by the would-be underwriters. The accounting firm retained over many years by the company assisted in the audit. Although there were no disputes as to the physical counts of goods on hand or as to methods of pricing, the underwriters' auditors concluded that the company's inventories were overstated by more than one million dollars. On the other hand, the company's accountants asserted that the new auditors were understating accounts payable by the same amount.

The dispute turned on the analysis of the transactions whereby the company acquired its raw cotton. In essence they were as follows: the company's cotton buyer would place an order for a firm amount and grade of cotton at a certain price (based on the New York cotton market) with one of several firms of cotton brokers in Boston. The broker would promptly segregate specific cotton in warehouses in the South and direct its shipment to the company. Title to this cotton was in the broker, subject to pledge evidenced by warehouse receipts in the hands of banks. The cotton arrived at the company's facility, but the shipping documents, including the receipts or bills of lading, went to the bank in Boston. By arrangement with the bank, the company unloaded the cotton, mingled it in its warehouse and sometimes started to process part of it immediately upon arrival. The company "classed" the cotton to see if it was up to contract specifications and on the ninth day after its arrival would give a check to the broker from whom the purchase had been made. The broker then paid the bank which surrendered the documents to the broker who then turned them over to the company.

The dispute hinged on whether cotton in the company's warehouse, or, in some cases, tumbling through its opening machinery, should or should not have been included in inventory while "title" to it remained in the bank.

In your opinion, what should be the "cut-off" point in such transactions, and how much if any of this cotton should appear in inventory on the company's financial statements?

Suppose that the company decided to acquiesce in the viewpoint of the auditors for the underwriters. Because the opening inventory was overstated by $900,000 and closing inventory was overstated by $1,100,000, the auditors for the underwriters have proposed the following journal entries to implement the changed policy:

Purchases	$900,000	
Opening Inventory		$900,0000

(To record as purchases in the current year goods previously treated as purchased in the prior year.)

Accounts Payable	$1,100,000	
Purchases		$1,100,000

(To reverse an earlier entry which erroneously treated these goods as purchased in the current year.)

Assuming that the price of cotton has remained constant throughout, to what extent would the change in policy affect the net income of the company for the period involved?

Problem 8.1B. On December 24, 20X1, X Corp. ordered goods in the amount of $10,000 from one of its suppliers for delivery in late January of 20X2. In accordance with its business practice with its suppliers, X included a check in the amount of 10% of the purchase price with its order. On December 29,

20X1, X learned that its order had been accepted and its check cashed. How should this transaction be recorded in the financial statements of X for 20X1?

Problem 8.1C. M Corp., a manufacturer of electronic business equipment, and D Co., which operates a large department store, have reached a tentative agreement that M will design and build a special computer for D to provide better inventory control. Because of D's unique requirements, the machine will be different from any that M has built before, and hence the parties have agreed that the price for the new machine should be equal to M's costs of building it plus a flat fee of $50,000. Your law firm serves as general counsel for D Co. and you have been asked to consider how the computation of M's costs should be approached in the formal contract, and whether there are any problems calling for special attention.

M maintains the following expense accounts:

Employment Costs
Wages & salaries, including
   vacation pay and sick leave
Social security taxes

Plant and Machinery Costs
Depreciation
Repair and maintenance
Plant protection

Selling
Advertising expense
Bad debt expense
Sales force compensation

General and Administration
Insurance
Property taxes
Utilities expense
Legal and accounting fees
Stockholder relations
   (meetings, annual
   reports, etc.)
Contributions & donations
Amortization of patents

Financing
Interest expense

2.   HOW TO PRICE INVENTORY

Once a business has determined what goods to include in ending inventory for the particular year, the business must decide how to price those items. Keep in mind that the business likely purchased merchandise or raw materials at several different prices during the year and must choose which of the different prices to use when valuing the items in ending inventory. Initially, this valuation aspect requires selecting an accounting method, or cost flow assumption, to assign costs to value the inventory items. Second, conservatism dictates that the business reduce this value to market, if cost exceeds market.

Conceptually, a business would most accurately match inventory expenses to revenues by specifically identifying the cost of each good it sells during the period. In most cases, however, a business cannot track a specific item from the time of purchase to the time of sale. When a business sells high volume, low cost goods, the venture usually cannot afford to use specific identification. Instead, most businesses choose, and consistently apply, one of several cost flow assumptions.

a. FLOW ASSUMPTIONS

Generally accepted accounting principles recognize several different cost flow assumptions, or accounting methods, for pricing inventory. These assumptions establish a set pattern of inventory flow and eliminate the need to specifically account for each piece of inventory as the business sells the inventory. Remember that the following methods incorporate various assumptions; accounting practice does not require that the cost flow assumption parallel the inventory's actual physical usage. A business may select one of several inventory flow assumptions or a combination of flow assumptions that most accurately reflects the income and closing inventory for the period. The consistency and disclosure principles, however, mandate that the business maintain that same assumption from period to period and properly disclose its method of inventory valuation in the notes to the financial statements. Inconsistent application of inventory methods could prevent financial statement users from obtaining the most accurate and comparable financial information about the business.

(1) Alternatives

To illustrate the different accounting methods for pricing inventories, assume that the Jones Shoe Company sells shoes at wholesale in a single style and price line. During its first year of operations, suppose that Jones Shoe purchases 8,000 pairs of shoes in four different lots at different prices and sells 5,000 pairs at $40 per pair. Accordingly, 3,000 pairs remain in inventory. At the end of the year, Jones Shoe's purchase records show the dates and prices of the various lots as follows:

Date	Amount	Unit Price	Total Price
January 1	2,000	$20.00	$ 40,000
March 1	3,000	22.00	66,000
June 1	2,000	23.00	46,000
November 1	1,000	21.00	21,000
Totals	8,000		$173,000

We will use this data to calculate the ending inventory under the specific identification; weighted average cost; first-in, first-out; and last-in, first-out methods of valuing inventories. In outlining these methods, we will illustrate only the first year of operations to avoid the problem of opening inventory. In reality, however, once a business adopts a method for pricing ending inventory for one accounting period, the ending inventory automatically becomes the opening inventory for the next period. In other words, the opening inventory becomes part of the goods available for sale in the next period.

a) SPECIFIC IDENTIFICATION

As we previously mentioned, specific identification of goods sold offers the most accurate way to reflect the costs of inventory, but the demanding record keeping requirements historically overwhelmed the typical business venture and prevented this method's widespread use. Accountants generally consider specific identification as appropriate where a business can practically separate and identify each individual item in inventory. A merchandiser selling a relatively small number of high value items, such as a car dealer, jeweler, or furrier, could effectively and efficiently use specific identification. In contrast, a seller of high volume low value goods, such as a grocery store or drug store, historically found specific identification cost prohibitive. Technological advancements involving scanners and electronic or readable codes, however, have enabled a growing number of enterprises to adopt specific identification.

Assume that at the end of the year, Jones Shoe's inventory records show that the company purchased the 3,000 pairs of shoes remaining in inventory on the following dates and at the previously given prices:

Pairs	Date	Unit Price	Total Price
300	January 1	$20.00	$ 6,000
1,100	March 1	22.00	24,200
900	June 1	23.00	20,700
700	November 1	21.00	14,700
Totals 3,000			$65,600

Using the specific identification method, the company would compute its gross profit, a term for sales less cost of goods sold, as follows:

Sales (5,000 pairs at $40 per pair)		$200,000
Less: Cost of Goods Sold		
Opening Inventory	$ –0–	
Purchases	173,000	
Goods Available for Sale	$173,000	
Less: Closing Inventory (from above)	65,600	$107,400
Gross Profit		$ 92,600

b) WEIGHTED AVERAGE COST

As previously discussed, businesses usually cannot afford to identify the cost of particular items as they are sold. A business's purchase records, however, do show the cost of the various lots of goods purchased during the year. Looking at our Jones Shoe Company example, again assume Jones Shoe sells 5,000 pairs. In view of the difficulty of determining which lots the 3,000 pairs of shoes still on hand at the end of the year actually came from, Jones Shoe may adopt a flow assumption for pricing these shoes in closing inventory.

The weighted average cost method of inventory valuation eliminates the need to specifically identify the items of inventory sold. Businesses holding relatively homogeneous items in inventory often find this average cost inventory valuation administratively convenient and particularly effective. Under the weighted average cost method, a business prices all items of inventory based upon the average cost of all similar goods available during the whole period. Under this method, Jones Shoe Company would compute the weighted average cost per unit based upon the total units available as follows:

$$\text{Weighted average cost} = \frac{\text{Total cost}}{\text{Total units purchased}}$$

$$= \frac{\$173,000}{8,000 \text{ Units}}$$

$$= \$21.625 \text{ per unit}$$

Based upon the weighted average cost per unit, Jones Shoe Company would value the 3,000 pairs of shoes left in the inventory at $21.625 a pair, for a total of $64,875. Under the weighted average cost method, Jones Shoe would compute its gross profit as follows:

Sales (5,000 pairs at $40 per pair)		$200,000
Less: Cost of Goods Sold		
Opening Inventory	$ –0–	
Purchases	173,000	
Goods Available for Sale	$173,000	
Less: Closing Inventory (from above)	64,875	$108,125
Gross Profit		$ 91,875

c) FIRST–IN, FIRST-OUT

To minimize spoilage and obsolescence, businesses normally expect to sell their oldest goods first. One flow assumption assumes that a business sells the goods in the order of their purchase. In other words, this alternative assumes that only the most recently purchased or produced goods remain unsold at the end of the period. Accountants refer to this method as *FIFO*, which serves as shorthand for the "first-in, first-out" flow assumption that underlies the method. Under the FIFO method, Jones Shoe Company carries its ending inventory of 3,000 pairs of shoes at $67,000. The company treats the ending inventory as including the last lot of 1,000 pairs which the company purchased at $21.00 per pair and 2,000 pairs from the next to the last lot purchased at $23.00 per pair.

If Jones Shoe Company adopts the FIFO inventory method, the company would value ending inventory at $67,000 and report $94,000 in gross profit as follows:

Sales (5,000 pairs at $40 per pair)		$200,000
Less: Cost of Goods Sold		
Opening Inventory	$ –0–	
Purchases	173,000	
Goods Available for Sale	$173,000	
Less: Closing Inventory (from above)	67,000	$106,000
Gross Profit		$ 94,000

Like merchandisers, manufacturers may also use the FIFO method in pricing their inventories. Of course, because a manufacturer's cost includes not only the purchase price of the component raw materials, but also labor expense and a portion of the overhead expenses for the period, manufacturers face additional challenges in determining the cost of various lots of manufactured goods. But once the manufacturer computes the costs of the various lots, the business prices the closing inventory based on the assumption that the business manufactured the unsold items most recently.

d) LAST–IN, FIRST-OUT

While FIFO tends to match a business's oldest inventory costs with current revenues, the "last-in, first-out" flow assumption, which accountants usually refer to as *LIFO*, adopts the exact opposite assumption. Regardless of the actual physical movement of goods, LIFO assumes that a business sells the most recently acquired goods first. To state this principle somewhat differently, the LIFO method presupposes that a business sells goods "off the top of the pile." LIFO, therefore, matches the business's most recent inventory costs with current revenues. Accordingly, a business prices the goods on hand in closing inventory as if the venture held those goods during the entire accounting period or acquired the goods in the earliest acquisition or acquisitions during the accounting period.

We should note that LIFO generally follows an unrealistic assumption regarding the physical flow of goods. Indeed, LIFO would accurately reflect that flow only in a case, for example, where a business piles goods as they arrive and sells or uses them from the top of the pile. A coal supplier could illustrate the flow assumption underlying LIFO. Even in that case, however, the coal supplier could not possibly sell goods which it purchased during a given year, but after the date of the last sale during the year. Once again, LIFO does not pretend to accurately reflect the flow of goods. Instead, LIFO presumes that the physical flow does not matter and stresses the importance of matching related current costs with current revenues. We should also note particularly that LIFO does not depart from the principle of using cost as the primary basis to price inventory. LIFO seeks only to provide a sound answer to the question of which inventory costs that a business incurred during the current period should be treated as "used up" during the current period, and hence charged to current expense.

Under the LIFO method, Jones Shoe Company would value its ending inventory of 3,000 pairs of shoes at $62,000. The company treats the ending inventory as including the first lot of 2,000 pairs which the company purchased at $20.00 per pair and 1,000 pairs from the second lot purchased at $22.00 per pair. If Jones Shoe Company adopts the LIFO inventory method, the company would report $89,000 in gross profit as follows:

Sales (5,000 pairs at $40 per pair)		$200,000
Less: Cost of Goods Sold		
Opening Inventory	$ –0–	
Purchases	173,000	
Goods Available for Sale	$173,000	
Less: Closing Inventory (from above)	62,000	$111,000
Gross Profit		$ 89,000

e) RETAIL METHOD

As discussed earlier, retailers may find some cost flow assumptions cumbersome for certain items. While specific identification may provide helpful financial information for high cost merchandise such as cars, jewelry or fur coats, the costs would outweigh the marginally useful information for lower cost items, like candy bars, canned vegetables and gallons of milk. The retail method of accounting for inventory eliminates the need to differentiate between products; the method allows the retailer to calculate the business's inventory based on a ratio of inventory costs to their retail prices. The retailer then uses retail prices and sales for the period to compile its ending inventory figure.

The retail method requires a business to keep records of the inventory valued at both cost and retail. The retailer then calculates the ratio of inventory cost to retail value. The enterprise calculates the ending inventory at retail by subtracting sales, at retail price, for the period from goods available for sale, again at retail price. The retailer then converts the ending inventory figure from retail to cost by multiplying the retail figure by the cost/retail ratio.

For example, assume Jones Shoe Company also operates an outlet store which sells shoes at retail. Further assume that the company owns inventory at the beginning of an accounting period which cost $100,000 and that it lists these items for sale at $150,000. During the period, Jones manufactures or purchases additional shoes which cost $1,100,000 and which the company prices to sell for $1,850,000. The sum of these amounts gives inventory available for sale which Jones Shoe purchased for $1,200,000, but plans to sell at retail for $2,000,000. Using these figures, Jones Shoe can calculate the ratio of cost to retail as follows:

$$\text{Ratio of cost to retail} = \frac{\text{Value of inventory at cost}}{\text{Value of inventory at retail}}$$

$$= \frac{\$1,200,000}{\$2,000,000}$$

$$= .60 \text{ or } 60\%$$

This percentage indicates that the cost of the inventory constitutes sixty percent (60%) of the retail price. Given this ratio, Jones Shoe can now calculate the ending inventory based on sales for the period. Assuming that Jones Shoe's sales during the period total $1,800,000, the company can estimate the ending inventory using the retail method as follows:

	Cost	Retail
Inventory at beginning of period	$ 100,000	$ 150,000
Purchases during the period	1,100,000	1,850,000
Totals	$1,200,000	$ 2,000,000
Sales during the period		1,800,000
Estimated ending inventory at retail:		$ 200,000

Based upon the calculated cost to retail ratio, the ending inventory figure at cost should equal sixty percent (60%) of the ending inventory at retail or $120,000 (60% of $200,000).

f) COMBINATION

Generally accepted accounting principles do not limit a business to only one cost flow assumption. Indeed, businesses often use different cost flow assumptions for different parts of their inventories. For example, a department store may use specific identification for its fine jewelry and fur coats, while selecting an alternative flow assumption, such as LIFO or FIFO, for its sock inventory. A business may adopt any combination of acceptable assumptions as long as the business applies them consistently from period to period and properly discloses the methods used in the financial statements.

(2) Critique and Basis for Selection

The different inventory flow assumptions offer various advantages and disadvantages. Again, we must remember that the actual physical flow may, and usually does, differ from the flow assumption which a business adopts.

a) ILLUSTRATION OF THE EFFECTS OF ALTERNATIVE METHODS

To recap, the different inventory methods produce different amounts for ending inventory, cost of goods sold, and gross profit for Jones Shoes Company. The following chart summarizes those differences.

Method	Ending Inventory	Cost of Goods Sold	Gross Profit
Specific Identification	$65,600	$107,400	$92,600
Weighted Average	64,875	108,125	91,875
FIFO	67,000	106,000	94,000
LIFO	62,000	111,000	89,000

You should conclude that the selection of an inventory method can significantly affect the financial statements. You should also notice that in periods of rising prices, LIFO produces a lower gross profit, and smaller net income, than FIFO. In contrast in deflationary periods, these results flip-flop; FIFO produces a smaller gross profit, and lower net income, than LIFO.

b) FIRST–IN, FIRST–OUT

FIFO prefers fair presentation on the balance sheet at the expense of the income statement. FIFO offers a significant advantage over the other inventory methods because the amount shown for inventory on the balance sheet usually reflects current market price. In addition, FIFO mirrors the actual physical movement of goods in most businesses. Finally, FIFO does not allow management to manipulate profits, as we will see below during the LIFO discussion.

FIFO, however, presents at least two serious disadvantages. First, FIFO does not match current costs with current sales. Under FIFO, the cost of goods sold reflects prices the business paid to acquire the oldest items in inventory. Second and related to the first, the FIFO method produces fictitious inventory profits during inflationary periods. In such periods, FIFO tends to understate the cost of goods sold.

c) LAST–IN, FIRST–OUT

Unlike FIFO, the last-in, first-out approach matches current costs with current sales, thereby producing higher cost of goods sold and lower profits in times of rising prices. Those results made LIFO particularly attractive for income tax purposes because the Internal Revenue Code allows taxpayers to use LIFO to compute taxable income only if they also use the method for financial accounting purposes.

Some accountants and financial analysts, however, prefer LIFO for financial accounting reasons. For one thing, LIFO produces a lower, and hence more conservative (albeit sometimes too much so for a fair presentation) balance sheet figure for inventory. In addition, LIFO results in a more meaningful presentation on the income statement by matching the current inventory costs with current sales revenues.

To illustrate, suppose that in 20X2 the Jones Shoe Company's inventory and purchase records show the following:

Date	Quanity	Unit Price	Total
Opening Inventory	3,000	FIFO	$ 67,000
February	2,000	$22	44,000
April	2,000	23	46,000
July	2,000	24	48,000
October	2,000	26	52,000
December	2,000	28	56,000
Totals	13,000		$313,000

Suppose further that Jones sold 4,000 pairs of shoes during the first half of the year at an average price of $30 per pair, and 4,000 pairs during the second half of the year at an average price of $35 per pair, for total sales revenues of $260,000. If Jones Shoe continued to carry closing inventory on the FIFO basis, the company would compute its gross profit as follows:

Sales		
4,000 pairs at $30 per pair	$120,000	
4,000 pairs at $35 per pair	140,000	$260,000
Less: Cost of Goods Sold		
Opening Inventory	$ 67,000	
Purchases	246,000	
Goods Available for Sale	$313,000	
Less: Closing Inventory at FIFO		
2,000 pairs at $28 per pair	$56,000	
2,000 pairs at $26 per pair	52,000	
1,000 pairs at $24 per pair	24,000	
Total Closing Inventory	$132,000	
Cost of Goods Sold		$181,000
Gross Profit		$ 79,000

Because Jones Shoe matched some of the lower inventory costs incurred before the middle of the year with the higher revenues obtained in the latter part of the year, the company derived a substantial part of the gross profit simply from the rising price level rather than from improvement in the company's competitive position or increased efficiency of operations.

In contrast, applying LIFO in the previous example would result in a closing inventory of $111,000, arrived at by pricing 3,000 pairs at the opening inventory figure of $67,000 and the remaining 2,000 pairs at the cost of the first 2,000 pairs purchased during the year, or $44,000. Jones Shoe would compute its gross profit under LIFO as follows:

Sales		$260,000
Less: Cost of Goods Sold		
Opening Inventory	$ 67,000	
Purchases	246,000	
Goods Available for Sale	$313,000	
Less: Closing Inventory at LIFO		
3,000 pairs from Opening Inventory	$67,000	
2,000 pairs at $22 per pair	44,000	
Total Closing Inventory	$111,000	
Cost of Goods Sold		$202,000
Gross Profit		$ 58,000

As we see, the increase in the current cost of goods sold expense which results from pricing the closing inventory on LIFO produces a lower gross profit figure. This lower figure probably better indicates the business's success in the rising price market.

LIFO's critics, however, point to several potential disadvantages. First, the lower amounts usually shown as ending inventory under LIFO, reflecting those early costs of inventory, can adversely affect financial ratios based on current assets, total assets or equity, such as the current ratio or the debt to equity ratio, which loan agreements frequently use. The following excerpts from the 2013 annual report for Exxon Mobil Corp. illustrate how LIFO can significantly understate the value of inventories that appear on a balance sheet and several other points that we will soon discuss.

(millions of dollars)	Dec. 31 2013	Dec. 31 2012
Current Assets:		
Inventories		
Crude oil, products and merchandise	$12,117	$10,836
Materials and supplies	4,018	3,706

* * *

NOTES TO CONSOLIDATED FINANCIAL STATEMENTS

* * *

1. Summary of Accounting Policies

* * *

Inventories. Crude oil, products and merchandise inventories are carried at the lower of current market value or cost (generally determined under the last-in, first-out method – LIFO). Inventory costs include expenditures and other charges (including depreciation) directly and indirectly incurred in bringing the inventory to its existing condition and location. Selling expenses and general and administrative expenses are reported as period costs and excluded from inventory cost. Inventories of materials and supplies are valued at cost or less.

* * *

3. Miscellaneous Financial Information

* * *

In 2013, 2012 and 2011, net income included gains of $282 million, $328 million and $292 million, respectively, attributable to the combined effects of LIFO inventory accumulations and drawdowns. The aggregate replacement cost of inventories was estimated to exceed their LIFO carrying values by $21.2 billion and $21.3 billion at December 31, 2013, and 2012, respectively.

Crude oil, products and merchandise as of year-end 2013 and 2012 consist of the following:

(billions of dollars)	2013	2012
Petroleum products	3.9	3.6
Crude oil	4.7	4.0
Chemical products	2.9	2.9
Gas/other	0.6	0.3
Total	$12.1	$10.8

Exxon Mobil Corp., Annual Report (Form 10-K) 64, 67-69 (Feb. 26, 2014). If Exxon Mobil used FIFO, rather than LIFO, to value inventories, the company's balance sheet would have reported those inventories at approximately $21.2 billion more than actually shown on the December 31, 2013 balance sheet.

To use LIFO for income tax purposes, federal tax law imposes two restrictions on taxpayers. Under the conformity requirement in section 472 of the Internal Revenue Code, a taxpayer can use LIFO for federal income tax purposes only if the taxpayer uses LIFO for general financial reporting purposes. I.R.C. § 472(c) (2012). A business, therefore, cannot avail itself of the tax savings which LIFO usually offers without applying LIFO to report earnings in its financial statements. Moreover, a taxpayer cannot apply the lower of cost or market rule discussed below to reduce the figure at which the taxpayer values inventory.

From a financial reporting standpoint, businesses can use *LIFO reserves* to disclose the excess of FIFO cost over LIFO cost. In fact, the SEC requires registrants to disclose the excess of the replacement or current cost over stated LIFO value. See Last–In, First–Out Method of Accounting for Inventories, Accounting Series Release No. 293, 46 Fed. Reg. 36,127 (July 14, 1981) (codified in the Codification of Financial Reporting Policies, § 205.02, *reprinted in* 7 Fed. Sec. L. Rep. (CCH) ¶ 72,993 (May 18, 1988)); *see also* Mark F. Dalton, Note, *An Examination of Some Considerations Relating to the Adoption and Use of the Last-in, First-out (LIFO) Inventory Accounting Method*, 28 Vand. L. Rev. 521, 534–45 (1975) (discussing and criticizing the conformity requirement). Businesses may refer to this excess as the "excess of current replacement cost over LIFO cost," the *LIFO inventory adjustment*, or the LIFO reserve in the notes to the financial statements. You may recall that Exxon Mobil's Form 10-K for 2013 specifically states that: "The aggregate replacement cost of inventories was estimated to exceed their LIFO carrying values by $21.2 billion and $21.3 billion at December 31, 2013, and 2012, respectively." Exxon Mobil Corp., Annual Report (Form 10-K) 69 (Feb. 26, 2014).

To further illustrate LIFO's effects, consider Exxon Mobil Corporation's financial results for 2007 through 2013. When oil prices increased rapidly during 2007, LIFO increased Exxon Mobil's costs, and therefore, reduced its income before taxes, by about $9.5 billion. If Exxon Mobil had used FIFO, rather than LIFO, to value its ending inventory, its income before income taxes would have increased from a then-record $70.5 billion to about $80 billion. The notes to Exxon Mobil's 2007 financial statements quantified the company's LIFO reserve, or the cumulative difference between the inventory's current replacement cost and its carrying amount on the balance sheet, at $25.4 billion. Exxon Mobil Corp., Annual Report (Form 10-K) 50, 56 (Feb. 28, 2008); *see also* David Reilly, *Big Oil's Accounting Methods Fuel Criticism*, Wall St. J., Aug. 8, 2006, at C1 (providing the LIFO reserve and an estimated net profit for 2005). By comparison, when oil prices fell during the second half of 2008, Exxon Mobil's LIFO reserve fell to $10.0 billion at December 31, 2008, which means that LIFO actually added $15.4 billion to the company's reported

$81.75 billion in income before taxes during 2008. Exxon Mobil Corp., 2008 Annual Report (Form 10-K) 58, 64 (Feb. 27, 2009). Then, as oil prices generally rose during the period from 2009 to 2012, when average worldwide realizations increased from $57.86 per barrel during 2009 to $100.29 per barrel in 2012, Exxon Mobil's LIFO reserve increased to $21.3 billion on December 31, 2012. Over that four year period, therefore, LIFO reduced the company's income before taxes by more than $11 billion. Exxon Mobil Corp., Annual Report (Form 10-K) 53, 68 (Feb. 27, 2013); Exxon Mobil Corp., Annual Report (Form 10-K) 62, 69 (Feb. 26, 2010). Finally, when average worldwide realizations dropped from $100.29 per barrel in 2012 to $97.48 per barrel in 2013, Exxon Mobil's LIFO reserve dropped to $21.2 billion on December 31, 2013. Exxon Mobil Corp., Annual Report (Form 10-K) 54, 69 (Feb. 26, 2014).

As a practical constraint, IFRS does not recognize LIFO as a permissible accounting method. IFRS requires the specific identification method to account for the individual costs of inventory items not ordinarily interchangeable and goods or services produced and segregated for specific projects. For other inventory items, particularly large quantities of interchangeable items, IFRS allows either FIFO or weighted average cost. *See* INVENTORIES, Int'l Accounting Standard No. 2, ¶¶ 23-25 (Int'l Accounting Standards Bd. 2001), *reprinted in* INT'L ACCOUNTING STANDARDS BD., INT'L FIN. REPORTING STANDARDS (AS ISSUED AT 1 JANUARY 2014), at A633 (2014).

Given the growing global trend toward IFRS, the massive national debt, and continuing federal deficits, LIFO's long-term future looks doubtful in the United States. The tax benefits that businesses with LIFO reserves currently enjoy seem unlikely to survive. Unless Congress eliminates the conformity requirement, the IASB decides to allow LIFO, or the SEC permits registrants to continue to use LIFO, a transition to IFRS would preclude taxpayers from using LIFO for federal income tax purposes and could generate more than $80 billion in additional federal income taxes over ten years. Even before the SEC announced its proposed roadmap for switching to IFRS, influential members of Congress from both major political parties sponsored legislation to repeal LIFO, first in 2005 for oil and gas companies, and more recently, for all businesses. All six of President Obama's budget proposals have contained provisions that would repeal the LIFO inventory accounting method, most recently for taxable years beginning after December 31, 2014. The last proposal would require taxpayers to write up their beginning LIFO inventory to its FIFO amount and to include their prior years' LIFO reserves in income ratably over ten years, beginning with the year of change. *See* DEP'T OF TREASURY, GENERAL EXPLANATIONS OF THE ADMINISTRATION'S FISCAL YEAR 2015 REVENUE PROPOSALS 93, 281 (2014), *available at* http://www.treasury.gov/resource-center/tax-policy/Documents/General-Explanations-FY2015.pdf; Thomas Jaworski, *LIFO Repeal: Would the New Revenue Be Worth the Corporate Resistance?*, 127 TAX NOTES 253 (Apr. 19, 2010); Lauren Gardner, *Move from GAAP to IFRS Could Spell Big Changes for Companies Using LIFO*, 6 Corp. Accountability Rep. (BNA) 964 (Sept. 12, 2008); Edward D. Kleinbard et al., *Is It Time to Liquidate LIFO?*, 113 TAX NOTES 237 (Oct. 16, 2006).

LIFO also gives a business's management the opportunity to manipulate reported profits. If a business voluntarily or involuntarily depletes its inventories, all the previously unrealized gains and losses from inventory appreciation appear in the accounting period in which the depletion occurs. As a result, LIFO produces earnings less reliable than under FIFO. Under LIFO, you may recall, the earliest inventory costs of the period in which the business adopted LIFO, starting with the opening inventory of that period, if any, determine the original LIFO cost figure. As long as the physical quantity of inventory at year-end in subsequent periods does not fall below the quantity at the end of the year in which the business adopted LIFO, that LIFO cost figure remains frozen on the balance sheet as a part of the asset Inventory. For example, if in the year an enterprise adopts LIFO its closing inventory contains ten units, and those ten units cost $10 each under LIFO, then as long as the enterprise owns at least ten units at the end of each succeeding year, the closing inventory will include ten units priced at that original LIFO cost of $10. If the physical quantity on hand at year-end expands, the business will price the excess over ten according to the LIFO principle as applied in the respective years in which the increase in volume occurred.

For a business which has used LIFO for many accounting periods, this treatment can cause the business to report the asset Inventory on the balance sheet on the basis of some very out-of-date costs. When the economy has experienced sustained inflation, the LIFO cost figure may fall far below the inventory's current market value. This very conservative representation of inventory on the balance may not bother creditors, who could only be pleasantly surprised to find, in case of financial difficulty, that the business can sell the inventory for more than the amount shown on the balance sheet; but, as we have noted, undue conservatism may present a misleadingly pessimistic view of the state of the business's affairs.

Of course, this preservation of old costs on the balance sheet does not affect the income statement, so long as the quantity of goods in the inventory at the end of each year equals or exceeds the quantity on hand at the close of the prior year. When a business increases the units in inventory, LIFO matches costs that the business incurred during the year against revenues for the current year. But suppose that the quantity on hand at the end of the year falls below quantity at the beginning, perhaps because the business voluntarily reduced operations or war, strikes, or the like caused an involuntary shortage. Then the business will match some of those old LIFO costs imbedded in the Opening Inventory figure against current revenues. In the typical case where current costs exceed LIFO costs, the reduction in inventory will create a much higher current net income figure than the business would have reported if the inventory quantity at year end had not fallen below the quantity at the beginning of the year.

To illustrate this problem which the liquidation of LIFO inventory can cause, suppose that Jones Shoe had adopted LIFO at the time of its organization in 20X1 and that shoes cost $10 per pair throughout that year. Suppose further, for simplicity, that the company bought 3,000 more pairs of shoes than it sold during that year, but that in each of the next eight years it purchased exactly as many pairs of shoes as the company sold. Accordingly, closing inventory for 20X9, and of course opening inventory for 20Y0, would equal $30,000, or 3,000 pairs of shoes priced under LIFO at $10 per pair. If Jones' purchases and sales for 20Y0 were exactly the same as indicated in the illustration on page 606, *supra*, gross profit for the year computed under LIFO would equal the same $58,000 shown in the illustration on page 607, *supra*:

Sales		$260,000
Less: Cost of Goods Sold		
Opening Inventory (on LIFO)	$ 30,000	
Purchases	246,000	
Goods Available for Sale	$276,000	
Less: Closing Inventory at LIFO		
3,000 pairs at $10 per pair	$ 30,000	
2,000 pairs at $22 per pair	44,000	
Total Closing Inventory	$ 74,000	
Cost of Goods Sold		$202,000
Gross Profit		$ 58,000

This result should cause no surprise: because the closing inventory in both cases equals the sum of opening inventory, either 3,000 pairs at $10 per pair in this example or 3,000 pairs at a $67,000 total cost on page 607, *supra*, plus $44,000 (the cost of the first 2,000 pairs of shoes purchased during the year), the cost of goods sold remains the same.

But suppose that Jones Shoe did not make any purchases in October and December, so that total purchases for the year amounted to only 6,000 pairs. In that event, the gross profit would be computed as follows:

Sales		$260,000
Less: Cost of Goods Sold		
Opening Inventory (on LIFO)	$ 30,000	
Purchases	138,000	
Goods Available for Sale	$168,000	
Less: Closing Inventory of		
1,000 pairs on LIFO	$ 10,000	
Cost of Goods Sold		$158,000
Gross Profit		$102,000

Thus although the company still sold 8,000 pairs of shoes for $260,000, LIFO reflects a much higher net income. This higher income figure results from the fact that LIFO matched against current revenues in the higher price-level era the older, much lower, LIFO inventory costs, which would have remained on the balance sheet, and would not have entered into the determination of net income, if the quantity of inventory at year-end had not dropped below the quantity in opening inventory.

Because LIFO liquidations can significantly affect reported results of operations, the SEC requires registrants to disclose any material amount of income that they realize from inventory liquidations. In Staff Accounting Bulletin No. 103, the SEC gives the following guidance:

F. LIFO Liquidations

Facts: Registrant on LIFO basis of accounting liquidates a substantial portion of its LIFO inventory and as a result includes a material amount of income in its income statement which would not have been recorded had the inventory liquidation not taken place.

Question: Is disclosure required of the amount of income realized as a result of the inventory liquidation?

Interpretive Response: Yes. Such disclosure would be required in order to make the financial statements not misleading. Disclosure may be made either in a footnote or parenthetically on the face of the income statement.

Staff Accounting Bulletin No. 103, Topic 11 (2003), http://www.sec.gov/interps/account/sab103.htm. Special rules apply to interim financial reports when an enterprise using LIFO liquidates a base period inventory during the fiscal year, but expects to replace the base period inventory by the end of the annual period. In that event, the interim reporting should not give effect to the LIFO liquidation, and the enterprise should include the expected cost of replacing the liquidated LIFO base in the cost of goods sold during the interim reporting period. FASB ASC ¶ 270-10-45-6(b) (a codification of Interim Financial Reporting, Accounting Principles Board Opinion No. 28, ¶ 14b (Am. Inst. of Certified Pub. Accountants 1973)).

Again, you should note that Exxon Mobil's Form 10-K for 2013 reveals that the company liquidated LIFO inventory layers in 2013, 2012, and 2011. Net income for those years included "gains of $282 million, $328 million and $292 million, respectively, attributable to the combined effects of LIFO inventory accumulations and drawdowns." Exxon Mobil Corp., Annual Report (Form 10-K) 69 (Feb. 26, 2014). With at least 4.335 billion shares outstanding at all times during those years and even assuming that Exxon Mobil reported the inventory gains after tax, those gains increased earnings per share no more than eight cents per share during any year in that period. *Id.* at 64.

LIFO critics have argued that to show an inflated net income figure for the period in which LIFO inventory was liquidated distorts the picture of both current operations and the trend of the business's fortunes. We must recognize this argument's merits, regardless of whether the business involuntarily reduced the inventory, as for example in the case of war scarcity, inadvertently decreased the inventory, or intentionally decided to liquidate the inventory, as for example if the business chose to reduce the scope of its operations. In any event, GAAP requires the business to include this extra net income from selling the low-cost LIFO inventory in the current income statement unless the liquidation was involuntary, the taxpayer intends to replace the liquidated inventory (though has not done so before year-end), and the taxpayer does not recognize gain for income tax reporting purposes. FASB ASC ¶ 605-40-25-3 (a codification of Accounting for Involuntary Conversions of Nonmonetary Assets to Monetary Assets, An Interpretation of APB Opinion No. 29, FASB Interpretation No. 30, ¶ 11 (Fin. Accounting Standards Bd. 1979)).

b. LOWER OF COST OR MARKET

Accounting standards require a departure from the cost basis for pricing inventory when damage, physical deterioration, obsolescence or other circumstances cause the utility of goods, and hence their market value, to fall below their cost. In such circumstances, FASB ASC Topic 330, *Inventory*, which codified ARB No. 43, requires the business to recognize a loss in the current period to reflect the decline in value. For example, Microsoft Corp. recorded an approximately $900 million loss during fiscal 2013 for "Surface RT inventory adjustments" when the company's tablet computer failed to sell. A business determines the loss by subtracting market value from cost.

To illustrate, suppose that a drop in the price level or some other reason has caused prices to decline at the end of an accounting period to a figure below the FIFO or weighted average cost figure for closing inventory. As we have seen, under the conservatism principle a business should not carry any current asset on the balance sheet at an amount greater than its current market value or realizable value. Historically, this balance sheet aspect of pricing inventory became paramount, leading to the classic doctrine of *lower of cost or market*, which ordains that businesses should carry inventory on the balance sheet at market value, as of the balance sheet date, if that figure falls below original cost. By pricing closing inventory at the lower value figure, the business increases the cost of goods sold expense for the period. While this treatment means that the cost of goods sold expense for the period exceeds the cost of the inventory that the business actually sold or used during the period, which arguably interferes with the matching of related costs and revenues, a diminution in the value of items on hand below their cost at the end of the accounting period represents at least a probable loss that the business should recognize in the current period under traditional principles of conservatism.

Although one often encounters the term "writing down" inventory from cost to market, you should realize that accrual accounting does not require the business to prepare a separate journal entry reducing closing inventory from the FIFO or weighted average cost figure to market. The business simply prices the closing inventory at the lower market figure at the time the accountant or bookkeeper records the entry debiting the Inventory account for the amount of the closing inventory and crediting the Cost of Goods Sold account for that same amount. The write-down notion arises from the fact that the enterprise originally included the goods at cost either in Opening Inventory or in Purchases, both of which the business will close to the debit side of the Cost of Goods Sold account. When the business includes the goods in closing inventory at a lower figure, cost of goods sold expense increases, which reduces net income by the amount of the difference between cost and market. Nevertheless, occasionally a business's management may desire a separate write-down entry to highlight a significant inventory loss. In that event, the business prices closing inventory at cost in the first instance, and then writes down the closing inventory by debiting a Loss on Inventory account for the difference between cost and market and crediting the Inventory account for that same amount.

Adopting the lower of cost or market basis for pricing closing inventory leads immediately to the question of what constitutes "market," or realizable, value. Where a business can obtain an actual market price quotation for the goods, businesses most often use the *current replacement cost* as the appropriate quotation for "market" at the close of the period. Thus, in the case of the Jones Shoe Company, if shoes cost $20 per pair at the end of year one, the company would carry the 3,000 pairs in closing inventory at $60,000 on the basis of lower of cost or market.

The use of replacement cost as the measure of "market" ignores the fact that in most cases the business will not involuntarily liquidate the goods. Under normal conditions, the business will sell the goods in the usual course of the company's business rather than in the replacement market. For this reason, some accountants have argued that a business should look to the market in which the business operates, rather than the replacement market, to value the goods. Under this view, the business should determine the appropriate "market" figure by estimating the goods estimated selling prices and subtracting any necessary costs to prepare the goods for sale and to complete their sale. For example, assume that Jones Shoe estimates that the company can sell the shoes included in closing inventory for at least $25 per pair, after spending an additional $2 per pair for selling expenses such as packaging and shipping. These accountants argue that a figure for estimated selling price less costs of sale, which they often call *net realizable value,* offers a more meaningful guide to market value than replacement cost. In the above example, because the $23 net realizable value exceeds actual cost, as determined by either FIFO or weighted average cost, even conservatism does not require the business to carry the shoes at less than actual cost.

Accountants premise using net realizable value as the measure of "market" on the notion that a business has not incurred a loss on closing inventory as long as the venture can sell its inventory during the following year at a price which will at least cover the original cost plus any additional expenses to complete the sale. On the other hand, if the selling price will most likely not cover that sum, then the business should recognize loss by pricing the closing inventory at net realizable value, thereby charging the loss to the current period while reflecting inventory on the balance sheet at a figure no higher than the amount that the business actually expects to realize from the inventory's eventual sale. To illustrate, assume that Jones Shoe estimates that the company will eventually sell the shoes in its closing inventory at the end of 20X1 for $20 per pair. Further assume that the company will incur $2 per pair in selling expenses. If the company uses net realizable value as the controlling "market," Jones Shoe would carry the shoes inventory at $18 per pair, even if replacement cost equals or exceeds historical cost.

Some accountants argue against using net realizable value, rather than replacement cost, as the test for determining market value because balance sheet conservatism gives the principal reason for pricing inventory at the lower of cost or market. Under this view, a business should price inventory assuming a forced and speedy liquidation. These accountants suggest replacement cost as a better measure.

One other school of thought as to the "market" value of inventory merits mention. Some accountants argue that because the economic significance or utility of inventory lies in the fact that a business can sell the inventory for a profit, a business should ask whether it can still realize the profit that it expected when it acquired the goods. For example, assume that the Jones Company originally acquired a pair of shoes for $20 and expected to sell the shoes for $25 after spending an additional $2 per pair. If the estimated selling price for such shoes still on hand at the end of the year had dropped to $23, the company would have to purchase such shoes for $18 to produce the same profit-making or economic utility. According to this approach, the company should treat the "market" value of the shoes as $18. Under this theory, a business should subtract not only the estimated selling costs but also the normal profit from the estimated selling price to determine the inventory's market value. Accordingly, accountants usually call this figure *net realizable value less normal profit.*

The Codification sets up a formula that incorporates all three bases discussed above for determining the "market" value of inventory. FASB ASC Topic 330, *Inventory*, again which codified ARB No. 43, defines market value as presumptively equal to current replacement cost, so long as that figure lies somewhere between a maximum of net realizable value and a minimum of net realizable value less expected or normal profit. We could graphically illustrate these limitations as follows:

net realizable value

net realizable value less normal profit

In other words, net realizable value serves as a ceiling which market value may not exceed, while net realizable value less normal profit constitutes a floor below which market value may not drop. Whenever replacement cost falls somewhere between the ceiling and the floor, ASC Topic 330 treats replacement cost as the proper test of market value. If replacement cost exceeds net realizable value, then Topic 330 sets net realizable value as the appropriate figure for market value. If replacement cost falls below net realizable value less normal profit, then the Codification establishes the latter as the figure for market value. We must emphasize that the principle of lower of cost or market only applies when cost exceeds the market value as so determined.

An enterprise can use at least three different ways to apply the lower of cost or market method for valuing inventories. Whichever technique an enterprise adopts, the enterprise must use the approach consistently from accounting period to period. First and most commonly, an enterprise can apply the lower of cost or market to each item in inventory. Second, the business may compare aggregate cost to aggregate lower of cost or market on a category-by-category basis. Third, an enterprise can apply the lower of total cost or total market to the entire inventory.

As we have already observed, the historical emphasis on balance sheet "conservatism" greatly influenced the principle that businesses should price inventory at the lower of cost or market. The more recent emphasis on the income statement, however, invites reconsideration of the doctrine of lower of cost or market. Some commentators have expressed concern that while pricing closing inventory at the lower of cost or market does produce a conservative balance sheet, it may result in a less meaningful or even misleading periodic picture of income from a business's operations. Before discussing that point, we should raise consistency concerns because the lower of cost or market requires an enterprise to recognize unrealized losses on inventory items, but to ignore unrealized gains. In addition, businesses often face great difficulty measuring net realizable value with any certainty. How should the business determine expected selling costs? How does the business determine a normal profit? In any event, the lower of cost or market approach presents some serious practical problems.

Most significantly, however, using the lower of cost or market can distort the income statement and, more particularly, the picture that consecutive income statements for the year of the inventory writedown and the succeeding year. To illustrate, assume that, at the beginning of 20X0, Russ Company purchases merchandise for $100,000. Further assume that the enterprise sold half the goods during the year for $80,000; that Russ sold the remaining half in 20X1 for $75,000; and that the inventory at the end of 20X0, which cost $50,000, would have cost $40,000 to replace. In the table that follows, we compare the gross profit for 20X0 and 20X1 under the lower of cost or market and the cost methods:

	Lower of Cost or Market	Cost
20X0:		
Sales	$ 80,000	$ 80,000
Cost of Goods Sold		
Purchases	$100,000	$100,000
Less: Ending Inventory	40,000	50,000
Cost of Goods Sold	$ 60,000	$ 50,000
Gross Profit	$ 20,000	$ 30,000
20X1:		
Sales	$ 75,000	$ 75,000
Cost of Goods Sold (Ending Inventory from 20X0)	40,000	$ 50,000
Gross Profit	$ 35,000	$ 25,000

Although the company has stated the ending inventory and the gross profit during 20X0 more conservatively under the lower of cost or market method than under cost method, the income statements for 20X0 and 20X1 under the lower of cost or market method show gross profit increasing from $20,000 to $35,000, which may convey a misleading impression to any reader who does not realize that the inventory write-down effectively transferred $10,000 in profits from 20X0 to 20X1.

The lower of cost or market method assumes that a decrease in selling prices will parallel the decrease in replacement cost. This assumption did not apply in the previous illustration, and frequently does not hold true in the real world. As a result, some accountants argue that an enterprise should not reduce an inventory's valuation to market unless the sales price has, or probably will, decrease accordingly. These accountants argue that net realizable value more meaningfully measures the market value of inventory than replacement cost.

Even if we assume that the selling prices decreased $10,000, an amount equal to the decrease in inventory valuation, so that sales in 20X1 total $70,000, we again encounter potentially misleading income statements:

	Lower of Cost or Market	Cost
20X0:		
Sales	$ 80,000	$ 80,000
Cost of Goods Sold		
Purchases	$100,000	$100,000
Less: Ending Inventory	40,000	50,000
Cost of Goods Sold	$ 60,000	$ 50,000
Gross Profit	$ 20,000	$ 30,000
20X1:		
Sales	$70,000	$ 70,000
Cost of Goods Sold (Ending Inventory from 20X0)	40,000	$ 50,000
Gross Profit	$30,000	$ 20,000

Once again, the figures in the Cost column seem to reflect the facts more accurately. The decrease in selling prices caused Russ Company to earn less profit in 20X1 than in 20X0. The Lower of Cost or Market column tells a strange story: the company generated more gross profit in 20X1 than in 20X0, despite the decrease in selling prices during 20X1. Presumably as a result, accountants have often exercised judgment and have not followed literally the rules originally set forth in ARB No. 43, and now codified in FASB ASC Topic 330, *Inventory*. DONALD E. KIESO ET AL., INTERMEDIATE ACCOUNTING 481 n.5 (15th ed. 2013).

The Codification instructs businesses to measure net losses on firm purchase commitments for additional inventory in the same way as losses on inventory already owned. If material, a net loss on firm purchase commitments should be recognized and separately disclosed in the income statement.

An early twentieth century divide case illustrates the need to recognize a decline in the value of inventory, whether the enterprise already holds the goods or has ordered them, at least when the enterprise faces a material prospective loss. *Branch v. Kaiser*, 291 Pa. 543, 140 A. 498 (1928), involved a corporation that sold groceries as a wholesaler. All of the shareholders were retail grocery stores that were also customers of the corporation. The corporation enjoyed considerable success until 1920, when the business suffered about a $1 million loss arise from a sudden and dramatic decline in the market price of a number of grocery items the company handled. For example, the market price of sugar fell from around twenty-eight cents per pound to as low as 5.5 cents. Between the company's inventory and future purchase commitments, this decline in price caused about a $500,000 loss on sugar alone. Although no one could reasonably blame the directors for the decline in the price of sugar, they decided to conceal the calamity that had befallen the company with the hope that future business would enable to the company to recoup its losses. The directors continued to carry the company's inventories at cost and to pay dividends, while giving no notice of the loss in the company's financial reports. This practice continued for four years with the directors "inflating" their purchases of new inventory to carry it at the old high 1920 prices, this in effect adopting a kind of informal LIFO system, but the company ultimately found itself in bankruptcy, and the court held the directors personally liable for the dividends the corporation paid after the losses occurred.

Although FASB ASC Topic 450, *Contingencies*, which codified SFAS No. 5 and which we discussed in Chapter VII, allows enterprises to accrue reserves for asset impairments, including inventory obsolescence, any such loss must qualify as both "probable" as of the balance sheet date and "reasonably estimated." As mentioned on page 531, *supra*, the SEC instituted cease-and-desist proceedings against Microsoft Corporation in 2002 for unsupported and undisclosed reserves. Among other reserves, Microsoft maintained a corporate level reserve account for inventory obsolescence that did not comply with SFAS No. 5, or, presumably its successor, FASB ASC Topic 450, *Contingencies*, because the company's senior financial officials did not properly assess whether inventory losses had occurred and did not reasonably estimate any losses. In fact, together the combined corporate level reserve and factually supported inventory reserve accounts at the operating level created a negative inventory amount for Microsoft at the end of fiscal 1997. To resolve the proceedings, Microsoft consented to a cease-and-desist order that found that the corporate level reserves during the four fiscal years at issue did not comply with GAAP. *In re* Microsoft Corp., Accounting and Auditing Enforcement Release No. 1563, [2001–2003 Transfer Binder] Fed. Sec. L. Rep. (CCH) ¶ 75,078 (June 3, 2002).

Special rules apply to inventory losses from market declines for interim financial reporting purposes. As a general rule, an enterprise should not defer these losses beyond the interim period in which the loss occurs. If the market goes back up, the business should recognize the gains from recovery of such losses on the same inventory in a later interim period of the same year. Such gains, however, should not exceed previously recognized losses. If an enterprise reasonably expects a market decline to recover in the fiscal year, the enterprise need not recognize such a temporary market decline in the interim period.

We have already noted that important differences exist between GAAP and federal income tax law. *Thor Power Tool Co. v. Commissioner*, 439 U.S. 522 (1979), provides another example. In that case, the Supreme Court held that the taxpayer could not write down its spare parts inventory for tax purposes even though GAAP required a writedown to qualify for an unqualified opinion. In its most significant case to date involving inventory methods for federal income tax purposes, the Supreme Court explained the vastly different objectives of tax and financial accounting:

> The primary goal of financial accounting is to provide useful information to management, shareholders, creditors, and others properly interested; the major responsibility of the accountant is to protect these parties from being misled. The primary goal of the income tax system, in contrast, is the equitable collection of revenue; the major responsibility of the Internal Revenue Service is to protect the public fisc. Consistently with its goals and responsibilities, financial accounting has as its foundation the principle of conservatism, with its corollary that "possible errors in measurement [should] be in the direction of understatement rather than overstatement of net income and net assets." In view of the Treasury's markedly different goals and responsibilities understatement of income is not destined to be its guiding light. Given this diversity, even contrariety, of objectives, any presumptive equivalency between tax and financial accounting would be unacceptable.

> * * *

> * * * [A] presumptive equivalency between tax and financial accounting would create insurmountable difficulties of tax administration. Accountants long have recognized that "generally accepted accounting principles" are far from being a canonical set of rules that will ensure identical accounting treatment of identical transactions. "Generally accepted accounting principles," rather, tolerate a range of "reasonable" treatments, leaving the choice among alternatives to management. Such, indeed, is precisely the case here. Variances of this sort may be tolerable in financial reporting, but they are questionable in a tax system designed to ensure as far as possible that similarly situated taxpayers pay the same tax. If management's election among "acceptable" options were dispositive for tax purposes, a firm, indeed, could decide unilaterally—within limits dictated only by its accountants—the tax it wished to pay. Such unilateral decisions would not just make the Code inequitable; they would make it unenforceable.

439 U.S. at 542–44 (footnotes omitted).

PROBLEMS

Problem 8.2A. The Jesse James Company ("JJC") was formed on June 1, 20X1. The following information is available from JJC's inventory records for the quarter ended September 30, 20X1 for a particular product which JJC purchases and resells to customers:

	Units	Unit Cost
Beginning inventory, July 1	800	$ 9.00
Purchases		
July 5, 20X1	1,500	10.00
July 25, 20X1	1,200	10.50
August 16, 20X1	600	11.00
September 26, 20X1	900	11.50

A physical inventory on September 30, 20X1 reveals 1,600 units remaining in inventory. Compute the amount of the ending inventory at September 30, 20X1 under each of the following inventory methods:

1. Specific identification assuming that the ending inventory includes 100 units from the beginning inventory, 200 units purchased on July 5, 300 units from those purchased on July 25, 400 units purchased on August 16, and 600 units from the September 26 purchase.

2. Weighted average cost

3. FIFO

4. LIFO

Problem 8.2B. Assume that immediately after beginning operations in 20X1, Company X purchased three units of inventory in a rising market, at prices of $5, $6 and $7 successively, and sold two of them during the year for a total of $16.

(a) Compute X's gross profit under both FIFO and LIFO.

(b) Assuming that X adopted LIFO in 20X1, and that during 20X2 X purchased two more units of inventory, at $8 and $9 successively, while selling two units for a total of $20, how much gross profit would X report in 20X2?

(c) Would the gross profit differ if X purchased a third item of inventory during 20X2, also at $9, while still selling only two items for a total of $20?

(d) How about if X purchased only one item during 20X2, at $8, while still selling two for $20?

(e) Now suppose that in 20X3, X, still on LIFO, starts with a single item of inventory, at a cost of $5, and during the year prices peak and turn downward, so that X purchases three items during 20X3, at successive costs of $10, $8, and $6, while selling two items for a total price of $18. Compute X's gross profit for 20X3.

Problem 8.2C. Dischord Music ("Dischord") was formed on January 1, 20X1. The following information is available from Dischord's inventory records for the quarter ended March 31, 20X1 for ear buds which Dischord purchases and resells to customers:

	Units	Unit Cost
Beginning inventory, January 1	2,000	$4.00
Purchases		
January 31, 20X1	1,000	4.20
February 15, 20X1	1,500	4.40
February 26, 20X1	3,000	4.60
March 7, 20X1	2,500	4.80
March 28, 20X1	1,000	5.00

A physical inventory on March 31, 20X1 reveals 4,800 ear buds remaining in inventory. If Dischord sells ear buds for $75,000 during the quarter, calculate the gross profit for the quarter ending March 31, 20X1 under each of the following inventory methods:

1. Specific identification assuming that the ending inventory includes 300 units from the beginning inventory; 500 units purchased on January 31; 700 units from those purchased on February 15; 1,400 units purchased on February 26; 1,200 units from the March 7 purchase; and 700 units from those purchased on March 28.

2. Weighted average cost

3. FIFO

4. LIFO

Problem 8.3A. Assume the following facts as to an item to be included in a closing inventory:

Cost	$500
Replacement Cost	350
Estimated Selling Price	600
Additional Cost of Disposal	200
Normal Profit	100

What is the appropriate amount at which this item should be carried in inventory:

(a) under the formula in FASB ASC Topic 330, *Inventory*?

(b) under the decision in *Branch v. Kaiser*, *supra* at page 619?

Problem 8.3B. Is there a lower of cost or market problem lurking in Problem 8.2B? Explain fully.

Problem 8.3C. Assume that the appropriate market value of the goods ordered in Problem 8.1B, on page 598, *supra*, is only $9,200 at the end of 20X1.

In the light of the requirements of ASC Topic 330, *Inventory*, explain which of the following entries you would make to reflect this fact in X's financial statements on that date:

(a) No entry

(b) Loss on Inventory Commitment $800
      Advance on Inventory Commitment $800

(c) Loss on Inventory Commitment $800
      Estimated Loss on Inventory Commitment $800

Problem 8.4A. Which inventory method did Amazon.com use to value its inventories as of December 31, 2012? Explain briefly how and where you found your answer.

Problem 8.4B. Which inventory method did Google use to value its inventories as of December 31, 2012? Explain briefly how and where you found your answer.

Problem 8.4C. Which inventory method did UPS use to value its inventories as of December 31, 2012? Explain briefly how and where you found your answer.

C.   CONSISTENCY

As we have seen, the consistency principle generally requires enterprises to treat the same economic events in the same way from accounting period to accounting period. Otherwise, users of financial statements cannot meaningfully compare an enterprise's financial statements with similar reports for previous periods. The following case involves the consistency requirement and also illustrates that an unjustified writedown of inventory violates generally accepted accounting principles just as much as a failure to recognize a necessary writedown.

Chick v. Tomlinson

Supreme Court of Idaho, 1975.
531 P.2d 573.

■ DONALDSON, JUSTICE.

In 1963, Carlyle Chick and H. Lowell Hatch, hereinafter called respondents, began working at appellant Lewis Korth Lumber Company for K. D. Tomlinson, appellant. * * *

In return for their efforts at Lewis Korth Lumber Company, respondents were to each receive $500 per month salary, certain expenses, and bonuses [equal to] 40% of all net profits above the first $25,000. The dispute is found in the determination and distribution of those funds.

Although the respondents were employed at Lewis Korth from 1963 to 1971, profits sufficient to fund the bonus program were made only in 1963, 1967, and 1968. The bonus for 1963 was $8,500 each while the 1967 figure was $6,500 each. Neither of these amounts is in question. However 1968 was an excellent year for the lumber business and the relatively large profits for that year are the basis for this dispute.

Appellant Tomlinson contends that the 1968 net profit figure was $77,326.82, which resulted in $20,930.72 available for distribution by the bonus plan, i.e. 40% of profits after the first $25,000.00. The trial court amended the net profit figure to $194,323.96, with $67,729.58 for distribution. The trial court arrived at this sum by disallowing deductions of $25,000 for Tomlinson's salary and of $20,000 for a bonus reserve fund taken by Tomlinson from the net profit. The trial court also disallowed an accounting procedure utilized by Tomlinson wherein the closing lumber inventory of Lewis Korth Lumber Company was intentionally understated by over one million board feet. This procedure had the effect of reducing the profit by $71,997.14, which was subsequently added back in by the trial court in arriving at its figure of $67,729.58, net profit for distribution.

* * *

The trial court's determination that Tomlinson's salary deduction and the bonus reserve deduction from the 1968 net profits be disallowed as contrary to the bonus agreement is * * * assigned as error. * * * During the several years of the respondents' employment at Lewis Korth Lumber Company, only in 1968 were these deductions taken. This unilateral, one-time attempt is sufficient evidence to support the trial court's determination that the deductions were not in accord with the agreement.

The trial court's revaluation of the 1968 lumber inventory is assigned as error. As we noted above, 1968 was a bumper year in the industry. Lewis Korth Lumber Company earned record profits. Tomlinson testified that traditionally such years are followed by large increases in costs as workers seek wage increases. In order to 'hedge' against this, Tomlinson continued, he ordered the closing inventory of the lumber lowered by over one million board feet. This was done allegedly to compensate for the lower price the then green lumber would demand the following spring, and had the net effect of lowering the 1968 profit figure by $71,997.14.

Appellant Tomlinson argues that the trial court disregarded the only expert testimony as to the acceptability of that accounting procedure. Victor Wakefield, a CPA, did testify as a witness for the appellant, and a segment of that testimony was as follows:

"Q: (By Mr. Givens) Now, do you, is the inventory based in board feet and dollar volume contained in your report, your inventory and adjusted inventory?

"A: (By Mr. Wakefield) It is an adjusted inventory.

"Q: And does that meet normal and accepted accounting practices?

"A: Well, the technical word, probably not, but by and large most any business has a tendency to put these hedges in in those years."

* * *

The trial court elected to place greater weight on the first part of the second answer and found the accounting procedure to be unacceptable.

In this the trial court was correct. Assuming arguendo that inventory adjustment was called for, placing one million board feet 'under the rock,' as Tomlinson termed it, is hardly the correct way to go about it. The position of the American Institute of Certified Public Accountants is as follows:

"STATEMENT 5

"A departure from the cost basis of pricing the inventory is required when the utility of the goods is no longer as great as its cost. Where there is evidence that the utility of goods, in their disposal in the ordinary course of business, will be less than cost, whether due to physical deterioration, obsolescence, changes in price levels, or other causes, the difference should be recognized as a loss of the current period. This is generally accomplished by stating such goods at a lower level commonly designated as Market.

"Discussion

.08 Although the cost basis ordinarily achieves the objective of a proper matching of costs and revenues, under certain circumstances cost may not be the amount properly chargeable against the revenues of further periods. A departure from cost is required in these circumstances because cost is satisfactory only if the utility of the goods has not diminished since their acquisition; a loss of utility is to be reflected as a charge against the revenues of the period in which it occurs. Thus, in accounting for inventories, a loss should be recognized whenever the utility of goods is impaired by damage, deterioration, obsolescence, changes in price levels, or other causes. The measurement of such losses is accomplished by applying the rule of pricing inventories at Cost or Market, whichever is lower. This provides a practical means of measuring utility and thereby determining the amount of the loss to be recognized and accounted for in the current period." APB Accounting Principles, § 5121.08 [now codified at FASB ASC ¶¶ 330-10-35-1 to -2].

By failing to adopt the procedure traditionally called "cost or market, whichever is lower" Tomlinson went beyond accepted accounting procedures, and the trial court correctly rejected the devaluation of the inventory.

* * *

Judgment affirmed in part, and reversed [on another issue] and remanded in part. Costs to appellants.

■ McQuade, C. J., and McFadden and Bakes, JJ., concur.

■ Shepard, J., sat but did not participate.

NOTES

1. As we saw earlier, GAAP requires an enterprise to disclose the accounting principles that the firm uses and the methods adopted to apply those principles. In addition, GAAP also generally prevents an enterprise from changing from one accounting principle to another unless the new principle qualifies as "preferable" to the old principle. FASB ASC ¶ 250-10-45-19 (a codification of Accounting Changes and Error Corrections—a replacement of APB Opinion No. 20 and FASB Statement No. 3, Statement of Fin. Accounting Standards No. 154, ¶ 21 (Fin. Accounting Standards Bd. 2005)). These requirements specifically applies to the principles and procedures which an enterprise adopts to state inventories. If an enterprise alters the basis for stating inventories, the enterprise must disclose the change's nature and effect, if material, as well as the justification, in the financial statements for the accounting period in which the change occurs. FASB ASC ¶ 330-10-50-1 (a codification of Restatement and Revision of Accounting Research Bulletins, Accounting Research Bulletin No. 43, Chapter 4, Statement 8 (Am. Inst. of Certified Pub. Accountants 1953)).

2. Under FASB ASC Topic 250, *Accounting Changes and Error Corrections*, which codified SFAS No. 154, income tax savings alone will not qualify a new accounting principle as "preferable." The new accounting principle must constitute an improvement in financial reporting. FASB ASC ¶ 250-10-55-1 (a codification of Accounting Changes Related to the Cost of Inventory—an Interpretation of APB Opinion No. 20, FASB Interpretation No. 1, ¶ 5 (Fin. Accounting Standards Bd. 1974)).

3. Lawyers frequently draft or negotiate written contracts that present issues regarding inventories. Since LIFO tends to minimize net income and current assets in an inflationary environment, while FIFO maximizes current assets and earnings in that same setting. If an agreement will give your client the right to a portion of an enterprise's income for some period during an inflationary period, you should consider specifying that the parties will use FIFO to compute income for purposes of the contract. If you represent someone selling a business for an amount based on the venture's net worth, you may want to insist that the parties use FIFO, or maybe even current value, when determining net worth to reflect more accurately the inventory's "real" value.

*

CHAPTER IX

LONG-LIVED ASSETS AND INTANGIBLES

A. IMPORTANCE TO LAWYERS

In Chapter I, we saw that a close relationship exists between deferred expenses and assets. Many assets which an enterprise uses in its operations benefit several, or even many, accounting periods. For example, a manufacturing enterprise may purchase production equipment that should last at least five years or a building to use as a sales office that should last even longer. The same manufacturing enterprise may also develop or purchase a patent for use in its operations. When such assets benefit several accounting periods, accountants increasingly refer to these assets, both tangible and intangible, as *long-lived assets*. The term long-lived assets, therefore, includes both tangible *fixed assets*, such as property, plant and equipment, which accountants sometimes refer to as *capital assets*, and *intangibles* like copyrights, patents and trademarks.

Long-lived assets function in the same way as other deferred expenses. The very reason why E. Tutt spent $2,000 for computer equipment for her law office, namely that the expenditure will provide benefit in future accounting periods, requires that she not treat the entire expenditure as an expense in the month she bought the computer. Rather, the expenditure reflects an unexpired cost, which E. Tutt should record as an asset. We also noted, however, that such an asset, like most tangible fixed assets other than land, will not last forever. Ultimately, E. Tutt will retire the computer. The computer may physically wear out or become technologically obsolescent. In any event, the $2,000 which E. Tutt paid to purchase the computer, less any salvage value, represents an expense which E. Tutt should offset against revenues during the computer's estimated useful life under the matching principle. Depreciation refers to the systematic allocation of a tangible asset's cost over its expected life.

An enterprise may also acquire natural resources, such as timber rights, mineral interests and oil and gas reserves, or intangible assets, including intellectual property, such as patents and trademarks, and benefits that arise from contractual or other legal rights, like customer lists and noncontractual customer relationships. These assets continue to grow in importance in today's economy. In addition, enterprises often purchase other businesses, and when the purchase price exceeds the cumulative net fair market values of the acquired business's individually identifiable assets and liabilities, the acquiring enterprise treats the excess as *goodwill*. Goodwill reflects the economic reality that the purchase price for "a whole business" often exceeds the sum of the value of its parts. Goodwill encompasses any economic resource that provides a competitive advantage, such as a solid reputation, strong brands, and supplier loyalty.

Because a fixed asset provides benefits for more than one accounting period, an enterprise should allocate the asset's cost among the different periods in a systematic and rational manner. Depreciation assigns the costs to acquire capital assets to the future periods that an enterprise expects to benefit from the services that those assets provide. Because land does not experience wear or tear, or undergo functional or economic obsolescence, however, businesses cannot depreciate land. The term *depletion* refers to a similar cost allocation process for natural resources found on or below land, such as timber or oil reserves, which accountants often describe as *wasting assets*. Unlike depreciation, depletion attempts to measure these assets' physical consumption.

Intangibles, including goodwill, do not possess physical substance but they do provide benefits over more than one accounting period. If legal, regulatory, contractual, or other factors limit an intangible's useful life, the owning enterprise must allocate the costs to acquire such a limited-life intangible from a third party among the different accounting periods that the owner expects to benefit from the intangible's acquisition. Such treatment seeks to match revenues with the expenses incurred to produce the revenues and most accurately presents the enterprise's financial results and condition. Accountants use the term *amortization* to describe this cost-allocation process for limited-life intangibles.

U.S. GAAP now generally exempts indefinite-life intangibles and goodwill from amortization. Instead, enterprises must test these assets for impairment at least annually. If the impairment test reveals that the asset's fair value exceeds its carrying amount, the enterprise must write-down the carrying value to fair value and charge the reduction against earnings for the current period.

To provide meaningfully comparative financial data, an enterprise must consistently apply the same depreciation, depletion and amortization methods from period to period. In addition, the enterprise must disclose information about the method of allocating the costs to acquire the underlying assets, the carrying amounts of goodwill and other intangible assets, and the estimated amortization expense for the next five years.

Accounting for long-lived assets and intangibles affects lawyers because the methods used to recognize and recover capital expenditures can directly impact an enterprise's financial position and results. Lawyers should recognize the importance of accounting for long-lived assets, both tangible and intangible, for several reasons, including the following:

● As we have already seen, lawyers frequently draft, negotiate or litigate contracts that often contain profit-sharing provisions. Accounting for long-lived assets and intangibles can affect these provisions in at least three different ways. First, accounting rules may determine whether an enterprise can treat an expenditure as an asset or must treat the cost as an expense. An entity or its owners or managers may try to treat actual expenses as capital expenditures which would therefore appear on the balance sheet as assets, thus overstating the enterprise's assets and profits. Alternatively, the entity or its owners or managers could manipulate the venture's profit or loss by expensing unexpired costs which will provide substantial benefits to subsequent accounting periods, thus increasing the entity's expenses and decreasing its profit. Second, depreciation, depletion and amortization expenses can significantly impact profit computations. Finally, write downs of long-lived assets and intangibles can greatly affect net income. Large write downs in the 1990s prompted the business community to use the term "Big Bath" to describe an enterprise's one-time recognition of expense or loss for supposedly worthless assets. Although these write downs significantly reduce current income, they improve the possibility of future income by negating the allocation of expenses to future periods. In a 1998 speech at the NYU Center for Law and Business, *supra* at 380 to 385, then SEC Chairman Arthur Levitt announced an action plan to combat accounting "illusions," including "'big bath' restructuring charges" and "creative acquisition accounting," which the Chairman also referred to as "merger magic." Under this latter technique, you may recall that acquiring companies increasingly treat large portions of the total consideration paid to acquire a target as purchasing "in-process research and development." See *supra* at 383. Because accounting rules in this country require enterprises to treat all research and development costs as expenses in the period incurred, acquirers then immediately write off these in-process research and development charges.

- The way that an enterprise treats certain costs can influence the taxes which the business or its owners owe. An enterprise can misstate financial statements by either overstating or understating repairs or amounts spent on research and development activities. Improperly treating capital expenditures which will benefit subsequent taxable periods as immediate expenses will increase the business's deductions and thereby decrease its taxable income and tax liability. Closely held businesses often treat long-term costs as repairs to avoid taxes, while publicly traded businesses may sometimes overstate earnings by treating regular expenses as capital expenditures.

- In the years ahead, businesses in the United States will likely spend hundreds of billions of dollars to clean up environmental problems. Should businesses treat these costs as expenses or as capital expenditures which will benefit future accounting or taxable periods?

- As the Internet emerges, enterprises have spent, and will continue to spend, enormous amounts to develop the content and the graphics on their Web sites. How should firms treat these costs for financial accounting purposes?

- Accounting for long-lived assets and intangibles advances different objectives in various situations. For tax accounting, public companies prefer to reduce taxable income and tax liabilities by increasing depreciation, depletion and amortization expenses in years of high income. On the other hand, for financial statement presentation, lower depreciation expenses increase earnings and improve earnings per share. For utility rate regulation purposes, depreciation, depletion, amortization and writeoffs can represent expenses lawfully included in service rates.

● As the accounting frauds at both WorldCom and HealthSouth Corp. illustrate, improperly treating operating expenses as long-lived assets overstates income. Like other financial frauds, intentionally understating expenses and overstating long-lived assets can create criminal liability.

● As we have seen, creditors and bankruptcy trustees can hold corporate directors personally liable for dividends they declare which exceed various legal limitations. An entity's depreciation method can affect the amount that the business can distribute to its owners in some states.

● The cost allocation issues present in accounting for long-lived assets and intangible assets can also affect the computation of damages in breach of contract and tort cases.

Like accounting for inventories in the previous chapter, accounting for long-lived assets and intangibles influences both the income statement and the balance sheet. On the income statement, depreciation, depletion and amortization match costs to acquire long-lived assets against revenues in the current period. Enterprises initially record long-lived assets at historical cost; depreciation, depletion and amortization allocate those costs among future periods. From a balance sheet perspective, long-lived assets often represent a substantial part of an enterprise's total assets.

As discussed in Chapter II, an enterprise's management often exercises judgment when applying generally accepted accounting principles. Accounting for long-lived assets requires managerial judgment involving significant estimates. As discussed below in greater detail, accounting for long-lived assets involves estimating both the assets' useful lives and any expected salvage values remaining after productive service. Additionally, depreciation, depletion and amortization expenses also represent non-cash expenditures, an important point to remember for income statement and cash flow analysis.

B. CLASSIFICATION OF EXPENDITURES: ASSETS VS. EXPENSES

The matching principle emphasizes offsetting costs against the corresponding revenues whenever reasonable and practicable. Accounting for long-lived assets and intangibles implements the matching principle by requiring the systematic and rational expensing of expenditures to acquire assets over the accounting periods that benefit from those expenditures. As an enterprise acquires long-lived assets and intangibles, the balance sheet displays the assets' historical costs. The income statement, in turn, absorbs the costs through depreciation, depletion and amortization expenses over the periods of future benefit as the assets help to generate revenues throughout their useful lives.

Accounting for expenditures related to long-lived assets and intangibles ultimately boils down to a single question: Does the expenditure produce benefits that the enterprise will enjoy in future accounting periods? If so, the enterprise has acquired an asset, whether tangible or intangible. Although the acquisition of a tangible asset typically provides an obvious answer, even intangible assets can benefit future accounting periods. When the enterprise acquires any asset, the so-called capital expenditure appears on the balance sheet. In later years, the asset's cost will flow through the income statement, either as depreciation, depletion or amortization expenses; as an impairment loss when the asset's expected future benefits no longer exist; or as an offset to the asset's selling price upon which the enterprise will recognize gain or loss at disposition. By comparison, if the original outlay represents an expense, the cost immediately and completely reduces net income or increases net loss on the income statement during the period incurred.

Accountants, unfortunately, have not developed an absolute test to resolve this characterization question. Nevertheless, the answers to the following questions generally help an enterprise to decide whether to treat an expenditure as an asset or expense:

- Does the expenditure create a new asset?

- Does the outlay restore an underlying asset to its original condition?

- Does the expenditure enable the enterprise to produce greater quantity or better quality products?

- Does the outlay extend an existing asset's useful life?

- How often does the expenditure recur?

In addition, the item's materiality can affect the determination. Many enterprises have adopted accounting policies that establish a threshold amount, say $5,000, necessary to recognize an asset or capital expenditure. An enterprise treats any related costs below that cumulative amount as expenses in the accounting period incurred. At that cumulative amount and beyond, the enterprise treats all related costs as capital expenditures. Such policies eliminate the need to capitalize and depreciate small items, such as brooms, trash cans, desk calculators, office chairs, and even laptop computers.

Accountants define *repairs* as costs incurred to maintain an asset's operating efficiency and expected useful life. Usually small in amount and recurrent in nature, accountants treat repairs as expenses because these expenditures predominately benefit only the current accounting period. Examples of repairs include maintaining buildings, changing machine oils and replacing minor equipment parts. As current expenses, these costs reduce current net income when incurred. The enterprise debits an expense account, such as Repair Expense, upon incurring such a cost and credits cash or a payable.

Capital expenditures, on the other hand, generally increase operational efficiency and productive capacity or extend an underlying asset's useful life.

Usually more significant in amount than repairs, these costs add to an enterprise's investment in the underlying asset. The enterprise debits the appropriate asset account upon incurring a capital expenditure. The resulting depreciation, depletion or amortization will reduce net income in those accounting periods that benefit from the capital expenditure.

Accountants sometimes divide capital expenditures into three categories: *additions*, *improvements* and *replacements*. Additions generally increase an asset's productive capacity. For example, constructing a new wing on an existing plant may increase the enterprise's ability to manufacture products. Although theoretically these expenditures create a new asset, the enterprise may debit the underlying asset, such as the Building account, upon incurring such expenditures. Both improvements and replacements involve substituting one asset for another. An improvement, which some accountants call a *betterment*, substitutes a better asset for an existing asset. In a replacement, in contrast, the enterprise supplants an existing asset with a like asset. To illustrate, installing a concrete floor in an area where a dirt floor previously existed usually involves an improvement, while substituting one wooden floor for another demonstrates a replacement. In both situations, however, the substitutions must extend or enhance the asset's useful life.

NOTES

1. Mischaracterizing a cost as an asset rather than an expense results in the enterprise overstating net income, assets and owners' equity on a dollar per dollar basis. Recall that WorldCom improperly treated $11 billion in operating expenses as assets. This fraud meant that the company understated expenses and overstated net income, assets and shareholders' equity.

2. U.S. GAAP requires enterprises to treat all research and development costs as expenses in the period incurred. *See generally* FASB ASC Topic 730, *Research and Development*, which codified ACCOUNTING FOR RESEARCH AND DEVELOPMENT COSTS, Statement of Fin. Accounting Standards No. 2 (Fin. Accounting Standards Bd. 1974) ("SFAS No. 2"). FASB reached its conclusion to require treatment as an expense based on several factors, including the high degree of uncertainty that usually exists regarding the future benefits of individual research and development projects and the lack of causal relationship between expenditures and benefits. FASB ASC ¶¶ 730-10-05-2 to -3 (which codified SFAS No. 2, ¶¶ 8, 39, 41).

Prior to 2007, U.S. GAAP required enterprises to expense certain in-process research and development ("IPR&D") acquired in a business combination. FASB ASC Topic 805, *Business Combinations*, which codified the rules promulgated in SFAS No. 141(R) in 2007 in an effort to promote further convergence with international accounting standards, requires acquirers to recognize and measure this IPR&D at acquisition-date fair value, to treat the intangible as indefinite-lived, and to periodically test the asset for impairment, until the acquirer completes or abandons the research and development efforts. FASB ASC ¶¶ 805-20-25-1, 805-20-30-1, 805-20-35-5 (codifications of SFAS No. 141(R), ¶¶ 66, B149–50).

As the effort to develop international accounting standards continues, see pages 162 to 168, *supra*, we should keep in mind that accounting practices in other countries, including English-speaking nations, permit the capitalization of at least some research and development costs. Paul E. Nix & David E. Nix, *A Historical Review of the Accounting Treatment of Research and Development Costs*, 19 ACCOUNTING HISTORIANS J. 51, 69–71 (1992). Among global luxury car manufacturers, for example, *The Wall Street Journal* reported that India's Tata Motors, which purchased JaguarLand Rover in 2008, capitalized about eighty percent of its research and development costs during its fiscal year ended March 31, 2013. Like IFRSs, accounting standards in India give enterprises discretion in accounting for such costs. By comparison, the article stated that Indian SUV-manufacturer Mahindra & Mahindra capitalized only forty-four percent of its research and development costs during the same fiscal year, while German auto company BMW, which follows IFRSs and uses the calendar year, had capitalized an average of only a third of such costs from 2008-2012. In further contrast, American and Japanese car companies must expense all their spending on research and development. *See* Abheek Bhattacharya, *It Pays to Look Under Tata's Hood*, WALL ST. J., Nov. 15, 2013, http://online.wsj.com/news/articles/SB100014240527023037896045791992108520438160.

3. The Codification also offers guidance as to whether enterprises should immediately charge various costs against current earnings or treat them as capital expenditures in efforts to eliminate inconsistencies in financial reporting. *See, e.g.*, FASB ASC Subtopic 350-40, *Intangibles—Goodwill and Other—Internal-Use Software* (codifying ACCOUNTING FOR THE COSTS OF COMPUTER SOFTWARE DEVELOPED OR OBTAINED FOR INTERNAL USE, Statement of Position 98-1 (Am. Inst. of Certified Pub. Accountants 1998)) (requiring enterprises to expense, as incurred, computer software costs incurred in preliminary project stages, similar costs stemming from research and development, training costs, maintenance costs, and many costs related to data conversion, while specifying capitalization for external direct costs of materials and services used to develop or acquire internal use software, payroll costs for employees who work directly on tasks related to the internal use software, and interest costs incurred while developing such software); FASB ASC Subtopic 350-50, *Intangibles—Goodwill and Other—Website Development Costs* (a codification of ACCOUNTING FOR WEB SITE DEVELOPMENT COSTS, Emerging Issues Task Force Issue No. 00-2 (Fin. Accounting Standards Bd. 2000)) (concluding that enterprises should capitalize initial development costs for Web graphics, but can expense changes to the graphics); FASB ASC Subtopic 720-15, *Other Expenses—Start-Up Costs* (codifying REPORTING ON THE COSTS OF START-UP ACTIVITIES, Statement of Position 98-5 (Am. Inst. of Certified Pub. Accountants 1998)) (mandating businesses to expense organization costs and costs related to start-up activities as incurred); FASB ASC Subtopic 720-35, *Other Expenses—Advertising Costs* (a codification of REPORTING ON ADVERTISING COSTS, Statement of Position 93-7 (Am. Inst. of Certified Pub. Accountants 1993)) (concluding that, except for direct-response advertising, enterprises must expense the costs of all advertising in the periods in which the enterprise incurs those costs or the first time that the advertising takes place, whichever the enterprise prefers and applies consistently).

4. Questions about whether to treat an expenditure as an expense or a capital expenditure can arise in various contexts. *See, e.g.*, Pashman v. Chemtex, Inc., 825 F.2d 629 (2d Cir. 1987) (holding that costs that an employer incurred to purchase a worthless ownership interest in a paint plant were not "capital expenditures," but that the employer could deduct that amount from revenues in determining net profits under employment agreement which awarded salesman ten percent of pretax profits on sales); Lege v. Lea Exploration Co., Inc., 631 So.2d 716 (La. App. 1994) (holding that the trial court properly treated amounts lessee incurred in reworking oil and gas well and in constructing saltwater disposal system as capital costs, rather than as operating expenses, in determining whether well was producing in paying quantities, so as to preclude lease cancellation).

These questions often arise in tax cases. *See, e.g.*, INDOPCO, Inc. v. Comm'r, 503 U.S. 79, 88 (1992) (holding that legal, investment banking, and other fees that the taxpayer incurred to facilitate its own acquisition in a friendly takeover represented "capital expenditures," rather than deductible expenses, because the payments produced "significant benefits that extended beyond the tax year in question"); Von–Lusk v. Comm'r, 104 T.C. 207 (1995) (upholding the Commissioner's determination that the taxpayer must capitalize property taxes and amounts incurred in meeting with government officials, obtaining building permits and zoning variances, performing engineering and feasibility studies, and drafting architectural plans related to raw land which the taxpayer planned to subdivide and use as lots upon which to build houses).

PROBLEM

Problem 9.1. The Americans with Disabilities Act of 1990 ("ADA") generally requires businesses classified as "public accommodations" to remove architectural barriers that prevent access to their facilities, or at least to make their services physically accessible to persons with disabilities to the extent "readily achievable." 42 U.S.C. § 12182 (2012). Assume that a corporation which operates a chain of fast-food restaurants spends $10 million to comply with the ADA. This amount includes costs to install ramps at doorways, remodel restrooms by widening toilet stalls and lowering sinks, and relocate drinking fountains at each restaurant. The expenditures do not extend the restaurants' estimated useful lives and actually reduce seating capacity in the restaurants. The corporation's labor agreement requires the corporation to contribute ten percent of its pretax income to a profit-sharing plan for certain employees. Can the business treat these costs to comply with the ADA as expenses?

C. Allocation of Capitalized Costs

In Chapter I, pages 75 to 76, *supra*, we introduced depreciation accounting during our discussion regarding deferral. You may want to review those materials at this time. In a nutshell, depreciation accounting attempts to allocate and distribute the costs to acquire a tangible asset, less any estimated salvage value, systematically and rationally among the different accounting periods that span the asset's expected useful life. This cost allocation essentially flows from the matching principle that requires enterprises to offset costs against the revenues that those costs generate.

Note that GAAP does not require an enterprise to apportion the costs to acquire a fixed asset, less salvage value, *ratably* over the asset's useful life. In other words, depreciation accounting need not allocate an equal amount to each accounting period. As we will see, some enterprises use activity, such as operating hours or units produced, to measure useful life. Even in those situations, an enterprise need not assign an equal amount to each operating hour or unit produced. As we shall see later in this chapter, systems involving non-ratable allocation of cost, for example, deducting larger amounts in the early years than in the later years, can also qualify as "rational." Nevertheless, ratable allocation, which accountants usually refer to as *straight-line depreciation* connoting the fact that the enterprise apportions cost evenly over an asset's useful life, remains the most common practice.

We should also emphasize two other preliminary points about depreciation. First, depreciation does not value fixed assets. In fact, depreciation accounting does not attempt to measure any decline in the market value which the assets shown on the balance sheet have suffered. Indeed, some depreciable assets, such as buildings, often appreciate in value. Second, although accountants usually use the term *accumulated depreciation*, depreciation accounting does not "accumulate" anything. Similarly, depreciation accounting does not guarantee that the enterprise will own sufficient resources to replace the fixed assets at the end of their useful lives. For example, assume that an investor organizes X Corp. on January 1 of Year 1 and purchases 1,000 shares of $100 par value common stock for par value. If X Corp. uses the proceeds from the stock issuance to buy a plant which cost the same amount, its balance sheet would reflect the following:

X Corp.
Balance Sheet, After Plant Acquisition

Plant	$100,000	Stated Capital	$100,000

If X Corp. assigns a fifty-year estimated useful life, without salvage value, to the plant, depreciation expense for Year 1 under the straight-line method would equal $2,000 ($100,000 cost/50 years estimated useful life). If X Corp. does not generate any income or incur any other expenses for the year, the Profit and Loss account for the year would show a $2,000 loss, and the balance sheet at the end of Year 1 would appear as follows:

X Corp.
Balance Sheet, End of Year 1

Plant	$100,000	Stated Capital	$100,000
Less: Accumulated			
Depreciation	2,000	Deficit	(2,000)
Total	$98,000	Total	$98,000

Given forty-nine similar years, even the most scrupulous application of depreciation accounting would not provide any "funds" to replace the plant at the end of its useful life. Only receipts that exceed expenditures can provide the funds necessary to replace fixed assets, or for any other purpose. In this context, depreciation accounting, like the allocation of any other asset involving a deferred expense, simply serves to show that the excess of receipts over actual cash expenditures does not constitute net income for accounting purposes.

To properly calculate depreciation during an accounting period, an enterprise must consider at least five factors: (1) costs to acquire the asset, (2) projected salvage value, (3) estimated useful life, (4) depreciation method and (5) actual time used during the accounting period. We will consider each factor in turn.

1. COSTS TO ACQUIRE AND RETIRE THE ASSET

Enterprises use the historical cost principle to record fixed asset acquisitions. As a result, historical cost provides the usual basis for determining depreciation. Keep in mind that, as mentioned earlier on page 631, *supra*, enterprises often adopt accounting policies that establish a threshold amount necessary to recognize an asset. An enterprise treats all related and cumulative costs above that amount as capital expenditures. Similar to accounting for inventories, historical cost represents the cash or cash equivalent price to acquire a fixed asset and bring the item to the location and condition of its intended use. Examples of expenditures considered part of a fixed asset's historical cost include purchase price, freight costs and installation charges. Once an enterprise determines an asset's historical cost, that cost figure appears on the balance sheet and also becomes the starting point for depreciation calculations.

a. SPECIFIC COSTS: DIRECT AND OVERHEAD COSTS

The costs to acquire property include not only any amounts necessary to purchase the asset, but also expenditures which ready the asset for its intended use. These expenditures can include both direct and certain indirect costs.

(1) Land and Buildings

In addition to the purchase price paid to the seller, the historical cost of land includes any other expenditures by the purchaser to acquire the land, such as the amount of any mortgages assumed, any real estate commissions, title insurance, legal fees, accrued property taxes, or surveyor fees. Although less obvious, the cost of land also includes any amounts incurred to bring the land to the condition necessary for its intended use, such as for clearing, grading or draining the property, or expenditures incurred to demolish old buildings before constructing a new facility on the property.

Accountants treat land separately from any buildings or improvements that may sit upon the land. The cost of a building includes all expenditures to acquire the facility and prepare the structure for its intended use. Construction-related costs often dominate building acquisition expenditures. For example, the direct costs associated with building acquisitions include expenditures for materials and labor, attorney's fees, architect's charges and building permits. When an enterprise constructs facilities for its own use, the cost of the facility also includes indirect or overhead charges. These costs include reasonable amounts for utilities, insurance, and depreciation of machines used to construct the facility.

A special but quite important example of an expenditure to ready property for its intended use involves interest on funds borrowed to finance an acquisition, being paid or accrued during a period of development or construction before the new property contributes to the production of revenues. The amounts of such expenditures can be very large, particularly in the real estate development field, or in the public utility business where expansion and new construction are virtually continuous. Until 1979, an enterprise's management could decide, within rather broad parameters, whether or not to defer such expenditures. Of course, U.S. GAAP did require each enterprise to follow a consistent practice.

In the mid–1970s, the SEC, concerned about the increasing number of companies that decided to defer interest in such circumstances, in effect imposed a moratorium which prevented any more companies, other than public utilities, from adopting the practice. Following its general, but not invariable, practice of deferring to the authoritative standard-setters for the profession, the Commission urged the FASB to consider the issue. In 1979, the FASB concluded that enterprises should defer interest incurred during a construction period prior to any contribution to revenues, and treat the interest as part of the historical cost of acquiring the asset, being a cost necessary to bring the asset to the desired condition for its intended use. The objective, according to the Board, was to get a better measure of the enterprise's total investment in the asset, while also charging a cost which will benefit future periods against the revenues of those periods.

The Board added that enterprises should not capitalize interest costs for inventories that the enterprise routinely manufactured, or for assets, including land, which are not undergoing activities to ready them for use. If the activity involved results in a structure, such as a plant, the Board concluded that an enterprise should treat the interest capitalized with respect to the land as part of the acquisition cost of the structure. Three members of the Board dissented on the ground that charging interest to expense when incurred results in more meaningful financial information, particularly with respect to the overall return on capital during each period. *See* CAPITALIZATION OF INTEREST COSTS, Statement of Fin. Accounting Standards No. 34 (Fin. Accounting Standards Bd. 1979), now codified at FASB ASC Subtopic 835-20, *Interest—Capitalization of Interest.*

(2) Equipment

As described above, the purchase price, freight charges and installation costs all enter into the historical cost for equipment. In addition, the cost for equipment includes any other expenditures necessary to bring the equipment to its operating location and to prepare the asset for its productive use, such as insurance premiums during transit, amounts paid to build special foundations, and outlays for trial runs.

b. SPECIAL ISSUES IN ASSET ACQUISITIONS

An enterprise may acquire an asset in several different ways which can raise special accounting issues. For example, an enterprise may issue an ownership interest in the enterprise in exchange for one or more assets. Alternatively, an enterprise may agree to make deferred payments when purchasing an asset. Sometimes, an enterprise will acquire numerous assets in a lump-sum purchase. Every once in a while, an enterprise will acquire an asset via gift. We briefly highlight the accounting issues that can arise in these situations.

(1) Issuance of Ownership Interests

An interesting issue arises when an enterprise issues an ownership interest, such as common shares, for the purchase of property. If actively traded, the market value of the ownership interest establishes the property's historical cost. If the markets do not actively trade an enterprise's stock, the enterprise uses the acquired property's fair market value to establish the asset's cost.

(2) Deferred Payment Contracts

Enterprises often acquire fixed assets through long-term financing and credit contracts using notes, mortgages or bonds. Proper accounting requires the enterprise to determine the obligation's present value on the acquisition date. The obligation's present value then represents the asset's cost for depreciation purposes.

(3) Lump-Sum Purchases

Enterprises sometimes acquire a group of assets in a single transaction. Such acquisitions require the acquiring enterprise to allocate the lump-sum purchase price to the various assets purchased. In this situation, the general practice allocates the total purchase price first to current assets and noncurrent investments in marketable securities and then among the remaining noncurrent assets, based on their relative fair values, as long as the allocated price does not exceed an asset's fair value.

To illustrate, assume that ABC Co. purchases several long-lived assets for $90,000. The assets purchased reflect the following characteristics:

	Book Value	Fair Value
Asset 1	$15,000	$ 10,000
Asset 2	10,000	20,000
Asset 3	20,000	30,000
Asset 4	30,000	40,000
	$75,000	$100,000

ABC Co. would allocate the $90,000 purchase price among the assets based on the relative fair values in the following manner.

	Cost
Asset 1	$9,000
Asset 2	18,000
Asset 3	27,000
Asset 4	36,000
	$90,000

By comparison, if ABC purchases the four assets for any amount which exceeds their $100,000 cumulative fair value in a transaction that qualifies as a "business combination," a term which we will discuss later starting on page 660, *infra*, the excess represents goodwill, which we will also describe in that same discussion.

(4) Acquisition by Gift

When an enterprise acquires an asset through a gift or nonreciprocal transfer, a situation common to not-for-profits, but rare in the business context, a strict application of the historical cost principle would require the enterprise to assign a zero cost to the asset. Accountants, however, typically use the asset's appraised value or fair market value to establish cost for subsequent depreciation calculations. In this situation, the enterprise would normally debit the particular asset account and might credit a Donated Capital account.

c. ASSET RETIREMENT OBLIGATIONS

Some tangible long-lived assets, such as nuclear power plants, strip and other mines, oil and gas wells and their production platforms, and landfills, require substantial decommissioning, clean-up, or removal costs when an enterprise retires such assets from service. Until a new accounting standard became effective, diverse accounting practices existed for these asset retirement obligations (AROs). Some enterprises accrued such obligations ratably over the related asset's useful life, either as a component of depreciation expense, with a corresponding increase to accumulated depreciation, or as a liability. Other enterprises did not recognize liabilities for AROs until the enterprise retired the underlying asset. These divergent accounting practices left it very difficult to compare the financial statements of enterprises that faced similar obligations but accounted for them differently.

Under FASB ASC Subtopic 410-20, Asset Retirement and Environmental Obligations—Asset Retirement Obligations, which codified SFAS No. 143, *Accounting for Asset Retirement Obligations,* an enterprise must record the fair value of a liability arising from a legal obligation associated with the retirement of a tangible long-lived asset in the period in which the enterprise can reasonably estimate the liability, capitalize the related costs as part of the long-lived asset's carrying amount, and allocate those costs to expense over the asset's useful life. The Codification defines a legal obligation as an obligation that an existing or enacted law, statute, ordinance, written or oral contract, or that the doctrine of promissory estoppel requires the enterprise to fulfill. The rules, however, do not apply to obligations that arise when an enterprise improperly operates an asset or decides to sell or otherwise dispose of an long-lived asset, and to certain lessee obligations. When the enterprise satisfies the obligation subject to the rules, the enterprise either discharges the liability for its recorded amount or recognizes a gain or loss on the satisfaction. In addition, the enterprise must describe AROs and reconcile changes in the components of such obligations. FASB ASC Subtopic 410-20 (a codification of Accounting for Asset Retirement Obligations, Statement of Fin. Accounting Standards No. 143 (Fin. Accounting Standards Bd. 2001)). The Codification also clarifies that an enterprise must immediately recognize a liability for a conditional asset retirement obligation when incurred, generally upon acquisition, construction, development, or normal operation, even though uncertainty about the timing or method of settlement may exist. Although an enterprise may consider the uncertainty in measuring the liability, the enterprise must recognize the ARO if the circumstances allow it to reasonably estimate the obligation. FASB ASC Subtopic 410-20 (codifying Accounting for Conditional Asset Retirement Obligations, FASB Interpretation No. 47 (Fin. Accounting Standards Bd. 2005)).

2. Salvage Value

As outlined above and discussed more fully below, depreciation accounting allocates the costs to acquire a fixed asset to the different accounting periods that benefit from the asset's use based on the asset's historical cost and estimated *salvage value*. If an enterprise anticipates recovering a portion of the acquisition cost at disposal, the enterprise should reduce the amount otherwise allocable to the different accounting periods expected to benefit from the asset's use.

Salvage value reflects the residual amount that an enterprise expects to receive upon the asset's disposition at the end of its anticipated useful life to the enterprise. In other words, salvage value represents an asset's estimated future trade-in value or selling price. If an enterprise expects disposal to involve additional removal or selling costs, the enterprise uses "net" salvage value to determine the costs to allocate to the various accounting periods. To illustrate, assume that Z Corp. purchases an asset for $100,000 and expects to sell the asset for $15,000 at the end of the asset's useful life in ten years. Further assume that Z Corp. expects to incur $1,000 in costs to remove the assets from its manufacturing facility and to pay a $1,500 commission on the sale. In these circumstances, Z Corp. would use a $12,500 net salvage value which represents the $15,000 estimated selling price minus the $1,000 removal costs and the $1,500 selling commission. Accordingly, Z Corp. would allocate $87,500, the difference between the $100,000 acquisition cost and the $12,500 net residual value, to the accounting periods that Z Corp. expects to benefit from the asset's use.

3.   USEFUL LIFE

Unlike many deferred expenses, such as prepaid insurance, an enterprise usually cannot precisely ascertain a tangible fixed asset's useful life or *service life* for several reasons. First, service lives often differ from physical lives. An asset may possess the physical capability to continue production for years longer than the estimated useful life, but most enterprises will not continue to use facilities when asset inefficiencies cause production costs to increase. Accountants, therefore, consider obsolescence estimations to assess useful lives. Fixed assets may become inadequate when an enterprise's production characteristics change or when a product's nature changes over time. In addition, new technologies may afford faster or more efficient production, rendering current facilities obsolete. In many cases, accountants simply select arbitrary useful lives. In some situations, an accountant may employ statistical methods and engineering studies in an attempt to determine more precisely an asset's useful life. An entity's past experience with similar assets, and perhaps the experiences of other businesses in the same industry, can also assist in determining the estimated useful service lives of assets. As a practical matter, management usually must resort to estimation, and businesses often maintain schedules of their useful life policies.

Most businesses express a fixed asset's useful life in units of accounting periods, such as years or months. Occasionally, however, a different measure may prove more convenient. For example, an enterprise may express a machine's useful life in terms of estimated hours of running time, in which event the amount which the enterprise treats as depreciation expense during any accounting period will depend upon the number of hours that the machine actually operated during the period. Alternatively, an enterprise might use the estimated total number of items that the machine will produce in its lifetime to measure useful life. In that event, the number of items produced in a particular accounting period will determine depreciation expense for the period.

If an enterprise typically uses capital assets for less than their normal life, the enterprise will use the actual useful life to the business for depreciation purposes. For example, an automobile rental company which rents cars for only one or two years and then sells them to a used car dealer would allocate the difference between cost and wholesale value to the accounting periods of actual use.

Although, as we have previously explained, enterprises cannot depreciate land for financial accounting purposes, they can depreciate *land improvements*, such as parking lots, fences, sidewalks and street lights, because these assets have limited useful lives.

Once an enterprise has determined an asset's useful life, the enterprise can calculate depreciation expense. But before beginning the calculation, the enterprise must select a depreciation method.

4. DEPRECIATION METHODS

As we defined the term earlier in the chapter, depreciation accounting employs methods that allocate the costs to acquire assets to different accounting periods in a "systematic and rational" manner. Over the years, accountants have used various techniques for this purpose. These techniques include the units-of-activity method, the straight-line method, and several accelerated methods, including the sum-of-the-years'-digits and declining-balance. To illustrate these methods, assume that Trahan Co. acquires an asset with the following characteristics:

Cost	$12,000
Projected salvage value	$2,000
Expected productive hours	20,000 hours
Estimated useful life	Four years

Accountants sometimes refer to the difference between cost and anticipated salvage value as the *depreciable base*. With a $12,000 cost and a $2,000 projected salvage value, Trahan Co. would use $10,000 as the asset's depreciable base.

a. UNITS-OF-ACTIVITY (OR UNITS-OF-PRODUCTION) METHOD

If depreciation of a fixed asset relies on a function of use or productivity instead of the more common passage of time, an enterprise may adopt an activity or unit method of accounting for depreciation that bases the asset's usefulness upon either an estimated output or number of hours of productive capacity. Notice that enterprises desiring to manipulate income levels can report lower depreciation expenses during periods of low productivity and higher depreciation charges in periods of higher productivity by either adopting or switching to activity or unit methods.

Based on the Trahan Co. data provided above, we can compute the depreciation expense per hour as follows:

$$\text{Depreciation charge per unit} = \frac{\text{Depreciable base}}{\text{Estimated useful life in units}}$$
$$= \frac{\$10,000}{20,000 \text{ hours}}$$
$$= \$.50 \text{ per hour}$$

If Trahan Co. uses the asset for 1,500 hours during the accounting period, the depreciation expense for the period equals 1,500 hours times $.50 per hour, or $750.

b.   STRAIGHT-LINE METHOD

The straight-line method allocates an equal amount of the depreciable base to each period in an asset's estimated useful life. Enterprises almost always use this method to amortize the costs to acquire intangibles and often apply this method to depreciate tangible assets for financial statement purposes because the method offers a computational advantage. The following formula represents the straight-line depreciation charge computation:

$$\text{Depreciation charge per accounting period} = \frac{\text{Depreciable base}}{\text{Estimated useful life in periods}}$$
$$= \frac{\$10,000}{\text{Four years}}$$
$$= \$2,500 \text{ per year}$$

Assuming Trahan Co. places the asset in service at the beginning of the first year and uses the asset during its entire estimated life, Trahan will record the same depreciation expense for each year as follows:

	Depreciation Expense
Year 1	$2,500
Year 2	2,500
Year 3	2,500
Year 4	2,500
	$10,000

c.   ACCELERATED METHODS

In 1947, the Committee on Accounting Procedure suggested in ARB No. 33, later Chapter 9 of ARB No. 43, that enterprises could use depreciation methods other than straight-line if the asset's expected economic usefulness justified the method. *See* RESTATEMENT AND REVISION OF ACCOUNTING

RESEARCH BULLETINS, Accounting Research Bulletin No. 43, ch. 9 (Am. Inst. of Certified Pub. Accountants 1953) (relevant portions now codified at FASB ASC ¶¶ 360-10-35-4 & -7). That pronouncement led numerous companies to experiment with accelerated depreciation, which allocates a greater share of an asset's total cost to the earliest years of its life when the asset enjoys the greatest, or at least most predictable, usefulness. These efforts ultimately led to more formal "declining charges" methods, under which the depreciation charge is highest in the first year and declines progressively each year thereafter.

Among the reasons advanced in support of accelerated depreciation methods was the fact that annual maintenance costs usually rise as an asset grows older. Therefore, declining depreciation charges result in the total expenses associated with an asset remaining reasonably level over the asset's useful life. Another justification suggested is that heavier depreciation charges at the outset tend to correspond with the decline in the realizable value of the asset, which is usually greatest in the earliest years of use. Such parallelism is viewed as a plus by all who favor having balance sheet figures correspond as closely to value as possible, though of course it is acknowledged that depreciation accounting does not seek to reflect diminution in realizable value as such. Finally, there is the point that most decisions about expansion of capacity, and maybe even ordinary replacement, are made on the basis of relatively short-term needs, because projections beyond that are regarded as too speculative to be useful. Since the anticipated benefits are more certain in the earliest years, it is appropriate to allocate a greater portion of the total cost of the asset to those years.

Accelerated depreciation received a substantial boost in 1954 when Congress approved declining charges methods for tax purposes in the Internal Revenue Code. Shortly after, the Committee on Accounting Procedure added its official imprimatur of approval to declining charges methods of depreciation as follows:

> The declining-balance method is one of those which meets the requirements of being "systematic and rational." In those cases where the expected productivity or revenue-earning power of the asset is relatively greater during the earlier years of its life, or where maintenance charges tend to increase during the later years, the declining-balance method may well provide the most satisfactory allocation of cost. The conclusions of this bulletin also apply to other methods, including the "sum-of-the-years'-digits" method, which produce substantially similar results.

FASB ASC ¶ 360-10-35-7 (essentially a codification of DECLINING-BALANCING DEPRECIATION, Accounting Research Bulletin No. 44, ¶ 2 (Am. Inst. of Certified Pub. Accountants 1954), which was revised in 1958 and superseded in 1987 in connection with accounting for differences in tax treatment not here material).

The two most commonly used accelerated depreciation systems, the "sum-of-the-years'-digits" method, and the "declining-balance" method are described below.

(1) Sum-of-the-Years'–Digits

The sum-of-the-years'-digits method produces a decreasing depreciation charge as a function of a declining fraction of the depreciable base, again cost less estimated salvage value. Each year's applicable fraction uses the remaining years of useful life as the numerator. For example, in the first year of an estimated four-year useful life, the asset has four years of useful life left, so the numerator equals four. The numerator drops to three in the second year because three years would remain in the asset's estimated useful life after the use in the first year, then to two in the third year, and finally to one in the fourth year.

For the denominator, accountants sum the digits associated with each year of estimated useful life. For an asset with a four year useful life, the denominator for each year's fraction stays constant at 10 (1+2+3+4 = 10); when an asset has a longer useful life, an accountant might use the formula n(n+1)/2 to determine the applicable denominator, as in 4(4+1)/2 = 10 or 10(10+1)/2 = 55.

To determine the applicable depreciation for each year, multiply the decreasing fraction by the constant depreciable base. The fraction for year 1, therefore, becomes four divided by ten or 4/10ths; year 2 is 3/10ths, year 3 equals 2/10ths, and year 4 gets the remaining 1/10th. Upon making the final calculation in year 4, the end of the asset's useful life, the balance remaining (historical cost less accumulated depreciation) should equal the estimated salvage value.

Based on the Trahan Co. data provided, the sum-of-the-years'-digits calculations for depreciation over the four year useful life are illustrated below:

	Fraction	Depreciation Base	Depreciation Expense
Year 1	4/10	$10,000	$ 4,000
Year 2	3/10	10,000	3,000
Year 3	2/10	10,000	2,000
Year 4	1/10	10,000	1,000
			$10,000

(2) Declining-Balance Methods

The declining-balance method also involves decreasing depreciation charges, but uses a constant depreciation rate based on a specified multiple of the straight-line rate. To illustrate, an asset with a four-year useful life allocates twenty-five percent of the depreciable base, or the historical cost less the estimated salvage value, to each year in the expected useful life under the straight-line method. Thus, the 150 percent declining balance method would assign 1.5 times the straight-line rate of twenty five percent, or 37.5 percent, of the asset's unallocated cost to depreciation each year. Similarly, the 200 percent declining balance method would treat twice the twenty-five percent straight line rate, or fifty percent of the remaining cost, as depreciation each year. Under the declining-balance methods, each year's depreciation reduces the remaining depreciable amount. The applicable rate does not change and applies to the remaining book value each year. Because the depreciable amount itself declines, the constant rate produces lower depreciation in each successive year.

Please note that contrary to previously described methods, the declining-balance method does not utilize salvage value to compute the depreciable amount. Instead, the declining-balance calculation continues until the depreciable amount of the asset drops to the estimated salvage value, at which time depreciation ceases with respect to that asset.

By applying the 150 percent declining depreciation method to Trahan Co. data, we determine the following results:

Year	Calculation	Depreciation Expense	Remaining Balance
0			$12,000.00
1	$12,000.00 x ¼ x 150%	$ 4,500.00	7,500.00
2	$7,500.00 x ¼ x 150%	2,812.50	4,687.50
3	$4,687.50 x ¼ x 150%	1,757.82	2,929.68
4	$2,929.68 x ¼ x 150%	929.68	2,000.00
	Total	$10,000.00	

You should note that except for the rule that depreciation cannot drop the remaining balance below the $2,000 salvage value, depreciation expense for Year 4 would have equaled $1,098.63 ($2,929.68 x 1/4 x 150%).

Similarly, we could apply the double declining depreciation method to Trahan Co. as follows:

Year	Calculation	Depreciation Expense	Remaining Balance
0			$12,000.00
1	$12,000.00 x ¼ x 200%	$ 6,000.00	6,000.00
2	$6,000.00 x ¼ x 200%	3,000.00	3,000.00
3	$3,000.00 x ¼ x 200%	1,000.00	2,000.00
4	$2,000.00 x ¼ x 200%	-0-	2,000.00
	Total	$10,000.00	

Once again, please note that but for the rule that depreciation cannot drop the remaining balance below the $2,000 salvage value, depreciation expense for Year 3 would have equaled $1,500 ($3,000 x 1/4 x 200%). In addition, because Trahan Co. has already allocated the entire $10,000 difference between the $12,000 purchase price and the $2,000 salvage value to depreciation expense in Years 1, 2 and 3, Trahan Co. cannot allocate any amount to depreciation expense in Year 4.

d. ILLUSTRATION OF THE EFFECTS OF THE DIFFERENT DEPRECIATION METHODS ON DEPRECIATION EXPENSE

To recap, the different depreciation methods produce different amounts for depreciation expense in different accounting periods. The following chart summarizes the timing differences in our relatively simple example:

Year	Straight Line Method	Sum-of-the-Years'-Digits Method	150% Declining Balance	200% Declining Balance
1	$2,500	$ 4,000	$ 4,500	$ 6,000
2	2,500	3,000	2,813	3,000
3	2,500	2,000	1,758	1,000
4	2,500	1,000	929	-0-
Totals	$10,000	$10,000	$10,000	$10,000

You should observe that the selection of a depreciation method can significantly affect the financial statements and especially net income for a particular accounting period. You should also note that the accelerated methods treat greater portions of an asset's cost as expense in the early accounting periods following the asset's acquisition.

As a general rule, an enterprise's management typically prefers to report as much net income as possible to the enterprise's owners for financial accounting purposes, which means that we would expect enterprises to use the straight-line method which minimizes depreciation expenses in the accounting periods immediately following a capital expenditure. Although slightly dated, the most recent AICPA annual surveys of the accounting practices used in the annual reports of at least 500 publicly traded, but non-regulated, industrial, merchandising and service companies confirm that almost all of the firms in the surveys selected the straight-line depreciation method for financial accounting purposes. As the following chart indicates, however, some companies used more than one method:

	Number of Entities		
	2011	**2010**	**2009**
Straight line.	490	492	488
Declining balance.	9	10	10
Sum of the years' digits.	2	2	3
Accelerated method–not specified.	9	13	17
Units of production.	12	15	16
Group/composite.	17	4	10

Am. Inst. of Certified Pub. Accountants, ACCOUNTING TRENDS & TECHNIQUES[:] U.S. GAAP FINANCIAL STATEMENTS–BEST PRACTICES IN PRESENTATION AND DISCLOSURE 416 (66th ed. 2012). Observe that in the text under the heading "Property, Plant and Equipment" in Note 1 to the financial statements on page 56 of Starbucks' Form 10-K for the fiscal year ending September 30, 2012, which appears in Appendix A on page 752, *infra*, the company states that it uses the straight-line method to depreciate fixed assets over estimated useful lives, generally ranging from two to fifteen years for equipment and thirty to forty years for buildings.

When drafting and negotiating agreements and legal documents implicating the income statement, the accounting estimates and method or methods for computing depreciation will likely represent very important variables. A lawyer should keep in mind that, in management's discretion, a single enterprise could use a number of different bases for computing depreciation for financial accounting purposes and, as described below, still others for tax purposes. To illustrate, an enterprise may depreciate some assets on an accelerated basis, while using the straight-line method to depreciate others. As another example, an enterprise could assign disparate useful lives to similar leasehold improvements located in different premises, based upon the length of the company's leases. As a final example, management may revise various accounting estimates. As a result, an agreement does well to establish some basic guidelines for computing depreciation. For example, a profit-sharing agreement with a labor union may require the enterprise to compute depreciation on a straight-line basis, using useful lives based upon a specified schedule, such as five years for motor vehicles, ten years for machinery and equipment, and forty years for buildings. In addition, an agreement may restrict the enterprise's ability to change accounting estimates. Many agreements attempt to address this issue by stating that the enterprise will compute depreciation on a basis consistent with past practices. Such language, however, does not adequately resolve issues which may arise when the enterprise purchases assets different in kind from those which the enterprise has previously utilized. Finally, some agreements may want to limit the amount that management can treat as repair expense during any particular accounting period. Terry Lloyd, *Financial Language in Legal Documents*, ACCOUNTING FOR LAWYERS 1994 at 302–03 (1994).

NOTE ON CHANGES IN ACCOUNTING PRINCIPLES AND ESTIMATES

You may recall from Chapter IV on pages 276 to 278, *supra*, that U.S. GAAP draws a distinction between changes in accounting estimates and changes in accounting principles. Depreciation accounting offers another opportunity to illustrate that distinction. As described above, depreciation accounting involves management's estimates as to an asset's salvage value and useful life. As with other estimates, an enterprise's management should periodically review estimated useful lives and salvage values to evaluate the continuing soundness of the previous assumptions affecting depreciation calculations. If necessary, management can, in its discretion, revise those estimates. By comparison, an enterprise can only change the depreciation method used for an asset, say from the straight-line method to an accelerated depreciation method, if the new method qualifies as "preferable."

FASB ASC Topic 250, *Accounting Changes and Error Corrections,* now contains the rules originally announced in APB Opinion No. 20, but later incorporated in SFAS No. 154, that address how an enterprise should handle revisions in salvage values or estimated useful lives and other changes in accounting estimates. Under the Codification, if management decides to revise estimated salvage values or useful lives, the enterprise will reflect those changes in the financial statements for the current and future periods only. The enterprise does not correct any previously issued financial statements. Most significantly, however, changes in useful life or salvage value need not satisfy the "preferability" requirement. FASB ASC Topic 250, *Accounting Changes and Error Corrections* (a codification of ACCOUNTING CHANGES AND ERROR CORRECTIONS—A REPLACEMENT OF APB OPINION NO. 20 AND FASB STATEMENT NO. 3, Statement of Fin. Accounting Standards No. 154 (Fin. Accounting Standards Bd. 2005)).

If management decides to extend an asset's useful life beyond the original estimate, the enterprise bases current and future depreciation calculations on the remaining depreciable amount over the remaining estimated useful life. For example, suppose that an enterprise spends $100,000 to purchase a machine which the enterprise expects to sell for $10,000 at the end of its expected six-year useful life. Assuming straight-line depreciation, the enterprise would treat $15,000 per year as depreciation expense [($100,000 cost less $10,000 salvage value) divided by six-year estimated useful life]. Further suppose that in the fourth year, and after treating $45,000 as depreciation expense during the first three years, management estimates that salvage value will remain at $10,000, but that the machine will last five more years, meaning that the machine will have a useful life totaling eight years rather than the six years originally estimated. Although the enterprise has overestimated depreciation and understated income for the first three years by treating $15,000 rather than $11,250 [($100,000 cost less $10,000 salvage value) divided by eight-year revised estimated useful life] as depreciation expense each year, U.S. GAAP precludes the enterprise from adjusting the previously reported results. Instead, the enterprise will calculate depreciation for the current and subsequent periods by dividing the asset's remaining book value less any salvage value by the asset's remaining estimated life. Depreciation expense for years four through eight, therefore, would equal $9,000 per year ([($100,000 cost less $45,000 accumulated depreciation for the first three years) less $10,000 salvage value] divided by five years). Under FASB ASC Topic 250, *Accounting Changes and Error Corrections*, the Codification requires the enterprise to disclose any material changes in estimates in the notes to the financial statements.

5. USE DURING ACCOUNTING PERIOD

Depreciable assets are often purchased during an accounting period or disposed of before the end of an accounting period. In either case, depreciation calculations are adjusted to consider the partial period of ownership. Under straight-line methods, the fraction of the year the asset was subject to depreciation is multiplied by the full-year straight-line amount. With the accelerated methods, the computation again originates with a full year's depreciation and is reduced to the fraction of the year the company held the asset.

This procedure results in full years' depreciation in future years, with a another partial year depreciation in the final year of the asset's useful life. For example, a 10 year asset purchased July 1, year 1 produces one-half year depreciation in year 1, full years' depreciation in years 2–10 and another one-half year depreciation in year 11.

NOTE ON TAX DEPRECIATION AND DEFERRED INCOME TAXES

As already mentioned, an enterprise's management typically prefers to report as much net income as possible to the enterprise's owners for financial accounting purposes while keeping taxable income, and hence income taxes, as low as possible. By using accelerated depreciation for tax purposes and straight-line depreciation for financial accounting purposes, an enterprise's management can usually accomplish these twin objectives. Unlike the conformity requirement which requires an enterprise to use LIFO for financial accounting purposes if the enterprise adopts that method for tax purposes, no such rule limits the selection of different depreciation methods for tax and financial accounting purposes.

For federal income tax purposes, the Modified Accelerated Cost Recovery System ("MACRS") in section 168 of the Internal Revenue Code sets forth the current rules for depreciating most tangible assets used in a trade or business or held for investment. 26 U.S.C. § 168 (2012). Keep in mind, however, that taxpayers cannot depreciate land. Section 168(b)(4) treats the salvage value for all eligible tangible property as zero; establishes its own set of useful lives for various types of assets, under the rubric of "applicable recovery period;" and adopts certain conventions for dealing with the acquisition and retirement of assets in the midst of a taxable year. To encourage economic growth and investment, section 168(c)(1) specifies recovery periods significantly shorter than most assets' expected useful lives. Those periods range from three years for certain race horses to fifty years for railroad grading or tunnel bores. Under section 168(b), the applicable recovery period generally determines the depreciation method. As a general rule, taxpayers can depreciate property having recovery periods which do not exceed ten years under the 200 percent declining-balance method, switching to the straight-line method when straight-line produces a larger deduction. If the recovery period does not exceed twenty years, taxpayers can use the 150 percent declining-balance method, again switching to straight-line when advantageous to do so. MACRS requires taxpayers to use the straight-line method to depreciate real property and related improvements. Finally, the applicable convention determines how much depreciation a taxpayer may claim in the years in which the taxpayer places an asset in service and retires the property from service. As general rules, MACRS requires taxpayers to use the half-year convention for personal property and the mid-month convention for real property. The half-year convention treats all property placed in service during any taxable year as placed in service on the mid-point of the taxable year. As a result, taxpayers can generally claim a half-year's depreciation on any depreciable personal property placed in service or sold during the year. The mid-month convention gives a taxpayer a half-month's depreciation on any real property placed in service or sold during the month.

An important complication, however, arises from using different depreciation methods for tax and financial accounting purposes. Although an enterprise can generally depreciate an asset faster for tax purposes than for financial accounting purposes, the enterprise cannot allocate any more than an asset's actual cost to the different accounting periods that benefit from the asset's use under any depreciation system. In other words, increased depreciation expenses in earlier accounting periods under an accelerated depreciation method will produce smaller depreciation expenses in later periods, relative to the straight-line method.

When an enterprise's income for financial accounting purposes exceeds its income for tax purposes, the government has essentially allowed the enterprise to defer some of its income tax expense to a later accounting period. To illustrate, let us return to the example involving the asset that Trahan Co. acquired on page 643, *supra*. Assume that the asset generates $7,500 in income each year, net of any expenses other than depreciation, and that the company pays income taxes at a forty percent rate. The following table shows the differences between the company's net income using the 200 percent declining-balance method to compute depreciation for tax purposes and the straight-line method for financial accounting purposes and the amounts for Year 1 in the summary chart on page 647, *supra*:

	Tax Purposes	Financial Accounting Purposes
Income Before Depreciation	$7,500	$7,500
Depreciation	6,000	2,500
Income Before Taxes	$1,500	$5,000
Income Taxes	600	2,000
Net Income	$ 900	$3,000

Even though the financial statements show $2,000 in income tax expense, Trahan Co. only actually owes the government $600 for Year 1. In some future accounting periods, however, the company's taxable income will exceed its income for financial accounting purposes by $3,500, the difference between the $6,000 in depreciation for tax purposes and the $2,500 for financial accounting purposes. Assuming that a forty percent tax rate will apply to all future periods, the tax laws allow the company to postpone the payment of $1,400 in income taxes. But to stay consistent with the lower depreciation expense and higher net income shown on the financial accounting statements, this $1,400 in additional taxes really belongs in Year 1 and Trahan Co. should accrue that amount as income tax expense, just as the company would record any other expense which the company has incurred, but not paid. In other words, for financial accounting purposes, the income tax expense for Year 1 should reflect both the $600 in income taxes that Trahan Co. actually owes now and the $1,400 in additional taxes which the tax laws allow the company to defer currently, but which the company will have to pay when depreciation for financial accounting purposes exceeds tax depreciation. Accordingly, Trahan Co. would record the following entry to reflect income tax expense and income taxes payable for Year 1:

Income Tax Expense	$2,000	
Income Taxes Payable		$600
Deferred Income Tax Liability		1,400

For this reason, a deferred income tax liability may appear on an enterprise's balance sheet, usually as a long-term obligation. Unlike other liabilities, however, a deferred income tax liability does not reflect a present obligation to pay taxes to the government. The enterprise's future taxable income will determine whether the enterprise will owe any amount as income taxes in the future. In addition, if the enterprise continues to purchase new assets, either to expand its operations or to replace older property, with the resulting much higher depreciation on those new assets for tax purposes during the earliest years of useful life, the total depreciation for financial accounting purposes may never exceed tax depreciation, and the income tax deferral may never reverse itself.

As the converse, when taxable income exceeds income for financial accounting purposes, the enterprise effectively prepays taxes. You may recall from Chapter VI on page 485, *supra*, that for tax purposes enterprises cannot deduct accrued liabilities until they satisfy the "all events test" and the economic performance requirements in section 461(h) of the Internal Revenue Code. As a result, enterprises frequently cannot deduct, for tax purposes, accrued warranty expenses that they include in their financial statements. To illustrate, assume that Neiers Company earns $750,000 in income, before $250,000 in warranty expense that we accrued on page 501, *supra*, and that the company pays income taxes at a forty percent rate. The following table shows the differences between the company's net income, without the warranty expense for tax purpose and with the expense for financial accounting purposes:

	Tax Purposes	Financial Accounting Purposes
Income Before Warranty Expense	$750,000	$750,000
Warranty Expense	–0–	250,000
Income Before Taxes	$750,000	$500,000
Income Taxes	300,000	200,000
Net Income	$450,000	$300,000

The tax laws require Neiers Company to pay $300,000 in income taxes to the government even though the company's financial statements only show $200,000 as income tax expense. How should the company treat the additional $100,000? If the company actually incurs the warranty expense in the future, its income for financial accounting purposes will exceed its taxable income in some future period, because the company has already subtracted the warranty expenses for financial accounting purposes. Assuming that a forty percent tax rate will apply to all future periods and that Neiers Company will ultimately spend the entire $250,000 on warranty expenses, such expenditures will reduce the company's future income tax liability by $100,000. In other words, the tax laws that prevent taxpayers from deducting warranty expenses until economic performance has occurred have forced the company to prepay $100,000 in income taxes. Once again, to achieve the proper matching for financial accounting purposes, the company should defer this amount, just as the company would defer any prepaid expense item. In other words, for financial accounting purposes, the $300,000 in income taxes payable should reflect both the $200,000 in income tax expense for the current year and the $100,000 prepayment that accountants often describe as a *deferred tax asset*. Under these assumptions, Neiers Company would record the following entry to reflect income tax expense and income taxes payable for the current year:

Income Tax Expense	$200,000	
Deferred Tax Asset	100,000	
Income Taxes Payable		$300,000

In such circumstances, a deferred income tax asset would appear on an enterprise's books. A deferred income tax asset, however, does not mean that the enterprise can claim a tax refund from the government. In fact, the tax savings from the accrued warranty expense may never actually materialize because the tax benefit will result only if the enterprise otherwise generates taxable income. In addition, the tax rates may change. Although beyond the scope of these materials, accounting for deferred income taxes represents one of the most complex and controversial issues in accounting. *See generally* FASBASC Topic 740, *Income Taxes* (a codification of ACCOUNTING FOR INCOME TAXES, Statement of Fin. Accounting Standards No. 109 (Fin. Accounting Standards Bd. 1992)).

When trying to figure out how to allocate tax expense from a later period to an earlier one, we might think about the simpler problem of allocating tax expense within the same period. Consider the case of L Corp., with income before taxes for the year in the amount of $5,000,000. Assuming a tax rate of forty percent, L's taxes for the year would be $2,000,000, and its net income would be $3,000,000. Suppose that during the year L suffers a catastrophe resulting in the loss of property carried on L's books at $1,000,000, for which there is no insurance. This loss would be reflected by a credit eliminating the property and a debit to some "Loss" account, which, as we have seen, is akin to an expense account and would be closed to Profit and Loss. As a result, L's income before taxes for the year would be $4,000,000, and, assuming the loss would also be deductible for tax purposes, L's taxes would be $1,600,000. But suppose that for accounting purposes this catastrophic loss qualified for extraordinary item treatment under ASC Subtopic 225-20, which codified APB No. 30: then on L's income statement the loss should be shown separately from the income from regular operations, so that a user of the financial statements can get a picture of how the enterprise would have fared without this unusual and non-recurring item. The theory of separating out such extraordinary items, it may be recalled, is that the user of the financial statements may be helped to make a more meaningful comparison of this year's performance with that of prior years (in which, presumably, such a loss did not occur), or to make a judgment about the prospects of the enterprise in future years (in which in all likelihood such a loss will not occur).

How should L's income statement portray this data? There are two obvious possibilities:

(a)

Income before Extraordinary Loss and Taxes	$5,000,000
Less: Extraordinary Loss	1,000,000
Income before Taxes	$4,000,000
Less: Taxes	1,600,000
Net Income	$2,400,000

(b)

Income before Extraordinary Loss and Taxes	$5,000,000
Less: Taxes	1,600,000
Income before Extraordinary Loss	$3,400,000
Less: Extraordinary Loss	1,000,000
Net Income	$2,400,000

Both of these approaches appear to separate out the extraordinary loss, and both of course reach the appropriate net income figure. In fact, however, neither one completely disengages the extraordinary item from the results of ordinary operations. Under alternative (a), the extraordinary loss is combined with the pretax income from ordinary operations, to produce the penultimate "Income before Taxes," from which the tax figure is then deducted. But the investor who wants to make some judgments about the future on the basis of how the enterprise fared during the current year in its ordinary operations will presumably want an after-tax figure in that regard, and will not find it readily available if alternative (a) is used.

Alternative (b) is even more troubling. Although it does purport to provide an after-tax figure for income before extraordinary items (which in effect is income from regular operations), that figure is of doubtful significance, if not downright misleading, because it is based upon a tax figure which is substantially affected by the existence of the extraordinary loss, being $400,000 lower than it would have been had no such loss occurred. In other words, the extraordinary item, though reflected separately itself, is still exerting a significant impact upon the after-tax income from regular operations because of the tax effects of the extraordinary loss; the result is a figure for after-tax income from regular operations which is not indicative of how the company would have performed in the absence of such an extraordinary loss.

What seems called for is an approach which will separate out not only the extraordinary loss itself but also its related tax effect, and associate that tax effect directly with the extraordinary item. As already mentioned on pages 282 to 283, that is exactly what GAAP does, in requiring that extraordinary items be listed on the income statement "net of tax"–that is, in the case of a loss, decreased by the tax saving, and if a gain, decreased by the tax burden. Thus, L Corp.'s income statement would appear as follows:

(c)

Income before Taxes	$5,000,000
Less: Taxes	2,000,000
Income before Extraordinary Loss	$3,000,000
Less: Extraordinary Loss, net of tax	600,000
Net Income	$2,400,000

But, perhaps not surprisingly, even this approach has its drawbacks. For example, looking just at presentation (c), would a reader readily discern what the gross loss suffered by L Corp. was? Is that an important figure? How about L's actual tax for the year?

NOTE ON DEPLETION

As defined earlier, depletion allocates the costs to acquire natural resources among the accounting periods in which an enterprise consumes those wasting assets, such as oil and gas reserves, mineral deposits, and timber rights. Like depreciation of long-lived assets, depletion seeks to defer the unexpired costs attributable to such wasting assets to the future accounting periods that will benefit from those expenditures. Unlike fixed assets, however, enterprises physically consume natural resources. Although a complicated and specialized subject, in a nutshell, depletion uses a system akin to the units-of-production depreciation method to allocate the capitalized costs to the accounting periods in which the enterprise consumes the underlying natural resources. The enterprise estimates the total number of recoverable units from the particular wasting asset and divides that number into the total capitalized costs, which includes acquisition, exploration, and in some cases, development costs, to obtain a per unit depletion cost. The enterprise computes the depletion expense for each accounting period by multiplying the number of units withdrawn during the period by the unit depletion costs.

For enterprises like oil and gas companies that must undertake exploration or other costly activity to locate desired wasting assets, a special problem exists: how to deal with the costs of unsuccessful efforts, like drilling wells that do not produce any oil. Generally speaking, U.S. GAAP recognizes two accounting methods, both based on historical costs. Enterprises can either capitalize expenditures for unsuccessful exploration or development as part of the costs of successful endeavors, often referred to as the *full cost* method, or write off costs attributable to unsuccessful efforts immediately, the so-called *successful efforts* method.

PROBLEMS

Problem 9.2. During its recently-ended fiscal year, Z Corp. paid $143,000 in real estate taxes, which the accounting department charged to current tax expense. Analysis at the end of the year revealed that $27,000 of this amount related to a new warehouse which the corporation built during the year, but had not placed in service by the end of the year.

(a) Which of the following year-end adjusting entries, if any, would you recommend?

a.	Warehouse Buildings	$27,000	
	Tax Expense		$27,000
b.	Deferred Expenses	$27,000	
	Tax Expense		$27,000
c.	Prepaid Taxes	$27,000	
	Tax Expense		$27,000

What other information, if any, would you like before resolving this question?

(b) Assume that Z Corp. had issued so-called "income bonds," which require the corporation to pay the specified interest only to the extent that its income statement shows "net earnings" during the year. Would the fact that the corporation had not earned the full amount of interest for the year affect your recommendation?

Problem 9.3. On August 1, Year 1, Bambi Corporation ("Bambi") purchased a new machine on a deferred payment basis. Bambi made a down payment of $1,000 and agreed to make four $2,500 quarterly installments beginning on November 1, Year 1. The cash equivalent price of the machine was $9,500. Bambi incurred and paid installation costs amounting to $300. Bambi estimates that the machine will produce 10,000 widgets over its useful life and have no salvage value. During the quarter ended October 31, Year 1, the machine produced 300 widgets. What should Bambi record as depreciation expense for the quarter ended October 31, Year 1 under the units-of-activity method? Explain briefly, showing your computations.

Problem 9.4. On February 1, Year 1, Jefferson Corporation ("Jefferson") purchased a new machine on a deferred payment basis. Jefferson made a down payment of $5,000 and agreed to make four quarterly installments of $7,500 beginning on November 1, Year 1. The cash equivalent price of the machine was $29,500. Jefferson incurred and paid installation costs amounting to $3,000. Jefferson estimates that the machine will produce 10,000 widgets over its useful life and have no salvage value. During the quarter ended October 31, Year 3, the machine produced 400 widgets. What should Jefferson record as depreciation expense for the quarter ended October 31, Year 3, under the units-of-activity method? Please show your computations.

Problem 9.5A. On January 1, Year 1, the Evans Corporation purchased a new machine for $350,000. The new machine has an estimated useful life of five years and an estimated salvage value of $50,000. Determine the amount of depreciation for Years 1 through 5 and show supporting computations under each of the following depreciation methods:

(1) Straight-line

(2) Sum-of-the-Years'-Digits

(3) 150% Declining-Balance

(4) 200% Declining-Balance

Problem 9.5B. On January 1, Year 1, Action Corporation purchased a new machine for $160,000. The new machine has an estimated useful life of ten years and an estimated salvage value of $10,000. Determine the amount of depreciation for Years 1 through 3 and show supporting computations under each of the following depreciation methods:

(1) Straight-line

(2) Sum-of-the-Years'-Digits

(3) 150% Declining-Balance

(4) 200% Declining-Balance

Problem 9.5C. On July 1, Year 1, the Madison Corporation purchased a new machine for $500,000. The new machine has an estimated useful life of five years and an estimated salvage value of $100,000. Determine the amount of depreciation for Years 1 through 6 and show supporting computations under each of the following depreciation methods:

(1) Straight-line

(2) Sum-of-the-Years'-Digits

(3) 150% Declining-Balance

(4) 200% Declining-Balance

Problem 9.6A. Which method and estimated useful lives did Amazon.com use to depreciate its property, plant and equipment during the fiscal year ended December 31, 2012? Explain briefly how and where you found your answers.

Problem 9.6B. Which method and estimated useful lives did Google use to depreciate its property, plant and equipment during the fiscal year ended December 31, 2012? Explain briefly how and where you found your answers.

Problem 9.6C. Which method and estimated useful lives did UPS use to depreciate its property, plant and equipment during the fiscal year ended December 31, 2012? Explain briefly how and where you found your answers.

Problem 9.7. D Corp. is a manufacturer of pollution control equipment, with its plant located in the Northeast. A couple of years ago, in anticipation of a likely increase in demand for its products, at least in the near term, D decided to expand its operations and undertook construction of a new facility in the Southeast, which would have approximately half the capacity of its existing plant. The new plant cost $2,500,000 and was expected to have a twenty-year life, with no salvage value; it was completed just in time for operations to get underway in earnest at the beginning of D's most recent fiscal year, which ended a couple of months ago. D's Northeastern plant was built fifteen years ago, at a cost of $3,000,000, and its estimated useful life was twenty years, with no salvage value.

D's management has taken note of the sixty-seven percent increase in the cost of adding to its plant capacity, and has accordingly decided that depreciation on the Northeastern plant for the year just ended should be based on the estimated current replacement cost of $5,000,000 rather than its $3,000,000 actual cost, producing depreciation expense for the year on that plant of $250,000 instead of $150,000. In addition, the management decided to charge extra depreciation on the new plant of three percent per year for each of the first three years of useful life, because of the expected intensive use of the new plant for at least that long; that made the depreciation expense on the new plant $200,000 for the year just ended.

Partly as a result of this additional depreciation expense, D's operating results for the year were somewhat disappointing, with net income at only $600,000, down from almost $1,000,000 the year before. However, there were other reasons for this sharp decline in profitability. Although D's production during the year was at record levels, fully utilizing the added capacity of the new plant, there was a distinct softening in the price for D's products, engendered by a very considerable increase in competition from the entry of a number of new firms into the industry. Thus D was able to maintain its share of a growing market only by accepting significantly lower prices and profit margins.

D has outstanding 100,000 shares of preferred stock, which are subject to an Article provision calling for dividends of up to $8 per share to be paid each year, but only if, and to the extent, earned. The Article provision also recites that D's "earnings shall be determined for each year in accordance with currently accepted accounting principles, after making all necessary charges for consumption of resources and other costs accrued and losses incurred during the year."

Assume that D's figures for the year would show the following:

Income before Depreciation		$1,050,000
Less:		
Regular Depreciation on Old Plant	$150,000	
Regular Depreciation on New Plant	125,000	275,000
Income before Extra Depreciation		$775,000
Less:		
Extra Depreciation on Old Plant	$100,000	
Extra Depreciation on New Plant	75,000	175,000
Net Income		$600,000

(1) The directors of D have announced that the dividend on the preferred stock for the year just ended will be $6 per share, and a group of preferred stockholders has consulted your law office as to whether they are entitled to a larger dividend. (In advising them, keep in mind the possible implications of GAAP rules on accounting changes, which are discussed at pages 276 to 278, 648, and 649 of the text.)

(2) Suppose that instead of attempting to charge extra depreciation expense on both of its plants, D charged only the normal depreciation on the old plant, but adopted the declining balance method of depreciation (using double the straight-line rate) on the new plant. How would the preferred stockholders make out in those circumstances?

D.   INTANGIBLE ASSETS AND GOODWILL

Accounting for intangible assets generally resembles accounting for other long-lived assets, but presents additional challenges. As we described in Chapter VI, accounting for deferred costs—an intangible asset—involves the same issues as depreciation accounting for tangible assets: the enterprise allocates the cost over the asset's useful life, or more precisely, the duration of the expected future benefits from the underlying expenditure. (For intangibles, accountants refer to this process of allocating costs as "amortization" rather than depreciation.) In addition, conservatism requires an enterprise to recognize an immediate loss for any non-temporary decline in value of both tangible and intangible assets. If an asset's carrying value, sometimes referred to as net book value, exceeds the asset's fair value, the enterprise must write down the asset on its financial accounting records.

Because intangibles lack physical qualities, documenting their existence, determining their useful lives, and estimating their value requires considerable judgment. In at least one respect, however, accounting for intangibles may offer fewer challenges. Because either contract law or statute often sets a specific period as the useful life for many intangible assets, enterprises frequently do not either need to estimate such useful lives or worry about a salvage value at the end of that life. For example, an underlying contract may establish the useful life for a deferred cost, such as prepaid insurance that the insured might surrender for a refund. By comparison, federal statutes define the durations for patents and copyrights. In those situations where an enterprise cannot readily determine an intangible asset's expected useful life, however, the accounting treatment becomes more challenging. To illustrate, serious doubt may exist as to whether the prospective future benefits will last beyond the current period, and if so, for how long. At the opposite end of the spectrum, the intangible's expected benefits might seem likely to last indefinitely because no foreseeable termination date appears, as with an established trademark.

FASB ASC Topic 350, *Intangibles—Goodwill and Other*, and Topic 805, *Business Combinations*, govern the financial accounting treatment for intangible assets. The Codification divides intangibles into three categories: intangible assets with finite useful lives, intangible assets with indefinite useful lives, and goodwill.

FASB ASC Topic 350, which codified SFAS No. 142, *Goodwill and Other Intangible Assets*, and related promulgations, defines the term "intangible assets" as "[a]ssets (not including financial assets) that lack physical substance" and notes that the term refers to intangible assets other than goodwill. The term "goodwill" means "[a]n asset representing the future economic benefits arising from other assets acquired in a business combination . . . that are not individually identified and separately recognized." FASB ASC § 350-10-20 (codifying GOODWILL AND OTHER INTANGIBLE ASSETS, Statement of Fin. Accounting Standards No. 142, ¶ F1 (Fin. Accounting Standards Bd. 2001)). In a nutshell, goodwill connotes any one or more of the many amorphous factors that contribute to the competitive advantage a business may enjoy, but which an enterprise cannot separate from the business as a whole. Such factors may include a good reputation, strong brands, effective management, solid relationships with suppliers, and a loyal employee base. Because goodwill remains the most amorphous of assets, and usually the one quickest to evaporate if financial difficulty develops, the Codification allocates the consideration in an acquisition to the identifiable assets first, leaving any excess of the total consideration over the fair market value of the other assets as small as possible, and reporting goodwill more conservatively on the balance sheet. We will take a closer look at the accounting treatment for goodwill shortly, after first discussing other intangible assets. Keep in mind, however, that under financial accounting rules goodwill can arise only in a business combination.

The financial accounting treatment for intangible assets and goodwill depends upon whether the enterprise purchased the intangible or internally developed it; whether any acquisition involved a business combination; and whether legal, regulatory, contractual, competitive, economic, or other factors limit the intangible's useful life to the enterprise.

An enterprise must recognize as an expense, when incurred, any costs to internally develop, maintain, or restore intangible assets, including goodwill, that do not qualify as specifically identifiable, that have indeterminate lives, or that inhere in a continuing business and relate to the entity as a whole. With regard to those costs that an enterprise incurs to develop internally specifically identifiable intangible assets, such as patents, trademarks, and franchises, FASB ASC Topic 350, *Intangibles—Goodwill and Other* codifies SFAS No. 142, which carried forward the provisions in APB Opinion No. 17, *Intangible Assets*, that previously allowed the enterprise, in its discretion but subject to the consistency principle, to either defer any costs involved, or in other words, to capitalize them and recognize an asset, or, alternatively, to treat them as expenses. If an enterprise elects to capitalize those costs, FASB ASC Topic 350, *Intangibles—Goodwill and Other*, now applies.

By comparison, an enterprise must capitalize the costs to acquire any intangible asset acquired from third parties, whether individually or with a group of other assets. The rules for initially recognizing and recording purchased intangibles depend upon whether the acquisition involved a business combination. FASB ASC Topic 805, *Business Combinations*, which codified SFAS No. 141(R) on that same topic, defines a business combination as a transaction or other event in which an acquirer obtains control of one or more businesses. The Codification explains control generally as "the direct or indirect ability to determine the direction of management and policies through ownership, contract, or otherwise." FASB ASC § 805-10-20 (a codification of SFAS No. 141(R), ¶ 3).

If the acquisition does not involve a business combination, an enterprise must initially capitalize the costs to acquire any intangible assets from third parties. If the acquisition involves a group of assets, the enterprise must allocate the cost of the entire group to the individual assets acquired, including any intangibles—other than goodwill, because non-combination transactions cannot give rise to goodwill—based on their relative fair market values. FASB ASC Topic 350, *Intangibles—Goodwill and Other*, acknowledges that recognition of intangible assets enhances the usefulness of financial statements in today's business environment, especially in non-combination transactions. In addition, the Codification expressly suggests that an acquired intangible might qualify for treatment as an identifiable asset even if it does not meet either the contractual-legal criterion or the separability criterion, giving as examples specially-trained employees or a unique manufacturing process related to an acquired manufacturing plant. The arm's length bargaining process underlying such transactions can provide reliable evidence as to an asset's existence and fair value.

If the acquisition involves a business combination, FASB ASC Topic 805, again which codified the rules in SFAS No. 141(R) on business combinations, generally requires an enterprise to recognize the assets acquired and liabilities assumed at their acquisition-date fair values. Enterprises must then recognize any remaining portion of the purchase price as goodwill, which the standard defines as the excess of the consideration transferred in the acquisition over the fair values of the assets acquired and liabilities assumed. In 2013, *The Wall Street Journal* reported that companies in the S&P 500 index were carrying $2 trillion in goodwill on their books, including more than $50 billion at AT&T Inc., Bank of America Corp., Berkshire Hathaway Inc., General Electric Co., and Procter & Gamble Co. *See* Emily Chasan & Maxwell Murphy, *Companies Get More Wiggle Room on Soured Deals*, WALL ST. J., Nov. 12, 2013, at B1.

As a disclosure requirement, an enterprise must provide information about goodwill and other intangible assets in the years subsequent to their acquisition. Required disclosures include material changes in the carrying amount of goodwill and intangible assets, the current carrying amounts of finite-lived and indefinite-lived intangibles by asset classes, and the estimated intangible amortization expense for the next five years.

1.   INTANGIBLE ASSETS (OTHER THAN GOODWILL)

The term "intangible assets" includes intellectual property, such as patents and trademarks; assets for deferred costs like prepaid insurance; certain computer software development costs; and other items that either (a) arise from contractual or other legal rights, regardless of whether the enterprise can transfer or otherwise separate those rights from the firm, or (b) exist separately from an enterprise's other assets because the enterprise can sell, transfer, license, rent, or exchange the intangible, regardless of whether the firm intends to do so. Intangibles arising from contractual or other legal rights include patents, trademarks, service marks, broadcast licenses, airline route authorities, and franchises. By comparison, customer lists, noncontractual customer relationships, unpatented technology, and databases satisfy the "separability" criterion.

a. FINITE-LIVED

Once an enterprise has permissibly capitalized a cost related to an intangible asset, whether that cost arises from an internally developed identifiable intangible or an acquisition from a third party, the subsequent accounting depends upon whether legal, regulatory, contractual, competitive, economic, or other factors limit the intangible's useful life to the enterprise. FASB ASC Topic 350, *Intangibles—Goodwill and Other*, requires an enterprise to amortize any intangible asset with a finite useful life over that period. The enterprise also must regularly evaluate any intangible asset being amortized to assess whether the original finite life determination remains sound. If the useful life has changed, the enterprise must adjust the amortization schedule as necessary. If the useful life no longer appears finite, the enterprise must cease amortization, and the accounting rules for indefinite-lived intangibles become applicable.

The Codification defines useful life as the period over which the enterprise expects the intangible asset to contribute directly or indirectly to the firm's future cash flows. If an enterprise cannot determine the precise useful life, the entity should use the best estimate to amortize the intangible. ASC Topic 350 offers additional guidance to assist enterprises in determining the useful life of intangible assets. In particular, the Codification lists the factors enterprises should use to develop assumptions about renewals or extensions related to the useful life of recognized intangible assets. FASB ASC ¶ 350-30-35-3 (a codification of DETERMINATION OF THE USEFUL LIFE OF INTANGIBLE ASSETS, FASB Staff Position No. FAS 142-3 (Fin. Accounting Standards Bd. 2008)).

(1) Impairment Review

In addition to amortizing any definite-lived intangible assets, FASB ASC Topic 360, *Property, Plant, and Equipment*, requires an enterprise to review such assets periodically for any impairment, especially whenever events or changes in circumstances indicate that the enterprise may not recover the asset's carrying amount from expected operating cash flows and proceeds at disposition. FASB ASC Topic 360 codifies the requirements for recognizing an impairment loss that originally appeared in SFAS No. 121, and that SFAS No. 144 reaffirmed. Topic 360, however, specifically does not apply to goodwill, indefinite-lived intangibles, and unproved oil and gas properties for which an enterprise has elected to use the successful-efforts accounting method.

For purposes of this impairment review, "the asset" may actually represent a group of assets, specifically the smallest group of related assets for which the enterprise can estimate identifiable future cash flows independent from those attributable to other groups of assets and liabilities. When events or changing circumstances suggest that the expected cash flows arising from the use and eventual disposition of "the asset," undiscounted and without interest charges, will not enable the enterprise to recover the asset's carrying amount, the enterprise must determine the asset's fair value and, if necessary, recognize an impairment loss. The impairment loss, if any, will equal the difference between asset's carrying amount and its fair value.

Although the balance sheet has never represented a current value statement, the "Impairment or Disposal of Long-Lived Assets" subsections of ASC Topic 360 essentially embraces that approach when accounting for impaired assets held for use in operations, including definite-lived intangibles. Those subsections set forth the circumstances in which an enterprise shall recognize an impairment loss on an asset or group of assets that the enterprise holds for use in its operations. As a starting point, the Codification lists various events or changes in circumstances that indicate that an enterprise should conduct an impairment review. These events and changes in circumstances include:

- A significant decrease in the asset's market value, for example, through technological obsolescence;

- A significant change in the extent or manner in which an enterprise uses the asset;

- A significant physical change in the asset;

- A significant adverse change in the legal factors or business climate that affects the asset's value;

- An adverse action or assessment by a regulator;

- An accumulation of costs that significantly exceeds the amount originally intended to acquire or construct the asset, for example, through cost overruns;

- A current period operating or cash flow loss combined with a history of such losses;

- A projection or forecast demonstrating continuing operating or cash flow losses; and

- A current expectation that the enterprise will more likely than not sell or otherwise dispose of the asset significantly before the end of its previously estimated useful life.

The Codification recognizes, at least implicitly, that an enterprise need not evaluate all assets every year, much less every quarter. As a result, enterprises retain some discretion in deciding when to conduct an impairment review.

(2) Cash Flows Analysis

Once an enterprise has identified events or circumstances that suggest that an impairment may have occurred, a cash flows analysis follows to determine whether an impairment actually exists. The enterprise must conduct this inquiry at the "lowest level" of identifiable cash flows. In the inquiry, an enterprise must estimate the future cash flows that the enterprise expects during the remaining useful life of the asset or asset group and upon its ultimate disposition. For this purpose, ASC Topic 360 establishes a "primary asset" approach that requires the enterprise to identify the principal long-lived tangible asset being depreciated or intangible being amortized. As the most significant component from which the asset group derives its cash-flow generating capacity, the primary asset determines the group's remaining useful life for evaluating cash flows.

Ultimately, a cash flows analysis seeks to determine the expected future cash inflows from the asset in question, and then subtracts the expected future cash outflows necessary to obtain the inflows. If the enterprise develops alternative courses of action to recover the carrying amount or identifies a range for the amount of estimated future cash flows, the "Impairment or Disposal of Long-Lived Assets" subsections of ASC Topic 360 endorse a probability weighted estimation approach to consider the alternative courses of action or range of estimates. If the asset's carrying amount exceeds the sum of the expected net cash flows, undiscounted and without interest charges, then the enterprise must recognize an impairment loss as described in the next section. If the sum of the expected net cash flows exceeds the asset's carrying amount, the enterprise cannot recognize an impairment loss.

(3) Impairment Loss

If the cash flow analysis requires an enterprise to recognize an impairment loss, the "Impairment or Disposal of Long-Lived Assets" subsections of ASC Topic 360, *Property, Plant, and Equipment*, further establish standards for measuring that loss. As a basic principle, the Codification requires the enterprise to determine the asset's fair value and to write-down the asset to that amount.

ASC section 820-10-37, which codified the fair value framework set forth in SFAS No. 157, defines "fair value" as "the price that would be received to sell an asset . . . in an orderly transaction between market participants at the measurement date." The Codification considers quoted market prices in active markets as the best evidence of fair value. For those assets without active markets, ASC Topic 820, *Fair Value Measurement*, requires an enterprise to estimate fair value based on the best information available in the circumstances. In this regard, the enterprise must consider the prices for similar assets and available valuation techniques. The Codification specifically authorizes the discounted cash flows method as long as the enterprise uses a discount rate that reflects the risks involved. Once again, Topic 820 allows an enterprise's management to exercise considerable discretion in estimating expected cash flows and selecting the appropriate discount rate.

If the asset's carrying value exceeds its fair value, the enterprise must write-down the asset to its fair value. The resulting write-down represents the impairment loss. After recognizing an impairment loss, ASC Topic 360, *Property, Plant, and Equipment*, requires the enterprise to treat the reduced carrying amount as the asset's new cost. Once an enterprise has recognized an impairment loss, the enterprise may not reverse or recover that loss if the impairment subsequently disappears. For a definite-lived intangible, the enterprise must then amortize the intangible's new cost over its remaining useful life. To illustrate, Topic 360 would require an enterprise to record a $50,000 impairment loss related to a patent as follows:

Loss for Long-Lived Asset Impairment	$500,000	
Patent		$500,000

Please keep in mind that while an enterprise compares an asset's carrying amount to the asset's fair value to determine the amount of the impairment loss, the enterprise does not use the asset's fair value to determine whether an impairment exists initially.

b. INDEFINITE-LIVED

ASC Topic 350, *Intangibles—Goodwill and Other*, provides that an enterprise may not amortize an intangible asset with an indefinite useful life, such as a trademark, a broadcast or liquor license, or a franchise. ASC § 350-30-35. The term "indefinite" means that no legal, regulatory, contractual, competitive, economic, or other factors limit the intangible's useful life to the enterprise. In other words, the expected cash flows from the intangible extend beyond the foreseeable horizon. ASC ¶ 350-30-35-4. Please note that the FASB deliberately used the term "indefinite," rather than "indeterminate," presumably because the later term conveys difficulty in estimating a useful life.

ASC section 350-30-35 requires an enterprise to evaluate regularly whether an indefinite-lived intangible's useful life has become finite, in which case the enterprise must recognize any loss in the current accounting period and amortize the adjusted carrying value over the intangible's remaining useful life. As set forth in the previous section, if an enterprise cannot determine a precise useful life, the Codification requires the enterprise to use its best estimate to amortize the intangible.

Rather than amortize an intangible that an enterprise expects to last for the indefinitely foreseeable future, ASC Topic 350 requires the enterprise to test the intangible for possible impairment in value at least annually, and more frequently if events or circumstances indicate a more likely than not probability that the intangible has suffered impairment. If the intangible asset's carrying amount exceeds its fair value, the enterprise must recognize an impairment loss equal to that excess.

Although the Codification always required enterprises to test indefinite-lived intangibles and goodwill for impairment at least annually, different rules applied to goodwill. Since 2012, ASC Topic 350 has set forth a two-step process for impairment testing for indefinite-lived intangibles--a qualitative assessment followed by a quantitative comparison. The 2012 amendments, however, give enterprises an option to skip the qualitative assessment for any indefinite-lived asset in any period and to proceed directly to calculating the intangible's fair value in the quantitative comparison. *See* INTANGIBLES—GOODWILL AND OTHER (TOPIC 350): TESTING INDEFINITE-LIVED INTANGIBLE ASSETS GOODWILL FOR IMPAIRMENT, Accounting Standards Update No. 2012-02 (Fin. Accounting Standards Bd.). Please keep in mind that these new rules *do not apply* to finite-lived intangibles, such as technology, copyrights, customer relationships, and covenants not to compete.

In the qualitative assessment, an enterprise evaluates the likelihood that events and circumstances have impaired the indefinite-lived intangible to determine whether or not the enterprise should apply the quantitative test and calculate the asset's fair value. Unless, after considering all relevant events and circumstances, the enterprise determines that a greater than fifty percent chance exists that an indefinite-lived intangible's carrying value exceeds its fair value, the process ends. Consequently and as a practical matter, the optional qualitative assessment often allows an enterprise to avoid the costs necessary to hire an outside valuation expert to calculate the indefinite-lived intangible's fair value.

If the qualitative assessment cannot rule out an impairment, the quantitative comparison measures the amount of the impairment, if any. If the intangible's fair value has declined below its carrying value, the enterprise must write down the asset to fair value and recognize the corresponding loss in the current accounting period. In essence, the asset's fair value becomes its new cost. If the asset's fair value subsequently increases, both the revenue recognition principle and conservatism bar the enterprise from subsequently writing up any recovery.

2.   GOODWILL

Until SFAS No. 142, again now codified in FASB ASC Topic 350, accounting literature identified two separate views about the nature of goodwill. The first view described goodwill as intangible resources arising from a business's competitive advantages. Under the second view, goodwill reflected expected earnings that exceeded a fair return on the assets invested in the business. *See, e.g.*, Accounting for Business Combinations and Purchased Intangibles, FASB Discussion Memorandum 46–50 (Fin. Accounting Standards Bd. 1976).

These different viewpoints lead to distinct methodologies for measuring goodwill in various legal contexts. Lawyers should recognize that these alternative approaches exist because the circumstances surrounding a particular legal problem may suggest using one methodology rather than the other to resolve the matter even though FASB ASC Topic 350 has adopted the first view for financial accounting purposes. Under that method, which accountants have historically referred to as the *residual method*, if X Corp.

pays $250,000 to acquire a business that owns identifiable assets worth $240,000, X would treated the residual amount, or the $10,000 difference between those two figures, as goodwill.

With regard to accounting treatment for goodwill arising from a business combination, FASB ASC Topic 350 currently prohibits public companies from amortizing goodwill. Instead, a public company must use at least a two-step quantitative process to test goodwill for impairment at least annually. Under the first step, the enterprise must screen for impairment by comparing the fair value of each reporting unit with its carrying value, including goodwill. The second step measures the amount of the impairment, if any. If a reporting unit's carrying amount exceeds its fair value, the enterprise must calculate the goodwill's implied fair value by hypothetically applying the acquisition method and measuring the unit's identifiable assets and liabilities as of the date of the impairment test in accordance with ASC Topic 805, *Business Combinations*. If the goodwill has become impaired, the enterprise must write-down the goodwill to its implied fair value and charge current income for the difference between the goodwill's carrying value and its implied fair value. Lawyers should keep in mind that any write-downs reduce equity and could cause an enterprise to violate a covenant in a loan agreement.

Readers of financial statements might view goodwill as a report card for acquisitions and for the executives who did the buying. When an enterprise writes down goodwill, management acknowledges that the enterprise overpaid in a business combination, whether because executives overestimated the financial benefits that would arise from the transaction, the costs to integrate the operations and cultures exceeded expected benefits, or economic or market conditions simply changed. Write-downs, for example, surged during the 2008 financial crisis.

Private companies complained about the quantitative procedure that required enterprises to calculate the fair value of each reporting unit at least annually. In response, FASB issued new rules in 2011 that simplify how both private and public firms test goodwill for impairment. Like the recent amendments for indefinite-lived assets, the new rules add an optional qualitative starting point that allows an enterprise to assess the likelihood that a reporting unit's carrying amount exceeds its fair value. The qualitative factors typically considered include the enterprise's financial performance, industry and economic changes, cost factors, legal and regulatory matters, and other company-specific issues. Unless, after considering all relevant events and circumstances, the enterprise determines that it is more likely than not that a reporting unit's carrying value exceeds its fair value, the enterprise need not perform the two-step, quantitative comparison. As with indefinite-lived intangibles, an enterprise may choose to skip the qualitative assessment for any reporting unit in any period and proceed directly to the quantitative comparison. Once again and practically speaking, therefore, the new rules eliminate the need for many enterprises to calculate the fair values of various reporting units at least annually. *See* Intangibles—Goodwill and Other (Topic 350), Testing Goodwill for Impairment, Accounting Standards Update No. 2011-08 (Fin. Accounting Standards Bd.).

Because the Codification requires judgments and projections, particularly after the amendments that allow enterprises to start with a qualitative assessment, management enjoys considerable leeway when deciding whether to write down goodwill and by how much. Readers should keep in mind that management might use pessimistic projections to write-off assets, including goodwill, acquired in an transaction that predecessors arranged, while adopting optimistic forecasts to avoid or minimize a potential impairment arising from their own acquisitions. When goodwill exceeds a company's market value, the market believes that the company should write-down goodwill, but no accounting rule requires an impairment loss in that situation. *See* Emily Chasan & Maxwell Murphy, *Companies Get More Wiggle Room on Soured Deals*, WALL ST. J., Nov. 12, 2013, at B1; Scott Thurm, *Buyers Beware: The Goodwill Games*, WALL ST. J., Aug. 14, 2012, at B1.

Preparers and auditors of private company financial statements continued to express concerns to the newly created Private Company Council (PCC) about the cost and complexity underlying the process for assessing goodwill impairment. In PCC's outreach to users of private company financial statements, the council learned that users often disregard goodwill and goodwill impairment losses in the analysis of a private company's financial condition and operating performance. Ultimately, PCC concluded that the benefits of the current accounting for goodwill after initial recognition by private companies did not justify the related costs.

Based on this PCC consensus, early in 2014 FASB issued an accounting standards update on accounting for goodwill that gives private companies an option to amortize goodwill on a straight-line basis over ten years. If a private company can demonstrate a shorter, and more appropriate, useful life, the company can amortize goodwill over that period.

Any private company that elects this alternative must adopt an accounting policy to test goodwill for impairment at either the entity level or the reporting unit level. Rather than test goodwill for impairment annually as non-electing enterprises must do, this election allows a private company to conduct such an evaluation only when a triggering event occurs that indicates that the fair value of the applicable entity or the reporting unit may have dropped below the its carrying amount. If a triggering event has occurred, the entity can elect either to perform the qualitative assessment or to proceed directly to a quantitative test to determine whether goodwill has been impaired. If any qualitative assessment concludes that goodwill more likely has not been impaired, the evaluation ends. Otherwise, the entity will apply the quantitative test and record an impairment only if the carrying amount of the entity or reporting unit exceeds its corresponding fair value. In that event, the goodwill impairment loss, which represents the difference between the applicable carrying amount and fair value, cannot exceed the goodwill's carrying amount.

Without jeopardizing relevant information for users of private company financial statements, FASB expects that the combination of the amortization method and the relief from the requirement to test goodwill for impairment at least annually will result in significant cost savings for many private companies that carry goodwill on their balance sheets for at least two reasons. First, amortization should reduce the likelihood that goodwill would suffer an impairment. As a result, private companies will likely test goodwill for impairment less frequently. Second, the ability to test for impairment at the entity-level and the elimination of the second step of the quantitative test that would otherwise require the hypothetical application of the acquisition method to measure the reporting unit's identifiable assets and liabilities as of the date of the impairment test in accordance with ASC Topic 805, *Business Combinations*, to calculate the goodwill's implied fair value should significantly reduce the cost of any impairment test.

If elected, a private company should apply the accounting alternative prospectively to goodwill that exists at the beginning of the period of adoption and to new goodwill recognized in annual periods beginning after December 15, 2014, and in interim periods within annual periods beginning after December 15, 2015. The guidance, however, also allows early application to any period for which a private company's annual or interim financial statements have not yet been made available for issuance. Intangibles—Goodwill and Other (Topic 350): Accounting for Goodwill (a consensus of the Private Company Council), Accounting Standards Update No. 2014-02 (Fin. Accounting Standards Bd. Jan. 2014).

NOTES

1. Goodwill often does not appear on an enterprise's balance sheet. Recall that an enterprise can only record an unidentifiable intangible, such as goodwill, when the enterprise purchases an existing business. Presumably, the "assets" of Starbucks Corporation include both going concern value and its customer loyalty, strong brands, and solid reputation arising from the company's trademarks, marketing success and emphasis on social responsibility above and beyond the $399.1 million in goodwill related to various acquisitions as set forth in Note 8 and that appears on the company's consolidated balance sheet as of September 30, 2012 in Appendix A on page 769, *infra*. Starbucks' going concern value, reputation, brands, customer and supplier loyalty, and emphasis on social responsibility, however, do not appear on the company's balance sheet for financial accounting purposes. Nevertheless, and as the principal case indicates, circumstances sometimes allow an enterprise, its owners, or an adversary to value goodwill or going concern value for other purposes.

2. As part of their joint project on business combinations, the FASB and IASB concluded that enterprises should not treat acquisition-related costs, such as legal, consulting, and due diligence costs, as includible in goodwill. The FASB and IASB believed that the consideration related to the underlying business combination does not include acquisition-related costs. Instead, such costs reflect separate transactions where the buyer pays for the services received. Under FASB ASC Topic 805, *Business Combinations*, which codified SFAS No. 141(R), enterprises now recognize all acquisition-related costs as expenses as incurred, except for any costs to issue debt or equity securities. FASB ASC ¶

805-10-25-23 (a codification of SFAS No. 141(R), ¶¶ 59, B365–66). In addition, the Codification requires acquirers to recognize and measure any IPR&D at acquisition-date fair value, to treat the intangible as indefinite-lived, and to test the asset periodically for impairment, until the enterprise completes or abandons the research and development efforts. FASB ASC ¶¶ 805-20-25-1, 805-20-30-1, 805-20-35-5 (codifications of SFAS No. 141(R), ¶¶ 66, B149–50).

3. Transactional lawyers in particular should understand how the new rules on business combinations, now codified in FASB ASC Topic 805, affect how entities negotiate and structure mergers and acquisitions. The new rules apply to any "business combination," defined as any transaction in which an acquirer obtains control of one or more "businesses." FASB ASC ¶ 805-10-15-3. The standards define "business" broadly as "[a]n integrated set of activities and assets that is capable of being conducted and managed for the purpose of providing a return." FASB ASC § 805-10-20. This expansive definition encompasses a wide variety of transactions.

In many mergers and acquisitions, the acquirer will issue equity interests, such as stock, options, or warrants, as part or all of the consideration in the transaction. The new rules can pose difficulties in estimating the purchase price when the acquirer uses equity-based consideration. The acquirer now measures the consideration transferred, including equity interests, at fair value on the "acquisition date." FASB ASC ¶ 805-30-30-7. The "acquisition date" refers to the date the acquirer obtains control of the acquiree, generally the closing date of the transaction. FASB ASC ¶¶ 805-10-25-6 to -7. The acquirer's stock price can change between the date the acquirer announces the transaction and the actual closing date. Therefore, the purchase price recorded could differ from the initial estimate of the purchase price based on the value of the acquirer's shares on the announcement date. Lawyers can expect acquirers concerned with minimizing such volatility to increase the use of cash consideration or to negotiate a "collar," a cap and floor on pricing, in the acquisition agreement.

The new standards could also impact how acquirers structure "earn outs." In a typical earn out, the acquirer agrees to pay additional consideration after the closing if the acquiree satisfies specified criteria, such as a target level of sales or earnings, within a set time frame. The acquirer and acquiree typically negotiate an earn out when the parties cannot agree on a purchase price that properly values the acquiree. Using the terminology of the business combinations standards, earn outs constitute "contingent consideration." The acquirer must recognize the fair value of any contingent consideration on the acquisition date regardless of the likelihood of the acquiree satisfying the earn out criteria. FASB ASC ¶ 805-30-25-5. Determining the fair value of contingent consideration can involve considerable complexity. The acquirer must determine the likelihood that the acquiree will meet the earn out requirements and discount the required payments appropriately.

The acquirer generally will classify earn outs requiring payment of cash as a liability and those involving share-based payments as equity. FASB ASC ¶ 805-30-25-6. The acquirer must remeasure contingent consideration classified as a liability at fair value at each reporting date until the resolution of the contingency, with changes in fair value recognized in earnings. Contingent consideration classified as equity does not require remeasurement; the acquirer accounts for the subsequent settlement within equity. FASB ASC ¶ 805-30-35-1. Cash earn outs, then, will subject the acquirer to considerable earnings volatility as the acquirer remeasures the contingent consideration liability at each reporting date. Lawyers can anticipate that acquirers seeking to minimize post-acquisition earnings volatility will avoid the use of earn outs, negotiate for a shorter earn out period, or use equity-based consideration in the earn out.

The new standards could also impact how acquirers plan due diligence for proposed and pending transactions. As mentioned in the previous note, acquirers must now expense acquisition-related costs in the period incurred. Such costs include professional fees for lawyers, bankers, accountants, and other advisors. FASB ASC ¶ 805-10-25-23. Acquirers must expense these costs in the period incurred, even if the acquirer announces or closes the transaction in a future period. Observers might anticipate an upcoming deal when an acquirer discloses acquisition-related costs without the formal announcement of a transaction. Lawyers can expect acquirers seeking to avoid early revelation of a potential upcoming transaction to delay the start of due diligence or to compress the time frame for completing such diligence to ensure that acquisition-related costs will appear in the same period as the announcement of the deal.

4. Lawyers representing clients in mergers and acquisitions can commit malpractice if they do not understand how *pushdown accounting* can affect transactions terms, including contingent consideration, puts, and related buy-sell agreements. Under pushdown accounting, an acquired entity establishes a new accounting basis in its separate financial statements, which reflects the acquisition cost, rather than the acquired firm's previous accounting. In one recent case, *Matsumura v. Benihana Nat'l Corp.*, 465 Fed. Appx. 23 (2d Cir. Mar. 5, 2012), the acquirer's use of push down accounting cost the sellers about $1.6 million when they exercised a put option on their remaining shares. When an acquirer incurs debt to finance the transaction, push down accounting allows the parent to record the debt on the newly acquired subsidiary's balance sheet. When Benihana National Corp. ("BNC") bought a controlling intereset in Haru, a company that owned a sushi restaurant chain, the plaintiff sellers retained a put option to sell their remaining shares in Haru, which they later exercised. Put options give the holder the right, but not the obligation, to sell property at a certain price, often called the strike price. When the holder exercises the put, the other party must buy at the strike price. Pursuant to a provision in a related stockholders' agreement, BNC subtracted Haru's debt from the numerator in the formula used to establish the strike price. Because push down accounting increased the amount of debt on Haru's balance sheet, and that debt lowered the strike price, the put option brought the sellers about $1.6 million less than they expected for their twenty percent stake in Haru. The Second Circuit affirmed the district court's ruling that using push down accounting to record the original $8.125 million purchase price as debt on Haru's books did not violate the stockholders' agreement.

Lawyers should keep in mind that the current U.S. GAAP offers only limited guidance for determining whether and when an acquired enterprise can apply pushdown accounting in its separate financial statements after an acquirer obtains control. In particular, section 805-50-S99 of the Codification contains some direction from the SEC staff, which technically does not apply to non-SEC registrants. In addition, considerable diversity in practice exists among non-registrants and the existing guidance does not address various issues that have arisen in practice for all entities. As a result, the Emerging Issues Task Force ("EITF") has undertaken a project to clarify when and how acquired entities can use pushdown accounting. Interested readers can monitor developments regarding Issue No. 12-F, "Recognition of New Accounting Basis (Pushdown) in Certain Circumstances," via the web page describing the recent and current issues before the EITF at http://www.fasb.org/cs/ContentServer?c=Page&pagename=FASB%2FPage%2FSectionPage&cid=1218220137528.

PROBLEMS

Problem 9.8A. Bio–Med, Inc. incurred $175,000 of research and development costs in its laboratory to develop a patent which the U.S. Patent Office granted on January 31, 201X. Legal fees and other costs associated with registration of the patent totaled $35,000. On October 31, 201X, Bio–Med, Inc. paid $50,000 for legal fees in a successful defense of the patent. Through November 1, 201X, how much may Bio–Med capitalize for the patent? Explain briefly.

Problem 9.8B. Mark Company brought a franchise from Brian Corporation on January 1, 20X1 for $200,000. Mark Company hired an independent consultant who estimated that the remaining useful life of the franchise was fifty years. The franchise's unamortized cost on Brian Corporation's books on December 31, 20X0 was $100,000. Mark Company has decided to amortize the franchise over the maximum period allowed under generally accepted accounting principles. What amount can Mark Company amortize for the year ended December 31, 20X1? Explain briefly.

Problem 9.8C. The Gunther Company acquired a gold mine for $1,000,000 at the beginning of 20X1. The company reasonably attributed $250,000 to the land value and $750,000 to the minerals in the mine. Geological surveys indicate that the mine will produce 10,000 ounces of pure gold. Gunther incurred $150,000 in development costs in 20X1, but did not extract any minerals. The company further estimates that it will spend $100,000 to reclaim the land and to comply with various environmental laws in 20X5 after removing all the gold. In Year 20X2, Gunther extracted and sold 1,500 ounces of gold from the mine. What amount should the company expense for 20X2? Explain briefly.

Problem 9.9A. Ivy Clothes, a small, but successful, proprietorship selling men's clothing and accessories, had the following balance sheet at the close of its most recent fiscal year:

Ivy Clothes
Balance Sheet
December 31, 201X

Assets		Liabilities & Proprietorship	
Cash	$ 50,000	Accounts Payable	$ 50,000
Inventory	105,000		
Building Fixtures	65,000	Proprietorship	170,000
Total	$220,000	Total	$220,000

Suppose the proprietor pays off her liabilities and sells all the rest of the assets of her business to a newly-organized corporation, Ivy Corp., for $200,000. Ivy Corp. pays the $200,000 in cash, out of the proceeds of its initial stock issue of $240,000. How should Ivy Corp. record this acquisition on its books? If relevant, assume that an investigation would reveal that the inventory's current replacement cost approximates its book value, but that it would cost $75,000 to replace the building fixtures in their current condition. How do these accounting decisions at the corporation's outset affect the determination of net income in the future?

Problem 9.9B. Y Corp., formed on January 1, paid a $10,000 bill for legal expenses incident to its formation. How should Y Corp. reflect this payment in its financial statements at the end of that year? Explain briefly.

Problem 9.9C. An airline company spent $750,000 during the current year to train personnel on new planes before the company put the planes into commercial use. How should the airline treat this expenditure in its financial statements?

E.   LEASE ACCOUNTING

You will recall from our discussion about revenue recognition in Chapter VI on pages 390 to 397, *supra*, that accountants focus on substance, rather than on form, in deciding whether an enterprise can recognize revenue in a particular exchange transaction. Questions about substance also often arise when an enterprise contracts to use property in exchange for consideration. Even though an agreement may establish a lessor-lessee relationship from a state law standpoint, if the contract transfers substantially all the benefits and risks that accompany ownership, then the Codification may require the parties to treat the "lease" as a purchase by the lessee, as well as either a sale or a financing by the lessor, for financial accounting purposes.

If an enterprise purchases an asset on credit, both the asset and the related liability appear on the enterprise's balance sheet. In some situations, the Codification requires enterprises to account for certain leases following similar rules. If a "lessee" must include the underlying asset and corresponding liability on its balance sheet, such treatment can adversely affect regulatory limits or various financial ratios, such as the debt-equity ratio, and could conceivably cause the enterprise to violate a financial covenant based on that ratio or tangible net book value. As we will see, lease accounting can also affect the lessee's net income in various accounting periods, particularly the periods immediately after the parties sign the "lease."

1.   CLASSIFICATION

Accountants generally classify leases into two basic categories for financial accounting purposes: *operating leases* and *capital leases*. Operating leases represent "true" leases in which the lessor conveys the right to use property, whether land, machinery, equipment or other property, for a stated period in exchange for some consideration. In contrast, capital leases represent installment purchases in substance. When a "lease" transfers substantially all the benefits and risks that accompany ownership, the parties should treat the transaction as though the lessee acquired the property and incurred an offsetting liability.

Generally accepted accounting principles in the United States require an enterprise to classify a lease at its inception. If, at that time, a noncancellable lease meets one or more of the following criteria, FASB ASC Topic 840, *Leases*, which codified SFAS No. 13, *Accounting for Leases*, and numerous pronouncements on lease accounting, requires the lessee to treat the arrangement as a capital lease:

(1) The lease transfers ownership of the property to the lessee.

(2) The lease contains a bargain purchase option.

(3) The lease term equals or exceeds seventy-five percent or more of the leased property's estimated economic life.

(4) The present value of the minimum lease payments, excluding insurance, maintenance, taxes and similar items, equals or exceeds ninety percent of the leased property's fair value.

If the beginning of the lease term occurs during the last twenty-five percent of the leased property's estimated economic life, the Codification does not use either the third or fourth criteria to classify the lease. In addition, the lessee generally uses its *incremental borrowing rate*, defined as the rate lenders would charge the lessee for a secured loan containing repayments terms similar to the payment schedule in the "lease," to determine the present value of the minimum lease payments under the fourth criterion. If the lessee knows the implicit interest rate that the lessor has used to compute the lease payments, however, and the implicit rate falls below the lessee's incremental borrowing rate, then the lessee may use the lessor's implicit rate. FASB ASC Topic 840, *Leases* (a codification of ACCOUNTING FOR LEASES, Statement of Fin. Accounting Standards No. 13 (Fin. Accounting Standards Bd. 1976)).

2. TREATMENT

If the transaction does not satisfy any of the four tests described above, then the lease qualifies as an operating lease. Lessees generally prefer to treat leases as operating leases for two reasons. First, an operating lease does not affect the lessee's balance sheet. In this regard, U.S. GAAP does not require the lessee to record an asset and related liability because the lessee does not "own" the underlying asset. For this reason, the business community sometimes refers to operating leases as "off-balance sheet financing." Second, the lessee expenses rent payments as incurred. In a capital lease, in contrast, the lessee must recognize both depreciation expense and interest expense arising from the lease transaction.

If a lessee wants to keep a lease off the balance sheet, the lessee can "negotiate" various factors that affect the criteria used to classify a transaction as either an operating lease or a capital lease. In this regard, for example, the lessee could "overestimate" the asset's economic life, which reduces the chance that the lease term will equal or exceed seventy-five percent of the asset's economic life. In the alternative, the lessee could overestimate the applicable interest rate or the asset's fair market value. The overstated interest rate produces a lower present value, which translates to lower chance of satisfying the "ninety percent test." Even if the transaction satisfies that criterion, the higher interest rate reduces the asset's fair market value, which the lessee must capitalize and record as a corresponding liability. Similarly, an overstated fair market value reduces the chance that the transaction will satisfy the same ninety percent test. Finally, the lessee may request a shorter lease term. The shorter the lease term, the less chance that the lessee will satisfy either the seventy-five or the ninety percent tests.

In the post-Enron effort to improve accounting standards, observers have increasingly criticized the accounting principles that govern leases, arguing that the ninety and seventy-five percent tests for capital leases illustrate arbitrary accounting rules that obscure financial statements. In 2004, *The Wall Street Journal* reported that "off-balance sheet" commitments for operating leases totaled $482 billion for companies in the Standard & Poor's 500 stock index alone, an amount equal to eight percent of the $6.25 trillion that those same companies reported as debt on their balance sheets. In addition to keeping these obligations off balance sheets, operating leases increase returns on assets and typically boost earnings by lowering depreciation expenses. Jonathan Weil, *How Leases Play a Shadowy Role in Accounting*, WALL ST. J., Sept. 22, 2004, at A1. Shortly after that article, the FASB voted to begin a comprehensive reconsideration of lease accounting as a joint project with the IASB. The project aims to ensure that enterprises recognize the assets and liabilities arising from lease contracts on their balance sheets, potentially eliminating the off-balance sheet treatment for operating leases and bringing an estimated $2 trillion in lease obligations onto balance sheets worldwide. In May 2013, the FASB issued a proposed accounting standards update, a revision of a 2010 exposure draft. After the comment period on the revised proposal closed in September 2013, the Boards have continued to redeliberate the proposals in the 2013 exposure draft.

Interested readers can use FASB's website to check the joint project's status via the page for Project Roster & Status at http://www.fasb.org/jsp/FASB/Page/SectionPage&cid=1218220137074.

a. OPERATING LEASES

In an operating lease, the lessee debits rent expense on a straight-line basis even if the contract requires the lessee to remit payments according to some other schedule. On the other side of the transaction, the lessor carries the leased asset on its balance sheet and depreciates the asset. Like the lessee, the lessor accrues revenues on a straight-line basis.

b. CAPITAL LEASES

If an enterprise purchases an asset on credit, the enterprise records the asset and corresponding liability on its balance sheet. In addition, the enterprise depreciates the asset over its estimated useful life and accrues interest on the related indebtedness. As the enterprise repays the debt, interest expense declines. Generally accepted accounting principles in the United States require a lessee to account for a capital lease following similar rules.

(1) Lessee

In a capital lease, the lessee accounts for the transaction as if the enterprise purchased the underlying asset. As a result, the lessee debits an asset and credits a liability for the present value of the minimum lease payments which the lease agreement requires the lessee to make during the lease or, if lower, the property's fair market value. Although the offsetting increases in assets and liabilities do not affect owners' equity, the additional debt will increase the debt to equity ratio. In addition, the lessee must record depreciation expense for the property and allocate the lease payments between interest expense and the liability's reduction.

To illustrate, suppose that a lessee enters into a capital lease to use an automobile for four years at $10,000 annual rent, payable at the end of each year. GAAP treats the transaction as though the lessee purchased the vehicle for four installment payments of $10,000. As we saw on pages 404-405, *supra*, the consideration is not $40,000, but the present value of the four $10,000 payments, discounted at an appropriate interest rate. Assuming an eight percent annual interest rate and rounded to the nearest ten dollars, the real purchase price was $33,120, and the straight-line depreciation expense based on a four-year estimated useful life and no salvage value would be $8,280. In addition, the lessee's expense for the period would include $2,650 (the 8% imputed interest rate times the $33,120 outstanding principal balance during the lease's first year). Thus, the total of the lessee's expenses for that first year would be $10,930, almost ten percent more than the $10,000 annual rent, which the lessee would treat as the expense for an operating lease.

(2) Lessor

From the lessor's standpoint, accountants divide capital leases into three categories: *operating leases, sales-type leases* and *direct financing leases*. As an initial matter, the rules governing lease accounting applicable to lessors mirror the revenue recognition requirements which we discussed in Chapter VI. If the lessor really has not transferred the risks and benefits related to ownership, the lessor should not remove the asset from its books. Even if the lessee must treat a lease as a capital lease for financial accounting purposes, the Codification requires the lessor to classify the lease as an operating lease if collectibility does not appear reasonably certain or the lessor has not substantially completed performance. To summarize, a lessor treats a transaction as an operating lease under three different circumstances: (1) if the transaction does not satisfy any of the four criteria described in ASC Topic 840, *Leases*, (2) collectibility does not appear reasonably certain, or (3) the lessor has not substantially completed performance.

If the transaction satisfies the requirements for revenue recognition, then the lessor will treat the lease as either a sales-type lease or a direct financing lease. The distinction between a sales-type lease and a direct financing lease turns on whether a difference exists between the leased property's fair market value at the lease's inception and the lessor's cost or book value. A sales-type lease involves a manufacturer's or dealer's profit or loss, while a direct financing lease does not. In a direct financing lease, therefore, the leased property's fair value equals the lessor's book value.

In a sales-type lease, the "lessor" recognizes revenue from the sale of the leased property. Because the lessor no longer owns the underlying asset, the lessor does not record depreciation on the asset. Instead, the lessor allocates receipts between periodic interest income and principal payments. In a direct financing lease, in contrast, the bank or other lender uses the effective interest method to recognize interest income over the lease's term.

PROBLEMS

Problem 9.10A. The Loebl Corporation has signed a noncancellable agreement to lease a $20,000 automobile from Fitzgerald Leasing Company for five years. Under the lease agreement, which implicitly contains a twelve percent annual interest rate that falls below the corporation's incremental borrowing rate, Loebl will make a $1,500 down payment and annual payments of $2,500 at the end of each year. At the end of the lease, Loebl can purchase the vehicle for $10,000. Fitzgerald estimates that the vehicle will last for eight years and will be worth $8,000 at the end of the lease. Can Loebl treat this lease as an operating lease? Explain briefly.

Problem 9.10B. On January 31, 201X, Morris Company leased a new machine from Graham Corp. At the inception of the ten year lease, which assumes a ten percent interest rate, compounded annually, and requires $50,000 annual rental payments at the beginning of each year, the parties estimated that the machine had a fifteen year economic life and a $400,000 fair market value. The lease did not contain a renewal option and provides that possession of the machine reverts to Graham Corp. when the lease terminates. At what amount, if any, should the machine appear on Morris Company's balance sheet? Explain briefly.

Problem 9.10C. Grey Company manufactures equipment for sale or lease. On November 30, 20X1, Grey leased equipment to White Corporation for a five-year period expiring November 30, 20X6, at which date White can purchase the equipment for $10. Equal payments of $40,000 are due under the lease on November 30 of each year, beginning with the first payment on November 30, 20X1. Although the normal sales price of the equipment is $175,000 and the present value of the lease payments is only $150,000, Grey's sales manager approved the lease because White had the cash to make the first lease payment on November 30, 20X1 and the sales manager was trying to meet sales projections. White paid the first $40,000 installment on November 30, 20X1. The equipment cost Grey $120,000 to manufacture and Grey does not have any warranty or service obligations under the lease. Given White's credit history, the collectibility of the remaining lease payments is reasonably assured. The equipment has an estimated life of ten years. For the fiscal year ending November 30, 20X1, how much income, if any, should Grey realize from the lease? Discuss how Grey should classify the lease agreement and briefly explain your conclusions.

F. WRITE–DOWNS AND THE "BIG BATH"

Under the historical cost model, the balance sheet presents long-lived assets at net book value, usually their actual cost or fair market value at the date of acquisition less accumulated depreciation, depletion, or amortization. Recall that accumulated depreciation, depletion, or amortization reflect that portion of a long-lived asset's original cost that the enterprise has allocated to the accounting periods that already have benefitted from the asset's use.

In the historical cost system, an enterprise's balance sheet reflects an adherence to decades of reliance on basic historical cost principles or modifying conventions: objectivity, consistency, and conservatism. Under this framework, long-lived assets remained on a balance sheet based on their original historic costs, unless an other-than-temporary decline in value occurred. For such non-temporary declines, an enterprise recorded an impairment to the asset's carrying value by debiting a loss account, such as *Loss Due to Equipment Obsolescence*, usually reported on the income statement in the Other Expenses and Losses section, and crediting either the asset account or the accumulated depreciation account for that respective asset, in this case the *Equipment* account or the *Accumulated Depreciation: Equipment* account, respectively. If the enterprise credited the accumulated depreciation account, the accounting records and financial statements would continue to show the asset's original cost. The enterprise would then allocate the remaining book value, less any estimated salvage value, to the future accounting periods that the enterprise then expected to benefit from the asset's use or consumption.

1.   The Problem

Such write-downs appeared straightforward, except that no standards existed to determine when an impairment had occurred, and, if so, to assess whether it would last, or to measure the impairment. This subjective "I'll know it when I see it" standard lacked consistency and comparability, giving an enterprise and its management much latitude and discretion when deciding impairment issues. As a result, enterprises followed diverse practices.

Based on this latitude, the expression "big bath" came to refer to situations in which an enterprise announced a enormous write-down or write-off during one accounting period. In 2002, for example, AOL Time Warner Inc., which has subsequently changed its name to Time Warner Inc., reported a $98.7 billion net loss, at the time the largest annual loss in corporate history and more than twice what analysts on Wall Street expected, after taking a $45.5 billion charge in the fourth quarter to write down the carrying value of its America Online unit. The huge fourth-quarter charge followed a $54 billion write-down in the first quarter, which had earlier generated the largest quarterly net loss in U.S. history, when the company reduced the carrying value of assets in the Time Warner businesses. *The Wall Street Journal* described the charges as "an effort by the company to get as much bad news as possible out of the way." Martin Peers & Julia Angwin, *AOL Reports Record Annual Loss and Says Ted Turner Will Resign*, Wall St. J., Jan. 30, 2003, at A1.

Less than five years before the disastrous 2001 merger between America Online Inc. and Time Warner, in October 1996, AOL announced a $385 million charge to reverse an accounting policy that had enabled the company to post quarterly profits by capitalizing massive marketing costs and amortizing them over up to two years rather than treating them as expenses. *The Wall Street Journal* described the 1996 charge as "more than five time as large as the total pretax earnings that AOL had reported for the past five fiscal years combined." Jared Sandberg, *America Online Plans $385 Million Charge*, Wall St. J., Oct. 30, 1996, at A3.

Such write-offs obviously can distort an enterprise's income statements, lumping losses into one quarter or year while improving past and future earnings. These items can also lead to lawsuits alleging securities fraud. Following AOL's 1996 announcement, disappointed investors filed a class action lawsuit against the company, alleging that the company and its officers violated federal securities laws. In June 1998, the company agreed to pay up to $35 million to settle the lawsuit, noting that insurance would cover a substantial portion of the settlement. In 2000, AOL consented to a cease-and-desist order and agreed to pay a $3.5 million civil penalty to resolve administrative proceedings alleging that the company improperly accounted for its advertising costs. The company did not admit or deny the charges. SEC v. America Online, Inc., Accounting and Auditing Enforcement Release No. 1258, [1999–2001 Transfer Binder] Fed. Sec. L. Rep. (CCH) ¶ 74,765 (May 15, 2000).

For years, critics attributed less than honorable motives to such announcements and often alleged that enterprises orchestrated the timing of these large, "one-time" losses. These critics claimed that, rather than recognizing the expense or loss when incurred, enterprises used the broad discretion allowed under then-existing standards governing accounting for impairments to accumulate such expenses or losses and to manipulate the stock market's reaction to such announcements. Investor Warren Buffet compared the financial statements that followed these write-offs to bogus golf scores. Imagine a golfer reporting an atrociously high score for his first round, say a 140, and then shooting in the eighties "for the next few rounds by drawing down against the 'reserve' established in the first round. 'On Wall Street, * * * they will ignore the 140—which after all, came from a "discontinued" swing—and will classify our hero as an 80 shooter (and one who never disappoints).' " Richard A. Oppel Jr., *Buffet Deplores Trend of Manipulated Earnings*, N.Y. TIMES, Mar. 15, 1999, at C2.

As a variation, repeated write-downs can also muddy an enterprise's income statements. In 1996, *The Wall Street Journal* observed that AT&T Corp.'s $14.2 billion in restructuring charges during the previous decade actually exceeded the $10.3 billion in total net income that the company reported during that same period. Randall Smith & Steven Lipin, *Odd Numbers[:] Are Companies Using Restructuring Costs To Fudge the Figures?*, WALL ST. J., Jan. 30, 1996, at A1. Another article reported that among the thirty companies in the Dow Jones industrials, the most commonly watched barometer of stock market performance, seven took material write-offs in four of the past five years, and that ten of the thirty companies reported charges that eliminated at least a quarter of their earnings over that period. Pablo Galarza & Michael K. Ozanian, *Forgive Nothing; Here's How to Deal with All Those Huge "Nonrecurring" Charges*, FIN. WORLD, Mar. 11, 1996, at 18.

With such drastic and dramatic expense recognitions, one might expect shareholders and the market to look unfavorably upon these announcements. After all, both shareholders and the market usually view losses as undesirable. On balance, however, investors found a silver lining, no longer viewing these charges as admissions of corporate mismanagement. Most investors considered these charges as an effort to remove unproductive assets from the balance sheet and to enable future earnings gains. Keep in mind that the write-offs did not involve any cash payment, but instead attempted to bring future income closer to future cash flows by reducing future depreciation, one of the largest non-cash expenses. As non-cash charges, these write-offs theoretically would not affect an enterprise's ability to pay dividends or its bills.

The SEC and all realized that "big baths" represented an area needing increased regulation. As early as 1995, the FASB announced new rules in the area via SFAS No.121, which SFAS No. 144 later superseded. *See* ACCOUNTING FOR THE IMPAIRMENT OF LONG-LIVED ASSETS AND FOR LONG-LIVED ASSETS TO BE DISPOSED OF, Statement of Fin. Accounting Standards No. 121 (Fin. Accounting Standards Bd. 1995). SFAS No. 121 established standards that attempted to determine when enterprises should recognize impairment losses and how they should measure such losses to increase comparability and uniformity. Unfortunately, SFAS No. 121 did not address those situations in which an enterprise decided to discontinue a portion of its operations. Although the pronouncement limited management's discretion, opportunities remained for management to manipulate write-offs and reported earnings. Staff accountants at the SEC soon questioned the way that registrants reported restructuring and asset impairments charges and suggested that firms were recognizing losses prematurely. *See* Restructuring and Impairment Charges, Staff Accounting Bulletin No. 100, 64 Fed. Reg. 67,154 (1999), *available at* http://www.sec.gov/interps/account/sab100.htm and *codified in* Topic 5: Miscellaneous Accounting, Section P. Restructuring Charges and Section CC. Impairments, Codification of Staff Accounting Bulletins (updated Mar. 2011), *available via* http://www.sec.gov/interps/account/sabcode.htm. About two years later, the SEC initiated public administrative proceedings against Kimberly-Clark Corp., alleging that the company improperly recorded $354 million in restructuring charges after its merger with Scott Paper Co. in December 1995. In subsequent years, Kimberly-Clark used a portion of the corresponding restructuring reserves to offset expenses in subsequent years, which increased the company's pretax income by about eleven percent in 1996 and lesser percentages in subsequent fiscal years. In 1999, the company voluntarily restated its financial statements after discussions with the SEC's Division of Corporation Finance. Without admitting or denying the SEC's allegations, the company consented to a cease-and-desist order. *In re Kimberly-Clark Corp.*, Accounting and Auditing Enforcement Release No. 1533, [2001–2003 Transfer Binder] Fed. Sec. L. Rep. (CCH) ¶ 75,048 (Mar. 27, 2002).

2.   The New Rules

For more than ten years, FASB worked to improve the accounting standards involving the impairment of long-lived assets. As a result, the Codification now limits an enterprise's ability to record large up-front write-downs and allows firms to recognize disposal or exit costs only as actually incurred.

In 2001, the FASB issued Statement of Financial Accounting Standards No. 144, *Accounting for the Impairment or Disposal of Long-Lived Assets*, now codified in the "Impairment or "Disposal of Long-Lived Assets" subsections of FASB ASC Topic 360, *Property, Plant, and Equipment*, to supersede SFAS No. 121, while still retaining many of its underlying rules. In addition to addressing the accounting for impairment of long-lived assets other than goodwill, other indefinite-lived intangibles, and unproved oil and gas properties for which an enterprise has elected to use the successful-efforts accounting method, SFAS No. 144 established a single accounting model for all disposals of long-lived assets. In that regard, the pronouncement expanded the rules in SFAS No. 121 to apply also to those disposals of segments of a business that another pronouncement, APB Opinion No. 30, *Reporting the Results of Operations-Reporting the Effects of Disposal of a Segment of a*

Business, and Extraordinary, Unusual and Infrequently Occurring Events and Transactions, previously addressed.

Next, in 2002 FASB issued new rules governing exit and disposal actions. In SFAS No. 146, *Accounting for Costs Associated with Exit or Disposal Activities*, now codified in FASB ASC Topic 420, *Exit or Disposal Cost Obligations*, the Board decided that future expenses arising from a plan to sell or abandon a fixed asset, such as a factory or corporate headquarters, must meet the definition of a liability before an enterprise can recognize them for financial accounting purposes. This promulgation nullified EITF Issue No. 94-3, *Liability Recognition for Certain Employee Termination Benefits and Other Costs to Exit an Activity (including Certain Costs Incurred in a Restructuring)*.

a. GENERAL RULES ON IMPAIRMENTS

FASB ASC Topic 360, *Property, Plant, and Equipment*, codifies the requirements for recognizing an impairment loss that originally appeared in SFAS No. 121, and that SFAS No. 144 reaffirmed, but specifically does not apply to goodwill and indefinite-lived intangibles. Via the "Impairment or Disposal of Long-Lived Assets" subsections, ASC Topic 360 also establishes a single accounting model for assets that an enterprise plans to sell. Accordingly, the Codification creates specific rules for long-lived assets that an enterprise holds (1) for use, (2) for disposal by other than sale, and (3) for disposal by sale.

(1) Assets Held for Use

As described in more detail on pages 662-665, *supra*, ASC Topic 360, *Property, Plant, and Equipment*, sets forth the circumstances in which an enterprise must recognize an impairment loss on an asset or group of assets that the enterprise holds for use in its operations. As a starting point, the "Impairment or Disposal of Long-Lived Assets" subsections of Topic 360 require an enterprise to test such assets other than indefinite-lived intangibles and goodwill for impairment periodically, especially whenever events or changes in circumstances indicate that the enterprise may not recover the asset's carrying amount. For purposes of this review, recall that "the asset" may actually represent the smallest group of related assets for which the enterprise can estimate identifiable future cash flows independent from those attributable to other groups of assets and liabilities.

You may recall that ASC Topic 360 first requires an enterprise to compare the undiscounted future cash flows associated with "the asset" to its net carrying value on the balance sheet. If the estimated undiscounted future cash flows exceed the asset's net carrying value, as usually occurs in this first prong, then no impairment exists. Please note that because the Codification specifies the use of undiscounted cash flows in the first prong, far fewer impairments exist than if the rules required enterprises to use discounted cash flows in that prong. If the asset's net carrying value exceeds those cash flows, however, then the enterprise next must discount the estimated cash flows back to the balance sheet date to determine the asset's fair value and, if necessary, recognize an impairment loss. Please also recall that because enterprises can depreciate, amortize, or deplete finite-lived assets, their carrying values decrease on an enterprise's balance sheet each accounting period, which further reduces the chances that an impairment will exist. The impairment loss, if any, will equal the difference between the asset's carrying amount and its fair value. Although the balance sheet does not claim to present a statement of current values, the Codification embraces that approach for impaired assets held for use in operations.

Lawyers should keep in mind that management enjoys considerable discretion in estimating expected future cash flows both from using an asset and from its disposition. In addition, the "lowest level of identifiable cash flows" raises some interesting possibilities. If net expected cash flows for some assets exceed their carrying amounts, can an enterprise use that excess to offset impairment losses attributable to other assets? The answer involves the proper grouping of assets. Specifically, enterprises must analyze assets, either individually or in small groups, at the "lowest level" at which the enterprise can separately identify independent cash flows. To illustrate, in response to the then-new rules in SFAS No. 121, PepsiCo Inc. wrote-off approximately $520 million, or seven percent of the assets related to the company's Taco Bell, Pizza Hut, and KFC restaurants, during the fourth quarter in 1995 even though the value of the restaurants as a group exceeded their combined book values. Because PepsiCo chose to identify cash flows on a restaurant-by-restaurant basis, the company could take the charge, which boosted earnings in subsequent accounting periods. After all, the write-offs reduced subsequent depletion and amortization charges, which allowed higher earnings in later years. When questioned, the company conceded that another restaurant operator might group its stores by regions which could result in a lower charge. Roger Lowenstein, *Earnings Not Always What They Seem*, WALL ST. J., Feb. 15, 1996, at C1.

Please note that the requirement that an enterprise use the "lowest level of identifiable cash flows" to test for impairment significantly affects accounting for natural resources. Prior to SFAS No. 121, for example, oil companies typically used a country-by-country grouping to evaluate assets for impairments. Under this method, profitable wells offset unsuccessful wells, reducing or eliminating any write-offs. SFAS No. 121, however, required these companies to evaluate wells on field-by-field basis or even an individual basis if the enterprise considers a well's cash flow "identifiable." This separation may differ from the methodology that an enterprise uses to amortize various costs related to the wells. For example, an enterprise may group assets by region or product for amortization purposes, whereas the "Impairment or Disposal of Long-Lived Assets" subsections of ASC Topic 360 continue the rules that originated in SFAS No. 121 and that require an enterprise to separate these assets for impairment analysis depending upon the "lowest level of identifiable cash flows."

(2) Assets Held for Disposal by Other than Sale

Apart from sale, an enterprise can dispose of long-lived assets via exchange; distribution to its owners, perhaps in a spinoff; or abandonment. The "Impairment or Disposal of Long-Lived Assets" subsections of FASB ASC Topic 360, *Property, Plant, and Equipment*, require an enterprise to treat any asset that it holds for disposal by other than sale as held for use until actually abandoned or transferred. As a result, the rules in the previous section apply while ASC Topic 360 treats the asset as held and used.

An enterprise abandons an asset when it ceases to use it. Temporary idling, however, does not give rise to an abandonment. If an enterprise commits to a plan to abandon an asset before the end of its previously estimated useful life, however, the enterprise must revise the depreciable life in accordance with FASB ASC Topic 250, *Accounting Changes and Error Corrections*, which codified SFAS No. 154 on those same subjects, to reflect the asset's use over its shortened useful life.

With regard to exchanges or spinoffs, ASC Topic 845, *Nonmonetary Transactions*, which codifies amendments to APB Opinion No. 29, *Accounting for Nonmonetary Transactions* in SFAS No. 144, requires an enterprise to immediately recognize an impairment loss if, on the date of the exchange or spinoff, the transferred asset's carrying amount exceeds its fair value. FASB ASC ¶¶ 360-10-35-47 to -49, 360-10-40-4, 360-10-45-15 (codifying ACCOUNTING FOR THE IMPAIRMENT OR DISPOSAL OF LONG-LIVED ASSETS, Statement of Fin. Accounting Standards No. 144, ¶¶ 27–29, C4 (Fin. Accounting Standards Bd. 2001)).

(3) Assets Held for Disposal by Sale

The "Impairment or Disposal of Long-Lived Assets" subsections of ASC Topic 360, *Property, Plant, and Equipment*, again which codify SFAS No. 144, require an enterprise to report all long-lived assets that it holds for disposal by sale, whether previously held and used or newly acquired, at the lower of the asset's carrying amount or fair value less the cost to sell. You may recall from the discussion in Chapter IV on pages 280 to 281, *supra*, the "Impairment or Disposal of Long-Lived Assets" subsections of ASC Topic 360, *Property, Plant, and Equipment*, specifically apply to discontinued operations, a term accountants use to describe components that an enterprise decides to sell or eliminate. An enterprise holds a long-lived asset for sale when, among other criteria, management commits to a plan to sell the asset, makes the asset available for immediate sale in its present condition subject only to usual and customary terms, and, subject to certain exceptions, expects the transfer to qualify for recognition as a completed sale within one year.

Unlike the treatment for assets that an enterprise plans to hold for use in operations, the "Impairment or Disposal of Long-Lived Assets" subsections of ASC Topic 360 require an enterprise to subtract the cost to sell from the amount that would otherwise appear on the enterprise's balance sheet. The cost to sell an asset generally includes the incremental direct costs necessary to transact the sale, such as broker commissions, legal and title transfer fees, and closing costs. Costs to sell would not include expected future losses arising from the asset's operation pending sale. In addition, once an enterprise decides to hold an asset for disposal by sale, the Codification precludes the enterprise from depreciating or amortizing the asset. Finally, the Topic 360 prohibits an enterprise from retroactively reclassifying assets as held for sale when the enterprise does not meet the requisite criteria until after the balance sheet date, but requires the enterprise to disclose certain information about the decision to hold for sale in the notes to the financial statements. FASB ASC ¶¶ 360-10-35-38 to -40, -43 to -45, 360-10-45-7 to -13 (codifications of ACCOUNTING FOR THE IMPAIRMENT OR DISPOSAL OF LONG-LIVED ASSETS, Statement of Fin. Accounting Standards No. 144, ¶¶ 30–40 (Fin. Accounting Standards Bd. 2001)).

b.   GENERAL RULES ON DISPOSAL ACTIVITIES

Under ASC Topic 420, *Exit or Disposal Cost Obligations*, which codified SFAS No. 146, *Accounting for Costs Associated with Exit or Disposal Activities*, an enterprise can only recognize and measure a liability arising from a restructuring, discontinued operation, plant closing, or other exit or disposal action, including obligations arising from lease terminations and employee severances, once the enterprise has actually incurred the liability. These rules, however, do not apply to costs to terminate a capital lease. FASB ASC Topic 420, *Exit or Disposal Cost Obligations* (a codification of ACCOUNTING FOR COSTS ASSOCIATED WITH EXIT OR DISPOSAL ACTIVITIES, Statement of Fin. Accounting Standards No. 146 (Fin. Accounting Standards Bd. 2002)).

Before SFAS No. 146, EITF Issue No. 94-3, *Liability Recognition for Certain Employee Termination Benefits and Other Costs to Exit an Activity (including Certain Costs Incurred in a Restructuring)*, allowed an enterprise to recognize liabilities and record associated expenses on the date the enterprise announced an exit plan, even though the "commitments" did not meet the definition of a liability in FASB Concepts Statement No. 6, *Elements of Financial Statements*, now codified at FASB ASC ¶ 410-20-25-1. Accordingly, enterprises could record large expenses at the time they announced a plant closing or corporate restructuring, even though employee turnover, sublease rental payment amounts, and other circumstances might reduce the actual amounts paid to consolidate facilities or relocate employees.

The Codification defines a liability as "probable future sacrifices of economic benefits arising from present obligations of a particular entity to transfer assets or provide services to other entities in the future as a result of past transactions or events." FASB ASC ¶ 410-20-25-1 (a codification of ELEMENTS OF FINANCIAL STATEMENTS, Statement of Fin. Accounting Concepts No. 6, ¶ 35 (Fin. Accounting Standards Bd. 1985)). In SFAS No. 146, now codified in ASC Topic 420, *Exit or Disposal Cost Obligations*, FASB concluded that an enterprise's commitment by itself to an exit or disposal plan does not create a present obligation to others that satisfies the definition of a liability for financial accounting purposes. When a commitment satisfies that definition, an enterprise should use fair value to measure the liability. The

Codification defines a liability's "fair value" as "the price that would be . . . paid to transfer [the] liability in an orderly transaction between market participants at the measurement date." FASB ASC § 820-10-35. In the unusual circumstance in which the enterprise cannot reasonably estimate the fair value, it must wait until it can reasonably estimate the fair value to recognize the liability. If the disposal activity does not involve a component of the entity that qualifies for treatment as a discontinued operation, the enterprise must treat the employee termination benefits and other costs as an expense related to continuing operations. In other words, an enterprise should report a disposal activity in continuing operations before income taxes unless the activity involves a discontinued operation.

The Codification also establishes rules for treating the liability for, and compensation expense related to, one-time termination benefits. If an employee must perform services during a legal notification period, often sixty days, or otherwise in the future to qualify for termination benefits, FASB ASC Topic 420 requires the enterprise to allocate the liability's fair value as of the date that an employee will stop rendering services ratably over the future service period. Consequently, the underlying liability will accumulate during the future service period, until the obligation reaches an amount equal to the estimated fair value on the date that the required services end. As a result, enterprises will often now recognize these exit and disposal costs in one or more accounting periods following a commitment to a plan, rather than at the date of commitment.

Finally, the Codification requires disclosures about any exit or disposal activity initiated during the accounting period and any subsequent period until the enterprise completes the activity. For each major type of cost, an enterprise must: (1) report by business segment the total amount that it expects to incur in connection with the exit, the amount incurred in the period, and the cumulative amount incurred to date; (2) reconcile the beginning and ending balances in the liability accounts, showing separately the changes during the period attributable to costs incurred and charged to expense, costs paid or otherwise settled, and any adjustments to the liability, and explaining the reasons for any adjustments; and (3) identify the line items in the income statement in which the costs appear. FASB ASC Topic 420 (a codification of ACCOUNTING FOR COSTS ASSOCIATED WITH EXIT OR DISPOSAL ACTIVITIES, Statement of Fin. Accounting Standards No. 146 (Fin. Accounting Standards Bd. 2002)).

Under FASB ASC Topic 805, *Business Combinations*, which you may recall codified SFAS No. 141(R), enterprises must apply these same rules to exit activities that arise from business combinations. Acquirers may recognize liabilities for exit activities or restructuring costs related to the business acquired only if those liabilities meet the recognition criteria now found in FASB ASC Topic 420, *Exit or Disposal Cost Obligations*, at the acquisition date. As suggested on page 682, *supra*, an enterprise's commitment to an exit plan does not, by itself, create a present obligation to others that meets the definition of a liability. When an enterprise actually incurs a liability for a cost associated with an exit or disposal activity, the enterprise must recognize and measure the cost at fair value. FASB ASC ¶¶ 420-10-25-1 to -3, 420-10-30-1 (a codification of SFAS No. 146). Amounts that the acquirer expects, but is not obligated, to incur do not meet the recognition criteria, and the enterprise should account for such costs separately in the post-combination financial statements, usually as expenses when incurred. The new standard, in essence, levels the playing field for restructuring costs, whether originating from an existing operating activity or an acquisition. FASB ASC ¶ 805-20-25-2 (a codification of SFAS No. 141(R), ¶ 13). The new rule would presumably preclude companies like Cendant Corp., which allegedly intentionally overstated merger reserves and then reversed those amounts in later periods to overstate pretax operating income by more than $500 million between 1995 and 1997, from using acquisition reserves to hide subsequent poor performance from investors. Lingling Wei, *Merger Loophole May Be Plugged*, Wall St. J., Aug. 13, 2004, at C3.

*

APPENDIX A

ILLUSTRATIVE FINANCIAL REPORTS AND STATEMENTS

1971 Seattle

Embracing our heritage and values while aiming higher than ever.

Starbucks Corporation Fiscal 2012 Annual Report

2012 Mumbai

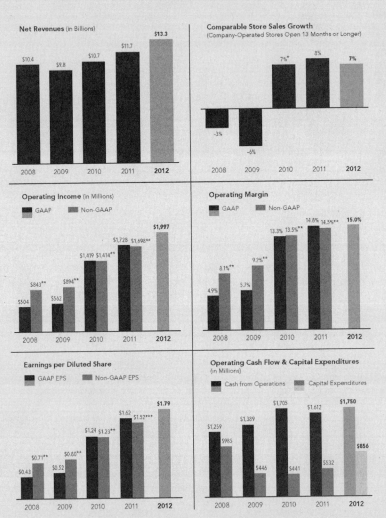

Fiscal 2012 Financial Highlights

Net Revenues (in Billions)

2008	2009	2010	2011	2012
$10.4	$9.8	$10.7	$11.7	$13.3

Comparable Store Sales Growth
(Company-Operated Stores Open 13 Months or Longer)

2008	2009	2010	2011	2012
-3%	-6%	7%*	8%	7%

Operating Income (in Millions)

■ GAAP ■ Non-GAAP

2008	2009	2010	2011	2012
$504 / $843**	$562 / $894**	$1,419 / $1,414**	$1,728 / $1,698**	$1,997

Operating Margin

■ GAAP ■ Non-GAAP

2008	2009	2010	2011	2012
4.9% / 8.1%**	5.7% / 9.2%**	13.3% / 13.5%**	14.8% / 14.5%**	15.0%

Earnings per Diluted Share

■ GAAP EPS ■ Non-GAAP EPS

2008	2009	2010	2011	2012
$0.43 / $0.71**	$0.52 / $0.80**	$1.24 / $1.23**	$1.62 / $1.52***	$1.79

Operating Cash Flow & Capital Expenditures
(in Millions)

■ Cash from Operations ■ Capital Expenditures

2008	2009	2010	2011	2012
$1,259 / $985	$1,389 / $446	$1,705 / $441	$1,612 / $532	$1,750 / $856

* 2010 comparable store sales growth was calculated excluding the additional week in September 2010.

** Non-GAAP measure. Excludes $339, $332 and $53 million in pretax restructuring and transformation charges in 2008, 2009 and 2010, respectively. Also excludes a benefit from the 53rd week in 2010 of approximately $59 million and a gain on the sale of properties in 2011 of $30 million.

*** 2011 excludes $0.10 of gain resulting from the acquisition of the company's joint venture operations in Switzerland and Austria and the gain on the sale of properties.

1971,

Our first store opens in Seattle's
Pike Place Market

Dear Shareholders,

It is an honor to write you this
year, not only because we have
achieved record financial
performance but because we
have once again done so by living
up to the heritage of our company,
balancing profits with a social conscience. Our
commitment to creating shareholder value through
the lens of humanity is truly a cornerstone of Starbucks
global strength, especially as we pursue the most
ambitious agenda in our company's history.

Two years ago, we embarked on a strategic plan, the
Blueprint for Profitable Growth, in which we would
leverage multiple channels of distribution. I am proud
to affirm that it is no longer theory but a true growth
engine. The measure of our success can be seen in the
past year's performance:

Starbucks consolidated global revenues reached a
record $13.3 billion, a 14 percent increase, with revenue
growth driven by a 7 percent rise in global comparable
store sales and a 50 percent rise in revenue from
Channel Development. Our operating income was
$2 billion, a 16 percent increase, with our consolidated
operating margin rising to 15 percent, up 20 basis
points from last year.

Starbucks record earnings-per-share growth continued,
up 10 percent in 2012 to $1.79 from last year's $1.62.
Through share repurchases and dividends, we returned
approximately $1.1 billion to shareholders.

While we are proud of our achievements, we have
learned never to take our success for granted, which is
why three primary attributes will continue to drive our
every decision and action. First, we will remain
committed to our coffee core. Second, we will exercise
relevant, timely, and courageous innovation. And third,

we will ceaselessly honor our values. I firmly believe that
the ability to adhere to these attributes is what defines
the most enduring organizations of our time, and as I
share them with you in the context of highlights from
Starbucks past year, I think you will agree that they
are key to our ongoing success.

Staying True to Our Core Purpose and Capabilities as We Grow

We will always be a coffee company
whose core business is to ethically
source and roast the highest-quality
arabica coffee in the world, as we
simultaneously create authentic
connections with our customers and the
communities we serve. I assure you we
are not deviating from this purpose but
rather enhancing it with extreme diligence.

Scaling the Starbucks Experience. Today, 42 years after
opening our first store in Seattle, Starbucks operates in
61 countries, and we recently had our most successful
launch ever, in India. I was in Mumbai when our doors
opened, and I personally witnessed, with our fantastic
business partner in India, Tata Global Beverages, the
unabashed affection and demand for Starbucks, a
definitive signal that our brand is resonating around
the world.

In the China and Asia Pacific region in 2012, we once
again posted strong annual returns, including 11
consecutive quarters of double-digit comparable store
sales growth. This success showcases how—with nearly
3,300 stores, plus hundreds more planned throughout
Asia Pacific—we are mastering the transferable ability
to scale our brand's core attributes and expertise, while
respecting and reflecting regional customs and cultures
so we may be locally relevant. When we strike this
delicate balance, we establish trust, which ensures the
company has opportunities for continued growth
everywhere we do business. That includes the 36
countries in EMEA, where revenues grew 9 percent last
year and where we continue to apply lessons of the
past to reconnect with our customers in this
economically challenged but important region.

As the equity of our brand thrives around the world, we
anticipate having 20,000 stores on six continents by
2014. Additionally, over the next five years, we plan to
open 3,000 new stores in the Americas region alone.
Unlike a period in our past, I assure you that our growth
today is highly disciplined.

Strengthening Connections. As always, our 200,000
partners (employees) are working hard, crafting perfect
beverages, and fostering the personal relationships
with customers that distinguish our brand. As consumer
behavior continues to shift, we are further translating
our connective spirit beyond the walls of our stores by
leveraging a combination of social and digital media,

our loyalty and Card program, and mobile technologies. It is hard to overstate the collective power of Starbucks 54 million Facebook fans, 3 million Twitter followers, 14.6 million loyalty program members, and 7 million users of our mobile applications, who pay this way 2 million times each week. We also gave our customers another quick, mobile way to pay by forging a partnership with Square. We will not stop innovating on this front, where our best-in-class digital reach, and more notably the authentic engagement we ignite daily with millions of consumers online, will continue to drive our core business.

Coffee and connection will always be the heart of Starbucks, yet our ability to reinvigorate our business around that heritage remains an unmatched competitive advantage.

Innovating with Timely Relevance, Courage, and Conviction

Last year also saw significant product innovation around our coffee core, most notably in the $8 billion premium single-cup category.

We reached a true milestone with the launch of the beautiful Verismo® System, a breakthrough technology that heralds the first time customers can make Starbucks® brewed or latte beverages in their homes. This is only the beginning as we embark on a multiyear plan to grow the Verismo brand into the leading platform in the single-cup space, where sales of our other, complementary single-serve offerings are also accelerating. In 2012 Starbucks VIA® Ready Brew sales grew significantly and we shipped nearly 500 million K-Cup® packs, garnering approximately 16 percent of the premium single-cup market.

Through creative new products, we are meeting more of our customers' needs. This summer we introduced Starbucks Refreshers™ beverages, delicious cold energy drinks made with natural green coffee extract, available in cans, as an instant beverage, and handcrafted in our stores. And we continue to delight with seasonal coffee beverages such as Pumpkin Spice and Peppermint Mocha, as well as Starbucks® Blonde roast, which we introduced for the 40-plus percent of U.S. coffee drinkers who prefer a lighter roast.

Meanwhile, three strategic acquisitions are bringing bold upgrades to our food and

2012, Mumbai, our first store in India

non-coffee beverage categories. With La Boulange® bakery products, we have begun the transformation of the selection, taste, and quality of the fresh food in our stores. Second, adding Evolution Fresh to our brand portfolio fulfills our commitment to health and wellness, and not just by bringing high-quality premium juices to our customers but by extending the Evolution Fresh brand to an exciting new store concept. With Evolution Fresh™ juice products currently in more than 2,200 Starbucks® stores as well as 1,500 grocery locations, we are on our way toward nationwide distribution.

Finally, with the acquisition of the high-end Teavana brand, we'll apply our competencies in retail operations and hot and cold beverage creation to expand Teavana's 300-store footprint as we reinvent the tea category, in part by bringing tea bars into Teavana stores and applying learnings from our own Tazo brand. Long term, our intent is to significantly grow Teavana's global store presence, transforming tea just as we have transformed coffee.

Our pace of innovation and creativity is rapid, and I assure you that every move is highly strategic and thoughtfully executed as we push for relevant, timely, and disciplined reinvention in our stores, in consumer product channels, and beyond.

Honoring Our Culture's Values and Guiding Principles

More than ever, today's consumers have an interest in and access to what companies stand for—their values. This is nothing new to Starbucks. We've been building a company with a conscience for four decades, and the reservoir of trust we have earned is perhaps our most precious asset. As we continue to execute our Blueprint for Profitable Growth to become a truly performance-driven global organization, we are committed to leading through the lens of humanity, not just when it is convenient or easy. This alone makes our partners incredibly proud.

At Starbucks our aspiration is nothing less than to be among the most enduring brands of our time. I am confident we are on that path, and I thank you for joining us on this journey.

Warm regards,

Howard Schultz

Howard Schultz
chairman, president
and chief executive officer

UNITED STATES SECURITIES AND EXCHANGE COMMISSION
Washington, DC 20549

Form 10-K

☒ ANNUAL REPORT PURSUANT TO SECTION 13 OR 15(d) OF THE SECURITIES EXCHANGE ACT OF 1934

For the Fiscal Year Ended September 30, 2012

or

☐ TRANSITION REPORT PURSUANT TO SECTION 13 OR 15(d) OF THE SECURITIES EXCHANGE ACT OF 1934

For the transition period from   to   .

Commission File Number: 0-20322

Starbucks Corporation
(Exact Name of Registrant as Specified in its Charter)

Washington	91-1325671
(State of Incorporation)	*(IRS Employer ID)*

2401 Utah Avenue South, Seattle, Washington 98134
(206) 447-1575

(Address of principal executive offices, zip code, telephone number)

Securities Registered Pursuant to Section 12(b) of the Act:

Title of Each Class	Name of Each Exchange on Which Registered
Common Stock, $0.001 par value per share	Nasdaq Global Select Market

Securities Registered Pursuant to Section 12(g) of the Act: None

Indicate by check mark if the registrant is a well-known seasoned issuer, as defined in Rule 405 of the Securities Act.   Yes ☒   No ☐

Indicate by check mark if the registrant is not required to file reports pursuant to Section 13 or Section 15(d) of the Act.   Yes ☐   No ☒

Indicate by check mark whether the registrant: (1) has filed all reports required to be filed by Section 13 or 15(d) of the Securities Exchange Act of 1934 during the preceding 12 months (or for such shorter period that the registrant was required to file such reports), and (2) has been subject to such filing requirements for the past 90 days.   Yes ☒   No ☐

Indicate by check mark whether the registrant has submitted electronically and posted on its corporate Web site, if any, every Interactive Data File required to be submitted and posted pursuant to Rule 405 of Regulation S-T (§ 232.405 of this chapter) during the preceding 12 months (or for such shorter period that the registrant was required to submit and post such files).   Yes ☒   No ☐

Indicate by check mark if disclosure of delinquent filers pursuant to Item 405 of Regulation of S-K (§ 229.405 of this chapter) is not contained herein, and will not be contained, to the best of the registrant's knowledge, in definitive proxy or information statements incorporated by reference in Part III of this Form 10-K or any amendment to this Form 10-K.   ☐

Indicate by check mark whether the registrant is a large accelerated filer, an accelerated filer, a non-accelerated filer, or a smaller reporting company. See the definitions of "large accelerated filer," "accelerated filer" and "smaller reporting company" in Rule 12b-2 of the Exchange Act. (Check one):

Large accelerated filer ☒	Accelerated filer ☐
Non-accelerated filer ☐ (Do not check if a smaller reporting company)	Smaller reporting company ☐

Indicate by check mark whether the registrant is a shell company (as defined in Rule 12b-2 of the Exchange Act).   Yes ☐   No ☒

The aggregate market value of the voting stock held by non-affiliates of the registrant as of the last business day of the registrant's most recently completed second fiscal quarter, based upon the closing sale price of the registrant's common stock on March 30, 2012 as reported on the NASDAQ Global Select Market was $41 billion. As of November 9, 2012, there were 743.6 million shares of the registrant's Common Stock outstanding.

DOCUMENTS INCORPORATED BY REFERENCE

Portions of the definitive Proxy Statement for the registrant's Annual Meeting of Shareholders to be held on March 20, 2013 have been incorporated by reference into Part III of this Annual Report on Form 10-K.

STARBUCKS CORPORATION
Form 10-K
For the Fiscal Year Ended September 30, 2012
TABLE OF CONTENTS

CAUTIONARY NOTE REGARDING FORWARD-LOOKING STATEMENTS

This Annual Report on Form 10-K includes "forward-looking" statements within the meaning of the Private Securities Litigation Reform Act of 1995. Forward-looking statements can be identified by the fact that they do not relate strictly to historical or current facts. They often include words such as "believes," "expects," "anticipates," "estimates," "intends," "plans," "seeks" or words of similar meaning, or future or conditional verbs, such as "will," "should," "could," "may," "aims," "intends," or "projects." A forward-looking statement is neither a prediction nor a guarantee of future events or circumstances, and those future events or circumstances may not occur. You should not place undue reliance on forward-looking statements, which speak only as of the date of this Annual Report on Form 10-K. These forward-looking statements are all based on currently available operating, financial and competitive information and are subject to various risks and uncertainties. Our actual future results and trends may differ materially depending on a variety of factors, including, but not limited to, the risks and uncertainties discussed under "Risk Factors" and "Management's Discussion and Analysis of Financial Condition and Results of Operations". Given these risks and uncertainties, you should not rely on forward-looking statements as a prediction of actual results. Any or all of the forward-looking statements contained in this Annual Report on Form 10-K and any other public statement made by us, including by our management, may turn out to be incorrect. We are including this cautionary note to make applicable and take advantage of the safe harbor provisions of the Private Securities Litigation Reform Act of 1995 for forward-looking statements. We expressly disclaim any obligation to update or revise any forward-looking statements, whether as a result of new information, future events or otherwise.

PART I

Item 1. *Business*

General

Starbucks is the premier roaster, marketer and retailer of specialty coffee in the world, operating in 60 countries. Formed in 1985, Starbucks Corporation's common stock trades on the NASDAQ Global Select Market ("NASDAQ") under the symbol "SBUX." We purchase and roast high-quality coffees that we sell, along with handcrafted coffee, tea and other beverages and a variety of fresh food items, through company-operated stores. We also sell a variety of coffee and tea products and license our trademarks through other channels such as licensed stores, grocery and national foodservice accounts. In addition to our flagship Starbucks brand, our portfolio also includes Tazo® Tea, Seattle's Best Coffee®, Starbucks VIA® Ready Brew, Starbucks Refreshers™ beverages, Evolution Fresh™, La Boulange bakery brand and the Verismo™ System by Starbucks.

Our objective is to maintain Starbucks standing as one of the most recognized and respected brands in the world. To achieve this goal, we are continuing the disciplined expansion of our global store base. In addition, by leveraging the experience gained through our traditional store model, we continue to offer consumers new coffee products in a variety of forms, across new categories, and through diverse channels. Starbucks Global Responsibility strategy and commitments related to coffee and the communities we do business in, as well as our focus on being an employer of choice, are also key complements to our business strategies.

In this Annual Report on Form 10-K ("10-K" or "Report") for the fiscal year ended September 30, 2012 ("fiscal 2012"), Starbucks Corporation (together with its subsidiaries) is referred to as "Starbucks," the "Company," "we," "us" or "our."

Segment Financial Information

Segment information is prepared on the same basis that our management reviews financial information for operational decision-making purposes. Beginning with the first quarter of fiscal 2012, we redefined our reportable operating segments to align with the three-region leadership and organizational structure of our retail business that took effect at the beginning of fiscal 2012.

The three-region structure includes: 1) Americas, inclusive of the US, Canada, and Latin America; 2) Europe, Middle East, and Africa, collectively referred to as the "EMEA" region; and 3) China / Asia Pacific ("CAP"). Our chief executive officer, who is our chief operating decision maker, manages these businesses, evaluates financial results, and makes key operating decisions based on the new organizational structure. Accordingly, beginning with the first quarter of fiscal 2012, we revised our reportable operating segments from 1) US, 2) International, and 3) Global Consumer Products Group to the following four reportable segments: 1) Americas, 2) EMEA, 3) CAP, and 4) Global Consumer Products Group. In the second quarter of fiscal 2012, we renamed our Global Consumer Products Group segment "Channel Development." Segment revenues as a percentage of total net revenues for fiscal year 2012 were as follows: Americas (75%), EMEA (9%), CAP (5%), and Channel Development (10%).

Concurrent with the change in reportable operating segments, we revised our prior period financial information to reflect comparable financial information for the new segment structure. Historical financial information presented herein reflects this change.

The Americas, EMEA, and CAP segments include both company-operated and licensed stores. Our Americas segment is our most mature business and has achieved significant scale. Certain markets within EMEA and CAP operations are in the early stages of development and require a more extensive support organization, relative to the current levels of revenue and operating income, than the Americas operations. The Americas and EMEA segments also include foodservice accounts, primarily in Canada and the UK. Our Americas segment also includes the retail and wholesale activities of Bay Bread, LLC (doing business as La Boulange), which was acquired in the fourth quarter of fiscal 2012.

Our Channel Development segment includes whole bean and ground coffees, premium Tazo® teas, Starbucks VIA® Ready Brew, Starbucks® coffee and Tazo® tea K-Cup® portion packs, a variety of ready-to-drink beverages, such as Starbucks Refreshers™ beverages, and other branded products sold worldwide through channels such as grocery stores, warehouse clubs, convenience stores, and US foodservice accounts.

Seattle's Best Coffee is reported in "Other" along with Evolution Fresh, Digital Ventures and unallocated corporate expenses that pertain to corporate administrative functions that support our operating segments but are not specifically attributable to or managed by any segment and are not included in the reported financial results of the operating segments. The Other category comprised approximately 1% of total net revenues.

Financial information for Starbucks reportable operating segments and Other is included in Note 17 to the consolidated financial statements included in Item 8 of this 10-K.

Revenue Components

We generate our revenues through company-operated stores, licensed stores, consumer packaged goods ("CPG") and foodservice operations.

Company-operated and Licensed Store Summary as of September 30, 2012

	Americas	As a % of Total Americas Stores	EMEA	As a % of Total EMEA Stores	CAP	As a % of Total CAP Stores	Total	As a % of Total Stores
Company-operated stores	7,857	61%	882	47%	666	20%	9,405	52%
Licensed stores	5,046	39%	987	53%	2,628	80%	8,661	48%
Total	**12,903**	**100%**	**1,869**	**100%**	**3,294**	**100%**	**18,066**	**100%**

The mix of company-operated versus licensed stores in a given market will vary based on several factors, including the ability to access desirable local retail space, the complexity and expected ultimate size of the market for Starbucks, and the ability to leverage the support infrastructure in an existing geographic region.

Company-operated Stores

Revenue from company-operated stores accounted for 79% of total net revenues during fiscal 2012. Our retail objective is to be the leading retailer and brand of coffee in each of our target markets by selling the finest quality coffee and related products, and by providing each customer a unique *Starbucks Experience*. The *Starbucks Experience* is built upon superior customer service as well as clean and well-maintained company-operated stores that reflect the personalities of the communities in which they operate, thereby building a high degree of customer loyalty.

Our strategy for expanding our global retail business is to increase our market share in a disciplined manner, by selectively opening additional stores in new and existing markets, as well as increasing sales in existing stores, to support our long-term strategic objective to maintain Starbucks standing as one of the most recognized and respected brands in the world. Store growth in specific existing markets will vary due to many factors, including the maturity of the market.

The following is a summary of total company-operated store data for the periods indicated:

	Net Stores Opened (Closed) During the Fiscal Year Ended[1]		Stores Open as of	
	Sep 30, 2012	Oct 2, 2011	Sep 30, 2012	Oct 2, 2011
Americas:				
US	161	(2)	6,866	6,705
Canada	42	37	878	836
Chile	6	5	41	35
Brazil	25	5	53	28
Puerto Rico	—	(2)	19	19
Total Americas	234	43	7,857	7,623
EMEA:				
UK	(7)	5	593	600
Germany	7	8	157	150
France	5	8	67	62
Switzerland	4	—	50	46
Austria	—	2	12	12
Netherlands	1	2	3	2
Total EMEA	10	25	882	872
CAP:				
China	130	58	408	278
Thailand	14	8	155	141
Singapore	8	8	80	72
Australia	2	(1)	23	21
Total CAP	154	73	666	512
Total company-operated	**398**	**141**	**9,405**	**9,007**

(1) Store openings are reported net of closures. In the Americas, 279 and 100 company-operated stores were opened during 2012 and 2011, respectively, and 45 and 57 stores were closed during 2012 and 2011, respectively. In EMEA, 27 and 41 company-operated stores were opened during 2012 and 2011, respectively, and 17 and 16 stores were closed during 2012 and 2011, respectively. In CAP, 161 and 87 company-operated stores were opened during 2012 and 2011, respectively, and 7 and 14 stores were closed during 2012 and 2011, respectively.

Starbucks company-operated stores are typically located in high-traffic, high-visibility locations. Our ability to vary the size and format of our stores allows us to locate them in or near a variety of settings, including downtown and suburban retail centers, office buildings, university campuses, and in select rural and off-highway locations. To provide a greater degree of access and convenience for non-pedestrian customers, we continue to selectively expand development of drive-thru stores.

Starbucks stores offer a choice of regular and decaffeinated coffee beverages, a broad selection of Italian-style espresso beverages, cold blended beverages, iced shaken refreshment beverages, a selection of premium Tazo® teas, distinctively packaged roasted whole bean and ground coffees, a variety of Starbucks VIA® Ready Brew soluble coffees, Starbucks® coffee and Tazo® tea K-Cup® portion packs, Starbucks Refreshers™ beverages, juices and bottled water. Starbucks stores also offer an assortment of fresh food items, including selections focusing on high-quality ingredients, nutritional value and great flavor. Food items include pastries, prepared breakfast and lunch sandwiches, oatmeal and salads. A focused selection of beverage-making equipment and accessories are also sold in our stores. Each Starbucks store varies its product mix depending upon the size of the store and its location. To complement the in-store experience, our US company-operated Starbucks stores also provide customers free access to wireless internet.

Retail sales mix by product type for company-operated stores:

Fiscal Year Ended	Sep 30, 2012	Oct 2, 2011	Oct 3, 2010
Beverages	75%	75%	75%
Food	19%	19%	19%
Packaged and single serve coffees	4%	4%	4%
Coffee-making equipment and other merchandise	2%	2%	2%
Total	100%	100%	100%

Starbucks Card

The Starbucks stored value card program is designed to increase customer loyalty and the frequency of store visits by cardholders. Starbucks Cards are accepted at company-operated and most licensed stores in North America. The cards are also accepted at a number of international locations. Customers who register their cards in the US, Canada, and certain other countries are enrolled in the My Starbucks Rewards™ program and can receive various benefits depending on the number of Stars earned in a 12-month period.

Licensed Stores

Product sales to and royalty and license fee revenues from our licensed stores accounted for 9% of total revenues in fiscal 2012. In our licensed store operations, we leverage the expertise of our local partners and share our operating and store development experience. Licensees provide improved, and at times the only, access to desirable retail space. Most licensees are prominent retailers with in-depth market knowledge and access. As part of these arrangements, we receive royalties and license fees and sell coffee, tea and related products for resale in licensed locations. Employees working in licensed retail locations are required to follow our detailed store operating procedures and attend training classes similar to those given to employees in company-operated stores. For our Seattle's Best Coffee brand, we use various forms of licensing, including traditional franchising.

Starbucks total licensed stores by country as of September 30, 2012 are as follows:

Americas		Europe/Middle East/Africa		China / Asia Pacific	
US	4,262	Turkey	171	Japan	965
Mexico	356	UK	168	South Korea	467
Canada	303	United Arab Emirates	99	China	292
Other	125	Spain	78	Taiwan	271
		Kuwait	65	Philippines	201
		Saudi Arabia	64	Malaysia	134
		Russia	60	Indonesia	133
		Greece	42	Hong Kong	131
		Other	240	New Zealand	34
Total	5,046	Total	987	Total	2,628

In the Americas, 351 and 296 licensed stores were opened during 2012 and 2011, respectively, and 81 and 564 licensed stores were closed during 2012 and 20 11, respectively. The 564 licensed stores that were closed in the Americas during fiscal 2011 include 475 Seattle's Best Coffee locations in Borders Bookstores. In EMEA, 139 and 111 licensed stores were opened during 2012 and 2011, respectively, and 38 and 32 licensed stores were closed during 2012 and 2011, respectively. In CAP, 354 and 264 licensed stores were opened during 2012 and 2011, respectively, and 60 and 71 licensed stores were closed during 2012 and 2011, respectively.

Consumer Packaged Goods

Consumer packaged goods includes both domestic and international sales of packaged coffee and tea as well as a variety of ready-to-drink beverages and single-serve coffee and tea products to grocery, warehouse club and specialty retail stores. It also includes revenues from product sales to and licensing revenues from manufacturers that produce and market Starbucks and Seattle's Best Coffee branded products through licensing agreements. Revenues from sales of consumer packaged goods comprised 8% of total net revenues in fiscal 2012.

Foodservice

Revenues from foodservice accounts comprised 4% of total net revenues in fiscal 2012. We sell Starbucks® and Seattle's Best Coffee® whole bean and ground coffees, a selection of premium Tazo® teas, Starbucks VIA® Ready Brew, and other coffee and tea related products to institutional foodservice companies that service business and industry, education, healthcare, office coffee distributors, hotels, restaurants, airlines and other retailers. We also sell our Seattle's Best Coffee® through arrangements with national accounts. The majority of the sales in this channel come through national broadline distribution networks with SYSCO Corporation, US Foodservice™, and other distributors.

Product Supply

Starbucks is committed to selling only the finest whole bean coffees and coffee beverages. To ensure compliance with our rigorous coffee standards, we control coffee purchasing, roasting and packaging, and the global distribution of coffee used in our operations. We purchase green coffee beans from multiple coffee-producing regions around the world and custom roast them to our exacting standards, for our many blends and single origin coffees.

The price of coffee is subject to significant volatility. Although most coffee trades in the commodity market, high-altitude *arabica* coffee of the quality sought by Starbucks tends to trade on a negotiated basis at a premium above the "C" coffee commodity price. Both the premium and the commodity price depend upon the supply and demand at the time of purchase. Supply and price can be affected by multiple factors in the producing countries, including weather, natural disasters, crop disease, general increase in farm inputs and costs of production, inventory levels and political and economic conditions. Price is also impacted by trading activities in the *arabica* coffee futures market, including hedge funds and commodity index funds. In addition, green coffee prices have been affected in the past, and may be affected in the future, by the actions of certain organizations and associations that have historically attempted to influence prices of green coffee through agreements establishing export quotas or by restricting coffee supplies.

We buy coffee using fixed-price and price-to-be-fixed purchase commitments, depending on market conditions, to secure an adequate supply of quality green coffee. Price-to-be-fixed contracts are purchase commitments whereby the quality, quantity, delivery period, and other negotiated terms are agreed upon, but the date, and therefore the price, at which the base "C" coffee commodity price component will be fixed has not yet been established. For these types of contracts, either Starbucks or the seller has the option to select a date on which to "fix" the base "C" coffee commodity price prior to the delivery date. Until prices are fixed, we estimate the total cost of these purchase commitments. Total green coffee purchase commitments as of September 30, 2012 were $854 million, comprised of $557 million under fixed-price contracts and an estimated $297 million under price-to-be-fixed contracts. As of September 30, 2012, approximately $125 million of our price-to-be-fixed contracts were effectively fixed through the use of futures contracts. All price-to-be-fixed contracts as of September 30, 2012 were at the Company's option to fix the base "C" coffee commodity price component. Total purchase commitments, together with existing inventory, are expected to provide an adequate supply of green coffee through fiscal 2013.

We depend upon our relationships with coffee producers, outside trading companies and exporters for our supply of green coffee. We believe, based on relationships established with our suppliers, the risk of non-delivery on such purchase commitments is remote.

To help ensure sustainability and future supply of high-quality green coffees and to reinforce our leadership role in the coffee industry, Starbucks operates Farmer Support Centers in six countries. The Farmer Support Centers are staffed with agronomists and sustainability experts who work with coffee farming communities to promote best practices in coffee production designed to improve both coffee quality and yields.

In addition to coffee, we also purchase significant amounts of dairy products, particularly fluid milk, to support the needs of our company-operated stores. For our largest markets, the US, Canada and the UK, we purchase substantially all of our fluid milk requirements from eight dairy suppliers. We believe, based on relationships established with these suppliers, that the risk of non-delivery of sufficient fluid milk to support our stores is remote.

Products other than whole bean coffees and coffee beverages sold in Starbucks stores include Evolution Fresh™ juices and a number of ready-to-drink beverages that are purchased from several specialty suppliers, usually under long-term supply contracts. Food products, such as pastries, breakfast sandwiches and lunch items, are purchased from national, regional and local sources. We also purchase a broad range of paper and plastic products, such as cups and cutlery, from several companies to support the needs of our retail stores as well as our manufacturing and distribution operations. We believe, based on relationships established with these suppliers and manufacturers, that the risk of non-delivery of these items is remote.

Competition

Our primary competitors for coffee beverage sales are quick-service restaurants and specialty coffee shops. In almost all markets in which we do business, there are numerous competitors in the specialty coffee beverage business. We believe that our customers choose among specialty coffee retailers primarily on the basis of product quality, service and convenience, as well as price. We continue to experience direct competition from large competitors in the US quick-service restaurant sector and the US ready-to-drink coffee beverage market. We also continue to face competition from well-established companies in many international markets.

Our coffee and tea products sold through our Channel Development segment compete directly against specialty coffees and teas sold through supermarkets, club stores and specialty retailers and compete indirectly against all other coffees and teas on the market. Starbucks also faces competition from both restaurants and other specialty retailers for prime retail locations and qualified personnel to operate both new and existing stores.

Patents, Trademarks, Copyrights and Domain Names

Starbucks owns and has applied to register numerous trademarks and service marks in the US and in additional countries throughout the world. Some of our trademarks, including Starbucks, the Starbucks logo, Seattle's Best Coffee, Frappuccino, Starbucks VIA and Tazo are of material importance. The duration of trademark registrations varies from country to country. However, trademarks are generally valid and may be renewed indefinitely as long as they are in use and/or their registrations are properly maintained.

We own numerous copyrights for items such as product packaging, promotional materials, in-store graphics and training materials. We also hold patents on certain products, systems and designs. In addition, Starbucks has registered and maintains numerous Internet domain names, including "Starbucks.com", "Starbucks.net", and "Seattlesbest.com."

Seasonality and Quarterly Results

Our business is subject to seasonal fluctuations, including fluctuations resulting from the holiday season. Cash flows from operations are considerably higher in the first fiscal quarter than the remainder of the year. This is largely driven by cash received as Starbucks Cards are purchased and loaded during the holiday season. Since revenues from Starbucks Cards are recognized upon redemption and not when purchased, seasonal fluctuations on the consolidated statements of earnings are much less pronounced. Quarterly results can also be affected by the timing of the opening of new stores and the closing of existing stores. For these reasons, results for any quarter are not necessarily indicative of the results that may be achieved for the full fiscal year.

Employees

Starbucks employed approximately 160,000 people worldwide as of September 30, 2012. In the US, Starbucks employed approximately 120,000 people, with 113,000 in company-operated stores and the remainder in support facilities, store development, and roasting and warehousing operations. Approximately 40,000 employees were employed outside of the US, with 38,000 in company-operated stores and the remainder in regional support facilities and roasting and warehousing operations. The number of Starbucks employees represented by unions is not significant. We believe our current relations with our employees are good.

Executive officers of the registrant

Name	Age	Position
Howard Schultz	59	chairman, president and chief executive officer
Cliff Burrows	53	president, Starbucks Coffee Americas and US
John Culver	52	president, Starbucks Coffee China and Asia Pacific
Jeff Hansberry	48	president, Channel Development and Emerging Brands
Michelle Gass	44	president, Starbucks Coffee EMEA
Troy Alstead	49	chief financial officer and chief administrative officer
Lucy Lee Helm	55	executive vice president, general counsel and secretary

Howard Schultz is the founder of Starbucks and serves as the chairman, president and chief executive officer. Mr. Schultz has served as chairman of the board since Starbucks inception in 1985 and he resumed his role as president and chief executive officer in January 2008. From June 2000 to February 2005, Mr. Schultz held the title of chief global strategist. From November 1985 to June 2000, he served as chief executive officer. From November 1985 to June 1994, Mr. Schultz also served as president.

Cliff Burrows joined Starbucks in April 2001 and has served as president, Starbucks Coffee Americas and US since October 2011. From March 2008 to October 2011, Mr. Burrows served as president, Starbucks Coffee US. He served as president, Europe, Middle East and Africa (EMEA) from April 2006 to March 2008. He served as vice president and managing director, UK prior to April 2006. Prior to joining Starbucks, Mr. Burrows served in various management positions with Habitat Designs Limited, a furniture and housewares retailer.

John Culver joined Starbucks in August 2002 and has served as president, Starbucks Coffee China and Asia Pacific since October 2011. From December 2009 to October 2011, he served as president, Starbucks Coffee International. Mr. Culver served as executive vice president; president, Global Consumer Products, Foodservice and Seattle's Best Coffee from February 2009 to September 2009, and then as president, Global Consumer Products and Foodservice from October 2009 to November 2009. He previously served as senior vice president; president, Starbucks Coffee Asia Pacific from January 2007 to February 2009, and vice president; general manager, Foodservice from August 2002 to January 2007.

Jeff Hansberry joined Starbucks in June 2010 and has served as president, Channel Development and Emerging Brands since June 2012. From October 2011 to June 2012, he served as president, Channel Development and president, Seattle's Best Coffee. From June 2010 to October 2011, he served as president, Global Consumer Products and Foodservice. Prior to joining Starbucks, Mr. Hansberry served as vice president and general manager, Popular BU for E. & J. Gallo Winery, a family-owned winery, from November 2008 to May 2010. From September 2007 to November 2008, Mr. Hansberry served as vice president and general manager, Value BU, and from April 2005 to August 2007, he served as vice president and general manager Asia, for E. & J. Gallo Winery. Prior to E. & J. Gallo, Mr. Hansberry held various positions with Procter & Gamble.

Michelle Gass joined Starbucks in 1996 and has served as president, Starbucks Coffee EMEA since October 2011. From September 2009 to October 2011, she served as president, Seattle's Best Coffee. Ms. Gass served as senior vice president, Marketing and Category from July 2008 to November 2008, and then as executive vice president, Marketing and Category from December 2008 to September 2009. Ms. Gass previously served as senior vice president, Global Strategy, Office of the ceo from January 2008 to July 2008, senior vice president, Global Product and Brand from August 2007 to January 2008 and senior vice president, U.S. Category Management from May 2004 to August 2007. Ms. Gass served in a number of other positions with Starbucks prior to 2004.

Troy Alstead joined Starbucks in 1992 and has served as chief financial officer and chief administrative officer since November 2008. Mr. Alstead previously served as chief operating officer, Starbucks Greater China from April 2008 to October 2008, senior vice president, Global Finance and Business Operations from August 2007 to April 2008, and senior vice president, Corporate Finance from September 2004 to August 2007. Mr. Alstead served in a number of other senior positions with Starbucks prior to 2004.

Lucy Lee Helm joined Starbucks in September 1999 and has served as executive vice president, general counsel and secretary since May 2012. She served as senior vice president and deputy general counsel from October 2007 to April 2012 and served as interim general counsel and secretary from April 2012 to May 2012. Ms. Helm previously served as vice president, assistant general counsel from June 2002 to September 2007 and as director, corporate counsel from September 1999 to May 2002. During her tenure at Starbucks, Ms. Helm has led various teams of the Starbucks legal department, including the Litigation and Brand protection team, the Global Business (Commercial) team and the Litigation and Employment team. Prior to joining Starbucks, Ms. Helm was a principal at the Seattle law firm of Riddell Williams P.S. from 1990 to 1999, where she was a trial lawyer specializing in commercial, insurance coverage and environmental litigation.

There are no family relationships among any of our directors or executive officers.

Global Responsibility

We are committed to being a deeply responsible company in the communities where we do business around the world. Our focus is on ethically sourcing high-quality coffee, reducing our environmental impacts and contributing positively to communities. Starbucks Global Responsibility strategy and commitments are integral to our overall business strategy. As a result, we believe we deliver benefits to our stakeholders, including employees, business partners, customers, suppliers, shareholders, community members and others. For an overview of Starbucks Global Responsibility strategy and commitments, please visit www.starbucks.com.

Available Information

Starbucks 10-K reports, along with all other reports and amendments filed with or furnished to the Securities and Exchange Commission ("SEC"), are publicly available free of charge on the Investor Relations section of our website at investor.starbucks.com or at www.sec.gov as soon as reasonably practicable after these materials are filed with or furnished to the SEC. Our corporate governance policies, code of ethics and Board committee charters and policies are also posted on the Investor Relations section of Starbucks website at investor.starbucks.com. The information on our website is not part of this or any other report Starbucks files with, or furnishes to, the SEC.

Item 1A. *Risk Factors*

You should carefully consider the risks described below. If any of the risks and uncertainties described in the cautionary factors described below actually occurs, our business, financial condition and results of operations, and the trading price of our common stock could be materially and adversely affected. Moreover, we operate in a very competitive and rapidly changing environment. New factors emerge from time to time and it is not possible to predict the impact of all these factors on our business, financial condition or results of operation.

• *Our financial condition and results of operations are sensitive to, and may be adversely affected by, a number of factors, many of which are largely outside our control.*

Our operating results have been in the past and will continue to be subject to a number of factors, many of which are largely outside our control. Any one or more of the factors set forth below could adversely impact our business, financial condition and/or results of operations:

- lower customer traffic or average value per transaction, which negatively impacts comparable store sales, net revenues, operating income, operating margins and earnings per share, due to:
- the impact of initiatives by competitors and increased competition generally;
- customers trading down to lower priced products within Starbucks, and/or shifting to competitors with lower priced products;
- lack of customer acceptance of new products or price increases necessary to cover costs of new products and/or higher input costs;
- unfavorable general economic conditions in the markets in which we operate that adversely affect consumer spending;
- declines in general consumer demand for specialty coffee products; or
- adverse impacts resulting from negative publicity regarding our business practices or the health effects of consuming our products;
- cost increases that are either wholly or partially beyond our control, such as:
- commodity costs for commodities that can only be partially hedged, such as fluid milk and high-quality *arabica* coffee;

10

- labor costs such as increased health care costs, general market wage levels and workers' compensation insurance costs;

- adverse outcomes of current or future litigation; or

- construction costs associated with new store openings and remodeling of existing stores;

- any material interruption in our supply chain beyond our control, such as material interruption of roasted coffee supply due to the casualty loss of any of our roasting plants or the failures of third-party suppliers, or interruptions in service by common carriers that ship goods within our distribution channels, or trade restrictions, such as increased tariffs or quotas, embargoes or customs restrictions;

- delays in store openings for reasons beyond our control, or a lack of desirable real estate locations available for lease at reasonable rates, either of which could keep us from meeting annual store opening targets and, in turn, negatively impact net revenues, operating income and earnings per share;

- the degree to which we enter into, maintain, develop, and are able to negotiate appropriate terms and conditions, and enforce, commercial and other agreements;

- the impact on our business, especially in our larger or fast growing markets, due to labor discord, war, terrorism (including incidents targeting us), political instability, boycotts, social unrest, and natural disasters, including health pandemics that lead to avoidance of public places or restrictions on public gatherings such as in our stores or cause a material disruption in our supply chain; and

- deterioration in our credit ratings, which could limit the availability of additional financing and increase the cost of obtaining financing.

• *Economic conditions in the US and certain international markets could adversely affect our business and financial results.*

As a retailer that is dependent upon consumer discretionary spending, our results of operations are sensitive to changes in macro-economic conditions. Our customers may have less money for discretionary purchases as a result of job losses, foreclosures, bankruptcies, increased fuel and energy costs, higher interest rates, higher taxes, reduced access to credit and lower home prices. Any resulting decreases in customer traffic and/or average value per transaction will negatively impact our financial performance as reduced revenues result in sales de-leveraging which creates downward pressure on margins. There is also a risk that if negative economic conditions persist for a long period of time or worsen, consumers may make long-lasting changes to their discretionary purchasing behavior, including less frequent discretionary purchases on a more permanent basis.

• *We may not be successful in implementing important strategic initiatives, which may have an adverse impact on our business and financial results.*

There is no assurance that we will be able to implement important strategic initiatives in accordance with our expectations, which may result in an adverse impact on our business and financial results. These strategic initiatives are designed to improve our results of operations and drive long-term shareholder value, and include:

- successfully leveraging Starbucks brand portfolio outside the company-operated store base, including our increased focus on international licensed stores;

- focusing on relevant product innovation and profitable new growth platforms;

- continuing to accelerate the growth of our Channel Development business;

- balancing disciplined global store growth and existing store renovation while meeting target store-level unit economics in a given market;

- timely completing certain supply chain capacity expansion initiatives, including increased roasting capacity and construction of a new soluble products plant and a new Evolution Fresh™ plant; and

- executing a multi-channel advertising and marketing campaign to effectively communicate our message directly to Starbucks consumers and employees.

11

- *We face intense competition in each of our channels and markets, which could lead to reduced profitability.*

The specialty coffee market is intensely competitive, including with respect to product quality, service, convenience, and price, and we face significant competition in each of our channels and markets. Accordingly, we do not have leadership positions in all channels and markets. In the US, the ongoing focus by large competitors in the quick-service restaurant sector on selling high-quality specialty coffee beverages could adversely affect our sales and results of operations. Similarly, continued competition from well-established competitors in our international markets could hinder growth and adversely affect our sales and results of operations in those markets. Increased competition in the US packaged coffee and tea and single-serve and ready-to-drink coffee beverage markets, including from new and large entrants to this market, could adversely affect the profitability of the Channel Development segment.

- *We are highly dependent on the financial performance of our Americas operating segment.*

Our financial performance is highly dependent on our Americas operating segment, as it comprised approximately 75% of consolidated total net revenues in fiscal 2012. If revenue trends slow or decline, our business and financial results could be adversely affected, and because the Americas segment is relatively mature and produces the large majority of our operating cash flows, could result in reduced cash flows for funding the expansion of our international business and for returning cash to shareholders.

- *We are increasingly dependent on the success of our EMEA and CAP operating segments in order to achieve our growth targets.*

Our future growth increasingly depends on the growth and sustained profitability of our EMEA and CAP operating segments. Some or all of our international market business units ("MBUs"), which we generally define by the countries in which they operate, may not be successful in their operations or in achieving expected growth, which ultimately requires achieving consistent, stable net revenues and earnings. The performance of these international operations may be adversely affected by economic downturns in one or more of our large MBUs. In particular, our Japan, UK, and China MBUs account for a significant portion of the net revenue and earnings of our EMEA and CAP segments and a decline in the performance of any of these MBUs could have a material adverse impact on the results of our international operations.

Additionally, some factors that will be critical to the success of the EMEA and CAP segments are different than those affecting our US stores and licensees. Tastes naturally vary by region, and consumers in some MBUs may not embrace our products to the same extent as consumers in the US or other international markets. Occupancy costs and store operating expenses can be higher internationally than in the US due to higher rents for prime store locations or costs of compliance with country-specific regulatory requirements. Because many of our international operations are in an early phase of development, operating expenses as a percentage of related revenues are often higher compared to more developed operations, such as in the US. Additionally, our international joint venture partners or licensees may face capital constraints or other factors that may limit the speed at which they are able to expand and develop in a certain market.

Our international operations are also subject to additional inherent risks of conducting business abroad, such as:

- foreign currency exchange rate fluctuations, or requirements to transact in specific currencies;
- changes or uncertainties in economic, legal, regulatory, social and political conditions in our markets;
- interpretation and application of laws and regulations;
- restrictive actions of foreign or US governmental authorities affecting trade and foreign investment, especially during periods of heightened tension between the US and such foreign governmental authorities, including protective measures such as export and customs duties and tariffs, government intervention favoring local competitors, and restrictions on the level of foreign ownership;
- import or other business licensing requirements;
- the enforceability of intellectual property and contract rights;

- limitations on the repatriation of funds and foreign currency exchange restrictions due to current or new US and international regulations;

- in developing economies, the growth rate in the portion of the population achieving targeted levels of disposable income may not be as fast as we forecast;

- difficulty in staffing, developing and managing foreign operations and supply chain logistics, including ensuring the consistency of product quality and service, due to distance, language and cultural differences, as well as challenges in recruiting and retaining high quality employees in local markets;

- local laws that make it more expensive and complex to negotiate with, retain or terminate employees;

- delays in store openings for reasons beyond our control, competition with locally relevant competitors or a lack of desirable real estate locations available for lease at reasonable rates, any of which could keep us from meeting annual store opening targets and, in turn, negatively impact net revenues, operating income and earnings per share; and

- disruption in energy supplies affecting our markets.

Moreover, many of the foregoing risks are particularly acute in developing countries, which are important to our long-term growth prospects.

- *Increases in the cost of high-quality* **arabica** *coffee beans or other commodities or decreases in the availability of high-quality* **arabica** *coffee beans or other commodities could have an adverse impact on our business and financial results.*

We purchase, roast, and sell high-quality whole bean *arabica* coffee beans and related coffee products. The price of coffee is subject to significant volatility and, although coffee prices have come down from their near-record highs of 2011, they are still above the historical average price of coffee and may again increase significantly due to factors described below. The high-quality *arabica* coffee of the quality we seek tends to trade on a negotiated basis at a premium above the "C" price. This premium depends upon the supply and demand at the time of purchase and the amount of the premium can vary significantly. Increases in the "C" coffee commodity price do increase the price of high-quality *arabica* coffee and also impact our ability to enter into fixed-price purchase commitments. We frequently enter into supply contracts whereby the quality, quantity, delivery period, and other negotiated terms are agreed upon, but the date, and therefore price, at which the base "C" coffee commodity price component will be fixed has not yet been established. These are known as price-to-be-fixed contracts. The supply and price of coffee we purchase can also be affected by multiple factors in the producing countries, including weather, natural disasters, crop disease, general increase in farm inputs and costs of production, inventory levels and political and economic conditions, as well as the actions of certain organizations and associations that have historically attempted to influence prices of green coffee through agreements establishing export quotas or by restricting coffee supplies. Speculative trading in coffee commodities can also influence coffee prices. Because of the significance of coffee beans to our operations, combined with our ability to only partially mitigate future price risk through purchasing practices and hedging activities, increases in the cost of high-quality *arabica* coffee beans could have an adverse impact on our profitability. In addition, if we are not able to purchase sufficient quantities of green coffee due to any of the above factors or to a worldwide or regional shortage, we may not be able to fulfill the demand for our coffee, which could have an adverse impact on our profitability.

In addition to coffee, we also purchase significant amounts of dairy products, particularly fluid milk, to support the needs of our company-operated retail stores. Although less material to our operations than coffee or dairy, other commodities including but not limited to those related to food inputs and energy, are important to our operations. Increases in the cost of dairy products and other commodities could have an adverse impact on our profitability.

13

• *Our success depends substantially on the value of our brands and failure to preserve their value could have a negative impact on our financial results.*

We believe we have built an excellent reputation globally for the quality of our products, for delivery of a consistently positive consumer experience and for our corporate social responsibility programs. The Starbucks brand has been highly rated in several global brand value studies. To be successful in the future, particularly outside of US, where the Starbucks brand and our other brands are less well-known, we believe we must preserve, grow and leverage the value of our brands across all sales channels. Brand value is based in part on consumer perceptions on a variety of subjective qualities. Even isolated business incidents that erode consumer trust, such as contaminated food, recalls or privacy breaches, particularly if the incidents receive considerable publicity or result in litigation, can significantly reduce brand value and have a negative impact on our financial results. Consumer demand for our products and our brand equity could diminish significantly if we or our licensees fail to preserve the quality of our products, are perceived to act in an unethical or socially irresponsible manner or fail to deliver a consistently positive consumer experience in each of our markets. Additionally, inconsistent uses of our brand and other of our intellectual property assets, as well as failure to protect our intellectual property, including from unauthorized uses of our brand or other of our intellectual property assets, can erode consumer trust and our brand value and have a negative impact on our financial results.

• *Our business depends in large part on the success of our business partners and suppliers, and our brand and reputation may be harmed by actions taken by third parties that are outside of our control.*

Our business strategy, including our plans for new stores, foodservice, branded products and other initiatives, relies significantly on a variety of business partners, and licensee and partnership relationships, particularly in our international markets. Licensees are often authorized to use our logos and provide branded beverages, food and other products directly to customers. We provide training and support to, and monitor the operations of, certain of these business partners, but the product quality and service they deliver may be diminished by any number of factors beyond our control, including financial pressures. We believe customers expect the same quality of products and service from our licensees as they do from us and we strive to ensure customers have the same experience whether they visit a company-operated or licensed store. Any shortcoming of a Starbucks business partner, particularly an issue affecting the quality of the service experience, the safety of beverages or food or compliance with laws and regulations, may be attributed by customers to us, thus damaging our reputation and brand value and potentially affecting our results of operations.

Our food and beverage products are sourced from a wide variety of domestic and international business partners in our supply chain operations, and in certain cases are produced or sourced by our licensees directly. We rely on these suppliers and vendors to provide high quality products and to comply with applicable laws. Our ability to find qualified suppliers and vendors who meet our standards and supply products in a timely and efficient manner is a significant challenge, especially with respect to goods sourced from outside the US. A vendor's or supplier's failure to meet our standards, provide products in a timely and efficient manner, and comply with applicable laws is beyond our control. These issues could negatively impact our business and profitability.

• *Failure to meet market expectations for our financial performance will likely adversely affect the market price and volatility of our stock.*

Failure to meet market expectations going forward, particularly with respect to operating margins, earnings per share, comparable store sales, operating cash flows, and net revenues, will likely result in a decline and/or increased volatility in the market price of our stock. In addition, price and volume fluctuations in the stock market as a whole may affect the market price of our stock in ways that may be unrelated to our financial performance.

- *The loss of key personnel or difficulties recruiting and retaining qualified personnel could adversely impact our business and financial results.*

Much of our future success depends on the continued availability and service of senior management personnel. The loss of any of our executive officers or other key senior management personnel could harm our business. We must continue to recruit, retain and motivate management and other employees sufficiently, both to maintain our current business and to execute our strategic initiatives, some of which involve ongoing expansion in business channels outside of our traditional company-operated store model. Our success also depends substantially on the contributions and abilities of our retail store employees whom we rely on to give customers a superior in-store experience. Accordingly, our performance depends on our ability to recruit and retain high quality employees to work in and manage our stores, both domestically and internationally. If we are unable to recruit, retain and motivate employees sufficiently to maintain our current business and support our projected growth, our business and financial performance may be adversely affected.

- *Adverse public or medical opinions about the health effects of consuming our products, as well as reports of incidents involving food-borne illnesses, food tampering or food contamination, whether or not accurate, could harm our business.*

Some of our products contain caffeine, dairy products, sugar and other active compounds, the health effects of which are the subject of public scrutiny, including the suggestion that excessive consumption of caffeine, dairy products, sugar and other active compounds can lead to a variety of adverse health effects. Particularly in the US, there is increasing consumer awareness of health risks, including obesity, due in part to increased publicity and attention from health organizations, as well as increased consumer litigation based on alleged adverse health impacts of consumption of various food products. While we have a variety of beverage and food items, including items that are coffee-free and have reduced calories, an unfavorable report on the health effects of caffeine or other compounds present in our products, or negative publicity or litigation arising from certain health risks could significantly reduce the demand for our beverages and food products.

Similarly, instances or reports, whether true or not, of unclean water supply, food-borne illnesses, food tampering and food contamination, either during manufacturing, packaging or preparation, have in the past severely injured the reputations of companies in the food processing, grocery and quick-service restaurant sectors and could affect us as well. Any report linking us to the use of unclean water, food-borne illnesses, food tampering or food contamination could damage our brand value and severely hurt sales of our beverages and food products, and possibly lead to product liability claims, litigation (including class actions) or damages. Clean water is critical to the preparation of coffee and tea beverages and our ability to ensure a clean water supply to our stores can be limited, particularly in some international locations. If customers become ill from food-borne illnesses, tampering or contamination, we could also be forced to temporarily close some stores. In addition, instances of food-borne illnesses, food tampering or food contamination, even those occurring solely at the restaurants or stores of competitors, could, by resulting in negative publicity about the foodservice industry, adversely affect our sales on a regional or global basis. A decrease in customer traffic as a result of these health concerns or negative publicity, or as a result of a temporary closure of any of our stores, as well adverse results of claims or litigation, could materially harm our business and results of operations.

- *Effectively managing growth both in our retail store business and our Channel Development business is challenging and places significant strain on our management and employees and our operational, financial, and other resources.*

Effectively managing growth can be challenging, particularly as we continue to expand into new channels outside the retail store model, increase our focus on our Channel Development business, and expand into new markets internationally where we must balance the need for flexibility and a degree of autonomy for local management against the need for consistency with our goals, philosophy and standards. Growth can make it increasingly difficult to ensure a consistent supply of high-quality raw materials, to locate and hire sufficient numbers of key employees, to maintain an effective system of internal controls for a globally dispersed enterprise and to train employees worldwide to deliver a consistently high quality product and customer experience.

- *As we pursue strategic acquisitions, divestitures or joint ventures, we may not be able to successfully consummate favorable transactions or successfully integrate acquired businesses.*

We have recently completed several acquisitions and we continue to evaluate potential acquisitions, divestitures, or joint ventures with third parties. These transactions create risks such as:

- disruption of our ongoing business, including loss of management focus on existing businesses;
- problems retaining key personnel;
- operating losses and expenses of the businesses we acquire or in which we invest;
- the potential impairment of tangible assets, intangible assets and goodwill acquired in the acquisitions;
- the difficulty of incorporating an acquired business into our business and unanticipated expenses related to such integration; and
- potential unknown liabilities associated with a business we acquire or in which we invest

In the event of any future acquisitions, we might need to issue additional equity securities, spend our cash, incur debt, or take on contingent liabilities, any of which could reduce our profitability and harm our business.

- *We rely heavily on information technology in our operations, and any material failure, inadequacy, interruption or security failure of that technology could harm our ability to effectively operate our business and expose us to potential liability and loss of revenues.*

We rely heavily on information technology systems across our operations, including for administrative functions, point-of-sale processing and payment in our stores and online, management of our supply chain, Starbucks Cards, online business and various other processes and transactions. Our ability to effectively manage our business and coordinate the production, distribution and sale of our products depends significantly on the reliability, integrity and capacity of these systems. We also rely on third party providers for some of these information technology systems and support. The failure of these systems to operate effectively, problems with transitioning to upgraded or replacement systems, or a breach in security of these systems could cause material negative impacts to our product sales, the efficiency of our operations and our financial results. Significant capital investments and other expenditures could be required to remedy the problem. Furthermore, security breaches of our employees' or customers' private data could result in a violation of applicable U.S. and international privacy and other laws, loss of revenues from the potential adverse impact to our reputation and our ability to retain or attract new customers, and could result in litigation, potential liability and the imposition of penalties.

- *The effect of changes to healthcare laws in the United States may increase the number of employees who choose to participate in our healthcare plans, which may significantly increase our healthcare costs and negatively impact our financial results.*

Since 1988 we have offered comprehensive healthcare coverage to eligible full-time and part-time employees in the US. We currently have relatively low minimum work hour requirements for our US employees to be eligible for healthcare coverage under our healthcare plans but for various reasons many of our eligible employees choose not to participate in our plans. However, many of such eligible employees who currently choose not to participate in our healthcare plans may find it more advantageous to do so when recent changes to healthcare laws in the United States become effective in 2014. Such changes include potential fees to persons for not obtaining healthcare coverage and being ineligible for certain healthcare subsidies if an employee is eligible for healthcare coverage under an employer's plan. If a large portion of current eligible employees who currently choose not to participate in our plans choose to enroll when or after the law becomes effective, it may significantly increase our healthcare coverage costs and negatively impact on our financial results.

• *Failure to comply with applicable laws and regulations could harm our business and financial results.*

Our policies and procedures are designed to comply with all applicable laws, accounting and reporting requirements, tax rules and other regulations and requirements, including those imposed by the SEC, NASDAQ, and foreign countries, as well as applicable trade, labor, healthcare, privacy, food, anti-bribery and corruption and merchandise laws. The complexity of the regulatory environment in which we operate and the related cost of compliance are both increasing due to additional or changing legal and regulatory requirements, our ongoing expansion into new markets and new channels, together with the fact that foreign laws occasionally conflict with domestic laws. In addition to potential damage to our reputation and brand, failure to comply with the various laws and regulations as well as changes in laws and regulations or the manner in which they are interpreted or applied, may result in civil and criminal liability, damages, fines and penalties, increased cost of regulatory compliance and restatements of our financial statements.

Item 1B. *Unresolved Staff Comments*

None.

Item 2. *Properties*

The significant properties used by Starbucks in connection with its roasting, distribution and corporate administrative operations, serving all segments, are as follows:

Location	Approximate Size in Square Feet	Purpose
Rancho Cucamonga, CA	265,000	Manufacturing
Carson Valley, NV	384,000	Roasting, distribution and warehouse
York County, PA	748,000	Roasting, distribution and warehouse
Sandy Run, SC	117,000	Roasting and distribution
Auburn, WA	351,000	Warehouse and distribution
Kent, WA	332,000	Roasting and distribution
Seattle, WA	1,000,000	Corporate administrative
Amsterdam, Netherlands	97,000	Roasting and distribution
Basildon, United Kingdom	142,000	Warehouse and distribution

We own our roasting facilities and lease the majority of our warehousing and distribution locations. As of September 30, 2012, Starbucks had approximately 9,400 company-operated stores, almost all of which are leased. We also lease space in various locations worldwide for regional, district and other administrative offices, training facilities and storage.

Item 3. *Legal Proceedings*

In the first quarter of fiscal 2011, Starbucks notified Kraft Foods Global, Inc. ("Kraft") that we were discontinuing our distribution arrangement with Kraft on March 1, 2011 due to material breaches by Kraft of its obligations under the Supply and License Agreement between the Company and Kraft, dated March 29, 2004 (the "Agreement"), which defined the main distribution arrangement between the parties. Through our arrangement with Kraft, Starbucks sold a selection of Starbucks and Seattle's Best Coffee branded packaged coffees in grocery and warehouse club stores throughout the US, and to grocery stores in Canada, the UK and

17

other European countries. Kraft managed the distribution, marketing, advertising and promotion of these products.

Kraft denies it has materially breached the Agreement. On November 29, 2010, Starbucks received a notice of arbitration from Kraft putting the commercial dispute between the parties into binding arbitration pursuant to the terms of the Agreement. In addition to denying it materially breached the Agreement, Kraft further alleges that if Starbucks wished to terminate the Agreement it must compensate Kraft as provided in the Agreement in an amount equal to the fair value of the Agreement, with an additional premium of up to 35% under certain circumstances.

On December 6, 2010, Kraft commenced a federal court action against Starbucks, entitled *Kraft Foods Global, Inc. v. Starbucks Corporation*, in the U.S. District Court for the Southern District of New York (the "District Court") seeking injunctive relief to prevent Starbucks from terminating the distribution arrangement until the parties' dispute is resolved through the arbitration proceeding. On January 28, 2011, the District Court denied Kraft's request for injunctive relief. Kraft appealed the District Court's decision to the Second Circuit Court of Appeals. On February 25, 2011, the Second Circuit Court of Appeals affirmed the District Court's decision. As a result, Starbucks is in full control of our packaged coffee business as of March 1, 2011.

While Starbucks believes we have valid claims of material breach by Kraft under the Agreement that allowed us to terminate the Agreement and certain other relationships with Kraft without compensation to Kraft, there exists the possibility of material adverse outcomes to Starbucks in the arbitration or to resolve the matter. Although Kraft disclosed to the press and in federal court filings a $750 million offer Starbucks made to Kraft in August 2010 to avoid litigation and ensure a smooth transition of the business, the figure is not a proper basis upon which to estimate a possible outcome of the arbitration but was based upon facts and circumstances at the time. Kraft rejected the offer immediately and did not provide a counter-offer, effectively ending the discussions between the parties with regard to any payment. Moreover, the offer was made prior to our investigation of Kraft's breaches and without consideration of Kraft's continuing failure to comply with material terms of the agreements.

On April 2, 2012, Starbucks and Kraft exchanged expert reports regarding alleged damages on their affirmative claims. Starbucks claimed damages of up to $62.9 million from the loss of sales resulting from Kraft's failure to use commercially reasonable efforts to market Starbucks® coffee, plus attorney fees. Kraft's expert opined that the fair market value of the Agreement was $1.9 billion. After applying a 35% premium and 9% interest, Kraft claimed damages of up to $2.9 billion, plus attorney fees. The arbitration hearing commenced on July 11, 2012 and was completed on August 3. Starbucks presented evidence of material breaches on Kraft's part and sought nominal damages from Kraft for those breaches. Kraft presented evidence denying it had breached the parties' Agreement and sought damages of $2.9 billion plus attorney fees. We expect a decision from the Arbitrator in the first half of fiscal 2013.

At this time, Starbucks believes an unfavorable outcome with respect to the arbitration is not probable, but as noted above is reasonably possible. As also noted above, Starbucks believes we have valid claims of material breach by Kraft under the Agreement that allowed us to terminate the Agreement without compensation to Kraft. In addition, Starbucks believes Kraft's damage estimates are highly inflated and based upon faulty analysis. As a result, we cannot reasonably estimate the possible loss. Accordingly, no loss contingency has been recorded for this matter.

Starbucks is party to various other legal proceedings arising in the ordinary course of business, including certain employment litigation cases that have been certified as class or collective actions, but, except as noted above, is not currently a party to any legal proceeding that management believes could have a material adverse effect on our consolidated financial position, results of operations or cash flows.

Item 4. Mine Safety Disclosures

Not applicable.

18

PART II

Item 5. *Market for the Registrant's Common Equity, Related Shareholder Matters and Issuer Purchases of Equity Securities*

SHAREHOLDER INFORMATION

MARKET INFORMATION AND DIVIDEND POLICY

Starbucks common stock is traded on NASDAQ, under the symbol "SBUX."

The following table shows the quarterly high and low sale prices per share of Starbucks common stock as reported by NASDAQ for each quarter during the last two fiscal years and the quarterly cash dividend declared per share of our common stock during the periods indicated:

	High	Low	Cash Dividends Declared
2012:			
Fourth Quarter	$ 54.28	$ 43.04	$ 0.21
Third Quarter	62.00	51.03	0.17
Second Quarter	56.55	45.28	0.17
First Quarter	46.50	35.12	0.17
2011:			
Fourth Quarter	$ 42.00	$ 33.72	$ 0.17
Third Quarter	40.26	34.61	0.13
Second Quarter	38.21	30.75	0.13
First Quarter	33.15	25.37	0.13

As of November 9, 2012, we had approximately 18,500 shareholders of record. This does not include persons whose stock is in nominee or "street name" accounts through brokers.

Future decisions to pay cash dividends continue to be at the discretion of the Board of Directors and will be dependent on our operating performance, financial condition, capital expenditure requirements, and other such factors that the Board of Directors considers relevant.

ISSUER PURCHASES OF EQUITY SECURITIES

The following table provides information regarding repurchases of our common stock during the quarter ended September 30, 2012:

Period(1)	Total Number of Shares Purchased	Average Price Paid per Share	Total Number of Shares Purchased as Part of Publicly Announced Plans or Programs	Maximum Number of Shares that May Yet Be Purchased Under the Plans or Programs (2)
July 2, 2012 — July 29, 2012	—	$ —	—	24,015,356
July 30, 2012 — August 26, 2012	5,265,260	46.44	5,265,260	18,750,096
August 27, 2012 — September 30, 2012	6,622,320	50.27	6,622,320	12,127,776
Total	11,887,580	$ 48.58	11,887,580	

(1) Monthly information is presented by reference to our fiscal months during the fourth quarter of fiscal 2012.

(2) The share repurchase program is conducted under authorizations made from time to time by our Board of Directors. On March 24, 2010 we publicly announced the authorization of up to an additional 15 million shares, on November 15, 2010 we publicly announced the authorization of up to an additional 10 million shares, and on November 3, 2011 we publicly announced the authorization of up to an additional 20 million shares. These authorizations have no expiration date.

On November 14, 2012, our Board of Directors authorized the repurchase of up to an additional 25 million shares, in addition to the 12.1 million shares that remained available for repurchase at September 30, 2012 under previous authorizations. As with previous authorizations, shares may be repurchased in open market transactions, including pursuant to a trading plan adopted in accordance with Rule 10b5-1 of the Securities Exchange Act of 1934. The timing, manner, price and amount of repurchases will be determined in the Company's discretion and the share repurchase program may be suspended, terminated or modified at any time for any reason.

Performance Comparison Graph

The following graph depicts the total return to shareholders from September 30, 2007 through September 30, 2012, relative to the performance of the Standard & Poor's 500 Index, the NASDAQ Composite Index, and the Standard & Poor's 500 Consumer Discretionary Sector, a peer group that includes Starbucks. All indices shown in the graph have been reset to a base of 100 as of September 30, 2007, and assume an investment of $100 on that date and the reinvestment of dividends paid since that date. The stock price performance shown in the graph is not necessarily indicative of future price performance.

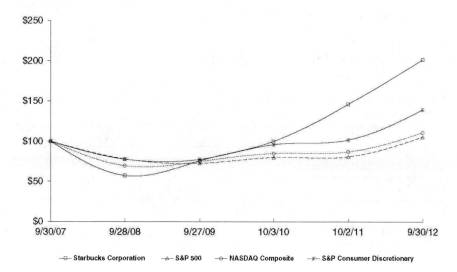

	9/30/2007	9/28/2008	9/27/2009	10/3/2010	10/2/2011	9/30/2012
Starbucks Corporation	100.00	57.10	75.69	99.93	145.94	201.33
S&P 500	100.00	78.02	72.63	80.01	80.93	105.37
NASDAQ Composite	100.00	69.59	74.90	84.99	86.87	110.79
S&P Consumer Discretionary	100.00	77.59	77.55	95.87	101.79	139.08

21

Item 6. *Selected Financial Data*

The following selected financial data are derived from the consolidated financial statements. The data below should be read in conjunction with "Management's Discussion and Analysis of Financial Condition and Results of Operations," "Risk Factors," and the consolidated financial statements and notes.

Financial Information (in millions, except per share data):

As of and for the Fiscal Year Ended[1]	Sep 30, 2012 (52 Wks)	Oct 2, 2011 (52 Wks)	Oct 3, 2010 (53 Wks)	Sep 27, 2009 (52 Wks)	Sep 28, 2008 (52 Wks)
Results of Operations					
Net revenues:					
Company-operated stores	$ 10,534.5	$ 9,632.4	$ 8,963.5	$ 8,180.1	$ 8,771.9
Licensed stores[2]	1,210.3	1,007.5	875.2	795.0	779.0
CPG, foodservice and other[2]	1,554.7	1,060.5	868.7	799.5	832.1
Total net revenues	$ 13,299.5	$ 11,700.4	$ 10,707.4	$ 9,774.6	$ 10,383.0
Operating income[3]	$ 1,997.4	$ 1,728.5	$ 1,419.4	$ 562.0	$ 503.9
Net earnings including noncontrolling interests	1,384.7	1,248.0	948.3	391.5	311.7
Net earnings (loss) attributable to noncontrolling interests	0.9	2.3	2.7	0.7	(3.8)
Net earnings attributable to Starbucks	1,383.8	1,245.7	945.6	390.8	315.5
EPS — diluted	1.79	1.62	1.24	0.52	0.43
Cash dividends declared per share	0.72	0.56	0.36	—	—
Net cash provided by operating activities	1,750.3	1,612.4	1,704.9	1,389.0	1,258.7
Capital expenditures (additions to property, plant and equipment)	856.2	531.9	440.7	445.6	984.5
Balance Sheet					
Total assets	$ 8,219.2	$ 7,360.4	$ 6,385.9	$ 5,576.8	$ 5,672.6
Short-term borrowings	—	—	—	—	713.0
Long-term debt (including current portion)	549.6	549.5	549.4	549.5	550.3
Shareholders' equity	5,109.0	4,384.9	3,674.7	3,045.7	2,490.9

(1) Our fiscal year ends on the Sunday closest to September 30. The fiscal year ended on October 3, 2010 included 53 weeks with the 53rd week falling in our fourth fiscal quarter.

(2) Includes the revenue reclassification described in Note 1. For fiscal years 2010, 2009, and 2008, we reclassified $465.7 million, $427.3 million, and $392.6 million, respectively, from the previously named "Licensing" revenue to "CPG, foodservice and other" revenue.

(3) Fiscal 2010, 2009, and 2008 results include pretax restructuring charges of $53.0 million, $332.4 million, and $266.9 million, respectively.

Comparable Store Sales:

Fiscal Year Ended	Sep 30, 2012 (52 Wks)	Oct 2, 2011 (52 Wks)	Oct 3, 2010 (53 Wks)	Sep 27, 2009 (52 Wks)	Sep 28, 2008 (52 Wks)
Percentage change in comparable store sales[4]					
Americas					
Sales growth	8%	8%	7%	(6)%	(4)%
Change in transactions	6%	5%	3%	(4)%	(4)%
Change in ticket	2%	2%	3%	(2)%	— %
EMEA					
Sales growth	—%	3%	5%	(3)%	1%
Change in transactions	—%	3%	6%	—%	(3)%
Change in ticket	—%	—%	(1)%	(3)%	4%
China / Asia Pacific					
Sales growth	15%	22%	11%	2%	8%
Change in transactions	11%	20%	9%	—%	4%
Change in ticket	3%	2%	2%	2%	3%
Consolidated					
Sales growth	7%	8%	7%	(6)%	(3)%
Change in transactions	6%	6%	4%	(4)%	(4)%
Change in ticket	1%	2%	3%	(2)%	— %

(4) Includes only Starbucks company-operated stores open 13 months or longer. For fiscal year 2010, comparable store sales percentages were calculated excluding the 53rd week. Comparable store sales exclude the effect of fluctuations in foreign currency exchange rates.

23

Store Count Data:

As of and for the Fiscal Year Ended	Sep 30, 2012 (52 Wks)	Oct 2, 2011 (52 Wks)	Oct 3, 2010 (53 Wks)	Sep 27, 2009 (52 Wks)	Sep 28, 2008 (52 Wks)
Net stores opened (closed) during the year:					
Americas					
Company-operated stores	234	43	(33)	(417)	561
Licensed stores[5]	270	(268)	111	101	558
EMEA[6]					
Company-operated stores	10	25	(64)	20	127
Licensed stores	101	79	100	98	153
China / Asia Pacific					
Company-operated stores	154	73	30	24	9
Licensed stores	294	193	79	129	261
Total	1,063	145	223	(45)	1,669
Stores open at year end:					
Americas					
Company-operated stores	7,857	7,623	7,580	7,613	8,030
Licensed stores	5,046	4,776	5,044	4,933	4,832
EMEA[6]					
Company-operated stores	882	872	847	911	891
Licensed stores	987	886	807	707	609
China / Asia Pacific					
Company-operated stores	666	512	439	409	385
Licensed stores	2,628	2,334	2,141	2,062	1,933
Total	18,066	17,003	16,858	16,635	16,680

(5) Includes the closure of 475 licensed Seattle's Best Coffee locations in Borders Bookstores during fiscal 2011.

(6) EMEA store data has been adjusted for the acquisition of store locations in Austria and Switzerland in the fourth quarter of fiscal 2011 by reclassifying historical information from licensed stores to company-operated stores, and the transfer of certain company-operated stores to licensees in the fourth quarter of fiscal 2012.

Item 7. *Management's Discussion and Analysis of Financial Condition and Results of Operations*

General

Our fiscal year ends on the Sunday closest to September 30. The fiscal year ended on October 3, 2010 included 53 weeks with the 53rd week falling in the fourth fiscal quarter. The fiscal years ended on October 2, 2011 and September 30, 2012 both included 52 weeks. Comparable store sales percentages for fiscal 2010 are calculated excluding the 53rd week. All references to store counts, including data for new store openings, are reported net of related store closures, unless otherwise noted.

Financial Highlights

- Total net revenues increased 14% to $13.3 billion in fiscal 2012 compared to $11.7 billion in fiscal 2011. The increase was due primarily to a 7% increase in global comparable store sales, 50% revenue growth in Channel Development, and 20% growth in licensed stores revenue. The comparable store sales growth in company-operated stores was comprised of a 6% increase in the number of transactions and a 1% increase in average ticket.

- Consolidated operating income was $2.0 billion in fiscal 2012 compared to $1.7 billion in fiscal 2011 and operating margin increased to 15.0% compared to 14.8% in fiscal 2011. The operating margin expansion was driven by increased sales leverage and the absence of charges in fiscal 2012 related to the Seattle's Best Coffee store closures in Border's bookstores, partially offset by higher commodity costs.

- EPS for fiscal 2012 was $1.79, compared to EPS of $1.62 reported in fiscal 2011, with the increase driven by the improved sales leverage, partially offset by the impact of higher commodity costs in fiscal 2012 and certain gains recorded in the fourth quarter of fiscal 2011, including a gain from a fair market value adjustment resulting from the acquisition of the remaining ownership interest in our joint venture in Switzerland and Austria as well as a gain on the sale of corporate real estate.

- Cash flow from operations was $1.8 billion in fiscal 2012 compared to $1.6 billion in fiscal 2011. Capital expenditures were approximately $856 million in fiscal 2012 compared to $532 million in fiscal 2011. Available operating cash flow after capital expenditures during fiscal 2012 was directed at returning approximately $1.1 billion of cash to our shareholders via share repurchases and dividends.

Overview

Starbucks results for fiscal 2012 reflect the strength of our global business model. We continue to execute on our new regional operating model which we implemented at the beginning of fiscal 2012. We now have four reportable operating segments: Americas; Europe, Middle East, and Africa ("EMEA"); China / Asia Pacific ("CAP") and Channel Development. Each segment is managed by an operating segment president.

Total net revenues increased 14% to $13.3 billion driven by global comparable store sales growth of 7% and a 50% increase in Channel Development revenue. This growth drove increased sales leverage and resulted in higher operating margin and net earnings compared to fiscal 2011. This helped mitigate the impact of higher commodity costs, mostly coffee, which negatively impacted operating income by approximately $214 million for the year, equivalent to approximately 160 basis points of impact on operating margin.

Our Americas business continued its strong momentum and contributed 75% of total net revenues in fiscal 2012. The revenue growth for the year was driven by an 8% increase in comparable store sales, comprised of a 6% increase in traffic and a 2% increase in average ticket. This sales growth, combined with a continued focus on operational efficiencies, drove increased sales leverage that offset the impact of higher commodity costs. Looking forward, we expect to continue driving sales growth and profitability through continued store efficiency efforts, new store development, and expanding our pipeline of new product offerings to increase revenues throughout all dayparts.

EMEA segment results reflect both the investments we have begun making as part of our transformation plan for the region, as well as the macro-economic headwinds we, and others, face there. This resulted in flat comparable store sales and operating income of $10 million for fiscal 2012, a decrease of $30 million compared to fiscal 2011. We started the year by putting in place a new leadership team that is focused on increasing the Starbucks brand presence, health and relevancy across the region, improving the profitability of the existing store base through a focus on revenue growth and operating costs, and identifying opportunities for new store growth through licensing arrangements. We expect the investments we are making as part of this transformation effort will result in improved operating performance as we progress on our plan towards mid-teens operating margin; however, this turnaround will take time to gain traction.

CAP segment revenues increased 31%, driven by new store growth and comparable store sales of 15%. This segment continues to grow rapidly and is becoming a more meaningful contributor to overall company profitability. We expect continued growth will be from a mix of new store openings and comparable store sales growth. China continues to be a significant growth opportunity for us as we remain on track to reach our goal of 1,500 stores in 2015. In addition, other key markets such as Japan, Korea, Thailand, Singapore and Indonesia all continue to be profitable and provide a solid foundation for continued growth in the region.

Our Channel Development segment represents another important, profitable growth opportunity for us. Channel Development results were a solid contributor to overall revenue growth with a 50% increase in revenues primarily due to sales of Starbucks and Tazo branded K-Cup® portion packs which launched at the start of fiscal 2012 and our transition to a direct distribution model for packaged coffee, which occurred during the second quarter of fiscal 2011. High commodity costs continued to be a significant drag on operating margin; however, despite these higher costs, operating income increased $61 million to $349 million for fiscal 2012. We expect continued innovation and new product offerings such as the Verismo™ system by Starbucks and Starbucks Refreshers™ beverages will drive further growth and profitability within this segment over time.

Fiscal 2013 — The View Ahead

For fiscal year 2013, we expect moderate revenue growth driven by mid single-digit increased comparable store sales, new store openings and strong growth in the Channel Development business. Licensed stores will comprise between one-half and two-thirds of new store openings.

We expect continued robust consolidated operating margin and EPS improvement compared to fiscal 2012, reflecting the strength of our global business and the pipeline of profitable growth initiatives.

We expect increased capital expenditures in fiscal 2013 compared to fiscal 2012, reflecting additional investments in store renovations, new store growth and manufacturing capacity.

Operating Segment Overview

Starbucks has four reportable operating segments: Americas, Europe, Middle East, and Africa ("EMEA"), China and Asia Pacific ("CAP") and Channel Development. Seattle's Best Coffee is reported in "Other," along with Evolution Fresh, Digital Ventures and unallocated corporate expenses that pertain to corporate administrative functions that support our operating segments but are not specifically attributable to or managed by any segment and are not included in the reported financial results of the operating segments.

The Americas, EMEA and CAP segments include company-operated stores and licensed stores. Licensed stores generally have a higher operating margin than company-operated stores. Under the licensed model, Starbucks receives a reduced share of the total store revenues, but this is more than offset by the reduction in its share of costs as these are primarily incurred by the licensee. The EMEA and CAP segments have a higher relative share of licensed stores versus company-operated stores compared to the Americas segment; however, the Americas segment has been operating significantly longer than the other segments and has developed deeper awareness of, and attachment to, the Starbucks brand and stores among its customer base. As a result, the more mature Americas segment has significantly more stores and higher total revenues than the other segments. Average sales per store are also higher in the Americas due to various factors including length of time in market and local income levels.

Starbucks store base in EMEA and CAP continues to expand and we continue to focus on achieving sustainable growth from established international markets while at the same time investing in emerging markets, such as China. Occupancy costs and store operating expenses can be higher in certain international markets than in the Americas segment due to higher rents for prime store locations or costs of compliance with country-specific regulatory requirements. Because many of our international operations are in an early phase of development, operating expenses as a percentage of related revenues are often higher compared to the Americas segment. International markets in the early stages of development require a more extensive support organization, relative to the current levels of revenue and operating income, than the Americas.

The Channel Development segment includes packaged coffee and tea, a variety of ready-to-drink beverages, single-serve coffee and tea products and other branded product operations worldwide, as well as the US foodservice business. In prior years through the first several months of fiscal 2011, we sold a selection of Starbucks and Seattle's Best Coffee branded packaged coffees and Tazo® teas in grocery and warehouse club stores throughout the US and to grocery stores in Canada, the UK and other European countries through a distribution arrangement with Kraft Foods Global, Inc. Kraft managed the distribution, marketing, advertising and promotion of these products as a part of that arrangement. During fiscal 2011, we successfully transitioned these businesses including the marketing, advertising, and promotion of these products, from our previous distribution arrangement with Kraft and began selling these products directly to the grocery and warehouse club stores. Our Channel Development segment also includes ready-to-drink beverages, which are primarily manufactured and distributed through The North American Coffee Partnership, a joint venture with the Pepsi-Cola Company. The proportionate share of the results of the joint venture is included, on a net basis, in income from equity investees on the consolidated statements of earnings. The US foodservice business sells coffee and other related products to institutional foodservice companies with the majority of its sales through national broad-line distribution networks. The Channel Development segment reflects a modest cost structure and a resulting higher operating margin, compared to the other reporting segments, which consist primarily of retail stores.

Acquisitions

See Note 2 to the consolidated financial statements in this 10-K.

RESULTS OF OPERATIONS — FISCAL 2012 COMPARED TO FISCAL 2011

Consolidated results of operations (in millions):

Revenues

Fiscal Year Ended	Sep 30, 2012	Oct 2, 2011	% Change	Sep 30, 2012	Oct 2, 2011
				% of Total Net Revenues	
Net revenues:					
Company-operated stores	$ 10,534.5	$ 9,632.4	9.4%	79.2%	82.3%
Licensed stores	1,210.3	1,007.5	20.1%	9.1%	8.6%
CPG, foodservice and other	1,554.7	1,060.5	46.6%	11.7%	9.1%
Total net revenues	**$ 13,299.5**	**$ 11,700.4**	**13.7%**	**100.0%**	**100.0%**

Consolidated net revenues were $13.3 billion for fiscal 2012, an increase of 13.7%, or $1.6 billion over fiscal 2011, primarily due to increased revenues from company-operated stores (contributing $902 million), driven by an increase in comparable store sales (approximately 7%, or $680 million). Also contributing to the increase were incremental revenues from net new company-operated store openings over the past 12 months (approximately $184 million).

Licensed store revenues contributed $203 million to the increase in total net revenues in fiscal 2012, primarily due to higher product sales to and royalty revenues from our licensees, resulting from improved comparable store sales and the opening of 665 net new licensed stores over the past 12 months.

CPG, foodservice and other revenues increased $494 million, primarily due to sales of Starbucks and Tazo branded K-Cup® portion packs launched in the CPG channel on November 1, 2011 (approximately $232 million). The benefit of recognizing full revenue from packaged coffee and tea under the direct distribution model (approximately $78 million) and an increase in foodservice revenues (approximately $50 million) also contributed.

Operating Expenses

Fiscal Year Ended	Sep 30, 2012	Oct 2, 2011	Sep 30, 2012	Oct 2, 2011
			% of Total Net Revenues	
Cost of sales including occupancy costs	$ 5,813.3	$ 4,915.5	43.7%	42.0%
Store operating expenses	3,918.1	3,594.9	29.5%	30.7%
Other operating expenses	429.9	392.8	3.2%	3.4%
Depreciation and amortization expenses	550.3	523.3	4.1%	4.5%
General and administrative expenses	801.2	749.3	6.0%	6.4%
Total operating expenses	11,512.8	10,175.8	86.6%	87.0%
Gain on sale of properties	—	30.2	—%	0.3%
Income from equity investees	210.7	173.7	1.6%	1.5%
Operating income	**$ 1,997.4**	**$ 1,728.5**	**15.0%**	**14.8%**
Supplemental ratios as a % of related revenues:				
Store operating expenses			37.2%	37.3%

Cost of sales including occupancy costs as a percentage of total net revenues increased 170 basis points, driven by increased commodity costs (approximately 160 basis points), primarily due to higher coffee costs.

Store operating expenses as a percentage of total net revenues decreased 120 basis points, due to increased Channel Development and licensed store revenues. Store operating expenses as a percent of company-operated store revenues decreased 10 basis points due to increased sales leverage.

Other operating expenses as a percentage of total net revenues decreased 20 basis points. As a percentage of net revenues excluding company-operated store revenues, other operating expenses decreased 350 basis points. This decrease was primarily driven by increased sales leverage (approximately 150 basis points), the absence of charges in fiscal 2012 related to the Seattle's Best Coffee store closures in Borders bookstores (approximately 80 basis points) and a shift in the timing of marketing spend (approximately 60 basis points).

Income from equity investees increased $37.0 million, primarily due to an increase in income from our North American Coffee Partnership (approximately $13 million), Japan (approximately $11 million) and Shanghai (approximately $10 million) joint venture operations.

The combination of these changes, along with increased sales leverage on depreciation and amortization (approximately 40 basis points) and general and administrative expenses (approximately 40 basis points), resulted in an increase in operating margin of 20 basis points over fiscal 2011.

Other Income and Expenses

Fiscal Year Ended	Sep 30, 2012	Oct 2, 2011	Sep 30, 2012	Oct 2, 2011
			% of Total Net Revenues	
Operating income	$ 1,997.4	$ 1,728.5	15.0%	14.8%
Interest income and other, net	94.4	115.9	0.7%	1.0%
Interest expense	(32.7)	(33.3)	(0.2)%	(0.3)%
Earnings before income taxes	2,059.1	1,811.1	15.5%	15.5%
Income taxes	674.4	563.1	5.1%	4.8%
Net earnings including noncontrolling interests	1,384.7	1,248.0	10.4%	10.7%
Net earnings (loss) attributable to noncontrolling interests	0.9	2.3	—%	—%
Net earnings attributable to Starbucks	**$ 1,383.8**	**$ 1,245.7**	**10.4%**	**10.6%**
Effective tax rate including noncontrolling interests			32.8%	31.1%

Net interest income and other decreased $21 million over the prior year, primarily due to the absence of the gain recognized in the fourth quarter of fiscal 2011 resulting from the acquisition of the remaining interest in our previous joint venture operations in Switzerland and Austria (approximately $55 million), partially offset by the recognition of additional income associated with unredeemed gifts cards in the second quarter of fiscal 2012 (approximately $29 million), following a court ruling related to state unclaimed property laws.

Income taxes for the fiscal year ended 2012 resulted in an effective tax rate of 32.8% compared to 31.1% for fiscal year 2011. The rate increased in fiscal year 2012 primarily due to tax benefits recognized in fiscal 2011 from the Switzerland and Austria transaction and the release of foreign valuation allowances. The effective tax rate for fiscal 2013 is expected to be approximately 33%.

Segment Information

Segment information is prepared on the same basis that our management reviews financial information for operational decision-making purposes. The following tables summarize the results of operations by segment *(in millions)*:

Americas

Fiscal Year Ended	Sep 30, 2012		Oct 2, 2011	As a % of Americas Total Net Revenues	
				Sep 30, 2012	Oct 2, 2011
Total net revenues	$ 9,936.0	$	9,065.0	100.0%	100.0%
Cost of sales including occupancy costs	3,885.5		3,512.7	39.1%	38.8%
Store operating expenses	3,427.8		3,184.2	34.5%	35.1%
Other operating expenses	83.8		75.8	0.8%	0.8%
Depreciation and amortization expenses	392.3		390.8	3.9%	4.3%
General and administrative expenses	74.3		60.8	0.7%	0.7%
Total operating expenses	7,863.7		7,224.3	79.1%	79.7%
Income from equity investees	2.1		1.6	—%	—%
Operating income	$ 2,074.4	$	1,842.3	20.9%	20.3%
Supplemental ratios as a % of related revenues:					
Store operating expenses				37.8%	38.1%

Revenues

Americas total net revenues for fiscal 2012 increased 10%, or $871 million, primarily due to increased revenues from company-operated stores (contributing $712 million), driven by an increase in comparable store sales (approximately 8%, or $626 million). Also contributing to the increase were incremental revenues from net new company-operated store openings over the past 12 months (approximately $100 million).

Licensed store revenues also contributed to the increase in total net revenues with an increase of $149 million in fiscal 2012 over the prior year period, primarily due to higher product sales to and royalty revenues from our licensees, resulting from improved comparable store sales and the opening of 270 net new licensed stores over the past 12 months.

Operating Expenses

Cost of sales including occupancy costs as a percentage of total net revenues increased 30 basis points, primarily driven by higher commodity costs (approximately 110 basis points), mainly coffee, partially offset by increased sales leverage on occupancy costs (approximately 70 basis points).

Store operating expenses as a percentage of total net revenues decreased 60 basis points. Increased licensed store revenues contributed approximately 30 basis points of the decrease. Store operating expenses as a percentage of company-operated store revenues decreased 30 basis points, primarily due to increased sales leverage (approximately 70 basis points), partially offset by higher debit card transaction fees (approximately 20 basis points).

Other operating expenses as a percentage of total net revenues was flat over prior year. As a percentage of net revenues excluding company-operated store revenues, other operating expenses decreased 100 basis points, primarily driven by increased sales leverage.

The combination of these changes, along with increased sales leverage on depreciation and amortization expense (approximately 40 basis points), resulted in an increase in operating margin of 60 basis points over fiscal 2011.

EMEA

Fiscal Year Ended	Sep 30, 2012	Oct 2, 2011	Sep 30, 2012	Oct 2, 2011
			As a % of EMEA Total Net Revenues	
Total net revenues	$ **1,141.3**	$ **1,046.8**	**100.0%**	**100.0%**
Cost of sales including occupancy costs	597.3	530.3	52.3%	50.7%
Store operating expenses	371.1	327.3	32.5%	31.3%
Other operating expenses	33.6	36.5	2.9%	3.5%
Depreciation and amortization expenses	57.1	53.4	5.0%	5.1%
General and administrative expenses	72.1	65.0	6.3%	6.2%
Total operating expenses	1,131.2	1,012.5	99.1%	96.7%
Income from equity investees	0.3	6.0	—%	0.6%
Operating income	$ **10.4**	$ **40.3**	**0.9%**	**3.8%**
Supplemental ratios as a % of related revenues:				
Store operating expenses			38.3%	36.1%

Revenues

EMEA total net revenues for fiscal 2012 increased 9%, or $95 million, primarily driven by increased revenues from company-operated stores (contributing $63 million), due to the acquisition of the remaining interest in our previous joint venture operations in Switzerland and Austria in the fourth quarter of fiscal 2011 (approximately $80 million), partially offset by unfavorable foreign currency fluctuations (approximately $33 million).

An increase in licensed store revenues of $27 million also contributed to the increase in total net revenues, primarily due to higher product sales to and royalty revenues from our licensees, resulting from the opening of 101 net new licensed stores over the past 12 months.

Operating Expenses

Cost of sales including occupancy costs as a percentage of total net revenues increased 160 basis points, primarily driven by higher costs related to the transition to a consolidated food and dairy distribution model in the UK that began in the first quarter of fiscal 2012 (approximately 180 basis points). These costs are expected to decline over time as the full benefits of the transition are realized. Also contributing to the decrease were costs related to store portfolio optimization initiatives occurring in the fourth quarter of fiscal 2012 (approximately 60 basis points), partially offset by increased sales leverage on occupancy costs.

Store operating expenses as a percentage of total net revenues increased 120 basis points. Store operating expenses as a percentage of company-operated store revenues increased 220 basis points, primarily driven by asset impairments related to underperforming stores (approximately 140 basis points). Also contributing to the decrease were costs related to store portfolio optimization initiatives occurring in the fourth quarter of fiscal 2012 (approximately 40 basis points).

Other operating expenses as a percentage of total net revenues decreased 60 basis points. Excluding the impact of company-operated store revenues, other operating expenses decreased 640 basis points, primarily driven by operational efficiencies.

Income from equity investees declined to $0.3 million in fiscal 2012, due to the acquisition of the remaining interest in our previous joint venture operations in Switzerland and Austria.

The above changes contributed to a decrease in operating margin of 290 basis points over the prior year.

China / Asia Pacific

Fiscal Year Ended	Sep 30, 2012	Oct 2, 2011	As a % of CAP Total Net Revenues Sep 30, 2012	Oct 2, 2011
Total net revenues	$ 721.4	$ 552.3	100.0%	100.0%
Cost of sales including occupancy costs	362.8	282.0	50.3%	51.1%
Store operating expenses	119.2	83.4	16.5%	15.1%
Other operating expenses	47.0	35.7	6.5%	6.5%
Depreciation and amortization expenses	23.2	18.1	3.2%	3.3%
General and administrative expenses	38.1	32.9	5.3%	6.0%
Restructuring charges	—	—	—%	—%
Total operating expenses	590.3	452.1	81.8%	81.9%
Income from equity investees	122.4	92.9	17.0%	16.8%
Operating income	$ 253.5	$ 193.1	35.1%	35.0%
Supplemental ratios as a % of related revenues:				
Store operating expenses			24.4%	23.1%

Revenues

China / Asia Pacific total net revenues for fiscal 2012 increased 31%, or $169 million, primarily driven by increased revenues from company-operated stores (contributing $128 million). The increase in company-operated store revenues was primarily due to the opening of 154 net new stores over the past 12 months (approximately $71 million) and an increase in comparable store sales (approximately 15%, or $53 million).

Also contributing to the increase in revenues was an increase in licensed store revenues of $41 million, due to increased royalty revenues from and product sales to licensees, primarily driven by 294 net new licensed store openings over the past 12 months.

Operating Expenses

Cost of sales including occupancy costs as a percentage of total net revenues decreased 80 basis points primarily driven by the accelerated growth of company-operated stores, which contribute a higher gross margin, in China (approximately 140 basis points), partially offset by increased commodity costs (approximately 120 basis points), mainly higher coffee costs.

Store operating expenses as a percentage of total net revenues increased 140 basis points. Store operating expenses as a percentage of company-operated store revenues increased 130 basis points, primarily driven by increased costs associated with the expansion efforts of company-operated stores in mainland China.

Income from equity investees increased $30 million, primarily driven by an increase in income from our Japan (approximately $11 million) and Shanghai (approximately $10 million) joint venture operations.

The combination of these changes, along with increased sales leverage on depreciation and amortization (approximately 10 basis points) and general and administrative expenses (approximately 70 basis points), resulted in an increase in operating margin of 10 basis points over fiscal 2011.

Channel Development

Fiscal Year Ended	Sep 30, 2012		Oct 2, 2011	As a % of Channel Development Total Net Revenues	
				Sep 30, 2012	Oct 2, 2011
Total net revenues	$ 1,292.2	$	860.5	100.0%	100.0%
Cost of sales	827.6		487.5	64.0%	56.7%
Other operating expenses	191.1		151.8	14.8%	17.6%
Depreciation and amortization expenses	1.3		2.4	0.1%	0.3%
General and administrative expenses	8.9		6.6	0.7%	0.8%
Total operating expenses	1,028.9		648.3	79.6%	75.3%
Income from equity investees	85.2		75.6	6.6%	8.8%
Operating income	$ 348.5	$	287.8	27.0%	33.4%

Revenues

Channel Development total net revenues for fiscal 2012 increased 50%, or $432 million, primarily due to sales of Starbucks and Tazo branded K-Cup® portion packs (approximately $232 million). The benefit of recognizing full revenue from packaged coffee and tea sales under the direct distribution model through the second quarter of fiscal 2012 (approximately $70 million) and increased foodservice revenues (approximately $33 million) also contributed.

Operating Expenses

Cost of sales as a percentage of total net revenues increased 730 basis points, primarily due to increased commodity costs (approximately 570 basis points), mainly coffee, and a shift in our product mix driven by the introduction of Starbucks and Tazo branded K-Cup® portion packs (approximately 140 basis points).

Other operating expenses as a percentage of total net revenues decreased 280 basis points, primarily due to increased sales leverage.

Income from equity investees increased $10 million over the prior year period, driven by increased income from our North American Coffee Partnership joint venture. Income from equity investees declined as a percentage of total net revenues (approximately 220 basis points) primarily due to the growth in segment revenues.

The combination of these changes resulted in a decrease in operating margin of 640 basis points over fiscal 2011.

Other

Fiscal Year Ended	Sep 30, 2012		Oct 2, 2011	% Change
Total net revenues	$	**208.6**	$ 175.8	**18.7%**
Cost of sales		140.1	. 103.0	36.0%
Other operating expenses		74.4	93.0	(20.0)%
Depreciation and amortization expenses		76.4	58.6	30.4%
General and administrative expenses		607.8	584.0	4.1%
Total operating expenses		898.7	838.6	7.2%
Gain on sale of properties		—	30.2	(100.0)%
Income from equity investees		0.7	(2.4)	nm
Operating loss	$	**(689.4)**	$ (635.0)	**8.6%**

Other includes operating results from Seattle's Best Coffee, Evolution Fresh, and Digital Ventures, as well as expenses pertaining to corporate administrative functions that support our operating segments but are not specifically attributable to, or managed by, any segment and are not included in the reported financial results of the operating segments.

Other total net revenues increased $33 million, primarily due to incremental revenues from Evolution Fresh, which was acquired during the first quarter of fiscal 2012.

Total operating expenses increased $60 million, primarily due to increased cost of sales resulting from higher commodity costs, primarily coffee, and higher general and administrative expenses to support the growth of the business.

RESULTS OF OPERATIONS — FISCAL 2011 COMPARED TO FISCAL 2010

Consolidated results of operations (in millions):

Revenues

Fiscal Year Ended	Oct 2, 2011		Oct 3, 2010	% Change	Oct 2, 2011	Oct 3, 2010
					% of Total Net Revenues	
Net revenues:						
Company-operated stores	$	9,632.4	$ 8,963.5	7.5%	82.3%	83.7%
Licensed stores		1,007.5	875.2	15.1%	8.6%	8.2%
CPG, foodservice and other		1,060.5	868.7	22.1%	9.1%	8.1%
Total net revenues	$	**11,700.4**	$ 10,707.4	9.3%	100.0%	100.0%

Consolidated net revenues were $11.7 billion for fiscal 2011, an increase of 9%, or $993 million over fiscal 2010. The increase was primarily due to an increase in company-operated store revenues driven by an 8% increase in global comparable stores sales (contributing approximately $672 million). The increase in comparable store sales was due to a 6% increase in number of transactions (contributing approximately $499 million) and a 2% increase in average value per transaction (contributing approximately $173 million). Also contributing to the increase in total net revenues was favorable foreign currency translation (approximately $126 million) resulting from a weakening of the US dollar relative to foreign currencies and an increase in licensed store revenues (approximately $106 million). This increase was partially offset by the impact of the extra week in fiscal 2010 (approximately $207 million).

Operating Expenses

Fiscal Year Ended	Oct 2, 2011		Oct 3, 2010	Oct 2, 2011	Oct 3, 2010
				% of Total Net Revenues	
Cost of sales including occupancy costs	$	4,915.5	$ 4,416.5	42.0%	41.2%
Store operating expenses		3,594.9	3,471.9	30.7%	32.4%
Other operating expenses		392.8	279.7	3.4%	2.6%
Depreciation and amortization expenses		523.3	510.4	4.5%	4.8%
General and administrative expenses		749.3	704.6	6.4%	6.6%
Restructuring charges		—	53.0	—%	0.5%
Total operating expenses		10,175.8	9,436.1	87.0%	88.1%
Gain on sale of properties		30.2	—	0.3%	—%
Income from equity investees		173.7	148.1	1.5%	1.4%
Operating income	$	**1,728.5**	$ **1,419.4**	**14.8%**	**13.3%**
Supplemental ratios as a % of related revenues:					
Store operating expenses				37.3%	38.7%

Cost of sales including occupancy costs as a percentage of total net revenues increased 80 basis points. The increase was primarily due to higher commodity costs (approximately 220 basis points), mainly driven by increased coffee costs. Partially offsetting this increase was lower occupancy costs as a percentage of total net revenues (approximately 70 basis points), driven by increased sales leverage.

Store operating expenses as a percentage of total net revenues decreased 170 basis points primarily due to increased sales leverage.

Other operating expenses as a percentage of total net revenues increased 80 basis points primarily due to higher expenses to support the direct distribution model for packaged coffee and tea (approximately 40 basis points) and the impairment of certain assets in our Seattle's Best Coffee business associated with the Borders bankruptcy in April 2011 (approximately 20 basis points).

The above changes contributed to an overall increase in operating margin of 150 basis points for fiscal 2011. Considering the impact from all line items, the primary drivers for the increase in operating margin for fiscal 2011 were increased sales leverage (approximately 300 basis points), the absence of restructuring charges in the current year (approximately 50 basis points) and the gain on the sale of corporate real estate in fiscal 2011 (approximately 30 basis points). These increases were partially offset by higher commodity costs (approximately 220 basis points).

Other Income and Expenses

Fiscal Year Ended		Oct 2, 2011		Oct 3, 2010	Oct 2, 2011	Oct 3, 2010
					% of Total Net Revenues	
Operating income	$	1,728.5	$	1,419.4	14.8%	13.3%
Interest income and other, net		115.9		50.3	1.0%	0.5%
Interest expense		(33.3)		(32.7)	(0.3)%	(0.3)%
Earnings before income taxes		1,811.1		1,437.0	15.5%	13.4%
Income taxes		563.1		488.7	4.8%	4.6%
Net earnings including noncontrolling interests		1,248.0		948.3	10.7%	8.9%
Net earnings (loss) attributable to noncontrolling interests		2.3		2.7	—%	—%
Net earnings attributable to Starbucks	$	**1,245.7**	$	**945.6**	**10.6%**	**8.8%**
Effective tax rate including noncontrolling interests					31.1%	34.0%

Net interest income and other increased $66 million over the prior year. The increase primarily resulted from the gain recorded in the fourth quarter of fiscal 2011 related to our acquisition of the remaining ownership interest in our joint venture operations in Switzerland and Austria (approximately $55 million).

Income taxes for the fiscal year ended 2011 resulted in an effective tax rate of 31.1% compared to 34.0% for fiscal 2010. The lower rate in fiscal 2011 was primarily due to a benefit from the Switzerland and Austria transaction and to an increase in income in foreign jurisdictions having lower tax rates.

Segment Information

The following tables summarize our results of operations by segment for fiscal 2011 and 2010 (*in millions*).

Americas

Fiscal Year Ended		Oct 2, 2011		Oct 3, 2010	Oct 2, 2011	Oct 3, 2010
					As a % of Americas Total Net Revenues	
Total net revenues	$	**9,065.0**	$	**8,488.5**	100.0%	100.0%
Cost of sales including occupancy costs		3,512.7		3,258.5	38.8%	38.4%
Store operating expenses		3,184.2		3,083.3	35.1%	36.3%
Other operating expenses		75.8		63.1	0.8%	0.7%
Depreciation and amortization expenses		390.8		392.9	4.3%	4.6%
General and administrative expenses		60.8		56.4	0.7%	0.7%
Restructuring charges		—		28.4	—%	0.3%
Total operating expenses		7,224.3		6,882.6	79.7%	81.1%
Income from equity investees		1.6		0.9	—%	—%
Operating income	$	**1,842.3**	$	**1,606.8**	**20.3%**	**18.9%**
Supplemental ratios as a % of related revenues:						
Store operating expenses					38.1%	39.2%

Revenues

Americas total net revenues for fiscal 2011 increased 7%, or $577 million. The increase was primarily driven by an increase in comparable store sales in our company-operated stores of 8% (contributing approximately $590 million), driven by a 5% increase in number of transactions and a 2% increase in average value per transaction. Also contributing to the increase was favorable foreign currency translation resulting from the weakening of the US dollar (approximately $51 million), primarily in relation to the Canadian dollar, and an increase in product sales to and royalty revenues from licensees (approximately $73 million), primarily due to improved comparable store sales and net new store openings. These increases were partially offset by the absence of the extra week in fiscal 2010 (approximately $162 million).

Operating Expenses

Cost of sales including occupancy costs as a percentage of total net revenues increased 40 basis points over the prior year. The increase was primarily due to higher commodity costs (approximately 140 basis points), mainly coffee, partially offset by increased sales leverage on occupancy costs (approximately 60 basis points).

Store operating expenses as a percentage of total net revenues decreased 120 basis points primarily due to increased sales leverage.

Also contributing to the increase in operating margin was the absence of restructuring charges in fiscal 2011 (approximately 30 basis points) and increased sales leverage resulting in lower depreciation and amortization expenses as a percentage of total net revenues (contributing 30 basis points). The combination of these changes resulted in an overall increase in operating margin of 140 basis points for fiscal 2011.

EMEA

Fiscal Year Ended	Oct 2, 2011	Oct 3, 2010	Oct 2, 2011	Oct 3, 2010
			As a % of EMEA Total Net Revenues	
Total net revenues	$ 1,046.8	$ 953.4	100.0%	100.0%
Cost of sales including occupancy costs	530.3	471.8	50.7%	49.5%
Store operating expenses	327.3	324.5	31.3%	34.0%
Other operating expenses	36.5	36.1	3.5%	3.8%
Depreciation and amortization expenses	53.4	50.6	5.1%	5.3%
General and administrative expenses	65.0	58.2	6.2%	6.1%
Restructuring charges	—	24.5	—%	2.6%
Total operating expenses	1,012.5	965.7	96.7%	101.3%
Income from equity investees	6.0	6.8	0.6%	0.7%
Operating income	$ 40.3	$ (5.5)	3.8%	(0.6)%
Supplemental ratios as a % of related revenues:				
Store operating expenses			36.1%	38.4%

Revenues

EMEA total net revenues for fiscal 2011 increased 10%, or $93 million. The increase was primarily driven by favorable foreign currency translation resulting from the weakening of the US dollar (approximately $35 million), primarily in relation to the British pound, the acquisition of the remaining interest in our previous joint venture operations in Switzerland and Austria in the fourth quarter of fiscal 2011 (approximately $28 million), and an increase in comparable store sales in our company-operated stores of 3% (approximately $24 million). An increase in royalty revenues from and product sales to licensees also contributed (approximately $20 million), due to improved comparable store sales and net new store openings. These increases were partially offset by the absence of the extra week in fiscal 2010 (approximately $18 million).

Operating Expenses

Cost of sales including occupancy costs as a percentage of total net revenues increased by 120 basis points compared to the prior year. The increase was primarily driven by higher higher commodity costs (approximately 160 basis points), mainly coffee, partially offset by increased sales leverage on occupancy costs (approximately 50 basis points).

Store operating expenses as a percentage of total net revenues decreased 270 basis points. Increased licensed stores revenues contributed approximately 40 basis points to the decrease. Store operating expenses as a percentage of company-operated store revenues decreased 230 basis points primarily due to fewer impairment charges in fiscal 2011 compared to fiscal 2010 (approximately 110 basis points), lower equipment maintenance costs (approximately 60 basis points) and increased sales leverage on salaries and benefits (approximately 40 basis).

Also contributing to the increase in operating margin was the absence of restructuring charges in fiscal 2011 (approximately 260 basis points). The combination of these changes resulted in an overall increase in operating margin of 440 basis points for fiscal 2011.

China / Asia Pacific

Fiscal Year Ended	Oct 2, 2011		Oct 3, 2010	Oct 2, 2011	Oct 3, 2010
				As a % of CAP Total Net Revenues	
Total net revenues	$	**552.3**	$ 407.3	100.0%	100.0%
Cost of sales including occupancy costs		282.0	213.4	51.1%	52.4%
Store operating expenses		83.4	64.1	15.1%	15.7%
Other operating expenses		35.7	30.0	6.5%	7.4%
Depreciation and amortization expenses		18.1	15.8	3.3%	3.9%
General and administrative expenses		32.9	27.4	6.0%	6.7%
Restructuring charges		—	0.1	—%	—%
Total operating expenses		452.1	350.8	81.9%	86.1%
Income from equity investees		92.9	73.1	16.8%	17.9%
Operating income	$	**193.1**	$ 129.6	35.0%	31.8%
Supplemental ratios as a % of related revenues:					
Store operating expenses				23.1%	25.4%

Revenues

China / Asia Pacific total net revenues for fiscal 2011 increased 36%, or $145 million. The increase was primarily driven by an increase in comparable store sales in our company-operated stores of 22% (contributing approximately $58 million), driven by a 20% increase in number of transactions and a 2% increase in average value per transaction. Also contributing to the increase in total net revenues was favorable foreign currency translation resulting from the weakening of the US dollar (approximately $40 million), the opening of 73 net new company-operated stores in the past 12 months (approximately $40 million), and an increase in royalty revenues from and product sales to licensees (approximately $17 million), due to improved comparable store sales and net new store openings. These increases were partially offset by the absence of the extra week in fiscal 2010 (approximately $9 million).

Operating Expenses

Cost of sales including occupancy costs as a percentage of total net revenues decreased by 130 basis points compared to the prior year, primarily due to increased sales leverage on occupancy costs.

Store operating expenses as a percentage of total net revenues decreased 60 basis points. Excluding the impact of licensed store revenues, store operating expenses decreased 230 basis points as a percent of company-operated store revenues in fiscal 2011 compared to fiscal 2010, primarily driven by lower compensation costs (approximately 210 basis points) as a percentage of total net revenues.

Other operating expenses as a percentage of total net revenues decreased 90 basis points. Increased company-operated store revenues contributed approximately 30 basis points to the decrease. Other operating expenses as a percentage of licensed store revenues decreased 60 basis points, primarily driven by lower compensation related costs (approximately 140 basis points), partially offset by increasing costs related to our expansion efforts into key emerging markets, primarily China.

Income from equity investees increased $20 million in fiscal 2011, driven by improved performance in our joint venture operations, primarily in Japan, Shanghai and Taiwan.

The changes in the above line items combined with increased sales leverage on general and administrative expenses (approximately 70 basis points) and depreciation and amortization (approximately 60 basis points) contributed to an overall increase in operating margin of 320 basis points in fiscal 2011.

Channel Development

Fiscal Year Ended		Oct 2, 2011		Oct 3, 2010	Oct 2, 2011	Oct 3, 2010
					As a % of Channel Development Total Net Revenues	
Total net revenues	$	860.5	$	707.4	100.0%	100.0%
Cost of sales including occupancy costs		487.5		383.2	56.7%	54.2%
Other operating expenses		151.8		115.6	17.6%	16.3%
Depreciation and amortization expenses		2.4		3.7	0.3%	0.5%
General and administrative expenses		6.6		4.5	0.8%	0.6%
Total operating expenses		648.3		507.0	75.3%	71.7%
Income from equity investees		75.6		70.6	8.8%	10.0%
Operating income	$	**287.8**	$	**271.0**	**33.4%**	**38.3%**

Revenues

Total Channel Development net revenues for fiscal 2011 increased 22%, or $153 million. The increase was primarily due to the benefit of recognizing full revenue from packaged coffee and tea sales under the direct distribution model for the majority of the year (approximately $70 million). On March 1, 2011, we successfully transitioned to a direct distribution model from our previous distribution arrangement with Kraft for the sale of packaged Starbucks® and Seattle's Best Coffee® coffee products in grocery and warehouse club stores throughout the US, and to grocery stores in Canada, the UK and other European countries. We successfully transitioned the Tazo® tea business to a direct distribution model in January 2011. Also contributing to the increase were improved revenues from US foodservice (approximately $26 million) and the expanded distribution of Starbucks VIA®

Ready Brew in fiscal 2011 (approximately $24 million), partially offset by the extra week in fiscal 2010 (approximately $16 million).

Operating Expenses

Operating margin decreased 490 basis points over the prior year primarily due to increased commodity costs (approximately 830 basis points), driven by higher coffee costs. Partially offsetting the increase in commodity costs was the benefit of price increases (approximately 200 basis points) and lower marketing expenses for Starbucks VIA® Ready Brew in 2011 (approximately 120 basis points).

Other

Fiscal Year Ended	Oct 2, 2011	Oct 3, 2010	% Change
Total net revenues	$ 175.8	$ 150.8	16.6%
Cost of sales	103.0	89.6	15.0%
Other operating expenses	93.0	34.9	166.5%
Depreciation and amortization expenses	58.6	47.4	23.6%
General and administrative expenses	584.0	558.1	4.6%
Total operating expenses	838.6	730.0	14.9%
Gain on sale of properties	30.2	—	nm
Loss from equity investee	(2.4)	(3.3)	(27.3)%
Operating loss	$ (635.0)	$ (582.5)	9.0%

Substantially all net revenues in Other are generated from the Seattle's Best Coffee operating segment. The increase in revenues for Seattle's Best Coffee was primarily due to the recognition of a full year of sales to national accounts added in the latter part of fiscal 2010 as well as new accounts added during fiscal 2011(approximately $20 million). This was partially offset by the impact of the closure of the Seattle's Best Coffee locations in Borders Bookstores.

Total operating expenses in fiscal 2011 increased 15%, or $109 million. This increase is the result of an increase of $59 million in other operating expenses primarily due to the impairment of certain assets in our Seattle's Best Coffee business associated with the Borders bankruptcy in April 2011 and an increase in marketing expenses. Also contributing was a $26 million increase in general and administrative expenses due to higher corporate expenses to support growth initiatives and higher donations to the Starbucks Foundation. These increases in operating expenses were partially offset by a gain on the sale of corporate real estate in fiscal 2011 (approximately $30 million).

SUMMARIZED QUARTERLY FINANCIAL INFORMATION (unaudited; in millions, except EPS)

	First	Second	Third	Fourth	Total
2012:					
Net revenues	$ 3,435.9	$ 3,195.9	$ 3,303.6	$ 3,364.2	$ 13,299.5
Operating income	556.0	430.4	491.6	519.6	1,997.4
Net earnings attributable to Starbucks	382.1	309.9	333.1	359.0	1,383.8
EPS — diluted	$ 0.50	$ 0.40	$ 0.43	$ 0.46	$ 1.79
2011:					
Net revenues	$ 2,950.8	$ 2,785.7	$ 2,932.2	$ 3,031.9	$ 11,700.4
Operating income	501.9	376.1	402.2	448.3	1,728.5
Net earnings attributable to Starbucks	346.6	261.6	279.1	358.5	1,245.7
EPS — diluted	$ 0.45	$ 0.34	$ 0.36	$ 0.47	$ 1.62

FINANCIAL CONDITION, LIQUIDITY AND CAPITAL RESOURCES

Investment Overview

Starbucks cash and short-term investments were $2.0 billion and $2.1 billion as of September 30, 2012 and October 2, 2011, respectively. As of September 30, 2012, approximately $703 million of cash was held in foreign subsidiaries. Of our cash held in foreign subsidiaries, $343 million is denominated in the US dollar. We actively manage our cash and short-term investments in order to internally fund operating needs domestically and internationally, make scheduled interest and principal payments on our borrowings, and return cash to shareholders through common stock cash dividend payments and share repurchases. Our short-term investments consisted predominantly of US Treasury securities, commercial paper, corporate bonds, and US Agency securities. Also included in our short-term investment portfolio are certificates of deposit placed through an account registry service, with maturities ranging from 91 days to one year. The principal amounts of the individual certificates of deposit do not exceed the Federal Deposit Insurance Corporation limits. Our portfolio of long-term available for sale securities consists predominantly of high investment-grade corporate bonds, diversified among industries and individual issuers, as well as certificates of deposits with maturities greater than 1 year.

Borrowing capacity

In November 2010, we replaced our previous credit facility with a new $500 million unsecured credit facility ("the credit facility") with various banks, of which $100 million may be used for issuances of letters of credit. The credit facility is available for working capital, capital expenditures and other corporate purposes, including acquisitions and share repurchases and is currently set to mature in November 2014. Starbucks has the option, subject to negotiation and agreement with the related banks, to increase the maximum commitment amount by an additional $500 million. The interest rate for any borrowings under the credit facility, based on Starbucks current ratings and fixed charge coverage ratio, is 0.85% over LIBOR. The specific spread over LIBOR will depend upon our long-term credit ratings assigned by Moody's and Standard & Poor's rating agencies and our fixed charge coverage ratio. The credit facility contains provisions requiring us to maintain compliance with certain covenants, including a minimum fixed charge coverage ratio, which measures our ability to cover financing expenses. As of September 30, 2012 and October 2, 2011, we were in compliance with each of these covenants.

Under our commercial paper program we may issue unsecured commercial paper notes, up to a maximum aggregate amount outstanding at any time of $500 million, with individual maturities that may vary, but not exceed 397 days from the date of issue. The program is backstopped by the credit facility and the combined borrowing limit is $500 million for the commercial paper program and the credit facility. Starbucks may issue commercial paper from time to time, and the proceeds of the commercial paper financing may be used for working capital needs, capital expenditures and other corporate purposes, including acquisitions and share repurchases. During fiscal 2012 and fiscal 2011, there were no borrowings under the credit facility or commercial paper programs. As of September 30, 2012 and October 2, 2011, a total of $18 million and $17 million, respectively, in letters of credit were outstanding under the revolving credit facility.

The $550 million of 10-year 6.25% Senior Notes also require us to maintain compliance with certain covenants, including limits on future liens and sale and leaseback transactions on certain material properties. As of September 30, 2012 and October 2, 2011, we were in compliance with each of these covenants.

Use of Cash

We expect to use our cash and short-term investments, including any potential future borrowings under the credit facility and commercial paper program, to invest in our core businesses, including new product innovations and related marketing support, as well as other new business opportunities related to our core businesses. We believe that future cash flows generated from operations and existing cash and short-term investments both domestically and internationally will be sufficient to finance capital requirements for our core businesses in those respective markets as well as shareholder distributions for the foreseeable future.

We consider the majority of undistributed earnings of our foreign subsidiaries and equity investees as of September 30, 2012 to be indefinitely reinvested and, accordingly, no US income and foreign withholding taxes have been provided on such earnings. We have not, nor do we anticipate the need to, repatriate funds to the US to satisfy domestic liquidity needs; however, in the event that we need to repatriate all or a portion of our foreign cash to the US we would be subject to additional US income taxes, which could be material. We do not believe it is practical to calculate the potential tax impact of repatriation, as there is a significant amount of uncertainty around the calculation, including the availability and amount of foreign tax credits at the time of repatriation, tax rates in effect, and other indirect tax consequences associated with repatriation.

We may use our available cash resources to make proportionate capital contributions to our equity method and cost method investees. We may also seek strategic acquisitions to leverage existing capabilities and further build our business in support of our growth agenda. Acquisitions may include increasing our ownership interests in our equity method and cost method investees. Any decisions to increase such ownership interests will be driven by valuation and fit with our ownership strategy. Significant new joint ventures, acquisitions and/or other new business opportunities may require additional outside funding.

As discussed further in Note 15, we are in arbitration with Kraft Foods Global, Inc. ("Kraft") for a commercial dispute relating to a distribution agreement we previously held with Kraft. As a part of those proceedings Kraft has claimed damages inclusive of a premium and interest for terminating the arrangement. We believe we have valid claims of material breach by Kraft under the Agreement. We also believe Kraft's claim is highly inflated and based upon faulty analysis. However, should the arbitration result in an unfavorable outcome, we believe we have adequate liquidity.

Other than normal operating expenses, cash requirements for fiscal 2013 are expected to consist primarily of capital expenditures for remodeling and refurbishment of, and equipment upgrades for, existing company-operated stores; systems and technology investments in the stores and in the support infrastructure; new company-operated stores; and additional investments in manufacturing capacity. Total capital expenditures for fiscal 2013 are expected to be approximately $1.2 billion.

During the first three quarters of fiscal 2011, we declared and paid a cash dividend to shareholders of $0.13 per share. In the fourth quarter of fiscal 2011 and the first three quarters of fiscal 2012 we declared and paid a cash dividend of $0.17 per share. Cash dividends paid in fiscal 2012 and 2011 totaled $513 million and $390 million, respectively. In the fourth quarter, we declared a cash dividend of $0.21 per share to be paid on November 30, 2012 with an expected payout of $157 million.

During fiscal years 2012 and 2011, we repurchased 12 million and 16 million shares of common stock ($593 million and $556 million, respectively) under share repurchase authorizations. The number of remaining shares authorized for repurchase at September 30, 2012 totaled 12.1 million. On November 14, 2012, our Board of Directors authorized the repurchase of up to an additional 25 million shares under our share repurchase program.

Cash Flows

Cash provided by operating activities was $1.8 billion for fiscal year 2012, compared to $1.6 billion for fiscal year 2011. The slight increase was primarily attributable to an increase in net earnings in fiscal 2012. This was partially offset by a net increase in our working capital accounts, due primarily to increased payments on accounts payable.

Cash used by investing activities totaled $1.0 billion for fiscal years 2012 and 2011. Net cash proceeds on investment maturities were offset by an increase in capital expenditures, primarily for remodeling and renovating existing company-operated stores and opening new retail stores, the absence of cash proceeds from the sale of corporate real estate in the prior year and cash paid to acquire Evolution Fresh and Bay Bread, LLC (doing business as La Boulange) in the first and fourth quarters of fiscal 2012, respectively.

Cash used by financing activities for fiscal year 2012 totaled $746 million, compared to $608 million for fiscal year 2011. The increase was primarily due to an increase in cash returned to shareholders through higher dividend payments in fiscal 2012.

The following table summarizes our contractual obligations and borrowings as of September 30, 2012, and the timing and effect that such commitments are expected to have on our liquidity and capital requirements in future periods (*in millions*):

Contractual Obligations[1]	Total	Less than 1 Year	1 - 3 Years	3 - 5 Years	More than 5 Years
Operating lease obligations[2]	$ 4,060.2	$ 787.9	$ 1,368.9	$ 934.9	$ 968.5
Purchase obligations[3]	911.0	727.9	170.0	13.1	—
Debt obligations[4]	722.0	34.4	68.8	618.8	—
Other obligations[5]	94.9	19.4	9.6	8.3	57.6
Total	$ 5,788.1	$ 1,569.6	$ 1,617.3	$ 1,575.1	$ 1,026.1

(1) Income tax liabilities for uncertain tax positions were excluded as we are not able to make a reasonably reliable estimate of the amount and period of related future payments. As of September 30, 2012, we had $78.4 million of gross unrecognized tax benefits for uncertain tax positions.

(2) Amounts include the direct lease obligations, excluding any taxes, insurance and other related expenses.

(3) Purchase obligations include agreements to purchase goods or services that are enforceable and legally binding on Starbucks and that specify all significant terms. Green coffee purchase commitments comprise 94% of total purchase obligations.

(4) Debt amounts include principal maturities and scheduled interest payments on our long-term debt.

(5) Other obligations include other long-term liabilities primarily consisting of asset retirement obligations, capital lease obligations and hedging instruments.

Starbucks currently expects to fund these commitments with operating cash flows generated in the normal course of business.

43

Off-Balance Sheet Arrangements

Off-balance sheet arrangements relate to operating lease and purchase commitments detailed in the footnotes to the consolidated financial statements in this 10-K.

COMMODITY PRICES, AVAILABILITY AND GENERAL RISK CONDITIONS

Commodity price risk represents Starbucks primary market risk, generated by our purchases of green coffee and dairy products, among other things. We purchase, roast and sell high-quality whole bean *arabica* coffee and related products and risk arises from the price volatility of green coffee. In addition to coffee, we also purchase significant amounts of dairy products to support the needs of our company-operated stores. The price and availability of these commodities directly impacts our results of operations and can be expected to impact our future results of operations. For additional details see Product Supply in Item 1, as well as Risk Factors in Item 1A of this 10-K.

FINANCIAL RISK MANAGEMENT

Market risk is defined as the risk of losses due to changes in commodity prices, foreign currency exchange rates, equity security prices, and interest rates. We manage our exposure to various market-based risks according to a market price risk management policy. Under this policy, market-based risks are quantified and evaluated for potential mitigation strategies, such as entering into hedging transactions. The market price risk management policy governs how hedging instruments may be used to mitigate risk. Risk limits are set annually and prohibit speculative trading activity. We also monitor and limit the amount of associated counterparty credit risk. In general, hedging instruments do not have maturities in excess of five years.

The sensitivity analyses disclosed below provide only a limited, point-in-time view of the market risk of the financial instruments discussed. The actual impact of the respective underlying rates and price changes on the financial instruments may differ significantly from those shown in the sensitivity analyses.

Commodity Price Risk

We purchase commodity inputs, including coffee, dairy products and diesel that are used in our operations and are subject to price fluctuations that impact our financial results. In addition to fixed-price and price-to-be-fixed contracts for coffee purchases, we have entered into commodity hedges to manage commodity price risk using financial derivative instruments.

The following table summarizes the potential impact as of September 30, 2012 to Starbucks future net earnings and other comprehensive income ("OCI") from changes in commodity prices. The information provided below relates only to the hedging instruments and does not represent the corresponding changes in the underlying hedged items *(in millions)*:

	Increase/(Decrease) to Net Earnings		Increase/(Decrease) to OCI	
	10% Increase in Underlying Rate	10% Decrease in Underlying Rate	10% Increase in Underlying Rate	10% Decrease in Underlying Rate
Commodity hedges	$ 10	$ (10)	$ 13	$ (13)

Foreign Currency Exchange Risk

The majority of our revenue, expense and capital purchasing activities are transacted in US dollars. However, because a portion of our operations consists of activities outside of the US, we have transactions in other currencies, primarily the Canadian dollar, British pound, euro, and Japanese yen. As a result, we may engage in transactions involving various derivative instruments to hedge revenues, inventory purchases, assets, and liabilities denominated in foreign currencies.

As of September 30, 2012, we had forward foreign exchange contracts that hedge portions of anticipated international revenue streams and inventory purchases. In addition, we had forward foreign exchange contracts that qualify as accounting hedges of our net investment in Starbucks Japan to minimize foreign currency exposure.

Starbucks also had forward foreign exchange contracts that are not designated as hedging instruments for accounting purposes (free standing derivatives), but which largely offset the financial impact of translating certain foreign currency denominated payables and receivables. Increases or decreases in the fair value of these derivatives are generally offset by corresponding decreases or increases in the US dollar value of our foreign currency denominated payables and receivables (*i.e.* "hedged items") that would occur within the period.

The following table summarizes the potential impact as of September 30, 2012 to Starbucks future net earnings and other comprehensive income ("OCI") from changes in the fair value of these derivative financial instruments due in turn to a change in the value of the US dollar as compared to the level of foreign exchange rates. The information provided below relates only to the hedging instruments and does not represent the corresponding changes in the underlying hedged items (*in millions*):

	Increase/(Decrease) to Net Earnings		Increase/(Decrease) to OCI	
	10% Increase in Underlying Rate	10% Decrease in Underlying Rate	10% Increase in Underlying Rate	10% Decrease in Underlying Rate
Foreign currency hedges	$ 8	$ (8)	$ 30	$ (30)

Equity Security Price Risk

We have minimal exposure to price fluctuations on equity mutual funds and equity exchange-traded funds within our trading portfolio. The trading securities approximate a portion of our liability under the Management Deferred Compensation Plan ("MDCP"). A corresponding liability is included in accrued compensation and related costs on the consolidated balance sheets. These investments are recorded at fair value with unrealized gains and losses recognized in net interest income and other in the consolidated statements of earnings. The offsetting changes in the MDCP liability are recorded in general and administrative expenses. We performed a sensitivity analysis based on a 10% change in the underlying equity prices of our investments as of September 30, 2012 and determined that such a change would not have a significant impact on the fair value of these instruments.

Interest Rate Risk

We utilize short-term and long-term financing and may use interest rate hedges to manage the effect of interest rate changes on our existing debt as well as the anticipated issuance of new debt. As of September 30, 2012 and October 2, 2011, we did not have any interest rate hedge agreements outstanding.

The following table summarizes the impact of a change in interest rates as of September 30, 2012 on the fair value of Starbucks debt (*in millions*):

		Change in Fair Value	
	Fair Value	100 Basis Point Increase in Underlying Rate	100 Basis Point Decrease in Underlying Rate
Debt	$ 674	$ 29	$ (29)

Our available-for-sale securities comprise a diversified portfolio consisting mainly of fixed income instruments. The primary objectives of these investments are to preserve capital and liquidity. Available-for-sale securities are recorded on the consolidated balance sheets at fair value with unrealized gains and losses reported as a component

45

of accumulated other comprehensive income. We do not hedge the interest rate exposure on our available-for-sale securities. We performed a sensitivity analysis based on a 100 basis point change in the underlying interest rate of our available-for-sale securities as of September 30, 2012, and determined that such a change would not have a significant impact on the fair value of these instruments.

APPLICATION OF CRITICAL ACCOUNTING POLICIES

Critical accounting policies are those that management believes are both most important to the portrayal of our financial condition and results and require the most difficult, subjective or complex judgments, often as a result of the need to make estimates about the effect of matters that are inherently uncertain. Judgments and uncertainties affecting the application of those policies may result in materially different amounts being reported under different conditions or using different assumptions.

We consider financial reporting and disclosure practices and accounting policies quarterly to ensure that they provide accurate and transparent information relative to the current economic and business environment. We believe that of our significant accounting policies, the following policies involve a higher degree of judgment and/or complexity:

Asset Impairment

When facts and circumstances indicate that the carrying values of long-lived assets may not be recoverable, we evaluate long-lived assets for impairment. We first compare the carrying value of the asset to the asset's estimated future undiscounted cash flows. If the estimated future cash flows are less than the carrying value of the asset, we measure an impairment loss based on the asset's estimated fair value. For retail assets, the impairment test is performed at the individual store asset group level. The fair value of a store's assets is estimated using a discounted cash flow model based on internal projections. Key assumptions used in this calculation include revenue growth, operating expenses and a discount rate that we believe a buyer would assume when determining a purchase price for the store. Estimates of revenue growth and operating expenses are based on internal projections and consider a store's historical performance, local market economics and the business environment impacting the store's performance. These estimates are subjective and can be significantly impacted by changes in the business or economic conditions. For non-retail assets, fair value is determined using an approach that is appropriate based on the relevant facts and circumstances, which may include discounted cash flows, comparable transactions, or comparable company analyses.

Our impairment loss calculations contain uncertainties because they require management to make assumptions and to apply judgment to estimate future cash flows and asset fair values, including forecasting asset useful lives. Further, our ability to realize undiscounted cash flows in excess of the carrying values of our assets is affected by factors such as the ongoing maintenance and improvement of the assets, changes in economic conditions, and changes in operating performance. During the past three fiscal years, we have not made any material changes in the accounting methodology that we use to assess long-lived asset impairment loss. For the foreseeable future, we do not believe there is a reasonable likelihood that there will be a material change in the estimates or assumptions that we use to calculate long-lived asset impairment losses. However, as we periodically reassess estimated future cash flows and asset fair values, changes in our estimates and assumptions may cause us to realize material impairment charges in the future.

Goodwill Impairment

We test goodwill for impairment on an annual basis during our third fiscal quarter, or more frequently if circumstances, such as material deterioration in performance or a significant number of store closures, indicate reporting unit carrying values may exceed their fair values. When evaluating goodwill for impairment, we first perform a qualitative assessment to determine if the fair value of the reporting unit is more likely than not greater than the carrying amount. If not, we calculate the implied estimated fair value of the reporting unit. If the carrying amount of goodwill exceeds the implied estimated fair value, an impairment charge is recorded to reduce the carrying value to the implied estimated fair value. The fair value of each of our reporting units is the price a willing buyer would pay for the reporting unit and is typically calculated using a discounted cash flow model. Key assumptions used in this calculation include revenue growth, operating expenses and a discount rate that we believe a buyer would assume when determining a purchase price for the reporting unit. Estimates of revenue growth and operating expenses are based on internal projections considering a reporting unit's past performance and forecasted growth, local market economics and the local business environment impacting the reporting unit's performance. The discount rate is calculated using an estimated cost of capital for a retail operator to operate the reporting unit in the region. These estimates are highly subjective judgments and can be significantly impacted by changes in the business or economic conditions.

Our impairment loss calculations contain uncertainties because they require management to make assumptions in the qualitative assessment of the reporting unit and require management to apply judgment to estimate the fair value of our reporting units, including estimating future cash flows, and if necessary, the fair value of a reporting units' assets and liabilities. Further, our ability to realize the future cash flows used in our fair value calculations is affected by factors such as changes in economic conditions, changes in our operating performance, and changes in our business strategies.

As a part of our ongoing operations, we may close certain stores within a reporting unit containing goodwill due to underperformance of the store or inability to renew our lease, among other reasons. We abandon certain assets associated with a closed store including leasehold improvements and other non-transferable assets. Under GAAP, when a portion of a reporting unit that constitutes a business is to be disposed of, goodwill associated with the business is included in the carrying amount of the business in determining any loss on disposal. Our evaluation of whether the portion of a reporting unit being disposed of constitutes a business occurs on the date of abandonment. Although an operating store meets the accounting definition of a business prior to abandonment, it does not constitute a business on the closure date because the remaining assets on that date do not constitute an integrated set of assets that are capable of being conducted and managed for the purpose of providing a return to investors. As a result, when closing individual stores, we do not include goodwill in the calculation of any loss on disposal of the related assets. As noted above, if store closures are indicative of potential impairment of goodwill at the reporting unit level, we perform an evaluation of our reporting unit goodwill when such closures occur.

During the past three fiscal years, we have not made any material changes in the accounting methodology that we use to assess goodwill impairment loss. For fiscal 2012, we determined the fair value of our reporting units was substantially in excess of their carrying values. Accordingly, we did not recognize any goodwill impairments during the current fiscal year. We do not believe there is a reasonable likelihood that there will be a material change in the estimates or assumptions that we use to test for impairment losses on goodwill in the foreseeable future. However, as we periodically reassess our fair value calculations, including estimated future cash flows, changes in our estimates and assumptions may cause us to realize material impairment charges in the future.

Self Insurance Reserves

We use a combination of insurance and self-insurance mechanisms, including a wholly owned captive insurance entity and participation in a reinsurance treaty, to provide for the potential liabilities for certain risks, including workers' compensation, healthcare benefits, general liability, property insurance, and director and officers' liability insurance. Key assumptions used in the estimate of our self insurance reserves include the amount of claims incurred but not reported at the balance sheet date. These liabilities, which are associated with the risks that are retained by Starbucks are not discounted and are estimated, in part, by considering historical claims experience, demographic, exposure and severity factors, and other actuarial assumptions. The estimated accruals for these liabilities could be significantly affected if future occurrences and claims differ from these assumptions and historical trends.

Our self-insurance reserves contain uncertainties because management is required to make assumptions and to apply judgment to estimate the ultimate cost to settle reported claims and claims incurred but not reported at the balance sheet date. Periodically, we review our assumptions to determine the adequacy of our self-insurance reserves.

During the past three fiscal years, we have not made any material changes in the accounting methodology that we use to calculate our self-insurance reserves. We do not believe there is a reasonable likelihood that there will be a material change in the estimates or assumptions that we use to calculate our self-insurance reserves for the foreseeable future. However, if actual results are not consistent with our estimates or assumptions, we may be exposed to losses or gains that could be material.

A 10% change in our self-insurance reserves at September 30, 2012 would have affected net earnings by approximately $10 million in fiscal 2012.

Income Taxes

We recognize deferred tax assets and liabilities based on the differences between the financial statement carrying amounts and the respective tax bases of our assets and liabilities. Deferred tax assets and liabilities are measured using current enacted tax rates expected to apply to taxable income in the years in which we expect the temporary differences to reverse. We routinely evaluate the likelihood of realizing the benefit of our deferred tax assets and may record a valuation allowance if, based on all available evidence, we determine that some portion of the tax benefit will not be realized.

In addition, our income tax returns are periodically audited by domestic and foreign tax authorities. These audits include questions regarding our tax filing positions, including the timing and amount of deductions taken and the allocation of income among various tax jurisdictions. We evaluate our exposures associated with our various tax filing positions; we recognize a tax benefit only if it is more likely than not that the tax position will be sustained on examination by the relevant taxing authorities, based on the technical merits of our position. For uncertain tax positions that do not meet this threshold, we record a related liability. We adjust our unrecognized tax benefits liability and income tax expense in the period in which the uncertain tax position is effectively settled, the statute of limitations expires for the relevant taxing authority to examine the tax position, or when new information becomes available.

Income generated in certain foreign jurisdictions has not been subject to US income taxes. We intend to reinvest these earnings for the foreseeable future. If these amounts were distributed to the US, in the form of dividends or otherwise, we would be subject to additional US income taxes, which could be material. Determination of the amount of unrecognized deferred income tax liabilities on these earnings is not practicable because such liability, if any, is dependent on circumstances existing if and when remittance occurs.

Deferred tax asset valuation allowances and our liability for unrecognized tax benefits require significant management judgment regarding applicable statutes and their related interpretation, the status of various income tax audits, and our particular facts and circumstances. Although we believe that the judgments and estimates discussed herein are reasonable, actual results could differ, and we may be exposed to losses or gains that could be material. To the extent we prevail in matters for which a liability has been established, or are required to pay amounts in excess of our established liability, our effective income tax rate in a given financial statement period could be materially affected.

Litigation Accruals

We are involved in various claims and legal actions that arise in the ordinary course of business. Legal and other contingency reserves and related disclosures are based on our assessment of the likelihood of a potential loss and our ability to estimate the loss or range of loss, which includes consultation with outside legal counsel and advisors. We record reserves related to legal matters when it is probable that a loss has been incurred and the range of such loss can be reasonably estimated. Such assessments are reviewed each period and revised, based on current facts and circumstances and historical experience with similar claims, as necessary.

Our disclosures of and accruals for litigation claims, if any, contain uncertainties because management is required to use judgment to estimate the probability of a loss and a range of possible losses related to each claim. Note 15 to the consolidated financial statements describes the Company's legal and other contingent liability matters.

As we periodically review our assessments of litigation accruals, we may change our assumptions with respect to loss probabilities and ranges of potential losses. Any changes in these assumptions could have a material impact on our future results of operations.

RECENT ACCOUNTING PRONOUNCEMENTS

See Note 1 to the consolidated financial statements in this 10-K for a detailed description of recent accounting pronouncements. We do not expect these recently issued accounting pronouncements to have a material impact on our results of operations, financial condition, or liquidity in future periods.

Item 7A. *Quantitative and Qualitative Disclosures About Market Risk*

The information required by this item is incorporated by reference to the section entitled "Management's Discussion and Analysis of Financial Condition and Results of Operations — Commodity Prices, Availability and General Risk Conditions" and "Management's Discussion and Analysis of Financial Condition and Results of Operations — Financial Risk Management" in Item 7 of this Report.

Item 8. *Financial Statements and Supplementary Data*

STARBUCKS CORPORATION
CONSOLIDATED STATEMENTS OF EARNINGS
(in millions, except per share data)

Fiscal Year Ended		Sep 30, 2012		Oct 2, 2011		Oct 3, 2010
Net revenues:						
Company-operated stores	$	10,534.5	$	9,632.4	$	8,963.5
Licensed stores		1,210.3		1,007.5		875.2
CPG, foodservice and other		1,554.7		1,060.5		868.7
Total net revenues		13,299.5		11,700.4		10,707.4
Cost of sales including occupancy costs		5,813.3		4,915.5		4,416.5
Store operating expenses		3,918.1		3,594.9		3,471.9
Other operating expenses		429.9		392.8		279.7
Depreciation and amortization expenses		550.3		523.3		510.4
General and administrative expenses		801.2		749.3		704.6
Restructuring charges		—		—		53.0
Total operating expenses		11,512.8		10,175.8		9,436.1
Gain on sale of properties		—		30.2		—
Income from equity investees		210.7		173.7		148.1
Operating income		1,997.4		1,728.5		1,419.4
Interest income and other, net		94.4		115.9		50.3
Interest expense		(32.7)		(33.3)		(32.7)
Earnings before income taxes		2,059.1		1,811.1		1,437.0
Income taxes		674.4		563.1		488.7
Net earnings including noncontrolling interests		1,384.7		1,248.0		948.3
Net earnings (loss) attributable to noncontrolling interests		0.9		2.3		2.7
Net earnings attributable to Starbucks	$	1,383.8	$	1,245.7	$	945.6
Earnings per share — basic	$	1.83	$	1.66	$	1.27
Earnings per share — diluted	$	1.79	$	1.62	$	1.24
Weighted average shares outstanding:						
Basic		754.4		748.3		744.4
Diluted		773.0		769.7		764.2
Cash dividends declared per share	$	0.72	$	0.56	$	0.36

See Notes to Consolidated Financial Statements.

STARBUCKS CORPORATION
CONSOLIDATED BALANCE SHEETS
(in millions, except per share data)

	Sep 30, 2012	Oct 2, 2011
ASSETS		
Current assets:		
Cash and cash equivalents	$ 1,188.6	$ 1,148.1
Short-term investments	848.4	902.6
Accounts receivable, net	485.9	386.5
Inventories	1,241.5	965.8
Prepaid expenses and other current assets	196.5	161.5
Deferred income taxes, net	238.7	230.4
Total current assets	4,199.6	3,794.9
Long-term investments — available-for-sale securities	116.0	107.0
Equity and cost investments	459.9	372.3
Property, plant and equipment, net	2,658.9	2,355.0
Other assets	385.7	409.6
Goodwill	399.1	321.6
TOTAL ASSETS	$ 8,219.2	$ 7,360.4
LIABILITIES AND EQUITY		
Current liabilities:		
Accounts payable	$ 398.1	$ 540.0
Accrued liabilities	1,133.8	940.9
Insurance reserves	167.7	145.6
Deferred revenue	510.2	449.3
Total current liabilities	2,209.8	2,075.8
Long-term debt	549.6	549.5
Other long-term liabilities	345.3	347.8
Total liabilities	3,104.7	2,973.1
Shareholders' equity:		
Common stock ($0.001 par value) — authorized, 1,200.0 shares; issued and outstanding, 749.3 and 744.8 shares, respectively (includes 3.4 common stock units in both periods)	0.7	0.7
Additional paid-in capital	39.4	40.5
Retained earnings	5,046.2	4,297.4
Accumulated other comprehensive income	22.7	46.3
Total shareholders' equity	5,109.0	4,384.9
Noncontrolling interests	5.5	2.4
Total equity	5,114.5	4,387.3
TOTAL LIABILITIES AND EQUITY	$ 8,219.2	$ 7,360.4

See Notes to Consolidated Financial Statements.

51

STARBUCKS CORPORATION
CONSOLIDATED STATEMENTS OF CASH FLOWS
(in millions)

Fiscal Year Ended	Sep 30, 2012	Oct 2, 2011	Oct 3, 2010
OPERATING ACTIVITIES:			
Net earnings including noncontrolling interests	$ 1,384.7	$ 1,248.0	$ 948.3
Adjustments to reconcile net earnings to net cash provided by operating activities:			
Depreciation and amortization	580.6	550.0	540.8
Gain on sale of properties	—	(30.2)	—
Deferred income taxes, net	61.1	106.2	(42.0)
Income earned from equity method investees, net of distributions	(49.3)	(32.9)	(17.2)
Gain resulting from acquisition of joint ventures	—	(55.2)	(23.1)
Stock-based compensation	153.6	145.2	113.6
Other	23.6	33.3	75.5
Cash provided/(used) by changes in operating assets and liabilities:			
Accounts receivable	(90.3)	(88.7)	(33.4)
Inventories	(273.3)	(422.3)	123.2
Accounts payable	(105.2)	227.5	(3.6)
Accrued liabilities and insurance reserves	23.7	(81.8)	(18.7)
Deferred revenue	60.8	35.8	24.2
Prepaid expenses, other current assets and other assets	(19.7)	(22.5)	17.3
Net cash provided by operating activities	1,750.3	1,612.4	1,704.9
INVESTING ACTIVITIES:			
Purchase of investments	(1,748.6)	(966.0)	(549.0)
Maturities and calls of investments	1,796.4	430.0	209.9
Acquisitions, net of cash acquired	(129.1)	(55.8)	(12.0)
Additions to property, plant and equipment	(856.2)	(531.9)	(445.8)
Cash proceeds from sale of property, plant, and equipment	5.3	117.4	5.1
Other	(41.8)	(13.2)	2.3
Net cash used by investing activities	(974.0)	(1,019.5)	(789.5)
FINANCING ACTIVITIES:			
(Payments)/proceeds from short-term borrowings	(30.8)	30.8	—
Purchase of noncontrolling interest	—	(27.5)	(45.8)
Proceeds from issuance of common stock	236.6	250.4	132.8
Excess tax benefit from exercise of stock options	169.8	103.9	36.9
Cash dividends paid	(513.0)	(389.5)	(171.0)
Repurchase of common stock	(549.1)	(555.9)	(285.6)
Minimum tax withholdings on share-based awards	(58.5)	(15.0)	(4.9)
Other	(0.5)	(5.2)	(8.4)
Net cash used by financing activities	(745.5)	(608.0)	(346.0)
Effect of exchange rate changes on cash and cash equivalents	9.7	(0.8)	(5.2)
Net increase (decrease) in cash and cash equivalents	40.5	(15.9)	564.2
CASH AND CASH EQUIVALENTS:			
Beginning of period	1,148.1	1,164.0	599.8
End of period	$ 1,188.6	$ 1,148.1	$ 1,164.0
SUPPLEMENTAL DISCLOSURE OF CASH FLOW INFORMATION:			
Cash paid during the period for:			
Interest, net of capitalized interest	$ 34.4	$ 34.4	$ 32.0
Income taxes	$ 416.9	$ 350.1	$ 527.0

See Notes to Consolidated Financial Statements.

STARBUCKS CORPORATION
CONSOLIDATED STATEMENTS OF EQUITY
(in millions)

	Common Stock		Additional Paid-In Capital	Retained Earnings	Accumulated Other Comprehensive Income/(Loss)	Shareholders' Equity	Noncontrolling Interest	Total
	Shares	Amount						
Balance, September 27, 2009	742.9	$ 0.7	$ 186.4	$ 2,793.2	$ 65.4	$ 3,045.7	$ 11.2	$ 3,056.9
Net earnings	—	—	—	945.6	—	945.6	2.7	948.3
Unrealized holding loss, net	—	—	—	—	(17.0)	(17.0)	—	(17.0)
Translation adjustment, net of tax	—	—	—	—	8.8	8.8	—	8.8
Comprehensive income						937.4	2.7	940.1
Stock-based compensation expense	—	—	115.6	—	—	115.6	—	115.6
Exercise of stock options, including tax benefit of $27.7	10.1	—	137.5	—	—	137.5	—	137.5
Sale of common stock, including tax benefit of $0.1	0.8	—	18.5	—	—	18.5	—	18.5
Repurchase of common stock	(11.2)	—	(285.6)	—	—	(285.6)	—	(285.6)
Net distributions to noncontrolling interests	—	—	—	—	—	—	(0.8)	(0.8)
Cash dividend	—	—	—	(267.6)	—	(267.6)	—	(267.6)
Purchase of noncontrolling interests	—	—	(26.8)	—	—	(26.8)	(5.5)	(32.3)
Balance, October 3, 2010	742.6	$ 0.7	$ 145.6	$ 3,471.2	$ 57.2	$ 3,674.7	$ 7.6	$ 3,682.3
Net earnings	—	—	—	1,245.7	—	1,245.7	2.3	1,248.0
Unrealized holding loss, net	—	—	—	—	(4.4)	(4.4)	—	(4.4)
Translation adjustment, net of tax	—	—	—	—	(6.5)	(6.5)	—	(6.5)
Comprehensive income						1,234.8	2.3	1,237.1
Stock-based compensation expense	—	—	147.2	—	—	147.2	—	147.2
Exercise of stock options, including tax benefit of $96.1	17.3	—	312.5	—	—	312.5	—	312.5
Sale of common stock, including tax benefit of $0.1	0.5	—	19.1	—	—	19.1	—	19.1
Repurchase of common stock	(15.6)	—	(555.9)	—	—	(555.9)	—	(555.9)
Cash dividend	—	—	—	(419.5)	—	(419.5)	—	(419.5)
Purchase of noncontrolling interests	—	—	(28.0)	—	—	(28.0)	(7.5)	(35.5)
Balance, October 2, 2011	744.8	$ 0.7	$ 40.5	$ 4,297.4	$ 46.3	$ 4,384.9	$ 2.4	$ 4,387.3
Net earnings	—	—	—	1,383.8	—	1,383.8	0.9	1,384.7
Unrealized holding loss, net	—	—	—	—	(26.4)	(26.4)	—	(26.4)
Translation adjustment, net of tax	—	—	—	—	2.8	2.8	—	2.8
Comprehensive income						1,360.2	0.9	1,361.1
Stock-based compensation expense	—	—	155.2	—	—	155.2	—	155.2
Exercise of stock options, including tax benefit of $167.3	16.5	—	326.1	—	—	326.1	—	326.1
Sale of common stock, including tax benefit of $0.2	0.3	—	19.5	—	—	19.5	—	19.5
Repurchase of common stock	(12.3)	—	(501.9)	(91.3)	—	(593.2)	—	(593.2)
Cash dividend	—	—	—	(543.7)	—	(543.7)	—	(543.7)
Non-controlling interest resulting from acquisition	—	—	—	—	—	—	2.2	2.2
Balance, September 30, 2012	749.3	$ 0.7	$ 39.4	$ 5,046.2	$ 22.7	$ 5,109.0	$ 5.5	$ 5,114.5

See Notes to Consolidated Financial Statements.

53

STARBUCKS CORPORATION

NOTES TO CONSOLIDATED FINANCIAL STATEMENTS
Fiscal Years ended September 30, 2012, October 2, 2011 and October 3, 2010

Note 1: Summary of Significant Accounting Policies

Description of Business

We purchase and roast high-quality coffees that we sell, along with handcrafted coffee and tea beverages and a variety of fresh food items, through our company-operated stores. We also sell a variety of coffee and tea products and license our trademarks through other channels such as licensed stores, grocery and national foodservice accounts.

In this 10-K, Starbucks Corporation (together with its subsidiaries) is referred to as "Starbucks," the "Company," "we," "us" or "our."

We have four reportable operating segments: Americas; Europe, Middle East, and Africa, collectively referred to as "EMEA;" China / Asia Pacific ("CAP") and Channel Development. Our Seattle's Best Coffee operating segment is reported in "Other" with Evolution Fresh, our Digital Ventures business and unallocated corporate expenses.

Additional details on the nature of our business and our reportable operating segments are in Item 1 of this 10-K.

Principles of Consolidation

The consolidated financial statements reflect the financial position and operating results of Starbucks, including wholly owned subsidiaries and investees that we control. Investments in entities that we do not control, but have the ability to exercise significant influence over operating and financial policies, are accounted for under the equity method. Investments in entities in which we do not have the ability to exercise significant influence are accounted for under the cost method. Intercompany transactions and balances have been eliminated.

Fiscal Year End

Our fiscal year ends on the Sunday closest to September 30. Fiscal years 2012 and 2011 included 52 weeks. Fiscal year 2010 included 53 weeks, with the 53rd week falling in the fourth fiscal quarter.

Estimates and Assumptions

Preparing financial statements in conformity with accounting principles generally accepted in the United States of America ("GAAP") requires management to make estimates and assumptions that affect the reported amounts of assets, liabilities, revenues and expenses. Examples include, but are not limited to, estimates for asset and goodwill impairments, stock-based compensation forfeiture rates, future asset retirement obligations, and inventory reserves; assumptions underlying self-insurance reserves and income from unredeemed stored value cards; and the potential outcome of future tax consequences of events that have been recognized in the financial statements. Actual results and outcomes may differ from these estimates and assumptions.

Cash and Cash Equivalents

We consider all highly liquid instruments with a maturity of three months or less at the time of purchase to be cash equivalents. Cash and cash equivalents are valued using active markets for identical assets. We maintain cash and cash equivalent balances with financial institutions that exceed federally insured limits. We have not experienced any losses related to these balances and we believe credit risk to be minimal.

Our cash management system provides for the funding of all major bank disbursement accounts on a daily basis as checks are presented for payment. Under this system, outstanding checks are in excess of the cash balances at certain banks, which creates book overdrafts. Book overdrafts are presented as a current liability in accounts payable on the consolidated balance sheets.

Short-term and Long-term Investments

Our short-term and long-term investments consist primarily of investment grade debt securities, including some auction rate securities, all of which are classified as available-for-sale. Also included in our available-for-sale investment portfolio are certificates of deposit placed through an account registry service. Available-for-sale securities are recorded at fair value, and unrealized holding gains and losses are recorded, net of tax, as a component of accumulated other comprehensive income. Available-for-sale securities with remaining maturities of less than one year and those identified by management at the time of purchase to be used to fund operations within one year are classified as short term. All other available-for-sale securities, including all of our auction rate securities, are classified as long term. Unrealized losses are charged against net earnings when a decline in fair value is determined to be other than temporary. We review several factors to determine whether a loss is other than temporary, such as the length and extent of the fair value decline, the financial condition and near term prospects of the issuer, and whether we have the intent to sell or will likely be required to sell before the securities anticipated recovery, which may be at maturity. Realized gains and losses are accounted for using the specific identification method. Purchases and sales are recorded on a trade date basis.

We also have a trading securities portfolio, which is comprised of marketable equity mutual funds and equity exchange-traded funds. Trading securities are recorded at fair value with unrealized holding gains and losses included in net earnings.

Fair Value

Fair value is the price we would receive to sell an asset or pay to transfer a liability (exit price) in an orderly transaction between market participants. For financial instruments and investments that we record or disclose at fair value, we determine fair value based upon the quoted market price as of the last day of the fiscal period, if available. If a quoted market price is not available for identical assets, we determine fair value based upon the quoted market price of similar assets or using a variety of other valuation methodologies. We determine fair value of our auction rate securities using an internally developed valuation model, using inputs that include interest rate curves, credit and liquidity spreads, and effective maturity.

The carrying value of cash and cash equivalents approximates fair value because of the short-term nature of these instruments. The fair value of our long-term debt is estimated based on the quoted market prices for the same or similar issues or on the current rates offered to us for debt of the same remaining maturities.

We measure our equity and cost method investments at fair value on a nonrecurring basis when they are determined to be other-than temporarily impaired. Fair values are determined using available quoted market prices or discounted cash flows.

Derivative Instruments

We manage our exposure to various risks within the consolidated financial statements according to a market price risk management policy. Under this policy, we may engage in transactions involving various derivative instruments to hedge interest rates, commodity prices and foreign currency denominated revenues, purchases, assets and liabilities. We generally do not enter into derivative instruments with maturities longer than five years.

We enter into fixed-price and price-to-be-fixed coffee purchase commitments. Price-to-be-fixed contracts are purchase commitments whereby the quality, quantity, delivery period, and other negotiated terms are agreed upon, but the date, and therefore price, at which the base "C" coffee commodity price component will be fixed has not yet been established. For these types of contracts, either Starbucks or the seller has the option to "fix" the base "C" coffee commodity price prior to the delivery date. For both fixed-price and price-to-be-fixed purchase commitments, we expect to take delivery of and to utilize the coffee in a reasonable period of time and in the conduct of normal business. Accordingly, these purchase commitments qualify as normal purchases and are not recorded at fair value on our balance sheets.

We record all derivatives on the balance sheets at fair value. For a cash flow hedge, the effective portion of the derivative's gain or loss is initially reported as a component of other comprehensive income ("OCI") and subsequently reclassified into net earnings when the hedged exposure affects net earnings. For a net investment hedge, the effective portion of the derivative's gain or loss is reported as a component of OCI.

Cash flow hedges related to anticipated transactions are designated and documented at the inception of each hedge by matching the terms of the contract to the underlying transaction. We classify the cash flows from hedging transactions in the same categories as the cash flows from the respective hedged items. Once established, cash flow hedges are generally not removed until maturity unless an anticipated transaction is no longer likely to occur. For discontinued or dedesignated cash flow hedges, the related accumulated derivative gains or losses are recognized in net interest income and other on the consolidated statements of earnings.

Forward contract effectiveness for cash flow hedges is calculated by comparing the fair value of the contract to the change in value of the anticipated transaction using forward rates on a monthly basis. For net investment hedges, the spot-to-spot method is used to calculate effectiveness. Under this method, the change in fair value of the forward contract attributable to the changes in spot exchange rates (the effective portion) is reported as a component of OCI. The remaining change in fair value of the forward contract (the ineffective portion) is reclassified into net earnings. Any ineffectiveness is recognized immediately in net interest income and other on the consolidated statements of earnings.

Certain foreign currency forward contracts, commodity swap contracts, and futures contracts are not designated as hedging instruments for accounting purposes. These contracts are recorded at fair value, with the changes in fair value recognized in net interest income and other on the consolidated statements of earnings.

Allowance for Doubtful Accounts

Allowance for doubtful accounts is calculated based on historical experience, customer credit risk and application of the specific identification method. As of September 30, 2012, October 2, 2011, and October 3, 2010, the allowance for doubtful accounts was $5.6 million, $3.3 million, and $3.3 million respectively.

Inventories

Inventories are stated at the lower of cost (primarily moving average cost) or market. We record inventory reserves for obsolete and slow-moving inventory and for estimated shrinkage between physical inventory counts. Inventory reserves are based on inventory obsolescence trends, historical experience and application of the specific identification method. As of September 30, 2012, October 2, 2011, and October 3, 2010, inventory reserves were $22.6 million, $19.5 million, and $18.1 million, respectively.

Property, Plant and Equipment

Property, plant and equipment are carried at cost less accumulated depreciation. Depreciation of property, plant and equipment, which includes assets under capital leases, is provided on the straight-line method over estimated useful lives, generally ranging from 2 to 15 years for equipment and 30 to 40 years for buildings. Leasehold improvements are amortized over the shorter of their estimated useful lives or the related lease life, generally 10 years . For leases with renewal periods at our option, we generally use the original lease term, excluding renewal option periods, to determine estimated useful lives. If failure to exercise a renewal option imposes an economic penalty to us, we may determine at the inception of the lease that renewal is reasonably assured and include the renewal option period in the determination of the appropriate estimated useful lives. The portion of depreciation expense related to production and distribution facilities is included in cost of sales including occupancy costs on the consolidated statements of earnings. The costs of repairs and maintenance are expensed when incurred, while expenditures for refurbishments and improvements that significantly add to the productive capacity or extend the useful life of an asset are capitalized. When assets are retired or sold, the asset cost and related accumulated depreciation are eliminated with any remaining gain or loss recognized in net earnings.

Goodwill

We test goodwill for impairment on an annual basis during our third fiscal quarter, or more frequently if circumstances, such as material deterioration in performance or a significant number of store closures, indicate reporting unit carrying values may exceed their fair values. When evaluating goodwill for impairment, we first perform a qualitative assessment to determine if the fair value of the reporting unit is more likely than not greater than the carrying amount. If not, we calculate the implied estimated fair value of the reporting unit. If the carrying amount of goodwill exceeds the implied estimated fair value, an impairment charge to current operations is recorded to reduce the carrying value to the implied estimated fair value.

As a part of our ongoing operations, we may close certain stores within a reporting unit containing goodwill due to underperformance of the store or inability to renew our lease, among other reasons. We abandon certain assets associated with a closed store including leasehold improvements and other non-transferable assets. Under GAAP, when a portion of a reporting unit that constitutes a business is to be disposed of, goodwill associated with the business is included in the carrying amount of the business in determining any loss on disposal. Our evaluation of whether the portion of a reporting unit being disposed of constitutes a business occurs on the date of abandonment. Although an operating store meets the accounting definition of a business prior to abandonment, it does not constitute a business on the closure date because the remaining assets on that date do not constitute an integrated set of assets that are capable of being conducted and managed for the purpose of providing a return to investors. As a result, when closing individual stores, we do not include goodwill in the calculation of any loss on disposal of the related assets. As noted above, if store closures are indicative of potential impairment of goodwill at the reporting unit level, we perform an evaluation of our reporting unit goodwill when such closures occur. During Fiscal 2012 and fiscal 2011 we recorded no impairment charges and recorded $1.6 million in fiscal 2010.

Other Intangible Assets

Other intangible assets consist primarily of trademarks with indefinite lives, which are tested for impairment annually or more frequently if events or changes in circumstances indicate that the asset might be impaired. Definite-lived intangible assets, which mainly consist of contract-based patents and copyrights, are amortized over their estimated useful lives, and are tested for impairment when facts and circumstances indicate that the carrying values may not be recoverable. Based on the impairment tests performed, there was no impairment of other intangible assets in fiscal 2012, 2011, and 2010.

Long-lived Assets

When facts and circumstances indicate that the carrying values of long-lived assets may not be recoverable, we evaluate long-lived assets for impairment. We first compare the carrying value of the asset to the asset's estimated future cash flows (undiscounted). If the estimated future cash flows are less than the carrying value of the asset, we calculate an impairment loss based on the asset's estimated fair value. The fair value of the assets is estimated using a discounted cash flow model based on forecasted future revenues and operating costs, using internal projections. Property, plant and equipment assets are grouped at the lowest level for which there are identifiable cash flows when assessing impairment. Cash flows for company-operated store assets are identified at the individual store level. Long-lived assets to be disposed of are reported at the lower of their carrying amount, or fair value less estimated costs to sell.

We recognized net impairment and disposition losses of $31.7 million, $36.2 million, and $67.7 million in fiscal 2012, 2011, and 2010, respectively, primarily due to underperforming company-operated stores. Depending on the underlying asset that is impaired, these losses may be recorded in any one of the operating expense lines on the consolidated statements of earnings: for retail operations, the net impairment and disposition losses are recorded in store operating expenses and for all other operations, these losses are recorded in cost of sales including occupancy costs, other operating expenses, or general and administrative expenses.

Insurance Reserves

We use a combination of insurance and self-insurance mechanisms, including a wholly owned captive insurance entity and participation in a reinsurance treaty, to provide for the potential liabilities for certain risks, including workers' compensation, healthcare benefits, general liability, property insurance, and director and officers' liability insurance. Liabilities associated with the risks that are retained by us are not discounted and are estimated, in part, by considering historical claims experience, demographic, exposure and severity factors, and other actuarial assumptions.

Revenue Recognition

Consolidated revenues are presented net of intercompany eliminations for wholly owned subsidiaries and investees controlled by us and for licensees accounted for under the equity method, based on our percentage ownership. Additionally, consolidated revenues are recognized net of any discounts, returns, allowances and sales incentives, including coupon redemptions and rebates.

Company-operated Stores Revenues

Company-operated store revenues are recognized when payment is tendered at the point of sale. Retail store revenues are reported net of sales, use or other transaction taxes that are collected from customers and remitted to taxing authorities.

Licensed Stores Revenues

Licensed stores revenues consist of product sales to licensed stores, as well as royalties and other fees paid by licensees to use the Starbucks brand. Sales of coffee, tea and related products are generally recognized upon shipment to licensees, depending on contract terms. Shipping charges billed to licensees are also recognized as revenue, and the related shipping costs are included in cost of sales including occupancy costs on the consolidated statements of earnings.

Initial nonrefundable development fees for licensed stores are recognized upon substantial performance of services for new market business development activities, such as initial business, real estate and store development planning, as well as providing operational materials and functional training courses for opening new licensed retail markets. Additional store licensing fees are recognized when new licensed stores are opened. Royalty revenues based upon a percentage of reported sales and other continuing fees, such as marketing and service fees, are recognized on a monthly basis when earned.

CPG, Foodservice and Other Revenues

CPG, foodservice and other revenues primarily consist of domestic and international sales of packaged coffee and tea as well as a variety of ready-to-drink beverages and single-serve coffee and tea products to grocery, warehouse club and specialty retail stores, sales to our national foodservice accounts, and revenues from sales of products to and license revenues from manufacturers that produce and market Starbucks and Seattle's Best Coffee branded products through licensing agreements. Sales of coffee, tea, ready-to-drink beverages and related products to grocery and warehouse club stores are generally recognized when received by the customer or distributor, depending on contract terms. We maintain a sales return allowance to reduce packaged goods revenues for estimated future product returns based on historical patterns. Revenues are recorded net of sales discounts given to customers for trade promotions and payments to customers for product placement in our customers' stores.

Revenues from sales of products to manufacturers that produce and market Starbucks and Seattle's Best Coffee branded products through licensing agreements are generally recognized when the product is received by the manufacturer or distributor. License revenues from manufacturers are based on a percentage of sales and are recognized on a monthly basis when earned. National foodservice account revenues are recognized when the product is received by the customer or distributor.

Stored Value Cards

Revenues from our stored value cards, primarily Starbucks Cards, are recognized when redeemed or when the likelihood of redemption, based on historical experience, is deemed to be remote. Outstanding customer balances are included in deferred revenue on the consolidated balance sheets. There are no expiration dates on our stored value cards, and we do not charge any service fees that cause a decrement to customer balances. While we will continue to honor all stored value cards presented for payment, management may determine the likelihood of redemption to be remote for certain cards due to long periods of inactivity. In these circumstances, if management also determines there is no requirement for remitting balances to government agencies under unclaimed property laws, card balances may then be recognized in the consolidated statements of earnings, in net interest income and other. For the fiscal years ended September 30, 2012, October 2, 2011, and October 3, 2010, income recognized on unredeemed stored value card balances was $65.8 million, $46.9 million, and $31.2 million, respectively. In fiscal 2012, we recognized additional income associated with unredeemed gift cards due to a recent court ruling relating to state unclaimed property laws.

Customers in the US, Canada, and the UK who register their Starbucks Card are automatically enrolled in the My Starbucks Reward program and earn points ("Stars") with each purchase. Reward program members receive various benefits depending on the number of Stars earned in a 12-month period. The value of Stars earned by our program members towards free product is included in deferred revenue and recorded as a reduction in revenue at the time the Stars are earned, based on the value of Stars that are projected to be redeemed.

Marketing & Advertising

Our annual marketing expenses include many components, one of which is advertising costs. We expense most advertising costs as they are incurred, except for certain production costs that are expensed the first time the advertising campaign takes place.

Annual marketing expenses totaled $277.9 million, $244.0 million, and $198.7 million in fiscal 2012, 2011, and 2010, respectively. Included in these costs were advertising expenses, which totaled $182.4 million, $141.4 million, and $176.2 million in fiscal 2012, 2011, and 2010, respectively.

Store Preopening Expenses

Costs incurred in connection with the start-up and promotion of new store openings are expensed as incurred.

Operating Leases

We lease retail stores, roasting, distribution and warehouse facilities, and office space under operating leases. Most lease agreements contain tenant improvement allowances, rent holidays, lease premiums, rent escalation clauses and/or contingent rent provisions. For purposes of recognizing incentives, premiums and minimum rental expenses on a straight-line basis over the terms of the leases, we use the date of initial possession to begin amortization, which is generally when we enter the space and begin to make improvements in preparation of intended use.

For tenant improvement allowances and rent holidays, we record a deferred rent liability on the consolidated balance sheets and amortize the deferred rent over the terms of the leases as reductions to rent expense on the consolidated statements of earnings.

For premiums paid upfront to enter a lease agreement, we record a deferred rent asset on the consolidated balance sheets and then amortize the deferred rent over the terms of the leases as additional rent expense on the consolidated statements of earnings.

For scheduled rent escalation clauses during the lease terms or for rental payments commencing at a date other than the date of initial occupancy, we record minimum rental expenses on a straight-line basis over the terms of the leases on the consolidated statements of earnings.

Certain leases provide for contingent rents, which are determined as a percentage of gross sales in excess of specified levels. We record a contingent rent liability on the consolidated balance sheets and the corresponding rent expense when specified levels have been achieved or when we determine that achieving the specified levels during the fiscal year is probable.

When ceasing operations in company-operated stores under operating leases, in cases where the lease contract specifies a termination fee due to the landlord, we record such expense at the time written notice is given to the landlord. In cases where terms, including termination fees, are yet to be negotiated with the landlord, we will record the expense upon signing of an agreement with the landlord. In cases where the landlord does not allow us to prematurely exit the lease, but allows for subleasing, we estimate the fair value of any sublease income that can be generated from the location and expense the present value of the excess of remaining lease payments to the landlord over the projected sublease income at the cease-use date.

Asset Retirement Obligations

We recognize a liability for the fair value of required asset retirement obligations ("ARO") when such obligations are incurred. Our AROs are primarily associated with leasehold improvements, which, at the end of a lease, we are contractually obligated to remove in order to comply with the lease agreement. At the inception of a lease with such conditions, we record an ARO liability and a corresponding capital asset in an amount equal to the estimated fair value of the obligation. The liability is estimated based on a number of assumptions requiring management's judgment, including store closing costs, cost inflation rates and discount rates, and is accreted to its projected future value over time. The capitalized asset is depreciated using the same depreciation convention as leasehold improvement assets. Upon satisfaction of the ARO conditions, any difference between the recorded ARO liability and the actual retirement costs incurred is recognized as an operating gain or loss in the consolidated statements of earnings. As of September 30, 2012 and October 2, 2011, our net ARO asset included in property, plant and equipment was $8.8 million and $11.8 million, respectively, and our net ARO liability included in other long-term liabilities was $42.6 million and $50.1 million, respectively.

Stock-based Compensation

We maintain several equity incentive plans under which we may grant non-qualified stock options, incentive stock options, restricted stock, restricted stock units ("RSUs") or stock appreciation rights to employees, non-employee directors and consultants. We also have employee stock purchase plans ("ESPP"). RSUs issued by us are equivalent to nonvested shares under the applicable accounting guidance. We record stock-based compensation expenses based on the fair value of stock awards at the grant date and recognize the expense over the related service period following a graded vesting expense schedule. For stock option awards we use the Black-Scholes-Merton option pricing model to measure fair value. For restricted stock units, fair value is calculated using the stock price at the date of grant.

Foreign Currency Translation

Our international operations generally use their local currency as their functional currency. Assets and liabilities are translated at exchange rates in effect at the balance sheet date. Income and expense accounts are translated at the average monthly exchange rates during the year. Resulting translation adjustments are recorded as a component of accumulated other comprehensive income on the consolidated balance sheets.

Income Taxes

We compute income taxes using the asset and liability method, under which deferred income taxes are provided for the temporary differences between the financial statement carrying amounts and the tax basis of our assets and liabilities. We routinely evaluate the likelihood of realizing the benefit of our deferred tax assets and may record a valuation allowance if, based on all available evidence, we determine that some portion of the tax benefit will not be realized. We recognize the tax benefit from an uncertain tax position only if it is more likely than not that the tax position will be sustained on examination by the relevant taxing authorities, based on the technical merits of our position. The tax benefits recognized in the financial statements from such a position are measured based on the largest benefit that has a greater than 50% likelihood of being realized upon ultimate settlement. Starbucks recognizes interest and penalties related to income tax matters in income tax expense.

Earnings per Share

Basic earnings per share is computed based on the weighted average number of shares of common stock outstanding during the period. Diluted earnings per share is computed based on the weighted average number of shares of common stock and the effect of dilutive potential common shares outstanding during the period, calculated using the treasury stock method. Dilutive potential common shares include outstanding stock options and RSUs. Performance-based RSUs are considered dilutive when the related performance criterion has been met.

Common Stock Share Repurchases

We may repurchase shares of Starbucks common stock under a program authorized by our Board of Directors, including pursuant to a contract, instruction or written plan meeting the requirements of Rule 10b5-1(c)(1) of the Securities Exchange Act of 1934. Under applicable Washington State law, shares repurchased are retired and not displayed separately as treasury stock on the financial statements. Instead, the par value of repurchased shares is deducted from common stock and the excess repurchase price over par value is deducted from additional paid-in capital and from retained earnings, once additional paid-in capital is depleted.

Recent Accounting Pronouncements

In July 2012, the FASB issued guidance that revises the requirements around how entities test indefinite-lived intangible assets, other than goodwill, for impairment. The guidance allows companies to perform a qualitative assessment before calculating the fair value of the reporting unit. If entities determine, on the basis of qualitative factors, that the fair value of the indefinite-lived intangible asset is more likely than not greater than the carrying amount, a quantitative calculation would not be needed. The guidance will become effective for us at the beginning of our first quarter of fiscal 2013. The adoption of this guidance will not have a material impact on our financial statements.

In September 2011, the FASB issued guidance that revises the requirements around how entities test goodwill for impairment. The guidance allows companies to perform a qualitative assessment before calculating the fair value of the reporting unit. If entities determine, on the basis of qualitative factors, that the fair value of the reporting unit is more likely than not greater than the carrying amount, a quantitative calculation would not be needed. We early-adopted this guidance effective for our fiscal 2012 annual goodwill impairment test, which we performed during the third fiscal quarter. The adoption of this guidance will result in a change in how we perform our goodwill impairment assessment; however, it will not have a material impact on our financial statements.

In June 2011, the FASB issued guidance that revises the manner in which entities present comprehensive income in their financial statements. The guidance requires entities to report the components of comprehensive income in either a single, continuous statement or two separate but consecutive statements. The guidance will become effective for us at the beginning of our first quarter of fiscal 2013. The adoption of this new guidance will result in a change in how we present the components of comprehensive income, which is currently presented within our consolidated statements of equity.

In May 2011, the FASB issued guidance to amend the fair value measurement and disclosure requirements. The guidance requires the disclosure of quantitative information about unobservable inputs used, a description of the valuation processes used, and a qualitative discussion around the sensitivity of the measurements. This guidance became effective for us at the beginning of our second quarter of fiscal 2012. The adoption of this new guidance did not have a material impact on our financial statements.

Reclassifications

Change in shared service allocations

Effective at the beginning of fiscal 2012, we implemented the previously announced strategic realignment of our organizational structure designed to accelerate our global growth strategy. A president for each region, reporting directly to our chief executive officer, now oversees the company-operated retail business working closely with both the licensed and joint-venture business partners in each market. The regional presidents also work closely with our Channel Development team to continue building out our brands and channels in each region.

In connection with the changes to our organizational structure and reporting, we have changed the accountability for, and reporting of, certain indirect overhead costs. Certain indirect merchandising, manufacturing costs and back-office shared service costs, which were previously allocated to segment level costs of sales and operating expenses, are now managed at a corporate level and will be reported within unallocated corporate expenses. These expenses have therefore been removed from the segment level financial results. In order to conform prior period classifications with the new alignment, the historical consolidated financial statements have been recast with the following adjustments to previously reported amounts (in millions):

| | Year Ended October 2, 2011 | | |
	As Filed	Reclass	As Adjusted
Total net revenues	$ 11,700.4	$ —	$ 11,700.4
Cost of sales including occupancy costs	4,949.3	(33.8)	4,915.5
Store operating expenses	3,665.1	(70.2)	3,594.9
Other operating expenses	402.0	(9.2)	392.8
Depreciation and amortization expenses	523.3	—	523.3
General and administrative expenses	636.1	113.2	749.3
Total operating expenses	10,175.8	—	10,175.8
Gain on sale of properties	30.2	—	30.2
Income from equity investees	173.7	—	173.7
Operating income	$ 1,728.5	$ —	$ 1,728.5

| | Year Ended October 3, 2010 | | |
	As Filed	Reclass	As Adjusted
Total net revenues	$ 10,707.4	$ —	$ 10,707.4
Cost of sales including occupancy costs	4,458.6	(42.1)	4,416.5
Store operating expenses	3,551.4	(79.5)	3,471.9
Other operating expenses	293.2	(13.5)	279.7
Depreciation and amortization expenses	510.4	—	510.4
General and administrative expenses	569.5	135.1	704.6
Restructuring charges	53.0	—	53.0
Total operating expenses	9,436.1	—	9,436.1
Income from equity investees	148.1	—	148.1
Operating income	$ 1,419.4	$ —	$ 1,419.4

There was no impact on consolidated net revenues, total operating expenses, operating income, or net earnings as a result of this change. Additional discussion regarding the change in our organizational structure and segment results is included at Note 17.

Change in revenue presentation

In the second quarter of fiscal 2011, concurrent with the change in our distribution method for packaged coffee and tea in the US, we revised the presentation of revenues. Non-retail licensing revenues were reclassified on the consolidated financial statements to the renamed "CPG, foodservice and other" revenue line, which includes revenues from our direct sale of packaged coffee and tea as well as licensing revenues received under the previous distribution arrangement. The previous "Licensing" revenue line now includes only licensed store revenue and therefore has been renamed "Licensed stores." For fiscal 2010, $465.7 million was reclassified from the previously named Licensing revenue to CPG, foodservice and other revenue. There was no impact to consolidated or segment total net revenues from this change in presentation.

Note 2:   Acquisitions

On July 3, 2012, we acquired 100% ownership interest in Bay Bread, LLC and its La Boulange bakery brand (collectively "La Boulange"), to elevate our core food offerings and build a premium, artisanal bakery brand. We acquired La Boulange for a purchase price of approximately $100 million in cash. The following table summarizes the allocation of the purchase price to the fair values of the assets acquired and liabilities assumed on the closing date (in millions):

	Fair Value at July 3, 2012
Property, plant and equipment	$ 18.1
Intangible assets	24.3
Goodwill	58.7
Other current and noncurrent assets	5.1
Current liabilities	(6.4)
Total cash paid	$ 99.8

The assets acquired and liabilities assumed are included in our Americas operating segment. Other current assets acquired primarily include cash, trade receivables, and inventory. In addition, we assumed various current liabilities primarily consisting of accounts payable and accrued payroll related liabilities. The intangible assets acquired as part of the transaction include the La Boulange trade name and proprietary recipes and processes. The La Boulange trade name was valued at $9.7 million and determined to have an indefinite life while the intangible asset relating to the proprietary recipes and processes was valued at $14.6 million and will be amortized over a period of 10 years. The $58.7 million of goodwill is deductible for income tax purposes and was allocated to our Americas operating segment.

On November 10, 2011, we acquired the outstanding shares of Evolution Fresh, Inc., a super-premium juice company, to expand our portfolio of product offerings and enter into the super-premium juice market. We acquired Evolution Fresh for a purchase price of $30 million in cash. The fair value of the net assets acquired on the acquisition date included $18 million of goodwill. Evolution Fresh is its own operating segment and is reported in "Other" along with our Seattle's Best Coffee operating segment, our Digital Ventures business, and unallocated corporate expenses.

In the fourth quarter of fiscal 2011, we acquired the 50% ownership interest in Switzerland and Austria from our joint venture partner, Marinopoulos Holdings S.A.R.L., converting these markets to 100% owned company-operated markets, for a purchase price of $65.5 million. As a result of this acquisition, we adjusted the carrying value of our previous equity investment to fair value, resulting in a gain of approximately $55 million which was included in net interest income and other on our consolidated statements of earnings. The fair value of 100% of the net assets of these markets on the acquisition date was $131.0 million and was recorded on our consolidated balance sheets. Included in these net assets were $63.8 million of goodwill and $35.1 million in definite-lived intangible assets.

In the third quarter of fiscal 2011, we acquired the remaining 30% ownership of our business in the southern portion of China from our noncontrolling partner, Maxim's Caterers Limited (Maxim's). We simultaneously sold our 5% ownership interest in the Hong Kong market to Maxim's.

In the first quarter of fiscal 2010, we acquired 100% ownership of our business in France, converting it from a 50% joint venture with Sigla S.A. (Grupo Vips) of Spain to a company-operated market. We simultaneously sold our 50% ownership interests in the Spain and Portugal markets to Grupo Vips, converting them to licensed markets.

In the fourth quarter of fiscal 2010, we acquired 100% ownership of our business in Brazil, converting it from a 49% joint venture with Cafés Sereia do Brasil Participações S.A of Brazil to a company-operated market.

In the fourth quarter of fiscal 2010, we acquired 100% ownership of a previously consolidated 50% joint venture in the US with Johnson Coffee Corporation, Urban Coffee Opportunities ("UCO").

The following table shows the effects of the change in Starbucks ownership interest in UCO and our business in South China on Starbucks equity:

Fiscal Year Ended	September 30, 2012	October 2, 2011	October 3, 2010
Net earnings attributable to Starbucks	$ 1,383.8	$ 1,245.7	$ 945.6
Transfers (to) from the noncontrolling interest:			
Decrease in additional paid-in capital for purchase of interest in subsidiary	—	(28.0)	(26.8)
Change from net earnings attributable to Starbucks and transfers to noncontrolling interest	$ 1,383.8	$ 1,217.7	$ 918.8

Note 3:   Derivative Financial Instruments

Foreign Currency

We enter into forward and swap contracts to hedge portions of cash flows of anticipated revenue streams and inventory purchases in currencies other than the entity's functional currency. Net derivative losses from cash flow hedges of $2.9 million and $11.1 million, net of taxes, were included in accumulated other comprehensive income as of September 30, 2012 and October 2, 2011, respectively. Of the net derivative losses accumulated as of September 30, 2012, $2.9 million pertains to derivative instruments that will be dedesignated as cash flow hedges within 12 months and will also continue to experience fair value changes before affecting earnings. Outstanding contracts will expire within 12 months.

We also enter into net investment derivative instruments to hedge our equity method investment in Starbucks Coffee Japan, Ltd., to minimize foreign currency exposure. Net derivative losses from net investment hedges of $33.6 million and $34.2 million, net of taxes, were included in accumulated other comprehensive income as of September 30, 2012 and October 2, 2011, respectively. Outstanding contracts will expire within 29 months.

In addition to the hedging instruments above, to mitigate the translation risk of certain balance sheet items, we enter into certain foreign currency swap contracts that are not designated as hedging instruments. These contracts are recorded at fair value, with the changes in fair value recognized in net interest income and other on the consolidated statements of earnings. Gains and losses from these instruments are largely offset by the financial impact of translating foreign currency denominated payables and receivables, which is also recognized in net interest income and other.

Coffee

Depending on market conditions, we also enter into futures contracts to hedge a portion of anticipated cash flows under our price-to-be-fixed green coffee contracts, which are described further in Note 1. Net derivative losses of $32.9 million, net of taxes, were included in accumulated other comprehensive income as of September 30, 2012 related to coffee hedges. Of the net derivative losses accumulated as of September 30, 2012, $26.9 million pertains to derivative instruments that will be dedesignated as cash flow hedges within 12 months and will also continue to experience fair value changes before affecting earnings. Outstanding contracts will expire within 15 months. There was insignificant coffee hedge activity in fiscal 2011.

Dairy

To mitigate the price uncertainty of a portion of our future purchases of dairy products, we enter into certain futures contracts that are not designated as hedging instruments. These contracts are recorded at fair value, with the changes in fair value recognized in net interest income and other. Gains and losses from these instruments are largely offset by price fluctuations on our dairy purchases which are included in cost of sales.

Diesel Fuel

To mitigate the price uncertainty of a portion of our future purchases of diesel fuel, we enter into certain swap contracts that are not designated as hedging instruments. These contracts are recorded at fair value, with the changes in fair value recognized in net interest income and other. Gains and losses from these instruments are largely offset by the financial impact of diesel fuel fluctuations on our shipping costs which are included in operating expenses.

The following table presents the pretax effect of derivative contracts designated as hedging instruments on earnings and other comprehensive income ("OCI") for fiscal years ending (*in millions*):

| | Foreign Currency | | Coffee | |
	Sep 30, 2012	Oct 2, 2011	Sep 30, 2012	Oct 2, 2011
Cash Flow Hedges:				
Gain/(Loss) recognized in earnings	$ (11.5)	$ (15.9)	$ (3.4)	$ —
Gain/(Loss) recognized in OCI	$ (2.5)	$ (12.1)	$ (39.8)	$ —
Net Investment Hedges:				
Gain/(Loss) recognized in earnings	$ —	$ —		
Gain/(Loss) recognized in OCI	$ 1.1	$ (12.0)		

The amounts shown in the above table as recognized in earnings for foreign currency and coffee hedges represent the realized gains/(losses) reclassified from OCI to net earnings during the year. The amounts shown as recognized in OCI are prior to these reclassifications.

The following table presents the pretax effect of derivative contracts not designated as hedging instruments on earnings for fiscal years ending (*in millions*):

| | Foreign Currency | | Coffee | | Dairy | | Diesel Fuel | |
	Sep 30, 2012	Oct 2, 2011	Sep 30, 2012	Oct 2, 2011	Sep 30, 2012	Oct 2, 2011	Sep 30, 2012	Oct 2, 2011
Gain/(Loss) recognized in earnings	$ (2.2)	$ 0.7	$ —	$ (0.9)	$ 7.8	$ 5.7	$ 3.1	$ 1.1

65

Notional amounts of outstanding derivative contracts (*in millions*):

	Sep 30, 2012	Oct 2, 2011
Foreign currency	$ 383	$ 499
Coffee	125	66
Dairy	72	10
Diesel fuel	$ 24	$ —

Note 4: Fair Value Measurements

Assets and Liabilities Measured at Fair Value on a Recurring Basis (in millions):

	Balance at September 30, 2012	Fair Value Measurements at Reporting Date Using		
		Quoted Prices in Active Markets for Identical Assets (Level 1)	Significant Other Observable Inputs (Level 2)	Significant Unobservable Inputs (Level 3)
Assets:				
Cash and cash equivalents	$ 1,188.6	$ 1,188.6	$ —	$ —
Short-term investments:				
Available-for-sale securities				
Agency obligations	80.0	—	80.0	—
Commercial paper	103.9	—	103.9	—
Corporate debt securities	84.3	—	84.3	—
Government treasury securities	459.7	459.7	—	—
Certificates of deposit	62.9	—	62.9	—
Total available-for-sale securities	790.8	459.7	331.1	—
Trading securities	57.6	57.6	—	—
Total short-term investments	848.4	517.3	331.1	—
Long-term investments:				
Available-for-sale securities				
Agency obligations	14.0	—	14.0	—
Corporate debt securities	61.3	—	61.3	—
Auction rate securities	18.6	—	—	18.6
Certificates of deposit	22.1	—	22.1	—
Total long-term investments	116.0	—	97.4	18.6
Total	$ 2,153.0	$ 1,705.9	$ 428.5	$ 18.6
Liabilities:				
Short-term derivatives:				
Foreign Currency	$ 10.1	$ —	$ 10.1	$ —
Coffee	8.8	—	8.8	—
Total short-term derivatives	18.9	—	18.9	—
Long-term derivatives:				
Foreign Currency	3.0	—	3.0	—
Total long-term derivatives	3.0	—	3.0	—
Total	$ 21.9	$ —	$ 21.9	$ —

	Balance at October 2, 2011	Fair Value Measurements at Reporting Date Using		
		Quoted Prices in Active Markets for Identical Assets (Level 1)	Significant Other Observable Inputs (Level 2)	Significant Unobservable Inputs (Level 3)
Assets:				
Cash and cash equivalents	$ 1,148.1	$ 1,148.1	$ —	$ —
Short-term investments:				
Available-for-sale securities				
Agency obligations	20.0	—	20.0	—
Commercial paper	87.0	—	87.0	—
Corporate debt securities	78.0	—	78.0	—
Government treasury securities	606.0	606.0	—	—
Certificates of deposit	64.0	—	64.0	—
Total available-for-sale securities	855.0	606.0	249.0	—
Trading securities	47.6	47.6	—	—
Total short-term investments	902.6	653.6	249.0	—
Long-term investments:				
Available-for-sale securities				
Corporate debt securities	67.0	—	67.0	—
Auction rate securities	28.0	—	—	28.0
Certificates of deposit	12.0	—	12.0	—
Total long-term investments	107.0	—	79.0	28.0
Total	$ 2,157.7	$ 1,801.7	$ 328.0	$ 28.0
Liabilities:				
Short-term derivatives:				
Foreign Currency	$ 20.1	$ —	$ 20.1	$ —
Coffee	1.2	—	1.2	—
Total short-term derivatives	21.3	—	21.3	—
Long-term derivatives:				
Foreign Currency	9.9	—	9.9	—
Total long-term derivatives	9.9	—	9.9	—
Total	$ 31.2	$ —	$ 31.2	$ —

Short-term and long-term derivatives are included in other accrued liabilities and other long-term liabilities, respectively.

Gross unrealized holding gains and losses on investments were not material as of September 30, 2012 and October 2, 2011.

Available-for-sale Securities

Available-for-sale securities include government treasury securities, corporate and agency bonds, commercial paper, certificates of deposit placed through an account registry service and auction rate securities ("ARS").

Level 1: For government treasury securities, we use quoted prices in active markets for identical assets to determine fair value.

Level 2: For corporate and agency bonds, for which a quoted market price is not available for identical assets, we determine fair value based upon the quoted market price of similar assets or the present value of expected future cash flows, calculated by applying revenue multiples to estimate future operating results and using discount rates appropriate for the duration and the risks involved. Fair values for commercial paper are estimated using a discounted cash flow calculation that applies current imputed interest rates of similar securities. Fair values for certificates of deposit are estimated using a discounted cash flow calculation that applies current interest rates to aggregate expected maturities.

Level 3: We determine fair value of our ARS using an internally developed valuation model, using inputs that include interest rate curves, credit and liquidity spreads, and effective maturity.

Proceeds from sales of available-for-sale securities were $5.0 million, $0.0 million, and $1.1 million in fiscal years 2012, 2011, and 2010, respectively. For fiscal years 2012, 2011, and 2010 realized gains and losses on sales and maturities were not material.

Certificates of deposit have maturity dates ranging from approximately one month to 2 years and principal amounts, that when aggregated with interest that will accrue over the investment term, will not exceed Federal Deposit Insurance Corporation limits. Certificates of deposit with original maturities of 90 days or less are included in cash and cash equivalents. The amounts invested in certificate of deposits that were included in cash and cash equivalents were $0.2 million and $4.2 million as of September 30, 2012 and October 2, 2011, respectively.

Long-term investments (except for ARS) generally mature within 3 years. ARS have long-dated maturities but provide liquidity through a Dutch auction process that resets the applicable interest rate at pre-determined calendar intervals. Our ARS are collateralized by portfolios of student loans, substantially all of which are guaranteed by the United States Department of Education. Due to the auction failures that began in 2008, these securities became illiquid and were classified as long-term investments. The investment principal associated with the failed auctions will not be accessible until:

- successful auctions resume;
- an active secondary market for these securities develops;
- the issuers replace these securities with another form of financing; or
- final payments are made according to the contractual maturities of the debt issues which range from 18 to 32 years.

We do not intend to sell the ARS, nor is it likely we will be required to sell the ARS before their anticipated recovery, which may be at maturity.

Trading Securities

Trading securities include equity mutual funds and exchange-traded funds. For these securities, we use quoted prices in active markets for identical assets to determine fair value, thus these securities are considered Level 1 instruments. Our trading securities portfolio approximates a portion of the liability under the Management Deferred Compensation Plan ("MDCP"), a defined contribution plan. The corresponding deferred compensation liability of $94.8 million and $84.7 million as of September 30, 2012 and October 2, 2011, respectively, is included in accrued compensation and related costs on the consolidated balance sheets. The changes in net unrealized holding gains/losses in the trading portfolio included in earnings for fiscal years 2012 , 2011 and 2010 were a net gain of $10.9 million, a net loss of $2.1 million, and a net gain of $4.1 million, respectively.

Derivative Assets and Liabilities

Derivative assets and liabilities include foreign currency forward contracts, commodity swaps and futures contracts. Where applicable, we use quoted prices in active markets for identical derivative assets and liabilities that are traded on exchanges. Derivative assets and liabilities included in Level 2 are over-the-counter currency forward contracts and commodity swaps whose fair values are estimated using industry-standard valuation models. Such models project future cash flows and discount the future amounts to a present value using market-based observable inputs, including interest rate curves and forward and spot prices for currencies and commodities.

Changes in Level 3 Instruments Measured at Fair Value on a Recurring Basis

Financial instruments measured using Level 3 inputs described above are comprised entirely of our ARS. Changes in this balance related primarily to calls of certain of our ARS. In fiscal 2012 and 2011, $10.7 million and $15.8 million, respectively, of our ARS were called at par.

Assets and Liabilities Measured at Fair Value on a Nonrecurring Basis

Assets and liabilities recognized or disclosed at fair value on a nonrecurring basis include items such as property, plant and equipment, goodwill and other intangible assets, equity and cost method investments, and other assets. These assets are measured at fair value if determined to be impaired.

During fiscal 2012 and 2011, we recognized fair market value adjustments with a charge to earnings for these assets as follows:

	Year Ended September 30, 2012		
	Carrying Value before adjustment	Fair value adjustment	Carrying value after adjustment
Property, plant and equipment [1]	$ 21.5	$ (14.4)	$ 7.1

	Year Ended October 2, 2011		
	Carrying Value before adjustment	Fair value adjustment	Carrying value after adjustment
Property, plant, and equipment [1]	$ 8.8	$ (5.9)	$ 2.9
Other assets [2]	$ 22.1	$ (22.1)	$ —

(1) These assets primarily consist of leasehold improvements in underperforming stores. The fair value was determined using a discounted cash flow model based on expected future store revenues and operating costs, using internal projections. The resulting impairment charge was included in store operating expenses.

(2) The fair value was determined using valuation techniques, including discounted cash flows, comparable transactions, and/or comparable company analyses. The resulting impairment charge was included in other operating expenses.

Fair Value of Other Financial Instruments

The estimated fair value of the $550 million of 6.25% Senior Notes based on the quoted market price (Level 2) was approximately $674 million and $648 million as of September 30, 2012 and October 2, 2011, respectively.

Note 5: **Inventories** *(in millions)*

	September 30, 2012		October 2, 2011	
Coffee:				
Unroasted	$	711.3	$	431.3
Roasted		222.2		246.5
Other merchandise held for sale		181.6		150.8
Packaging and other supplies		126.4		137.2
Total	$	1,241.5	$	965.8

Other merchandise held for sale includes, among other items, serveware and tea. Inventory levels vary due to seasonality, commodity market supply and price fluctuations.

As of September 30, 2012, we had committed to purchasing green coffee totaling $557 million under fixed-price contracts and an estimated $297 million under price-to-be-fixed contracts. As of September 30, 2012, approximately $125 million of our price-to-be-fixed contracts were effectively fixed through the use of futures contracts. Until prices are fixed, we estimate the total cost of these purchase commitments. We believe, based on relationships established with our suppliers in the past, the risk of non-delivery on such purchase commitments is remote.

Note 6: **Equity and Cost Investments** *(in millions)*

	September 30, 2012		October 2, 2011	
Equity method investments	$	393.9	$	334.4
Cost method investments		66.0		37.9
Total	$	459.9	$	372.3

Equity Method Investments

As of September 30, 2012, we had a 50 percent ownership interest in each of the following international equity investees: Starbucks Coffee Korea Co., Ltd.; President Starbucks Coffee Taiwan Ltd.; Shanghai President Coffee Co.; Berjaya Starbucks Coffee Company Sdn. Bhd. (Malaysia); and Tata Starbucks Limited (India). In addition, we had a 39.6 percent ownership interest in Starbucks Coffee Japan, Ltd. These international entities operate licensed Starbucks retail stores. We also have licensed the rights to produce and distribute Starbucks branded products to The North American Coffee Partnership with the Pepsi-Cola Company. We have a 50 percent ownership interest in The North American Coffee Partnership, which develops and distributes bottled Frappuccino® beverages, Starbucks DoubleShot® espresso drinks, Seattle's Best Coffee® ready-to-drink espresso beverages and Starbucks Refreshers™ beverages.

Our share of income and losses from our equity method investments is included in income from equity investees on the consolidated statements of earnings. Also included in this line item is our proportionate share of gross margin resulting from coffee and other product sales to, and royalty and license fee revenues generated from, equity investees. Revenues generated from these related parties, net of eliminations, were $190.3 million, $151.6 million, and $125.7 million in fiscal years 2012, 2011, and 2010, respectively. Related costs of sales, net of eliminations, were $111.0 million, $83.2 million, and $65.3 million in fiscal years 2012, 2011, and 2010, respectively. As of September 30, 2012 and October 2, 2011, there were $33.0 million and $31.9 million of accounts receivable from equity investees, respectively, on our consolidated balance sheets, primarily related to product sales and royalty revenues.

As of September 30, 2012, the aggregate market value of our investment in Starbucks Japan was approximately $400 million, determined based on its available quoted market price, which exceeds its carrying value of $201 million.

Summarized combined financial information of our equity method investees, which represent 100% of the investees' financial information (*in millions*):

Financial Position as of	September 30, 2012	October 2, 2011
Current assets	$ 603.1	$ 476.9
Noncurrent assets	735.3	651.4
Current liabilities	411.2	340.1
Noncurrent liabilities	119.7	80.2

Results of Operations for Fiscal Year Ended	September 30, 2012	October 2, 2011	October 3, 2010
Net revenues	$ 2,796.7	$ 2,395.1	$ 2,128.0
Operating income	353.5	277.0	245.3
Net earnings	286.7	231.1	205.1

Cost Method Investments

As of September 30, 2012, we had a $41 million investment of equity interests in entities that develop and operate Starbucks licensed retail stores in several global markets. We have the ability to acquire additional interests in some of these cost method investees at certain intervals. Depending on our total percentage of ownership interest and our ability to exercise significant influence over financial and operating policies, additional investments may require a retroactive application of the equity method of accounting.

During the fourth quarter of fiscal 2012, we made a $25 million investment in the preferred stock of Square, Inc. In addition, in conjunction with a commercial agreement with Square, we also received warrants to purchase common stock of Square that are subject to certain vesting conditions.

Note 7: Supplemental Balance Sheet Information (*in millions*)

Property, Plant and Equipment, net	Sep 30, 2012	Oct 2, 2011
Land	$ 46.2	$ 44.8
Buildings	225.2	218.5
Leasehold improvements	3,957.6	3,617.7
Store equipment	1,251.0	1,101.8
Roasting equipment	322.8	295.1
Furniture, fixtures and other	836.2	757.8
Work in progress	264.1	127.4
Property, plant and equipment, gross	6,903.1	6,163.1
Less accumulated depreciation	(4,244.2)	(3,808.1)
Property, plant and equipment, net	$ 2,658.9	$ 2,355.0

On August 8, 2011, we completed the sale of two office buildings for gross consideration of $125 million. As a result of this sale, we recognized a $30.2 million gain within operating income on the consolidated statements of earnings in fiscal 2011.

Other Assets

	Sep 30, 2012	Oct 2, 2011
Long-term deferred tax asset	$ 97.3	$ 156.3
Other intangible assets	143.7	111.9
Other	144.7	141.4
Total other assets	$ 385.7	$ 409.6

Accrued Liabilities

	Sep 30, 2012	Oct 2, 2011
Accrued compensation and related costs	$ 381.6	$ 364.4
Accrued occupancy costs	126.9	148.3
Accrued taxes	138.3	109.2
Accrued dividend payable	157.4	126.6
Other	329.6	192.4
Total accrued liabilities	$ 1,133.8	$ 940.9

Other Long-Term Liabilities

	Sep 30, 2012	Oct 2, 2011
Deferred rent	$ 201.9	$ 215.2
Unrecognized tax benefits	78.4	56.7
Asset retirement obligations	42.6	50.1
Other	22.4	25.8
Total other long-term liabilities	$ 345.3	$ 347.8

Note 8: Other Intangible Assets and Goodwill

Other intangible assets *(in millions)*:

	Sep 30, 2012	Oct 2, 2011
Indefinite-lived intangibles	$ 87.7	$ 68.6
Definite-lived intangibles	72.3	54.2
Accumulated amortization	(16.3)	(10.9)
Definite-lived intangibles, net	56.0	43.3
Total other intangible assets	$ 143.7	$ 111.9
Definite-lived intangibles approximate remaining weighted average useful life in years	10	11

Amortization expense for definite-lived intangibles was $4.5 million, $2.2 million, and $1.2 million during fiscal 2012, 2011, and 2010, respectively. Amortization expense is estimated to be approximately $6 million each year from fiscal 2013 through fiscal 2017, and a total of approximately $26 million thereafter.

Changes in the carrying amount of goodwill by reportable operating segment *(in millions)*:

	Americas	EMEA	China / Asia Pacific	Channel Development	Other	Total
Balance at October 3, 2010[1]						
Goodwill prior to impairment	$ 163.6	$ 3.1	$ 74.8	$ 23.8	$ 5.7	$ 271.0
Accumulated impairment charges	(8.6)	—	—	—	—	(8.6)
Goodwill	$ 155.0	$ 3.1	$ 74.8	$ 23.8	$ 5.7	$ 262.4
Acquisitions	—	63.8	—	—	—	63.8
Purchase price adjustment of previous acquisitions	—	—	—	—	—	—
Impairment	—	—	—	—	—	—
Other[2]	(0.7)	(3.9)	—	—	—	(4.6)
Balance at October 2, 2011[1]						
Goodwill prior to impairment	$ 162.9	$ 63.0	$ 74.8	$ 23.8	$ 5.7	330.2
Accumulated impairment charges	(8.6)	—	—	—	—	(8.6)
Goodwill	$ 154.3	$ 63.0	$ 74.8	$ 23.8	$ 5.7	$ 321.6
Acquisitions	70.5	—	—	—	7.0	77.5
Purchase price adjustment of previous acquisitions	—	—	—	—	—	—
Impairment	—	—	—	—	—	—
Other[2]	2.5	(3.0)	0.5	—	—	—
Balance at September 30, 2012						
Goodwill prior to impairment	$ 235.9	$ 60.0	$ 75.3	$ 23.8	$ 12.7	$ 407.7
Accumulated impairment charges	(8.6)	—	—	—	—	(8.6)
Goodwill	$ 227.3	$ 60.0	$ 75.3	$ 23.8	$ 12.7	$ 399.1

(1) In conjunction with the change in reportable operating segments, we reclassified goodwill by segment as of October 2, 2011 and October 3, 2010.

(2) Other is primarily comprised of changes in the goodwill balance as a result of foreign exchange fluctuations.

Note 9: Debt

Revolving Credit Facility and Commercial Paper Program

In November 2010, we replaced our previous credit facility with a new $500 million unsecured credit facility ("the credit facility") with various banks, of which $100 million may be used for issuances of letters of credit. The credit facility is available for working capital, capital expenditures and other corporate purposes, including acquisitions and share repurchases and is currently set to mature in November 2014. Starbucks has the option, subject to negotiation and agreement with the related banks, to increase the maximum commitment amount by an additional $500 million. No borrowings were outstanding under the credit facility at the end of fiscal 2012 or fiscal 2011. The interest rate for any borrowings under the credit facility, based on Starbucks current ratings and fixed charge coverage ratio, is 0.85% over LIBOR. The specific spread over LIBOR will depend upon our long-term credit ratings assigned by Moody's and Standard & Poor's rating agencies and our fixed charge coverage ratio. The credit facility contains provisions requiring us to maintain compliance with certain covenants, including a minimum fixed charge coverage ratio, which measures our ability to cover financing expenses.

Under our commercial paper program we may issue unsecured commercial paper notes, up to a maximum aggregate amount outstanding at any time of $500 million, with individual maturities that may vary, but not exceed 397 days from the date of issue. The program is backstopped by the credit facility and the combined borrowing limit is $500 million for the commercial paper program and the credit facility. We may issue commercial paper from time to time and the proceeds of the commercial paper financing may be used for working capital needs, capital expenditures and other corporate purposes, including acquisitions and share repurchases. No borrowings were outstanding under the commercial paper program at the end of fiscal 2012 or fiscal 2011.

As of September 30, 2012 and October 2, 2011, a total of $18 million and $17 million, respectively, in letters of credit were outstanding under the respective revolving credit facility.

Long-term Debt

In August 2007, we issued $550 million of 6.25% Senior Notes ("the notes") due in August 2017, in an underwritten registered public offering. Interest is payable semi-annually on February 15 and August 15 of each year. The notes require us to maintain compliance with certain covenants, which limit future liens and sale and leaseback transactions on certain material properties. As of September 30, 2012 and October 2, 2011, we were in compliance with each of these covenants. As of September 30, 2012 and October 2, 2011, the carrying value of the notes, recorded on the consolidated balance sheets, was $549.6 million and $549.5 million, respectively.

Interest Expense

Interest expense, net of interest capitalized, was $32.7 million, $33.3 million, and $32.7 million in fiscal 2012, 2011 and 2010, respectively. In fiscal 2012, 2011, and 2010, $3.2 million, $4.4 million, and $4.9 million, respectively, of interest was capitalized for asset construction projects.

Note 10: Leases

Rental expense under operating lease agreements *(in millions)*:

Fiscal Year Ended	Sep 30, 2012	Oct 2, 2011	Oct 3, 2010
Minimum rentals	$ 759.0	$ 715.6	$ 688.5
Contingent rentals	44.7	34.3	26.1
Total	$ 803.7	$ 749.9	$ 714.6

Minimum future rental payments under non-cancelable operating leases as of September 30, 2012 *(in millions)*:

Fiscal Year Ending	
2013	$ 787.9
2014	728.5
2015	640.4
2016	531.5
2017	403.4
Thereafter	968.5
Total minimum lease payments	$ 4,060.2

We have subleases related to certain of our operating leases. During fiscal 2012, 2011, and 2010, we recognized sublease income of $10.0 million, $13.7 million, and $10.9 million, respectively.

Note 11: Shareholders' Equity

In addition to 1.2 billion shares of authorized common stock with $0.001 par value per share, we have authorized 7.5 million shares of preferred stock, none of which was outstanding at September 30, 2012.

Included in additional paid-in capital in our consolidated statements of equity as of September 30, 2012 and October 2, 2011 is $39.4 million related to the increase in value of our share of the net assets of Starbucks Japan at the time of its initial public stock offering in fiscal 2002.

Share repurchase activity *(in millions, except for average price data)*:

Fiscal Year Ended	Sep 30, 2012	Oct 2, 2011
Number of shares acquired	12.3	15.6
Average price per share of acquired shares	$ 48.15	$ 35.53
Total cost of acquired shares	$ 593.2	$ 555.9

As of September 30, 2012, 12.1 million shares remained available for repurchase under the current authorization. On November 14, 2012, our Board of Directors authorized the repurchase of up to an additional 25 million shares under our share repurchase program.

During fiscal years 2012 and 2011, our Board of Directors declared the following dividends *(in millions, except per share amounts)*:

	Dividend Per Share	Record date	Total Amount	Payment Date
Fiscal Year 2012:				
First quarter	$0.17	February 8, 2012	$128.2	February 24, 2012
Second quarter	$0.17	May 9, 2012	$129.0	May 25, 2012
Third quarter	$0.17	August 8, 2012	$129.1	August 24, 2012
Fourth quarter	$0.21	November 15, 2012	$157.4	November 30, 2012
Fiscal Year 2011:				
First quarter	$0.13	February 9, 2011	$97.4	February 25, 2011
Second quarter	$0.13	May 11, 2011	$97.8	May 27, 2011
Third quarter	$0.13	August 10, 2011	$97.4	August 26, 2011
Fourth quarter	$0.17	November 17, 2011	$126.6	December 2, 2011

Comprehensive Income

Comprehensive income includes all changes in equity during the period, except those resulting from transactions with our shareholders. Comprehensive income is comprised of net earnings and other comprehensive income. Accumulated other comprehensive income reported on our consolidated balance sheets consists of foreign currency translation adjustments and the unrealized gains and losses, net of applicable taxes, on available-for-sale securities and on derivative instruments designated and qualifying as cash flow and net investment hedges.

Comprehensive income, net of related tax effects *(in millions)*:

Fiscal Year Ended	September 30, 2012	October 2, 2011	October 3, 2010
Net earnings attributable to Starbucks	$ 1,383.8	$ 1,245.7	$ 945.6
Unrealized holding gains/(losses) on available-for-sale securities, net of tax (provision)/benefit of $(0.3), $(0.3), and $0.1, respectively	0.4	0.4	(0.2)
Unrealized holding losses on cash flow hedging instruments, net of tax benefit of $4.3 $4.5, and $6.6, respectively	(37.9)	(7.7)	(11.3)
Unrealized holding gains/(losses) on net investment hedging instruments, net of tax (provision)/benefit of $(0.4), $4.5, and $4.0, respectively	0.6	(7.6)	(6.8)
Reclassification adjustment for net losses realized in net earnings for cash flow hedges, net of tax benefit of $4.3, $6.1, and $0.8, respectively	10.5	10.5	1.3
Net unrealized loss	(26.4)	(4.4)	(17.0)
Translation adjustment, net of tax (provision)/benefit of $(3.3), $0.9, and $(3.2), respectively	2.8	(6.5)	8.8
Total comprehensive income	$ 1,360.2	$ 1,234.8	$ 937.4

Components of accumulated other comprehensive income, net of tax *(in millions)*:

Fiscal Year Ended	Sep 30, 2012	Oct 2, 2011
Net unrealized gains/(losses) on available-for-sale securities	$ (0.1)	$ (0.5)
Net unrealized gains/(losses) on hedging instruments	(72.1)	(45.3)
Translation adjustment	94.9	92.1
Accumulated other comprehensive income	$ 22.7	$ 46.3

As of September 30, 2012 and October 2, 2011, the translation adjustment was net of tax provisions of $6.6 million and $3.3 million, respectively.

Note 12: Employee Stock and Benefit Plans

We maintain several equity incentive plans under which we may grant non-qualified stock options, incentive stock options, restricted stock, restricted stock units ("RSUs"), or stock appreciation rights to employees, non-employee directors and consultants. We issue new shares of common stock upon exercise of stock options and the vesting of RSUs. We also have an employee stock purchase plan ("ESPP").

As of September 30, 2012, there were 24.6 million shares of common stock available for issuance pursuant to future equity-based compensation awards and 8.1 million shares available for issuance under our ESPP.

Stock based compensation expense recognized in the consolidated financial statements *(in millions)*:

Fiscal Year Ended	Sep 30, 2012	Oct 2, 2011	Oct 3, 2010
Options	$ 46.2	$ 60.4	$ 76.8
Restricted Stock Units ("RSUs")	107.4	84.8	36.8
Total stock-based compensation expense recognized in the consolidated statement of earnings	$ 153.6	$ 145.2	$ 113.6
Total related tax benefit	54.2	51.2	40.6
Total capitalized stock-based compensation included in net property, plant and equipment and inventories on the consolidated balance sheets	2.0	2.1	1.9

Stock Option Plans

Stock options to purchase our common stock are granted at the fair market value of the stock on the date of grant. The majority of options become exercisable in four equal installments beginning a year from the date of grant and generally expire 10 years from the date of grant. Options granted to non-employee directors generally vest over one to three years. Nearly all outstanding stock options are non-qualified stock options.

The fair value of each stock option granted is estimated on the grant date using the Black-Scholes-Merton ("BSM") option valuation model. The assumptions used to calculate the fair value of options granted are evaluated and revised, as necessary, to reflect market conditions and our experience. Options granted are valued using the multiple option valuation approach, and the resulting expense is recognized over the requisite service period for each separately vesting portion of the award. Compensation expense is recognized only for those options expected to vest, with forfeitures estimated at the date of grant based on our historical experience and future expectations.

The fair value of stock option awards was estimated at the grant date with the following weighted average assumptions for fiscal years 2012, 2011, and 2010:

Fiscal Year Ended	Employee Stock Options Granted During the Period		
	2012	2011	2010
Expected term (in years)	4.8	5.0	4.7
Expected stock price volatility	38.2%	39.0%	43.0%
Risk-free interest rate	1.0%	1.6%	2.1%
Expected dividend yield	1.5%	1.7%	0.1%
Weighted average grant price	$ 44.26	$ 31.46	$ 22.28
Estimated fair value per option granted	$ 12.79	$ 9.58	$ 8.50

The expected term of the options represents the estimated period of time until exercise, and is based on historical experience of similar awards, giving consideration to the contractual terms, vesting schedules and expectations of future employee behavior. Expected stock price volatility is based on a combination of historical volatility of our stock and the one-year implied volatility of Starbucks traded options, for the related vesting periods. The risk-free interest rate is based on the implied yield available on US Treasury zero-coupon issues with an equivalent remaining term. The dividend yield assumption is based on the anticipated cash dividend payouts. The amounts shown above for the estimated fair value per option granted are before the estimated effect of forfeitures, which reduce the amount of expense recorded on the consolidated statements of earnings.

The BSM option valuation model was developed for use in estimating the fair value of traded options, which have no vesting restrictions and are fully transferable. Our employee stock options have characteristics significantly different from those of traded options, and changes in the subjective input assumptions can materially affect the fair value estimate. Because our stock options do not trade on a secondary exchange, employees do not derive a benefit from holding stock options unless there is an increase, above the grant price, in the market price of our stock. Such an increase in stock price would benefit all shareholders commensurately.

Stock option transactions from September 27, 2009 through September 30, 2012 *(in millions, except per share and contractual life amounts)*:

	Shares Subject to Options	Weighted Average Exercise Price per Share	Weighted Average Remaining Contractual Life (Years)	Aggregate Intrinsic Value
Outstanding, September 27, 2009	63.6	$ 14.75	6.7	$ 442
Granted	14.9	22.28		
Exercised	(9.6)	11.94		
Expired/forfeited	(8.2)	18.73		
Outstanding, October 3, 2010	60.7	16.52	6.6	611
Granted	4.3	31.46		
Exercised	(16.1)	14.40		
Expired/forfeited	(3.6)	18.06		
Outstanding, October 2, 2011	45.3	18.57	6.4	848
Granted	3.4	44.26		
Exercised	(13.6)	15.99		
Expired/forfeited	(2.0)	20.67		
Outstanding, September 30, 2012	33.1	22.19	6.1	945
Exercisable, September 30, 2012	18.4	19.96	5.0	567
Vested and expected to vest, September 30, 2012	32.0	21.92	6.0	923

The aggregate intrinsic value in the table above is the amount by which the market value of the underlying stock exceeded the exercise price of outstanding options, is before applicable income taxes and represents the amount optionees would have realized if all in-the-money options had been exercised on the last business day of the period indicated.

The following is a summary of stock options outstanding at the end of fiscal 2012 (shares in millions):

	Options Outstanding			Options Exercisable	
Range of Prices	Number of Options	Weighted Average Remaining Contractual Life	Weighted Average Exercise Price	Number of Options	Weighted Average Exercise Price
Under $10.00	9.0	6.0	$ 8.65	5.0	$ 8.65
$10.01 - $20.00	3.6	3.7	15.14	3.3	15.22
$20.01 - $30.00	10.8	6.0	23.14	6.5	23.91
Over $30.00	9.7	7.1	36.36	3.6	32.89
	33.1	6.1	$ 22.19	18.4	$ 19.96

As of September 30, 2012, total unrecognized stock-based compensation expense, net of estimated forfeitures, related to nonvested stock options was approximately $35 million, before income taxes, and is expected to be recognized over a weighted average period of approximately 2.3 years. The total intrinsic value of stock options exercised was $440 million, $323 million, and $118 million during fiscal years 2012, 2011, and 2010, respectively. The total fair value of options vested was $59 million, $126 million, and $108 million during fiscal years 2012, 2011, and 2010, respectively.

RSUs

We have both time-vested and performance-based RSUs. Time-vested RSUs are awarded to eligible employees and entitle the grantee to receive shares of common stock at the end of a vesting period, subject solely to the employee's continuing employment. Our performance-based RSUs are awarded to eligible employees and entitle the grantee to receive shares of common stock if we achieve specified performance goals for the full fiscal year in the year of award and the grantee remains employed during the subsequent vesting period. The fair value of RSUs is based on the closing price of Starbucks common stock on the award date. Expense for performance-based RSUs is recognized when it is probable the performance goal will be achieved.

RSU transactions from September 27, 2009 through September 30, 2012 *(in millions, except per share and contractual life amounts)*:

	Number of Shares	Weighted Average Grant Date Fair Value per Share	Weighted Average Remaining Contractual Life (Years)	Aggregate Intrinsic Value
Nonvested, September 27, 2009	4.4	$ 11.55	1.6	$ 88
Granted	2.3	22.27		
Vested	(0.7)	16.35		
Forfeited/cancelled	(0.6)	12.27		
Nonvested, October 3, 2010	5.4	13.55	1.1	141
Granted	5.4	31.06		
Vested	(1.7)	9.40		
Forfeited/cancelled	(0.8)	25.68		
Nonvested, October 2, 2011	8.3	23.11	0.8	309
Granted	4.1	44.05		
Vested	(4.2)	18.93		
Forfeited/cancelled	(0.9)	35.56		
Nonvested, September 30, 2012	7.3	34.68	0.9	366

As of September 30, 2012, total unrecognized stock-based compensation expense related to nonvested RSUs, net of estimated forfeitures, was approximately $80 million, before income taxes, and is expected to be recognized over a weighted average period of approximately 2.0 years.

ESPP

Our ESPP allows eligible employees to contribute up to 10% of their base earnings toward the quarterly purchase of our common stock, subject to an annual maximum dollar amount. The purchase price is 95% of the fair market value of the stock on the last business day of the quarterly offering period. The number of shares issued under our ESPP was 0.4 million in fiscal 2012.

Deferred Stock Plan

We have a deferred stock plan for certain key-employees that enables participants in the plan to defer receipt of ownership of common shares from the exercise of nonqualified stock options. The minimum deferral period is 5 years. As of September 30, 2012 and October 2, 2011, 3.4 million shares were deferred under the terms of this plan. The rights to receive these shares, represented by common stock units, are included in the calculation of basic and diluted earnings per share as common stock equivalents. No new initial deferrals are permitted under this plan; the plan permits re-deferrals of previously deferred shares.

Defined Contribution Plans

We maintain voluntary defined contribution plans, both qualified and non-qualified, covering eligible employees as defined in the plan documents. Participating employees may elect to defer and contribute a portion of their eligible compensation to the plans up to limits stated in the plan documents, not to exceed the dollar amounts set by applicable laws.

Our matching contributions to all US and non-US plans were $59.8 million, $45.5 million, and $23.5 million in fiscal years 2012, 2011, and 2010, respectively.

Note 13: Income Taxes

The components of earnings before income taxes were as follows *(in millions)*:

Fiscal Year Ended	Sep 30, 2012	Oct 2, 2011	Oct 3, 2010
United States	$ 1,679.6	$ 1,523.4	$ 1,308.9
Foreign	379.5	287.7	128.1
Total earnings before income taxes	$ 2,059.1	$ 1,811.1	$ 1,437.0

Provision for income taxes *(in millions)*:

Fiscal Year Ended	Sep 30, 2012	Oct 2, 2011	Oct 3, 2010
Current taxes:			
Federal	$ 466.0	$ 344.7	$ 457.5
State	79.9	61.2	79.6
Foreign	76.8	37.3	38.3
Total current taxes	622.7	443.2	575.4
Deferred taxes:			
Federal	49.2	111.6	(76.0)
State	(0.7)	8.3	(9.3)
Foreign	3.2	—	(1.4)
Total deferred taxes	51.7	119.9	(86.7)
Total provision for income taxes	$ 674.4	$ 563.1	$ 488.7

Reconciliation of the statutory US federal income tax rate with our effective income tax rate:

Fiscal Year Ended	Sep 30, 2012	Oct 2, 2011	Oct 3, 2010
Statutory rate	35.0%	35.0%	35.0%
State income taxes, net of federal income tax benefit	2.5%	2.5%	2.5%
Benefits and taxes related to foreign operations	(3.3)%	(3.1)%	(2.5)%
Domestic production activity deduction	(0.7)%	(0.8)%	(0.9)%
Other, net[1]	(0.7)%	(2.5)%	(0.1)%
Effective tax rate	32.8%	31.1%	34.0%

(1) Fiscal 2011 includes a benefit of 0.9% related to the acquisition of the remaining ownership interest in Switzerland and Austria.

US income and foreign withholding taxes have not been provided on approximately $1.5 billion of cumulative undistributed earnings of foreign subsidiaries and equity investees. We intend to reinvest these earnings for the foreseeable future. If these amounts were distributed to the US, in the form of dividends or otherwise, we would be subject to additional US income taxes, which could be material. Determination of the amount of unrecognized deferred income tax liabilities on these earnings is not practicable because of the complexities with its hypothetical calculation, and the amount of liability, if any, is dependent on circumstances existing if and when remittance occurs.

Tax effect of temporary differences and carryforwards that comprise significant portions of deferred tax assets and liabilities *(in millions):*

	Sep 30, 2012	Oct 2, 2011
Deferred tax assets:		
Property, plant and equipment	$ 62.7	$ 46.4
Accrued occupancy costs	72.0	55.9
Accrued compensation and related costs	66.9	69.6
Other accrued liabilities	15.7	27.8
Asset retirement obligation asset	20.1	19.0
Deferred revenue	43.7	47.8
Asset impairments	38.5	60.0
Tax credits	14.6	23.0
Stock based compensation	131.8	128.8
Net operating losses	99.2	85.5
Other	80.9	58.6
Total	$ 646.1	$ 622.4
Valuation allowance	(154.2)	(137.4)
Total deferred tax asset, net of valuation allowance	$ 491.9	$ 485.0
Deferred tax liabilities:		
Property, plant and equipment	(89.0)	(66.4)
Intangible assets and goodwill	(34.0)	(25.2)
Other	(44.8)	(18.1)
Total	(167.8)	(109.7)
Net deferred tax asset	$ 324.1	$ 375.3
Reported as:		
Current deferred income tax assets	$ 238.7	$ 230.4
Long-term deferred income tax assets (included in Other assets)	97.3	156.3
Current deferred income tax liabilities (included in Accrued liabilities)	(1.3)	(4.9)
Long-term deferred income tax liabilities (included in Other long-term liabilities)	(10.6)	(6.5)
Net deferred tax asset	$ 324.1	$ 375.3

We will establish a valuation allowance if either it is more likely than not that the deferred tax asset will expire before we are able to realize the benefit, or the future deductibility is uncertain. Periodically, the valuation allowance is reviewed and adjusted based on our assessments of the likelihood of realizing the benefit of our deferred tax assets. The valuation allowance as of September 30, 2012 and October 2, 2011 is primarily related to net operating losses and other deferred tax assets of consolidated foreign subsidiaries. The net change in the total valuation allowance for the years ended September 30, 2012 and October 2, 2011, was an increase of $16.8 million and $49.3 million, respectively. During fiscal 2011, we recognized approximately $32 million of previously unrecognized deferred tax assets in certain foreign jurisdictions, with a corresponding increase to the valuation allowance due to the uncertainty of their realization.

As of September 30, 2012, Starbucks has utilized all of its foreign tax credits and no longer has a foreign tax credit carryforward. Starbucks has a capital loss carryforward of $7.1 million, with an expiration date of 2015, and foreign net operating losses of $318 million, with the predominant amount having no expiration date.

Taxes currently payable of $50.8 million and $30.1 million are included in accrued liabilities on the consolidated balance sheets as of September 30, 2012 and October 2, 2011, respectively.

Uncertain Tax Positions

As of September 30, 2012, we had $75.3 million of gross unrecognized tax benefits of which $39.7 million, if recognized, would affect our effective tax rate. We recognize interest and penalties related to income tax matters in income tax expense. As of September 30, 2012 and October 2, 2011, we had accrued interest and penalties of $5.5 million and $6.2 million, respectively, before the benefit of the federal tax deduction, recorded on our consolidated balance sheets.

The following table summarizes the activity related to our unrecognized tax benefits *(in millions)*:

	Sep 30, 2012	Oct 2, 2011	Oct 3, 2010
Beginning balance	$ 52.9	$ 68.4	$ 49.1
Increase related to prior year tax positions	8.8	4.4	35.0
Decrease related to prior year tax positions	—	(32.3)	(21.4)
Increase related to current year tax positions	20.0	26.0	14.1
Decrease related to current year tax positions	(1.1)	(0.8)	(8.1)
Decreases related to settlements with taxing authorities	(0.5)	(5.0)	—
Decreases related to lapsing of statute of limitations	(4.8)	(7.8)	(0.3)
Ending balance	$ 75.3	$ 52.9	$ 68.4

We are currently under routine audit by various jurisdictions outside the US as well as US state taxing jurisdictions for fiscal years 2006 through 2011. We are no longer subject to US federal or state examination for years prior to fiscal year 2009, with the exception of seven states. We are subject to income tax in many jurisdictions outside the US. We are no longer subject to examination in any material international markets prior to 2006.

There is a reasonable possibility that the unrecognized tax benefits will change within 12 months, but we do not expect this change to be material to the consolidated financial statements.

Note 14:   Earnings per Share

Calculation of net earnings per common share ("EPS") — basic and diluted *(in millions, except EPS)*:

Fiscal Year Ended	Sep 30, 2012	Oct 2, 2011	Oct 3, 2010
Net earnings attributable to Starbucks	$ 1,383.8	$ 1,245.7	$ 945.6
Weighted average common shares and common stock units outstanding (for basic calculation)	754.4	748.3	744.4
Dilutive effect of outstanding common stock options and RSUs	18.6	21.4	19.8
Weighted average common and common equivalent shares outstanding (for diluted calculation)	773.0	769.7	764.2
EPS — basic	$ 1.83	$ 1.66	$ 1.27
EPS — diluted	$ 1.79	$ 1.62	$ 1.24

Potential dilutive shares consist of the incremental common shares issuable upon the exercise of outstanding stock options (both vested and non-vested) and unvested RSUs, calculated using the treasury stock method. The calculation of dilutive shares outstanding excludes out-of-the-money stock options (i.e., such options' exercise prices were greater than the average market price of our common shares for the period) because their inclusion would have been antidilutive. Out-of-the-money stock options totaled 0.2 million, 0.1 million, and 7.9 million as of September 30, 2012, October 2, 2011, and October 3, 2010, respectively.

Note 15:   Commitments and Contingencies

Legal Proceedings

In the first quarter of fiscal 2011, Starbucks notified Kraft Foods Global, Inc. ("Kraft") that we were discontinuing our distribution arrangement with Kraft on March 1, 2011 due to material breaches by Kraft of its obligations under the Supply and License Agreement between the Company and Kraft, dated March 29, 2004 (the "Agreement"), which defined the main distribution arrangement between the parties. Through our arrangement with Kraft, Starbucks sold a selection of Starbucks and Seattle's Best Coffee branded packaged coffees in grocery and warehouse club stores throughout the US, and to grocery stores in Canada, the UK and other European countries. Kraft managed the distribution, marketing, advertising and promotion of these products.

Kraft denies it has materially breached the Agreement. On November 29, 2010, Starbucks received a notice of arbitration from Kraft putting the commercial dispute between the parties into binding arbitration pursuant to the terms of the Agreement. In addition to denying it materially breached the Agreement, Kraft further alleges that if Starbucks wished to terminate the Agreement it must compensate Kraft as provided in the Agreement in an amount equal to the fair value of the Agreement, with an additional premium of up to 35% under certain circumstances.

On December 6, 2010, Kraft commenced a federal court action against Starbucks, entitled *Kraft Foods Global, Inc. v. Starbucks Corporation*, in the U.S. District Court for the Southern District of New York (the "District Court") seeking injunctive relief to prevent Starbucks from terminating the distribution arrangement until the parties' dispute is resolved through the arbitration proceeding. On January 28, 2011, the District Court denied Kraft's request for injunctive relief. Kraft appealed the District Court's decision to the Second Circuit Court of Appeals. On February 25, 2011, the Second Circuit Court of Appeals affirmed the District Court's decision. As a result, Starbucks is in full control of our packaged coffee business as of March 1, 2011.

While Starbucks believes we have valid claims of material breach by Kraft under the Agreement that allowed us to terminate the Agreement and certain other relationships with Kraft without compensation to Kraft, there exists the possibility of material adverse outcomes to Starbucks in the arbitration or to resolve the matter. Although Kraft disclosed to the press and in federal court filings a $750 million offer Starbucks made to Kraft in August 2010 to avoid litigation and ensure a smooth transition of the business, the figure is not a proper basis upon which to estimate a possible outcome of the arbitration but was based upon facts and circumstances at the time. Kraft rejected the offer immediately and did not provide a counter-offer, effectively ending the discussions between the parties with regard to any payment. Moreover, the offer was made prior to our investigation of Kraft's breaches and without consideration of Kraft's continuing failure to comply with material terms of the agreements.

On April 2, 2012, Starbucks and Kraft exchanged expert reports regarding alleged damages on their affirmative claims. Starbucks claimed damages of up to $62.9 million from the loss of sales resulting from Kraft's failure to use commercially reasonable efforts to market Starbucks® coffee, plus attorney fees. Kraft's expert opined that the fair market value of the Agreement was $1.9 billion. After applying a 35% premium and 9% interest, Kraft claimed damages of up to $2.9 billion, plus attorney fees. The arbitration hearing commenced on July 11, 2012 and was completed on August 3. Starbucks presented evidence of material breaches on Kraft's part and sought nominal damages from Kraft for those breaches. Kraft presented evidence denying it had breached the parties' Agreement and sought damages of $2.9 billion plus attorney fees. We expect a decision from the Arbitrator in the first half of fiscal 2013.

At this time, Starbucks believes an unfavorable outcome with respect to the arbitration is not probable, but as noted above is reasonably possible. As also noted above, Starbucks believes we have valid claims of material breach by Kraft under the Agreement that allowed us to terminate the Agreement without compensation to Kraft. In addition, Starbucks believes Kraft's damage estimates are highly inflated and based upon faulty analysis. As a result, we cannot reasonably estimate the possible loss. Accordingly, no loss contingency has been recorded for this matter.

Starbucks is party to various other legal proceedings arising in the ordinary course of business, including certain employment litigation cases that have been certified as class or collective actions, but, except as noted above, is not currently a party to any legal proceeding that management believes could have a material adverse effect on our consolidated financial position, results of operations or cash flows.

Note 16: Restructuring Charges

The restructuring efforts we began in fiscal 2008 to rationalize our store portfolio and the non-retail support organization were completed in fiscal 2010. On a cumulative basis we closed 918 stores on a global basis as part of this effort.

Restructuring charges by type of cost for fiscal 2010 were as follows (*in millions*):

| | | By Type of Cost | | |
	Total	Lease Exit and Other Related Costs	Asset Impairments	Employee Termination Costs
Costs incurred and charged to expense in fiscal 2010	$ 53.0	$ 53.0	$ 0.2	$ (0.2)
Accrued liability as of October 3, 2010[1]	$ 89.2	$ 89.2	$ —	$ —
Cash payments	(27.1)	(27.1)	—	—
Other	0.5	0.5	—	—
Accrued liability as of October 2, 2011[1]	$ 62.6	$ 62.6	$ —	$ —
Cash payments	(18.7)	(18.7)	—	—
Other	(5.3)	(5.3)	—	—
Accrued liability as of September 30, 2012[1]	$ 38.6	$ 38.6	$ —	$ —

(1) The remaining liability relates to lease obligations for stores that were previously closed where Starbucks has been unable to terminate the lease or find subtenants for the unused space.

For fiscal 2010, $28.4 million, $24.5 million and $0.1 million of restructuring charges were recorded to the Americas, EMEA, and CAP segments, respectively.

Note 17: Segment Reporting

Segment information is prepared on the same basis that our management reviews financial information for operational decision-making purposes. Beginning with the first quarter of fiscal 2012, we redefined our reportable operating segments to align with the three-region leadership and organizational structure of our retail business that took effect at the beginning of fiscal 2012.

The three-region structure includes: 1) Americas, inclusive of the US, Canada, and Latin America; 2) Europe, Middle East, and Africa, collectively referred to as the "EMEA" region; and 3) China / Asia Pacific ("CAP"). Our chief executive officer, who is our chief operating decision maker manages these businesses, evaluates financial results, and makes key operating decisions based on the new organizational structure. Accordingly, beginning with the first quarter of fiscal 2012, we revised our reportable operating segments from 1) US, 2) International, and 3) Global Consumer Products Group to the following four reportable segments: 1) Americas, 2) CAP, 3)

EMEA, and 4) Global Consumer Products Group. In the second quarter of fiscal 2012, we renamed our Global Consumer Products Group segment "Channel Development." Segment revenues as a percentage of total net revenues for the year ended 2012 were as follows: Americas (75%), EMEA (9%), China / Asia Pacific (5%), and Channel Development (10%).

Concurrent with the change in reportable operating segments, we revised our prior period financial information to reflect comparable financial information for the new segment structure. Historical financial information presented herein reflects this change.

Americas

Americas operations sell coffee and other beverages, complementary food, packaged coffees, single serve coffee products and a focused selection of merchandise through company-operated stores and licensed stores. The Americas segment is our most mature business and has achieved significant scale.

Europe, Middle East, and Africa

EMEA operations sell coffee and other beverages, complementary food, packaged coffees, single serve coffee products and a focused selection of merchandise through company-operated stores and licensed stores. Certain markets within EMEA operations are in the early stages of development and require a more extensive support organization, relative to the current levels of revenue and operating income, than Americas.

China / Asia Pacific

China /Asia Pacific operations sell coffee and other beverages, complementary food, packaged coffees, single serve coffee products and a focused selection of merchandise through company-operated stores and licensed stores. Certain markets within China / Asia Pacific operations are in the early stages of development and require a more extensive support organization, relative to the current levels of revenue and operating income, than Americas.

Channel Development

Channel Development operations sell a selection of packaged coffees as well as a selection of premium Tazo® teas globally. Channel Development operations also produce and sell a variety of ready-to-drink beverages, Starbucks VIA® Ready Brew, Starbucks® coffee and Tazo® tea K-Cup® portion packs, Starbucks® ice creams, and Starbucks Refreshers™ beverages. The US foodservice business, which is included in the Channel Development segment, sells coffee and other related products to institutional foodservice companies.

Other

Other includes Seattle's Best Coffee, Evolution Fresh, Digital Ventures, and unallocated corporate expenses that pertain to corporate administrative functions that support the operating segments but are not specifically attributable to or managed by any segment, and are not included in the reported financial results of the operating segments.

Revenue mix by product type *(in millions)*:

Fiscal Year Ended	Sep 30, 2012		Oct 2, 2011		Oct 3, 2010	
Beverage	$ 7,838.8	59%	$ 7,217.0	62%	$ 6,750.3	63%
Food	2,092.8	16%	2,008.0	17%	1,878.7	18%
Packaged and single serve coffees	2,001.1	15%	1,451.0	12%	1,131.3	10%
Other[1]	1,366.8	10%	1,024.4	9%	947.1	9%
Total	$ 13,299.5	100%	$ 11,700.4	100%	$ 10,707.4	100%

(1) Other includes royalty and licensing revenues, beverage-related ingredients, packaging and other merchandise.

Information by geographic area *(in millions)*:

Fiscal Year Ended	Sep 30, 2012	Oct 2, 2011	Oct 3, 2010
Net revenues from external customers:			
United States	$ 10,177.5	$ 8,966.9	$ 8,335.4
Other countries	3,122.0	2,733.5	2,372.0
Total	$ 13,299.5	$ 11,700.4	$ 10,707.4

No customer accounts for 10% or more of our revenues. Revenues are shown based on the geographic location of our customers. Revenues from countries other than the US consist primarily of revenues from Canada, UK, and China, which together account for approximately 64% of net revenues from other countries for fiscal 2012.

Fiscal Year Ended	Sep 30, 2012	Oct 2, 2011	Oct 3, 2010
Long-lived assets:			
United States	$ 2,767.1	$ 2,587.1	$ 2,807.9
Other countries	1,252.5	978.4	821.6
Total	$ 4,019.6	$ 3,565.5	$ 3,629.5

Management evaluates the performance of its operating segments based on net revenues and operating income. The accounting policies of the operating segments are the same as those described in the summary of significant accounting policies in Note 1. Operating income represents earnings before net interest income and other and income taxes. Management does not evaluate the performance of its operating segments using asset measures. The identifiable assets by segment disclosed in this note are those assets specifically identifiable within each segment and include net property, plant and equipment, equity and cost investments, goodwill, and other intangible assets. Corporate assets are primarily comprised of cash and investments, assets of the corporate headquarters and roasting facilities, and inventory.

The tables below presents financial information for our reportable operating segments and Other for the years ended September 30, 2012, October 2, 2011, and October 3, 2010 including the reclassifications discussed in Note 1 (*in millions*):

	Americas	EMEA	China / Asia Pacific	Channel Development	Other	Total
Fiscal 2012						
Total net revenues	$ 9,936.0	$ 1,141.3	$ 721.4	$ 1,292.2	$ 208.6	$13,299.5
Depreciation and amortization expenses	392.3	57.1	23.2	1.3	76.4	550.3
Income (loss) from equity investees	2.1	0.3	122.4	85.2	0.7	210.7
Operating income/(loss)	2,074.4	10.4	253.5	348.5	(689.4)	1,997.4
Total assets	2,199.0	467.4	656.6	88.8	4,807.4	8,219.2
Fiscal 2011						
Total net revenues	$ 9,065.0	$ 1,046.8	$ 552.3	$ 860.5	$ 175.8	$11,700.4
Depreciation and amortization expenses	390.8	53.4	18.1	2.4	58.6	523.3
Income (loss) from equity investees	1.6	6.0	92.9	75.6	(2.4)	173.7
Operating income/(loss)	1,842.3	40.3	193.1	287.8	(635.0)	1,728.5
Total assets	1,841.9	398.2	540.0	54.7	4,525.6	7,360.4
Fiscal 2010						
Total net revenues	$ 8,488.5	$ 953.4	$ 407.3	$ 707.4	$ 150.8	$10,707.4
Depreciation and amortization expenses	392.9	50.6	15.8	3.7	47.4	510.4
Income (loss) from equity investees	0.9	6.8	73.1	70.6	(3.3)	148.1
Operating income/(loss)	1,606.8	(5.5)	129.6	271.0	(582.5)	1,419.4
Total assets	1,837.9	475.8	442.0	54.1	3,576.1	6,385.9

The following table reconciles the total of operating income in the table above to consolidated earnings before income taxes (*in millions*):

Fiscal Year Ended	Sep 30, 2012	Oct 2, 2011	Oct 3, 2010
Operating income	$ 1,997.4	$ 1,728.5	$ 1,419.4
Interest income and other, net	94.4	115.9	50.3
Interest expense	(32.7)	(33.3)	(32.7)
Earnings before income taxes	$ 2,059.1	$ 1,811.1	$ 1,437.0

Note 18:   Subsequent Event

In the first quarter of fiscal 2013, we signed an agreement to acquire 100% of the outstanding shares of Teavana Holdings, Inc., a specialty retailer of premium loose-leaf teas, authentic artisanal teawares and other tea-related merchandise, for approximately $620 million in cash. The acquisition is expected to close by December 31, 2012, subject to regulatory approval and customary closing conditions.

REPORT OF INDEPENDENT REGISTERED PUBLIC ACCOUNTING FIRM

To the Board of Directors and Shareholders of Starbucks Corporation
Seattle, Washington

We have audited the accompanying consolidated balance sheets of Starbucks Corporation and subsidiaries (the "Company") as of September 30, 2012 and October 2, 2011, and the related consolidated statements of earnings, equity, and cash flows for each of the three years in the period ended September 30, 2012. These financial statements are the responsibility of the Company's management. Our responsibility is to express an opinion on these financial statements based on our audits.

We conducted our audits in accordance with the standards of the Public Company Accounting Oversight Board (United States). Those standards require that we plan and perform the audit to obtain reasonable assurance about whether the financial statements are free of material misstatement. An audit includes examining, on a test basis, evidence supporting the amounts and disclosures in the financial statements. An audit also includes assessing the accounting principles used and significant estimates made by management, as well as evaluating the overall financial statement presentation. We believe that our audits provide a reasonable basis for our opinion.

In our opinion, such consolidated financial statements present fairly, in all material respects, the financial position of Starbucks Corporation and subsidiaries as of September 30, 2012 and October 2, 2011, and the results of their operations and their cash flows for each of the three years in the period ended September 30, 2012, in conformity with accounting principles generally accepted in the United States of America.

We have also audited, in accordance with the standards of the Public Company Accounting Oversight Board (United States), the Company's internal control over financial reporting as of September 30, 2012, based on criteria established in *Internal Control — Integrated Framework* issued by the Committee of Sponsoring Organizations of the Treadway Commission and our report dated November 16, 2012 expressed an unqualified opinion on the Company's internal control over financial reporting.

/s/ Deloitte & Touche LLP

Seattle, Washington
November 16, 2012

89

Item 9. *Changes in and Disagreements with Accountants on Accounting and Financial Disclosure*

Not applicable.

Item 9A. *Controls and Procedures*

Disclosure Controls and Procedures

We maintain disclosure controls and procedures that are designed to ensure that material information required to be disclosed in our periodic reports filed or submitted under the Securities Exchange Act of 1934, as amended (the "Exchange Act"), is recorded, processed, summarized and reported within the time periods specified in the SEC's rules and forms. Our disclosure controls and procedures are also designed to ensure that information required to be disclosed in the reports we file or submit under the Exchange Act is accumulated and communicated to our management, including our principal executive officer and principal financial officer as appropriate, to allow timely decisions regarding required disclosure.

During the fourth quarter of fiscal 2012, we carried out an evaluation, under the supervision and with the participation of our management, including our chief executive officer and our chief financial officer, of the effectiveness of the design and operation of our disclosure controls and procedures, as defined in Rules 13a-15(e) and 15d-15(e) under the Exchange Act. Based upon that evaluation, our chief executive officer and chief financial officer concluded that our disclosure controls and procedures were effective, as of the end of the period covered by this report (September 30, 2012).

There were no changes in our internal control over financial reporting (as defined in Rules 13a-15(f) and 15d-15(f) of the Exchange Act) during our most recently completed fiscal quarter that materially affected or are reasonably likely to materially affect internal control over financial reporting.

The certifications required by Section 302 of the Sarbanes-Oxley Act of 2002 are filed as exhibits 31.1 and 31.2, respectively, to this 10-K.

Report of Management on Internal Control over Financial Reporting

Our management is responsible for establishing and maintaining adequate internal control over financial reporting. Internal control over financial reporting is a process to provide reasonable assurance regarding the reliability of our financial reporting for external purposes in accordance with accounting principles generally accepted in the United States of America. Internal control over financial reporting includes maintaining records that in reasonable detail accurately and fairly reflect our transactions; providing reasonable assurance that transactions are recorded as necessary for preparation of our financial statements; providing reasonable assurance that receipts and expenditures are made in accordance with management authorization; and providing reasonable assurance that unauthorized acquisition, use or disposition of company assets that could have a material effect on our financial statements would be prevented or detected on a timely basis. Because of its inherent limitations, internal control over financial reporting is not intended to provide absolute assurance that a misstatement of our financial statements would be prevented or detected.

Management conducted an evaluation of the effectiveness of our internal control over financial reporting based on the framework and criteria established in *Internal Control — Integrated Framework*, issued by the Committee of Sponsoring Organizations of the Treadway Commission. This evaluation included review of the documentation of controls, evaluation of the design effectiveness of controls, testing of the operating effectiveness of controls and a conclusion on this evaluation. Based on this evaluation, management concluded that our internal control over financial reporting was effective as of September 30, 2012.

Our internal control over financial reporting as of September 30, 2012, has been audited by Deloitte & Touche LLP, an independent registered public accounting firm, as stated in their report which is included herein.

REPORT OF INDEPENDENT REGISTERED PUBLIC ACCOUNTING FIRM

To the Board of Directors and Shareholders of Starbucks Corporation
Seattle, Washington

We have audited the internal control over financial reporting of Starbucks Corporation and subsidiaries (the "Company") as of September 30, 2012, based on criteria established in *Internal Control — Integrated Framework* issued by the Committee of Sponsoring Organizations of the Treadway Commission. The Company's management is responsible for maintaining effective internal control over financial reporting and for its assessment of the effectiveness of internal control over financial reporting, included in the accompanying Report of Management on Internal Control over Financial Reporting. Our responsibility is to express an opinion on the Company's internal control over financial reporting based on our audit.

We conducted our audit in accordance with the standards of the Public Company Accounting Oversight Board (United States). Those standards require that we plan and perform the audit to obtain reasonable assurance about whether effective internal control over financial reporting was maintained in all material respects. Our audit included obtaining an understanding of internal control over financial reporting, assessing the risk that a material weakness exists, testing and evaluating the design and operating effectiveness of internal control based on the assessed risk, and performing such other procedures as we considered necessary in the circumstances. We believe that our audit provides a reasonable basis for our opinion.

A company's internal control over financial reporting is a process designed by, or under the supervision of, the company's principal executive and principal financial officers, or persons performing similar functions, and effected by the company's board of directors, management, and other personnel to provide reasonable assurance regarding the reliability of financial reporting and the preparation of financial statements for external purposes in accordance with generally accepted accounting principles. A company's internal control over financial reporting includes those policies and procedures that (1) pertain to the maintenance of records that, in reasonable detail, accurately and fairly reflect the transactions and dispositions of the assets of the company; (2) provide reasonable assurance that transactions are recorded as necessary to permit preparation of financial statements in accordance with generally accepted accounting principles, and that receipts and expenditures of the company are being made only in accordance with authorizations of management and directors of the company; and (3) provide reasonable assurance regarding prevention or timely detection of unauthorized acquisition, use, or disposition of the company's assets that could have a material effect on the financial statements.

Because of the inherent limitations of internal control over financial reporting, including the possibility of collusion or improper management override of controls, material misstatements due to error or fraud may not be prevented or detected on a timely basis. Also, projections of any evaluation of the effectiveness of the internal control over financial reporting to future periods are subject to the risk that the controls may become inadequate because of changes in conditions, or that the degree of compliance with the policies or procedures may deteriorate.

In our opinion, the Company maintained, in all material respects, effective internal control over financial reporting as of September 30, 2012, based on the criteria established in *Internal Control — Integrated Framework* issued by the Committee of Sponsoring Organizations of the Treadway Commission.

We have also audited, in accordance with the standards of the Public Company Accounting Oversight Board (United States), the consolidated financial statements as of and for the fiscal year ended September 30, 2012, of the Company and our report dated November 16, 2012 expressed an unqualified opinion on those financial statements.

/s/ Deloitte & Touche LLP

Seattle, Washington
November 16, 2012

91

Item 9B. *Other Information*

On November 13, 2012 the Starbucks Board of Directors approved an amendment to Article X of the Company's amended and restated bylaws (as amended, the "Amended Bylaws") to read as follows:

ARTICLE X. AMENDMENTS

These bylaws may be altered, amended or repealed, and new bylaws may be adopted, by the Board of Directors or shareholders by action taken in the manner provided by the WBCA, the Articles of Incorporation and these bylaws.

Prior to the amendment, Article X of the Company's amended and restated bylaws read as follows: "These bylaws may be altered, amended or repealed, and new bylaws may be adopted, by the Board of Directors only upon a vote of two-thirds of the Board of Directors."

The Amended Bylaws became effective on November 13, 2012. The Amended Bylaws are attached hereto as Exhibit 3.2.

PART III

Item 10. *Directors, Executive Officers and Corporate Governance*

Information regarding our executive officers is set forth in Item 1 of Part 1 of this Report under the caption "Executive Officers of the Registrant."

We adopted a code of ethics applicable to our chief executive officer, chief financial officer, controller and other finance leaders, which is a "code of ethics" as defined by applicable rules of the SEC. This code is publicly available on our website at www.starbucks.com/about-us/company-information/corporate-governance. If we make any amendments to this code other than technical, administrative or other non-substantive amendments, or grant any waivers, including implicit waivers, from a provision of this code to our chief executive officer, chief financial officer or controller, we will disclose the nature of the amendment or waiver, its effective date and to whom it applies on our website at http://www.starbucks.com/about-us/company-information/corporate-governance or in a report on Form 8-K filed with the SEC.

The remaining information required by this item is incorporated herein by reference to the sections entitled "Proposal 1 — Election of Directors" and "Beneficial Ownership of Common Stock — Section 16(a) Beneficial Ownership Reporting Compliance," "Corporate Governance — Board Committees and Related Matters" and "Corporate Governance — Audit Committee" in our definitive Proxy Statement for the Annual Meeting of Shareholders to be held on March 20, 2013 (the "Proxy Statement").

Item 11. *Executive Compensation*

The information required by this item is incorporated by reference to the sections entitled "Executive Compensation," "Compensation of Directors," "Corporate Governance — Compensation Committee" and "Compensation Committee Report" in the Proxy Statement.

Item 12. *Security Ownership of Certain Beneficial Owners and Management and Related Shareholder Matters*

The information required by this item is incorporated by reference to the sections entitled "Equity Compensation Plan Information" and "Beneficial Ownership of Common Stock"in the Proxy Statement.

Item 13. *Certain Relationships and Related Transactions, and Director Independence*

The information required by this item is incorporated by reference to the section entitled "Certain Relationships and Related Transactions" and "Corporate Governance — Affirmative Determinations Regarding Director Independence and Other Matters" in the Proxy Statement.

Item 14. *Principal Accounting Fees and Services*

The information required by this item is incorporated by reference to the sections entitled "Independent Registered Public Accounting Firm Fees" and "Policy on Audit Committee Pre-Approval of Audit and Permissible Non-Audit Services of the Independent Registered Public Accounting Firm" in the Proxy Statement.

PART IV

Item 15. *Exhibits, Financial Statement Schedules*

(a) The following documents are filed as a part of this 10-K:

1. Financial Statements

The following financial statements are included in Part II, Item 8 of this 10-K:

- Consolidated Statements of Earnings for the fiscal years ended September 30, 2012, October 2, 2011, and October 3, 2010;
- Consolidated Balance Sheets as of September 30, 2012 and October 2, 2011;
- Consolidated Statements of Cash Flows for the fiscal years ended September 30, 2012, October 2, 2011, and October 3, 2010;
- Consolidated Statements of Equity for the fiscal years ended September 30, 2012, October 2, 2011, and October 3, 2010;
- Notes to Consolidated Financial Statements; and
- Reports of Independent Registered Public Accounting Firm

2. Financial Statement Schedules

Financial statement schedules are omitted because they are not required or are not applicable, or the required information is provided in the consolidated financial statements or notes described in Item 15(a)(1) above.

3. Exhibits

The Exhibits listed in the Index to Exhibits, which appears immediately following the signature page and is incorporated herein by reference, are filed as part of this 10-K.

SIGNATURES

Pursuant to the requirements of Section 13 or 15(d) of the Securities Exchange Act of 1934, the registrant has duly caused this report to be signed on its behalf by the undersigned, thereunto duly authorized.

STARBUCKS CORPORATION

By: /s/   Howard Schultz

Howard Schultz
chairman, president and chief executive officer

November 16, 2012

POWER OF ATTORNEY

Know all persons by these presents, that each person whose signature appears below constitutes and appoints Howard Schultz and Troy Alstead, and each of them, as such person's true and lawful attorneys-in-fact and agents, with full power of substitution and resubstitution, for such person and in such person's name, place and stead, in any and all capacities, to sign any and all amendments to this Report, and to file the same, with all exhibits thereto, and other documents in connection therewith, with the Securities and Exchange Commission, granting unto said attorneys-in-fact and agents, and each of them, full power and authority to do and perform each and every act and thing requisite and necessary to be done in connection therewith, as fully to all intents and purposes as such person might or could do in person, hereby ratifying and confirming all that said attorneys-in-fact and agents, or any of them or their or such person's substitute or substitutes, may lawfully do or cause to be done by virtue thereof.

Pursuant to the requirements of the Securities Exchange Act of 1934, this report has been signed below by the following persons on behalf of the registrant and in the capacities indicated as of November 16, 2012.

Signature	Title
By: /s/ Howard Schultz Howard Schultz	chairman, president and chief executive officer
By: /s/ Troy Alstead Troy Alstead	chief financial officer and chief administrative officer (principal financial officer and principal accounting officer)
By: /s/ William W. Bradley William W. Bradley	director
By: /s/ Robert M. Gates Robert M. Gates	director
By: /s/ Mellody Hobson Mellody Hobson	director

	Signature	Title
By:	/s/ Kevin R. Johnson Kevin R. Johnson	director
By:	/s/ Olden Lee Olden Lee	director
By:	/s/ Joshua Cooper Ramo Joshua Cooper Ramo	director
By:	/s/ James G. Shennan, Jr. James G. Shennan, Jr.	director
By:	/s/ Clara Shih Clara Shih	director
By:	/s/ Javier G. Teruel Javier G. Teruel	director
By:	/s/ Myron E. Ullman, III Myron E. Ullman, III	director
By:	/s/ Craig E. Weatherup Craig E. Weatherup	director

INDEX TO EXHIBITS

Exhibit Number	Exhibit Description	Incorporated by Reference				Filed Herewith
		Form	File No.	Date of First Filing	Exhibit Number	
2.1	Agreement and Plan of Merger, dated as of November 14, 2012, among Starbucks Corporation, Taj Acquisition Corp. and Teavana Holdings, Inc.	8-K	0-20322	11/15/2012	2.1	
3.1	Restated Articles of Incorporation of Starbucks Corporation	10-Q	0-20322	5/12/2006	3.1	
3.2	Amended and Restated Bylaws of Starbucks Corporation (As amended and restated through November 13, 2012)	—	—	—	—	X
4.1	Form of Indenture	S-3 ASR	333-145572	8/20/2007	4.1	
4.2	Form of Note for 6.25% Senior Notes due 2017	8-K	0-20322	8/23/2007	4.2	
4.3	Form of Supplemental Indenture for 6.25% Senior Notes due 2017	8-K	0-20322	8/23/2007	4.3	
10.1*	Starbucks Corporation Amended and Restated Key Employee Stock Option Plan — 1994, as amended and restated through March 18, 2009	8-K	0-20322	3/20/2009	10.2	
10.2*	Starbucks Corporation Amended and Restated 1989 Stock Option Plan for Non-Employee Directors	10-K	0-20322	12/23/2003	10.2	
10.3*	Starbucks Corporation 1991 Company-Wide Stock Option Plan, as amended and restated through March 18, 2009	8-K	0-20322	3/20/2009	10.3	
10.3.1*	Starbucks Corporation 1991 Company-Wide Stock Option Plan — Rules of the UK Sub-Plan, as amended and restated through November 20, 2003	10-K	0-20322	12/23/2003	10.3.1	
10.4*	Starbucks Corporation Employee Stock Purchase Plan — 1995 as amended and restated through April 1, 2009	10-Q	0-20322	2/4/2009	10.6	
10.5	Amended and Restated Lease, dated as of January 1, 2001, between First and Utah Street Associates, L.P. and Starbucks Corporation	10-K	0-20322	12/20/2001	10.5	
10.6*	Starbucks Corporation Executive Management Bonus Plan, as amended and restated effective November 8, 2011	10-Q	0-20322	5/2/2012	10.2	

Exhibit Number	Exhibit Description	Incorporated by Reference				Filed Herewith
		Form	File No.	Date of First Filing	Exhibit Number	
10.7*	Starbucks Corporation Management Deferred Compensation Plan, as amended and restated effective January 1, 2011	10-Q	0-20322	2/4/2011	10.2	
10.8*	Starbucks Corporation 1997 Deferred Stock Plan	10-K	0-20322	12/23/1999	10.17	
10.9	Starbucks Corporation UK Share Save Plan	10-K	0-20322	12/23/2003	10.9	
10.10*	Starbucks Corporation Directors Deferred Compensation Plan, as amended and restated effective September 29, 2003	10-K	0-20322	12/23/2003	10.10	
10.11*	Starbucks Corporation Deferred Compensation Plan for Non-Employee Directors, effective October 3, 2011	10-K	0-20322	11/18/2011	10.1	
10.12*	Starbucks Corporation UK Share Incentive Plan, as amended and restated effective November 14, 2006	10-K	0-20322	12/14/2006	10.1	
10.13*	Starbucks Corporation 2005 Long-Term Equity Incentive Plan, as amended and restated effective March 23, 2011	10-Q	0-20322	5/6/2011	10.1	
10.14*	2005 Key Employee Sub-Plan to the Starbucks Corporation 2005 Long-Term Equity Incentive Plan, as amended and restated effective November 15, 2005	10-Q	0-20322	2/10/2006	10.2	
10.15*	2005 Non-Employee Director Sub-Plan to the Starbucks Corporation 2005 Long-Term Equity Incentive Plan, as amended and restated effective September 13, 2011	10-K	0-20322	11/18/2011	10.17	
10.16*	Form of Stock Option Grant Agreement for Purchase of Stock under the Key Employee Sub-Plan to the Starbucks Corporation 2005 Long-Term Equity Incentive Plan	10-Q	0-20322	5/2/2012	10.1	
10.17*	Form of Stock Option Grant Agreement for Purchase of Stock under the 2005 Non-Employee Director Sub-Plan to the Starbucks Corporation 2005 Long-Term Equity Incentive Plan	8-K	0-20322	2/10/2005	10.5	
10.18*	Form of Restricted Stock Unit Grant Agreement under the 2005 Non-Employee Director Sub-Plan to the Starbucks Corporation 2005 Long-Term Equity Incentive Plan	10-K	0-20322	11/18/2011	10.20	

| Exhibit Number | Exhibit Description | Incorporated by Reference | | | | Filed Herewith |
		Form	File No.	Date of First Filing	Exhibit Number	
10.19*	2005 Company-Wide Sub-Plan to the Starbucks Corporation 2005 Long-Term Equity Incentive Plan, as amended and restated on September 14, 2010	10-K	0-20322	11/22/2010	10.20	
10.20*	Form of Stock Option Grant Agreement for Purchase of Stock under the 2005 Company-Wide Sub-Plan to the Starbucks Corporation 2005 Long-Term Equity Incentive Plan	10-Q	0-20322	8/10/2005	10.2	
10.21	Credit Agreement dated November 17, 2010 among Starbucks Corporation, Bank of America, N.A., as Administrative Agent, Swing Line Lender and L/C Issuer, and the other Lenders from time to time a party thereto.	8-K	0-20322	11/19/2010	10.1	
10.22	Commercial Paper Dealer Agreement between Starbucks Corporation and Banc of America Securities LLC, dated as of March 27, 2007	8-K	0-20322	3/27/2007	10.1.1	
10.23	Commercial Paper Dealer Agreement between Starbucks Corporation and Goldman, Sachs & Co., dated as of March 27, 2007	8-K	0-20322	3/27/2007	10.1.2	
10.24*	Letter Agreement dated February 19, 2008 between Starbucks Corporation and Arthur Rubinfeld	10-Q	0-20322	5/8/2008	10.1	
10.25*	Letter Agreement dated February 21, 2008 between Starbucks Corporation and Clifford Burrows	10-Q	0-20322	5/8/2008	10.3	
10.26*	Letter Agreement dated November 6, 2008 between Starbucks Corporation and Troy Alstead	8-K	0-20322	11/12/2008	10.1	
10.27*	Form of Time Vested Restricted Stock Unit Agreement (US) under Starbucks Corporation 2005 Long-Term Equity Incentive Plan	10-K	0-20322	11/18/2011	10.30	

		Incorporated by Reference				
Exhibit Number	Exhibit Description	Form	File No.	Date of First Filing	Exhibit Number	Filed Herewith
10.28*	Form of Time Vested Restricted Stock Unit Agreement (International) under Starbucks Corporation 2005 Long-Term Equity Incentive Plan	10-K	0-20322	11/18/2011	10.31	
10.29*	Form of Performance Based Restricted Stock Unit Agreement under Starbucks Corporation 2005 Long-Term Equity Incentive Plan	10-K	0-20322	11/18/2011	10.32	
10.30*	Letter Agreement dated November 30, 2009 between Starbucks Corporation and John Culver	10-Q	0-20322	2/2/2010	10.3	
10.31*	Letter Agreement dated September 1, 2009 between Starbucks Corporation and Annie Young-Scrivner	10-K	0-20322	11/18/2011	10.36	
10.32*	Letter Agreement dated May 5, 2010, between Starbucks Corporation and Jeff Hansberry	10-K	0-20322	11/18/2011	10.37	
10.33*	Letter Agreement dated August 9, 2011 between Starbucks Corporation and Michelle Gass	10-K	0-20322	11/18/2011	10.38	
10.34*	Letter Agreement dated September 16, 2011 between Starbucks Corporation and Michelle Gass	10-K	0-20322	11/18/2011	10.39	
12	Computation of Ratio of Earnings to Fixed Charges	—	—	—	—	X
21	Subsidiaries of Starbucks Corporation	—	—	—	—	X
23	Consent of Independent Registered Public Accounting Firm	—	—	—	—	X
31.1	Certification of Principal Executive Officer Pursuant to Rule 13a-14 of the Securities Exchange Act of 1934, As Adopted Pursuant to Section 302 of the Sarbanes-Oxley Act of 2002	—	—	—	—	X
31.2	Certification of Principal Financial Officer Pursuant to Rule 13a-14 of the Securities Exchange Act of 1934, As Adopted Pursuant to Section 302 of the Sarbanes-Oxley Act of 2002	—	—	—	—	X
32**	Certifications of Principal Executive Officer and Principal Financial Officer Pursuant to 18 U.S.C. Section 1350, As Adopted Pursuant to Section 906 of the Sarbanes-Oxley Act of 2002					

Exhibit Number	Exhibit Description	Incorporated by Reference				Filed Herewith
		Form	File No.	Date of First Filing	Exhibit Number	
101	The following financial statements from the Company's 10-K for the fiscal year ended September 30, 2012, formatted in XBRL: (i) Consolidated Statements of Earnings, (ii) Consolidated Balance Sheets, (iii) Consolidated Statements of Cash Flows (iv) Consolidated Statements of Equity (v) Notes to Consolidated Financial Statements	—	—	—	—	X

* Denotes a management contract or compensatory plan or arrangement.

**Furnished herewith.

Market Information

Starbucks common stock is traded on the NASDAQ Global Select Market ("NASDAQ"), under the symbol SBUX. The following table shows the quarterly high and low sale prices per share of Starbucks common stock for each quarter during the last two fiscal years and the quarterly cash dividend declared per share of its common stock during the periods indicated:

Fiscal 2012	High	Low	Cash Dividends Declared
Fourth Quarter	$54.28	$43.04	$0.21
Third Quarter	62.00	51.03	0.17
Second Quarter	56.55	45.28	0.17
First Quarter	46.50	35.12	0.17

Fiscal 2011	High	Low	Cash Dividends Declared
Fourth Quarter	$42.00	$33.72	$0.17
Third Quarter	40.26	34.61	0.13
Second Quarter	38.21	30.75	0.13
First Quarter	33.15	25.37	0.13

The company's U.S. Securities and Exchange Commission filings may be obtained without charge by accessing the Investor Relations section of the company's website at http://investor.starbucks.com, at http://sec.gov, or by making a request to Investor Relations through the address, phone number or website listed below.

Starbucks Coffee Company
Investor Relations, Mailstop: EX4
PO Box 34067
Seattle, WA 98124-1067
(206) 318-7118
http://investor.starbucks.com

Independent Auditors
Deloitte & Touche LLP

Transfer Agent
Computershare
PO Box 43006
Providence, RI 02940-3006
(888) 835-2866
https://www-us.computershare.com/investor

Annual Meeting of Shareholders
March 20, 2013
10:00 a.m. PDT
Marion Oliver McCaw Hall
Seattle, WA
Live webcast at http://investor.starbucks.com

Global Responsibility
Starbucks is committed to being a deeply responsible company in the communities where it does business around the world. The programs and goals that address these commitments are integral to the company's overall business strategy and can be reviewed in the annual Global Responsibility report. Please see Starbucks fiscal 2012 report, available online, this spring at http://www.starbucks.com/GRreport.

Board of Directors and Senior Leadership Team

Board of Directors
Howard Schultz
  Starbucks Corporation, chairman, president and chief executive officer
William W. Bradley
  Allen & Company LLC, managing director
Robert M. Gates
  Former Secretary of Defense
Mellody Hobson
  Ariel Investments, LLC, president
Kevin R. Johnson
  Juniper Networks, Inc., chief executive officer
Olden Lee
  PepsiCo, Inc., retired executive
Joshua Cooper Ramo
  Kissinger Associates, Inc., vice chairman
James G. Shennan, Jr.
  Trinity Ventures, general partner emeritus
Clara Shih
  Hearsay Social, Inc., chief executive officer
Javier G. Teruel
  Colgate-Palmolive Company, retired vice chairman
Myron E. Ullman, III
  U.S. and International retail chief executive officer (retired)
Craig E. Weatherup
  Pepsi-Cola Company, retired chief executive officer

Senior Leadership Team
Howard Schultz chairman, president and chief executive officer *
Troy Alstead chief financial officer and chief administrative officer *
Adam Brotman senior vice president, chief digital officer
Clifford Burrows president, Starbucks Coffee Americas and U.S. *
John Culver president, Starbucks Coffee China and Asia Pacific *
Curtis Garner senior vice president, chief information officer
Michelle Gass president, Starbucks Coffee EMEA *
Jeff Hansberry president, Channel Development and Emerging Brands *
Lucy Lee Helm executive vice president, general counsel and secretary *
Kalen Holmes executive vice president, Partner Resources
Arthur Rubinfeld chief creative officer, president, Global Development and Evolution Fresh Retail
Craig Russell senior vice president, Global Coffee
Blair Taylor senior vice president, chief community officer
Vivek Varma executive vice president, Public Affairs

* executive officer

Updated Financial Information
Please visit http://investor.starbucks.com to find the latest financial information publicly available for the company.

Keurig and K-Cup are trademarks of Keurig, Incorporated, used with permission. K-Cup® packs for use in Keurig® K-Cup® Brewing Systems.

The artwork on the cover is inspired by the Siren from our original store's logo in Seattle's Pike Place Market. The second illustration comes from the interior of our first store in Mumbai, India. These drawings evoke the *Starbucks Experience*, treasured in Seattle since 1971 and now around the world.

STARBUCKS

Exhibit 21

SUBSIDIARIES OF STARBUCKS CORPORATION

The list below excludes certain subsidiaries which, considered in the aggregate as a single subsidiary, would not constitute a significant subsidiary under SEC rules as of September 30, 2012.

Entity Name	Organized Under the Laws of:
Alki Limited Partnership	United Kingdom
AmRest Coffee Sp. z o. o.	Poland
AmRest Coffee s.r.o.	Czech Republic
AmRest Kavezo Kft.	Hungary
Bay Bread LLC (dba La Boulange)	Delaware
Beijing Starbucks Coffee Co., Ltd.	China
Berjaya Starbucks Coffee Company Sdn. Bhd.	Malaysia
Cafe Sirena S. de R.L. de C.V.	Mexico
Café Sirena S.R.L.	Argentina
Chengdu Starbucks Coffee Company Limited	China
Coffee Concepts (Southern China) Limited	Hong Kong
Coffee House Holdings, Inc.	Washington
Corporacion Starbucks Farmer Support Center Columbia	Columbia
Emerald City C.V.	Netherlands
Evolution Fresh, Inc.	Delaware
Guangdong Starbucks Coffee Company Limited	China
High Grown Investment Group (Hong Kong) Ltd.	Hong Kong
Hubei Starbucks Coffee Company Limited	China
Koffee Sirena LLC	Russia
Marinopoulos Coffee Company Bulgaria EOOD	Bulgaria
Marinopoulos Coffee Company Cyprus Limited	Cyprus
Marinopoulos Coffee Company III S.R.L.	Romania
Marinopoulos Coffee Company S.A.	Greece
North American Coffee Partnership	New York
Olympic Casualty Insurance Company	Vermont
President Coffee (Cayman) Holdings Ltd.	Cayman Islands
President Starbucks Coffee (Shanghai) Company Limited	China
President Starbucks Coffee Corporation Taiwan Limited	Taiwan (Republic of China)
Qingdao American Starbucks Coffee Company Limited	China
Rain City C.V.	Netherlands
SBI Nevada, Inc.	Nevada
SCI Europe I, Inc.	Washington
SCI Europe II, Inc.	Washington
SCI Investment, Inc.	Washington
SCI UK I, Inc.	Washington
SCI Ventures, S.L.	Spain
Seattle Coffee Company	Georgia
Seattle's Best Coffee LLC	Washington
Shaya Coffee Limited	Cyprus
SoCal Bakery LLC	Delaware
Starbucks (China) Company Limited	China

Starbucks (Shanghai) Supply Chain Co., Ltd.	China
Starbucks Asia Pacific Investment Holding II Limited	Hong Kong
Starbucks Asia Pacific Investment Holding III Limited	Hong Kong
Starbucks Asia Pacific Investment Holding Limited	Hong Kong
Starbucks Brasil Comércio de Cafés Ltda.	Brazil
Starbucks CPG International, G.K.	Japan
Starbucks Capital Asset Leasing Company, LLC	Delaware
Starbucks Card Europe Limited	United Kingdom
Starbucks Coffee (Dalian) Company Limited	China
Starbucks Coffee (Liaoning) Company Limited	China
Starbucks Coffee (Shenzhen) Ltd.	China
Starbucks Coffee (Thailand) Ltd.	Thailand
Starbucks Coffee Agronomy Company S.R.L.	Costa Rica
Starbucks Coffee Argentina S.R.L.	Argentina
Starbucks Coffee Asia Pacific Limited	Hong Kong
Starbucks Coffee Austria GmbH	Austria
Starbucks Coffee Canada, Inc.	Canada
Starbucks Coffee Chile S.A.	Chile
Starbucks Coffee Company (Australia) Pty Ltd	Australia
Starbucks Coffee Company (UK) Limited	United Kingdom
Starbucks Coffee Deutschland GmbH	Germany
Starbucks Coffee Development (Yunan) Company Limited	China
Starbucks Coffee EMEA B.V.	Netherlands
Starbucks Coffee France S.A.S.	France
Starbucks Coffee Holdings (UK) Limited	United Kingdom
Starbucks Coffee International, Inc.	Washington
Starbucks Coffee Japan, Ltd.	Japan
Starbucks Coffee Korea Co., Ltd.	South Korea
Starbucks Coffee Netherlands B.V.	Netherlands
Starbucks Coffee Puerto Rico, LLC	Delaware
Starbucks Coffee Singapore Pte Ltd	Singapore
Starbucks Coffee Switzerland A.G.	Switzerland
Starbucks Coffee Trading Company Sarl	Switzerland
Starbucks Farmer Support Center Ethiopia Plc.	Ethiopia
Starbucks Farmer Support Center Rwanda Ltd.	Rwanda
Starbucks Farmer Support Center Tanzania Ltd.	Tanzania
Starbucks Holding Company	Washington
Starbucks Manufacturing Corporation	Washington
Starbucks Manufacturing EMEA B.V.	Netherlands
Starbucks New Venture Company	Washington
Starbucks Singapore Investment Pte.	Singapore
Starbucks Switzerland Austria Holdings B.V.	Netherlands
Starbucks-Marinopoulos SEE B.V.	Netherlands
Tata Starbucks Limited	India
The New French Bakery, Inc.	California
Torrefazione Italia LLC	Washington

Torz and Macatonia Limited	United Kingdom
Xi'an Starbucks Coffee Company Limited	China

Exhibit 31.1

CERTIFICATION PURSUANT TO RULE 13A-14 OF THE SECURITIES EXCHANGE ACT OF 1934
AS ADOPTED PURSUANT TO SECTION 302 OF THE SARBANES-OXLEY ACT OF 2002

I, Howard Schultz, certify that:

1. I have reviewed this Annual Report on Form 10-K for the fiscal year ended September 30, 2012 of Starbucks Corporation;

2. Based on my knowledge, this report does not contain any untrue statement of a material fact or omit to state a material fact necessary to make the statements made, in light of the circumstances under which such statements were made, not misleading with respect to the period covered by this report;

3. Based on my knowledge, the financial statements, and other financial information included in this report, fairly present in all material respects the financial condition, results of operations and cash flows of the registrant as of, and for, the periods presented in this report;

4. The registrant's other certifying officer(s) and I are responsible for establishing and maintaining disclosure controls and procedures (as defined in Exchange Act Rules 13a-15(e) and 15d-15(e)) and internal control over financial reporting (as defined in Exchange Act Rules 13a-15(f) and 15d-15(f)) for the registrant and have:

    (a) Designed such disclosure controls and procedures, or caused such disclosure controls and procedures to be designed under our supervision, to ensure that material information relating to the registrant, including its consolidated subsidiaries, is made known to us by others within those entities, particularly during the period in which this report is being prepared;

    (b) Designed such internal control over financial reporting, or caused such internal control over financial reporting to be designed under our supervision, to provide reasonable assurance regarding the reliability of financial reporting and the preparation of financial statements for external purposes in accordance with generally accepted accounting principles;

    (c) Evaluated the effectiveness of the registrant's disclosure controls and procedures and presented in this report our conclusions about the effectiveness of the disclosure controls and procedures, as of the end of the period covered by this report based on such evaluation; and

    (d) Disclosed in this report any change in the registrant's internal control over financial reporting that occurred during the registrant's most recent fiscal quarter (the registrant's fourth fiscal quarter in the case of an annual report) that has materially affected, or is reasonably likely to materially affect, the registrant's internal control over financial reporting; and

5. The registrant's other certifying officer(s) and I have disclosed, based on our most recent evaluation of internal control over financial reporting, to the registrant's auditors and the audit committee of the registrant's board of directors (or persons performing the equivalent functions):

    (a) All significant deficiencies and material weaknesses in the design or operation of internal control over financial reporting which are reasonably likely to adversely affect the registrant's ability to record, process, summarize and report financial information; and

    (b) Any fraud, whether or not material, that involves management or other employees who have a significant role in the registrant's internal control over financial reporting.

November 16, 2012

/s/ Howard Schultz

Howard Schultz
chairman, president and chief executive officer

Exhibit 31.2

CERTIFICATION PURSUANT TO RULE 13A-14 OF THE SECURITIES EXCHANGE ACT OF 1934
AS ADOPTED PURSUANT TO SECTION 302 OF THE SARBANES-OXLEY ACT OF 2002

I, Troy Alstead, certify that:

1. I have reviewed this Annual Report on Form 10-K for the fiscal year ended September 30, 2012 of Starbucks Corporation;

2. Based on my knowledge, this report does not contain any untrue statement of a material fact or omit to state a material fact necessary to make the statements made, in light of the circumstances under which such statements were made, not misleading with respect to the period covered by this report;

3. Based on my knowledge, the financial statements, and other financial information included in this report, fairly present in all material respects the financial condition, results of operations and cash flows of the registrant as of, and for, the periods presented in this report;

4. The registrant's other certifying officer(s) and I are responsible for establishing and maintaining disclosure controls and procedures (as defined in Exchange Act Rules 13a-15(e) and 15d-15(e)) and internal control over financial reporting (as defined in Exchange Act Rules 13a-15(f) and 15d-15(f)) for the registrant and have:

    (a) Designed such disclosure controls and procedures, or caused such disclosure controls and procedures to be designed under our supervision, to ensure that material information relating to the registrant, including its consolidated subsidiaries, is made known to us by others within those entities, particularly during the period in which this report is being prepared;

    (b) Designed such internal control over financial reporting, or caused such internal control over financial reporting to be designed under our supervision, to provide reasonable assurance regarding the reliability of financial reporting and the preparation of financial statements for external purposes in accordance with generally accepted accounting principles;

    (c) Evaluated the effectiveness of the registrant's disclosure controls and procedures and presented in this report our conclusions about the effectiveness of the disclosure controls and procedures, as of the end of the period covered by this report based on such evaluation; and

    (d) Disclosed in this report any change in the registrant's internal control over financial reporting that occurred during the registrant's most recent fiscal quarter (the registrant's fourth fiscal quarter in the case of an annual report) that has materially affected, or is reasonably likely to materially affect, the registrant's internal control over financial reporting; and

5. The registrant's other certifying officer(s) and I have disclosed, based on our most recent evaluation of internal control over financial reporting, to the registrant's auditors and the audit committee of the registrant's board of directors (or persons performing the equivalent functions):

    (a) All significant deficiencies and material weaknesses in the design or operation of internal control over financial reporting which are reasonably likely to adversely affect the registrant's ability to record, process, summarize and report financial information; and

    (b) Any fraud, whether or not material, that involves management or other employees who have a significant role in the registrant's internal control over financial reporting.

November 16, 2012

/s/ Troy Alstead
Troy Alstead
chief financial officer and chief administrative officer

Exhibit 32

CERTIFICATIONS PURSUANT TO 18 U.S.C. SECTION 1350
AS ADOPTED PURSUANT TO SECTION 906 OF THE SARBANES-OXLEY ACT OF 2002

In connection with the Annual Report of Starbucks Corporation ("Starbucks") on Form 10-K for the fiscal year ended September 30, 2012, as filed with the Securities and Exchange Commission on November 16, 2012 (the "Report"), Howard Schultz, chairman, president and chief executive officer, and Troy Alstead, chief financial officer and chief administrative officer of Starbucks, each hereby certifies, pursuant to 18 U.S.C. Section 1350, as adopted pursuant to Section 906 of the Sarbanes-Oxley Act of 2002, that, to his knowledge:

(1)   the Report fully complies with the requirements of Section 13(a) or 15(d) of the Securities Exchange Act of 1934; and

(2)   the information contained in the Report fairly presents, in all material respects, the financial condition and results of operations of Starbucks.

November 16, 2012

/s/ Howard Schultz
_____
Howard Schultz
chairman, president and chief executive officer

November 16, 2012

/s/ Troy Alstead
_____
Troy Alstead
chief financial officer and chief administrative officer

Starbucks Reports Record Fourth Quarter and Fiscal 2012 Results
Q4 Revenues up 11% to a Record $3.4 Billion
Q4 EPS of $0.46; Up 24% After Excluding Non-Routine Gains in Prior Year
Strong Traffic Drives 7% US Comparable Store Sales Growth; 6% Global Growth
Channel Development Revenue Grows 32%
Board Raises Quarterly Cash Dividend 24% on Strength of Business and Outlook

SEATTLE; November 1, 2012 – Starbucks Corporation (NASDAQ: SBUX) today reported financial results for its 13-week fiscal fourth quarter and 52-week fiscal year ended September 30, 2012. When comparing with prior year results, note that fiscal 2011 included non-routine gains related to the sale of corporate real estate and the acquisition of the company's joint venture operations in Switzerland and Austria. A reconciliation of select FY11 GAAP measures to non-GAAP measures is included at the end of this document.

Fiscal Fourth Quarter 2012 Highlights:

- Total net revenues increased 11% to a fourth-quarter record of $3.4 billion
- Global comparable store sales increased 6% driven by a 5% increase in traffic and a 1% increase in average ticket
  - Americas comparable store sales increased 7% driven by 5% growth in traffic and 2% growth in average ticket
- Operating margin expanded 60 basis points to 15.4% over the prior year's operating margin of 14.8%, which included a 100 basis point benefit from a non-routine gain in Q4 FY11
  - Operating margin expanded 160 basis points when compared to prior year non-GAAP operating margin of 13.8% after excluding the non-routine gain in Q4 FY11
- EPS was $0.46 per share compared to the prior year EPS of $0.47 per share, which included $0.10 relating to non-routine gains in Q4 FY11
  - Fourth quarter EPS of $0.46 grew 24% over Q4 FY11 non-GAAP EPS of $0.37 per share, which excluded the non-routine gains in Q4 FY11
  - EPS includes charges of $0.02 per share related to store portfolio optimization initiatives in Europe
- The Board of Directors declared a cash dividend of $0.21 per share, a 24% increase from $0.17 per share

Fiscal Year 2012 Highlights:

- Total net revenues increased 14% reaching a record $13.3 billion
- Global comparable store sales increased 7% driven by a 6% increase in traffic and a 1% increase in average ticket
  - Americas comparable store sales increased 8% driven by a 6% increase in traffic and a 2% increase in average ticket
- Channel Development revenue grew 50% to $1.3 billion
- The company opened 1,063 net new stores globally
- Operating margin improved 20 basis points to 15.0% over the prior year's operating margin of 14.8%, which included a non-routine gain in FY11, despite 160 basis points of impact due to higher commodity costs in FY12
  - Operating margin expanded 50 basis points when compared to prior year non-GAAP operating margin of 14.5% after excluding the non-routine gain from FY11

- more -

- EPS increased 10% to $1.79 per share compared to the prior year EPS of $1.62 per share which included $0.10 relating to non-routine gains in FY11
  - EPS of $1.79 grew 18% over the prior year non-GAAP EPS of $1.52, excluding the non-routine gains in FY11
- Operating cash flow totaled $1.7 billion
- Starbucks returned approximately $1.1 billion to shareholders through share repurchases and dividend payments

"Our Q4 and overall 2012 fiscal year performance demonstrates the strength of our business and brand," said Howard Schultz, chairman, president and chief executive officer, Starbucks Coffee Company. "The resiliency and relevance of our U.S. retail business, acceleration of the Channel Development business and expansion in Asia all contributed significantly to our strong results. I am incredibly proud of our 200,000 Starbucks partners around the world who have contributed to the success of the company and I am optimistic about achieving our aspirations for the future."

"Our excellent fourth quarter and full fiscal year results reflect the strength of our business and the solid execution by our partners, specifically illustrated in the fourth quarter by strong traffic growth, continued momentum in Channel Development, and rapid earnings growth," stated Troy Alstead, chief financial officer. "By delivering relevant innovation to our customers while increasing focus on execution and operating efficiencies, we drove sales growth and expanded profit margins. On the strength of our business in fiscal 2012 and the momentum we carry into the new fiscal year, we remain confident in our fiscal 2013 outlook of continued strong profitable growth on a global scale."

- Page 3 -

Fourth Quarter Fiscal 2012 Summary

Comparable Store Sales[1]	Quarter Ended Sep 30, 2012		
	Sales Growth	Change in Transactions	Change in Ticket
Consolidated	6%	5%	1%
Americas	7%	5%	2%
EMEA	(1%)	0%	(1%)
CAP	10%	7%	2%

(1) Includes only Starbucks company-operated stores open 13 months or longer.

Operating Results	Quarter Ended		
($ in millions, except per share amounts)	Sep 30, 2012	Oct 2, 2011	Change
Net New Stores [1]	415	(15)	430
Revenues	$3,364.2	$3,031.9	11%
Operating Income	$519.6	$448.3	16%
Operating Margin	15.4%	14.8%	60 bps
EPS	$0.46	$0.47	(2%)

(1) Net new stores includes the addition of 20 La Boulange company-operated cafés in the fourth quarter of fiscal 2012 and the closure of 248 licensed Seattle's Best Coffee locations in Borders Bookstores in the fourth quarter of fiscal 2011.

Consolidated net revenues reached a fourth-quarter record $3.4 billion in Q4 FY12, an increase of 11% over Q4 FY11. The increase was primarily due to a 6% increase in global comparable stores sales, 32% revenue growth in Channel Development and 14% revenue growth in licensed stores. The 6% increase in comparable store sales was comprised of a 5% increase in the number of transactions and a 1% increase in average ticket.

Consolidated operating income increased 16% to a record $519.6 million, compared to $448.3 million for the same period a year ago. Operating margin expanded 60 basis points to a record 15.4% this quarter, compared to 14.8% in the same period last year. Operating margin expanded 160 basis points from 13.8% after excluding the non-routine gain in the prior year. Increased sales leverage was the primary driver of margin expansion.

Q4 Americas Segment Results

($ in millions)	Quarter Ended		
	Sep 30, 2012	Oct 2, 2011	Change
Net New Stores[1]	250	(124)	374
Revenues	$2,511.7	$2,296.4	9%
Operating Income	$536.3	$444.2	21%
Operating Margin	21.4%	19.3%	210 bps

(1) Net new stores includes the addition of 20 La Boulange company-operated cafés in the fourth quarter of fiscal 2012 and the closure of 248 licensed Seattle's Best Coffee locations in Borders Bookstores in the fourth quarter of fiscal 2011.

Net revenues for the Americas segment were $2.5 billion in Q4 FY12, an increase of 9% over Q4 FY11. The increase was primarily due to a 7% increase in comparable store sales, comprised of a 5% increase in the number of transactions and a 2%

- more -

- Page 4 -

increase in average ticket. Also contributing to the increase were incremental revenues from 504 net new store openings over the past 12 months.

Operating income increased to $536.3 million in Q4 FY12, compared to $444.2 million for the same period a year ago. Operating margin increased 210 basis points to 21.4% in Q4 FY12 primarily due to increased sales leverage.

Q4 EMEA Segment Results

($ in millions)	Quarter Ended		
	Sep 30, 2012	**Oct 2, 2011**	**Change**
Net New Stores	33	28	5
Revenues	$283.7	$290.1	(2%)
Operating Income / (Loss)	($6.5)	$2.5	nm
Operating Margin	(2.3%)	0.9%	(320) bps

Net revenues for the EMEA segment were $283.7 million in Q4 FY12, a decrease of 2% over Q4 FY11 primarily driven by unfavorable foreign currency exchange and partially offset by 29% revenue growth in licensed stores.

The EMEA segment had an operating loss of $6.5 million in Q4 FY12, compared to operating income of $2.5 million for the same period a year ago. Operating margin decreased 320 basis points to -2.3% compared to 0.9% in the prior-year period. The margin contraction was driven by costs related to store portfolio optimization initiatives in Europe, which had 410 basis points of impact. Excluding these costs, operating margin expanded as a result of improved operational efficiencies.

Q4 China/Asia Pacific Segment Results

($ in millions)	Quarter Ended		
	Sep 30, 2012	**Oct 2, 2011**	**Change**
Net New Stores	132	81	51
Revenues	$198.0	$161.2	23%
Operating Income	$65.2	$58.5	11%
Operating Margin	32.9%	36.3%	(340) bps

Net revenues for the China/Asia Pacific segment were $198.0 million in Q4 FY12, an increase of 23% over Q4 FY11. The increase was primarily due to incremental revenues from 154 net new company-operated store openings over the last 12 months and a 10% increase in comparable store sales. The increase in comparable store sales was attributable to a 7% increase in number of transactions and a 2% increase in average ticket.

Operating income increased 11% to $65.2 million in Q4 FY12, compared to $58.5 million for the same period a year ago. Operating margin decreased 340 basis points to 32.9% in Q4 FY12 compared to 36.3% in the prior-year period. The margin decline was primarily due to increased spending to support accelerated store growth in China.

- more -

- Page 5 -

Q4 Channel Development Segment Results

(\$ in millions)	Quarter Ended		
	Sep 30, 2012	Oct 2, 2011	Change
Revenues	\$318.5	\$242.2	32%
Operating Income	\$100.8	\$80.3	26%
Operating Margin	31.6%	33.2%	(160) bps

Channel Development net revenues were \$318.5 million in Q4 FY12, an increase of 32% over Q4 FY11. The increase was primarily due to sales of Starbucks- and Tazo-branded K-Cup® portion packs.

Channel Development operating income was \$100.8 million in Q4 FY12 compared to \$80.3 million for the same period a year ago. Operating margin declined by 160 basis points to 31.6% in Q4 FY12 compared to 33.2% in the prior-year period. The margin contraction was mainly due to shifts in product mix and higher commodity costs, primarily coffee.

Full Year Financial Results

Comparable Store Sales[1]	Year Ended Sep 30, 2012	Change in	
	Sales Growth	Transactions	Change in Ticket
Consolidated	7%	6%	1%
Americas	8%	6%	2%
EMEA	0%	0%	0%
CAP	15%	11%	3%

(1) Includes only Starbucks company-operated stores open 13 months or longer.

(\$ in millions, except per share amounts)	Year Ended		
	Sep 30, 2012	Oct 2, 2011	Change
Net New Stores[1]	1,063	145	918
Revenues	\$13,299.5	\$11,700.4	14%
Operating Income	\$1,997.4	\$1,728.5	16%
Operating Margin	15.0%	14.8%	20 bps
EPS	\$1.79	\$1.62	10%

(1) Net new stores for fiscal 2012 includes the addition of 20 La Boulange company-operated cafés in fiscal 2012 and the closure of 475 licensed Seattle's Best Coffee locations in Borders Bookstores in fiscal 2011.

Consolidated net revenues reached a record \$13.3 billion in FY12, an increase of 14% over FY11. The increase was primarily due to a 7% increase in global comparable stores sales, consisting of a 6% increase in the number of transactions and a 1% increase in average ticket, 50% revenue growth in Channel Development, and 20% growth in licensed stores revenue.

Consolidated operating income grew 16% to a record \$2.0 billion in FY12, compared to \$1.7 billion in FY11. Operating margin expanded 20 basis points to a record 15.0% in FY12 compared to 14.8% in FY11. The operating margin expansion was 50 basis points when excluding the non-routine gain in the prior year. This improvement was primarily due to increased sales leverage. Increased commodity costs, mainly coffee, negatively impacted operating income and operating margin in FY12 by approximately \$214 million and 160 basis points, respectively.

- more -

Fiscal 2013 Targets

Starbucks has updated its fiscal 2013 targets as follows:

- The company is further accelerating its store growth target through the opening of approximately 1,300 net new stores globally, representing 22% growth over fiscal 2012.
  - o Maintaining its growth target of approximately 600 net new stores in the Americas, with the majority of those in the U.S. Of the approximately 600 stores, approximately half of the additions will be licensed stores.
  - o Accelerating growth in China/Asia Pacific to approximately 600 net new stores, with licensed stores comprising approximately half of the new additions. Of the approximately 600 stores, slightly more than half will be in China.
  - o Maintaining growth of approximately 100 net new stores in EMEA (Europe, Middle East, Russia and Africa), with licensed stores comprising more than two thirds of the new stores.
- Starbucks continues to target approximately 10% - 13% revenue growth, driven by mid-single-digit comparable store sales growth, approximately 1,300 net new store openings, and continued strong growth in the Channel Development business.
- The company now expects full-year consolidated operating margin improvement of approximately 100 basis points over FY12 results.
- Reflecting the strength of its global business and the pipeline of profitable growth initiatives, Starbucks is raising its earnings per share target to a range of $2.06 to $2.15, representing growth in the range of 15% - 20%, and consistent with its long-term outlook.
- Capital expenditures are now expected to be approximately $1.2 billion for the full year, reflecting the increase in new store growth and an increase in production capacity to support recently-announced initiatives.

Company Updates

- Starbucks Coffee Company and its joint venture partner in India, Tata Global Beverages Limited, opened the first three Starbucks stores in India in October, located in Mumbai. Starbucks now operates retail stores in 61 countries around the world.
- The company opened its 700th store in China as it continues to execute against its significant growth plans in the CAP region.
- The Verismo™ System by Starbucks was introduced and is now available at more than 6,400 locations including participating Starbucks retail stores in the US, Canada and select international markets, Verismo.com, and specialty retailers in the US and Canada.
- Starbucks announced a partnership with Square, Inc. to provide enhancements to its mobile payment platform.
- In August, Starbucks announced plans to open a high-tech juicery that will significantly expand the production and distribution capacity of Evolution Fresh™ juices.
- Evolution Fresh opened new retail locations in downtown Seattle and San Francisco. The San Francisco opening is the first outside of the Seattle area.
- Starbucks announced a partnership with Umoe Restaurant Group to open stores in Scandinavia. The first high street locations are expected to open in 2013 in Sweden and Norway.
- Starbucks hosted approximately 10,000 store managers in Houston on Oct 3-6 for its 2012 Global Leadership Conference.
- The Board of Directors declared a cash dividend of $0.21 per share, an increase from $0.17 per share, payable on November 30, 2012, to shareholders of record as of November 15, 2012.
- The company repurchased approximately 12 million shares of common stock in fiscal 2012; approximately 12 million shares remain available for purchase under previous authorizations.

- Page 7 -

Conference Call

Starbucks will be holding a conference call today at 2:00 p.m. Pacific Time, which will be hosted by Howard Schultz, chairman, president and ceo, Michelle Gass, president, Starbucks Coffee EMEA and Troy Alstead, cfo. The call will be broadcast live over the Internet and can be accessed at the company's web site address of http://investor.starbucks.com. A replay of the call will be available via telephone through 9:00 p.m. Pacific Time on Friday, November 2, 2012 by calling 1-855-859-2056, reservation number 99153013. A replay of the webcast will also be available via the Investor Relations page on Starbucks.com through approximately 5:00 p.m. Pacific Time on Friday, November 30, 2012 at the following URL: http://investor.starbucks.com.

The company's consolidated statements of earnings, operating segment results, and other additional information have been provided on the following pages in accordance with current year classifications. This information should be reviewed in conjunction with this press release. Please refer to the company's Annual Report on Form 10-K for the fiscal year ended October 2, 2011 for additional information.

About Starbucks

Since 1971, Starbucks Coffee Company has been committed to ethically sourcing and roasting the highest quality *arabica* coffee in the world. Today, with stores around the globe, the company is the premier roaster and retailer of specialty coffee in the world. Through our unwavering commitment to excellence and our guiding principles, we bring the unique *Starbucks Experience* to life for every customer through every cup. To share in the experience, please visit us in our stores or online at www.starbucks.com.

Forward-Looking Statements

This release contains forward-looking statements relating to certain company initiatives, strategies and plans, as well as trends in or expectations regarding, earnings per share, revenues, shareholder value, operational improvements and efficiencies, diversified business model, changes to the organizational and leadership structures, business momentum, growth and growth opportunities overall and of specific businesses, markets and channels, sales leverage, store traffic, average ticket, overall performance of new and existing stores, loyalty programs, operating margins, profits, capital expenditures, operating costs, charges, comparable store sales, store openings and closings, the strength, health and potential of our business and brand, product innovations, store experience, tax rate and commodity costs and their impact. These forward-looking statements are based on currently available operating, financial and competitive information and are subject to a number of significant risks and uncertainties. Actual future results may differ materially depending on a variety of factors including, but not limited to, coffee, dairy and other raw material prices and availability, costs associated with, and the successful execution of, the company's initiatives, strategies and plans, the acceptance of the company's products by our customers, fluctuations in U.S. and international economies and currencies, the impact of competition, the effect of legal proceedings, and other risks detailed in the company filings with the Securities and Exchange Commission, including the "Risk Factors" section of Starbucks Annual Report on Form 10-K for the fiscal year ended October 2, 2011. The company assumes no obligation to update any of these forward-looking statements.

Contacts:

Starbucks Contact, Investor Relations:
JoAnn DeGrande
206-318-7118
investorrelations@starbucks.com

Starbucks Contact, Media:
Zack Hutson
206-318-7100
press@starbucks.com

- more -

- Page 8 -

STARBUCKS CORPORATION
CONSOLIDATED STATEMENTS OF EARNINGS
(unaudited, in millions, except per share data)

	Quarter Ended			Quarter Ended	
	September 30, 2012	October 2, 2011	% Change	September 2012	October 2, 2011
				As a % of total net revenues	
Net revenues:					
Company-operated stores	$ 2,665.9	$ 2,470.4	7.9 %	79.2 %	81.5 %
Licensed stores	305.3	266.8	14.4	9.1	8.8
CPG, foodservice and other	393.0	294.7	33.4	11.7	9.7
Total net revenues	**3,364.2**	**3,031.9**	**11.0**	**100.0**	**100.0**
Cost of sales including occupancy costs	1,459.2	1,314.5	11.0	43.4	43.4
Store operating expenses	989.9	922.9	7.3	29.4	30.4
Other operating expenses	111.9	103.7	7.9	3.3	3.4
Depreciation and amortization expenses	141.7	137.1	3.4	4.2	4.5
General and administrative expenses	203.8	192.3	6.0	6.1	6.3
Total operating expenses	2,906.5	2,670.5	8.8	86.4	88.1
Gain on sale of properties	-	30.2	(100.0)	-	1.0
Income from equity investees	61.9	56.7	9.2	1.8	1.9
Operating income	**519.6**	**448.3**	**15.9**	**15.4**	**14.8**
Interest income and other, net	26.3	65.7	(60.0)	0.8	2.2
Interest expense	(6.4)	(9.8)	(34.7)	(0.2)	(0.3)
Earnings before income taxes	539.5	504.2	7.0	16.0	16.6
Income taxes	180.2	145.9	23.5	5.4	4.8
Net earnings including noncontrolling interest	359.3	358.3	0.3	10.7	11.8
Net earnings attributable to noncontrolling interest	0.3	(0.2)	nm	0.0	(0.0)
Net earnings attributable to Starbucks	**$ 359.0**	**$ 358.5**	**0.1 %**	**10.7 %**	**11.8 %**
Net earnings per common share - diluted	$ 0.46	$ 0.47	(2.1) %		
Weighted avg. shares outstanding - diluted	773.5	768.5			
Cash dividends declared per share	$ 0.21	$ 0.17			

Supplemental Ratios:

Store operating expenses as a percentage of company-operated stores revenue	37.1 %	37.4 %
Effective tax rate including noncontrolling interest	33.4 %	28.9 %

- more -

- Page 9 -

STARBUCKS CORPORATION
CONSOLIDATED STATEMENTS OF EARNINGS
(unaudited, in millions, except per share data)

	Year Ended			Year Ended	
	September 30, 2012	October 2, 2011	% Change	September 2012	October 2, 2011
				As a % of total net revenues	
Net revenues:					
Company-operated stores	$ 10,534.5	$ 9,632.4	9.4 %	79.2 %	82.3 %
Licensed stores	1,210.3	1,007.5	20.1	9.1	8.6
CPG, foodservice and other	1,554.7	1,060.5	46.6	11.7	9.1
Total net revenues	**13,299.5**	**11,700.4**	**13.7**	**100.0**	**100.0**
Cost of sales including occupancy costs	5,813.3	4,915.5	18.3	43.7	42.0
Store operating expenses	3,918.1	3,594.9	9.0	29.5	30.7
Other operating expenses	429.9	392.8	9.4	3.2	3.4
Depreciation and amortization expenses	550.3	523.3	5.2	4.1	4.5
General and administrative expenses	801.2	749.3	6.9	6.0	6.4
Total operating expenses	11,512.8	10,175.8	13.1	86.6	87.0
Gain on sale of properties	-	30.2	(100.0)	-	0.3
Income from equity investees	210.7	173.7	21.3	1.6	1.5
Operating income	**1,997.4**	**1,728.5**	**15.6**	**15.0**	**14.8**
Interest income and other, net	94.4	115.9	(18.6)	0.7	1.0
Interest expense	(32.7)	(33.3)	(1.8)	(0.2)	(0.3)
Earnings before income taxes	2,059.1	1,811.1	13.7	15.5	15.5
Income taxes	674.4	563.1	19.8	5.1	4.8
Net earnings including noncontrolling interest	1,384.7	1,248.0	11.0	10.4	10.7
Net earnings attributable to noncontrolling interest	0.9	2.3	(60.9)	0.0	0.0
Net earnings attributable to Starbucks	**$ 1,383.8**	**$ 1,245.7**	**11.1 %**	**10.4 %**	**10.6 %**
Net earnings per common share - diluted	$ 1.79	$ 1.62	10.5 %		
Weighted avg. shares outstanding - diluted	773.0	769.7			
Cash dividends declared per share	$ 0.72	$ 0.56			

Supplemental Ratios:

Store operating expenses as a percentage of company-operated stores revenue	37.2 %	37.3 %
Effective tax rate including noncontrolling interest	32.8 %	31.1 %

- more -

- Page 10 -

Segment Results
The tables below present reportable segment results net of intersegment eliminations *(in millions):*

Americas		September 30, 2012	October 2, 2011	% Change	September 30, 2012	October 2, 2011
					As a % of Americas total net revenues	
Quarter Ended						
Net revenues:						
Company-operated stores	$	2,294.2 $	2,112.2	8.6 %	91.3 %	92.0 %
Licensed stores		202.2	178.6	13.2	8.1	7.8
Foodservice and other		15.3	5.6	173.2	0.6	0.2
Total net revenues		**2,511.7**	**2,296.4**	**9.4**	**100.0**	**100.0**
Cost of sales including occupancy costs		972.0	910.4	6.8	38.7	39.6
Store operating expenses		857.6	805.5	6.5	34.1	35.1
Other operating expenses		24.4	20.2	20.8	1.0	0.9
Depreciation and amortization expenses		100.8	98.4	2.4	4.0	4.3
General and administrative expenses		20.6	17.7	16.4	0.8	0.8
Total operating expenses		1,975.4	1,852.2	6.7	78.6	80.7
Income from equity investees		-	-	-	-	-
Operating income	$	**536.3** $	**444.2**	**20.7 %**	**21.4 %**	**19.3 %**

Supplemental Ratios:

	September 30, 2012	October 2, 2011
Store operating expenses as a percentage of company-operated stores revenue	37.4 %	38.1 %

		September 30, 2012	October 2, 2011	% Change	September 30, 2012	October 2, 2011
Year Ended						
Net revenues:						
Company-operated stores	$	9,077.0 $	8,365.5	8.5 %	91.4 %	92.3 %
Licensed stores		825.8	676.7	22.0	8.3	7.5
Foodservice and other		33.2	22.8	45.6	0.3	0.3
Total net revenues		**9,936.0**	**9,065.0**	**9.6**	**100.0**	**100.0**
Cost of sales including occupancy costs		3,885.5	3,512.7	10.6	39.1	38.8
Store operating expenses		3,427.8	3,184.2	7.7	34.5	35.1
Other operating expenses		83.8	75.8	10.6	0.8	0.8
Depreciation and amortization expenses		392.3	390.8	0.4	3.9	4.3
General and administrative expenses		74.3	60.8	22.2	0.7	0.7
Total operating expenses		7,863.7	7,224.3	8.9	79.1	79.7
Income from equity investees		2.1	1.6	31.3	0.0	0.0
Operating income	$	**2,074.4** $	**1,842.3**	**12.6 %**	**20.9 %**	**20.3 %**

Supplemental Ratios:

	September 30, 2012	October 2, 2011
Store operating expenses as a percentage of company-operated stores revenue	37.8 %	38.1 %

- more -

- Page 11 -

EMEA	September 2012	October 2, 2011	% Change	September 2012	October 2, 2011
				As a % of EMEA total net revenues	
Quarter Ended					
Net revenues:					
Company-operated stores	$ 233.2	$ 250.4	(6.9) %	82.2 %	86.3 %
Licensed stores	40.4	31.3	29.1	14.2	10.8
Foodservice	10.1	8.4	20.2	3.6	2.9
Total net revenues	**283.7**	**290.1**	**(2.2)**	**100.0**	**100.0**
Cost of sales including occupancy costs	153.2	152.9	0.2	54.0	52.7
Store operating expenses	97.1	91.0	6.7	34.2	31.4
Other operating expenses	7.6	11.6	(34.5)	2.7	4.0
Depreciation and amortization expenses	14.2	15.8	(10.1)	5.0	5.4
General and administrative expenses	18.1	16.3	11.0	6.4	5.6
Total operating expenses	290.2	287.6	0.9	102.3	99.1
Income from equity investees	-	-		-	-
Operating income / (loss)	$ **(6.5)**	$ **2.5**	**nm %**	**(2.3) %**	**0.9 %**

Supplemental Ratios:

Store operating expenses as a percentage of company-operated stores revenue				41.6 %	36.3 %

Year Ended					
Net revenues:					
Company-operated stores	$ 968.3	$ 905.5	6.9 %	84.8 %	86.5 %
Licensed stores	139.5	112.2	24.3	12.2	10.7
Foodservice	33.5	29.1	15.1	2.9	2.8
Total net revenues	**1,141.3**	**1,046.8**	**9.0**	**100.0**	**100.0**
Cost of sales including occupancy costs	597.3	530.3	12.6	52.3	50.7
Store operating expenses	371.1	327.3	13.4	32.5	31.3
Other operating expenses	33.6	36.5	(7.9)	2.9	3.5
Depreciation and amortization expenses	57.1	53.4	6.9	5.0	5.1
General and administrative expenses	72.1	65.0	10.9	6.3	6.2
Total operating expenses	1,131.2	1,012.5	11.7	99.1	96.7
Income from equity investees	0.3	6.0	(95.0)	0.0	0.6
Operating income	$ **10.4**	$ **40.3**	**(74.2) %**	**0.9 %**	**3.8 %**

Supplemental Ratios:

Store operating expenses as a percentage of company-operated stores revenue				38.3 %	36.1 %

- more -

China/Asia Pacific (CAP)	September 30, 2012		October 2, 2011	% Change	September 30, 2012	October 2, 2011
					As a % of CAP total net revenues	
Quarter Ended						
Net revenues:						
Company-operated stores	$	138.5	$ 107.8	28.5 %	69.9 %	66.9 %
Licensed stores		59.5	53.4	11.4	30.1	33.1
Total net revenues		**198.0**	**161.2**	**22.8**	**100.0**	**100.0**
Cost of sales including occupancy costs		100.1	83.7	19.6	50.6	51.9
Store operating expenses		35.2	26.4	33.3	17.8	16.4
Other operating expenses		14.6	9.5	53.7	7.4	5.9
Depreciation and amortization expenses		6.7	4.9	36.7	3.4	3.0
General and administrative expenses		8.0	8.8	(9.1)	4.0	5.5
Total operating expenses		164.6	133.3	23.5	83.1	82.7
Income from equity investees		31.8	30.6	3.9	16.1	19.0
Operating income	$	**65.2**	$ **58.5**	**11.5 %**	**32.9 %**	**36.3 %**

Supplemental Ratios:
Store operating expenses as a percentage of company-operated stores revenue   25.4 %   24.5 %

Year Ended						
Net revenues:						
Company-operated stores	$	489.2	$ 361.4	35.4 %	67.8 %	65.4 %
Licensed stores		232.2	190.9	21.6	32.2	34.6
Total net revenues		**721.4**	**552.3**	**30.6**	**100.0**	**100.0**
Cost of sales including occupancy costs		362.8	282.0	28.7	50.3	51.1
Store operating expenses		119.2	83.4	42.9	16.5	15.1
Other operating expenses		47.0	35.7	31.7	6.5	6.5
Depreciation and amortization expenses		23.2	18.1	28.2	3.2	3.3
General and administrative expenses		38.1	32.9	15.8	5.3	6.0
Total operating expenses		590.3	452.1	30.6	81.8	81.9
Income from equity investees		122.4	92.9	31.8	17.0	16.8
Operating income	$	**253.5**	$ **193.1**	**31.3 %**	**35.1 %**	**35.0 %**

Supplemental Ratios:
Store operating expenses as a percentage of company-operated stores revenue   24.4 %   23.1 %

- more -

- Page 13 -

Channel Development	September 30, 2012	October 2, 2011	% Change	September 2012	October 2, 2011
				As a % of Channel Development total net revenues	
Quarter Ended					
Net revenues:					
CPG	$ 235.0	$ 162.2	44.9 %	73.8 %	67.0 %
Foodservice	83.5	80.0	4.4	26.2	33.0
Total net revenues	**318.5**	**242.2**	**31.5**	**100.0**	**100.0**
Cost of sales	201.2	139.6	44.1	63.2	57.6
Other operating expenses	43.8	47.0	(6.8)	13.8	19.4
Depreciation and amortization expenses	0.3	0.5	(40.0)	0.1	0.2
General and administrative expenses	2.2	1.9	15.8	0.7	0.8
Total operating expenses	247.5	189.0	31.0	77.7	78.0
Income from equity investees	29.8	27.1	10.0	9.4	11.2
Operating income	$ **100.8**	$ **80.3**	**25.5 %**	**31.6 %**	**33.2 %**
Year Ended					
Net revenues:					
CPG	$ 952.1	$ 553.2	72.1 %	73.7 %	64.3 %
Foodservice	340.1	307.3	10.7	26.3	35.7
Total net revenues	**1,292.2**	**860.5**	**50.2**	**100.0**	**100.0**
Cost of sales	827.6	487.5	69.8	64.0	56.7
Other operating expenses	191.1	151.8	25.9	14.8	17.6
Depreciation and amortization expenses	1.3	2.4	(45.8)	0.1	0.3
General and administrative expenses	8.9	6.6	34.8	0.7	0.8
Total operating expenses	1,028.9	648.3	58.7	79.6	75.3
Income from equity investees	85.2	75.6	12.7	6.6	8.8
Operating income	$ **348.5**	$ **287.8**	**21.1 %**	**27.0 %**	**33.4 %**

- more -

- Page 14 -

Other	September 30, 2012		October 2, 2011	% Change
Quarter Ended				
Net revenues:				
Licensed stores	$	3.2	$ 3.5	(8.6) %
CPG, foodservice and other		49.1	38.5	27.5
Total net revenues		**52.3**	**42.0**	**24.5**
Cost of sales		32.7	27.9	17.2
Other operating expenses		21.5	15.4	39.6
Depreciation and amortization expenses		19.7	17.5	12.6
General and administrative expenses		154.9	147.6	4.9
Total operating expenses		228.8	208.4	9.8
Gain on sale of properties		-	30.2	(100.0)
Income from equity investees		0.3	(1.0)	nm
Operating loss	$	**(176.2)**	$ **(137.2)**	**28.4** %
Year Ended				
Net revenues:				
Licensed stores	$	12.8	$ 27.7	(53.8) %
CPG, foodservice and other		195.8	148.1	32.2
Total net revenues		**208.6**	**175.8**	**18.7**
Cost of sales		140.1	103.0	36.0
Other operating expenses		74.4	93.0	(20.0)
Depreciation and amortization expenses		76.4	58.6	30.4
General and administrative expenses		607.8	584.0	4.1
Total operating expenses		898.7	838.6	7.2
Gain on sale of properties		-	30.2	(100.0)
Income from equity investees		0.7	(2.4)	nm
Operating loss	$	**(689.4)**	$ **(635.0)**	**8.6** %

- more -

- Page 15 -

STARBUCKS CORPORATION
CONSOLIDATED BALANCE SHEETS
(in millions, except per share data)
(unaudited)

	September 30, 2012	October 2, 2011
ASSETS		
Current assets:		
Cash and cash equivalents	$ 1,188.6	$ 1,148.1
Short-term investments	848.4	902.6
Accounts receivable, net	485.9	386.5
Inventories	1,241.5	965.8
Prepaid expenses and other current assets	196.5	161.5
Deferred income taxes, net	238.7	230.4
Total current assets	4,199.6	3,794.9
Long-term investments – available-for-sale securities	116.0	107.0
Equity and cost investments	459.9	372.3
Property, plant and equipment, net	2,658.9	2,355.0
Other assets	385.7	409.6
Goodwill	399.1	321.6
TOTAL ASSETS	$ 8,219.2	$ 7,360.4
LIABILITIES AND SHAREHOLDERS' EQUITY		
Current liabilities:		
Accounts payable	$ 398.1	$ 540.0
Accrued liabilities	1,133.8	940.9
Insurance reserves	167.7	145.6
Deferred revenue	510.2	449.3
Total current liabilities	2,209.8	2,075.8
Long-term debt	549.6	549.5
Other long-term liabilities	345.3	347.8
Total liabilities	3,104.7	2,973.1
Shareholders' equity:		
Common stock ($0.001 par value) - authorized, 1,200 shares; and outstanding, 749.3 and 744.8 shares, respectively, (includes 3.4 common stock units in both periods)	0.7	0.7
Additional paid-in-capital	39.4	40.5
Retained earnings	5,046.2	4,297.4
Accumulated other comprehensive income	22.7	46.3
Total shareholders' equity	5,109.0	4,384.9
Noncontrolling interests	5.5	2.4
Total equity	5,114.5	4,387.3
TOTAL LIABILITIES AND EQUITY	$ 8,219.2	$ 7,360.4

- more -

- Page 16 -

STARBUCKS CORPORATION
CONSOLIDATED STATEMENTS OF CASH FLOWS
(unaudited and in millions)

	Year Ended September 30, 2012	Year Ended October 2, 2011
OPERATING ACTIVITIES:		
Net earnings including noncontrolling interests	$ 1,384.7	$ 1,248.0
Adjustments to reconcile net earnings to net cash provided by operating activities:		
Depreciation and amortization	580.6	550.0
Gain on sale of properties	-	(30.2)
Deferred income taxes, net	61.1	106.2
Income earned from equity method investees, net of distributions	(49.3)	(32.9)
Gain resulting from acquisition of joint ventures	-	(55.2)
Stock-based compensation	153.6	145.2
Other	23.6	33.3
Cash provided/(used) by changes in operating assets and liabilities:		
Accounts receivable	(90.3)	(88.7)
Inventories	(273.3)	(422.3)
Accounts payable	(136.0)	227.5
Accrued liabilities and insurance reserves	23.7	(81.8)
Deferred revenue	60.8	35.8
Prepaid expenses, other current assets and other assets	(19.7)	(22.5)
Net cash provided by operating activities	**1,719.5**	**1,612.4**
INVESTING ACTIVITIES:		
Purchase of investments	(1,748.6)	(966.0)
Maturities and calls of investments	1,796.4	430.0
Acquistions, net of cash acquired	(129.1)	(55.8)
Additions to property, plant and equipment	(856.2)	(531.9)
Cash proceeds from sale of property, plant and equipment	5.3	117.4
Other	(41.8)	(13.2)
Net cash used by investing activities	**(974.0)**	**(1,019.5)**
FINANCING ACTIVITIES:		
Proceeds from short-term borrowings	-	30.8
Purchase of noncontrolling interest	-	(27.5)
Proceeds from issuance of common stock	236.6	250.4
Excess tax benefit from exercise of stock options	169.8	103.9
Cash dividends paid	(513.0)	(389.5)
Repurchase of common stock	(549.1)	(555.9)
Minimum tax witholdings on share-based awards	(58.5)	(15.0)
Other	(0.5)	(5.2)
Net cash used by financing activities	**(714.7)**	**(608.0)**
Effect of exchange rate changes on cash and cash equivalents	9.7	(0.8)
Net increase/(decrease) in cash and cash equivalents	40.5	(15.9)
CASH AND CASH EQUIVALENTS:		
Beginning of period	1,148.1	1,164.0
End of the period	**$ 1,188.6**	**$ 1,148.1**
SUPPLEMENTAL DISCLOSURE OF CASH FLOW INFORMATION:		
Cash paid during the period for:		
Interest, net of capitalized interest	$ 34.4	$ 34.4
Income taxes	$ 416.9	$ 350.1

- more -

- Page 17 -

Supplemental Information

The following supplemental information is provided for historical and comparative purposes. The U.S. data is included as a transitional tool to provide insight into the U.S. business, as it was previously a reportable segment and is now the largest component of the Americas segment:

Fourth Quarter 2012 U.S. Supplemental Data

(S in millions)	Quarter Ended		
	Sep 30, 2012	Oct 2, 2011	Change
Comparable Store Sales Growth	7%	10%	
Change in Transactions	5%	7%	
Change in Ticket	2%	3%	
Revenues	$2,204.7	$2,029.8	9%
Operating Income	$497.3	$411.6	21%
Operating Margin	22.6%	20.3%	230 bps

Fiscal Fourth Quarter 2012 Store Data

The company's store data for the periods presented are as follows:

	Net stores opened/(closed) during the period				Stores open as of	
	Quarter Ended		Year Ended			
	Sep 30, 2012	Oct 2, 2011	Sep 30, 2012	Oct 2, 2011	Sep 30, 2012	Oct 2, 2011
Americas:						
Company-operated stores[1]	151	39	234	43	7,857	7,623
Licensed stores[2]	99	(163)	270	(268)	5,046	4,776
	250	(124)	504	(225)	12,903	12,399
EMEA:						
Company-operated stores[3]	3	5	10	25	882	872
Licensed stores[3]	30	23	101	79	987	886
	33	28	111	104	1,869	1,758
CAP:						
Company-operated stores	59	21	154	73	666	512
Licensed stores	73	60	294	193	2,628	2,334
	132	81	448	266	3,294	2,846
Total	415	(15)	1,063	145	18,066	17,003

[1] Includes the addition of 20 La Boulange company-operated cafés in the fourth quarter of fiscal 2012.

[2] Includes the closure of 248 and 475 licensed Seattle's Best Coffee locations in Borders Bookstores in the fourth quarter of fiscal 2011 and the full year ending October 2, 2011, respectively.

[3] EMEA store data has been adjusted for the acquisition of store locations in Austria and Switzerland in the fourth quarter of fiscal 2011 by reclassifying historical information from licensed stores to company-operated stores, and the transfer of certain company-operated stores to licensees in the fourth quarter of fiscal 2012.

- more -

- Page 18 -

Non-GAAP Disclosure

In addition to the GAAP results provided in this release, the company provides non-GAAP operating margin and non-GAAP earnings per share (non-GAAP EPS) for fiscal 2011. These non-GAAP financial measures are not in accordance with, or an alternative for, generally accepted accounting principles in the United States. The GAAP measure most directly comparable to non-GAAP operating margin and non-GAAP earnings per share (non-GAAP EPS) are operating margin and diluted net earnings per share, respectively.

The fiscal 2011 non-GAAP financial measures provided in this release exclude non-routine gains from the sale of properties and the acquisition of the company's joint venture operations in Switzerland and Austria in fiscal 2011. The company's management believes that providing these non-GAAP financial measures better enables investors to understand and evaluate the company's historical and prospective operating performance. More specifically, for historical non-GAAP financial measures, management excludes the non-routine gains in fiscal 2011 because it believes that the impact of non-routine gains do not reflect expected future expenses and do not contribute to a meaningful evaluation of the company's future operating performance or comparisons to the company's past operating performance.

These non-GAAP financial measures may have limitations as analytical tools, and these measures should not be considered in isolation or as a substitute for analysis of the company's results as reported under GAAP. Other companies may calculate these non-GAAP financial measures differently than the company does, limiting the usefulness of those measures for comparative purposes.

STARBUCKS CORPORATION
RECONCILIATION OF SELECTED GAAP MEASURES TO NON-GAAP MEASURES
(unaudited)

	Quarter Ended October 2, 2011		Year Ended October 2, 2011	
Consolidated				
Operating margin, as reported (GAAP)	14.8	%	14.8	%
Gain on sale of properties	(1.0)		(0.3)	
Non-GAAP operating margin	13.8	%	14.5	%
Diluted EPS, as reported (GAAP)	$ 0.47		$ 1.62	
Gain on sale of properties	(0.02)		(0.02)	
Gain from Switzerland and Austria transaction	(0.07)		(0.07)	
Non-GAAP Diluted EPS	$ 0.37		$ 1.52	

#

APPENDIX B

PRESENT AND FUTURE VALUE TABLES

Table I: Future Value of $1.00

$$f = p(1 + r)^n, \text{ where } r = \text{interest rate}; n = \text{number of compounding periods}; p = \$1.00.$$

Periods = n	1%	2%	3%	4%	5%	6%	7%	8%	9%	10%	12%	15%
1	1.01000	1.02000	1.03000	1.04000	1.05000	1.06000	1.07000	1.08000	1.09000	1.10000	1.12000	1.15000
2	1.02010	1.04040	1.06090	1.08160	1.10250	1.12360	1.14490	1.16640	1.18810	1.21000	1.25440	1.32250
3	1.03030	1.06121	1.09273	1.12486	1.15763	1.19102	1.22504	1.25971	1.29503	1.33100	1.40493	1.52087
4	1.04060	1.08243	1.12551	1.16986	1.21551	1.26248	1.31080	1.36049	1.41158	1.46410	1.57352	1.74901
5	1.05101	1.10408	1.15927	1.21665	1.27628	1.33823	1.40255	1.46933	1.53862	1.61051	1.76234	2.01136
6	1.06152	1.12616	1.19405	1.26532	1.34010	1.41852	1.50073	1.58687	1.67710	1.77156	1.97382	2.31306
7	1.07214	1.14869	1.22987	1.31593	1.40710	1.50363	1.60578	1.71382	1.82804	1.94872	2.21068	2.66002
8	1.08286	1.17166	1.26677	1.36857	1.47746	1.59385	1.71819	1.85093	1.99256	2.14359	2.47596	3.05902
9	1.09369	1.19509	1.30477	1.42331	1.55133	1.68948	1.83846	1.99900	2.17189	2.35795	2.77308	3.51788
10	1.10462	1.21899	1.34392	1.48024	1.62889	1.79085	1.96715	2.15892	2.36736	2.59374	3.10585	4.04556
11	1.11567	1.24337	1.38423	1.53945	1.71034	1.89830	2.10485	2.33164	2.58043	2.85312	3.47855	4.65239
12	1.12683	1.26824	1.42576	1.60103	1.79586	2.01220	2.25219	2.51817	2.81266	3.13843	3.89598	5.35025
13	1.13809	1.29361	1.46853	1.66507	1.88565	2.13293	2.40985	2.71962	3.06580	3.45227	4.36349	6.15279
14	1.14947	1.31948	1.51259	1.73168	1.97993	2.26090	2.57853	2.93719	3.34173	3.79750	4.88711	7.07571
15	1.16097	1.34587	1.55797	1.80094	2.07893	2.39656	2.75903	3.17217	3.64248	4.17725	5.47357	8.13706
16	1.17258	1.37279	1.60471	1.87298	2.18287	2.54035	2.95216	3.42594	3.97031	4.59497	6.13039	9.35762
17	1.18430	1.40024	1.65285	1.94790	2.29202	2.69277	3.15882	3.70002	4.32763	5.05447	6.86604	10.76126
18	1.19615	1.42825	1.70243	2.02582	2.40662	2.85434	3.37993	3.99602	4.71712	5.55992	7.68997	12.37545
19	1.20811	1.45681	1.75351	2.10685	2.52695	3.02560	3.61653	4.31570	5.14166	6.11591	8.61276	14.23177
20	1.22019	1.48595	1.80611	2.19112	2.65330	3.20714	3.86968	4.66096	5.60441	6.72750	9.64629	16.36654
22	1.24472	1.54598	1.91610	2.36992	2.92526	3.60354	4.43040	5.43654	6.65860	8.14027	12.10031	21.64475
24	1.26973	1.60844	2.03279	2.56330	3.22510	4.04893	5.07237	6.34118	7.91108	9.84973	15.17863	28.62518
26	1.29526	1.67342	2.15659	2.77247	3.55567	4.54938	5.80735	7.39635	9.39916	11.91818	19.04007	37.85680
28	1.32129	1.74102	2.28793	2.99870	3.92013	5.11169	6.64884	8.62711	11.16714	14.42099	23.88387	50.06561
30	1.34785	1.81136	2.42726	3.24340	4.32194	5.74349	7.61226	10.06266	13.26768	17.44940	29.95992	66.21177
32	1.37494	1.88454	2.57508	3.50806	4.76494	6.45339	8.71527	11.73708	15.76333	21.11378	37.58173	87.56507
34	1.40258	1.96068	2.73191	3.79432	5.25335	7.25103	9.97811	13.69013	18.72841	25.54767	47.14252	115.8048
36	1.43077	2.03989	2.89828	4.10393	5.79182	8.14725	11.42394	15.96817	22.25123	30.91268	59.13557	153.1519
38	1.45953	2.12230	3.07478	4.43881	6.38548	9.15425	13.07927	18.62528	26.43668	37.40434	74.17966	202.5433
40	1.48886	2.20804	3.26204	4.80102	7.03999	10.28572	14.97446	21.72452	31.40942	45.25926	93.05097	267.8635
50	1.64463	2.69159	4.38391	7.10668	11.46740	18.42015	29.45703	46.90161	74.35752	117.3909	289.0022	1,083.66
100	2.70481	7.24465	19.21863	50.50495	131.5013	339.3021	867.7163	2,199.76	5,529.04	13,780.6	83,522.3	1.17 mil.

Table II: Future Value of Annuity of $1.00 in Arrears

$$F = [\,((1 + r)^n - 1]/r, \text{ where } r = \text{interest rate}; n = \text{number payments.}$$

No. of Payments = n	1%	2%	3%	4%	5%	6%	7%	8%	9%	10%	12%	15%
1	1.00000	1.00000	1.00000	1.00000	1.00000	1.00000	1.00000	1.00000	1.00000	1.00000	1.00000	1.00000
2	2.01000	2.02000	2.03000	2.04000	2.05000	2.06000	2.07000	2.08000	2.09000	2.10000	2.12000	2.15000
3	3.03010	3.06040	3.09090	3.12160	3.15250	3.18360	3.21490	3.24640	3.27810	3.31000	3.37440	3.47250
4	4.06040	4.12161	4.18363	4.24646	4.31013	4.37462	4.43994	4.50611	4.57313	4.64100	4.77933	4.99338
5	5.10101	5.20404	5.30914	5.41632	5.52563	5.63709	5.75074	5.86660	5.98471	6.10510	6.35285	6.74238
6	6.15202	6.30812	6.46841	6.63298	6.80191	6.97532	7.15329	7.33593	7.52333	7.71561	8.11519	8.75374
7	7.21354	7.43428	7.66246	7.89829	8.14201	8.39384	8.65402	8.92280	9.20043	9.48717	10.08901	11.06680
8	8.28567	8.58297	8.89234	9.21423	9.54911	9.89747	10.25980	10.63663	11.02847	11.43589	12.29969	13.72682
9	9.36853	9.75463	10.15911	10.58280	11.02656	11.49132	11.97799	12.48756	13.02104	13.57948	14.77566	16.78584
10	10.46221	10.94972	11.46388	12.00611	12.57789	13.18079	13.81645	14.48656	15.19293	15.93742	17.54874	20.30372
11	11.56683	12.16872	12.80780	13.48635	14.20679	14.97164	15.78360	16.64549	17.56029	18.53117	20.65458	24.34928
12	12.68250	13.41209	14.19203	15.02581	15.91713	16.86994	17.88845	18.97713	20.14072	21.38428	24.13313	29.00167
13	13.80933	14.68033	15.61779	16.62684	17.71298	18.88214	20.14064	21.49530	22.95338	24.52271	28.02911	34.35192
14	14.94742	15.97394	17.08632	18.29191	19.59863	21.01507	22.55049	24.21492	26.01919	27.97498	32.39260	40.50471
15	16.09690	17.29342	18.59891	20.02359	21.57856	23.27597	25.12902	27.15211	29.36092	31.77248	37.27971	47.58041
16	17.25786	18.63929	20.15688	21.82453	23.65749	25.67253	27.88805	30.32428	33.00340	35.94973	42.75328	55.71747
17	18.43044	20.01207	21.76159	23.69751	25.84037	28.21288	30.84022	33.75023	36.97370	40.54470	48.88367	65.07509
18	19.61475	21.41231	23.41444	25.64541	28.13238	30.90565	33.99903	37.45024	41.30134	45.59917	55.74971	75.83636
19	20.81090	22.84056	25.11687	27.67123	30.53900	33.75999	37.37896	41.44626	46.01846	51.15909	63.43968	88.21181
20	22.01900	24.29737	26.87037	29.77808	33.06595	36.78559	40.99549	45.76196	51.16012	57.27500	72.05244	102.4436
22	24.47159	27.29898	30.53678	34.24797	38.50521	43.39229	49.00574	55.45676	62.87334	71.40275	92.50258	137.6316
24	26.97346	30.42186	34.42647	39.08260	44.50200	50.81558	58.17667	66.76476	76.78981	88.49733	118.1552	184.1678
26	29.52563	33.67091	38.55304	44.31174	51.11345	59.15638	68.67647	79.95442	93.32398	109.1818	150.3339	245.7120
28	32.12910	37.05121	42.93092	49.96758	58.40258	68.52811	80.69769	95.33883	112.9682	134.2099	190.6989	327.1041
30	34.78489	40.56808	47.57542	56.08494	66.43885	79.05819	94.46079	113.2832	136.3075	164.4940	241.3327	434.7451
32	37.49407	44.22703	52.50276	62.70147	75.29883	90.88978	110.2182	134.2135	164.0370	201.1378	304.8477	577.1005
34	40.25770	48.03380	57.73018	69.85791	85.06696	104.1838	128.2588	158.6267	196.9823	245.4767	384.5210	765.3654
36	43.07688	51.99437	63.27594	77.59831	95.83632	119.1209	148.9135	187.1021	236.1247	299.1268	484.4631	1,014.35
38	45.95272	56.11494	69.15945	85.97034	107.7095	135.9042	172.5610	220.3159	282.6298	364.0434	609.8305	1,343.62
40	48.88657	60.40198	75.40126	95.02552	120.7998	154.7620	199.6351	259.0565	337.8824	442.5926	767.0914	1,779.09
50	64.46318	84.57940	112.7969	152.6671	209.3480	290.3359	406.5289	573.7702	815.0836	1,163.91	2,400.02	7,217.72
100	170.4814	312.2323	607.2877	1,237.62	2,610.03	5,638.37	12,381.70	27,484.50	61,422.70	137,796	696,011	7.83 mil.

Table III: Present Value of $1.00

$p = f/(1 + r)^n$, where r = discount (interest) rate; n = number of periods until payment; f = $1.00.

Periods = n	1%	2%	3%	4%	5%	6%	7%	8%	9%	10%	12%	15%
1	.99010	.98039	.97087	.96154	.95238	.94340	.93458	.92593	.91743	.90909	.89286	.86957
2	.98030	.96117	.94260	.92456	.90703	.89000	.87344	.85734	.84168	.82645	.79719	.75614
3	.97059	.94232	.91514	.88900	.86384	.83962	.81630	.79383	.77218	.75131	.71178	.65752
4	.96098	.92385	.88849	.85480	.82270	.79209	.76290	.73503	.70843	.68301	.63552	.57175
5	.95147	.90573	.86261	.82193	.78353	.74726	.71299	.68058	.64993	.62092	.56743	.49718
6	.94205	.88797	.83748	.79031	.74622	.70496	.66634	.63017	.59627	.56447	.50663	.43233
7	.93272	.87056	.81309	.75992	.71068	.66506	.62275	.58349	.54703	.51316	.45235	.37594
8	.92348	.85349	.78941	.73069	.67684	.62741	.58201	.54027	.50187	.46651	.40388	.32690
9	.91434	.83676	.76642	.70259	.64461	.59190	.54393	.50025	.46043	.42410	.36061	.28426
10	.90529	.82035	.74409	.67556	.61391	.55839	.50835	.46319	.42241	.38554	.32197	.24718
11	.89632	.80426	.72242	.64958	.58468	.52679	.47509	.42888	.38753	.35049	.28748	.21494
12	.88745	.78849	.70138	.62460	.55684	.49697	.44401	.39711	.35553	.31863	.25668	.18691
13	.87866	.77303	.68095	.60057	.53032	.46884	.41496	.36770	.32618	.28966	.22917	.16253
14	.86996	.75788	.66112	.57748	.50507	.44230	.38782	.34046	.29925	.26333	.20462	.14133
15	.86135	.74301	.64186	.55526	.48102	.41727	.36245	.31524	.27454	.23939	.18270	.12289
16	.85282	.72845	.62317	.53391	.45811	.39365	.33873	.29189	.25187	.21763	.16312	.10686
17	.84438	.71416	.60502	.51337	.43630	.37136	.31657	.27027	.23107	.19784	.14564	.09293
18	.83602	.70016	.58739	.49363	.41552	.35034	.29586	.25025	.21199	.17986	.13004	.08081
19	.82774	.68643	.57029	.47464	.39573	.33051	.27651	.23171	.19449	.16351	.11611	.07027
20	.81954	.67297	.55368	.45639	.37689	.31180	.25842	.21455	.17843	.14864	.10367	.06110
22	.80340	.64684	.52189	.42196	.34185	.27751	.22571	.18394	.15018	.12285	.08264	.04620
24	.78757	.62172	.49193	.39012	.31007	.24698	.19715	.15770	.12640	.10153	.06588	.03493
26	.77205	.59758	.46369	.36069	.28124	.21981	.17220	.13520	.10639	.08391	.05252	.02642
28	.75684	.57437	.43708	.33348	.25509	.19563	.15040	.11591	.08955	.06934	.04187	.01997
30	.74192	.55207	.41199	.30832	.23138	.17411	.13137	.09938	.07537	.05731	.03338	.01510
32	.72730	.53063	.38834	.28506	.20987	.15496	.11474	.08520	.06344	.04736	.02661	.01142
34	.71297	.51003	.36604	.26555	.19035	.13791	.10022	.07305	.05339	.03914	.02121	.00864
36	.69892	.49022	.34503	.24367	.17266	.12274	.08754	.06262	.04494	.03235	.01691	.00653
38	.68515	.47119	.32523	.22329	.15661	.10924	.07646	.05369	.03783	.02673	.01348	.00494
40	.67165	.45289	.30656	.20829	.14205	.09722	.06678	.04603	.03184	.02209	.01075	.00373
50	.60804	.37153	.22811	.14071	.08720	.05429	.03395	.02132	.01345	.00852	.00346	.00092
100	.36971	.13803	.05203	.01980	.00760	.00295	.00115	.00045	.00018	.00007	.00001	.00000

Table IV: Present Value of Annuity of $1.00 in Arrears

$P = (1 - 1/[1 + r]^n)/r$, where r = discount (interest) rate; n = number of payments.

No. of Payments = n	1%	2%	3%	4%	5%	6%	7%	8%	9%	10%	12%	15%
1	.99010	.98039	.97087	.96154	.95238	.94340	.93458	.92593	.91743	.90909	.89286	.86957
2	1.97040	1.94156	1.91347	1.88609	1.85941	1.83339	1.80802	1.78326	1.75911	1.73554	1.69005	1.62571
3	2.94099	2.88388	2.82861	2.77509	2.72325	2.67301	2.62432	2.57710	2.53129	2.48685	2.40183	2.28323
4	3.90197	3.80773	3.71710	3.62990	3.54595	3.46511	3.38721	3.31213	3.23972	3.16987	3.03735	2.85498
5	4.85343	4.71346	4.57971	4.45182	4.32948	4.21236	4.10020	3.99271	3.88965	3.79079	3.60478	3.35216
6	5.79548	5.60143	5.41719	5.24214	5.07569	4.91732	4.76654	4.62288	4.48592	4.35526	4.11141	3.78448
7	6.72819	6.47199	6.23028	6.00205	5.78637	5.58238	5.38929	5.20637	5.03295	4.86842	4.56376	4.16042
8	7.65168	7.32548	7.01969	6.73274	6.46321	6.20979	5.97130	5.74664	5.53482	5.33493	4.96764	4.48732
9	8.56602	8.16224	7.78611	7.43533	7.10782	6.80169	6.51523	6.24689	5.99525	5.75902	5.32825	4.77158
10	9.47130	8.98259	8.53020	8.11090	7.72173	7.36009	7.02358	6.71008	6.41766	6.14457	5.65022	5.01877
11	10.36763	9.78685	9.25262	8.76048	8.30641	7.88687	7.49867	7.13896	6.80519	6.49506	5.93770	5.23371
12	11.25508	10.57534	9.95400	9.38507	8.86325	8.38384	7.94269	7.53608	7.16073	6.81369	6.19437	5.42062
13	12.13374	11.34837	10.63496	9.98565	9.39357	8.85268	8.35765	7.90378	7.48690	7.10336	6.42355	5.58315
14	13.00370	12.10625	11.29607	10.56312	9.89864	9.29498	8.74547	8.24424	7.78615	7.36669	6.62817	5.72448
15	13.86505	12.84926	11.93794	11.11839	10.37966	9.71225	9.10791	8.55948	8.06069	7.60608	6.81086	5.84737
16	14.71787	13.57771	12.56110	11.65230	10.83777	10.10590	9.44665	8.85137	8.31256	7.82371	6.97399	5.95423
17	15.56225	14.29187	13.16612	12.16567	11.27407	10.47726	9.76322	9.12164	8.54363	8.02155	7.11963	6.04716
18	16.39827	14.99203	13.75351	12.65930	11.68959	10.82760	10.05909	9.37189	8.75563	8.20141	7.24967	6.12797
19	17.22601	15.67846	14.32380	13.13394	12.08532	11.15812	10.33560	9.60360	8.95011	8.36492	7.36578	6.19823
20	18.04555	16.35143	14.87747	13.59033	12.46221	11.46992	10.59401	9.81815	9.12855	8.51356	7.46944	6.25933
22	19.66038	17.65805	15.93692	14.45112	13.16300	12.04158	11.06124	10.20074	9.44243	8.77154	7.64465	6.35866
24	21.24339	18.91393	16.93554	15.24696	13.79864	12.55036	11.46933	10.52876	9.70661	8.98474	7.78432	6.43377
26	22.79520	20.12104	17.87684	15.98277	14.37519	13.00317	11.82577	10.80998	9.92897	9.16095	7.89566	6.49056
28	24.31644	21.28127	18.76411	16.66306	14.89813	13.40616	12.13711	11.05108	10.11613	9.30657	7.98442	6.53351
30	25.80771	22.39646	19.60044	17.29203	15.37245	13.76483	12.40904	11.25778	10.27365	9.42691	8.05518	6.56598
32	27.26959	23.46833	20.38877	17.87355	15.80268	14.08404	12.64656	11.43500	10.40624	9.52638	8.11159	6.59053
34	28.70267	24.49859	21.13184	18.41120	16.19290	14.36814	12.85401	11.58693	10.51784	9.60857	8.15656	6.60910
36	30.10751	25.48884	21.83225	18.90828	16.54685	14.62099	13.03521	11.71719	10.61176	9.67651	8.19241	6.62314
38	31.48466	26.44064	22.49246	19.36786	16.86789	14.84602	13.19347	11.82887	10.69082	9.73265	8.22099	6.63375
40	32.83469	27.35548	23.11477	19.79277	17.15909	15.04630	13.33171	11.92461	10.75736	9.77905	8.24378	6.64178
50	39.19612	31.42361	25.72976	21.48218	18.25593	15.76186	13.80075	12.23348	10.96168	9.91481	8.30450	6.66051
100	63.02888	43.09835	31.59891	24.50500	19.84791	16.61755	14.26925	12.49432	11.10910	9.99927	8.33323	6.66666

INDEX

References are to Pages

ACCOUNTING RESEARCH BULLETINS
See Accounting Principles

ACCOUNTING SERIES RELEASES
See Securities and Exchange Commission

ACCOUNTING STANDARDS BOARD
See American Institute of Certified Public Accountants

ACCOUNTING STANDARDS CODIFICATION
See Financial Accounting Standards Board

ACCOUNTING STANDARDS DIVISION
See American Institute of Certified Public Accountants

ACCOUNTING STANDARDS DIVISION EXECUTIVE COMMITTEE
See American Institute of Certified Public Accountants

ACCOUNTS PAYABLE
See Liabilities

BALANCE SHEET

BIG BATH

BONDS AND DEBT INSTRUMENTS

BONDS PAYABLE

BOOK VALUE

CREDIT
　See Bookkeeping

CURRENT ASSETS
　See Assets

CURRENT LIABILITIES
　See Liabilities

CURRENT RATIO
　See Financial Ratio

DATA SECURITY
　See Contingencies

DEBIT
　See Bookkeeping

DEBT COVERAGE
　See Financial Ratios

DEBT SECURITIES
　See Bonds and Debt Instruments

DEBT TO EQUITY
　See Financial Ratios

DEBT TO TOTAL ASSETS
　See Financial Ratios

MODIFYING CONVENTIONS

MONETARY UNIT ASSUMPTION
See Assumptions

NATURAL RESOURCES
See Long-Lived Assets

NET BOOK VALUE
See Financial Ratios

NET SALES
See Sales

NET WORTH
See Equity

NO-PAR STOCK
See Shares

NONCONTROLLING INTERESTS
See Equity

NONMONETARY TRANSACTIONS
See Financial Statement Analysis
See Revenue Recognition

NONRECURRING ITEMS
See Financial Statement Analysis
See Income Statement

NOTES PAYABLE
See Income Statement
See Liabilities

NOTES RECEIVABLE
See Assets

NOTES TO FINANCIAL STATEMENTS
See Financial Statements

OBJECTIVITY PRINCIPLE
See Accounting Principles

OPERATING AGREEMENT
See Limited Liability Companies

OPERATING LEASES
See Leases

OUTSTANDING SHARES
See Shares

OWNER'S EQUITY
See Equity

PAR VALUE
See Shares

WORK PRODUCT PROTECTION
See Contingencies

WORK-IN-PROCESS INVENTORY
See Inventory

WORKING CAPITAL
See Financial Ratios

WORKING PAPERS AND WORKPAPERS
See Auditing

WORKING TRIAL BALANCE
See Bookkeeping

WORKSHEET
See Bookkeeping

WRITE-DOWNS